FROMMER'S

HONEYMOON DESTINATIONS

RISA WEINREB

2ND EDITION

PRENTICE HALL

New York □ London □ Toronto □ Sydney □ Tokyo □ Singapore

Copyright © 1988, 1990
by Risa Weinreb

All rights reserved
including the right of reproduction
in whole or in part in any form

Published by Prentice Hall Trade Division
A Division of Simon & Schuster Inc.
15 Columbus Circle
New York, NY 10023

ISBN 0-13-332677-2
ISSN 1041-8687

Manufactured in the United States of America

*Although every effort was made to ensure the accuracy
of price information appearing in this book,
it should be kept in mind that prices
can and do fluctuate in the course of time.*

CONTENTS

PART TWO

MEXICO

PART THREE

THE CARIBBEAN, THE BAHAMAS, AND BERMUDA

MAPS

IN APPRECIATION

I am deeply grateful to all the talented, dedicated people who worked hard and long to make this book informative, accurate, and fun to use.

First and foremost, a great big "thank you" goes to the various contributing editors, who scouted the Western Hemisphere for the best honeymoon hideaways and romantic restaurants. All are experienced travel writers, and I think you'll find it interesting to get to know a bit about them.

Naomi Black (New England Country Inns, Bonaire, Curaçao, St. Martin) frequently writes for *Modern Bride* magazine and is the author of several travel books.

Robin D. Hill (Florida) has written both the Florida and Alabama vacation guides for the states' Departments of Tourism, and frequently covers Florida for *Modern Bride* and other national magazines.

Barbara A. Koeth (Martinique, Guadeloupe) is a freelance writer and photographer who specializes in writing about off-the-beaten-track adventures.

Marty Wentzel (Oahu, Kauai restaurants) calls Honolulu her home. She often writes for *Modern Bride, Discover Hawaii, Aloha Magazine,* and *Pleasant Hawaii,* and covers Hawaii's delicious culinary scene for *RSVP* magazine.

I would also like to thank the various writers who researched the original edition of this book: Yvette Cardoza and Bill Hirsch (Cayman Islands), Rachel Jackson Christmas (The Bahamas), Laura Del Rosso (Mexico), Richard Gehr (New York City), Robert F. Miller (Puerto Rico), and Elizabeth Tener (Barbados).

Many, many thanks (plus *mille grâces* and *muchas gracías* go to all the helpful, hard-working people at the various tourist boards and visitors bureaus for the assistance they have extended. I owe a special debt of gratitude to Cele Goldsmith Lalli, Editor in Chief, and Howard Friedberg, Publisher, at *Modern Bride* magazine, for encouraging me to produce the original edition of this book. On a personal note, I could not have accomplished any of this without the support of my editor, Marilyn Wood, and the rest of the Travel Team at Simon & Schuster/Prentice Hall.

Finally, I owe special recognition to my family and friends for the patience and understanding they tendered during my work on this book, which caused me to miss many dinner dates and special events. Kitty Hawk deserves an extra tidbit for providing comic relief. And, most of all, I'd like to thank my best friend, Steen Hansen, for sharing the spirit of romance and adventure

To my parents—the original romantics.

AN INVITATION TO READERS

This guide to honeymoons is my best effort to help you plan that special trip. If you find an establishment that's geared for romance and is not included in this book, I'd like to hear about it, so it may be added to the next edition. If, on the other hand, you find a restaurant, hotel, or attraction that is *not* up to my description (chefs *do* change and hotels *do* deteriorate), please write me about that as well. Any additional honeymoon tips you may come up with will also be appreciated. And if you find this guide to be especially helpful, do drop me a line about *that*. Write to me at Prentice Hall Travel, 15 Columbus Circle, New York, NY 10023.

A DISCLAIMER

Although every effort was made to ensure the accuracy of the prices and travel information appearing in this book, it should be kept in mind that prices can and do fluctuate in the course of time, and that information does change under the impact of the varied and volatile factors that affect the travel industry, including natural disasters—hurricanes, earthquakes, and the like.

FROMMER'S HONEYMOON DESTINATIONS

Ever since Adam and Eve, lovers have tried to return to the Garden of Eden. For most couples, the closest they'll ever come is their honeymoon.

Honeymoons rank among the oldest of human rituals. The word "honeymoon" itself is derived from a custom of the early Anglo-Saxons, who celebrated weddings by drinking mead (fermented honey) for the period of time between full moons—about 30 days.

Although the word is an ancient one, honeymoons themselves are a fairly recent invention. At first only the rich and famous could afford them. In one of the first honeymoons to gain widespread attention, Napoleon's younger brother, Jerome, came to America and took his bride, Betsy Patterson, to Niagara Falls in the early 1800s. The modern honeymoon was born.

Not so long ago, marriages were arranged, and honeymoons were important getting-acquainted periods. Today, even after the "sexual revolution," 98% of all newlyweds take honeymoons to symbolize a deeper commitment to each other for a variety of reasons.

In this book, we've taken the point of view of unabashed romantics. We've focused on places and activities that most stir the heartbeats of honeymooners. It's not meant to be the most complete guidebook on the market. It doesn't list every historic old fort or musty museum. But what the book does have is detailed information about the most popular honeymoon destinations in the United States, Mexico, and the Caribbean. For each destination area, we'll discuss:

ROMANTIC INTERLUDES

What are the most sensuous—and fun—pastimes for couples in love? We'll give you the inside scoop on secluded beaches prime for picnics-for-two, sunset perches, idyllic day-cruises . . . as well as rollicking amusement parks, active volcanoes, free concerts, and hot-air-balloon rides. You'll notice that throughout this book, we use "vacation" as a synonym for "honeymoon"—we believe this trip should be fun!

HONEYMOON HOTELS AND HIDEAWAYS

Your choice of accommodations matters more on your honeymoon than on any other trip you'll ever take. You will want to spend every moment in memorable romantic surroundings. In recognition of the fact that every couple harbors different boudoir fantasies, we've included a wide range of where-to-stay options. Sexy little love nests and high-rise pleasure palaces. Thatch-roofed hales and porticoed great houses in the tropics. And because the most romantic room of all is one you can afford, we've also sought out the most attractive budget properties.

ROMANTIC RESTAURANTS

Because there comes a time when you can't live on love alone, we'll point out some of the most delectable dining possibilities. Once again, our selections are skewed toward the eclectic. You'll find high-toned meccas of classic cuisine as well as Formica lunch counters that serve the best slice of Neapolitan pizza in town. Whatever you crave, you'll surely find something to satisfy your appetite.

PRACTICAL FACTS

In addition, since even starry-eyed lovers need to know what plane to catch and what travel documents they need, there's a full section covering everything from telephone area codes to the rainy seasons.

Some Important Topics

Prices: Every effort has been made to assure that all price information was accurate at the time the book went to press. Unfortunately, it is a fact of life that rates constantly change—almost always in an upward direction. Consult your travel agent or the establishment for the most up-to-date information.

Hotel Rates: Whenever possible, we have listed the honeymoon package rate. However, many hotels also have other packages (tennis, diving, sailing), as well as longer or shorter stays that couples might find attractive. In addition, hotels frequently change the components of their honeymoon packages. Ask your travel agent for details.

Restaurants: Write-ups either list typical prices of menu items, or else give an approximate cost for a complete dinner for two people. In the latter case, prices are based on a couple ordering a moderately priced appetizer, entrée, dessert, and coffee. Cost of drinks is not included.

Honeymoon Hotline: We'd like to get feedback from our readers. Your comments and suggestions about this book will be invaluable in planning future volumes. Also, we'd appreciate receiving your own personal reviews of the hotels and restaurants we've covered—as well as letting us know about any new romantic hideaways you've found. Future honeymooners will thank you for sharing your joy. Send your responses to: Risa Weinreb, c/o Frommer Books, Prentice Hall Travel, 15 Columbus Circle, New York, NY 10023.

A popular wedding toast goes: "May you enjoy your work as much as your vacations; and may you love each other always with loyalty, trust, and joy." It is our hope that you begin fulfilling all the promise of your futures together on your honeymoon.

PLANNING YOUR HONEYMOON

1. HONEYMOON CHECKLIST
2. CHOOSING YOUR DESTINATION
3. ALL ABOUT TRAVEL AGENTS
4. A GLOSSARY OF TRAVEL TERMS

Making a schedule. Setting the date. Choosing the wedding dress. Deciding where to have the reception. These count among your most important wedding arrangements. Now another series of crucial decisions await—planning your honeymoon. Just as you have a schedule for mailing your invitations and finalizing the seating plan, you need a calendar for making your honeymoon arrangements.

1. Honeymoon Checklist

By planning your trip ahead, you can make sure you'll select the honeymoon destination that's right for you; get the most convenient airline reservations at the cheapest price; and reserve the most romantic room at your favorite resort. Here's a checklist:

6 to 12 Months Beforehand
☐ Start discussing what sort of honeymoon destination you want—a beach, the country, the ski slopes? What kind of ambience—elegant, casual?
☐ Ask family and friends about their recommendations, not only for destinations, but also about travel agents.
☐ Get travel brochures from tourist boards, hotels, and your travel agent.

4 to 6 Months Beforehand
☐ Make your airline, hotel, and car rental reservations. (Note: Do this even further in advance if you will be traveling during peak season, such as the Christmas

holidays in the Caribbean.) Send any deposits necessary.
□ Get passports and/or visas, if needed.

2 to 4 Months Beforehand
□ Check that you have received all your confirmations.
□ Consider your luggage requirements and purchase any new pieces needed.
□ Analyze your wardrobe. Shop for clothes for your honeymoon.
□ Check that the camera you intend to take is in good working order.

1 Month Beforehand
□ Reconfirm all your arrangements through your travel agent.
□ If you will be driving your own car to your destination, take it in to the service station for a complete mechanical check-up.

1 to 2 Weeks Beforehand
□ Reconfirm all your arrangements through your travel agent.
□ Pack everything except the clothes and toiletries you will need for the coming week. Is everything clean, ironed, and repaired?
□ Purchase traveler's checks.
□ Arrange to stop the mail delivery, newspaper, etc., while you are away.

1 to 2 Days Beforehand
□ Reconfirm all your arrangements through your travel agent.
□ Pack your remaining items.
□ Be sure you have your passports, airline tickets, traveler's checks, hotel confirmation, rental car confirmation, credit cards.
□ Bon voyage!

---

2. Choosing Your Destination

"Where should we go on our honeymoon?" That's probably the question that's uppermost in your mind (and, incidentally, it's the question couples most frequently ask me when they find out that I'm a travel writer). The answer is, "That depends."

And what it depends on is what you both like to do. What do you want from your honeymoon? Relaxation? Adventure? New scenery? Every newlywed couple has a unique honeymoon style. The knack of creating a perfect honeymoon (or a perfect vacation in the years to come) comes from planning a trip around your interests. Start by discussing what each of you wants from the trip. Here are some main areas to consider:

SETTING
What kind of setting do you want? Shall it be a cosmopolitan whirl of theater, museums, and shopping in a big city—or a beachy retreat on a tropical isle with only the coconut palms for company? A secluded cabin by a mountain lake—or a self-contained resort with tennis courts, a golf course, gourmet restaurants, and discos right on the property? Talk about all your interests and desires. If you have different hobbies, don't despair. Some locations can satisfy both your inclinations. There are big cities within an hour's drive of the ski slopes, and Caribbean islands with both duty-free shopping and world-class scuba-diving, places that offer both game-fishing

and gambling, and country villages where quaint stores sell museum-quality furniture from around the world. With a little research, you can uncover the locale that's right for you both.

WHEN TO GO

When are you going? If you're heading to a beach resort, you want sunshine. At the ski slopes, you need snow. What places offer peak conditions during the time you'll be on your honeymoon? Some resort areas have "seasons," meaning that the weather varies at different times of the year. Sometimes the seasonality is obvious: Vermont in the summer is quite different from Vermont in the winter. Other times, variations are subtle: California weather along the coast tends to be sunniest in autumn; diving conditions in the Caribbean are usually clearest from April to June. Seasonality might have nothing to do with the weather, but rather with special events and cultural activities. New York's music, dance, and theater scene is liveliest in winter; Barbados hosts its celebrated "Crop Over" festival in August. In the introduction to all the areas covered by this book, we've given an accurate assessment of the annual weather, so read carefully before you go.

Don't write off a place just because it's the so-called "off" season. Some destinations—particularly in the U.S. Sunbelt, Hawaii, Mexico, and the Caribbean —have virtually the same weather all year. In the Caribbean, for example, many islands have only a 5° temperature difference between the winter and the summer. By going during the low season, you can save up to 50% on airline and hotel prices over the high season. Another advantage: In the low season, you'll find fewer crowds on beaches, in stores, and in restaurants.

THE TIME FACTOR

How much time do you have? Your schedule strongly influences your honeymoon choice. If you have only a week, you should not spend a full day traveling each way, or head to a far-away destination where you'll experience a lot of jet lag. The time factor can also determine how you travel—for example, if your honeymoon locale can be reached easily either by car or plane. Flying will usually save you time; driving will save you money. Which works best for you?

THE COST

How much can you afford? Enter Reality. Exactly how much money do you want to spend on your honeymoon? This is a very personal decision—no two couples earning, let's say, $40,000 a year are going to spend their money the same way. Some will go all out on a honeymoon splurge. Others, saving to buy a house, a car, or furniture will opt for a more modest expenditure. It's up to you, as a couple, to set priorities. It might be interesting for you to know, however, how much a "typical" honeymoon might cost. According to the latest figures from *Modern Bride* magazine, the average couple spent $1,240 on a honeymoon within the continental United States; $2,784 on a trip outside (which would also include Hawaii and the U.S. Virgin Islands).

Obviously, how much you're willing to allocate will determine which honeymoon destinations you can realistically consider. What is not so obvious is that on vacation there are different ways to spend money. Some couples will devote a large chunk of their budget to flying to an exotic location, then stay in cheap digs once they get there. Others want to stay in the best hotel in town—even if the "town" in question is only a 60-mile drive from where they grew up. What do you two want to do?

Often, honeymoon budgeting is the first time a couple has to sit down and discuss their financial facts of life. This can cause some strains and tensions in your relationship. To help avoid the rough spots, see the section on "Coping with Honeymoon Stress."

Making a Budget

Let's get down to the nitty-gritty here. You've scribbled out all the dollar figures on paper and have a good idea how much you can spend on your trip. Can you afford that dream honeymoon? Use the chart below to calculate approximate expenses.

Want to make your money go even further? Here are some tried-and-true tips for cutting costs.

1. Travel during the off-season, if possible. Air fares and hotel rates can be up to 50% cheaper. See the individual destination chapters in this book for details about when each area offers its lowest rates.
2. Book your airline tickets in advance. Special discount fares can save you over 80% on many routes. Many airlines only make 10% to 15% of their seats available at the lowest fare; by booking early, you have a better chance of getting these low rates. Ask your travel agent or check in your local newspaper for airline ads promoting bargain rates.
3. To save some money on meals, have some picnic lunches with wine and cheese. Who ever said economizing can't be romantic?

3. All About Travel Agents

Whether you know exactly where you want to go—or if you're still casting about for helpful suggestions—a travel agent can help you plan and arrange all the honeymoon details. Important to know: In most cases, using a travel agent is free. Agents earn money through commissions on airline tickets, car rentals, and hotel reservations. All you might have to pay for would be special services, such as long-distance telephone calls. Ask the travel agent in advance.

A good travel agent will be up-to-date on the latest vacation information: air fares, hotels, special packages. In addition, because most of them have computer hook-ups with airlines, hotels, and rental car agencies, they can make reservations quickly and easily. Travel agents can not only book flights and hotels; they can also reserve theater tickets and sightseeing tours, and advise you about the climate and customs of a country. In brief, they are your personal travel advisers.

Remember to stay open to suggestions. An agent can often recommend a destination you had not thought of but which might be just right for your honeymoon.

How can you find a good travel agent? Your best bet is to ask family and friends for recommendations. Also, look for someone who is a member of ASTA (American Society of Travel Agents) or is a CTC (Certified Travel Counselor). In particular, the CTC designation helps assure expertise. To qualify, an agent must have been in the business for at least five years, and must have passed an eighteen-month course.

4. A Glossary of Travel Terms

"Super APEX" is not Clark Kent's alter ego, and a MAP is not something you buy from Rand McNally. Like any other business, travel uses trade lingo, slang, and abbreviations. Here's a rundown of some of the most common terms you'll encounter when talking with your travel agent or reading through brochures. Many are also used in this book. If you have any specific questions, ask your travel agent or contact the program operator directly

EXPENSES

Transportation
Main transportation
(air, ship, car): $ _____

Airport transfers: $ _____

Gas/tolls/parking: $ _____

Rental car: $ _____

Taxis: $ _____

              TOTAL TRANSPORTATION: $ _____

Accommodations
Room rate: $ _____

Tips: $ _____

Misc. (laundry, taxes, etc.): $ _____

              TOTAL ACCOMMODATIONS: $ _____

Food (per couple)
Breakfast
$ _____ per day × _____ days $ _____

Lunch
$ _____ per day × _____ days $ _____

Dinner
$ _____ per day × _____ days $ _____

              TOTAL FOOD: $ _____

Amusements and Entertainment
Sports equipment/fees $ _____

Movies/theater/concerts $ _____

Admission fees $ _____

Nighclubs/discos $ _____

              TOTAL ENTERTAINMENT: $ _____

Shopping and Gifts
              TOTAL SHOPPING: $ _____

Miscellaneous
              TOTAL MISCELLANEOUS: $ _____

              TOTAL EXPENSES: $ _____

Airlines

Nonstop flight: The plane flies from one place to another with "no stops."

Direct flight: The plane will stop en route to pick up additional passengers, but you do not need to change planes to reach your final destination.

Connecting flight: You will need to change planes in order to get where you want to go.

Hotels

Concierge desk: A special-service desk at many fine hotels, staffed by an employee who can help make airline and restaurant reservations, arrange sightseeing excursions, and perform other personal services.

Double-occupancy rate: Price per person, based on two people sharing a room.

Double-room rate: Price per room, based on two people sharing the room.

Guaranteed late arrival: In most cases, a hotel will hold a room only until 6 p.m. To assure your room will be waiting no matter what time you arrive, you can arrange a guaranteed late arrival. It requires that you give a credit card number. If you fail to arrive that night, the room cost will still be charged to your credit card.

Honeymoon packages: Plans that offer accommodations—plus such goodies as air transportation, car rental, or sightseeing jaunts—in one neat "package." Often, the programs offer extremely good value, giving you all the honeymoon features you want at a comparatively inexpensive price. As with any present, however, you want to make sure this package gives you something of real value—not mere gift wrapping.

When you glance through this book, you'll see that honeymoon packages vary widely. In general, you'll get one of the best rooms in the house (with king-size bed and a great view) and a welcoming gift (such as a fruit basket or bottle of champagne). Other features run the full gamut: from sunset cocktail cruises to scuba-diving lessons. Usually, the room rate offers you significant savings over the "rack" rate (the standard price for the accommodations). When evaluating different honeymoon packages, try to put a dollar value on all those bonus items you're getting. How much do those flowers cost? The tennis court fee? Even more important—will you take advantage of all the opportunities?

Oceanfront: Means that the room directly overlooks the water.

Oceanview: While you will have some view of the water, the room won't completely front it.

Service charges: In some locales, a fixed percentage (usually 10% to 15%) is added to hotel and/or meal bills. This eliminates the need for tipping.

Taxes: Federal and local taxes can also be levied against hotel and restaurant bills.

Meals

EP (European Plan): No meals are included in your room rate.

CP (Continental Plan): Room rate includes a continental breakfast, generally bread or croissants, jam, and coffee or tea.

BP (Bermuda Plan): Named for the country where it was first popularized, this option includes a full breakfast: juice, eggs, bread, coffee, tea, etc.

MAP (Modified American Plan): Includes breakfast and either lunch or dinner. Also known as half-board or half-pension.

AP (American Plan): Includes breakfast, lunch, and dinner daily. Also known as full-board or full-pension.

PREPARING TO GO AWAY

1. CHOOSING YOUR ACCOMMODATIONS
2. GETTING THERE
3. THE PRACTICALITIES
4. SOME SPECIAL TIPS FOR HONEYMOONERS

Where you stay is more important on your honeymoon than on any other trip. After all, many of you have been planning this vacation since you were five years old—all you needed was the right roommate. Now that you've found him or her, you want to share each moment together in the most romantic surroundings possible.

1. Choosing Your Accommodations

The perfect honeymoon hideaway—where can it be found? Here once again we get into personal preferences—the "right" hotel is the one that suits both of you. Before making your room reservations, you should consider what kind of accommodations you would prefer. High-rise hotel? Cozy little love nest? Here are some of your options.

HOTELS
Skyscrapers with mirrored windows, plant-filled atriums, and clear-glass elevators that ascend, like bubbles, to distant penthouses. Gargoyled grand hotels where red carpets cascade down the entrance stairs. Hotels certainly come in all shapes and sizes. What they usually have in common is a deluxe atmosphere emphasizing personal service in all its manifestations: porters, a concierge, bellhops, room service. In addition, you'll generally find many amenities right in-house: boutiques, rental car offices, beauty salons, laundry services. Usually, they are located in cities.

SELF-CONTAINED RESORTS
Often these are hotels as well, but they can also be low-rise villas, condos, or cottages. What differentiates them from just plain hotels? The fact that everything necessary for human survival—and even a honeymoon's survival—is located right on the property. A multiplicity of tennis courts, golf courses, swimming pools with waterfalls and swim-up bars, discos, enough restaurants that you need never dine in

the same one twice even if you stay there for a week—that's what you'll find at these resorts, which are actually complete worlds unto themselves.

MOTELS

At motels or motor lodges, you can drive up and park your car right outside your door. Convenience and economy are the usual bywords here.

CONDOMINIUMS AND VILLAS

Enjoy all the comforts of a home—while away on your honeymoon. Condos and villas have become an increasingly popular option for couples because they combine the privacy and spaciousness of a residence (bedroom, bathroom, kitchen, living and dining areas) with all the services of a hotel—front desk, porters, daily maid service, and sports facilities such as tennis courts and swimming pools. In particular, the kitchen facilities come in handy.

INNS

These can range from historic old lodgings where George Washington slept to modern structures that bear a striking physical (if not semantic) resemblance to a hotel. For the purposes of this book, we'll consider an inn a small hotel that also has a dining room that serves meals to the public.

BED-AND-BREAKFASTS

Usually, "B&Bs" are private residences that take in paying guests, offering both a bedroom and breakfast (either full or continental). Settings can range from gingerbread-trimmed Victorian mansions to an extra bedroom in a city apartment. Be aware that not all B&B accommodations offer a private bath—sometimes you'll have to share the one down the hall.

ACCOMMODATIONS CHECKLIST

No matter what type of accommodations you prefer, keep the following points in mind when deciding where to stay.

1. **Location:** What is it near—sightseeing, shopping, the beach? Although centrally located properties are convenient, they usually charge higher rates.
2. **Ground transportation:** How do you get from the airport to the hotel? How much will it cost you? Does the hotel offer guests free transfers? How long will the journey take?
3. **Amenities:** Does the property have the facilities you want (such as tennis courts, swimming pools, restaurants, a health spa)? How good are the facilities? Are the tennis courts lit for night play? What brand of exercise equipment is in the gym? How much will it cost you to use the facilities?
4. **Rooms:** What kind of view does the room have? Make sure you reserve a room with a double, queen-, or king-size bed.
5. **Meals:** Does the room rate include any meals? Which ones? Hotel meal plans generally will save you money, but you miss out on the fun of trying out new places.
6. **Confirmation:** Make sure you get a written confirmation for your room, specifying all the details: honeymoon package, dates, view, even the king-size bed.
7. **Guaranteed late arrival:** As mentioned earlier, most hotels will hold rooms only until 6 p.m. It's a good idea to guarantee late arrival using your credit card; especially if you encounter unforeseen travel delays, you want that room ready!

2. Getting There

BY AIR
Here's a guide to help you plan your travel by air.

Making Reservations
The easiest way to make airline reservations is through a travel agent. Most agents have on-line computer hook-ups to the airlines, and so have instant access to information about fares and seat availability. Travel agents are also up-to-date on rate information, and can fully explain any restrictions, requirements, or cancellation penalties. Once again, using a travel agent is generally free.

If you want to do it yourself, you can get flight information from the Official Airline Guide (OAG), a book available at many libraries. The OAG lists all domestic and international flights with their airport departure and arrival times. Many airlines in the United States have toll-free "800" numbers you can call for reservations and information. To get the number, call 800/555-1212. In order to find out which airlines fly to which cities or countries, you can call the area tourist board.

Fares
First the good news: It probably costs less to reach your preferred destination than ever before. Now the bad news: Air fares and airline routes change at such a dizzying rate, even travel agents and airline reservations agents have trouble keeping up with the latest events. Your best bet for assuring that you get the low-down on low fares: Skim the daily newspapers for advertisements about new promotions and ask your travel agent for details about requirements and restrictions.

In general, rates will vary depending on whether you fly first class or economy/coach, and how far in advance you purchase your tickets. APEX (Advance Purchase Excursion) fares are usually the cheapest. As the name implies, you must buy your tickets a specified number of days in advance. Other restrictions often apply, such as staying a minimum number of days, staying over a weekend, etc. In addition, you might be liable for a penalty if you change or cancel your plans.

Air fares are usually most expensive during high ("peak") season, especially during holiday periods. Low ("off") season rates can often be up to 50% lower. In "shoulder" seasons (airline parlance for those periods in between high and low seasons), air fares will be somewhere in the middle. Traveling during the week also affects air fares. It usually costs less to fly to a resort destination Monday through Thursday than on weekends. (It's often the opposite when you're flying to major cities that are popular business destinations: It's cheaper on the weekends.) In addition, evening or overnight ("red-eye") flights are generally the cheapest of all.

Airline Check-in
Plan to arrive at the airport at least an hour in advance of departure time for domestic flights, two hours in advance for international flights. This gives you plenty of time to check in your luggage and make seat selections. A time-saving tip: Get your boarding passes in advance if possible. You can get them through your travel agent for flights on most of the major airlines. This is a big advantage, because if a flight is overbooked, passengers without boarding passes get bumped first.

Baggage
According to current airline regulations, each person is usually permitted to check in two pieces of luggage weighing a total of 44 pounds. If your baggage weighs

more, you may have to pay a penalty. Tag each bag you check with your name and home phone number. (Many police officers advise against including your home address, which could tip off burglars. You can put your complete address inside the suitcase.) For an added safety precaution, lock each bag. When you hand over your baggage, make sure the ticket on each piece corresponds with your flight number and final destination. Also verify that you have a claim ticket for each bag.

The smartest travel tip we can give you: Always, always take essentials with you in a carry-on bag. (For honeymooners, essentials mean not only toiletries, medications, and eyeglasses, but also bathing suits and contraceptives.) Carry-on baggage must fit securely underneath the seat or in the overhead compartment. Each airline has different size requirements, so check with your travel agent in advance. Often you can carry on hanging garment bags, which can either be hung in airplane closets or placed in the overhead compartments.

Best of all, follow the advice of frequent fliers. Don't check in any baggage at all—just take a carry-on bag and hanging garment bag. If you pack the right clothes, you should be able to travel for a month—or more.

TRAVEL BY CAR

Obviously, driving is not an option if you live in Des Moines and will be honeymooning in the Cayman Islands. But it's something to consider if your destination is within 1,000 miles of home. When you drive, getting there is half the fun. On the way to your final destination, you can explore charming old towns, make detours to historic houses, and stop for picnics by secluded waterfalls.

Your Own Car Versus a Rental Car

If you're not going too far, and if your own vehicle is in good shape, you'll probably want to save money and use your own car. Important: Take your car in for a complete mechanical check-up about a month before the wedding. The last last-minute worry you want is a balky transmission or other mishap. If you'll be driving long distances, consider renting a car. Not only does this save wear-and-tear on your own vehicle, but you can have a bit of fun and splurge on a luxury or sports model, such as a convertible.

If you'll be flying to your honeymoon destination, ask your travel agent whether or not you should rent a car. It's a virtual necessity in many vacation areas. Many airlines and hotels often have special fly/drive or fly/stay rates that give you extremely low rates for a rental vehicle. Even if you plan on spending most of your honeymoon at your resort hotel, you might want to rent a car for a day. It's the best way to get acquainted with a new area.

Most rental car companies will ask for a major credit card. Renting a car without one demands considerable advance planning. You'll have to undergo a credit check and furnish bank references, proof of employment, and other financial disclosures. You'll also have to pay the full rental amount in advance, plus an additional deposit that will be refunded when you return the car.

Important: Most rental car companies require you to be at least 21 years of age to rent a car—and even 25, under certain circumstances. You must have a valid driver's license. Call the rental car company's toll-free 800 number if you have any questions.

Here's a rundown of factors that influence rental car rates.

Make, size, model: The bigger the car and the more loaded with features, the more it will cost. You'll usually find the cheapest rate on a subcompact.

Equipment: Features such as air conditioning and automatic transmission cost extra in some destinations. If you want either of these options, make sure your request is noted on your reservation.

Locale: It simply costs more to rent a car in some places.

Drop-off charge: If you rent a car in one state or city, and return it in another, you may have to pay a fee. This can be as much as $75.

Length of rental: Because of special deals, it sometimes costs less to rent a car for a week than for five days; weekday rentals can run less than those on weekends. Ask your travel agent for details.

Peak seasons: Just as with airline seats, it costs more to rent a car during the high season.

Unlimited mileage versus mileage charge: With unlimited mileage, you can drive as far as you like without paying a per-mile fee. Mileage charges generally run anywhere from 10 to 30 cents per mile, which really adds up if you intend to drive far.

Collision damage waiver: You'll hear varying viewpoints about its necessity. The cost is usually less than $10 per day. More important, you may already be covered if you rent a car using a major credit card such as American Express; check in advance with your credit card company. In general, we recommend coverage if you'll be traveling long distances in the United States; it is essential when driving in foreign countries such as Mexico.

Corporate discounts: Many large companies receive corporate discounts from rental car companies. Often, employees can benefit from these discounts even if they are using the car for vacation travel. Ask your company travel representative for details.

3. The Practicalities

HOW TO GET A PASSPORT

You must apply in person at one of the 13 passport agencies in the United States (see addresses below), the county clerk's office, or a major post office. Bring with you:

1. The application, available at major post offices.
2. Two photos taken within the past six months.
3. An official birth certificate with a raised seal, which you can obtain from the Department of Health in the area where you were born. Allow plenty of time; it often takes four to six weeks to obtain the birth certificate.

The passport application fee is $42. It generally takes three weeks to process, but can sometimes take longer.

Passport Renewals

Save time by renewing your passport by mail. You can do so if your current passport was issued within the last 12 years, and it was issued after your sixteenth birthday. You can obtain the proper forms at one of the passport offices or a major post office; you will also need two new photos. Renewal fee is $35; it takes about three weeks to receive the new passport.

Two good services to know about are **Passport Plus,** 677 Fifth Ave., New York, NY 10022 (tel. 212/759-5540, or toll free 800/367-1818), and **Travel Agenda, Inc.,** 119 West 57th St., New York, NY 10019 (tel. 212/265-7887). They operate nationwide and can help you obtain all travel documents, from passports to visas. Fees vary: A passport renewal runs from $35 (plus the $35 renewal fee) for one-week service, to $150 for emergency delivery. Call them for complete details.

A Word to the Bride

If you already have a passport under your maiden name, it will remain valid for your honeymoon. If your airline tickets are in your married name, bring a copy of your marriage certificate with you. (Immigration officials check whether the name on the passport and on the airline ticket are the same.) If you will be using your husband's last name after marriage, you can have your passport amended by mail. This service is free.

Passport Offices

The following are the locations and phone numbers for passport agencies in the United States. Outside of these areas, main post offices will be able to process applications.

Boston: John F. Kennedy Building, Room E-123, Government Center, Boston, MA 02203 (tel. 617/565-6990).

Chicago: Kluczynski Federal Building, 230 S. Dearborn St., Suite 380, Chicago, IL 60604 (tel. 312/353-7155).

Honolulu: New Federal Building, Room C-106, 300 Ala Moana Blvd., P.O. Box 50185, Honolulu, HI 96850 (tel. 808/541-1919).

Houston: One Allen Center, 500 Dallas St., Houston, TX 77002 (tel. 713/653-3160).

Los Angeles: 11000 Wilshire Blvd., Room 13100, Los Angeles, CA 90024 (tel. 213/209-7070).

Miami: Federal Office Building, 51 S.W. First Ave., 16th Floor, Miami, FL 33130 (tel. 305/536-4681).

New Orleans: 701 Loyola Ave., Room T12005, New Orleans, LA 70113 (tel. 504/589-6161).

New York: 630 Fifth Ave., Room 270, New York, NY 10111 (tel. 212/541-7700).

Philadelphia: 600 Arch St., Room 4426, Philadelphia, PA 19106 (tel. 215/597-7482).

San Francisco: 525 Market St., Suite 200, San Francisco, CA 94105 (tel. 415/974-7972).

Seattle: Federal Building, 915 Second Ave., Room 992, Seattle, WA 98174 (tel. 206/442-7941).

Stamford: One Landmark Square, Broad and Atlantic Streets, Stamford, CT 06901 (tel. 203/325-4401).

Washington, D.C. (main office): 1425 K Street NW, Washington, DC 20524 (tel. 202/647-0518).

TIPS ABOUT TIPPING

Le pour-boire. La propina. Although the amount and the nature of the acknowledgment may vary in different countries, it is customary to reward excellent service. Here are some guidelines for how much and who to tip in the United States. Customs vary in different countries; see the "Practical Facts" section for each area.

Transportation

Taxi: 15% to 20% of the fare; plus 50 cents to $1 per suitcase.
Hotel limousine driver: 10% to 15% of the fare. If the service is complimentary, 50 cents to $1 per bag.
Private limousine: 10% to 15% of the fare.
Train: Sleeping-car attendants, $1 per day; dining-car waiter, 15% of the bill.

Hotels

Bellhops: 50¢ to $1 per bag.
Doorman: 50¢ to $1 for getting a cab.
Parking attendant: 50¢ to $1.
Maid: $1 per day.

Restaurants

Waiter: 15% to 20% of bill.

Wine steward: 5% of wine cost.
Maître d': $1 to $10, depending on service rendered.

Miscellaneous
Beach or pool attendant: $1 per couple per day.
Sightseeing guide (group tour): $2 per couple.

In several foreign countries and in some U.S. hotels, resorts, and restaurants, a service charge of 10% to 15% is automatically added to bills. Additional tipping is not necessary. If you have any queries, ask in advance.

HANDLING FOREIGN CURRENCY
Whether you'll be looking after pounds or pesos, the following pointers will help smooth the way when dealing with foreign currencies:

□ Exchange rates for the U.S. dollar can fluctuate daily. You'll usually get the best rate of exchange at a national bank; rates tend to be less favorable at hotels, restaurants, and shops.

□ Never change money on the street. Fast-talking con artists with nimble fingers often give unwary tourists the wrong change—or even wrap a single bill of foreign currency around a wad of cardboard.

□ Try to change money only as you need it. You lose money every time you convert currency.

□ Very useful: a small pocket calculator or currency converter. It's the fast, accurate way to keep track of how much something costs in dollars.

MAKING PHONE CALLS FROM ABROAD
Americans enjoy some of the lowest telephone rates in the world. As a consequence, it often costs far more than you would expect to call home from a foreign country. In addition to the higher phone rates, many hotels outside the United States add a substantial surcharge to the cost of the call—sometimes as much as 100% to 300%. To avoid excessive telephone charges:

1. Always ask the hotel about telephone surcharges before you place a call.
2. If dialing from your hotel, call your party and ask them to call you back. The call costs less if placed from the United States. You can reimburse the person for the cost when you return home.
3. If you can, place your call from a pay phone at a telephone or post office. These offices do not levy surcharges.
4. Charging your call to an international calling card can also save you money. You can get these cards free from your local telephone company.
5. Find out if your hotel participates in American Telephone and Telegraph's TELEPLAN. Under this program, participating hotel chains, such as Hilton International and Marriott, agree to add only a reasonable surcharge for calls. To find out if your hotel is a member of TELEPLAN, call toll free 800/874-4000.

SHOPPING TIPS
A word hovering on many honeymooners' lips is "bargains." The Caribbean islands are especially well known for offering savings on many luxury items. Depending on which island you visit, you might encounter one of the following shopping opportunities. "Duty-free" shopping means that the country does not tax imported goods (or taxes them at a very low rate). "In-bond" shopping is similar in principle, in that no duties are levied on imports. It operates slightly differently, though, since it treats the imported goods as if they never entered the country. Usually, the in-bond merchandise you buy will be delivered to your airplane or cruise ship when you depart; you will not be able to take it with you directly from the store.

Meanwhile, some countries will not tax imports from their mother countries, although they will levy duties on merchandise from other nations. This means that you can usually find good values on English goods on British islands, French goods on islands such as Martinique and Guadeloupe, etc. You might want to consult *A Shopper's Guide to the Caribbean* for further details and tips (published by Prentice Hall Press, New York).

You'll find good shopping values not only in the duty-free ports of the Caribbean, but also in diamond merchants' stalls along 47th Street in Manhattan, the factory outlets of the Poconos, even on the racks of swank Beverly Hills boutiques during clearance sales. Another potential source of bargains: airport duty-free stores. Wherever you shop, here are some pointers for assuring that what you buy is a really good value.

1. **Have shopping priorities.** Be firm with yourselves. Plan in advance exactly what items you most want—and concentrate your search on them.
2. **Comparison shop in advance.** This is a corollary of no. 1 above. Before your honeymoon journey, check the price range of items you want in stores back home. That way, when you get to the alleged bargain center of the universe, you'll know exactly how much of a good value you're actually getting.
3. **Research specific items.** If you're looking to fill in your china or crystal pattern, know that not all stores carrying famous lines (such as Wedgwood and Waterford) carry all patterns. To find out which store carries the pattern you want, contact the local tourist board.
4. **Beware of fakes.** Counterfeits have become big business worldwide. Check merchandise carefully. Be on the lookout for shoddy workmanship. Items like cameras or watches should carry serial numbers.
5. **Shop around.** Be aware that just because one store offers the best price on jewelry, it isn't necessarily the bargain leader on liquor.
6. **Haggle.** In many places, prices are negotiable.
7. **Ask about warranties and service.** You can't always get them at duty-free or discount outlets—something to consider.
8. **Always buy it because you like it, not because it's a bargain.** That way, it will continue to give you pleasure in years to come.

CLEARING U.S. CUSTOMS

If you honeymoon abroad, you will have to clear U.S. Customs when you return. By knowing the basic rules and regulations, you'll be able to pass through smoothly.

1. All returning Americans must fill out a Customs form that you'll receive on your return flight or cruise ship. For convenience, you can also get the declaration form from your travel agent before you leave and fill it in as you make purchases.
2. From most countries, you are permitted to return with $400 worth of goods per person duty free. You can make a simple oral declaration to the Customs inspector; you do not need to enumerate your purchases. Your $400 allowance is based on the retail value of the articles; the goods must be for your personal use. Exceptions: From the U.S. Virgin Islands, your duty-free allowance is $800 per person. From Puerto Rico, you can bring back an unlimited amount of goods, except for alcohol, for which you must prove that taxes have been paid.
3. Liquor and cigarettes: If you are 21 or older, your exemption includes one liter of alcohol and one carton of cigarettes. If you are returning from the U.S. Virgin Islands, your exemption includes one gallon of alcohol and 1,000 cigarettes.
4. If you buy more, you will have to pay Customs duty. You'll be charged a flat

rate of 10% (5% if you are returning from the U.S. Virgin Islands) on the first $1,000 worth of purchases over the exemption. You will need to make a written declaration—a complete list of everything you've bought and how much you paid.

5. Keep all your sales receipts handy to support your statements. Since Customs officials can ask to inspect your bags, pack all your new purchases together in one suitcase.
6. Customs officers are usually kind to people who exceed the $400 limit, and will try to include the items subject to the highest duty in the exemption.
7. Fruits, flowers, and plants are either prohibited or strictly regulated. Narcotics are forbidden.
8. Over and above your duty-free allowance, you can also send gifts to family and friends—up to $100 per person per day, duty free. You cannot mail perfume, liquor, or tobacco.
9. For complete details about U.S. Customs regulations, send for the free booklet *Know Before You Go,* available from the U.S. Customs Service, 1301 Constitution Ave., NW, Washington, DC 20229.

EATING RIGHT

Any change in your familiar routine—from the excitement of the wedding to traveling halfway around the globe—can cause stomach jitters.

The best way to stay healthy is by eating right. Here are some tips:

1. The general rule is: If you can't peel it, boil it, or cook it, don't eat it.
2. In areas where the water is a problem, drink only purified water. Use the purified water for brushing your teeth; avoid drinks with ice cubes (beer is a good substitute).
3. Do not eat raw vegetables. Peel all fruits. Avoid raw or rare meat (even if you take it that way back home).
4. Avoid dairy products such as milk or cheese.
5. Stay away from buffets, where foods are prepared in advance and are exposed to the air for a long time.

ABOUT DRUGS

In a word—don't. Marijuana, hallucinogens, and other drugs are illegal in every country covered in this book. You can be dealt with very severely for possession of even a small quantity, and being an American citizen won't prevent you from being jailed: You are subject to the laws of the country you are visiting. Forget it.

ABOUT CRIME

Whenever you're traveling in an unfamiliar city or country, stay alert. Be aware of your immediate surroundings. Wear a moneybelt and don't sling your camera or purse over your shoulder; wear the strap diagonally across your body. This will minimize the possibility of your becoming a victim of crime, and possibly marring your honeymoon. Every society has its criminals. It's your responsibility to be aware and be alert even in the most heavily touristed areas.

4. Some Special Tips for Honeymooners

IF YOU'RE REMARRYING . . .

Whether or not either of you has been married previously, much of the advice that appears on the previous pages applies to you. Nonetheless, couples who are remarrying have some special needs.

One factor to consider is the wedding itself. Whatever their previous marital history, couples today are free to plan a wedding that suits their lifestyle and social circle. Often, people who eloped the first time or had a very simple ceremony will choose an all-out party to celebrate their new happiness. Someone who has already been through a splashy reception might prefer a more quiet, intimate event. One idea previously married individuals might want to consider is getting married at their honeymoon locale. The paradisiacal setting—a tropical beach, hidden waterfall, or bounteous garden—seems fitting for the new life that's beginning. Psychologically, it also frees couples from any family pressures or unstated objections regarding the marriage. One bride we talked with who had been married previously told us, "The first time I was married, I went along with a lot of the ideas my parents had about the wedding. This time, the marriage ceremony is what *we* want." For more information about combining your wedding with your honeymoon, see the next section, "Getting Married There."

It should go without saying, but we'll mention it anyway. Do not honeymoon where either of you has been with an ex-spouse. Dr. Maryellyn Duane, a New York City psychologist who specializes in family and marital practice, stresses, "Don't do it the way you did it the first time. Try to do something different and something that speaks to the uniqueness of your own relationship, and get away as much as you can from the memories of 'what was.' " People who have been married before should be prepared for feeling a twinge of sadness even as they plan for their new happiness. It's a natural emotion, and yet a complicated one, that might cause some insecurities if you share it with your new spouse. Instead, therapists recommend talking it out with a close friend, your parents, or a professional.

Someone who is marrying for the first time who is tying the knot with a divorced person will experience some different anxieties. Cele Goldsmith Lalli, editor in chief of *Modern Bride* magazine, says, "It's only natural that the one who hasn't been would be concerned about living up to previous expectations. You just have to put all of that out of your mind. This is a new life, this is a different relationship, and there is no basis for comparison. You have nothing to be concerned about if you just concentrate on being yourself."

If either of you has children by a previous marriage, the question of taking them along on your trip may already have come up. The response of the experts varies from "no—never" to a qualified "perhaps." The general feeling is that the partners need some time to be together as a couple. But each situation is different, and each couple should decide what works best for their family. Mrs. Lalli adds, "In general, it is better to go away together and get some distance and objectivity—and relaxation—and not have to deal with these responsibilities that are going to be such a demanding part of your everyday lives together. And there will be plenty of time in the future for family vacations."

GETTING MARRIED THERE

If you are planning to get married at your honeymoon locale, pay particular attention to:

1. **Time frames:** Some places require that you be in the area for a certain number of days before a license can be issued or a wedding performed.
2. **Fees:** This can range from about $5 to several hundred.
3. **Identification:** Do you have to produce either proof of identity or proof of age? What documents are acceptable? Driver's license? Certified birth certificate? Passport?
4. **Local rules:** These can be quite different from what you're accustomed to back home. In Bermuda, for example, a marriage notice must be published in the newspapers two weeks before a license can be issued.
5. **Other documentation:** If either one of you is divorced or widowed, you usually have to furnish the official certificate. If you will be marrying in a

non-English-speaking country, you probably will need a translated, notarized copy of the papers.

Arranging a wedding long distance can be simplified if you contact a local specialist. In many areas, you can consult a wedding service. Often, your best bet will be telephoning the social activities director of the hotel where you will be staying and discussing your plans. The hotel can frequently handle all the details, from arranging for the officiant to ordering flowers—even finding someone to videotape the ceremony.

Wherever you choose to marry, try to incorporate local customs into your wedding. In the U.S. Virgin Islands, this might mean hiring a steel band for the music. In Hawaii, you can wear the traditional maile leis that symbolize long life, health, and prosperity. You'll add special meaning to this most special event.

COPING WITH HONEYMOON STRESS

You're madly in love. The air fare you have just paid to reach your honeymoon destination outstrips the annual budget of several small nations, and your suite outglitters anything on *Lifestyles of the Rich and Famous*. Yet you have just burst into tears because your partner announces that s/he is heading down to the beach to play volleyball with the gang instead of going antiques shopping with you. Is it all over?

Relax—you're dealing with honeymoon stress.

Honeymoon stress is just the flip side of taking The Trip of a Lifetime. For most couples, the honeymoon is the most significant vacation they'll ever have. And, as with anything that is important—and that also costs a lot of money—you want it to be perfect. Worse, you're constantly worrying whether everything measures up. (Please note that "everything" also often includes your new mate.) This feeling of tension can manifest itself several different ways: anything from arguing over inconsequential matters to sudden, inexplicable attacks of sheer dumbness—like forgetting to take your airline tickets when you head for the airport. The factors contributing to honeymoon stress are varied:

□ **The wedding.** When most couples start planning their honeymoons, they little anticipate how downright exhausted they'll be by the time the wedding night rolls around. Between the nervous tension about details that might go awry—plus the sheer joy when the ceremony and reception turn out as gloriously as planned— you'll be emotionally frazzled by the day after the wedding. This fatigue makes you susceptible; petty annoyances that would not usually upset you get under your skin instead.

□ **The commitment of marriage.** Even for couples who have lived together before marriage, the honeymoon marks the official start of a transition from single to married life. Stuart R. Johnson, a marital and family therapist in New Haven, Connecticut, points out that even today, "Marriage is a lot more than a piece of paper, psychologically speaking." Marriage represents a major commitment, and each party feels—and fears—that he or she is surrendering some of his or her independence. "There are two fundamental human issues that make marriages work or not work," Mr. Johnson continues. "They come down to how do people deal with intimacy— not just sex, but anything they do together: love, companionship, problem solving, playing. Autonomy is the other issue—the sense of being a separate person and doing autonomous activities . . . careers and work, but also separate hobbies." On their honeymoon, couples are first beginning to grapple with this issue of "we" versus "I," the fact that it is impossible to meld two separate individuals into one entity. Until a workable balance is established, there will be strains in the relationship.

□ **Getting to know each other.** During courtship, couples are often distracted from their relationship by career pressures and other responsibilities. The honeymoon gives people a chance really to concentrate on each other. Also during courtship, most men and women stay on their best behavior and try to please each other. They worry that if certain of their traits or quirks are uncovered—an inability to calculate a waiter's tip, crankiness in the morning—their mate won't love them anymore. Likewise, each partner will learn new things about the person he or she married.

□ **Defining new roles.** As mentioned at the beginning of this introduction, honeymoon planning is often the first time a couple discusses nitty-gritty finances with each other. One partner may tend to be an epicurean spendthrift, the other wants to save for a rainy day. Naturally, they'll run into conflicts. In addition, while the couple travels together, each partner will start to assume new responsibilities. One person might become the car driver, the other the map reader. Someone will be the budget planner, the other the tour guide. Until these roles are clearly defined, couples will encounter some rough spots.

□ **Exaggerated expectations.** So much time and energy have gone into planning this trip that couples tend to expect too much from it: perfect weather, complete compatibility, a string of magic moments. Mr. Johnson points out, "The image of the honeymoon is wall-to-wall intimacy. It captures all the romantic mythology about intimacy: 'We become as if we are one.' Well, that's nonsense. Two human beings are not one." The problem is compounded by movies and television soap operas, which present an unrealistic image of love and romance. American culture is so imbued with these myths that even people who wouldn't be caught dead watching these programs accept the myths of unmitigated sweetness and light that Hollywood presents. Of course, life and love just don't work like that, and often the honeymoon is the first glimpse of that reality.

□ **"Great sexpectations."** Perhaps the biggest myth surrounding honeymoons concerns the sexual relationship; couples expect not only the hearts and flowers of intimacy, but also the rockets and fireworks of passion as well. And although couples put tremendous pressure on themselves for peak sexual performance, conditions for a loving relationship are far from optimal. The wedding planning, ceremony, and reception sap a lot of energy out of people—they're absolutely zonked by their wedding night.

□ **Travel is stressful.** People who don't travel much often believe that trips unfold in complete pleasure. Not true. Travelers constantly worry about catching that flight, paying with foreign currencies, finding that left-hand turn to the hotel. When you add in the anxieties associated with the wedding, you'll often find that extremely well-organized, experienced travelers will suddenly pull real bloopers and forget to take their wallets, hotel confirmations, passports, or other necessities.

It's important for honeymooners to realize that feeling stress is not necessarily bad—it's part of the growing pains involved in forming a deeper relationship. Dr. Duane comments, "When stress is actually due to change, it can be very, very productive. It means that you are having deep, emotional feelings. It's a process of growth and change. So how can a honeymoon not be a time of stress?"

Although some anxiety is natural, there are ways to help assure that stress won't interfere with a happy honeymoon.

□ **Consider delaying your honeymoon departure.** In all likelihood, you'll be pooped the day after the wedding. By postponing your departure by at least a day, you can catch up with your sleep and spend time with wedding guests visiting from out of town. In many cases, delaying your honeymoon for several weeks or months may be the smartest way to give yourselves the honeymoon you always dreamed of, especially if both of you also face substantial career pressures. It just may be too difficult to take the time away from work for planning the wedding and for the honeymoon, too. Cele Lalli recommends, "If it is too complicated to take your honeymoon right after the wedding, you should postpone such an important trip to a little later time when you can do it without conflict."

□ **Do your honeymoon your way.** Plan your trip around what you would like to do, instead of what you think you ought to do or what is romantic to do. One couple, for example, spent their honeymoon cross-country skiing with friends. It was comfortable, natural—and, most important, it felt right for them.

□ **Make a list of items you must bring with you.** Do this several weeks before your departure so that last-minute anxiety attacks won't numb you into forgetfulness.

□ **Consider choosing a resort area that's especially popular with honeymooners.** Most newlyweds discover that they enjoy being with other just-marrieds, because they all have so much in common. From her conversations with couples from around the country, Mrs. Lalli finds that newlyweds "really will enjoy being with others who are on their honeymoon, because you can share the interesting wedding experiences that all of you have had—it can make everything more fun." Many of the most popular resorts for honeymooners offer a wide range of social activities—from party boats to volleyball games. With so much to do, you'll have plenty of new events to talk about.

□ **Plan a realistic budget.** Be practical about what you can afford, but also allow some money for splurges. When we've asked married couples what they would have done differently on their honeymoon, some of the most common responses were: "Gee, I wish we'd paid extra to get an oceanfront room"; "I wish we'd taken that helicopter tour"; "I love the poster that we took home—but we should have bought the original watercolor painting of the beach we always went to." Don't shortchange your honeymoon memories.

□ **Relax.** Enjoy every moment of the honeymoon trip for what it is. Don't let inflated expectations or overambitious planning interfere with the real fun you're having. You don't have to schedule activities for every moment. A honeymoon is a time to get away and unwind. Also, don't put pressure on yourselves to have the greatest sex of your lives. Dr. Duane reminds newlyweds, "Any sexual relationship is something a couple has to work on. Defocus the sex, and instead find other activities you enjoy doing in common. You'll find that sex will come more naturally then."

□ **Communicate.** Since the honeymoon marks the transition into married life, there's no better time to start good habits—like talking things over. If you feel uncomfortable when your spouse automatically assumes all responsibility for travel finances, or rejected if he or she doesn't share your enthusiasm for pre-Mayan artifacts, talk about it. Communication forms a stronger basis for a relationship than sulking.

□ **Each of you should have some time alone.** Realize that you don't have to spend every moment together. You have different interests—indulge them. While one of you goes to the baseball game, the other can scope out the shopping mall. Private time doesn't even mean that you have to be apart. You can have that same feeling of space while sitting on the beach together, each reading a book.

□ **Keep your sense of humor.** If things go wrong on your journey, remember that the mishaps will probably turn into the funniest stories you'll tell in years to come. And that's good advice for both traveling . . . and marriage.

THE UNITED STATES

NEW ENGLAND INNS

New England's heart and soul lie along its back roads, where general stores still sell sodas in long slender bottles and pretzel rods for a penny. Time hasn't stood still; it's just accommodated itself to Yankee stubbornness. Whether you're in the dramatic Green Mountains of Vermont or the coast off Cape Cod, you'll begin to understand why New England has managed to keep its rural ways despite the sprawl of its big cities. The people are tied to the land—to the cranberry bogs, to the birch trees, to the sunken meadows. A visit to the inns and bed-and-breakfasts of these northern states means spending time just observing the passing of the seasons, even subtle changes from day to day.

Whole books have been written about the wide range of charming inns this region offers. Since we cannot possibly cover them all in this volume, we have instead focused on what we consider to be the most romantic honeymoon locales in Connecticut, Massachusetts, and Vermont.

1. Practical Facts

GETTING THERE
Although airline, bus, and train services are all available to take you into New England, most of the small towns are accessible by car only. If you are traveling to Martha's Vineyard or Nantucket, however, consider leaving your car behind and bringing—or renting—a bicycle instead.

By Air
To southern Connecticut: The closest major airport, Bradley International, is located in Windsor Locks, just north of Hartford and about 40 miles from East Haddam. Over a dozen airlines fly into Bradley. **Business Express, The Delta Con-**

nection, one of Delta's commuter airlines (tel. toll free 800/345-3400), also flies into Tweed Airport in New Haven (about 40 miles from the East Haddam/Chester area) and into the Groton/New London Airport (approximately 25 miles away).

To northwestern Connecticut and the Berkshires: Bradley International Airport in Windsor Locks is a little over 50 miles from the Salisbury area; the Albany, N.Y., airport, about 75 miles.

To Cape Cod: Airports in Hyannis and Provincetown provide regularly scheduled service to the Cape. The most popular airlines are Delta's **Business Express** and the **Continental Express** (tel. toll free 800/525-0280) from Boston and New York.

To the islands: Several small airlines serve the islands. **Tri Air** (tel. 508/771-4888, or toll free 800/247-3113 in Massachusetts) and **Nantucket Airlines** (tel. 508/790-0300, or toll free 800/635-8787 in Massachusetts) hop from Hyannis to Nantucket. **Edgartown Air** (tel. 508/627-9631, or toll free 800/637-9631 in Massachusetts) leaves Hyannis for Martha's Vineyard.

To Vermont: Although Rutland State Airport had regularly scheduled flights—and may have them again soon—as we go to press, the best way to get to Vermont by air is via **Continental** (tel. toll free 800/525-0280), **United** (tel. toll free 800/241-6522), or **USAir** (tel. toll free 800/428-4322) to Burlington International Airport.

By Bus

Greyhound and **Bonanza** bus lines, in conjunction with smaller, regional bus companies, have a fairly extensive network that runs throughout New England. Contact Bonanza (tel. toll free 800/556-3815), an independent working out of Providence, R.I., for information to Lee, Lenox, and Hyannis, Mass., and Canaan, Conn. Greyhound goes to Lee, Lenox, and Stockbridge, Mass., and New Haven, Conn.; in addition, they also have schedule and fare information for **Vermont Transit** (tel. toll free 800/451-3292 and 800/642-3133 in Vermont), a part of Greyhound that runs up to Manchester and Ludlow.

By Train

To southern Connecticut: The closest stop is in Old Saybrook, although you can take **Amtrak** (tel. toll free 800/872-7245) into New London or New Haven.

To northwestern Connecticut and the Berkshires: From Boston, you can get off the Lake Shore Limited in Pittsfield, which is just a hop away from Lenox and Lee. From New York, the only train to the area stops in Albany.

To Cape Cod: Amtrak runs a reservations-only Metroliner to Hyannis from Washington, New York, and Providence in season on weekends, but the schedule changes often, so be sure to call before you make even tentative plans to visit the area.

To Vermont: Amtrak's service to Vermont may very well be a bus; whether train or motor coach, the stops are at Bellows Falls and White River Junction. The Montrealer train was scheduled to begin running again in 1989, but details at press time were still vague.

By Boat

To Nantucket and Martha's Vineyard: The **Woods Hole, Martha's Vineyard and Nantucket Steamship Authority** (tel. 508/540-2022) offers year-round ferry service running from Hyannis to Nantucket and from Woods Hole (on Cape Cod) to Martha's Vineyard. Schedules vary seasonally, as does the availability of getting car reservations. If you must bring your car over during the summer high season, call as far in advance as possible; the ferry often becomes booked months ahead of time, especially on holiday weekends.

Hy-Line Cruises (tel. 508/778-2600) has first-class and regular-class service for passengers to Nantucket and single-class service between the islands, summer season only. **Bay State Cruises** (tel. 617/723-7800) also provides summer crossings from Boston to Nantucket, the Vineyard, and Provincetown. For information on boats from Montauk, N.Y.; New London, Conn.; and other ports, contact the islands' information offices.

Bicycles are welcome on all boats.

GETTING AROUND

Public transportation is almost nonexistent in most small towns. A **car** is the only way to take advantage of New England—except on the islands, where bicycles may be your best option. Be advised that most gas stations in small towns close down by 7 p.m., and even along main highways, many service stations close by 10 p.m. Keep an eye on your gas gauge.

By Taxi

Taxis can be prohibitively expensive for touring, but drivers can be arranged through most tourist offices; the charge for two hours usually hovers around $25 or $30.

By Rental Car

The major rental car companies have offices scattered throughout New England, including facilities at the main airports. Call **Hertz** (tel. toll free 800/654-3131), **Avis** (tel. toll free 800/331-1212), **Budget** (tel. toll free 800/527-0700), or **National Rental Car** (tel. toll free 800/227-7368) for more specific information.

WEATHER

New England's temperate weather means mild springs, warm but not blistery summers, and crisp, cool autumns. If you're by the shore, winter temperatures log in around 25° to 30°. Head to Vermont, though, and the nights can be bitter cold, plummeting below zero. In Vermont, there's an extra season that usually falls in April: mud season. As the thaw sets in, rivers rise and the unpaved roads turn to unpassable mud. Venture to the north country only if you have a four-wheel-drive vehicle at your disposal.

CLOTHING

Although dress is casual in the countryside, there's a general trend for clothing to become more fashionable the closer you get to New York City. Jeans and comfortable shirts are acceptable for traveling, but bring along dinner clothes for evenings at gourmet restaurants. Most innkeepers dress casually and expect that their guests will do the same.

TIME

All the New England states are on Eastern Standard Time in winter and go on Daylight Saving Time in the summer.

TELEPHONES

The area code for Connecticut is 203; for Vermont, 802. In Massachusetts, the area code for the Berkshires is 413; for Cape Cod and the islands, 508. Most inns and bed-and-breakfasts have a house phone that guests can use. In many cases, however, the phone is also used for reservations, so keep your calls brief. It is easiest to use a credit card.

SHOPPING

New England offers a cornucopia of crafts and antiques at stores that are as quaint and charming as the towns in which they stand. On the other extreme, however, are the fabulous outlet stores—in Manchester Center, Vt., and Hyannis, Cape Cod—that offer no-nonsense bargains on clothing, tableware, and the like.

Take a special side trip to a local event: a harvest fair, fruit celebration, or school fund-raiser. (Schedules are available from the tourism offices.) The shopping's sure to include homemade crafts and baked goods—and you just might find that white elephant that endears you to the area forever.

ABOUT ACCOMMODATIONS

Inns. Bed-and-breakfasts. Bed-and-breakfast inns. They all sound alike, and in many cases, they are alike. Much to the dismay of travelers, there are no standardized definitions that outline the facilities and amenities of these unique accommodations.

As a general rule, most **inns** have a dining room that offers meals to the outside public. Professionally run **bed-and-breakfast inns** usually don't serve afternoon or evening meals, and if they do, it's to guests only. The owners also tend to keep their living quarters separate from that of their guests. **Bed-and-breakfasts** that are mom-and-pop operations, in most cases, tend to have community rooms that are shared, and only open up guest rooms on an irregular schedule. They don't offer as much privacy and comfort as the bed-and-breakfast inns.

In many cases, the terms "bed-and-breakfast" and "inn" will be used interchangeably once it is established that a place offers dinner. All of the accommodations listed in this book provide good mattresses, private baths, and a special, unique touch that you can't get anywhere else.

Deposit and cancellation policies: Most inns and bed-and-breakfasts follow strict rules concerning deposits and necessary cancellations. A deposit equal to 50% of the cost of your stay is not unusual. If you must cancel at the last minute, you will probably be required to pay a small service charge (approximately $10) in addition to the full sum. Notify innkeepers as soon as you know of a change in your plans, because most hosts will refund your money if they can rent the room.

Peak season: Definitions differ from one inn to the next. In Massachusetts and Connecticut, peak seasons are usually summer and autumn; in Vermont, autumn and winter.

Minimum stays: Partly as a reminder that guests tend to relax only after they've stayed more than one night and partly as good business practice, many inns have instituted a minimum stay policy. Many innkeepers require a two-night stay for peak season weekends and three-day holidays. Don't be put off by the rules. Hopping from inn to inn is not necessarily as pleasant as it may sound. Stay an extra day, and you'll enjoy your honeymoon so much more.

What to expect: Good bedding and a private bath to start. No room phones, no television, and no children. Beyond that the amenities vary dramatically from inn to inn. Air conditioning, often not provided, is not really very important when you're out in the country. Most of the houses have wonderful cross breezes. If you're fussy about heat in the cool seasons, ask in advance if the room has individual temperature controls. Most inns lack this luxury, but then again, most innkeepers are happy to raise or lower the heat if you ask. Breakfasts are included in the room rate; taxes and gratuities are not.

Breakfasts: In general, the breakfasts served are above average. Hosts bring out finished products based on the secret recipes of who knows how many generations back. To clarify the terms used here, **continental** means the basics: coffee or tea, muffins or breads or croissants, and juice. An **expanded continental** breakfast is an enlargement on the theme; in addition to what you get in a continental breakfast, you usually can choose from cold cereals, granola, cheeses, and fruit. **Full** breakfast denotes a hot meal, usually some sort of egg dish, pancakes, French toast, or the like, plus everything on the continental breakfast. Sometimes it even includes an appetizer such as a baked pear or fruit compote.

Rates and payments: Room rates may change with the seasons. Also, prices may vary for different rooms at the same inn or B&B, depending on views, size, and amenities. Few places have honeymoon packages; however, if you let your hosts know in advance that you are newlyweds, they will often have a chilled bottle of champagne waiting in your room when you arrive.

Regarding payment, be aware that not all inns and B&Bs accept credit cards. Some will honor "plastic" for the room deposit, but not the complete payment. Ask in advance.

DINING OUT

When you make your room reservation, don't be surprised if innkeepers ask you where you will want to dine, even if it's months in advance. Some of the finest restaurants outside of New York, Chicago, and San Francisco are in New England's tiny inn towns. Make your reservations as soon as possible and confirm them once you arrive at your destination.

New England's gourmet restaurants generally change their menus seasonally, adding more fresh fish in the summer and game in the winter. Let the maitre d' know you're on your honeymoon. He or she may know of a special dessert or appetizer that's not on the menu but that can be whipped up just for you.

HOW TO GET MARRIED IN NEW ENGLAND

Bed-and-breakfasts and inns thrive on romance, and the majority of innkeepers are willing and eager to help with wedding plans. Newlyweds-to-be should take advantage of innkeepers' knowledge if they wish to be married or have their reception at the inn. The locals know the best florists, caterers, bakers, etc.

In Connecticut: Couples must obtain a certificate from the Registrar of Vital Statistics in the town in which the marriage is to be celebrated. The certificate will be issued four days after filing with proof of identity and marital status and with physician's statement (a rubella test for brides-to-be under 50 and capable of pregnancy is the only necessary test). The marriage must be solemnized within 65 days.

In Massachusetts: You must file your notice of intention to marry at least three days before the marriage ceremony. You both have to go in person to the clerk or registrar of any town in the state. Both members of the couple must submit to a medical exam no more than 30 days before filing. The license will be issued 3 or more (but not more than 60) days after filing. If you plan to ask a nonresident clergyman to perform the ceremony, you may need special permission. Ask the clerk or registrar in advance if this will be a problem.

In Vermont: You must file for a marriage certificate from the town clerk of the groom's hometown, or if he is not a resident, from the bride's hometown. Nonresidents must file in the town where the ceremony will be performed and must provide an affidavit that the proposed marriage is not contrary to the laws of their home states. Both members of the couple must have a premarital medical examination within 30 days before application. After the marriage certificate is obtained, three days must elapse before the ceremony can take place.

In all three states, waivers from the various requirements may be obtained from the probate judge for the area in which the marriage will be solemnized.

FOR FURTHER INFORMATION

Contact the **New England Vacation Center,** 630 Fifth Avenue, New York, NY 10020 (tel. 212/307-5780).

For Connecticut: Contact **The Connecticut Tourism Office,** 865 Brook Street, Rocky Hill, CT 06067-3405 (tel. 203/258-4290). **Connecticut Valley Tidewater Commission,** 70 College St., Middletown, CT 06457 (tel. 203/347-6924). **Litchfield Hills Visitors Commission,** P.O. Box 1776, Marbledale, CT 06777 (tel. 203/868-2214).

For Massachusetts: Contact **The Spirit of Massachusetts,** Division of Tourism, 100 Cambridge St., 13th floor, Boston, MA 02202 (tel. 617/727-3201, or toll free 800/447-MASS). **Berkshire Visitors Bureau,** Berkshire Common Plaza Level, Dept. MA, Pittsfield, MA 01201 (tel. 413/443-9186). **Cape Cod Chamber of Commerce,** Dept. MA, Hyannis, MA 02601 (tel. 508/362-3225).

For Vermont: Contact the **Vermont Chamber of Commerce,** Box 37, Montpelier, VT 05601 (tel. 802/828-3236). **Ludlow Area Chamber of Commerce,** 196 Main St., P.O. Box 333, Ludlow, VT 05149 (tel. 802/228-5318). **Manchester and the Mountains Chamber of Commerce,** Adams Park Green, Rte. 7, P.O. Box 928, Manchester, VT 05255 (tel. 802/362-2100).

CONNECTICUT

2. Connecticut's River Towns

Often overlooked by tourists, the villages of East Haddam, Chester, Deep River, and Ivoryton offer a taste of past eras. Situated in Middlesex County on the Connecticut River, which bisects the state, all are within a five- to ten-minute drive north of the beautiful and beach-studded Long Island Sound. The location encouraged shipbuilding and ivory trade, which helped shape the character of the towns. Many of the residents here are relearning the history that surrounds them. Attractions include the Goodspeed Opera House, known for its musical revivals, and its neighbor, the Goodspeed-at-Chester, which stages new musical productions.

East Haddam, spurred to growth by the theater, is the busiest of the four towns; Chester, with its restored buildings and mill river is the quaintest; and Ivoryton, the grandest. But for a real glimpse of the area before tourism, stroll through Deep River. Bordered by New Haven, New London, and Hartford counties, this little cutout of Connecticut retains its small-town feel even though it is only a short drive away from the state's biggest cities. Sports enthusiasts can take advantage of good bicycling roads, canoeing on the Connecticut, and swimming at the lakes or in the Sound.

SHOPPING

Best bets in southeastern Connecticut include the **Essex-Saybrook Antiques Village** on Middlesex Turnpike in Old Saybrook (tel. 388-0689), which represents 85 dealers, and **Brush Factory Antiques** on Deep River Road in Centerbrook (tel. 767-0845), a cooperative of 23 dealers. Stroll the gift and clothing shops along Chester's main street; and if you don't mind driving into a more crowded and touristy area, **Olde Mistick Village** in Mystic—no more than half an hour away off exit 90 on I-95. More than 60 stores in an 18th-century setting comprise the village, among them **Franklin's General Store** (featuring handmade items), **Bestemors Scandinavian Gifts, Mystick Pewter Shop, Ye Olde 1776 Shoppe** (for scrimshaw), and the **Rocking Horse Shop** (with—what else?—rocking horses, plus other gifts).

ROMANTIC INTERLUDES

This deceptively quiet river valley offers romantic adventure aloft, afloat, and aground.

Rise above the Connecticut River Valley in a **seaplane.** From the small three-seater you can see Selden's Creek, Gillette Castle, and Long Island Sound. Plan to take off in the morning so you can land in the river before the pleasure boats come out (May to November, weekdays). Or opt for a land plane and go any time you

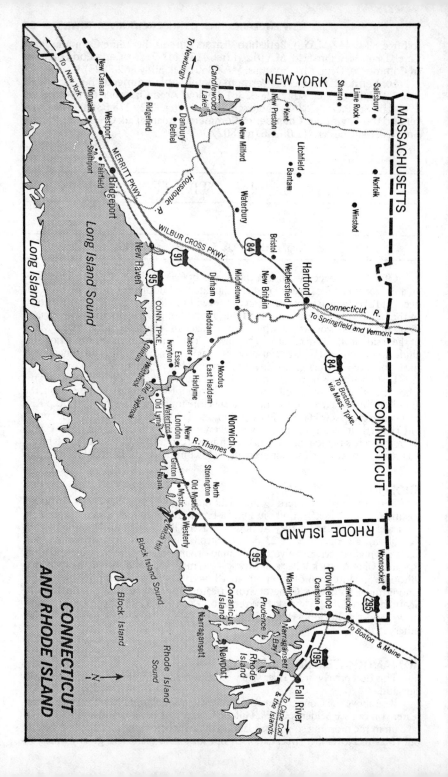

CONNECTICUT AND RHODE ISLAND

desire. Contact **Eagle Aviation** for information about the $35-per-couple, 20-minute rides, which leave from the Goodspeed Airport at Goodspeed Landing (tel. 873-8568).

All aboard! The **Valley Railroad** (tel. 767-0103) takes you back in time to circa 1910 as you chug along from Essex to Chester in restored vintage steam-train cars. Experience first-class travel in the Pullman parlor car *Wallingford* with its revolving plush seats, carpets, leaded-glass partitions, and music. The train connects with a riverboat at Deep River for an hour-long ride past Gillette Castle and by the Goodspeed Opera House. The schedule varies seasonally. Allow two hours and ten minutes for the train and cruise, which costs $14.90 ($1.95 less if you opt for the more simple bench-seating cars). Arrive 45 minutes ahead of time for the best seats. The train runs during the spring, summer, and fall, and around the Christmas holidays, weather permitting.

Built of native stone and southern white oak, **Gillette Castle** stands atop a rocky ridge that overlooks the Connecticut River. The building resembles a child's turreted sand castle—on a grand scale. Walking trails snake through the 122-acre property, which includes a picnic area and a very romantic arched stone bridge. Stop at **The Wheatmarket** (tel. 526-9347) in Chester before you go, and pick up their Lover's Picnic, typically a hefty lunch of brie cheese, country pâté, celeriac salad, marinated mushrooms, French bread, and sparkling cider ($20 for two people). If you haven't already discovered it, take the **Chester-Hadlyme** ferry ($1.25 for car with two passengers) back across the river. A wonderfully picturesque road leads from the ferry toward Rte. 9A.

Imagine paddling up to a silent, wooded cove that's all your own for the day. The placid **Connecticut River** is dotted with islands and private inlets perfect for newlyweds equipped with a bottle of champagne and a treat-laden picnic basket. For $28 to $30 for the two of you, **Down River Canoes** (tel. 345-8355) will provide the boat and arrange to pick you up at the end of the day. If you don't mind company, ask about their overnight canoe trip that highlights a candlelit waterfront steak or shad-and-clam bake.

For a tamer trip on the Connecticut, reserve a lunch or dinner cruise aboard the luxury yacht *The Camelot* (tel. 345-4507). The lunch trip leaves Haddam at noon for a 2½-hour trip to the tunes of Dixieland jazz ($19.75 per person plus tax and tip). The three-hour evening cruise features live entertainment and dinner dancing ($37.75 per person plus tax and tip). There's also an all-you-can-eat Sunday brunch buffet for $24.75 per person.

IDYLLIC INNS AND BED-AND-BREAKFASTS

The romantic settings of southern Connecticut serve as backdrops to the wonderful array of homey places to stay.

Riverwind, 209 Main St., Deep River, CT 06417 (tel. 203/526-2014). Situated by the village green, this 1850s clapboard house embodies warmth and whimsy. Innkeeper Barbara Barlow, who hails from Smithfield, Va., has captured the magic that comes from combining Yankee ingenuity with southern graciousness. The eight guest rooms, all with impeccable private baths, ooze charm and coziness; decorated with country American crafts and beautiful antiques, each room offers something special—for instance, a canopied bed or a maple four-poster that rises 2½ feet above the polished pine floors. The Champagne and Roses Suite—awash with roses—is particularly special with its Japanese steeping tub, a private balcony in the treetops overlooking the rose garden, and champagne nightly for honeymooners. Candlelit buffet breakfasts feature such delicious baked goods as blueberry pound cake and an incredibly good coffee cake, and when there's a chill outside, guests can curl up by the 12-foot keeping-room fireplace or one of the three other hearths in Riverwind's common rooms. As one visitor wrote in the guest diary: "Every detail is perfect." Rates: $80 to $135 per couple per night.

Stonecroft Inn, 17 Main St., East Haddam, CT 06423 (tel. 203/873-1754).

This gracious, Federal-style inn sits on a low rise just down the street from the Goodspeed Opera House. An atmosphere of refined relaxation predominates. Guests take their cues from Connecticut Yankee Bonnie Baskin, who returned to her home state after running a B&B in Seattle. Stonecroft is awash in the subtle colors of the Federal era, the appointments complementing the walls with a certain graciousness. Although five of the six rooms are well suited to newlyweds (one of them has twin beds), Four-Poster and Fireside are the two unofficial honeymoon hideaways; whether you choose the chintz-covered canopied bed or the one with the quilted headboard, Bonnie will place a bride's basket bouquet on your door and champagne inside the room if she knows you're on your honeymoon. Working fireplaces in many of the rooms are a special bonus here. Rates: $75 to $90 per couple per night with full breakfast.

A stately addition to the area's bed-and-breakfasts, **Selden House,** 20 Read St., Deep River, CT 06417 (tel. 203/526-9195), emphasizes a simple, almost spare, elegance. The details of the house are splendid—lovely moldings, pocket doors in the living room, original hardware. An inviting living room highlights an autumn-colored Oriental rug, a Chinese silk Empire sofa, and chairs carved by the man who designed Mount Rushmore. The eight rooms, which are more plainly furnished, still reflect the house's gracefulness, especially the spacious room no. 1, which has a nice-size working fireplace. Outside, on the land's four acres, a beautiful weeping cherry tree stands within sight of terraced stone steps, and you'll find many perfect places for a wedding ceremony or an evening drink before dinner. In 1990, two large suites with working fireplace will be added in the carriage house, and the plans for bringing back the old gardens should be well on the way to completion. Rates: $75 to $110 per couple per night.

Copper Beech Inn, Main Street, Ivoryton, CT 06426 (tel. 203/767-0330). Guests have a choice of accommodations at this fine inn, once the residence of an ivory magnate. First-time inn visitors may feel more comfortable in the recently remodeled carriage house, which includes nine capacious rooms characterized by crisp, reproduction colonial furniture, king-size beds, televisions, and whirlpool tubs. Old hands will prefer the four accommodations in the main house. These uniquely furnished older rooms each convey a different mood, influenced by the wonderful beds: Take your choice among brass, white wicker, Hitchcock, or a four-poster. Sally and Eldon Senner bought the inn in the summer of 1988 and have kept it in shipshape order. Rates: $85 to $145 per couple per night with continental breakfast.

ROMANTIC RESTAURANTS

Some of the finest restaurants in Connecticut are clustered here by the Connecticut River. Most couples dress for dinner, although no code dictates such formality.

Fine Bouche, 79 Main St., Centerbrook (tel. 767-1277). Chef-owner Steven Wilkinson takes his job seriously, and it's reflected in the consistent quality and character of the extraordinary good French menu he's prepared. Specialties change every six to eight weeks and might include a succulent quail stuffed with a chicken and truffle mousse, salmon filet with a cream and chervil sauce, and crisp but moist sautéed duck breast with black currants and cassis. Wilkinson's desserts are equally enticing, as is his wine list, which offers an array that begins under $10 and includes an excellent selection of rare wines as well. The food is so good you may not even notice the simple but romantic surroundings, complete with fireplace. Five-course prix-fixe dinner, $38; à la carte appetizers from $5.50 to $7.50, entrées from $17.50 to $25, plus wine. Make reservations several weeks in advance if possible. Open Tuesday through Sunday 5:30 to 9:30 p.m.

Restaurant du Village, 59 Main St., Chester (tel. 526-5301). Tucked into a row of winsome buildings on Chester's main street, this small, formal restaurant epitomizes French country charm. White linens, Laura Ashley service plates, and a diminutive bouquet share the glow from small votive candles. In warm weather the

French doors open out onto the red-brick path that leads to the entrance. The doors open at 5:30 p.m. to serve the pretheater crowd. Try the mussels in curry cream sauce to start if it's offered as a special. This is French country cooking at its best. Dinner without drinks comes to about $70 for two. Open Wednesday through Sunday from 5:30 to 10 p.m.; from January through March, Friday through Sunday only.

Fiddlers Seafood Restaurant, 4 Water St., Chester (tel. 526-3210). A treasure trove for seafood-lovers! Each day's specials can be mesquite-grilled, poached, or pan sautéed on request. In addition there are 13 standard fish and shellfish entrées, ranging from whole lobster to a well-sauced pan-fried filet of sole. A rare treat is the broth-based Rhode Island clam chowder. Desserts change daily, but the chocolate terrine appears often and shouldn't be passed up. The setting is cheery and sweet: candlelight, a nosegay of fresh flowers, and blue scallop shells hand-stenciled on the walls. Dinner for two with appetizer and dessert: about $45. Lunch, about $12 for two. Open for lunch Tuesday through Saturday from 11:30 a.m. to 2 p.m. Dinner hours: Tuesday through Thursday from 5:30 to 9 p.m.; Friday from 5:30 to 9:30 p.m.; Saturday from 5:30 to 10 p.m.; and Sunday from 4 to 9 p.m.

Copper Beech Inn, Ivoryton (tel. 767-0330), voted Most Romantic in the county by readers of *Connecticut* magazine. Fine French food, good wine list, and scrumptious desserts. Chef Rob Chiovaloni prepares the elegant fare. Entrées priced from $23.50. Open for dinner during the week from 6 to 8:30 p.m.; on Friday and Saturday from 5:30 to 9:30 p.m.

For more inexpensive treats try the **Gourmet Galley** in Westbrook (tel. 399-5751), where you'll be eating al fresco and very casually under a yellow-and-white-striped tent. Breakfast—from $1.25 to $3.85—highlights homemade muffins, french toast, and the like. The Gourmet Galley roasts its own turkey too; sandwiches from $2.95, salads from $1.50. Open from 7 a.m. to 2:30 p.m. from April 1 to the end of May; until 11 p.m. from June through August; call to verify the hours before you go.

---

3. North of the Litchfield Hills

Litchfield, judged by some to be the prettiest example of an 18th-century New England village, has been "discovered" in the past decade; but travel north to the old resort towns of Lakeville, Salisbury, and Norfolk and you'll find yourself in countryside that's punctuated with cascading streams, village greens surrounded by stately mansions, and a quietness that lends itself to romance.

Tucked into the top northwest corner of Connecticut near the Housatonic River, these small towns share a border with New York to the west and Massachusetts to the north, a location that led people to dub the area the "Connecticut Berkshires." In fact, the Indian name for the river means "Place Beyond the Mountains." And although the peaks may not be as lofty as they are across the state line, their beauty is just as compelling.

While warm weather brings musicians and tourists to Music Mountain in Falls Village and the summer home of the Yale School of Music in Norfolk, Lime Rock Park in Lime Rock attracts serious car-racing fans, especially during the major summer holidays. For those travelers who want to take a more active role, the sporting activities here include skiing, canoeing on the Housatonic, and horseback riding in addition to the year-round hiking.

SHOPPING

If you're looking for auto art, you can't beat northwestern Connecticut, which claims to have the largest collection of contemporary automotive artwork in the world at **Auto Art** in West Cornwall (tel. 672-6055 for an appointment). Other

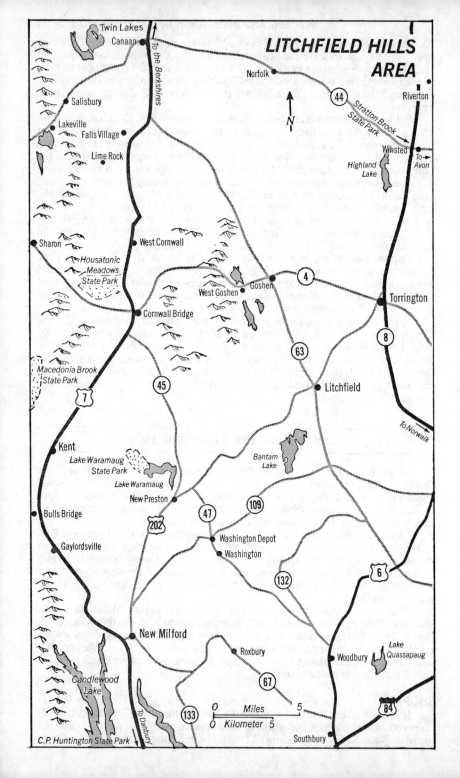

LITCHFIELD HILLS AREA

Twin Lakes
Canaan
To the Berkshires
Norfolk
Riverton
44
Stratton Brook State Park
Salisbury
Winsted
To Avon
Lakeville
Falls Village
Highland Lake
Lime Rock
N
Sharon
West Cornwall
Housatonic Meadows State Park
West Goshen
Goshen
4
Torrington
Cornwall Bridge
8
63
Macedonia Brook State Park
7
45
Litchfield
To Norwalk
Kent
Lake Waramaug State Park
Bantam Lake
Lake Waramaug
New Preston
202
47
109
Bulls Bridge
Washington Depot
Washington
Gaylordsville
132
6
New Milford
Roxbury
Woodbury
Lake Quassapaug
67
Candlewood Lake
84
133
Miles
0   5
Kilometer
0   5
To Danbury
C.P. Huntington State Park
Southbury

notables include the **Cornwall Bridge Pottery Store** near the covered bridge in West Cornwall (tel. 672-6545), open Wednesday through Sunday; and **Friendship Artisans,** a crafts gallery in Salisbury that features traditional floor cloths, jewelry, leather, and other unique goods from New England craftspeople (tel. 435-2433). The **Designing Woman,** also at Salisbury Square (tel. 435-9760), has custom-designed needlepoint canvases and yarn.

ROMANTIC INTERLUDES

Spend some time traveling the unmarked roads really to appreciate this corner of Connecticut. You'll fall in love all over again.

Connecticut's two **covered bridges** still open to automobile traffic are easily reached from Salisbury. West Cornwall, along Rte. 128, boasts one of native oak that was built in 1837; the other, **Bull's Bridge,** in Kent on Rte. 7, dates back to the Revolution. Although you can see both by car, you may want to stop in at the **Village Store** in Salisbury (tel. 435-9459) to rent a bike ($10 for the day) or call **Clarke Outdoors** in West Cornwall (tel. 672-6365) for a canoe. Clarke will take you up to Falls Village and let you wend your way down through calm and easy white water on the Housatonic (class I and II), past the red-hued covered bridge in West Cornwall and down to their pick-up point. Remember to pack a picnic!

A dark-burgundy and gold-pinstripe reproduction of a French **vis-à-vis** drawn by a **draft horse** will take you around the back roads of Norfolk for $40 to $50 for two. **Horse & Carriage Livery** (tel. 542-6085) will make arrangements to provide a picnic basket and a bottle of wine or champagne on request, or you can bring your own for the hour-long ride. Proprietor Beth Denis also gathers folks for hay rides and private sleigh rides according to the season.

Capture the sunset from the pavilion atop **Dennis Hill** (two miles south of Norfolk on Rte. 272), a 1,627-foot elevation that affords a sweeping view of the countryside. Haystack Mountain, one mile north of Norfolk on Rte. 272, commands an equally impressive vista from its 34-foot-high stone tower. Visit the latter on a clear evening and you can see Long Island Sound.

INNS AND BED-AND-BREAKFASTS

Wake up to the sound of wind in the trees or to the smell of breakfast and you'll never want to stay in a hotel again.

Blackberry River Inn, P.O. Box 326, Rte. 44, Norfolk, CT 06058 (tel. 203/542-5100). Not many people have had to deal with the vagaries of a tornado, but after a twister struck, Kim and Bob Zuckerman faithfully restored the beautiful exterior of this unusual 1763 inn listed in the National Register of Historic Places. In 1989, the inn took on new colors: light gray with white trim and blackberry-colored shutters. Making the inn even more special are the 17 acres of grounds that in winter become cross-country ski territory. Kim is gradually doing over all the rooms with bold Louis Nicole florals, giving the accommodations an extra dose of cheeriness. Even though there is a bridal suite, the fireplace rooms in the main house are best suited to romance. Blackberry River Inn has a wonderfully lived-in feel; you won't mistake your surroundings for a museum. Instead, you can put your feet up under you on the big couches or linger in the sunroom where breakfast is served. The restaurant serves up good food—and at reasonable prices. Rates: $65 to $150 per couple per night.

Yankee magazine called **Greenwoods Gate,** Greenwoods Road East, Norfolk, CT 06058 (tel. 203/542-5439), New England's most romantic bed-and-breakfast, and there's a softness in its elegance that sets the stage for romance the way few other settings do. Deanne Raymond decorated this former private residence with a confident hand, falling back on sensibilities that once led her to the Parsons School of Design. Here, amid the Ralph Lauren patterns, you'll find eyelet linens and Battenburg lace as well as homey quilts and puffed-up down comforters. Each room in this colonial-era house has an all-embracing feel; beautiful antiques—small and large—give special depth to the rooms. Honeymooners will especially love the light E. J. Trescott Suite and the loft-enhanced Levi Thompson Suite, which sports its own steam room and whirlpool bath. Breakfasts are equally impressive: freshly squeezed orange juice, private-blend coffee, and full entrées supplemented with homemade muffins. Rates: $120 to $150 per couple per night.

Mountain View Inn, Rte. 272, Norfolk, CT 06058 (203/542-5595). The marriage of Victoriana and Americana succeeds in this country manse (seven guest rooms) within walking distance of the timeless Norfolk green. The living room tempts guests to stay up and linger until the wee hours of the morning. Lit predominantly by the fireplace, the textured red wallpaper reflects a warmth that is carried through in the tapestry fabrics of the loveseat and parlor chairs. The low light picks up the glow of the wood in the Eastlake rocker as well. The reigning mood is casual, though, as guests chat or read. You can request white eyelet linens for an extra touch of romance. Breakfast is served in a wrap-around multiwindowed enclosed porch. Dining room. Rates: $60 to $100 per couple per night with expanded continental breakfast.

For a more rustic environment, try the **Ragamont Inn,** Rte. 44, Salisbury, CT 06068 (tel. 203/435-2372). Suite no. 11 has a simple charm, with a private parlor that overlooks the main street. Strong colonial reds and browns predominate, so don't opt for this if you want soft pastels. Yet the wallpaper and curtains match the sofa, loveseat, and chair for an overall restful effect. The bedroom of this suite is down a short private hall away from what little traffic noise there is. The restaurant, renowned for its German and Swiss food, is nicely set off from the guests' common rooms. No credit cards accepted. Rates: $58 to $85 per couple per night with breakfast.

ROMANTIC RESTAURANTS

Casual is the keynote in this corner of the state, where many celebrities come to relax.

Ragamont Inn, Rte. 44, Salisbury (tel. 435-2372). Nestled between two white-columned facades, the awning-covered patio dining area refreshes visitors after a full day's sightseeing. The decor inside, a lush splash of verdant leaves, continues the warm-weather theme. You're given no menus here, only the always-changing specials that are written up each day on blackboards. The Swiss and German cuisine draws an interesting crowd. Owner Rolf Schenkel dishes up some very good veal entrées as well as raclette, Sauerbraten, and Hasenpfeffer. The menu is varied to suit less adventurous palates. Lunch offerings range between $6 and $12.50; a complete dinner for two is about $45. Open May to November: from noon to 2 p.m. Tuesday through Saturday; 11:30 a.m. to 2 p.m. for Sunday brunch. Dinner runs from 5:30 to 9 p.m. Tuesday through Thursday; 5:30 to 10 p.m. on Friday; 6 to 10 p.m. on Saturday; and 5 to 9 p.m. on Sunday.

Freshfields, Rte. 128, West Cornwall (tel. 672-6601), is the area's answer to nouvelle cuisine. Chef Randy Nichols, a former instructor at the Culinary Institute in Vermont, has come up with excellent and unpretentious fare. The menu changes often, using the best of seasonal foods; fresh fish is delivered three times a week. Occasionally diners will be treated to complimentary sample appetizers. The mâché, duck, and wild mushroom salad surpassed our expectations, as did the rack of lamb. And care was taken to choose an unusual house wine—a Rutherford Hills chardonnay—when last we visited. Don't miss the Mile High Pie, though! The service is congenial, and the airy surroundings are quite pleasant, with butcher-block tables, stoneware bud vases, and lace curtains. Lunch is about $14 for two. Sunday brunch runs from $12.95 to $18.95; complete dinner for two, about $45 plus wine. Call to confirm dining times.

Holley Place, Pocketknife Square at Holley Street, Lakeville (tel. 435-2727). Sophisticated and friendly, this factory-turned-restaurant makes a bold, utterly romantic design statement with its buff-colored granite walls. Tracklights and a sky-light give depth to the stone's texture, while pastel peach linens and floral Villeroy & Boch china soften the effect. The tavern room is less intimate and attracts a more informal crowd. It's great for lunch. A Culinary Institute of America graduate works the kitchen here, turning out good, solid continental fare. Grilled dishes and desserts are his specialties. Appetizers from $3.95 to $8.50; entrées from $11.25 to $22.95; desserts from $3.25 to $5.95. Open for dinner on Wednesday and Thursday from 5:30 to 9 p.m.; on Friday and Saturday from 5:30 to 10 p.m.; and on Sunday from 5 to 9 p.m.

Pleasant outdoor dining at **Chez Riette,** Rte. 44, Lakeville (tel. 435-2889), includes French fare for dinner and salads and pasta for lunch. Prices are reasonable, hovering between $6 and $13.50 per person in the afternoon, $13.50 to $21.50 for entrées at night. From April to January the restaurant is open from 11:30 a.m. to 3 p.m. and from 5 to 10 p.m. From January through March the doors are closed on Tuesday and Wednesday, and lunch is served only on weekends.

Chiwalla on Main Street in Salisbury (tel. 435-9758) offers a taste of the unusual. In short, Mary O'Brien left New York City, met a maharajah's son in India who taught her about fine tea tasting, and has now opened up a fine tea house. Chiwalla's "lots of different nibbles and a sideboard full of goodies" include dim sum, tomato pie, and sausage in puff pastry, plus heart-shaped shortbread and homemade scones. Mary will be bringing "the Châteaux Margaux of teas" to her lovely 200-year-old house. À la carte prices range from $2.75 to $6 for the teas; $2 to $6 for the savories and goodies. Open from 10 a.m. to 6 p.m.

MASSACHUSETTS

4. The Berkshires of Massachusetts

Midway up the western border of Massachusetts, right where the turnpike cuts through, is a series of rolling hills and valleys renowned for their beauty, culture, and history.

Sophisticated and cosmopolitan, Lenox and Stockbridge have welcomed elegant visitors for over a century. The unusually well-maintained towns are beautifully restored, with many summer "cottages" still standing as private residences. In contrast, neighboring Lee is more of a working class town. It is also the home of the Jacob's Pillow Dance Festival and the 15,710-acre October Mountain State Forest.

The whole area comes alive in the summer, so much so that traffic slows down to a halt sometimes along the main streets. You'll escape the cities here but not the charged energy that marks these towns as preeminent vacation spots.

SHOPPING

The Berkshires are a veritable gold mine for antiques of every kind. Stopping in to browse is part of the fun. Also look in on the **Hancock Shaker Village** outside of Pittsfield (tel. 443-0188) for teas, stencils, and reproductions of Shaker furniture. At the **Norman Rockwell Museum** on Main Street in Stockbridge (tel. 298-3822) you'll find prints and reproductions for sale in the gift shop. If you don't buy the handmade dinnerware, vases, or silk flowers at **Great Barrington Pottery** in Housatonic (tel. 274-6259), you can at least tour the Japanese gardens and ceremonial tea house.

Don't miss **L&R Wise Goldsmiths** on Church Street in Lenox, who do custom goldwork and gem sculpture (tel. 637-1589). **Design Works** (tel. 232-4235) also

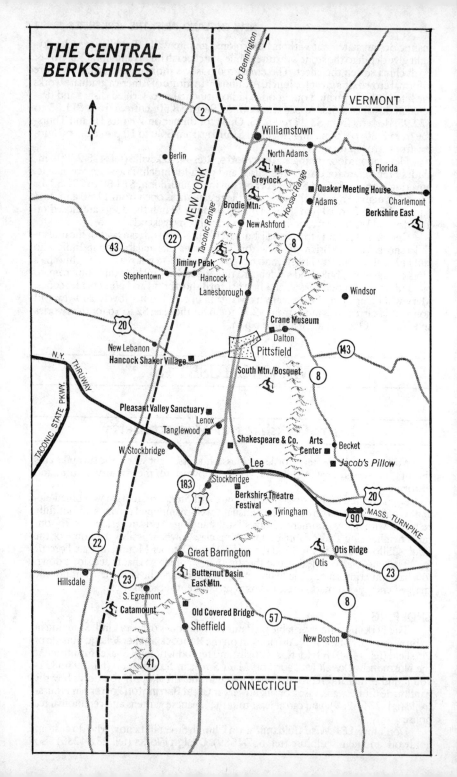

features handmade items in their store in West Stockbridge—a full line of American contemporary crafts.

ROMANTIC INTERLUDES

Romance in the Berkshires begins with al fresco cultural events.

Shakespeare at the Mount. Bring your picnic to the house that Edith Wharton built. A magnificent but aging beauty, this mansion in Lenox stands as a backdrop for outdoor professionally staged Shakespeare during the summer. Make your reservations as far in advance as possible. As darkness descends the night becomes magical, and you'll feel that you've entered another era. Admission is $3.50 per person for a tour of the premises (tel. 637-1899), from $10 to $22.50 per person for tickets to the shows (tel. 637-1197).

World renowned as the summer home of the Boston Symphony Orchestra, **Tanglewood** (tel. 637-1940) pampers its listeners with much more. The estate includes beautiful vistas of the Stockbridge Bowl, a formal labyrinth of hedges, and, most important, an expanse of perfectly tended lawn where lovers can stretch out and dream as they listen to music under the stars. Arrive early to avoid the heaviest traffic, and bring a warm wrap, because the night air can get chilly. You can now order your tickets through Ticket Master (call information if you're in the New York City area or Boston; otherwise, call toll free 800/877-1414). Tickets for the lawn, where you can bring a picnic, range from $7 to $8.50, while tickets in the shed cost from $11 to $46; prices for special events vary.

Matthew Arnold described the view from **Chesterwood** as "beautiful and soul-satisfying." The turn-of-the-century Georgian Revival-style house overlooks the Housatonic River and Monument Mountain. But it's the wooded nature trail that makes the estate extraordinary. Daniel Chester French, sculptor of the "Seated Lincoln" in the Lincoln Memorial, laid out the walking path with stone benches and pieces of his sculpture. The cool woods contrast with the brilliant garden adjacent to the house and artist's studio. The National Trust for Historic Preservation maintains the property, which is open May through October (tel. 298-3579). A small admission fee is charged.

If you're hardy, take the right-hand trail from the parking lot to the top of Great Barrington's **Monument Mountain,** just 2½ miles south of Stockbridge. You won't need anything but each other to appreciate the stunning views in all directions.

Experience a picnic! Besides the great cottage estates, the Berkshires have a wealth of quiet, treed forests perfect for picnics. **Crosby's** on Church Street in Lenox (tel. 637-3396), which was once known for its terrific take-out food, now caters almost exclusively. They will, however, pack a special picnic for about $12 per person, but you must call at least two days in advance to order.

INNS AND BED-AND-BREAKFASTS

Even though inns line the street in downtown Lenox, you'll have to make your reservations far in advance of your arrival date if it's in the summer or during fall foliage. You'll be glad you did.

The Inn at Stockbridge, Rte. 7, Stockbridge, MA 01262 (tel. 413/298-3337). Don and Lee Weitz have turned this dignified, white-columned Georgian home into a delightful, classic bed-and-breakfast inn. Formal Williamsburg-style appointments in the dining room give way to an airy parlor with chintz-covered couches and a piano. Guests often curl up in front of the fire in the second living room. Upstairs, the house is just as lovely. Decor varies from a Laura Ashley-type dusty-blue room with white wicker furnishings to an ecru and turquoise Chinese-inspired room. Lee pays scrupulous attention to all details; her extraordinarily good breakfast, for example, is served on Spode, Wedgwood, or other bone china. Don and Lee *love* weddings and newlyweds, and if you're staying awhile, will help to make your honeymoon memorable. Rates: $65 to $165 per couple per night including full breakfast.

Haus Andreas, R.R. 1, Box 605-B, Stockbridge Road, Lee, MA 01238 (tel. 413/243-3298). Hosts Lilliane and Gerhard Schmid split their time between the formal bed-and-breakfast here at the Haus and The Gateways, their larger, more imposing inn and restaurant in Lenox, so you may not see much of them. Their absence is filled with amenities not found in most inns: a swimming pool, volleyball, tennis, croquet, and badminton on the property; a nine-hole public golf course across the street; and a tandem bicycle, yours for the asking. Built by a Revolutionary War soldier, the house stands as an eloquent reminder of the beauty of the summer cottages of the area. Many of the eight air-conditioned rooms have views of the orchard and mountains, and two have fireplaces. Rates: $60 to $195 per couple per night, including continental breakfast.

Wheatleigh, P.O. Box 824, Lenox, MA 01240 (tel. 413/637-0610), is most definitely not a charming inn. This luxurious, imposing estate was fashioned after a 16th-century Italian palazzo as a wedding present from father to daughter. Although it doesn't quite follow the rules for inclusion, Wheatleigh stands as an exception in every sense of the word. For a truly patrician experience, stay in one of the terraced rooms—with fireplace—that overlook the Stockbridge Bowl. Grand proportions may intimidate the fainthearted, but for the cavalier romantic, this place is heaven. Air conditioning. Dining room. Rates: $85 to $425 per couple per night with continental breakfast.

ROMANTIC RESTAURANTS

From a renovated barn to an Italian palazzo, Berkshire restaurants cultivate romance in a variety of settings. Although there are no requirements, you'll probably feel more at ease if you dress for dinner.

Candlelight Inn, 53 Walker St., Lenox (tel. 637-1555). Chef Vincent Rawl brings new American cuisine to the Berkshires in this inn off the main street in Lenox. Shrimp scampi with Dijon mustard and a sautéed chicken breast with ginger, dill, and brie liven up a menu that's sure to include a rack of lamb and New York strip steak as well. Fresh raw vegetables in summer come compliments of the house. As the name hints, dinner is by candlelight. Ask to be seated near the window on the enclosed porch, where you can see the semicircular drive and the goings-on of the street beyond. Appetizers range from $6 to $9, entrées from $15 to $25. From July 1 through the foliage season, the restaurant is open daily for lunch from noon to 2:30 p.m.; Sunday brunch begins at 11:30 a.m. The rest of the year, lunch is served only on weekends. From July 1 through Labor Day, dinner is served daily from 5 to 9:30 p.m.; through the foliage season, daily from 6 to 9:30 p.m.; the rest of the year, on Saturday and Sunday from 6 to 9:30 p.m.

Federal House, Rte. 102, South Lee (tel. 243-1824). Some of the best food in the Berkshires can be found in the three intimate dining rooms of this tidy white-pillared, red-brick house. The chef, Ken Algren, began his career as a pastry chef and has since worked at Stonehenge in Connecticut and Windows on the World in New York. His oysters in beer batter are an elegant rendering of an American classic and demonstrate the magic he can let loose from the kitchen. The setting is subdued and tasteful and terribly romantic. Bouquets of fresh flowers adorn all the tables and the mantels of the restaurant's two fireplaces. Good wine list. Complete dinner from about $65 per couple plus drinks. Open daily for dinner from 5:30 to 10 p.m., July 1 through Labor Day; Tuesday through Sunday from 6 to 9 p.m., the rest of the year.

There's no mistaking **Embree's,** Main Street, Housatonic (tel. 274-3476). It's the only lit facade in the whole town. From the outside, as you peer in through the floor-to-ceiling plate-glass windows, Embree's looks enticingly warm and inviting. And it is. Unique vegetarian specials head off the choices, which also might include, depending on the season, roast duck pie, curried ground lamb with custard and chutney, and lemon chicken. For traditionalists, there's a superb pot roast. Entrées are priced from $10 to $20. Open July through October, Wednesday through Sunday from 6 p.m.; off-season, Embree's is also closed on Wednesday.

Dine in ultimate luxury amid Italian-inspired splendor at **Wheatleigh,** Hawthorne Road, in Lenox (tel. 637-0610). The cuisine is "new classic French." Prix-fixe dinner costs $58 per person and includes pre-appetizer, appetizer, entrée, dessert, and hot beverage. Their wine list is extensive; in addition, they serve champagne by the glass. From July 1 to August 31, the restaurant serves dinner daily from 5:30 to 9:30 p.m.; closed Monday from September 1 to June 30.

Truc Orient Express, behind Main Street in W. Stockbridge (tel. 232-4204), serves up great, authentic Vietnamese food. Lunch ranges from $4.50 to $6.75 per person. Dinner for two should run about $30. Open daily from 11 a.m. to 3 p.m. for lunch and from 3 to 10 p.m. for dinner in season. In winter, the restaurant is closed on Monday and shuts an hour early at dinner.

Exposed beams and collections of old tools set the scene at the **Old Mill,** Rte. 23 in South Egremont (tel. 528-1421). The menu changes but always includes fresh fish, veal, chicken, and beef. Lunch from $9 to $12.50; dinner entrées from $12 to $22. From Memorial Day to Columbus Day, the restaurant is open on Saturday and Sunday from 11:30 a.m. to 2 p.m. and from 5 to 10:30 p.m.; Monday through Friday from 5 to 9:30 p.m. only. After Columbus Day, the restaurant closes on Monday.

Sebastian's, just down the road from the Old Mill on Rt. 23 (tel. 528-3469), satisfies cravings with good homemade pasta and desserts. Appetizers from $3.50, pastas and entrées from $10.95, except on Thursday, when pastas are a special $7.95. Open in season Thursday through Monday from 5 p.m. to closing; call for winter hours.

Head for the **Shaker Mill Tavern,** Rte. 102 in West Stockbridge (tel. 232-8565), for burgers ($4.50 to $5.50) and a look at the "scene." Open daily from 11:30 a.m. to 1 a.m.; closed Wednesday in winter.

---

5. Cape Cod

Separated from the mainland by the Bourne and Sagamore bridges, within commuting distance from Boston, the Cape has been described as a flexed arm with Rte. 6 besecting the upper arm, Rte. 6A running the length of the inner arm, and Provincetown at the end of the curled fingers. The more placid waters of the bay lap against the towns of Sandwich, Barnstable, Dennis, and Brewster. Falmouth and Chatham, with Hyannis in between, carve out the area from shoulder to elbow on the outer arm; Nantucket Sound crashes onto the shore there. But it's at the stretch from Chatham to Truro, the outer arm from elbow up, that promises the most dramatic surf.

The Cape attracts a crowd of summer visitors every year. Yet the bay side retains a peaceful, unpretentious atmosphere, especially along the Old Kings Highway, Rte. 6A, which parallels the busier Rte. 6. Only those going to or from the slumbering towns from Sandwich to Orleans pass by. The roadway—lined with cranberry bogs, salt ponds, and tidy weather-worn shingled houses—also boasts unobtrusive crafts shops, old bookstores, galleries, and antique stores. Beyond the bay side are quiet pockets with the charm and atmosphere of eras past: Centerville, Wellfleet, Eastham, Truro, to name a few. Glorious white-sand beaches complement intriguing estuarine marshes, so visitors can either swim or hike, or both. Golf, tennis, bicycling, boat charters, and the like fill out Cape life.

SHOPPING

Cape Cod has its own recent history of craftspeople. One of the more interesting shops is **Scargo Pottery** in Dennis (tel. 385-3894), run by the Holl family.

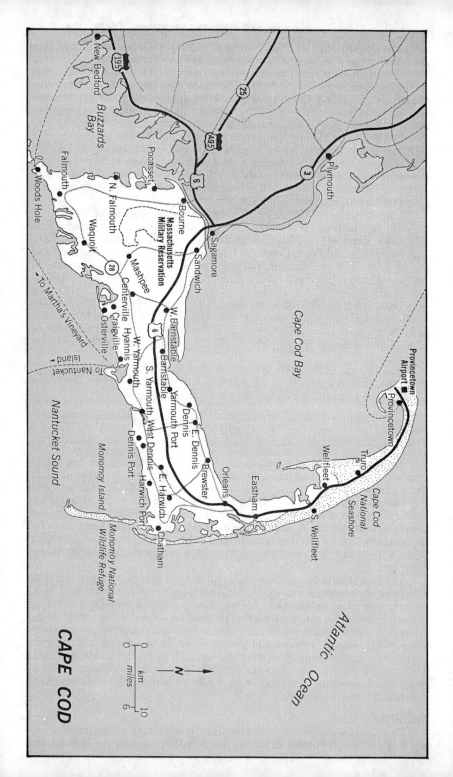

CAPE COD

New Bedford

Buzzards Bay

Pocasset

N. Falmouth

Falmouth

Woods Hole

Waquoit

Massachusetts Military Reservation

Bourne

Mashpee

Centerville

Craigville
Osterville

Hyannis

W. Yarmouth

S. Yarmouth, West Dennis

Dennis Port

Harwich Port

E. Harwich

Chatham

Dennis

E. Dennis

Yarmouth Port

Barnstable

W. Barnstable

Sandwich

Sagamore

Cape Cod Bay

Plymouth

To Nantucket Island

To Martha's Vineyard

Nantucket Sound

Monomoy Island

Monomoy National Wildlife Refuge

Brewster

Orleans

Eastham

S. Wellfleet

Wellfleet

Truro

Cape Cod National Seashore

Provincetown Airport

Provincetown

Atlantic Ocean

N

km
miles

0
0

6
6 10

Birdfeeders fashioned to look like Italian castles, paintings, and sculpture sit side by side with dishes and flameware pottery. You can get an assortment of antiques at very reasonable prices at **Barnstable Village Antiques,** a cooperative of eight dealers whose tastes range from prints to silver to linens (tel. 362-8538), and braided rugs at the **Cape Cod Braided Rug Co.** in South Dennis (tel. 398-0089).

Routes 132 and 28 in Hyannis and Rte. 28 in East Falmouth have a lion's share of outlet stores: **Quoddy Moccasin, Van Heusen, Dansk, Kitchen Etc.** (with Noritake, Pfaltzgraff, and Oneida at 10% to 60% off) to name a few.

ROMANTIC INTERLUDES

Great beaches and quiet, wooded landscapes make Cape Cod a honeymooner's haven.

In mid-April through early May, the herring run upriver to the spawning pools by **the old grist mill** in Brewster. It's fascinating! The rest of the year, however, the tranquility of the two pools soothes the soul. Stone walkways and fragrant greenery make this an ideal spot for an early-morning walk when the mist is just beginning to rise.

A 40-mile stretch of protected seashore awaits you at the **National Seashore.** The most impressive white-sand beaches are Race Point near Provincetown and Coast Guard near Orleans. When you tire of the unremitting sun, take the surprisingly beautiful swamp hike along the Atlantic White Cedar Swamp Trail or the Nauset Marsh Trail. Visitor centers are located off Rte. 6 in Eastham and by the dunes in Provincetown.

For **whale watching** the Dolphin Fleet offers morning, afternoon, and sunset trips to watch these magnificent, awesome creatures (tel. 255-3857, or toll free in Massachusetts 800/826-9300). Right whales, called thus because whalers thought they were the "right" whale to kill, humpbacks, and finbacks appear often. The lesser known, more slender minkes show up periodically, and once in a great while sei whales grace the waters. The *Ranger V* has a similar schedule (tel. 487-3322, or toll free in Massachusetts 800/992-9333). Both operate out of Provincetown from April through October. Prices are competitive, about $15 per person.

Go to Ocean Street in Hyannis to pick up the classic gaff-rigged ketch the *Spray,* a beautiful 56-foot replica of the boat that Joshua Slocum sailed when he completed the first successful solo circumnavigation of the globe in 1895. The **moonlight sail** leaves the docks on Fridays and Saturdays at about 8:30 p.m. in the summer. **Windsong Charters** (tel. 775-1630) schedules other two-hour sails throughout the day.

Two of the newer entrepreneurs on the Cape, Mike Meunier and his partner Bob have opened a sea-kayak store in West Barnstable. Although they primarily sell the graceful boats, **Atlantic Sea Kayak Co.** will rent single and double kayaks, Scuppers, and Keowees (little kayaks) for $35 on weekends. For a little extra, they'll throw in a temporary roof rack and hints on where to go. Call 362-6896 from 8 a.m. to 4 p.m. during the week for more information.

Just $2.50 will get you into the **Cape Cod Museum of Natural History** (on Rte. 6A in Brewster; tel. 896-3867) for a respite from the sun or the rain. The nonprofit museum boasts two floors of exhibits—including a working beehive—and over 200 acres of preserved land that guests can meander through either unaccompanied or with a trail guide on a scheduled walk. Open from May 1 to Columbus Day from 9:30 a.m. to 4:30 p.m., Monday through Saturday; from 12:30 p.m. to 4:30 p.m., Sunday. From Columbus Day to May 1, the museum is closed on Monday.

Known primarily for its magnificent gardens, the **Heritage Plantation of Sandwich** (tel. 888-3300), located a mile from town on Grove Street, is also home to an impressive array of Americana. Gary Cooper's 1930 Duesenberg and one of the few American-made Rolls-Royces highlight a collection of over 30 mint-condition vintage cars. In addition, a carousel, scrimshaw, and wooden decoys draw oohs and ahs from passersby. The $6 admission allows you to tour the grounds as well as the collections. Open daily from 10 a.m. to 5 p.m., mid-May to late October.

INNS AND BED-AND-BREAKFASTS

The quiet side of the Cape, on the bay, specializes in lovers' retreats hidden away from heavy traffic and touring families, but honeymoon hideaways punctuate the Cape.

With **Charles Hinckley House,** Box 723, Barnstable Village, MA 02630 (tel. 508/362-9924), Miya and Les Patrick may very well have the best bed-and-breakfast in New England. Miya has used her unerring sense of style to complement Les's restoration of the circa 1809 colonial building with antiques and handcrafted accessories. Romance, relaxation, and a homespun elegance characterize the inn. Miya attends to the smallest details, from toiletries and thick-piled cotton bath towels in the bathrooms to her trademark flower on the breakfast plate. Her vision extends into the stunning front-yard wildflower garden, which provides many of the blooms in the house. But that doesn't satisfy Miya; she orders in striking exotic blossoms and adds them to the bouquets. Care and thoughtfulness are apparent at every level. Although all five guest rooms are well heated and have working fireplaces, when the cold weather sets in, Miya still changes the linens from the pressed sheets and handcrafted quilts to flannel bed dressings and down comforters. Honeymooners are treated to a bottle of champagne, and if they wish, breakfast in bed. Rates: $98 to $135 per person per night with a full breakfast.

Beechwood, 2839 Main St., Rte. 6A, Barnstable, MA 02630 (tel. 508/362-6618). Just a few miles up from the Charles Hinckley House, this 1853 Queen Anne–style Cape "cottage" has been restored to Victorian splendor. Owners Anne and Bob Livermore delight in the romance of the Victorian age. They serve afternoon tea each day in the elegant fire-lit parlor, and their full breakfasts feature goodies such as raspberry-filled almond muffins and blueberry pancakes. The Rose and Marble Rooms each have a fireplace to banish the evening's chill. A huge canopied four-poster dominates the former, while a substantial brass bed and gold upholstered Empire sofa lend romance to the latter. The downstairs Lilac Room is another favorite among newlyweds, decked out in Waverly fabrics and sporting a brass king-size bed and wonderful old claw-foot tub. Each room is furnished as a silent tribute to passion. Hanging out and relaxing are the big pastimes. You may be tempted to go no farther than the wrap-around veranda. Rates: $85 to $135 per couple per night.

You'll be positively charmed by the **Inn at West Falmouth,** P.O. Box 1111, West Falmouth, MA 02574 (tel. 508/540-7696), which captures the feel of an old English manor house. Built in 1900, the three-story shingled inn sits high on a hill with views looking out to Buzzards Bay. Five of the nine rooms are appointed with queen-size canopied beds, five have fireplaces and balconies, and all enjoy direct-access telephones, private Italian marble baths, and whirlpool tubs. Chintz-covered, overstuffed furniture complements the English, French, and Oriental antiques that innkeeper Lewis Milardo collected after his apprenticeship at a prominent *pensione* in Rome. In the European tradition, you'll be happily pampered here. Extras includes bicycles, a heated swimming pool, a clay tennis court. Rates: $135 to $185 per couple per night, including continental breakfast with home-baked muffins and fresh-brewed coffee.

The Inn at Fernbrook, 481 Main St., Centerville, MA 02632 (tel. 508/775-4334), once sat on 17 exquisite acres landscaped by Frederick Law Olmsted, designer of Boston's Public Garden and New York's Central Park. Just half a mile from Craigville Beach, the stately house now stands on a smaller plot of land, but its graciousness and greatness are retained. Besides an old-fashioned, romantic heart-shaped rose garden and a wisteria arbor, the property boasts a wealth of unusual trees: Japanese cork, black walnut, red hickory, white dogwood, and Chinese katsura, among many others. Inside is a house that epitomizes the notion of good taste. The inventor of Technicolor entertained here, as did Cardinal Spellman, who hosted such notables as John F. Kennedy and Richard Nixon. The suites, three rooms, and cottage that comprise the bed-and-breakfast include a chapel–turned–guest room with a 17-foot-high ceiling; a beautiful lace-canopy four-poster bed; a turret room; and a more casual suite with a loft. Homemade muffins accompany a typical breakfast of broiled grapefruit, freshly squeezed orange juice, and baby Dutch pancakes with sliced strawberries and sausage. Innkeepers Brian Gallo and Sal DiFlorio take great pride in their 1881 Queen Anne Victorian, for it is indeed a treasure. Rates: $95 to $170 per couple per night.

ROMANTIC RESTAURANTS

Super-casual to formally romantic, Cape Cod's restaurants love honeymooners.

The Cranberry Moose, Rte. 6A, Yarmouth Port (tel. 362-8153 or 362-3501), came under new ownership in the summer of 1988, when Marietta Hickey, formerly of La Cipollina, returned to the Cape after a respite in Hawaii. She's carrying on the restaurant's floral tradition, bringing in eight or nine new arrangements every Thursday. The blooms set off the new white Rosenthal china and white linens. The food is still good too; most of the menu changes weekly, but you'll almost always find a good veal chop, rack of lamb, or duck, and lots of fresh fish—and occasionally a cranberry mousse. Marietta hired Brett Lancaster as chef—he graduated second in his class from the Culinary Institute of America—and her careful choices also extend to the wine list. Its 125 selections have been narrowed down from the approximately 1,500 types of wine Marietta tasted before making her final decisions. Appetizers run from $4.50 to $10.50, entrées from $17 to $35. Open daily from 5:30 to 10 p.m., mid-May to mid-October. Off-season, the restaurant opens for lunch and Sunday dinner, although they're closed on Tuesday; call for specifics.

The Regatta, 217 Clinton St., Falmouth (tel. 548-5400), is blissfully romantic. The views of moonlight and the ocean set the scene as much as the soft pinks and mauve of the decor. Creative American food is the hallmark, with fresh fish featured nightly. If you visit in July or August, you may find the special roast lobster stuffed with crabmeat soufflé and served with beurre blanc. Don't pass it up! A "dessert trilogy" allows you to sample three of the most popular sweets. All in all, a gem. Appetizers run from $4 to $8, entrées from $16 to $26, plus dessert and wine. No hard liquor or beer. Open from 5:30 to around 10 p.m., Memorial Day through September.

The Regatta at Cotuit, 4631 Falmouth Rd.–Rte. 28, Cotuit (tel. 428-5715). The Bryans have done it again! This time in a 200-year-old Georgian mansion with nine dining rooms. Featuring "New American Grill" foods, this second Regatta has its own distinct personality. From Cotuit oyster chowder and conch fritters to grilled seafood sausage with lemon pasta to a seared filet mignon in cabernet sauce, the food excels. Many herbs come from right out back, the organically grown vegetables from the New Alchemy Institute down the road. Damask cloths and Limoges china set the scene, as does period wallpaper. Six- and seven-course tasting menus cost $26 and $36, while à la carte entrées run from $12.50 to $26 in season. Open from 5:30 to around 10 p.m., Memorial Day to mid-October. Off-season, the restaurant closes Tuesday, but call for specifics.

Chillingsworth, Rte. 6A, Brewster (tel. 896-3640). Reserve your table weeks —if not months—in advance of your visit and request one of the smaller, more intimate dining rooms. If you're lucky, you'll get the table for two in front of the fireplace. This is an old sea captain's house—approximately 250 years old—and some of the original wallpaper has even been left intact. People ooh and aah over the Limoges china, but it's the nouvelle cuisine that keeps them returning. The menu, which changes often, is in French, but the waiters and waitresses have their recitation, which explains what may be unfamiliar to you. The five-course dinners are prix-fixe, ranging from $39.50 to $49 depending on your entrée. From Memorial Day to

June, the restaurant has two seatings—from 6 to 6:30 p.m. and from 9 to 9:30 p.m., on weekends only. From June to mid-September, it's open daily except Monday; through Columbus Day, the doors are open Thursday through Sunday; through Thanksgiving, on Friday and Saturday. Early and late in the season, the seatings may vary slightly, so call first to double check.

The Mooring, 230 Ocean St., Hyannis (tel. 775-4656), is a civilized stop for harborside dining by the Hy-Line boat docks. Sandwiches, seafood, chicken, and beef run from $4.25 up at lunch, from $5.50 up at dinner. Open daily from 11:30 a.m. to 10:30 p.m.; dinner starts at 5 p.m.

If you're in Hyannis for the Melody Tent summer theatre, plan to eat at **The Paddock** at the West Main rotary (tel. 775-7677) next door. They'll reserve a special table or do something out of the ordinary for you if you let them know you're newlyweds. Sandwiches at lunch from $4.50; dinner entrées from $13.75 to $22.95. Open April 1 to mid-November from 11:45 a.m. to 2:30 p.m. and from 5 to 10 p.m.

Kadee's in East Orleans (tel. 255-6184) should satisfy anyone who likes fresh seafood. They offer some of the best inexpensive sea fare on the Cape; they also run a fish market next door and an adjacent miniature golf course (open from 11:30 a.m. to 10:30 p.m., from $2 to $3 a game). Lunch prices range from $5.50 to $12.50, with dinners running from $6.50 to $15.95. Wine, beer, and champagne coolers only.

For an informal lunch after walking on the beach, stop in at **The Marshside,** Bridge Street off of Rte. 6A in East Dennis (tel. 385-4010). Sandwiches, snacks, and seafood salads are their specialty: most items under $10. Open from 7 a.m. to 9 or 10 p.m., depending on the season. Generous gourmet deli sandwiches, terrific take-out fare, and a great selection of imported beers are for the asking at the **Dennis Village Mercantile,** Rte. 6A in Dennis (tel. 385-3877), which is open Monday through Saturday from 7:30 a.m. to 5:30 p.m., and on Sunday from 8:30 a.m. to 2:30 p.m. And if **Kate's** drive-in on 6A in Brewster is open, stop for homemade ice cream and the best lobster roll on the Cape.

6. Nantucket and Martha's Vineyard

Sister islands that sit off the coast of southern Cape Cod, Nantucket and Martha's Vineyard have long attracted the wealthy and the famous, old-money patrons and new intellectuals, and a host of sea-loving vacationers who passionately argue the merits of one island over the other.

Nantucket, with no traffic lights, no fast-food businesses, and a building code that maintains a standard weathered-shingle look for all structures, is the smaller of the two. Tourism entrenches itself along the cobblestoned main street of Nantucket Town but barely brushes the rose-covered trellises of tiny 'Sconset and the other residential areas of Madaket and Dionis. Take to the moors to feel as if you've traveled back in time. The Maria Mitchell Science Center (tel. 228-0898) leads guided walking tours into backcountry that few passing tourists see. The ubiquitous green bearberry covers much of the ground; bayberry, blackberry, scrub oak, and pitch pine add dimension to the textured landscape. As on the Vineyard, bicycles become the favored mode of transportation, especially in the summer, when the town streets are crowded with day-trippers in their autos.

Martha's Vineyard—the summer haunt of celebrities such as John Hersey, William Styron, Carly Simon, and Mike Wallace—is larger and less easy to categorize. Conservatives tend to favor Edgartown; bohemians, Vineyard Haven. And a small community of Wampanoag Indians dominates Gay Head. The Vineyard, though larger than Nantucket, maintains a trim profile—just 20 miles long and 9 miles wide—and is still good bicycling territory for the willing tourist.

Maritime traditions continue: lighthouses boom their messages to passing

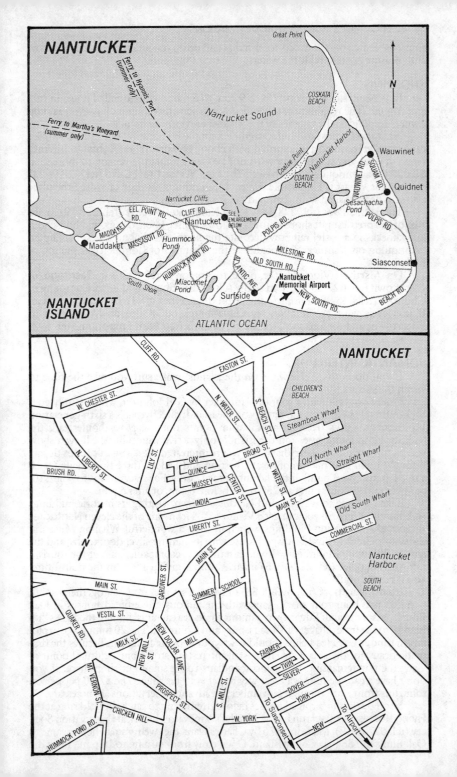

ships, fishermen ply the waters for fish that end up on restaurant tables the same day, and pleasure boats speckle the waters.

SHOPPING

In general, stores are open from 9 a.m. to 5 p.m., with extended hours in July and August. The reliability of scheduled hours sometimes lapses, however, as shop owners respond to the vagaries of the weather and visiting friends.

Nantucket's most striking souvenir is a simple yet beautiful tightly hand-woven caned basket, covered and adorned with ebony or ivory. These **lightship baskets** range in price and size from upward of $100 for a miniature version to more than $3,000 for an antique covered basket. **The Four Winds Craft Guild** (tel. 228-9623) on Straight Wharf is a reputable dealer representing a number of artists; the place also sells heart-shaped scrimshaw and sailor's valentines.

The **Lion's Paw** (tel. 228-3837) and **Nantucket Accent** (tel. 228-1913) are two of the prettiest gift shops in town. Pillows, quilts, hooked rugs, and household knickknacks in a pastel rainbow decorate the boutiques. For antiques, pick up an "Antiquing on Nantucket" brochure at the Chamber of Commerce at the top of Main Street.

On Martha's Vineyard, the place to go for tasteful gifts is **Tashtego** in Edgartown (tel. 627-4300); head to the **Allen Farm Sheep and Wool Company** in Chilmark (tel. 645-9064) for handmade products as beautiful to touch as to look at. If jewelry is what you're after, try **Claudia** (tel. 627-8306) on Main Street in Edgartown; and for antiques, try West Tisbury's **Red Barn Emporium** (tel. 693-0455).

ROMANTIC INTERLUDES

If you do nothing else while on the islands, make sure you take the time to watch the sun set.

Orient yourself with a tour of Nantucket by Gail Johnson, whose family goes back indirectly to the first ten settlers on the island; directly, she's a sixth-generation Nantucketer. Gail's lively historical tour points out the Macy homestead, the Sankaty Head lighthouse, and the island's only active windmill. She'll even show you pictures of the cranberry harvest if you're interested. **Gail's Seanic Rides** depart from the town information office at Chestnut and Federal three times daily (at 10 a.m., 1 p.m., and 3 p.m.) at the height of the season. For reservations for the $10-per-person, 1½-hour tour, call 257-6557 before 8 a.m. or after 6 p.m.

Take the time to walk around Nantucket town, visiting its historic buildings and museums. For $6 you can get a Visitor's Pass from any of the eleven **Nantucket Historical Association** buildings, which include a wonderful Whaling Museum; the stately Greek Revival Hadwen House with its sterling silver doorknobs; and the almost 200-year-old Old Mill. If you'd rather go accompanied, ask at the tourism information office (tel. 228-0925) if Mr. Young is giving a tour in the near future. You'll be glad you did.

Island Transport (tel. 693-0058) of Martha's Vineyard puts together a solid, narrated two-hour tour that begins with the famous gingerbread houses in Oak Bluffs; passes through Edgartown, famous for its sea captains' homes; then goes "up island" to the little villages of West Tisbury and Chilmark. The 20 minutes of exploration time at Gay Head cliffs should whet your appetite to return. Besides the dramatic beauty of the area, Gay Head is an interesting stop from a cultural point of view; the few remaining Wampanoag Indians run a small gift shop there. If you don't have a car, the tour is a great way to get your bearings. The $7.50-per-person tour runs from April through November; no advance reservations are necessary.

Stroll by the gingerbread houses before attempting to catch the gold ring at the **Flying Horses carousel** run by the Martha's Vineyard Historical Preservation Society (tel. 627-8017). Made in 1876 by Charles Dare, the twenty small horses came to Oak Bluffs in 1884 via Coney Island. Open daily from 10 a.m. to 10 p.m., from the end of May through Labor Day. Rides are $1 each. Cotton candy, popcorn, and other snacks are on hand.

If you'd rather ride a real horse—western style—call **Eastover Farms** in West Tisbury (tel. 693-3770). They've developed six different routes that vary from a half-hour walk/ride through woods and fields for $15 per person to a one-and-a-half-hour walk/trot/canter excursion along South Beach (*behind* the dunes from June 15 through September 15) for $35 per person. Other trails wind around Watcha Pond, meander through pretty fields, or take you through a state forest. As newlyweds, you'll probably pass up the sunrise ride, but Eastover's sunset and moonlight rides can be pretty special. Overall, prices range from $15 to $55 per person.

INNS AND BED-AND-BREAKFASTS
It's crucial to make plans early, as the nicest accommodations can be booked a year in advance.

On Nantucket
Wauwinet, P.O. Box 2580, Nantucket, MA 02554 (tel. 617/228-0145, or toll free 800/426-8718). The sandy shore of Nantucket Harbor defines the back-yard boundary of this elegant 40-room inn, while out front, just steps from the entry, a seemingly endless length of Atlantic beach stretches to Great Point, the isolated northern tip of the island. By virtue of its location alone, Wauwinet would prove to be a great inn. Yet a certain graciousness—of service, structure, and style—marks the Wauwinet at every level of detail. Sisal carpeting covers the floors; the simplicity follows through to a beachy blend of simple antique pine and white-wicker furniture. So as not to distract, the armoire unobtrusively hides a TV, VCR, and toaster oven. Turn-down service, a morning newspaper outside the door, and a free shuttle van into town supplement the courteous attention here. Besides water sports, Wauwinet boasts a tupelo- and sassafras-lined path to two Har-tru tennis courts, bicycles, volleyball, and croquet. "Wauwinet Interlude" honeymoon package: Five days/four nights (CP): $1,528 to $1,865 per couple. Includes water-view accommodations; welcome bottle of champagne, caviar, and hors d'oeuvres; a candlelight dinner with wine at Topper's; breakfast in bed the first morning, continental breakfast thereafter; keepsake champagne flutes, long-stemmed roses, and a box of chocolate truffles. Two- and three-night packages are also available. Open from the end of April to the end of October.

Jared Coffin House, 29 Broad St., Nantucket, MA 02554 (tel. 508/228-2405), is really a complex of five houses. The main Jared Coffin House dates from 1845, and it is there that guests check in and first relax in the three antiques-strewn formal parlors. Across the street, the 1842 Harrison Gray House and the 1821 Henry Coffin House play host to many honeymooners because all of the rooms—12 in the former, 6 in the latter—have canopied queen-size beds. Reproductions outnumber antiques, but the overall feel is one of crisp, clean formality. The location is ideal for visitors who want to be within walking distance of town but far enough away to be out of earshot. Rates: $100 to $175 per couple per night from May 1 to November 1; reduced rates in winter except for holidays and special events.

On Martha's Vineyard
Captain Dexter House, 100 Main St., P.O. Box 2457, Vineyard Haven, MA 02568 (tel. 508/693-6564). If you decide to go to Martha's Vineyard for a brief visit, you might want to stay at this pretty, restored sea captain's house, which is conveniently located around the corner from the ferry landing yet separated from town by enough distance to maintain a quiet atmosphere. The Captain Harding Room is a favorite with honeymooners, with a lace canopy adorning the reproduction rice-carved four-poster bed and a very comfortable loveseat positioned next to the fireplace. The bay window on the opposite side of the room overlooks the exten-

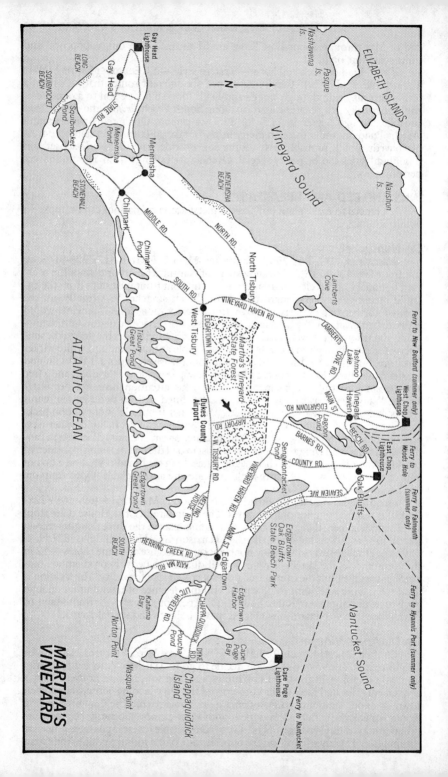

MARTHA'S VINEYARD

sion of the town's main street and the harbor beyond. Throughout the eight guest rooms and common rooms, there's an ample scattering of antiques, which complement the ambience of the 1843 house. Continental breakfast includes freshly-squeezed orange juice and freshly baked breads and muffins. Rates: $55 to $145 per couple per night.

Charlotte Inn, 27 South Summer St., Edgartown, MA 02539 (tel. 508/627-4751). Owners Gerret and Paula Conover have been welcoming guests here for 18 years. Upon arrival, you'll undoubtedly head for the front desk, a barrister's table originally made in Scotland. From there you'll be shown to one of the 25 charming rooms that comprise this lovely inn, steeped in the protocol of old-world hospitality. Choose among accommodations in one of three old whaling captains' houses or in two newer buildings that are equally inviting. Fireplaces warm two queen-bedded suites with high ceilings and private entrances—perfect for honeymooners who want to splurge; on the opposite side of the spectrum are two cozy chambers that share a bath. In between are the other 21 rooms (3 of which also have fireplaces), each with a personality designed to please. English and country antiques blend in with other appointments for a mix that takes the best from the past and the present. Rates: $75 to $335 per couple per night.

ROMANTIC RESTAURANTS

Take note that outside of Edgartown and Oak Bluffs, Martha's Vineyard is a dry island, so you may want to bring a bottle of champagne or wine to your restaurant of choice; most provide a corking service and glasses. Also, a few places on Nantucket do have a dress code, so ask as you make your reservations. One final note: Not all establishments accept credit cards.

On Nantucket

Most seasoned summer residents would agree that **Chanticleer,** 9 New St. in Siasconset (tel. 257-6231), serves the most elegant classical French cuisine on the island. Its rose-covered trellises, the leitmotif of 'Sconset, provide a charming backdrop to the noted fare. French chef Jean-Charles Berruet, who has owned the restaurant for 20 years, was once the private chef for the owner of *Gourmet* magazine. Lunch for two costs about $50; prix-fixe dinner, $50 per person. Open Mother's Day through Columbus Day from noon to 2 p.m. and from 6:30 to 9:30 p.m.; closed Wednesday.

Topper's, at the Wauwinet Inn (tel. 228-8768), has one of the best views of the setting sun, so go for a drink at least, if not for dinner. As at the inn, the service is top-notch. And the food is wonderful. The salad, for instance, might combine lamb's lettuce, endive, radicchio, and dandelion greens; the bread arrives warm and toasted. The menu does change seasonally. Summer specialties set the mouth watering: lobster and crab cakes, corn soup with roasted red-pepper cream, jumbo shrimp wrapped in veal bacon on crispy pasta, and grilled chicken with rice-paper shrimp rolls, to name a few. Lunch is just as inventive. Dinner for two hovers around $100; lunch ranges from $6 to $16 per person. Open noon to 9:30 p.m. from the end of April to the end of October.

Jared's, at the Jared Coffin House (tel. 228-2400), is a picture of Victorian finery dressed in large swaths of coral fabric. Its atmosphere resembles that of an old English tea room; the food represents a sampling of good continental-style cuisine. Scallops in a pastry shell, chicken breast stuffed with rock shrimp, and filet of beef join duck, veal, lamb, and fish on the menu. Choose between a prix-fixe meal for $29.95 that comes with salad and dessert or à la carte entrées from $20.95 to $24.95. Open daily from 6 to 9 p.m. in season; call for the off-season schedule.

De Marco, 9 India St. (tel. 228-1836), is known for its gourmet Italian food such as mozzarella in carrozza, fennel-seed and garlic-seasoned lamb chunks sautéed with artichoke hearts, and grilled veal chop with sun-dried tomatoes, leeks, and pine nuts in a port and raspberry sauce. The comfortable restaurant also cooks up home-made pastas from $14 to $20; other entrées from $19 to $29; antipasti from $5 to $8. Open daily from 6 to 11 p.m., early June to Labor Day; but call first to confirm.

Thick, creamy chowder, endless shoestring potatoes, folk music, and specialty beverages attract youthful locals and tourists to **The Brotherhood,** "an 1840 Whal-ing Bar" at 23 Broad St. (no reservations or telephone). Champagne specialties run $4 to $5; soups, half sandwiches, and sandwiches go for $2.25 and up. There aren't many tables for two, but you'll have fun making friends at the long wooden tables. Open Monday through Thursday from 11:30 a.m. to 11 p.m.; on Friday and Satur-day to midnight; on Sunday from noon to 11 p.m. **The Juice Bar** tantalizes passers-by with the smell of hand-rolled waffle cones and cups for their yummy homemade ice cream. Try the two-person ice-cream sandwich: your choice of ice cream lovingly squashed between two freshly baked toll-house cookies. Prices start at $2, not in-cluding their baked goods and freshly squeezed fruit and vegetable juices. Open from 8 a.m. to 11 p.m. (to 8 p.m. in the shoulder season), May to Columbus Day.

On Martha's Vineyard
The Black Dog Tavern, Beach Road, Vineyard Haven (tel. 693-9223), is long on personality and atmosphere. Locals, tourists, and summer residents haunt its wa-terside dining room, which serves throughout the day. Typical lunch offerings—fresh fish and chips, stir-fried vegetables, burgers, and more—run from about $3 for soups to about $8 for heartier fare. In summer all the vegetables are local and the fish are as fresh as can be. Tuna, swordfish, and delicious filets may come with a simple lemon-butter sauce, a hollandaise, or a spicy blanket of jalapeño peppers. Dinners range from $5.95 to $19 per person. Open daily from mid-May through October, 6:30 a.m. to 10 p.m.; off-season hours are 7 a.m. to 9 p.m., usually seven days a week, although they may be closed on Tuesday.

L'Etoile, at the Charlotte Inn, 27 South Summer St., Edgartown (tel. 627-5187). This most romantic of restaurants is actually a plant-filled Victorian conser-vatory punctuated with antique brass and old British still lifes and equestrian paint-ings. Candlelit seating in the garden becomes all the more romantic when surrounded by bougainvillea and other blooms bursting with color. The menu changes monthly, but typical offerings range from roasted rack of lamb to a goat-cheese and sun-dried-tomato flan with roasted garlic and red zinfandel sauce; count on there always being lobster and scallops on the menu, accompanied by heavenly scented cornbread and sea beans, a type of seaweed. Prix-fixe dinner: $42 to $46, depending on the season. From July to Labor Day, the restaurant is open daily from 6:30 p.m. to 9:45 p.m. During shoulder seasons—Memorial Day to July 1, and September and October—dinner is served Wednesday through Sunday. In winter, dinner is served Thursday through Saturday. Sunday brunch is served year-round from 10:30 a.m. to 12:30 p.m. Closed January. Make your summer reservations at least two weeks in advance.

Louis' Tisbury Café in Vineyard Haven receives kudos from locals. It's proba-bly the best eatery on the island for your money's worth. Homemade pastas, vege-tarian lasagna, char-grilled lamb, and linguine lobster diavolo (entrées from $9.75 to $18) tempt diners, while subs and pizzas ($3.75 to $10) lead the take-out menu. From April through December, open daily from 11:30 a.m. to closing—which var-ies seasonally; from January through March, open for dinner Thursday through Monday from 5:30 p.m. on. The view—and the fresh pies ($2.50 to $3.00 a slice) —are what draw people to **The Aquinnah Shop** at Gay Head (tel. 645-9654). They also have a good Quahog chowder for $1.95 to $3.50. Open from Easter to Novem-ber 1, Monday through Thursday from 9 a.m. to 8 p.m.; on Friday, Saturday, and Sunday from 8 a.m. to 9 p.m. **Homeport** (tel. 645-2679) in Menemsha is known for its seafood and its "back-door dinners," which are exactly what they sound like. You pick up your take-out by the back door and head to the nearest beach. Or you can eat inside. Open May 1 to October 15, daily from 5 to 10 p.m.; take-out open from 5 to 9:30 p.m. A complete dinner with appetizer, salad, entrée, and dessert will run about $22 per person.

VERMONT

7. Manchester and the Mountains

Just before southern Vermont classifies as mid-Vermont, about half an hour northeast of Albany, N.Y., Manchester and the mountains greet you with picture-postcard perfection.

Manchester Village is a tidy town of white clapboard houses with black shutters, a requisite white-steepled church, and a gracious resort that fronts the wide main street of the town. Equinox Mountain, rising to 3,816 feet, provides a dramatic backdrop. The effect is simple elegance; the atmosphere, dignified yet casual. Townspeople take their afternoon constitutionals, stopping at the rare-books store or the stencil shop by the Equinox hotel.

Depending on the season, visitors usually take off early in the morning for the ski slopes, the hiking trails, or the back roads. The lingerers tend to golf, fish on the world famous Battenkill, or stroll along main street with the oldtimers.

SHOPPING

Vermont, too, is known for its factory outlets. In Manchester, you can get **Ralph Lauren, Anne Klein, Dexter** shoes, and more. You can also satisfy your antiques cravings at **Carriage Trade Antiques Center, Danby Antiques Center,** or any one of a score of others. Ask your hosts for their favorite shops. Woodcarver Bill Herrick works out of his own shop, **Pierre's Gate** (tel. 362-1766). For antique clocks, try the **Clock Emporium** (tel. 362-3328); for miniatures and dolls, the **Enchanted Doll House** (tel. 362-1327); and for baskets, **Basketville** (tel. 362-1609). Fly fishermen will appreciate the **Orvis** store (tel. 362-1300) with its range of fishing tackle and hunting accessories.

ROMANTIC INTERLUDES

Sports enthusiasts as well as antique hunters call this place paradise.

It doesn't take long before you're **cross-country skiing** along groomed and mapped trails enjoying the winter sunshine. One of the prettiest alpine centers is at **Hildene,** Robert Todd Lincoln's estate (tel. 362-1788) right in Manchester; trail fees vary from $5 to $7; equipment rental is $10 daily. At **Wild Wings** (tel. 824-6793) you can stop in for complimentary hot bouillon after you've explored their 12 miles of groomed and primitive trails. Trail fees range from $5 to $7; equipment rental, which includes use of the grounds, from $10 to $15. **Viking,** one of the largest centers, has extensive trails in Londonderry (tel. 824-3933) and charges from $7 to $10, and $17 for a weekend pass; equipment rental, $12. They also offer guided bike tours in the summer for $45 a day, which includes bike rental and lunch.

From mid-May through October, the lovely 412-acre estate that belonged to Robert Todd Lincoln—Abraham Lincoln's son—is open to the public for **tours and picnics** on the grounds (admission to the grounds is free; $5 for house tour). With sweeping views of the mountains and about three miles of hiking and nature trails, **Hildene** (tel. 362-1788) is much more than a historic home. The formal garden, gazebo, and observatory shouldn't be missed. Brides often choose the terrace for their receptions. It's located in Manchester.

What more need be said? In the light of day or under the glow of a full moon,

horsedrawn rides give lovers a chance to snuggle together. **Village Carriage Company** (tel. 518/692-7686)—situated in front of the Equinox hotel in Manchester Village—has coachmen who come attired in top hat and tails to take you to your chosen restaurant or for a ride (approximately $50 to $60 per carriage per hour). There's also a 20-minute ride for only $20 per couple. For a more countrified jaunt, call **Windhill Farm Stable and Tack Shop** (tel. 362-2604). They'll take you out on the trail for $12 an hour per person. When it snows, call them for a sleigh ride: just $35 for the two of you.

INNS AND BED-AND-BREAKFASTS

The area around Manchester has blossomed with bed-and-breakfasts in the past decade.

1811 House, Rte. 7A, Manchester Village, VT 05254 (tel. 802/362-1811). Anglophiles take heart. Mary and Jack Hirst and Pat and Jeremy David have created a superbly put together, sophisticated bed-and-breakfast complete with English pub and after-hunt atmosphere. Guests help themselves to drinks on the honor system, then head to the basement for a game of pool or table tennis. There's a stunning collection of antique furniture, dishware, and prints, many pieces of which come from the owners' families. All the double-bedded rooms are appropriate for honeymooners, but the six fireplace suites are exceptionally lovely, all but one with queen- or king-size four-poster canopied beds. Expect a hearty breakfast with eggs and bacon, french toast, or the like. Rates: $100 to $160 per couple per night includes a 15% service charge.

The Inn at Sunderland, R.R. 2, Box 2440, Arlington, VT 05250 (tel. 802/362-4213). Peggy and Tom Wall migrated to Vermont from Washington, D.C., where they met, married, and decided they wanted to work together. This cheerful, tidy bed-and-breakfast is the result. In 1986, they added five rooms to the original house, including one accessible to handicapped guests, to bring the total room count to ten. Both old and new rooms contain a comfortable mix of Victorian-era antiques and modern accoutrements. The house and hosts make lounging around a pleasure. Peggy puts out a boursin cheese spread and offers refreshments in the early evening; it's a nice way to share stories about the day's adventures. If Peggy knows you're honeymooners, she prepares a silver tray with a split of champagne and crystal flutes. Rates: $75 to $95 per couple per night with full breakfast.

ROMANTIC RESTAURANTS

Vermont's varied restaurants make eating out a pleasure for many nights running.

The Arlington Inn, Rte. 7A, Arlington (tel. 375-6532). A refined air permeates this beautifully restored Greek Revival mansion, Victorian embellishments adding a richness to the crisp interior. Chef-owner Paul Kruzel shows off his Culinary Institute of America training with such specials as lobster-and-corn chowder and venison in a maple-chestnut sauce. The printed menu, which changes every six months, offers less adventurous but equally good choices. Entrées from $13.95; Sunday brunch from $6.25. Open daily from 5:30 to 9 p.m.; Sunday brunch from noon to 2:30 p.m. Call to verify lunch hours during the summer season.

The Black Swan, Rte. 7A, Manchester (tel. 362-3807). Ask for the dining room with exposed brick walls and country wreaths tied with pretty bows. The decor and food together bespeak years of experience, which chef-owner Richard Whisenhunt has: Le Cirque in New York and Le Club in San Francisco are his alma maters. The sweetbreads of veal and the lobster-and-truffle pasta hint at the inventiveness here. If you crave a soufflé or baked Alaska with dinner, you can request these treats in advance when you make your reservation; tell them it's your honeymoon. Appetizers run from $3.50 to $7, entrées from $14 to $19. Open daily except Wednesday from June 1 to November 1, 5:30 to 9 p.m.; Thursday through Monday from December 1 to May 30.

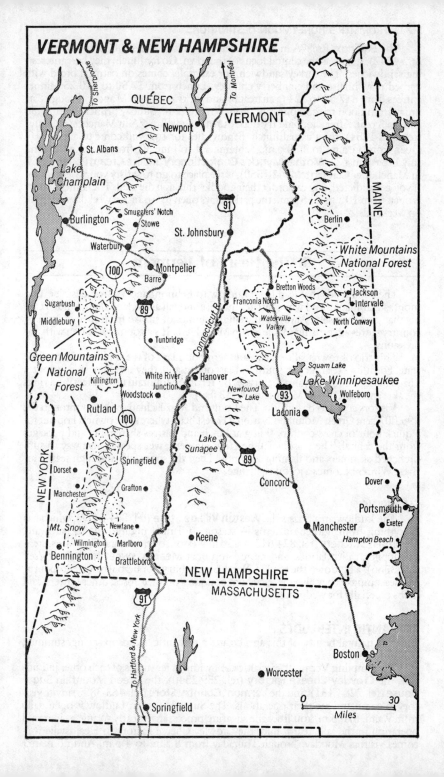

VERMONT & NEW HAMPSHIRE

To Sherbrooke

QUÉBEC

To Montréal

VERMONT

MAINE

N

Newport

St. Albans

Lake
Champlain

Smugglers' Notch

Burlington

Stowe

Waterbury

Montpelier

Barre

100

89

Sugarbush

Middlebury

Green Mountains
National
Forest

Killington

Woodstock

Rutland

100

Dorset

Manchester

Mt. Snow

Newfane

Wilmington

Marlboro

Bennington

Brattleboro

NEW YORK

91

To Hartford & New York

St. Johnsbury

91

Berlin

White Mountains
National Forest

Bretton Woods

Jackson

Franconia Notch

Intervale

Waterville
Valley

North Conway

Connecticut R.

Tunbridge

White River
Junction

Hanover

Squam Lake

Lake Winnipesaukee

Newfound
Lake

93

Wolfeboro

Laconia

Springfield

Lake
Sunapee

89

Grafton

Concord

Dover

Portsmouth

Keene

Manchester

Exeter

Hampton Beach

NEW HAMPSHIRE

MASSACHUSETTS

Boston

Worcester

0   30

Miles

Springfield

The Equinox, Rte. 7A in Manchester Village (tel. 362-4700, or toll free 800/ 362-4747), stands as the central focus of the town. Go for lunch; they have interesting sandwiches. The turkey sandwich, for example, comes on oatmeal bread with herbed mayonnaise and cranberry chutney. Lunch from $7.50 to $10.25; dinner entrées from $17.50 to $24 (a chateaubriand for two). Open Monday through Saturday from noon to 2:30 p.m. and from 6 to 10 p.m.; Sunday brunch from 11:30 a.m. to 3 p.m. After shopping try the **Gourmet Deli,** Rte. 7A in Manchester Center (tel. 362-1254), for a casual lunch. Sandwiches for two will come to about $10. Open from 11 a.m. to 3:30 p.m., September 1 to June 30; from 8 a.m. to 6 p.m., July 1 to August 31. **Mother Myrick's Confectionery and Ice Cream Parlor,** Rte. 7 in Manchester Center (tel. 362-1560), is *the* place to go to satisfy your sweet tooth. If you get addicted, you can order their goodies through the mail. The confectionery is open from 10 a.m. to 6 p.m.; the parlor stays open to 9 p.m. on weekdays, 10 p.m. on weekends.

8. The Heart of Vermont

The rural roads that lead from Ludlow to Belmont and Weston describe Vermont: sugar maples and white birches that rise and fall as the land does, hidden cabins that give themselves away by the single plumes of smoke from their chimneys, country stores advertising Maple Syrup Made Here. It's a countryside rich with impressions.

This trio of towns falls on the southern boundary of the middle region of the state. Forming a triangle just south and east of Rutland, they are connected by routes 155, 103, and 100—an area that passes by Terrible Mountain (2,844 feet) and rings the ski center at Okemo Mountain (3,343 feet).

Visitors come to be outside. The Long and Appalachian trails run through the 295,007-acre Green Mountain National Forest here, where store owners hop out for a quick hour of cross-country skiing at lunch and natives share news and packages from the capital. The seasons fall heartily; pungent, wet springs give way to sun-drenched summers and flaming autumns. Then the snow falls and high season arrives. Winter becomes a joyful challenge.

SHOPPING

The Ludlow area boasts the **Weston Village Store** (tel. 824-5477), which has everything from fiddlehead ferns in season to flannel nightgowns to hardware. **Mountain Stitchery** (tel. 824-6431), also in Weston, offers natural fiber yarns, stencil supplies, calico fabrics, and more. Stop in at **Meadowsweet Herb Farm** (tel. 492-3566), a bit down the road in North Shrewsbury, for herb wreaths, potpourri, and seasonings. They also make custom bouquets of dried roses, other flowers, and herbs especially for weddings.

ROMANTIC INTERLUDES

The natural beauty of this area creates a romantic backdrop spring, summer, fall, and winter.

Try sampling Vermont specialties. All within a few miles of each other in Ludlow, the **Crowley Cheese Factory** (tel. 259-2340), the **Green Mountain Sugar House** (tel. 228-7151), and the **Vermont Country Store** (tel. 463-3855) invite visitors to come and see their operations. The Sugar House in Ludlow is open daily from 9 a.m. to 6 p.m. You'll see the sugaring process in the early spring, a cider-mill operation in the fall. Year-round, the Crowley Cheese Factory in Healdsville welcomes visitors Monday through Thursday from 8 a.m. to 4 p.m. And no matter what time of year you go into the Country Store, you'll be able to snitch a taste of the crisp, crumbly Vermont Common Crackers that have helped make the store famous.

Whether you're Christian, Jewish, Muslim, Buddhist, or atheist, the **Weston Priory,** a monk's retreat nestled amid the Green Mountains near Ludlow, is worth a trip. Call (tel. 824-5409) for the hours of service. The brothers, who can usually be found outside wearing jeans and working the land, are world-renowned for their singing. Bring a picnic. The roads leading to and from the priory are some of the most photographed in Vermont.

Pick a perfect summer weekend day to call **Kinhaven Music School** (tel. 824-9592) in Weston for their schedule of free concerts. You'll feel a part of a small community as you listen to classical music played by very able, polished students. The drive and the grounds are beautiful, so bring a snack and a blanket if not a full picnic.

INNS AND BED-AND-BREAKFASTS

Skiing is the number one attraction in this corner of the state, so for relative quiet head to the mountains in the summer.

Rowell's Inn, R.R. 1, Box 269, Simonsville, VT 05143 (tel. 802/875-3658). When most people think of a classic New England inn, they probably conjure up someplace very much like Rowell's, which is about as far from Ludlow as it is from Manchester. The house dates from 1820, but the Tavern Room—now equipped with a small pool table and a dart board—goes all the way back to 1790. Lee and Beth Davis are congenial hosts who have sprinkled bits of their past throughout the inn: Beth's grandmother's wedding dress sits at the top of the stairs, for instance, and family portraits hang in the dining room. Even the antiques look at home here. Each of the five guest rooms has a unique appeal, but in room no. 1 you'll be able to curl up on a loveseat in front of a working fireplace. When you're sitting down to one of Beth's five-course dinners—rock Cornish game hen, pork tenderloin, or the like—take a look at the striped cherry-and-maple floor; it's known as a wedding floor because it shows the marriage of two woods. Rates: $120 to $140 per couple with a full country breakfast and dinner. The inn also operates as a bed-and-breakfast midweek from mid-November through March, with rates from $70 to $90 per couple per night.

Governor's Inn, 86 Main St., Ludlow, VT 05149 (tel. 802/228-8830). Innkeeper Deedy Marble will fuss over you, to be sure, if you reveal you're honeymooning. She'll even leave an extra gift by your pillow next to the chocolates from Harbor Sweets. The former governor's mansion, a late-19th-century Victorian, is chock-full of collections, including the Marbles' impressive array of framed magazine articles about the inn. Among the treasures are a beautiful assortment of teacups and Deedy's grandmother's wedding china, a set of 1876 Limoges china that commemorates the birth of Princess Margaret Rose. Hand-painted slate fireplaces, original tilework, and stained glass enhance this distinguished house, in which heirloom antiques fill the eight guest rooms. Between the memorabilia and the built-in details, there's an unimpeachable sense of being taken back to another era. The tea that Deedy and Charlie, her husband, set out every afternoon helps too. Rates: $170 to $180 per couple with five-course country breakfast and six-course dinner. (The inn does not serve dinner on Tuesday and gives guests a credit for that night only.)

Black River Inn, 100 Main St., Ludlow, VT 05149 (tel. 802/228-5585). "We don't sell rooms. We sell romance," commented innkeeper Tom Nunan. The 1835 house has a cozy, lived-in feel. Guests gather around the fireplace in the tasteful, comfy living room, or wander down to the Black River out back. Each guest room commands a distinct personality. The imposing first-floor Lincoln Room gets its name from the four-poster bed our former president once slept in. For added privacy, choose the quiet, floral-motif Romance Room, with brass bed, spool chest, and sloped-ceiling bathroom. A sitting area in every room serves as your breakfast nook in the morning. In the Maple Room, the table stands in front of the window looking down on the stream. The real warmth of this understated inn, however, comes from its hosts, Marilyn and Tom. Their openness and friendliness make this a very special place. Rates: $140 for two, including breakfast and dinner. Ask about weekend packages.

ROMANTIC RESTAURANTS

Some of the finest romantic atmospheres in all of New England are here.

The Inn at Weston, Rte. 100, Weston (tel. 824-5804). The scenic drive from Belmont or Ludlow to Weston is an appropriate predinner treat. Take a few minutes to explore the town before you go in to dine. The atmosphere is relaxed and casual in this 1848 farmhouse, which is also an inn with six charming guest rooms. The menu changes every six months, but typical choices include Vermont veal, scampi with sun-dried tomatoes, and gingered duckling. For dessert, you may have trouble picking just one item from the six on the dessert tray; the maple cheesecake is particularly good. Wine list with 50 entries. Appetizers run from $3 to $6.25, entrées from $13 to $22. Call for hours.

Nikki's, Pond Street at the foot of Okeno, Ludlow (tel. 228-7797). The locals tend to go here for a casual but elegant dinner. Stained-glass artwork and wide pine floorboards set the ambience as much as the glass-globed "candles." Owner Robert Gilmore heartily recommends the mixed grill—a tasty combination of breast of chicken, jumbo shrimp, and sweet Italian sausage cooked with herb butter. Nikki's has earned an award-winning reputation from its use of compound butters, fresh seafood (delivered three times a week), and black Angus beef. For a special treat, sample a number of wines by the glass; Nikki's offers an extensive wine list as well as eight vintage wines from its Cruvinet. Brunch for two costs about $15. Dinner appetizers are priced between $3.25 and $6.95, entrées ranging from $10.95 to $19.95. Dinner from 5 to 9:30 p.m. during the week; from 5 to 10 p.m. on Friday and Saturday; Sunday brunch from 11 a.m. to 3 p.m.

For an intimate meal with more than a modicum of friendliness, reserve a table at the **Black River Inn,** 100 Main St. in Ludlow (tel. 228-5585). The 7 p.m. seating features a single-entrée menu for $22.50 that changes every day. Possible dishes: ginger-basted swordfish in a yellow-pepper sauce, carrot and coriander soup, trivegetable terrine, lime–macademia nut torte. Fresh fish is delivered twice a week. Closed Wednesday. Both the Black River Inn and neighboring **Governor's Inn,** 86 Main St. in Ludlow (tel. 228-5585), will try to accommodate special diet requests (allergies, low cholesterol, etc.) if you call well in advance. Deedy and Charlie Marble have become expert amateurs, if such can be the case, with eleven national culinary awards to their credit. Complementing the graciously presented single-entrée meal are sterling silver service and Waterford crystal. It's $40 per person for the meal, which is served at a 7 p.m. seating. Closed Tuesday.

If you're on the road, stop in at **The Village Green Deli** on the green in Chester (tel. 875-3898). Antiques, charm, and a community jigsaw puzzle make this little spot an especially nice way station. Lunch for two about $12.

CALIFORNIA

Over 300 years before Horace Greeley wrote, "Go West, young man, go West," long before James Marshall culled some sparkling nuggets out of the American River, and before dream-weavers such as Samuel Goldwyn, Cecil B. deMille, and Louis M. Mayer began spinning celluloid fantasies, 16th-century writers had dreamed of a land of gold. "Know then, that west of the Indies, but to the East of Eden, lies California . . . [this] island, the most rugged in the world, abounds in gold," novelist Garci Ordóñez de Montalvo had penned.

So from the very beginning, California has beckoned as the place of the dream, the land of the myth. Over the years, its romantic magnetism has continuously lured newcomers. The same promise of riches and fame that brought grizzled old prospectors westward still draws hopeful young starlets from Duluth, or Coral Gables, or Albany, who stalk the beach at Malibu waiting to be discovered. The vocabulary remains the same: strike it rich; getting that one big break; finding a pot of gold. Even its nickname recognizes that glittering image: California is known as "The Golden State." This mother lode of promise—this newness and the spirit of good things to come—is what makes California such a treasure trove for honeymooners.

California's cities and towns offer honeymooners a wide array of experiences. You can gawk at the stars while dining at an "in" West Hollywood bistro—or watch the whales spy-hop and breach while you cruise the Pacific. Go to San Francisco's Chinatown for dim sum, nibble pastries at a thatch-roofed Danish bakery (complete with a stork nesting in the chimney) in Solvang, or munch an enchilada along Olvera Street in Los Angeles at a fiesta to celebrate the Cinco de Mayo. Head for a big-city swirl of theater, concerts, and art galleries; spend some time with Mickey, Minnie, and friends at Disneyland; or retreat to a mountain spa and soak your cares away at the mineral springs. Whatever you do, spend a lot of time staring off at the Pacific Ocean. As you contemplate the surging waters from the edge of a rocky, wave-tossed promontory—at Point Reyes, for example, or the Monterey Peninsula—you'll surely find something awe-inspiring in the knowledge that you are standing at the brink of the North American continent, upon the last substantial chunk of terra firma for 8,000 miles . . . an endless, golden vista for two honeymooners.

Because of California's tremendous expanse and diversity, this chapter concentrates on what are probably the state's most popular travel destinations: the sights along Highway 1 from San Francisco south to Laguna Beach, the route known as the California Coast Drive.

1. Practical Facts

GETTING THERE
Convenient air connections from all over the world and a first-rate system of highways make California easy to reach from anywhere in the world.

By Air
To San Francisco and Napa Valley: **San Francisco International Airport (SFO)** is located some 14 miles south of the city, near San Mateo. The **SFO Airporter** (tel. 673-2433) provides 24-hour-a-day transportation from SFO to major downtown hotels. Fare for the 30-minute ride is $5.50 per person. A taxi from the airport to SFO will run about $30.

To Los Angeles: **Los Angeles International Airport (LAX)** is located south of the city. If you're not renting a car, you can get ground transportation via **Eden Airport Express** (tel. 213/459-0465), **Flightline Corporation Airport Shuttle** (tel. 213/971-8265), **Prime Time Shuttle** (tel. 818/905-8787), and **SuperShuttle, Inc.** (toll free 800/325-3948). Fares will run about $30 per couple, but vary according to your destination. Not all companies serve all areas of L.A., so ask in advance.

Elsewhere: There are local airports in Monterey, Santa Barbara, and Palm Springs.

Practically every major airline, plus a bevy of the smaller ones, serves SFO and LAX. In addition, passengers to these cities often benefit greatly from the airline price wars, which often make it cheaper to fly from New York to the West Coast than to Chicago or Phoenix. Check the daily newspapers and ask your travel agent for up-to-date information about the latest air fares and purchase requirements.

By Rail
Amtrak serves both Los Angeles (Union Station, 800 North Alameda St.) and San Francisco (in Oakland, 16th Street Station). The rail line also offers extensive service within California. For a complete brochure, call Amtrak: toll free 800/USA-RAIL.

By Car
The major highways leading to California are Interstate 10 from Phoenix to L.A., Interstate 15 from Las Vegas to L.A., and Interstate 80 from Salt Lake City into San Francisco. Route 5 is the fastest route from San Francisco to L.A.; Highway 1 (see details that follow) is the most scenic.

By Bus
The major line serving California is **Greyhound** (tel. toll free 800/237-8211).

GETTING AROUND
The Beach Boys were right when they harmonized, "She'll have fun, fun, fun 'til her daddy takes her T-bird away." Most California good times are predicated on having your own wheels

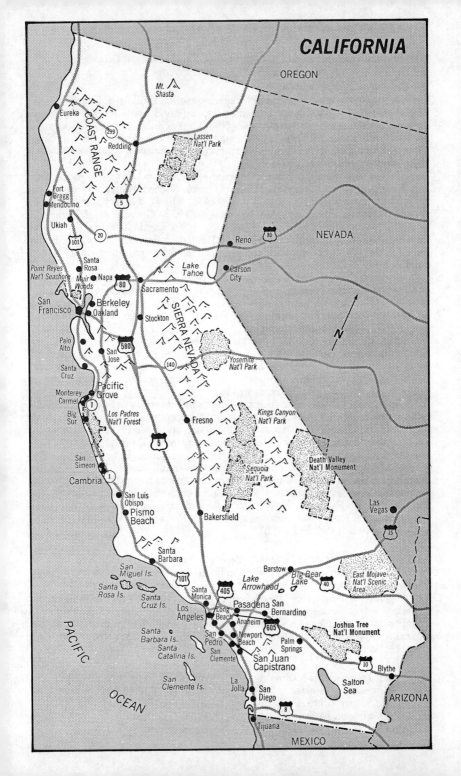

By Air
The main intra-California airlines are **AirCal** and **PSA.**

By Car
Definitely the modus operandi for getting around California. The state is the largest rental car market in the United States, and good deals on hired wheels are common. **Alamo** (tel. toll free 800/327-9633), for example, charges $96 per week for a subcompact car, with no mileage charge. If you'll be doing the California Coast Drive between Los Angeles and San Francisco (or vice versa), you'll have to pay a drop-off charge of about $100.

If you're any kind of driving enthusiasts, spend the bucks to rent a good sports car. **National** rents Camaros for $345 per week (7-day advance reservation required). Or if you want to bring back the Fabulous Fifties or Groovy Sixties, you can rent a "California Classic" car from National—a 1957 Chevy Bel Air, for example, or a '62 Chrysler 300-H (it belonged to the late singer Karen Carpenter) for $55 per day (plus 30 cents a mile, no drop-off charge). You must be a member of their Emerald Club for frequent renters. For complete details and current rates, call National: toll free 800/328-4300.

Or, for the ultimate romance (and to impress the local movie kingpins), you can rent a Corvette, Porsche, or Rolls-Royce. A 'Vette convertible goes for about $1,110 per week, plus 50¢ a mile; the Porsche Carrera convertible for around $1.410 per week, plus 50¢ per mile. (The first 200 miles are free.) Call **Autoexotica** at 415/673-4653 in San Francisco.

If you don't want to drive, but do want to see the California coast, consider the **California Parlour Car Tours** (tel. 415/474-7500). Their three-day San Francisco/Los Angeles tour, including the Monterey Peninsula, San Simeon, Solvang, and Santa Barbara, costs about $425 per person, which covers hotel accommodations and all meals on tour. Highly recommended.

San Francisco is the only city covered in this chapter with a well-developed **public transportation network.** Most beloved of all, of course, are the cable cars, with their tinkling bells and hairpin turns (see the details under San Francisco "Romantic Interludes"). The San Francisco Municipal Railway (MUNI) operates both the trolleys (fare: $2.25) and buses (fare: $1), exact change required. Route information is published in the Yellow Pages telephone directory, or call tel. 673-MUNI. The Bay Area Rapid Transit system (BART) is one of the most modern train systems in the world. It connects San Francisco with the East Bay area, including Oakland (tel. 788-BART). San Francisco also has a large fleet of taxi cabs, which you can usually hail right on the street. You can also call for a pickup. Contact **Allied Taxi** (tel. 826-9494) or **Veterans** (tel. 552-1300).

ABOUT THE CALIFORNIA COAST DRIVE Welcome to one of the most famous roadways in the world—California's Highway 1, officially known as the Cabrillo Highway. This switchbacked, two-lane highway skims the California coast from just south of Los Angeles to a bit north of Mendocino, a slender gray ribbon perched, just barely, between steep mountain flanks and a sheer plummet to the Pacific Ocean.

For maximum pleasure, count on spending at least three to four days on the drive, meaning you'll spend two to three overnights en route. Approximate driving distances between main places of interest are:

San Francisco to Monterey	185 miles (highway/good road)
Monterey to Big Sur	30 miles (very winding)
Big Sur to San Simeon	63 miles (very winding)
San Simeon to Santa Barbara	156 miles (good road)
Santa Barbara to Los Angeles	92 miles (highway)

On the winding stretches, figure that you will average no more than 35 mph, allowing for curves and stops at the scenic overlooks.

WEATHER

Since the state is so large, you might reasonably expect that different areas have different climates. True—but California is also known for its multiple microclimates, which produce such phenomena as the dense fog in San Francisco proper—and brilliant sunshine in Sausalito, just a few miles away. Here's an overview of weather patterns.

Northern California (San Francisco, Napa Valley, and the Monterey Peninsula)

You basically have a wet, cool season (December through February) and a dry, warm season (April through October), with fairly even temperature distribution throughout the year. The average daily high in San Francisco is 55° in January, 72° in July. What messes up any generalities, however, is the famous fog, which often envelops San Francisco and much of the northern coast in a damp, white blanket during the summer. This gives rise to such famous remarks as Mark Twain's: "The coldest winter I ever spent was a summer in San Francisco." Often the nicest months of all are September and October, which tend to have the sunniest weather along the coast. Napa tends to be warmer than San Francisco in the summer, cooler in the winter.

Southern California (Santa Barbara and Los Angeles)

Once again, count on experiencing a variety of microclimates, based on the interaction between the cool Pacific Ocean, warm land mass, and mountains. The wet season tends to be November through March, while the driest months are June through September. The average daily high runs about 65° in January, 84° in August. You can enjoy beach weather all year (many Californians spend Christmas Day at the beach); but the swimming season (for all but the wet-suit-clad surfer boys) runs from April to October. North of Santa Barbara, most people consider the ocean too cold for swimming.

CLOTHING

Casual clothing is the rule here. At night, even the fanciest restaurants will usually require only a jacket for men, no tie. California lives up to its reputation for liberalism and tolerance in manners of dress: In San Francisco, it is not uncommon to see three-piece-suited financiers frequenting the same establishments as sandal-wearing members of the counterculture.

Given the whimsical vagaries of California climate, the best advice is to dress in layers. During Northern California winters, you will need a warm coat and wool clothing; in Southern California, tropical-weight wools and a light overcoat are the most you'll require. From November through March, an umbrella is a good idea for all of California.

TIME

California is in the Pacific time zone, and observes daylight savings time in the summer. When it is noon in Los Angeles, it is 3 p.m. in New York.

TELEPHONES

The area codes for the places covered in this chapter are: San Francisco, 415; Napa Valley, 707; Carmel/Monterey, 408; Santa Barbara, 805; Greater Los Angeles area, 213 and 818; Palm Springs, 619.

SHOPPING

You name it, you can find it in California—everything from Alcatraz key chains to a Georgian dining table that seats 20. See the shopping section of each destination for details.

ABOUT ACCOMMODATIONS

Sleek big-city hotels where you might run into a famous rock star in the elevator. Tiny bed-and-breakfast inns, with crocheted antimacassars on the sofas and real Tiffany lamps. Very plush mountainside villas, where the floor-to-ceiling plate-glass windows overlook the blue Pacific. These are just a few of the honeymoon choices you'll find in California. Be sure to make your reservations as far in advance as possible, especially if you'll be honeymooning from May through October, the most popular tourist months along the coast.

If you're interested in B&Bs, you can get a free directory, *Bed and Breakfast Inns,* published by Yellow Brick Road, in cooperation with the California Office of Tourism. The guide lists 300 different inns. To order a copy, send a self-addressed, stamped (39¢) legal-size envelope to: **California Office of Tourism,** Dept. BBC, 1121 L St., Suite 103, Sacramento, CA 95814.

DINING OUT

The freshest natural ingredients, perfectly prepared—that summarizes the appeal of California cookery, which has practically reinvented the concept of American cuisine. Dedicated chefs use an international repertoire of cooking techniques to prepare foods—from stir-frying to mesquite-grilling. Because California is an important agricultural state, you'll be able to choose from a bounty of just-harvested produce: tender young green-leaf lettuce, baby carrots, vine-ripened tomatoes. You'll find that menus at the best restaurants change almost daily, to take advantage of fresh seasonal fruits, vegetables, fish, and game. To accompany your meal, choose a bottle of California wine, which is now internationally recognized to rank with the finest French bordeaux and burgundies.

HOW TO GET MARRIED IN CALIFORNIA

A garden gazebo overlooking the crashing waves of the Pacific . . . a red-roofed mission church . . . a gilded ballroom with crystal chandeliers . . . even a hot-air balloon. These are just a few of the places you can say "I do" in California. In order to be married in California, you both must have proof of age and identification, as well as a health certificate issued within the last 30 days. If either of you is divorced, you must furnish proof of the final judgment. You both must appear in person at the County Clerk's office for the license to be issued; fee is $35 (out-of-state checks are not accepted). The marriage license is valid for 90 days, and the marriage can be performed anywhere in the state of California. For complete details, contact the County Clerk in the area in which you wish to get married. In addition, the guest relations director at many hotels and inns can help you make complete wedding arrangements.

FOR FURTHER INFORMATION

Contact the following tourist offices: **California Office of Tourism,** 1121 L St., Suite 103, Sacramento, CA 95814 (tel. 916/322-2881); **Carmel Business Association,** Vandervort Court, San Carlos and 7th, P.O. Box 4444, Carmel-by-the-Sea, CA 93921 (tel. 408/624-2522); **Greater Los Angeles Visitors and Convention Bureau,** Manulife Plaza, 515 South Figueroa St., 11th Floor, Los Angeles, CA 90071 (tel. 213/624-7300); **Monterey Peninsula Visitors and Convention Bu-**

reau, P.O. Box 1770, Monterey, CA 93942 (tel. 408/649-1779); **Napa Chamber of Commerce,** 1556 First St., P.O. Box 636, Napa, CA 94559 (tel. 707/226-7455); **San Francisco Convention and Visitors Bureau,** 201 Third St., Suite 900, San Francisco, CA 94103 (tel. 415/974-6900); **Santa Barbara Conference and Visitors Bureau,** 222 East Anapamu St., Santa Barbara, CA 93101 (tel. 805/966-9222).

---

2. San Francisco

The screech of the gulls and the mournful wail of foghorns. A sprightly cling-clang of the cable-car bells. The warm aroma of baking sourdough bread, the briny steam rising from boiling crab pots, the foamy spurt of espresso into a china cup. Cadences of foreign tongues spoken on city streets—Chinese on Grant Avenue, Italian on the bocce courts in North Beach, Spanish at the bodegas in the Mission District. Yes, even if you were blindfolded, you would immediately know that you have arrived in San Francisco.

If the sounds and smells alone don't win you over, the sights of San Francisco certainly will. Pastel-painted Victorian mansions snuggle together, side by side. The burnished towers of the Golden Gate Bridge soar above the pale-white fog. Impossibly crooked streets, such as Lombard, zigzag down the hillside, and steep sidewalks clamber to the top of Nob Hill. ("When you get tired of walking around San Francisco, you can always lean against it," goes one local joke.) No wonder San Francisco has been voted the city that Americans would most like to visit, and "I Left My Heart in San Francisco" is viewed less as a theme song than as a statement of fact.

San Francisco sits at the top of a 32-mile-long peninsula located between the Pacific Ocean and San Francisco Bay. Its steep contours derive from the fact that it is built on over 40 hills (7 principal ones). Although the city proper has about 700,000 residents, about 5.8 million reside in the greater San Francisco Bay Area, making it the fourth largest metropolis in the country. Make your way to the top of Coit Tower, or other of San Francisco's vantage points, and you'll get a sense of what makes the city tick. In contrast to the quaint, gingerbread-trimmed Victorian houses, you'll see the sleek skyscrapers of the financial district. You'll quickly realize how important nautical activity is to San Francisco. At the piers of the Embarcadero at the northeastern part of the city, huge container ships from all over the globe tie up, helping maintain the city's reputation as a "window on the world." Along Fisherman's Wharf, trawlers and crab-fishing boats tug gently at their lines. Glancing over toward the Marina, you'll see much smaller vessels—sailboats, their shrouds pinging against the masts, seemingly eager to go zipping off across the sparkling blue bay.

Today, San Francisco reigns as the premier business nexus of the western United States. (Perhaps prophetically, much of the financial district was constructed on landfill made up of scuttled vessels that had brought prospectors west for the Gold Rush.) In addition, the city is a major center for the arts, known for its M.H. de Young Memorial Museum, Asian Art Museum, San Francisco Symphony, San Francisco Ballet, and San Francisco Opera. As you walk its streets (San Francisco is a city for strollers), you'll feel tempted to agree with Will Rogers, who remarked, "Cities are like gentlemen. They are born, not made. I bet San Francisco was a city from the very first time it had a dozen settlers."

One final pointer: Never, ever refer to it as 'Frisco, the sure mark of an insensitive out-of-towner. San Francisco is always called "The City," because to the many people who love it, there can be no other.

SHOPPING

Whether you're looking for souvenirs or future family heirlooms, you'll enjoy prowling the streets of San Francisco. Conveniently, many stores cluster together on certain streets or in distinct shopping areas, making it fun to browse. Following are some of the areas you will want to investigate.

San Francisco cherishes its past, and old buildings find new uses as up-to-date boutiques and restaurants. The brick complex of **Ghirardelli Square** (Beach Street between Polk and Larkin) was originally constructed as a woolen mill during the Civil War; it was later converted into a chocolate factory. Today, it has been beautifully refurbished and houses over 80 shops and restaurants. Here you'll find clothing stores such as **Aca Joe** and **Benetton,** and **The Sharper Image** for state-of-the-art electronic gadgets. Other standouts include **Folk Art International** for Mexican and South American crafts, **Xanadu Gallery** for African tribal art and artifacts, and **Light Opera** for exquisite glass perfume bottles, paperweights, and kaleidoscopes sculpted with bits of stained glass.

The Cannery (Beach Street at Leavenworth) is another renovated building—this time, Del Monte's circa-1894 produce cannery. Stand-out shops here include **Kachina** for Native American Indian arts and crafts, **Accession** for handicrafts from around the world. **Play** features kites and imaginative toys for children of all ages. **Compositions in Art and Wood** is a gallery exhibiting items from some of the finest American and European craftspeople, priced from $20 to $10,000. Hint: From the Cannery's many outdoor terraces and walkways, you'll have superb views of the bay and the Golden Gate Bridge.

More mass than class, **Pier 39** (at Pier 39 on the waterfront) is definitely the place to go for souvenirs. One store of note is the **NFL Shop,** which features jackets, sweats, caps, and banners all emblazoned with the logos of all the NFL teams.

Bargain-hunters, get ready to feel that surge of adrenalin! **Cost Plus** (Bay and Taylor Streets, near Fisherman's Wharf) has been a San Francisco tradition for years. The store carries over 100,000 items from 48 different countries: brass jugs from India, perfumed soaps from China, bright piñatas from Mexico. There's a lot of junk—but a lot of good buys too.

San Francisco's answer to New York's Fifth Avenue or Beverly Hills' Rodeo Drive, the **Union Square** area is where you'll find the toniest meccas for shopping nirvana. It's bounded by Powell, Stockton, and Post Streets, and Geary Avenue. Right on the square, you'll find outposts of **Macy's, Neiman-Marcus, I. Magnin, Saks,** and **Bullock & Jones.** On neighboring streets, cruise past boutiques for **Louis Vuitton, Ellesse, Dunhill, Brooks Brothers,** and **Gucci. La Ville du Soleil** (444 Post St.) is especially winsome, with everything from 18th-century armoires, porcelains, and baskets to toys and unusual candles.

Don't miss **Maiden Lane,** a charming alleyway right off the square that has garnered some of the poshest shops of all: **Chanel, Cartier, Diane Freis,** as well as art galleries such as **Circle** and **Maiden Lane,** and **Orientations** for fabulous Oriental art and antiques.

The newest San Francisco shopping mecca is dazzling **San Francisco Centre,** part ultra-mall, part Disney World. This eight-story fashion extravaganza is located at the corner of Market and Fifth Streets, just two blocks south of Union Square. Even if you don't want to shop, you'll want to ride the unusual spiral escalators. But how could you resist browsing a bit when you have excellent boutiques to chose from, including **Adrienne Vittadini** and **Ann Taylor,** as well as **Wet Seal** for kicky women's sportswear, **Avventura** for men's shoes. The top three floors house a **Nordstrom** department store.

North Beach, definitely the up-and-coming neighborhood for shopping trends, is located just north of Chinatown and south of Fisherman's Wharf. Best street for browsing: Grant Avenue. Try **Donna** (1424 Grant) for fashionable womenswear, and the **Primal Art Center** (1422 Grant) for exotic jewelry and masks, predominantly from West Africa. **East/West Leather** (1400 Grant) carries butter-soft leather jackets for women and men, as well as a fine selection of handmade western boots, including designs by Tony Lama. If your tastes encompass the absurd, don't miss **The Shlock Shop** at 1418 Grant, which carries a rummage-worthy hodgepodge of old Salvation Army hats, rare beer cans, British bobby hats. "Neat junk," says the owner, a bohemian painter. He also has a superb selection of Panama hats.

Union Street (most specifically the stretch between Gough and Fillmore Streets) has burgeoned into *the* place to shop, dine, and be seen among the city's smart set. Shoppers will encounter a myriad of high-quality boutiques carrying everything from patchwork quilts (at **Yankee Doodle Dandy**) to art deco sconces (**Paris 1925**, upstairs at 1954 Union). You'll also find fine antique furniture (**Jason Adams**, 1869 Union; and **Annalisa Wolfe**, 1861 Union) and elegant men's sportswear (**Lorenzini**, 2149 Union).

Our favorite discovery of all is the **Smile Gallery** (1750 Union). Owner Deborah West has a real eye for unusual, beautiful, fun objects. The gallery carries whimsical snake-motif screens by Arlene Elizabeth (she calls herself the "screen queen"), wooden sculptures by William Accorsi, and button jewelry by Cheryl Woody (actor Bill Cosby is one of her fans). Prices start at about $10 and zoom to about $2,000 or so, but everything is worth seeing.

ROMANTIC INTERLUDES

There are two ways to view San Francisco—as unabashed tourist and as intimate friend. Here are some recommendations that should allow honeymooners to appreciate both sides of this memorable city.

The cable cars are the nation's only mobile national monuments, with a design virtually unchanged since Andrew Hallidie invented them in 1873. Three routes still operate, including the Powell-Mason line, which terminates near Fisherman's Wharf; and the California Street line, which climbs through Chinatown to Van Ness. But, as the long waiting lines will demonstrate, the best ride of all is on the Powell-Hyde line. You board at the corner of Powell and Market Streets, then hang on as the cable car chugs resolutely up and over Nob Hill and Russian Hill, making several gasp-producing hairpin turns. Finally, the car gets up to about 9½ mph as it hurtles down to Aquatic Park, bells clanging joyfully, affording its human companions a magnificent view of San Francisco Bay. You can buy tickets at the automatic vending machines at the most popular stops; fare is $2.25 per person (have exact change).

Well before dawn, the fishing fleet casts off from **Fisherman's Wharf** every day. Much of the fresh catch with which the ships return—petrale sole, rockfish—appears on the menus of the famous restaurants that line the wharf, including Alioto's, Tarantino's, Sabellas, and others. The whole wharf pulsates with activity: crabs boil in giant cauldrons, caricaturists will sketch your portrait for $5, and street performers—from mimes to string quartets—will entertain. Across the street, feel like a kid again with visits to the Ripley's Believe It Or Not! Museum and the Guinness Museum of World Records.

Romantic it's not—but it sure is a heck of a lot of fun. Known as "The Rock," **Alcatraz** (tel. 546-2805) served as a maximum security federal penitentiary from 1934 to 1963; today it is operated by the National Park Service. Over the years, it housed such notorious criminals as the "Bird Man of Alcatraz," "Machine-Gun" Kelly, and Al Capone. Join up with one of the hour-long park ranger tours. The rangers will regale you with legends of the lockhouse, clang the cell doors open and shut, and even lock you up in solitary confinement—for only 30 seconds, but it feels like an eternity.

To reach Alcatraz, take the ferry operated by the Red & White Fleet. It leaves from Pier 41 and costs $5.50 per person. In summer, you must buy your tickets several days in advance. You can also purchase tickets through Ticketron outlets.

Chinatown is one of the largest Chinese communities outside of the Orient. For maximum visual impact, enter by the Chinatown Gate, Grant Avenue at Bush Street. Most of the tourist shops and restaurants line Grant Avenue, but to get a glimpse of the "real" Chinatown, head over to Stockton. Here, fresh produce such

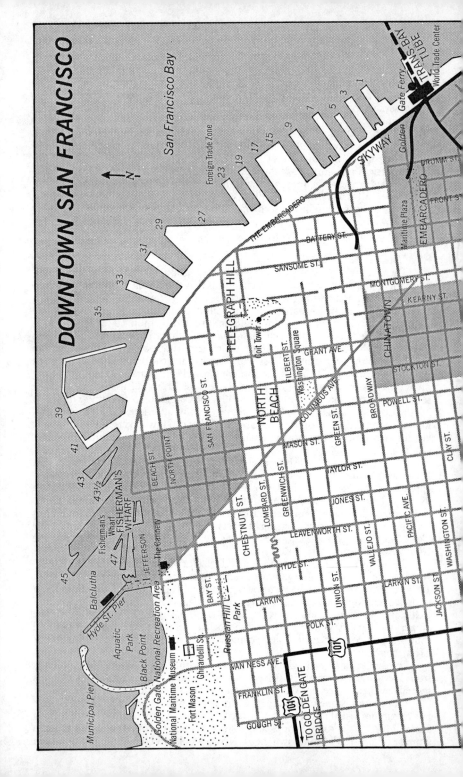

as bok choy, long beans, and winter melon spills over from the sidewalk stalls, and live carp swim in tanks in the fish markets. Back on Grant, browse through the various stores, which sell everything from T-shirts to fine antiques. **Chinatown Import-Export** (736 Grant) features an especially good selection of carved ivory and jade, as well as furniture. If you like doing your own Chinese cooking, **The Wok Shop** (804 Grant) is the stop for pot, cleavers, and bamboo steamers. **Canton Bazaar** (616 Grant) has it all—fashions, rugs, antiques, cloisonné, porcelain, furniture, and screens. When you get hungry, try **Brandy Ho's Hunan Food** (217 Columbus at Pacific) or **Pot Sticker** (150 Waverly Place), which is known for its fried dumplings.

Take a break in a real urban oasis: **Golden Gate Park** is three miles long, a half mile wide, and lush with stands of redwoods and eucalyptus, dells of rhododenrons, and exotic trees from around the world. Drop in at the Morrison Planetarium for the laser show, the Conservatory of Flowers Botanical Gardens, or explore the bicycle paths, bridle paths, and jogging trails that tread their way across the 1,000 acres of green expanse. For hand-in-hand strolls, your best bet is the Japanese Tea Garden, with wishing pools, carp ponds, a bronze Buddha, and a small tea house (fortune cookies were invented here). Or rent a small rowboat at Stow Lake (tel. 752-0347), then head over to Strawberry Hill Island, in the middle, for a picnic. And children of all ages will delight in the 1912-vintage Hershel-Spillman Carousel.

San Francisco has a fine selection of **museums,** most notably:

M.H. de Young Memorial Museum, Golden Gate Park (tel. 750-3600, or 750-3659 for a recording). The oldest and largest museum in the West, the de Young is well known for its permanent collection, including works by El Greco, Rembrandt, and Gainsborough. The museum also has hosted many of the major traveling exhibitions, such as the Impressionists and King Tut. Open Wednesday through Sunday, 10 a.m. to 5 p.m.; admission $4.50 per person (also permits entry into the Asian Art and Legion of Honor museums on the same day). Call to verify holiday hours.

Asian Art Museum—The Avery Brundage Collection, Golden Gate Park, next to the de Young (tel. 668-8921). Rotates exhibits from its extensive collections, such as exquisite jade miniatures from China, 18-inch-tall vases carved from a solid piece of rock crystal, earthenware horses from Japan, bronze gods and goddesses from Nepal, Thailand, and Cambodia. Open Wednesday through Sunday, 10 a.m. to 5 p.m.; admission $4.50 per person.

California Palace of the Legion of Honor, Lincoln Park (tel. 750-3600 or 750-3659 for a recording). A bronze cast of Rodin's "The Thinker" stands at the entrance to this museum that features a European collection: decorative arts, as well as fine paintings by Corot, Degas, Fragonard, Manet, Monet, and Renoir. Open Wednesday through Sunday, 10 a.m. to 5 p.m.; admission $4.50 per person.

San Francisco's diversity is most evident in its wide range of excellent small museums, which offer something for all tastes and interests.

American Carousel Museum, 633 Beach St., across from The Cannery (tel. 928-0550). It's a scene from everyone's childhood dream—prancing horses, fanciful cats, stately giraffes. They're all on display at this captivating museum that honors the traditions and art of the merry-go-round. The docents are extremely friendly and knowledgeable, setting the jaunty band organs into noisy motion or explaining restorations on view in the workshop. Open daily from 10 a.m. to 5 p.m.; admission $2.25.

The Mexican Museum, Building D, Fort Mason (tel. 441-0404). Did you know that piñatas probably originated in China, and were brought by Marco Polo to Italy, and then by the conquistadors to Mexico? That's just some of the information you might encounter at this museum devoted to Mexican and Mexican-American art. Also visit La Tienda, the museum's superb crafts boutique, where you can buy items such as black pottery from Oaxaca or glassware from Tlaquepaque, all reasonably priced. Open Wednesday through Sunday, noon to 5 p.m.; admission $2.25.

Wells Fargo History Museum, 420 Montgomery St. (tel. 396-2619). How many people could you cram onto a stagecoach? (Eighteen—nine inside and nine on top, hanging on for dear life.) How long did it take for a letter to go cross-country in the 1850s? (About 32 days.) These are just a few of the tidbits you'll pick up at the Wells Fargo History Museum, a treasure trove of Gold Rush memorabilia, including an authentic stagecoach used on the Great Overland Mail Route. Open Monday through Friday, 9 a.m. to 5 p.m. (closed bank holidays). Admission is free.

If you enjoy the **performing arts,** the city provides plenty of choices.

San Francisco Opera, Opera House, Van Ness Avenue and Grove Street (tel. 864-3300). Regular season at the 3,535-seat hall runs from September to December, attracting world-class stars. Be advised—tickets are very hard to get.

San Francisco Ballet, Opera House, Van Ness Avenue and Grove Street (tel. 762-BASS). The oldest permanent company in the United States, the San Francisco Ballet performs in the Opera House. The season runs late January to May; artistic director is Helgi Tomasson.

San Francisco Symphony, Davies Symphony Hall, Van Ness Avenue and Grove Street (tel. 431-5400). Under music director Herbert Blomstedt, the orchestra just celebrated its 77th anniversary. The season runs from October through May, and features special festivals.

Theater offerings range from major productions straight from Broadway to experimental productions by new playwrights. One of the most interesting companies is the **American Conservatory Theatre (ACT),** recognized as one of America's finest resident theater companies (tel. 673-6440).

To get an idea of what's playing where, pick up a copy of the Sunday *San Francisco Chronicle*.

Some ticket outlets you should know about: **BASS** has several convenient ticket centers in the city; for information or to charge by phone, call 762-2277. **Ticketron** also has multiple outlets; for information or to charge by phone, call 392-SHOW. **STBS** (San Francisco Ticket Box Office Service) sells half-price day-of-performance tickets for selected music, dance, and theater events. They're located on the Stockton Street side of Union Square. Cash only, no reservations or telephone sales accepted. Open Tuesday through Saturday, noon to 7:30 p.m. For recorded information, call 433-STBS.

If you want to get the best scenic vistas of San Francisco, here are some options.

Harbor cruises. What better way to see the city by the bay than from the bay? Cruises aboard sleek passenger sightseeing vessels afford ringside views of all the famous points of interest: the Golden Gate and Bay bridges, Alcatraz, Fisherman's Wharf, Fort Point, and Sausalito. Stand on deck amid sea breezes, or relax on one of the glass-enclosed observation decks. Different itineraries are available; fares run from $9 to $16.50 per person. Contact the **Blue & Gold Fleet** (tel. 415/781-7877) or the **Red & White Fleet** (tel. 415/546-2896). Or how about taking your dream date on a dinner/dance cruise across the bay? During the summer months, the Blue & Gold Fleet features Friday and Saturday-night sailings at 8 p.m. from West Marina, $35 per person including a delectable buffet of mesquite-grilled specialties.

Fort Point National Historic Site was completed in 1861 to defend San Francisco harbor (presumably against attacks by Confederate privateers), though not one of its 149 original cannon was ever fired in anger. Here you get right under the Golden Gate Bridge, giving you one of the best vantage points to admire the graceful mile-long span that symbolizes the city.

Vista Point is a scenic overlook just across the Golden Gate Bridge in Marin County. This is the best location for getting photos of the two of you with San Francisco shimmering in the background (for the best light, go in the afternoon).

Mrs. Lillie Hitchcock Coit, an honorary member of Knickerbocker Number Five Fire Company, donated $100,000 to build **Coit Tower** (top of Lombard Street on Telegraph Hill) to honor the city's firefighters. From the top of the 210-foot observation platform, the 360° views take in downtown San Francisco, the Bay Bridge, the Embarcadero, Angel Island, and the Golden Gate Bridge. Admission is $2. Downstairs, there's also an excellent gift shop with beautiful posters and classy T-shirts.

Photography buffs will want to get one of the classic shots of San Francisco: a row of pastel-painted Victorian houses, eaves covered with curlicued trim, contrasting with the futuristic San Francisco skyline, highlighted by the Transamerica and Bank of America towers. The place to go is **Alamo Square,** looking towards Steiner Street.

Get above it all with a **helicopter** flight above the city. **Commodore Helicopters** will take you aloft for four minutes for a gull's-eye perspective of the bay and Golden Gate Bridge. The trip costs $22 per person (tel. 332-4482).

Nostalgia buffs won't want to miss soaring above San Francisco in a beautifully restored 1940s Douglas DC-3. You can take wing with **Sentimental Journeys** (tel. 667-3800, or toll free 800/634-1165 in California), which offers different sightseeing itineraries aboard the roomy craft. Big-band music plays in the background to set the mood, and since the plane travels at a maximum altitude of 1,500 feet, you'll enjoy fantastic views. A one-hour sky tour costs $110 per person and departs from the North Field, Oakland International Airport.

Slightly raffish, distinctly prosperous with an artsy undercurrent, **Sausalito** often draws comparisons to the hilltop villages along the Riviera. It's located just across the bay from San Francisco in Marin County. Sausalito was originally a summer community for wealthy San Franciscans, who would moor their houseboats here. Today, the houseboats remain down at the waterfront, but are now joined by pricey wood-and-glass houses cantilevered out over the hillsides. Along the bayside promenade called Bridgeway, you'll find trendy boutiques—a wonderful place to browse for arts and crafts and unusual clothing. Stop for lunch or dinner at one of the waterside restaurants, such as Scoma's or Ondine's.

Getting here is half the fun: Drive your car across the Golden Gate Bridge (the passenger gets to appreciate the spectacular city views), or take the **Golden Gate Ferries** from the Ferry Building at the foot of Market Street (tel. 332-6600) or the **Red & White Fleet** from Pier 41 at Fisherman's Wharf (tel. 546-2896). Fare is about $3.50 per person.

Part of the fun of a vacation in San Francisco is getting out of the city and exploring some of the beautiful natural settings that surround it.

A day in the country is no farther than a ferry-ride to **Angel Island State Park,** a green dot in the bay just off Tiburon in Marin County. The entire 750-acre island is uninhabited except for some 200 deer and a few resident park rangers. It offers excellent hiking—follow North Ridge Trail to the top for panoramic views of the bay. Most fun of all—rent bikes in San Francisco and take them along to pedal the route that circles the island. Bring a picnic lunch with some sourdough bread and Napa Valley cabernet; no food is sold on the island.

The Red & White Fleet ferries to Angel Island run from Pier 43½ and Tiburon; tel. 546-2896 for schedules. The round-trip fare is $8 per person.

Stinson Beach. If the sun's out and you want to feel the sand scrunch under your toes, Stinson offers nearly a mile of beach, perfect for surfcasting, picnics, or a game of Frisbee (only the relentlessly hardy will swim here). Located north of San Francisco in Marin County off Highway 1 (tel. 415/383-1644).

See the oldest living things on earth—the famous sequoias that stand up to 200 feet tall, measure some 16 feet in diameter . . . and are about 1,200 years old. In the 500-acre **Muir Woods** preserve (tel. 388-2595), marked trails wind their way past ferns, groves of oaks, and madronas. About 15 miles north of San Francisco off Highway 1, the park is open daily from 8 a.m. until sunset.

Mount Tamalpais (tel. 388-2070). Located just beyond Muir Woods, Mount Tam, as it is known familiarly hereabouts, soars 2,600 feet up. Drive to the summit, or follow one of the well-marked hiking trails. On a clear day, you can see over 100 miles.

Point Reyes National Seashore (tel. 663-1092). Follow Highway 1 about 40 miles north of San Francisco to this stunning peninsula thrust out into the Pacific, a place of windswept, foggy beauty. The 67,000-acre recreational area encompasses secluded beaches, rocky cliffs, grassy bluffs, all reachable by 150 miles of hiking trails. First stop by the Bear Valley Visitor Center for a map, and then set off. In particular, walk down the 312 steps to the historic lighthouse, with a seaside deck that provides an excellent vantage point for viewing the gray whales that migrate past here from December through April.

HONEYMOON HOTELS AND HIDEAWAYS

Thankfully for visitors, San Francisco is a compact 46.6 square miles, so no matter what hotel you choose, it's close to a cable-car line or other public transportation, or a short cab ride from restaurants, attractions, and nightlife. Some areas are both convenient and especially romantic, Union Square, Nob Hill, and Pacific Heights among them. (The hotels listed below are located in those three areas.)

You'll find hotels in San Francisco less expensive than those in New York, but more costly than those in many other U.S. cities. Boosting the price is the city's 11% hotel tax, a fact to consider in figuring your honeymoon cost.

It's advised that you reserve well in advance during the peak convention months of October and November, especially at the major chain hotels, which cater to this business. However, reservations are recommended at any time of the year.

For the *San Francisco Convention & Visitors Bureau Lodging Guide,* covering 330 motels and hotels in all categories, as well as pensions and inns, send $1 for postage and handling to SFCVB, P.O. Box 6977, San Francisco, CA 94101.

Expensive

Guests ooh and aah at the magnificence of **The Sherman House,** 2160 Green St., San Francisco, CA 94123 (tel. 415/563-3600), a stunning white mansion considered the most luxurious small hotel in San Francisco. It is the result of the dream of Manouchehr Mobedshahi, an Iranian-born businessman who purchased the Pacific Heights landmark in 1980 and spent four years meticulously restoring it, the carriage house, and the formal gardens. The mansard-roofed house was originally built by Leland Sherman, founder of the Sherman Clay Music Company and a lover of the arts. Sherman's guests included stars of opera and stage—Enrico Caruso among them—who performed to high society in the home's three-story recital hall. The 15 rooms and suites are individually furnished in Biedermeier, English Jacobean, or French Second Empire antiques. Each room contains a marble, wood-burning fireplace, as well as beds canopied in rich tapestry fabrics and covered with feather-down comforters. Bathrooms are lovely, with black marble whirlpool baths and a mini-TV set above the vanity. In the middle of the formal gardens, the Carriage House contains three suites, all in romantic pastel colors. The spacious Garden Suite opens onto its own private flower garden and gazebo. Like most rooms, it has views of the Golden Gate Bridge and the bay. At mealtime, you'll want to try out the fine restaurant. Rates (EP): $240 to $370 per couple per night; $550 to $710 for a suite. Honeymoon package: None.

The Fairmont Hotel, atop Nob Hill, 950 Mason St. at California Street, San Francisco, CA 94108 (tel. 415/772-5000; reservations: toll free 800/527-4727). The Fairmont's regal facade is familiar to millions as the site of the St. Gregory in the TV series *Hotel.* The grande dame of Nob Hill hotels has retained its grand character, with musicians' balconies and boxes along one side of the lobby, still splendid with its marble columns, gold-leaf trim, and velvety red carpeting. The hotel contains seven restaurants and San Francisco's best-known supper club, the Venetian Room, which attracts big-name entertainers. Rooms contain such added touches as terry bathrobes, bath accoutrements, chocolates on the pillows, and in-room movies. The main building's guest rooms are slightly larger than those in the modern tower addition, but many tower rooms have better views. For honeymooners with infinite budgets, there's always the Fairmont's historic eight-room penthouse suite, which boasts the biggest price tag of any hotel accommodation in San Francisco— $5,500 per night. For those of more modest means, there's a honeymoon package (EP): $195 per couple per night in the main building or $235 per night in the tower, including a deluxe room, champagne and chocolates on arrival, personalized matches, and a breakfast in bed for two. Rates are $165 to $200 per night thereafter, and upgrades to suites are offered, if available.

Campton Place, 340 Stockton St., San Francisco, CA 94108 (tel. 415/781-5555; reservations: toll free 800/647-4007 nationwide; 800/235-4300 in California), has combined the luxury of a large, top-of-the-line hotel with the friendly, personal service of a small inn, making it a favorite of visiting celebrities and dignitaries. Impeccably groomed and courteous doormen set the mood at the entrance to the marble-floored lobby, which is decorated with Oriental art and a large crystal chandelier. Guest rooms are just as elegant, resembling rooms in a private home furnished by a top interior designer. There are king-size beds with beige down bedspreads, armoires hiding TV sets, remote-control lighting, and limited-edition artwork. Baths are in Roman travertine marble, with brass fixtures whose shine proves they are polished daily. The hotel provides such services as a valet to assist with packing and unpacking, immediate pressing, prompt shoe shining, and turndown service. The restaurant at Campton Place is consistently ranked in the city's top ten, and the cozy little bar serves cocktails mixed and hand-shaken in the traditional manner. The location a few steps from Union Square can't be beat. Honeymoon package: None. Rates (EP): $210 to $285 per couple per night. Two-room suites start at $500.

The Mandarin Oriental, 222 Sansome St., San Francisco, CA 94102 (tel. 415/885-0999; reservations: toll free 800/622-0404 in the U.S.; 800/526-6566 in Canada). One of the world's most acclaimed hotel companies opened its first U.S. hotel in San Francisco in mid-1987 and it quickly garnered accolades as one of the city's most sumptuous properties. Although in the bustling financial district, the Mandarin's twin towers rise so high you'll feel you are floating in the clouds above it all. The hotel's 160 rooms actually occupy the 38th through 48th floors of the third-highest building in San Francisco. (The lobby and restaurant are on the ground and second floors.) Italian marble in several shades, Oriental furnishings with a European touch, brass and chandeliers set the scene in the lobby and guest rooms. The bathrooms, lined with marble, have some of the best views in San Francisco: floor-to-ceiling windows overlooking the city line one side of each bathtub. Just so your feet won't get cold stepping on all this marble, the maid each evening sets out silk slippers from Thailand on an Irish linen mat at the side of the bed. Honeymoon package: Three days/two nights (EP): $600 per couple. Includes a Mandarin room with king-size bed, chilled champagne, room service breakfast one morning, and personalized stationery. Available add-ons are a dinner at Silks with a special menu, a tour of San Francisco with a Rolls-Royce and a romantic picnic, a bay sailing trip on a private yacht or a helicopter ride over the bay. Regular rates: $255 to $275 per couple per night for superior and deluxe rooms; $340 for Mandarin rooms; $440 and up for suites.

The Huntington Hotel, 1075 California St., San Francisco, CA 94108 (tel. 415/474-5400; reservations: toll free 800/227-4683). Set in a choice location atop Nob Hill, the Huntington Hotel exudes old-world charm. The ample size of the rooms, combined with the friendly, attentive service of the staff, makes guests feel as if they have their own home in the heart of San Francisco. From the moment you enter the elegant lobby, with the Queen Anne furniture, travertine marble floor, and stately grandfather clock, you'll feel very well taken care of indeed. No two rooms are furnished alike, but all are thoughtfully and sumptuously decorated: plump cushions on a damask sofa, English hunting prints to cheer the walls, antique vases, imported silk draperies, ankle-deep carpeting. But it's the staff that truly makes the hotel special. For example, Mary, the elevator operator, has worked for the Huntington for 43 years (she always gets a hello call from Luciano Pavarotti before he checks in). Downstairs, the Big Four restaurant is rated one of the tops in the city. Honeymoon package: None. Rates: $140 to $190 per couple per night for a room; $240 to $500 for a suite.

Four Seasons Clift Hotel, 495 Geary St., San Francisco, CA 94102 (tel. 775-4700, or toll free 800/332-3442). Wood paneling, crystal chandeliers, and a pastoral, Boucher-style oil painting that could easily have adorned Marie Antoinette's bedchamber at Versailles set the luxurious mood from the moment you enter this grande dame of San Francisco hotel society. Located near the theater district and Union Square, the Clift is known for its attentive service, with a very high staff-to-room ratio and a penchant for gratifying guests' every whim. One New Year's Eve, for example, the concierge zipped around town trying to track down a cowbell, a conga drum, and six drumsticks for some party-bound guests. Rooms reveal tasteful elegance: English-style furnishings, cozy sofas, chintz fabrics. Although some of the more inexpensive accommodations are somewhat smallish, all coddle visitors with perks such as plush terry bathrobes and a bathroom amenities basket scaled for people, not elves—big bar of soap, big bottle of shampoo, and lots more. Downstairs, the Clift has two excellent gathering places: the swooningly romantic French Room restaurant and the Redwood Room cocktail lounge, graced with the original art deco wood panels and Gustav Klimt prints. Honeymoon package: None. Rates: $180 to $275 per couple per night for a room; $325 to $715 for a suite. Lower-priced weekend packages are available.

Moderate

Casa Madrona Hotel, 801 Bridgeway, Sausalito, CA 94965 (tel. 415/332-0502). Casa Madrona's baby-blue Cape Cod–style cottages and flower-covered latticed arbors climb a steep hill above the picturesque town of Sausalito. A sailboat marina, the bay, and the city of San Francisco are the views from its hideaway-like rooms. The three parts of the hotel are connected by red-brick pathways and steps: an 1885 Victorian-style Italianate mansion with 13 cozy rooms furnished with antiques, floral-printed wallpaper, white wicker, and claw-foot bath tubs; the cottages, the three most romantic hideaways in Sausalito; and the Casa Madrona, 17 suite-like rooms individually decorated in such wide-ranging styles as art nouveau, French country, rustic mountain cabin, Southwest, Parisian artist's loft, elegant Oriental, and frilly Victorian. Of the cottages, La Tonnelle is the most romantic, with wood-burning stove, a tile tub for two, and a garden deck. In the Casa Madrona, several suites are recommended for honeymooners, but with their fireplaces and sweeping views from private balconies or decks, all are suitable. Some examples are Château Charmant, with melon and peach tones, canopied bed, elevated bathtub, and fireplace. Kathmandu transports you to an exotic mountain hideaway with secret alcoves, mirrors, a tub for two, and huge cushions for whiling away the hours. The hotel also has a hot tub under a vine-covered arbor that can be reserved for a private party of two. Also sumptuous is the Casa Madrona restaurant, with sweeping views, peach-and-white decor, and roll-back glass roof for an al fresco feeling. The hotel is in the heart of Sausalito's waterfront. Ferries to San Francisco depart just a few hundred yards from its doorstep. Honeymoon package: None. Rates (EP): $90 to $200 per couple per night in the Victorian House; $155 to $175 for the cottages; $150 to $330 for Casa Madrona suites.

"Not your ordinary hotel," proclaims **The Mansion,** 2220 Sacramento St., San Francisco, CA 94115 (tel. 415/929-9444), in its brochure, and that becomes delightfully clear at every turn in this Victorian fantasyland. Once in the grand foyer of the 1887 Queen Anne building, guests can see the eclectic collection of furnishings, murals, and fanciful artifacts, all from the creative—some say offbeat—mind of owner Bob Pritikin. His pig paintings and "porkabilia"—the largest such collection in the world—are on display everywhere. The usually packed weekend magic/music concerts in the Music Room feature Pritikin himself, billed as America's Foremost Concert Saw Player. This is in addition to the nightly appearance of the Mansion's ghost, Claudia, who, seated in her Victorian wheelchair, is pushed to the keyboard of a grand piano to play classical selections. For more romance and fun, there are the flower gardens, the billiard room with a live macaw looking on, a nickel-odeon with drums and tambourines, and valuable Turner and Reynolds paintings to feast your eyes upon. The hotel's candlelit dining room is supervised by master chef David Coyle, formerly personal chef to the duke and duchess of Bedford. Rooms run the gamut size-wise, from the tiny Tom Thumb Room, just barely big enough for two people standing, to the large, opulent Josephine Room, a favorite of such celebrities as Barbra Streisand and Robin Williams. Some rooms have marble fire-places, private terraces, and even ceilings that slant to the floor. Freshly picked flow-ers and colorful murals dominate many of them. The hotel is in a residential area four blocks from a cable-car line. Honeymoon package: None. Rates (BP) range from $100 per couple per night for the Tom Thumb Room to $220 per couple for the Josephine Room. Full breakfast and the music/magic shows are included.

The Inn at Union Square, 440 Post St., San Francisco, CA 94102 (tel. 415/397-3510), may be the narrowest hotel in San Francisco; wink as you walk past it and you'll miss its elegant entrance. But once you've seen the sumptuously deco-rated rooms and experienced the quiet graciousness of the staff, you won't want to pass it up. The Inn at Union Square is one of San Francisco's many refurbished downtown hotels, transformed in the last five years to an intimate hostelry that cap-tures the style of a European inn. Its rooms have been decorated individually by the owner's wife, San Francisco interior designer Nan Rosenblatt. Some are in warm neutral tones, others burst with color and prints. Most rooms contain king-size, four-poster beds with goose-down pillows, Georgian furniture, and comfortable sit-ting areas. The sixth-floor suite has its own fireplace, bar, whirlpool bath, and sauna. The hotel doesn't have a lobby per se, but each floor has its own cozy lounge with fireplaces, where guests are served flaky croissants, fresh juice, fruit, and coffee each morning, plus cucumber sandwiches, cakes, and tea in the afternoon—all included in the room price. The hotel is a half block west of Union Square and the Powell Street cable cars. Honeymoon package: None. Rates (CP) begin at $115 per couple per night for the smallest rooms with king-size beds: $155 to $180 for larger rooms and suites with king-size beds and sitting areas. It's $330 for the lavish penthouse suite.

The Union Street Inn, 2229 Union St., San Francisco, CA 94123 (tel. 415/346-0424), a tranquil six-room bed-and-breakfast, has all the charm of a 19th-century Edwardian home, yet it's smack in the midst of San Francisco's most fash-ionable residential area and trendiest shopping district. Owner Helen Stewart bought the 85-year-old house in 1978 and lovingly decorated the living room and each of the six guest rooms (all with private baths) with antiques, Oriental carpeting, and bric-a-brac. In the main house, the most sumptuously romantic room is the New Yorker, with a canopied queen-size bed, elegant English armoire, and a sexy salmon-colored chaise longue. But the inn's pièce de résistance is the Carriage House, actual-ly a suite with a plant-shrouded Jacuzzi bathtub that can be entered from the bed-room or bathroom. A skylight opens above the tub for viewing the stars or sky. Difficult to believe that just beyond the brick path and through the quiet garden are some of San Francisco's best restaurants and nightlife. Honeymoon package: None. Rates (CP): $250 per couple per night for the Carriage House; other rooms are $150 to $180. Rates include a continental breakfast of muffins and French pastries.

Petite Auberge, 863 Bush St., San Francisco, CA 94108 (tel. 415/928-6000). White Swan Inn, 845 Bush St., San Francisco, CA 94108 (tel. 415/775-1755). These two French and English "sisters," practically side by side on the lower slopes of Nob Hill, are romantic reminders of England and France, transported here by businessman–turned–hotel owner Roger Tost. When you enter the Petite Au-berge, you'll feel transported to the French countryside by the calico-printed wallpa-per, antiques, a carousel horse, and fresh-cut flowers everywhere. The inn's 26 rooms are individually decorated with quaint print wallpaper, curtains, and down comforters, French-style antiques, a collection of novels by the beds, and wood-burning fireplaces (in all but eight rooms). You'll have company—cuddly teddy bears, which share the queen-size beds in all rooms. The 27-room English-style White Swan offers the added warmth of a flower garden, curved bay windows, and handsome English antiques. The library, living room, and dining room are decorated in rich, warm woods. All rooms have fireplaces. In both hotels, guests are served bountiful breakfasts of freshly squeezed juices, fresh fruit, egg dishes, and homemade breads and pastries. Afternoon tea is provided in both inns' sitting rooms: A fire is usually crackling in the fireplace at both hotels to ward off the chills of foggy afternoons. The hotels are within easy walking distance of Union Square, Nob Hill, and the cable-car lines. Honeymoon packages: Petite Auberge: $220 to $280 per couple per night (regular rates: $115 to $215 per couple per night). White Swan: $225 to $340 per couple per night (regular rates: $160 to $275 per couple per night). At both inns, package includes a bottle of California champagne, two engraved champagne flutes, a teddy bear, and a souvenir key ring.

Kimco Hotels (tel. 415/397-5572; reservations: toll free 800/669-7777). About ten years ago, Bill Kimpton was the first entrepreneur to see the wisdom of taking old, run-down downtown San Francisco hotels and refurbishing them as intimate, European-style inns. His idea paid off handsomely, and today the seven properties in his Kimco group have become some of the most popular of San Francisco's "boutique hotels." Although each has a different theme, they share several elements in common. All are centrally located right near Union Square and the theater district, each lobby has a cozy sitting area off the lobby, most offer a complimentary continental breakfast and afternoon wine in the lobby, and all are reasonably priced. Downstairs at each hotel, you'll find some of San Francisco's premier restaurants, including Masa's at the Vintage Court and The Palm at the Juliana. The properties are:

Monticello Inn, 80 Cyril Magnin St., San Francisco, CA 94102 (tel. 415/392-8800). This historic 1906 structure has been decorated with a colonial-era theme, with Chippendale-style furnishings and canopied beds. Modern comforts include honor bars and remote-controlled color TVs. Honeymoon package: None. Rates: $110 to $180 per couple per night.

Vintage Court, 650 Bush St., San Francisco, CA 94108 (tel. 415/392-4666). In keeping with the hotel's name, everything takes on a wine-country motif here, with rooms named after different California wineries and a burgundy-hued color scheme predominating. Rooms have cozy chintz fabrics, and complimentary wines are served nightly in the lobby. Honeymoon package: None. Rates: $105 per couple per night.

Juliana, 590 Bush St., San Francisco, CA 94108 (tel. 415/392-2540). With only 107 rooms, the Juliana achieves an intimate, at-home feel. Stylishly decorated in soothing pastels, rooms feature minirefrigerators and remote-control color TVs, with VCRs available on request. The junior suites, with their sunny window seats, are perfect for honeymooners. Honeymoon package: $110 per couple per night for a junior suite (weekends only). Regular rates: $105 to $140 per couple per night.

Bedford, 761 Post St., San Francisco, CA 94109 (tel. 415/673-6040). Housed in a completely renovated 1933 building, this hotel is known for its personal service. Many rooms have canopied beds, decked out in airy, floral-patterned pastels. All rooms have VCRs, with movie rentals available in the lobby. Honeymoon package: None. Rates: $100 to $165 per couple per night.

Villa Florence, 225 Powell St., San Francisco, CA 94102 (tel. 415/397-7700). You'll almost feel as if you've been whisked off to Italy, thanks to the colonnaded entryway, a lobby mural depicting 16th-century Florence, and springtime-fresh room décor. Honeymoon package: None. Rates: $110 to $180 per couple per night.

Galleria Park, 191 Sutter St., San Francisco, CA 94104 (tel. 415/781-3060). The lobby is a stunner, with its art nouveau–design etched-glass entryway and eight-foot-tall wood-burning hearth. But the real perk for fitness enthusiasts is the roof-top jogging track. Honeymoon package: None. Weekend rates: $88 per couple per night. Regular rates: $120 per couple per night for a room, $150 to $385 per couple per night for a suite.

The Prescott, 545 Post St., San Francisco, CA 94102 (tel. 415/563-0303). Kimco's newest hotel is also the most luxurious, with concierge service, nightly turn-down, and complimentary wine and hors d'oeuvres served nightly in the wood-paneled library. Rooms feature Empire-style furnishings, including a bow-front armoire and columned cherry-wood headboard. Honeymoon package: None. Rates: $155 to $190 per couple per night.

Inexpensive

Hotel Beresford Arms, 701 Post St., San Francisco, CA 94109 (tel. 415/673-2600; reservations: toll free 800/533-6533). A grand old lobby with carved, molded ceilings and red-velvet upholstered Victorian love seats greets guests at this reasonably priced 90-room hotel. Standard rooms have queen-size beds with white cotton bedspreads, attractive dark-wood furniture, modern bathrooms with sliding glass doors opening onto the tubs, small refrigerators, and color TVs. Suites have whirlpool baths, bidets, and full kitchens. Every morning, complimentary coffee and pastries are served in the lobby. The location is excellent, two blocks from Union Square and from the theater district. Honeymoon package: None. Rates (EP): $77 per couple per night for standard rooms; $88 to $105 for suites. If this hotel is full, you might try its sister hotel, the Beresford, a block away on Sutter. Rates are the same.

The King George Hotel, 334 Mason St., San Francisco, CA 94102 (tel. 415/781-5050; reservations: toll free 800/227-4240 nationwide; 800/556-4545 in California; and 800/345-4240 in Canada), is a 143-room charmer. Refurbished several years ago in an English country motif, it has retained its inn-style character even though a renovation in mid-1987 gave it a more sophisticated look. The lobby has floor-to-ceiling drapes and Corinthian columns. Rooms are now bright, airy, and elegant, with cream-colored walls, cherry-wood furniture, and floral print bedspreads. The rooms are on the small side, but quite adequate and comfortable. A great place to relax after a day of sightseeing or shopping at Union Square (a block away) is at the hotel's Bread and Honey Tearoom above the lobby, serving traditional afternoon high tea (pastries) to the accompaniment of live classical piano music. Honeymoon package: $120 per couple per night. Includes all taxes; flowers, champagne, and chocolates upon arrival; discount on high tea at the hotel; San Francisco bay cruise; cocktails at Pier 39; and more.

The Bed and Breakfast Inn, Four Charlton Court, San Francisco, CA 94123 (tel. 415/921-9784). This plant-covered turn-of-the-century building with creaky floors was opened as a bed-and-breakfast inn by Robert and Marily Kavanaugh in 1975. Although it's in the popular shopping and restaurant district of Union Street, the inn is just off Union on a tiny alleyway that will take you back to the narrow mews of old London. The inn has only nine rooms, four of which share bathrooms. The five with private baths are quite appropriate for anyone's romantic dreams, especially The Mayfair, a private flat with living room, kitchen, latticed balcony, and spiral staircase to the bedroom loft. One of the most charming rooms, often recommended for honeymooners, has a large Jacuzzi bathtub lined with a mirror. The queen-size bed is in a cozy alcove, decorated in dainty Laura Ashley prints. Guests can enjoy the garden, brew a cup of tea in the library, and share the continental breakfast in the English country–style dining room. Honeymoon package: None. Rates (CP): $75 to $95 per couple per night for "pension" rooms with shared baths; $120 to $135 for rooms with private baths, telephones, and TVs; and $205 for the flat with spiral staircase.

The Cartwright, 524 Sutter St., San Francisco, CA 94102 (tel. 415/421-2865; reservations: toll free 800/227-3844), has many loyal guests who cite its friendly, almost familial service, moderate rates, and excellent location a block from Union Square and on the cable-car line as reasons for their repeat visits. A recent renovation has significantly upgraded the hotel, turning the lobby into an elegant showpiece and adding romantic brass and carved-wood beds, floral-print bed-spreads, and newly tiled baths to each of its 114 rooms. The new decor is the work of Aroline Adams, who owns the hotel with her husband, Jerome (their children and son-in-law are also involved in the family-owned hotel). Rooms have small refrigera-tors, fresh flowers, large bathtubs and showers, color TVs, and telephones. Compli-mentary tea is served in the lobby from 4 to 6 p.m. The hotel's Town and Country Tea Room serves breakfast and lunch in a country setting with blue-and-white floral print tablecloths, white rattan chairs, and hardwood floors. Honeymoon package: None. Rates (EP): $92 to $110 per couple per night.

    Hotel Diva, 440 Geary St., San Francisco, CA 94102 (tel. 415/885-0200, or toll free 800/553-1900). This is not just another pretty place. Outside, first impres-sions come from the Day-Glo–painted handprints in the sidewalk—souvenirs from visiting "divas" such as Leontyne Price, Anjelica Huston, and Talia Shire. Inside, there's nary a Laura Ashley fabric to be seen. Instead, hit videos play on the color monitors, and the polished stainless-steel lobby would not look out of place in the space shuttle. Rooms are decorated in the furniture equivalent of fashion forward, with austerely elegant gray carpeting and shiny white Italian-design bathrooms, plus first-rate stereos, remote-control color TVs, and VCRs for mediaholics. A compli-mentary continental breakfast includes orange juice, croissants, and coffee or tea, served in the lounge on each floor. But it's the personal service that really wins the hearts of celebrity regulars, who include Mel Gibson, Francis Ford Coppola, and others. For example, although the hotel has no honeymoon package, a manager is quick to point out, "Just let us know you're celebrating something special. We'll make your stay memorable." Rates (CP): $110 to $130 per couple per night.

Very Inexpensive

    Grant Plaza, 465 Grant Ave., San Francisco, CA 94108 (tel. 415/434-3883; reservations: toll free 800/472-6899 nationwide; 800/472-6805 in California). This small gem at the entrance of Chinatown inevitably gets listed in most budget guides to San Francisco. But besides being a bargain, the Grant Plaza is pretty, spot-lessly clean, and attractively decorated. Its lobby of chandeliers, elegant burgundy carpeting, and potted plants belies the budget price. The rooms are a bit small, but all feature furnishings that you'd find in a hotel whose rates are three times these. All rooms have color TVs, private baths, and direct-dial telephones. Unfortunately, the corner rooms (with the best views) have twin beds, but queen-size beds are available in others. Don't miss the cozy sitting area on the top floor, under the domed stained-glass skylight. The hotel does not have a bar or restaurant, but it is a five-minute walk from the Union Square shopping area and the theater district, and a ten-minute stroll from the nightlife and restaurants of North Beach. Cable cars are a block away. Honeymoon package: None. Rates (EP): $40 to $70 per couple per night.

ROMANTIC RESTAURANTS

    San Francisco is one of the world's great dining cities, a place where there's one restaurant for every 164 residents—many of whom seem to live to eat, rather than eat to live. San Francisco's renowned chefs take pride in using only the freshest in-gredients (many work with farmers who grow produce exclusively for their restau-rants). Often, the lettuce in your dinner salad had the fresh dew on it only that morning; a petrale sole was just off-loaded a few hours earlier at Fisherman's Wharf.

Expensive

    Located in one of San Francisco's most fashionable hotels, **Campton Place Restaurant,** 340 Stockton (tel. 781-5155), offers a plush setting in the Grand Euro-pean manner. When you enter, you'll feel as if you're sinking ankle-deep into the thick carpeting. Mirrors strategically placed hither and yon catch reflections. You can dine by the windows, in straight-backed chairs, or against the wall, ensconced in a cushy banquette. A spotlight draws attention to the huge floral display in a celadon vase; Wedgwood china gleams on the tables. If the decor is classic, the food is innovative American, featuring regional specialties in season: poached lobster served with blue-corn cakes, or a grilled quail served with matchstick-thin sweet potato sticks. All perfectly prepared and impeccably served. Lunch, about $80 to $100 per couple, served Monday through Friday, 11:30 a.m. to 2:30 p.m.; Saturday, noon to 2:30 p.m. Dinner for two with wine could easily run $150 or more; served daily from 5:30 to 10 p.m. Sunday brunch served from 8 a.m. to 2:30 p.m.

Moderate

Square One, 190 Pacific at Front (tel. 788-1110). The decor is Italian modern —terra-cotta tiles, blond-wood furniture, soft, soothing shades of beige, taupe, and pastels all around. But what really gets your libido racing here is the food. Run by Joyce Goldstein, who used to manage the Chez Panisse Café in Berkeley, Square One has rapidly zoomed to the top rank of San Francisco's restaurant galaxy. The menu changes daily to take advantage of seasonal specialties, and Goldstein delights in adapting spices and techniques from different countries—perhaps a Brazilian churrasco, or an Algerian chick-pea soup lushly seasoned with saffron. The Italian dishes equal those served in the finest restaurants in Tuscany: pollo all'arrabbiata, a grilled baby chicken in a marinade of garlic, hot peppers, tomatoes, and olive oil; or farfalle (bow-shaped pasta) served with prosciutto, artichokes, mushrooms, peas, and onions. Every day Square One features a different home-baked Italian bread, such as a crusty panmarino, lustily spiced with rosemary. The staff is congenial and knowledgeable about the extensive (and reasonably priced) wine list. Don't miss the outstanding desserts, such as a frozen peach sorbet, with the flavor of fresh-harvested fruit. Lunch, $40 to $50 per couple, served daily from 11:30 a.m. to 2:30 p.m.; dinner, $60 to $80 per couple plus drinks, from 5:30 to 9:30 p.m. on weekdays, to 10 p.m. on weekends.

Greens, Building A at Fort Mason (tel. 771-6222), is certainly one of the most intriguing restaurants in San Francisco—and one of the most beautiful. Set in a former army fort warehouse, the room retains a high-tech approach with gray industrial-type carpeting and the original high ceiling. Colorful abstract art brightens the walls, and natural-wood tables soften the hard-edge feel. But the pièce de résistance is the view through the floor-to-ceiling windows—a postcard-perfect outlook over the marina to the Golden Gate Bridge. The restaurant is run by a Zen Buddhist group (only in San Francisco would you find Buddhists operating a first-class restaurant in what once was an army supply depot). You'll know the ingredients are fresh—many of the vegetables are grown on the group's own farm near Muir Woods. The cuisine can best be described as haute vegetarian, with dishes so richly satisfying and zestily flavorful that you'll never notice the lack of meat. At lunch, you might be able to start off with mesquite-grilled polenta, served with warm Gorgonzola cheese and walnuts on a bed of lettuce, or a picked-from-the-garden salad. Greens' pastas are excellent, such as linguine gently tossed with lentils, ricotta cheese, sweet peppers, garlic, and herbs. For dessert, try a blackberry tart or chocolate-nut torte. At night, Greens turns the lights down to highlight the bay views. Selections might include mesquite-grilled brochettes with mushrooms, cherry tomatoes, peppers, and potatoes, or pizza with zucchini, tomatoes, red onions, fontina, and pesto. Lunch, $20 to $30 per couple, served daily from 11:30 a.m. to 2:15 p.m.; dinner, $30 to $40 per couple, from 6 to 9:30 p.m. Several times a week, they also offer a gourmet five-course prix-fixe dinner for $33 per person.

Fog City Diner, 1300 Battery St. at the Embarcadero (tel. 982-2000), is the place that originated the concept of "grazing"—downing a bevy of tasty appetizer-size portions rather than just one entrée. Go light with crab cakes, or hunker down seriously with a grilled skirt steak. And you've never seen such a glamorous diner—

looking like a railroad car dressed for a night on the town, with a razzle-dazzle neon-lighted stainless-steel facade outside, counterpointed by hand-rubbed Honduran mahogany booths inside. An extraordinary bar, made from Mexican onyx illuminated from underneath, provides a popular gathering place. Open daily from 11:30 a.m. to 11 p.m.; entrées priced from $6.50 to $16.50.

Bix, 56 Gold St. at Montgomery (tel. 433-6300). This ultrahot new restaurant recaptures the Gatsby-like glamor of the 1930s, complete with a huge mural depicting a Jazz Age club. White-jacketed bartenders concoct perfect Manhattans and impeccable martinis at the wildly popular bar. Set in a quiet alleyway near the financial district, the restaurant was started by the creators of the Fog City Diner, as well as the megasuccessful Mustards and Tra Vigne in Napa Valley (see Napa Valley "Romantic Restaurants" section). Here, the atmosphere recalls a swank supper club, with mellow mahogany paneling, art deco–design railings that look seaworthy enough for an ocean liner, and live jazz music bebopping in the background. The menu heads back to the basics—entrées include pork chops with mashed potatoes and peas, lamb chops with mint and onions—but all is artfully prepared. Open for lunch Monday through Friday, from 11:30 straight on, at $30 to $40 per couple. Dinner nightly, 6 to 10 p.m., about $55 per couple plus drinks.

Susie Kate's, 2330 Taylor St. (tel. 776-KATE). We'd like to be the first on the block to tell you about what's probably the best undiscovered restaurant in San Francisco. Simply decorated with vintage cooking implements and named after the chef-owner's grandmother, Susie Kate's specializes in down-home, downright delicious southern cooking. Recipes span Dixie from Georgia (represented by a meltingly tender southern-fried chicken) to N'Awlins (a rousing jambalaya accompanied by dirty rice). Dinners include soup or salad, as well as liberal helpings of fresh cornbread and buttermilk biscuits, plus homemade corn relish. House-baked desserts might include pecan pie or chocolate-chocolate bourbon pie. Dinner for two, $30 to $40 plus drinks, served Monday through Saturday, 5 to 10 p.m. Also open for Sunday brunch, 10:30 a.m. to 2:30 p.m.

Zuni Cafe & Grill, 1658 Market St. at Franklin (tel. 552-2522). Very modern and very chic, Zuni is located west of downtown, near the Civic Center. For seating, you have a choice of a table in the airy two-tiered dining room or (in nice weather) on the sidewalk terrace—a prime perch for people watching. The sublime food is perhaps the definitive rendition of Mediterranean cuisine, California style—or is it Californian cuisine, Mediterranean style? Innovative dishes include fusilli (spiral-shaped pasta) with charred tomatoes, hot pepper, pancetta, and bread crumbs; and a savory risotto studded with sweet morsels of lobster and suffused with sage. Open Tuesday through Sunday, 7:30 a.m. to midnight (to 11 p.m. on Sunday). Lunch, about $40 per couple; dinner, $60 to $70 per couple.

Corona Bar & Grill, 88 Cyril Magnin St. (tel. 392-5500). Our friend, the restaurant maven, was one of the first to recommend this place highly. "It draws a real lively crowd," she said. "Lots of fun—and great food." It's just that animated atmosphere that's packing them in at this excellent eatery downstairs from the Monticello Inn. New Mexico meets nouveau California in both the decor, which includes Santa Fe motifs and Indian masks, and the menu. You'll be hard put to choose among the tempting appetizers: quesadillas with shiitake mushrooms and Roquefort, or fresh oysters afloat in peppered tequila. The entrées are highlighted by a rack of lamb mole and a tamarind-glazed duck with shoestring yams. Open Monday through Saturday for lunch and dinner, 11:30 a.m. to 11 p.m.; Sunday, dinner only, 5 to 11 p.m. Prices run $30 to $50 per couple.

Cliff House, 1090 Point Lobos at Ocean Beach (tel. 386-3330), has been a favorite place to watch the sunset, as well as the surfers and seals. While the sunsets are spectacular, the food is just OK, so drop by for cocktails only.

Very Inexpensive

Who says you have to spend a lot of money to dine well—and romantically?

The best two meals in town are, if not free, about $7.50 per person. All along Fisherman's Wharf, sidewalk stands such as the **Lighthouse, Borruso's,** and **Guardino's** sell "walk-away" cocktails of shrimp or the famous Dungeness crab (about $3) and clam chowder ($2.75). When accompanied with some sourdough bread, it makes for a satisfying meal. For dessert, point your toes toward the **Ghirardelli Chocolate Manufactory,** where you can down an ice-cream soda, sundae, or the definitive chocolate malted, topped with a dollop of whipped cream. Good to the last slurp.

Or enjoy a lunch of dim sum (appetizers) in Chinatown at a restaurant such as **Tung Fong** (808 Pacific off Stockton; tel. 362-7115). Waiters push a trolley laden with tasty choices: spring rolls, barbecued chicken tidbits, steamed dumplings, and bow (puffy buns stuffed with ingredients such as black mushrooms and peppers)—just point to make your selections. The waiters are extremely helpful and will identify any items you don't recognize. Each dish costs about $2; figure on three per person. They serve from noon to 2:30 p.m. daily. Then saunter up Grant Avenue toward the nearby Italian quarter in North Beach and polish off a cappuccino and gelato (ice cream) in a sidewalk café. If you prefer your dim sum in a more eye-catching, Hong Kong–elegant milieu, try **Harbor Village** at Embarcadero Four (tel. 398-8883).

San Francisco's most popular pizza parlor must be **North Beach Pizza,** 1499 Grant Ave. at Union Street (tel. 433-2444). In addition to your usual toppings, such as pepperoni or mushrooms ($9.50 for a medium pie), they offer some gourmet exotica, such as Verdi's Special, with spinach, fresh pesto, onions, and feta cheese ($15). They also serve excellent pasta ($8 to $9 per person, including soup and salad), plus hearty favorites such as veal parmigiana ($10, including soup or salad). Open Sunday through Thursday, 11 a.m. to 1 a.m.; Friday and Saturday, 11 a.m. to 3 a.m.

---

3. Napa Valley

Whether inspired by the scenery, the local vintage, or the fact that he was stopping over on his honeymoon, Robert Louis Stevenson became one of Napa Valley's earliest tourism boosters, describing the region as "a bower of green and tangled thicket, still fragrant and still flower bespangled." He was also one of the area's most clairvoyant visitors, predicting that "the smack of California earth shall linger on the palate of your grandson."

One hundred years later, Stevenson has been proved right. Napa Valley is probably the best-known wine-growing region in America. Flanked by the Mayacamas and Vaca mountain ranges, the peaceful green valley is dotted with wood-frame houses, stone wineries, and acre after acre of well-ordered vineyards. Located some 44 miles north of San Francisco (about an hour's drive), the region stretches about 30 miles from Carneros to Calistoga. In between, road signs identify towns whose names grace many a wine label: Oakville, Yountville, Rutherford, and St. Helena.

ROMANTIC INTERLUDES

Napa Valley is not only America's premier wine-growing area, it is also one of California's largest tourist attractions.

Wine-tasting tours rank high on every visitor's list. Thanks to Napa's consistent, sunny weather and rich volcanic soil, the area produces wines that equal or surpass the great vintages of France. With nearly 140 area wineries from which to choose, you should plan in advance which ones you want to visit. For the most interesting variety, combine visits to some of the larger producers with stops at some smaller operations. After a tour explaining wine-making techniques, guests are usually invited to sample some of the house vintages (several companies have started to charge a small fee for tastings).

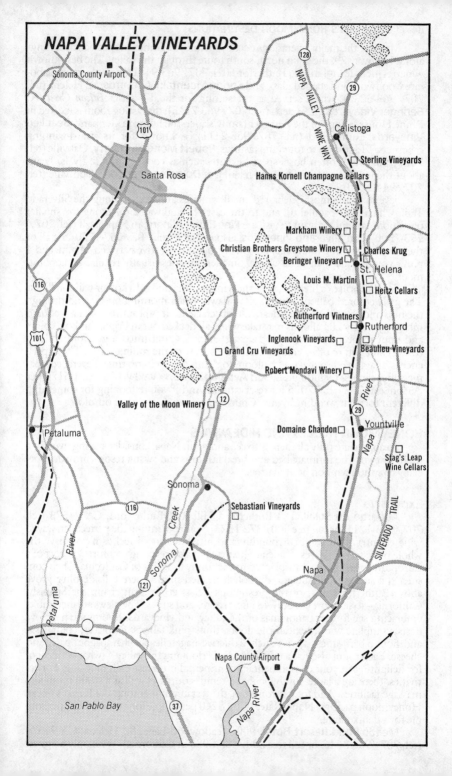

NAPA VALLEY VINEYARDS

Sonoma County Airport

Santa Rosa

Calistoga

Sterling Vineyards

Hanns Kornell Champagne Cellars

Markham Winery

Christian Brothers Greystone Winery

Charles Krug

Beringer Vineyard

St. Helena

Louis M. Martini

Heitz Cellars

Rutherford Vintners

Rutherford

Inglenook Vineyards

Beaulieu Vineyards

Grand Cru Vineyards

Robert Mondavi Winery

Valley of the Moon Winery

Petaluma

Domaine Chandon

Yountville

Stag's Leap Wine Cellars

Sonoma

Sebastiani Vineyards

Napa

Napa County Airport

San Pablo Bay

NAPA VALLEY WINE WAY

SILVERADO TRAIL

Napa River

Sonoma Creek

Petaluma River

Napa River

Many of the major operations occupy historic buildings in spectacular settings along Highway 29, the main north-south route through the valley. The best-known wineries include **Inglenook**, Rutherford (tel. 707/963-9411), notable for its elaborate woodwork and stained glass; and **Spring Mountain Vineyards**, St. Helena (tel. 707/963-5233), which served as the setting for the TV series *Falcon Crest*. At **Beringer Vineyards**, St. Helena (tel. 707/963-7115), the tasting room is located in Rhine House, a copy of the Beringer family's ancestral home in Germany. **Beaulieu Vineyards**, Rutherford (tel. 707/963-2411), is known for its award-winning cabernets. In addition to tours and tastings, **Robert Mondavi Winery**, Oakville (tel. 707/963-9611), often hosts special events, such as concerts and festivals. Learn about the intricacies of champagne making at **Domaine Chandon**, Yountville (tel. 707/944-2280).

Several of the most celebrated small wineries are located along the Silverado Trail, which runs parallel to, and to the east of, Highway 29. Among the smaller operations you might want to visit are **Pine Ridge Winery**, in Napa itself (tel. 707/253-7500), and **Silverado Vineyards**, also in Napa (tel. 707/257-1770). At all of the wineries, visiting hours vary seasonally, but if you arrive between 11 a.m. and 4 p.m., you're usually in good shape. Smaller wineries usually require an appointment.

For the thrill of a lifetime, view the wine country aboard a hot-air-balloon flight. The gaily colored balloons soar aloft at dawn, when morning mists wind through the hills and the air is crystal-clear. The spectacle itself is beautiful—on a weekend morning, nearly 20 balloons may take wing, all decked out in bright rainbow colors and zippy stripe, herringbone, and zigzag patterns. Climb into the gondola (balloon basket) and you're off—enjoying an eagle's view of the rolling valley. The experience is guaranteed to make a "balloon dog" out of you in no time. Several companies offer flights, including **Balloon Aviation of Napa Valley**. They cost $170 per person; call 707/252-7076 for reservations. And if you're looking for something different for your wedding, owner Chuck Foster can marry you both aloft.

HONEYMOON HOTELS AND HIDEAWAYS

To appreciate fully all there is to see and do in Napa, consider staying over for a night or two. The intimate bed-and-breakfast inns and swank resorts provide especially cozy honeymoon headquarters.

Expensive

Auberge du Soleil, 180 Rutherford Hill Rd., Rutherford, CA 94573 (tel. 707/963-1211, or toll free 800/372-1323). You're planning the perfect getaway to wine country. You want surroundings so intimate, you'll feel as if you have the whole place to yourselves. You crave luxury, but also relaxing comfort . . . sort of a European country inn, transplanted to the sunny foothills of California. Then consider the sumptuous Auberge du Soleil, nestled in a 33-acre hillside olive grove above Rutherford. Part of the prestigious Relais et Château chain, the Spanish-California–style resort has only 48 guest rooms and suites. The views are incredible, embracing see-forever panoramas of the valley and vineyards. Rooms are true love nests, complete with Mexican tile floors, think-pink fabrics, fireplaces, color TVs, and honor bars stocked with such seductive bagatelles as champagne, pâté, and cheese. Each room also has a private deck overlooking the valley—what better spot for delighting in your complimentary continental breakfast each morning. For activities, there are a large, lovely pool and tennis courts, as well as a steam room and massage facilities. And for gastronomes, the restaurant is among California's finest. Honeymoon package: None. Rates (CP): $240 per couple for a room; $425 per couple for a deluxe suite.

Meadowood Resort Hotel, 900 Meadowood Lane, St. Helena, CA 94574 (tel. 707/963-3646, or toll free 800/458-8080 in California). With only 58 guest accommodations set on 256 wooded acres of an exclusive country club, Meadowood offers honeymooners plenty of privacy. Set at the northern end of the valley along a vineyard-bordered country lane, the resort is a magical enclave of emerald-green lawns and proud California oak trees. Imagine Martha's Vineyard come to Napa Valley vineyards and you get the picture of the pretty wood-frame cottage accommodations, graced by dormer windows and white-railed porches. Some overlook the pool or tennis courts; others, the undulating fairways. Niceties include wood-burning fireplaces, terry-cloth robes, easy-to-brew coffee makers, and stocked refrigerators. The resort is one of the centers of wine-country life, and annually hosts the prestigious Napa Valley Wine Auction. It's a perfect choice for sports-lovers, with a swimming pool (heated April through November), six tennis courts, a nine-hole golf course, and, for those wicket-ly inclined, two regulation croquet courts. The croquet lawns are impeccably manicured, drawing top international competitors for the annual tournaments. (Neophytes can take lessons from the resident pro.) The fresh California cuisine is excellent at both the gourmet Starmont Restaurant and Fairway Bar and Grill. Honeymoon package: None. Rates (EP): $225 (weekdays) to $280 (weekends) per couple for a room; $235 (weekdays) to $315 (weekends) per couple for a suite.

Silverado, 1600 Atlas Peak Rd., Napa, CA 94558 (tel. 707/257-0200). Ensconced on 1,200 acres threaded with silver streams and dappled with oak, redwood, and eucalyptus groves, Silverado is a place for couples who enjoy the finer things in life—and want them close at hand. The self-contained resort occupies one of Napa's most historic estates, originally built by General John Franklin Miller, one of California's first U.S. Senators. The Italianate mansion he constructed, La Vergne, now houses the Club's reception area and dining room. Clustered in white-painted low-rise cottages with shingled roofs, accommodations are tastefully appointed with wood-burning fireplaces, wet bars, and patios or balconies. Since all of the units are condominiums, they reflect the spaciousness and grace of the private residences they actually are. You'll find plenty to do right on the property. Tee off on two 18-hole Robert Trent Jones Jr.–designed championship golf courses. Hone your backhand on one of the 20 hard-surfaced tennis courts. Find privacy at one of the eight swimming pools located throughout the resort. Rent bicycles and pedal along oak-shaded lanes. You're near all of the valley's best vineyards and restaurants —or enjoy the resort's three excellent restaurants and two cocktail lounges. Honeymoon package: None. Rates (EP): $160 to $180 per couple for a studio; $190 to $215 per couple for a one-bedroom suite.

ROMANTIC RESTAURANTS

Next to wining, dining is Napa Valley's favorite pastime. The following restaurants are so immensely successful, they often book up weeks in advance, so call for reservations even before you arrive in California.

Expensive

Auberge du Soleil, 180 Rutherford Hill Rd., Rutherford (tel. 963-1211). What shall we praise first? Should it be the view from the dining terrace, where you have the entire glorious extravaganza of Napa Valley laid out at your feet? Or should it be the rhapsodical cuisine, which brings flavors together with all the exuberance of fireworks on the Fourth of July? You couldn't ask for a more marvelous setting than this perch at the plush Auberge du Soleil resort. Although the indoor dining room is romantic enough to spark marriage proposals all over again, with French country–style cane chairs and columns hewn from polished tree trunks, definitely opt for a table out on the patio in nice weather. The food rises to the level of the surroundings, with deftly prepared French-Californian dishes such as a seafood sausage with crustacean coulis, or a classic rack of lamb spiced with rosemary. Time your dinner reservation so you can catch the last glow of sunset flaming behind the mountains.

By dessert time, the stars will be twinkling out good night. Open daily for lunch, 11:30 a.m. to 2 p.m.; $60 to $80 per couple. Dinner served from 6 to 9 p.m.; the four-course prix-fixe meal is $55 per person.

Domaine Chandon, California Drive at Highway 29, Yountville (tel. 944-2892). If we had to choose the perfect setting for a wine-country lunch, it would be the sunny terrace at this superb French restaurant *chez* one of California's finest sparkling-wine houses. Screened by a pergola, the patio overlooks rolling green lawns and neat rows of vines. Start off with a warm chèvre salad or seafood terrine, then try a magret of duck in cabernet sauce with a purée of yams and garlic; or a bowl of steamed seafood, served in its own juices and accented with light cream and snipped chives. To accompany your meal, enjoy one of the excellent house sparkling wines, available either by the bottle or by the glass. Although the food is equally good at dinner, you cannot eat outside, and the indoor dining room is a bit formal. During the summer (May through October), the restaurant serves lunch daily from 11:30 a.m. to 2:30 p.m. and dinner Wednesday through Sunday from 6 p.m. to 9 p.m. During the winter (November through April), the restaurant is closed Monday and Tuesday. Lunch will run $80 to $100 per couple plus champagne.

Miramonte, 1327 Railroad Ave. near Hunt, St. Helena (tel. 963-3970). Located in a restored turn-of-the-century hotel in charming St. Helena, Miramonte weaves the seductive mood of a European country inn, with flickering candlelight, fresh flowers, and an unusual chandelier made from stag horn. The restaurant spotlights the talents of Udo Nechutnys, a disciple of renowned French chef Paul Bocuse. He creates memorable dishes, such as a scallop mousse flecked with finely grated orange peel and served with a white wine–and–spinach sauce; or breast of Muscovy duck, served rare with a red currant–and–raspberry sauce and accompanied by black mushrooms. For dessert, go light with some fresh figs marinated in cabernet, or try the rich chocolate Bavarian cream, enhanced by a slightly bitter edge of coffee beans. Miramonte serves dinner only, Wednesday through Sunday, 6 to 9:30 p.m. The five-course prix-fixe meal costs $55 per person. Personal checks with identification are accepted; credit cards are not.

Moderate

Mustards Grill, 7399 St. Helena Highway 29, Yountville (tel. 944-2424). We've had some of our best meals ever (that's anywhere-in-the-world, at-any-price ever) at this friendly, unpretentious bistro in the heart of Napa Valley. The restaurant was created by the same people who started Tra Vigne in St. Helena and Fog City Diner and Bix in San Francisco. Up front, there's a gregarious bar scene. Inside, the decor captures the cozy appeal of a Left Bank café, with an art deco–tinged black-and-white-tile floor and burnished wood wainscotting. The simplicity of the setting makes way for the real star—which is chef Cindy Pawlcyn's extraordinary cuisine. Textures, flavors, colors, and even temperatures create culinary contrasts. Although the menu varies to take advantage of harvest bounty, usual standout items include a warm crêpe appetizer topped with caviar, crème fraîche, and snipped chives. For your entrée, try one of the wood-grilled specialties, such as quail or steaks, all garnished with unusual vegetables and sauces, such as a tomato-mango salsa. Don't miss dessert—especially the sneak preview of heaven, which manifests itself as a sublime crème brûlée topped with the thinnest, most luscious crinkle of caramelized sugar. Open daily for lunch and dinner, 11:30 a.m. to 10 p.m. About $45 to $55 per couple, plus drinks (the in-depth wine list is quite reasonably priced).

Tra Vigne, 1050 Charter Oak at St. Helena Highway, St. Helena (tel. 963-4444). The sister restaurant to Mustards, Tra Vigne gives Italian cuisine a California accent—and the result soars. Set in a historic stone building in St. Helena, the restaurant is stunning, with ash-wood tables, 15-foot-tall windows looking out over a brick courtyard, and, seemingly, acres of wood floors. Classic Italian recipes gain verve when married to fresh California produce, such as the grilled radicchio with black olive and zinfandel sauce, or al dente fettuccine tossed with grilled artichoke, sweet corn, and chervil. Absolutely everything is made on the premises—breads, pastas, gelati . . . even prosciutti and cheeses. Open daily from noon to 10 p.m.; $55 to $65 per couple, plus drinks.

4. Monterey, the Monterey Peninsula, and Carmel

For residents as well as vacationers, the Monterey Peninsula and the towns along its shores represent the best of California's coast drive. Here, all the images that embody California seem to swirl together in one massive montage of splendid scenery. Two-hundred-year-old red-roofed adobe structures line Monterey's broad streets. The indomitable Lone Cypress clings tenaciously to its rocky promontory off the 17-Mile Drive. Along the coast where the Pacific Ocean whips furiously into the cliffs, the pencil-thin outline of Highway 1 spirals its way along the shore. Although this is one of California's most historic regions, large stretches of terrain remain untouched. Yet in seaside towns such as Carmel and Monterey, civilization—in the form of gourmet restaurants, art galleries, and Bach festivals—reaches a chic refinement comparable to that of European communities along the Riviera.

Located about 120 miles south of San Francisco and 330 miles north of Los Angeles, the Monterey Peninsula forms the southernmost nub of Monterey Bay. Roughly rectangular in shape, the peninsula embraces four distinct communities. Moving counterclockwise around the peninsula, they are Monterey, Pacific Grove, Pebble Beach, and Carmel-by-the-Sea. Although each retains a distinct personality, you'll find it easy to travel from one to another. Only three miles separate Carmel from Monterey, so have no hesitations about flitting from one to another—perhaps visiting the Monterey Bay Aquarium in the morning, lunching and shopping in Carmel, then spending the night at a B&B in Pacific Grove.

ABOUT ACCOMMODATIONS

Although accommodations on the Monterey Peninsula embody romance, the amorous ambience does not come cheap. Count on spending between $70 and $140 a night at a charming bed-and-breakfast inn, about $200 to $350 at one of the renowned resort hotels.

If you will be staying on the Monterey Peninsula during the weekend, be aware that many of the bed-and-breakfasts require a minimum stay of two nights. Also, since the region ranks as a popular weekend getaway for folks from San Francisco and Los Angeles, the choicest properties book up fast for Fridays, Saturdays, and Sundays. Reserve your room several months in advance, especially if you will be honeymooning during the summer.

Honeymoon packages are the exception, rather than the rule, on the Monterey Peninsula. Unless otherwise noted, prices quoted are per couple per night. When making room reservations, let the hotel know that you are on your honeymoon—often, you'll receive a complimentary bottle of champagne.

ROMANTIC DINING

Superb—that describes dining on the peninsula known for just-caught seafood, just-picked fruits and vegetables, and just simply marvelous views of the ocean. Some Monterey specialties to know about: petrale sole and Monterey Bay shrimp. Do not hesitate if either appear on the menu.

Picnicking

For lovers such as you, the most romantic meal will undoubtedly be a picnic on one of the secluded beaches that line the coast from Carmel to Big Sur. Picnic etiquette is simple. All beaches have public access; be cautious that incoming tides don't strand you on some tenuous sandy promontory; and take all your garbage with you for disposal back at your hotel. Many stores and delis in Carmel and Monterey specialize in picnic provisioning.

WINE-TASTING ROMANTIC INTERLUDES

Although Monterey County is one of the finest up-and-coming wine-growing regions in California, viniculture in the region has a long tradition. Over 200 years ago, Franciscan friars planted the first vineyards in California near Monterey. Thanks to the rich soil and sun-kissed climate, about 35,000 acres of vineyards flourish in the county. Among the properties open to visitors: **Jekel Vineyards** in Greenfield (tel. 707/674-5522); **J. Lohr Winery** in San Jose (tel. 707/288-5057); The **Monterey Vineyard** in Gonzales (tel. 707/675-2481); and **Château Julian** in Carmel Valley (tel. 707/624-2600). Call for hours and appointments.

MONTEREY

In 1602, Spanish explorer Sebastián Vizcaíno discovered this broad, curving harbor. Because of its excellent anchorages and fine weather, Monterey served as the capital of Alta California—first for the Spanish, then for the Mexicans. It was not replaced as the number one city until a little shanty town up north—then named Yerba Buena, now called San Francisco—struck it rich during the Gold Rush. Reflecting the region's dependence on the sea, the town first served as port for trading schooners unloading their wares after a perilous journey around Cape Horn. Between the wars, Monterey ruled as the sardine-packing capital of the world, an era immortalized in John Steinbeck's novel *Cannery Row*. Today, Monterey continues to be a zesty blend of the old and the new.

Shopping

Monterey's Cannery Row also has an excellent selection of shops. **Sea Fantasies** (400 Cannery Row) is known for its "treasures from the sea," such as shell jewelry and vases. **Bayside Trading Co.** (225 Cannery Row) displays arts and crafts from all over the world, and **Windborne Kites** (585 Cannery Row) carries hundreds of rainbow-hued kites and wind socks.

Top name brands at savings of up to 70%—that's what you'll find at the new **American Tin Cannery** factory outlets, Ocean View Boulevard and Eardley Avenue, just around the corner from the Monterey Bay Aquarium (tel. 372-1442). Technically, the address places the shopping complex in Pacific Grove, but its proximity to Cannery Row means you'll probably want to make it part of your shopping foray there. Direct-to-you outlets include the **Van Heusen Factory Store, Bass Shoe Outlet, Royal Doulton** (firsts, seconds, and closeouts), **Harvé Benard,** and lots more. Open Monday through Saturday, 10 a.m. to 6 p.m.; Sunday, 11 a.m. to 5 p.m.

Romantic Interludes

Get a feel for Monterey's Spanish colonial past along the **"Path of History,"** a three-mile self-guided walking tour. The marked route takes you past dozens of beautifully preserved 18th- and 19th-century whitewashed adobe structures with red tile roofs and graceful black wrought-iron balconies. The historic houses that are open to the public include Larkin House (510 Calle Principal), built in the 1830s and considered one of the finest examples of Monterey colonial-style architecture; the Custom House (near Fisherman's Wharf), which was constructed in 1827 and now contains a museum of early California history; and Colton Hall and the Old Jail (Pacific between Madison and Jefferson), where California's first constitution was written in 1849. Also stop by Stevenson House (530 Houston St.), a former hotel where Robert Louis Stevenson lived. Most are open daily from 10 a.m. to 4 p.m.

From the 1920s to about 1946, Monterey was the sardine capital of the Western Hemisphere, with 16 canneries packing over 240,000 tons of sardines annually. The period is vividly recorded in John Steinbeck's novel *Cannery Row,* which de-

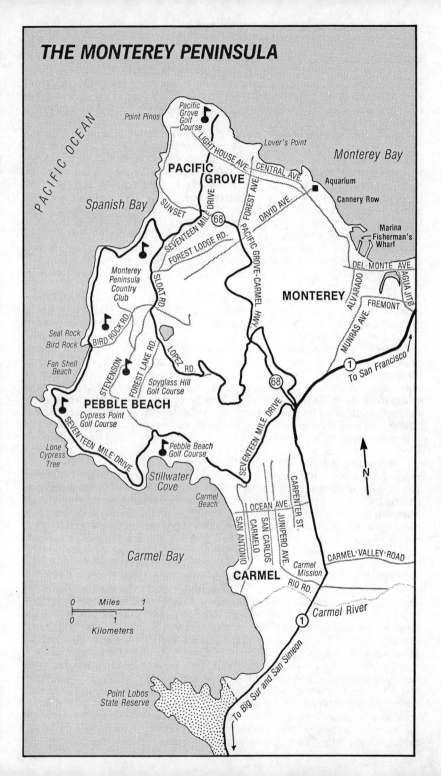

picts the raucous lives of the factory workers, fishermen, and hustlers. For reasons that are not completely understood, the sardines disappeared from area waters in 1948, and the old canneries went bankrupt. Today, the Row has been reborn—this time, as a fashionable stretch of restaurants and boutiques, where art galleries have replaced brothels, and pastel-painted bookstores occupy former bars where sailors once brawled. It's a fun spot for strolling and browsing, still filled with plenty of salty atmosphere.

Built, appropriately enough, around the old Hovden sardine cannery at the end of the row, the $40-million **Monterey Bay Aquarium** is the newest star on the peninsula and the largest aquarium in the United States. Most of all, it's a heck of a lot of fun, and the next best thing to being 20,000 leagues under the sea. Get eye-to-eye with bizarre denizens of the deep, such as wolf eels, giant sea stars, and the chambered nautilus, and meet strangely named creatures, such as the rubberlip sunperch and a striped "convictfish." The most impressive exhibit is unquestionably the three-story-tall kelp forest aquarium, where leopard sharks and schools of silvery sardines cruise. Feeding times are 11:30 a.m. and 4 p.m. Then, find out what's more fun than a barrel of monkeys—which is a tankful of playful sea otters. These aquatic clowns float on their backs and use small stones to whack open clams, which they hold on their tummies. Try to visit them at feeding time, 11 a.m., 2 p.m., and 4:30 p.m. daily.

The Monterey Bay Aquarium (tel. 375-3333) is open daily (except for Christmas Day) from 10 a.m. to 6 p.m.; admission is $7.50 per person. Tickets can also be bought in advance through Ticketron or the Aquarium. For parking, there's a new public garage on Foam Street (at Prescott).

Monterey's **Fisherman's Wharf** area still throbs with nautical sound effects. Sea lions bark and beg for tidbits, halyards ping against sailboat masts, foghorns blast across the bay, gulls squeal and cry. The wharf itself has a good-times, carnival atmosphere, complete with an organ grinder and his monkey and souvenir shops where you can buy T-shirts or a starfish. From here, you can leave on a deep-sea fishing expedition or go on a whale-watching cruise. Most fun of all—invest $1 and feed the sea lions that hang around the pilings. Each crafty old beggar has his own technique. Some emit a series of short, ear-piercing barks; others sound off in one long, mournful bellow.

When was the last time you could fall in love with a heroine (sigh!), scowl at a mustache-twirling villain (hiss!), and cheer the clean-cut hero (hurrah!)? Audience involvement is part of the fun when the **Troupers of the Gold Coast** present authentic 19th-century melodramas at the First Theatre in California, Scott and Pacific Streets in Monterey (tel. 375-4916). Performances are held in the long, low adobe building on Pacific Street that in 1848 became the first theater in California to host a paid performance. Showtime is 8 p.m. sharp on Friday and Saturday nights; tickets are $6 per person, and the box office is open Wednesday through Saturday.

Honeymoon Hotels and Hideaways

"A perfect inn for every detail!" "Romantic . . . and we've been married for 34 years." These are just a few of the rave reviews earned by the **Old Monterey Inn,** 500 Martin St., Monterey, CA 93940 (tel. 408/375-8284). The Tudor-style, half-timbered manse is set amid 1¼ acres of park-like gardens on a quiet residential street not far from the "Path of History." The house is a historic one too, built in 1929 by Monterey's first mayor, Carmel Martin Sr. Owners Ann and Gene Swett have created a gracious retreat that makes you feel as if you've been magically whisked to the English countryside. Throughout the house, you'll find carefully chosen antiques and family heirlooms—a Victorian sideboard in the parlor, the original handmade copper fireplace hood in the breakfast room. While each of the ten rooms (many with skylights, stained glass, and wood-burning fireplaces) weaves a different romantic charm, all feature modern private baths. Favorite accommodations for honeymooners include the Library Room, with its bookcases lined with old encyclopedias and classics, plus a private deck ($182 per couple per night); and the Garden Cottage, a private bungalow away from the main house, with bay windows overlooking the rose garden and a king-size bed done up all in white, accented with antique-lace pillow shams ($204 per couple per night). Breakfast is a lavish affair, with treats such as fresh fruit compote, a mushroom and artichoke soufflé, apple crêpes, and home-made olallieberry jam. There are also afternoon tea (accompanied by memorable chocolate-chip cookies) and evening hors d'oeuvres. Honeymoon package: None. Rates: $143 to $215 per couple per night.

Hotel Pacific, 300 Pacific St., Monterey, CA 93940 (tel. 408/373-5700, or toll free 800/225-2903 nationwide; 800/554-5542 in California). Something old, something new—that's what you'll find at this recently opened hotel near Fisherman's Wharf and Cannery Row. The elegant architecture and decor fit right in with historic Monterey: entrance fountain, Mexican tile floors, and adobe-style walls. But the amenities are thoroughly up-to-date, including remote-control color TV, honor bar, nightly turn-down service with Swiss chocolates placed on your pillow . . . even a second TV in the tiled bathroom. Every room is a suite—and a large one, at that, with wood-burning fireplace, private patio or balcony, separate sitting area where you can really spread out, and a canopied four-poster bed. Personal service is the watchword here. There's no check-in counter in the lobby; instead, registration takes place while you're comfortably seated at the concierge desk. The hotel can even arrange for a chauffeured Rolls-Royce to pick you up at Monterey airport (an additional $40 per couple). In the downstairs Salon, you can enjoy a continental breakfast in the morning, and tea, wine, and cheese in the afternoon—all complimentary to guests. Honeymoon package: None. Rates (including continental breakfast): $142 to $252 per couple, depending on view. Let them know in advance that you're honeymooners, and you'll receive a complimentary bottle of champagne.

The Mariposa Inn, 1386 Munras Ave., Monterey, CA 93940 (tel. 408/649-1414), is a real charmer—modern, sophisticated, sensuous—a whole new deluxe breed of motor inn. And the reasonable prices make it one of the best deals on the peninsula. The 51-unit lodge is built Spanish-style, surrounding a tranquil garden courtyard where daisies, primroses, and dahlias bloom in abundance. The central location, high up on Carmel Hill, places the Mariposa conveniently near shopping, restaurants, and attractions. Someone who really cares about your comfort put this place together. Period pieces such as English-style highboys counterpoint the mostly modern furnishings. The color palette soothes—soft beiges, restful blues, and warm mauves. Most rooms have fireplaces. In the garden, there's a heated pool open April through December, and a hot tub open all year. Rates: $73 to $86 per couple per night for deluxe queen-bedded rooms with fireplaces; $105 per couple for executive suites, with mirrored wet-bar, minifridge, sitting area, and fireplace; $155 per couple for honeymoon suites, complete with an ardently proportioned whirlpool spa surrounded by mirrors, a king-size bed, a double shower, a fireplace, and more.

Casa Munras, 700 Munras Ave., Monterey, CA 93940 (tel. 408/375-2411, or toll free 800/222-2558). A large heated swimming pool in the garden courtyard, brass beds topped off with comforters, and history dating back over 150 years—these help make Casa Munras a personable motel. The Casa occupies the original site of the hacienda belonging to Don Estebán Munras, last Spanish diplomat to California. Two-story adobe buildings with shingle roofs surround a colorful garden with fragrant roses and giant-size calla lilies. Accommodations, although not fancy, reflect cheerful, contemporary good taste, and the rooms with king-size beds and fireplaces offer honeymooners exceptionally good value. The Casa is located near the "Path of History" and an easy five blocks' walk from Fisherman's Wharf. The Casa Cafe serves breakfast, lunch, and dinner daily, and locals congregate at the Casa Bar for happy-hour cocktails. Honeymoon package: None. Rates: $76 to $130 per couple for regular rooms with king-size brass beds, fireplaces, and color TVs; $165 per couple for poolside suites with living rooms, king-size brass beds, corner fireplaces, color TVs, and large bathrooms. (December through April, the Casa sometimes offers special reduced rates. Ask!)

Colton Inn, 707 Pacific St., Monterey, CA 93940 (tel. 408/649-6500, or toll free 800/255-3050). This cozy motor lodge is located in downtown Monterey, right near the famous "Path of History," and the low adobe structure blends right in with the buildings where California history was made. The rooms are looking in tip-top shape after a recent refurbishment, and everything is impeccably clean and comfortable. Many have king-size beds and fireplaces. Honeymoon package: None. Rates: $64 to $70 per couple weekdays, $75 to $80 per couple weekends. But the real find is room no. 100, with a fireplace, king-size bed—and a private enclosed patio with a hot tub overlooking lush greenery and a rushing stream. It's the only one at the inn—and it goes for $110 to $155 a night.

Romantic Restaurants

Fresh Cream, 100 Pacific in Heritage Harbor (tel. 375-9798). California is generally regarded as having the best restaurants in the nation. Then, what are the best restaurants in California? This delectable dining spot run by chef-owner Robert Kincaid makes everyone's top ten list. Light and airy, the setting exudes fresh-as-springtime romance. Lanterns cast a warm glow on two rosebuds entwined in a vase, spotlights softly illuminate artwork on the walls, as well as a splendiferous five-foot-tall flower arrangement. The friendly, helpful staff explains all the specialties of the evening . . . perhaps some garlicky baked mussels, meltingly tender under a toasty gratin; or sautéed lobster and sea scallops, with snow peas, shiitake mushrooms, and sesame sauce. The roast duck breast with cassis sauce is a paragon of its breed, with a crisp brown skin that's good to the last crunch. For dessert, plan ahead and order the warm tarte tatin (apple pie), served atop a cool crème anglaise swirled with raspberry sauce. As a going-away treat, there's a perfect strawberry, hand-dipped just moments before in caramel. Dinner for two, about $80 per couple plus wine. Open Tuesday through Sunday, 6 to 10 p.m.; reservations required.

Stained-glass windows, weathered cedar-board walls, fresh flowers, and mirrors weave a romantic mood at the **Whaling Station Inn,** 763 Wave St., Monterey (tel. 373-3778), right near Cannery Row. The chef has a way with both the local veggies and the homemade pastas. The varied menu highlights mesquite-grilled dishes. Dinner for two, about $70 per couple plus drinks. Open for dinner daily from 5 to 10 p.m.

Set in an 1840s adobe house right on Monterey's "Path of History," the **Old House,** 500 Hartnell St., Monterey (tel. 373-3737), is one of the peninsula's most beautiful restaurants, with the warm, elegant feel of a French country inn. You'll be served on fine Villeroy et Boch china, and drink California wine from crystal goblets. The menu highlights French recipes, prepared with fresh ingredients from Salinas and Carmel Valley, considered the "breadbasket" of California. Sample entrées include California abalone, Idaho trout, beef Wellington, and other specialties. Dinner for two, about $70 plus wine. The Old House serves dinner only, from 6 p.m. to 10 p.m. (except Monday).

For seafood-by-the-bay, choose one of Monterey's Fisherman's Wharf establishments. **Domenico's** (tel. 372-3655) has big glass windows overlooking the harbor. Fresh fish entrées range from $12 to $22. Open daily for lunch, 11:30 a.m. to 2:30 p.m. (to 3 p.m. on weekends); dinner, 5 to 10 p.m.

The two-level **Wharfside Restaurant and Lounge** (tel. 375-3956) also has terrific views. The place specializes in pasta and seafood dishes such as bouillabaisse ($18) or homemade shrimp ravioli ($15), plus landlubber treats such as New York–cut steak ($18). Open daily from 11 a.m. to 9 p.m.

Looking for a quick bite while sightseeing on the Wharf? Various stands and vendors sell Dungeness crab for $3.75 per pound, shrimp or crab walkaway cocktails for $2.25. If you prefer to munch while sitting down, stop in at the **Abalonetti Cafe** (no phone), serving tender squid 'n' chips ($4.50), creamy clam chowder ($1.65), and other delights from the deep. Open daily from 11 a.m. to 4 p.m. Next door, the **Abalonetti Restaurant** (tel. 375-5941) has a more extensive menu that highlights calamari, be it baked with eggplant or tossed atop spaghetti alla napoletana. They also feature petrale sole, rock cod, pasta, chicken, and steaks. Dinner for two, about $40. Open from 11 a.m. to 9 p.m., except Tuesday.

PACIFIC GROVE

This town is one of the best-kept secrets on the Monterey Peninsula. Many visitors come to the area frequently—sometimes even for years—without following Lighthouse Avenue beyond the hustle and bustle of Cannery Row to this peaceful community at the northernmost point of the peninsula.

The area is probably best known as "Butterfly Town, U.S.A." because of the millions of monarch butterflies that winter here each year—some from places as distant as Alaska and Mexico. Since butterflies are rather finicky creatures that like only certain trees, many of them congregate in the cypress and eucalyptus branches in George Washington Park. You can look, but don't touch—the butterflies are strictly protected by law.

At the turn of the century, Pacific Grove prospered as a Methodist summer community. Because of the strong religious beliefs that governed the town, many strict laws stayed on the books for a long time. Until the 1930s, everybody—including married couples—was required to sleep with the window shades up. Liquor could be bought only with a prescription, until a referendum ended Pacific Grove's dubious distinction of being California's last dry town in 1969. Today, Pacific Grove has attracted many young adults, drawn by the friendly, hometown feeling. The town is also the setting for several of the peninsula's hottest new restaurants.

What remain from Pacific Grove's past are many fine Victorian buildings, graced by gables, turrets, and leaded-glass windows. Several houses have been restored as bed-and-breakfast inns, enabling honeymooners to dwell in the charm of another era.

Honeymoon Hotels and Hideaways

A good choice for honeymooners who crave seclusion and privacy, Pacific Grove also gives easy access to the main tourist sights.

Seven Gables Inn, 555 Ocean View Blvd., Pacific Grove, CA 93950 (tel. 408/ 372-4341). This is it—our vote for the most romantic bed-and-breakfast inn on the Monterey Peninsula. The house, a multigabled 1886 showplace, commands unobstructed views of Monterey Bay and Lover's Point. Inside, you'll see a world of frothy Victorian fantasy—Oriental carpets, lace doilies, stained glass, fringed lampshades, crystal chandeliers, canopied beds, armoires, bombé chests, knickknacks, needlepoint pillows, gilded wall sconces—all assembled with love by the Flatley family, innkeepers on the peninsula since 1958. Many of the pieces are of museum quality, including a real Tiffany window. There are 14 rooms, each one unique. The Cypress Room, for example, has a sitting area in the bay window, from which you enjoy a 180° view of Monterey Bay. The Lover's Point Room, overlooking the promontory, features a canopied bed and marble-topped sink. All rooms offer ocean views and spiffy modern private bathrooms; fabrics, towels, and wallcoverings are plushly new. No smoking.

At breakfast time, no one goes away hungry from the ample continental spread of fresh-squeezed orange juice, fresh fruit, and hot-from-the-oven croissants and muffins. At 4 p.m., high tea is served, and Mrs. Flatley tempts all young lovers with her homemade fudge, cookies, and cakes. Honeymoon package: None. Rates: Prices range from $95 to $165 per couple per night, depending on the size of the room. Since each room is so different, you should call the Flatleys to discuss the various layouts, and choose the one that best fulfills your honeymoon daydreams.

The Green Gables Inn, 104 Fifth St., Pacific Grove, CA 93950 (tel. 408/375-

2095). As you walk in the door, you'll hear strains of classical music and smell the warm, sweet aroma of baking bread. Teddy bears cavort in armchairs, a fire blazes in the hearth, and sunlight streams through the stained-glass window. Immediately, you'll fall under the spell of this half-timbered, step-gabled 100-year-old house set on the edge of the Pacific. The guest accommodations include five rooms and a suite in the main house, and five bedrooms in the adjacent Carriage House. The rooms in the main house offer the most atmosphere, with period details such as mirrored commodes, claw-foot bathtubs, wrought-iron bedsteads, and four-poster beds. Some have fireplaces, and most have private baths. The Carriage House rooms offer more privacy. Each has a fireplace, a color TV, and a private bath; although they too are furnished with traditional English-style pieces, the feeling is more modern. In the morning, breakfast is served in the dining room overlooking Monterey Bay; in the afternoon, guests gather in the parlor for afternoon tea, sherry, and wine, accompanied by hors d'oeuvres and music from the player piano. Rates: Main house rooms range from $132 per couple for the Gable Room with queen-size bed, ocean view, and shared bath to $165 per couple for the Lacey Suite with queen-size bed, sitting room with fireplace, and private bath with antique tub. Carriage House rooms are all $130 to $140 per couple. Ask about their special honeymoon package, which includes a bottle of California champagne, two engraved champagne flutes, a teddy bear, and a brass key ring (a replica of your room key).

"So romantic—you're going to love it." "A real winner." These are just some of the rave reviews recorded in the **Gosby House Inn,** 643 Lighthouse Ave., Pacific Grove, CA 93950 (tel. 408/375-1287), guest book. Located in the heart of downtown Pacific Grove, this Victorian structure was built in 1887 and has been operating as a hotel since 1894. It has been placed on the National Register of Historic Places, and is operated by the same group that runs Green Gables Inn.

In the front parlor, English- and French-style period furnishings surround the fireplace. A glass cabinet displays a fine collection of antique dolls. More contemporary teddy bears pose here and there—on mantelpieces, Queen Anne armchairs, bannisters. Rooms reflect the intimacy of European country inns: polished natural woods, wrought-iron headboards, fluffy comforters, mirrored armoires, and delicate floral wallpapers. Fine details abound—even the tissue caddy is edged in lace. Each room is different: most have private baths, some have fireplaces. The room price includes a hearty breakfast buffet (with fresh fruits and juices, granola, muffins, eggs or quiche), plus afternoon tea. Rates: For a room with a queen-size bed, from $110 to $138 per couple, depending on view, availability of a private bath, and fireplace. Ask about their special honeymoon package, which includes a bottle of California champagne, two engraved champagne flutes, a teddy bear, and a brass key ring (a replica of your room key).

When the **Centrella,** 612 Central Ave., P.O. Box 51157, Pacific Grove, CA 93950 (tel. 408/372-3372), opened in 1889, the local newspaper hailed it as the "largest, most commodious, and pleasantly located private boarding house in 'The Grove.'" That description remains true today. Completely restored, the Centrella enthralls honeymooners with its hand-rubbed oak and maple furnishings, beveled glass windows, and wainscotted hallways. It is listed on the National Register of Historic Places. The inn is very centrally located—just one block from town, only two blocks from the beach. Period decor sets the mood in the bedrooms—wrought-iron headboards, wicker sofas and chairs, floral chintz bedspreads with ruffled pillows, lace curtains. The rooms are a bit small, but there's a good reason—after the recent million-dollar renovation, practically everyone has a private bath. Several rooms have king-size beds—reserve these in advance. Also request a room facing the garden, with giant ferns, creamy white calla lilies, colorful impatiens, and a huge monkey tree holding court in garden center. Which brings us to the garden cottages, each entered by its own wooden gate. The two-room cottages provide a veritable home away from home, with overstuffed sofas, wicker tables, a fireplace, and a TV in the sitting room, and a wrought-iron bed and antique furnishings in the bedroom.

"Remember the Romance" honeymoon package: $132 per couple per night. Includes deluxe accommodations; a bottle of champagne upon arrival; dinner at the Fandango restaurant (see "Romantic Restaurants," which follows); a full buffet breakfast; turn-down service featuring cordials, truffles, and a long-stemmed rose; and late check-out. Available Sunday through Thursday nights only.

Romantic Restaurants

The next best thing to a trip to the Riviera is dinner at **Fandango,** 223 17th St., Pacific Grove (tel. 373-0588). Owners Pierre and Marianne Bain have created a cozy bistro where friendliness and good food are specialties of the house. Enhancing the intimacy, the restaurant has several different dining areas, including the stone-walled wine cellar and secluded card room. Especially nice for honeymooners is a table for two by the fireplace in the main dining room. Even if you aren't all that hungry when you first enter this bistro, the warm aromas of sautéeing garlic, simmering tomatoes, and heady herbes de Provence emanating from the kitchen will soon render you ravenous. The menu captures all the sunny flavors of the Mediterranean: Basque-style shrimp tossed with spinach, tomatoes, and garlic and served over pasta; couscous algérois, from a recipe that's been in the family for 150 years; an individual rack of lamb, mesquite-grilled and served pink inside, crusty outside from its herbal marinade. For dessert, your sweet tooth will swoon over the meringue with ice cream and hot-fudge sauce, or a cold Grand Marnier soufflé. Lunch, about $25 per couple; dinner, $45 per couple plus drinks (there's a four-course prix-fixe dinner for $22 per person). Lunch served Monday through Saturday, 11 a.m. to 2 p.m. Dinner served nightly from 5:30 to 10 p.m. Sunday brunch runs from 9 a.m. to 2:30 p.m.

Gernot's Victoria House, 649 Lighthouse, Pacific Grove (tel. 646-1477). Located in a grand old Victorian house, complete with stained glass and a turret, this restaurant provides an elegant setting for savoring fine continental cuisine. Cut crystal sparkles on the tables, lace curtains frame the bay windows. The Austrian-born owner takes particular pride in the wienerschnitzel served with lingonberry compote ($17.50), plus unusual dishes such as wild boar simmered in red wine with mushrooms and onions ($22). There's also a daily seafood special ($18). The price of the entrée also includes homemade soup and salad. Open Tuesday through Sunday for dinner only, 5:30 to 9:30 p.m.

Melac's Old Europe, 663 Lighthouse, Pacific Grove (tel. 375-1743). Brick walls, lace café curtains, and sprightly pink accents make this bistro owned by Janet and Jacques Melac a charming choice for lunch or dinner. The lunch menu is light and delightful, with dishes such as a salad of fresh grilled chicken, served with baby salad greens and artichoke bottoms and topped with a hazelnut-oil vinaigrette. Dinner options are more elaborate and deftly flavorful. Start off with the prawns à la mexicana, marinated with jalapeño peppers, or the lobster ravioli. Favorite entrées include the sea bass feuilleté, baked with thin-sliced veggies in a flaky puff pastry, or the steak au Roquefort, flamed with cognac. Lunch, about $25 per couple; dinner, $50 per couple plus drinks. Lunch served Tuesday through Friday, 11:30 a.m. to 2:30 p.m.; dinner, Tuesday through Saturday, 5:30 to 9:30 p.m.; Sunday brunch, 10:30 a.m. to 3:30 p.m.

Central 1-5-9, 159 Central Ave., Pacific Grove (tel. 372-2235). One of the peninsula's hottest new restaurants, Central 1-5-9 is known for an imaginative cuisine that accents regional American dishes with zesty Oriental and American Southwest spices. "Cooking of the Americas," chef David Beckwith and manager Ric Myroth call it. A Sunday brunch favorite, for example, is the lobster quesadilla, served with tomatillo sauce. The menu changes every few months to take advantage of seasonal specialties. Choices might include grilled petrale sole, a chicken and fennel sausage, or tai-pei rabbit with polenta and vegetables. All the ice creams, breads, and biscotti are homemade. The restaurant itself is modern, yet very inviting at the same time, with a fire blazing in the hearth and jazz music playing in the background. Extensive California wine list. Lunch, $20 per couple; dinner, $45 per couple plus drinks. Open for lunch Monday through Friday, 11:30 a.m. to 2 p.m.; dinner nightly, 6 to 10 p.m.; Sunday brunch, 10:30 a.m. to 2:30 p.m.

Old Bath House, 620 Ocean View Blvd., Pacific Grove (tel. 375-5195). Appropriately enough for honeymooners, this shingled building with a tall turret is located near Lover's Point in Pacific Grove. The interior is warm, cozy, and inviting, with rich wood paneling, etched glass, and an antique Victorian bar where you'll certainly want to sip a cocktail before dinner. For an appetizer, start with some pasta —perhaps linguine in a zesty red clam sauce or pasta primavera with fresh vegetables and cream. As your entrée, choose from a medley of veal dishes, such as saltimbocca alla romana, topped with prosciutto and mozzarella, or roast rack of lamb. Dinner for two will run about $50 per couple plus wine. Open for dinner only: Monday through Friday, 5 to 10:30 p.m.; Saturday, from 4 p.m.; Sunday, from 3 p.m.

Pepper's, 170 Forest Ave., Pacific Grove (tel. 372-3463). With its eye-catching neon sign and bright bunches of dried peppers hanging on the walls, Pepper's has become a local favorite for dishes from south of the border—both Mexican and Latin American. Everything from the tortillas to the salsas is made fresh daily, there are daily seafood specials, and a wide range of domestic and Mexican beers (as well as California wines) are available. Lunch, about $10 per couple; dinner, $20 per couple plus bebidas (drinks). Open weekdays from 11:30 a.m. to 10 p.m.; Saturday from 4 to 11 p.m.; Sunday from 4 to 10 p.m.; closed Tuesday.

PEBBLE BEACH

In this private community that skirts the western edge of the peninsula, blue-blood cars (Jaguars, Porsches, and every conceivable model of Mercedes-Benz) crowd the parking lot at the local post office, and million-dollar price tags are not uncommon on the mansions that stand behind formidable wrought-iron gates. The area, which is also known as the Del Monte Forest, encompasses over 5,300 acres, including that spectacular stretch of scenery known as the 17-Mile Drive.

Romantic Interludes

Schedule several hours for this leisurely ride, and bring along your camera to record some truly memorable scenic images.

Called "the slowest way between Carmel and Monterey," the two-lane **17-Mile Drive** meanders its way along the western coast of the Monterey Peninsula. It is part of the privately owned Pebble Beach/Del Monte Forest property. The route follows the former trails along which horsedrawn carriages brought vacationers to the original Del Monte Hotel in Monterey. Watch the antics of gulls and cormorants, seals and sea lions off Seal and Bird Rocks (the beach area has tables and benches perfect for a picnic lunch). From the Cypress Point Lookout, you can often see over 20 miles down the California coast, all the way to the Point Sur Lighthouse. Finally, there's the Lone Cypress, the symbol of the Monterey Peninsula, which stands grandly on nearly barren rock facing the sea. Along the route, the road winds past the emerald-green Pebble Beach Golf Links and palatial mansions surrounded by cypress, oaks, and sycamores.

There are four entrances to the 17-Mile Drive: at Highway 1, Carmel, Pacific Grove, and the country club. The road is privately owned; a $5.50 entrance fee per car helps maintain the route as well as the open spaces.

Honeymoon Hotels and Hideaways

Honeymooners who love the sporting life should choose exclusive Pebble Beach, where world-class golf, tennis, and equestrian facilities lie right outside your doorstep.

After over 70 years, **The Lodge at Pebble Beach,** 17-Mile Drive, Pebble Beach, CA 93953 (tel. 408/624-3811), still reigns as the grand resort of the Monterey Peninsula. The Lodge occupies a choice site on the brink of the Pacific Ocean within the private 5,328-acre Del Monte Forest, overlooking the Pebble Beach Golf Links, Carmel Bay, and the Santa Lucia Mountains.

From the moment a liveried attendant swings open the heavy wooden door in the columned entryway, you'll enter a world of old-world gentility and graciousness. Old-world spaciousness, too, for the Lodge dates from a time when ample proportions were the rule, rather than the exception. Six-foot-tall hearths, full-grown ficus trees, and overstuffed sofas grace the Terrace Lounge—all practically dwarfed by the 20-foot-high ceilings. Guest accommodations occupy low, two-story buildings, all nicely spread out (there are only 161 rooms, 140 of which have working fireplaces). Each room is different—most have balconies, some also have ocean views.

Sports-lovers will be in jock heaven. Golfers can tee off on their choice of four Pebble Beach courses, where they enjoy reduced greens fees. During their stay, guests have membership privileges at the Beach and Tennis Club, with its 14 courts and heated swimming pool. At the Pebble Beach Stables, horseback riders can mount up and explore the 34 miles of bridle paths that wind through every corner of the Del Monte Forest. Pebble Beach is also known for its full calendar of special events. One favorite: the August Concours d'Elegance vintage car show. The active life helps work up an appetite, and the Lodge has four fine restaurants to choose from, including the elegant Cypress Room for breakfast, lunch, and dinner (see description that follows). Rates: $250 to $360 per couple per night for king-bedded rooms, depending on view and amenities, such as fireplaces.

The **Inn and Links at Spanish Bay,** 2700 17-Mile Drive, Pebble Beach, CA 93953 (tel. 408/647-7500, or toll free 800/654-9300). How do you top a classic hotel? By creating a new classic—and that's exactly what the Pebble Beach Company has done with its Inn and Links at Spanish Bay, which opened in late 1987.

Perched on 236 acres between the Del Monte Forest on one side and the churning Pacific Ocean on the other, the inn coddles guests with standards of elegance that most mere hostelries can only dream of duplicating. Personal service—which many frequent travelers believe to have gone the way of the steamer trunk and biplane—is alive and well here. A concierge personally escorts guests to their room, explaining hotel layout and services, which include five restaurants and lounges. Rooms in fact have room—lots of it, with two plump, oversize armchairs cozying up to the fireplace, a writing desk spacious enough to pen letters home on, and (with most rooms) a good-size balcony or terrace. The honor bar is stuffed with not just the usual munchies such as peanuts and potato chips, but also jelly beans, pretzels, and chocolate-chip cookies. The scotch is Chivas, the splits of champagne Taittinger.

But it's the bathroom that shows the most careful thought. Has unpacking revealed wrinkles in your clothes? Not to worry—every room comes with a garment steamer. Something need mending? The sewing kit features prethreaded needles, no less. What's ensconced in that small lacquer box? Cotton balls and swabs. You probably haven't been as well taken care of since Mom tucked you in at night. (But then, did Mom leave delectable chocolate truffles on your pillow?)

For couples who believe in exercising their bodies as well as their good taste, the complete fitness facilities include eight tennis courts, aerobics studio, exercise room, large pool suited for serious lap swimming, plus separate men's and women's massage, steam room, and sauna facilities. But the star attraction is the new Links at Spanish Bay, an 18-hole course designed by Tom Watson, Robert Trent Jones Jr., and Frank "Sandy" Tatum to be reminiscent of Scotland's St. Andrews. There's even "The Lone Piper of Spanish Bay," a kilt-garbed bagpiper who plays ancient Highlands tunes across the hills and dales each evening towards sunset. Honeymoon package: None. Rates (EP): $220 to $330 per couple per night, plus a $15 per room charge that covers gratuities (except in the restaurants).

A Romantic Restaurant

The Cypress Room, The Lodge at Pebble Beach, 17-Mile Drive (tel. 624-

3811). Overlooking the 18th green, Carmel Bay, and the silhouette of Point Lobos in the distance, this elegant restaurant provides the perfect setting for the exquisite beauty of the Monterey Peninsula at breakfast, lunch, and dinner. A pianist plays softly on the baby grand piano, tall potted palms add an aura of old-world grandeur, and a color scheme culled from Nature's palette—sea-foam greens and sunset mauves—enhances the landscape views. The inventive menu highlights the best of American regional cuisine: a rare breast of pheasant, or homemade ravioli stuffed with crab meat. In season, dinner appetizers might include Pacific oysters on the half shell or a cream of artichoke soup. As an entrée, try the seafood brochette with garlic butter or the New York steak with zinfandel sauce—both excellent. Open daily for breakfast, 7 to 10:30 a.m.; lunch, 11:30 a.m. to 2:30 p.m.; dinner, 6:30 to 10:30 p.m.; Sunday buffet brunch, 10:30 a.m. to 2:30 p.m. Lunch runs about $40 per couple; dinner about $60 per couple plus drinks.

CARMEL-BY-THE-SEA

Why is this seaside town, less than a square mile in size, known throughout the world? When actor Clint Eastwood was elected Carmel's mayor in 1986, it didn't increase the town's celebrity but seemed more like a logical consequence of it.

Perhaps Carmel is best explained by enumerating what it doesn't have. No buildings more than two stories tall. No neon signs. No courthouse or jail. Few sidewalks and even fewer street lamps. Instead of street numbers, houses are identified by location (such as "on Monte Verde, between Seventh and Eighth") or evocative names (such as "The Grey Whale" or "Sea Spirit"). Residences range from tiny dollhouse-like cottages covered with climbing roses to ultramodern wood-and-glass showplaces on the oceanfront Scenic Road. Trees are protected by a special 1916 ordinance that created an extensive urban forest that now requires the ministrations of a city forester and several full-time employees. (A local cartoon depicts a burning house, with the frantic owner screaming, "Never mind the house—save the trees!")

The word "Carmel" means "at rest," and true to its name, the village offers enchanted ways to do nothing at all. Linger on Carmel Beach, a long pure-white crescent of sand that draws you to lounge, stroll, or sunbathe. The surf is always high; sandpipers on spindly legs always play a mad game of tag with the breaking waves. Sunsets are crimson wonders, with vistas stretching from Point Lobos to Pebble Beach.

Shopping

Despite the popularity of tennis, golf, horseback riding and the like, Carmel's number one sport is, unquestionably, shopping. (A local poster jokes: "Carmel. Population, 4,102. Gift shops, 17,210.") While not really in the thousands, the actual count of shops, galleries, and boutiques numbers about 100. The most amazing thing about this mercantile abundance is that none of the shops carry schlock—all the goods are absolutely first-rate. Most of the shops are clustered along Ocean Avenue and the neighboring cross streets from Mission to Casanova. Here are some establishments you might want to check out.

Carmel Bay Company (Ocean at Lincoln) offers great stuff for your new home, as well as posters, tote bags, and garden supplies. **Laub's Country Store** or the **Varsity Shop** (both on Ocean at San Carlos) is the place to pick up classy Carmel T-shirts. **Amourette** (Dolores, off Ocean) carries some of the nicest naughty lingerie you can imagine. **Handworks** (Dolores, off Ocean) carries exquisite crafts items: handwoven scarfs for $45; ceramic clocks decorated with bunnies or teddy bears, $50; turquoise or mother-of-pearl letter knives, $25; and original prints from $125. **Ladyfingers** (Dolores, off Ocean) offers one-of-a-kind jewelry, with many pieces designed by local artists, including some stunning rings and earrings using gold and semiprecious stones, from $50 to $450. **The Village Straw Shop** (Lincoln, off Ocean) displays straw goods from as far away as Botswana and Sri Lanka, priced from $5 to $50. **Great Things Antiques** (on Ocean between Lincoln and Dolores) features top-of-the-line heirlooms, from major pieces such as English sideboards or a dining room table big enough to seat 18, to candlesticks, sherry decanters, and biscuit tins (the latter items in the $65 to $100 price range). Other top choices for antiques include **Luciano** (on San Carlos between Fifth and Sixth), which carries highly unusual pieces, and **Pierre Deux** (at the Pine Inn on Ocean and Monte Verde), which specializes in French country. Fashion-forward dressers will want to browse at **Roxy** (corner of Ocean and San Carlos). An art center, Carmel is known for its galleries, including **Hanson** (Ocean and San Carlos) and **Simic** (San Carlos and Sixth). If you love ceramics, don't miss Karen Gelff's fanciful hand-painted designs at the **Peppercorn** (in Doud Arcade on Ocean at San Carlos).

Romantic Interludes

Here are two special places, one evoking the spirit of old California and the other the natural beauty of its spectacular shoreline.

Step back in time at the **Basilica of Mission San Carlos Borromeo del Rio Carmelo**—best known simply as the Carmel Mission. Footsteps echo down the Mexican tile aisles, water splashes in the garden fountain—sounds unchanged for over 200 years. The mission is closely associated with Padre Junípero Serra, the Franciscan friar who nurtured the establishment of 21 different California missions. From the time of its founding on June 3, 1770, Carmel served as Father Serra's headquarters. He is buried at the foot of the church altar. The Carmel Mission is one of only two basilicas in the entire western United States; it is possible that the Church will soon elect Father Serra to sainthood.

Despite its celebrity, Carmel Mission is a simple place. Hand-lettered signs identify the various exhibits that trace the mission's history. Stop by the gift shop to see if they have any of the folk art from La Palma, El Salvador, in stock. The town craftspeople create brightly painted wooden ornaments that would look just right on your Christmas tree. Carmel Mission is open weekdays from 9:30 a.m. to 4:30 p.m.; Sundays from 10:30 a.m. to 4:30 p.m. Suggested donation is $1.

Just south of Carmel Bay is the spot that Robert Louis Stevenson praised as "the most beautiful meeting of land and sea on earth"—**Point Lobos.** In this 1,276-acre preserve, you can hike past stands of cypress twisted by the ocean winds, stand atop jagged cliffs, stroll along hidden coves and lagoons. Just offshore, sea lions and spotted harbor seals bark a noisy welcome from their rocky perches. From mid-December through mid-April, you can often watch gray whales migrating to their spawning waters off Baja California. The reserve makes a wonderful place for a picnic, especially in the white sand beaches at Whaler's Cove and Weston Beach. Open daily from 9 a.m. to 5 p.m. There's an entrance fee of $2.50 if you come by car; no admission if you walk or bike in. At the entrance, you can pick up a map of the preserve.

Honeymoon Hotels and Hideaways

Highlands Inn, P.O. Box 1700, Highway 1 South, Carmel, CA 93921 (tel. 408/624-3801; reservations: toll free 800/538-9525 nationwide; 800/682-4811 in California), is that very rare entity—the perfect hotel in the perfect place. Carmel Highlands, just a stone's throw from Carmel proper, is one of the most beautiful spots on earth, a place where wind-bowed Monterey cypresses, rocky cliffs, and Pacific surf come together in a boisterous celebration of land and sea. Highlands Inn's two-storied, cedar-shingled villas harmonize with this setting, conveying the feel of an ultrasophisticated mountain lodge. The rooms are accented with light, natural oak trim and beams that bring a little bit of the outdoors inside. Furnishings are high-tech without being hard-edged. Two cushions are positioned invitingly by the fireplace; a comfortable, well-lit couch makes you want to curl up for a good read . . . or a good backrub. Two thick terry-cloth bathrobes hang in the closet—typical of the thoughtful amenities you'll find here. In the morning, you'll wake up to the sound of the surf, with sunshine streaming through the pine trees. Perhaps order breakfast from room service, served on your own private balcony.

The inn's lobby and lounge areas occupy the golden granite building that was the original lodge, which has been lightened by natural woods and brightened with skylights and picture windows to take advantage of the panoramic views. What remains from the original, however, are the ample proportions and the two massive stone fireplaces at each end of the lounge. No wonder Highlands Inn attracts so many honeymooners. Many couples also choose to be married at the inn's rose-covered gazebo, overlooking cypress trees, pines, and the endless Pacific Ocean. Superb bar and restaurant—see details that follow. Honeymoon package: None. Rates: Rooms are from $193 per couple per night. One-bedroom spa suites with whirlpools are $275 to $325 per couple. From December through April, Highlands Inn sometimes offers midweek reduced rates. Call for details.

Tickle Pink, 155 Highlands Dr., Carmel Highlands, CA 93923 (tel. 408/624-1244). Take a superb location on a bluff overlooking Point Lobos. Add oceanview decks for sunbathing, spacious accommodations for lounging, and flowers blooming from window boxes and planters. Color it all pink—and you've got this sweetheart of a retreat for honeymooners. Located at the start of the Coast Highway drive to Big Sur, just four miles from Carmel-by-the-Sea, and right next door to Highlands Inn, Tickle Pink is known for personal, personable service. The lodge has just undergone top-to-toe refurbishment. All rooms boast large picture windows and private balconies facing the ocean. Furnishings are modern and comfortable, and fabrics employ soft pastel colors, patterned into shell or floral motifs. The black-and-white-tiled bathrooms have an art deco look, and the room rates offer you the most view for the money on the peninsula. Honeymoon package: None. Rates: $142 per couple for rooms with king-size beds; $175 per couple for fireplace rooms; $220 to $270 per couple for one-bedroom suites. All rooms have minirefrigerators and color TVs; rates include complimentary continental breakfast and the morning newspaper.

La Playa Hotel, Camino Real at 8th, Carmel-by-the-Sea, CA 93921 (tel. 408/624-6476), is the only full-service resort hotel in the center of Carmel. Set in a quiet residential area just two blocks from the beach and four blocks from the downtown shops and galleries, this dazzling Mediterranean-style resort would look right at home on the French Riviera or Italy's Amalfi coast. The villa blossomed from a mansion built in 1904 by a Carmel artist. In 1984, it was completely restored and refurbished, from brick patio to red-tiled roof. The lobby creates a regal first impression, with Mexican tile floors, antiques, hand-loomed area rugs, and white marble fireplace flanked by two statues (which come from Hearst Castle). Built into the gentle hillside, landscaped terraces descend, palazzo-style, to the heated pool in the center of the garden courtyard.

In keeping with the architecture, the 75 rooms contain Mediterranean-style furnishings (curlicued chairs, low chests, marble-topped side tables), with many wood pieces specially hand-carved with La Playa's mermaid logo. Bathrooms compensate for their smallish proportions with pampering amenities—soaps, shampoos, and lotion from Neutrogena, plus a hairdryer. You have your choice of outlooks—ocean, gardens, patio, or the neighboring private houses—there isn't really a bad view. All rooms have color TVs and mini-refrigerators. If you want to splurge, consider La Playa's two suites. The Executive Suite stars a huge black marble fireplace in the living room, a 100-of-your-most-intimate-friends-size patio with views stretching all the way to Pebble Beach, and a whirlpool tub (the apartment was designed as a private apartment for the former owners). The Penthouse boasts even more expansive ocean views and opulent features such as a marble bathroom and gilt mirrors. La Playa is known for friendly, personalized service, and the concierge in the lobby can help you with golf, tennis, or dining arrangements. La Playa's own Spyglass restaurant is also excellent. Rates: $110 to $195 per couple for double rooms, depending on view; $300 to $400 per couple for suites.

The Stonehouse Inn, 8th below Monte Verde, P.O. Box 2517, Carmel-by-the-Sea, CA 93921 (tel. 408/624-4569). Step into another era, when young bohemian writers such as Sinclair Lewis and Jack London would gather at this unique country house built from stones hand-shaped by local Indians. Josephine "Nana" Foster, the original owner, often invited notable artists living in the San Francisco Bay Area to stay in her Carmel residence. Today, the house has been exquisitely restored to turn-of-the-century elegance, with antiques, comfy quilts, and silk flowers. The six bedrooms, each different, are named after some of Nana Foster's most celebrated guests. The Jack London room, all done up in moss greens and dusty roses, features gabled ceilings and a splendid ocean view, for $110 per couple. (We wonder a bit about what the author of *The Call of the Wild* and *The Sea Wolf* would think about the lodger who recorded in the guestbook, "The Jack London room is cool!") The tranquil Lola Montez room offers a four-poster bed, gabled ceiling, and garden view, for $88 per couple. All rooms share baths. Breakfast is a hearty affair, with hot entrées such as quiche or soufflés, homemade bread, fresh-ground coffee, and seasonal fruits served up in the sunny, greenhouse-like breakfast room. In the afternoon, guests gather around the large stone hearth for wine, sherry, and hors d'oeuvres. (Ask the manager to show you the secret safe built into the fireplace.) The sun porch entices you to curl up with a good book, or you can wander through the charming garden with stone pathways and a white minigazebo. Just two blocks from the center of Carmel. Honeymoon package: None. Rates: $88 to $116 per couple. No smoking is permitted.

The **Happy Landing,** Monte Verde between 5th and 6th, P.O. Box 2619, Carmel-by-the-Sea, CA 93921 (tel. 408/624-7917). Tudor half-timbered cottages painted a sweetheart pink . . . an enchanted garden . . . that's what you'll find at this fairy-tale hideaway just steps away from the heart of Carmel. Originally built as a family retreat, it has operated as an inn since the 1940s. Rooms surround a garden courtyard that also thinks pink, with rosy-hued blossoms of geraniums, fuchsias, and snapdragons. Flagstone paths lead to a small pond and white-trellised gazebo—a favorite spot for weddings. Each of the accommodations has unique charm. Room no. 1 is especially captivating, with its brass bed, open-beamed cathedral ceiling, hand-painted sink, and needlepoint footstool by the fireplace. There's also a special honeymoon cottage. All rooms have private baths. When you get hungry in the morning, just raise the front curtains—the staff will bring you breakfast in bed, which might include fresh-squeezed orange juice, piping-hot muffins, and a fruit cup. In the afternoon, guests gather around the stone fireplace in the lobby for tea, best sipped when seated in one of the tall, elaborately carved armchairs fit for King Henry VIII. Honeymoon package: None. Rates: $105 to $150 per couple per night.

Sea View Inn, Camino Real between 11th and 12th, P.O. Box 4138, Carmel-by-the-Sea, CA 93921 (tel. 408/624-8778). Located on a quiet residential street a few minutes' stroll from downtown Carmel, this gray-shingled Victorian is one of the oldest and finest inns in town, in operation since 1906. Everything is maintained to absolute perfection: fabrics are crisp, pillows plump, towels stacked neatly in the bathrooms awaiting your pleasure. Most rooms have a private bath; three have ocean views. No. 7 holds special romance, with its snug sitting alcove and chinoiserie bed decked out with a bold blue-and-white canopy. Breakfast is home-cooked and ample, with a hot entrée such as quiche and sausages on Sunday mornings. You'll also enjoy afternoon tea around the brick hearth in the parlor, or sitting out on the front veranda watching the passing scene. Honeymoon package: None. Rates: From $77 (queen-size bed with a shared bath) to $110 (king-size bed with private bath) per couple.

Located in the heart of Carmel just a few steps from Ocean Avenue, the **Sundial Lodge,** Monte Verde at Seventh Street, P.O. Box J, Carmel-by-the-Sea, CA 93921 (tel. 408/624-8578), has a charming brick courtyard bright with petunias, cyclamens, daisies, and primroses. Rooms are all different and are undergoing refurbishment—verify with management that you are getting one of the new ones. From some, you can glimpse the Pacific glimmering through the treetops. All accommodations have color TVs and private bathrooms (some have showers but no tubs). The continental breakfast includes homemade rolls, and afternoon tea or sherry warms the spirit. Rates: $99 to $138 per couple.

Although the **Sandpiper Inn,** 2408 Bayview at Martin Way, Carmel-by-the-Sea, CA 93923 (tel. 408/624-6433), sits a scant 50 yards from Carmel Beach, you'll feel more as if you're a guest in a country house in the Scottish Highlands, because the owner-hosts are Scottish-born Graeme and Irene Mackenzie. The greeting "ceud mile failte"—"a hundred thousand welcomes"—hangs over the parlor door, and that accurately describes the warm atmosphere. Decor is homey, not high fashion, but that's exactly what charms the guests, many of whom are repeat visitors. Quilted floral bedspreads and authentic antiques grace the 13 rooms in the main house and the two private cottages. The inn is quiet and secluded, and there are no room telephones or television—on purpose. At night, you can fall asleep to the sound of the surf crashing against Carmel Point. Rates: $122 to $155 per couple for oceanview or fireplace rooms; from $155 per couple for corner rooms with king-size beds. Includes continental breakfast and afternoon sherry.

Romantic Restaurants

A menu that changes to take advantage of the day's catch and fresh-from-the-garden vegetables. A strikingly modern yet welcoming decor where the emphasis is on quiet conversation, fine dining, intimate service (there are only 13 tables). That describes **Crème Carmel,** San Carlos between Ocean and Seventh, Carmel (tel. 372-3463). Proprietors Cynthia and Craig Ling (he's also the chef) work with favorite French dishes, lightening and enlivening them from a Californian point of view. Their cuisine is classic, never quirky. Daily specials might include a prawn and goat cheese tart appetizer with jalapeño-shallot sauce, browned jumbo scallops with julienned vegetables and caviar on a melt-in-your-mouth Maui onion crêpe, or loin of lamb roasted with rosemary and garlic. For dessert, treat yourselves to the chocolate soufflé with whipped cream, or strawberries in puff pastry with a homemade ice cream flecked with vanilla beans . . . accompanied, perhaps, by one of their fine California dessert wines. Dinner for two, about $70 per couple plus drinks. Open nightly for dinner, 5:30 to 10 p.m.

Casanova, Fifth between San Carlos and Mission, Carmel (tel. 625-0501). What's your definition of a romantic restaurant? One where French and Italian love songs croon in the background? Where you can sit at a table in a garden courtyard, surrounded by twittering birds by day, twinkling candles at night? Then head over to Casanova, which features French and Italian cuisine. The setting is especially seductive at lunch, when you can enjoy savory light fare such as cannelloni stuffed with spinach and ricotta cheese, or a grilled marinated chicken breast. In addition to pastas, the dinner menu spotlights some more substantial entries, such as a filet mignon with béarnaise sauce or broiled salmon. Lunch, about $22 per couple; dinner (includes salad, appetizer, entréa), about $50 per couple plus drinks. Open daily for breakfast, 8 to 11 a.m.; lunch, 11:30 a.m. to 3 p.m.; dinner, 5:30 to 10:30 p.m.; plus Sunday brunch, 9 a.m. to 3 p.m.

Anton & Michel, Mission between Ocean and Seventh, Carmel (tel. 624-2406). You couldn't ask for a dreamier setting than this elegant restaurant built facing a garden courtyard with a fountain and pool. Inside, the pale pastel furnishings are counterpointed by original oil paintings on the wall (on loan and for sale by local art galleries). Anton & Michel's is a delectable choice for Sunday brunch, when the menu features dishes such as omelets, a seafood crêpe, or fettuccine with shrimp and pesto (about $20 per couple). Try to reserve a table outside in nice weather. Lunch will run about $25 per couple; dinner (there's a four-course prix-fixe option), about $65 per couple plus drinks.

You are indeed at the very edge of the Pacific, at **Pacific's Edge,** Highland Inn,

Carmel Highlands (tel. 624-3801), with the ocean dramatically framed by towering Monterey cypresses that are spotlit at night. Through the floor-to-ceiling glass windows, you see it all—the gnarled trees, tempestuous surf, gyring gulls. And thanks to the two-tiered seating levels, every table enjoys a panoramic view. The excellent food matches the splendid setting with a menu that takes advantage of the seasonal bounty of the Monterey Peninsula: tender young lettuce from Watsonville, Castroville artichoke, Monterey salmon, local pheasant, duckling, and free-range chicken. Dishes are innovative, such as the basil-cured salmon with Maui onion marmalade, or veal chop with roasted shallots and fresh berries. The attentive waiters are knowledgeable about the wine list, which features the finest labels from Napa and Sonoma, as well as showcasing a different local Monterey County vintage each week. Dinner for two, about $80 plus drinks. Open for lunch, 11:30 a.m. to 2 p.m.; dinner, 6 to 10 p.m.

Robata Grill & Sake Bar, at the Barnyard shopping center, Highway 1 and Carmel Valley Road (tel. 624-2643). This place neither looks nor acts like most Japanese restaurants. Yes, it's got Oriental lanterns and samurai kites, but it also incorporates California country style, with wooden floors and open-beam ceilings. You can dine at the sushi bar—or on an outside terrace around a huge central fireplace. Start with the yakitori (chicken on a skewer) or the "Castroville Ten"—local mushrooms and artichokes fried up as tempura. For the entrée, the salmon teriyaki is a big favorite, as are the various combination plates. Part of the fun of dining at Robata's is the lively atmosphere—it's extremely popular with locals. "Our favorite restaurant," several couples said. Dinner for two, about $35 per couple. Open for dinner: Monday through Thursday, 5 to 10 p.m.; Friday and Saturday, 5 p.m. to 11 p.m.; Sunday, 4:30 to 9:30 p.m.

At happy hour time, mosey on over to **The Hog's Breath Inn** (Carmel, on San Carlos between Fifth and Sixth; tel. 625-1044)—owner Clint Eastwood sometimes drops by.

Picnic Suppliers

California Market at Highlands Inn (tel. 624-3801) sells upscale goodies such as prosciutto, pâté, brie, and chocolate mousse cake. They also turn out a mean roast beef sandwich.

Pick up dessert at one of the superb bakeries that line Carmel's Ocean Avenue. **Carmel Bakery** carries scones, breads shaped like crocodiles, and marzipan goodies. **Monterey Baking Company** features individual chocolate walnut tarts, almond-flavored jam drops with raspberry or apricot preserves, and wonderful breads baked fresh daily.

CARMEL VALLEY

This peaceful rolling valley is one of the Monterey Peninsula's booming areas. Just a ten-minute drive from downtown Carmel, it offers vineyards, golf courses, horseback riding trails, and sunny weather most of the year.

Honeymoon Hotels and Hideaways

Stonepine, 150 East Carmel Valley Rd., Carmel Valley, CA 93924 (tel. 408/659-2245). Come to your own private château in the heart of Carmel Valley. Built in 1930 as one of the country homes of the Crocker family (of the San Francisco–based banking empire), Stonepine is perhaps the closest America has to the great castle hotels of Europe. Centuries-old columns from ancient Rome grace the loggia that faces formal gardens. The Mediterranean-style main villa features a turret (which houses a grand circular wrought-iron stairway); a living room so large that a grand piano is dwarfed in its corner; and early 19th-century oak paneling in the library (a wedding gift to the original owners). Upon request, the resort's own Phantom V Rolls-Royce can pick you up at the Monterey airport.

If you've ever yearned to live like the landed gentry in some *Masterpiece Theatre* series, this is your opportunity. Guests enjoy full use of the house and its grounds—all 330 acres. Meals are served in splendor, on Limoges and Royal Crown Derby, Waterford and Baccarat. There are eight bedrooms in the main house (Château Noël), four accommodations in the Paddock House near the equestrian center. All rooms have private whirlpool tubs; many feature wood-burning fireplaces. For sheer drop-dead opulence, you can't top the Taittinger Suite, a symphony of champagne tones—from the satin bedspreads to the his-and-hers marble bathrooms. Feeling a bit cramped despite the marathon dimensions of your room? Then press the secret panel and ascend the hidden stairway to your very own tower and sitting area.

The oldest working Thoroughbred-breeding farm west of the Mississippi, Stonepine continues its equine traditions. Its stables are among the nation's largest breeding establishments for magnificent Belgian draft horses. Guests can explore the resort grounds on a horse-drawn carriage excursion, or saddle up (English or western style) for trail rides through the countryside—or for dressage lessons. In addition, Stonepine boasts a polo field, heated swimming pool, exercise room, tennis court, croquet lawn, archery range, and soccer field. Honeymoon package: None. Rates (including continental breakfast): $160 to $550 per couple per night.

Carmel Valley Ranch Resort, One Old Ranch Rd., Carmel, CA 93923 (tel. 408/625-9500, or toll free 800/4-CARMEL). Perched in the Santa Lucia foothills on 1,700 acres, this plush retreat provides the best of both worlds for honeymooners. You're only ten minutes from the elegant shops and lively restaurants of Carmel—but can also glimpse a doe and fawn treading gently across a lawn, see a red-tail hawk soaring on a thermal, and stroll through gardens with enough colorful blossoms to put a rainbow to shame.

If you're seeking privacy and seclusion, this is the place. Entry to the resort is by private gate; the restaurants and lounges are open exclusively to resort guests and club members. There are only 100 accommodations, clustered in low gray villas that seem part of the hillsides, nestled under stately California oak trees. Each of the accommodations is a very spacious suite, with separate living room, wood-burning fireplace, cathedral ceilings, fully stocked wet bar, two remote-control color TVs, and large deck with sweeping views of the valley, mountains, or golf course. Some have private outdoor spas. The California color palette is soothing—sage green, dusky rose, oak gray—and homey touches make you feel right at ease—Mexican baskets, kachina dolls, a small bleached-wood china cupboard, and handmade Amish quilts on the beds. Watercolors by artist Doris Ewing brighten the walls. The multitalented Ewing also designed the restaurant china and the stunning floral-motif area rugs in the main lodge. She is also the head gardener, responsible for coaxing 250 different varieties of flowers into blooming perfection. The resort is an excellent choice for sports-lovers, with its 18-hole Pete Dye–designed championship golf course, tennis club with 12 courts, and free-form pool with adjoining spa. Honeymoon package: None. Rates (EP): $205 to $300 per couple per night for a one-bedroom suite; $410 for a spa suite.

5. Big Sur

"Hill curves—next 74 miles" reads the yellow, diamond-shaped road sign as you drive south on Highway 1 past the Carmel River. Well, you can't say they didn't warn you. You are about to embark on the most incredibly scenic portion of the California coast drive—the stretch from Carmel to San Simeon, including the sinuous curves through Big Sur.

The area called Big Sur lies about 26 miles from Carmel—roughly a 45-minute drive. Here, Highway 1 sidewinds the coastal cliffs, looking exactly like it does in all those movies and car commercials. A two-lane ribbon of asphalt. Spindly silver bridges that look as if they were spun by drunken spiders. Nothing between you and

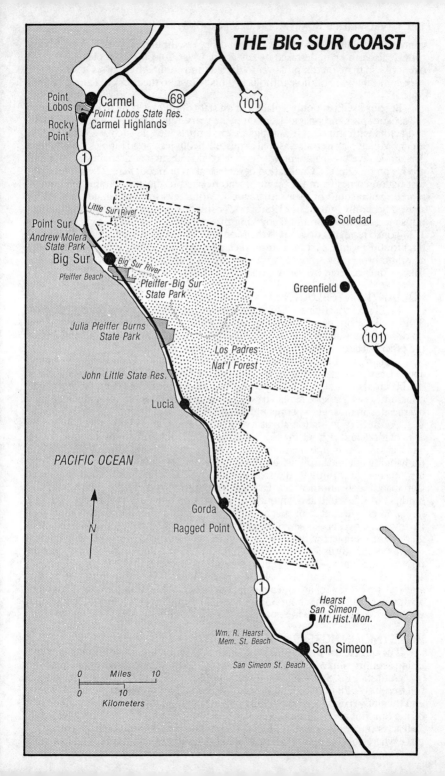

THE BIG SUR COAST

Point Lobos
Carmel
Point Lobos State Res.
Carmel Highlands
Rocky Point

68

101

Soledad

Little Sur River
Point Sur
Andrew Molera State Park
Big Sur
Big Sur River
Pfeiffer Beach
Pfeiffer-Big Sur State Park

Greenfield

Julia Pfeiffer Burns State Park

Los Padres Nat'l Forest

John Little State Res.

101

Lucia

PACIFIC OCEAN

N

Gorda
Ragged Point

1

Hearst San Simeon Mt. Hist. Mon.

Wm. R. Hearst Mem. St. Beach
San Simeon
San Simeon St. Beach

0   Miles   10

0   10
Kilometers

106 □ FROMMER'S HONEYMOON DESTINATIONS

yonder blue Pacific but a sheer 1,000-foot drop. Yes, the drive is breathtakingly beautiful. It also can be undertaken by any good driver. And there are plenty of scenic overlooks so that you can pull over to the side and admire the views. Often you can park your car at one of these turnoffs and hike down to the rocky beaches at water's edge.

Big Sur itself isn't only a place—it's a state of mind, a style of life, a tribute to the artistic spirit and imagination. Over the years, it has attracted writers, painters, and actors with impeccable avant-garde credentials, people such as Orson Welles, Henry Miller, Jack Kerouac, as well as miscellaneous jeans-clad hippies looking for a live-and-let-live environment where they could pursue an alternate lifestyle and groove on the sunsets. Civilization never has taken firm root here. The name of this vast region comes from the Spanish, who referred to the entire unmapped, unexplored region south of their settlement in Monterey as El Sur Grande. Electricity arrived here only in the early 1950s; power still does not reach into some mountainous recesses. You won't find anything that remotely resembles a town: the area's 1,200 or so residents drive up to the Monterey Peninsula when they need a new oil filter for the pickup, or some pâté for their pantry. The region offers contrasts: rocky coastline broken by smooth, white beaches . . . dense redwood forests and sun-baked ridges covered by bristly chaparral . . . hot springs and tide pools.

ROMANTIC INTERLUDES

In Big Sur, activity—like swimsuits in the hot tubs—is purely optional. Snooze all day on the sun deck or go off on a hike—it's up to you. However, if you do decide you want to explore actively, rather than just mellowing out and letting the experience come to you, you have several appealing options.

Vast areas of Big Sur have been set aside for public use. One of the best ways to appreciate the Ventana Wilderness Area and the Los Padres National Forest is along the hundreds of miles of hiking trails. You might encounter deer, raccoons, and opossum, as well as spot red-tail hawks, golden eagles, owls, and kingfishers soaring overhead. You must get a permit and should buy a trail map; both are available at the U.S. Forest Service Station about two miles north of the Ventana inn. A favorite both of locals and visitors, Pfeiffer Beach has jagged rock formations, tall sand dunes, and a lagoon. Although the water is too rough for swimming, this is a terrific beach for hanging out and strolling. Nearby, Pfeiffer Big Sur State Park has many easy hiking trails leading through the redwoods, as well as a river where you can swim. Garrapata Beach, another local favorite, has beautiful trails leading to the surf and hidden caves. Located at the mouth of the Big Sur River, Andrew Molera State Park has another fine stretch of beach (you have to wade across the river to get there). Partington Cove, about seven miles south of Big Sur, is the quintessential smuggler's cove, complete with a 200-foot tunnel that was officially used to ship tanbark —and unofficially used for . . . ? Esalen Institute, the center of the human potential movement, is a private facility, but its natural hot springs are open to the public from 1 p.m. to 5 a.m. You can also make an appointment to visit for an outstanding massage (tel. 667-2335 for arrangements). Search for pieces of California jade that often wash up at Jade Beach, about 35 miles south of Big Sur (it's a fun place to stop if you're driving down to San Simeon and Hearst Castle).

HONEYMOON HOTELS AND HIDEAWAYS

The spectacular Big Sur region is practically synonymous with Ventana, a very unique country inn where couples come to relax, renew, and discover one another.

Ventana, Big Sur, CA 93920 (tel. 408/667-2331 or 624-4812; reservations: toll free 800/628-6500 in California). The Spanish word *ventana* means a window, and this aptly named retreat not only provides an opening onto the awesome vistas of Big Sur, but also offers a peaceful perspective inward, into the soul. Located on 240 acres on a ridge some 1,200 feet above the sapphire-blue Pacific, Ventana is a place where couples seek total escape amid magnificent landscapes. The two-story cedar buildings with their latticework fronts harmonize with the golden foothills dotted with thickets of green oaks and bays. Around the villas, lush flower beds add brilliant splashes of color—alyssums, daisies, zinnias, pansies, and row upon row of regal calla lilies. Take a deep breath: Not only pine, but also bay laurel, sage, and wild basil perfume the air.

Through its thoughtful design, Ventana proves that rustic and luxurious need not be contradictory. Inside, the accommodations carry out the look of an elegant mountain lodge. One of the walls is built from rough-hewn cedar planks; a handmade quilt covers the bed. In the corner, the wood-burning stove stands with logs already arranged, just waiting the touch of a match. Every room is different; some face the Santa Lucia mountains, others the Pacific. Each has a cozily secluded terrace or balcony where two wooden rocking chairs await, highly conducive to hand holding, sunset watching, and planning out the next 50 years of your life together. When you sit out here at night, you can see millions of stars glittering against the black velvet sky, because there's no major town for miles.

There's a large heated swimming pool set up with lap lanes for serious swimmers. On the clothes-optional sun deck, you can bronze yourselves while overlooking the shimmering ocean, balmy breezes caressing your bodies. And, finally, unwind in the Japanese-style hot tubs or saunas, both tactfully separated into areas for men, women, and couples. Ventana has no (and never will have) tennis courts, golf courses, or video games. It offers instead a quiet, reflective oasis set in the scenic grandeur of Big Sur. Honeymoon package: None. Rates (CP): $160 to $170 per couple per night for a standard room (no fireplace); $300 to $385 per couple per night for a deluxe room with fireplace and private hot tub. Both include a lavish continental breakfast with a medley of fresh fruits (kiwi, cantaloupe, pineapple, watermelon), bowls of strawberries and cream, granola, and home-baked banana bread and strudel, served warm and honey-sweet from the oven. Also included are afternoon wine and cheese.

ROMANTIC RESTAURANTS
Both of Big Sur's memorable restaurants take maximum advantage of the superb views.

Ventana, one mile south of Big Sur State Park (tel. 667-2331). If ever one were to rank the great scenic vistas of the world, the view from Ventana's restaurant would belong, without question, in the top ten. Poised on the edge of a summit about 1,000 feet above the Pacific, the restaurant panoramas embrace over 50 miles of seacoast. And fortunately for serious gastronomes, the cuisine soars as well. At lunch, you'll want to dine on the broad wooden deck, looking south down the coast. Dinner is served both on the deck and in the high-ceilinged, skylit dining room with the unusual floor (made from six-inch blocks of solid wood). At both lunch and dinner, the menu pays full homage to California's bountiful harvests. For dinner, start off with a crunchy garden salad or fresh oysters on the half shell. As your main course, try the roast leg of lamb or grilled duck breast, accompanied by kiwifruit, broccoli, cauliflower, Mexican corn, and a wild-rice pancake. Every day, the chef offers different fish specialties. For dessert, chocoholics will want to sample the chocolate mousse pie with pralines and just a hint of orange. Lunch, from $35 per couple; dinner, about $70 per couple plus drinks. Open for lunch, 11:30 a.m. to 2:30 p.m.; dinner, 6 to 9:30 p.m.

Nepenthe, three miles south of Big Sur State Park (tel. 667-2345). There's no place else on earth quite like it. Yuppies from San Francisco and L.A. sit next to hippies who dropped out during the 1960s—and decided never to go back. Red BMW's sporting "Life is a cabernet" license-plate holders park next to rusting VW beetles. Somehow, all the juxtapositions work, and Nepenthe ranks as one of the most popular ports of call on the California coast drive.

Nepenthe has always been unusual. The house was designed by Rowan Maiden, a student of Frank Lloyd Wright's, using native materials—adobe and redwood.

Lolly and Bill Fassett, the original owners, wanted the house to be an island of no care, and so chose the name Nepenthe, from the Greek word meaning "no sorrow." During the 1940s, Orson Welles and Rita Hayworth lived on the property for a time. During the 1950s, novelist Henry Miller dwelled on nearby Partington Ridge.

Both of Nepenthe's restaurants offer unsurpassed views of the Big Sur coastline and pine-covered mountains. Since the food is fine, but definitely secondary to the mood and the view, both are best recommended for brunch or lunch. The self-service Cafe Amphora, downstairs, has a huge sun deck where you can improve your pallor while munching bagel sandwiches with lox or turkey melt, or whole-grain sandwiches such as a turkey and avocado twosome ($6 to $8). They also concoct excellent fruit smoothies (with banana or strawberry) for $3.50. Open daily from 10 a.m. to 4 p.m. Nepenthe restaurant upstairs offers table service. It has both an outdoor deck and a small, enclosed dining area perfect for cooler weather. Lunch choices include soups, salads, burgers, and quiche (about $7 to $8). Open for lunch, 11:30 a.m. to 4:30 p.m.; dinner, 5 to 9 p.m.

When you can pry yourselves off the sun deck, check out Nepenthe's Phoenix boutique, a treasure trove of gifts and handicrafts.

---

6. San Simeon and Area

At the southernmost reaches of the vast Big Sur region, on the top of a ridge named La Cuesta Encantata (the enchanted hill), stands a real-life castle that surpasses in richness all the citadels of our dreams—Hearst Castle.

Hearst Castle, east of Highway 1, San Simeon, CA 93452 (tel. 805/927-2000 for information only; see details about reservations at the end of this section). "Pleasure is worth what you can afford to pay for it," declared publishing magnate William Randolph Hearst. And at a time when a loaf of bread cost 4¢, and Hearst was earning some $50,000 a day, he spent $3 million to build what is truly a palace, combining Italian, Spanish, Moorish, and French architectural styles. The castle contains over 115 rooms, and could sleep over 80 people, both in the main house and mansion-like guest "cottages." Hearst heirs donated the castle to the state of California in 1958, and the Department of Parks and Recreation runs four different tours covering various parts of the property. For first-time visitors, the best tour is no. 1, which includes a guest house, the esplanade and gardens, the ground floor of the castle (Casa Grande), the assembly room, the dining room, the theater, and the Roman-style pool. You'll be truly flabbergasted by what you see.

At one time, the Hearst family owned 40 miles of prime California seacoast, which they used as a cattle ranch. (About 90,000 acres still belong to the family.) The sprawling dimensions led houseguest W. C. Fields to remark, "You know, you could send your kids out to play, and they'd be grown up when they came back." Hearst started constructing the castle in 1919, and he devoted the better part of 30 years to building the estate and adding to its rich furnishings, spending about one million depression-era dollars a year on collecting art treasures from around the world. The effect is dazzling: the Neptune pool with its white and black marble design, and statuary carved from Carrara marble; the assembly room paneled with 500-year-old Italian choir stalls; intricate tapestries designed by Rubens; a 1710 wine bucket made from over 30 pounds of pure silver. In this opulent setting, at the height of his power, Hearst entertained luminaries from the worlds of politics (Jimmy Walker, Winston Churchill, and Calvin Coolidge); royalty (the duke and duchess of Windsor); and Hollywood (Carole Lombard, Cary Grant, Jean Harlow, and Charlie Chaplin).

Because of the tremendous popularity of Hearst Castle, it is absolutely essential that you purchase tickets in advance. Each of the four tours costs $11 per person.

You can make telephone reservations seven days a week, from 9 a.m. to 6 p.m., by calling 619/452-1950 nationwide; toll free 800/444-7275 in California only. Reservations can be made up to eight weeks in advance; Visa and MasterCard are accepted.

HOTELS AND RESTAURANTS

The castle itself is a don't-miss sight, but the immediate area is not all that interesting. Unless you're a scion of the Hearst family and can stay at the castle, try to plan your route so that you will sleep elsewhere, such as Morro Bay (see details below). In San Simeon itself, the only accommodations are roadside motels and small hotels; the new Holiday Inn is definitely the pick of the bunch. You will probably have to stop for a bite in the area. There is a completely dependable snackbar near the admission gates, as well as some equally predictable coffee shops in San Simeon. Better yet—pack your own picnic.

The **Inn at Morro Bay,** Morro Bay, CA 93442 (tel. 805/772-5651, or toll free 800/321-9566). A sudden splashing in the water catches your attention. You look up just in time to glimpse a stately blue heron skimming the bay's surface, its catch of the day held triumphantly in its bill. Blue herons—as well as peregrine falcons and sea otters—are just some of your neighbors when you stay at the Inn at Morro Bay. Located 19 miles south of Hearst Castle next to Montana de Oro State Park, the inn is nestled right on the bay, a tranquil harbor backdropped by Morro Rock (*morro* means "fortress" in Spanish). At low tide, you can walk across to the sand dunes that form a natural breakwater between the harbor and the Pacific. Set in two-story units, the stylish rooms feature French provincial furnishings, brass beds, color TVs, minifridges, and terraces. There's a heated pool right on the property, and a challenging 18-hole golf course just across the way. The restaurant is excellent, and you'll find no better view of the sunset than the one from the cocktail lounge. Rates (EP): $150 to $170 per couple per night. The extra-large Honeymoon Suite is $260 per couple per night.

---

7. Santa Barbara

"God gave us the land, but the people made the city." Carved in Spanish over the entryway to the courthouse, these words crystallize all that is special about Santa Barbara. The setting—a long crescent-shaped indentation in the coastline, cupped in the embrace of the Santa Ynez Mountains—equals that of any village on the Amalfi coast or the Côte d'Azur. The city of Santa Barbara, happily, is in keeping with its spectacular setting, a town of white adobe houses with red-tile roofs, all of which rise and fall over the curves of the foothills.

Located 335 miles south of San Francisco and 90 miles north of Los Angeles, Santa Barbara lies at the heart of Southern California. With its red-tile roofs, terrazzo walkways, and long beachside boulevard lined with palm trees, Santa Barbara looks like a sleepy Spanish mission town. But in its own conservative way, it resembles Los Angeles, New York, and London. This is a major power center. The area has always appealed to captains of industry such as the Armours and the Firestones, as well as to weekend escapists from the Hollywood movie mills, such as John Travolta, Robert Mitchum, Michael Douglas, and Bo Derek. But recently, when a local boy named Ronald Reagan made good, Santa Barbara became the site of the White House West, and Cabinet officials, reporters, and Secret Service people became ubiquitous sights in the city's restaurants and shops. An interesting contrast: Although Santa Barbara shares Southern California's outdoor lifestyle—sailing, fishing, surfing, horseback riding—it has always nurtured the mind. The University of California has a campus here. The year-round roster of cultural attractions includes the Santa Barbara Ballet, live theater, rows and rows of art galleries, lectures and special events at the university, the Symphony Orchestra, and the Brooks Institute photography exhibits, to name just a few. Every sunny Sunday (and most of them are), there's the Santa Barbara Arts and Crafts Show, held under the fronds of Palm Park. Throughout the year, various events and festivals are scheduled: polo matches, the Summer Solstice Parade, whale-watching trips, film festivals, chili cook-offs, the Semana Nautica land and sea sporting event. . . . The list just goes on.

The city was named by the Spanish explorer Sebastián Vizcaíno, who sailed into the broad harbor on December 4, 1603—the feast of Santa Barbara. By 1786, it had become a major Spanish stronghold, with soldiers stationed at El Presidio; the gracious Mission Santa Barbara overlooked everything from its hillside perch. Much of the city remains beautifully preserved, including several fine old adobes, made from the local clay. To appreciate Santa Barbara's fine architecture best, follow the marked 90-minute "Red Tile Tour" that leads past some of the most historic sites: the "Historic Adobe" was the headquarters of Colonel John C. Frémont after he captured the city from the Mexicans in 1846; and La Caneda Adobe and El Cuartel, part of the original Spanish fortifications at El Presidio. To get the best view of Santa Barbara and its yacht harbor, head out to the end of Stearns Wharf, the oldest operating wharf on the West Coast.

As you stroll through Santa Barbara or loll on its 30 miles of unspoiled beaches, you might notice an interesting phenomenon. Somehow, the sunshine always seems, well, sunnier here than elsewhere along the California coast. A friend finally explained why. Santa Barbara has the only beach that faces due south, allowing full frontal sunbathing all day. I still prefer my original explanation. Sheer magic.

SHOPPING

Santa Barbara is a place for people who appreciate the finer things of life, such as great art, sleek polo ponies, and clothes that you won't see on every other man and woman in the street. An added bonus: Many stores are open on Sunday. For some of the best and most atmospheric browsing, head over to **El Paseo,** Spanish for "the street" (808 to 810 State St.), a picturesque shopping arcade built in and around the 1827 adobe home that belonged to the De la Guerra family. Here, **Neville and Hon** displays Southeast Asian and primitive art; **Astra Gallery** sells original art priced from $150; and **Nature's Own** carries shells, minerals, and gems. Save lots of time for what is indeed rubber-stamp paradise, **Stampa Barbara** (tel. 962-4077). Here, owner Gary Dorothy has a selection of over 30,000 rubber stamps, with designs that will please cat and dog fanciers, car fiends, airplane mavens, computer buffs, you name it. Prices for the stamps range from $4 to $17.50. **Victoria Court** (1221 State St.) is another appealing shopping arcade, with interesting boutiques such as **Tyger Tyger** for clothing, jewelry, and gifts; and **Zad** for women's accessories.

Other excellent areas for shopping include **upper State Street** (the 800 to 1300 numbers), where you'll find shops such as **Tienda Ho** (1017 State St.) for reasonably priced imports from Bali, and **Elizabeth Fortner Gallery** (1114 State St.) for fine crafts and wearable art—many pieces are of museum quality. **Great Pacific Ironworks** (also at 1114 State St. in the La Arcada Center) has a tremendous selection of fashion-right active sportswear for men and women from Patagonia and others. **Ruth Walters** (916-C State St.) and **P.S. Limited** (1100 State St.) both carry exquisite handcrafts from around the world, including fine pieces by local artists. Perhaps the most elegant shops are found in the Montecito enclave. If you're looking for something different in jewelry, head for **Silverhorn** (1155 Coast Village Rd.), where Michael and Carol Ridding create very beautiful, very modern designs using quartz glass and rough-cut gemstones. **Angel** (1221 Coast Village Rd.) highlights very fashion-forward women's sportswear, and **O Tatu** (1187 Coast Village Rd.) carries unusual crafts and gifts.

Whether women want something eye-catching for strolling along the beachfront, or assertive Power Dressing for the boardroom, they'll find something

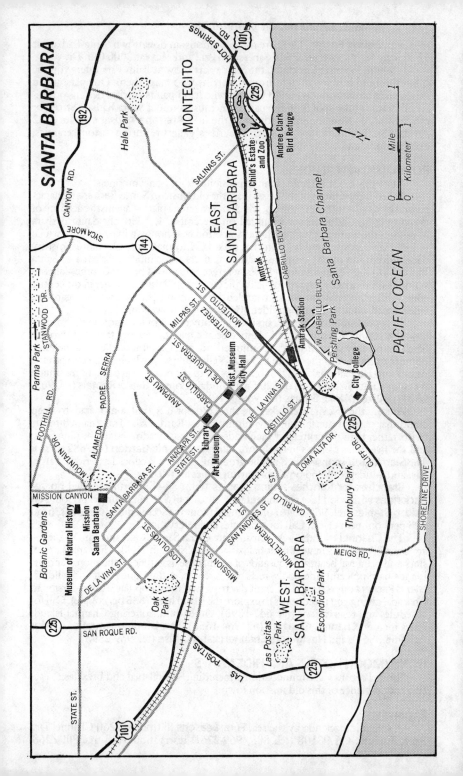

to suit at **Wendy Foster.** There are three locations: in downtown Santa Barbara at 1120 State St.; Montecito at 516 San Ysidro Rd.; and Mesa at 2000 Cliff Dr.

If you're interested in crafts, the Sunday art show at Palm Park offers you the opportunity to buy works right from the artists who make them. One person you might want to check out is **Judith Geiger,** who hand-paints fanciful designs on china silk. Her regular spot is on the park corner just south of Santa Barbara Street, or call 569-3323. Near the park, stop in at the new **Anacapa Artisans Gallery,** 32 Anacapa St. (tel. 962-1585), a cooperative artists' gallery featuring custom ceramics, exotic woods, and blown glass.

ROMANTIC INTERLUDES

A city this beautiful holds infinite possibilities for honeymooners.

Called "The Queen of the Missions," the old **Mission Santa Barbara** is characterized by its two matching towers, which pose a serene picture against a backdrop of the eucalyptus-clad foothills. Founded on December 4, 1786, the Santa Barbara Mission is the tenth of the Spanish missions. Today, it houses a fine museum, which you can visit on a self-guided tour that makes California's Spanish colonial history come alive. One of the most fascinating artifacts on exhibit is a sketch of Santa Barbara in 1793, drawn by John Sykes, who accompanied Captain George Vancouver on his exploratory voyage up the Pacific coast. You'll want to linger in the central courtyard, with its fountain surrounded by towering palms, and lush gardens, where small, hand-lettered signs identify the various flowers and herbs.

To appreciate Santa Barbara best, choose other ways of locomotion than a car.

The county has several well-planned scenic **bike paths** that take you through Santa Barbara, Goleta, Montecito, Summerland, and Carpinteria. Perhaps the most popular route of all is the 9.6-mile Goleta Valley Bikeway, which connects with the Atascadero Recreational Trail that branches off to the beach. You can rent mountain bikes for about $7 per hour, or $20 for a half-day. Contact **Beach Rentals** (tel. 963-2524) or **Bike 'n' Hike Sports** (tel. 969-0719).

Among the favorite area **hikes** are the Cold Springs Trail, a moderate-to-steep climb that passes waterfalls and swimming holes; Rattlesnake Trail (named for its twists rather than the critters), which leads to a grassy meadow edged by pine trees; and the five miles of trails in the **Santa Barbara Botanic Garden** (tel. 682-4726). The **Sierra Club** sponsors free public group hikes every Wednesday, Friday, Saturday, and Sunday; call 966-6622 for starting times and details.

Branchwater Ranches Riding Stables (tel. 688-4658) runs guided **horseback rides** with good lake and mountain views, from $20 per hour per person. **San Ysidro Stables** (tel. 969-5046) offers guided tours of scenic mountain trails, from $25 per hour per person. Call for schedules and reservations.

The **Channel Islands**—Anacapa, Santa Cruz, Santa Rosa, and San Miguel— are one of America's newest national parks, established in 1980. They are places of stark and primeval beauty. Thousands of elephant seals gather on the shores, and the islands have peaceful tide pools, reefs, caves, coves, and unique plant and wildlife. **Island Packers** offers several different day trips. The most popular is the excursion to Anacapa, giving you three hours to explore the island itself ($35 per couple). Call for schedules and reservations (tel. 642-1393). Other outfits offering Channel Islands tours include **Channel Charters** (tel. 964-1656), **Sea Landing Aquatics Center** (tel. 963-3564), and **Navigators Channel Island Cruise** (tel. 969-2393).

HONEYMOON HOTELS AND HIDEAWAYS

Santa Barbara's accommodations, including several bed-and-breakfasts, capture the ambience of this old mission town.

Expensive

A splendid hacienda by the sea, **Four Seasons Biltmore,** 1260 Channel Dr., Santa Barbara, CA 93108 (tel. 805/969-2261; reservations: toll free 800/268-

6282), reigns as the queen of Santa Barbara after a $16-million renovation. Opened in 1927 as part of the original Biltmore chain, the hotel captures the spirit of the Roaring '20s—but in keeping with the Southern California setting. Built Spanish-style with tranquil green courtyards, the two-story white stucco buildings sprawl across from Butterfly Beach, the red-tile roofs, open archways, and wrought-iron grillwork harmonizing with the hazy blue Santa Ynez Mountains in the distance. Towering palm trees and fragrant eucalyptus dot the 21 acres of the property. The drop-dead gorgeous lobby has a Spanish feel, with its high, exposed-beam ceilings, Mediterranean furnishings, archways, and iron-grillwork door. There are 228 guest rooms offering views of the ocean, pool, gardens, or mountains. Many rooms have balconies or private patios, vaulted ceilings, and ceiling fans; some have fireplaces. Floral prints in either sunny California colors or soft earth tones brighten the decor, which has a substantial, if a bit stolid, feel.

Biltmore guests have full privileges at the Coral Casino Beach and Cabana Club just across the street, which has an Olympic-size pool, private beach, cocktail lounge, and dancing. The Coral Casino is also slated to add health spa facilities by 1990. On the property are three lighted tennis courts, a swimming pool, and a putting green; golf can be arranged. Honeymoon package: Three days/two nights (some meals): $440 (weekdays) to $550 (weekends) per couple. Includes deluxe accommodations, a bottle of champagne, dinner for two at oceanview La Marina restaurant, and more.

El Encanto Hotel and Garden Villas, 1900 Lasuen Rd., Santa Barbara, CA 93103 (tel. 805/687-5000; reservations: toll free 800/346-7039 in California only). The name, meaning "the enchanted one," says it all. El Encanto is situated on ten gardened acres on a hilltop in Santa Barbara's very exclusive Riviera district.

The most romantic accommodations are the cottages, which make you think that you're sleeping in an English garden. Springtime flowers seem to be everywhere —on the wallpaper and matching bedspread—unfurling petals of blue, pink, peach, and coral. Touches of brass add glamour, on the headboard, desk lamps, and drawer-pulls on the English-style furnishings. Baskets of silk flowers create a pleasing trompe l'oeil effect against the floral wallpaper. Windows are all around, covered with louvers so you can let in daylight and the garden views when you wish. Unusual for a hotel room, the lighting is well designed, with a combination of strategically placed lamps and track lighting allowing you to control the scheme for romance. Standard rooms offer similar nice touches, though on a smaller proportioned scale.

The pride of El Encanto must be the magnificent gardens, centered around a brick-columned pergola overhung with vines and surrounded by regal blue-and-gold bird of paradise plants. There are a tennis court and a solar-heated swimming pool on site, and the resort can arrange golf privileges nearby. For dining with a view, try the excellent restaurant. "Some Enchanted Evening" honeymoon package: $198 per couple. Includes one night's lodging in deluxe accommodations with fireplace, two sunset cocktails, dinner for two at El Encanto's dining room (includes wine), European breakfast in bed, tax, and gratuity. Offered October 15 through June 15, Sunday through Thursday only, subject to availability. Regular rates (EP): $110 to $330 per couple per night, depending on size, views, and lavishness of furnishings.

Hideaway is the word that comes to mind when describing the **San Ysidro Ranch,** 900 San Ysidro Lane, Montecito, CA 93108 (tel. 805/969-5046), in the foothills of the Santa Ynez Mountains and the very exclusive Montecito residential area. After all, if you can't find seclusion at a resort that has only 43 rooms—and 540 acres of prime real estate—where else could you? Among your escapist predecessors were Winston Churchill (who wrote one of his books here), Laurence Olivier and Vivien Leigh (who married here), and John and Jacqueline Kennedy (who honeymooned here). The ranch has a colorful history, having begun life in 1893 as a way station for Franciscan monks, who sold their homemade wine here. In the late 1920s, the spread was purchased by actor Ronald Colman.

A member of the Relais et Château group, the ranch was purchased by the owners of Napa Valley's posh Auberge du Soleil in 1987. The new management intends to perfect the resort into "the best little inn" in America, primping and refining rooms and gardens while maintaining the ranch's down-home friendliness. There is no "typical" room—each has a unique personality. The cottages have different names and fascinating pasts: Somerset Maugham penned several of his short stories in "Geranium;" Sinclair Lewis wrote in the closet at "Oak" (he found the beautiful views too distracting). The seductive decor might include a plump chintz sofa, curtained bed, and a Jacuzzi bubbling nicely on the outdoor deck surrounded by latticework. Whichever cottage you choose, a sign will be hanging on the door, with your surname carved in wood. San Ysidro is that kind of place.

Cozy as these nests might be, you should take advantage of your awesome surroundings. Ride off into the hills on a sleek quarter horse from the stables ($25 per hour). See if you can keep your eye on the ball on the tennis courts (you'll find yourself gazing off at the Pacific or the mountains instead). Mix yourself a drink at the honor bar in the hacienda lounge and swim a few laps in the heated pool (preferably not in that order). Home on the range has never been so sweet. Honeymoon package: None. Rates (EP): $176 per couple for rooms to about $470 per couple for a private cottage with Jacuzzi. If your ménage includes the family horse, equine guests are boarded for $33 per night (AP). Includes gourmet hay.

Moderate

The **Bayberry Inn,** 111 West Valerio St., Santa Barbara, CA 93101 (tel. 805/682-3199). With its beautiful silk wall coverings, sparkling beveled mirrors, crystal chandeliers, and fine Victorian antiques, the Bayberry is a real showstopper. Add in the ample amenities showered on guests (such as a complimentary carafe of sherry in your room) and you'll understand why the inn ranks among the crème de la crème of Santa Barbara B&Bs. Set on a quiet residential street just a few blocks from the center of Santa Barbara, the Bayberry also features a lovely garden, framed by pink camellias, calla lilies, orange trees, and an impeccable emerald-green lawn. Rooms coddle you with Victorian elegance: down pillows, fluffy comforters, and canopied beds (each with its own small crystal chandelier for light from above). All rooms have queen-size beds and private baths; some have fireplaces, private decks, or whirlpool tubs. No smoking anywhere on the grounds. Honeymoon package: None. Rates (BP): $82 to $138 per couple per night. Ask about special low midweek rates from September 2 through early June.

The **Cheshire Cat,** 36 West Valerio St., Santa Barbara, CA 93101 (tel. 805/569-1610). If Alice had been staying at this winsome B&B, she'd have had no need to wander off to find Wonderland. From the moment you enter the cozy Victorian house with the twin bay windows, you'll lead a fairy-tale existence. Upon your arrival, you'll find chocolates and liqueurs in your room; the ample morning breakfast (which might include an egg "puff" and homemade banana bread) is served on Wedgwood. Conveniently located near downtown, the inn occupies two of Santa Barbara's oldest homes, both meticulously restored and enhanced with Laura Ashley wallpapers and fabrics. Each of the rooms is named after a beloved Lewis Carroll character. All have private baths, some boast extras such as fireplaces, private patios, or spas. For example, the Cheshire Cat Suite features a sunken Jacuzzi tub, color TV, VCR, and a plump stuffed Cheshire Cat grinning from the bay window seat. Alice's Suite, all done up in pink and ivory with ruffled pillows and wicker furniture, has its own private patio overlooking the gardens and mountains. Honeymoon package: None. Rates (BP): $130 to $187 per couple per night. Ask about special midweek rates.

The **Old Yacht Club Inn,** 431 Corona Del Mar, Santa Barbara, CA 93103 (tel. 805/962-1277). A friend—not a visitor—that's what you'll feel like when you stay at the Old Yacht Club Inn. Set in a 1912-vintage California craftsman house, this B&B is just half a block from the beach and Santa Barbara's pleasurable oceanfront promenade. The inn itself is filled with fine antiques and family heirlooms belonging to innkeeper-owners Lucille Caruso, Nancy Donaldson, and Sandy Hunt. In late afternoon, guests gather in the living room for a glass of wine or cup of tea around the large brick fireplace, or perhaps to play favorite tunes on the turn-of-the-century piano, with a tall stack of sheet music on the stand. Accommodations are located both in the main house and the Hitchcock House next door (where each room has a private entry). Most rooms have a private bath. Favorite choices for honeymooners include the Castellamare Room (main house), with whirlpool tub and French doors opening to a balcony; and the large Belle Caruso Suite (Hitchcock House), with a deco-design etched-glass shower door and a patchwork quilt on the king-size bed.

In the morning, you'll awaken to the aroma of fresh-brewed coffee, served along with home-baked breads and tasty omelets. But perhaps the biggest treats are the gourmet dinners (generally offered on Saturday nights exclusively for inn guests, at extra cost). Chef Nancy (her recipes have been featured in national magazines) serves up an elegant five-course prix-fixe affair that is frequently topped off by her famous chocolate cheesecake. Honeymoon package: None. Rates (BP): $72 to $132 per couple per night.

The **Tiffany Inn**, 1323 De la Vina St., Santa Barbara, CA 93101 (tel. 805/963-2283). It looks very much like you want your perfect B&B to look, an airy Victorian (built in 1898) with large diamond-pane bay windows and bright flowers coloring the borders out front. Innkeeper-owners Carol and Larry MacDonald have perfectly restored this gem of a house located near many of Santa Barbara's most exclusive shops and restaurants. Rooms (most with private baths and fireplaces) feature exquisite antiques that the MacDonalds have collected over the years. In particular, there's a one-of-a-kind quilt hanging by the main stairway that incorporates ribbons from Texas state fairs dating back to 1862. Continental breakfast is usually served on the back porch facing the garden; every afternoon about 5 p.m., guests sit on the chintz sofas and Queen Anne armchairs in the living room for wine, cheese, and conversation. For steal-away privacy, couples can ensconce themselves in the aptly named Honeymoon Suite, entered through a secluded garden. The suite features 1880s-era furniture, including a fine walnut armoire, brass canopied bed with white eyelet quilt, wood-burning fireplace, and whirlpool tub. Honeymoon package: None. Rates (BP): $93 to $170 per couple per night.

ROMANTIC RESTAURANTS

Santa Barbarans claim their city has the most restaurants per capita in the United States. And, we may add, some of the best and most reasonably priced. Because of its proximity to the great fishing waters, the seafood particularly merits a "10." Try fresh albacore tuna, swordfish, rockfish, white bass, or Pacific lobster. But when they appear on the menu, head straight for the Santa Barbara shrimp, generally served with their roe—definitely a foretaste of heaven.

Expensive

The Stonehouse, San Ysidro Ranch, 900 San Ysidro Lane, Montecito (tel. 969-5046). According to legend, San Ysidro (Spanish for Isadore) was so kind to suffering peasants that a guardian angel was sent from heaven to till the fields while Isadore ministered to the sick and needy. Today, a new miracle of sorts is taking place at San Ysidro Ranch, where chef Marc Ehrler is gladdening the palates of gastronomes with absolutely superb cuisine. Ehrler, who previously was chef to the French ambassador in Washington, D.C., and worked at Maxim's in Paris and New York, has a genuine love affair going with the fresh produce for which the Santa Barbara area is known. Local farmers bring him the pick of their crop: baby lettuce, yellow raspberries for a tart, etc. Bacon for quiche Lorraine is prepared in the chef's own smokehouse; herbs for marinades and sauces come from the garden out back.

Menus constantly change to take advantage of the fresh ingredients that pique

Ehrler's imagination: jumbo sea scallops, served with tiny green lentils and a white pepper sauce; or lamb tenderloin balanced by a fresh raspberry sauce. The Stonehouse building provides a perfect showcase for the cuisine. A former citrus-packing house, it features thick whitewashed stone walls, open beamed ceilings, as well as a patio for outdoor dining. Open daily for breakfast (8 to 10 a.m.; about $20 per couple), lunch (noon to 2 p.m.; $40 per couple), and dinner (6 to 9:30 p.m.; $80 per couple plus wine). The Stonehouse also serves a lavish Sunday brunch with everything from a melt-in-your-mouth seafood salad to savory crab cakes and a dessert table headlined by a swooningly decadent chocolate mousse. Served on Sundays from 10:30 a.m. to 2 p.m.; $32 per person prix-fixe.

Michael's Waterside Inn, 50 Los Patos Way, Montecito (tel. 969-0307). The decor is unmistakably French, with floral-print portières framing the windows, and crisp white linens on the table. And the cuisine features classic French techniques enlivened with innovative California twists, such as serving cultured abalone with a limpid buerre blanc sauce tinged with fresh dill, squab with a wine sauce based on a local cabernet, or roast duck combined with Santa Barbara olives. There's no innovation just for innovation's sake—these recipes are well thought out and the textures and flavors marry beautifully. The three-course prix-fixe dinner, from $20 to $30 per person, includes appetizer, entrée, and dessert (such as the ambrosial crêpe soufflé with raspberries). Open nightly for dinner, 6 to 9:30 p.m. (to 10 p.m. on Friday and Saturday). Sunday brunch is served from 11 a.m. to 2 p.m.

Norbert's, 920 de la Vina, Santa Barbara (tel. 965-6012). Set in a beautifully refurbished California bungalow with pink walls, archways, and only 13 tables, Norbert's offers gourmet dining at its most intimate. In addition to an à la carte menu that highlights seasonal specialties, they offer a seven-course "signature menu," served in appetizer-size portions to give you a range of tastes. A sample dinner might start off with an herb salad topped with a chèvre crêpe and duck foie gras, followed by local lobster and shrimp. The next dish might be a scaloppine of king salmon, then a strawberry sorbet as an intermezzo. For the main course, savor a lamb medallion grilled with thyme. To round out the meal, there's a selection of cheeses, plus a tangerine gratin with poppyseed ice cream for dessert. About $50 to $55 per person. For calorie-counters, there's a gourmet fitness menu for $40 to $45 per person. Open for dinner Thursday through Monday, 5:30 to 9 p.m.

Moderate

The Palace Café, 8 East Cota St. (off State), Santa Barbara (tel. 966-3133). For a little bit of Dixieland gone west, head on over to the happening Palace Café. The decor sets a trendy New Orleans mood, with posters and paintings celebrating jazz, catfish festivals, Mardi Gras, and a bright neon sign heralding Louisiana's own Dixie beer. Best of all, the food delivers that real New Orleans flavor, with good ol' southern delicacies such as crawfish, soft-shell crabs, and redfish airlifted in daily. Appetizers spotlight such yummies as black-bean soup with andouille sausage, or crab claws dipped in a spicy batter, deep-fried, and served with a smooth rémoulade sauce. For entrées, recommendations include the real thing jambalaya, packed with prawns, chicken breast, crawfish, andouille sausage, and served on a bed of "dirty" rice, and the crawfish étouffée, thickened with a dark roux. Pace yourselves so you can last till dessert, most notably the Key lime pie. The place is always packed, so be prepared to wait. Dinner for two, about $40 to $50. Open nightly from 5:30 to 9:30 p.m.

Paradise Café, 812 Anacapa St., Santa Barbara (tel. 966-2428). The building looks as if it stepped straight out of a movie, with its original 1940s wall murals and neon signs. Take advantage of the balmy Santa Barbara climate, and eat on their large patio or veranda. The specialty here is oak-grilled steaks and fresh fish, priced from $9.50 for red snapper to $16 for a 22-ounce T-bone steak. Dinner entrées come complete with garlic bread, soup or salad, vegetables, rice, or shoestring potatoes. Open Monday through Saturday, 11 a.m. to 11 p.m.; Sunday, 8:30 a.m. to 11 p.m.

Montecito Cafe, 1295 Coast Village Rd., Montecito (tel. 969-3392). Light, lively, and fun, this is a popular gathering place for Santa Barbarans. The decor is French country with a modern Californian touch, accented by colorful original artwork on the walls (exhibits constantly change). Start off with some goat-cheese pancakes, topped by gravlax and caviar; or a roast sweet-pepper salad accompanied by grilled lamb sausage. For your entrée, there's a crisp vegetable salad with grilled baby salmon, or grilled chicken breast served with roasted Anaheim chiles, red onion, and tomato. Excellent, reasonably priced wine list. Dinner for two, about $30 per couple. Open Tuesday through Sunday for lunch, 11:30 a.m. to 2:30 p.m.; dinner, 5:30 to 10 p.m.

Brigitte's, 1327 State St., Santa Barbara (tel. 966-9676). When you need your pasta fix, head for this stylish café with brick walls and the flags of the world unfurled overhead. Favorite appetizers include the spinach salad with bay scallops and pesto —big enough for two to share. Follow through with one of the pasta specials, or a heartier entrée such as the leg of lamb with thyme and grilled red-onion sauce. Because it is located in the heart of downtown, Brigitte's is an especially nice choice for lunch when you're shopping on State Street. Open Monday through Saturday, 11:30 a.m. to 2:30 p.m., and 5 to 10 p.m.; Sunday, dinner only, 5 to 10 p.m.

For fresh seafood at reasonable prices, try **Salmon Wellingtons,** 214 State St. (tel. 966-0260), or **Andria's Harbor Side,** 336 West Cabrillo St. (tel. 962-8159), both of which have the same owners. Salmon Wellingtons is smaller and a bit more elegant, the Harbor Side a little more lively. In addition to the fresh catch of the day, menus offer pasta, chicken, and steak dishes. As the name suggests, the specialty of both houses is the salmon Wellington, the fish topped off with herb butter and baked in a puff pastry. Dinner for two will run about $45 plus drinks. Salmon Wellingtons is open nightly for dinner, 5 to 10 p.m., and also for Sunday brunch, 10:30 a.m. to 2:30 p.m. Andria's Harbor Side is open daily for breakfast, 6 to 10:30 a.m.; lunch, 11 a.m. to 4 p.m.; and dinner, 4:30 to 10 p.m. (to 11 p.m. on Friday and Saturday).

Or how about something more intimate—such as a picnic for two? For an elegant spread, check out **Pierre Lafond** gourmet caterers. This is al fresco dining with class—you get a picnic basket along with a checkered tablecloth, utensils, and glassware. Selections include chicken salad stuffed into fresh croissants, served with cucumber-and-dill salad, fresh fruit, and lemon bars. Also an avocado stuffed with seafood and crème fraîche, plus Montrachet pasta salad, Niçoise olives, pâté, brie, baguette, fresh fruit, and white-chocolate brownies. Complete picnics range from $22 to $33 per person; there is a $20 deposit (with $17 refund) when you return the basket. Please try to order two days in advance. Pierre Lafond has two locations: in Montecito at 516 San Ysidro Rd. (tel. 565-1502), and on the Mesa, 2000 Cliff Dr. (tel. 965-5138). Open daily from 7 a.m. to 8 p.m. Where should you have your feast? A top choice is at Goleta Beach, just north of Santa Barbara, which has picnic tables scattered around the beach area.

Inexpensive

La Super-Rica Taqueria, 622 North Milpas (at the corner of Alphonse), Santa Barbara (tel. 963-4940). To say that this is only a taco stand is like commenting that Michelangelo just painted ceilings. This family-run restaurant serves some of the best Mexican food north of the border. (Santa Barbara resident Julia Child, the chef and author who popularized French cooking in the United States, is a frequent patron.) Even though the restaurant doesn't have its name or address outside, it's easy to recognize—it's the little blue-trimmed building with the line of eager diners outside. You order your meal by number from the chalkboard. Favorites include the no. 12—Pechuga Suiza, grilled chicken breast with melted cheese and two fresh-made tortillas; and the no. 16 Especial, a roasted chile pasilla stuffed with cheese and combined with charbroiled marinated pork and served with three tortillas. Daily specials might include chiles rellenos or vegetable enchiladas. A meal might run $10 to $15 per couple—no kidding! Open daily from 11 a.m. to 8 p.m. (to 9 p.m. on Friday and Saturday).

What could be more romantic than dining alongside the beach, with your table just a hop, skip, and jump away from the sand and sea? Santa Barbara features two fun, casual choices. **The Brown Pelican,** 2981½ Cliff Dr., in Arroyo Burro State Park just north of Santa Barbara (tel. 687-4550), is set right on Henery's Beach, one of the area's most popular strands. Nothing fancy—just good burgers and crisp salads, about $15 to $20 per couple. Open daily from 7 a.m. to 8 p.m. Right in Santa Barbara, the **East Beach Grill,** 1118 East Cabrillo (tel. 965-8805), is known for its beachside breakfasts ($5 to $10 per couple) and casual lunches, such as hamburgers, chili dogs, and deli sandwiches ($5 to $10 per couple). You can even take time out for a swim or volleyball game between courses. Open Monday through Friday for breakfast, 6 to 11 a.m.; and lunch, 11:30 a.m. to 3 p.m. On Saturday and Sunday, breakfast is served from 7 to 11:30 a.m.; lunch from noon to 3 p.m.

8. Los Angeles and Environs

Freeways. Surfers. Movie stars. U.C.L.A. Dodger Stadium. Valley Girls. Palm trees. Swimming pools. A sign that spells out H-O-L-L-Y-W-O-O-D. It seems only fitting that Los Angeles presents itself in montage images. Not only is L.A. linked, twin-like, with the movie industry, but also the city itself isn't so much a place as it is places, 140 different cities and communities loosely stitched together, like a patchwork quilt: Beverly Hills, Westwood, and Bel Air; Burbank, Hollywood, and Century City; Santa Monica, Venice, and Marina del Rey, and all the other cityscapes and townlets.

With a population of about 13.6 million, Greater Los Angeles is the second largest metropolitan area in the country. Los Angeles County itself is huge, encompassing over 4,083 square miles, surrounded on one side by the San Gabriel Mountains, on the other by the Pacific Ocean. Its lowest point lies some nine feet below sea level; its tallest, Mount Baldy, towers some 10,080 feet above it. The experiences it offers are as wide as all humanity. There's the surfing, of course, at the beaches that gave the Beach Boys their name: Surfrider in Malibu, as well as Manhattan Beach, Hermosa Beach, and Redondo Beach. Yet just a two-hour drive away, Big Bear Lake offers top-notch downhill skiing. You can give yourselves over shamelessly to celebrity gawking, driving past the homes of the stars on Beverly Drive, getting the best of *Jaws* on the Universal Studios tour, and poking each other in the ribs in excitement when you see "you know, what's his name?" sit down at an adjoining table at Ma Maison, The Ivy, or whatever new spot the rich and famous have chosen to frequent this month. And despite such put-downs as Gertrude Stein's "There is no there, there," Los Angeles actually has a downtown, a rather spectacular one, a futuristic core of silver skyscrapers that glitter like a mirage when you approach the city from the San Diego Freeway. If you're coming to L.A. for the first time, you will probably increase the number of Rolls-Royces, Jaguars, and Porsches you have seen in your life at least tenfold—and that's just in the parking lot of the Hotel Bel-Air. But L.A. is also one of the most "happening" art scenes in the country, and perhaps the world, with the new Museum of Contemporary Art (MOCA) downtown and the rapidly growing collection at the Getty Museum in Malibu, where practically every *objet* seems to be sporting a just-typed "recent acquisition" tag.

On your visit, make it a point to get to know L.A.'s various neighborhoods, to develop a sense for what makes swank Bel-Air different from posh Beverly Hills (Bel-Air is where the really, really rich live). Spend each day poking around a different area. Perhaps start off in downtown L.A., strolling through the state historic park along Olvera Street, the oldest thoroughfare in town. Stop in at the Avila Adobe, home of one of the pueblo's early mayors. Sample L.A.'s ethnic neighborhoods, with visits to Chinatown, Little Tokyo, Koreatown, and the *corazón* of the Mexican neighborhood, the Grand Central Market. Pack your beach towels and drive off to

Malibu, Zuma, or the string of shores that stretch all along the county's coast. Celebrate L.A.'s romance with the road by driving—follow winding, two-lane Mulholland Drive, which climbs 1,400 feet into the Hollywood Hills, or Coldwater Canyon Drive, deep into the hills.

Los Angeles is a city with a wonderfully romantic past—and a tremendously vibrant, energetic future. Even the most active honeymooners are sure to run out of time before they run out of things to do.

SHOPPING

Whatever your taste—from classic European haute couture to the latest beach bunny craze—you're sure to get that shopping adrenaline pumping overtime in L.A.

The shopping area par excellence is the aptly named **"Golden Triangle,"** bounded by Wilshire Boulevard, Santa Monica Boulevard, and Cañon Drive. The most famous address in this gilded district is **Rodeo Drive** (pronounce it Row-DAY-o), ranked right up there with rue du Faubourg St. Honoré in Paris and Fifth Avenue in New York. You'll find stores by all the worldwide celebrities—**Cartier** and **Van Cleef & Arpel** for jewelry; **Gucci, Hermès,** and **Louis Vuitton** for leather goods and handbags; plus boutiques showcasing **Armani, Fendi, Maud Frizon, Chanel,** and more. Don't miss the **Rodeo Collection,** a four-tier, open-air complex at 421 Rodeo Dr. Top shops include **Gianni Versace** and **Sonia Rykiel** for men's and women's designer wear; **Ana Izax,** a gallery specializing in primitive art as well as contemporary pieces by Warhol and others; and **Arlene Altman** for one-of-a-kind pieces of jewelry—pricey but very beautiful. **Boulemiche** (corner of Rodeo and Little Santa Monica) carries very appealing womenswear and designer jeans; **Ixi:z** (474 North Rodeo) features extremely fashion-forward clothes for men—both shops have realistic, yes-you-can-buy-it prices. Finally, there's that uniquely L.A. nirvana, **Bijan,** where $700 shirts and $13,000 fur coats are sold by appointment only. Around the corner on Wilshire Boulevard, you can browse through the classic department stores such as **Saks, I. Magnin,** and **Neiman-Marcus.**

When shopping on Rodeo Drive, bring plenty of quarters to feed the meters at the municipal parking lots—they're generally your best, cheapest bet for stationing your car.

Then dress up in your tightest jeans, tallest boots, and pinkest hair and head on over to **Melrose Avenue** in West L.A.. The stretch running between Doheny Drive and Highland Avenue has become L.A.'s newest hot spot. Check out **Harvey's Tropical Sun Rattan** (7365-67 Melrose), **Off the Wall** (7325 Melrose), and **Art Deco L.A.** (7300 Melrose) for antiques and off-beat collectibles. You might walk off with anything from a barbershop chair to your very own Coke machine. **Hollywood Neon** (7456 Melrose) features original neon designs. At **Cottura** (7215 Melrose), you'll discover fabulous hand-painted ceramics from Italy and Southern Europe.

For very elegant, sophisticated clothes for men and women, browse at **Ecru** (7428 Melrose), a favorite of stars such as Amy Irving, Jodie Foster, Richard Dreyfus, and Corbin Bernsen. You'll find more classics for women at **Kanji** (7320½ Melrose), and skin-tight, outrageous soap opera–star type of wear at **Neo80** (7356½ Melrose). Want to get real close to your favorite celebrity? **A Star Is Worn** (7303 Melrose) carries clothes and costumes worn by luminaries such as Cher, Joan Collins, and Catherine Oxenberg. Looking for souvenir T-shirts? **Vacationville** (7372 Melrose) carries designs ranging from the camp to the downright weird.

Not far away from the Melrose scene, browse through **Beverly Center** at 8500 Beverly Blvd. The gigantic reddish-colored building with the pink-and-purple stripes houses **Bullock's** and **The Broadway** department stores, designer boutiques, specialty food stores, and 14 movie theaters. At street level, you'll find the West Coast branch of the **Hard Rock Café,** which is practically always packed. Finally, you may be wondering what that blue glass building at the corner of San Vicente and Melrose is. The answer: the **Pacific Design Center,** a/k/a the "Blue Whale." Most

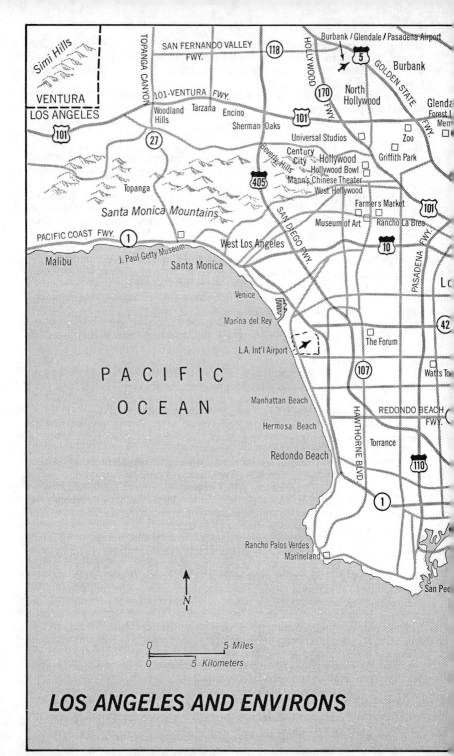

LOS ANGELES AND ENVIRONS

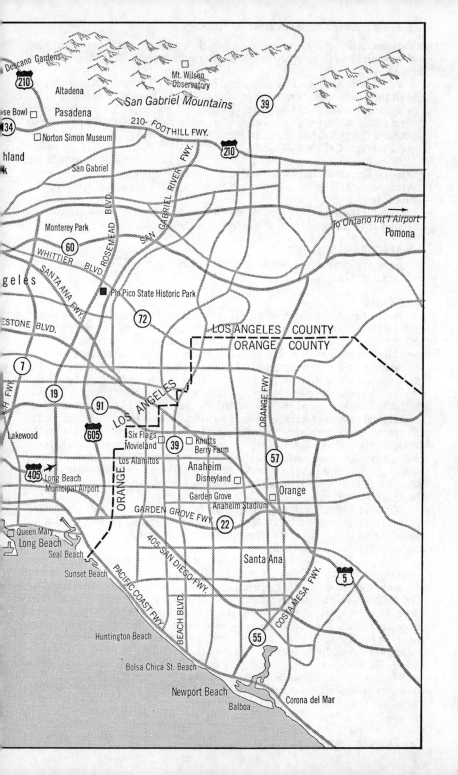

of the interior design showrooms are open to the trade only, but if you are working with a decorator to furnish your new home, he or she can probably arrange an intro- duction.

While mainstreamers have discovered Melrose in full force, trend-surfers have moved their supersonic tastes over to nearby **La Brea Avenue.** Everything old is new again at the **American Rag Cie.** (150 South La Brea), L.A.'s hottest vintage clothing store. La Brea is also the center of the avant-garde art scene at galleries such as **Richard/Bennett** (830 North La Brea), **Richard Green** (834 North La Brea), and the **Wenger Gallery** (828 North La Brea).

If your tastes run toward the more pragmatic, i.e., something to wear to the beach or office, you'll find a whole string of appealing boutiques along Main Street in Santa Monica. Favorites include **Motto** for him (2908 Main) and **Jerico** for her (2804 Main).

If you're really into shopping, check out *The Serious Shopper's Guide to Los Angeles* (Prentice Hall Press, New York) for further information.

ROMANTIC INTERLUDES

From star gazing to fine art, beaches to horse racing, you'll find plenty of thrills and excitement in L.A.

Star Tours

Scrape the phoney tinsel off Hollywood and you'll find the real tinsel under- neath, pianist Oscar Levant said. To most visitors, Los Angeles means a chance to visit the scene of the dream, the heart of the motion picture and television indus- tries. Here are some ways for you to make the most of your time in Tinsel Town.

Mann's Chinese Theatre, 6925 Hollywood Blvd. (tel. 213/464-8111). For many years, some of the most glamorous movie openings took place at Grauman's Chinese Theatre (now called Mann's). From the time of the first premiere (Cecil B. deMille's *King of Kings* in 1927) it became the tradition for Hollywood celebrities to leave their footprints sealed in concrete in the courtyard. Here you can gaze at the signatures and footprints of luminaries such as Marilyn Monroe, Judy Garland— 169 at latest count. Some left an even more personal impression: Al Jolson left knee prints, John Barrymore stamped in his profile, and Betty Grable registered her fa- mous legs. And be on the lookout for the new, $300-million **Hollywood Prome- nade,** a major retail, entertainment, hotel, and office complex slated to open next to the theater in 1991.

Walk of Fame, Hollywood Boulevard between Sycamore and Gower, and Vine between Sunset and Yucca. Right near Mann's Chinese Theatre, stroll along the sidewalks inlaid with more than 1,500 stars representing celebrities from the worlds of film, radio, television, and music.

Set in the Hollywood Hills on the slopes of Mount Lee, the **Hollywood sign** is looking good these days, after a recent refurbishment.

Universal Studios, 100 Universal City Plaza, Universal City, CA 91608 (tel. 818/777-3794), is located on the Hollywood Freeway at Lankershim or Cahuenga. Get behind the scenes at this working movie studio, where classic films have been made since 1915. The 5½-hour tour includes a tram ride through the famous back lot and a visit to the Entertainment Center, where you'll be treated to five action- packed live shows. In the back lot, you'll see the sets for movies such as *Back to the Future, The Sting,* and *Earthquake.* For the biggest highlights, you'll enter the amaz- ing world of special effects, featuring a shark attack by the great white of *Jaws.* Then get set to quake, rattle, and roll at "Earthquake—The Big One," which simulates the effects of a tremblor measuring 8.3 on the Richter Scale. The lights go out; a massive beam splinters, "trapping" the tram; the earth buckles, sending a flood of 60,000 gallons of water toward the tram . . . it happens 200 times a day at the stu- dio. Other new attractions at Universal include "Streets of the World," a 4.5-acre shooting set; and "Star Trek Adventure," certain to delight trekkies. Open summer and holidays, 8:30 a.m. to 5 p.m.; winters, 10 a.m. to 3:30 p.m. on weekdays and 9:30 a.m. to 3:30 p.m. on weekends. Admission is $18.75 per person.

NBC Television Studio Tour, 3000 West Alameda Ave., Burbank, CA 91523 (tel. 818/840-3537). Originally designed to show visiting VIPs how TV programs were made, the network now opens the studios to the public on a 75-minute walking tour. This is truly a backstage visit: What you see depends on what exactly is in production that day. You'll view set construction, wardrobe, dressing rooms, the KNBC News Studio, and the set of *The Tonight Show.* New for visitors—a special-effects set, where you might be chosen to fly like Superman over the L.A. skyline. Tours depart at regular intervals all day. Weekdays: 8:30 a.m. to 4 p.m. Saturdays: 10 a.m. to 4 p.m. Sundays: 10 a.m. to 2 p.m. Closed Easter, Thanksgiving, Christmas Day, New Year's Day. Admission is $6.75.

Live TV show tapings. If you'd like to watch a taping of a live network TV show, you can pick up free tickets daily at various locations. The best-known program is that run by **NBC,** 3000 West Alameda Ave., Burbank, CA 91523, tel. 818/840-3537. The ticket counter is open Monday through Friday, 8:30 a.m. to 5 p.m.; Saturday and Sunday, 9:30 a.m. to 4 p.m. If you're interested in tickets to *The Tonight Show,* these are available only on the date of the show and are limited to two tickets per person. Seating for all shows is on a first-come, first-served basis. Broadcast tickets (including *The Tonight Show*) can also be obtained by mail at the above address. Include the name of the show, number of tickets, date desired, and be sure to enclose a stamped, self-addressed envelope.

Other free tickets to TV tapings are also available. If you are interested in seeing a particular show, the studios recommend calling ahead to be assured of schedules and ticket availability. You can obtain tickets through: **ABC-TV,** 4151 Prospect Ave., Hollywood, CA 90027 (tel. 213/557-4396); ticket window open Monday through Friday, 9 a.m. to 5 p.m. **CBS-TV,** 7800 Beverly Blvd., Los Angeles, CA 90036 (tel. 213/852-4002); ticket window open Monday through Friday, 9 a.m. to 5 p.m.; Saturday and Sunday, 10 a.m. to 5 p.m. **Paramount TV Audience Shows,** 860 North Gower, Hollywood, CA 90038 (tel. 213/468-5575); tickets available at the Paramount Visitor Center Monday through Friday, 10 a.m. to 4 p.m. You can also get tickets for major shows through **Audience Associates,** 1680 Vine St. at Hollywood Boulevard, Hollywood, CA 90028 (tel. 213/467-4697); **Audiences Unlimited** at Fox TV Center, 5746 Sunset Blvd. (tel. 818/506-0043); and at the **Greater Los Angeles Visitors Bureau's Information Centers** located in Hollywood and Downtown.

Movie stars' homes. At various L.A. bookstores and from miscellaneous entrepreneurs hawking their wares from the back of 1967 station wagons, you can pick up a $6 map of where different movie stars live or once lived. Although you probably won't run into Ann-Margret mowing the front lawn, it's a fun way to drive through some of the posh neighborhoods, such as Beverly Hills, Bel Air, and Brentwood. Some of the best routes for eyeballing the palatial real estate: Beverly Drive through Beverly Hills (this is the road with all the palm trees that you see in movies such as *Beverly Hills Cop*), Stone Canyon Road in Bel Air, and Mulholland through Hollywood.

Hollywood on Location, 8644 Wilshire Blvd., Beverly Hills, CA (tel. 213/659-9165). Lights, action, camera! If you really want to see the stars, this may be your best bet in town. Every weekday morning at 9:30 a.m., Hollywood on Location releases a list telling you where movie and TV crews are filming that day—and night. For $30, you get a list of locations and a very detailed map pinpointing each location. The location list contains the name of each TV series and movie filming that day, the stars in it, gives the exact address and location, and also describes the scheduled type of filming, stunts, and special effects you might see. On most days, you'll have a roster of more than 40 different locations, practically always within ten miles of the Hollywood on Location office in Beverly Hills. You make up your own schedule based on the productions you most want to watch.

Go to the Beach

You'll have fun, fun, fun if you spend the day frolicking on one of the fine Southern California **beaches.**

Once known as the Gold Coast, **Santa Monica** was the first great L.A. beach. The area has undergone a sizable renaissance recently and is once again a fashionable residential and resort area. In addition to playing some beach blanket bingo down on the sand, stroll down the landmark Santa Monica pier (tel. 213/458-8900), originally built in 1909. Its most beloved attraction is the colorful carousel, original-ly built in 1922, with its brightly painted horses and glittery mirrors. Exhibits trace the history of the pier, and there are also some marvelous pre–video-era amusement games for 25¢, such as the Iron Claw, Estrella's Prophesies, and a Personality Tester. When you get the munchies, you can buy walkaway shrimp or crab cocktails on the pier, about $3 each. To our mind, much of the appeal of Santa Monica comes from the broad, palm-lined park that runs along the cliff above the beach, a green prome-nade that recalls the boulevards that line the waterfront in Cannes and Nice. A per-fect spot for strolling, roller skating, picnicking, and sunset watching.

Malibu isn't just one beach, but rather is a 27-mile-long stretch of sands edging the Pacific north of Santa Monica. It is best known as Hollywood-by-the-sea, a popu-lar residential area for celebrities such as Barbra Streisand, Johnny Carson, Sissy Spacek, Warren Beatty, and Goldie Hawn. Although the rich and famous generally keep to their own hot tubs behind the gates, the beach (and bathing-suit-clad bodies) make the trip well worthwhile. Check out the section known as Surfrider Beach, just north of Malibu Pier, said to be the original Beach Boys' hangout. The waves attract some of the best surfers.

Well, you just know **Venice** has to be a bit off the wall, since its original develop-er, Abbot Kinney, originally envisioned turning this area of marshy tidal flats into a second Venice, Italy, complete with singing gondoliers. The canal-cum-lagoon idea never quite took hold—but then, with Venice, you'll never know. It still might. Venice has long been a refuge for Southern California bohemia—from Alan Gins-berg and Jack Kerouac in the 1950s to Janis Joplin in the early 1970s. Among its major contributions to humankind have been the Frisbee, the skateboard, and the resurrection of roller skates. Today, Main Street, U.S.A., it decidedly ain't. Part ba-zaar, part bizarre, the waterfront sidewalk is lined with hawkers and gawkers, cruis-ing bodybuilders in full flex, musicians, sword swallowers, fortune-tellers, and broken-bottle jumpers. You can buy a watch for $1.99, or sunglasses for $3.99. To blend in with the crowd, you can rent roller skates ($3.50 per hour) or bikes ($4 per hour) from one of the shacks at the beach. You might see a swami on roller skates, or a beachboy on a skateboard, being towed by his mastiff. Oh yes, by the way, there's also a beach. Note: Although somewhat outlandish, Venice is safe by day. At night, things get a bit raunchy, so shove off before sunset.

The most popular strand for Valley Girls and their sun-bleached-blond surfer boyfriends is **Zuma Beach,** north of Santa Monica. **Manhattan Beach** is young and sporty, attracting surfers, joggers, bicycle riders, and volleyball players. **Hermosa Beach,** just south, is fairly similar, with a tad more locals (it's hard to find a parking spot). **Redondo Beach,** south of Hermosa, is where California surfing first made its debut in 1907, and is known as the best winter-surfing spot.

The Museums

Perhaps the biggest happening on the cultural front has been the emergence of L.A. as a formidable power in the art world, with several area **museums** making major acquisitions and undertaking expansions.

The **J. Paul Getty Museum,** 17985 Pacific Coast Hwy., Malibu (tel. 213/458-2003), occupies ten acres of the 65-acre Getty estate in fashionable Malibu. It is generally considered to be the richest museum in the world, with an endowment of over $2.3 billion. The setting is grand enough. Getty designed his museum after a second-century Roman palazzo, complete with colonnaded walkways, pools, and fountains. The first floor of the museum houses an extraordinary collection of Greek and Roman art. On the second floor, you'll find works by Rembrandt, Cézanne, Van Dyck, Goya, and others. Since the museum must spend $100 million a year, you can count on finding new treasures sporting the "recent acquisition" tag by the time you visit. The museum is open Tuesday through Sunday, 10 a.m. to 5 p.m. Admission and parking are free. However, the quirky feature is that you must call in advance to reserve a parking space: absolutely no "drive-ins" are permitted.

The **Museum of Contemporary Art (MOCA),** 250 South Grand Ave. at California Plaza, Downtown L.A. (tel. 213/626-6222). The splendidly designed building by Japanese architect Arata Isozaki only opened in December 1986, and it has become one of the most talked-about museums in the world. Outside, the museum is breathtaking, faced with rough-cut sandstone and composed of carefully arranged geometric shapes, with arches and pyramids. Inside, the wide-open, white-painted galleries with their light-wood floors provide the perfect setting for works by Robert Rauschenberg, Claes Oldenburg, Louise Nevelson, and Eric Fischl. Open Tuesday to Sunday, 11 a.m. to 6 p.m. (to 8 p.m. on Thursday and Friday). Closed Thanksgiving, Christmas, and New Year's Day. Admission is $4.50 per person.

The **Temporary Contemporary,** 152 North Central Ave., Los Angeles (tel. 213/626-6222). This cavernous police warehouse in Little Japan served as the temporary home for MOCA until it moved into its permanent home in late 1986; the locale proved so popular that the Temporary Contemporary will continue to be a museum in its own right, spotlighting the latest innovations in postmodern art. Open Tuesday to Sunday, 11 a.m. to 6 p.m. (to 8 p.m. on Thursday and Friday). Closed Thanksgiving, Christmas, and New Year's Day. Admission is $4.50 per person.

Los Angeles County Museum of Art, 5905 Wilshire Blvd., Los Angeles (tel. 213/857-6000). With the opening of the exuberant, art deco–design Robert O. Anderson Building, LACMA has gained new vitality and is attracting interesting special exhibitions. Permanent installations include pre-Columbian, Far Eastern, American, and European art. Open Tuesday through Friday, 10 a.m. to 5 p.m.; Saturday and Sunday, 10 a.m. to 6 p.m. Closed Monday and most holidays.

Gene Autry Western Heritage Museum, Griffith Park, 4700 Zoo Dr., Los Angeles (tel. 213/460-5698). This new, $25-million museum focuses on the history of the American West, from the early forays of the Spanish conquistadors through the present day. Costumes, paintings, firearms, historic documents, and more are on display. Located immediately adjacent to the Greater Los Angeles Zoo.

Two new museums of interest are scheduled to open in 1990. The **Armand Hammer Museum of Art and Cultural Center,** in the Westwood section of Los Angeles, will house a $250-million art collection. The **J. Paul Getty Center,** occupying a panoramic 110-acre hilltop site in West L.A., will provide permanent facilities for the Center for the History of Art and the Humanities, the Conservation Institute, as well as a new museum building.

Back to Nature

Despite all this talk of celluloid fantasies, you should remember that Los Angeles features natural attractions as well. For a whale of a good time, head off on a whale-watching expedition. Each year from December through March, gray whales head along the coast of California to their mating and calving waters in the Sea of Cortés in Mexico. On their journey they pass through the Catalina Channel, which provides an excellent observation point for viewing these 40-ton "gentle giants." Whale-watching cruises led by a trained naturalist are sponsored by the Cabrillo Museum and the American Cetacean Society of Los Angeles. For details, contact **Cabrillo Museum,** 3720 Stephen White Dr., San Pedro, CA 90731 (tel. 213/548-

7562), or the **San Pedro Peninsula Chamber of Commerce,** Box 167, San Pedro, CA 90733 (tel. 213/832-7272).

Or escape to an island for the day—Catalina Island, that is. Measuring only 22 miles long, 8 miles wide, Catalina offers complete recreational facilities ranging from horseback riding to golf. Much of the land is virtually unspoiled. The island is only 90 minutes away via the sleek vessels of **Catalina Express,** Berth 95, P.O. Box 1391, San Pedro, CA 90733 (tel. 213/519-1212). The round-trip ride is $30 per person.

Other Attractions

Disneyland, 1313 South Harbor Blvd., P.O. Box 3232, Anaheim (tel. 714/999-4000). Mickey, Minnie, and all your favorite Disney characters are waiting to greet you at this magical land filled with fantasy and adventure. Attractions include the new Splash Mountain, a half-mile-long journey in a hollowed-out log boat that takes you through backwoods swamps and hurtles down the world's longest flume drop. The ride features more than 100 different animated characters. At Space Mountain in Tomorrowland, climb aboard a thrilling roller-coaster ride that seems to hurl you through outer space. See if the spirits move you in the Haunted Mansion. And even if you'd sooner buckle than swash, you'll be yo-ho-hoing with the best of the buccaneers at Pirates of the Caribbean. Disneyland is open daily: weekdays, 9:30 a.m. to 7 p.m.; Saturday, 8:30 a.m. to midnight; Sunday, 9 a.m. to midnight. Admission is $22 per person. Anaheim is about a 45-minute drive south of L.A.

The Hollywood Bowl, a shell in the Hollywood Hills, is the summer home of the Los Angeles Philharmonic, and also hosts a summer concert series. For a schedule of concert dates, call 213/850-2000.

Whatever your favorite **sport,** you can probably find top-flight events in Los Angeles. Baseball fans should check out the schedule at Dodger Stadium (tel. 213/224-1500). The gigantic Forum sports arena in Inglewood is home to the Los Angeles Lakers basketball team and L.A. Kings hockey team (tel. 213/673-1300 for ticket information). The Coliseum, which hosted the track and field events for the 1984 Olympics, is where the Los Angeles Raiders football team plays (tel. 213/322-5901). And you can see the sport of kings at its finest at Santa Anita Park in Arcadia (racing late December through mid-April, October to November; tel. 818/574-7223) or at Hollywood Park (racing late April to mid-July, mid-November to late December; tel. 213/419-1500).

HONEYMOON HOTELS AND HIDEAWAYS

It is only fitting that the movie capital of the world would dream up some of the most captivating accommodations imaginable. But like everything else in L.A., romance has its price. Do not expect anything smacking of seductive ambience for under $70 per couple per night. Since L.A. is so spread out, your biggest decision in choosing a hotel should be location: Where do you envision spending most of your time? Beverly Hills and West Hollywood are centrally located both to downtown and Burbank—and provide the most recognizable L.A. addresses, the places where Rolls-Royces purr curbside, hopefuls have themselves paged by the pool, and moguls cut deals in penthouse suites. Westwood attracts L.A.'s young guard of actors and rock stars, as well as an arty and literary crowd that gathers around U.C.L.A. (it also has great movie theaters, a neighborhood feeling, and real sidewalks where you can stroll). Probably because it's right at the beach, Santa Monica has a more relaxed, laid-back feeling. You might be able to watch the sunset from your window, then stroll along the main street, where many of L.A.'s hottest new restaurants are located.

One other eccentricity of L.A. lodging nomenclature should be noted: the "bungalow." This resembles nothing you might have inhabited at summer camp. Just as Marie Antoinette enjoyed playing a shepherdess at the Trianon in Versailles,

Hollywood's royalty has a fondness for retreating into pastoral splendor in these elegant minimanses and villas found at several of Beverly Hills' swankiest hotels. If you want to splurge, you've come to the right place.

Unless indicated, none of the following hotels have honeymoon packages. Rates quoted are per couple per night.

For honeymooners on a tight budget, your best bet is one of the clean and dependable inns and motels in downtown L.A., especially the very good Best Western properties: **The Best Western Dragon Gate Inn,** 818 N. Hill St., Los Angeles, CA 90012 (tel. 213/617-3077), and **Best Western Hollywood,** 6141 Franklin Ave., Hollywood, CA 90028 (tel. 464-5181), or toll free 800/528-1234. Rates run about $60 per couple per night.

Very Expensive

Hotel Bel-Air, 701 Stone Canyon Rd., Los Angeles, CA 90077 (tel. 213/472-1211). The setting is enchanted. Swans glide and preen in the lagoon, backdropped by the blush-pink Spanish mission–style buildings with the red-tile roofs. Long corridors lined with archways wind through gardens where the dominant color is pink: primroses, hibiscus, azaleas, magnolias, roses, impatiens. The lemon trees sprout absolutely massive fruits. In the distance, rugged mountains seem to cup the palm trees, the fountains, the porticos, the pools, setting you off from the rest of the world. Incredibly, this secluded Shangri-la is only one mile from Rodeo Drive in Bel-Air, probably the most exclusive residential enclave in Los Angeles.

After a $6-million refurbishment under the knowledgeable eye of Caroline Hunt Schoellkopf, whose Rosewood Hotels bought the property for $23 million in 1983, the Bel-Air radiates the savoir faire of a truly great hotel. Rosewood kept the best of the old Bel-Air—the personalized service and attention to detail—and completely renovated the hotel rooms and bungalows. Each of the 92 rooms is different. Many are done in ice-cream pastels: pistachio, strawberry, lemon, peach. Appointments might include marble sinks, gold-tone faucets, Mexican-tile floors, dhurrie rugs. Even the least expensive room has its own private terrace, screened from view by cascades of flowers. You'll enjoy complete seclusion: The property meanders over 11 park-like acres with splashing fountains, a gazebo, and a luxuriant green backdrop of ferns, palms, California sycamores, and live oaks. The restaurant has also been redone in French country style, in shades of pink and beige, and the California-style cuisine is excellent. In nice weather, tables are set up on the terrace overlooking Swan Lake. The hotel's oval swimming pool is heated year-round, and the concierge can arrange for tennis, golf, and other sports activities. A 3:1 staff-guest ratio assures that your wish is—truly—their command. Rates (EP): $250 to $395 per couple per night for rooms; $425 to $1,430 per couple per night for suites.

Regent Beverly Wilshire, 9500 Wilshire Blvd., Beverly Hills, CA 90212 (tel. 213/275-5200; reservations: toll free 800/545-4000 nationwide). Warren Beatty lived here for a while. Paul Newman and Joanne Woodward like one of the suites. When you check into this hotel, you aren't just getting a place to stay—you're living a legend. Part of the prestigious Regent Hotel chain, the Beverly Wilshire would merit star billing just for its location, right at the intersection of Wilshire Boulevard and Rodeo Drive.

Originally built in 1927, the hotel looks in tip-top shape after a $65-million renovation of its Wilshire Wing, which is earning oohs and aahs from *tout* Hollywood. The spacious lobby is once more a place for grand entrances, with its restored bronze and crystal chandelier, mahogany-and-ebony front desk, marble floors and columns. The accommodations have been entirely rebuilt and refurnished—70 rooms were eliminated for the sake of added amenities. In a concept borrowed from the Regent's luxurious hotel in Hong Kong, there's a steward posted on every floor to handle requests. Instead of awkward "Do Not Disturb" signs, each room has an illuminated "Privacy" button. The accommodations themselves are spectacular, done up in tones of wheat, peach, rose, and celery. Special double-glazed windows keep out the sounds of rush hour on Wilshire Boulevard. Best of all are the huge all-new bathrooms (another Regent hallmark worldwide), lined in what seems like acres of beige marble, with a deep soaking tub, separate glass-enclosed shower, plus mini-TV so that you don't have to miss a moment of the morning news while you perform your ablutions. In addition to plush bathrobes and hairdryers, amenities include a teak shoehorn, a leather-handled clothes brush, a loofah scrub. The Wilshire Wing has also been enhanced by a new dining room, lobby lounge (where there's live jazz every afternoon), and corner café (serving ice-cream sodas and sundaes—the plate-glass windows are perfect for ogling the gleaming cars passing on Wilshire). Meanwhile, sleeping accommodations of the hotel's Beverly Wing are currently undergoing the same impeccable renovation. Three other hotel features should be mentioned: the palazzo-type Don Quixote pool, where handpainted Mexican tiles recount the tale of Cervantes' knight-errant; the masseur; and the health spa. "Romantic Interlude" honeymoon package: Three days, two nights (BP): $500 per couple. Includes luxurious suite, breakfast in bed daily, a bottle of chilled champagne with fresh strawberries (replenished each day), complimentary valet parking, complimentary use of sauna and swimming pool, fresh flowers and a box of "sweets" in your room. Available for Friday and Saturday arrival. Regular rates: $300 per couple per night for a deluxe room; $440 to $550 for a one-bedroom suite.

When celebrities want to get away—in the best of circles—they head over to the landmark **Beverly Hills Hotel,** 9641 Sunset Blvd., Beverly Hills, CA 90210 (tel. 213/278-1487 or 213/276-2251), built in 1912, affectionately known as the "Pink Palace." Set on a 16-acre enclave right in the heart of Beverly Hills, the hotel has the secluded feel of a country resort. Thanks to the park-like setting, you'll enjoy many sports right on the property. And the Beverly Hills pool is famous as an out-door conference room, a place where agents and producers often must wipe suntan oil off their palms before shaking hands on a deal.

The guest register includes Clark Gable and Carole Lombard, F. Scott Fitzger-ald, Marilyn Monroe—and, more recently, Eddie Murphy, Debra Winger, Lee Iacocca, and Mike Wallace. Michael J. Fox held his wedding reception here. You might run into Martin Scorcese being interviewed by cable TV in the dining room, or Paloma Picasso doing a photo shoot in the garden.

The hotel's current owners are primping, painting, and renovating, to embel-lish the ample proportions and gracious details of this 75-year-old hotel. Many ac-commodations have fireplaces, private patios, terraces, and kitchens; all now have fully stocked bars. The most attention is being lavished on the private "bungalows," more like private homes. No. 5, for example, has been exquisitely redone, with its black-and-white marble foyer, oak-mantle fireplace, dining room table that seats eight, and hand-painted Mexican tile stairway. (It's a favorite of Liz Taylor, who stayed here with all her husbands except the first, Nicky Hilton, who preferred to check in at one of his family's hotels.) During the ongoing remodeling of the hotel, however, the quality of the rest of the rooms is very uneven; you or your travel agent should check very carefully that you will be given refurbished quarters. The restora-tion and refurbishment notwithstanding, the Beverly Hills traditions are being pre-served: The corridors in the main hotel will still be lined with the flamboyant palm-frond wallpaper, and a welcoming fire always blazes in the lobby hearth. Standard rooms (EP): $237 to $335 per couple per night. Suites (EP): $410 to $3,500 per couple per night.

Expensive

If the Beverly Hills Hotel is the bastion of Los Angeles' old guard, the **Westwood Marquis Hotel and Gardens,** 930 Hilgard Ave., Los Angeles, CA 90024 (tel. 213/208-8765; reservations: toll free 800/421-2317 nationwide), is the gathering place par excellence for the new crew of celebrities: superstars such as Whitney Houston, Dustin Hoffman, Tom Cruise, Jimmy Connors, and Jack

Nicklaus. As the name implies, the 15-story hotel is located in the highly fashionable Westwood area, a stone's throw from Beverly Hills, Bel-Air, and Century City. This is an all-suite hotel in the grand European tradition, intimately scaled and opulently decorated with fine marble, Oriental rugs, tapestries, oil paintings, huge vases filled with spectacular floral displays, and an eclectic assemblage of objets d'art. If you arrive during afternoon high tea, you'll be greeted with the relaxing sounds of softly tinkling harp music.

Individually decorated, each of the 256 suites is sophisticated and plush, with different accent pieces and colors: peach, champagne, and sea-foam green. Often, you'll find chinoiserie: bamboo-backed chairs, Chinese vase lamps, lacquer cabinets and chests. If you're preparing for a big night on the town, the bathroom has plenty of mirrors, as well as a separate makeup vanity. We counted three phones in our suite (including one in the bathroom), handy for accepting calls from agents and producers. Each suite has a separate dining area, so a room service breakfast can be enjoyed in leisurely comfort.

A special pride of the hotel is the beautiful garden leading to the pool area. The hotel has full health spa facilities, with separate men's and women's saunas, steam rooms, and treatment centers with hydrotherapy, massages, and facials. Both the Dynasty Room and Garden Terrace restaurants are excellent. And the ultimate luxury: The hotel offers complimentary limousine service to surrounding areas, including Rodeo Drive. The Westwood Marquis has attractive weekend packages, for Friday or Saturday arrival for one or two nights. One-bedroom suite (BP): $210 per couple per night. Includes full American breakfast, bottle of California champagne, complimentary valet parking, and late checkout. Regular rates for a suite are $240 to $360 per couple per night.

Four Seasons Hotel, 300 South Doheny Dr. at Burton Way, Los Angeles, CA 90048 (tel. 213/273-2222; reservations: toll free 800/332-3442). L.A.'s newest star isn't appearing on the silver screen or a weekly TV series. Instead, it's an elegantly lavish, understated yet drop-dead gorgeous new hotel that is wowing the Hollywood glitterati. In the lobby area, Empire-style furniture perfectly complements the intricately inlaid marble floors. European antiques mingle with American contemporary art. Although the Four Seasons is a grand hotel in the majestic and luxurious sense, it is intimately scaled. Public areas are divided into smaller chambers, giving a feeling of gracious warmth. The hotel's owners are also in the floral and landscaping businesses, and they take particular pride in the elaborate five-foot-tall displays that blossom in bowls and vases throughout the property. Out of doors, the Wetherly Gardens flourish with a formal finesse reminiscent of Versailles. All this just one block from Beverly Hills.

Architecturally, the hotel resembles a sleek 16-story château. Each room has tall French doors opening onto a small railed terrace. Fine touches abound—marble-topped desks and nightstands, cabinets veneered with exotic woods, piles of throw pillows on the sofas, thick terry robes awaiting in the marble bathroom (which also has a small color TV). The minibar in each room stocks only top-of-the-line brands: Absolut vodka, Chivas scotch, Toblerone chocolates. Decor ranges from floral-accented traditional to striking lacquer contemporary. There's 24-hour-a-day room service—as well as pressing and seamstress service. Sporting types can take advantage of the beautiful pool area surrounded by palm trees, with exercise equipment nearby for al fresco workouts. Tennis club privileges can be arranged. Service anticipates guests' needs, with a concierge to handle special arrangements, as well as complimentary limousine service to Rodeo Drive. Right in the hotel, you can savor three fine restaurants, including Gardens for gourmet cuisine. Though there is no honeymoon package, the weekend "Beverly Hills" package (usually available Friday, Saturday, and Sunday nights) would appeal to newlyweds. It includes superior accommodations, chilled bottle of champagne, fresh-cut flower bouquet, full breakfast, complimentary valet parking: $200 per couple for the first night; $150 per couple for each extra night. Regular room rates: $265 to $390 per couple per night.

Sunset Marquis Hotel and Villas, 1200 North Alta Loma Rd., Los Angeles, CA 90069 (tel. 213/657-1333; reservations: toll free 800/692-2140 nationwide; 800/858-9758 in California). The lettering on the entrance canopy is so discrete, you might drive by without noticing that the hotel is there. And that's the way the friendly, low-key management and the illustrious celebrity clientele prefer things at the Sunset Marquis Hotel and Villas. With its oh-so-choice West Hollywood location, the hotel attracts a hip crowd, especially movers and shakers in the music industry. Bookstall racks feature *Harpers, Queen, Variety,* and *Billboard.* Gold records hang over the bar, a tribute from rock 'n' rollers who call this place home when they're in L.A.: Phil Collins, Genesis, Cyndi Lauper, Whitney Houston. At the outdoor café and pool areas, moguls gather to close deals as well as catch some rays. Underscoring its close association with the entertainment field, the hotel recently added a $750,000 recording studio to its facilities. Why do the big names choose the Sunset Marquis? In part, because they enjoy the hotel's luxurious yet unstuffy outlook. It's also due to the superb service, including a concierge at your beck and call 24 hours a day. But much of the appeal also comes from the property's oasis-like setting on six verdant acres complete with emerald-green lawns, palm trees, terraced flower beds, exotic parrots chirping in cages, plus tables tucked here and there for an impromptu picnic.

All the accommodations are one- and two-bedroom suites, furnished in California Modern elegance and plush with features such as wet bars or kitchens, remote-control color cable TVs, and VCRs upon request. If you want to splurge, consider one of the one-bedroom Mediterranean villas with all the comforts of home—and then some. No. 1 North, for example, has a refrigerator for chilling the Dom Pérignon, glass-block windows for privacy, and a deep whirlpool tub for two ($410 per night). Another villa even comes with its own baby grand piano ($495 per night). Private parking and butler service are available. Rates: $190 to $300 per couple per night for one-bedroom suites; $355 to $415 per night for junior villas; $495 to $575 per night for one-bedroom villas.

L'Ermitage Hotels (reservations: toll free 800/424-4443). Luxurious . . . innovative . . . comfortable . . . It's hard to decide how to begin any description of these seven elegant Los Angeles hotels founded by the Ashkenazy brothers, Arnold and Severyn. Instead of feeling as if you're lodging in a hotel, you'll feel much more as if you're staying in a posh apartment lent you by friends—that is, if your friends have the taste and the megabucks to buy superb original art by the likes of Renoir, Utrillo, Chagall, and Van Gogh. The hotels are situated in all the best neighborhoods, such as Beverly Hills and West Hollywood. Although none has a honeymoon package, the weekend packages offer exceptionally good values. Each property also offers guests free limousine service in the immediate neighborhood. Here's a rundown on the collection:

L'Ermitage Hotel, 9291 Burton Way, Beverly Hills, CA 90210 (tel. 213/278-3344), well merits its "Hotel de grande classe" designation. You'll find every conceivable pampering amenity: 24-hour room service; gilt-framed original oil paintings from the English, French, Dutch, and Russian schools; a private bar where complimentary caviar and pâté are served each evening; and even someone to help you pack or unpack, upon request. You'll have fresh flowers in your room, and chocolates and cordials by your pillow each night. The hotel is situated in a tranquil residential section of Beverly Hills; rooms face either tree-lined Burton Way or the Hollywood Hills. The lobby resembles an elegant French country inn, a motif that is carried out in the furnishings of the various suites, each of which has a fireplace. One of the hotel's biggest attractions is the multileveled rooftop garden, with swimming pool, mineral-water whirlpool, and huge trees in planters. At night the entire deck is illuminated with hundreds of tiny white lights. There's also the very elegant Café Russe, reserved exclusively for hotel guests. The personal service is legendary here, and the staff takes special pride in fulfilling requests. Like the time the Very Famous Celebrity asked to have a Very Expensive diamond bracelet delivered to his girlfriend on a tray of caviar . . . Weekend package: Three days/two nights (CP): $495 per couple. Includes continental breakfast, fruit basket, and complimentary parking. Regular rates: From $280 per couple per night for an executive suite.

Nestled between West Hollywood and Beverly Hills, the **Bel Age Hotel,** 1020 N. San Vicente Blvd., West Hollywood, CA 90069 (tel. 213/854-1111), pays homage to la Belle Époque—the splendid early years of the 20th century. The lobby is graciously French, with tall potted palms, Oriental carpets, and light-wood paneling. Each suite features hand-carved furniture, gilt-framed paintings, a private terrace with views of the Hollywood Hills, Los Angeles, or Beverly Hills, and a kitchenette. There's a lovely roof garden with swimming pool and whirlpool spas, and the Bel Age restaurant serves fine Russian cuisine. Because of its intimacy and luxury, the hotel attracts many visiting celebrities. A friend of ours did admit to a twinge of excitement when encountering Michael J. Fox in the restaurant. Weekend package: Three days/two nights (EP): $365 per couple. Includes Sunday brunch, fruit basket, and more. Regular rates: From $275 per couple per night.

Mondrian Hotel, 8440 Sunset Blvd., West Hollywood, CA 90069 (tel. 213/650-8999). Imagine a colorful Mondrian design splashed over the exterior of a white concrete hotel, and you'll get the picture of the very modern, ultra-elegant Mondrian Hotel. You can't beat the Sunset Boulevard location, right at the heart of L.A.'s trendy Sunset Plaza district, near the Pacific Design Center, "restaurant row" on La Cienega Boulevard, and the boutiques of Melrose Avenue. Many celebrities —especially rock musicians—stay here. The 188 rooms use the bright, primary colors that Dutch painter Piet Mondrian was known for; the eye-catching combination of black couches, red lacquer tables, gray carpeting, and original artwork has won the hotel many design awards. Every suite has a kitchenette and a wet bar, and some have extra-deep whirlpool tubs. For breakfast, lunch, and dinner, the Cafe Mondrian serves French-Californian cuisine. The health spa facilities are excellent, with a heated, ground-level swimming pool, exercise machines, men's and women's sauna and steam rooms, and massage rooms. Weekend package: Three days/two nights (EP): $310 per couple. Includes Sunday brunch, fruit basket, and more. Regular rates: From $165 per couple for rooms; from $225 per couple for suites.

Le Dufy, 1000 Westmount Dr., West Hollywood, CA 90069 (tel. 213/657-7400). Soft, Impressionist-painter tones of gray, rose, salmon, and blue; hand-screened bedspreads that could have been designed by Jackson Pollock; a corner fireplace—these are just a few of the ingratiating touches you'll savor at Le Dufy. The lobby is small, but a true knockout, with a lavish use of pink marble, blond-wood furniture, a massive cocktail table incorporating a concrete slab, and brass railings and fixtures to add the right sparkle. The all-suite hotel is a big favorite with movie and record company executives, because of its proximity to the major studios as well as to the fashionable restaurants on La Cienega and the shops on Melrose. The junior suites are compact but beautifully appointed with pastel fabrics, light woods, and original art in soft, rainbow colors. Almost all the junior suites have mirrored ceilings in the bedroom. In addition, guests enjoy a complimentary fruit basket and beverage upon arrival. On the landscaped roof garden, you can swim in the heated pool, soak in the whirlpool spa, or perfect your tan on the sun deck. Weekend package: Three days/two nights (CP): $240 per couple. Includes continental breakfast, parking, and evening turn-down service. Regular rates: From $175 per couple per night.

Le Parc, 733 North West Knoll, West Hollywood, CA 90069 (tel. 213/855-8888), is an especially fitting choice for sports-minded couples. On the rooftop overlooking L.A. and the Hollywood Hills, there's a lighted tennis court surrounded by the flags of the world. Use is free to guests—just sign up. At the rooftop pool area, you might find movie executives taking calls or making deals in the cozy, low-key setting brightened with flowers and citrus trees. There's also a health spa with sauna and exercise equipment. Each of the 154 spacious suites has a fireplace, wet bar, separate dressing area, private balcony, and a VCR; you can choose your evening's entertainment from their library of tapes at a nominal charge. Set on a very quiet residential street in West Hollywood, Le Parc is just one block from La Cienega restaurants and one block from the boutiques and galleries on Melrose Avenue. Weekend package: Three days/two nights (CP): $240 per couple. Includes a fruit basket upon arrival, continental breakfast, and complimentary parking. Regular rates: From $190 per couple per night.

Valadon, 900 Hammond St., West Hollywood, CA 90069 (tel. 213/855-1115). Painted a bright, bubblegum pink, Valadon stands out from its residential neighbors on a quiet tree-lined street in West Hollywood. The lobby is hung with canvasses by Maurice Utrillo, whose mother, Suzanne Valadon, is the namesake of the hotel. Art nouveau touches abound: curvaceous wood moldings in the elevators, swirling trim on corridor mirrors. Your suite features a sunken living room with fireplace, color TV with VCR, small kitchenette, and terrace. Thoughtful touches make you feel right at home—a clock radio with cassette player by the bed, ample portions of shampoo and body lotion provided in the bathroom. To make the hotel a "resort de ville"—a complete retreat—Valadon also features a complete gym, rooftop tennis court (open until 10 p.m.), and very nice heated pool area with sun deck and whirlpool spa facing toward the Hollywood Hills and Beverly Hills. And for exploring the neighborhood, there's a fleet of bicycles. Weekend package: Three days/two nights (CP): $265 per couple. Includes continental breakfast daily, fruit basket, complimentary parking, and more. Regular rates: From $175 per couple per night.

Le Rêve, 8822 Cynthia St., West Hollywood, CA 90069 (tel. 213/657-7400). As its name implies, Le Rêve offers a tranquil, relaxed setting near Sunset Boulevard, Beverly Hills, and the fine shopping on Melrose. The split-level suite features a kitchenette, large bathroom, private balcony, fireplace, and remote-control color TV. The decor is French country in feel, with natural pine furnishings and crisp chintz upholstery. Save some time to relax on the rooftop garden with its heated pool, mineral spa, and wrap-around view of the city. Weekend package: Three days/two nights (CP): $190 per couple. Includes continental breakfast, fruit basket, complimentary parking, and more. Regular rates: From $105 per couple per night.

Loews Santa Monica, 1700 Ocean Ave., Santa Monica, CA 90401 (tel. 213/458-6700; reservations: toll free 800/223-0888). Finally, you can come out and play in L.A. In the land of surfin' safaris and suntan contests, the new Loews Santa Monica is L.A.'s first luxury hotel right on the beach. And a very nice beach, indeed, just two blocks from the famed Santa Monica pier. First impressions mean quite a lot, and the hotel greets guests with artful panache. The pink–and–sea-green facade is in keeping with Santa Monica's fine, art deco residences. The marble-floored lobby is topped off by a five-story glass atrium; huge plate-glass windows let in postcard-perfect views of the ocean. Music from the grand piano in the lounge enhances the seductive mood. In feeling, the place is casual: There's no dress code, and you can walk right from the hotel elevators onto the beach. Rooms enhance the beachside setting, with a color scheme that borrows hues from a Pacific sunset. Accommodations feature bleached-oak furniture, marble-topped dressers, and original works by local California artists on the walls. In the pink-and-gray marble bathrooms, you'll find terry-cloth bathrobes, TVs, hairdryers, and makeup mirrors. Many rooms have ocean views as well as private patios or balconies. In addition to 24-hour room service, guests have their choice of two restaurants: the casual Coast Cafe and the more intimate Riva for Italian seafood specialties. As part of the extensive health club facilities (sauna, steam room, aerobics classes, and massage rooms), there's a heated indoor/outdoor swimming pool domed by a bubble. Down at the beach, you can rent bicycles or skates from the sports pavilion. Tennis and golf privileges can be arranged. Rates: "B, B, & B" package (Bed, Breakfast, and Beach): $125 per couple per night, available for Friday, Saturday, and Sunday nights. Includes room and full breakfast. Regular rates: $192 to $275 per couple per night. Also inquire about new honeymoon packages.

The **Biltmore,** 506 South Grand Ave., Los Angeles, CA 90071 (tel. 213/624-

1011; reservations: toll free 800/421-8000 nationwide; 800/252-0175 in California). This is what a grand hotel is supposed to be. A huge lion-head fountain in the lobby. A three-story-tall arcade surrounding the restaurant. Twelve-foot-high doorways surmounted by carvings representing the angels of Los Angeles. Trompe l'oeil murals of columns and gardens behind the reception desk. It was here that the Oscar was born . . . here that the Beatles, trying to elude frenetic fans during their first U.S. tour, landed on the roof in a helicopter. Returned to its original 1920s grandeur after a $40-million restoration project, the Biltmore is the crown jewel of L.A.'s revitalized Downtown, located near the Museum of Contemporary Art, the L.A. Stock Exchange, the Los Angeles Theatre Center, and burgeoning new clubs and discos. This is indeed *L.A. Law* territory—in fact, many scenes of the popular TV series have been shot here, as well as segments of *Murder, She Wrote* and the films *Beverly Hills Cop* and *The Poseidon Adventure.*

The rooms are spacious (as part of the renovation, the original 1,000 rooms were reconfigured into 700). Amid the urban setting, the accommodations provide a peaceful oasis. A garden of flowers adorns the bedspreads, big mirrors in the bathroom give you plenty of room for primping. The junior suites are really huge, with comfy twin sofas in the sitting area. Each room features a writing desk, color TV discreetly ensconced in an armoire, and pampering amenities tray in the bathroom. In addition to 24-hour room service, you'll find five restaurants and lounges, including Bernard's (for award-winning gourmet cuisine) and the happening Grand Avenue Bar (featuring live jazz Monday through Friday, 5 to 9 p.m.). Best of all, there's the Biltmore Health Club, featuring aerobics classes, Nautilus equipment, and an exuberantly opulent art deco swimming pool that rivals William Randolph Hearst's at San Simeon. Honeymoon package (CP): $179 per couple per night. Includes junior suite, complimentary parking, free use of health club and pool, late check-out, continental breakfast, and champagne upon arrival. The Biltmore's special weekend packages also offer exceptionally good values. For example, the "Renaissance Weekend"—at $85 per couple per night—includes standard accommodations plus complimentary parking and use of the health club and pool.

Ma Maison Sofitel, 8555 Beverly Blvd., Los Angeles, CA 90048 (tel. 213/278-5444; reservations: toll free 800/221-4542). Right at the crossroads of Beverly and La Cienega Boulevards, there's a hotel that's as refreshing as a stay in the French countryside—the Ma Maison Sofitel, which opened in December 1988. The lobby is very grand, with its marble floors and gleaming brass-bannistered stairway. Rooms capture the warmth of Provence, with floral-patterned fabrics, Riviera-hued prints on the wall, and a large, mirrored armoire. Each accommodation features minibar and remote-control color TV; some rooms have terraces. The bathroom is not only large, it is also thoughtfully laid out (in the tub, there's even a roomy ledge to hold your shampoo and other niceties). Even the amenities have French flair—they're from Lancôme. Best of all is the state-of-the-art telephone: Part magic box, part private secretary, it also acts as an answering machine. The executive king rooms are especially nice, with a separate sitting area furnished with two comfy armchairs and a second TV. Health spa facilities include Nautilus equipment and a heated outdoor swimming pool. In addition to the hotel's elegant namesake restaurant, Ma Maison, the La Cajole café features more casual dining. Though no honeymoon package is available, there's a plush three-day/two-night weekend package for $800 per couple. Includes private limousine service to and from the airport, suite accommodations, one dinner in Ma Maison, one breakfast in La Cajole, use of private limousine for two hours, and a massage or facial. Regular rates: $175 to $210 per couple for a room.

Located right at the end of Wilshire Boulevard on the beach in Santa Monica, the **Miramar Sheraton Hotel,** 101 Wilshire Blvd., Santa Monica, CA (tel. 213/394-3731; reservations: toll free 800/325-3535), has been a longtime favorite of people who want to be right on the water in Santa Monica. The rooms at this two-wing, ten-story property have just been beautified as part of a top-to-toe renovation project. Each now features an honor bar and a color cable TV. The accommodations in the Palisades wing have an English feeling, with Queen Anne–style chairs and a black-and-gray marble bathroom; the Ocean Tower incorporates California-style decor, with bleached-oak furniture, a pink-and-champagne color scheme, and beige marble in the bathroom. Views in both towers overlook either the Santa Monica Mountains or the Pacific Ocean. The large lobby area is also slated for refurbishment soon. On the property, you'll find all the amenities you'd expect of this fine hotel chain, including a large outdoor swimming pool you can really swim laps in, shops, a beauty salon, and rental car and airline desks. The best amenity of all is Adrienne Miley, the chief concierge. She literally knows L.A. like the back of her hand and can recommend fun, romantic escapades such as renting bikes and heading for the string of beaches south of Santa Monica. Honeymoon package: None. Room rates (EP): $165 to $187 per couple per night, depending on view and availability of a terrace. Suites run $210 to $300 per couple per night.

Moderate

Good value at a great location—that's what you'll find at the **Del Capri Hotel,** 10587 Wilshire Blvd., Los Angeles, CA 90024 (tel. 213/474-3511), located right on choice Wilshire Boulevard in Westwood. The two-story hotel surrounds a central courtyard with a heated, free-form pool. This perennial favorite of Angelenos in the know has gotten all prettied up as part of a major refurbishment program. Stylish new furnishings use light, sunny colors drawn from nature, such as sea-foam green and tea-rose pink. Most bathrooms feature a combination whirlpool/bathtub, and the dressing mirror comes with Hollywood-style bulbs around the perimeter. Beds are adjustable, so you can sit up and read. The number of king-size beds is limited, so make sure you state your preferences in advance. Also new—a complimentary shuttle service to whisk you to Westwood, Beverly Hills, and Century City. Honeymoon package: None. But if you advise the friendly staff that you are newlyweds, they'll usually proffer a bottle of champagne. Rates (CP): $97 per couple per night for a room; $115 to $125 per couple per night for a suite. Includes continental breakfast.

Hotel Shangri-La, 1301 Ocean Ave., Santa Monica, CA 90401 (tel. 213/394-2791), is a true art deco gem, facing out over Palisades Park, the beach, and the ocean in lively Santa Monica. Built in 1939 as an apartment house, the hotel retains its art deco features. Every room has a beautiful view of the Southern California coastline. If you want something really special, choose the Penthouse ($380 per couple per night), which has an unbelievably long terrace that wraps around the building and views that stretch all the way to Malibu. Inside, mirrored walls reflect the panorama of sky and ocean. Colors come in wonderful seaside shades of pink and aqua. The suite has a fully equipped kitchen, marble master bathroom, and a mirrored headboard in the bedroom. Every room is different—some have balconies, some face directly over the ocean—but all have deco touches, such as the custom-made furniture done all in curves and angles, etched mirrors, shell-design lamps. Even the studio rooms have plenty of panache. The hotel also has a garden courtyard, with imported Italian tile, charming gazebo, and refreshing fountain. Owned and managed by the Adaya family, the Shangri-La has become a favorite hideaway for stars who want a low-key yet elegant atmosphere. Cyndi Lauper, Lauren Hutton, Diane Keaton, Gene Hackman, and Brooke Shields have all stayed here. Rates (CP): $105 per couple per day for a studio; $135 to $150 per day for a one-bedroom suite, depending on view and availability of terrace. Includes continental breakfast and afternoon tea. If you let the Adayas know that you're honeymooners, they will generally offer you special amenities.

Moderately Inexpensive

Bay View Plaza Holiday Inn, 530 West Pico Blvd., Santa Monica, CA 90405 (tel. 213/399-9344; reservations: toll free 800/HOLIDAY), is quite a wonderful place—extremely modern, designed somewhat like a step pyramid, and just a five-minute walk from the Santa Monica beach. Thanks to all those sharp angles, every room overlooks the mountains or the Pacific Ocean (you can see all the way to Catalina on clear days). To get in the California groove, choose one of the minisuites, four of which have a Jacuzzi-with-a-view on the terrace. Some of the suites are English-style; others have light rattan furnishings. Standard rooms are cheerful and breezy, with contemporary light-wood furnishings and seashore colors, such as beige, blue, dusty mauve, and sea-foam green. The hotel has two swimming pools and an art gallery selling watercolors and posters by local artists. All in all, it adds up to a well-thought-out hotel. Rates (EP): $83 per couple per night for an economy room; $137 per couple per night for a superior room; $275 per couple per night for the Jacuzzi suite.

La Maida, 11159 La Maida St., North Hollywood, CA 91601 (tel. 818/769-3857). Many bed-and-breakfasts offer guests freshly squeezed orange juice, but how many give them the opportunity to pluck their own oranges from trees in the garden, or to brunch on eggs laid by the inn's own chickens? Those are just some of the extra-special touches you'll find at La Maida, a landmark Italianate villa near Universal City and Burbank. Throughout the inn, you'll find antiques and fascinating objects gathered by the current owner during her worldwide travels: a silver tea service, Victorian sideboard, Chinese lacquer table. Most spectacular of all are the 97 intricate stained-glass windows crafted by the owner herself. Guests enjoy not only their own airy quarters, but the villa's public areas as well, including a spacious living room with baby grand piano, flower-filled gardens accented by fountains, and the swimming pool. The inn also plans to add a gym.

Rooms (all with private bath) are set in either the main house or three neighboring cottages. Choicest lodgings for honeymooners include La Streletzia (Bird of Paradise) suite, with a wood-burning fireplace, huge bathroom with Roman whirlpool tub, and front porch overlooking a Japanese-style fern garden with goldfish pond ($240 per couple per night). Cipresso ($170 per night) is also captivating, with its four-poster bed swathed in filmy muslin, its small balcony, and its bathroom's amazing blue, black, and white tile floor of basket-weave design (original to the house). Fresh-cut flowers in your room, evening apéritifs, and turn-down service are all complimentary. In addition to a lavish continental breakfast, the resident chef can prepare you a gourmet dinner on request ($35 per person). And if you're planning on getting married while in L.A., there's a charming white gazebo in the garden. Rates: $93 to $240 per couple per night.

Terrace Manor, 1353 Alvarado Terrace, Los Angeles, CA 90006 (tel. 213/381-1478). As you turn off Pico Boulevard onto Alvarado Terrace, it's almost as if you've fallen through a time warp. A row of Victorian houses stands proudly in a scene virtually unchanged for the past 100 years. This is the setting for Terrace Manor, a Tudor-style bed-and-breakfast that's on the National Register of Historic Places. Owners Sandy and Shirley Spillman have exquisitely restored the 1902 building. In addition to its tiger-oak paneling and columned fireplace, the house is graced with splendid stained- and leaded-glass windows (thanks to the original owner, who ran a glass factory). There are only five accommodations, each with private bath (some baths are adjacent to rooms). The Sewing Room ($70 per couple) contains an elaborately carved oak bedstead, a dressing table converted from an old sewing machine stand, plus an old dressmaker's mannequin and a pair of high-button shoes to add atmosphere. Perhaps Lydia's Room ($100 per couple) is the most romantic, with its king-size brass-and-iron bed and Victorian settee. The Spillmans really coddle their guests, treating them to a breakfast that might include french toast or blintzes, tucking them in with cookies or fudge at night. The inn has also hosted many weddings, in either the sitting room or the garden, shaded by lemon and loquat trees and wisteria vines. If innkeeper Sandy Spillman looks familiar, that's because he is moonlighting from his other career as a professional actor and magician (he's been known to perform sleight of hand at the breakfast table). Which leads to a unique perk for inn guests. Spillman, a member of Hollywood's famed Magic Castle private club, can make reservations for you to attend the spellbinding dinner-show. Rates: $65 to $100 per couple per night.

Eastlake Inn, 1442 Kellam Ave., Los Angeles, CA 90026 (tel. 714/250-1620). Just a few minutes from the hurly-burly of downtown L.A., the Angelino Heights area is a peaceful enclave of restored Victorian mansions—including this entrancing bed-and-breakfast built in 1887. Turn-of-the-century clothes adorn mannequins in the front hall; an old wooden telephone with crank handle hangs on the wall; and many windows still have their original "flashed glass" colored panels. Because of the soft red-pine floors, no high heels can be worn inside. There are nine rooms, some with private baths. Each has unique charm. The sunny Skylight Suite ($137 per couple) has a queen-size bed, white wicker chairs, and a claw-foot tub outfitted with a shower head. Although North Star does not have a private bath, it does feature cherubs soaring over the canopied bed, as well as a prime view of the famous Hollywood sign ($110 per couple). In the morning, breakfast might include fresh juice and fruit, selection from the cheeseboard, coffees and teas, croissants, and soft-boiled eggs. Try to check out nearby Echo Park Lake—15 acres of green lawns, jogging trails, and a lake where you can fish for carp or cruise languidly in a paddleboat. Rates: $72 to $165 per couple per night.

In Laguna Beach

Located about 60 miles south of Los Angeles, Laguna Beach is a popular weekend retreat for Angelenos, thanks to the five-mile-long strip of beach. The frontage is well utilized by all ilk of beach-goers—joggers, surfers, volleyball players, dog walkers, bikinied beach-party lasses, all seemingly blessed with sun-bleached hair, even tans, and toothpaste-commercial-caliber teeth.

For over 150 years, Laguna Beach has been known as an artists colony, hosting several festivals annually. The most unusual event—not only in Laguna Beach but perhaps in the world—must be the **Pageant of the Masters** held in July and August, when a cast of thousands (literally) poise themselves in tableaux and re-create various Old Master paintings. All year-round, you can enjoy the perfect Southern California weather (85° in the summer, 70° in the winter), and browse through the art galleries and shops in town.

The Ritz-Carlton, 33533 Shoreline Dr., Laguna Niguel, CA 92677 (tel. 714/240-2000; reservations: toll free 800/241-3333 nationwide; 800/821-3101 in California). Putting on the Ritz, Southern California–style, means checking into the Ritz-Carlton Hotel, spectacularly perched on a 150-foot-high bluff over the ocean. With its red-roofed, Mediterranean-style architecture and marble terraces that spread out over the hillside, the hotel would look suitably at home in either St. Tropez or Positano. Reminiscent of the grand hotels of Europe, the columned lobby area has leather armchairs and a giant-size lounge gallery with a high, vaulted ceiling, marble floors, and an Oriental carpet that seems to run for the length of a football field. Throughout the hotel, a $2-million collection of 18th- and 19th-century American and European art and antiques is on display (the works even have their own curator and information pamphlet). In spite of all this old-world splendor, the hotel is a virtual youngster, having first opened its doors in 1984.

Pamper yourselves by staying in accommodations on the top Club Floor, where a concierge ministers to your every need—from mixing a cocktail to setting up an appointment with the masseur. In the morning, you can help yourself to a lavish continental breakfast; in the afternoon, enjoy tea and crumpets while looking out over the Pacific. On the Club Floor, rooms are very large and very luxurious, with a king-size, four-poster bed and French country furnishings, elegantly done in cream, Wedgwood blue, and green. On your balcony, you can sit and watch the sunset over the Pacific. For sheer, unmitigated glamour, you can't outdo the opulent bathroom, where shiny chrome fixtures and crystal chandeliers enhance the gray-and-white marble floors and walls. Although the standard rooms are not quite as expansive, they too have marble bathrooms and French country decor. The staff-to-guest ratio is about 1:1, including a full-time member of the housekeeping staff whose main responsibility is to fluff pillows and stamp the distinctive Ritz Carlton lion's-head logo in the ash urns.

Follow the winding paths down through the gardens to the beach (you can also hop the free jitney). The hotel is located on a stretch called Salt Creek Beach, popular with area surfers who bob out beyond the breakers, waiting for the perfect wave. The Ritz-Carlton has an excellent fitness center, with exercise equipment and frequent aerobics classes; there are also tennis courts, two outdoor swimming pools, and two Jacuzzis. When you work up an appetite, the three restaurants are excellent. On a typically balmy California day, you can't ask for anything nicer than lunch on the Café Terrace, shaded by a pergola and overlooking the main pool. "Celebration" visit: $220 to $770 per couple per night, depending on room category. Includes bottle of domestic champagne with gift of champagne flutes, chocolate truffles, use of the fitness center, and valet parking.

In Greater Palm Springs

With streets sporting the well-known names of Frank Sinatra, Bob Hope, and Gerald Ford, you just know that the Palm Springs area has to be a favorite oasis for celebrities. Year-round luscious temperatures (average 88° by day, 55° by night) and proximity to Los Angeles (less than a two-hour drive away) are just some of the region's natural attractions. Add in top-notch sports facilities (including over 70 golf courses) and world-class shopping and dining, and you have a resort empire that can't be beat.

Don't give in to the temptation of not budging from your poolside lounge chair, because there is so much to see and do here. For an unbeatable sensation in winter, travel 8,500 feet up, from sunstruck wilderness to the snowcapped San Jacinto Mountains, in only 15 minutes aboard the **Palm Springs Aerial Tramway** (tel. 325-1391); admission, $13.25 per person. Go hiking through **Palm, Andreas,** and **Murray Canyons** (known as the Indian Canyons), where palm-shaded oases contrast with unusual rock formations. Saddle up for a desert horseback ride with **Smoketree Stables** (tel. 327-1372); or a jeep tour with **Desert Off-Road Adventures** (tel. 619/773-3187), $70 per person for a three-hour expedition. And any time of year, call the 24-hour **Activities Hotline** (tel. 619/322-4636) to find out what's new each week.

La Quinta Hotel, Golf & Tennis Resort, 49-499 Eisenhower Dr., P.O. Box 69, La Quinta, CA 92253 (tel. 619/564-4111; reservations: toll free 800/854-1271 nationwide; 800/472-4316 in California). The guest roster reads like a Who's Who of Hollywood's golden era, with a guest registry that includes the names of Greta Garbo, Bette Davis, Charlie Chaplin, Clark Gable, and Marlene Dietrich. They were just some of the luminaries who flocked to a tiny, six-cottage hideaway nestled in the Santa Rosa Mountains some 20 miles from the nearest town—a soon-to-be-discovered outpost called Palm Springs. Sixty years later, La Quinta maintains her reign as the queen of the desert resorts. The rich and famous continue to check in, among them Johnny Carson, Cheryl Tiegs, and Donna Mills. The property is newly groomed and manicured after a $45-million renovation project that added 41 new cottages and a splashy shopping/dining complex on the 45-acre property. But still, the resort exudes a feeling of spacious privacy—after all, there are 19 public pools and 19 spas to choose from. Accommodations are located in individual Spanish-style casitas, with red-tile roofs, white stucco walls, and blue shutters. Rooms are really large—over 500 square feet. The Spanish- and Mexican-design furnishings (including some fine antiques) are accented by bright red and blue fabrics. Many accommodations have fireplaces, decorated with hand-painted Mexican tiles (in some suites, there's even a second fireplace in the bathroom). Golfers will want to tee off on the La Quinta Hotel Golf Club's challenging Dunes Course, designed by Pete Dye; tennis players can hone their game on 30 courts serving up a choice of grass, clay, and hard surfaces. At mealtime, guests have three choices: the award-winning California gourmet cuisine of La Mirage; the lighter fare of Morgan's (with its spirit of the Roaring '20s); and the Mexican specialties (including melt-in-your-mouth homemade tortillas) of the Adobe Grill. Room rates (EP): $88 to $275 per couple per night in summer; $205 to $385 per couple in winter. Suites are also available.

ROMANTIC RESTAURANTS

The trend in L.A., as elsewhere in the state, is toward what has become known as California cuisine: ultrafresh ingredients, cooked to enhance the natural flavors. In addition, L.A. restaurants tend to mix some of the dramatic flair of show business into their recipes: Dining out in L.A. is part food, part theater. People do not so much eat to live, as eat to look at who else is dining there. The "hot" new restaurant changes just about as rapidly as the "hot" new star. For our restaurant recommendations, we've concentrated on places that are romantic, serve good food, are "in"—and have earned their fashionable reputations over a bit of time. Reservations are practically always necessary.

Expensive

The Ivy, 113 North Robertson, Beverly Hills (tel. 213/274-8303). As refreshing as a stay in sunny Provence, The Ivy will enthrall you with its authentic 18th- and 19th-century antiques, collection of vintage cowboy hats, roses picked from the gardens of the owners, and excellent food (many of the herbs used are grown in these same gardens). You'll be tempted to order one of everything on the menu—appetizers such as Cajun crayfish or pizza with four types of mushrooms, or entrées such as the zingy pepper shrimp. Every night, they feature different specials from their mesquite grill. Fabulous desserts. Lunch about $60 per couple; dinner, $80 to $100 plus drinks. Open Monday through Saturday for lunch, 11:30 a.m. to 2:45 p.m.; dinner, 6 to 10:45 p.m.

Rockenwagner, 1023 West Washington Blvd., Venice (tel. 213/399-6504). The superb food and sexy ambience of Rockenwagner—perhaps L.A.'s best "undiscovered" restaurant—outshine those of many more trendy establishments. This small bistro (only 15 tables) has a winsome, eclectic decor that manages to harmonize such disparate elements as ceramic angel heads, whale murals, and Santa Fe–style mirrors. But the pièce de résistance, romantically speaking, is the enclosed terrace in the back, a secret garden where ivy scampers up trellises, and bouquets of flowers peek out from vases moored to the walls. Like the decor, the menu brings together diverse ingredients and makes them all work; the excellent roast breast of guinea hen, for example, is served with a leek tart and truffle sauce, the aromatic truffles perfectly complementing the crisp skin and sweet leeks. Save room for dessert, such as the raspberry soufflé or chocolate sandwich filled with mocha mousse and topped with hazelnut sauce. Dinner for two, about $80 to $100 per couple, served from 6 to 9:30 p.m. nightly.

Chinois on Main, 2709 Main St., Santa Monica (tel. 213/392-9025). Superstar chef Wolfgang Puck has single-handedly invented nouvelle chinoise cuisine—and the dazzling results will surely leave your taste buds swooning. East meets West in the glamorous decor, with a wooden Buddha enthroned over the bar and orchids spotlighted behind a plate-glass window. Similarly, the menu brings together Oriental and Californian influences. Stir-fry garlic chicken nests atop radicchio leaves; a tangy Shanghai risotto incorporates lobster, ginger, and thin-sliced scallions. Dessert might be an amazing crème brulée trio, flavored with ginger, mandarin orange, and chocolate-mint. Open for lunch Wednesday through Friday, noon to 1:45 p.m.; $60 to $70 per couple. Dinner served Monday through Saturday, 6 to 10:30 p.m.; $80 to $100 per couple.

Ma Maison, 8555 Beverly Blvd., Los Angeles (tel. 213/655-1991). Like a great movie star making an Oscar-winning comeback, Ma Maison has returned to the forefront of the L.A. restaurant scene. This doyenne of celebrities in the '70s and early '80s has reopened in a sumptuous new locale at its namesake, the Ma Maison Sofitel hotel. "We're better than ever," reports Patrick Terrail, the guiding spirit behind both the original Ma Maison and this shining reincarnation. Ma Maison II is "dedicated to California sunshine," as Terrail puts it, with French country decor as well as a sliding glass roof that rolls back for under-the-stars dining. Back on the menu are such Ma Maison signature dishes as its potato-cum-escargot appetizer and chicken salad entrée, and back in the graceful armchairs are such Hollywood glitterati as Suzanne Pleshette, Swifty Lazar, and Ed McMahon, and new superstars including Michael Jackson and Darryl Hannah. Lunch, $60 to $80 per couple; dinner, $80 to $100 per couple plus drinks. Open Monday through Saturday, 11:30 a.m. to 2:30 p.m.; 5:30 to 10:30 p.m.

West Beach Cafe, 60 North Venice Blvd., Venice (tel. 213/823-5396). Although the setting doesn't exude romance (it's hard-edge modern, with neon lights, narrow-slat blinds, and white-painted cinderblock walls), the excellent food should set your libido racing. The menu changes weekly to take advantage of what's fresh, but you can expect savory dishes, such as a saffron-braised Norwegian salmon served with leeks and fresh herbs, or the restaurant's own version of risotto simmered with four cheese. Open for breakfast Tuesday through Friday, 8 to 11:30 a.m. ($15 per couple); lunch, Tuesday through Sunday, 11:30 a.m. to 2:30 p.m. ($20 to $40 per couple); dinner, Tuesday through Sunday, 6 to 10:45 p.m. ($70 to $100 per couple). Closed Monday.

Moderate

Citrus Restaurant, 6703 Melrose Ave., Los Angeles (tel. 213/857-0034). The phone keeps ringing, as ardent prospective diners try to coax reservations out of the maître d'. Through the windows fronting the open-view kitchen, you can eye *toques blanches* bobbing on the heads of chefs hard at work, julienning, reducing, and flambéing. Smartly togged men and women emerge from the polished Jaguars and Mercedes Benzes parked curbside. Such is the scene at Citrus, one of the hottest dining addresses in L.A. Fortunately, Citrus's superb food has earned the restaurant more than flash-in-the-frying-pan success. The cuisine of chef Michel Richard (a protégé of the renowned French pastry chef Gaston Lenôtre) continually soars to new heights . . . the perfectly turned roast duck with cabernet sauvignon sauce, or sautéed scallops crunchfully topped with deep-fried Maui onion rings. The setting enhances the food, a garden-like milieu created by the skylight, white umbrellas, patio furniture, and spectacular five-foot-tall flower arrangements. Open Monday through Friday for lunch, noon to 3 p.m., $40 to $50 per couple; and Monday through Saturday for dinner, 6:30 to 11 p.m., $60 to $80 per couple plus drinks. Closed Sunday.

Restaurant Katsu, 1972 Hillhurst, Los Angeles (tel. 213/665-1891). Outside, no sign identifies the restaurant. Inside, the stark, avant-garde decor of black walls and cube tables contrasts with the vintage rock 'n' roll throbbing softly on the sound system. But nothing upstages the extraordinary Japanese food at Katsu. The sushi is truly exceptional—rosy maguro (tuna) and translucent yellowtail, as well as some unusual delicacies, such as pickled halibut topped with roe, served atop a lemon wedge. Sit at the counter so you can watch the sushi chef at work, combining the precision of a Swiss watchmaker with the artistic flair of a Matisse. Other dishes are also first-rate, such as a roast duck served with shiitake mushrooms. Open Monday through Friday for lunch, noon to 2 p.m., $20 to $25 per couple; Monday through Saturday for dinner, 6 to 9:45 p.m., $30 to $50 per couple. (There's also a multicourse deluxe dinner for $38.50 per person.)

Ivy at the Shore, 1541 Ocean Ave., Santa Monica (tel. 213/393-3113). Believe it or not, sunny Los Angeles has never had many sidewalk cafés. Ivy at the Shore fills that gap in style with a bistro right in the center of all the Santa Monica action. Seated on a white wicker chair on the terrace, you'll be able to gaze at the passing parade as well as the palm-lined promenade, beach, and Pacific Ocean. Indoors, the seating is equally charming, with rattan furnishings, 1930s pink floral-print fabric on the rattan chairs, and ceiling fans. The food is truly excellent, with many mesquite-grilled dishes, as well as pastas and pizzas. Every day, fresh fish is flown in from New Orleans: gulf shrimp, lump crabmeat, and redfish. And you probably never have tasted anything as delicious as their tropical drinks made from scratch: If you order a piña colada, the barman slices up a pineapple, adds fresh coconut and rum, and whips it up in the blender. Lunch, $40 to $50 per couple; dinner, $60 to $80 per couple. Serving daily from 11:30 a.m. to 3:15 p.m., and from 5:30 to 11 p.m.

If only the tables could talk . . . **The Polo Lounge,** the Beverly Hills Hotel on Sunset Boulevard, Beverly Hills (tel. 213/276-2251), has acted as Hollywood's unofficial club–cum–conference room ever since Will Rogers, Darryl Zanuck, and Spencer Tracy used to pile in here after playing a few chukkers on an adjacent polo field. It was here that the concept of the "power breakfast" and the "power lunch" originated, here that W. C. Fields reserved a table for two and arrived accompanied by a carnivorous plant. This famous rendezvous has three different seating areas. The Green Room, right in front of the entrance, is where the superstars and the main power brokers sit—when they want to be seen. If they don't want to be seen, they'll opt for the pink-and-white Patio, surrounded by flowers. For seclusion, patrons choose the Loggia, separated from the main area by a glass partition. For us mere mortals, the nice thing about the Polo Lounge (and the whole Beverly Hills Hotel, for that matter) is the fact that it's a friendly place. If you come here, you won't get the best table in the house, but at least you'll be treated with respect and courtesy. It's a nice way to step into a favored milieu of the rich and famous. The food is good enough, but remember that you've come here for the atmosphere. Breakfast, about $40 per couple. Lunch: sandwiches, from $12.25; salads, from $15; hot entrées, $16 and up. Open from 7 a.m. to 1 a.m.

Fennel, 1535 Ocean Ave., Santa Monica (tel. 213/394-2079). Here, the casual greeting "What's cooking?" is often replaced by the query "Who's cooking?" since this stylish restaurant rotates its chef every month. Each guest chef runs a well-known restaurant in France, and all share a penchant for making the most of California's bountiful fresh produce. Ingredients come together with artful panache: A salad combines veal sweetbreads and scallops with French beans and mushrooms; leg of lamb marries beautifully with a subtle garlic flan. The desserts are real diet-busters—especially the rich chocolate tart with pistachio sauce. And as a side dish, there's a ringside view of the strollers along the beachfront promenade. Lunch or dinner will run $60 to $80 per couple plus drinks. Open Tuesday through Sunday for lunch, noon to 2:45 p.m.; for dinner, 6 to 9:30 p.m.

Opera, 1551 Ocean Ave., Santa Monica (tel. 213/393-9224). Another bright, airy café in the heart of the beach boulevard action, Opera earns bravos for its innovative California cuisine. Memorable appetizers include the seared peppered carpaccio, served with roasted eggplant and pinenut sauté. For seafaring entrées, there's an aromatic bouillabaisse, while turf-lovers should head for the tender New York steak served with a creamy potato gratin. Lunch (summer only), $40 per couple, noon to 2:30 p.m. Dinner, $60 to $80 per couple, 6 to 11:30 p.m.

72 Market Street, at (you've guessed it) 72 Market St., Venice (tel. 213/392-8720). High-tech in decor, with a weathered copper facade and glass-brick-walled interior, this restaurant also attracts the "in" crowd, thanks to its celebrity ownership, which includes actors Dudley Moore and Tony Bill. The menu is known for its homey touches—one signature dish is meatloaf, served with spinach and mashed potatoes. In addition to a full roster of steaks and seafood, the menu features daily specials, such as linguine with sausage and peppers. Lunch, $30 to $40 per couple, served from 11 a.m. to 2:30 p.m. Dinner, $60 to $80 per couple, served from 6 to 10:30 p.m. (to 11:30 p.m. on weekends).

Chaya Brasserie, 8741 Alden Dr., Los Angeles (tel. 213/859-8833). Casual yet stylish, Chaya has plenty of flair, with lively bar action up front, French-style café chairs, and a flourishing stand of bamboo at stage center that soars up toward a skylight. For starters, try the halibut sashimi or Dungeness crab served with sliced avocado. As for an entrée, habitués in the know swear by the savory grilled chicken in Dijon-mustard sauce. Open Monday through Friday for lunch, 11:30 a.m. to 2:30 p.m., $40 to $50 per couple. Dinner served Monday through Sunday, 6 to 10:30 p.m., $60 to $70 per couple plus drinks.

The drive down to **Gladstone's 4 Fish,** 17300 West Pacific Coast Hwy., Pacific Palisades (tel. 213/454-3474), is beautiful, leading you to the westernmost tip of Sunset Boulevard. Gladstone's is an "in" spot, noisy, wildly animated—and its outdoor deck overlooks the Pacific. As the name implies, the specialties of the house are the denizens of the deep. Start with fried calamari or a rich, creamy chowder, then check out what the fisherman has brought back that day—it might be salmon, trout, or yellowtail grilled over mesquite charcoal. For shellfish-lovers, there's Maine lobster fresh from the tank. For the finale, sip espresso and share a hot-fudge sundae, chocolate-chip cheesecake, or strawberry shortcake. Open daily from 7 a.m. to 11 p.m., serving breakfast ($15 per couple), lunch ($30 to $40 per couple), and dinner ($40 to $50 per couple).

Rebecca's, 55 North Venice Blvd., Venice (tel. 213/306-6266). Even in a city known for its special effects, it's hard to top the drop-dead decor of Rebecca's, complete with an illuminated marble facade and larger-than-life wall murals. The restaurant attracts an exuberant, party-happy crowd nightly for a Mexican-accented menu that stars quesadillas and fajitas, plus specials such as a charred tuna in cilantro salsa. When the time comes to collect your just desserts, share a chocolate bread pudding or lime-curd tart. Dinner for two, $35 to $60 per couple (there's a $16.50 per person minimum). Open 6 to 10:45 p.m. (to 11:30 p.m. weekends).

Pastel, 421 North Rodeo Dr., Beverly Hills (tel. 213/274-9775). Looking for a light lunch and good people-watching as a break from your Rodeo Drive shopping? Try Pastel, located downstairs at the Rodeo Drive Collection. Although you can eat indoors as well, the prime tables are on the courtyard terrace, shaded by umbrellas and surrounded by fountains. Chatter from nearby tables might negotiate points, or casting for a new movie. The menu highlights pastas and salads, including an especially toothsome lobster salad that mingles crunchy broccoli, carrots, and string beans on a medley of fresh greens. Lunch for two, about $30 to $40 per couple. Open daily from 11:30 a.m. to 11 p.m.

Inexpensive

Back in the 1950s, when car tail-lights sported fins, *Leave It to Beaver* episodes ran on prime-time network TV, and McDonald's was a nursery-rhyme farm, not a purveyor of hamburgers, there existed an All-American wonderland of shiny vinyl booths and clean-cut Formica tables known as the neighborhood diner. The diner is back, Beverly Hills style, at **Ed Debevic's,** 134 North La Cienega Blvd., Beverly Hills (tel. 213/659-1952). Waiters and waitresses sporting name tags such as Toots and Delbert hand over the wise-cracking menu, studded with flip remarks such as "vegetable club sandwich (Mother says eat your vegetables)." Despite the retro atmosphere, the chow is definitely upscale—they even make their own hamburger buns. It's extremely popular and they accept no dinner reservations, so be prepared to wait—especially on Friday and Saturday nights, when lots of celebrities drop in. Open daily from 11:30 a.m. to midnight; about $10 to $20 per couple.

Neither of the following restaurants in Santa Monica is fancy—in fact, if you were just strolling by, you might feel a bit dubious about walking in on your own. But both offer excellent eats at low prices. **Chez Jay,** 1657 Ocean Ave. (tel. 213/395-1741), is the quintessential neighborhood joint, right down to the sawdust on its wood-plank floors. Lunch choices range from hamburgers and omelets to filet of sole and steamed clams; about $10 to $20 per couple. Dinner gets more elaborate, with entrées such as stuffed chicken breast or broiled lobster tail; about $30 to $60 per couple. Open daily (except Christmas) from noon to 2 p.m. and from 6 to 11 p.m. Set in a simple white building across from the beach, **The Lobster,** corner of Ocean Avenue and Colorado (tel. 213/394-9751), has been around for years (and so, from the well-worn looks of it, has the interior decor). A terrific seafood lunch or dinner will run about $20 to $30 per couple. Open Tuesday through Sunday, 11:30 a.m. to 9 p.m.

FLORIDA

Florida is exactly as you'd expect . . . and *nothing* like it. There are miles of sugar-white shoreline and swaying palms, but also underground caves, moss-draped cypress, and the Everglades, a last haven for near-extinct animals and birds. Spend a day lazing on the gulf doing nothing, or try everything from billfishing to spelunking to wagering on a jai alai match. Float into cloudless skies with your love in the gondola of a hot-air balloon, or dive below the depths for an underwater spectacle of reefs, colorful tropical fish, and sunken wrecks.

Located in the southeastern United States, Florida is the southernmost state; subtropical with plenty of warmth and winter sunshine. Its proximity to the rest of the South makes it a great place to find cotton plantations, Civil War battlegrounds, and down-home cooking such as southern-fried chicken and grits. It is a peninsula surrounded by the Atlantic on the east coast and the Gulf of Mexico on the west; no other state can boast as many miles of shoreline and sunny beaches.

Florida is not one destination; it is many destinations, each with its own ambience and charm.

Driving around Florida is as diverse and scenic as a trip across the entire United States—Pensacola is separated from Key West by 900 miles. The road between Miami and Key West and any route from Orlando south will find you surrounded by Everglades sawgrass, acres of fragrant orange groves, or tall cypress eerily draped in Spanish moss. Coastal roads feature water views, resort towns, and high-rise condominiums, but inland, discover Indian reservations, natural springs, waterfalls, and underground caverns. One of the best ways to see Florida is to *not* plan too much and stop along the road when you see something interesting. The destinations in this chapter are just starting points for finding *your* place in the sun.

Take a bumpy airboat ride through wild marshland in the morning, visit a southern plantation in the afternoon or climb to the top of a century-old lighthouse for incredible vistas, have dinner in an old castle while cheering on your favorite knight in a jousting competition, then kick up your heels as a New Orleans jazz band cranks out 1920s Dixieland tunes. And that's only one day!

Florida has all you plan a honeymoon for—and more. Hundreds of miles of

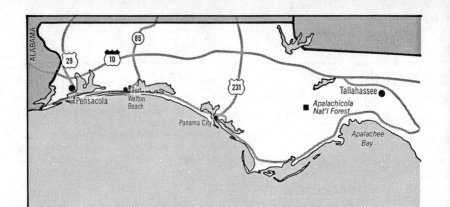

ALABAMA

29

10

85

231

Pensacola

Fort Walton Beach

Panama City

Tallahassee

Apalachicola Nat'l Forest

Apalachee Bay

GULF OF MEXICO

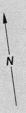

N

| 0 | miles | 30 |
| 0 | kms | 50 |

FLORIDA

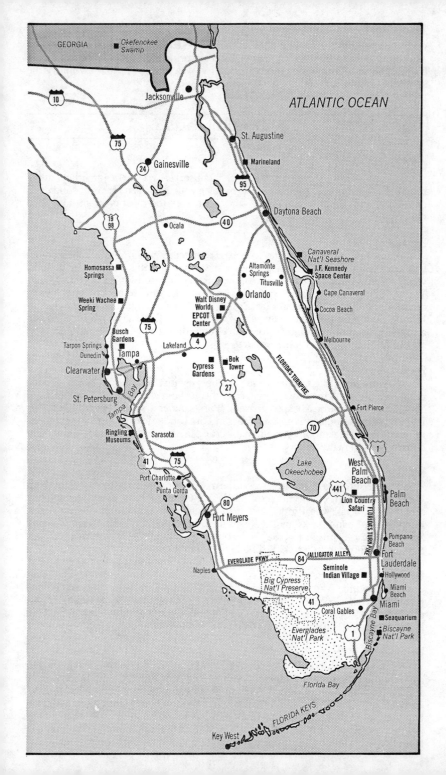

warm beaches and the hush of history; shady woodlands and endless water sports; Mickey Mouse and Ernest Hemingway; baseball spring training and Florida Cracker homes; and enough sunshine to last an eternity. Welcome to Florida—come for the beaches, stay for the fun!

---

1. Practical Facts

GETTING THERE

Florida is easy to reach, thanks to frequent service via the major airlines and a top-notch network of interstate highways. Keep your eyes open for year-round deals on air fare and rental car packages—they're usually the most economical way to travel.

By Air

Many airlines offer packages to one or more cities within Florida. Remember that rates will probably be higher during the winter months and holiday periods, when throngs of northerners crowd hotels and resorts to escape the cold. Disney World/EPCOT packages are especially popular, so be sure to check for specials and availability of flights well in advance. Nearly every major airline flies to *somewhere* in Florida. To reach cities other than Miami, Orlando, or Tampa, you may need to hop a connecting commuter flight once you're here. Almost all commuter airlines operate out of Miami International Airport.

By Cruise Ship

A cruise from the Bahamas or the Caribbean with a final destination in Florida can be a truly romantic way to begin or end your honeymoon. Ports are located in Tampa/St. Petersburg, at Cape Canaveral (Port Canaveral, servicing Orlando), West Palm Beach, Miami, and Port Everglades in Fort Lauderdale. If you'd like to spend more of your honeymoon on land, many cruise lines offer day trips and dinner sails departing from many cities.

By Train

For a leisurely ride, **Amtrak** serves the midwestern, northeastern, and southern United States with connections to the West. Pull into one of over a dozen cities served by Amtrak: Clearwater, Deerfield Beach, Fort Lauderdale, Delray Beach, Hollywood, Miami, Jacksonville, Kissimmee, Lakeland, Orlando, Ocala, Sanford, Sebring, West Palm Beach, St. Petersburg, and Tampa. For information, call Amtrak's toll-free number: 800/424-1111.

By Bus

Greyhound/Trailways provides transportation from other states and throughout Florida. Many smaller companies (i.e., **Gray Line**) have buses strictly for touring purposes. To find out about bus schedules to and around Florida, call your local Greyhound station.

Driving Your Own Car

If you live within 300 miles or so of Florida, you could save money on air fares and rental cars by driving yourself. Access to Florida is a breeze from Interstates 10 and 65 from the west, I-75 or I-95 from the north. Welcome Centers at all major entrance points offer maps, information, and brochures on sights, attractions, restaurants, and hotels as well as a free glass of Florida citrus juice. Plan where you're going to stop if you're driving to south Florida from anywhere—it's a 900-mile trek from Pensacola in the Panhandle to Key West on Florida's southernmost tip!

GETTING AROUND

When you make your hotel reservation, ask about complimentary transportation to major shopping malls and attractions. Many hotels have them, especially in the Orlando area. Often hotels (not just in large cities) have shuttles to and from the airport. If you really want to do some serious sightseeing, a rental car is almost a must. It's usually inexpensive and, let's face it, it's fun!

By Taxi

Taxis may be your best bet for areas where parking is a problem. If you're hailing a cab in Orlando, Miami, Tampa, or other major tourist centers, be aware that "special events fares" for Broadway plays, gallery openings, and symphony concerts may add up to $5 to the cost of the ride.

By Rental Car

The deals are sweeter in Florida than in any other state. Some of the larger companies give you unlimited mileage and many other driver benefits. If you plan on visiting more than one destination in Florida, this may be the best way to get around. Here's a rundown on the kind of deals you might be able to find; they change frequently, so ask your travel agent for the latest scoop. **National Car Rental** (tel. toll free 800/CAR-RENT) has a weekly rate of $89.98 for an economy car with unlimited mileage if you book seven days in advance. **Avis** (tel. toll free 800/331-1212) offers an economy car with unlimited mileage for $115; some blackout dates and restrictions apply. Rent a car from **Hertz** (tel. toll free 800/654-3131) in Orlando for $89 to $109 per week for an economy car; $149 to $169 for a midsize car; both have unlimited mileage. Watch out for a $40-per-week surcharge during holiday periods. Rates also vary depending on where in Florida you rent and if you return the car to the same destination.

WEATHER

From Pensacola in the north to Key West in the south, temperatures can vary as much as 20° on any given day. In the summertime, temperatures range from warm to hot, so your bikinis and shorts should be sufficient wherever you travel in the state (average is 76° in the north, 81° in the south). In the winter, however, it is always best to prepare for the occasional cold snap that occurs as far south as Miami. Winters average 55° in the north, 68° in the south. In south Florida, rain is common in June and July, a factor you may consider when planning picnics or other outdoor activities. Tropical storm season is June through November.

CLOTHING

Lightweight clothing, swimsuits, and sandals are good choices for your Florida honeymoon. You'll also want to pack a good pair of walking shoes. A lightweight jacket or sweater and a pair of long pants will come in handy during the winter months or for restaurants where air conditioning may be chilly. For most restaurants, attractions, and hotels, casual attire is accepted and expected. However, many restaurants in the more upscale hotels require jackets for gentlemen, and sometimes even ties are requested, so it's best to be prepared.

TIME

Florida spans two time zones—Central and Eastern, with most of the state being in the Eastern time zone. If you're entering Florida on I-10 from the west, you'll be on Central time for about two hours into the state.

TELEPHONES

Calling Florida will be easier if you know which area code belongs to which part of the state. All of northwest Florida over to Daytona Beach on the east coast uses

904. Tampa–St. Pete and all down the west coast is 813. A new area code has been added in central Florida. All of the central east coast and south to Miami and the Keys remains in the 305 area; Orlando and its fringes are now 407. If you aren't sure of the area code and the local phone book doesn't help you, just try the call and a recording will tell you the proper area code.

SHOPPING

If you're looking for T-shirts, ashtrays, or painted sand-dollar clocks, you'll find such souvenirs at drug stores, in malls, and in assorted shops on assorted beaches. Some real finds might be a bushel basket of real Florida citrus (many places will ship to your home so that you don't have to carry it with you), or some rare shells you've collected yourself. Since Florida is dotted with shipping ports, shopping almost anywhere has an international flair. Coconut Grove's **Mayfair Mall** near Miami is a mecca for goods from all over the world, as is **Park Avenue** in Winter Park near Orlando and the Vacation Kingdom's **EPCOT Center,** featuring authentic art objects, dolls, toys, and souvenirs from ten different countries around the world.

ABOUT ACCOMMODATIONS

Although not all Florida hotels have honeymoon packages, the wide range of vacation packages more than compensates. Summer rates can offer especially attractive deals in some resort areas; prices can drop by 30% to 50%. Where applicable, we've listed both low- and high-season rates in this chapter. A 15% tax will be added to your room rate.

DINING OUT

Nearly all of Florida is "come as you are," restaurants included, even the more expensive establishments. The occasional restaurant may require a jacket for men, sometimes even a tie, but if you're planning to pay $100 or more for a night out, you'll both probably want to dress up anyway.

Florida is part of the South, so along with the best international cuisine you'll find traditional favorites like corn bread, biscuits, and red-eye gravy. Of course, you must try any number of seafood delicacies cooked hundreds of different ways: Grouper, flounder, snapper, gulf shrimp, pompano, and oysters are standard fare in many restaurants.

HOW TO GET MARRIED IN FLORIDA

To obtain a marriage license, you both need a blood test in Florida and proof of U.S. citizenship, such as a birth certificate. After the license is issued, you must wait three days before the actual ceremony can take place. Contact the city hall in the particular area in which you wish to marry.

How about a wedding at sea? If you'll be traveling to or from Florida aboard a cruise ship, many captains are licensed to officiate at weddings. If your perfect wedding involves a ship of smaller dimensions, some paddle wheelers or yachts can be chartered for the wedding and the reception. Outdoor gazebos at hotels and parks are favorite settings for weddings for many couples, but probably the number one choice in Florida is the beach. Sunset makes an especially nice setting. At many hotels, the social director can assist you in making all the arrangements.

FOR FURTHER INFORMATION

There are more than 200 chambers of commerce throughout the state that can provide you with maps, restaurant and hotel guides, brochures, and any other pertinent information you need on the areas you'll be visiting. For general information, write to the **Florida Chamber of Commerce,** P.O. Box 5497, Tallahassee, FL 32301 (tel. 904/222-2831). Chambers of Commerce for the areas listed in this chapter follow:

Coconut Grove Chamber of Commerce, 3437 Main Hwy., Coconut Grove, FL 33133 (tel. 305/444-7270).

The Florida Upper Keys Chamber of Commerce, Key Largo, FL 33037 (tel. 305/451-1414).

Islamorada Chamber of Commerce, Islamorada, FL 33036 (tel. 305/664-4503).

Key Biscayne Chamber of Commerce, 95 W. McIntyre St., Key Biscayne, FL 33149 (tel. 305/361-5207).

Greater Key West Chamber of Commerce, 402 Wall St., Key West, FL 33040 (tel. 305/294-2587).

Lower Keys Chamber of Commerce, Big Pine Key, FL 33043 (tel. 305/872-2411).

Marco Island Chamber of Commerce, P.O. Box 913, Marco Island, FL 33937 (tel. 813/394-7549).

Greater Marathon Chamber of Commerce, Marathon, FL 33050 (tel. 305/743-5417).

Miami-Dade Chamber of Commerce, 6255 Northwest Seventh Ave., Miami, FL 33150 (tel. 305/751-8648).

Miami Beach Chamber of Commerce, 1920 Meridian Ave., Miami Beach, FL 33139 (tel. 305/672-1270).

Orlando Area Chamber of Commerce, P.O. Box 1234, Orlando, FL 32802 (tel. 305/425-1234).

Sanibel/Captiva Island Chamber of Commerce, Causeway Road, Sanibel Island, FL 33957 (tel. 813/472-1080).

2. Sanibel and Captiva Islands

Exotic, unhurried, meticulously preserved and teeming with wildlife, the barrier islands of Sanibel and Captiva are truly a tropical paradise—a wonderfully diverse destination to "get away from it all." Residents fought hard to keep their islands isolated from the rest of Florida, but since the causeway linking the islands to the mainland opened in 1963, thousands can now visit these two pearls of the Gulf of Mexico.

The two islands are located north of Fort Myers and south of Tampa. Sanibel is the larger of the two (12 miles long and 3 miles wide), extending in an east-west direction into the Gulf of Mexico; Captiva is only six miles long and two miles wide. They are connected to the mainland by a $3 toll bridge.

You won't find a lot of glitz and glitter here; the islands' real appeal lies in their solitude and amazing variety of wildlife. Resorts offer a return to civilization, but honeymooners with a real love of outdoor life will find Sanibel and Captiva most appealing. In order to protect its fragile natural splendor, Sanibel seceded from Lee County and set up its own government, which immediatley put a stop to high-rise development. Sanibel Island is also home to the J. N. "Ding" Darling National Wildlife Refuge, the wonders of which will be discussed later, and is the best place for shelling in the Western Hemisphere.

ROMANTIC INTERLUDES
Just walking hand in hand along the shoreline with the surf washing over your bare feet conjures up a picture of romance in anyone's book, but keep your eyes open for the beautiful and strange birds and other wildlife all around you.

For a day of shelling, the islands are a conchologist's (shell collector's) delight; there are almost more shells than sand on Sanibel. Bring a bucket and wire scoop and at low tide dig in for lion's paws, tulips, cowries, jingles, sand dollars, and calico scallops (only two live samples per person, please). The tides wash them ashore by the thousands. Pick up a shelling guide at any one of the local shops to identify your finds. You'll probably be in good company; hundreds of bent-over diggers can be seen engaging in the popular posture called the "Sanibel stoop."

You'll spot brown pelicans, gulls, Louisiana herons, and other tropical birds all over the islands, but nowhere is the bird and wildlife watching better than in the 5,000-acre **J. N. "Ding" Darling National Wildlife Refuge** on Sanibel Island, named for political cartoonist and naturalist J. N. "Ding" Darling. Bring along a camera, a pair of binoculars, some insect repellent, and a bird book to identify such local inhabitants as the roseate spoonbill, snapping up a meal of fish with its spatula-shaped beak, and "snake" birds, which can swim underwater but must air-dry their wings before flying. There's also a five-mile drive through a mangrove swamp. Rent a canoe at **'Tween Waters Inn** on Captiva Island (tel. 472-5161) or the **Tarpon Bay Marina** (tel. 472-3196) and see the refuge from a different angle. Rentals average $10 for a half day. Canoe trails twist and turn and the current can be swift at times, so this journey may be better left to experienced boaters.

Breakfast, lunch, sightseeing, and romantic sunset dinner cruises are a honeymoon couple's delight from **Fort Dearborn Cruises** at South Seas Plantation (tel. 472-5111). Travel to **Useppa Island,** where the glamour of a bygone era is relived at a historic island resort, now a private club. **Cabbage Key** is laid-back, friendly, fun, and relatively unpopulated (25 people live here full time). Perched atop an ancient Calusa Indian shell mound, the historic **Cabbage Key Inn** offers the best views of the island's natural splendors. Your options include:

□ Captiva breakfast cruise (9 to 10 a.m.): $15 per person.

□ Island luncheon cruise (10:30 a.m. to 3 p.m.): This scenic 1½-hour trip crosses Pine Island Sound to Cabbage Key or Useppa Island, with a stop for lunch at one of the historic resorts. The $20-per-person price does not include lunch.

□ Captiva sightseeing cruise (3:30 to 4:30 p.m.): Sightseeing, sunshine, and tropical libations combine in a nice afternoon cruise of the surrounding waters. The cost is $15 per person; drinks are extra.

□ Island dinner cruise (6 to 10:30 p.m.): Sunset cruise to Cabbage Key or Useppa Island. The $20-per-person price does not include drinks and dinner.

Very much worth the drive over to Fort Myers is the **Thomas A. Edison Home,** 2350 McGregor Blvd., Fort Myers (tel. 334-3614). The 1886 winter home of Thomas Alva Edison is jammed with original furnishings and his numerous inventions, such as his lightbulbs, toaster, and large collection of gramophones. The adjacent laboratory appears untouched, waiting for the inventor to return. The botanical gardens include an assortment of over 6,000 plants and trees. Edison was especially fond of banyans—their gnarled trunks make for interesting photographs. Open Monday through Saturday, 9 a.m. to 4 p.m.; Sunday, 12:30 to 4 p.m. Admission: $5 per person.

HONEYMOON HOTELS AND HIDEWAYS

From luxury hotels to furnished condominiums to private villas, the islands of Sanibel and Captiva welcome you to their tropical hideaways. Where applicable, prices shown reflect the spread between low- and high-season rates.

On Sanibel

Moderate: Tucked cozily among royal palms and surrounded by shimmering crystal waters and an endless blue sky, the **Casa Ybel Resort,** 2255 West Gulf Dr., Sanibel Island, FL 33957 (tel. 813/481-3636; reservations: toll free 800/237-8906 nationwide; 800/282-8906 in Florida), blends perfectly with these romantic islands in southwest Florida. As you step onto the footbridge leading to the resort's entrance, the reflection of the picturesque Thistle Lodge in the serene pond below welcomes you to "a little slice of paradise." Your warmly furnished one-bedroom villa will make you feel instantly at home; but once you walk out onto your private balcony to a view of a sun-washed white beach, palm trees, and emerald water dotted with pleasure craft, you'll know you've landed in a truly enchanted place. All villas are furnished with fully equipped kitchens and beachfront screened-in balconies. Rent sailboats, catamarans, bicycles, and beach cabanas for a whole honeymoon's worth of outdoor activity. Or there's a refreshing swim in the pool, an invigorating set of tennis, or a leisurely round of golf to be enjoyed. "Romantic Retreat" honeymoon package: Four days/three nights (EP): $410.30 per couple; additional night (EP): $121. Includes luxurious one-bedroom villa with private balcony facing the Gulf of Mexico (living/dining/kitchen area and separate kitchen and bedroom), champagne and tropical fruit basket on arrival, $25 dinner certificate at the award-winning Truffles restaurant at the Thistle Lodge, half day's use of bicycles plus picnic lunch, souvenir insulated cooler bag, tennis, and one day's use of beach cabanas. Eight day/seven night package (EP): $855 per couple.

Sundial Beach & Tennis Resort, 1246 Middle Gulf Dr., Sanibel Island, FL 33957 (tel. 813/472-4151; reservations: toll free 800/237-4184 nationwide). The waters of the Gulf of Mexico lap gently to the beach just steps away from your very own island hideaway. Four-story, balconied buildings are hidden from the shell-strewn sands by dense tropical vegetation and playful fountains. This resort is so complete, you'll never have to leave. Play golf or tennis, take a dip in one of the Sundial's five pools, dine to the music of the surf with the gulf as a backdrop, or sip drinks poolside. The Sanibel trolley can transport you on shopping or sightseeing excursions several times a day.

Tropical water colors and a contemporary island-style flair are setting the tone after Sundial's recent $1.2-million renovation and expansion. Hot-pink, royal-blue, and tropical-teal canopies will accent the new exterior, along with extensive tropical gardens. In the meantime, Windows on the Water Restaurant offers panoramic gulf views and seafood specialties; live entertainment and exotic tropical drinks are served up nightly in Morgan's Lounge; Morgan's Deli tempts you with huge sandwiches, salads, and take-out specialties, while Noopies, an authentic Japanese steakhouse, prepares Oriental cuisine tableside. "Tropical Fantasy Honeymoon": Four days/three nights (EP): $397.10 to $707.30 per couple, depending on season; additional night (EP): $104.50 to $207.90 per couple. Includes one-bedroom garden suite, welcome bottle of chilled champagne with souvenir glasses and fruit basket, romantic Sanibel Island excursion with full day's use of bicycles plus picnic lunch, unlimited tennis, "sunset" cocktails, two Sundial beach towels, use of beach cabanas, $100 worth of Island Discount Coupons, and a coupon for a free night at Sundial on your first anniversary. Eight-day/seven-night package (EP): $815.10 to $1,538 per couple, depending on season.

Island-lovers can take advantage of the resort atmosphere without spending a fortune at the **West Wind Inn,** 3345 West Gulf Dr., Sanibel Island, FL 33957 (tel. 813/472-1541; reservations: toll free 800/824-0476 nationwide; 800/282-2831 in Florida). Sun-drenched days and tropical night breezes beckon newlyweds to laze in a beach cabana by the pool, sip an island drink at the tiki pool bar, and explore Sanibel's galleries and shops by bicycle. All rooms include kitchenettes and private balconies with gulf views. "Sanibel Island Honeymoon": Five days/four nights (EP): $308 per couple. Champagne is served up in your room complete with a beautiful rose . . . and you keep the glasses! Also included are a welcome cocktail at the tiki bar, continental breakfast each day, one-day bicycle rental, and discounts on sailboats, windsurfers, even suntan lotion. Seven-day/six-night package (EP): $478 per couple.

Victorian charm is the watchword at **Sanibel Cottages,** 2341 West Gulf Dr., Sanibel Island, FL 33957 (tel. 813/481-3636; reservations: toll free 800/237-

8906). With its laid-back island atmosphere and elegant two-bedroom "Old Florida" retreat—the decor and style born in the glory days of the 1920s—this is the perfect place to be in love. Bay windows overlook whitewashed terraces and a grassy lawn with a footbridge and gazebo. Suites come with fully equipped kitchens, as well as window seats; paddle fans, muted colors, lots of gingerbread woodwork, and oversize tubs with whirlpools top off your private retreat for two. Honeymoon package: None. Room rates (EP): $154 to $291 per couple per night; $1,001 to $1,963.50 per couple per week.

The **Tortuga Beach Club,** 959 East Gulf Dr., Sanibel Island, FL 33957 (tel. 813/481-3636; reservations: toll free 800/237-8906), is a slice of the Caribbean right here in Florida. The two-bedroom villas are lushly landscaped and splashed with bright tropical flowers. The Beach Club's central pool and spa with game room and clubhouse provide an opportunity for socializing in the sun with fellow vacationers. All 54 town-house suites are two-bedroom, two-bath affairs with fully equipped kitchens; wicker and tropical shades blend with the landscape. Honeymoon package: None. Seasonal room rates (EP): $137.50 to $269.50 per couple per night.

Song of the Sea, 863 East Gulf Dr., Sanibel Island, FL 33957 (tel. 813/472-2220; reservations: toll free 800/237-8906). You may feel more as if you're somewhere in the Mediterranean rather than Florida at this old-world inn with whitewashed walls, red tile roofs, and sculptures scattered throughout the grounds. Swim in the heated pool while playful stone cherubs and delicately carved seahorses look on. Relax with a good book from the lending library or treat yourselves to a luxurious soak in the Jacuzzi. After a stroll around the grounds or a few hours of beachcombing in search of shells, cook some juicy steaks or fresh gulf seafood on one of the gas barbecue grills. Rent a boat and catch a breeze for a moonlight sail around Sanibel's Lighthouse Point. Tennis and golf are two privileges you may enjoy as a guest of Song of the Sea, and rented bicycles offer a different perspective of the island. Efficiencies and apartments are modestly but beautifully furnished in soft colors; some offer separate living rooms, fully equipped kitchens, and gulf-front screened balconies. Honeymoon package: None. Seasonal room rates (EP): Efficiency apartment: $74.80 to $154 per couple per night. One bedroom apartment (EP): $91.30 to $176 per couple per night.

On Captiva

South Seas Plantation Resort & Yacht Harbour, P.O. Box 194, Captiva Island, FL 33924 (tel. 813/472-5111; reservations: toll free 800/237-6000 nationwide; 800/282-6158 in Florida), spreads over 330 acres on the northern tip of the island. Accommodations range from hotel rooms to one-bedroom villas to four-room houses right on the beach. The new Harbourside Village deluxe hotel rooms are especially honeymoon-right, overlooking the yacht harbor and Pine Island Sound. The feeling is tropical and islandy, with wicker headboards, rattan chairs, shell-motif pastel fabrics, and a green carpet that matches the palm trees outside. All the rooms have balconies facing the gulf, the marina, or tiny Pine Island. For a ringside view of the famous gulf sunset, choose a one-bedroom beach villa. Each is uniquely decorated, and you can walk right out to the beach. Go shelling on the resort's 2½ miles of private beach, swimming in one of 17 pools scattered around the property, shopping in one of 17 specialty shops in Chadwick Square, or hiking around the miles of resort trails. Play tennis on one of 22 courts or tee off on the resort's own nine-hole golf course. Try a new challenge by spending the day on a deep-sea fishing charter. Learn to sail, windsurf, or jet ski. Or spend a day on the *Silver Lady* boat excursion to legendary Useppa Island and Boca Grande. Since South Seas Plantation encompasses most of Captiva Island, and includes two restaurants and two lounges, you may find that all of your dining and entertainment desires can be met right on the grounds. "Tropical Honeymoon" package: Seven days/six nights (EP): $1,042 to $1,191 per couple for the Harbourside Village hotel room; $1,339 to $1,504 per couple for the Beach Villa suite. Additional night (EP): $192 per couple for the Harbourside Village hotel room, $236 for the Beach Villa suite. Includes champagne and fruit delivered to your suite, use of bicycles for one day, complimentary beach towels, one day's use of beach cabanas, welcome cocktails, and a romantic cruise to a nearby historic island. A huge range of packages is available; call for details.

Started in 1926 with one cottage, **'Tween Waters Inn,** Captiva Road, Captiva Island, FL 33924 (tel. 813/472-5161; reservations: toll free 800/223-5865 nationwide; 800/282-7560 in Florida), has changed hands and expanded, but has kept the original flavor and charm of 1920s Florida. The inn is situated on a narrow strip of land between the gulf and Pine Island Sound; hence its name. Lushly landscaped with native trees and flowers, the popular inn has undergone extensive renovation to offer honeymooners the expected and unexpected amenities of modern resort hotels. The bayside marina provides rental of boats, canoes, and bicycles, and to see this island in all its splendor, try all the boats, bikes, and footpaths you can find. Half-day shelling charters are available from the marina for $160. The crew will take you to Johnson Shoals and Cayo Costa for four hours of shelling on these lovely barrier islands. 'Tween Waters Inn caters to those who crave the outdoors *and* those who prefer the civilized bounty of finely prepared cuisine in a dining room built early in the century. The Old Captiva House Dining Room is open daily for breakfast, lunch, and dinner, and if you'd like, an MAP meal plan (full American breakfast and dinner) is available for just $29 per person per day. Honeymoon package: None. Consider, however, "The Captiva Escape" package: Four days/three nights (EP): $261.25 per couple for a room; $302.50 for a waterview efficiency; $371.25 for an apartment—all with late check-out (3 p.m.). "The Captiva Getaway" package —five days/four nights (EP)—works this way: Stay Friday, Saturday, and Sunday, then Monday or Thursday is free; $313.50 per couple for a room; $363 for a waterview efficiency; $445.50 for an apartment.

Off Captiva

What used to be the winter home of mystery writer Mary Roberts Rinehart is now the **Cabbage Key Inn,** P.O. Box 200, Pineland, FL 33945 (tel. 813/283-2278). The charming 1936 home and adjacent guest cottages are accessible only by boat, but Cabbage Key has other swank residences to explore, plus a restaurant, a lounge, and a marina. Tranquility reigns on this island hideaway (population: 25), but remember that civilization is just a short trip across the water. Cabbage Key is totally devoid of commercialization, but therein lies its charm; here is a perfect slice of "Old Florida" in which to bask, love, and while away your days. Honeymoon package: None. Room rates: Six guest rooms are available in the main house (two with private bath) for $49.50 (EP) per couple per night; three guest cottages have two bedrooms, full kitchens, living areas, baths, patios, and docks for $137.50 (EP) per couple per night, with a two-night minimum.

ROMANTIC RESTAURANTS AND NIGHTSPOTS

Take a break from your busy vacation schedule to enjoy dinner and cocktails in a quaint, romantic setting on these tropical isles.

Expensive

Voted one of America's Top 100 Restaurants by *Florida Trend* is **The Bubble Room,** 15001 Captiva Dr., Captiva Island (tel. 472-5558). Their slogan here is "Every day is Christmas at The Bubble Room," and no matter where your honeymoon adventures take you, you'll never see anything else like this again. The pink, yellow, purple, and green restaurant exterior with uneven rooflines and old tin soft-drink signs gets its name from the hundreds of old-style bubble Christmas lights that adorn the walls inside. If there is a theme, amid the antique toys, old trains that run around a track overhead, movie star photos, and piped-in big-band music, it has to be '30s and '40s nostalgia. Even the dining tables themselves are display cases filled with trinkets and memorabilia. Highlights include Santa's workshop from Macy's department store (circa 1929) and a six-foot stuffed Mickey Mouse hanging from the rafters, one of the first of the "Steamboat Willie" toys. While you're staring in awe at The Bubble Room's amazing collection, don't overlook the real reason the place has gotten so much attention—the food, described by manager Jeffrey Scavo as "hearty middle American home-style cooking with huge portions." Try the "Eddie Fisherman"—a filet of local black grouper topped with a sweet nut-crumb topping and baked in a brown paper bag ($18.95). As much fun to read about as to eat is the "Porky Pig à la Bobby Philips" (who, we're told, dines here on occasion and was the original voice of Porky Pig). "Porky" consists of three thick, slow-cooked and then roasted pork loin chops brushed with garlic and Key lime juice, served with baked banana and guava shells stuffed with cream cheese ($18.95)! The Bubble Room complements its entrées with a fine selection of wines, specialty drinks, and over 20 homemade desserts. Open for lunch from 11 a.m. to 2 p.m., dinner from 5 to 10 p.m., every day except Christmas and Superbowl Sunday. Absolutely a honeymoon have-to!

Moderate to Inexpensive

Truffles at The Thistle Lodge, Casa Ybel Resort (tel. 472-3145). Over a century ago, the Reverend George Barnes built the Victorian gingerbread Thistle Lodge as a wedding gift for his daughter. With its turrets and balconies, fine-trimmed lawn and lush foliage, there could be few places on earth better suited for an evening tête-à-tête. The chef takes foods indigenous to this area—Sanibel shrimp, shark, yellowtail, pecans, and oranges—and creates menus to capture "the taste of Florida." Many specialties such as the Cajun beef Wellington and the creole onion soup rely heavily on the blackening techniques and roux sauces of New Orleans. Menus change monthly to reflect the freshest ingredients. Luncheon is served Monday through Saturday from 11 a.m. to 2 p.m. Sandwiches, soups, and specialty menu items are priced in the $5 to $12 range. Dinner is served from 6 to 10 p.m., with entrées priced between $18 and $28. Brunch on Sunday is an event in itself, featuring seafood crêpes Punta Rassa, Belgian waffles, and café Orleans with praline liqueur and Kahlúa. Brunch is served from 10 a.m. to 2 p.m. and costs $14.95 prix fixe. And if you'd like to be married here, the Thistle Lodge staff would be more than happy to assist you with everything from flowers to limousines.

The Mucky Duck, Andy Rosse Lane, Captiva Island (tel. 472-3434). This English-style pub at the gulf's edge opened in 1976 and quickly gained a reputation for excellence in dining. The warm, cozy feel of The Mucky Duck fits in beautifully with those spectacular water views; it's a local hangout, so don't be surprised if other diners or staff members walk up to your table and start a conversation. The lunch menu ranges from something on the light side (shrimp salad, fruit plate) to real rib-stickers like Scottish-style meat pie or Sam's Samwich with ham, turkey, and Swiss on rye, about $3.75 to $8. Dinner gets dressed up when the chef pulls out all the stops to create roast duckling à l'orange, steak and sausage pie, and Polynesian chicken; prices range from $11 to $16. The Mucky Duck's famous New England clam chowder is not to be missed. Lunch hours are from 11:30 a.m. to 2:30 p.m.; dinner is from 5 to 9:30 p.m. Choose a delicate wine with your meal or a hearty mug of imported beer. No reservations are ever needed and The Mucky Duck takes cash or traveler's checks only.

Stars twinkling over gulf waves—that's the view from **Windows on the Water** at the Sundial Beach and Tennis Resort, 1451 Middle Gulf Dr., Sanibel Island (tel. 472-4151). The panorama is yours for breakfast, lunch, or dinner in a setting of tropical enchantment and exemplary service. Wake up to a glorious breakfast buffet, served Monday through Sunday from 7:30 to 10:30 a.m. Sunday features a special champagne brunch (from 11 a.m. to 2 p.m.) for $13.95 per person. Dinner entrées lean heavily on fresh-from-the-gulf seafood done in unusual ways by the expert chef: shrimp and scallop sausage; mixed grill with seafood sausage; shrimp, scallops, and fresh fish served with a roasted garlic, orange beurre blanc ($17.95); or lump crabmeat vol-au-vent—deviled lump crab encased in puff pastry and served with lobster beurre blanc ($15.95). If you *love* spicy food, though, one of Windows on the Water's very best dishes has to be a Tex-Mex delight—chicken fundido ($9.95). The chicken is braised with onions, tossed with cheddar cheese and sour cream, rolled in a flour tortilla and deep-fried, then served with a rice-stuffed pepper and a heap of guacamole on the side. Olé! The Florida Key lime pie is one of the best in the state; mile-high and served on raspberry sauce, it's guaranteed to make your tastebuds tingle! Top that off with a cup of espresso or cappuccino for a fun, filling, and moderately priced dining experience. Dinner is served from 5:30 to 9:30 p.m., then the adjoining lounge offers gulf views and soft dance music into the night.

The Old Captiva House at 'Tween Waters Inn, Captiva Island (tel. 472-5161). Rustic and quaint inside and out, The Old Captiva House is set in one of the original parts of the hotel. It's clean and pleasant, but if the decor doesn't bowl you over, the food certainly will. Dinners like Florida flounder Véronique (baked in a white wine sauce and topped with white grapes) or medallions Rossini (center-cut filet mignon sautéed in white wine and topped with tomato and mozzarella cheese sauce) include a salad, fresh breads, vegetables, and potato or linguine. All you add is your beverage and dessert. Prices range from $10.95 to $18. The Old Captiva House opens at 7 a.m. for breakfast and closes at midnight.

Chadwick's at South Seas Plantation, Captiva Island (tel. 472-5111). "Tropical" is the key word at this recently redone restaurant. Huge paintings of parrots, toucans, and hibiscus flowers decorate the walls; bright greens and pinks spike interest in the furnishings. Seafood is the specialty here, especially at the all-you-can-eat seafood buffet on Friday nights ($22.50 per person). Help yourself from heaping platters of grouper, shrimp, oysters, and red snapper. Every Tuesday, there's a Hawaiian-style luau ($18 per person), and on Sundays there's a champagne brunch from 9 a.m. to 2 p.m. A live band plays on Friday and Saturday nights at Chadwick's Lounge.

3. Marco Island

Still one of Florida's last frontiers, Marco Island is beautifully remote from the more populated tourist centers that dot the west coast of Florida. The Calusa Indians called this serene island home for 2,000 years and archaeologists are still uncovering artifacts dating back to 500 B.C. Modern man has left his mark on the island, as the high-rise hotels and condominiums attest. But this certainly hasn't dissuaded the locals from moving right in and making themselves at home—bald eagles are sighted occasionally and some have even returned to the island to rear their young.

Take Florida 41 south of Fort Myers for a nice taste of rural Florida. Then follow Florida 953 or 951 onto tiny Marco Island, only about four miles long from stem to stern and so narrow the Jolly Green Giant could straddle it (about a half mile across). Once you cross the bridge, it seems you're far from the mainland— gleaming sugar-white beaches contrast with sparkling emerald and turquoise gulf waters, and lush scrub brush and tall trees seem to grow out of the snowy-white sands.

This is the place where the Ten Thousand Islands begin, a conglomerate of mangrove trees that, because of their enormous root system, pick up pieces of shell, driftwood, and other debris and eventually form their own islands. The islands are great fun to explore by boat, but bring along a guide, as the maze of trees can be confusing.

ROMANTIC INTERLUDES

Far from the big city crowds, Marco Island offers you a chance to get back to nature and enjoy a quiet respite without going too far from civilization.

For a taste of the Everglades wilderness without actually venturing in, **Collier-Seminole State Park** (tel. 394-3397) has 6,500 acres of marshland for canoeing (a favorite spot is the 13-mile loop trail at the Blackwater River) and hiking. A catwalk winds its way through the mangrove swamps. Camping facilities are available and the fishing is fabulous! Admission: $2.50 per person. Follow U.S. 41 (the Tamiami Trail) 16 miles east to find the park.

Ready for a real adventure? Welcome to the wildest part of Florida—**The Everglades.** Spend a day or two exploring this magnificent subtropical wilderness. Everglades National Park takes up most of Florida's southern tip; at 1.4 million acres, that's more area than the entire state of Delaware. Once you venture by boat into the vast sea of marshland and sawgrass, watch carefully for the incredible variety and sheer numbers of plant, bird, and reptile species you are about to encounter. In an environment hostile to man, the alligators, bald eagles, and snowy egrets live harmoniously. It's your chance to see what Florida would be like had man never intervened.

Boat tours are available so you can spend more time watching and picture taking and less time navigating. Everglades tours can be found at Everglades National Park from the **National Park Service** in Everglades City (tel. 695-2591, or toll free 800/233-1821 nationwide; 800/455-7724 in Florida), or from **Eden of the Everglades,** where you can talk to Ervin Stokes in Everglades City (tel. 695-2800). Air-boat rides are offered through **M. Douglas House,** Everglades City (tel. 642-5777, or toll free 800/282-9194).

The pretty little **Marco Island Trolley** (tel. 394-2120) will delight you with a 1½-hour tour of this largest of the Ten Thousand Islands. Trolleys leave from all major hotels and shopping areas 11 times a day (every 45 minutes), but don't fret if it's not exactly on schedule; you're running on island time now. One of your stops will be the Calusa Indian burial mounds, where 6,000-year-old artifacts have been uncovered. Relax and enjoy the ride while spotting pelicans, spoonbills, and perhaps even a dolphin or two (bring binoculars!). The trolley costs $5 per person and runs Monday through Saturday.

HONEYMOON HOTELS AND HIDEAWAYS

It's the best of two worlds: the open wilderness beyond Marco Island and the bustling civilization of cottages and towering hotels that line the beach. Where applicable, prices shown reflect the difference between low- and high-season rates.

Expensive

There's never a dull moment at **Marriott's Marco Island Resort,** 400 South Collier Blvd., Marco Island, FL 33937 (tel. 813/394-2511; reservations: toll free 800/228-9290 nationwide; 800/GET-HERE in Florida), with activities like sailing, fishing, waterskiing, windsurfing, minigolf, or tennis on one of 16 courts. Stroll or swim along the 3½ miles of private beach or swim in one of three pools. Volleyball games are organized regularly if you care to join in the fun. If you go out for a day of birdwatching or deep-sea fishing, chances are you'll be ready for a romantic dinner for two when you get back—you have five restaurants to dine in, from elegant to casual. Just for fun, ask for extra everything on your sundae at the Ice Cream Parlor next to the health club (is that a hint?). Many of the rooms overlook the Gulf of Mexico, others the pool or garden area. Each room is tastefully appointed in soft, pleasant pastel hues and light woods, and each has a separate dressing room with vanity, cable TV and in-room movies, radio, refrigerator, minibar, and coffee maker. And every room has a private balcony. In addition to the tower rooms, there are Hawaiian-style lanais with direct access to the beach. "Island Honeymoon" package: Four days/three nights (EP): $825 per couple. Includes a room with king-size bed, breakfast for two in your room, a bottle of champagne and selection of imported cheeses to welcome you, and a quiet dinner for two in the lavish Marco Dining Room. A six-day/five-night package is available for $1,155 (EP) per couple; and an eight-day/seven-night package costs $1,485 (EP).

At the **Marco Beach Hilton,** 560 South Collier Blvd., Marco Island, FL 33937 (tel. 305/394-5000; reservations: toll free 800-HILTONS nationwide), you'll have ringside seats for some of the most spectacular sunsets on the gulf. Imagine waking to fresh tropical breezes blowing into your room off your private gulf-front balcony. Your honeymoon suite has its own TV with Home Box Office—even a phone in the bathroom. Spend your days sunning, shelling, shopping, surfing, swimming, or enjoying any number of activities the Hilton can help you set up. Honeymoon package: Three days/two nights (EP): $229.90 per couple; additional night (EP): $118 per couple. Includes a standard room with private balcony, welcome champagne and cocktails, a rose, daily continental breakfast, and souvenir sun visors.

Moderate

The Olde Marco Inn, 100 Palm St., Marco Island, FL 33937 (tel. 813/394-3131), provides the comfort and fine dining one would expect at an elegant resort, but preserves the hospitality and charm of the 19th-century wayside inn it once was. The inn is currently owned by Marion Blomeier, a former German concert singer, who has made restoring the inn a life's work. She has included such museum pieces as a 2,000-prism cranberry-colored glass chandelier, original Audubon prints, and wildlife prints by Ray Harin, a former guest at the inn. If you arrive by boat, dock at the pier, where you can fish or enjoy the great sunsets. A new addition to the inn is the Boat House (tel. 813/642-7700) adjacent to the inn just off the Marco River at the entrance to Collier Bay. The lovely guest house, built in keeping with the historic white facade of the inn, features 20 guest rooms with custom-designed interiors. Built-in sitting nooks, overstuffed pillows, and queen- and king-size beds with percale sheets create a cozy tropical ambience. French windows and doors with wooden shutters bring in maximum light and air, while paddle fans, rattan furnishings, and plenty of olive plants provide guests with the warm, friendly atmosphere of a bygone era. More modern conveniences like the cable TV, computer module capability, and direct-dial phones with an automatic wake-up feature remind you that you're not so far away from civilization. Honeymoon package: None. Standard rate (EP) is $115 and up per couple per night, including continental breakfast.

Combine the comfort of a condominium with the amenities of a resort hotel and you've got the **Eagle's Nest Beach Resort,** 410 South Collier Blvd., Marco Island, FL 33937 (tel. 813/481-3636; reservations: toll free 800/237-8906 nationwide). One- and two-bedroom villas are grouped around a tropical garden pool and two spas. French doors open onto screened terraces in the villas, terra-cotta tile floors set off the wood cabinetry, and tropical prints are warmed by natural wicker furnishings. Tennis, racquetball, an exercise and weight room, and a dry sauna are on the premises, while several restaurants and lounges with live entertainment are a short walk away. Honeymoon package: None. Seasonal room rates (EP): $132 to $214.50 per couple per night; weekly rates from $847 to $1,424.50.

You may spend as much time in your room as out when you stay at the **Radisson Suite Resort,** 600 South Collier Blvd., Marco Island, FL 33937 (tel. 813/394-4100; reservations: toll free 800/228-9822 nationwide). The 222 richly appointed suites all have private balconies overlooking the gulf for a cozy breakfast for two of croissants and coffee. Whip up a honeymoon feast in your own kitchen, equipped with refrigerator, dishwasher, and all the trimmings. After dinner, relax in the comfortable living room with a view of the water—and HBO and the Disney Channel on your TV. If you're ready to step out, the Radisson mixes romance with adventure in three restaurants and a piano lounge. "Romantic Adventure" honeymoon package: Four days/three nights (EP): $700 per couple in winter; $427.90 in summer. Includes welcome cocktails, a fruit basket, unlimited use of the whirlpool, exercise room and heated pool, breakfast for two in your room or one of the restaurants, a chilled bottle of champagne, pool towels, and parking. Six-day/five-night package (EP): $1,028.50 per couple in winter; $709.50 in summer. Eight-day/seven-night package (EP): $1,367.30 per couple in winter; $920.70 in summer.

Inexpensive

Glorious sunsets, quaint gazebos, and southern-style hospitality welcome you to **The Beach Club of Marco Hotel,** 901 South Collier Blvd., Marco Island, FL 33937 (tel. 813/394-8860; reservations: toll free 800/323-8860 nationwide; 800/237-8402 in Florida). One-bedroom apartments afford sunset views from private terraces; rooms are tastefully decorated in sunset colors and modern furnishings. Dishes, linens, color TVs, and AM/FM radios make staying in a treat. Outdoor barbecue grills offer another dimension to your honeymoon vacation. Honeymoon package: None. Seasonal room rates (EP): $77 to $143 per couple per night; $462 to $924 per week.

ROMANTIC RESTAURANTS AND NIGHTSPOTS

From quiet and intimate to upbeat and stirring, Marco Island is filled with great eateries and nightclubs, all with those intoxicating gulf views surrounding them.

Moderate

Folks come from all over to dine at **O'Shea's,** 1081 Bald Eagle Dr. (tel. 394-7531). This huge eatery is popular both for its fine food and for its view of Marco Island—the back of the building is glass and overlooks the harbor and marina. Besides a raw bar (4 to 6 p.m. daily) serving shrimp, oysters, clams, and spicy hot chicken wings, there is a Sunday brunch (10:30 a.m. to 2:30 p.m.; $6.95) that just won't quit: freshly squeezed fruit juices; fresh-baked muffins, biscuits, bagels, and pastries; eggs Benedict; roast beef; three vegetables; hash browns—you name it, they've probably got it. Dinner begins at 5 p.m., offering hearty meat-and-potato fare, chicken, fresh seafood, and nightly specialties priced from $6.95 to $12.95. A late-night menu begins at 10 p.m., and a band entertains nightly in the lounge. O'Shea's is also the proud owner of Rosie O'Shea's, an authentic Mississippi paddle wheeler, making luncheon, sightseeing, and moonlight dinner excursions daily. The boat is actually a floating restaurant offering live entertainment with your meal. They also book weddings and receptions on board and can accommodate up to 150 passengers. Call O'Shea's main number for details.

Set in the middle of a small entertainment district on Marco Island, you'll discover the **Cafe de Marco** at the Port of Marco Shopping Village, 244 Palm St. (tel. 394-6262). It's hard to put a name on the eclectic decor, which encompasses stained glass, Tiffany lamps, beamed ceilings, giant stuffed fish on the walls, modest captain's chairs, and tables graced with tiny lanterns. The restaurant is cozy and attracts a horde of locals as well as tourists; there's a nice feeling inside, as if you may have been here before. But the real excitement begins with the food, appetizers including oysters Moscow (on the half shell with horseradish cream and caviar) and stone crab claws. Fresh from Marco waters come such delicacies as grouper, snapper, frogs' legs, lobster, swordfish, and scallops. The grouper Fresca is first sautéed; then simmered in garlic butter and wine with mushrooms, shrimp, shallots, celery, tomatoes, and green peppers; and finally served on a bed of spinach fettuccine. Wonderful! The pride put into every dish is evident and makes for a superb meal for a moderate price (about $50 to $60 per couple).

Dress up for this evening's romantic dinner for two. **Sandcastles Restaurant** at the Marco Beach Hilton (tel. 394-5000) is elegant and intimate with lovely pool views. Low lighting and the white linen and burgundy color scheme offer a romantic setting. Choose the upper balcony for truly intimate dining. Fresh seafood is the specialty here, with exotic treats like swordfish, coconut fried shrimp, or the catch of the day served one of six different ways. Veal, filet mignon, juicy New York sirloin, and breast of chicken round out the menu, painstakingly prepared, elegantly presented, and overwhelmingly enjoyed. Take your time to savor the scenery both inside and out, and linger over after-dinner drinks. Dinners, which will cost a bit over $25 per person, are served between 5:30 and 10 p.m. Sunday through Thursday; one hour later on the weekends. Reservations and jackets are requested.

When you hear strains of "In the Mood" and other classics, you may find it hard to keep your seat, but there's plenty of time to do everything on the island, and dinner at the **Marco Dining Room** at Marriott's Marco Island Resort (tel. 394-2511) should be savored slowly. The cool gray-green color scheme and softly lit chandeliers provide just the proper backdrop for the tuxedoed waiters who come complete with white gloves. Many of the restaurant's specialty dishes are prepared tableside so that you may dine, listen to some great dance music, and watch the chef's floor show all at once! You'll spend about $70 per couple on your dinner, not including dessert and cocktails. Try a glass or bottle of excellent wine from the Marco Dining Room's considerable list. Dinner is served from 6:30 to 11 p.m., with reservations required.

Olde Marco Inn, 100 Palm St. (tel. 813/394-3131). This lovely restored 1883 inn gets more beautiful every week. All of the six dining rooms are decorated in Victorian-era furnishings, curtains, and table settings from the summerhouse setting of the veranda to the formal wood-paneled Audubon Room with its original prints and crystal wall sconces. The continental menu compliments the period ambience. Start your meal with an appetizer of stone-crab claws or marinated Icelandic herring. Fresh fish might include snapper, grouper, shrimp, scallops, stone-crab claws, or whatever comes off the boat that day. Then there are favorites such as southern-fried chicken, wienerschnitzel, or veal Madagascar. Ask about the specialty entrées of the evening. Dinner, including appetizer, soup, and entrée, will run close to $60 per couple. Open for dinner only from 5:30 to 10 p.m. Monday through Saturday; 5 to 10 p.m. on Sunday. Entertainment is provided nightly in both the piano lounge and the Crystal Room for dance music. Reservations for dinner requested.

Inexpensive

The **Paradise Cafe** at the Marco Beach Hilton (tel. 394-5000) is completely glass-enclosed, decked out in soft turquoise and rose with wrought-iron chairs and plants. On the far end, oldtime beach chairs overlook the Hilton's pool. Start each island morning off with a continental breakfast or select from heartier fare. Eggs sandcastle is a thinly sliced filet mignon on an English muffin topped with poached eggs and béarnaise sauce. You'll spend between $5 and $9 for your main breakfast course. Appease your luncheon hunger with a meal of French onion soup and a fiesta salad (beef, beans, cheese, guacamole, and all the trimmings in a tortilla shell), seafood salad (shrimp, scallops, crabmeat, and whitefish), or bite into a grouper sandwich or order the catch of the day grilled or blackened in Cajun spices. Lunch entrées range from $4.95 to $11.95. The Paradise Cafe is open daily from 7 a.m. to 10 p.m.

Beer steins, diagonally paneled windows, plate art, and Lederhosen accent the authentic German menu at **The Bavarian Inn,** opposite the Marco Beach Hilton (tel. 394-7233). Fill up a stein of foamy brew and toast great dishes like sauerbraten, Yaeger schnitzel, Kasseler rippschen, and roast kalbshaxe; waiters will happily help with pronunciations! Serving 4:30 to 10 p.m.; the midnight menu is in effect from 10 p.m. to 1 a.m. Complete dinners are all in the $12 to $20 per person range, sans beer.

4. Central Florida, Disney World, and EPCOT

Up until the 1970s, visitors escaped to Central Florida for the cool serenity of moss-draped cypress, clear natural springs, and sprawling horse farms. Then a man with a vision bought 27,400 acres of swamp land—twice the size of Manhattan— and transformed it into the largest tourist attraction in the world: Walt Disney World and EPCOT Center, jointly known as the Vacation Kingdom. Now Florida Cracker homes and thoroughbred farms coexist with technological wonders of the 21st century. Add to that Central Florida's multitude of spectacles—Sea World, Cypress Gardens, and throngs of other razzle-dazzle attractions—and you just may have the most action-packed and delightfully diverse honeymoon vacation this side of the Milky Way.

Nothing in Disney's world has been left out or left to chance. Each attraction, hotel, restaurant, shop—even landscaping and maintenance—has been planned down to the last detail for visitors from all over the world, honeymooners being no exception. Certainly Disney must have had romance in mind when he designed lazy boat rides through mysterious Louisiana bayous, grottos, and lagoons, cascading waterfalls, even waterside dining with a simulated night sky overhead, complete with the reflected twinkle from Disney-manufactured fireflies.

Orlando is to Central Florida what Mickey Mouse is to the Magic Kingdom— the very center of things and the star attraction. The area is bordered by shady, sleepy southern towns with friendly-sounding names: Fellowship, Lake Placid, Winter Haven, and Kissimee (pronounce it Kiss-SIM-ee). It is about 90 miles from Florida's east and west coasts, which is why it has become such a popular place to live. And for vacations, well, need I say more? There are sure to be all the right ingredients in Central Florida for a memorable honeymoon. It's a place everyone can afford and an experience no one should miss.

ROMANTIC INTERLUDES

If you don't see another thing on your Central Florida honeymoon, take in **The Walt Disney World Vacation Kingdom** (Walt Disney World and EPCOT Center), P.O. Box 40, Lake Buena Vista, FL 32830 (tel. 407/824-4321). Perhaps the eighth wonder of the world, it can be the centerpiece for an entire vacation. There is so much to see and do, a week would not be too long to spend here. Couples will find romantic boat cruises, dining in several different "countries" with authentic cuisine, goods from around the world, fascinating and informative exhibits, and of course, the fun and child-like innocence of Disney character parades, haunted houses, and roller coasters. You're almost guaranteed a perfect honeymoon!

The best time to visit is any time school is in session—early spring or late fall. Crowds thin out a bit at these times, making your stay more enjoyable and lines shorter. A one-day Worldpass, which entitles you to visit either Walt Disney World *or* MGM Studios *or* EPCOT, is $30.65 per person. Four-day Worldpassports good for admission to all three attractions are $102.45 per person; five-day passes are $118.25 per person. If you plan to stay at one of the hotels owned by Walt Disney World, you may get a few dollars off the price of your ticket.

Whole guidebooks have been written about Walt Disney World and EPCOT (pick up a copy of *Frommer's Orlando, Disney World, & EPCOT* or *The Unofficial Guide to Walt Disney World,* both published by Prentice Hall, if you need one). What we've done here is focus in on the attractions that most appeal to fun, action-loving honeymooners like yourselves.

By no means for kids only, **Walt Disney World** is a thrill-a-minute entertainment showcase that provides rides, live entertainment, restaurants, and shopping every day of the year. Begin at Main Street, U.S.A., a look at turn-of-the-century

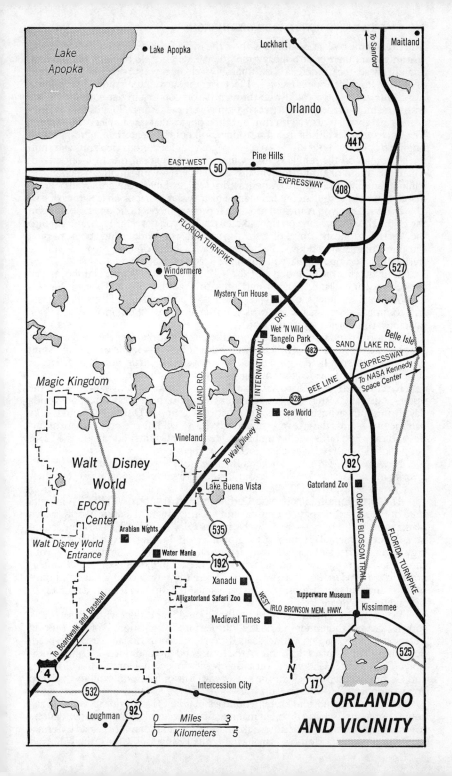

America. Come back at 3 p.m. to witness the Main Street Character Parade. If you visit in the summer or at holiday time, the parade goes electric at 9 and 11 p.m. Straight ahead, the Cinderella Castle officially welcomes you to the wonderful world of Disney, its golden spires rising 181 feet over the surrounding moat. Take off into Adventureland, where you'll ride through bayou country in flat-bottomed boats with eerie moss-draped cypress trees hanging overhead. Stop by Pirates of the Caribbean, a real crowd pleaser, with rum-guzzling pirates that jeer and leer at passersby. The Enchanted Tiki Birds are a fun stopping-off point, an entertaining respite with singing tropical birds set inside a tiki hut. Watch out for curious elephants and smiling crocodiles on the Jungle Cruise. Climb aboard a log raft ride in Frontierland, where the sound of steamboat whistles is interspersed with singing, dancing, and banjo strumming in a salute to America's first settlers. Liberty Square's Hall of Presidents relives our turbulent but fascinating history through look-alike figures of past U.S. leaders. Then you're invited to a dinner party with 999 frolicking holograms in the Haunted House. Hang on tight to each other as you travel through, and get into the "spirit" as ghosts dance, play the organ, and sing while flying about, passing through doors and windows. Before you leave Liberty Square, there's a vintage stern-wheeler waiting to take you down the Rivers of America.

Your favorites of childhood are back—Peter Pan, Snow White, Dumbo, and all the rest in Fantasyland, plus an in-depth, down-under look at Captain Nemo's 20,000 Leagues Under the Sea. Then take a slow boat to China, Holland, Mexico, and countless other faraway places as you sing along to "It's a Small World." We guarantee you'll never forget the words!

Tomorrowland is more than simply a dream of what *could* be: Part of the exhibit has been transformed into a roller-coaster ride at 65 mph—in the dark! Planets and stars whirl past your head within the elaborate Space Mountain ride. While here, be sure to check out the video tour of America in the 360° theater.

River Country and Discovery Island charge additional admission fees, but the flumes, rafts, and water slides can certainly be a refreshing break on a hot Florida day! Bring your swimsuit; towels are provided. Getting to Discovery Island is only half the fun—cross the lake by boat and step into a wildlife preserve with giant turtles and over 500 birds, including bald eagles. River Country admission is $12.46 per person; Discovery Island charges $7.95 per person.

New to see and do . . . Mickey's Birthdayland, a special salute to the world's favorite mouse. Mickey's All-American Birthday Parade gets under way every afternoon down Main Street, U.S.A.

The **Experimental Prototype Community of Tomorrow (EPCOT)** presents state-of-the-art technology in unusual and exciting ways. At Future World, watch plants grow without soil—up to twelve inches a day!—in Kraft's The Land, an innovative experimental greenhouse for growing crops in space. Exxon's World of Energy begins with a movie in the round, then suddenly, one wall moves away, your theater seat starts to move, and all at once you're back in the times of giant *Tyrannosaurus rex*, *Pterodactylus*, and *Stegosaurus*. There they are, looming huge and ominous, munching on treetops. You can even smell the dirt and feel the dampness of the rain forest climate.

Don't miss "Captain EO," the multimillion-dollar thriller with Michael Jackson and a cast of thousands in Kodak's Journey into Imagination. World of Motion puts you in a car, while a tunnel-shaped movie screen moves at incredible speed; Spaceship Earth displays the home of the future and great advances in communications; The Living Sea lets you in on a fish-eye view of ocean floor life; and Horizons and Communicore will delight the senses with lots of hands-on exhibits that keep you wondering, "How do they do that?"

Take a whirlwind tour of ten countries in EPCOT's World Showcase. Each country presents itself in a different manner, from spectacular films to native dancers to street vendors to lazy boat rides. Take in the sights and sounds of Canada, Germany, France, Mexico, Morocco, Japan, the United Kingdom, China, the U.S., and

Norway, "Land of the Midnight Sun," the newest addition to World Showcase. Take plenty of time to browse and buy goods and souvenirs in each country's shops —the section of art objects and handcrafted dolls is as complete and authentic as if you'd actually visited each country. Lastly, our story, an "American Adventure," is told in part by Ben Franklin and Mark Twain. Once you see them walk, gesture, and talk, you'll find it hard to believe they aren't the genuine article.

Look for Disney's newest attraction—**Pleasure Island,** a nighttime entertainment complex on Buena Vista Lagoon. Designed around a mythical 19th-century tale of shipbuilder Merriweather Adam Pleasure, Pleasure Island features seven themed nightclubs to suit all musical tastes and a variety of shops and restaurants to complete the six-acre complex. Shopping and dining excursions are free; there's a $16.50 cover charge at the nightclubs after 6 p.m.

Now the glamour and sizzle of Hollywood have come to Central Florida with the opening of **Disney's MGM Studios** at Walt Disney World (tel. 407/824-4321). Florida has become the third-largest film-producing state in the U.S., after California and New York, and hopes to surpass both of the film giants with this studio and a Universal Studio, also opened in 1989. Visitors to MGM Studios can walk along a re-created Hollywood Boulevard of the 1930s with its own Chinese Theatre, art deco buildings, and shops selling Hollywood trinkets. Tours offer a glimpse of three sound stages where TV shows and films are produced, rides and shows based on Hollywood films such as the flash flood at Catastrophe Canyon, the streets of New York, and The Great Movie Ride. During your visit, you'll also see a special-effects set, meet and talk with Disney animators, and perhaps even be a star at the Disney Television Theatre! Admission is $32 per person; call for tour times.

Nearby, check out **Sea World,** 7007 Sea World Dr. (look for the I-4 Sea World exit), Orlando, FL 32821 (tel. 407/351-3600), the largest marine-life theme park in the world. The shows are the big attraction here, with skillful waterskiing exhibitions, talented seals, choreographed dolphins, and Shamu, the killer whale, trained to perform tricky maneuvers and high jumps with his human entourage. There's more entertainment in store with the "New Friends" whale and dolphin show, 60s-themed waterski show, feeding demonstrations, Japanese pearl-diving exhibitions, and the Shark Encounter, where you can view the creatures from moving sidewalks that glide past the huge shark tanks. But most fun of all is undoubtedly the Penguin Encounter, which showcases about 300 of the dapper black-and-white birds, whose "formal attire" would rival the best-dressed wedding party. Six thousand pounds of manufactured "snow" falls on the exhibit daily. Don't miss it! Open 8:30 a.m. to 10 p.m., later in summer and on holidays. Admission: $23.95 per person; a week-long pass costs $28.95. Parking is free.

Cypress Gardens, P.O. Box 1, west of U.S. 27 on Rte. 540 at Cypress Gardens Boulevard in Winter Haven, FL 33880 (tel. 813/324-2111), is a bit off the beaten path. Cypress Gardens was created over 50 years ago from a cypress swamp. Exotic flowers and clear reflecting pools, in a maze of nature trails, make up the gardens. The waterski shows are some of the best in the state. You'll want to spend the better part of a day here drinking it all in. Open 9 a.m. to 6 p.m., 365 days a year. Waterski shows are at 10 a.m., noon, 2 p.m., and 4 p.m. Admission is $16.95 per person and parking is free.

There's a cozy little town just north of the crowds and feverish pace of Orlando where you may want to spend a whole day. In fact, some folks who visit **Winter Park** go back home, pack the rest of their belongings, and return to stay. Streets are quiet and shady with turn-of-the-century homes adorned with graceful lattice-work gables and porches. Man-made canals weave finger-like through the city. For a leisurely tour of the "Venice of America," hop aboard an excursion boat on one of three lakes. Call the **Winter Park Chamber of Commerce** (tel. 407/644-8281) for a list of boat excursions, times, and prices.

Because of its proximity to Orlando, the town can no longer be called rural— **Park Avenue** is now an exclusive shopping district. After shopping, walk over to

Rollins College to view the well-known **Walk of Fame,** 800 stones inscribed with the names of famous people, brought from their homes and birthplaces. There's also **Mead Botanical Gardens,** a quiet place to walk and picnic while viewing native Florida flora.

A good day trip by car (about two hours from Orlando), the lure of **Busch Gardens** (The Dark Continent), I-275 to the Busch Boulevard exit, 3000 Busch Blvd., Tampa, FL 33612 (tel. 813/971-8282), is not its free beer (although that may cause you to linger a bit); it is the wild giraffes, wildebeests, antelopes, elephants, and zebras that roam the veldt just as they would in Africa. Be sure to bring a camera for some great close-ups in this park, where animals roam free separated from the public by a large moat. Boat rides offer another perspective of these jungle-like habitats. Open from 9:30 a.m. to dusk. Admission, $20.95 per person; parking is $2.

From the folks who brought you Sea World and Cypress Gardens, **Boardwalk and Baseball,** exit 23 off of I-4, Orlando (tel. 407/648-5151), offers a different type of theme park. Reminiscent of Coney Island or Atlantic City, every ride, show, and attraction in the park is connected by a wooden boardwalk. The other half of the name comes in with daily exhibition baseball games in February, March, and April, when Boardwalk and Baseball hosts the Kansas City Royals during spring training. For hard-core baseball fans, there are also batting cages, pitching machines, baseball memorabilia exhibits, and baseball films. For everybody else, Boardwalk and Baseball offers 30 thrill rides, including roller coasters, log flumes, and ferris wheels. Live shows are featured several times daily. New at the park are the majestic Royal Lippizzan Stallions and the Studio One Super Spoof Comedy Game Show, where you can try your skills as a contestant! You'll also enjoy the IMAX Theatre with its 70-foot screen and panoramic short films. Admission is $18.95 per person, which is all-inclusive with the exception of the games on the midway. Parking is free.

After nearly a century of silence, the whistle of a paddle-wheel steamer returns to the St. John's River in the form of the riverboat *Grand Romance,* 433 North Palmetto Ave., Sanford (tel. 407/321-5091, or toll free 800/423-7401). All cruises sail from the downtown harbor in historic Sanford, midway between Orlando and Daytona Beach. The *Grand Romance* is fully climate-controlled, with a library/parlor area, marble fireplace, a grand balcony, a panoramic lounge, and a separate third-deck party room, perfect for weddings and receptions. The captain has performed many ceremonies and would be happy to do yours on board. The ship's wedding coordinator makes all arrangements for meals, hors d'oeuvres, cake, beverages, entertainment, decorations, and anything else you need for a perfect wedding "steamboat-style." Cruises are from 11 a.m. to 2 p.m. on Sunday, Wednesday, and Saturday ($26.25 per person); from 11 a.m. to 3 p.m. on Monday, Tuesday, Thursday, and Friday ($35 per person); and from 7:30 to 11 p.m. every Friday and Saturday—the "Moonlight Magic" dinner-dance cruise ($35 per person on Friday; $40 on Saturday). Also available is a two-day River Adventure, which includes all meals and lodging for $223 per person.

Dating back to boat trips in 1875, **Silver Springs,** State Road 40 near Ocala (tel. 904/236-2121), was Florida's first attraction. The park is set around a series of underground springs, teeming with fish, alligators, and a host of other freshwater creatures. The water is 99.9% pure, so go ahead and scoop up a handful. The jungly natural vegetation is home to raccoons, Florida crocodiles, and a variety of other native wildlife, supplemented with Silver Springs' own additions of Rhesus and spider monkeys, African giraffes, zebras, and colorful parrots and macaws. *Sea Hunt,* the '60s TV series with Lloyd Bridges, and about 120 other movies and TV shows have been filmed in this tranquil place. Glass-bottomed boats (they were invented here) let you observe underwater amazements, while the Jungle Boat Safari takes you on a floating zoo adventure past exotic emus (flightless birds), ostriches, llamas, and cranes. It's a theme park, but its natural setting and distance from major tourist centers (about an hour outside of Orlando) keep the crowds manageable, so your day is relaxed and you can see all you want to see without waiting in long lines. Open

365 days a year, rain or shine, from 9 a.m. to 5 p.m. with extended summer hours. Admission $14.95 per person.

HONEYMOON HOTELS AND HIDEAWAYS

Whether you go all the way or sleep cheap, Central Florida has the largest variety of accommodations in all of Florida—your opportunity to find that one perfect place for romance in a land of magic and fun. Stay right on the Disney grounds in one of several "official" Walt Disney World hotels, or stay for less (usually) in the surrounding towns of St. Cloud, Kissimmee, or Winter Park.

Expensive

The good folks at Disney have outdone themselves with their sparkling turn-of-the-century-style resort **The Grand Floridian,** P.O. Box 10,100, Lake Buena Vista, FL 32830-0100 (tel. 407/W DISNEY). Not since early Floridian magnates Henry Flagler, Addison Mizner, and George Merrick created astonishing resort hotels such as the Breakers in Palm Beach, the Boca Raton Hotel and Club in Boca Raton, and The Biltmore in Coral Gables has there been this kind of old Florida sophistication and detail brought to a resort hotel. Three giant stained-glass domes grace the five-story lobby ceiling, and a chamber orchestra plays daily on the second-floor balcony; at night, a tuxedoed musician positions himself at the grand piano in the very center of the lobby. Bellboys in golf caps and knickers drive you to your room in miniature trolleys. And all about you, gables, turrets, breezy verandas, and lots of gingerbread grace the whitewashed and red-roofed buildings. The Grand Floridian is a marvel, with 900 rooms in several buildings built around a central lodge, designed after the century-old Hotel del Coronado near San Diego. Most rooms are drenched in sun-washed tones of peach and white and boast light woods, armoires, marble vanities, and paddle fans. Honeymoon package: None. If you choose a suite over a room, you will stay in one of the buildings adjoining the main lodge. Six honeymoon suites are all in the main building, and in addition to the endless space, you'll be treated to a panoramic view, a four-poster bed, and concierge service, combining the graciousness of a bygone era with the technological wizardry of today. Room rates (EP): Garden view: $203.50 to $225.50 per couple per night. Honeymoon suites (EP): $330 to $352 per couple per night. Other accommodations and packages are available; call Walt Disney World reservations (tel. toll-free 800/874-7624).

An oasis in a world of fun, Disney's **Contemporary Resort** at Walt Disney World, P.O. Box 10,100, Lake Buena Vista, FL 32830-0100 (tel. 407/W DISNEY), is a sightseer's delight with its 90-foot floor-to-ceiling mural on the Grand Canyon Concourse. Oversize rooms, with two queen-size beds, extra-spacious bathrooms, and 21st-century conveniences, are tastefully adorned in muted blues and earth tones. Private balconies overlook either shimmering Bay Lake or Disney's Magic Kingdom. The pleasures of shopping are made to order right inside the resort, where you can indulge yourself in Disney logo sportswear, swimsuits, jewelry, and a wealth of fun souvenirs. Honeymoon package: None. Room rates (EP): $165 to $187 per couple per night; $220 to $242 for a room in the tower.

Comparable to any of Florida's most luxurious accommodations, **Disney's Village Resort** at Walt Disney World, P.O. Box 10,100, Lake Buena Vista, FL 32830-0100 (tel. 407/W DISNEY), gives you a choice of a villa or a suite in a wooded setting on a private lake. Each unit has been individualized. You might get an airy town house or a rustic villa with a loft. Or how about a circular tree house hidden back in the woods for the honeymoon night? Most accommodations will have full kitchens with microwaves, or you'll get a refrigerator, wet bar, and hot-pot with coffee, cups, and stirrers. You're just a short walk away from infinite shopping and dining possibilities at Walt Disney World Village, and a great view of EPCOT's geodesic dome is visible from just about anywhere on the grounds. Honeymoon package: None. Rates (EP): $159.50 to $187 per couple per night for a club suite; $203.50 to $231 per night for a one-bedroom villa.

A "suite" honeymoon at Walt Disney World Village would surely have to include the all-suite **Pickett Suite Resort,** P.O. Box 22811, Lake Buena Vista, FL 32830-9990 (tel. 407/934-1000; reservations: toll free 800-PICKETT nationwide). The one-bedroom suite has a separate bedroom and living/dining area, hairdryers, two remote-controlled color TVs, coffee/tea makers, a wet bar, a stocked refrigerator, and a microwave. The daily breakfast buffet comes with your suite, as does access to the Pickett's health club, heated pool, and lighted tennis courts. "Magical Honeymoon" package: Four days/three nights (EP): $729.30 per couple. Your luxurious one-bedroom suite comes with a king-size bed, full breakfast buffet daily, a bottle of champagne with special keepsake glasses, and two one-day Passports to the Magic Kingdom, EPCOT, or the Disney MGM Studio Theme Park. A six-day/five-night package includes a four-day World Passport for $1,202.30 (EP) per couple, and the eight-day/seven-night package for $1,601.60 (EP) gives you a five-day World Passport.

Moonlight on the waves, sipping cool drinks while gentle ocean breezes tempt you to fall in love all over again—cruises just seem to appeal to people in love. **Premier Cruise Lines,** the official cruise line of Walt Disney World, 101 George King Blvd., Cape Canaveral, FL 32920 (tel. 407/783-5061), can make fairy-tale honeymoons come true with their combination cruise and Walt Disney package. "Honeymoon Magic at Sea" package (EP): Eight days/seven night cruise from $1,309 per couple. Take off on the *Star/Ship Majestic, Atlantic,* or *Oceanic* from Port Canaveral, just 45 minutes from Orlando. You'll be welcomed aboard with chilled champagne in your stateroom, compliments of the captain. A different theme with its own international menu awaits you each night at dinner. There's even a midnight buffet *every night!* Nightclub revues, a special honeymooner's cocktail party, visits by Disney characters, and a special "Honeymoon-at-Sea" certificate are all part of the package. If you visit Walt Disney World Resort before or after your honeymoon cruise, you'll get three nights of accommodations at an Orlando hotel, seven days rental of a Budget or Alamo rental car with unlimited mileage, a three-day WorldPassport to Walt Disney World's Magic Kingdom and EPCOT, plus a tour of Spaceport USA at the NASA Kennedy Space Center—free. Important: You must book six months in advance and stay at one of the Disney properties. A deluxe honeymoon package can be added to the cost of the cruise for just $203.50 (EP) per couple more. You'll get a luxury suite at an Orlando hotel, luxury rental car, two crystal wine glasses, fresh flowers in your stateroom, honeymoon T-shirts, and a keepsake photo and photo album.

With 1,503 guest rooms and a sweeping panoramic view, **Marriott's Orlando World Center,** World Center Drive, Orlando, FL 32830 (tel. 407/239-4200; reservations: toll free 800/228-9290 nationwide; 800/843-3755 in Florida), rates as the largest and certainly one of the most diverse resort hotels in all of Florida. Each room has a private balcony. Furnishings are contemporary, done up in soothing tones of peach and gray, with a separate sitting area. There are 10 restaurants, an 18-hole golf course on the grounds, 12 lighted tennis courts, palms, waterfalls, a lagoon, 4 pools, whirlpools, and more amenities to discover for yourselves as guests of this palatial honeymoon retreat. The views are spectacular. The free-form pool contains a half-million gallons of water, and the World Center would, of course, have to have its own shops that are as unique and diverse and extravagant as those at the Walt Disney World Shopping Village. "World Honeymoon Package": Four days/three nights (EP): $638 per couple. Includes a deluxe suite with private balcony; welcome champagne and chocolates; one-day tickets to the Magic Kingdom, EPCOT, or the Disney/MGM Studio Theme Park; transportation to and from the parks; and a candlelight dinner at the Regent Court restaurant or from room service. Additional night, standard room, is $187 (EP) per couple; suite $275 (EP).

For an upbeat but romantic atmosphere; for fancy accommodations and fanciful nights; for sheer unexcelled delights on a grand scale, spend a night or two or seven at the **Stouffer Orlando Resort,** 6677 Sea Harbor Dr., Orlando, FL 32821 (tel. 407/351-5555; reservations: toll free 800/822-4200). The lobby of this world-class honeymoon haven is breathtaking. Ten stories of rooms with private balconies flank a 65,000-square-foot atrium capped by giant skylights. Take a ride up one of the seven glass elevators really to appreciate the view. Look down upon diners in the café-like L'Orangerie. Exotic birds, fish, and plants add to the tropical setting amid pools and waterfalls. You might guess that all the rooms and suites here provide the ultimate in comfort and luxury. Honeymoon packages: "The Wedding Night": Two days/one night (EP): $222 per couple; additional night (EP): $218. Includes oversize room with king-sized bed, or exclusive Club Level Floor accommodations featuring bathrobes, makeup mirrors, a hairdryer, personalized concierge service, complimentary cocktails, hors d'oeuvres, continental breakfast daily at the Club Level Lounge, and nightly turn-down service. Both types of rooms receive chilled champagne with keepsake glasses upon arrival, room service breakfast, special certificate for return stay on your first anniversary. "The Grand Honeymoon" package: Three to seven nights (EP): $907 to $1,574 per couple. Additional night (EP): $218 per couple. All of the above plus dinner for two in the Atlantis or Haifeng restaurant, and $200 in Stouffer currency to use for attraction tickets, gift shop purchases, or for dining and entertainment in any of the eight restaurants and lounges.

Made for romance, the **Hyatt Regency Grand Cypress,** One Grand Cypress Boulevard, Orlando, FL 32819 (tel. 407/239-1234; reservations: toll free 800/233-1234 nationwide), is an alluring paradise for just-wedded bliss. Soft colors, lush gardens, ponds, lagoons, grottos, a rope bridge, waterfalls, and colorful sailboats on the Hyatt's private lake make a lasting first impression. Step into a multistory lobby where giant coconut palms tower over the marble reception desk. Check into one of 750 rooms, meticulously appointed for total comfort. Get into the swing right away at the 45-hole Jack Nicklaus Signature Golf Course, the 9-hole pitch-and-putt course, or one of the championship tennis courts. A health and fitness center, aerobics classes, bicycles, a 20-station par course, nearly five miles of jogging trails, and an equestrian center are all part of the fun. Honeymoon package: Two days/one night (EP): $393.80 per couple. Includes a one-bedroom executive suite, use of health club and recreation facilities, a bottle of champagne on arrival, and breakfast in bed.

The royal ducks have moved to Orlando at **The Peabody Orlando,** 9801 International Dr., Orlando, FL 32819 (tel. 407/352-4000; reservations: toll free 800/COCONUT nationwide). A new flock of ducks has stolen some of the Memphis Peabody's thunder—now there are two of these grandiose hotels, known worldwide for their impeccable attention to detail. *And* their ducks, which arrive each morning to frolic in the lobby fountain. The 891 guest rooms and suites are a visual treat—soft, muted shades of peach and beige and a touch of mint blend subtly with the day's fading sky. Remote-control cable TV, bathroom TV and hairdryer, and imported soaps will make you feel pampered. "Again and Forever" honeymoon package: Two days/one night: $181.50 per couple. Toast your honeymoon with welcome champagne, breakfast in bed or at the Peabody's Bee Line Diner, and receive a souvenir of your stay. The four-day/three-night package for $638 (EP) per couple adds a one-day pass to the Magic Kingdom and EPCOT, transportation to the attractions, and a welcome cocktail. The eight-day/seven-night package, $1,177 (EP), offers a four-day pass to the Magic Kingdom and breakfast each day.

Moderate

Along with the Buena Vista Plaza and Hotel Royal Plaza, the **Hilton** at Walt Disney World Village, 1751 Hotel Plaza Blvd., Lake Buena Vista, FL 32830 (tel. 407/827-4000; reservations: toll free 800-HILTONS), is an "official" Walt Disney World hotel, meaning there is a quality of service and satisfaction that must be maintained, so the only surprises will be good ones. Adjacent to the Walt Disney World Shopping Village, the ten-story hotel is as luxurious as it is convenient. Complimentary transportation to the Magic Kingdom and EPCOT Center is available for all guests. Built on 23 acres, the Hilton is designed to complement its lush surroundings, encircling a picturesque waterfall and fountain. Enter through the palm-lined drive past a tropical background and two ponds. Rooms feature soothing colors and plush furnishings plus state-of-the-art telephones that control everything from the TV to the room temperature. Two swimming pools, tennis courts, golf, a health club, six restaurants, and lounges are available to you during your stay. There's horseback riding and sailing nearby that the Hilton will be happy to set up for you. Honeymoon package: None. "Stay and Play" package: Four days/three nights (EP): $631.40 per couple. Includes standard room plus breakfast each day; two tickets to the Magic Kingdom, EPCOT, or Disney's MGM Studio Theme Park; and free transportation to and from the parks. Additional night (EP): $165 to $214.50 per couple.

Las Palmas Inn, 6233 International Dr., Orlando, FL 32819 (tel. 407/351-3900; reservations: toll free 800/327-2114 nationwide; 800/432-1175 in Florida), is located in the "heart of the entertainment district," within walking distance of 150 shops and restaurants, and is also conveniently close to Disney World, EPCOT, and all the rest. Refreshingly tranquil, the newly decorated hotel has a breezy Mediterranean feel to it, with its white stucco walls and red-tile roof. Soak up those warm Florida rays at the palm-studded courtyard pool or have a drink in the poolside cabana. The staff here is anxious to arrange every detail beforehand to assure you of a memorable honeymoon. Guests are treated to transportation to nearby attractions, and if you'd like to play a round of golf or a fast set of tennis, Las Palmas can get you there too. Honeymoon packages: "Magic Moments": Three days/two nights (EP): $125 per couple. Includes deluxe accommodations with use of resort amenities, one-day Passport for admission to either the Magic Kingdom or EPCOT Center, one-day admission to Sea World. "Magic Memories": Seven days/six nights (EP): $315 per couple. Similar to "Magic Moments," but also includes a three-day Passport to both the Magic Kingdom and EPCOT Center.

Remodeled, refurbished, and rededicated, the 27-acre **Sheraton Lakeside Inn** at Walt Disney World Main Gate, 7711 U.S. 192 West, Kissimmee, FL 32741 (tel. 407/828-8250; reservations: toll free 800/422-8250 nationwide), extends a special welcome to newlyweds. The 651 deluxe rooms are surrounded by amenities such as two heated Olympic-size pools, an 18-hole miniature golf course, four tennis courts, and free paddleboats for a romantic trip around the Sheraton's private lake. The sparkle at Sheraton Lakeside is designed for love: New are an intimate lounge, a lakeview restaurant, a deli, and a buffet restaurant. All rooms are redecorated in soft colors and light woods, and they now have refrigerators (to keep the champagne cold?). "Honeymoons Forever" package: Five days/four nights (EP): $515 per couple in winter; $443 in summer. Includes a welcome split of champagne, one dinner and one breakfast in one of the restaurants, a welcome cocktail, and one-day passes to both the Magic Kingdom and EPCOT. Eight-day/seven-night package (EP): $891 per couple in winter; $760 in summer. Add to the above tickets to either Wet-n-Wild or Cypress Gardens, a rental car for seven full days, and a Walt Disney World three-day Passport.

If a spacious suite with a wood-burning fireplace, whirlpool, and a full kitchen with dishwasher, coffee maker, and popcorn popper can stir visions of fun-filled honeymoon days and nights, step into the all-suite **Residence Inn by Marriott-Kissimmee,** 4786 West Irlo Bronson Memorial Highway, Kissimmee, FL 32741 (tel. 407/396-2056; reservations: toll free 800/468-3027 nationwide; 800/648-7408 in Florida). Suites are L-shaped with 500 square feet of room to sprawl. Pinks, grays, light woods, and lots of potted palms create a homey environment. Many of the suites offer views of Lake Cecile. Honeymoon package: Eight days/seven nights (EP): $1,087.90 per couple. Includes luxurious studio suite with fruit basket, surprise honeymoon gift, bottle of champagne, and daily continental breakfast buffet; three-day interchangeable World Passport to EPCOT Center and the Magic Kingdom, two one-day admissions to Sea World, and two one-day admissions to Water Mania (the exciting new water park in Kissimmee); waterskiing, jet skiing, bumper boating, sailing, paddleboating, and canoeing on Lake Cecile; and seven-day car rental. Lakeview suites at no extra charge based on availability. Also, the Residence Inn asks you to mention any other special requests that would make your honeymoon stay more enjoyable.

Inexpensive

Setting the style for great little hotels, **The Floridian of Orlando,** 7299 Republic Dr. (International Dr.), Orlando, FL 32819 (tel. 407/351-5009; reservations: toll free 800/445-7299 nationwide; 800/237-0730 in Florida), might be a cozy getaway for couples on a budget. Not fancy, but spotless and comfortable in pastels and wicker. Honeymoon package: None. If you alert the hotel that you're on your honeymoon, you could be treated to a few surprises! Room rates (EP): Standard room $97 per couple per night; suites range from $93 to $130 per night. Two restaurants, a poolside bar, and a lounge offer ample dining opportunities, but you're also right in the hub of "entertainment central" for dining, shopping, and sightseeing.

ROMANTIC RESTAURANTS AND NIGHT SPOTS

We'll concentrate on the best spots in the greater Orlando area, including everything from New Orleans jazz to Shakespeare-flavored fare. Remember, this is only a very small sampling. From wherever you're staying in the area, you more than likely have access to at least 50 different places to eat and drink. All these restaurants are located in the 407 telephone area code.

Expensive

You'll find the charming **Christini's Ristorante Italiano** in a quiet corner of Orlando at The Marketplace, 7600 Dr. Phillips Blvd. (tel. 345-8770). The maitre d' welcomes you warmly, then escorts ladies to their tables. Christini himself visits each table to make sure everything meets with your approval. Italian songs are played softly on the accordion while you dine on sumptuous fare such as carpaccio, rack of lamb, lobster Vesuvio, and an abundant selection of pasta dishes. Italian bronze and porcelain figurines create an elegant border between the two tiers of seating, with light-oak furnishings set off by tones of muted green and mauve. Along with your entrée, you're served warm Italian bread with eggplant spread. Try a hot appetizer of baked stuffed clams or fresh mushroom caps filled with prosciutto, artichokes, mozzarella, and parmesan. For the finale, Christini recommends his own ricotta cheesecake with strawberry coulis. Dinner for two, including wine, averages $80 to $100 per couple. Serving dinner from 6 p.m. to midnight. Reservations are always recommended, as is proper attire.

Villa Nova, 839 North Orlando Ave., Winter Park (tel. 644-2060), has been an Orlando tradition since 1948. The menu is classic northern Italian, meaning sauces are very light and cooked for mere minutes. Your surroundings are classically elegant, with fanlight windows, arched doorways, and museum pieces blended with low-slung leather chairs and warm sunset colors. You'll find fancy dishes such as duckling and squid, but your favorites are here, too, prepared in interesting ways. Start with fried jumbo shells filled with lobster mousse for $6.95, or slices of charred sirloin, served cold with parmesan shavings, virgin olive oil and mustard sauce ($6.95). Pasta is a must—the northern versions won't fill you up, so there's room for the entrée, maybe even dessert! Share a plate of spinach ravioli with brown butter, sage, walnuts, and parmesan cheese ($8.95). Entrées to make your mouth water are chicken breasts filled with Italian sausage and sautéed, then placed on Madeira sauce and grilled eggplant and topped with Alfredo sauce for $12.95. Or there's fresh loin of tuna rolled in pasta sheets, with a julienne of vegetables, fresh herbs, and basil cream ($15.95). Open Monday through Saturday, 6 to 11 p.m.; Sunday, 5 to 9 p.m.

"The best slow dancing" and "best fast dancing" lounge, according to *Central Florida Magazine,* is **Cheek to Cheek,** the back room of the Villa Nova restaurant, 839 North Orlando Ave., Winter Park (tel. 644-2060). Live entertainers crank out contemporary and Top 40 tunes Tuesday through Saturday; performers have included Phoebe Snow, Kenny Rankin, Bonnie Raitt, Leon Russell, and Doc Severinsen, among others. Ladies are treated to free champagne, and the $3 cover charge is waived Tuesday through Thursday. Call the VIP Concert Ticket Line at 407/647-4477 for concert information. If you dine at the Villa Nova, there's no cover charge. The intimate atmosphere is highlighted by geometric designs and huge plants lit from within. Open Tuesday through Saturday, 8 p.m. to 2 a.m.

Smack in the middle of Winter Park's most exclusive shopping district, is found the café-like **Park Plaza Gardens,** 319 Park Avenue South, Winter Park (tel. 645-2475). The New Orleans–courtyard setting is casual and friendly, and highly regarded for its power lunches, Sunday champagne brunches, and elegant candlelight dinners. Since 1984, Park Plaza Gardens has appeared on *Florida Trend*'s list of Top 100 Restaurants. Lobster, shrimp, scallops, and red snapper poached in white vermouth, scaloppini of veal rolled around shrimp, and filet of beef tenderloin are all prepared creatively and presented in exemplary fashion. Entrées range from $15.95 to $28.50. For those watching their health, the restaurant presents five entrées recommended by the American Heart Association. Breakfast is served Monday through Saturday from 8 to 11 a.m.; lunch from 11:30 a.m. to 3 p.m.; dinner Sunday through Thursday from 6 to 10 p.m. and Friday and Saturday from 6 to 11 p.m.; Sunday brunch from 11 a.m. to 3 p.m.

Pricey but nice, the **Royal Orleans,** 8445 International Dr. in Mercado Festival Center (tel. 352-8200), offers superb Louisiana-heritage cuisine (entrées $16 to $22), 50 fine wines, and impeccable service for a special night out. The menu changes monthly to maintain the finest and freshest products at the peak of their season. The terraced courtyard serves hot chocolate New Orleans style, chicory coffee, and beignets (French doughnuts with powdered sugar). Dinner served nightly from 5 to 11 p.m.

Moderate

"Let the good times roll" as you cavort through the **Church Street Station,** 129 West Church St., Orlando (tel. 422-2434), an all-inclusive dining and entertainment complex created from old warehouses. Located in historic downtown Orlando, Church Street Station is one stop you must make. Any night of the week, any day of the year, you're guaranteed some great Dixieland jazz, high-stepping dancing girls, and terrific dining. **Apple Annie's Courtyard** serves up crispy salads, deli sandwiches, fresh fruit and frozen ice cream specialty drinks at moderate prices, along with a heavy dose of folk and bluegrass music (open nightly from 8:20 p.m. to 2 a.m.). **Lili Marlene's Aviator's Pub and Restaurant** is the place for aviator memorabilia, aged steaks, and fresh Florida seafood (open for lunch from 11 a.m. to 4 p.m.; dinner from 5:30 p.m. to midnight). Expect to pay around $15 apiece for lunch; dinner entrées range from $16 to $25. The rip-roarin', foot-stompin' **Rosie O'Grady's Good Time Emporium** comes complete with Red Hot Mamas, Rosie O'Grady's Good Time Jazz Band, cancan and bar-top dancers. **The Gay 90's** sandwich parlor serves stacked sandwiches and Rosie's authentic Red Hots (hot dogs); food served from 4:30 to 11 p.m. Eat 'em raw at **Crackers** (oysters, shrimp, and clams), or try the delectable blackened gator, the andouille sausage jambalaya, or a Cedar Key salad with sugar dates, peaches, and pineapple. Luncheons average about $15; for dinner you'll spend anywhere from $25 to $40 each. Belly up to the bar in the **Cheyenne Saloon and Opera House,** famous for its barbecue (lunch, about $20 per couple; dinner, about $40 to $50). At 8:30 p.m., 10 p.m., 11:30 p.m., and 1:00 a.m., the Cheyenne Stampeders and the Cheyenne Cloggers perform; dance lessons are offered free every Monday. Get swept up in the light and video extravaganza at **Phineas Phogg's Balloon Works,** where there's dancing to the latest hits from 7 p.m. to 2 a.m. nightly. Admission to all of the nightly shows is $14.95 per person. For an inspired honeymoon adventure, book a champagne balloon flight, available daily, weather permitting. Along with the hot-air-balloon flight, you're treated to free admission to Church Street Station, a complimentary Church Street Station champagne glass, a souvenir gift packet, and a champagne brunch in Lili Marlene's restaurant after the flight! Total package: $140 per person plus tax. Call 407/422-2434 for bookings.

If you're staying in the Kissimmee area (that's closest to Disney World), and even if you're not, you may still opt for a drive to **Medieval Times,** 4510 Vine St., Kissimmee (tel. 396-1518), a castle-looking structure where a night's (knight's?) fare may include roasted chicken flambé, spare ribs, pastries, and a hearty mug of ale. Seating is by reservation only (those coming early get the best seats) in an arena-type hall where jousting exhibitions, javelin throwing, and sword fighting make up your dinnertime entertainment. The $25-per-person price includes your dinner, beverages, show, and tax. The castle opens at 6 p.m., with the two-hour show beginning at 6:45 p.m.

At **King Henry's Feast,** 8984 International Dr. at Plaza International, Orlando (tel. 351-5151; reservations: toll free 800/347-8181), another full evening's fun awaits you in an English manor house with its own tower and moat. The king's six wives are portrayed in paintings on the walls of the entrance hall. The theme is King Henry's surprise birthday feast as he seeks out a seventh bride—one that won't, um, lose her head. Wenches serve up jugs of free beer and wine, and refer to red-bibbed diners as "m'Lord" and "m'Lady." The evening begins with a welcome mead (wine and honey) reception, moves on to a five-course banquet consisting of the Lord Mayor's soup, Suffolk salad, mix'd Normandy berries, main roasts, and young wife's pudding, then the real entertainment begins. Sing-alongs, magic shows, dancing, singing, and balancing acts are the main attractions, with all performers clad in period costumes. The singing and carrying-on get louder and generally wilder as the evening wears on. Showtime begins promptly at 7:30 p.m. and lasts up to three hours. Admission price is $24.95 per person. Twenty-four-hour advance reservations requested.

"Bienvenu!" "Welcome!" At **Mardi Gras,** at Mercado Festival Center, 8445 International Dr., Orlando (tel. 351-5151; reservations: toll free 800/347-8181), you will enjoy an evening of southern hospitality, carnival excitement, and the delicacies of an authentic New Orleans–style dinner all rolled into one. The evening starts off with a traditional mint julep or famous hurricane cocktail, followed by a four-course lightly seasoned creole dinner including cream of broccoli soup, fruit ambrosia, seafood casserole or baked chicken breast, corn-and-tomato vegetable casserole, and a great praline parfait dessert prepared by New Orleans chef James "Beany" Macgregor. A New Orleans jazz band performs during dinner, then a one-hour cabaret show features a 22-member cast with elaborate costumes and sterling choreography. The show combines a medley of Caribbean, Latin American, and West Indian Mardi Gras numbers. Showtime is 8 p.m. and reservations are essential. Admission is $24.95 per person.

Another in a series of themed restaurants owned by "Orlando Entertains," this newest undertaking, the **Fort Liberty Wild West Dinner Show and Trading Post,** 5260 West Hwy. 192 near I-4, Kissimmee (tel. 351-5151; reservations: toll free 800/347-8181), cost $4 million to build and seats 500 in a realistic 11-acre western complex with a stockade and western memorabilia. Fort Liberty features the essence of American pioneer days, complete with western music and food, and a medicine man and his traveling entertainment show. The evening starts off with a five-course western banquet with unlimited beer and soft drinks served by cowpokes and rustlers in authentic costume. After dinner comes the hootin', hollerin' 12-performer show. Be prepared to participate and sing along with songs everybody knows. Showtimes vary according to season and last about two hours. Open daily; reservations are requested. Admission price is $24.95 per person.

Wonderful seafood, large portions, great desserts, and a fun, relaxed ambience keep folks coming back to **Charlie's Lobster House** at Mercado Mediterranean Shopping Village, 8445 International Dr., Orlando (tel. 352-6929). The diverse seafood menu includes shrimp, lobster, oysters, clams, scallops, mussels, and some of the most succulent crab you've ever encountered. Fresh fish and crab cakes round out the assorted entrées. Key lime pie is done to perfection, as are all of Charlie's lip-smacking desserts. Dine in wide, comfortable banquettes with tiny lanterns on each table. It's intimate enough for quiet conversation, and the personable staff adds to the fun with top-notch service and lively commentary. Dinner entrées range from $15 to $20, including salad. Open daily for lunch and dinner, 10 a.m. to 10 p.m.

5. Miami/Miami Beach

Miami is as different from Miami Beach as a Jeep is from a BMW: Both can be very exciting, but in very different ways.

The two are next-door neighbors. If you're driving south along the coast, you can follow Interstate 95 or U.S. 1 from Fort Lauderdale south into Miami, or take A1A south for the island route: Sunny Isles, Bal Harbour, and on into beautiful Miami Beach. It is only about ten miles long but those are about the most visitor-oriented, fun-filled, nightlife- and attraction-packed ten miles you'll ever see. Miami Beach is linked to Miami by several causeways, giving you easy access from four different points.

Key Biscayne is an island south of the beach, with Virginia Key and Fisher Island in between. It can only be reached by the Rickenbacker Causeway through Virginia Key from U.S. 1 in south Miami. The Key is only a couple of miles long, but offers water views all around and *seclusion* in this busy tourist town. The famous Tamiami Trail (U.S. 41), connecting Florida's east and west coasts, is a direct route from Miami to Coral Gables southeast of Miami. Here and in most of Miami, you'll want to brush up on your Spanish—it's the second language here and may make it easier for you when dealing with taxi drivers, airport porters, and waiters. South of Coral Gables on Biscayne Bay is glitzy, wealthy Coconut Grove.

If you've never considered Miami and its most famous beach as a honeymoon destination, think again. The upbeat, thriving feel of a resort city on the move is back, offering tourists sunshine, accommodations, and nightlife.

ROMANTIC INTERLUDES

There is an enormous amount of sightseeing (and driving!) to be done in and around Miami. You may want to get a rental car so you won't miss a thing!

Built as a winter refuge for Evanston, Illinois, native John Deering, the incredible **Vizcaya Museum and Gardens,** 3251 South Miami Ave. (tel. 579-2813), a mansion-turned-museum, took two years (1914–1916) and 1,000 people to build. Deering, not to be confused with John Deere of tractor fame, earned his great wealth as cofounder and vice president of International Harvester Company. Because the mansion overlooks Biscayne Bay, he named the property "Vizcaya," a Basque word meaning elevated place. Deering used the palatial home as a showcase for his European and Oriental art pieces. As you take the guided tour through the home you will learn, among many other things, of the 150 types of marble used in the floors, shipped here from all over the world.

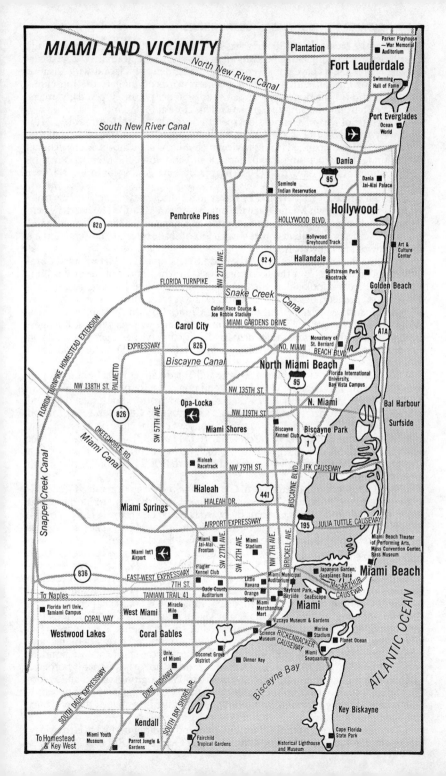

The entire estate, once 180 acres, has shrunk to only 30, but the entrance roads are still dense with jungle-like vegetation, in contrast to the neatly landscaped gardens. It is possible to have your wedding in the gardens of Vizcaya with advance permission of the museum and some planning to accommodate the museum's many restrictions. The house-and-garden tour is $6 per person. Open daily except December 25 from 9:30 a.m. to 5 p.m. Gardens close at 5:30 p.m.

For a taste of Miami's wilder side, spend a day at the **Miami Metrozoo**, 12400 Southwest 152nd St. (tel. 251-0400). Over 100 species of animals, birds, and reptiles roam cageless, separated from the viewing public by large moats. Many exhibits are still under construction, but when it's all said and done, the Metrozoo may be Florida's finest. Open daily from 10 a.m. to 5:30 p.m. Admission price is $6 per person.

The **Bill Baggs State Park** in Key Biscayne is a shady, peaceful place away from the bustle of downtown Miami (take the causeway from Miami). The big draw here is the view of land, sea, and sky from the top of a restored 1830s lighthouse (122 steps up!). Other than that, it's quiet—with lots of shade trees and flowers. And it's open to the public at no charge.

Just past the Latin side of town, the middle-class suburb of Miami called **Coral Gables** gets its name from the hard coral rock on which most of the city is built (actually it's a coral look-alike called Miami oolite). George Merrick, turn-of-the-century entrepreneur, began this community as a peaceful diversion from city life. The combination of Mediterranean, French, Chinese, South African, and Dutch-influenced architecture you'll find here is more like art, with its whimsical gingerbread and palatial facades. It might help to identify the styles and get around if you pick up a map at City Hall, 405 Biltmore Way (tel. 442-6441), before you begin your tour.

The **Venetian Pool** at Almeria Avenue and Toledo Street must be at the top of your sightseeing list. Designed by Merrick and now open for public use, this lovely pool is surrounded by waterfalls, caves, lagoons, and grottos. For hours, days, and fees for the pool, contact the **Coral Gables Chamber of Commerce**, 50 Aragon Ave. (tel. 446-1657). Merrick's own gabled house of coral is close by, appropriately called **Coral Gables House**, 907 Coral Way (tel. 442-6593). Admission is $1 per person. Open Wednesdays from 1 to 4 p.m. The main entrance to the city, **"La Puerta del Sol,"** and the newly renovated **Biltmore Hotel** (see hotel listings) also merit your time.

You'll need to rent a car for **Coral Castle**, 28655 U.S. 1, Homestead (tel. 248-6344), but you will never again see anything like it, and the drive to Homestead is scenic with lots to do and see along the way. Take the beach road (U.S. 1) or the Florida Turnpike to Homestead, about 35 miles south of Miami. The "castle" was built by one 97-pound Latvian immigrant for his "Sweet Sixteen," a woman who remains a mystery, but supposedly jilted Edward Leedskalnin on their wedding day. This massive structure took him 15 years to build (1925–1940) and is made entirely from coral rock. How he completed it remains a mystery. Leedskalnin used no heavy machinery and worked entirely solo, moving pieces of coral weighing several tons each. Open from 9 a.m. to 9 p.m. daily. Admission is $6.50 per person.

Slip into the Florida of 50 years ago in Miami Beach's **Art Deco District,** filled with blocks of oceanfront buildings splashed in shades of pink, light blue, ocean green, coral, and yellow. Look for portholes, spires, eyebrow awnings, and breakfronts—Depression-era creations designed to lift the spirits of a despondent populace. Now on the National Register of Historic Places, the district is bordered by Ocean Drive on the south, 9th Street north to Washington Avenue, and east to 13th Street. Here, tuxedos and designer jeans can co-exist in the same elegant restaurant, where a feeling of vitality and rebirth breathes life into an area that was once cast aside.

The best way to get a feel for the excitement and glamour of this era is to stop by the **Miami Design Preservation League**, 1236 Ocean Dr., Room 11 (tel. 672-

1836). Each Saturday at 10:30 a.m., the MDPL conducts 90-minute walking tours of the district for $5 a person. If you don't happen to be in the area on a Saturday, stop by their office for self-guided tour maps. A tip for camera buffs: Try experimenting to create some dramatic effects. Look for portholes, curved balconies, glass-block windows, and lots of neon—all typically used in this district where construction began after the hurricane of 1926 and ended just before World War II.

Experience how the Miccosukee Indians existed (and still do) in the heart of the Everglades at the **Miccosukee Indian Village,** 25 miles west of Miami on the Tamiami Trail (U.S. 41), P.O. Box 440021, Miami (tel. 223-8388). Alligator wrestling, doll making, and other demonstrations are offered, but the real thrills here come from the tailbone-bruising airboat rides through part of the 286,000 acres of Everglades wilderness. You'll stop at a Miccosukee hammock-style camp, occupied for more than 125 years. Open daily from 9 a.m. to 5 p.m. Admission to the village is $5 per person; airboat rides are an additional $6 per person for a half-hour ride (and worth every penny!). A restaurant on the grounds serves up authentic Everglades dishes such as frogs' legs, catfish, and fry bread.

Biscayne National Park doesn't get a lot of visitors, even though it's America's newest national park. It could be because you can't see it from the road—the park is 95 percent under water! But now, thanks to the **Biscayne Aqua-Center, Inc.,** P.O. Box 1270, Homestead (tel. 247-2400), there's a new way to see the park, once accessible only to scuba-divers. A new 53-foot glass-bottomed boat takes visitors on cruises along 20 miles of living coral reef; it also makes snorkeling and scuba trips. The park asks that you set up your trip to the reef at least seven days in advance, and in exchange, they promise you a honeymoon adventure unmatched for its colorful marine life, scenery, and lively narrative. Snorkeling/scuba trips are Tuesday, Thursday, and Saturday from 10:30 a.m. to 2:15 p.m. The snorkeling trip is $20 per person, with equipment included; the scuba trip is $25 per person, with gear rental extra. Glass-bottomed boat tours happen daily (weather permitting) from 2:30 to 5:30 p.m.; a second trip, from 10:30 a.m. to 1:30 p.m., is scheduled on Monday, Wednesday, and Friday. The cost is $14.62 per person.

HONEYMOON HOTELS AND HIDEAWAYS

In town or on the beach, you're never very far from a wealth of shops, restaurants, and those great views of the ocean and the bay. Where applicable, prices shown reflect the spread between low- and high-season rates.

In Miami

EXPENSIVE: The **Hotel Intercontinental Miami,** 100 Chopin Plaza, Miami, FL 33131 (tel. 305/577-1000; reservations: toll free 800/33-AGAIN), seizes the opportunity to lure lovers of a fast-paced lifestyle by offering panoramic views from every floor. Its strategic location close to downtown and a quick taxi ride to almost anywhere allows honeymooners to take full advantage of attractions in town and on the beach. The centerpiece of the huge lobby is Sir Henry Moore's marble sculpture *The Spindle,* soaring 18 feet into the domed atrium. Elsewhere, look for marble from Italy, granite from Brazil and Africa, black mahogany from Central America, English oak, and Asian teak, all used as backdrops for 18th-century Belgian tapestries and a collection of rare English prints. Rooms are spacious with a Far Eastern feel—red sculpted chairs, black armoires painted with Oriental designs, and deep floral prints on bedspread and curtains. Fully stocked refrigerators and the Lancôme soap, shampoo, and conditioner amenities give the place tip-to-toe class. There's no beach, but the good-size pool helps compensate. "Just the Beginning" honeymoon package: Two days/one night (EP): $258.50 per couple. Includes luxury accommodations (upgraded to a suite if available), a bottle of champagne, limousine transportation to the airport or the Port of Miami, in-room breakfast, nightly turndown service, and a $50 gift certificate for a major department store.

Beyond your wildest expectations is the **Doral Resort and Country Club,**

4400 Northwest 87th Ave., Miami, FL 33178-2192 (tel. 305/592-2000; reservations: toll free 800/327-6334 nationwide; 800/FOR-A-TAN in Florida). When you check into the Doral Resort and Country Club, the Doral Ocean Beach Resort, or the Doral Saturnia International Spa Resort, all in the Miami area, you get three vacations for the price of one. Motorcoach service will take you to the other properties, and signing privileges let you enjoy the activities, the facilities, and the variety of all three. The Doral Resort and Country Club is an exclusive (and yes, expensive) 2,400-acre golf and tennis resort with a new equestrian center. All rooms are newly redecorated—natural wicker and glass tables, with neutral colors throughout—and private terraces afford spectacular views of Miami. Two telephones, clock radios, twin vanities, hairdryers, refrigerators, and lots of extras assure the two of you top-to-toe pampering. Honeymoon package: None. Seasonal rates (EP): $187 to $242 per couple per night for a standard room; $209 to $264 for a superior room; $286 to $352 for a junior suite.

MODERATE: If you want to get caught up in the excitement of this vibrant city, the **OMNI International Hotel,** Biscayne Boulevard at 16th St., Miami 33132 (tel. 305/374-0000; reservations: toll free 800/228-2121 nationwide), will capture you and carry you away on a roller-coaster ride of big-city magic. Like a sparkling jewel over the Miami skyline, the OMNI is part of a complex of 125 shops, boutiques, restaurants, and nightclubs overlooking Biscayne Bay, just five minutes from the Port of Miami. Rooms are newly redecorated in deep greens and soft beiges, teamed with comfortable modern furnishings. "OMNIMoon in Miami" honeymoon package (EP): $141.90 per couple per night. Includes deluxe accommodations with bay view, welcome bottle of champagne, and full breakfast in bed. One bedroom suite available for $196.90 per couple per night.

You'll find the **Sheraton River House** at the Miami International Airport, 3900 Northwest 21st St., Miami, FL 33142 (tel. 305/871-3800; reservations: toll free 800/325-3535 nationwide). While right in the center of a bustling airport in this exciting city, the Sheraton's grounds are surprisingly tranquil, framed by the Miami River, large trees, and park-like landscaping. You might see planes arriving and departing from your window, but mostly what you'll notice are the green fairways of the golf course, open space, and trees that reach almost five stories. Soundproof rooms are open with free-flowing space, dressed in warm shades of orange, gold, and light wicker. "Beautiful Beginnings" honeymoon package: Two days/one night (EP): $108.90 per couple. Includes deluxe accommodations (upgraded to a minisuite, if available), chilled bottle of champagne on arrival, full American breakfast served in your room each day, check-out extended to 4 p.m. Three-day/two-night package (EP): $203.50 per couple.

On Miami Beach

Along that most famous strip of beach, palm trees, and block after block of towering condominiums is a respite of lush greenery, cool waterfalls, and serene grottos at **The Alexander Hotel,** 5225 Collins Ave., Miami Beach, FL 33140 (tel. 305/865-6500; reservations: toll free 800/327-6121 nationwide). With a splash of fun and a dash of joie de vivre, the Alexander heralds the completion of one of the most extensive renovations on Miami Beach. The one- and two-bedroom luxury suites with private terraces all have ocean views, as well as separate living and dining rooms and kitchens. A free-spirited feeling governs in a wash of stripes, a bouquet of florals, and a rainbow of pastels. Linens, silks, and chintzes invite you to make yourself at home, while the staff will do everything to make your stay a pleasant one, from delivering groceries to your room to chartering a boat to sewing on a button. Honeymoon package: None. Rates (EP): $236.50 to $522.50 per couple per night for a one-bedroom suite.

The Fontainebleau Hilton, 4441 Collins Ave., Miami Beach, FL 33140 (tel. 305/538-2000; reservations: toll free 800/HILTONS nationwide). When this massive Miami Beach landmark was first constructed in the 1950s, no sign announced its name at the driveway entrance: If you didn't *know* this was the famed Fontainebleau, no one was going to tell you. After the recent $25-million facelift, there's finally an identifying marker. Now under the management of Hilton, the Fontainebleau still sets the standards for quality service and luxury on the Beach. The ornate lobby is somewhat overwhelming with its huge fountains, full-size trees, and tiny shimmering lights. Everything the Fontainebleau does is a spectacle, though, which has kept it a favorite for so many years. The rooms have all been re-done recently, and they positively exude elegance, with reproduction antiques, plush carpeting, and rich pastel fabrics.

The hotel has recently opened its own health club and spa and is one of the few on the Beach with tennis courts: seven of them, all lit for night play. The grotto swimming pool is made as intimate as a 140-foot pool can be by the tropical foliage, giant rocks, and cascading waterfalls. In its restaurants, the hotel maintains a staff of the finest chefs in the state. The Steak House and Poodle Lounge are very much in the art deco style with black everything and bald-headed female mannequins floating on pedestals. The Dining Galleries is also an art gallery—the hotel has purchased priceless paintings, furniture, and sculpture to enhance its posh decor. Honeymoon package: None. Room rates (EP): $159.50 to $209 per couple per night.

The Beach's resurgence of visitors in the past few years has prompted hotels to renovate, expand, and provide their guests with every possible convenience during their stay. Your lovely room at the **Doral-on-the-Ocean,** 4833 Collins Ave., Miami Beach, FL 33140 (tel. 305/532-3600; reservations: toll free 800/327-6334 nationwide), is decorated in soft pastels and cozy furnishings and includes minirefrigerator, hair dryer, makeup mirror, remote-control color TV, and two phones. You'll have access to tennis, the aqua sports club, and the health and fitness center. Honeymoon package: None. Junior suites are recommended for honeymooners, though. These oversize rooms have king-size beds. Junior suite rates: $195 to $210 per couple per night.

In Coconut Grove

The **Grand Bay Hotel,** 2669 S. Bayshore Dr., Coconut Grove, Miami, FL 33133 (tel. 305/858-9600; reservations: toll free 800/327-2788 nationwide), ranks among the top 15 hotels in the world according to a list compiled by *Lifestyles of the Rich and Famous.* The lobby decor features the finest marble, inlaid woods, highly polished brass, shimmering chandeliers, and elegant clusters of cozy seating. Even though guests pass through constantly, it's still a wonderfully serene spot for reading or afternoon tea. Custom-designed rooms each have different furnishings in a variety of color schemes so on a return visit you'll again be surprised. Pool, no beach. "La Romantica" honeymoon package: Four days/three nights (EP): $531 per couple. Includes deluxe bayview accommodations with a private balcony, a glass of freshly squeezed Florida orange juice, a bottle of chilled French champagne, breakfast on your balcony or in the Grand Cafe, health club privileges, sauna, and Jacuzzi. The "Una Notte" (One Night) package (EP): $308 per couple. Includes a junior suite, a full breakfast, valet parking, and a bottle of champagne.

Each room of the **Mayfair House,** 3000 Florida Ave., Coconut Grove, Miami, FL 33133 (tel. 305/441-0000; reservations: toll free 800/433-4555 nationwide; 800/341-0809 in Florida), is a work of art, from the salmon-and-black marble foyer to the French and Oriental period pieces gracing the Mayfair Grill and Bar. The rooftop garden bar and pool overlook Biscayne Bay. The suite-size rooms have expensive antiques, Oriental rugs, and original oil paintings. Headboards are beautifully carved, and separate sitting areas provide a cozy place for relaxing or reading. Strawberries are served in your suite every afternoon. Sip champagne from your private Japanese hot tub, then slip into silky "yukata" robes to enjoy a lingering breakfast or a rainbow-colored sunset from your patio. "Honeymoon Suite" package: Two days/one night (EP): $165 to $203.50 per couple. Includes Mayfair suite with pri-

vate terrace and Japanese hot tub, glass of champagne on arrival, welcome fruit bas-
ket and bottle of champagne, souvenir Mayfair kimonos, breakfast in the Mayfair
House Grill from 7 to 11 a.m., as well as guest membership in the private Ensign
Bitters club, daily newspaper, caviar and pâté served from 4 to 6 p.m. in the Tiffany
Lounge and from 6 to 7 p.m. in the Mayfair House Grill Bar, and shopping dis-
counts.

In Coral Gables

Towering, majestic . . . the magnificent old **Biltmore Hotel,** 1200 Anastasia
Ave., Coral Gables, FL 33134 (tel. 305/445-1926; reservations: toll free 800/445-
2586 nationwide), once the tallest building in the South, has come to life after a
major multimillion-dollar renovation. George Merrick's dream hotel, erected in
Coral Gables in 1926, still boasts the largest hotel pool in the country (there's no
beach, however). A pool, incidentally, where Johnny Weismuller taught and Ginger
Rogers, Bing Crosby, and Judy Garland swam. The Spanish-style loggias, facade,
and courtyard walkways are now proudly gleaming in tones of sienna and aqua.
Doormen still greet guests as griffins playfully watch from atop stairwells. The original flavor of opulence and luxury has been carried throughout the hotel, from bellhops to room service. Spacious rooms have been preserved as much as possible—
wood beams or painted ceilings have been kept, and tapestries, Oriental rugs, and
antiques brought in to capture the old hotel flavor. Every room is different, but elegant, in a classical, traditional style. Plumbing and vanity areas have been updated
for modern travelers. Honeymoon package: Two days/one night (EP): $209 per
couple. Includes suite accommodations, French champagne on arrival, full American breakfast served in your room, and welcome cocktails. Additional night (EP):
$176 per couple.

ROMANTIC RESTAURANTS AND NIGHT SPOTS

Whether you prefer an ambience that is wonderfully romantic or playfully
whimsical, choose your place for a special night out with crystal and linens or a
good-time atmosphere for a less expensive meal. Many of the finest restaurants are
located in Miami-area hotels.

On Miami Beach

EXPENSIVE: The beautifully restored 1941 art deco hotel has turned its lobby into a
showplace called the **Carlyle Grill** (inside the Carlyle Hotel), 1250 Ocean Dr., Miami Beach (tel. 534-2135). Pastel walls feature original sconces on either side of the
fireplace, a huge black curved bar (formerly the reception desk), and curved bronze
mirrors. Sit by the window for an ocean view or enjoy your lunch under umbrellas
on the veranda. For starters, try a hearts-of-palm salad or escargots. Quiche Lorraine,
chicken crêpes, or London broil are main course features. With Miami Beach's large
Jewish population, you'll find kosher-style deli favorites everywhere—roast beef or
corned beef on rye are two popular items. Luncheon entrées are priced between $6
and $12. Dinner at the Carlyle is a fancier affair with frogs' legs, lobster tails, cornish
hen, or duckling to choose from, priced from $70 to $100 per couple for a full meal
with wine. Open for breakfast at 7 a.m.; lunch is served from noon to 3 p.m.; dinner
from 6 p.m. on.

For the one night of your honeymoon stay you want to feel catered to, your
every whim satisfied, reserve your table at **Dominque's Famous French Restaurant**
(inside the Alexander Hotel), 5225 Collins Ave., Miami Beach (tel. 861-5252). Tables have individual lighting controls to suit your preferences and are set with the
finest china, silver, crystal, and linens; live piano music provides a fitting backdrop.
Try for a table near the bay windows overlooking a fountain cascading over coral
grottos into two lagoon pools. Past that—the white sands of Miami Beach. Start
with exotic appetizers such as buffalo sausages, diamondback rattlesnake salad, and
alligator tail. Of course, there's also plenty of regular fare. A sampling of entrées in-

cludes grilled salmon with watercress-and-dill sauce; Maine lobster; prime New York sirloin steak stuffed with escargots and garlic butter; and the house specialty—marinated rack of lamb. For dessert, house sorbet, glacés, rich pastries, or the special pistachio soufflé created for *Miami Vice* star Don Johnson. Dinners will cost around $120 per couple, more with drinks. Open 7:30 a.m. to 2:30 p.m. for breakfast and lunch; 6 to 11 p.m. for dinner. Reservations are requested. Dress up.

For your one "sky's the limit" honeymoon dining adventure in Miami, make it the **Café Chauveron,** 9561 East Bay Harbour Dr., Bay Harbor Island (tel. 866-8789). Host Roger Chauveron remains true to the classic French recipes that have won him so much acclaim. The restaurant is a bastion of romantic old-world opulence: soft antique lighting, dark woods, and private leather-backed banquettes add flourish to two-tier waterfront dining. The menu is in French with subtitles, but the prices are very American, running from $20 up to about $45 for your entrée. Be assured, though, that while you are dining, your every wish is their command. And indeed, you will feel as if you are in an enchanted place. Specialties of the house include pâté of wild duck and pheasant, pike dumplings, and the old-fashioned seafood stew of Marseilles (bouillabaisse). Expect the very height of gracious service, presentation with a flourish, and masterfully prepared courses. Open Monday through Friday from 11:30 a.m. to 2 p.m. for lunch; 6 to 11 p.m. for dinner. Reservations are required. So are jackets.

"New Wave *Miami Vice* dazzle" describes both the food and the decor at **Chef Allen's,** 19088 NE 29th Ave., North Miami Beach (tel. 935-2900). Let's start with pastel-pink walls, black-lacquer chairs, a pink neon tube snaking across the ceiling, and glass-block walls. Cuisine combines Florida and California favorites; blackening and mesquite grilling are two popular methods of preparation. Before you order dinner, order dessert—specifically the soufflé with crème de cocoa. It takes time to prepare, and knowing what's in store for later, you'll want to save room! Happily, Chef Allen's provides diners with a guide to South Florida's game fish, so you'll feel comfortable ordering something new. Menus change weekly to keep customers coming back. Pastas, fresh fish, lamb, veal, chicken, and mesquite-grilled dishes are light and "fun." Chef Allen Susser says he doesn't want people to come away from their meal too stuffed, so entrées and side dishes are prepared without heavy sauces and creams. Prix-fixe regional menus available for $35 per person. Most entrées run $15 to $20. Open for lunch Monday through Friday, 11:30 a.m. to 2 p.m.; dinner, 6 to 11 p.m. daily.

MODERATE: The Tropics inside the Edison Hotel, 960 Ocean Dr., Miami Beach (tel. 531-5335). Delightfully colorful and fun, this avant-garde art deco–flavored restaurant is a gathering place for artists and socialites from early morning right into the wee hours. The huge floor-to-ceiling windows flood the place with the warm Miami sunshine, especially lovely at sunrise. The chefs have found a fun way to serve food too: Your lox, bagels, and cream cheese may be served on a platter with carrot and carved green-pepper palm trees. Breakfast items are $4 to $8 each; luncheon $5 to $10. Dinner is a little of everything—chicken flambé with cognac, paella, blackened lamb, or fettuccine with onions, pepper, cured ham, and cream. The service is first-class. Dinners are priced from $35 to $65 per couple. Breakfast is served from 7 a.m. to noon; lunch from noon to 3 p.m.; and dinner from 7 p.m. to midnight daily. On weekends, appetizers are served until 3 a.m. Enjoy live entertainment from 10 p.m. until 2 a.m. nightly and a weekend brunch Saturday and Sunday from 10 a.m. until 4 p.m.

"The First Eating House on Miami Beach," **Joe's Stone Crab Restaurant,** 227 Biscayne St., Miami Beach (tel. 673-0365), has upheld a tradition for great food in elegant surroundings since 1913. A huge stone fireplace and fancy chandeliers are focal points of the spacious dining room. French doors on two sides offer lovely garden views of a fountain and blooming hibiscus. Have whatever you want here as long as it's stone crab, the hearty little crab now on the endangered list; fishermen are only allowed to break off the claws and then must throw the crabs back to grow others. Actually, Joe's offers other seafood delights and meat and poultry items, but if you've never sampled the delicate flavor of cold claws drenched in drawn butter, it would be almost criminal at least not to try them while you're here. Something to remember before you walk into Joe's—they require long pants or skirts, and tank tops are a no-no too. If you do slip up, Joe's will lend you sweat pants and/or long-sleeve shirts to wear during your meal, which will cost about $32 per couple (the meal, not the clothes). Open for lunch from 11:30 a.m. to 2 p.m. Tuesday through Saturday; 5 to 10 p.m. daily for dinner (closed mid-May to October). Make reservations (lunch included) or get in line early for this popular Miami Beach stop.

The Twenties inside the Sheraton Bal Harbour, 9701 Collins Ave., Bal Harbour (tel. 865-7511), set in an award-winning art deco room, serves delicious continental entrées like dry-aged steaks and fresh seafood. Dinners at The Twenties will run from $20 to $25 per person. Menu selections have Prohibition-era names like Bonnie and Clyde (surf and turf), Flapper Snapper, and the Great Gatsby (chateaubriand for two). Open for dinner from 5:30 to 10:30 p.m.

The Sheraton also has one of the finest nightly floor shows in the area. "Masquerade" is their 32nd-anniversary show featuring fast-paced original choreography and exotic costumes. Shows are Tuesday through Saturday at 8 p.m., with a Sunday matinee at 2 p.m. Cost is $20 per person for just the show (includes one drink), or you may dine during the show for about $70 per couple. Reservations are required.

Eating at **The Dining Galleries** inside the Fontainebleau Hilton Resort, 4441 Collins Ave., Miami Beach (tel. 538-2000), is like dining in a museum. There are European statues, original oils, and an 1882 grand piano from Hamburg that was once owned by the late Liberace. Many of the dishes are named after works in the gallery. Try "The Three Graces," three small medallions of veal tenderloin enhanced with three different sauces (sorrel, villeroy, and tomato fondue) for $24.50. Or the "Chicken Rosa di Maggio"—a sautéed breast of chicken with fresh poached oysters and roasted sweet peppers in a delicate sauce choron. Entrées are priced from $18.95 to $28.95, which includes vegetable; other courses are à la carte. Open daily. Make reservations for dinner from 6 p.m. until midnight or join them for a champagne brunch on Sunday between 10 a.m. and 3 p.m.

Adjoining The Dining Galleries, **The Poodle Lounge and Steak House** inside the Fontainebleau Hilton (tel. 538-2000) has been "deco-ized." In true 1930s fashion, almost everything is black, including the walls, carpet, tables, and chairs. The stark white napkins really stand out. On each table, a single flower floats in a glass vase lit by an overhead light. Dinner is hearty and delicious; there are a few gourmet specialties, but meat-and-potato people will also find lots to like. The blackened pompano has to be their finest offering and comes heartily recommended ($20.95). Duckling, pork steak, veal, prime rib, New York strip, and lamb chops are all good eating; dinner may land in the $60 to $100 per couple range. Open for dinner daily from 6 p.m. to midnight; the lounge stays open until 3 a.m.

The Bayview inside the Biscayne Bay Marriott (tel. 374-3900) has a lovely one —from the second floor overlooking the marina. It's casual and comfortable all day and all night, serving breakfast, a lunch buffet Monday through Friday, Sunday brunch, and a daily Early Bird Dinner Buffet. Continental specialties, deli sandwiches, and homemade desserts are served. Prices are comfortable too: Complete dinners range from $36 to $74 per couple. Open daily for breakfast from 7 to 10 a.m.; lunch from 11:30 a.m. to 2 p.m.; dinner from 7 to 10 p.m., and Sunday champagne brunch from 11 a.m. to 2:30 p.m.

INEXPENSIVE: At **Wolfie's 21,** Collins Avenue and 21st Street (tel. 538-6626), the walls are decked with photos of Clark Gable, Frank Sinatra, and Judy Garland. Whether they were here or not doesn't really matter. The atmosphere is early deli, the waitresses look as if they have worked here since the turn of the century, and the food is good and cheap—you can get out of here with a full meal for about $8 per person. Late nights are when Wolfie's comes alive—theatergoers and other social-scene types stop in for kosher-style favorites while an accordion player serenades from 11 p.m. to 1 a.m. on weekends. Joseph Nevel, owner of Wolfie's, can be seen strolling around the place, making sure his guests are enjoying themselves. Open 24 hours every day.

South Florida's newest and hottest innovative nightclub, **Facade,** at 3509 Northeast 163rd St., North Miami Beach (tel. 947-9988), is a multimillion-dollar light, sound, and video extravaganza. Six bars overlook the sunken dance floor, where a ten-piece band plays Top 40 favorites nightly. "Glowing" hostesses serve you from neon trays. They call this decor "Greek Art Deco." At the back of Facade, **Rinaldo's Backstage Restaurant** offers northern Italian gourmet specialties from 5:30 p.m. to 6 a.m. in an atmosphere of magnificent imported chandeliers and custom–hand-painted murals. A special late-night-snack and breakfast menu is served from 2 to 6 a.m. Dine on caviar, pasta, calamari, Norwegian salmon, or baby lamb chops, all in the $15 to $27 price range. Pastas are in the $9 to $15 range. Facade is open nightly, 9 p.m. to 6 a.m.

In Miami and Vicinity

EXPENSIVE: A favorite spot for a special night out is **The Pavilion Grill** at the Hotel Intercontinental Miami, 100 Chopin Plaza, Miami (tel. 577-1000). Look around at the rich French and Italian interior, with its rosewood and green marble, leather booths, and upholstery. The menu offers regional dishes from all 50 states: cactus leaves from Texas, king crab from Alaska, wild rabbit from Wyoming. And you didn't think anything from your own turf could taste so heavenly! How about fresh Florida lobster rolled up in a chicken breast and mesquite grilled ($21.95), or Key West tuna steamed in ginger, sake, and chili peppers ($20.95)? A full dinner with wine will run about $120 per couple on the average.

MODERATE: **Le Grand Cafe** at the Grand Bay Hotel, 2669 South Bayshore Dr., Coconut Grove (tel. 858-9600) is an intimate, charming spot. Rattan tables and chairs are umbrella-covered and, along with lush plants and Impressionist-inspired prints, give an outdoor garden ambience. Try one of the unusual dishes here, such as black linguini with calamari; terrine of fresh foie gras as an appetizer; or one of the other Mediterranean menu items. A dinner for two will be about $50. The Sunday brunch is a lavish spectacle, served from 11:30 a.m. to 3 p.m. Breakfast is served Monday through Saturday, 7 to 11 a.m.; lunch 11:30 a.m. to 3 p.m.; and dinner daily from 6 to 11 p.m.

The **Cafe at the Biltmore** inside the Biltmore Hotel, Coral Gables (tel. 445-1926), serves up very good, moderately priced meals, with enough variety that you wouldn't get tired of the food or the ambience of the place even if you ate here every day. Try huevos rancheros or Belgian waffles for breakfast, with breads and croissants made in the Biltmore bakery daily. Lunch can be plain—Biltmore hamburger with bacon and cheese ($8.95)—or fancy—sautéed Norwegian salmon on Noilly Prat Italian parsley sauce. For your honeymoon dinner here, don't be surprised if the maitre d' sends over a bottle of wine or serves the champagne himself, toasting your good health and a happy life together. Appetizers are priced from $5 to $12, with entrées in the $8.95 to $23.95 range. Top it all off with a steaming cup of cappuccino for a relaxing end to a fine meal. Breakfast served from 6:30 to 11 a.m.; lunch from 11 a.m. to 2:30 p.m.; late lunch, 2:30 to 6 p.m.; and dinner, 6 to 11 p.m.

A favorite of both visitors and locals for casual fun, entertainment, great food and views of tropical Biscayne Bay, **Monty Trainer's Bayshore Restaurant, Lounge, Raw Bar, and Marina,** 2560 South Bayshore Dr., Coconut Grove (tel. 858-1431), is the gateway to the Grove, by land or by sea. The indoor restaurant has a nautical setting with dark-pine paneling and shipboard memorabilia. The 30-plus entrées are mostly seafood specialties, but MT's ribs, prime rib, and sirloin are the finest corn-fed midwestern beef available, aged three to four weeks. Delectable entrées such as island mahimahi Coconut Grove–style or amandine, paella, or conch will run about $15; meat and poultry are a little less than that. A full meal will run about $70 per couple. After dinner, visit the lovely MT's Lounge and Indoor Garden Patio, then stroll over to the Bay Front Bar at Monty Trainer's Outdoor Raw Bar and Marina, where you can enjoy a drink under a grass tiki hut or dance under the stars. There's live entertainment every night of the week. Open daily from 11 a.m. to 3 a.m.; open on weekends for breakfast at 8 a.m.

Since 1933, **East Coast Fisheries,** 360 West Flagler St., Miami (tel. 373-5515), has been a landmark on the Miami River. They catch and ship fresh seafood world-wide. The restaurant is somewhat noisy, as fish is continuously being brought into the kitchen, and the food is prepared in an open-air kitchen in full view of diners; there's also a fish market in operation on the main floor near the dining room. It's happy chaos, however, and once you've dipped into a just-caught Florida lobster oozing with butter, bluefish broiled in garlic butter sauce, or one of 38 other seafood types, you won't mind the din so much. The extensive menu is printed in Spanish and English, but no matter which language you order in, it's all "muy bueno." Full lunches or dinners (same menu) run about $30 for two without drinks; lobster and stone crab are about $10 higher. Open daily from 11 a.m. to 10 p.m.

If you enjoy the flavor of southern cooking, but never much cared for the "come as you are" atmosphere of most "grits and cornbread" establishments, the upscale **Savannah Moon** (tel. 238-8868) is a sure-fire winner. Roomy booths draped in soft pastel fabric, light woods, and mirrored columns begin an evening of visual and culinary surprises. Live piano music creates the necessary romantic atmosphere. Try a bottle of fine wine—the few selections are artfully chosen and reasonably priced. Begin your meal with a Carolina turnover, filled with delicate crawfish meat and artichoke hearts and covered with a light barbecue sauce. It'll be tough not to get carried away with a bread basket filled with biscuits, corn muffins, and fennel bread, but save yourself for main courses such as caveached grouper ($18.95), topped with spiced grapes; or Georgian roast duckling ($16.75), marinated in peach-brandy sauce and served with a delicate peach purée. Desserts change nightly, but most are worth trying—blackberry cobbler and chess pie, a nut-and-chocolate confection, top the list of patrons' favorites. Dinner for two with wine will be in the neighborhood of $70 to $80 since everything at Savannah Moon is à la carte. Lunch is a less lavish production, with sandwiches, burgers, and specialties such as Kentucky bourbon steak ($9.95) and crab-and-corn pie ($6.50). Open for lunch Monday through Friday from 11:30 a.m. to 2:30 p.m.; dinner served Tuesday through Sunday from 6 to 11 p.m. A special late-night menu is available from 11 p.m. to 2 a.m.

INEXPENSIVE: **The Royal Palm Court,** Hotel Intercontinental Miami, 100 Chopin Plaza, Miami (tel. 577-1000), is located in the grand lobby and is a terrific spot for a cozy brunch. Try the tempting Bayfront, snow crab and diced bell peppers topped with Swiss cheese. For lunch or dinner, there are club sandwiches and burgers along with specialties such as salmon coulibiac and Hungarian-style stuffed cabbage. Menu items are in the $10 to $13 range. There is also a nice selection of American and French wines and domestic and imported beers. Open daily from 6 a.m. to 11 p.m.

6. The Florida Keys

Once you drive south from Miami, say goodbye to the glamour of big-city life, so long to buildings over three stories tall, and ta-ta to any hopes of being in a hurry. The drive from Miami to Key West is delightful, and there's a back road to take if you're so inclined. As you approach Miami from the north, look for exit 4 to Homestead and Key West. This is the West Dade Tollway (821), which connects with U.S.

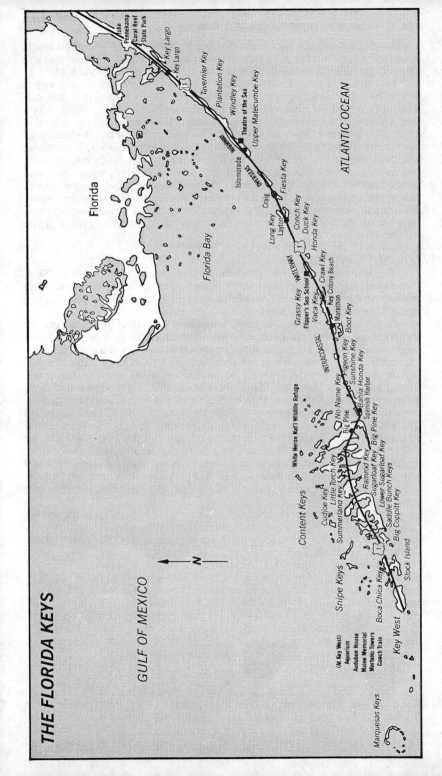

THE FLORIDA KEYS

GULF OF MEXICO

Florida

Florida Bay

ATLANTIC OCEAN

N

Marquesas Keys

(At Key West)
Aquarium
Audubon House
Maine Memorial
Martello Towers
Conch Train

Key West

Snipe Keys

Boca Chica Keys

Stock Island

Content Keys

Cudjoe Key
Little Torch Key
Summerland Key

Ramrod Key
Sugarloaf Key
Lower Sugarloaf Key

Saddle Bunch Keys
Big Coppitt Keys

White Heron Nat'l Wildlife Refuge

No Name Key
Big Pine

Big Pine Key

Bahia Honda Key
Spanish Harbor

INTRACOASTAL

Pigeon Key
Sunshine Key

Boot Key

Marathon

Key Colony Beach

Vaca Key

Crawl Key

Grassy Key
Flipper's Sea School

WATERWAY

Honda Key
Duck Key

Conch Key

Long Key
Layton
Craig

Fiesta Key

OVERSEAS

Islamorada

HIGHWAY

Upper Matecumbe Key

Theatre of the Sea

Windley Key

Plantation Key

Tavernier Key

Key Largo

John
Pennekamp
Coral Reef
State Park

Key Largo

1 at Florida City leading to Key Largo. You may want to take the Card Sound Bridge Road (toll: $1) at Florida City; it's a little longer but more scenic. Take your time and stop a lot on your way to the islands that make up the rest of the Florida Keys.

Flip on U.S. 1 (104.7 FM) on your car radio, the Keys' own station, as you approach the Overseas Highway. The road was once Henry Flagler's seagoing railroad; he built the Casa Marina Resort in Key West so that his wealthy friends would have a place to stay at the end of the line. A mighty hurricane ended the railroad in 1935. Now a highway vaults from key to key on legs of concrete and steel, connecting dozens of tiny "islets" with such fetching names as Islamorada, Matecumbe, and Bahia Honda. The scenery changes from the sawgrass of the Everglades to water, water, and more water. Crystalline and pure, deep green, aquamarine, and sometimes even indigo—it's what make the Keys so very special. Herons, spoonbills, egrets, and ospreys are sighted almost as frequently as sailboats, shrimpers, and deluxe yachts skimming the emerald waters. Don't just drive through—stop often, savor constantly, and make your honeymoon trip through the Keys a memory you will cherish always.

ROMANTIC INTERLUDES

Your search for honeymoon thrills can be a daily adventure in the Florida Keys. If you've never tried snorkeling, be sure to learn how while you're here so you won't miss out on the "other side of Keys life." It takes no special skill, and the bounty of sealife will surprise and amaze you.

Discover the *other* Florida at **John Pennekamp Coral Reef State Park** on Key Largo (tel. 451-1621), one of the only underwater parks in the world. The living coral reef is 74 miles long, and all around it are schools of brightly colored fish, waving sea fans, and anemones whose graceful fingers seem to beckon you to take a closer look. Barnacle-covered shipwrecks are home to an endless variety of marine life. Pick up a waterproof fish-identification book at the dive shop to assist you with the inhabitants' names. Snorkeling trips from the park take you to shallow reefs three times daily on the 49-passenger *El Capitan;* the 9:00 a.m., noon, and 3 p.m. trips cost $20 per person, including all of your equipment. Half-day trips leave at 9:30 a.m. and 1:30 p.m. for $35 per person; and full-day trips depart at 10:00 a.m. for $48 a head (be sure to bring the sunscreen!). Scuba trips are also available to certified divers. A glass-bottomed boat with an undersea viewing room cruises the reefs at 9 a.m., noon, and 3 p.m. daily for about $12. The park asks that reservations be made in advance for any trip, as Pennekamp is the most popular snorkeling and scuba spot in the Keys.

As the only key other than Key West with a historic district, little **Tavernier** (population 2,500) has a few nicely restored homes and churches dating back to the early part of the century. For a self-guided tour map, stop by the **Old Church Visitor Center** at Mile Marker 91.5.

Bahia Honda, or "deep bay," has become well known for its abundant trees and beautiful wildflowers. The entire key is a **State Recreation Area** (tel. 872-2353), and the closest beach to Key West. From one of the beaches, the old East Coast Railroad trestle is still visible as part of the old Bahia Honda Bridge. There's a state park entry fee of $2.50 for drivers and $1.50 per passenger, but if you bring a beach towel, suntan lotion, a cooler, and snorkeling equipment, you're set for the day. Hike the nature trail to see tropical plants brought here from the West Indies by waves, wind, and birds. Several rare species include the satinwood tree, the spiny catesbaea, and the dwarf morning glory. The park opens at 8 a.m. and closes at sunset year-round.

Right around sunset, drive down to **Big Pine Key,** where suddenly the vegetation looks more like northern Carolina than tropical Florida. Scientists believe that this key may have been the remnant of an Appalachian upheaval millions of years ago. Enjoy the drive through the tall pines as you follow the main road to **No Name Key.** Go all the way to the end of the road . . . and stop. Be patient and as quiet as you can. Before long the tiny **Key deer** will appear along the side of the road. Have your camera ready, but please, no feeding! This is the last habitat of the endangered Key deer, a subspecies of the white-tailed deer. There are only 300 in existence. A full-size Key deer is about as big as a German shepherd.

HONEYMOON HOTELS AND HIDEAWAYS

A virtual smorgasbord of earthly delights awaits key-hopping newlyweds. Big hotel chains are few and far between, so to be sure of getting a clean, quality room at a good price, see our recommendations below.

Expensive

A sparkling new classic in the Keys tradition is the renovated **Cheeca Lodge,** Mile Marker 82, P.O. Box 527, Islamorada, FL 33036 (tel. 305/664-4651; reservations: toll free 800/327-2888 nationwide). More than $2 million has been invested in updating, expanding, and redecorating. And the facelift has worked: Cheeca Lodge is now one of the Keys' premier resorts, with tropical gardens, two freshwater swimming pools, a saltwater lagoon, several ponds, three 9-hole golf courses, and its own 1,000-foot stretch of beach fronting some of the world's best fishing waters (just ask President Bush; it's his favorite fishing hole). Islamorada, or "the purple isle," is named for the violet waters, colored by millions of tiny coastal snails and the vibrant masses of purple morning glories that bloom *everywhere*. At the lodge entryway, towering date palms, red hibiscus, and the pink blush of bougainvillea set the scene for what's inside. Wicker and rattan furniture with overstuffed silk cushions in sea green, mustard, light blue, and, of course, violet, make a comfy place to watch sailboats on the Atlantic while cockatiels, parrots, and other South American birds squawk and sing in the lobby's aviary. Custom-made guest-room furniture is British colonial—teak-stained nightstands and dressers, bamboo and wicker headboards and chairs. Color schemes feature either periwinkle blue and strawberry, or green and hot orange. Honeymoon package: Four days/three nights (EP): $709.50 per couple in winter; $627 per couple in summer. Additional night (EP): $236.50 per couple. Includes a one-bedroom suite with VCR, ceiling fans, screened-in porch, bathrobes, hairdryers, and full kitchen, plus one complimentary dinner and a bottle of wine at either of the two gourmet restaurants, a bottle of champagne on arrival, and fresh flowers in your room. A seven-day/six-night package (EP): $1,287 per couple in winter; $1,123 in summer.

Just the two of you on your very own private island, where the cares of the world are washed away by gentle ocean waves; a thatched-roof hut is your private hideaway. **Little Palm Island,** Mile Marker 28.5, Route 4, P.O. Box 1036, Little Torch Key, FL (tel. 305/872-2524; reservations: toll free 800/GET-LOST nationwide), is as close as you may ever come to that fantasy. Accessible only by boat, this exclusive resort occupies all five acres of Little Munson Island, which, according to local legend, has hosted Presidents Roosevelt, Truman, Kennedy, and Nixon over the years. It's a 15-minute boat ride from the Shore Station on Little Torch Key; Key West is only 30 miles away. Little Palm Island's centerpiece is the Great House, which has the only TVs and telephones on the island, plus a lounge and an indoor/outdoor restaurant with spectacular sunset views. Thirty luxury suites are scattered about the island, hidden among hundreds of coconut palms. Each of the fourteen two-unit thatched-roof suites includes a master bedroom, wet bar with coffee maker, well-stocked refrigerator, and private wrap-around sun deck with a hammock in which to laze away the warm Florida days. A private outdoor shower is right outside each unit, next to a separate entryway leading to a fully equipped bathroom with Mexican tiles and a whirlpool. Interiors are plush and tropical, furnished in rattan and wicker furniture and paddle fans. Bicycles, massage services, and every type of water sport are available on the island and are included in the price of the room. Honeymoon package: None. "Extended Weekender Package": Four days/three nights (EP): $973.50 to $1,089 per couple. Includes deluxe accommodations, all meals plus a special Sunday brunch with live entertainment, and use of all recreational amenities and facilities. Stay must begin on a Thursday, Friday, or Saturday. "Mid-Week Package": Five days/four nights (valid between Sunday and Thursday): $1,166 to $1,298 per couple. Includes deluxe accommodations; all meals, plus a Wednesday-night Caribbean-style "Jump-Up," complete with entertainment; and use of all facilities. Additional night (EP): $433.50 per couple!

Moderate

Hawk's Cay Resort and Marina, Mile Marker 61, Duck Key, FL 33050 (tel. 305/743-7000; reservations: toll free 800/327-7775 nationwide; 800/432-2242 in Florida), just keeps getting better. The rambling 60-acre West Indies–style resort has spent $1 million on improving all 177 guest rooms, suites, public areas, and meeting rooms. Furnishings are wicker-work rattan with a salmon-and-teal color scheme; artwork compliments the tropical motif. This is the first phase of an expansion that will eventually include 400 villas. A pool deck with heated Jacuzzis, a saltwater lagoon, and a private beach are only the beginning. Feel free to run about in just your bikini—Hawk's Cay isn't a bit pretentious; the staff wants you to feel at home in the casually elegant surroundings. "Perfect Beginning" honeymoon package: Four days/three nights (EP): $528 to $940.50 per couple for waterview accommodations; $709.50 to $1,122 per couple for a captain's suite. Package includes a lavish 60-item breakfast buffet each day, complimentary champagne, a fruit and cheese basket, nightly turn-down service, three daily dolphin and sea lion shows, and two hours of tennis court time. A six-day/five-night package (EP): $880 to $1,567.50 per couple for waterview accommodations; $1,182.50 to $1,870 per couple for a captain's suite. You'll receive all of the above amenities plus a Tropical Reef Adventure. Eight-day/seven-night package (EP): $1,232 to $2,194.50 per couple for waterview accommodations; $1,655.50 to $2,618.00 for a captain's suite. Includes all the above, plus a Florida Keys Nature Tour.

Find lots of fellow sybarites at **Holiday Isle Resort and Marina,** 84001 Overseas Hwy., Islamorada, FL 33036 (tel. 305/664-2321; reservations: toll free 800/327-7070 nationwide; 800/432-2875 in Florida). Drink in the sights, the sounds, and the sensations of this tropical isle, and you're sure to find lots of fun-loving folks doing the same thing. Scuba-diving, snorkeling, sailing, windsurfing, waterskiing, and jet skiing are all available right here, plus they'll teach you how! Honeymoon package: Four days/three nights (EP): $660 to $709.50 per couple. Your accommodations are in the King Neptune Honeymoon Suite, a spacious deluxe room in white and sun-washed tropical shades with a king-size bed, private Jacuzzi, and private balcony overlooking the Atlantic Ocean. Package includes iced champagne in your suite on arrival, a gift certificate for breakfast for two, a $50 dinner gift certificate for two in the Horizon Room Restaurant on the 6th floor (with a great view of the ocean), two welcome cocktails, and fresh-cut flowers in your room. A six-day/five-night package (EP): $1,006.50 to $1,089 per couple; an eight-day/seven-night package (EP): $1,100 to $1,336.50 per couple.

ROMANTIC RESTAURANTS AND NIGHTSPOTS

Resort restaurants are always a good bet in the Keys, but you may do just as well turning off the main road and heading for the "mom and pop" variety. These attract mostly locals because they don't advertise, so you're sure to run into at least one favorite dish served with some local lore.

Food for every mood! That's what awaits the two of you at **The Atlantic's Edge** at the Cheeca Lodge, Mile Marker 82, Islamorada (tel. 664-4651). A sweeping azure ocean fronts the plantation-style dining room where shades of peach, fanlight windows, and crystal chandeliers set the stage for what's to come. Fresh local fish is the staple for unique dishes, complemented by the restaurant's forte: its wonderful sauces. For example, they start with fresh grouper or pompano, sauté it, bake it with banana and tomato concassea, then top it with lemon-butter sauce. If you're looking for a break from fish (it's hard to get away from it in Florida), The Atlantic's Edge also has choice veal, prime rib, New York strip, and filet mignon. Expect to spend about $70 per couple for dinner. Open daily at 4 p.m.; closing is seasonal. Make reservations in peak seasons.

While you're in the upper Keys, ask around for a great place for a romantic dinner, and you'll hear the name **Snook's Bayside Club,** Mile Marker 99.9, Key Largo (tel. 451-3857), more than any other. Snook's is a private club, but if you're not a member, they'll ask you to sign a guestbook before seating you. Dine inside or out; both locations overlook the water. Outdoors, you have a ringside seat for sunsets on Florida Bay as tall palms provide shade from the day's last burst of sun. Inside, a huge stone fireplace and multilevel seating create intimate spots for a cozy dinner. Seafood is a treat, and the yellowtail stuffed with crabmeat is not to be missed. Start with the wilted spinach salad with hot bacon dressing; mandarin oranges and water chestnuts make this unusual salad a savory experience. Lobster au gratin, prime rib, aged steak, and loaves of warm bread top off an unparalleled meal. Dinner for two is $60 on the average; wine and drinks are extra. Open daily from 4:30 to 11 p.m.; reservations are suggested.

Dine on the rooftop with nothing but the moon, the stars, the ocean, and each other at the **Horizon Rooftop Restaurant** at Holiday Isle Resort and Marina, Mile Marker 84, Islamorada (tel. 664-2321). The food is gourmet, but the atmosphere is casual and relaxed. You're in the Keys now, where sandals are accepted and expected. The walls are glass for spectacular views all around from six floors up. Start with a drink—a tropical rum runner or piña colada—then slip down slithery oysters on the half shell or deep-fried conch fritters. Full Bahamian conch dinners come three different ways—dipped in egg and sautéed with lemon and parsley butter; dipped in egg and sautéed with shallots and garlic butter in a brandied brown sauce; or fried. All are about $14. Tropical dinners run the gamut from fresh fish cooked any number of ways to lobster, chicken, veal, steak, and pasta dishes. Your complete dinner shouldn't be more than $50 for both of you with drinks. Open daily for lunch and dinner, 11 a.m. to 11 p.m.

A host of dining possibilities exist at **The Quay,** Mile Marker 102.5, Key Largo (tel. 451-0943); Mile Marker 84, Marathon (tel. 289-1810); and 12 Duval St., Key West (tel. 294-4446). Fresh local Keys seafood and indoor or outdoor patio dining are what make The Quay's restaurants special spots for newlyweds. Indoor seating is on rattan with soft pink and white touches; tropical fish dart about the huge lounge aquariums. Enjoy your dinner by the water as you watch the sun sink into the Gulf of Mexico. Feast on nature's bounty—yellowtail snapper prepared ten different ways, conch steak, lobster, salmon, stone crab, and raw oysters. Prime rib, rack of lamb, and veal Oscar are also available, as well as a tempting assortment of desserts. Dinner for two will be in the neighborhood of $70 with drinks. Open daily year-round for dinner, 4 to 11 p.m.; lounges stay open into the night, depending on season.

7. Key West

"It's not the end of the earth, but you can see it from here" is a good description of Key West. The little island at the end of the road is 100 miles from Miami, 90 miles from Cuba, and as far as you can get from just about anywhere in the United States.

To become a "conch" (pronounced konk), a Key West native, you first must pack away your watch, slip off your shoes, and give up any hopes of following a set itinerary. Relish this most amazing place frequented by the likes of Audubon, Hemingway, Tennessee Williams, and Jimmy Buffett. Soon after you arrive, you'll be operating on "island time," during which the locals follow only the position of the sun to know when to open their shops or return from a day of conch fishing. Or, as

Tennessee Williams once wrote, "Time past has a lovely habit of remaining time present in Key West."

ROMANTIC INTERLUDES

Time past and time present have a lovely way of blending with the scenery here; take your time and enjoy the sights, sounds, and sensations of Key West.

See the sights of old and new Key West while listening to a charming narration of the island's bizarre and unscrupulous history on a **Conch Tour Train.** Hear tales of pirates, buried treasure, and wreckers, those who made a fortune plundering vessels loaded with jewels and money. The 1½-hour tour takes you through Old Town, the heart of Key West; the Old Lighthouse; and past the homes of John James Audubon, Ernest Hemingway, and Harry Truman. Tours board at 501 Front St., Mallory Square, and 3850 North Roosevelt Blvd. The trains run seven days a week between 9 a.m. and 4 p.m. Price is $7.50 per person (tel. 294-5161).

An intimate and old Key West way to sightsee is a **horse-drawn carriage** just for two. The tour lasts 45 minutes, costs $11.50 per couple, and can be boarded at Front and Whitehead Streets from 9 a.m. until dark.

Yes, the famed novelist gave us *For Whom the Bell Tolls, A Farewell to Arms,* and *The Snows of Kilimanjaro* from the second-floor study of the pool house, but few remnants of his actual presence remain. Ernest Hemingway purchased this Spanish-colonial home in 1931, but took all of his personal effects with him when he moved to Cuba ten years later. Still, the rooms are furnished in "Hemingwayesque" style— bare floors, limited and modest furnishings, and, of course, *lots* of books and Hemingway photos. You'll hear about the legendary six-toed cats that roamed about the house and of which Hemingway became enamored. Descendants still pad through the shady yard looking for handouts from the visitors. The **Ernest Hemingway Museum** is located at 907 Whitehead St. (tel. 294-1575); admission is $5 per person. Open daily from 9 a.m. to 5 p.m.

John James Audubon (1785–1851), one of America's great painters and ornithologists, spent some time in Key West, and the **Audubon home** still stands on Whitehead and Greene Streets (tel. 294-2116). During his stay in the Keys, Audubon, a native of Saint-Dominigue (now called Haiti), was thrilled by the spectacular water birds, many new to him. Eighteen species were added to his monumental work, *Birds of America,* including the great white heron and the white-crowned pigeon, both Key West natives. The 1830s home and tropical gardens can be rented for weddings and receptions. The home is furnished with early-19th-century Key West pieces. Open daily from 9:30 a.m. to 5 p.m.; admission is $4.50 per person.

If you're not a snorkeler, the *Fireball* **glass-bottomed boat** is the next best thing to being there. View a living coral reef teeming with exotic plant and aquatic life from the safety of your vessel. The sunset cruise is spectacular, but times vary according to sunsets, so check beforehand. Price is $12 per person for a two-hour cruise leaving the gulf end of Duval Street (tel. 296-6293). Daytime trips depart at about 9:30 a.m., 11:30 a.m., 2 p.m. and 4 p.m., varying a bit at different times of the year.

At sunset, it has become a Key West tradition to see what type of characters **Mallory Pier** has stirred up on any given day. Long-haired, unshaven guitar players, dapperly dressed tap dancers, prophets, psychics, vegetarians, conch-shell peddlers, even folks like us can be found there. The performers are merely a prelude of the main attraction—a hint of pink streaks through the deep blue, fanning out into lavender before bursting into reds, golds, and oranges. A particularly memorable sunset will elicit a standing ovation from the crowd. And best of all . . . it's free.

Key West may be the end of the road, but it's by no means the end of Florida. Sixty-eight miles west of Key West is the massive, hexagonally shaped **Fort Jefferson on Garden Key in the Dry Tortugas.** The citadel saw little fighting; instead, it served as a prison after the Civil War. Among its most famous inmates was Dr. Samuel Mudd, who had set the broken leg of John Wilkes Booth. He was not aware that

Booth had just assassinated President Abraham Lincoln, but that's what makes the story even more moving. Dr. Mudd was officially pardoned (a little late) during the Carter presidency. There is a large plaque on the wall of the fort honoring his tireless care of prisoners ill with malaria. The fort is just one highlight of the four-hour sea-plane trip that leaves at 8:30 a.m. and 12:30 p.m. You can also enjoy some excellent snorkeling (gear is provided), birdwatching, or swimming. En route the planes fly at low altitude so you are able to take pictures of marine life—sharks, stingrays, por-poises, and the giant sea turtles after which Ponce de Léon named the islands ("Las Tortugas"). Cost for the half-day trip is $115 per person, but longer trips—all day or overnight camping—are available for $240 per person. Contact the **Key West Sea-plane Service** (tel. 294-6978) for reservations.

Some of us sit around and tell stories of sunken wrecks and a king's ransom in buried treasure; Mel Fisher and his crew have sought the wrecks out and gone after the alleged treasure. And treasure they found—aboard ships like the *Nuestra Señora del Atocha* and the *Santa Margarita,* which sank in the Straits of Florida during a violent hurricane in 1622. The treasure is beyond compare: heavy, ornate gold chains, solid gold bars, a gold "poison cup," a 23-piece gold belt studded with ru-bies and diamonds, a stupendous emerald crucifix—adding up to more wealth than you'll probably see in a lifetime. The greatest treasure find of all time is on exhibit at the **Mel Fisher Heritage Society Museum,** 200 Greene St., Key West (tel. 294-2633). Open daily from 10 a.m. to 6 p.m. Admission is $5 per person.

In the heart of Key West's Old Town district, stop in at the **Wrecker's Muse-um,** 322 Duval St. (tel. 305/294-9502). Apart from being the oldest house (1829) in Key West, somewhat of an accomplishment on an island visited by hurricanes nu-merous times in the last 150 years, the museum is furnished with shipwreck salvage, a practice that was quite legal in the 1820s and 1830s and made the fortunes of many such "wreckers." The antiques are lovely, but the tales of "wrecking" hold the real fascination. Open daily from 10 a.m. to 4 p.m.; admission is $2 per person.

HONEYMOON HOTELS AND HIDEAWAYS

Capture the charm of Old Key West in Old Town or one of the newer resorts. No matter where you stay, nothing is far away. Where applicable, rates quoted reflect the spread between low- and high-season rates.

Moderate to Expensive

One of Key West's most lavish beachfront resorts, **The Reach,** Simonton Street at the Ocean, Key West, FL 33040 (tel. 305/296-5000; reservations: toll free 800/874-4118 nationwide; 800/423-9953 in Florida), touts itself as "outrageously ro-mantic." Victorian gingerbread Key West architecture washed in subtle peach and white looks stunning against the deep blue of the ocean. She's a beauty outside, and indoors you'll find all the nice extras that take a resort hotel from pleasant to perfect: sunny terraces for an intimate breakfast for two; wicker and pine furniture for a spa-cious and airy feel; white walls, neutral shades of upholstery, and white lamps; Mexi-can tile floors and Indian dhurrie rugs; an alarm that wakes you to a fresh pot of coffee. The attentive European-style service and light, breezy feel of the place can only be described as a 24-hour celebration. Choose works by your favorite authors while your "librarian" dispenses tea and sherries in the lending library. "Romancing the Reach" honeymoon package: Four days/three-nights (EP): $462 to $660 per couple. Additional night: $137.50 to $203.50 per couple. Warm your spirits by day and let the balmy breezes stir your soul by night in your deluxe oceanview room with private balcony. Package includes a welcome bottle of champagne and breakfast in bed for two the first morning.

If you want more room than a hotel and more privacy than a guesthouse, **Ocean Key House,** Zero Duval Street, Key West, FL 33040 (tel. 305/296-7701; reservations: toll free 800/328-9815 nationwide; 800/231-9864 in Florida), of-fers space and intimacy in their brand-new all-suite accommodations. Right on the

Gulf of Mexico, just steps from the charm of historic Key West, the Ocean Key House is pure luxury without being stuffy. The open-air lobby sets the mood of the place with a long inlaid wood reception desk with a huge arched window behind it and lots of plants all around. Rooms are downright luscious, with nothing left out. Decorated in soft peaches, pinks, and neutrals, the white furniture and live plants carry the island theme. Private balconies overlook the waterfront—a rather spectacular view to wake up to because it's where the Atlantic Ocean and the gulf meet. Sip champagne in your private Jacuzzi, cook up a feast in your own gourmet kitchen, or swim in the sparkling pool with the gulf as a backdrop. For avid boating enthusiasts, sightseeing and fishing boats are available at the Ocean Key House Marina. "Suite-Heart Days" honeymoon package: Three days/two nights (EP): $547.80 per couple. Includes a deluxe one-bedroom, gulf-view suite with private balcony, Jacuzzi, fully equipped kitchen, living/dining area, minibar, and satellite TV (VCRs available for rent), welcome champagne, daily continental breakfast, sunset cruise, welcome special at the Dockside Bar and Raw Bar, shopping and entertainment coupon book, and souvenir T-shirts. Four-day/three-night package (EP): $821.70 per couple; six-day/five-night package (EP): $1,369.50 per couple.

Exalt your spirit in Key West's newest resort fantasy, the **Hyatt Key West,** 601 Front St., Key West, FL 33040 (tel. 305/296-9900; reservations: toll free 800/ 233-1234 nationwide). Contemplate Atlantic sunrises and Gulf of Mexico sunsets from your airy balconied room. Wicker is the word in furnishings, along with oak wainscotting and paddle fans. Nick's Coastal Cafe at the Hyatt reflects Key West's cultural diversity in a mix of Caribbean and Italian cuisine, enjoyed indoors or out by the water. There are two more restaurants, a pool, and a charter boat to take you on a deep-sea adventure. "Spirit of Romance" honeymoon package: Four days/ three nights (EP): $416.90 to $691.90 per couple. Extra night (EP): $119.90 to $218.90 per couple. Includes a deluxe king-bedded air-conditioned guest room with paddle fan, servi-bar, and balcony overlooking the gulf; welcome tropical fruit, a bottle of chilled champagne delivered to your room on arrival, dinner for two with a bottle of wine in either Nick's Grill or Nick's Coastal Cafe; and use of the health club. Upgrade to a gulf-front King Salon for an additional $72.60 (EP) per couple.

Marriott's Casa Marina Resort, Reynolds Street on the Ocean, Key West, FL 33040 (tel. 305/296-3535; reservations: toll free 800/228-9290 nationwide; 800/235-4837 in Florida). The original 1921 Spanish Renaissance La Casa Marina was created by Henry Morrison Flagler to give the tourists who rode the Overseas Railroad a place to stop and visit at the end of the line. The railroad, destroyed by a 1935 hurricane, has been replaced by a highway, but visitors still flock to this elegant resort, which has been a haven for politicians, movie stars, artists, and socialites. Many additions have been made as the resort grew up, with modern amenities added to keep pace with today's traveler. Breakfast on a patio by the ocean or wander around the 13-acre estate grounds. Sun on the beach or sail away from the private pier. Your room combines the lovely posh surroundings of the old resort with the amenities of the new one. Thick carpets and pastel wallpaper complement the natural wicker furniture. Think of the rich, the powerful, and the influential who must have gazed in the heavy mirrored vanity before you. Many of the nice old touches have been left alone—paddle fans, tall columns, high-beamed ceilings. "Honeymoon on Kokomo Beach" (named after the Beach Boys' hit song) (EP): $172.70 per couple for first night; $120 per couple for each additional night. Includes a deluxe island-view room, champagne on arrival, daily breakfast for two, and a sunset cruise on a large catamaran or schooner.

Holiday Inn La Concha Resort Hotel, 430 Duval St., Key West, FL (tel. 305/ 296-2991; reservations: toll free 800/HOLIDAY nationwide; 800/227-6151 in Florida). The grande dame of Old Key West, this 1925 hotel marks the place where Tennessee Williams put his final touches on *A Streetcar Named Desire.* In the heart of the historic district, La Concha has spared no expense making every detail in renovation historically accurate. Pinks, violets, whites, and beiges blend with deep-green awnings and marble stairways to create the elegantly casual ambience. Sunset colors accent The Top's lounge and rooftop garden, where guests may watch Atlantic sunrises and gulf sunsets from the island's tallest building. Rooms are adorned with 1920s antique furnishings, poster beds, chenille bedspreads, and white-lace curtains billowing with fresh sea air. "The Romance of the 1920s" honeymoon package: Three days/two nights (EP): $324.50 per couple. Includes a bottle of chilled champagne, breakfast in bed one morning, a tour of Key West on the Old Town Trolley, and a sunset cruise on a glass-bottomed boat. New in the honeymoon package at La Concha is the extra-nice addition of a half-day bicycle rental and box lunch, so that sweethearts can enjoy an intimate picnic at nearby Fort Taylor State Park.

The nicest little hotel in Key West has got to be the newly restored **Marquesa,** 600 Fleming St., Key West, FL 33040 (tel. 305/292-1919; reservations: toll free 800/792-7637 nationwide). This is not a place for couples who want to walk barefoot through the lobby. The 1884 building is a marvel of architectural reconditioning, interior design, and first-class amenities. In fact, James Bond (Timothy Dalton) and some of the cast and crew of *License to Kill* filled the hotel in August of 1988 while filming the movie in Key West. What they found delighted them: marble baths, antique furnishings, Caswell-Massey toiletries, window seats and ceiling fans, and colors of cool, tropical blues and pinks. In the morning, after a dip in the solar-heated pool, guests can dine on toasted granola, fresh-squeezed orange juice, and banana-coconut-pecan toast. Don't miss the Mira Restaurant inside the hotel for exquisite ambience (see "Romantic Restaurants" section). It's owned by the same folks who brought you Louie's Backyard. Honeymoon package: None. Seasonal room rates (EP): mid-December to April: $165 per couple for a standard room; $236.50 for a suite. May to mid-December, standards are $99 per couple; suites are $154 and up.

Guesthouses

If you'd like to experience living in one of these grand old Key West homes for a day or a week, they are filled with lots of charm and Old South graciousness; most are very affordable. It's a great way to go if you don't have a great amount of money to spend, and many of the homes offer breakfast as part of the deal. In addition, the managers will truly bend over backward for honeymoon couples.

Surround yourselves in a sea of Victorian tranquility at **La Mer,** 506 South St., Key West, FL 33040 (tel. 305/296-5611; toll free 800/354-4455 in Florida). For pure romantics, La Mer has the charm, the beauty, and the privacy that capture the spirit of old Key West. The 11-room guesthouse is a 1900 Victorian "Conch" house (lots of breezy porches and gingerbread woodwork) in the very heart of the Old Town historic district. Guest rooms, however, are tropical and contemporary with queen- or king-size beds, mauve and floral patterns, and rattan furniture. Some have kitchenettes; all have private baths. Honeymoon package: None. Room rates (EP): $108.90 to $152.90 per couple per night in summer; $147.40 to $207.90 in winter. Rates also vary according to views.

Heron House, 512 Simonton St., Key West, FL 33040 (tel. 305/294-9227), is actually three restored homes, the oldest of which was built in 1856. Renovation has included making rooms larger (there are just 17) with a light and airy spaciousness that gently blends old and new. Stroll around the shady grounds; there's a park right across the street, and the beach is only three blocks away. Heron House is located in a residential area so it's far from the noise and crowds in the busier tourist areas. Honeymoon package: None. Room rates (EP): $71.50 to $137.50 per couple per night in summer; $93.50 to $170.50 in winter. All rooms have private baths.

Pat Hoffman is the gracious proprietor of the **Merlinn Guest House,** 811 Simonton St., Key West, FL (tel. 305/296-3336). Each room is individually decorated to perfection with wood-beam ceilings, Bahama fans, and polished wood floors. Every room has a private bath. Breakfast is served daily on the deck overlooking the guesthouse's small pool. Vegetable quiche, fresh biscuits, juice, and coffee are just a few of the menu items you might find waiting when you awaken. Complimentary cocktails and hors d'oeuvres welcome you to this quiet and pleasant place. Honeymoon package: None. Standard rates (EP): $64.90 to $86.90 per couple per night; room with queen-size bed (EP): $71.50 to $95.70; an apartment with kitchen, dining area, and separate bedroom (EP): $86.90 to $113.30. Two accommodations of note here are the patio house, with a kitchen and sitting area and a king-size bed under a large skylight; and "The Treehouse" honeymoon suite on the second floor, jutting out from the rest of the house so it is actually set into the trees. It has a queen-size bed with a mosquito net canopy and a private sun deck. Both accommodations are $86.90 to $121 (EP) per night.

ROMANTIC RESTAURANTS AND NIGHTSPOTS

Historic hangouts abound if you want to follow the footsteps of the greats, but there's also plenty of history in resort restaurants. The ocean or gulf views can also pick you up at several local nightspots.

Moderate

Four plant-filled, candlelit dining rooms plus the enclosed Buttery Garden Room at **The Buttery,** 1208 Simonton St. (tel. 294-0717), offer diners as much variety in seating as eating. Managers Toni and Paul have revamped this beautiful old building from scratch. The garden room is glass-enclosed to keep diners comfortable, and French doors, high ceilings, and skylights keep that open outdoor-like atmosphere. The Audubon Room is very formally decorated with a crystal chandelier and Queen Anne chairs upholstered in silk brocade. The Fountain Room is a misnomer; the fountain fell into disrepair and has been removed, but the room now has a tropical feel to it, with parroted upholstery, lots of palms, and rattan chairs and tables. The Cape Cod and Buttery rooms are earthy with deep-wood paneling and captain's chairs; a second dining room has lace curtains and antiques. An intimate table in the corner of this room is a favorite spot for wedding proposals! Try gamberetti de mare with Key West shrimp, Buttery steak Richardo, or the catch of the day prepared any of six different ways. Entrées priced from $18 to $24. Open at 7 p.m. daily.

Henry's at Casa Marina Resort (296-3535) is named for 1920s railroad tycoon Henry Morrison Flagler. Fine dining touches abound, such as butter served on chilled lemon leaves and salads presented with chilled forks on cloth napkins. Entrées including yellowtail snapper, drunken lobster, and steak Diane are favorites, but save room for conch chowder and Key lime pie. Entrées are priced from $17.95 to $32.95. Sultry piano music plays in the natural rattan and burgundy dining area while you eat, the moon glistens on the ocean waves, paddle fans whirr, and there you are with your favorite person in the world. Enjoy! Open from 7:30 a.m. to 11 p.m. After dinner, enjoy live entertainment in the Calabash Lounge from 9 p.m. until 2 a.m. A truly "honeymoonish" night out.

La Terraza De Marti, 1125 Duval St. (tel. 294-8435). Called "La-Te-Da" for short, this European-style hotel in the historic district is better known for its superb cuisine than its modest accommodations. Breeze through an entryway adorned with bougainvillea and passion flowers to the dining area with a double-decker porch overlooking a truly gem-like pool. If you prefer, dine outdoors at one of several intimate poolside tables. Get a delicious start on your day with croissants with brie and tropical fruit or eggs served nine incredible ways from Benedict with oyster (Key West style) to five layers of omelets and fillings baked in cream custard. You might guess that luncheon and dinner menus are equally as tempting and exotic. The tea dance is a Sunday-afternoon highlight. Among 18 dinner entrées are lobster boreale, poulet rôti champagne (roast chicken with forcemeat stuffing of chicken and pork in champagne-and-celery cream sauce), and lamb Montmorencey (grilled and sliced, dressed with a port-and-garlic sauce with fresh cherries). Breakfast entrées $6.50 to $19; luncheon $7.50 to $15.75; dinner $8.95 to $23. Open seven days.

Built in 1909, **Louie's Backyard,** 700 Waddell Ave. (tel. 294-1061), is listed on the National Register of Historic Places. Patrons may dine seaside in the shade of flowering sea-grape trees under the stars or in one of Louie's elegant dining rooms, where period furnishings mingle with 1980s wicker and plants. Louie's four-star rating from the *Miami Herald* is well deserved. Begin your meal with a glass of wine or champagne ($3.25 to $7.00) and an appetizer of grilled shrimp and chorizo (spicy sausage) with blistered peppers, onions, and sherry vinegar ($9), or a bowl of Bahamian conch chowder ($5.25). The next course might be a vegetable plate of roasted peppers, squash and zucchini terrine ($7), light pasta, or antipasto. Delectable entrées include grilled quail with duck liver stuffing and port sauce ($22.50), and a thick filet of grouper (a fleshy, delicate fish) with black beans, lime, and plantains ($21). The best is yet to come: Louie's lime cheesecake with crushed strawberries in Bonny Doon's strawberry wine ($5), or a pavé of chocolate with pistachio cream, so thick and heavy that it comes by the slice ($5.50). A quick calculation will have you spending about $90 for dinner for two, served from 6 to 10:30 p.m. in winter, from 7 to 11 p.m. in summer. Louie's also serves Sunday brunch from 11:30 a.m. to 3 p.m. It's about $30 per person, depending on how hungry you are (includes an alcoholic eye-opener). Lunch is served daily from 11:30 a.m. to 3 p.m. for around $25 per person. There's a separate menu in the upstairs dining room, featuring "Nuevo Cubano" cuisine, with an average price of $25 per person. The Afterdeck Bar, a transom's height above the water on the third deck, delivers Louie's own specialty drinks, wines, and apéritifs from 11:30 a.m. to 2 a.m.

A Mallory Pier sunset will put you in the mood for the **A & B Lobster House,** 700 Front St., Key West, (tel. 294-2536). Ride the elevator to the main dining room or walk around the building to the raw bar directly on the water. The upstairs room offers a wonderful view of the harbor; the interior features polished terrazo floors and a carpeted gazebo in the center. From the restaurant, you can buy a ride on a sailing schooner, take a sunset cruise, or visit a coral reef. All boats are privately owned and dock at the A & B Marina.

Did we mention food? In addition to all the sights and sails, there's a tremendous selection of exotic specialty drinks (there's even a separate menu just for them) and good, good food at moderate prices. Shrimp scampi, lobster tail, London broil, stuffed flounder, grouper, yellowtail, chicken, prime rib, conch, scallops, stone-crab claws, and filet mignon give everyone a choice of their favorites. Entrées start at $10.95 and range all the way up to $24.95 for a whole lobster tail with New York strip steak. Dinners come with everything but the kitchen sink and the dessert—can you possibly leave without a slice of THE Key lime pie? The main dining room serves Monday through Saturday from 5 to 10 p.m. The raw bar serves daily from 10:30 a.m. to 10 p.m.

People watching is a popular pastime for diners at **Claire,** Gingerbread Square, 900–904 Duval St., Key West (tel. 296-5558). All seating areas are great for views: either indoors, in the garden, on the porch, or on the deck. Tables are covered with white paper and customers are issued crayons to doodle. Try one of Claire's regular favorites, such as fettuccine "Marco Polo"—stir-fried broccoli, snow peas, red peppers, fresh ginger, soy, and Parmesan alone or with your choice of tofu, breast of chicken, or Key West shrimp. Daily specials might include cream of zucchini soup with romano basil butter, yellowtail, grouper, Florida spiny lobster, dolphin, or snapper. Complete dinners should run around $60 per couple. Dinner menu in effect from 5:30 p.m. to 2 a.m.; late-night menu from midnight to 1:30 a.m.

Inexpensive

Dine directly on South Beach on the ocean side of Key West in **The Eatery,** 1405 Duval St. (tel. 294-2727), a delightful home-style buffet restaurant. The brick floor and the whitewashed walls with natural cedar frames and latticework combine with paddle fans and greenery to create an authentic Key West feel. Huge windows on the front and side of The Eatery look out onto the ocean. Haitian and palm-weave artwork by local talent is proudly displayed on the walls. This is an "all-you-can-eat" buffet restaurant, so come hungry. Breakfast—served Monday through Saturday, 8 to 11 a.m.; on Sunday, 8 a.m. to 2 p.m.—might include baked apples, home fries, or chipped beef in gravy ($5.75 per person). Dinner selections include local fresh fish, baby back ribs, conch chowder, or fritters, and a selection of five vegetables for about $11.95 per person. Open daily from 8 a.m. to 9 p.m.; dinner buffet served from 5 to 9 p.m.

When it was known as the Midget Bar, **Sloppy Joe's** at the corner of Greene and Duval (tel. 294-5717) was a place where Hemingway spent many hours downing a few cold beers or picking a fist fight. The new Sloppy Joe's, with its loud Top 40 music and carnival atmosphere, is now a trendy hangout for college students on vacation, but a plaque in the bar blatantly announces that Hemingway *was here*. Meanwhile, **Captain Tony's Saloon** looks more like a Sloppy Joe's—in fact, it was the original at 428 Greene St. (tel. 294-1838). Business cards and newspaper clippings adorn the walls. This place has got atmosphere by the ladleful and a trip to Key West isn't complete until you've at least walked through Captain Tony's and read one newspaper clipping dating back to the early 1930s.

HAWAII

1. PRACTICAL FACTS
2. OAHU
3. MAUI
4. KAUAI
5. THE BIG ISLAND

You decide: Your honeymoon in Hawaii can be an action-packed adventure or a calm, beachside reverie.

Located in the Pacific Ocean 2,397 miles southwest of San Francisco, Hawaii is a sparkling string of four major tourist islands, four smaller islands, and some tiny volcanic outcroppings. Oahu is the most visited, but Maui, Kauai, and the big island of Hawaii—collectively known as the "Neighbor Islands"—also hold countless honeymoon possibilities. All four islands lie within just 236 miles of one another, yet each one is quite different from the next.

On Oahu's south coast, Waikiki shimmers with all the hustle and bustle of a cosmopolitan city, while the island's north shore boasts miles and miles of pristine beaches and backcountry towns. On Maui, resplendent resort areas such as Kaanapali, Kapalua, and Wailea rise in dramatic contrast to the gently rolling pasturelands of heavenly Hana. On the large island of Hawaii (generally referred to as the Big Island, to distinguish it from the name of the entire state), you can shiver at the summit of a 10,000-foot-high volcano or bask on world-famous black-sand beaches. On Kauai, a hike through the wilderness of the Na Pali (cliffs) coast is set off by lazy days on golden beaches. The options are many, the choice is all yours.

The ethnic mix—Japanese, Filipino, Samoan, Caucasian, Thai, and Chinese—contributes an array of international flavors so that Hawaii combines the exotica of a foreign country with the easy familiarity of the United States. Everything and everyone are extremely accommodating in the 50th state. Rainbow-hued tropical fish are so friendly they'll eat right out of your hand, and the air and water temperatures always seem to be exactly perfect. All year long, heady flowers bloom, waterfalls rush down the sides of volcanic cliffs, and the colors of earth, sea, and sky are vibrant. Activities and lodgings abound on the isles, and tours and transportation are generally quite easy to arrange.

Most of all, Hawaii's gracious people make it the epitome of heaven on earth. The natural warmth and friendliness of the islanders will embrace you with what is known as the "aloha spirit." From the lei of flowers that you receive upon arrival to the helpful tips from a passerby, the aloha spirit springs freely from this rich land and its one million residents, making Hawaii a harbor of love.

1. Practical Facts

Although Hawaii is some 2,400 miles from the North American mainland, it is the 50th of the United States. Absolutely no border formalities are required for Americans—it's as easy as going from New York to New Jersey. Since farming is a major Hawaiian industry, an agricultural inspection takes place at the airport to prevent certain fruits and flowers from entering or leaving Hawaii. For details, contact the **Department of Agriculture,** 1428 South King St., Honolulu, HI 96814 (tel. 808/548-2211).

GETTING THERE

The most convenient transportation to Hawaii is by air, although cruise ships do dock as well.

By Air

From New York it takes about ten hours to fly to Hawaii, from California, about five hours. **United, American, Delta, Continental, Northwest, Pan American, Transamerica,** and **TWA** provide service into Honolulu and some Neighbor Islands, and a local airline, **Hawaiian Air,** now offers flights from the West Coast to Hawaii. The principal island airports are in Kahului on Maui, Lihue on Kauai, and both Kona and Hilo on the Big Island. In addition to Hawaiian Air, major interisland carriers are **Aloha Air, United, Air Molokai,** and **Big Island Air.** Flights from Honolulu to Maui take 30 minutes, to Kauai 20 minutes, and to the Big Island 40 minutes. These flights depart from the interisland terminal directly adjacent to the main terminal. Interisland flights from Honolulu are particularly convenient if you want to fly to the Kapalua/West Maui Airport (near Kaanapali on Maui), Hana (Maui), or Princeville Airport (on Kauai's north shore).

By Sea

American Hawaii Cruises, 550 Kearny St., San Francisco, CA 94108 (tel. toll free 800/227-3666), offers all-inclusive interisland excursions on glittering "love boats" that depart Honolulu on Saturdays and stop at the Big Island, Kauai, and Maui. A wide range of different cruise options is available, including the "Elegant Honeymoon" six-night package, which gives you two nights' accommodations at the Hawaiian Regent hotel in Waikiki, and four nights aboard the S.S. *Constitution.* At the Hawaiian Regent, you'll get limousine transfers from the airport to the hotel, accommodations in a junior suite, welcome champagne and a pineapple, and full American breakfast daily. Aboard the S.S. *Constitution,* you'll receive a floral lei greeting, welcome champagne, a souvenir photo of both of you with the captain, a Fern Grotto cruise in Kauai, and a cabin with a double bed. Rates (BP at hotel, FAP aboard ship): $2,090 to $2,970 per couple, depending on your cabin selection.

GETTING AROUND OAHU

On Hawaii's most populated island, Oahu, for $11 per couple an **airport shuttle bus** will take both of you plus your luggage the nine miles into Waikiki.

Taxis are used less frequently in Honolulu than in other major U.S. cities, but they'll take you where you need to go if you phone ahead. Two such companies are **Charleys** (tel. 531-1333) and **Aloha State** (tel. 847-3566). The fare runs about $17 from the airport to Waikiki.

For 60¢ in exact change, you can go just about anywhere on Oahu's efficient public transportation system, dubbed **"TheBus"** (tel. 531-1611).

With so many sights in so many places, Oahu begs to be seen by car. **Renting a car** is not necessary in order to get around, but it's certainly nice to have one available for that early morning spin to the beach or an impulsive moonlight drive.

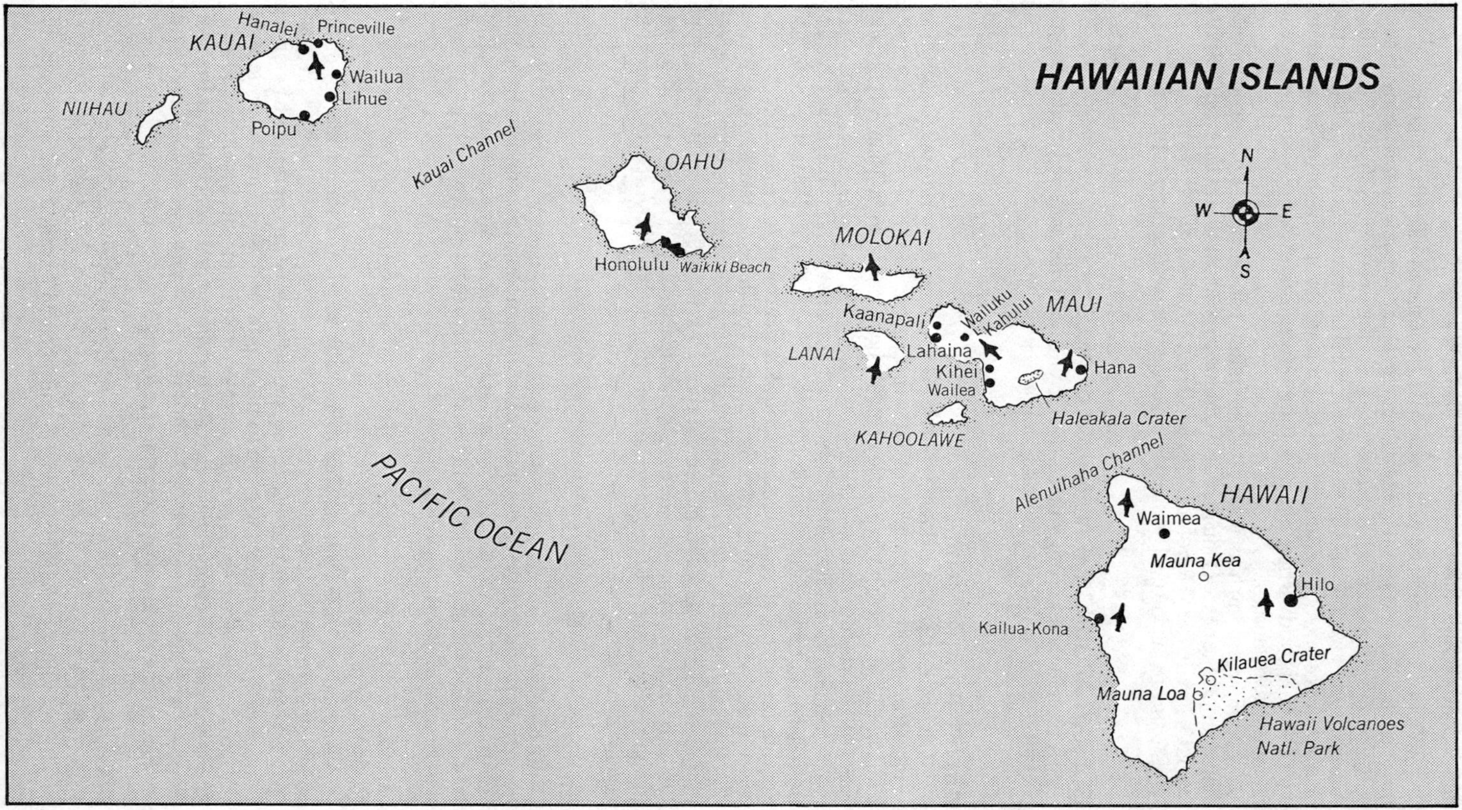

HAWAIIAN ISLANDS

N
W — E
S

PACIFIC OCEAN

NIIHAU

KAUAI
Hanalei
Princeville
Wailua
Lihue
Poipu

Kauai Channel

OAHU
Honolulu Waikiki Beach

MOLOKAI

LANAI
Kaanapali

KAHOOLAWE

MAUI
Wailuku
Kahului
Hana
Lahaina
Kihei
Wailea
Haleakala Crater

Alenuihaha Channel

HAWAII
Waimea
Hilo
Mauna Kea
Kilauea Crater
Mauna Loa
Kailua-Kona
Hawaii Volcanoes Natl. Park

To rent a car you must be 18 years old and have a valid driver's license and a major credit card. A wide variety of major rental-car companies stands ready to help you, and the competition has kept prices fairly low, between $35 and $45 a day. Automatic shift usually costs a few dollars more than manual shift. Rentals generally offer insurance on your car, and several have money saving "fly/drive" deals tied in with U.S. mainland carriers as well as the interisland airlines. Ask your travel agent for complete details.

For $55 to $65 an hour (two-hour minimum) you can hire a Rolls-Royce chauffeured limousine to see Oahu in style. Write ahead to **Silver Cloud Limousine Service,** P.O. Box 15773, Honolulu, HI 96830 (tel. 808/524-7999).

Be sure to buckle up, because Hawaii's seat-belt law is strictly enforced.

GETTING AROUND THE NEIGHBOR ISLANDS

Although there are other alternatives, a rental car is the preferred mode of transportation for visitors to Maui, Kauai, and the Big Island.

Airport Transportation

On Maui, a **Gray Line Hawaii shuttle** from Kahului Airport to the Kaanapali or Wailea Beach resort area costs about $20 a couple (tel. 808/877-5507). Between 9 a.m. and 5 p.m., there's a free **trolley shuttle** between the West Maui Airport and Kaanapali hotels and condos.

On Kauai, both **Gray Line Hawaii** and **TransHawaiian** run regular shuttles from the main Lihue Airport to the major island resort areas. Costs run about $20 per couple from the airport to Poipu; about $48 per couple to Princeville.

On the Big Island, no shuttles are available; you'll have to take a taxi.

By Taxi: On Maui, a cab ride from Kahului Airport to Kaanapali runs about $37 for two. On Kauai, to get from Lihue Airport to Princeville costs about $52, from Lihue to Poipu beach, about $26.50. On the Big Island, it's $17.50 to $27.50 from Keahole Airport to the Kona resorts, and $5.50 from the Hilo Airport to your Hilo hotel.

Island Buses

Hilo's **Hele-On** bus makes a morning and afternoon trip around the town (tel. 935-8241). Buses also operate between some of the major attractions of the Big Island, Monday through Friday, but the schedule is usually not convenient for tourists. No public buses run on Maui or Kauai.

Rental Cars

A rental car offers you maximum mobility to explore the far reaches of the Neighbor Islands.

On Maui, Kauai, and the Big Island, the major rental car companies have offices that are either immediately adjacent to the airport or within a free van ride away. Fly/drive deals offered through interisland airlines include cars for under $20 a day. If you really plan to explore the island, sign up with a rental agency such as **Tropical-Rent-A-Car** (tel. toll free 800/367-5140) that offers a flat rate and unlimited free mileage. Tropical's super-saver rates start as low as $97 per week.

LANGUAGE

In Hawaii, the English language is enlivened with many Hawaiian words that are used in everyday conversation. Instead of compass directions, say *mauka* (toward the mountains) or *makai* (seaward). *Mahalo* means thanks, and *pau* means finished. For the most romantic accommodations, get a hotel room with a *lanai* (balcony). Call your new mate *ipo* (sweetheart). If you forget all of that, just say *aloha,* which means everything from hello and goodbye to "I love you."

MONEY

Most of Hawaii's banks are open Monday to Friday from 8:30 or 9 a.m. until 3 p.m. (6 p.m. on Friday). Major credit cards and traveler's checks are widely accepted. Personal checks from out of town require at least two pieces of identification.

WEATHER

The Hawaiian weather report sounds like a broken record: sunny skies, light showers over the mountains, high in the mid to upper 80s. There are just two seasons. Summer runs from May to October, and while temperatures climb into the 90s during the warmest months of August and September, constant trade winds keep the climate comfortable. Winter (November through April) brings cooler weather, ranging from 65° at night to 85° during the day, along with 20- to 30-foot waves that often pound the north shores of all the islands. It rains more frequently during winter, but the sun returns quickly, and you can count on nice beach weather just about every day of the year.

CLOTHING

The word for Hawaiian fashion is casual. Dress tends to reflect the comfortable lifestyle of this easygoing place. Bring bathing suits, sports clothes, informal shirts and shorts, and sandals or informal shoes, and you'll be covered for almost every occasion. Don't forget your sunglasses, which are imperative in this bright climate. For an evening out, women should bring a summery dress or a skirt and blouse, and men should bring slacks, a light jacket, a tuck-in shirt, and dress shoes. A handful of the finer restaurants require men to wear jackets and ties, and casual eateries generally insist that all diners wear shirts and shoes. Be sure to leave room in your suitcase so that you can buy some traditional aloha fashions. These colorful Hawaiian fabrics are turned into casual dress shirts for men, long and short muumuus (loose-fitting dresses) for women, and action-wear for everyone.

TIME

Hawaii's days are long and luxurious, so there is no need here for daylight saving time. In winter, Hawaii is five hours behind the U.S. East Coast: When it is noon in New York, it is 7 a.m. in Hawaii. In summer, when the mainland goes on daylight saving time, there is a six-hour time difference: When it is noon in New York, it is 6 a.m. in Hawaii.

TELEPHONES

The area code for the entire state is 808. A call to any number within each island is considered a local call and costs 25¢ from a pay phone. Higher rates apply to interisland calls. For directory assistance dial, 1-411. In an emergency dial, 911.

SHOPPING

A variety of international goodies is available in this Pacific melting pot, and souvenir prices range from $2 for a strand of shiny black nuts from the kukui tree to

$3,000 for an elegant Oriental rug. Hawaii's pride and joy, however, are goods created in the islands. These local products reflect the spirit of the islands and offer cherished mementos of your Hawaiian honeymoon.

Koa and rosewood are prized island woods that make beautiful souvenirs such as bowls, furniture, and sculptures. Tapa, or bark cloth, is stenciled with handsome designs and used as a wall hanging or decorative covering. Other natural materials are used to create fascinating woven goods such as baskets of coconut fronds and hats of *lauhala* (pandanus). Feather bands are worn to add color to the brim of a hat, and leis made of seeds, shells, and nuts last a lifetime. The most precious keepsakes are the leis and necklaces made from the tiny, delicately colored shells gathered on Niihau, the island that is *kapu* (off-limits) to people not of Hawaiian blood. The necklaces are very expensive—about $350 for a simple choker, and up into the thousands for a shell lei. All of these items are available at arts and crafts stores in the major cities and towns, as well as at outdoor fairs held frequently on the weekends.

Delectable local edibles make great souvenirs because they literally capture the flavor of the isles. Macadamia nuts are grown and packaged on the Big Island, as is Kona coffee, a gourmet brew, but you can buy these products in any grocery store on any island. (You'll often find the cheapest prices at the local Woolworth's outlet.) Several distributors make it easy to ship home a carton or two of juicy Hawaiian pineapples and papayas. Often you can find a coupon or bargain on this service by looking in the free publications distributed in Waikiki street stands and at Neighbor Island airports.

If you want to send home some Hawaiian-bred flowers such as orchids, anthuriums, and proteas, the major flower shops can handle that for you. A dozen of each cost about $22 to $40 including shipping. It's fun to watch the lei-stringers in the flower shops, and even more fun to buy and bring home one of these traditional garlands of love, priced anywhere from $5 to $30. If you want to surround yourselves with the heady scents of Hawaii's blooms on a more permanent basis when you return home, you can choose from one of the several lines of locally produced tropical perfumes and colognes sold in hotel gift shops.

For the widest selection of resort wear, visit the major department stores. A smaller, more select, and usually more expensive variety is available in hotel fashion boutiques. For specific store recommendations, refer to the information about the appropriate islands.

ABOUT ACCOMMODATIONS

Each island features a diversity of accommodations. They range from the clean yet simple hotels off the beach with the basic amenities (air conditioning, television, telephone, comfortable beds, bathroom with shower, wall-to-wall carpeting, room service, and a small pool) to the luxurious beachfront apartment-hotels that pull out all the stops (ocean views off the lanai, a kitchenette, refrigerator, bar, stereo, king-size beds, sitting area, whirlpool, cable television and movies, turn-down service, and so on).

Condominiums are becoming increasingly popular among honeymooners who are looking for all the comforts of home. In Hawaii, quite often the condo is more than just an apartment. Not only does it offer spacious accommodations and a fully equipped kitchen, complete with an oven, large refrigerator, and all your cooking needs, but it also features the amenities of a fine hotel, such as maid service, bell and front desks, sports facilities, and fine restaurants. It's a luxurious way to set up housekeeping on your honeymoon, and costs about the same as comparable hotel accommodations.

DINING OUT

Hawaii has every type of cuisine imaginable, from seaside snacks to continental feasts. The influence of many different cultures makes each meal an international treat, be it shave ice for two (a snow cone laced with exotic Hawaiian fruit syrups) or

Japanese sashimi (bite-size slices of tender raw fish enhanced with rice, vegetables, and tangy mustard).

For starters, there are American, Hawaiian, Korean, Chinese, Japanese, Thai, Italian, Vietnamese, Indian, and Filipino eateries spread across the islands. Go ahead, dig in! Begin your meal with a hearty round of *pupus* (appetizers), which can be anything from crispy *gau gee* (meat-filled dumplings) to spicy Portuguese sausage with fresh pineapple. Your entrée can come laced with a fiery teriyaki sauce or graced with a garnish of rich macadamia nuts. Traditional dishes become culinary works of art when prepared with one of Hawaii's homegrown foods, like the sweet Maui onion, so mild you can eat it all by itself. And fresh coconut ice cream and Kona coffee make the most decadent of desserts.

Ah, and the fresh fruit! Juicy pineapples and papayas, lovely green kiwi and star fruits, generous guavas and passion fruit, sweet bananas and quenching mountain apples tempt you both. Honeymoon when the mangoes are ripe and you'll insist on eating one with every meal.

Then, of course, there's Hawaiian food, best sampled at one of the many fine commercial luaus. The featured attraction is kalua pig, succulent and smoky after having been cooked for hours in an *imu* (underground oven). Try a little of everything, from the zesty lomilomi salmon, marinated with onions and tomatoes, to a thick taro pudding called *poi*, which Hawaiians love to eat with their fingers.

Sample as much of the fresh fish as possible, because it's bound to be a prize catch. One of the most delectable dishes from Hawaiian seas is *opakapaka*, a pink snapper which is tender and tempting whether it's broiled, fried, or served as sashimi. Equally magnificent is *mahimahi*, a white dolphin fish that often appears as the catch of the day. *Uku* and *onaga* are other types of snapper, *ahi* and *aku* are two popular types of tuna, and *ono* is a kind of mackerel. *Ulua* is a highly prized jack fish that is often the key ingredient in the tantalizing local chowder, and Hawaii's lobster, shrimp, and prawns taste as delicate as any.

Most restaurants take reservations, and many of the finest are found in hotels. If you order wine with your meal, be advised that the drinking age in Hawaii is 21.

HOW TO GET MARRIED IN HAWAII

Nearly one-quarter of the couples who marry in Hawaii are visitors, testimony to the alluring magic of the islands. Your Hawaiian wedding is all the more special when you incorporate traditional local touches. The bride wears the *holoku*, or formal Hawaiian gown with a long train, and the man dons a long-sleeved white shirt and white pants with a colored sash around his waist. The favorite wedding lei is made of *maile*, an aromatic green leaf often interwoven with delicate white pikake blossoms. And no wedding in paradise is complete without the beloved strains of "The Hawaiian Wedding Song."

A permit for getting married in Hawaii costs $9 and is valid for 30 days. You must be at least 20 years old, and the bride-to-be must show proof of a rubella test. If you plan to get married on Oahu, apply in person to the **Hawaii Department of Health,** 1250 Punchbowl St., in Honolulu. The office is open from 8 a.m. to 4 p.m., Monday through Friday, except holidays. There are approximately 50 agents statewide who can be contacted for marriage permits on all the Neighbor Islands. For a complete information package, write to the **State Department of Health,** P.O. Box 3378, Honolulu, HI 96801 (tel. 808/548-5862 or 808/548-6479).

Most couples choose to marry in one of the splendid beach or garden settings of their hotel. In that case, the marriage license is issued right at the hotel, and the hotel staff takes care of all the details, including paperwork, officiant, music, cake, flowers, photography, and the reception.

FOR FURTHER INFORMATION

The Hawaii Visitors Bureau is a goldmine of information about every activity under the sun. Contact them on Oahu: 2270 Kalakaua Ave., Honolulu, HI 96815 (tel. 808/923-1811). Mainland offices include New York, 441 Lexington Ave., Rm. 1407, New York, NY 10017 (tel. 212/986-9203); Chicago, 180 N. Michigan Ave., Suite 1031, Chicago, IL 60601 (tel. 312/236-0632); San Francisco, 50 California St., Suite 450, San Francisco, CA 94111 (tel. 415/392-8173); Los Angeles, 3440 Wilshire Blvd., Los Angeles, CA 90010 (tel. 213/385-5301).

2. Oahu

If you tend to equate Oahu with Waikiki, guess again! It's true that Waikiki is a stimulating amalgam of sights and delights, but its famous beach area is only a tiny portion of the island Hawaiians call "The Gathering Place."

Third largest in the Hawaiian chain, Oahu is more than just a cosmopolitan sprawl. Stretched along the island's southeastern shore, the state's capital city of Honolulu is where about 80% of Hawaii's people live and work. It takes 15 minutes to drive from the Honolulu Airport to downtown Honolulu, and another 10 minutes to Waikiki, which is part of Honolulu.

Honolulu presents a charming mix of the old and new, from the modest homes of the first missionaries and America's only royal palace, to dazzling skyscrapers and fashionable shopping malls. Luxurious ocean liners still dock at historic Aloha Tower, while salty fishermen show off today's big catch at bustling Fisherman's Wharf.

Rising above it all are the magnificent Koolau Mountains, rugged reminders of the island's volcanic beginnings and the setting for much Hawaiian history and legend. In the hillsides of the Nuuanu Pali, King Kamehameha and his army fought off Oahu warriors in the famous Battle of Nuuanu (1795), conquering the enemy and unifying the islands under his rule. At the Nuuanu Pali Lookout, stop for magnificent panoramas of the island and ocean.

On the other side of the mountains, Oahu's north shore abounds with ancient fish ponds and haunting *heiaus* (sacred places). Ivory sands and shady beach parks invite lovers to picnic, swim, and linger in the serenity of the north shore, the "flip side" of Honolulu. World famous surfing havens like Sunset Beach and the Banzai Pipeline attract championship riders to perpetuate a sport once reserved for Hawaii's royalty. And to the west are the Waianae Mountains, steadfast guardians of the pristine sugarcane and pineapple fields that have played a dominant role in Hawaii's economy.

After your day tours of Oahu, you'll most likely be drawn back to Waikiki, an effervescent hub flanked by what's called "life's greatest beach" and an unmistakable dormant volcano called Diamond Head. Today, nearly all of Oahu's visitors stay in Waikiki, and with good reason. The best restaurants on the island are here, as are the top draws in Hawaii's entertainment field. Despite its large number of day- and nighttime attractions, Waikiki is compact, and getting around by foot is easy. In fact, the beach is never more than a few blocks away from all the hotels. TheBus runs regularly up and down its streets, and the oldtime Waikiki trolley picks up and deposits visitors with turn-of-the-century charm.

Waikiki is conveniently adjacent to the Honolulu Zoo, the Waikiki Aquarium, and tree-lined Kapiolani Park, a favorite spot for jogging, kite flying, and picnics for two. This is the home of the free Kodak Hula Show, which traces the history of the hula, as well as the Kapiolani Bandstand, site of numerous free community concerts. Also in Kapiolani Park is the Waikiki Shell, an outdoor amphitheater where, for a moderate admission, you can enjoy entertainment by a variety of artists, from the Honolulu Symphony to international stars such as Al Jarreau, Bill Cosby, the Beach Boys, and Chick Corea. Its sloping green lawns are perfect for relaxing under the stars, sipping some wine, and gazing at the silhouette of Diamond Head as music fills the air. Check the newspapers for concert dates.

Waikiki is there for your pleasure; indulge yourselves!

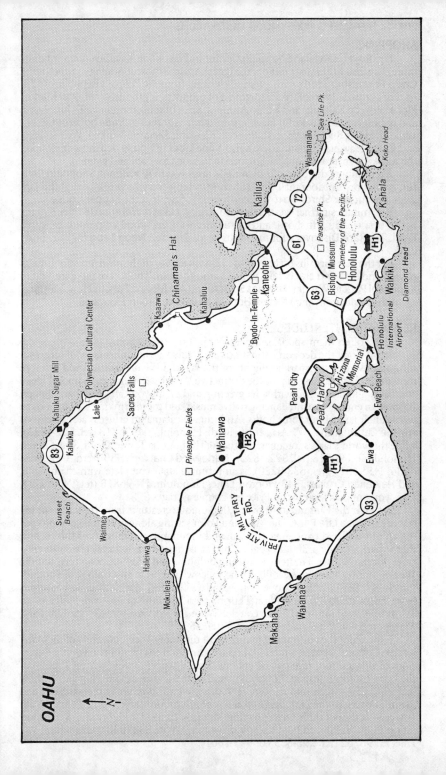

SHOPPING

The **Royal Hawaiian Shopping Center** in Waikiki on Kalakaua Avenue boasts more than 280,000 square feet of excellent shops, the most appealing of which is the **China Friendship Store,** with gifts and clothing from the People's Republic of China. For a crowded yet colorful assortment of products, try the **International Market Place** between Kalakaua and Kuhio Avenues, a riot of souvenir stands, T-shirt shops, and upbeat eateries. Colorful Hawaiian-wear awaits at the **Andrade hotel outlets** in Waikiki: Hyatt Regency Waikiki, Princess Kaiulani, Sheraton Waikiki, Waikiki Parc, and Royal Hawaiian Hotel. There's also a fine **Liberty House** department store on the Kalakaua strip, with quality Polynesian fashions for men and women.

A ten-minute drive west from Waikiki takes you to **Ala Moana Shopping Center,** an indoor/outdoor mall with 155 shops selling everything from delightful Japanese products at **Shirokiya** to Hawaiian-style footwear at the **Slipper House.**

Five minutes farther west, **Ward Centre** and **Ward Warehouse** offer elegant boutiques, trendy gift shops, and a gourmet wine and food emporium called **R. Field.** Try **Rare Discovery** for luxurious keepsakes, and **Neon Leon** for zany postcards.

For the best bargains on handmade Hawaiiana, watch the newspaper for listings of weekend **arts and crafts fairs** in parks around town. The best of these are held in **Kapiolani Park** in Waikiki; **Thomas Square** and **Ala Moana Park** in Honolulu; and the **Bishop Museum** and **Mission Houses Museum,** also in Honolulu.

ROMANTIC INTERLUDES

Oahu offers many special moments for just the two of you.

Stroll along the deck on a **sunset dinner cruise** as the amber glow of early evening gives way to the sparkling lights of the Waikiki skyline. What could be more romantic? Most cruises sail past the distinctive Waikiki shoreline to Diamond Head and back, and lavish you with a lei greeting and an all-you-can-drink bar. Dinner, Polynesian entertainment, dancing to live music, and more drinking follow, and the whole affair lasts about three hours. An intimate catamaran cruise is available from **Aikane Catamarans,** 677 Ala Moana Blvd., Honolulu, HI 96813 (tel. 522-1533), while the world's largest catamaran is the **Ali'i Kai,** Aloha Tower, Pier 8, Street Level, Honolulu, HI 96813 (tel. 522-7822). **Tradewind Charters,** 350 Ward Ave., Honolulu, HI 96814 (tel. 533-0220), is an intimate affair complete with champagne, and **Hawaiian Cruises,** 343 Hobron Lane, Honolulu, HI 96815 (tel. 947-9971), takes you out on a large yacht. Price per couple averages $75.

Fat Fred the Penguin joins over 2,000 unique creatures from the sea at the extraordinary **Sea Life Park.** The Makapuu Point setting alone is magnificent, providing an unparalleled panorama of ocean and mountains. Highlights of this 62-acre theme park include a 300,000-gallon reef tank filled with tropical Hawaiian creatures, Ocean Science Theater showcasing dolphins and adorable penguins, and the Whaler's Cove, where two 1,600-pound killer whales perform a routine of astounding stunts. Sea Life Park is open on Monday, Tuesday, Wednesday, and Saturday from 9:30 a.m. to 5 p.m., and on Thursday, Friday, and Sunday from 9:30 a.m. to 10 p.m. Admission is $17 per couple. Write for information to: Sea Life Park, Makapuu Point, Waimanalo, HI 96795 (tel. 259-7933).

Experience the culture and traditions of the South Pacific courtesy of the **Polynesian Cultural Center,** a top-rated visitor attraction that features authentic recreations of villages from seven island nations. Special attractions include the Pageant of the Long Canoes, meals at the Gateway Restaurant, and an exhilarating dinner show featuring 150 singers and dancers. The complete package for two costs $124 and includes entry to the park, admission to the afternoon and evening shows, an all-you-can-eat dinner buffet, a lei greeting, an escorted tour, and round-trip transportation from Waikiki, an hour's scenic drive away. Write 55370 Kamehameha Hwy., Laie, HI 96762 (tel. 293-3333 or 923-1861).

The romance of old Hawaii endures in the forest splendor of the 1,800-acre **Waimea Falls Park** valley, once the site of an ancient community. Located on the north shore, the park entices lovers of all ages to smell the flowers and wander back to the 45-foot waterfall. Each month there are free full-moon strolls.

Wedding packages are available in the botanical gardens, including traditional Hawaiian leis for the bride and groom, Hawaiian melodies, champagne, a minister, a photographer, and use of either a Rolls-Royce limousine for four hours or a Lincoln Town Car for three days.

General admission to Waimea Falls Park is $17 for two, and it is open daily from 10 a.m. to 5:30 p.m. Write to: 59-864 Kamehameha Hwy., Haleiwa, HI 96712 (tel. 638-8511).

A pristine crescent of sand ringed by lacy palms and unbelievably blue water beckon you to **Hanauma Bay,** Oahu's premier snorkeling and skin-diving spot. The fish are tame in this underwater volcanic crater, and they swim right up to you if you offer them frozen peas. Hanauma Bay, which also offers bathroom and snack bar facilities, is a 20-minute drive from Waikiki. If you don't want to drive, **Steve's Diving Adventures** takes you there and back and provides equipment, beach mats, and fish food for $14 per couple. Contact them at 1860 Ala Moana Blvd., Honolulu, HI 96815 (tel. 947-8900).

Built in 1882, **Iolani Palace** has been restored to the initial splendor envisioned by its first occupant, King David Kalakaua, the "Merry Monarch" whose penchant for opulence helped dub his reign the "Champagne Dynasty." Guided tours are scheduled from 9 a.m. to 2:15 p.m., Wednesday through Saturday, and the cost for two is $8. Your tour guide will provide you with slippers to protect the highly polished floors. The bandstand on the grounds adds a charming touch to this regal attraction, and every Friday at 12:15 p.m. the Royal Hawaiian Band performs there for your picnicking pleasure. Write to: P.O. Box 2259, Honolulu, HI 96804 (tel. 522-0832).

There's no view more precious than from atop **Diamond Head,** the famous extinct volcano rising 760 feet above town. From Waikiki you can drive through a tunnel into the crater. It's an easy half-hour hike up the inside trail, which culminates in 99 steps and a diversion through some wartime bunkers. Go when the gates open at 6 a.m. and the early morning lights make the whole ocean glimmer. Later in the day, the panoramic mountains reflect the rosy hues of the sunset. For details write **Hawaii State Parks and Recreation,** P.O. Box 621, Honolulu, HI 96809 (tel. 548-7455).

HONEYMOON HOTELS AND HIDEAWAYS

Be it a modest beach bungalow or the island's most luxurious suite, Oahu's variety of lodgings fits the bill for a honeymoon of any size and shape.

Expensive

Originally a private beachfront estate, **Halekulani,** 2199 Kalia Rd., Honolulu, HI (tel. 808/923-2311; reservations: toll free 800/367-2343), has been accommodating discriminating travelers to Waikiki Beach since 1917. The carefully restored main building, dating back to 1931, remains the focal point of the new Halekulani today. Steeped in nostalgia, this 456-room oasis links the elegance of the past with that of the present, and its five interconnecting buildings surround tranquil gardens and a century-old kiawe tree. White doves strut over gracious lawns lined with coconut palms, the beautiful pool is lined with an intricate mosaic depicting an orchid blossom, and the freshly swept beach offers a deck-chair view of the ocean and Diamond Head. Each room is tastefully furnished in accents of white, beige, blue, and gray, and has central air conditioning, separate sitting areas with lounge chairs, a tiled lanai, a love seat, a coffee table, three telephones, a refrigerator, a wet bar, and a color cable TV. "Romance Package": Four days/three nights: $919 per couple; eight days/seven nights: $1,849. Includes flowers and French champagne upon arrival, oceanview room, one room-service breakfast for two, use of the fitness room, a take-home gift of Halekulani bathrobes, delivery of the local paper each morning, plus such regular Halekulani offerings as maid service and aerobics classes.

The world's rich and famous have often chosen the **Kahala Hilton,** 5000 Kahala Ave., Honolulu, HI 96816 (tel. 808/734-2211; reservations: toll free 800/367-2525), as their Hawaiian host, for its peaceful beachside location in the prestigious Kahala area and its private, protected environment. It's still only ten minutes to Waikiki via the shuttle bus. Dolphins, penguins, and sea turtles cavort in the glistening lagoon, and tiny songbirds serenade you as you dine on the Hala Terrace, where you just might rub elbows with the likes of Henry Kissinger, Queen Elizabeth, Sylvester Stallone, and Linda Evans. *Magnum P.I.* used to film a part of each episode by the oceanside terrace. Most of its 370 rooms have lanais offering fine views of Kahala Bay or the Koolau mountains. Spacious living quarters are designed in bright island colors and feature his-and-her dressing areas, refrigerators and well-stocked minibars, cable TVs, clock radios, house slippers, and his-and-her robes. Honeymoon package: Four days/three nights: $627 per couple (mountain view, no balcony), $753 per couple (mountain view with balcony), and $914 per couple (ocean view). Includes full American breakfast served daily and complimentary champagne.

Meet "the first lady of Waikiki," the **Sheraton Moana Surfrider,** 2365 Kalakaua Ave., Honolulu, HI 96815 (tel. 808/922-3111; reservations: toll free 800/334-8484), a superb hostelry that opened in 1901. Fronting the ivory sands of Waikiki Beach, the white colonial-style hotel is somewhat dwarfed by the surrounding high-rises, but it remains equally convenient to the exciting shopping, dining, and sightseeing attractions of the area. A $50-million renovation has preserved the original charm of this classic South Seas retreat, which means that the rooms are smaller than their modern counterparts. The conservative decor has decidedly Hawaiian overtones, including tropical-style rattan chairs and other furnishings made out of local koa wood. Rooms are newly outfitted with state-of-the-art electronic controls for the cable television, radio, do-not-disturb indicator, and even the lock on the door. Touches of old-style island hospitality include a fresh-flower lei greeting upon arrival, valet parking, and a personal escort to your room. The H-shape of the design creates a center courtyard dominated by a century-old banyan tree, and the original oceanside veranda has been restored as a gathering place for conversation and cocktails. Honeymoon package: None (although honeymooners are greeted with a complimentary bottle of champagne). Standard rates (EP): $340 to $520 per couple per night for rooms; from $750 per couple per night for suites.

Moderate to Inexpensive

The centerpiece of the **Hyatt Regency Waikiki,** 2424 Kalakaua Ave., Honolulu, HI 96815 (tel. 808/923-1234; reservations: toll free 800/228-9000), is its open-air Great Hall Atrium, with three cascading waterfalls, gardens of tropical foliage, and a custom-designed 45,000-pound chandelier suspended from a height of six floors. Oriental art prints decorate the walls of each 425-square-foot guest room, which is designed in warm earth tones and features air conditioning, wall-to-wall carpeting, private balcony, color TV, enclosed bathroom, twin mirrors, and a combination desk/game table with chairs. You can get almost anything you need from the many shops and boutiques in the hotel, and you can keep busy with the elaborate Hawaiian activities program. The hotel's central location makes Waikiki sightseeing a snap. There's an award-winning restaurant, Hawaiian melodies in the atrium, and dancing in one of Honolulu's hottest discos, Spats. "The Spirit of Splendor" honeymoon package: Four days/three nights: $610 per couple; $185 per couple for additional night. Includes oceanfront room, champagne upon arrival, and breakfast in bed the first morning. Upgrade available to include dinner at Bagwells 2424 and use of the Regency Club.

Spread over 20 acres, the **Hilton Hawaiian Village,** 2005 Kalia Rd., Honolulu, HI 96815 (tel. 808/949-4321; reservations: toll free 800/445-8667), commands the largest hotel beachfront in Waikiki. Catamaran sails are offered daily from the Hilton's private dock, and outrigger canoes, Hobie cats, surfboards, and snorkeling gear make this an outdoor-lover's nirvana. An entire city-within-the-city has been created here, to the extent that you may never need to venture beyond its 100 shops and services, 9 restaurants, 13 lounges, and 4 swimming pools. The open-air lobby is surrounded by feathery palms, blossoming trees, cascading waterfalls, an outdoor stage, a multilevel swimming pool, pristine lagoons, colorful fish, and exotic birds. Now nearly all the 2,522 rooms have some sort of ocean view, although the best views are from the Rainbow or Ocean Tower. Rooms are done in delicious shades of raspberry or aqua, with beige rugs and furniture designed in rattan and bamboo. For a feeling of true exclusivity, ask to stay in the pricey yet plush corner or penthouse suites of the Ocean Tower, which pamper you with a state-of-the-art exercise room, private sun deck, swimming pool, and bar. Honeymoon package: Five days/four nights (EP): $475 to $676 per couple. Includes a deluxe oceanview room in the Diamond Head, Tapa, or Rainbow Tower, plus a bottle of Le Domaine champagne, two souvenir champagne glasses, and a gift certificate for one night's free stay on a return visit. Upgrade to the Alii Tower: Five days/four nights (EP): $999 per couple. Added to the above package are limousine transportation to and from the airport, a lei greeting, one breakfast in bed for two, nightly turn-down, complimentary use of health club facilities, afternoon pupus, and a choice of the Don Ho show or a twilight dinner sail.

The New Otani Kaimana Beach Hotel, 2863 Kalakaua Ave., Honolulu, HI 96815 (tel. 808/923-1555; reservations: toll free 800/421-8795). An ideal setting smack-dab on the nicest beach in Waikiki makes this a highly recommended honeymoon haven. It's off the beaten track, across from scenic Kapiolani Park and right near Diamond Head. Recent renovations have turned the lobby into a bright and cheerful gathering place with open-air views straight out to the water. Rooms and suites include paintings by local artist Pegge Hopper; shades of lavender, blue, taupe, and other pastels; brass planters, tape decks, balconies, and small refrigerators. Some rooms even have kitchenettes, and the best rooms feature breathtaking ocean vistas. There's dining in the Miyako, a fine Japanese restaurant, and the more casual Hau Tree Lanai is an outdoor eatery right next to Kaimana Beach's bevy of sunbathers and sapphire waters. Honeymoon package: $175 per couple per night. Includes accommodations in an oceanfront superior room, a convertible rental car, free parking, a bottle of champagne upon arrival, and more.

Affectionately dubbed the "Pink Palace," the legendary **Royal Hawaiian Hotel,** 2259 Kalakaua Ave., Honolulu, HI 96815 (tel. 808/923-7311; reservations: toll free 800/634-4747), is a pastel fairyland set right on the beach. Inaugurated in 1927, it is the second oldest of Waikiki's hotels, and it has been beautifully maintained in trademark stucco style. In the original building, gardenview rooms open up to groves of flowers and coconut palms, oceanview rooms offer a spacious old-world charm, and deluxe oceanview rooms are the largest and most luxurious, complete with a sitting room. Built in 1969, the Royal Tower offers private lanais and oceanfront views. All rooms have double doors, air conditioning, color TV with first-run movies, refrigerators, and electronic safes. A wide range of dining is available, including the elegant Monarch Room, a celebrated dinner showroom. For the ultimate trip into Hawaii's romantic past, go tea dancing each Sunday. Choose from 579 rooms and suites. Honeymoon package: Four days/three nights (EP): $848 per couple. Includes a fresh-flower lei greeting, a deluxe garden room, a round-trip limousine ride between the airport and hotel, a breakfast briefing, a split of champagne, and a basket of fresh tropical fruit.

Located in the "country" on the west coast of the island, a 30-minute drive from the airport and an hour-plus from Waikiki, the **Sheraton Makaha Resort and Country Club,** P.O. Box 896, Makaha, HI 96792 (tel. 808/695-9511; reservations: toll free 800/634-4747), combines easy access to Honolulu attractions with the serenity of a summer estate. Just minutes away via Sheraton's free shuttle service awaits the world-famous Makaha Beach, home of annual surfing championships. The weather is usually pleasant here, with comfortable tradewinds ideal for golf, tennis, water sports, biking, jogging, and horseback riding. Gardens surround the 200 guest rooms and suites, which feature views of either the Makaha Coast or the rugged Waianae Mountains. The architecture is Polynesian, with two-story cottages, high ceilings, open-air pavilions, and an elegant use of natural woods that blend into the country setting. Your room features a private lanai, individually controlled air conditioning, a telephone, a refrigerator, and a color TV, and the hotel includes two restaurants and a lounge, a fountain-fed swimming pool, gift shops, and Waikiki shuttle service. Honeymoon package: Four days/three nights (EP): $468 per couple. Includes a deluxe flower lei greeting, a gardenview room, three days' use of a Hertz convertible rental car with unlimited mileage, a split of champagne, a full American breakfast for two, and a basket of fresh tropical fruit.

Located on an 808-acre oceanfront resort on Oahu's scenic north shore, **Turtle Bay Hilton and Country Club,** P.O. Box 187, Kahuku, HI 96731 (tel. 808/293-8811; reservations: toll free 800/445-8667), offers a Neighbor Island atmosphere while remaining accessible to Honolulu, just a scenic hour's drive away. There are three wings of 486 rooms and suites, and from your private lanai you get a magnificent view of the bay. The simple yet gracious room furnishings are done in wicker, brass, pastels, and light-colored woods, with prints of tropical flowers on the walls and plenty of living space. Five restaurants and three cocktail lounges offer superb ocean views, as do the two swimming pools, the adjacent private cottages, the 18-hole golf course, and the tennis courts. Honeymoon package: Four days/three nights (EP): $595 per couple. Includes a lei greeting, complimentary champagne, a complimentary in-room breakfast for two, unlimited tennis, surfing or windsurfing lessons, a gift certificate for one night's stay upon return visit, and an Aloha Remembrance gift.

ROMANTIC RESTAURANTS

Whatever you hunger for, you're sure to satisfy your appetite at one of Oahu's long list of fine restaurants and night spots. Unless otherwise noted, all these restaurants are in the Waikiki area.

Expensive

Treat yourselves like royalty at the oceanside **Michel's at the Colony Surf,** 2895 Kalakaua Ave. (tel. 923-6552), set right on the beach for panoramic views of the ocean. Sterling silver, beveled glass, white linen, and fresh orchids on each table are naturally illuminated by Hawaiian sunshine by day and Waikiki moonlight by night. This is one of the very few places on Oahu where men must wear dinner jackets. Lunch includes outstanding salads, sandwiches, soufflés, and hot entrées. One of many highlights of the Sunday brunch is the baked avocado with crabmeat for $20. Dinner's highlights include a fine lobster bisque laced with cognac, opakapaka Véronique, veal Oscar, and duckling flambé. Breakfast for two costs about $22, lunch $30, brunch $35, dinner $100, plus drinks. Open for breakfast Monday through Saturday from 7 to 10 a.m. and on Sunday from 7 to 9:30 a.m.; lunch Monday through Saturday from 11:30 a.m. to 2 p.m.; dinner nightly from 5:30 to 10 p.m. Sunday brunch is from 11 a.m. to 2 p.m.

Maile Restaurant, 5000 Kahala Ave. (tel. 734-2211). Dine and dance amid tropical flowers, plants, and fountains as the waves gently lap on the nearby shore at the Kahala Hilton's signature restaurant, located about 15 minutes from Waikiki. The restaurant is noted for its formal elegance, extensive wine list, and unquestionably superb continental cuisine spiced with touches of Hawaii and the Orient. For

$96 per couple, the four-course table d'hôte dinner regales you with the best of the best, from escargots bourguignon, to grilled salmon, roast duck, and delectable dessert soufflés. À la carte dinners for two add up to about $120 plus drinks. Live entertainment is featured in the Maile Lounge, and jackets are requested of the men. Open for dinner nightly, with seatings at 6:30 p.m., 7 p.m., 7:30 p.m., and 8:30 p.m.

French continental cuisine with hints of the Orient awaits at **Bagwells,** 2424 Kalakaua Ave. (tel. 923-1234). The sun-bleached decor features aquatic overtones, with four elevated dining areas for semiprivate affairs. The centerpiece of the room is a 12-foot floor-to-ceiling glass fountain with water flowing down both sides. Appetizers include broiled marinated Kahuku prawns on a pineapple fondue, and a favorite entrée is double breast of chicken stuffed with Boursin cheese. For dessert, the Grand Marnier soufflé is not to be missed. Order à la carte or get the Chef's Surprise, six mystery courses created each day by chef On-Jin Kim. Pianist Paul Conrad plays classical and popular tunes on a white baby grand. Dinner for two is $100 plus drinks. Open for dinner seven days a week from 6 to 10 p.m., with music nightly.

Moderate

Ranked among the world's top Italian restaurants, the **Trattoria,** 2168 Kalia Rd. (tel. 923-8415), a Waikiki landmark, serves an extensive menu of traditional and exotic fare in a setting as sumptuous as the food. High ceilings and chandeliers add a distinctly European flair to the atmosphere, and a handsome Italian troubadour strolls from table to table. Your intimate candlelit meal might include fresh island mahimahi Veronica, a sautéed island fish served with lemon sauce and seedless grapes. Trattoria also offers a unique presentation of manicotti glazed in a rich cream and tomato sauce. Dinner for two ranges from $32 to $52 plus drinks. Open for dinner nightly from 5:30 to 11 p.m.

At **Hy's Steak House,** 2440 Kuhio Ave. (tel. 922-5555), tuxedoed waiters cater to your every need. Specializing in charbroiled steaks of distinction, Hy's is also famed for its broiled lobster tail, the kiawe-broiled rack of lamb, fresh opakapaka, and a superb steak tartare. After dinner, slip into the softly lit rosewood lounge for an after-dinner drink by the piano bar. Dinner for two costs from $50 to $60 plus drinks. Open for dinner nightly from 6 to 11 p.m., with pupus served in the lounge until 1 a.m.

Designed with plush red carpeting and jet-black leather, **Nick's Fishmarket,** 2070 Kalakaua Ave. (tel. 955-6333), is a favorite haunt for Honolulu's elite as well as out-of-town celebrities. Mood lighting, comfy booths, and impeccable table settings of the finest china put stars in the eyes of lovers. The menu promises such gifts of the sea as broiled fresh ulua amandine, cherrystone clams, swordfish, and ono. The aptly named Special Salad costs $5.95, and it's big enough to share. Get decadent over bananas flambé, the best in town. Nick's lounge is an upbeat forum for local talent, and you might even catch a star or two in the audience. Dinner for two is $60 plus drinks. Open for dinner nightly from 6 to 11 p.m.

Another hot spot for celebrities is **Keo's Thai Cuisine,** 625 Kapahulu Ave. (tel. 737-8240). The bamboo and brass decor accented by striking arrangements of purple orchids is soothing, but the food's the real story here. Start with spring rolls wrapped in lettuce and fresh mint, garnished with cucumber and a piquant sauce. Keo's Evil Jungle Prince is a classic entrée, seasoned with just the right degree of intensity of hot peppers, fresh basil, and coconut milk. Spicy green papaya salad, crispy fried beef, and ginger shrimp are just a few of the consistently delicious offerings of this crowning achievement. Dinner for two is $30 to $40 plus drinks. Open for dinner nightly from 5:30 to 11 p.m.

A favorite with the locals, **Tahitian Lanai,** 1811 Ala Moana Blvd. (tel. 946-6541), is a casual tropical restaurant next to the Hilton Lagoon offering informal dining amid fresh ocean breezes. Breakfast, lunch, and dinner are all fun here. Morning fare features a great eggs Benedict and very special banana muffins. Lunch and dinner offerings of note are a robust French onion soup, Tahitian-style chicken, Hawaiian combination plate, and ahi Tahitienne. For a sweet taste of the islands, top it off with fresh pineapple wedges. For two, breakfast ranges from $7 to $16; lunch from $10 to $20; dinner from $20 to $56. Behind the restaurant is the Papeete piano bar, and there's Dixieland jazz on Sunday afternoons from 2 to 5 p.m. Open daily for breakfast from 7 to 11 a.m.; lunch from 11 a.m. to 2:30 p.m.; late lunch from 2:30 to 5:30 p.m.; dinner from 6 to 10 p.m.

Designed to resemble the dining room of a splendid ocean liner, **Captain's Table**, 2570 Kalakaua Ave. (tel. 922-2511), in the Holiday Inn Waikiki, takes you on an excursion through Hawaii's unique seas, offering fresh ono sautéed with capers and lemon butter, broiled salmon with dill sauce, and other fine seafood. Try the stuffed grape leaves as an appetizer, or perhaps the herbed cream cheese that is served with lavosh crackers. Veal marsala, Malaysian-style lamb chops, and Australian lobster tail broaden this cosmopolitan menu for a meal you want to linger over for a good long time. The Captain's Table lounge offers live entertainment nightly. For two, Japanese- and American-style breakfasts run about $20; brunch costs $35; dinner is $40 to $80 plus drinks. Open daily for breakfast from 6 to 9 a.m. and for dinner from 6:30 to 10 p.m. Sunday brunch runs from 10 a.m. to 2 p.m.

Get a taste of Hawaiian *paniolo* (cowboy) traditions at **Hawaiian Hoe-Down Country Barbecue**, Heeia Park, Kaneohe (tel. 922-3377): high-kicking saloon girls, cowboy hula, singers, and callers. Dance the two-step and the cotton eye Joe. The dinner spread includes an all-you-can-eat barbecue buffet with kiawe-broiled ribs, teriyaki chicken, corn on the cob, salad, baked beans, mai tais, beer, and lots more. It costs $77 per couple, including drinks, hotel pickup, and round-trip transportation. The gala get-together happens each Tuesday and Thursday, with Waikiki pick-up between 4 and 4:30 p.m.; return between 9 and 9:30 p.m.

Set on a private estate a half-hour's drive from Waikiki, **Germaine's Luau**, southwest shore (tel. 949-6626), offers traditional Hawaiian fun. Hosting as many as 800 people per night, this outdoor affair is far from intimate, but it does offer a healthy dose of the aloha spirit and an entertaining introduction to the luau. An all-you-can-drink bar warms things up as you watch the procession of the royal court and the ceremonial lifting of the pig from its imu. You sit at long, rectangular tables where the food just keeps on coming: kalua pig, fried chicken, lomilomi salmon, mahimahi, macaroni and tossed salads, fresh pineapple spears, banana bread, and *haupia* (coconut) pudding. As the stars twinkle over the Pacific, a spellbinding Polynesian revue wraps up the evening with island songs and dances plus zany comedy. The luau costs $79 for two, including transportation from Waikiki (pick-up at 4:30 p.m.) and it's held nightly.

Restaurant Suntory, Royal Hawaiian Shopping Center (tel. 922-5511), is the place to try Japanese cuisine at its best. Choose from the Sushi Bar, the Teppanyaki Room (seafood, beef, or lobster cooked in a hearty stew), or the Shabushabu Room (specializing in tempura, which is fish and vegetables deep-fried in a light batter). Teppanyaki dinners cost from $70 to $80 per couple plus drinks. Lunch is served daily from 11:30 a.m. to 2 p.m., dinner from 6 to 9:45 p.m.

Rise above it all at one of Honolulu's elevated eateries, such as **Windows of Hawaii**, 1441 Kapiolani Blvd. (tel. 941-9138), a revolving restaurant high above Ala Moana Shopping Center. Brunch for two costs $30 including champagne; dinner for two costs $40 to $60 plus drinks. Saturday and Sunday brunch is served from 10 a.m. to 2 p.m.; open for lunch Monday through Friday, 11 a.m. to 2 p.m.; dinner nightly, 5 to 10 p.m.

Inexpensive

How about dinner on the beach at **Shore Bird Beach Broiler**, 2169 Kalia Rd. (tel. 922-2887)? This broil-your-own eatery sits right on Waikiki Beach, a great spot for a fun night out. You're the chefs, and you stand around big open fires cooking your meal while gazing at the panorama of sand and sea, just a stone's throw away.

Ribs, kebobs, chicken, and fish are the featured attractions, and all dinners come with an exceptionally generous salad bar. Dinners run from $12 to $25 for two plus drinks. Afterward, boogie down in Waikiki's only beachfront disco, complete with two dance floors and a ten-foot video screen. Open daily for dinner from 5 to 10:30 p.m.

Eggs 'n' Things, 1911 Kalakaua Ave. (tel. 949-0820). Most visitors don't know about it, and most locals love it. This cramped, casual breakfast nook serves up phenomenal breakfasts at cheap prices, including a $1.75 early riser special of three pancakes and two eggs. Fancy crêpes and omelets cost about $12 for two, plus coffee. It's open at odd hours for a late breakfast or a midnight snack (from 11 p.m. to 2 p.m. the next day).

If your tastes run to Chinese food, go to **Maple Garden,** 909 Isenberg St. (tel. 941-6641), a bright dining room with comfy booths and smiling waitresses who regale you with smoky Szechuan duck, sautéed scallops with snow peas, and an eggplant with garlic sauce to write home about. Dinner for two costs $25 plus drinks. Open daily for lunch from 11 a.m. to 2 p.m.; dinner from 5:30 to 10 p.m. Or try **Pizzeria Uno,** 2256 Kuhio Ave. (tel. 926-0646), whose second-story balcony juts out over the busy Kuhio Avenue scene, making for fun people-watching while you munch tasty pizza. Pizzas range from $6 to $12. Open daily from 11 a.m. to midnight.

---

3. Maui

Ever since Maui, the legendary demigod, snared the sun and demanded longer days, his island namesake has been the sunniest link in the Hawaiian chain. In fact, it

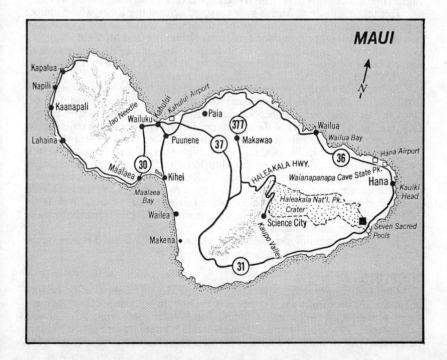

feels as if he may have cast a spell over the whole island, for Maui is filled with a magic that begs you to extend the honeymoon just a little bit longer.

The most visited of the Neighbor Islands is actually formed by two volcanoes connected by an isthmus. Maui is the second-largest Hawaiian island, with an area of 729 square miles. Just to the west lie the islands of Molokai, Lanai, and Kahoolawe, which are considered part of Maui country.

Maui's east and west sections are as different in attractions as the people who visit them. Some head west toward seaside Lahaina, once the capital of all of Hawaii and a bustling whaling village, and now a popular forum for sightseeing, shopping, and dining. North of Lahaina lie the sun-drenched shores of Kaanapali, where a once-thriving old Hawaiian community has given way to glistening condos and hotels of Maui's most popular vacation area. Backed by the towering West Maui Mountains, the resort invites the active to swing golf clubs and tennis racquets while the serene sip refreshing mai tais by a stretch of sand and sea once prized by Hawaiian *alii* (royalty). Whether you go in for shopping or windsurfing by day, dining or disco dancing by night, it all adds up to Kaanapali, the most cosmopolitan pocket on the Valley Isle.

Beyond Kaanapali, the public beaches of Honokowai, Kahana, and Napili offer more secluded spots for swimming, snorkeling, picnicking, collecting shells, and napping to the sound of gentle waves. Farther north awaits Kapalua, which means "arms embracing the sea," a peaceful, ultra-elegant resort area hosting a classy hotel, fancy condominiums, and a tasteful array of European-style shops.

Compared to the west, eastern Maui is larger and more diverse, with its fields of sugar and pineapple flanking the "big cities" of Kahului and Wailuku. You'll most likely fly into the airport in Kahului, home of several busy shopping centers, Maui Community College, botanical gardens, and a zoo. Wailuku's pride and joy is Iao Valley State Park, where King Kamehameha defeated enemy forces in the bloody battle of 1790. Jutting high above the park is Iao Needle, an impressive 2,250-foot cinder cone, accompanied by an even higher peak called Puu Kukui, at 5,788 feet.

Heading south along Maui's west coast, you encounter Kihei, whose remote beaches were created with only the two of you in mind, and whose golf courses offer panoramic views of the nearby islands of Lanai, Kahoolawe, and Molokini. Nearby is Wailea, where desert cactus and barren landscapes of the early 1900s have been transformed into an exclusive resort area brimming with hotels, condominiums, shopping, land and water sports, and swinging night life.

At the easternmost corner of Maui awaits Hana, country home of just a few small accommodations and all the peace and quiet you may seek. Winding roads take you past homes and churches built in the 1800s, and families still farm and fish these reaches in the manner of their ancestors. Hiking and horseback trails beckon you to explore Hawaii's past in this region so aptly dubbed "heavenly Hana."

Inland stretch Maui's soothing, green highlands, where rough-and-tumble paniolos ride the upcountry ranges and white-face Hereford cattle graze in seemingly endless pasturelands. Above it all reigns 10,000-foot Haleakala, the dormant volcano whose crater embraces a vast lunar landscape. As he gazed upon the warm reds, greens, and purples of the sunrise across the lava and cinder cones, Mark Twain called Haleakala "the sublimest spectacle I ever witnessed, and I think the memory of it will remain with me always."

Just like that cunning demigod Maui, you will wish you could command the sun to shine forever during your honeymoon on the Valley Isle.

SHOPPING

On Maui, the place to get your matching "Just Mauied" T-shirts is **Sgt. Leisure** in Lahaina. As the former whaling capital of the isles, this quaint port features many shops with nautical overtones, including **The Whaler** (866 Front St.), **Lahaina Scrimshaw** (718 and 845 Front St.), and **Lahaina Printsellers** (at Seamen's Hospital and the Wharf). You'll find some of the most beautiful island treasures at the **Sea**

and Shell Gallery on Front Street, including gracefully curved nautilus shells plucked from Pacific seas. And although it might seem a bit incongruous here in the tropics, Lahaina is one of the world's leading centers for fine art, with galleries carrying works by renowned artists such as Norman Rockwell, Leroy Neiman, R. C. Gorman, and Salvador Dalí. The best galleries include **Dyansen** (844 Front St.), **Grycner** (758 Front Street), and **Center Art Galleries** (802 Front St.).

The area's newest mercantile attraction is the **Lahaina Cannery Shopping Center,** an air-conditioned mall with 50 stores and restaurants set in a replica of the original Baldwin Packers Pineapple Cannery. Noteworthy shop stops include the **Maui Dive Shop** for swimwear and snorkel gear, **Dolphin Gallery** for art and collectibles, **Blue Ginger Designs** for clothes and gifts made from colorful Hawaiian fabrics, and **Kite Fantasy** for kites so beautiful that they're really airborne art.

A maritime theme dominates in nearby Kaanapali at **Whaler's Village,** an elegant minimall boasting the most elaborate selection of scrimshaw **(Lahaina Scrimshaw)**. You can also add to your antique map collection with a selection from **Lahaina Printsellers.** Also check out **Hobie Sports** for Hawaiian shirts and red-hot jams for both men and women; **Crazy Shirts** and **Maui Beach Club** for your souvenir T-shirts; **Sea and Shell Gallery** for treasures from the deep; and **Foreign Intrigue** for beautiful womenswear spiced with a hint of the exotic.

Many of the fancy resorts have their own **shopping arcades,** the most glamorous of which are found at the Hyatt Regency Maui and Westin Maui. **The Shops** at Kapalua are also appealing, though pricey; its most distinctive boutique is **Distant Drums** featuring the arts and crafts of the Pacific Basin from Peru to Sri Lanka. Pieces range from museum-quality carvings to inexpensive take-me-homes for $5.

You get the most for your money at one of the island's large shopping centers, such as Kahului's **Kaahumanu Shopping Center** on Kaahumanu Street, with 50-plus stores. In Kihei, try the **Rainbow Connection** for elegant keepsakes; it's in a shopping center called **Azeka's Place** on Route 35.

Some of the most inventive island arts and crafts can be found in the local shops of Paia, including **Exotic Maui Woods** and **Paia Trading Company,** both on Hana Highway. And a must for Hana honeymooners is **Hasagawa General Store** on Highway 36, a legendary landmark where you can get just about anything you need (and plenty of things you've never heard of before).

ROMANTIC INTERLUDES

Go ahead! Bicycle down a volcano, then luxuriate in a seaside resort. On Maui, the emphasis is on variety.

On the west coast, the picturesque seaside town of **Lahaina** recalls the golden years of whaling in Hawaii. Just 15 minutes from Kaanapali, this beautifully restored historic burg brings to life the 1850s, when as many as 100 ships anchored in the original Hawaiian capital. It also reflects the efforts of the prim and proper missionaries who lived in Lahaina in the 1830s. The Baldwin House, the old prison, and several other simple homes and churches are preserved by the Lahaina Restoration Foundation. Now a National Historic Landmark, the city brims with narrow streets and old homes alongside colorful boutiques and delightful open-air restaurants and nightclubs, which are particularly lively in the evenings.

There's lots to do and see in Lahaina, day or night. Visit the **Pioneer Inn,** a whimsical 1901 homestead full of nautical memorabilia, and the *Carthaginian,* a restored 19th-century whaling vessel turned into a floating museum. Then hold hands in the shade of the world's largest-known **banyan tree,** measuring a quarter-mile in circumference and covering four city blocks.

For $16.50 per couple, a restored sugarcane train takes you from Kaanapali Resort to Lahaina, with a singing conductor as your guide. Contact **Lahaina-Kaanapali & Pacific Railroad,** Box 816, Lahaina, HI 96761 (tel. 661-0089).

What's more fun than a barrel of monkeys? How about a pod of frisky humpback whales cavorting just a few feet from your boat? Each year from late November through May, several hundred of these gentle giants head south to Hawaii from their summer feeding waters in the Bering Sea to mate and calve. Often, you can observe the whales spy-hopping (poking their heads out of the water, seemingly to take a peek at you) or breaching (hurling their entire bodies out of the water in a grand backflopping leap). Although you can frequently spot whales from your hotel's beach, your best opportunity for viewing the leviathans up close is aboard a whale-watching cruise. Excursions are offered by the **Pacific Whale Foundation** in Kihei (tel. 879-8811), **Ocean Activities Center** in Kihei (tel. 879-4485), and **Aloha Activities Center** at Whaler's Village in Lahaina (tel. 661-3815). Costs run about $27.50 per person.

Did you ever wonder how pineapples grow, or want to learn how macadamia nuts are harvested? You can find out on a tour of the **Maui Tropical Plantation,** Highway 30 in Waikapu near Kahului (tel. 244-7643). At this lush 60-acre facility, you'll hop aboard a tram to ride through fields of sugarcane, papaya, guava, coffee, and more. Afterward, you can sample many of these just-harvested exotic delicacies at the Plantation Restaurant, and buy "edible souvenirs" to take home with you at the Made-in-Maui Marketplace store. Admission is free to the Marketplace and restaurant; there's a charge for some activities. Open daily from 9 a.m. to 5 p.m.

Molokini Island, a tiny crescent just a short boat ride off Maui's southern shore, is actually the top of a dormant volcano and the home of exotic Hawaiian fish by the hundreds. Hop on a half-day snorkel cruise out of Maalaea Harbor, Kihei, or Lahaina and treat yourselves to an underwater adventure straight out of Jacques Cousteau. Butterfly fish frolic along with ulua, palani, taape, and other pretty swimmers. Most Molokini tours include equipment, lessons, breakfast, and lunch. **Dive Maui,** Lahainaluna Marketplace, Lahainaluna Road, Lahaina, HI 96761 (tel. 667-2080), charges about $120 per couple for snorkelers, $170 for scuba-divers for a two-tank dive.

Get up *real* early, fill a thermos with coffee, borrow blankets from your hotel, and prepare yourselves for an unrivaled sunrise from the top of a 10,023-foot-high dormant volcano. Translated "House of the Sun," **Haleakala** boasts a crater that is 20 miles in circumference, 19 square miles in area, and 3,000 feet deep. That's big enough to hold all of Manhattan Island! Allow yourselves at least 2½ hours to drive from Kaanapali to the observatory (two hours from Wailea). There's a $3.50-per-person admission fee to the park; call 572-7749 for a recorded message on weather and road conditions.

After sunrise, you can hike along more than 30 miles of trails through the 28,665-acre national park, which includes three cabins in the crater (available by advance lottery). Or take a guided horseback trip past the indigenous silversword, an eerie plant related to the sunflower. **Pony Express Tours,** P.O. Box 507, Makawao, HI 96768 (tel. 667-2202), offers full-day horseback tours of the crater for $265 a couple, and half-day tours for $175. Yet another option for "doing" Haleakala is to join a bicycle tour from the summit to the beach with **Maui Mountain Cruisers,** P.O. Box 1356, Makawao, HI 96768 (tel. 572-0195, or toll free 800/232-6284); **Cruiser Bob's Haleakala Downhill,** 505 Front St. Lahaina, HI 96761 (tel. 667-7717); or **Maui Downhill,** 440A Alamaha St., Kahului, HI 96732 (tel. 871-2155). It costs about $190 per couple, including breakfast.

A taste of Hawaii-gone-by lingers on in "Heavenly **Hana."** To get there, follow the road east from Kahului, take off your wristwatches, and set aside a whole day to drive the 50 miles past lush pasturelands, glorious rain forests, lacy waterfalls, sparkling bays, and breathtaking sea cliffs. All along the way you feel compelled to park the car, snap giddy pictures, smell the flowers, dunk in bracing mountain pools, and forget the rest of the world. If the surf's up, stop to watch daredevil windsurfers tackle the huge waves near Paia.

Once in Hana, plan to spend the night. A few small condominiums and a gracious hotel have been designed and landscaped to blend into Hana's simple beauty. This is truly the "old country" of Maui, where life is unhurried and people take pride in their heritage. You can visit the simple, touching burial site of Hana resident Charles Lindbergh and swoon over the views from the top of Mount Lyons. Just beyond the town you can visit the frothy cascades of Wailua Falls as well as Seven Sacred Pools, a series of ponds dancing down to the sea—remote swimming spot indeed.

Where else but Hawaii could you find such ambrosia as pineapple wine? On the cool upper slopes of Haleakala is the **Tedeschi Winery,** P.O. Box 953, Ulupalakua, HI 96790 (tel. 878-6058). Acres of pineapples and grapes are cultivated and transformed into a well-respected line of **fine wines.** Drive on Highway 37, the mountain road beyond Kula, to the Ulupalakua Ranch, whose owner joined forces with vintner Emil Tedeschi about ten years ago. The result of their union must be sampled firsthand, and at free daily wine tastings you can do just that. Toast each other in the tasting room, a former jail built in 1856, and be sure to try Tedeschi's pink champagne. Cheers!

HONEYMOON HOTELS AND HIDEAWAYS

Maui's major resort areas offer wonderful options for a honeymoon supreme.

Expensive

Kapalua Bay Hotel and Villas, One Bay Dr., Kapalua, HI 96761 (tel. 808/669-5656; reservations: toll free 800/367-8000). The ultimate in seclusion and luxury, Kapalua offers 23,000 acres by the sea, where palm and pine trees preside over two championship golf courses (a third is slated to open in 1990), tennis courts, glittering beaches, and a wealth of gourmet restaurants and elite boutiques. A grand vaulted lobby overlooks verdant lawns that roll down to the water's edge, and throughout the hotel you find native plants and flowers of all shapes and sizes. Your room is decorated in soothing shades of periwinkle blue and cream, accented by light woods, including mahogany paddle fans, wicker chairs, and rattan headboards. The 194 rooms afford breathtaking views of Kapalua Bay as well as the neighboring isles of Molokai and Lanai. Within each room you'll find such South Seas touches as high ceilings and shutters leading to your roomy lanai. Lavish marble bathrooms add glamour. If you opt for one of the condominium villas, your hosts pull out all the stops: sunken tiled baths, complete kitchens, and daily maid service, for starters. Honeymoon package: Four days/three nights (EP): $1,120 per couple. Includes oceanview hotel room, basket of fruit, champagne, midsize rental car, dinner for two, and a pair of designer kimonos.

The **Westin Maui,** 2365 Kaanapali Parkway, Lahaina, HI 96761 (tel. 808/667-2525; reservations: toll free 800/228-3000). Dare you? You dare. Your fingers relax their grip and you're off, accelerating down the 150-foot slide that deposits you—splash!—into the true-blue swimming pool. The water slide is only one of many great entrances for which the Westin Maui is known. Guests are picked up at the West Maui airport by a complimentary stretch limousine. The lobby reverberates with the whoosh of a 20-foot waterfall. Extravagant touches in the 761 rooms and suites include silk bedspreads and draperies. All rooms have air conditioning, remote-control color TVs, minibars, and private lanais facing either the Pacific, Royal Kaanapali Golf Course, or West Maui mountains.

The Westin Maui occupies 12 oceanfront acres on Kaanapali, Maui's most popular beach, a three-mile stretch of sand once reserved for the Hawaiian royalty. Action is definitely centered on the swimming pool complex, which features waterfalls and a swim-through grotto with a Jacuzzi, as well as the aforementioned water slide. (There's also a 20-foot version for a more gentle approach.) You'll want to make friends with the exotic avian assemblage that includes talkative macaws and cockatoos, as well as high-stepping flamingos. A $2-million art collection gathers treasures and antiquities from China, Bangkok, Hong Kong, and Indonesia, including reproductions of the terra-cotta army excavated in Xian, China; local Hawaiian artists such as Herb Kane are also represented. The Westin Maui also offers a nonstop whirl of activities: whale-watching cruises, snorkeling trips, and sunset champagne sails, as well as hula and lei-making instruction. Sports enthusiasts can enjoy the 36-hole Royal Kaanapali golf course, 11 tennis courts, a health club, and aerobics classes.

If you grew up thinking that orchids are exclusively for prom night, you'll be astounded by the quantity of purple vanda orchids that festoon drinks and vases at the resort's eight restaurants and lounges. Time your reservations at romantic Sound of the Falls so that you can watch the sun set behind the islands of Molokai and Lanai. Specializing in fresh island seafood and tropical drinks such as the Nautilus (served in a pearly spiral shell), the Villa Restaurant overlooks waterfalls and the black-swan lagoon. Honeymoon package: Four days/three nights (BP): $975 per couple (mountainview accommodations); $1,165 per couple (oceanview). Eight days/seven nights (BP): $2,090 per couple (mountainview); $2,540 per couple (oceanview). Includes full American breakfast daily, a bottle of champagne and chocolate-dipped strawberries upon arrival, one dinner for two at Sound of the Falls. The Westin Maui can also make all arrangements for your wedding in Hawaii. Call for details.

In a word, the **Hyatt Regency Maui,** 200 Nohea Kai Dr., Lahaina, HI 96761 (tel. 808/661-1234; reservations: toll free 800/228-9000), is spectacular. A tropical fantasyland by the sea in Kaanapali, it encompasses 18 exotic acres graced with flamingos, swans, peacocks, penguins, and parrots, who strut amid Japanese gardens, underground grottoes, and graceful waterfalls. A rope bridge crosses a stream linking the gardens to the hotel, and the half-acre swimming pool features a grand 130-foot waterslide and a sunken bar. Quiet elegance characterizes each of the 815 rooms, which offer lounging areas, private phones, full bathrooms, air conditioning, color TVs, and local artworks as well as views of the mountains or ocean. Honeymoon package: Four days/three nights (EP): $985 per couple. Includes oceanfront accommodations, a bottle of champagne upon arrival, breakfast in bed for two.

Although a bit more low-key than the neighboring Hyatt Regency, the **Maui Marriott Resort,** 100 Nohea Kai Dr., Lahaina, HI 96761 (tel. 808/667-1200; reservations: toll free 800/831-9290), is equally luxurious. Spread across 15 oceanfront acres along Kaanapali Beach, it is surrounded by extensive landscapes laced with waterfalls, coconut groves, and two swimming pools with cascades. The hotel meets the sea in an open grouping of low-rise wings along its own stretch of golden sand. The beach is the focal point here, and the Marriott offers free sailing, surfing, and windsurfing demonstrations for fun in the sun. Designed to complement the softly colorful lithographs of Hawaiian artist Pegge Hopper, the decor of the 720 rooms has been recently refurbished. Each room has its own private lanai and ocean view, mirrored closet doors, a king-size bed, sitting area, refrigerator/bar, and color TV. Come evening time, sip exotic drinks in the Makai Bar. Honeymoon package: (EP): $245 to $320 per couple per night, depending on view. Includes rental car, champagne and logo glasses upon arrival, and free breakfast buffet.

Kaanapali Beach Hotel, 2525 Kaanapali Pkwy., Lahaina, HI 96761 (tel. 808/661-0011; reservations: toll free 800/367-5170), is a casual beachside resort ideally situated between the ocean and two superb golf courses, just four miles from Lahaina and adjacent to Whalers Village Shopping Center. Its 431 rooms and four wings embrace a courtyard with a whale-shaped swimming pool. Each room has a private lanai from which you can see pristine Neighbor Islands on an azure sea or glorious panoramas of the West Maui mountains. Rooms feature air conditioning, color TVs, refrigerators, ironing boards, daily maid service, telephone message alert, special shampoos and hand lotions, and full tubs with shower. In the evenings the courtyard fills with friendly folks for open-air dining and dancing under the stars. (All accommodations are slated to be completely refurbished soon.) This resort has many attractions, but the most appealing quality lies in its warm, Hawaiian feeling. There's a free hula show every night, and daily sessions of lei making, storytelling, and more. "You couldn't take this hotel and plunk it down anywhere else but Hawaii," remarked one of the guests here. Honeymoon package: Four days/three nights (EP): $550 per couple. Eight days/seven nights (EP): $1,155 per couple. Includes deluxe oceanview room, Hawaiian fruit basket with champagne, two embossed fluted glasses, *Maui on My Mind* gift book, champagne sunset cruise.

If you both love the sun, you'll find plenty of it at **Maui Prince Hotel,** 5400 Makena Alanui Dr., Kihei, HI 96753 (tel. 808/874-1111; reservations: toll free 800/321-6284), at Makena Beach Maui's south shore. The 1,000 well-landscaped acres make for a sports-lover's paradise, with endless opportunities for oceanside golf and tennis, swimming and sailing in calm waters, and sunning on a white-sand beach. You may find yourselves lingering in the stunning 30,000-square-foot courtyard, whose cascading waterfalls, fish ponds, rock gardens, foot bridges, and Hawaiian ferns, orchids, and anthuriums create a Garden of Eden in your own backyard. Take your choice of four fine restaurants, but when you both feel impetuous, you can call on the 24-hour room service and order a treat from the particularly diverse menu. Each of the 300 cheery rooms and suites has an ocean view, air conditioning, TV, phone, and plenty of room for relaxing after an active day outside. Honeymoon package: Four days/three nights (EP): $735 per couple. Includes tropical fruit basket and Maui champagne, souvenir Yukata robes, and choice of one of the following: golf for two (greens fees and cart included) on one day, tennis for two on two days, a snorkel cruise for two to Molokini Island, or two days' use of a midsize rental car.

The advantages of **Kaanapali Alii,** 50 Nohea Kai Dr., Lahaina, HI 96761 (tel. 808/667-1400; reservations: toll free 800/642-6284), are many. It's "your place" on the beach, a large one- or two-bedroom condominium apartment with fully equipped kitchen, washer/dryer, and plush, elegant furnishings. Daily maid and bell services are provided, and freshwater pools, saunas, three grass tennis courts, and an exercise room enhance this oceanside experience. Plenty of privacy on your own balcony, perfect for that breezy breakfast or a drink at sunset. The hotel occupies an especially choice location between the high-action Westin and Hyatt resorts on a prime stretch of Kaanapali beachfront. Honeymoon package: Four days/three nights (EP): $990 per couple (garden-view accommodations); $1,120 per couple (oceanview). Includes one-bedroom deluxe condominium, champagne and Maui chocolates upon arrival, helicopter tour, sunset cocktail cruise, deluxe compact rental car.

Built around its own tropical gardens on 15 sloping acres, **Stouffer's Wailea Beach Resort,** 3550 Wailea Alanui Dr., Wailea, HI 96753 (tel. 808/879-4900; reservations: toll free 800/468-3571) is a 347-room beachfront resort that urges you to celebrate the senses. Come alive with a splash in the south Maui surf, and gaze in awe at the majestic stillness of Haleakala. Run your hands over the smooth furnishings of your room, which is designed in koa, a rich Hawaiian hardwood, and spoil yourselves with such complimentary amenities as your custom-designed refreshment center, digital clock, air conditioning, plush carpeting, in-room refrigerator, and color TV with a daily selection of movies. For an unforgettable treat, ask to be served the gourmet candlelight dinner for two on your private lanai. Honeymoon package: Four days/three nights: From $890 per couple. Includes oceanview room, air-conditioned compact car, dinner for two and champagne upon arrival.

Getting you to unwind and enjoy life Hawaiian-style is what the **Hotel Hana Maui,** Hana, HI 96713 (tel. 808/248-8211; reservations: toll free 800/321-4262), does best. In a remote region beneath Haleakala's east face, the Hotel Hana Maui consists of many one-story bungalows scattered over 50 acres of broad green lawn and pastures. Everywhere there are vistas of the volcano, with its deep-cut valleys and rain forests of koa and bamboo. Below, beaches of black and gold sand curve among lava cliffs glistening with spray. The hotel's spacious 108 rooms and suites, many with open lanais, are inspired by plantation life and decorated with discreetly elegant rattan furniture and cool tropical prints. The management really emphasizes hospitality by inviting guests to the plantation house for cocktails with the general manager and his wife. No television except in the lounge, but there's a library with comfy couches and chairs, jigsaw puzzles, and other simple pleasures. The new dining room includes a covered lanai that looks out to Hana Bay, and the Paniolo Bar's fourth side opens to a view of mountain pastures. Sign up for one of the resort's guided trail rides through the misty mountains and down to the beach. Honeymoon package (FAP): $490 per couple per night (minimum four nights). Includes garden-view accommodations, all meals, transfers to and from the Hana Airport, barbecue cookout, champagne and fresh fruit basket upon arrival, a one-hour horseback ride, a picnic lunch, Jeep adventure tours, tennis, use of snorkeling gear, beach equipment, and bicycles.

Moderate

What could be better for two people in love than a private bungalow on the beach at **Papakea Beach Resort,** 3543 Honoapiilani Hwy., Lahaina, HI 96761 (tel. 808/669-4848; reservations: toll free 800/367-5637). These one-bedroom, oceanview condominiums in Honokowai, just north of Kaanapali, are ideal if you're looking for an informal home away from home, framed by coconut palms and adjacent to waters so clear you can count your toes. It's so nice to have all the comforts of home at your fingertips, such as a blender to whip up something tropical, and a complimentary assortment of basics such as coffee, tea, salt, pepper, sugar, and a juicy Maui pineapple to get you started. Ceiling fans keep you cool (there's no air conditioning). Cook in your own private kitchen or do a little outdoor barbecuing by one of the swimming pools. Three night-lit tennis courts, putting greens, two whirlpool spas, and four saunas will keep you amply entertained. Honeymoon package: Four days/three nights (EP): $610 per couple. Includes a car, champagne, and a fruit basket upon arrival.

At **Royal Lahaina Resort,** 2780 Kekaa Dr., Lahaina, HI 96761 (tel. 808/661-3611; reservations: toll free 800/621-2151), each of the 520 guest rooms is designed in pastels, with plants and rattan and wicker furnishings setting a tropical island scene. Intimate garden and oceanfront cottages are perfect for a private honeymoon, and you'll find it all amid 30 landscaped acres right on Kaanapali Beach. The hotel has earned a five-star ranking as a tennis resort. Honeymoon package: Four days/three nights (EP): $700 per couple. Includes a deluxe oceanview room in the Lahaina Kai Tower, in-room champagne breakfast, admission to the Royal Lahaina Luau, champagne sunset sail, and *Maui on My Mind* gift book. Seven-night package available for $1,425 per couple.

Maui Inter-Continental Wailea, P.O. Box 779, Wailea, HI 96753 (tel. 808/879-1922; reservations: toll free 800/33-AGAIN), a deluxe 21-acre vacation resort, sprawls across both lush, green hills and a magnificent crescent of south shore beach, from which you can see the neighboring islands of Lanai and Kahoolawe. The outdoors is the key here. The open-air lobby is lush with ferns, palms, lava-rock walls, and island woods, and each of the 600 rooms uses rattan and bamboo furnishings. The rooms are quite comfortable, and feature private balconies, color TVs, air conditioning, radios, room service, laundry, and valet. Special honeymoon suites are available. If you love tennis, this is the place for you; it is called "Wimbledon West" because of its superior 14-court tennis facility (including three grass courts). Honeymoon package: Four days/three nights (EP): $530 per couple. Includes oceanview accommodations, three days' use of a rental car, a bottle of champagne upon arrival. "Orchid Rendezvous": Four days/three nights (BP): $963 per couple. Includes suite accommodations, three days' use of a rental car, breakfast daily (including room service and gratuity), dinner for two with a bottle of wine at La Pérouse, a bottle of champagne and a fruit basket, two sun visors, two beach towels, and one beach bag.

ROMANTIC RESTAURANTS

Whether you dine by candlelight or sup by the sea, Maui offers whatever your hearts desire.

Expensive
Sound of the Falls, Westin Maui, Kaanapali (tel. 667-2525). The restaurant is drop-dead gorgeous, with a grand 30-foot-long entrance stairway that would have inspired Fred Astaire to new choreographic heights. Open to the cooling trade winds, the dining room looks out toward Molokai and Lanai over illuminated palm trees, over islets where flamingos balance precariously on one slender leg, and over swans floating languidly across a lagoon. Fresh orchids on your table and oversize dinner plates with marbleized rims enhance the elegant mood. Oriental and French influences combine to produce the savory cuisine, including tea-smoked duckling breast with thyme and tomato paste, or a sautéed veal cutlet with Thai herbs in a green lemon sauce. The three-course prix-fixe dinner costs $38.50 per person. Open nightly from 6 to 10 p.m.

    Swan Court, Hyatt Regency Maui, Kaanapali (tel. 661-1234). Yes, swans really do swim by you in this dreamy al fresco dining room by a peaceful pond. Come here to linger, and linger some more, under the hypnotic spell of Japanese gardens, trickling waterfalls, and muted stained glass. This is one of the most romantic dining experiences you'll discover on Maui. Swoon over such joys as shrimp bisque with cognac, roast duck glazed with honey and macadamia nuts, fresh fish with ginger butter, and veal with morel mushrooms. Dinner costs about $80 to $100 per couple plus drinks. The daily breakfast buffet covers several tables with tantalizing international fare, from fresh island fruit to tailor-made omelets created according to your whims. It's a beautiful way to start your day in paradise, and costs $28.50 per couple. Open daily for breakfast from 6:30 to 11:30 a.m. (till 1:30 p.m. on Sunday). Dinner hours are 5 to 11 p.m. daily.

    Named after the French explorer who discovered La Perouse Bay in 1786, **La Pérouse,** Maui Inter-Continental Wailea (tel. 879-1922), has been designed with the eclectic decor of Oriental silk tapestries, unusual seashells, a horned candelabra from Africa, and a ceramic fountain bowl. Equally varied is the fine bill of fare that might include a special callaloo crabmeat soup made with taro leaves, coconut milk, and chunks of crab. Try hukilau and tiger prawns en papillote, the day's catch and prawns steamed with spinach, herbs, and brandy. Be sure to sample the wilted salad made with Maui's own Kula spinach, and Caesar salad prepared at your tableside—for two, of course. Fine wines. A concert pianist plays pretty background music. Dinners for two range from $80 to $100 plus drinks. Open nightly from 6:30 to 10 p.m.

Moderate
Avalon, 844 Front St., Lahaina (tel. 667-5559). It seems as if fleets of jets and hundreds of farmers have worked around the globe to garner the exotic ingredients for your delectable meal on this garden terrace just off Front Street. Recipes might feature coquitos (like miniature coconuts) from Chile, raspberries airlifted in from New Zealand, and Maui's own sweet onions. Savory dishes utilize a mélange of spices and flavors ranging from Mexican to Indonesian—what the restaurant describes as "Pacific Basin cuisine." With so many tempting appetizers to choose from, you'll probably have trouble making up your mind—an excellent reason for selecting the hot assorted pupus, which include heavenly Maui onion rings, spiced snow peas, spring rolls, and more. Main course highlights include corn-fed New York cut steak and a crispy-fried snapper with Oriental spices. Dinner for two, $30 to $50 plus drinks. Open daily from 11 a.m. to midnight.

    A quaint country inn setting complements the fine French food at **La Bretagne,** 562-C Front St., Lahaina (tel. 661-8966). Pretty checkered tablecloths, tidy tile floors, and fresh cut flowers set the tone as you discover the joys of the Maui onion, prepared here in a tart and served as an appetizer. We recommend the breaded veal in mustard seed sauce, along with the superb duck with blueberry sauce. The French desserts are marvelous, especially when topped off by a rich café français. Dinner costs $40 to $60 for two plus drinks. Open nightly from 6 to 10 p.m.

Mama's Fish House, 799 Kiaholo Pl., Paia (tel. 579-9672). The drive to this sleepy town is well worth it when this beachfront restaurant is your goal. The spic-and-span dining room done in a Hawaiian-Tahitian motif offers ocean views and fresh island fish in creative preparations. It's hard to beat the Pacific abalone, flown in from Baja California and made to perfection by the same chef for years. Chilled papaya coconut soup is an island delicacy, and the catch of the day is usually outstanding. Desserts roll by on a cart filled with such treats as lemon cheesecake and banana crisp. Dinner for two runs about $50 per couple plus drinks. Open daily from 11 a.m. to 2:30 p.m., 5 to 10 p.m.

By all means, don't miss **Longhi's,** 888 Front St., Lahaina (tel. 667-2288), a popular café fashioned in a fantastic two-tiered black-and-white design. Set across from the ocean, Longhi's presents smashing views of Lahaina harbor and the glorious Pacific, particularly as the day gives way to a vermilion sunset. Instead of handing out printed menus, waiters recite the dishes with dramatic flair, regaling you with such possibilities as fresh opakapaka, prawns amaretto, pasta with pesto, and Gorgonzola cheese bread. Come here for brunch and feast on a medley of continental delights such as Italian sausage frittata and homemade sweet rolls. Dinner for two costs $70 plus drinks. Open daily from 7:30 a.m. to 10 p.m.

A country party, island-style! That's **Maui's Tropical Plantation Barbecue,** Waikapu Valley (tel. 244-7643). Recalling Hawaii's plantation days, this sunset shindig starts out with an old-fashioned horse-drawn hayride through fields of pineapple, sugarcane, macadamia nuts, bananas, and tropical flowers. An all-you-can-drink selection of beer, wine, and mai tais loosens you up for the square dancing and socializing, followed by a big paniolo feast: Portuguese bean soup, chili con carne, steaks from the grill, a salad bar, and your choice of apple cobbler, macadamia nut cream pie, or pineapple cake. It's a one-of-a-kind celebration of island food and hospitality on a 120-acre plantation. Held every Monday, Wednesday, Thursday, and Friday, it costs $88 per couple, plus $26.50 for round-trip transportation from Kaanapali, Lahaina, Kihei, Wailea, and Kahului.

Looking for a light lunch beachside, cocktails and pupus at sunset, or a dinner under the stars? Try **Leilani's** (tel. 661-4495) or **El Crab Catcher** (tel. 955-4911), both on the Kaanapali beach near Whalers Village. Take your choice of a tasty array of sandwiches, steaks, and fresh island fish. Lunch runs $15 to $20 per couple; dinner, $40 to $50 per couple. Open daily from 11:30 a.m. to 10:30 p.m.; to midnight for drinks.

Work off that big dinner with some dancing in **Spats II,** Hyatt Regency Maui, Kaanapali (tel. 661-1234). It's a disco with Roaring '20s speakeasy decor. Also in the Hyatt is **Drums of the Pacific,** a big Polynesian revue offered for cocktails ($55 per couple) or as a dinner show ($85 per couple). **The Old Lahaina Luau,** 505 Front St., Lahaina (tel. 667-1998), takes place on the beach and comes complete with Hawaiian dancers, Polynesian food, crafts demonstrations, and plenty of aloha spirit. It takes place Tuesday through Saturday starting at 5:30 p.m.; cost is $85 per couple.

Inexpensive

Heading for Hana? Pick up your picnic lunch at **Picnics Maui,** 30 Baldwin Ave. in Paia (tel. 579-8021). They've got everything from sandwiches ($4 to $5 per person) to more elaborate box lunches, complete with macadamia nut chocolates and a tablecloth ($7.50 to $20 per person). Open daily from 7:30 a.m. to 3:30 p.m.

4. Kauai

Remember the "special island" that beckoned in *South Pacific*? The movie could have been filmed only on Kauai, a legendary "Bali Hai" that beckons every

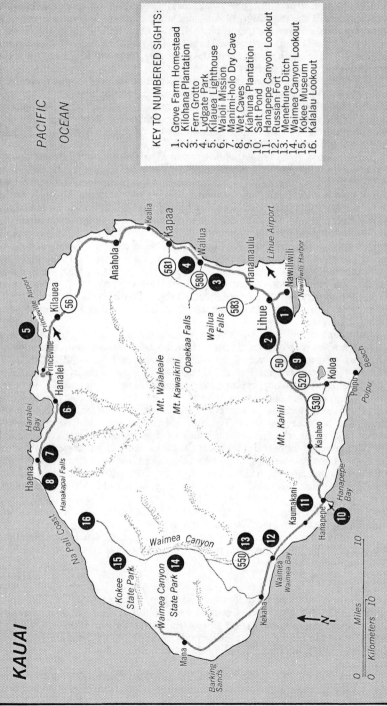

KAUAI

PACIFIC OCEAN

KEY TO NUMBERED SIGHTS:

1. Grove Farm Homestead
2. Kilohana Plantation
3. Fern Grotto
4. Lydgate Park
5. Kilauea Lighthouse
6. Waioli Mission
7. Manimi-holo Dry Cave
8. Wet Caves
9. Kiahuna Plantation
10. Salt Pond
11. Hanapepe Canyon Lookout
12. Russian Fort
13. Menehune Ditch
14. Waimea Canyon Lookout
15. Kokee Museum
16. Kalalau Lookout

Kealia
Kapaa
Anahola
Wailua
581
Kilauea 56
Princeville Airport
Princeville
Hanalei
Hanalei Bay
Haena
Hanakapiai Falls
Na Pali Coast

Mt. Waialeale
Mt. Kawaikini
Opaekaa Falls
Wailua Falls
583
580
Hanamaulu
Lihue Airport
Lihue
Nawiliwili
Nawiliwili Harbor
50
520
530
Koloa
Poipu
Poipu Beach
Mt. Kahili
Kalaheo

Kaumakani
Hanapepe
Hanapepe Bay
Waimea
Waimea Bay
550
Kekaha
Mana
Barking Sands

Waimea Canyon
Kokee State Park
Waimea Canyon State Park

N

0   Miles   10
0   Kilometers   10

day, every night, whispering love songs from the mountains to the sea.

Kauai is the northernmost of Hawaii's major islands, and the fourth largest. It is also the oldest of the populated islands, and some eight million years of nature's handiwork have sculpted the jagged pinnacles and furrowed the emerald cliffs that characterize Kauai's stunning beauty. The island is dominated by 5,240-foot Mount Waialeale, which rises from the great Alakai Swamp, source of Kauai's seven main rivers and home to rare plants and birds.

The island is steeped in ancient folklore, particularly tales of the *menehunes*. According to legend, the menehunes were an industrious race of little people, like leprechauns, who performed prodigious feats of construction. They supposedly labored in the secrecy of night, accepting in payment for their efforts only one shrimp per worker. The Menehune Fishpond in Nawiliwili and Menehune Ditch in Waimea are said to be two of their construction projects.

You can see both these sites while touring Kauai. Because of the island's compact proportions (about 33 miles long and 25 miles wide), sightseeing by car is easy. One main road runs around Kauai, ending on each side of the breathtaking 13-mile Na Pali coast in sheer-faced cliffs that rise 3,000 feet out of the sea. The lush, moist northern areas from Lihue up to Haena are steeped in the past, from the spiritual dry and wet caves of the gods near Ke'e Beach, to the banks of the Wailua River where the first Polynesians made their homes. Lining the northern coastline are quiet coves of sea and sand, including Lumahai Beach ("Nurses Beach" in *South Pacific* and dreamy Hanalei Beach Park, offering overpowering views of the Na Pali Coast.

Southern Kauai is almost always sunny and is well loved for its generous gifts of sand and sea. From windsurfing to boogie-boarding, water sports abound at Poipu Beach, the number one resort area of the south shore. Poipu boasts a string of gleaming hotels and condominiums that are interspersed with eateries and miles of ivory beaches.

Just inland from Poipu awaits Koloa, the island's oldest sugar plantation and a quaint little town with renovated historic buildings. Open-air restaurants, tiny boutiques with colorful resort wear, a tempting family-owned bakery and ice creamery, and a mom-and-pop general store called Sueoka's are some of the irresistible attractions of Koloa, whose name, appropriately enough, means "long cane."

Heading west you find Hanapepe's fascinating salt ponds, the only ones of their kind in all Hawaii. Here saltmakers evaporate seawater to create salt just as their ancestors have for over 200 ye rs. The old Hawaiian towns of Hanapepe, Lawai, Kalaheo, and Eleele stretch along the southern shoreline and offer plenty of local color in their casual shops and tidy residential communities. Farther west is Waimea, which was a favorite vacation spot for Hawaii's ancient royalty as well as site of Capt. James Cook's first landing in Hawaii in 1778. Yes, there are more excellent beaches to the west, where the isolated reaches of Barking Sands and Polihale invite you to stroll together down endless sands. Meanwhile, in the "high country" above Waimea, unusually cool forests invite outdoor lovers to camp, fish, and hike on the brink of a gaping chasm called Waimea Canyon.

Whatever your pleasure, each adventure is a delight on Kauai, your special island, where "some enchanged evening" happens every night.

SHOPPING

The compact capital of Lihue offers a fairly large range of shopping alternatives thanks to its large **Kukui Grove Center**. Here you'll find good prices on prints by local artists **(Stone's Gallery)** and aloha wear **(Robert's)**. Its **Woolworth's** and **Long's Drugs** can handle your sundries needs, and **See You In China** presents a fine selection of gifts and crafts, including tie-dyed dresses and handmade muumuus starting at $50.

Wailua is home of the **Market Place at Coconut Plantation,** another enormous shopping emporium where you can find everything from elegant Niihau shell jewelry **(Kauai Gold)** to Hawaiian posters **(The Poster Shop).** Farther north in Hanalei, find more fine island crafts at **Pua & Kawika's Place** in the **Ching Young Village Shopping Center.** While in Hanalei, check out the **Native Hawaiian Cultural Center,** where arts and crafts are sold by native Hawaiians.

You'll find some of the most congenial browsing in **Old Koloa Town,** a restored sugar-plantation village dating back to the 1830s. Stop at **Crazy Shirts** for your souvenir T-shirts, or **Swim Inn** or **That Tropical Feeling** for fashion-forward swimwear. **Safari Pomare** features classic and contemporary-style safari clothing—all in natural fabrics—for both men and women, while **Pendragon** carries striking custommade jewelry.

The stores in Poipu's **Kiahuna Shopping Village** also merit a glance, especially **Paradise Express** for superhot beach fashions and **Pearly Shells** for a wide variety of shell items, from lamps to wind chimes.

ROMANTIC INTERLUDES

By land, sea, or air, Kauai is fun to explore. Try a little of each activity on the Garden Isle, a truly appropriate nickname for this South Pacific haven.

Whirlybirds give you a tremendous look at places that would otherwise be inaccessible on Kauai. Within an hour you can see all the highlights, from hidden valleys of Waimea Canyon to the cascades of Mount Waialeale. Zoom over the Poipu coastline and ancient salt ponds of the south, or marvel from above at Lumahai Beach, where *South Pacific* was filmed. A one-hour tour costs about $270 per couple, and features narration, appropriate background music, and personal microphones for communication with the pilot. Reliable operations include **Kenai,** P.O. Box 3270, Lihue, HI 96766 (tel. 245-8591); **Papillon,** P.O. Box 339, Hanalei, HI 96714 (tel. 826-6591, or toll free 800/652-6650); **Na Pali Helicopters,** P.O. Box 831, Lihue, HI 96766 (tel. 245-6959); and **Menehune Helicopter Tours,** 3222 Kuhio Hwy., Lihue HI 96766 (tel. 245-7705). Kauai's newest flightseeing adventure is an excursion to Niihau, called "The Forbidden Island" because it is generally off-limits except to Hawaiians. The trip flies over the island and sets down on a deserted strand, a beachcomber's paradise ($200 per person). A combination Kauai/Niihau flight costs $260 per person. Contact **Niihau Helicopters,** P.O. Box 370, Makaweli, HI 96769 (tel. 338-1234 or 335-3500).

Kauai's only navigable river is the Wailua, and its banks are rich with blossoming ginger and burgeoning palms. Today you can chug up this idyllic waterway on a charming riverboat. Your destination is **Fern Grotto,** a series of yawning lava tubes curtained with giant tropical plants. This natural amphitheater provides a truly inspirational setting for couples in love, who can listen to "The Hawaiian Wedding Song" echoing through the ferns. Jolly entertainers strum ukuleles and croon happy Hawaiian melodies as you cruise up to the grotto and back. Cost is $20 per couple. Contact **Smith's Motor Boat Service,** P.O. Box 174, Kapaa, HI 96746 (tel. 822-4111). The Smith's twilight torchlight trip creates an especially romantic vision of this hallowed Hawaiian treasure, and various wedding packages are also available.

The **trail to Hanakapiai Beach** winds through groves of guavas and bananas, wanders past babbling brooks, and offers some of the island's most precious scenery. The two-mile trek makes the perfect day hike, beginning at Ke'e Beach on the north shore and ending at a prized beach flanked by razor-edged cliffs. The first mile of this ancient Hawaiian trail takes you up, up, up, but the climb is worth it, for from the edge of windswept cliffs you get a thrilling look at the Na Pali Coast. Then you head a mile down into Hanakapiai Valley, site of crystal ocean waters, perfect sands, enormous shade trees, and a bracing mountain stream. If you're looking for more adventure, follow the side trail from the beach into the lush hanging valley with its cascading waterfalls. Wild orchids, pungent guavas, sweet mangoes, and mountain apples surround you.

Another way to explore the inaccessible reaches of the Na Pali coast is on board a **Zodiac,** an inflatable rubber raft with a lot of power. Sit on the sides of the boat and let your able captain take you on a thrilling adventure, maneuvering into sea caves, across exotic reefs, and, if you're lucky, past schools of dolphins, flying fish, and sea turtles. Wear a swimsuit, bring your camera, and get ready for a rollicking ride! **Na Pali Zodiac Expeditions,** P.O. Box 456, Hanalei, HI 96714 (tel. 826-9371), offers half-day trips with snorkeling for $130 per couple. All-day trips with snorkeling plus a stop for lunch on a secluded beach go for $285 per couple.

"The Grand Canyon of the Pacific." That's what Mark Twain called **Waimea Canyon,** ten miles long, one mile wide, and 2,800 feet deep. Every lookout along Waimea Canyon Road inspires a slightly different reaction to this wonder of the world, and the layers of earth and vegetation seem to change colors throughout the day as the sunlight plays games with its ridges and ledges. Waimea Canyon Road ends at an equally awesome perch: the Kalalau Lookout, 4,120 feet above sea level. Dramatic cliffs, dense rain forests, shining waterfalls, and the never-ending sea spread out before you. On the way back down the hill, stop at delightful **Kokee Lodge** for a cozy drink by the roaring fireplace (tel. 335-6061). Open daily from 8:30 a.m. to 5:30 p.m., to 10 p.m. on Fridays and Saturdays.

Where do you go to really get away from it all? At the end of the main road (Highway 50) heading west there's a small marker pointing you left. Follow the signs along a bumpy cane-haul road, and sure enough, you'll find it: **Polihale Beach,** a remote state park flanked by mammoth cliffs and crashing surf. It's almost always sunny at this big beach, so bring along your visor for a beach experience par excellence. Buy your picnic provisions in Waimea, a half-hour's drive away, because Polihale is untouched by commercial enterprise. And if you're looking for the ultimate camping destination, pick up a free permit from **Kauai County—Parks Permit Section,** 4444 Rice St., Lihue, HI 96766 (tel. 245-1881), and head west to this beach on the brink of the wilderness.

HONEYMOON HOTELS AND HIDEAWAYS

The oldest inhabited Hawaiian island offers some of the newest and most delightful accommodations this side of the Pacific, and they are grouped in three areas. The first-class resorts in sunny Poipu are ideally situated on a stretch of sandy beaches with gentle surf. Heading north takes you to the Wailua-Kapaa hub, a series of small country towns and fine oceanside accommodations near the Wailua River and Fern Grotto. The third destination is the Princeville and Hanalei area, where toney resorts overlook Hanalei Bay and the spires of the Na Pali coast.

Expensive

Stouffer Waiohai Beach Resort, 2249 Poipu Rd., Box 174, Koloa, HI 96756 (tel. 808/742-9511; reservations: toll free 800/HOTELS-1). This handsome seaside resort in Poipu is one of Hawaii's best hotels, hands down. Silk, bronze, teak, mahogany, and etched glass accent the interiors, which include flowering courtyards and garden-like restaurants. The resort is uniquely shaped like a "W" to maximize the number of oceanview rooms, and your room is fashioned in the bold colors of the isles along with warm rattan and wood. The resort looks lovelier than ever after a recent $4.5-million renovation. Each of the 426 suites and rooms features a wet bar, refrigerator, sitting area, and big private balcony. Bathrooms are spacious, with large closets and, most memorable of all, brass sinks. This place is dreamy; curl up with a couple of good books in the browsing library, then sip a love potion at the sunken island bar. Honeymoon package: Four days/three nights (EP): From $755 per couple. Includes deluxe oceanside accommodations, rental car, picnic lunch, keepsake beach towels, complimentary bottle of champagne, and lei greeting upon arrival.

The **Westin Kauai at Kauai Lagoons,** Kalapaki Beach, Lihue, HI 96766 (tel. 808/245-5050, or toll-free 800/228-3000). You know the old expression about how "getting there is half the fun"? At the Westin Kauai, getting around the 800-acre property adds to the pleasure. Guests can hire a 19th-century–style horse-drawn carriage to explore the ten miles of bridle paths, or mahogany taxi-boats or outrigger canoes (complete with paddler) to ply the mile of waterways past islands where monkeys jabber and zebra and gemsbok graze.

Set along the half-mile expanse of Kalapaki Beach, the 847-room Westin is the first megaresort on Kauai. As in Hawaii's other opulent new properties, the pièce de résistance is the freshwater swimming pool. The Westin's is a circular, scallop-edged aquatic wonderland covering about half an acre. This is a place for good splashy fun, with waterfalls, slides, fountains, and five Jacuzzis. The Westin's other pool—the Palace Court Reflecting Pond—is for gazing, not swimming. Eight pairs of black and white swans float across its expanse, backdropped by seven life-size marble horses carved in China, and a fountain that shoots water 60 feet into the air. Inside the hotel, show-stopping pieces such as Thai-style bronze lions highlight the Westin Kauai's $2.5-million collection of Oriental and Pacific art. All of the rooms are air-conditioned and have minibars and refrigerators. Most have views of the Pacific or Nawiliwili Bay; some have a lanai.

Whether you're seeking a hole in one, an ace serve, or the perfect wave, the Westin Kauai has good sports for you. Golfers can tee off on two 18-hole Jack Nicklaus–designed courses: the recreational Kauai Lagoons layout and the tournament-class Kiele Lagoons. The eight tennis courts (all lighted) include a 600-seat exhibition stadium. Stay fit at the European health spa or the 25-meter-lap pool. Aquaphiles can enjoy everything from boogie-boarding to scuba lessons. After you've worked up an appetite, the Westin Kauai has 12 restaurants and lounges from which to choose. And if you're considering getting married in Hawaii, the Westin has a stunning wedding gazebo, set by a 40-acre lagoon overlooking the Pacific. Honeymoon package: Four days/three nights (BP): $1,110 per couple (pool view); $1,135 per couple (beach front). Includes a bottle of champagne and chocolate-dipped strawberries in your room upon arrival, breakfast daily, and one dinner for two at Inn on the Cliffs.

Kauai Hilton and Beach Villas, 4331 Kauai Beach Dr., Lihue, HI 96766 (tel. 808/245-1955; reservations: toll free 800/445-8667). The swimming pools themselves are worth seeing, a veritable fantasyland of waterfalls and fountains that play around volcanic rock formations at this resort located midway between Wailua and Lihue. Set on 25 oceanside acres filled with lush gardens, exotic birds, and gentle palms, the 350-room hotel—built in a dramatic horseshoe shape—has one main building of five floors and three adjacent buildings of two, three, and four floors. Reflecting the plantation-style architecture of the past, the main lobby is airy, with soaring floor-to-ceiling windows framing views of the gardens, pools, and the blue Pacific. Hotel rooms are fashioned in muted tones of mulberry ice, deep raspberry, and sea foam against an off-white background, and offer private lanais, sitting rooms, air conditioning, telephones, refrigerators, and color TVs. In addition, the 150 one- and two-bedroom villas offer large living areas, fully equipped kitchens, and laundry facilities. Honeymoon package: Three days/two nights (BP): $480 per couple. Includes deluxe oceanview accommodations, full American breakfast daily (including gratuities), champagne upon arrival, Fern Grotto river cruise for two, nightly turn-down service.

Draped down a cliff by Hanalei Bay, the sprawling **Sheraton Mirage Princeville Hotel,** P.O. Box 3069, Princeville, HI 96722 (tel. 808/826-9644; reservations: toll free 800/325-3535), on Kauai's north shore, is terraced in order to give maximum exposure to the spectacular views of the bay and mountain peak known as Bali Hai in the distance. The hotel is just completing a $60-million top-to-toe renovation and is slated to reopen early in 1990 as one of the most luxurious properties in Kauai. Designed to increase the hotel's spaciousness and enhance the spectacular vistas, the remodeling enlarged many rooms, expanded the pool area, added a new poolside restaurant, and refurbished three preexisting restaurants. The resort remains a favorite of golfers, who can tee off on the famous 27-hole Makai Golf Course, where every tee provides magnificent panoramas of the mountains and ocean. At the new 18-hole Prince Golf Course, a $5-million clubhouse has opened, featuring a health spa and tennis complex. Rates (EP) run $264 (pool view) to $495 (oceanfront) per couple per night. Honeymoon package rates have not been set as we go to press; check with your travel agent or the hotel.

Moderate

Kiahuna Plantation, 2253 Poipu Rd., Koloa, HI 96756 (tel. 808/742-6411; reservations: toll free 800/367-7052). Looking for a beach house for two? Look no further than this Poipu condominium resort. The 200 shoreside acres are dotted with 333 lovely one- and two-bedroom cottages, and the best of these are perched right by the water. Warm greens and yellows brighten your cottage, and bamboo furniture adds a naturally tropical touch. Kiahuna spares no expense to make you comfortable, from the all-electric, fully equipped kitchens to the daily maid service. Although every room has a color TV, Kiahuna encourages you to get outside and experience the glories of Poipu. Its famed 18-hole championship golf course was designed by Robert Trent Jones Jr., and ten tennis courts (not lighted) make this the perfect place for the active set. Brennecke Beach is nearby for swimming, snorkeling, and scuba-diving, and the resident surfing coach stands by to offer advice. Honeymoon package: Four days/three nights (EP): $765 per couple. Includes accommodations in a one-bedroom oceanview suite, a flower lei greeting, champagne upon arrival, a fruit basket, and a rental car.

Location is the big draw for the **Stouffer Poipu Beach Resort,** 2251 Poipu Rd., Koloa, HI 96756 (tel. 808/742-1681; reservations: toll free 800/468-3571), a casual little getaway whose three buildings, with a total of 137 guest rooms, are tucked away under a grove of palms right on Poipu Beach. Whether you face the pool, the ocean, or the mountains, all the rooms offer the same amenities, including open-air balconies, large dressing rooms, and small refrigerators. Best of all, your room features a well-equipped kitchenette, so you can fix a snack and get back outside quickly. If you prefer, breakfast, lunch, and dinner are offered in the restaurant, and a steak fry heats things up every Tuesday. Wrap up your nights by dancing cheek-to-cheek in the Poipu Beach Club as the waves crash right outside the windows. Honeymoon package: None. Regular rates (EP): $95 to $155 per couple (low season); $100 to $175 per couple (high season).

Coco Palms Resort Hotel, P.O. Box 631, Lihue, HI 96766 (tel. 808/822-4921; reservations: toll free 800/542-2626), a 45-acre resort, is nestled in a secluded coconut grove where Hollywood movie moguls have made several fantasy films. In fact, hundreds of couples get married and renew their vows at the newly restored Chapel in the Palms, originally built on the grounds for the movie *Sadie Thompson.* Set across from a one-mile stretch of white-sand beach where the Wailua River meets Wailua Bay, Coco Palms offers 390 guest rooms, junior suites, suites, and thatched-roof cottages, interspersed with crystal lagoons and lava-rock waterfalls. An evening torch-lighting ceremony outside recalls the days when ancient Hawaiian royalty strolled these hallowed grounds. Guest rooms have been newly refurbished in a cool, white-on-pastel motif, with island rattan furnishings, and include exotic touches such as giant clam-shell basins in the bathrooms, plus air conditioning, color TVs, and refrigerators. Some cottages offer tropical lanais and private garden hot tubs. Honeymoon package: Four days/three nights: $485 per couple. Includes superior accommodations, champagne on arrival, a fresh fruit basket, a remembrance gift from the staff, and an invitation to the manager's cocktail party.

With its unspoiled beauty and quiet serenity, **Hanalei Bay Resort,** P.O. Box 220, Hanalei, HI 96714 (tel. 808/826-6522; reservations: toll free 800/657-7922), is the perfect setting for pure relaxation. This sloping complex on Kauai's north shore features one-, two-, and three-bedroom low-rises that wind their way down to Hanalei Beach encompassing 20 acres. Explore the glorious gardens laced with gurgling streams. The resort itself boasts condominium apartments at their very best, including electric kitchens, large baths and living areas, rattan furniture, and island art on the walls. Princeville's lauded tennis and golf facilities are within walking distance, and if you're feeling even more active, horseback riding, snorkeling, and boogie-boarding are easily arranged. Ready to take it easy? Then grab your towels and loll around one of the swimming pools, or sip mai tais on the cocktail terrace on the top level. Honeymoon package: Four days/three nights (EP): $495 per couple. Includes one-bedroom oceanview suite, Princeville Airport transfers, one candlelight dinner for two, free tennis, lei greeting, and champagne.

ROMANTIC RESTAURANTS

Kauai has scores of good restaurants, from mom-and-pop shops to fancy-dress establishments.

Expensive

Tamarind, Waiohai Resort, Poipu (tel. 742-9511). Deluxe dining in a world-class hotel means jackets for the men, but that's part of the attraction of this plush restaurant. A blend of mirrors and brass works perfectly in tandem with earth colors of rusts and browns to create an atmosphere of tropical decadence. Settle back in your cushy bentwood chairs and enjoy the formal presentation, from fine cut-glass and gold-rimmed dishes to fresh flowers on every table. Order a different pâté each night: It's always superb. Impeccable service accompanies such entrées as lamb marinated in mustard and garlic, or lobster and scallops in puff pastry. Duckling, veal, and jumbo shrimp are all a real treat here. Be sure to save room for a temptation from the dessert and espresso carts. À la carte dinners cost about $100 per couple plus drinks. Your dinner concludes with a complimentary liqueur served in a tiny chocolate cup. On Sundays, folks flock to the breezy Waiohai Terrace for a lavish champagne brunch featuring hundreds of items—from pineapples and papayas to omelets and fresh island seafood. All you can eat for $23.50 per person. Open nightly for dinner from 6 to 10 p.m.

Gaylord's, Kilohana Plantation (tel. 245-9593). The centerpiece of a 19th-century sugar plantation, Gaylord's focuses on serving continental food in an al fresco fantasyland. Scattered casually around a courtyard, the tables look out to opulent gardens of exotic flowers and plants, creating an appetizing setting for marvelous meals. Piped-in classical music serenades you as you sample the made-to-order dishes. Baked brie in phyllo is an excellent beginning, and star entrées include the venison in blueberry-juniper sauce, sautéed Alaskan salmon laced with a caviar-lime butter sauce, and roast duck accompanied by sauces of peppercorns, port wine, and Madeira. For brunch, try "Auntie's cheese blintzes" with raspberry sauce and sour cream, served with a thick slice of smoked ham. Lunch for two costs about $25 plus drinks; dinner is $60 per couple plus drinks. Open for lunch Monday through Saturday, 11 a.m. to 4 p.m.; dinner, 5:30 to 9:30 p.m.; Sunday brunch, 10 a.m. to 3 p.m.

Sheraton Coconut Beach Luau, Coconut Plantation, Waipouli (tel. 822-3455). Hailed by many as Kauai's best luau, this open-air feast for the senses takes place in a scenic coconut grove. A torch-lighting ceremony and shell-lei greeting kick things off, along with the lifting of the pig from the underground imu where it has been cooking for hours. The buffet features traditional luau offerings like lomilomi salmon, teriyaki beef, chicken long rice, mahimahi, sweet potatoes, and, of course, the pig itself. After dinner the seaside sky lights up with a musical extravaganza starring some of the island's freshest young singers and dancers. The whole affair costs $66 for two. It takes place from 6:30 p.m. on, nightly except Monday.

Moderate

One look at **Bull Shed,** 796 Kuhio Hwy., Waipouli (tel. 822-3791), and you'll understand why it's an island tradition. The rustic A-frame restaurant is cradled by the curving shoreline and offers dreamy views of the sparkling Pacific. Inside, an airy design of exposed wood gives the place a relaxed, homey feeling, and it's easy to find a large table where the two of you can quaff some cocktails and gaze at the waves. Specializing in steak and seafood, Bull Shed offers such fine entrées as fresh fish, tenderloin fillet, steak and lobster combination, prime rib, and New Zealand rack of lamb. The salad bar is big and impressive. Hot rolls and rice come with the dinners, which cost about $30 for two. Open daily from 5:30 to 10 p.m.

Come as you are to **Brennecke's Beach Broiler,** Poipu (tel. 742-7588), right across from Poipu Beach Park. Settled in on the second floor, you get wonderful aerial views of the water while you dive into scrumptious seafood. Colorful petunias and geraniums decorate the pretty flower boxes by the window, beyond which lies that resplendent Poipu shoreline. You can actually see the cooks kiawe-broiling your yummy meals, which range from fresh fish to beach burgers, plus a variety of pastas, buckets of fresh clams, luscious island fruit, and great exotic drinks. Save room for the desserts—creamy homemade ice cream and delicious island sherbets in flavors like guava and mango. Light lunches cost $16 per couple. Dinner costs about $28 to $36 per couple plus drinks. Open daily for lunch from 11:30 a.m. to 3 p.m.; dinner from 5 to 10:30 p.m.

Since 1948 **Green Garden,** Hanapepe (tel. 335-5422), located in a family home, has served a menu of local favorites with a spirit of aloha. And what a garden it is! There are orchids on every table and an assortment of lush, tropical plants raised by the owner herself. You can order just about anything here: home-style soups, salads, vegetables, rolls, sandwiches, steaks, Chinese food, and more. Kiawe-broiled selections run from $11 to $28 for two, served with soup, salad, coffee or tea. Other dinners range from $12 to $40 per couple. Best of all is the *lilikoi* (passion fruit) chiffon pie, a legend in these parts. A perfect stop on your way to Waimea Canyon. Open daily from 7 a.m. to 2 p.m.; dinner served nightly (except Tuesday) from 5 to 9 p.m.

Once a plantation home and now a botanical wonderland, **Plantation Gardens,** Kiahuna Plantation, Poipu (tel. 742-1695), welcomes honeymooners into a tropical setting filled with white wicker furniture and offers wonderful open-air views of the surrounding gardens, ponds, and palm trees. The fresh catch of the day is the best choice here, be it onaga, opakapaka, ulua, ono, or mahimahi. Try it stuffed with crabmeat! Caesar salad is a super way to start, and the chicken teriyaki with vegetables and rice is tasty. Entrées cost between $22 and $50 per couple, and dinner comes with salad, soup, veggies, and bread. Plantation Gardens is well known for its Naughty Hula pie, a sinfully sweet dessert with macadamia nuts. Settle into the Poi Pounder Room after dinner for a drink amid Polynesian artifacts, or outside in the garden bar. Open daily for dinner from 5:30 to 10 p.m.

Casa di Amici, 2484 Kanake St., Kilauea (tel. 828-1388). Honeymooners will be ecstatic when they experience Casa di Amici, truly a world-class Italian restaurant. Translated "house of friends," it's an atmospheric little spot that lures lovers to share a bottle of red wine over the house antipasto as flickering candlelight warms the dark-wood furnishings. This relatively new establishment has won rave reviews for its authentic cuisine. Proceed to one of the fine pasta dishes, perhaps tossed with butter, white pepper, cream, nutmeg, and parmesan cheese. Outstanding among the entrées is the veal and prosciutto sautéed in white wine, butter, and lemon juice and sprinkled with provolone cheese, as well as the fresh prawns with garlic, capers, and tomatoes on linguine. Dinner for two costs about $50 plus drinks. Open for lunch Monday through Saturday from 11 a.m. to 3:30 p.m.; dinner daily from 5 to 9:45 p.m.

Duke's Canoe Club, Westin Kauai, Nawiliwili (tel. 246-9599), is filled with water-sports memorabilia. Canoes hang in the rafters, surfboards lean against the wall, and oldtime pictures recall island days of the 1930s when Hawaii's own Duke Kahanamoku was an Olympic swimming champ. Dine above a lava rock garden and sip a beer as the ocean waves serenade you through the open windows. In one room, Duke's features casual meals like burgers, sandwiches, and salads, all under $20 per couple. Upstairs, fresh fish, steaks, and ribs are featured, with entrées for two ranging from $20 to $40. Try the shrimp Hanalei, sautéed in butter and wine with a touch of parmesan cheese sprinkled on top. Dessert-lovers go crazy over the hula pie, with a chocolate wafer crust, macadamia nut ice cream, and fudge sauce. Open nightly for dinner from 5 to 10 p.m.

Inexpensive

A rustic inn, **Kokee Lodge,** Kokee State Park (tel. 335-6061), offers hearty breakfasts and lunches daily, enough to fuel you for those invigorating walks through the surrounding high country. Situated midway between Waimea Canyon and Kalalau Lookout, the lodge is set in a grove of pine trees—with a dozen furnished cabins nearby for those who decide to stay. Dinner, which is available on the weekends for about $25 per couple, includes steak, ribs, Cornish game hens stuffed with mushrooms and rice, mahimahi, and vegetarian fettuccine. Mud pie is high on the dessert list, and cocktails are best around the fireplace in the lounge. For two, breakfast costs $10, and lunch is $15. Open daily for breakfast and lunch from 8:30 a.m. to 3:30 p.m.; dinner served on Friday and Saturday from 6:30 to 9:30 p.m.

For good fun and great food in a casual setting, try **Koloa Broiler,** Koloa (tel. 742-9122), with the big open windows. You cook your own entrée, be it barbecued chicken, mahimahi, steak, beef kebobs marinated in dry vermouth, or hamburgers, all of which come with a salad bar, sourdough bread, and baked beans. A couple of burgers at lunch adds up to $8, while dinner prices range from $18 to $26 for two. Relax in the roomy rustic bar before and after your meal, and they'll whip up the best mai tai you've ever tasted. Open daily from 11 a.m. to 10 p.m.

Banana Joe's, Kilauea (tel. 828-1092), is a tropical fruit farm with such sightseeing refreshers as fruit frosties, which are $3 for two, and cut pineapple for $1 a pound. While you're visiting this roadside stand, take a tour of Joe's glorious groves. Open daily from 7 a.m. to 7 p.m. **Tropical Taco,** Kapaa Shopping Center (tel. 822-3622), makes inexpensive Mexican food with a creative Hawaiian touch. Dig into all your favorites: enchiladas, tostadas, tacos, and burritos. For dessert, try a tortilla with apple pie filling and cheese. Dinner for two costs $16 plus drinks. Open daily from 11 a.m. to 9:30 p.m. And continuing its long-standing tradition of offering the best breakfasts on the island is **The Eggbert's,** 4483 Rice St., Lihue (tel. 245-6325), where the eggs Benedict are renowned. Omelets are made to your specification, and begin at $8 for two. Open for breakfast and lunch Monday through Saturday from 7 a.m. to 3 p.m., on Sunday from 7 a.m. to 2 p.m.; dinner Wednesday through Saturday from 5:30 to 9:30 p.m.

NIGHTLIFE

When you're ready to boogie, try **Park Place,** Harbor Village Shopping Center, Nawiliwili (tel. 245-5775), with the largest dance floor on Kauai. Top 40 tunes and a video system enliven the triangular bar, where happy hour lasts all the way to midnight on Wednesday night. Among the late-night offerings at the Westin Kauai, the **Paddling Club** (tel. 245-5050) features nightly high-energy music in a five-level disco. Or you can boogie to live tunes any night of the week at the **Drum Lounge** (tel. 742-1661) at the Sheraton Kauai.

Another longtime Kauai favorite is **Club Jetty** in Nawiliwili (tel. 245-4970) which features live entertainment Wednesday through Saturday. In Hanalei, you can experience Old Hawaii at **Tahiti Nui** (tel. 826-6277). Friday and Saturday nights there's live entertainment, ranging from Hawaiian tunes strummed on the ukulele to rock bands from Honolulu. Shell necklaces and primitive paintings of hula dancers hang on the wall, and "Auntie Louise," a Tahitian, helps make sure everyone has fun. Be sure to stop by the Sheraton Coconut Beach's **Paddle Room,** where a beloved local group, Na Kaholokula, serenades you with tender songs of the islands.

5. The Big Island

Located in the south of the Hawaiian archipelago, this isle is roughly twice as large as all the other islands combined. Although the island's official name is Hawaii, it is referred to as the Big Island, to differentiate it from the state. Because it is also the youngest of the Hawaiian chain, the Big Island bubbles and breathes through its active volcanoes, which occasionally send rivers of molten lava down to the sea. This is a vital, vivid landscape filled with rushing waterfalls, teeming rain forests, fields ripe with fruits and flowers, and pastures full of horses and cattle. You can bet that such a diverse island holds an equally wide variety of activities and accommodations for your honeymooning pleasure.

The Big Island was created by five volcanoes: Mauna Kea, Kohala, Hualalai, Mauna Loa, and Kilauea, the latter two of which are still active today. Mauna Loa ("long mountain") stands at 13,677 feet, and its extinct neighbor Mauna Kea ("white mountain") is the world's tallest seamount, peaking at 13,796 feet. These two monoliths rise from the center of the island, and around them circle six very distinctive districts. Allow plenty of time for your explorations: Because the Big Island is about 93 miles by 73 miles, it takes most of a day to drive around it.

When you explore the Big Island, you're discovering Hawaii's sacred past. You can see it in the petroglyphs carved into rocks along the Kona Coast. You can feel it at a 13th-century leeward landmark called Mookini, which was the birthplace of King Kamehameha the Great, unifier of the islands, and at Pu'u Kohola Heiau, built by the king himself. You can sense it at the Kau beaches, where Polynesian explorers landed their canoes as early as A.D. 550. You can hear it in the legends of the volcanoes, and see it in the dances through which island residents honor the gods.

How do you explore such a vast and varied island?

Perhaps you'll want to begin with a tour of the county seat of Hilo, a charming combination of the old and the new. Get up with the fishermen and catch the multiethnic action at the Suisan Market fish auction. Poke around the **Hawaii Tropical Botanical Garden,** full of exotic plants and flowers. Find out nutty secrets about growing macadamias at the Mauna Loa orchards, and pick up some free samples of those tasty little gems. Browse through the shops of downtown Hilo, then learn about the island's steadfast missionaries at the Lyman House Museum.

Another day you'll want to take a drive up the Hilo Coast to jungles thick with monster-size heliconia, bamboo, ginger, bird of paradise, and the star of the show, a 420-foot cascade called Akaka Falls. Farther north is Waipio Valley, a broad, deep rain forest surrounded by 2,000-foot-high cliffs.

It's a totally different world on the expansive Kohala-Kona coast, where world-class resorts rise up amid fields of ancient lava flows. Play golf and tennis on championship courses by the sea. Visit Hulihee Palace in Kailua Village, where King David Kalakaua used to vacation. Stop by Kealakekua Bay, where Capt. James Cook died in 1779. Nearby, observe the workings of the Royal Kona Coffee Mill and Museum, and share a cup of that exceptional brew. Catch the marlin of your dreams in the fabled waters of Kona, site of an annual international deep-sea fishing contest. Doze on beaches of green and ivory, and be back in time for sunset from your oceanview suite. More Big Island adventuring takes you to the summit of steaming Kilauea Volcano, where you can walk and drive around primitive lava landscapes.

If you're looking for a "horse of a different color," you'll want to mosey around the pasturelands of Waimea, with its rolling hills and soft pine trees. Learn about the life of the paniolo, eat a hearty country meal, and watch a rip-snortin' rodeo,

HAWAII — THE BIG ISLAND

N

Upolu Point — Kapaau
Hawi
NORTH KOHALA
Kohala Coast
Waipio
270
Waipio Valley
Honokaa
Hamakua
250
Waimea
Laupahoehoe
19
Coast
QUEEN KAAHUMANU HWY.
Akaka Falls
Mauna Kea
Honomu
190
BELT RD.
Boiling Pots
Hilo Bay
HAWAII
19
SADDLE RD.
Hilo
Mt. Hualalai
Rainbow
Falls
Keahole Airport
200
Kailua-Kona
Kee'au
Kealakekua
130
Kapoho
Napoopoo
Mauna Loa
Pahoa
Kealakekua Bay
Kilauea Crater
Black Sand
Beach
Pu'uhonua o Honaunau
Nat'l Hist. Park
Kaimu
Kalapana
CHAIN OF CRATERS RD.
Kealia
K A U
Manuka Park
Hawaii Volcanoes
Nat'l Park
Pahala
Punaluu
11
Naalehu
Kelae
(South Point)

Hawaiian-style. It's all waiting for you on the Big Island, where super-big thrills enliven your vacation for two.

SHOPPING

Even though Hilo is the second-largest city in the Hawaiian Islands and is the capital of the Big Island, it retains an easygoing, folksy feel. The city has been undergoing a renaissance recently, with many interesting boutiques, art galleries, and antique shops opening in refurbished buildings, especially **"The Keawe Collection,"** a bevy of shops along Keawe Street between Waianuenue Avenue and Haili Street. Sally Mermel calls her establishment **The Most Irresistible Shop in Hilo,** and souvenir-lovers will agree after perusing her various goods: ceramics, postcards, hand-screened T-shirts for $20, koa wood products, books, local jams, and so on. The quaint old downtown section of Hilo also features the **Potter's Gallery** (95 Waianuenue Ave.), where absolutely top-notch paintings, pottery, and glass by Big Island artists and craftspeople are all for sale. Another real find for antiques collectors is **Louise Dumaine Antiques** (140 Keawe St.), which features a particularly fine selection of Depression glass and art deco jewelry, all at prices far lower than you would pay on the U.S. mainland.

Posters, books, slides, postcards, and other memorabilia relating to Kilauea are assembled at the **Hawaii Volcanoes National Park Visitor Center.** Next door is the **Volcano Arts Center,** absolutely the best place in Hawaii for paintings, sculptures, jewelry, and trinkets by top island craftspeople.

Many interesting new shops have opened in Waimea, especially the browseworthy boutiques at **Parker Square Center.** The **Gallery of Great Things** is just that, carrying exquisite arts and crafts such as handmade koa-wood bowls, tribal masks from New Guinea, and fabulous batiks; prices start at about $8 and go way, way up. **Fiberarts** carries fine crafts, including beautiful Hawaiian quilts. You're also sure to find something that strikes your fancy at the **Waimea General Store,** which carries Hawaiian white honey, a wide selection of Hawaiian books, pretty ceramic teapots, and more.

When in Kona don't miss the **Kona Arts & Crafts Gallery,** offering one-of-a-kind artworks small and large. Also in Kona is the **Shellery,** presenting a dazzling selection of gifts from the sea, as well as the **Coral Factory,** home of colored coral jewelry. Both these stores are located in the **Kona Inn Shopping Village.** The shopping arcade in the Hotel King Kamehameha is a fun place to scout out souvenirs, including **Gifts for All Seasons,** which boasts a unique combination of goods from Hawaii and the Philippines. Also check out the boutiques at the snazzy new **Waterfront Row** complex.

If you're driving along the Hamakua coast, stop at the townlet of Kukuihaele. Here, the **Waipio Woodworks Art Gallery** carries a wide variety of works by island artists: not only finely crafted wood items, but also pottery, stuffed toy nenes (Hawaiian geese), cards, and other gifts. Then step back in time at the village of Honokaa, a typical old sugarcane town where two-story wooden storefronts line the main street. Inveterate rummagers will love **Seconds to Go,** Highway 19 (tel. 775-9212), which stocks second-hand items ranging from 1950s-era ski boots to Depression glass.

ROMANTIC INTERLUDES

This island of life is erupting with romantic escapades to fill your days and nights.

Kilauea, the world's largest active volcano, is surrounded by legends and lore that enhance an already dramatic landscape. The fiery goddess Pele is said to live in the seething abyss, and her moods regulate the changes in climate and geography. As you stroll along some of the 130 miles of paths around this national park, it's easy to get caught up in the stories attached to the area. The **Kilauea Visitor Center,** Volcano, HI 96718 (tel. 965-8936), fills you in on the history of the volcano, and an observatory displays the seismographic equipment used in detecting the tremors. If your timing is right, you'll get a chance to see Pele do her thing during one of the frequent eruptions. Park rangers will direct you to the safest spot for viewing her pyrotechnics. There's even a **volcano hotline** (tel. 967-7977). Wear warm clothes when you visit the volcano. It tends to get very chilly at 4,000 feet! Also, be sure not to take rocks from the park; it's considered to be very bad luck to do so. In fact, in the visitor center you can peruse a whole display of letters written by people who brought lava rocks home and suffered the consequences. The visitor center is open daily from 7:45 a.m. to 5 p.m.

The best way to watch the volcano in action, and to tour the Big Island in general, is by **whirlybirds** that will spirit you away to such far reaches as Puu Oo vent, a real hot spot which is miles off the beaten track. Flightseeing also offers rare aerial views of the 442-foot Akaka Falls, sea cliffs, ancient Hawaiian ruins, and panoramic ranchlands. The cost ranges from $300 to $580 per couple, including in-flight narration by a knowledgeable pilot and background music to sweeten the views. Try **Kenai Helicopters,** P.O. Box 4118, Kailua-Kona, HI 96745 (tel. 329-7424), and **Big Island Air,** P.O. Box 1476, Kailua-Kona, HI 96745 (tel. 329-4868).

Set at the base of Mount Hualalai, an 8,721-foot dormant volcano, the sunny port of **Kona** is full of sightseeing goodies. King David Kalakaua fell in love with the area and summered at **Hulihee Palace,** a beautifully restored building now open as a museum. Open daily from 9 a.m. to 4 p.m.; admission is $4.50 per person. It also has an excellent gift shop. Hawaii's missionaries also cherished Kona, where they built their first church, **Mokuaikaua.** You can still visit this prim little New England–style house of worship, which dates back to 1827. South of town, take a turn through **Puuhonua o Honaunau** (the Place of Refuge), where ancient lawbreakers retreated for protection from their crimes. This highly spiritual site has been restored and preserved as a national historical park, and it offers demonstrations of traditional Hawaiian arts, crafts, and games.

Head up the hill to the **Royal Kona Coffee Mill and Museum,** where that wonderfully rich bean is grown and harvested. Go down to the sea for a visit to **Kealakekua Bay,** where Capt. James Cook was killed in 1779. Then stroll through **Kona Gardens,** a botanical park full of tropical plants, sacred sites, crafts demonstrations, and assorted displays of Hawaiiana. Contact **Kona Coast Activities,** P.O. Box 5397, Kailua-Kona, HI 96740 (tel. 367-5105).

From the first Spanish immigrants, called *espagnol,* came the first Hawaiian cowboys, called paniolos, that rare breed of cowpokes who work the tropical ranges. In the shadow of Mauna Kea in little Waimea town you'll find the **Parker Ranch,** whose 224,000 acres make it one of the largest privately owned spreads in America. Here the paniolos sing Hawaiian songs, wear aloha shirts, and sports flowers in their hatbands, while leading the rough-and-tumble life of six generations. The 15-minute presentation at the Parker Ranch Visitor Center fills you in on the days when John Palmer Parker jumped a whaling ship and spearheaded this 140-year-old legacy. The ranch itself recently opened for tours, giving you an up-close look at cow-punching, Hawaiian style. Sightseeing covers Mana Hale, the original homestead founded by John Palmer Parker; Puukalani Stables; Puuopelu, the art-filled mansion belonging to the ranch's current owner, Richard Smart; and working field areas where white-faced Hereford cattle graze. Tours run Monday through Saturday, 9 a.m. to 3 p.m.; admission is $16.50 per person. Contact Parker Ranch, P.O. Box 458, Kamuela, HI 96743 (tel. 885-7655).

Down the road from Waimea is the **Kamuela Museum,** at the intersection of Routes 19 and 250 (tel. 885-4724). The collection is a treasure trove for anyone interested in Hawaiian history, with many pieces that originally belonged to early missionaries and Hawaiian royalty. Some of the more unusual pieces include feathered helmets worn by native warriors and *pohaku po wa* (the Hawaiian stone version of brass knuckles), as well as touching photographs of Hawaii's kings and queens. Open daily from 8 a.m. to 5 p.m.; admission $2.75 per person.

How about some sight-*seaing*? New to the Big Island, **Atlantis Submarines** can take you 40 to 60 feet below the surface off the Kona Coast in a Jules Verne-esque 46-passenger submarine, the $2.5-million *Atlantis IV*, for a narrated 35- to 45-minute underwater cruise. There are four dives a day, Tuesday through Saturday, at noon, 1 p.m., 2 p.m., and 3 p.m.; you must check in for your trip a half-hour in advance at the Hotel King Kamehameha in Kailua-Kona. The excursion costs $64 per person. Contact Atlantis, Shop L, Hotel King Kamehameha, 75-5660 Palani Road, Kailua-Kona (tel. 329-6626).

Each day at about 8 a.m., scores of fisherfolk leave Kailua-Kona pier in search of buried treasure: **fish,** that is, and lots of 'em! The waters off the Kona coast are world-famous for their abundance of *opakapaka, ulua, ono, ahi, mahimahi,* and the grand prize, the Pacific blue marlin, tipping the scales as high as 1,000 pounds. Charter a boat to share with others or for your very own. While you're at sea, take time to catch a few rays, snap some photos, eat your picnic lunch, and drink some beer. And don't forget to work on those great "fish stories" you'll tell the folks back home. Contact the **Kona Activities Center,** P.O. Box 1035, Kailua-Kona, HI 96740 (tel. 329-3171), or the **Kona Charters Skippers Association,** 75-5663 Palani Rd., Kailua-Kona, HI 96740 (tel. 367-8047). They'll set up the two of you for a full day for about $500 exclusive, and $125 shared, including tackle and bait.

Green sand? No kidding! Deposits of olivine crystals add a definite emerald hue to **Green Sand Beach,** a southeastern destination near South Point Park. Summer makes the best time to swim here, as the winter seas can be rough, but all year long you can sunbathe in privacy on green sand. All it takes is a two-mile hike from the boat ramp.

Gorgeous **black-sand beaches** line the east coast from South Point up to Kalapana, including Punaluu Beach Park, Harry K. Brown Beach Park, Isaac Hale Beach Park, and Kaimu Beach Park. On the west coast, two miles of black sand grace Kiholo Bay, and Honomalino offers good swimming and snorkeling. Richardson's black-sand beach is the finest of its kind on Hilo Bay.

Don't miss a Jeep excursion into **Waipio Valley.** Deep in this six-mile-long valley, the twin waterfalls of Hiilawe tumble down to a river that in olden times was so well stocked, men caught fish with their bare hands. It's a place of awesome, deserted beauty, where the *mana* (spirit) of old Hawaii still resides. The narrow road (accessible only to four-wheel-drive vehicles) spirals down a sheer-faced cliff to a spectacular black-sand beach punctuated by 2,000-foot mountains on each side. Wild horses and pigs roam the valley, where hibiscus flowers grow as big as platters, and huge elephant-ear plants shade the Wailoa River. **Waipio Valley Shuttle** (tel. 775-7121) can take you there for a 1½-hour tour; $22 per person.

The **Hamakua Coast,** the Big Island's north shore, is one of the great scenic drives of Hawaii. As you follow Highway 19, the vistas constantly change: lacy waterfalls, wide-open sugarcane fields, narrow gorges lush with groves of ohia and pine trees. Especially breathtaking: the curves around verdant gulches such as Kaawelili and Maulua. If you're looking for a good picnic spot, try the wave-pounded lava peninsula at Laupahoehoe Point and Beach Park, or the beaches at Waikaumalo and Kolekole.

HONEYMOON HOTELS AND HIDEAWAYS

Everything's big on the Big Island, including the selection of places to stay. By far the most unusual destination is the Volcano House, the sole hotel by Kilauea caldera and a perfect base of operations as you explore the national park.

The Kona and Kohala coast is the resort center of the island. Enjoying more sunny days than anywhere else in Hawaii, the breezy Kohala coast makes a predictably perfect locale for your honeymoon. Its stunning beaches and gentle waves are ideal for water sports of all kinds, such as swimming, snorkeling, sailing, and surfing, while the cool countryside of Waimea is just 12 miles away for hiking, horseback riding, hunting, and exploring. Nearby, sports buffs are lured to Kona's waters in particular for deep-sea fishing, which is the best in the whole state.

Expensive

Kona Village Resort, P.O. Box 1299, Kaupulehu-Kona, HI 96745 (tel. 808/325-5555; reservations: toll free 800/367-5290). Very few maps show Kaupulehu. Like all the best places, it's hidden, and its charm lies in what it does NOT have: big shopping arcades, tour groups, and crowds. Instead, this hypnotic haven drips with old-fashioned charm, as it creates a historic Polynesian village around a picturesque bay. The 125 plush thatched cottages (called *hales*) surround peaceful lagoons and Kaupulehu's natural sandy beach. No room phone, no radio, no TV, but instead, a wide range of amenities in secluded surroundings. Recreational facilities include sailboats, outrigger canoes, snorkeling gear, tennis, and excursions on the resort's 27-foot glass-bottomed boat. At day's end, torches are lit along the beach and flames flicker on the bay: beautiful! Honeymoon package: Five days/four nights (FAP): $1,875 per couple. Includes all meals, round-trip transportation from Keahole-Kona Airport, lei greeting, welcoming rum punch, champagne upon arrival, breakfast, lunch, and dinner daily, three-hour snorkeling sail to a secluded beach or two one-hour massages, unlimited use of tennis courts, glass-bottomed boat trips, and an 11-by-14-inch art reproduction of your "Honeymoon Hale."

Since its opening in 1965, the **Mauna Kea Beach Hotel,** P.O. Box 218, Kohala Coast, HI 96743 (tel. 808/882-7222; reservations: toll free 800/228-3000), has maintained an international reputation for excellence that has attracted a steady flow of discriminating guests such as Robert Wagner, Meryl Streep, Steven Spielberg, and George Lucas. Best-selling author Danielle Steele, a recent visitor, enjoyed the Mauna Kea so much that she used it as a honeymoon setting in a recent novel. The award-winning design of this ultimate retreat capitalizes on a hillside location, with terracing used to make the most of panoramic views of Kaunaoa Bay. Interior walkways and courtyards open to refreshing trade winds, and throughout the buildings and grounds you see over 1,000 ancient and contemporary works of art from Asia and the Pacific, including a majestic 7th-century Indian Buddha and 30 stunning handmade Hawaiian quilts. Your room is brightened by rainbow-inspired decor and large, floral lithographs by Hawaii's Lloyd Sexton, and as you stand arm in arm on your private lanai you get views of the Kohala coastline, the Kohala Mountains, or Mauna Kea. An 18-hole golf course covers an ancient lava flow and offers panoramas of the Pacific from every green. The lovely white-sand beach is regarded as perhaps the island's finest. Honeymoon package: Six days/five nights (MAP): $2,190 per couple. Includes oceanview or beachfront guest room, breakfast and dinner daily, private limousine transfers from Kona's Keahole Airport, champagne upon arrival, tropical fruit basket, two *yukatas* (Japanese summer robes) as mementos. The Mauna Kea's expert staff can also help make all wedding arrangements.

Commanding a three-mile shoreline of bays and beaches, the **Mauna Lani Bay Hotel,** P.O. Box 4000, Kohala Coast, HI 96743 (tel. 808/885-6622; reservations: toll free 800/367-2323), is far away from other hotels. Pick your own secluded cove and make the rest of the world go away! Done in a bold contemporary design, this arrow-shaped, six-story hotel points to the crystal-clear waters of Makaiwa Bay, where swimming, diving, and boating are all excellent. Shady coconut and milo trees, springwater pools, lush green golf courses, and a sea of brilliant bougainvillea turn the chocolate-covered lava landscape into a rich oasis of luxury. You'll be fascinated by the 12 acres of ancient fish ponds, once reserved for Hawaiian royalty, filled with mullet, awa, and lemon butterflies—the next best thing to being underwater. Your room is fashioned with soft beige carpeting, teak and rattan furnishings, mahogany shutters—all beneath a 9½-foot-high ceiling. Comfort is the word here, with soft chairs, a couch, a marble coffee table, an oversize remote-control color TV, a dry bar and refrigerator, a clock radio, a guest-room safe, a spacious closet, a private lanai, and air conditioning.

The resort offers five superb restaurants, including the new Canoe House, where you can savor dining and dancing under the stars. For sports-lovers, there's the 18-hole championship golf course rated one of the best in the world by *Golf* magazine, ten tennis courts, and a new health spa facility complete with Nautilus equipment and aerobics classes. Honeymoon package: Four days/three nights (EP): $1,075 per couple. Includes an oceanview room, limousine transfers from the Kona airport, champagne and a fruit basket upon arrival, and a special gift. MAP (includes breakfast and dinner) available for an additional $110 per couple per day. Wedding packages also available.

Hyatt Regency Waikoloa, One Waikoloa Beach Resort, Big Island, HI 96743 (tel. 808/885-1234; reservations: toll free 800/228-9000). Not many hotel lobbies are big enough to accommodate twin arched bridges, a clutch of eight-foot-tall Chinese vases, a tram, a boat landing, and a lagoon. That gives you some sense of the grandiose scale of the new Hyatt Regency Waikoloa. Set on 62 acres on Waiulua Bay on the sunny Kohala coast, it is the most expensive hotel ever built, costing about $360 million. The construction statistics alone are staggering: Some 3,350 palm trees were trucked in to create a lush tropical oasis amid the black lava rock of the coastline; tons of sand were brought in on barges from Kauai and Oahu to form a beach. The larger-than-life proportions become evident from the moment you check in. After you saunter down the grand entrance stairway, you have three choices about how to get to your room. Settle into an air-conditioned tram, hop aboard a launch that cruises down a mile of waterways, or stroll along walkways flanked by Oriental and Pacific art worth $3 million.

For guests, the centerpiece of the resort is a three-quarter-acre swimming pool, complete with Jacuzzis, waterfalls, and a 170-foot slide. A second area has pools linked by a "river," so idle lotusland dreamers can float from one to another. Hyatt Regency Waikoloa carries the "fantasy resort" concept one step further by giving vacationers a chance to live out their dreams. Want to be a paniolo (cowboy) for a day? Swim with the resort's tame Atlantic bottlenose dolphins? It's possible as part of the resort's special guest programs (ask about dates and prices). Of course, Hyatt Regency Waikoloa supplies the full range of more usual pastimes: complete watersports facilities; a state-of-the-art health club; eight tennis courts; four nearby golf courses, plus a new $16-million course designed by Tom Weiskopf and Jay Morrish that is scheduled to open any minute. At meal times, the selection is equally wide. The resort has 13 lounges and 7 restaurants serving Italian, Japanese, continental, steak-and-seafood, and Polynesian cuisine. Afterward, head for Spats disco for dancing. Honeymoon package: Four days/three nights (EP): $990 per couple. Includes oceanfront accommodations, champagne, and one breakfast in bed for two.

Moderate

Set at the edge of Keauhou Bay near Kona, the **Kona Surf Resort,** 78-128 Ehukai St., Kailua-Kona, HI 96740 (tel. 808/322-3411; reservations: toll free 800/367-8011), covers 15 acres of natural and man-made delights. Rivers of ancient lava laid the foundation for this seaside resort, a modern white design enlivened by emerald shade trees and thousands of flowering plants. An open-air design invites paradise inside as well, as waterfalls dance down lava rocks and unhindered breezes rustle giant ferns. The hotel goes out of its way to make your honeymoon fun, with a fabulous pool-slide, fitness programs, water sports, jogging and hiking trails, Hawaiian arts and crafts, golf at the 27-hole Keauhou championship course, three Laykold tennis courts, and volleyball. Although the hotel does not have a good swimming beach, there are freshwater and saltwater pools. After a sauna and massage, slip into your private sunken bathtub and talk about tomorrow's plans. Each of the 530 rooms, recently refurbished, features a private lanai, color TV, radio, courtesy coffee-maker, and all-day room service. The hotel has just added a Hawaiian-style wedding chapel—you can even arrive for the ceremony in a festively decorated outrigger canoe. Honeymoon package: Four days/three nights (EP): $550 per couple.

Includes oceanfront room, champagne breakfast on your first morning, $40 food and beverage credit, special gift.

Named after the great king who lived and died on the Big Island, the **Hotel King Kamehameha,** 75-5660 Palani Rd., Kailua-Kona, HI 96740 (tel. 808/329-2911; reservations: toll free 800/367-5170), in the heart of Kailua-Kona, is rich in Hawaiiana, and it houses an extensive collection of artifacts, including a restored *heiau* (shrine). Two six-story towers flank an air-conditioned shopping arcade, and the property looks pretty spiffy after its recent refurbishment. To the east, Mount Hualalai rises up more than 8,000 feet, while at its foot the sandy coves of Kamakahonu Bay offer the best swimming, scuba-diving, snorkeling, and sunbathing in town. Your room offers a private balcony, air conditioning, refrigerator, TV, and sitting area, as well as delightful touches such as framed prints of old Kona. Diehard tennis fans rave about the hotel's video machine for stroke analysis, and the 18-hole Keauhou-Kona Golf Course is a short drive away. Honeymoon package: Four days/three nights: $520 per couple. Includes deluxe oceanview room, chilled champagne, tropical fruit basket, one breakfast for two, plus dinner for two at Moby Dick's or a dinner and show at the hotel's bayside luau.

Kona Hilton Beach and Tennis Resort, P.O. Box 1179, Kailua-Kona, HI 96745 (tel. 808/329-3111; reservations: toll free 800/445-8667). The rugged lava-rock rim of Kailua Bay sets the scene for this hotel's unique architecture, with sweeping balconies following the contour of the mountains. Lush landscapes of exotic plants and fish-filled ponds await outside, while inside, the 452 guest rooms and suites have been recently redone in soft pastels, with koa-wood room dividers and louvered closets. From your private lanai you can see the gardens, Kailua Bay, or Kailua-Kona village, and your room comes with air conditioning, refrigerator, color TV with a movie channel, coffeemaker, and his-and-her dressing areas. Dine and dance by the sea in one of the four restaurants and lounges. For tennis enthusiasts, there's a four-court Laykold complex, lighted for night play, and tennis pros are available for lessons. For beach-blanket potatoes, the private sandy lagoon and freshwater pool are perfect for swimming and sunning. All in all, it adds up to a very friendly and appealing resort in a terrific location—so close to Kona that you can walk to town. Honeymoon package: Four days/three nights (BP): $540 per couple ($670 per couple including a rental convertible). Includes deluxe oceanview accommodations, full American breakfast daily, nightly orchid turn-down service, champagne and chocolates upon arrival, plus a special gift.

Inexpensive

Volcano House, P.O. Box 53, Hawaii Volcanoes National Park, Volcano, HI 96718 (tel. 808/967-7321). Overlooking the very rim of creation, this one-of-a-kind hotel perches on the edge of active Kilauea crater, and is just a few steps away from the visitor center. It offers a large lounge furnished with deep-leather couches and chairs, with a floor-to-ceiling lava-rock fireplace that welcomes guests and warms the chill of the air at 4,200 feet above sea level. Of the 37 rooms, all the deluxe and most of the superior accommodations front the crater, while the lower-priced rooms are located in a separate building. The rooms are smallish, and their country-inn decor is simple and attractive, with wall-to-wall carpeting but no TV, radio, or (needless to say) air conditioning. A steam-vent sauna helps you unwind in natural style. Honeymoon package: None. Rates (EP): $65 to $90 per couple per night.

ROMANTIC RESTAURANTS

From fresh-grown fruits and vegetables to filet mignon for two, the Big Island boasts a bonanza of fine foods served in restaurants both casual and cosmopolitan. Bon appetit!

Expensive

Dining Pavilion, Mauna Kea Beach Hotel, Kohala Coast (tel. 882-7222). This freestanding wood-frame structure seats 300 guests throughout three levels, and the open-air design offers you glorious views of Kaunaoa Bay. There's a fascinating blend of the foreign and familiar here. For instance, Thai china table settings reflect the restaurant's international scope, while rose-colored linens remind you that nearby Waimea is the rose capital of Hawaii. The daily menu reflects the market's best offerings, and every evening you can choose from such continental masterpieces as a hearty wienerschnitzel and tender veal medallions with butter noodles. You'll love the imaginative preparations of island foods, such as leg of lamb with Maui onions, banana and papaya soup, and sautéed mahimahi with capers and limes. Dinner costs about $80 to $100 for two plus drinks. Folks flock in from miles around to eat their fill at the big luncheon buffet by the sea, which costs $44 per couple. Open daily from 7 to 10 a.m.; 11:30 a.m. to 2:30 p.m.; 6:30 to 9 p.m.

Moderate

The Pottery, 75-5995 Kuakini Hwy., Kona (tel. 329-2277). As the name implies, this homespun restaurant is a pottery as well, and on the wood-paneled walls are displays of handmade bowls, teapots, platters, and other ceramic delights that you can purchase at meal's end. Try something out of the steak kiln, or order the Cornish game hen, presented to you in a clay pot. All entrées come with salad, rice or potato, bread, and fresh vegetables. Look at your coffee mug, because it just may be a collector's item. Dinner for two in this creative hideaway costs from $20 to $40 plus drinks. Open nightly from 6 to 9:30 p.m.

Huggo's, 75-5828 Kaha Kai Dr., Kona (tel. 329-1493). Dine by the water's edge and savor the expansive views of the waves washing up on the black lava rocks. Some say there's no better place to watch the sunset over Kailua Bay. One thing's certain: Huggo's offers the perfect forum for scrumptious seafood like oysters on the half shell, or such fresh catches of the day as opakapaka and mahimahi. Another favorite is barbecued shrimp, as well as steaks, prime rib, and lobster. The super salad bar has a great variety of accompaniments, and the dressings are especially unique. Weekends you'll find live musical entertainment in the lounge. Dinner ranges from $20 to $50 for two plus drinks. Open daily from 11:30 a.m. to 9:30 p.m.

Fisherman's Landing, at the Kona Inn Shopping Village, Kailua-Kona (tel. 326-2555). Watch the Kona sunset blaze across the sky from the deck at this popular restaurant right on the waterfront. Flaming torches frame views of passing cruise ships and fishing boats moored in the harbor. Many of the preferred dinner entrées come right from these waters: fresh-caught opakapaka, onaga, or ono, kiawe boiled and served with rice pilaf, fresh veggies, and your choice of sauces. The menu also includes steak, veal, and chicken dishes. Main courses (which include soup or salad) run $20 to $22. Open daily for lunch, 11:30 a.m. to 2 p.m.; dinner, 5:30 to 10 p.m. (to 10:30 p.m. on Friday and Saturday).

The Jolly Roger, at Waterfront Row, Kailua-Kona (tel. 329-1344). For food, fun, and sunset fanfare, you can't beat this lively new gathering place on the Kona waterfront. Mosey on over for a hearty breakfast (would you believe a steak and four pancakes, topped by a farm-fresh egg?) or an array of dinner specialties such as teriyaki steaks or fresh seafood. Make a night of it—there's live entertainment each evening from 9 p.m. Open daily from 6:30 a.m. to 10:30 p.m.; dinner for two, $20 to $40 per couple.

Edelweiss, Highway 19 near Waimea (tel. 885-6800). Imagine an alpine lodge transported to the misty highlands of Waimea and you pretty much have the picture of this charming inn, completely lined with wood. Run by German-born Hans-Peter Suger (who was chef at some of the Big Island's finest hotels), the restaurant features specialties such as wienerschnitzel, roast pork with sauerkraut, and duck bigarade (with orange sauce). Open for lunch, 11:30 a.m. to 1:30 p.m.; about $15 per couple. Dinner, 5 to 9:30 p.m.; $40 to $50 per couple. Closed Monday.

Kona Hilton Luau, 75-5852 Alii Dr., Kailua-Kona (tel. 329-3111). A treasured Hawaiian tradition comes alive on the majestic Kona coastline. This open-air affair begins with an aloha shell-lei greeting and a good-hearted hour of *okole maluna!* (bottom's up!) in a romantic coconut grove. The featured entrée—roast kalua pig —is raised from the ground during the imu ceremony, and then you dine on the celebrated Hawaiian and Oriental delicacies of the luau feast, from "three-finger" poi to yummy haupia pudding. Flames of torchlight flicker against the night sky as the Polynesian revue captivates you with South Pacific songs and dances. For two, it costs $80. Held every Monday, Wednesday, and Friday starting at 6 p.m.

The SS James Makee, Kona Surf Resort, Kona (tel. 322-3411), invites you to gaze at the glorious sunset while sipping cocktails from the terrace. Dinner in the restaurant is notable for its fresh catch of the day, as well as for its Parker beef dinner special: a roundup of salad, steak, potatoes, vegetable, and beverage—all for $17.50. Friday and Saturday nights, there's a special seafood and roast beef buffet. Open nightly from 6 to 10 p.m.

Parker Ranch Broiler, Waimea (tel. 885-7366), takes you to the world of the paniolo with "90/10" hamburgers ($10 for two) plus steak sandwiches, "Very Portuguese" bean soup, and missionary seafood chowder. Dinner runs about $30 per couple, and you can dine by views of lush green pastures. Open daily from 11 a.m. to 2 p.m.; 5:30 to 9 p.m.

Inexpensive

KK Tei, 1550 Kamehameha Hwy., Hilo (tel. 961-3791). A taste of the Orient comes to the Big Island capital. Choose from several surroundings, including a serene Japanese garden where you sit on the floor and a more traditional dining room. American food is available, but we recommend going the Japanese route at this superb teahouse. Tempura and teriyaki entrées are good here, and all dinners come with such side dishes as miso soup, delectable sushi, and steaming rice. Indulge yourselves in a glass of hot sake (rice wine) and warm up your special honeymoon dinner. Price for two is about $20 plus drinks. Open for lunch Monday through Saturday from 11 a.m. to 2 p.m.; dinner nightly from 5 to 9 p.m.

Old Kailua Cantina, 75-5669 Alii Dr., Kona (tel. 329-8226). Kailua Bay is your view at this al fresco restaurant, where meals are memorable. Kick up your heels with a pitcher of margaritas to start things off in south-of-the-border style. Ever tried a margarita with fresh bananas? Or pineapple? How about papaya? At $10.50 a pitcher, this is the place to experiment. Chips and salsa are complimentary, and there's a wide choice of Mexican beers. Try the shrimp quesadilla appetizer, a tasty combination of seafood and spice. The Mauna Loa burrito is made with spicy pork, rice, beans, and cheese in a flour tortilla, and fresh island fish, meat, and chicken dishes are all available. Dinner costs about $20 per couple plus drinks. Open daily from 11 a.m. to 11 p.m.

Teshima Restaurant, Kealakekua-Kona (tel. 322-9140). For comfy decor and local-style dining, try this little gem on Highway 11, open since 1943. As soon as you walk in, you're treated like family. Relax in your booth over such Japanese dishes as shrimp tempura and teishoku with miso soup. They stuff a giant omelet full of spicy Portuguese sausage and fried rice, a popular combination with regular guests. Sashimi is particularly good here, but you can order just about anything and be guaranteed of the Teshima touch. Dinner for two costs $20 per couple, plus drinks. Open daily for lunch, 11 a.m. to 2 p.m.; dinner, 5 to 10 p.m.

When driving along the Hamakua Coast, stop for a bite at **Herb's Place,** Highway 19, Honokaa (tel. 775-7236). The decor's not fancy, but it's a real favorite with the *kama'ainas* (oldtimers) in this atmospheric sugar-plantation town. The food is excellent and heartily portioned: sandwiches, plate lunches (terrific stuffed cabbage), and a delicious saimin. About $10 per couple. Open Monday through Friday, 5:30 a.m. to 8:30 p.m.; on Saturday, 8 a.m. to 8:30 p.m. Closed Sunday.

For a lunch on the south coast, try **Punalu'u Black Sands Restaurant,** on Highway 11 south of Pahala (tel. 928-8528). The restaurant is set along a crescent-shaped black-sand beach, backed by palm trees and a lagoon where ducks paddle tranquilly. Sip a cool tropical drink and enjoy the ample luncheon buffet ($10 per person), served daily from 10 a.m. to 1 p.m. Or choose from the regular menu, served from 10:30 a.m. to 8:30 p.m.

NEW YORK CITY

Paris may well be the loveliest of cities, Rome the most eternal, but New York is certainly the sexiest and most energetic. Something about its dense vitality demands that it be shared with another, preferably beloved, person.

When people refer to New York City, they usually mean just the borough of Manhattan, and so will we in this chapter. Actually, New York City is comprised of five boroughs, of which Manhattan is but one (the others are Queens, Staten Island, the Bronx, and Brooklyn). Manhattan is the most densely populated part of New York City, with eight million inhabitants residing on an island 12 miles long and 3 miles wide.

So beautiful from so many angles, New York's charms defy simple description. Something resembling perspective, however, may be attained from the Observation Deck of the Empire State Building. Look toward the south and you'll see old New York: Greenwich Village, Chelsea, the Lower East Side, SoHo, Little Italy, and Chinatown. Farther on, the concrete and glass canyons of the financial district confront you along with the World Trade Center's twin towers. Past Battery Park at Manhattan's southern tip you'll spy the Statue of Liberty in all her proud, newly restored glory. Ellis Island, the entry point into the United States for more than ten million immigrants, lies beside it.

To the east, Brooklyn and Queens; to the west, the state of New Jersey. As you look north past the metallic forest of steel spires known as midtown, the lush, green rectangle of Central Park asserts itself, an 840-acre pastoral oasis amid the concrete-towered isle. To the right of Central Park, you can view the Fifth Avenue and Park Avenue apartments of the Upper East Side's well-heeled residents. To the park's left, the Upper West Side bustles with the vigor of a newly settled frontier as an ever-increasing army of yuppies settles in, bringing with them dozens of chic restaurants and fashion-conscious boutiques. Just beyond the northwest corner of Central Park, Columbia University and the Cathedral Church of St. John the Divine mark the lower boundary of Harlem. Gazing even farther north, you may be able to see Fort Tryon Park, home of the Cloisters, and across the Harlem River, the Bronx (also known as "DA BRONX!").

You could plan your entire honeymoon around just a single aspect of New York's many possibilities. A couple could spend a week exploring just a few of its 150 museums (not to mention its 400 art galleries), for example. Or attending Broadway, off-Broadway, and off-off-Broadway shows staged at more than 350 theaters. Or listening to jazz in intimate Greenwich Village clubs, or tasting their way through Chinatown, or shopping fashionable Fifth Avenue—the options are unlimited.

Most honeymooners, however, will probably want to mix and match, combining the town's more popular tourist spots—such as the Empire State Building, the Statue of Liberty, the Staten Island Ferry—with such relaxing delights as an afternoon in the Cloisters, coffee in an outdoor café in Central Park, or a quiet drink in a secret former speakeasy (ask for Chumley's Bar on Bedford Street in the West Village). It's amazing how romantic even the most public of settings can be in New York. Please don't feel as if you should skip the city's best-known attractions simply because you've heard about them your entire life; each and every one is famous for good reason.

At night New York City becomes a mecca of culture and pleasure. Between the aesthetic options offered by its hundreds of stages, theaters, and concert halls, as well as its enormous gastronomic possibilities and nightclubs that don't warm up until well after midnight (such as Tunnel or the Palladium), honeymooners will quickly realize why New York is called "the city that never sleeps."

1. Practical Facts

In this section you'll find out some basic New York City information—

GETTING THERE

New York is a major transportation nexus. You'll have no trouble reaching it from anywhere in the world.

By Air

The three large airports that serve New York City, in order of their proximity to midtown Manhattan, are LaGuardia Airport in northern Queens, John F. Kennedy (JFK) International Airport in southeastern Queens, and Newark International Airport in New Jersey. Such major airlines as **American, United, TWA, Continental, and Pan Am** frequently offer low-cost fares from all parts of the country.

From JFK to Manhattan, you can either take the JFK Express ("Train to the Plane"), a bus/subway combination ($7 per person) that leaves every 20 minutes and stops at many points from southern to northern Manhattan (tel. toll free 800/AIR-RIDE); the Carey Transportation motorcoach ($9 per person; tel. 718/632-0500), which leaves at least every 30 minutes and stops at both the Port Authority Bus Terminal's AirTransCenter, 42nd Street and Eighth Avenue, and Grand Central Station, 42nd Street and Park Avenue; or a taxi (between $20 and $30 for the cab ride).

From LaGuardia to Manhattan, you should take either the Carey motorcoach ($6.50 per person; tel. 718/632-0500), which goes to the Port Authority Terminal and Grand Central Station at least every 30 minutes, or catch a taxi at one of the two stands outside the main LaGuardia terminal ($10 to $15 for the cab ride).

From Newark, the Olympia Trails Coach (tel. 212/964-6233) leaves about every 15 minutes for the World Trade Center in lower Manhattan and Grand Central Station ($7.50 per person). Taxi fare is about $30 to $40.

Information on transportation to all three New York City–area airports is available from the Port Authority of New York and New Jersey (tel. toll free 800/AIR-RIDE).

By Train

Trains entering Manhattan from cities all over the country terminate either at

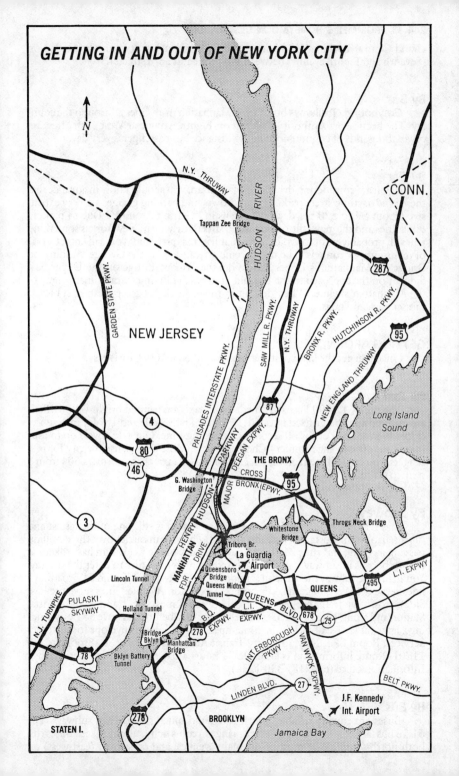

GETTING IN AND OUT OF NEW YORK CITY

Grand Central Terminal (42nd Street and Park Avenue) or at Pennsylvania Station (Seventh and Eighth avenues between West 31st and 33rd streets).

By Bus

Greyhound/Trailways buses serve Manhattan from cities all around the country. The hectic Port Authority building on Eighth Avenue at West 45th Street receives thousands of commuter and long-distance bus passengers every day.

By Car

If you are considering driving to Manhattan, you should know in advance that there is *no* daytime street parking in midtown, and parking garages are very expensive (about $9 to $20 per day); see details in "Getting Around." Due to parking difficulties and the generally overcrowded streets, driving in New York is something you will probably want to avoid. Since Manhattan is an island, you will enter by one of its bridges or tunnels. The most scenic arrivals are via the George Washington Bridge on Manhattan's Upper West Side, the Triboro Bridge on the Upper East Side, or on the approach to the Lincoln Tunnel, all offering extraordinary views of the Manhattan skyline. When driving in town watch out for pedestrians, bicycle messengers, and taxis.

GETTING AROUND

Once you get the hang of it, getting around New York City is easy.

By Taxi

The nearly 12,000 licensed "medallion" taxis are painted bright yellow. Taxis are metered and charge fixed rates: $1.15 for the first ⅛ mile and 15¢ for each subsequent ⅛ mile and/or for 60 seconds of standing time. One fare covers up to four passengers (five in the roomier "Checker" cabs). Most taxis cruise the city for passengers; you can hail them on the street. All licensed taxis charge an extra 50¢ from 8 p.m. to 6 a.m.

By Subway

At $1.15 per ride, the New York subway system is still one of the fastest and most reliable transportation bargains around. The system carries over three-million passengers daily, and runs 24 hours a day every day of the week. Purchase tokens at change booths in subway stations and insert them in turnstiles to enter the subway. You'll find the subway most useful for north-south trips (the 1, 2, and 3 "Broadway" lines serve the West Side; the 4, 5, and 6 "Lexington Avenue" lines serve the East Side); crosstown trains are also available between Times Square and Grand Central Station and along 14th Street. Get a free subway map before you leave home by sending a large (at least six-by-eight-inch) stamped, self-addressed envelope to Customer Services, Room 875, New York City Transit Authority, 370 Jay St., Brooklyn, NY 11201. Route information is available 24 hours a day from the New York Transit Information office (tel. 718/330-1234).

By Bus

Buses are equally reliable, a little safer, and much slower than subways. The $1.15 bus fare is payable only by exact change in coins or by subway token. Buses run both north-south along most of the main avenues, and crosstown (east-west) on such major streets as 14th, 34th, 42nd, 57th, and through Central Park on 68th, 79th, and 86th streets. Most midtown bus stops have route maps, and complete route maps may be found in most subway stations and in several of the easily obtainable New York pocket atlases.

By Car

Public transportation is a much more efficient, relaxing, and colorful way to enjoy the city. But if you want to bring a car into Manhattan, the parking lots on the West Side and Upper East Side (above 66th Street) are much less expensive than midtown and hotel lots. Parking in the theater district can cost anywhere from $10 to $20 for a couple of hours, not necessarily including the city's 14% parking tax. If you park on the street, carefully read the red-and-white signs that explain parking restrictions. An illegally parked car will be heavily fined, and if towed will cost you at least $125.

If you need to rent a car, you can do so either at the airport or midtown. Sample rental car rates from Avis for a compact car run about $260 a week with unlimited free miles; about $56 per day with no mileage fee for the first 300 miles. Various specials and discounts may also be available, so check with your travel agent. On weekends during the summer months, rental cars in Manhattan are usually reserved at least a week in advance, so make sure you plan ahead.

WEATHER

What kind of weather do you want? New York has it all, ranging from temperatures in the 20s and 30s (often accompanied by wind, rain, and snow) during the winter months (December through February) to the 80s and 90s during the humid summer (mid-June through September). Spring and autumn provide the most acclimate weather for appreciating the city.

CLOTHING

Dress corresponds to where you go and what time of year you go there. Bring your shorts and swimsuits for the summer, but in the winter you'll want to bundle up in overcoats, scarves, gloves, and a hat. Otherwise, wear whatever makes you feel comfortable, but remember that certain tonier dining spots may require gentlemen to wear a jacket and tie.

TIME

New York is on Eastern Standard Time, and observes Daylight Saving Time during the summer months.

TELEPHONES

The area code for Manhattan and the Bronx is 212; in the other boroughs it's 718. Local calls on pay phones cost 25¢. For directory information in Manhattan and the Bronx, dial 411; for the outer boroughs, dial 718/555-1212. The emergency number for police, fire, or ambulance assistance is 911.

SHOPPING

New York sells at least one of just about everything under the sun.

Macy's in midtown West 34th Street and Broadway (tel. 695-4400), the world's largest department store, is a good place to start a shopping expedition, with a dozen floors of reasonably priced clothing and housewares for a wide range of tastes. **Bloomingdale's,** East 60th Street and Lexington Avenue (tel. 705-2000), has an upscale selection of (mostly) women's clothing, plus men's clothes, housewares, and home furnishings, with prices competitive with Macy's. **Saks,** 49th Street and Fifth Avenue (tel. 753-4000), is another fashion institution. The best department store sales take place around the major holidays.

New York's garment district, along Seventh Avenue in the 30s, offers excellent fashion bargains. Other popular shopping streets for fashion (and more) include **Fifth Avenue** in the 50s, with **Tiffany's, Cartier,** and other famous names; and **Madison Avenue** between 61st and 86th streets, known for upscale boutiques such as **Pierre Balmain, Yves Saint Laurent,** and **Kenzo.** Chic one-of-a-kind fashions will be found in the many small boutiques in **SoHo** (the area south of Houston Street). **Chinatown** contains dozens of small shops that offer a large range of inexpensive gifts and souvenirs. On the **Upper West Side,** the streets of the major avenues (Broadway, Amsterdam, and Columbus) are lined with boutiques, bookstores, gift shops, and toy stores.

Music fans shouldn't pass up **Tower Records,** 692 Broadway at West 4th Street and 66th Street and Broadway (tel. 505-1500 for information), whose two branches lay claim to being the largest record stores in the world. Likewise, the **Strand,** just up the street at 829 Broadway at East 12th Street (tel. 473-1452), is one of the world's biggest book stores, with eight miles of used books and half-priced reviewers' copies.

Many electronics and clothing stores offer name-brand goods at a substantial discount. For jewelry, shop 47th Street between Fifth Avenue and Avenue of the Americas (Sixth Avenue). Electronic goods such as cameras, stereos, TVs, and videocassette recorders are sold substantially below list price at **Uncle Steve's,** 343 Canal (tel. 226-4010), **47th Street Photo,** 67 West 47th St. (tel. 398-1410), and by **The Wiz** and **Crazy Eddie** chains. (Note: Be advised, discounted electronics items are sometimes sold without manufacturers' warranties.)

Discount women's clothing is available at the **S & W Designers Apparel Discount Center,** 287 Seventh Ave. (tel. 924-6656), and in the many **Bolton's** outlets.

The **Odd Lot Trading Co., Third Avenue Bazaar,** and **Duane Reade** drugstores all offer large selections of miscellaneous discounted, discontinued, and/or slightly damaged goods.

THEATER

Amid New York's hundreds of theaters, something is bound to appeal to any taste. Ticket prices run from about $60 for the best Broadway seats on a weekend, down to $10 or less for off-off-Broadway productions. The TKTS booths in Times Square and Two World Trade Center (tel. 354-5800), however, are one of New York's best bargains, since they sell half-price tickets for a wide selection of its older productions and previews on the day of the show. The booths open at 10 a.m. for matinee performances (Wednesdays at 2 p.m. and Sundays at 3 p.m.), and at 3 p.m. for evening performances. There is a service charge of $1.50 per ticket. Most theaters are dark on Monday.

HOW TO GET MARRIED IN NEW YORK

You can get married 24 hours after obtaining a marriage license for $10 from the Marriage License Bureau in the Municipal Building downtown, 1 Centre St. at Chambers Street (tel. 269-2900). No blood test or physical is necessary, but you should have original identification, such as a valid driver's license, passport, or birth certificate. If either of you is between the ages of 18 and 23, original proof of age is required. If you are 16 or 17 years old, your parents need to be present to sign a consent form. The bureau is open Monday through Friday from 9 a.m. to 4 p.m

You must wait a full 24 hours before the marriage ceremony. Marriages can be performed for $5 in the City Clerk's office, 1 Centre St., Monday through Friday from 9 a.m. to 4 p.m.

FOR FURTHER INFORMATION

Contact: **New York Convention & Visitors Bureau,** Two Columbus Circle, New York, NY 10019 (tel. 212/397-8222). An information center located near Times Square, 158–160 West 42nd St., is open Wednesday through Friday from 9 a.m. to 6 p.m., and Saturday and Sunday from 10 a.m. to 6 p.m.

---

2. Romantic Interludes

The only problem honeymooners may have in New York is deciding what romantic activities might have to be postponed for their next visit—there's too much to do in a short period of time.

CRUISING NEW YORK

Take one of the **Circle Line's** Manhattan circumnavigations and get the big picture on the Big Apple. The double-decked boats depart every 45 minutes from Pier 83 at 42nd Street and Twelfth Avenue for the leisurely 2¾-hour trip ($16.50 per person), complete with well-informed guides. There's a snack counter and bar on board. Contact: **Circle Line Sightseeing Yachts, Inc.,** Pier 83, West 43rd Street and Twelfth Avenue, New York, NY 10036 (tel. 563-3200).

A MEDIEVAL MUSEUM

Almost no New York vista is more romantic than the sight of the sun setting over New Jersey as seen from the **Cloisters** (tel. 923-3700), a branch of the Metropolitan Museum located close to the northern tip of Manhattan, in Fort Tryon Park, overlooking the Hudson River. Constructed in medieval style, the Cloisters was pieced together in 1938 from parts of a 12th-century chapter house, parts of cloisters from five medieval monasteries, a Romanesque chapel, and a 12th-century Spanish apse. Medieval festivals and concerts are held intermittently during the nonwinter months. Admission is a donation. Open Tuesday through Sunday, 9:30 a.m. to 4:45 p.m. (November through February) or until 5:15 p.m. (March through October). To get to the Cloisters by subway, take the IND Eighth Avenue A train to 190th Street–Overlook Terrace, exit by elevator, then either take the no. 4 bus or walk through Fort Tryon Park to the museum. For those who wish to avoid the subways, the Madison Avenue bus no. 4, "Fort Tryon Park–The Cloisters," goes right to the door of the museum.

A LITTLE NIGHT MUSIC

Spend a romantic musical evening in Greenwich Village, the world's jazz capital. All prices that follow are per person. Begin at the **Village Vanguard,** Seventh Avenue just below West 11th Street (tel. 255-4037), $13.25 cover and $6.50 minimum, a classic basement mecca where the cream of the straight-ahead jazz crop still checks in regularly. Then mosey down the street to **Sweet Basil Jazz Restaurant,** Seventh Avenue and Bleecker Street (tel. 242-1785), $13 to $16.50 per-person cover charge, and $7 per-person minimum at a table (no minimum at the bar), a comfortable, sophisticated room that takes the genre's new sounds seriously. **The Blue**

Note, Sixth Avenue and West 3rd Street (tel. 475-8592), $15 to $30 cover charge and $5 minimum; **Bradley's,** University Place between West 10th and West 11th streets (tel. 473-9700), $5.50 to $11 cover and $9 minimum; and the **Village Gate,** Bleecker and Thompson streets (tel. 475-5120), variable cover, should also be on your jazz agenda. Slightly farther south, **S.O.B.,** which stands for Sounds of Brazil, Varick and West Houston streets (tel. 243-4940), $17 cover and no minimum, specializes in music from the Caribbean, Africa, and—of course—Brazil.

Uptown, the Algonquin Hotel's **Oak Room,** West 44th Street between Fifth and Sixth avenues (tel. 840-6800), about $25 cover and $16 minimum, a warm, masculine bastion of tradition; and the **Carlyle Café** in the Carlyle Hotel, Madison Avenue and East 76th Street (tel. 744-1600), $30 cover and two-drink minimum, provide unequaled opportunities to enjoy romantic music in beautiful settings. No matter who is appearing during your stay—the great Bobby Short, George Shearing, and Michael Feinstein are all regulars in one or the other of these rooms—you'll hear the standards of such great composers as Cole Porter, Noël Coward, Irving Berlin, and the Gershwins sung and played at their sentimental best.

VIEWS FROM ON HIGH

New York City's most popular tourist attraction is still **The Empire State Building,** Fifth Avenue at 34th Street (tel. 736-3100), $4 admission. Open daily from 9:30 a.m. to 11:30 p.m., it offers an unmatchable view of the city and surrounding environs. It's especially romantic on a clear evening, when Manhattan turns into an unbelievable light show. There's a great souvenir shop on the 86th floor.

Downtown, the twin towers of the **World Trade Center** offer amazing views of Manhattan and its environs. In the southern skyscraper, Tower 2, the 107th floor observation deck is open from 9:30 a.m. to 11:30 p.m. (tel. 466-7377; $4 per person admission). In Tower 1, you can either dine (at considerable expense) in the famous 107th floor Windows on the World (tel. 938-1111) or enjoy grilled entrées, snack on hors d'oeuvres, or just have a romantic late-night dessert or drink in the equally fabulously positioned Hors d'Oeuverie (tel. 938-1111), which features numerous appetizers such as crab fritters, chicken yakitori, and Thai spring rolls (all in the $5.50 to $13.50 range) as well as one or two entrées such as Korean short ribs (kalbi) or grilled Mexican chorizo with refried beans and tostadas. Hours are Monday through Saturday from 4 p.m. to 1 a.m., and on Sunday from noon to 9 p.m. During lunch Monday through Friday, the Hors d'Oeuverie is a private club, but nonmembers are admitted for an $8 surcharge. The adjoining City Lights Bar is open the same hours.

A WALK IN THE PARK

On a warm spring or summer day, **Central Park** becomes a magnet for young New Yorkers. However, the **Conservatory Gardens** on Fifth Avenue at 104th Street is a well-kept New York horticultural secret and perfect for a romantic stroll. Open from 8 a.m. to a half hour before dusk, this unpopulated piece of paradise is surrounded by rose bushes and features a large floral centerpiece whose beds are changed seasonally. The spring tulips are a floral marvel. A visit to the Conservatory Gardens is like being in another world.

Central Park proper is a green 2½-mile sanctuary amid the concrete jungle of Manhattan. Designed in 1856, its pedestrian and bike paths, tunnels and bridle paths form maze-like patterns in which many remarkable treasures are hidden. The **Central Park Zoo,** for example, is open daily from 10 a.m. to 5 p.m. Or pack a picnic and just wander around and visit such attractive spots as the elliptical **Conservatory Pond** with its fairy-tale motif, **Central Park Lake** (where you can rent paddleboats during the day), the **Great Lawn,** the **Reservoir,** the **Victorian Carousel** (10:30

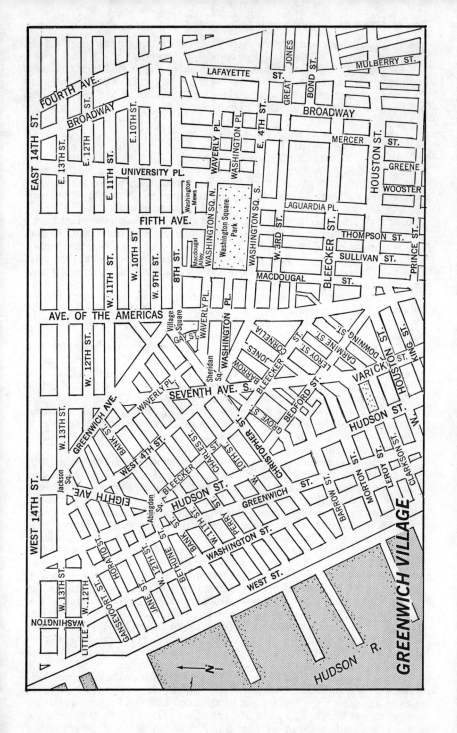

a.m. to 6 p.m.), and the newly renovated **Wollman ice skating rink** (open during the winter only; tel. 517-4800 for skate rental information).

Or pick up a bottle of champagne, a couple of glasses, and take a leisurely **moonlight carriage ride** through the park—or any other time of day, for that matter. Carriages park along 59th Street, and the legally set rates are $18.50 for the first half hour, $5.50 for each additional 15 minutes.

ROMANCE ON A BUDGET

Although the best things in life may not be free, they needn't cost a fortune either. New York offers many inexpensive or free staples of civilized life that are at least as enjoyable as its pricier attractions. For a mere 25¢, the **Staten Island Ferry** departs from the South Ferry Terminal adjacent to Battery Park every half hour for a 30-minute round trip to Staten Island and back, passing Governors Island, the Statue of Liberty, and Ellis Island, as well as giving a unique view of lower Manhattan.

During the summer months, Joseph Papp presents free **Shakespeare-in-the-Park** performances in Central Park's Delacorte Theater (tel. 861-7277). You usually have to get on line early in the afternoon for tickets (one per person) to these first-class productions, some of which (*The Mystery of Edwin Drood,* for example) have graduated to become full-scale Broadway hits.

The **Statue of Liberty,** which recently celebrated its anniversary with a highly publicized makeover, is still a must-see attraction. For $3.50 per person, take the 1½-hour tour, which leaves from Battery Park every half hour between 9 a.m. and 5 p.m. (tel. 269-5755).

You could spend days rambling about in the **American Museum of Natural History** on Central Park West at West 79th Street (tel. 769-5100), the world's largest natural-history museum, with its collection of some 35 million artifacts. Its most famous attractions include the Star of India star sapphire, a crosscut hunk of a giant sequoia tree, various reconstructed dinosaur skeletons, and a gigantic model of a blue whale hovering over the museum's Wednesday-evening cocktail bar. Also, don't miss the **Naturemax Theater**'s giant film screen or the **Hayden Planetarium.** The museum is open from 10 a.m. to 5:45 p.m., and 10 a.m. to 9 p.m. on Wednesday, Friday, and Saturday. $4 suggested contribution.

New York's newest attraction is also one of its oldest—the 200-year-old **South Street Seaport.** An 11-block enclave fronting the East River between the Brooklyn Bridge and the financial district, the area was the center of the city's shipping activity during the 18th and 19th centuries. Today, the brilliantly restored complex presents amazing juxtapositions of sights and sounds: cobblestoned streets and elegant brick buildings backdropped by soaring skyscrapers on Wall Street; screeching gulls, chugging steamships, and the ebullient rhythms of a Dixieland band. Visit the **South Street Seaport Museum** (tel. 669-9424), where you can tour the 347-foot *Peking,* said to be the second-largest sailing ship still in existence. Open daily from 10 a.m. to 6 p.m.; admission, $5.50 per person. Browse through the elegant boutiques along **Schermerhorn Row,** or the dozens of fine shops and restaurants at the **Fulton Market and Pier 17 Pavilion shopping malls.** Lively entertainment— mimes, jugglers, fire-eaters—energize the scene, and the activity continues late into the night. For evening fun, drop in at **Caroline's,** Pier 17 (tel. 233-4900), one of the city's hottest comedy clubs. Take a good look at the audience—stars such as Robin Williams often drop by to banter with the headliners. Cover runs $14 to $16.50 per person, two-drink minimum.

What's at the core of the Big Apple? The next best thing to being a native New Yorker is **Adventure on a Shoestring.** This 27-year-old organization showcases many of the city's finest freebies and paltry-priced activities for participants. Although annual membership costs $44 per person, nonmembers can attend the group's fascinating walking tours for $5.50 each. Strolls might explore SoHo, Greenwich Village, or—yummiest of all—Chinatown, with a stop for an extraordinary, extraordinarily low-cost lunch or dim sum. For schedules and information, contact them at 300 West 53rd St., New York, NY 10019 (tel. 265-2663).

---

3. Honeymoon Hotels and Hideaways

New York has many famous and beautiful romantic hotels, but lodgings aren't exactly a bargain. Though the city boasts nearly 175,000 hotel rooms, they tend to be either small, expensive, or both. But don't let room sizes dissuade you, since you'll want to spend most of your time outside, seeing and doing things you won't find anywhere else in the world. Accommodations range from luxurious suites overlooking Central Park to rooms in hotels famous for their literary clientele. Whichever you choose, remember to request a corner room; a long look down a midtown avenue is always inspirational.

In addition to the city's 8.25% sales tax, a 5% city occupancy tax and up to $2 per room will also be charged.

New York **bed-and-breakfast** services, such as **Urban Ventures,** P.O. Box 426, New York, NY 10024 (tel. 594-5650), or **City Lights Bed and Breakfast,** P.O. Box 20355, Cherokee Station, New York, NY 10028 (tel. 737-7049), offer such romantic lodgings as fireplace rooms in beautiful Upper East and West Side brownstones, artsy lofts, or quiet, private little apartments in Greenwich Village. Rates range from about $70 to $150 per couple per night, depending on the plushness of the accommodations.

The hotels listed below offer color TVs, air conditioning, and telephones in all rooms. Reservations are highly recommended.

Weekends are relatively slow for New York hotels, and many offer bargain rates at that time. Some of the best of these are noted below. Some hotels also offer theater packages, with the price of two tickets included in the room rate. This tends to be seasonal, and you should call the hotel for information.

All rates given are European Plan, i.e., meals not included.

EXPENSIVE

Recently remodeled, the 80-year-old **Plaza,** 59th Street and Fifth Avenue, New York, NY 10019 (tel. 212/759-3000, or toll free 800/228-3000), continues to attract newlyweds who equate honeymoons with old-world elegance. The Plaza's 800 rooms decorated in French provincial style rise above a labyrinthine complex of lobbies, restaurants, shops, and banquet rooms. Request one of the many rooms that offer a unique view of the length of Central Park. Such famous Plaza restaurants as the warm Oak Room, the Oyster Bar, the Palm Court, and the stately Edwardian Room are worth a visit, not necessarily for their food—better can often be found elsewhere—as much as for what they represent in hotel mythology. Honeymoon package: $385 per couple per night (available weekends only). Includes breakfast for two, champagne upon arrival, and a deluxe room. Regular rates: $260 to $530 per couple per night.

The Waldorf-Astoria, 100 East 50th St., New York, NY 10022 (tel. 212/355-3000; reservations: toll free 800/HILTONS). Everything in this Hilton Hotel–chain flagship seems larger than life—even the plush, marble-pillared main lobby is introduced by a smaller lobby that welcomes the visitor with ethereal harp music. Actually, the Waldorf-Astoria is two hotels: From the 20th floor up, it becomes the more expensive Waldorf Towers, with prices beginning at $285 per couple per night. The Waldorf-Astoria's elegant rooms are nice and big themselves—with comfortable mauve European decor, enormous marbled bathrooms, and wonderful views of Park Avenue—and the entire place recently underwent a $110-million restoration. The Waldorf's famous restaurants are an international potpourri of moods, and include the glamorous art deco Cocktail Terrace and the Bull and Bear

CENTRAL PARK

1. Arsenal
2. Wollman Rink
3. Dairy
4. Chess and Checkers
5. Carousel
6. Delacorte Clock
7. Children's Zoo
8. Zoo
9. Tavern on the Green
10. The Mall
11. Naumburg Bandshell
12. Frick Museum
13. Bethesda Fountain
14. Cherry Hill Fountain
15. Loeb Boathouse
16. New-York Historical Society
17. American Museum of Natural History
18. Hayden Planetarium
19. Shakespeare Gardens
20. Delacorte Theater
21. Swedish Cottage
22. Metropolitan Museum of Art

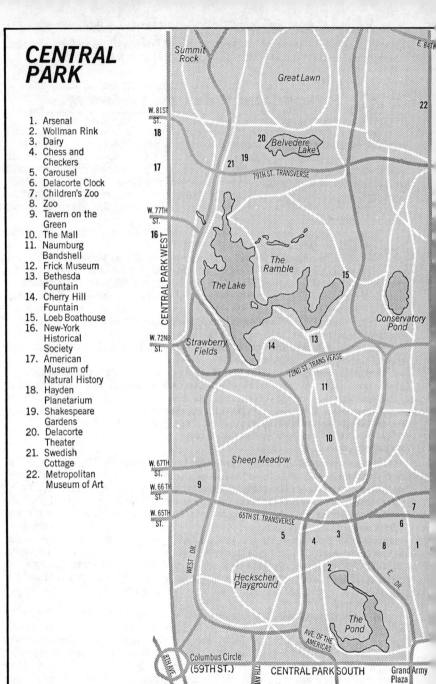

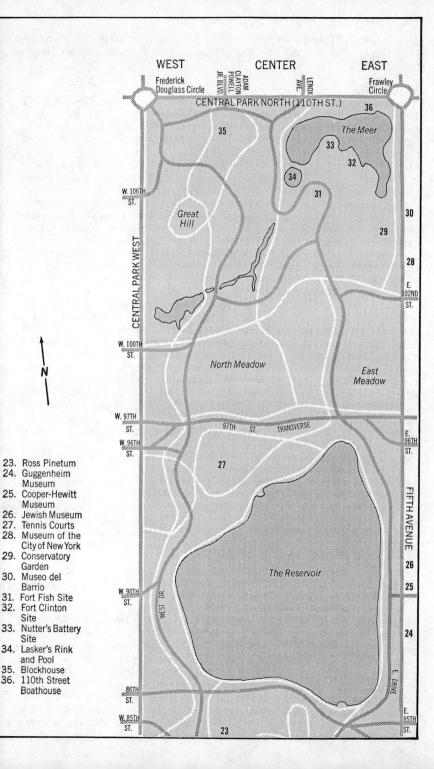

WEST   CENTER   EAST

Frederick Douglass Circle   ADAM CLAYTON POWELL JR. BLVD.   LENOX AVE.   Frawley Circle

CENTRAL PARK NORTH (110TH ST.)

36

The Meer

35

33

32

34

31

W. 106TH ST.

Great Hill

30

29

28

E. 102ND ST.

W. 100TH ST.

N

North Meadow

East Meadow

CENTRAL PARK WEST

W. 97TH ST.

97TH   ST.   TRANSVERSE

E. 96TH ST.

W. 96TH ST.

27

23. Ross Pinetum
24. Guggenheim Museum
25. Cooper-Hewitt Museum
26. Jewish Museum
27. Tennis Courts
28. Museum of the City of New York
29. Conservatory Garden
30. Museo del Barrio
31. Fort Fish Site
32. Fort Clinton Site
33. Nutter's Battery Site
34. Lasker's Rink and Pool
35. Blockhouse
36. 110th Street Boathouse

FIFTH AVENUE

26

The Reservoir

25

W. 90TH ST.

WEST DR.

24

E. DRIVE

86TH ST.

E. 85TH ST.

W. 85TH ST.

23

254 □ FROMMER'S HONEYMOON DESTINATIONS

steak restaurant. Honeymoon package: None. Standard rates: $210 to $640 per couple per night. Weekend rates start at $170 per couple per night, including continental breakfast.

MODERATE

New York's chicest new hotel, **Morgans,** 237 Madison Ave., New York, NY 10016 (tel. 212/686-0300; reservations: toll free 800/334-3408), is a study in tasteful simplicity. From the smartly tailored clerks and bellhops to the clean, well-lighted rooms, everything about Morgans is *just so.* Decorated in pastels and grays, the small, quiet midtown hotel has gone all out to assure that its rooms look nothing like those of any other commercial hotel. For example, you'll find a black toothbrush in your black-and-white bathroom with a clear Plexiglas shower door; instead of bedspreads, beds are covered with comforters made from Brooks Brothers cotton shirting material; and all rooms have window seats. Although the hotel offers no special honeymoon packages, it is small enough that the staff will treat newlyweds to a complimentary bottle of champagne and special care. All rooms come with fresh flowers, complimentary continental breakfast, the *New York Times* delivered to your door, complimentary admission to the Palladium (one of New York's popular clubs), audio and video cassette recorders (and use of the hotel's extensive video library), a refrigerator, and full turn-down service. Daily rates are from $235 per couple, and a weekend rate of $145 per couple per night is available.

A very romantic and beautiful hotel, **The Barbizon,** 140 East 63rd St., New York, NY 10021 (tel. 212/838-5700, or toll free 800/223-1020), is designed to complement the building that houses it, a Manhattan landmark built in 1927. The hotel has an interesting past, having been a women's residence hotel. Grace Kelly and Liza Minnelli were just a few of the young ladies who stayed here while waiting to make it big in the Big City. Today, completely refurbished, and decorated in various shades of pink and ochre, the Barbizon's rooms are intimate yet relaxing, and reflect the soothing charms of the early-20th-century Barbizon school of Impressionist painting. Surrounding the marbled lobby is a small shopping pavilion, the Barbizon Restaurant, and Cafe Barbizon, all designed to combine European elegance with American activity (Bloomingdale's, for instance, is just a few blocks away). Honeymoon package: None. Standard rates: $130 to $190 per couple per night. The weekend package offers rooms for as little as $105 per couple per night.

New York's Murray Hill neighborhood still contains many fine 19th-century brownstones. The 248-room **Shelburne Murray Hill,** 303 Lexington Ave., New York, NY 10019 (tel. 212/246-1300, or toll free 800/637-8483), evokes the Victorian era from the moment you walk in the door and take in the lobby's Persian rugs, antique furnishings, and crystal chandeliers. The rooms themselves are quite large by New York standards, and are furnished in extremely comfortable grandmotherly elegance. All the rooms and suites contain surprisingly large walk-in kitchens, and many also have balconies you can walk out on. The hotel is also close to Grand Central Station and the Madison and Fifth Avenue shopping districts. Honeymoon package: None. Standard rates: $190 to $210 per couple per night. Weekend rates range from $105 to $130 per couple per night.

Lyden Gardens, 215 East 64th St., New York, NY 10021 (tel. 212/355-1230, or toll free 800/637-8483). Located on a quiet, dignified Upper East Side street, this little-known hotel is apparently protected from public acclaim by its regular guests, who probably wish to keep it to themselves. Walking into any of the rooms, you'll be amazed at their size and comfort, with large sofas and dining room tables that seem more appropriate in a home than in a hotel room. The decor is tasteful and relaxed, and the afternoon light filters pleasantly into most rooms. All Lyden Gardens rooms contain kitchens so fully equipped that you'll be tempted to eat all your meals in the hotel; it seems a perfect place to be alone together in. Honeymoon package: None. Standard rates: $185 to $215 per couple per night. Weekend rates run $110 to $130 per couple per night

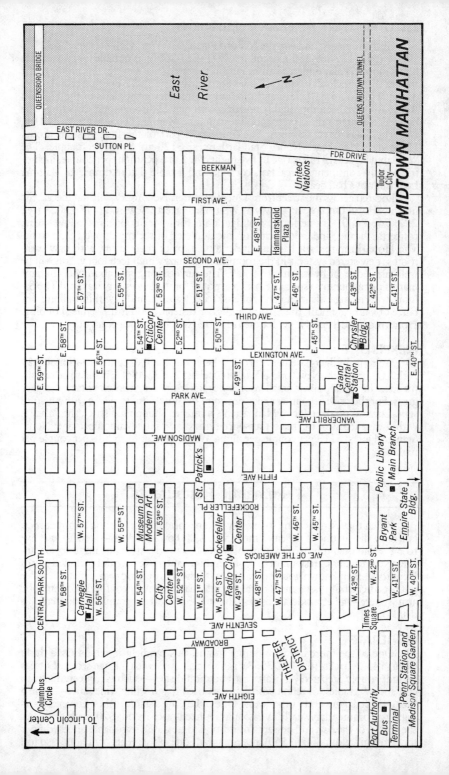

Glittery, glossy, and *big,* the **Milford Plaza,** 270 West 45th St., New York, NY 10036 (tel. 212/869-3600, or toll free 800/221-2690), is notable for two aspects honeymooners may find irresistible: First, it's located smack-dab in the middle of the theater district, close to Sardi's, Times Square, and the TKTS booth. Second, most of the Milford's 1,310 clean and modern rooms offer great views of the Hudson River. All have been thoroughly updated with new bathrooms and carpeting. The hotel also contains three pretty good restaurants: Mamma Leone's, Celebrity Deli, and The Stage Door Canteen. The property is part of the Best Western group. Honeymoon package: None. Standard rates: $120 to $165 per couple. The "Lullabuy" package offers one to five nights for $110 per night per couple, including a daily continental breakfast, cocktail, and a table d'hôte dinner at Mamma Leone's (not a bad deal).

Located across the street from Lincoln Center, New York's cultural mecca, the no-frills **Hotel Empire,** Broadway at West 63rd Street, New York, NY 10023 (tel. 212/265-7400), is a perfect low-budget hotel for honeymooners who love opera, concerts, theater, and enjoy being on the doorstep of the trendy West Side scene. The Hotel Empire itself has just undergone a major renovation, with new bathrooms, new stereo systems in the rooms, and a snazzy high-tech lobby. You will be well taken care of by its attentive staff. The surrounding neighborhood contains many fine restaurants (such as Fiorello's, noted for its delicious pizzas, and The Saloon, with its gigantic menu and roller-skating waiters), and is within walking distance of Carnegie Hall, the Broadway theater district, and Fifth Avenue shopping. Honeymoon package: None. Rates: $110 to $180 per couple per night.

INEXPENSIVE

We're in budget-basement territory here, but the **Palace International,** 429 Park Avenue South, New York, NY 10016 (tel. 212/532-4860), is still to be recommended for clean, albeit small rooms decorated in very contemporary designer grays. For the price, it's rather a nice deal, and the hotel aims to please with a helpful staff. Located on the edge of Manhattan's midtown shopping district, the Palace is within easy access of the main transportation routes. Honeymoon package: None. Standard rates: $115 per couple per night. Weekend rates from $88 per couple per night.

4. Romantic Restaurants

When they're not eating to live—you can grab a decent hot dog on any corner, or a tasty slice in one of the city's more than 1,000 pizza parlors—New Yorkers live to eat. From quaint bistros to unusual ethnic discoveries to luxurious four-star cuisine, New York has a restaurant for you. In this chapter, we have not included any of New York's well-known gourmet palaces with the statospheric prices; instead, we've put together a tasty assortment of restaurants that offer excellent food and romantic atmosphere—all at moderate prices (about $45 to $80 per couple for dinner, plus drinks).

MODERATE

One of the more intimate dining rooms, this candlelit jewel, **Le Café de la Gare,** 143 Perry St. (tel. 242-3553), is a special Greenwich Village secret. Entrées include simply prepared yet hearty fish and meat dishes—such as trout stuffed with cod and vegetables, or rabbit with cabbage, bacon, and white wine sauce—from a menu that changes every other week. One of Le Café's staple dishes, however, is its highly recommendable garlicky cassoulet. A fixed-price menu ($20) includes soup, the special of the day, and dessert. In addition to Le Café's reasonable prices (dinner for two runs about $50 to $60), the restaurant doesn't serve its own liquor, so feel

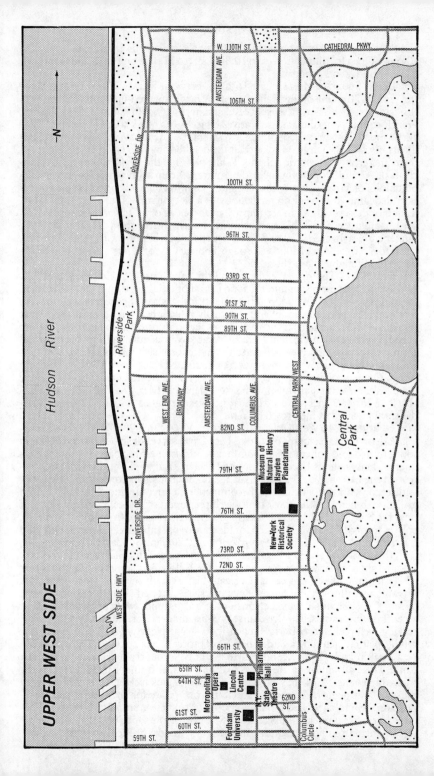

UPPER WEST SIDE

—N—

Hudson River

WEST SIDE HWY.

RIVERSIDE DR.

Riverside Park

RIVERSIDE DR.

WEST END AVE.

BROADWAY

AMSTERDAM AVE.

COLUMBUS AVE.

CENTRAL PARK WEST

Central Park

Columbus Circle

W. 110TH ST.

CATHEDRAL PKWY.

106TH ST.

100TH ST.

96TH ST.

93RD ST.

91ST ST.

90TH ST.

89TH ST.

82ND ST.

79TH ST.

76TH ST.

73RD ST.

72ND ST.

66TH ST.

65TH ST.

64TH ST.

62ND ST.

61ST ST.

60TH ST.

59TH ST.

Museum of Natural History

Hayden Planetarium

New-York Historical Society

Metropolitan Opera

Lincoln Center

N.Y. State Theatre

Philharmonic Hall

Fordham University

free to bring in your own bottle of wine. Not all credit cards are accepted, so ask in advance. Open for dinner from 6 to 10:30 p.m. (to 11 p.m. on Friday and Saturday). Closed Sunday and Monday.

Union Square Café, 21 East 16th St., between Broadway and Fifth Avenue (tel. 243-4020). One of the highlights of the newly spruced-up Union Square area, this handsome café—with its split-level architecture, warm lighting, fresh flowers, French country antiques, and attentive service—has quickly become one of New York's most highly regarded midrange restaurants. The restaurant takes fresh ingredients, many of which are purchased at the neighboring farmers' market, and turns them into creatively eclectic delights. While perusing the menu, nibble the lusty Sicilian olives and crunchy homemade croutons. Begin with a rich spaghettini alla puttanesca or a trusty, crusty duck confit, then move on to such toothsome entrées as grilled lamb steak, venison medallions, or a filet mignon of tuna. An unusual selection of dessert wines can accompany an apple tart or an Italian pear torte. A superb hamburger is available at lunchtime. Lunch entrées from $9.50 to $18.25, dinner entrées from $17.50 to $25.50. Open for lunch Monday through Saturday, noon to 3 p.m.; dinner Monday through Thursday, 6 to 11 p.m.; Friday and Saturday, 6 to midnight. Closed Sunday.

Omen, 113 Thompson St., between Prince and Spring, SoHo (tel. 925-8923). At this fine Japanese restaurant, the food is so subtle and good, and the rural Oriental ambience—lots of wood, bamboo, and brick—is so out of whack with the area that one feels both physically and spiritually replenished after a meal. And what meals! Since the menu makes no distinction between entrées and appetizers, you are encouraged to mix and match. Here are some recommended options: avocado and shrimp with miso sauce, seafood and chicken stew, spinach and shiitake mushrooms with sesame, scallops with lemon juice, or marinated chicken with white radish and carrot. Omen soup is a warming winter favorite, and the restaurant also serves very good sashimi. Wash it all down with sake or Japanese beer. Prix-fixe meals are available for $25 to $27 per person; à la carte items range from $6.50 to $22. Open Tuesday through Sunday, 5:30 to 10:30 p.m.

Quatorze, 240 West 14th St., Greenwich Village (tel. 206-7006). This charming Parisian-style restaurant on funky 14th Street serves delicious bistro cuisine in sophisticated and romantic surroundings—handsome tile floors, warm red banquettes, brass railings, and white-jacketed waiters. You might begin with local oysters on the half shell or the house salad, a traditional bistro concoction of chicory with bacon and hot vinaigrette. Recommended entrées include the half-chicken grilled with herbs or the consistently well-prepared fish dishes. For dessert, don't miss the house specialty, Chocolate Regal. Appetizers range from $5.50 to $9.50, entrées from $17.50 to $25. Open for lunch Monday through Friday, noon to 2:30 p.m.; dinner Monday through Saturday, 6 to 11:30 p.m.; Sunday, 5:30 to 11 p.m.

The Black Sheep, 344 West 11th St., West Greenwich Village (tel. 242-1010). Located about as far west as you can get in the Village, in a storefront on the corner of Washington Street, this casually elegant bistro recalls the time when New York was still a small town and horse-drawn carriages clattered along the cobblestoned streets. Classical guitar music strums in the background, while bright modern art accents the brick walls. The five-course prix-fixe dinner offers extremely good value, serving well-prepared country French food—and plenty of it. For openers, the crudité platter, including a garden harvest of broccoli, artichokes, and carrots, could be a meal in itself. Your second course might be a country pâté or green lasagna. Entrées take advantage of fresh seasonal offerings, and might include a perfectly roasted free-range chicken, sautéed yellowtail, or a pink rack of lamb, piquant with mustard and pepper. A green salad clears your palate for the dessert specials— perhaps a white chocolate mousse, chocolate truffle, or strawberry biscuit. Five-course prix-fixe dinner, from $25.50 to $34 per person. Open nightly for dinner, 6 to 11 p.m.; to midnight on Friday and Saturday; Sunday brunch, noon to 4 p.m.

Looking for restaurants in the theater district? Here are two that fill the bill.

Pietrasanta, 683 Ninth Ave. at 47th Street (tel. 265-9471), is one of those homey, family-style Italian trattorias where you feel that Mama—and maybe even Grandmama—is stirring the sauces in the kitchen. Start off with some garlicky fried ravioli, then choose among the extensive pasta, veal, and chicken dishes. The reasonable prices (about $6 to $8 for pastas) extend to the Italian and California offerings on the wine list, and portions are *molto grande*. A cozy dinner for two will run $25 to $40 per couple plus drinks. Open daily from 11:30 a.m. to 11 p.m. (to midnight on Friday and Saturday).

Down-home cooking, southern style—that's what you'll find at **Jezebel,** 630 Ninth Ave. at 45th Street (tel. 582-1045). The setting has all the front-porch welcome of Dixie, with white wicker furnishings, piano shawls casually draped here and there, and oodles of potted plants. If you're hankering for some soul food, this is the place: creamy she-crab soup, cornbread and biscuits, zingy fried chicken, and pork chops with gravy and okra. For dessert, try the pecan pie or banana pudding. Dinner for two, about $60 per couple plus drinks. Open for dinner from 5:30 p.m. to midnight.

Darbar, 44 West 56th St., between 5th and Sixth Avenues (tel. 432-7227). A passage to India right in midtown Manhattan—that describes this sumptuous dining room fit for a maharajah. Hand-woven tapestries, elaborate mirrors, and hammered copperwork adorn the walls; delicately carved wooden screens separate alcoves into intimate retreats. For an appetizer, try the murgh ki chaat (chicken with potatoes and onions in a pungent tamarind sauce) or one of the extraordinary breads (the crisp-puffed puris are lighter than air). Entrées cover specialties from the entire Subcontinent: Try one of the subtle chicken dishes from Kashmir or a torrid lamb vindaloo from Goa. Or order one of the succulent, moist dishes barbecued in the tandoor. Don't miss dessert, especially some of the cool, creamy homemade ice creams in exotic flavors such as mango. There's a complete lunch special for $20.95; dinner will run about $60 to $80 per couple plus drinks. Open daily for lunch, noon to 3 p.m.; dinner, 5:30 to 11 p.m.

The Gotham Bar and Grill, 12 East 12th St., between Fifth Avenue and University Place (tel. 620-4020), serves expensive but delicious and perfectly presented sausages, chops, and salads in a large, comfortably postmodern room that manages to evoke activity and intimacy simultaneously. The favorite restaurant of many food writers. Entrées from $26.50 to $32. Open for lunch Monday through Friday, noon to 2:30 p.m.; dinner Monday through Thursday, 6 to 10:30 p.m.; Friday and Saturday, 6 to 11:15 p.m.; Sunday, 5:30 to 9:45 p.m.

Oysters—raw and pan-roasted—are the specialty of the **Grand Central Oyster Bar and Restaurant** in the lower level of Grand Central Station (tel. 490-6650), a spacious room and adjacent masculine bar that remains the epitome of New York dignity and sophistication. Lunches and dinners begin at about $40 per couple and mount rapidly to the $80 to $100 range. Open Monday through Friday, 11:30 a.m. to 9:30 p.m.

INEXPENSIVE

Would you believe two 1¼-pound lobsters for $16.95? How about a bluefish filet for $6.75? And you also get all the salad you can eat, fresh garlic bread, fresh veggies, and spuds. **Cockeyed Clams,** 1678 Third Ave. at East 94th Street, Upper East Side (tel. 831-4121), keeps its prices low by operating its own fishing boats. (For landlubbers, they also raise their own cattle on a farm upstate, allowing the restaurant to offer a 16-ounce sirloin steak with all the trimmings for $11.95.) The decor is a funky nautical mixture of lobster traps, fish netting, operating room lights on ships, and who knows what else. The same management also operates **Hobeau's Restaurant,** 882 First Ave. at East 50th Street (tel. 421-2888), which has similar decor and prices. No reservations accepted, so be prepared for a wait. Open daily from 11 a.m. to 3 a.m.

Gigantic portions of Brazilian favorites are served in large tureens at **Cabana**

SOHO, LITTLE ITALY, AND CHINATOWN AREA

BLEECKER STREET

WEST HOUSTON STREET

KING STREET

CHARLTON STREET

VANDAM STREET

SPRING STREET

PRINCE STREET

SPRING STREET

SOHO

SULLIVAN STREET

THOMPSON STREET

AVENUE OF THE AMERICAS

VARICK STREET

HUDSON STREET

WEST BROADWAY

WOOSTER STREET

GREENE STREET

MERCER STREET

BROADWAY

CROSBY STREET

BROOME STREET

CANAL STREET

HOWARD STREET

DESBROSSES STREET

VESTRY STREET

LAIGHT STREET

GREENWICH STREET

HUBERT STREET

BEACH STREET

N. MOORE STREET

LISPENARD STREET

WALKER STREET

WHITE STREET

FRANKLIN STREET

FRANKLIN STREET

TRIBECA

LEONARD STREET

LAFAYETTE STREET

To Brooklyn Battery Tunnel

HARRISON STREET

JAY STREET

WORTH STREET

**LOWER
BROADWA**

Carioca, 123 W. 45th St., midtown (tel. 581-8088), an intimate wood-paneled up-stairs room filled with lovers, families, and local workers enjoying a late meal at the bar. Try the feijoda completa, Brazil's native dish, which combines delicious Portu-guese sausage and black beans. Before dinner, sample a caiparinja, a powerful and tasty concoction of crushed limes and cane liquor. Entrees $10.50 to $17.50. Open daily for lunch, noon to 3 p.m.; dinner, 4 to 11 p.m.

Known in the neighborhood as "the place with the line in front," the **Cucina Stagionale,** 275 Bleecker St., Greenwich Village (tel. 924-2707), modestly serves large portions of healthy Italian food at surprisingly low prices. The restaurant itself feels like an Italian grandmother's dining room, and as with most grandmothers, you'll have to bring your own wine since no liquor is served. Appetizers from $2 to $5.95, entrées $6.50 to $10.95. Open daily noon to midnight.

VIII

PENNSYLVANIA: THE POCONOS

1. PRACTICAL FACTS
2. ROMANTIC INTERLUDES
3. HONEYMOON HOTELS AND HIDEAWAYS

Welcome to the only area in the world where resorts devote themselves primarily to newlyweds and honeymoons—the Poconos.

Maybe it's the mountains, their pinnacles softened by towering oaks and hemlocks. Maybe the reason is the sparkling lakes, ranging from little ponds by the willows where ducks paddle, to wide blue expanses that invite vacationers to waterski or sail. Whatever the cause, the fact remains—the Poconos reign as "Honeymoon Capital of the World," attracting some 275,000 honeymoon couples annually from around the world.

What people commonly refer to as "the Poconos" is actually a collection of several mountains, part of the Appalachian chain, tucked in over 2,400 square miles in northeastern Pennsylvania. The region is bounded by the New York border to the north, the Delaware River to the east, and the Lehigh River on the southwest. The whole scenic area lies eminently close to major East Coast cities—about 75 miles from New York and 85 miles from Philadelphia. As you might expect, the name "Pocono" comes from an Indian word meaning "a stream between the mountains"—a very accurate description of the landscapes you'll encounter.

In a sense, the modern honeymoon was "invented" in the Poconos. Until the 1940s, only the very rich and famous could afford them. Then Rudolf Van Hoevenberg started promoting stays at his farm on the hill to newlyweds—and the whole loving tradition began. Nature provided the mountains and streams, but the Pocono resorts created the glamour and excitement. Each Pocono resort provides a self-contained world for honeymooners, with everything—from sports to nightclubs—right on the property. The Pocono properties not only invented the honeymoon, they created the concept of the "all-inclusive resort." The price you pay for your room covers everything: meals (some do not include lunch), social activities, nighttime entertainment, and all the sports facilities, equipment, and action a body can handle. Since the packages are all inclusive, planning a honeymoon budget is easy. You'll know how much your honeymoon will cost before you even leave home. Once you arrive at your honeymoon hotel, you can relax and enjoy the resort facilities completely, without worrying about how much it costs for a tennis game or Sunfish sail.

The sports options are especially extensive. In summer, lakes beckon for waterskiing, sailing, canoeing, and swimming. You can also swim and splash in large outdoor pools, many of which carry out the romantic motif by being shaped like wedding rings, bells, or hearts. Go bicycle riding along country roads, or play a round of golf—most resorts either have their own courses or can arrange for guests to play nearby. In winter, try snowmobiling, ice skating, or some of the best skiing in the East—both downhill and cross-country. Consider learning a new sport. Since the honeymoon package includes all equipment and instruction, it's a particularly good time to start. All year round, you can enjoy swimming, tennis, basketball, volleyball, and badminton, thanks to the modern indoor and outdoor facilities. You'll also find pool tables, video-game arcades, and health spas complete with state-of-the-art fitness equipment, whirlpools, saunas, and more.

Okay, enough about sports. What really makes the Poconos famous are the rooms, which are glittery, plush, and available with every amenity imaginable— saunas, sun lamps, and in-room swimming pools (too small for swimming laps, but ample for a splashing good time). And, of course, those famous heart-shaped tubs and whirlpools, with plenty of room for two people to luxuriate amid the bubbles. Beds are generally king-size, round or heart-shaped, surrounded by canopies, columns, and mirrors. Most rooms have a color TV, a log-burning fireplace, and a minirefrigerator where you can chill a bottle of champagne for a nightcap.

Razzle-dazzle nightlife adds more sophistication to a Poconos honeymoon. Each evening, there's a different show, from magicians and belly dancers to live bands, Las Vegas–style revues, maybe even a big-time headliner such as Tom Jones, Susan Anton, or Soupy Sales. At the disco, the band or theme varies each night— from New Wave to a down-home country hoedown.

Since most of the other resort guests are honeymooners also, the atmosphere is friendly and sociable. You'll find it easy to get to know other couples, since a social director makes introductions and arranges activities. Every day, the resorts schedule a full agenda: water polo, men's beauty contests, skeet-shooting instruction, plus competitions such as Trivial Pursuit or The Newlywed Game. Couples can join in the fun if they like, but there's never any pressure to participate.

Finally, a word about "Poconos people"—the folks who work at the resorts. Throughout the region, there's a long-term tradition of caring for guests with personal attention. The honeymoon hotels are still run by the families that founded them: the Wilkinses at the Caesars Resorts, the Fardas at the Summit, the Poalillos at Penn Hills, and Emil Wagner and Carl Martens at the Mount Airy properties. Many staff members have worked at the same hotels for years. Both the resort owners and the employees will do everything possible to assure your honeymoon happiness.

1. Practical Facts

GETTING THERE
The Poconos are easy to reach from throughout the United States.

By Air
Newark, Wilkes-Barre/Scranton, and Allentown are the main airports serving the region. Newark is a major hub, and airlines such as **United, American,** and **Continental** offer convenient nonstop and direct flights from the entire country. From the airport, all the honeymoon resorts can arrange ground transportation—even stretch limousines. Ask the resort for complete details when you or your travel agent make the room reservations.

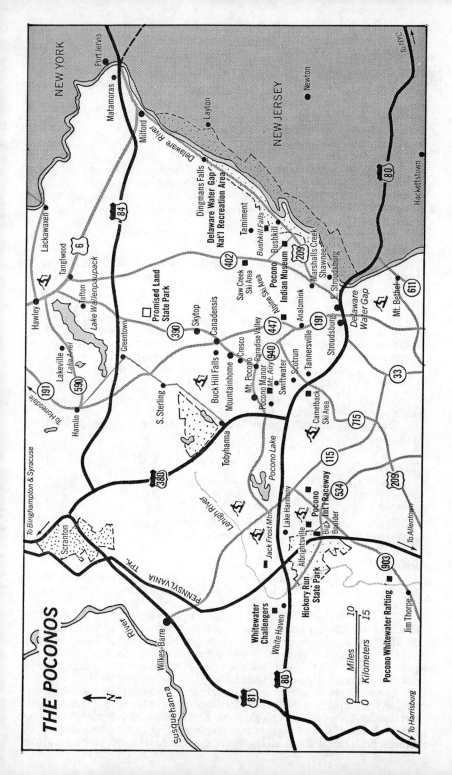

THE POCONOS

N

NEW YORK

Port Jervis
Matamoras
To NYC

Lackawaxen
Tanglwood
Hawley
Lakeville
Lake Ariel
Tafton
Lake Wallenpaupack

To Honesdale

Hamlin

Greentown

Promised Land State Park

S. Sterling

Tobyhanna

Pocono Lake

Lehigh River

Scranton

Wilkes-Barre

Susquehanna River

To Binghampton & Syracuse

PENNSYLVANIA TPK.

Whitewater Challengers

White Haven

Jack Frost Mtn.

Lake Harmony

Albrightsville

Hickory Run State Park

Pocono Whitewater Rafting

Jim Thorpe

To Harrisburg

Milford
Delaware River

Layton

Dingmans Falls
Delaware Water Gap Nat'l Recreation Area
Tamiment
Bushkill Falls
Bushkill
Marshalls Creek
Shawnee
Stroudsburg
E. Stroudsburg
Delaware Water Gap
Mt. Bethel

Saw Creek Ski Area
Alpine Ski Area
Pocono Indian Museum
Analomink

Skytop
Canadensis
Cresco
Paradise Valley
Mt. Pocono
Pocono Manor
Mt. Airy
Swiftwater
Scotrun
Tannersville
Buck Hill Falls
Mountainhome

Camelback Ski Area

Pocono Int'l Raceway
Big Boulder

NEW JERSEY

Newton

Hackettstown

To NYC

To Allentown

Miles   0   10
Kilometers   0   15

Interstate roads: 81, 80, 380, 84, 611, 402, 209, 191, 390, 940, 447, 33, 715, 115, 534, 903

By Car

The Pocono resorts are less than a two-hour drive from many East Coast cities. The main interstate highways are **Routes 80 and 84** from New York. From Philadelphia, take the Northeast Extension of the Pennsylvania Turnpike to **Route 209 east.**

By Bus

Greyhound/Trailways serves the area.

GETTING AROUND

Because the resorts are self-contained, you'll find practically everything you want right on the property. But to appreciate truly the scenic mountain region and explore the back country roads, you'll need a car. If you arrive by air, you can rent cars at both Allentown and Newark airports; rates run about $240 for six days, with unlimited mileage.

WEATHER

The climate resembles that of nearby New York and Philadelphia, but will be about 10° cooler because of the elevation.

CLOTHING

By day, choose casual activewear and sportswear. Jeans are best for rugged sports such as horseback riding or skiing, while sneakers see you through everything from tennis to hiking. For evening, dress ranges from calico shirts for country evenings to sequins for gala champagne dinners. Many resorts also plan special "theme nights" during the week—Hawaiian night, toga parties, etc. Ask about the schedule before you go; you might want to bring along something appropriate.

TIME

The Poconos are in the Eastern Time zone, and observe Daylight Saving Time in the summer.

TELEPHONES

The area code for the Poconos is 717.

TIPPING

To cover tips, a 15% service charge will generally be added to your hotel bill. If so, you will not have to tip hotel employees individually.

SHOPPING

First stop should probably be the gift boutique at your resort, which stocks items from all over the world: antiques, pewter candlesticks, wicker baskets, and cut crystal.

The region is also known for its antiques shops. Our number one favorite is the **Theo. B. Price Country Store** in Cresco, owned by Maryann and Micky Miller (tel. 595-2501). Out on the front porch, you'll be greeted by life-size soft sculptures and various tempting knickknacks. You could spend hours browsing through the quilted pillows ($22 to $40), baskets (some priced under $10), and magnificent carved swan and duck decoys (from $120).

Candles make popular honeymoon mementos; you can buy them for about 50% off regular prices at the **Pocono Candle Shop** (East Stroudsburg) and **American Candle** (Bartonsville) factory outlets. At the **Holley Ross Pottery,** on Route 191 in LaAnna, you can watch free pottery-making demonstrations Monday through Friday at 11 a.m. and 3:30 p.m., then browse through their selection of soup crocks, quiche dishes, ceramic cannisters, and other gifts. Open daily May through mid-December (tel. 676-3248).

Homemade candy is another treat. At **Callie's Candy Kitchen,** on Route 390 in Mountainhome (tel. 595-2280), the sweet smell of chocolate wafts into your nostrils the moment you walk in. It's a child's fantasy, with giant lollipops, gummy bears, peanut-butter ribbon candy, and more. Chocoholics should head straight for the Pocono Mountain Bark—dark, milk, or light chocolate laced with raisins, walnuts, coconut, or peanuts. The **Ella C. Ehrhardt General Store** in Newfoundland (no phone) sells old-fashioned penny candies—you'll have fun picking out an assortment.

Another good place to shop for gifts and souvenirs is **Memorytown, U.S.A.,** just off Route 940 in Mount Pocono. At the **Country Store,** you'll find homemade preserves, bags of spices, penny candies, pottery—even an antique spinning wheel. The **Red Corner Cupboard** carries dolls, brass items, carved wooden ducks ($20 to $30), cookie and muffin molds shaped like fruit and animals, and some captivating mechanical banks. Also stop by **Pocono Mineral and Gem** in Colony Village, south of Canadensis on Route 447. Here, the jewelry displays create the effect of underground caves, with fine pieces made from semiprecious stones such as amber, turquoise, amethyst, and malachite sparkling in the depths. Prices start around $20 and climb well over $100.

Also check out the nearby city of Stroudsburg, which is one of the factory-outlet capitals of the world. Savings run from 20% to 60%. For the widest selection, head over to the **Pocono Outlet Complex** at 9th and Ann Streets. Best bets include the **Stroud Handbag Outlet** for handbags, wallets, attaché cases, and leather goods, and **The Potting Shed** for silk and dried flowers, as well as houseplants. The **Workout ROM** features women's activewear, including a large selection of leotards and tights from Danskin. Whatever your sport, you'll find a shoe that fits at **Sneak Preview,** which carries sneakers by Pony, Converse, and Nike. In addition to ribbons, the **American Ribbon Factory Outlet** has a wide selection of baskets.

DINING OUT

Some of the Pocono resort honeymoon packages are Full American Plan (FAP), including breakfast, lunch, and dinner daily. Other resorts offer the Modified American Plan (MAP), including breakfast and dinner daily. Soda, wine, and cocktails are not included. See the individual resort listings for details.

Practically all the resorts offer free breakfast in bed daily, including specials such as Bloody Mary or champagne breakfasts. The three-course dinners are usually table d'hôte, giving you a choice among various selections for your appetizer, main course, and dessert. There are also theme dinners, such as Italian night with wine, international buffets, champagne dinners, Wild West barbecues, weiner roasts, and Hawaiian night, complete with leis and hula skirts. Most seating is at tables of from four to five honeymoon couples; you can also generally get a table for two if you prefer.

Since the Pocono honeymoon packages include meals, you will probably not be dining away from your resort. If you do go out, you'll find several absolutely top-notch restaurants in the area. **Fanucci's** on Route 611 in Swiftwater (tel. 839-7097) does terrific pasta, seafood, and veal dishes. Entrées for dinner priced from $10 to $18. Open daily from 4 to 11 p.m. Another favorite for Italian food is **Peppe's** in the Eagle Valley Mall near East Stroudsburg (tel. 421-4460). Try the cannelloni bolognese or the striped bass marechiare, a house specialty. Entrées from $8.75 to $22. Open daily for lunch, 11:30 a.m. to 2:30 p.m.; dinner, 5:30 to 10:30 p.m. **The Inn at Tannersville** on Route 611 (tel. 629-3131) is the place for thick, juicy, charbroiled steaks; prices range from $3.25 for a hamburger to $9.50 for an eight-ounce steak. Open daily from 10:30 a.m. to 2 a.m. For lobster, try the **Beaver House** at 1001 N. 9th St. in Stroudsburg (tel. 424-1020); you can choose your lobster from a tank out front, and they often have four-pounders. A complete dinner with a 1½-pound lobster runs $26.25. Open Monday through Saturday, 11:30 a.m. to 10:30 p.m.; Sunday, 1 to 8 p.m. At harvest time, stop at one of the many roadside stands for just-picked fruits and vegetables. They'll stay crisp and crunchy in the refrigerator in your room—or take some home as an edible souvenir of your honeymoon.

SPECIAL EVENTS

The Poconos pack in four full seasons of activity, and there are several annual events you should know about. Late May to early June is mountain laurel time, when the delicate pale-pink blossoms cover the hillsides and valleys. Many Pocono towns plan **Laurel Blossom Festivals** with fairs and crafts shows timed to coincide with the peak displays of the flowers. Late September through early November, the Poconos blaze into full fall foliage, with hues of crimson, orange, and gold. One of the most peaceful ways to view the spectacle is on a float trip along one of the region's rivers: the Delaware, Lehigh, or Lackawaxen. (See details under "Romantic Interludes," which follows.) The autumn is also harvest season, and many of the ski areas stage **Oktoberfests,** complete with German-style oompah bands, folk dancers, and Bavarian foods. From the last week in February through the first week in March, the **Pocono Winter Carnival** celebrates with ski races, skating parties, ice-skating exhibitions, torchlight ski parades, snow-sculpture contests, and more. Contact the **Pocono Mountains Vacation Bureau** (see address below) for a complete calendar of events.

HOW TO GET MARRIED IN THE POCONOS

If you want to combine your honeymoon with a Poconos wedding, here's how to do it. Both parties must be over the age of 18. You both must appear at the Prothonotary Office at the Monroe County Courthouse at the same time. Bring with you the signed results of your blood tests (which can be performed in your home state), as well as a certified copy of the final divorce decree, if either of you was previously married. There is a three-day waiting period before the license can be issued; the fee is $15. Contact the **Monroe County Courthouse,** Stroudsburg, PA 18360 (tel. 717/424-5100).

FOR FURTHER INFORMATION

Contact the **Poconos Mountain Vacation Bureau,** Box PR, 1004 Main St., Stroudsburg, PA 18360 (tel. 717/421-5791).

---

2. Romantic Interludes

Here are some special pastimes for lovers at and around the various Pocono resorts.

Most of the resorts have **photographers** who can snap candid pictures for your honeymoon scrapbook. Favorite poses include embracing in the woods, or toasting with champagne at a candlelight dinner. Most fun of all: Don bathing suits, pour in some bubble bath, start running the water, and call the photographer—he or she will photograph you up to your necks in bubbles in your heart-shaped tub. Five-by-seven color photos cost about $8 each.

The **resort gift boutique** makes a great place to purchase your honeymoon souvenirs. Best bets: his 'n' hers sweatshirts imprinted with the resort name, or a stuffed animal for a bedroom mascot.

What better way to savor the beautiful Pocono scenery than on a **picnic lunch?** Head for **Bushkill Falls,** called "the Niagara of Pennsylvania," where sparkling waters tumble down a 100-foot cliff and then race through a boulder-strewn gorge. It's on Route 209 in Bushkill. Open daily from April through November, from 9 a.m.

to 5 p.m. (tel. 588-6682). Closed in winter. Or visit the **Delaware Water Gap.** Perhaps the best-known landmark in the Poconos, it is a spectacular 1,200-foot gorge cut by the Delaware River through the Kittatinny Mountains. Explore the various hiking trails and take photos from the scenic overlooks. You'll find parking and a Visitor Center just east of Stroudsburg on Route 80.

The **Lehigh** and the **Delaware,** two of the mightiest rivers in the East, course through the Poconos. The Lehigh is more challenging, with several roiling Class III rapids for thrilling white-water rafting; the Delaware generally offers more tranquil runs perfect for canoeists. White-water rafting trips, including rafts, paddles, and experienced guide, run about $50 to $75 per couple. Contact **Jim Thorpe River Adventures** in Jim Thorpe (tel. 325-2570), or **Whitewater Challengers** in White Haven (tel. 443-9532). Both also offer peaceful float trips—excellent for viewing fall foliage. For canoe rentals as well as raft trips, contact **Kittatinny Canoes** in Dingman's Ferry (tel. 828-2338), owned and operated by the Jones family for over 32 years.

From about mid-April through November, theater-goers flock to the Poconos for **summer-stock productions** of long-run Broadway hits such as *West Side Story, Evita,* and *My Fair Lady.* Check out the performance schedules at **Shawnee Playhouse** in Shawnee-on-Delaware (tel. 421-1500) and **Pocono Playhouse** in Mountainhome (tel. 595-7456). Ticket prices run about $15.50 to $18.50 per person.

Each season, **Pocono Raceway** in Long Pond stages a calendar of major events for NASCAR stock cars, motorcycles, Indy cars—even big-rig truck races. Races are usually held on Sundays, admission $35 to $150 per person, depending on the event. For a season schedule, contact Pocono Raceway, Box 500, Long Pond, PA 18334 (tel. 717/646-2300; toll free 800/RACEWAY) for ticket information.

If you want to try your own hand at the wheel, head over to **Pocono Action Park** in Tannersville (tel. 629-4411). Strap on your seat belt in the $12,000 Lola T-506s, wait until the light tree flashes green, and then zoom off, testing your skills and reflexes on a half-mile course of hairpin turns and straightaways ($2.50 per lap). Pocono Action Park also features bumper boats, baseball batting cages, and a "Water World" with twister flumes and water slides. Open daily in season Monday through Friday, 11 a.m. to 5 p.m.; Saturday, 11 a.m. to 6 p.m.; Sunday noon to 6 p.m. Admission is free; you just pay for the rides.

With 16 major **ski areas** and over 120 different trails, the Poconos is one of the East's major centers for downhill skiing. All have extensive snow-making facilities. **Camelback** is the largest area, with 25 trails and 11 lifts. Other choices include **Big Boulder, Jack Frost,** and **Shawnee,** all open for night skiing as well. **Alpine Mountain** in Analomink (tel. 595-2150), with a 500-foot vertical drop, has four lifts, including a quad chair, with 14 trails and slopes for all levels, from novices to experts.

Horseback ride along pine-fringed mountain trails—it's a leisurely way to appreciate the scenery. Some of the resorts have stables on the premises; at others, the hotel social director can arrange trail rides. Most resort honeymoon packages do not include horseback riding, which costs about $16.50 per person for one hour in the saddle. Among the riding stables you can contact: **El-J Riding Stable** near Mount Pocono (tel. 839-8725), **Carsons** in Mt. Pocono (tel. 839-9841), **Shawnee Stables** in Shawnee-on-Delaware (tel. 421-9763), and **R.J.D. Stables** in Lake Ariel near Hamlin (tel. 698-6996).

---

3. Honeymoon Hotels and Hideaways

Choosing where to stay is probably the most important decision you can make when planning a Pocono honeymoon. Look for a place that features your favorite sports—and fulfills your heartfelt romantic fantasies.

The Pocono honeymoon packages are all-inclusive: The price of the room you choose determines the total cost of the honeymoon package. The basic honeymoon package runs six days/five nights, with arrival on Sunday and departure on Friday. Other packages are usually available; check with the specific resort for details. Make reservations early: The most popular rooms are the most luxurious ones, and these often book up a year in advance. Most resorts require a deposit of $75 to $100 with your reservation. During the winter, some resorts offer special reduced rates; ask your travel agent.

Rates quoted do not include the 6% Pennsylvania state tax, which will be added to your bill. A 15% service charge to cover gratuities will also generally be added.

Some of the resorts are owned and operated by the same company. Since accommodations and honeymoon packages are often similar at all hotels under the same ownership, we have grouped them together.

CAESARS RESORTS

These four resorts have all the glitter and glamour of their sister hotels in Las Vegas and Atlantic City. Over the past three years, the company has spent some $25 million refurbishing the properties and adding new facilities. As the star attraction, all four resorts feature the ultradeluxe "Champagne Towers." These multilevel suites have perhaps the ultimate fantasy—a whirlpool bath shaped like a champagne glass, with plenty of room for both of you and oodles of bubbles. The suite also has a heart-shaped swimming pool, sauna and massage table, combination shower/steam bath for two, round king-size bed, fireplace, and sunken living room with cushy furnishings done up in shades of burgundy, mauve, and pink.

Key A Round Club: No matter which Caesars Pocono resort you stay at, you are welcome to use the facilities at all four, giving you a chance to experience their different atmospheres. Just show your room key to identify yourselves as Caesars guests. To get around, guests at Pocono Palace, Paradise Stream, and Brookdale can hop the "Caesars Chariot" shuttle that runs among these three resorts.

Honeymoon package: At all four resorts, if you stay for four nights or more, you'll receive a bottle of champagne, a decanter of bubble bath, a honeymoon photo album, and a fire log. At certain times of the year, the package also includes free ski-lift tickets for two. And every morning, you can have breakfast in bed—free. Ask about Caesars' dazzling new rooms scheduled to debut in spring 1990.

Cove Haven, Lakeville, PA 18438 (reservations: tel. 717/226-2101, or toll free 800/233-4141). "We give you three big A's—for atmosphere, accommodations, and activities," one honeymoon couple wrote in the guest book at Cove Haven, the flagship of Caesars resorts in the Poconos. Their comments accurately describe the unique features of this sophisticated resort in a countryside setting. The atmosphere is very secluded, about a 40-minute drive north of the other three Caesars properties. Thanks to its location on the shores of Lake Wallenpaupack, Pennsylvania's largest lake, Cove Haven is a perfect choice for couples who love water sports: waterskiing, speed-boat rides, paddleboats, and sailing are all on the agenda. In fact, whatever your favorite sports activity you can probably find it somewhere on the 110-acre property. On land, you can tee off on the driving range, play tennis, or go bicycle riding. In winter, you can enjoy downhill skiing, snowmobiling, tobagganing, as well as ice skating in the indoor Ice Palace. Even when it snows, you can enjoy the semitropical paradise of the indoor Harbourside Health Club with a heated pool; whirlpools surrounded by grottos, plants, and waterfalls; exercise equipment; saunas; steam baths; tanning tents; and a game room. In the year-round Sports Palace, you'll find three tennis courts, four racquetball courts, electronic games, and bocce ball—remember, all equipment (even the balls) is included.

If you love nightlife as well as the sporting life, the million-dollar Champagne Palace Nightclub features spectacular light shows, multilevel stages, a large dance floor, and live entertainment seven nights a week.

Cove Haven is the largest of the Caesars Pocono resorts, but it retains a close-knit, personable feeling. This is the kind of place where the staff—everyone from the bar waitress to the power-boat captain—will soon greet you by name. But your best friend will probably be "Honest Phil," the long-time social director. Phil has the knack of making people feel welcome, and he helps the different honeymoon couples get to know each other. And honeymoon history buffs will be intrigued to learn that the heart-shaped tub was "invented" at Cove Haven in 1963 by Morris Wilkins.

Accommodations: Cove Haven offers a wide range of rooms priced to appeal to all pocketbooks. Although the rooms do not have lake views, the sumptuous furnishings establish them as cozy love nests. All accommodations have color cable TV and air conditioning. The rates quoted are Modified American Plan (MAP) including breakfast and dinner daily. The Champagne Towers: Needless to say, the duplex champagne glass you see the instant you walk in the door gets all the attention, but the plush upholstery and thick carpeting will make you feel pampered, even when you're not up to your neck in bubbles. Six days/five nights: $1,395 per couple. The Garden of Eden–Apple: You get a triangular private pool surrounded by mirrors and wall murals, as well as your own sauna. In the sunken bedroom, you'll find a round king-size bed with mirrored headboard, and a fireplace to complete the romantic mood. Six days/five nights: $1,180 per couple. The Ultra-Modern: These split-level accommodations are absolutely huge, featuring a sunken living room with log-burning fireplace, round king-size bed surrounded by mirrors, and a sunken, Roman-style whirlpool bath. Six days/five nights: $890 per couple. Many different rooms and lengths of stay are available.

The **Paradise Stream Resort,** Mount Pocono, PA 18344 (reservations: tel. 717/226-2101, or toll free 800/233-4141), provides elegance in a woodland setting. Throughout the resort, a Garden of Eden theme predominates. You can get snacks at the Poison Apple Deli, and every night there's top-caliber entertainment in the Red Apple Lounge and Nightclub.

The resort offers a full range of sports. Go swimming in the outdoor Olympic-size pool, play tennis, or get back to nature with a canoeing, fishing, or paddleboating excursion on Lake Eden. During the winter, you can zoom off on a snowmobile, ice skate on the pond out front, or head for the nearby ski slopes (you each get a free lift ticket). All year round, you can stay in shape at the new Carnivale Racquet and Swim Club, with new indoor pool and racquetball courts. Also new: the exotic Parrot Lounge and Jungle Cafe, lush with a tropical motif.

Accommodations: Paradise Stream's low-rise units are nicely spread out over the property. You have many different rooms to choose from, including the Champagne Towers. All have color cable TV and air conditioning. Rates quoted are MAP, including breakfast and dinner daily. Champagne Towers: Glass walls and mirrors maximize the views in this four-level townhouse design with the champagne glass–shaped whirlpool. Six days/five nights: $1,395 per couple. Garden of Eden–Apple: All private for you—a swimming pool heated to a cozy 90°, living room, and sunken bedroom with a round king-size bed surrounded by a mirrored headboard. Six days/five nights: $1,180 per couple. Lakeside Villa: Your own private cottage on the edge of Lake Eden. Outside, your private balcony overlooks the shimmering waters; inside, there's a round king-size bed, a cathedral ceiling . . . and a heart-shaped tub for two. Six days/five nights: $990 per couple. Many other rooms and packages are also available.

Pocono Palace, Marshalls Creek, PA 18335 (reservations: tel. 717/226-2101, or toll free 800/233-4141). The long driveway winds past pine trees to this intimate resort, nestled in a country club–like setting on 350 green, rolling acres. Here the outlook is definitely sporting. There's a regulation nine-hole golf course right on the property. And you never pay any greens fees, no matter how many times you play. You can also hone your skills on the driving range or putting green—and there's an excellent pro shop. Tennis players will want to round up another couple for a game of mixed doubles. Water sports are right on your doorstep, since the resort surrounds 25-acre Echo Lake—a perfect choice for waterskiing, speed-boat rides, paddleboat cruises, or sailing. If you want to relax, settle into one of the chaise longues on the private sandy beach. In addition to the lake, you can swim in the new outdoor heated pool, or soak your cares away in the warm, bubbling whirlpool. And if your honeymoon fantasies include horseback riding through the woods, Pocono Palace has its own stable of well-schooled mounts. In winter, the undulating golf course turns into a snowmobiler's dream, and there are new cross-country trails. Downhill racers each receive a free lift ticket for the nearby slopes.

Carrying out the Roman theme, the resort has the Noshorium for snacks, and the Gladiator Lounge and Nightclub for dazzling evening entertainment. When you want to work out, head for the Natatorium, with an indoor heated pool, state-of-the-art gym with Universal exercise equipment, and tanning machines.

Accommodations: In this woodsy setting, you'll find many different room choices, all with air conditioning and color TV. Rates quoted are MAP, including breakfast and dinner daily. Champagne Towers: After a full day in the great out-doors, you'll love your great indoors, with the champagne glass–shaped whirlpool for complete relaxation. Six days/five nights: $1,395 per couple. Fantasy Apple: Your own spacious triplex apartment, with a glass skylight illuminating your own private pool. A circular stairway leads to the round king-size bed, and you have a private balcony overlooking the woods and Echo Lake. Six days/five nights: $1,180 per couple. Capri Suite: Just for you: a round king-size bed, log-burning fireplace, and a heart-shaped whirlpool bath surrounded by eye-catching floor-to-ceiling mirrors. Six days/five nights: $890 per couple. Many other rooms and packages are also available.

Brookdale on the Lake, Scotrun, PA 18355 (reservations: tel. 717/233-4141, or toll free 800/233-4141). When you honeymoon at Brookdale, you'll feel as though you're staying at a private country estate. The resort encompasses over 250 acres of woodlands and meadows, all centered around storybook Brookdale Lake, a tranquil spot where swans glide among the willows. You can sail, canoe, set off in paddleboats, or stroll hand in hand along the shore and across a covered bridge. For a relaxing time, borrow some fishing rods—the lake is well stocked with trout. Then sun yourselves on the large outdoor patio deck around the heated pool that looks out over the marina and lake. And tennis players would have trouble imagining a more attractive setting than the two lakeside courts. In winter, explore the woods aboard snowmobiles or head over to Brookdale's own Frosty Mountain—perfect for tobogganing. Several major downhill ski areas are nearby, and each of you gets a free lift ticket. After a day on the slopes, jump into the heated pool at the indoor spa with floor-to-ceiling windows facing the lake, or warm yourselves through with a sauna. Recently, Brookdale has added a new, indoor ice-skating rink, expanded the dining room and gift shop, and created a new, million-dollar nightclub. The atmosphere at Brookdale is very friendly—after you've been here a day or so, the staff will greet you by name. Saxy Sal, the social director for over seven years and leader of the house band, really knows how to get people to mingle, and you'll soon be teaming up with other couples for volleyball or softball.

Accommodations: Whether you crave elegant sophistication or country charm, you'll find accommodations to please at Brookdale. Rates are MAP, including breakfast and dinner daily. Champagne Towers: What's your fantasy? Curling in front of a blazing fire . . . splashing in your own heart-shaped pool . . . or sipping champagne while lolling in a whirlpool shaped like a champagne glass? You can do it all here. Six days/five nights: $1,395 per couple. Lakeview Villa: This huge sumptuous apartment (almost like a four-room suite) is done up in muted tones of burgundy and champagne, with brass accents adding an art deco touch. Your private balcony overlooks the lake, and there's a whirlpool bath for two surrounded by mirrors galore. Six days/five nights: $990 per couple. Brooklodge Suite: Newly redesigned, these accommodations have very sophisticated, modern furnishings, decorated in warm beige and taupe tones. The rooms feature round beds with mirrored headboards and whirlpool baths, and are conveniently located in the main lodge building. Six days/five nights: $890 per couple. Many other rooms and packages are also available.

MOUNT AIRY/STRICKLAND'S/POCONO GARDENS

These three resorts, all under the same ownership, all offer different ambiences and accommodations. Guests at any one have access to the restaurants and extensive facilities at the others. If you love lavish shows and entertainment, take note that hotel guests pay no cover charge to attend the nightclub shows starring famous headliners at Mount Airy Lodge.

Honeymoon package: If you stay at least four nights, you get free skiing, equipment, and instruction; free golf, cart, and equipment rental; and free horseback riding, depending on weather conditions.

Mount Airy Lodge, Mount Pocono, PA 18344 (reservations: tel. 717/839-8811, or toll free 800/441-4410). Julio Iglesias, Sergio Franchi, Jack Jones, Corbett Monica, Bobby Rydell—these are just a few of the big-name stars that regularly appear at Mount Airy Lodge, a sumptuous 1,500-acre sports and entertainment complex in the heart of the Poconos. The sports facilities are extensive, including a challenging 18-hole golf course. There are two Olympic-size pools: one outdoors on the sundeck, the other indoors in the sports palace, which also has a health club, ice rink, and massage rooms. You can also get wet in the sparkling lake, the setting for waterskiing, sailing, paddleboating, plus sheer relaxation on a white-sand beach. Try out your serve on 21 tennis courts, indoors and out (they're open 24 hours a day). Or hit the trails—the lush country paths surrounding Mount Airy—on horseback or bicycle. Still want more? Add in volleyball, basketball, archery, billiards, Ping-Pong, and skeet shooting—you'll have trouble fitting it all in. Come winter, there are seven ski slopes right on the property, with two double-chair lifts, and complete snowmaking. You can also cross-country ski, snowmobile, or ice skate.

At night, curtain's up—and Mount Airy turns on its full glamour. After a full-course dinner, check out the talent lineup in the Crystal Room, then move to the disco beat in the Club Suzanne. Then, perhaps a nightcap in the intimate Royal Lounge, before heading back to your suite.

Accommodations: Mount Airy gives you one of the widest choices of any Pocono resort, and several other rooms and packages are also available. Rates quoted are FAP, including breakfast, lunch, and dinner daily. The Palace Suite: This suite features one of the largest in-room pools in the Poconos, with a totally private garden patio just outside the sliding-glass doors. There are also a valentine-red whirlpool tub lavishly backdropped by mirrors, Swedish sauna, drapery-framed round king-size bed, fireplace, and soft blue colors to create a seductive mood. Six days/five nights: $1,265 per couple. The Monarch: Recently redone in pale slate-blues and dusty pinks, the Monarch charms honeymooners with its circular king-size bed, heart-shaped whirlpool tub, oak-mantel fireplace, and very contemporary glass-and-chrome-accented living room. Six days/five nights: $1,155 per couple. Golden Suites: Very regal indeed, with a gold crown supporting the canopy over the king-size platform bed, sunken heart-shaped tub, crystal chandelier, French-style furnishings, and gold wall coverings. Six days/five nights: $1,075 per couple.

Strickland's Mountain Inn and Cottages, Mount Pocono, PA 18344 (reservations: tel. 717/839-7155, or toll free 800/441-4410). It's a woodland setting, 400 acres dense with evergreens and rhododendrons. Many of the accommodations are built of wood and glass, and snuggle into the slopes like ski chalets; decks and skylights take advantage of the sunshine and views. In addition, Strickland's roster of sports activities will tempt you into the Great Outdoors. You have a choice of three outdoor heated pools, or there's a tranquil private lake just right for paddleboats. Go bike riding or horseback riding, play a few sets of tennis, or challenge each other to archery, handball, or bocce. Try to improve your handicap on the nine-hole golf course—or aim for a hole-in-one at miniature golf. In winter, let it snow, because Strickland's offers sledding, snowmobiling, and cross-country skiing. For downhill skiing, you have full use of Mount Airy's extensive lifts and slopes. Strickland's also has a large indoor sports pavilion for tennis, racquetball, ice skating, and roller skating, as well as a comfortably heated indoor pool. Pinball wizards can try their skills on a slew of video games. With all this activity, you'll really appreciate the meals served in Strickland's dining room, where huge hearths and stained-glass windows add to the hearty mountain atmosphere. After dinner, though, you'll feel as if you're in the Big City, with entertainment by live bands or a New York–style revue.

Accommodations: Many of the most attractive accommodations harmonize with the mountain setting, using natural materials such as fieldstone, cedar, and redwood to create a mood of alpine elegance. Rates quoted are FAP, including breakfast, lunch, and dinner daily. Several other rooms and packages are also available. The Timberline: For your honeymoon—your own cozy trilevel chalet nestled in the woods. Downstairs sofas flank the fieldstone fireplace, and plank walls contribute a cozy, rustic feel. Upstairs you have a loft bedroom with mirrored ceiling, king-size bed, and a second fieldstone fireplace. There are also a Swedish sauna, sunken black whirlpool bath, and an oh-so-private deck for nude sunbathing, if you wish. Six days/five nights: $1,155 per couple. The Skytop: A private wood-and-glass mountain villa with a floor-to-ceiling stone fireplace in the living room and bedroom, outdoor balcony, and king-size bed illuminated by skylights. You'll also be pampered with a heart-shaped tub for two and private sauna. Six days/five nights: $1,210 per couple. Forest Chateau: Settle into your own cozy cottage for total privacy. The natural-stone fireplace casts its warm glow over the Mediterranean-style furnishings in the living room; there's a round king-size bed in your bedroom, sunken black tub for two in the bath, and a redwood terrace for sunning. Six days/five nights: $1,020 per couple.

Pocono Gardens, Mount Pocono, PA 18344 (reservations: tel. 717/595-7431, or toll free 800/441-4410). The feeling is very much that of an Italian villa: white ballustrades edge the terraces of the main building, columns frame arching windows, and marble statues stand in little nooks in the greenery. It's all very grand and glamorous. And very sporting, we should add, since Pocono Gardens not only has its own extensive facilities, but also shares those of Mount Airy Lodge, just minutes away. Right at Pocono Gardens, you can swim in the outdoor Olympic-size heated pool, play tennis, croquet, volleyball, and softball. Pocono Gardens has its own private clear-blue lake where you can cruise aboard a sailfish, canoe, or paddleboat, or stretch out your towels on a small white-sand beach. Nearby, there are waterskiing, 18 holes of golf, and horseback riding. In winter, the Poconos turn into a true wonderland, and you can enjoy favorite winter pastimes such as skiing (both downhill and cross-country), snowmobiling, and ice skating, both indoors and outside on the large lake. You'll want to spend lots of time around the indoor pool—shaped like an engagement ring and surrounded by statues and wrap-around windows that let in the views of the snow-covered pine trees. At night, Pocono Gardens' dining room always has a festive air, with its marble columns and mirrors. Afterward, there's star-studded entertainment every evening, and live music for dancing.

Accommodations: Each of Pocono Gardens' varied accommodations comes with air conditioning and a color TV. Several other rooms and packages are also available. Rates quoted are FAP, including breakfast, lunch, and dinner daily. The Amorata: This room is similar to the Palace Suite at Mount Airy. Your private pool is large, and just outside the sliding glass doors you have a secluded garden terrace. Other features include a sauna, round bed framed by a gilt-and-blue-velvet headboard, and heart-shaped whirlpool bath, artfully set off with mirrors. Six days/five nights: $1,265 per couple. The Sorrento-Capri II: Decorated in shades of blue, white, and gold, and accented by provincial-style furnishings, this suite has a distinct Italianate ambience—enhanced by the mirrored Roman whirlpool bath. Six days/

five nights: $1,155 per couple. Roman Forum Suite: Definitely for lovers of the dramatic, this room stars a round king-size bed set on a platform, backed by draperies and highlighted by mirrors overhead. In the bath, there's a heart-shaped whirlpool with mirrors and a crystal chandelier to add elegant finesse. Six days/five nights: $1,020 per couple.

SUMMIT RESORT

Owned by the Farda family, who have been part of the hospitality industry in the Poconos since 1952, the **Summit Resort,** Tannersville, PA 18372 (reservations: tel. 717/629-0203, or toll free 800/233-8250), offers practically every activity you can think of right on the property. Although all facilities are ultramodern, the Summit has the friendliness you can only find at a family-run resort.

The setting: a lush, green hillside above a large lake. The options: just about endless, what with tennis, bicycling, and boating, as well as horseback riding, archery, and water sports. That describes the Summit, a couples resort that believes in helping you live out your honeymoon dreams. Much of the action focuses on the main Summit Resort Center, a sleek wood-and-glass hilltop chalet. Here, all under one roof, you'll find the dining room, Moorish-motif Scheherezade Nightclub, and complete indoor sports facilities, including tennis courts, golf-driving range, basketball, ice skating, roller skating, complete fitness center, and large heated pool. Outdoors, you'll probably spend lots of time around the completely remodeled pool area with a waterfall, sundeck, sliding pond, and large whirlpool. During the winter, the Summit turns into a snowy wonderland, so grab your mittens and go tobogganing or snowmobiling. And the Summit is located near all the Pocono ski mountains—Camelback is just up the road.

You'll soon get to know the other honeymoon couples, thanks to the social director, who runs the Monday morning orientation tour of the property, and hosts Summit's own version of *The Newlywed Game.* Every day, the activity board lists a full swirl of events—picnic lunches, basketball games, trivia contests, skeet-shooting matches, or bowling derbies. Mealtime is something to look forward to, especially since the Summit menu includes entrées such as sirloin steak, roast prime rib of beef, and chicken cacciatore. If you have an attack of the munchies between meals, head over to the snackbar with café-style tables.

Honeymoon package: If you stay for four nights or longer, you'll receive a bottle of champagne, a bottle of bubble bath, a fire log, a honeymoon photo albumn, a Summit "Love Potion" cocktail (you also get to keep the glasses), and a horseback ride along scenic trails.

Accommodations: You have a varied choice of honeymoon headquarters, all with air conditioning and color TV. Rates quoted are FAP, including three meals a day. Other rooms and packages are also available. Fantasia II: Soft earth tones set the seductive mood in this lavish suite. There's a private glass-enclosed pool with mirrored walls and a woodland mural, fireplace, round king-size bed with mirrored canopy, heart-shaped whirlpool tub backed with mirrors, plus a private steam bath and sauna. Six days/five nights: $1,095 per couple. Montserrat Villa: Here, you get not only a heart-shaped whirlpool, but a heart-shaped bed as well, in most units. Each suite is located in its own spacious villa, featuring a very secluded outdoor sundeck. Six days/five nights: $920 per couple. Shasta Penthouse: Decorated in shades of blue and rust, these accommodations feature a king-size bed, a private balcony facing the Summit grounds, and a Roman-style sunken tub in the bathroom. Six days/five nights: $698.50.

PENN HILLS

In the mid-1940s Charles A. Poalillo Sr. and his wife Frances came to the Pocono Mountains to retire. Instead, they discovered a small inn set by a lovely waterfall. They bought the property—and began developing **Penn Hills Resort,**

Analomink, PA 18320 (reservations: tel. 717/421-6464, or toll free 800/233-8240). Today, honeymooners still love strolling through the woodlands to gaze at Rainbow Falls, and the Poalillo family maintains its tradition of friendly hospitality.

At Penn Hills Resort, honeymoon couples constantly find that they're able to enjoy the best of all worlds. The resort occupies over 500 acres, so there are plenty of woods and forests for hiking—and yet the accommodations are very chic and sophisticated. Penn Hills is located close to all the shops and factory outlets of Stroudsburg—and also right on a nine-hole golf course, Evergreen Park, and near its own ski mountain, Alpine.

Sports-lovers will appreciate the enormous variety of Penn Hills' facilities: tennis courts, par course fitness cluster, softball, bocce ball—even a large outdoor swimming pool shaped like a wedding bell. There are two private lakes; one, Lake Pocahontas, has small Paradise Island, an idyllic setting for paddleboating, canoeing, rowing, fishing, and other aquatic endeavors. You can enjoy many of your favorite sports all year, thanks to the large indoor sports arena, with volleyball, badminton, basketball, mini-golf, and a tennis court. You can even ice skate year-round at the indoor Ice-A-Rama. When it snows, Penn Hills looks just like a Christmas card, and couples can take advantage of a wide range of winter sports. The resort is an excellent choice for skiers, since it owns Alpine Mountain, just three miles from the resort. Alpine has a 500-foot vertical drop, 14 trails and slopes, four lifts, and 100% snowmaking capability. (Ask about the special ski packages.) Cross-country skiers can snap into bindings on the latest equipment and whoosh off along the stream and through the pine forests. Or you can turn into a kid again at the snow area complete with toboggan, sleds, and skibobs. Then head for something tropical —the indoor pool, sauna, or whirlpool. It's always easy to round up a team for softball, or opponents at tennis, because social director Ernie Camlet introduces everybody around.

Whatever season you visit, you'll enjoy dining in the Garden Terrace, a greenhouse-like dining room overlooking the woods and lakes of the golf course. Penn Hills has always been known for its good food, especially Italian dishes, including some Poalillo family recipes. At night, everyone heads over to the Reflections nightclub and disco, with live entertainment nightly, and dance music ranging from Golden Oldies to New Wave.

Honeymoon package: Ask about their different plans, which might include champagne, a honeymoon photo album, and more.

Accommodations: This is just a small sampling of the rooms and package plans available at Penn Hills. All rates are Modified American Plan (MAP), including breakfast and dinner daily; all rooms have air conditioning and color cable TV. Penthouse Towers: This triplex town house is nestled into the mountainside, overlooking the swimming pool and gardens. In addition to the heart-shaped bath, there's an enticing round bed encircled with Roman pillars, a log-burning fireplace, all accented with a passionate red. Six days/five nights: $1,110 per couple. Mountain Terrace Villa: Your own individual mountainside chalet, decorated in nature's tones of beige, brown, and russet. The spacious suite has five separate living areas, a round platform bed with circular mirror above, a fireplace, and a totally private terrace facing the woods. Six days/five nights: $1,110 per couple. Riviera Towers: These roomy accommodations have recently been redone in soft browns and beiges, with colorful modern art on the walls. Each has a playground-size king-size bed, and either a heart-shaped tub or combo steambath/whirlpool in the private bathroom. All have balconies overlooking the wedding-bell pool. Six days/five nights: $885.

PART TWO

MEXICO

IX

INTRODUCING MEXICO

1. PRACTICAL FACTS

A tropical breeze wafts across the tiled terrace as a pitcher of margaritas is laid out and the sun starts its steady decline. The soft strains of a singer caressing Spanish words—*"mi amor, mi vida"*—drift from the cantina below. The lapping waves carry in the tiny boat of the last fisherman with his catch.

The scene may seem familiar because you have been dreaming about spending your honeymoon in a place like Mexico, where the pace is unhurried, the people warm and hospitable, the food delicious and fresh, the music both soft and spirited, and the beaches long stretches of pure sand bordered by the sapphire blue of the Pacific or the crystal-clear turquoise of the Caribbean.

Mexico, the United States' southern neighbor, is a vast and rugged country encompassing mountain ranges, plateaus, jungles, deserts, colonial towns, and futuristic skyscraper-crowded cities. Nevertheless, it is its 6,212 miles of coastline—fronting the Gulf of Mexico and the Caribbean on the east, and the Pacific Ocean on the south and west—that draw most of the four million visitors from the United States each year. A large percentage are honeymooners who delight in Mexico's abundance of sun and sand.

The history of Mexico goes back hundreds of years, to about 1,500 B.C., when the Olmec Mesoamerican culture was first established in the Gulf Coast area. Thousands of ruins of ancient cities still dot the countryside, mute witnesses to the rise and fall of the sophisticated civilizations built by the Olmecs and their successors, the Mayans and the Aztecs. Today, the story of their achievements and downfall is still being unraveled by archeologists.

In 1519, the arrival of the Spanish conqueror Hernán Cortés dramatically changed Mexico's course of history. Over a period of 30 years, Cortés and his Spanish troops took over the Aztec nation and all that is today Mexico, infusing old-world culture into the New World.

The early 19th century saw the drive for independence from Spain, led by Father Hidalgo and Captain Ignacio Allende. In 1821, this goal was finally achieved. The early years of the Mexican republic were turbulent. Government corruption and the need for land reform sparked the Mexican Revolution of 1911 to 1920, directed by leaders such as Pancho Villa and Emiliano Zapata. Reforms and the new constitution generated by this movement helped create the modern Mexico, a politically stable and democratic republic.

This history, the mixture of charming Latin culture, the ancient wonders of the Mayas and Aztecs, and plush new hotels and modern conveniences combine to make Mexico romantic. For starters, there's the pace of life. Mexicans say that Americans live to work, while Mexicans work to live. You'll see this zestful approach to life in the Mexicans' relaxed attitude toward time and their passionate embrace of good food, love songs, and laughter. Then there are the historical remnants, seen in the Spanish-style buildings with their wrought-iron grillwork, ceramic pots and tiles, archways and bougainvillea-draped terraces, and the vestiges from the more ancient period of the Mayas and the Aztecs with the great temples and pyramids that have endured for generations. All this and 20th-century hotels and restaurants too.

Mexico is also for honeymooners who love the outdoors. The ocean affords opportunities for waterskiing, scuba-diving, snorkeling, sailing, and parasailing. On land, you can try tennis courts, golf courses, horseback riding into the jungle or along the beach, or exploring highways and byways of the land by four-wheel-drive vehicles.

Mexico's resorts have managed to maintain their individualism without becoming sterile chrome-and-glass cities on beaches. Whichever destination you choose, you'll be sure to find romance—in this case defined as warm, sunny weather; long, clean beaches; friendly people; a relaxed pace; lively music and delicious food—all available alongside the luxuries of the modern age.

---

1. Practical Facts

ENTERING AND LEAVING

Americans need proof of U.S. citizenship, such as a valid passport. An authorized birth certificate or a voter registration card is also acceptable. You need to obtain a tourist card (available at travel agencies, Mexican consulates, and airlines serving Mexico) before you arrive. The cards are free and valid for 90 days. Make sure to keep the tourist card with you during your trip, as it's required by law; and you must present both it and your proof of U.S. citizenship upon leaving the country. Canadians must have a passport. Mexico has a departure tax of $10 per person, payable in either dollars or pesos at airport check-in counters.

GETTING THERE

As each year passes, more opportunities open up for traveling to Mexico from the United States.

By Air

There are nonstop flights from several U.S. cities to Mexico on **Alaska, American, Continental, Delta, Northwest,** and **United,** plus the two Mexican airlines, **Mexicana** and **Aeromexico.** They fly from major U.S. cities directly to all the resorts mentioned in this book, or are sometimes routed through Mexico City, the hub of the country's air traffic. (For example, if you're flying from New York to Ixtapa, you'll probably need to connect to another flight in Mexico City; if you're flying from Los Angeles to Cancún, you'll probably also connect in Mexico City.) In recent years, numerous U.S. tour companies have contracted with airlines for charter flights to Mexican resorts. These generally cost less than regularly scheduled flights, but you won't have a lot of schedule flexibility. Check with your travel agent.

By Sea

Many luxury cruise ships sail to Mexico. Some stop at Mexican ports on their way around the world or through the Panama Canal; others sail year-round from Los Angeles or other West Coast ports. Check with your travel agent for itineraries.

GETTING AROUND

With inexpensive taxis and a variety of other transportation, getting around in Mexico is easy.

By Taxi

Taxis are so inexpensive and abundant in Mexico that they may be cheaper and easier than renting a car. There are no set rates for taxis and few have meters, so your best bet is to establish the price before you get into the car. (Your hotel doorman can help negotiate.) In some cities, you find that there are usual "going rates" between popular destinations; these are often posted at the front desk of your hotel.

Rental Cars

Major U.S. rental car companies, such as **Avis, Budget, Dollar, Hertz,** and **National** have offices in major resort cities, both at the airports and in town. Renting a car in Mexico is often more expensive than doing so in the United States (one of the few things in Mexico that costs more than back home). The sample rental rate for a Volkswagen bug with standard transmission runs about $50 a day. But the high cost of car rentals makes hiring a taxi a cost-saving option: In many cases, it can be cheaper to hire a taxi for an all-day excursion. In order to rent a car in Mexico, you'll need a valid U.S. driver's license, a credit card, and your tourist card. Car insurance is extra and mandatory since your U.S. policy is not recognized. The advantage of booking through U.S. companies is that you can reserve the car in advance and a 24-hour emergency service may be available.

Renting and driving four-wheel-drive vehicles is a lot of fun in Mexico, allowing you to explore off-road areas which are inaccessible to regular cars. Mexican highways and roads between major destinations are generally in good condition, but it is not recommended you drive outside of cities at night—even the Mexicans avoid it if they don't have to—because of animals and other hazards that often block roads.

LANGUAGE

Spanish is the official language, but you'll be able to get along fine in the resort areas even if you don't know a word. Still, you might want to invest in a Spanish phrase book since it adds to the fun to learn a word or two, such as *"gracias"* (thank you) or *"cuánto"* (how much). Mexicans are usually thrilled when other North Americans make an attempt to communicate in their language, and will help you improve your vocabulary rapidly.

MONEY

As of this writing, the Mexican currency—the peso—is continuing a controlled devaluation in relation to the U.S. dollar; good news for U.S. travelers, who will continue to find low prices in restaurants and shops. The exchange rate "floats" on the international money market, and will fluctuate almost daily. You'll find the current exchange rate posted at banks, hotels, airports, and money exchange houses; banks usually offer the most favorable rates. Pesos come in various denominations, both notes and coins.

Traveler's checks are your best bet; change them a little at a time as you need the money. (Make sure you have proof of identity with you.) Although traveler's checks are readily cashed in the major resort areas listed in this book, they are not widely accepted in small towns well off the beaten tourist track. Most hotels and restaurants accept major credit cards; they usually do not take personal checks. Since the peso is indicated by the dollar sign ($), the same as for U.S. and Canadian currency, pay particular attention to prices quoted in stores.

Mexico has instituted a value added tax—called the IVA—which places a 15% surcharge on all goods and services except surface transportation. Think of it as a 15% sales tax.

Tipping in Mexico is almost the same as in the United States. Give waiters/ waitresses 10% to 20%, porters the equivalent of 25¢ per bag. Chambermaids who clean your room are generally tipped 25¢ to 50¢ a day. Tips to cab drivers are optional.

WEATHER

In general, Mexico has a dry season (November through April) and a rainy season (May through October), but travel in both periods is encouraged—it can always rain in the dry season too, and you'll find the rain in the "rainy" season usually consists of afternoon showers, which cause little inconvenience. The beach resorts are tropical almost all year round, with humidity and temperature rising in the summer months and becoming cooler in the winter.

CLOTHING

Casual and fun are the key words throughout Mexico, but some resorts have definite differences. Acapulco, for example, is dressy compared to Cozumel, where informal is the byword. Few restaurants at the resorts require men to wear a tie and jacket, but there are elegant establishments at which gentlemen feel more comfortable in an open-necked shirt and jacket. Women should bring along some fun evening wear—nothing too fancy—for the nicer restaurants and discotheques. For the day, bring cotton clothing, comfortable walking shoes, and several bathing suits. Although shorts are fine at the beach, do not wear them on shopping expeditions to town or in more conservative inland areas.

TIME

Mexico does not change to Daylight Saving Time. Most of the country is on Central Time, including all the resorts in this chapter. During the summer when Daylight Saving Time is in effect in the United States, Mexico is one hour later than Los Angeles and two hours earlier than New York: When it is noon in Mexico, it is 11 a.m. in Los Angeles and 2 p.m. in New York. During the winter months, the Mexican resorts are two hours ahead of Los Angeles and one hour behind New York.

TELEPHONES

To call Mexico from the United States, dial 011-52, and the local area code and number. For long-distance telephone calls within Mexico, dial 91 plus the area code and the number. Area codes for the major resorts are: Acapulco, 748; Huatulco, 958; Puerto Vallarta, 322; Manzanillo, 333; Ixtapa/Zihuatanejo, 743; Cancún, 988; and Cozumel, 987. Use pay phones for local calls—they accept 100-peso coins.

Placing long-distance telephone calls from your hotel may be the most convenient method to call home, but it is expensive, since the telephone company charges a 50% tax on international calls plus a surcharge. For dialing direct to the United States, dial 95, area code, and number. An alternative is going to the local Larga Distancia office in each city where operators place the calls for you. You can also make collect calls from your hotel (dial 96 plus the area code and number) and you'll avoid the tax.

The Mexican phone system functions quite well, but due to a shortage of lines it will sometimes take some time to place a call to the U.S. from your hotel.

SHOPPING

The variety and quality of merchandise found in Mexico can be overwhelming. The resorts are home to so many modern shopping malls, tiny boutiques and open-air markets that vacationers often find themselves divvying up their days between sunning and shopping. Visitors may expect to find lovely handcrafts—the serapes,

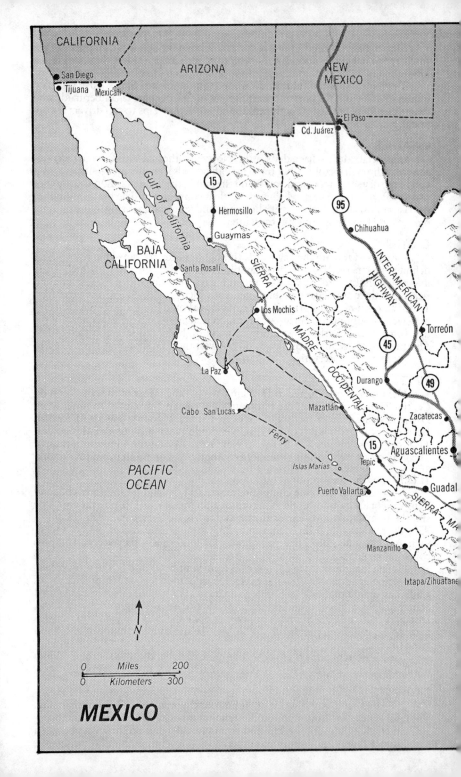

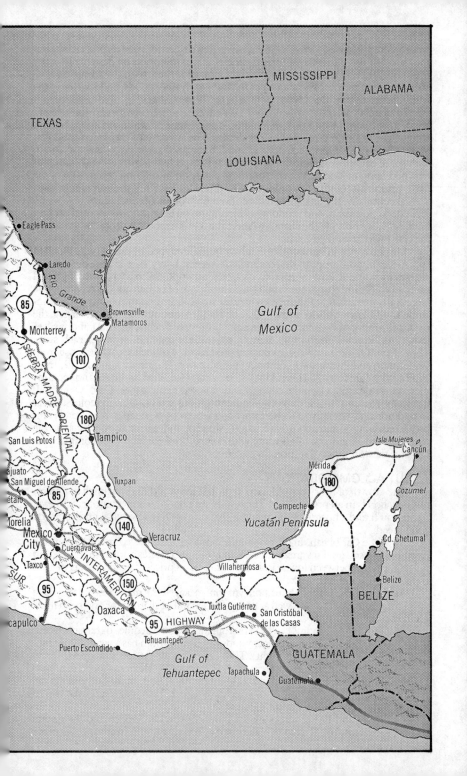

embroidered blouses, ceramic vases, silver jewelry, and copper products—but they're often also pleasantly surprised to come across low prices on designer items by the likes of Ralph Lauren and Gucci. Right alongside the artisans' markets in Mexico are some of the best-known names in clothing, leather goods, and jewelry in the world, at prices considerably lower than in the United States.

In general, stores are open from 10 a.m. to 2 p.m., then closed for "siesta" break to reopen at 4 or 5 p.m. Evening is a good time to stroll and shop, because stores close at 7 or 8 p.m., just before dinner. The strength of the American dollar makes shopping a favorite activity and you'll be amazed at the prices you can obtain with some patient bargaining, a practice that is expected in markets and stalls, but frowned upon in stores. As a rule of thumb, start off by offering about 50% of the asking price; although the vendor won't agree, this launches the bargaining give-and-take. Usually, the final price will be about 65% of the original price.

Markets, bazaars, and vendors hawking wares on beaches yield some of the best buys, and also provide the chance to meet the locals, often the people who created the crafts with their own hands.

Mexico is rich in **handcrafts** that have been developed by people who blended Indian skills and European designs and techniques. Every state in the country specializes in a unique kind of jewelry, ceramics, artwork, embroidery, weavings, and such, so you'll find some resorts will have a profusion of certain goods. Yet most have large crafts markets that feature merchandise from all around the country. These include hand-blown glass from the village of Tlaquepaque outside of Guadalajara, the carved furniture of Patzcuaro, the onyx and pottery of Puebla, and the famous silver jewelry of Taxco. Pottery, for example, reflects the different styles of each state. Those from Oaxaca and Chiapas display pre-Hispanic influences, while those from Guanajuato and Puebla have a distinct Spanish flavor. Imaginary figures made from papier-mâché are found all over. Piñatas, important for Mexican fiestas and ceremonies, are made from clay pots covered with colored tissue paper. Cute, whimsical, nativity scenes—available all year—come in various sizes and bright colors. As far as traditional clothing, you'll see leather and woven belts, serapes, sombreros, embroidered blouses and rebozos (Mexican shawls), and native dresses such as the Mexican wedding dress, all in white with colorful embroidery. (For complete details, see the "Shopping" section for each resort area).

ABOUT ACCOMMODATIONS

The growth of tourism to Mexico in the last ten years has given birth to numerous new hotels in all price ranges. The results are a boon to honeymooners: In each resort you'll find a host of modern hotels that provide all the services and comforts you'll need.

As in the Caribbean, high season in Mexico runs from December 15 through April 15; low season rates are about 30% to 50% lower. Rates quoted in this section reflect the range between low-season and high-season prices. The federal tax of 15% is not included unless noted.

Ask your travel agent about honeymoon packages. At many resorts they give you a substantial saving—as well as perks such as chilled champagne and fresh flowers in your room.

Beachfront hotel rooms can be extra romantic, with balconies or terraces facing the ocean. Make sure your travel agent finds out if your room has a view (sometimes they cost $10 to $20 more per night). They can be booked at special request.

As in other popular resort areas around the world, Mexican hotels may have problems with overbookings in high season. For this reason, make sure you get the receipt for your room deposit from your travel agent. Take it along on the trip to present at the hotel desk if any problems arise.

Christmas and Easter weeks are the most crowded in Mexico and the resorts burst at the seams. You'll need to make reservations six months in advance for other high-season dates.

DINING OUT

You may know it as the home of enchiladas, but you'll be pleasantly surprised by the range of delicious food in Mexico. Like the cuisines of France and Italy, Mexican cuisine consists of regional specialties. The Pacific resorts boast sumptuous fish and seafood: haddock, clams, oysters, lobster with palm hearts, stuffed snapper, shrimp in beer batter, *ceviche* (fish and seafood marinated in lime juice), and seafood grilled over mesquite or charcoal. There are also good, simple favorites such as steaks, spareribs, and kid grilled over coals, and beef and lamb skewered together and served over a bed of rice. The Yucatan is a mecca for Mexican gourmets. *Papadzul* is a classic of the area: a tortilla dipped in pumpkin seed sauce and filled with crumbled hard-boiled egg. Other specialties are lobster and shellfish, pompano, fish filet pit-roasted in banana leaves, and *panuchos*—small fried tortillas filled with black beans, onions, hard-boiled eggs, and shredded roast suckling pig. For dessert, there's coconut dishes and almond cake and, as everywhere in Mexico, the delicious flan, or egg custard.

You will be pleasantly surprised by the quality of Mexican wines, especially the whites from Baja California. And Mexican beers need little introduction, having won international awards for their flavor and quality. Neither does tequila, one of the oldest drinks in the country, its origins dating to pre-Hispanic times. Traditionally, it is drunk straight with a lick of salt and a bite of lime. More to most Americans' tastes are margaritas—tequila mixed with lime juice and orange liqueur in a glass rimmed with salt.

Restaurants are some of the liveliest and most romantic aspects of a Mexican honeymoon. You'll come across old haciendas turned into elegant dining rooms, thatch-roofed beachfront eateries serving fresh shrimp swathed in butter and garlic, and American-style coffeeshops where ham, eggs, and orange juice dominate the breakfast menu. Dinner is eaten late by American standards—most Mexicans head out to restaurants around 9 p.m. and vacationers seem to follow suit. Reservations are rarely required, except in the most elegant and popular of spots. Check with hotel desks for information.

The food, beer, and tequila are quite tempting, but be careful not to overdo it. That's the best advice to prevent the mild traveler's diarrhea that hits some visitors to Mexico on their first trip. It's best to eat and imbibe lightly the first few days while your system adapts to a new climate and food. Drink only purified water. Most major hotels have water purification plants, so it's safe to drink the water and brush your teeth with it; other hotels provide bottled purified water in the rooms. Whenever in doubt in restaurants, ask for mineral water (agua mineral), or stick with beer, wine, and name-brand bottled soft drinks. Avoid ice cubes not made from purified water as well as fruits and vegetables you cannot peel. Don't be tempted by the food sold at street stands—that's where most Americans get their cases of Montezuma's Revenge. If it happens to befall you, take an ounce of liquid Pepto-Bismol or the equivalent in tablets every half hour for four hours. Lomotil and Kaopectate are other helpful agents; before you go, ask your doctor's opinion of these treatments. Don't let health concerns stand in your way of having a good time. Eating and drinking are an integral part of the Mexican vacation experience.

HOW TO GET MARRIED IN MEXICO

Mexican government officials in the United States advise not trying to tie the knot in Mexico unless you have patience and are planning to spend at least a week in the country. It may take that long to make an appointment with a civil judge and have the blood tests, the two basic steps needed to get married. After the ceremony, you'll need to register your marriage at a U.S. consulate or embassy in Mexico (check before you leave to make sure there's one at your destination). Then, when you return home, you'll need to file the certified copy of the marriage certificate at your county courthouse. Brides and grooms who have been divorced in the United

States need to clear an added hurdle: They'll need to bring a certified copy of their divorce decree—translated into Spanish—to Mexico to present to the civil judge. To save time and energy in making these arrangements, check with the hotel you'll be staying at in Mexico before you leave. Some, such as romance-oriented Las Hadas and Las Brisas, can make all the arrangements necessary for a wedding ceremony as well as a champagne reception.

FOR FURTHER INFORMATION
Contact the **Mexican Government Tourism Offices** at the following addresses: In New York: 405 Park Ave., Suite 1002, New York, NY 10022 (tel. 212/755-7261). In Los Angeles: 10100 Santa Monica Blvd., Suite 224, Los Angeles, CA 90067 (tel. 213/203-8191). In Chicago: 70 East Lake St., Suite 1413, Chicago, IL 60601 (tel. 312/606-9013). In Houston: 2707 North Loop West, Suite 450, Houston, TX 77008 (tel. 713/880-5153). In Washington, D.C.: 1615 L St. NW, Suite 430, Washington, DC 20036 (tel. 202/659-8730).

X

MEXICO'S PACIFIC COAST RESORTS

1. ACAPULCO
2. HUATULCO
3. IXTAPA/ZIHUATANEJO
4. MANZANILLO
5. PUERTO VALLARTA

Every evening, a similar scene unfolds in dozens of seaside towns all along Mexico's Pacific coast. A fiery sun eases its way toward a glassy sea, its crimson rays seeming to enkindle both the wavelets and the sky. The sun moves slowly at first, then seems to accelerate toward the horizon, as if it, too, were subject to the laws of gravity. Finally, the perfect red circle . . . semicircle . . . sliver plops itself into the ocean.

From bars and hotel-room terraces, beach blankets, and yachts, a round of applause and hurrahs breaks out, along with toasts over frosty margaritas and ice-cold *cervezas* (beers). Another lousy sunset in Paradise, as the popular T-shirts sold by El Set, a restaurant in Puerto Vallarta, put it.

But as honeymooners soon discover, ringside views of the sunset are only part of the pleasure of a holiday on Mexico's western shore. With over 4,500 miles of coastline along the Pacific Ocean and the Sea of Cortés, Mexico offers choices to suit all inclinations—from total escape to nonstop partying.

1. Acapulco

Acapulco is one of the rare resort destinations that lives up to its reputation. You'll feel as if you've been plunked down into a glossy color postcard. The Bahía de Acapulco (Acapulco Bay) flaunts one of the most famous stretches of beachfront hotels in the world. As with Waikiki, Ipanema, or Cannes, photographs of its hotel skyline are instantaneously identifiable even by people who have never been there. The splendid setting borders on the awesome: Golden sands surround the sapphire-blue bay, all cupped by the green, jungly Sierra Madre Mountains that tumble seaward on three sides.

Acapulco is located on Mexico's Pacific coast, about 150 miles south of Mexico City. Acapulco life centers on the Costera Miguel Alemán, better known as the "strip," the broad avenue that threads its way along the coast. Many of the finest hotels front the Costera on one side, the beach on the other. Other honeymoon haciendas perch in the cliffs above the city, or to the east or west of town.

The city was founded in 1530 by the Spanish conquistadors. The beautiful harbor first served as a major port for Spanish trading ships carrying rare goods from the Orient—fine silks, porcelain, and ivory. During the 1950s, the first resort hotels were built toward the city's west end near Caleta and Catetilla beaches, and the influx of celebrities earned the city its nickname as "The Riviera of the West."

More so than other Mexican resorts, Acapulco has distinct tourist seasons. High season runs December through Easter; it's when most of the bejeweled jet-setters drop by their cliffside villas, and when parties, nightclubs, and restaurants throb most fervently. (It's also when you'll have the toughest time making reservations and squeezing yourselves into the discos.) But even Acapulco's off-season packs in more than enough action to satisfy the most energetic honeymooners, with plenty of sunshine, nightlife—and the pleasant addition of some elbow room.

There are really two, almost completely different, cities—Acapulco by day and Acapulco by night. When the sun shines (which averages about 350 days a year), Acapulco dedicates itself with full-blown hedonism to the delights of sand and sea. After dark, Acapulco transforms itself into party central, a town that greets each evening as if it were Mardi Gras. Couples sip cocktails on terraces before heading to some hilltop restaurant to dine—late—with the lights of the city spread out below their feet. And after dinner, they make a fashionably late arrival at the disco—several discos, actually, because club hopping characterizes the nighttime scene. "When," you may ask, "do we get time to sleep?" Most Acapulco revelers we know would never hit the beach before 1 p.m.—just in time for their afternoon siesta. If you want rest and relaxation, go elsewhere. If you want to dance and party to the max, Acapulco is the perfect choice.

SHOPPING

As you would expect, you'll find a staggering selection. Your best finds will be resortwear—from skimpy bikinis for the beach to tinselly minidresses for the discos. Most of the finest shops line the Costera, especially from the point across the avenue from the Americana Condesa del Mar hotel west to El Morro beach. Here's where you'll find **Izod, Ellesse, Calvin Klein,** and **Cartier.** For casual duds, check out **ACA Joe, Fiorucci,** and **Ruben Torres.** Women looking to enhance their bikini wardrobe should check out **Cocaine** and **Acapulco Pacifico,** also on this stretch of the Costera. **Diva** carries elegant womenswear; **Karistos** is a good bet for silver jewelry. Looking for classy T-shirts? Try **Poco Loco** or **Bye-Bye.**

For the most elegant resortwear, the no. 1 choice is the **La Vista** shopping mall near Las Brisas. The pink stucco buildings house an upscale selection of shops, including **Benamy** for silver, **Girasol** for embroidered cotton dresses, **Ares** for sportswear, and **Gucci** for leather goods.

Art-lovers will want to stop by the studio of **Pal Kepenyes,** an internationally renowned sculptor who works in metal (primarily bronze) and precious stones. He also creates jewelry—one-of-a-kind pieces that are real showstoppers (wearable art, really). Prices start at about $125; call 4-37-38 for an appointment.

If you're looking for inexpensive crafts and souvenir T-shirts, head for the **Mercado de Artesanías** (Artisans' Market) in Papagayo Park. They have some of the best prices in town on a wide selection of wares from throughout Mexico: onyx carvings, pottery, leather goods and silver jewelry. **Artesanías Finas Acapulco,** on Horacio Nelson around the corner from Baby 'O disco, also carries a good assortment of handcrafts. Prices are fixed in both of these stores; there's no bargaining over price. The place you can try out your haggling skills is at the **Mercado Municipal,** the public flea market. Here you'll find embroidered dresses, inexpensive silver-plate bracelets, and colorful papier-mâché birds.

ROMANTIC INTERLUDES

Night or day, lovers will find plenty of ways to amuse themselves in Acapulco. Most of the major hotels have concessions for parasailing, waterskiing, windsurfing, and sailing. Here are more options that really showcase the city's magic.

Acapulco's renown originally grew from that glorious crescent of **beach** that curves its way around the bay practically nonstop. Each section is known by its own name—about 23 different beaches in all. The search for the perfect beach by day makes as popular a pastime as club hopping at night. All beaches are public in Mexico, so the hotels have no control over them. As of this writing, the most fashionable stretch of Acapulco Bay for the sea-and-be-seen set is **La Condesa,** which connects the Hyatt Continental and El Presidente hotels. Thatch-roofed *palapas* (sun shelters) offer respite from the heat, and casual seaside cafés such as Paradise and Beto's (see "Restaurants" section) make for lively lunch spots. The surf is a bit rough here, however. **Icacos beach** lies toward the eastern curve of the bay near the Hyatt Regency and La Palapa hotels. Waters are calmer here, and the scene a bit less frenetic. **Revolcadero beach,** to the south of town near the Princess and Pierre Marques hotels, is another broad, tawny favorite. Be careful of the big breakers. Perhaps the most romantic option here is renting horses to ride along the shoreline. For sunset watching, head for **Pie de la Cuesta** about seven miles to the northwest of the city. Although you won't want to swim here (the surf is downright treacherous), you can stake out a hammock at water's edge, wrap your fingers around a cool tropical drink, and watch el sol dip slowly beneath the horizon. On the other side of the beach is peaceful **Laguna de Coyuca,** a freshwater lagoon that attracts birds such as herons, cormorants, and egrets. You can rent canoes or rowboats to skim the glassy surface of the lagoon, perhaps taking out some time for swimming or fishing. The cab fare from Acapulco proper is about $17 round trip; ask the driver to wait for you. Remember that throughout Mexico, the sun is strong—use protective sun lotions.

If you prefer active **water sports,** you're in plenty of luck. For scuba-diving, contact **Divers de Mexico,** on the Costera (tel. 2-13-98). Deep-sea fishing excursions can be arranged at **Pesca Deportiva** near the downtown docks. Or try parasailing from one of the concessions on many of the beaches (about $10 for a .ride).

Several different companies offer scenic **bay cruises** departing from the dock area on the *malecón* (promenade) daily. For example, the *Vagabundo* glass-bottomed boat takes you to **La Roqueta,** an uninhabited island at the center of the bay that offers good swimming and snorkeling. En route, you'll pass over the underwater shrine of Our Lady of Guadalupe, patron saint of fishermen. The cruise, including drinks and lunch on board, costs about $10 per couple.

Acapulco is also an old town, a favorite lair of conquistadors and marauding pirates in the 16th century. Get a sense for its past at **Fort San Diego,** a 17th-century stronghold that's now a museum recounting the history of the area from pre-Columbian times to the Spanish conquest. See models of the Spanish galleons and a royal carriage, then stroll out onto the ramparts for an impressive vista of the entire bay. Open from 11 a.m. to 5 p.m.; admission costs 25¢. Closed Monday.

Also explore **Acapulco Traditional,** the old part of town centered near Caleta Beach. Sit in the shade in the *zócalo* (town square), and visit the Cathedral. Nearby, discover the pastoral aspect of Acapulco in the 52 green, leafy acres of **Papagayo Park.**

The **cliff divers,** or *las clavadistas* as they are called in Spanish, plunge 150 feet into a wave-tossed gorge surrounded by jagged rocks at La Quebrada, to the west of town. Yes, it's very touristy—but it's a don't-miss Acapulco attraction, demanding split-second timing on the part of the divers. One of the best perches for watching the spectacle is the terrace at the El Mirador hotel (admission fee is $5 per person plus drinks; arrive early to get the best seats). There's an afternoon show at 1 p.m., and several evening shows, usually at 7:15, 8:15, 9:15, and 10:30 p.m. The evening shows are by far the most dramatic, illuminated by torchlight and bonfires. For the exact schedule, check at your hotel.

And who more than honeymooners would more enjoy cuddling up in *las calandrias,* charming **horse-drawn buggies** festooned with colorful balloons that clop down the Costera. Nicest time of all is at twilight, cooled by sea breezes and accented by the diamond-bright lights of the city. You can find buggies for hire all along the Costera, especially in front of the major hotels. About $20 for a half-hour ride.

If you want to experience a dazzling Mexican spectacle, *las corridas* (the bull-fights) are held most Sundays during the winter season at **Cajetilla Stadium** and at other times during the year. Be advised that because of the bloodshed, this spectacle is not suitable for everybody, and animal lovers might prefer spending the afternoon at the **dolphin shows** at the **CICI aquarium** or the **zoo** in **Parque Papagayo.** You can make arrangements for bullfight tickets at your hotel front desk.

HONEYMOON HOTELS AND HIDEAWAYS

Whatever season you visit, Acapulco's popularity makes it imperative that you make hotel reservations several months in advance. The off-season (approximately April through the beginning of December) represents a real travel bargain, with rates about 15% to 50% lower than in winter. Please note that winter rates are often MAP (including both breakfast and dinner), while EP (no meals) is available in summer. Price spreads reflect the difference between low- and high-season rates. Because the meal plans may vary between winter and summer, the difference in room rates can appear greater than is customary for Mexican hotels.

Expensive

Las Brisas, Carretera Escenica Clemente Mejia Avila 5255, Acapulco, Guerrero 39868, Mexico (tel. 748/4-16-50; U.S. reservations: toll free 800/228-3000), is romance—the most seductive resort in Mexico, and quite possibly the world. Certainly no setting could surpass this balmy perch on the hillsides above Santa Lucia Bay, Acapulco dramatically laid out beneath you. Accommodations are in white *casitas* (the Spanish word for small houses), carefully snuggled into the cliffs so as to maximize both views and privacy. Don't let the diminutive "ita" word-ending fool you, however. Rooms in the mlnivillas are graciously ample, with cool marble floors and sliding louvered doors opening onto the balcony and private pool. Perhaps it's the pools that lovingly establish Las Brisas' fairy-tale appeal. Lined with turquoise tiles, they are true oases, perfect for cooling refreshment, large enough so that you can swim a couple of strokes. Every morning, your maid arrives with a basketful of tulipan (hibiscus) blossoms, which she gently positions on the surface. Although the rooms are air-conditioned, the cooling breezes that give Las Brisas its name usually keep temperatures comfortable.

When you finally budge from your room, you'll discover that the 110-acre Las Brisas is a complete, self-contained resort. All the pleasures of Acapulco lie a mere ten minutes away, and right on the property, Las Brisas offers boutiques, five tennis courts, and its own discotheque. One of the nicest spots for sun-bronzing is its private La Concha Beach Club, centered around a seawater pool carved into the rocky hillside. The pool forms a natural aquarium, and colorful tropical fish are real amigos, loving to swim right up to you and inquisitively nudge your toes. Las Brisas has three excellent restaurants on the property: The Deli for casual dining, El Mexicano for creative regional cuisine, and Bella Vista, known for its white-glove service and dazzling views of Acapulco Bay. And there's room service 24 hours a day. Honeymoon package: Seven days/six nights (CP): $1,400 per couple, low season. Includes casita with a private pool, welcome cocktails, basket of seasonal fruit, continental breakfast, use of a Las Brisas pink-and-white jeep, bottle of champagne, and more. Honeymoon package available April to December only; but other, different, packages are available. The guest relations staff at Las Brisas is also very experienced at handling all arrangements for couples who want to get married in Mexico; contact them for complete details.

Moderate

Villa Vera Hotel and Racquet Club, Lomas del Mar 35, Acapulco, Guerrero, Mexico (tel. 748/4-03-33; U.S. reservations: toll free 800/233-4895 or 800/241-0767). At the swim-up bar, the sound of clinking glasses mingles with the beat of a Bruce Springsteen record. A huge inflatable dragon floats across the pool. As you stretch out on a blue-and-white-striped towel on a lounge chair, you can see, through your toes, the Acapulco skyline and blue bay. Welcome to La Dolce Vita, Mexican style—Villa Vera.

Poised on a steep hillside above the city, Villa Vera provides an enclave of classy escape, ten acres of tropical gardens just minutes' drive from downtown. The hotel evolved from a private home; the villas originally accommodated the owner's friends. Thanks to a 1:1 staff/guest ratio, personalized service is still very much maintained, and since there are only 80 accommodations, the atmosphere remains distinctly club-like. Rooms, suites, and villas are tucked here and there in white buildings around the gardens. Furnishings are tasteful, comfortable rather than opulent. Superior rooms have two queen-size beds, cool marble floors, and green and white spreads. Each suite layout is different: Some have king-size beds; others feature huge balconies overlooking the bay or a private pool. Every room features a minirefrigerator, air conditioning, and a TV. All are currently being refurbished as part of a multimillion-dollar facelift. The "racquet club" portion of the hotel name comes from the three clay courts (lit for night play), as well as resident pro and pro shop. But the main attraction of staying at Villa Vera is plugging into Acapulco's high-voltage social swirl. As one bronzed, gold-bechained playboy sighed, "Villa Vera is Acapulco." Honeymoon package: Eight days/seven nights (CP): $715 per couple (suite); $1,020 per couple (villa), low season. Includes bottle of wine and fruit basket upon arrival, continental breakfast daily, welcome cocktails, T-shirts, candlelight dinner on your last night, special gift, and more. High-season rates (BP): $180 per couple per night for a superior room; $365 per night for a villa with private pool.

At first glance, **Acapulco Princess,** P.O. Box 1351, Acapulco, Guerrero, Mexico (tel. 748/4-31-00; U.S. reservations: toll free 800/223-1818 nationwide; 800/442-8418 in New York State; 212/582-1800 in New York City), is overwhelming and rather magical at the same time, built to resemble a massive Mayan pyramid set on the broad plain east of Acapulco. Cascades of bougainvillea tumble over the terrace railings, palm trees and ponds grace the atrium lobby, a rope bridge crosses the jungled lagoon, and flamingoes strut in the glades. The Acapulco Princess is a true self-contained resort, occupying 380 acres of gardens alongside Revolcadero beach, about 25 minutes from Acapulco. It's a complete world, with 8 international restaurants, 4 bars, a pair of 18-hole golf courses, a disco, 11 tennis courts (9 lighted), an elegant shopping arcade, and one of the world's great swimming pools, with inlets, lagoons, a waterfall, and a swim-up bar. Rooms face either the golf course or the ocean; oceanview rooms are more expensive but definitely worth it. They are absolutely huge, with beige marble floors, queen- or king-size beds with colorful parrot-design bedspreads, rattan headboards, and never-ending views of the blue Pacific. Honeymoon package: Eight days/seven nights (MAP): $940 to $1,105 per couple per night, low season. Includes breakfast and dinner daily, welcome cocktails, bottle of domestic champagne, souvenir photo and honeymoon gift, his-and-hers T-shirts, use of chaise longue at pool, and all applicable taxes. Three-night packages, extra nights, and upgrades to suites are all available. High-season rates (MAP): $400 to $520 per couple per night.

Acapulco Plaza Holiday Inn, Costera Miguel Alemán 123, Acapulco, Guerrero, Mexico (tel. 748/5-80-50; U.S. reservations: toll free 800/HOLIDAY). This three-towered hotel is one of the largest on the strip with 1,000-plus rooms. Occupying a prime stretch of El Morro beach, just west of La Condesa, it features six restaurants, two freshwater pools, four tennis courts, a health club, arcades and arcades of boutiques, a disco, and live entertainment—making it a perfect in-town setting for action-loving honeymooners. Down at the beach, you can indulge in parasailing, scuba-diving, windsurfing, or waterskiing. The lobby itself is a tropical fantasy, with rushing waterfalls as well as parrots and peacocks adding to the sound effects. Half of the guest rooms are suites, and they come highly recommended, with a balcony overlooking Acapulco Bay, marble bathroom, and louvered partition between bedroom and living room. Decor is light and tropical, with rattan chairs and mauve-and-pink floral upholstery. All rooms offer air conditioning, color TVs, balconies, and minibars, and room service runs 24 hours a day. Part of the Holiday Inn chain. Honeymoon package: Eight days/seven nights (BP): $950 per couple, low season. Includes deluxe room with king-size bed, welcome drinks, and fresh flowers upon arrival, full breakfast including one breakfast in bed with champagne, one dinner. Suite rates are from $158 per couple per night. High-season rates (EP): $145 per couple per night for a deluxe room.

Hyatt Regency Exelaris Acapulco, Costera Miguel Alemán 1, Acapulco, Guerrero, Mexico (tel. 748/4-28-88; U.S. reservations: toll free 800/228-9000), located along the far eastern edge of Acapulco Bay on relatively tranquil Icacos beach, this luxury, 23-story property offers understated elegance. The circular marble lobby is a knockout, with columns and huge potted plants. You'll find all the amusements you could want right on the property, with six restaurants and bars, sauna and massage room, three tennis courts, and a sprawling free-form pool with a swim-up bar and little footbridges. Any sport you want—from parasailing to waterskiing—is available down at the beach. The spacious rooms face either the water or the Costera; each features air conditioning, a minibar, private balcony, and color TV. The color scheme is bright with yellows, reds, and greens; rugs adapt an Indian-type design. For the most pampering, opt for a room on the Regency Club level, where you'll enjoy amenities such as an oceanview room, complimentary continental breakfast, an open wine bar in the afternoons, and complimentary hors d'oeuvres. Honeymoon package: Eight days/seven nights (BP): $1,060 per couple, low season. Includes deluxe room, breakfast daily, bottle of champagne and flowers in your room upon arrival, fruit basket, one dinner for two, special gifts, and more. High-season rates (EP): $170 to $200 per couple per night.

Hyatt Continental Acapulco, Costera Miguel Alemán S/N, P.O. Box 214, Acapulco, Guerrero 39580, Mexico (tel. 748/4-09-09; U.S. reservations: toll free 800/228-9000). This is the action-loving sister resort to the Hyatt Regency Exelaris, located right on the beach in the heart of Acapulco's sun-and-fun strip. By day, activity focuses on the pool, one of the largest in Acapulco, complete with a water slide and its very own island. You can also plunk your beach chaise under a palm tree or palapa on El Morro beach. Rooms in the two towers feature marble floors, niceties such as satellite color TVs and servi-bars, and stunning ocean views—a parasail might go drifting by just a few feet from your balcony railing. Everything you need is right on the property: a fitness center, four bars, three restaurants, a water-sports concession, and more. For extra pampering, opt for the Regency Floor rooms, where you'll be treated to a fruit basket upon arrival, continental breakfast daily, afternoon cocktails, the services of a concierge, and more. Honeymoon package: Eight days/seven nights (BP): $750 per couple, low season. Includes upgrade to Regency Club accommodations if available, full American breakfast daily, domestic champagne and fruit basket, one dinner with domestic champagne, catamaran dinner cruise, special gifts, and more. High-season rates: $115 to $175 per couple per night.

Fiesta Americana Condesa Acapulco, Costera Miguel Alemán 1220, Acapulco, Guerrero, Mexico (tel. 748/4-28-28; U.S. reservations: 212/949-7250 in New York State; toll free 800/223-2332 nationwide). Right in the center of the action—that's where you'll be if you stay at this stylish high-rise on Acapulco's prime beach for people watching. Just across the Costera, you'll find top shops; all the favorite beach bars and restaurants are nearby. The Condesa itself is looking quite spiffy these days after a recent refurbishment. The modern rooms have color TVs, air conditioning, servi-bars, telephones, and balconies with great views of the bay. You'll probably spend lots of time basking down at the marble pool deck, poised on gigantic boulders above La Condesa beach and shaded by palm trees. Down at the beach, more boulders act as natural breakwaters to gentle the surf. There's a tour desk to arrange scuba-diving, snorkeling, fishing, and other excursions. Take your pick of five restaurants and three bars. Honeymoon package: Eight days/seven nights (BP): $835 per couple, low season. Includes deluxe room with king-size bed, breakfast daily (including a champagne breakfast in bed), one dinner, fresh flowers in your room upon arrival. High-season rate: $143 per couple per night.

Inexpensive

Maralisa Hotel, Enrique el Esclavo S/N, P.O. Box 721, Acapulco, Guerrero, Mexico (tel. 748/5-66-77 or 748/5-67-30; U.S. reservations: toll free 800/421-0767 nationwide; 800/252-0327 in California), is *it*—the real "find" in Acapulco, a true gem-like property that will have you whistling mariachi tunes as you lounge around the pool. The four-story white hotel is built surrounding a courtyard, Spanish style; small, balustraded balconies face the palm tree–lined terrace, gazebo/bar, and small pool. Wonder of wonders, the Maralisa is set on one of the prettiest stretches of El Morro beach, just off the Costera on a quiet side street. Another big bonus: Since the Maralisa is the sister hotel of that darling of the jet set, the Villa Vera, you share tennis and pool privileges. The rooms are simple but scrupulously clean, all with TV and air conditioning, and recently refurbished. Honeymoon package: None. Double room (EP): From $50 to $75 per couple per night.

ROMANTIC RESTAURANTS

Whether your tastes run to Dom Pérignon or Corona, Acapulco has the restaurant to suit your moods—from funky eateries on the beach to elegant continental showplaces that pull out all the stops.

Moderate

El Campanario, Paraiso S/N Fracc. Condesa (tel. 4-88-30). Set in a ritzy residential neighborhood in the hillsides above La Condesa beach, this restaurant resembles a fairy-tale castle, with turrets and the tall tower that gives it its name (which means bell tower). The magic begins the moment you arrive and wend your way up the stone stairway, past a rushing waterfall and flaming torches. Piano music tinkles in the background, a perfect counterpoint to the panoramic views of Acapulco. You'll dine seated in heavy oak chairs that make you feel like a returning conquistador. The menu highlights both continental and Mexican specialties; we went Latin, and enjoyed superb ceviche, Aztec soup, red snapper (huachinango), and chicken serrano (served with mildly spiced pepper), plus an excellent flan for dessert. Dinner for two, about $60 per couple. Open daily from 7:30 p.m. to midnight.

Madeiras, Scenic Highway near Las Brisas (tel. 4-43-78). Make your reservations several days in advance for this elegant continental dining spot on a cliff overlooking the city. (To take maximum advantage of the views, have cocktails on the terrace first.) Your four-course dinner will be served by candlelight, to the sound of live music. Entrées include a delectable filet mignon with green peppercorn butter or a sea bass infused with oranges and Cointreau. Chocoholics should be aware that there is a luscious chocolate torte for dessert. Four-course prix-fixe dinner, about $22 per person. Open daily from 7 p.m. to midnight.

Grazziel, Scenic Highway near Las Brisas Hotel (tel. 4-81-43). Pretty and pink, Grazziel is top choice when you're looking for savory Italian cuisine with a five-star view of Acapulco. Set on a cliff overlooking the bay, the restaurant features appetizers such as a seafood cocktail and prosciutto and melon (both about $7). Try the fettuccine Alfredo ($8) or pepper steak, the house specialty ($12), then go for a fiery finale with the crêpes Suzette ($7.50). Open daily from 6:30 p.m. to 1 a.m.

Palenque, Scenic Highway across from Fantasy disco (tel. 4-59-98). Celebrate with a real fiesta at this hilltop restaurant-in-the-round with panoramic vistas of the bay. First dine on Mexican specialties such as garlic shrimp ($17) or charbroiled sirloin ($15), then watch the lively show that breaks loose each evening at 9:30 p.m., complete with skirt-twirling folkloric dancers, mariachi and marimba bands. If you just want to come by for drinks and the show, that's fine too—there's no cover charge. Open daily from 7 p.m. to midnight.

Carlos 'n' Charlie's Bar & Grill, Costera Miguel Alemán (tel. 4-12-85). As the long lines will attest, this is probably the most popular spot on the strip. The atmosphere is simultaneously casual and outrageous—you never know when your waiter is going to pop up next to you on the dance floor, wearing a gorilla mask and waving a two-foot long unmentionable rubber object he has fastened somewhat below his midsection. The menu features good food and plenty of it: seafood, steaks, salads, and ribs. Dinner for two runs about $30 per couple. No reservations; open from 6 p.m. to 1 a.m.

Inexpensive

While away an afternoon at one of the lively beach bars such as **Paradise,** Costera Miguel Alemán at La Condesa beach (no phone). This thatch-roofed restaurant located on one of the most popular sections of La Condesa beach provides the perfect hangout. Once you wander in for lunch, you'll probably end up spending the whole afternoon, dancing to the live music and making new friends as you down frosty cervezas. Seafood is the specialty here—platterfuls of red snapper or garlicky shrimp. A complete lunch will run about $20 to $40 per couple. Open daily from noon to midnight. Other similar beach bars on the strip are **Beto's Safari Bar,** where a lolling lion cub adds authentic jungle atmosphere; **Barbarroja** (Redbeard's) with a pirate motif; and the **Langosta Loca.**

NIGHTLIFE

According to a recent count, you could hit a different **disco** in Acapulco every night for three months. Acapulco clubs run the complete gamut, from cozy little boîtes to lavish dance palaces.

The in-spot for the past few seasons has been **Fantasy,** where duplex floor-to-ceiling windows have a drop-dead view of Acapulco at night, lights sparkling like a contessa's necklace. Overhead, a galaxy of mirrored balls glitters; and the special effects roster includes soap bubbles, confetti, balloons, and giant video screens that replay the scene on the floor. Most spectacular of all—the fireworks that send down a shower of sparks that seems to merge with the city lights below. Be sure to ask for one of the special drinks, such as 7-Up with tequila (it foams up, and you chug-a-lug it down). Located in the La Vista shopping mall near Las Brisas (tel. 4-67-27).

Two new clubs are vying for queen-of-the-night partying honors. Both **News** and **Eve** on the Costera dazzle with light shows that take it to the max. **Baby 'O,** with its distinctive "melted cave" facade on the Costera in town, is a perennial favorite (tel. 4-74-74). Most of the discos open around 10 p.m., but the dance fever doesn't warm up in earnest until after midnight. Dancing until dawn is not a cliché here—often, the last reveler will not depart before sunup. The admission fee generally runs about $20 to $40 per couple, so be sure to allow plenty of room in your budget for boogeying.

2. Huatulco

About 450 years ago, Spanish conquistadors erected a large wooden cross along a golden stretch of coastline, imprinted with sapphire bays and studded with rocky islets. The cross became famous among the local Zapotec Indians, who believed it possessed magical powers. When English pirate Thomas Cavendish staged a fiery attack on the coast, he tried—and failed—to destroy the cross. "A miracle," the Indians murmured. Soon, the region became known as Huatulco, meaning "the place where the tree is adored" in Indian dialect.

Today, a new miracle is unfolding along this 20-mile expanse of tawny beaches and limpid coves. Here, where only a few dozen fishermen once dwelled in thatch-roofed palapas, and plump pelicans snoozed peacefully on boulders, a glittering new vacation paradise is taking shape. With its luxury hotels and bountiful natural beauty, Huatulco figures to be the first great resort of the 21st century. The locale earns rave reviews for both its outstanding scenery (cupped at the base of the western Sierra Madre mountains) and near-perfect weather (averaging about 82° year-round).

The resort-in-the-making encompasses nine bays and some 20 miles of shore-line, including four miles of beaches. It is located on the Pacific Ocean about 335 miles southeast of Acapulco and 229 miles south of Oaxaca, the Spanish colonial-suffused town that is the state capital (see "Romantic Interludes"). Huatulco is the newest, biggest project of FONATUR, the department of the Mexican government that also developed the megasuccessful Ixtapa and Cancún resorts.

Even if you're not one of those folks who constantly strive to keep up with the Joneses, you'll enjoy the thrill of being among the first to experience Huatulco. It's a chance to visit a tourist magnet projected to attract over 800,000 vacationers annually by the year 2000—and have the whole place practically to yourselves right now.

ROMANTIC INTERLUDES

Although the Pacific Ocean is not generally known for the jewel-like hues of the Caribbean, the **bays** at Huatulco gleam with the variegated blues most often seen in a peacock's tail: sapphire and cobalt, indigo and turquoise. The waters are clear as tequila, sheltered by coral reefs and cays that act as natural breakwaters. The sand is fine, gilt-toned, as if it, too, has been burnished by the sun.

This dynamic duo of sea and sand inspires a whole array of ocean-attuned pastimes ranging from kayaking to windsurfing. There's also good snorkeling and scuba-diving, with wells, caves, and shipwrecks to explore. Underwater visibility often exceeds 100 feet. Arrangements can be made at hotel water-sports concessions; scuba trips run about $30 to $60.

Hop aboard one of the day sails or snorkeling cruises that ply Huatulco's bays. Ask to visit **La Entrega**, a broad, dead-calm cove reachable only by boat. It's a perfect place for some leisurely snorkeling, followed by a picnic lunch. Nearby, view **La Bufadora**, a blowhole. Or anchor at tranquil **Maguey Bay**, where casual palapa restaurants sell grilled shrimp, fish, and octopus right on the beach. Excursions are available through Club Med or one of the charter boats in Santa Cruz (about $50 per person for a day trip).

Meanwhile, nature-lovers can explore miles of **trails**, keeping an eye out for albatross, woodpeckers, iguanas, wildcat, and deer. Over 80% of Huatulco's 52,000 acres are set aside as an ecological reserve.

While Huatulco is the resort in the future, you can step back into the past in **Oaxaca**. This gracious mountain plateau city is only a half-hour flight—and some 300 years—removed from the go-go vacation bustle of Huatulco. Here, raven-haired senoras sell fragrant gardenia bouquets in the main square, and wrought-iron grillwork frames the windows of 17th-century mansions.

Stop in at the **Church of Santo Domingo,** with its magnificent gilded altar; and the **Stouffer Presidente,** set in a restored 16th-century convent. Lunch at one of the al fresco restaurants facing the zocalo, such as El Asador Vasco or Mi Casita. Try the local specialties: chicken mole, served in a delectable sauce made from over 50 ingredients; and mezcal, a potent, tequila-like liquor. Lunch or dinner, about $20 to $30 per couple.

Every Saturday Indians from neighboring pueblos throng to the **Mercado Juárez** and **Mercado de Artesanías** to sell their wares: black Oaxaca pottery, geometric-design blankets, red habañero peppers, whose fiery color matches their piquancy. Round out your trip with a visit to the **ruins of Monte Alban and Mitla,** two awe-inspiring Mixtec and Zapotec sites nearby. Various hotel tour desks offer day trips to Oaxaca; prices run about $165 per person.

ROMANTIC HOTELS AND RESTAURANTS

Here's your chance to live out a Robinson Crusoe–like fantasy of being the first to discover a tropical paradise. With less than half a dozen hotels now open, you'll enjoy plenty of elbow room. To date, the entire restaurant scene is located in the hotels, which offer a wide choice of dining spots.

Club Med—Huatulco, Domicilio Conocido, Bahía de Tangolunda, Santa Cruz, Huatulco, Mexico (tel. 958/1-03-95; U.S. reservations: toll-free 800/CLUB MED). If you think you have to turn in your Club Med membership on the day you say "I do," think again. Founded in 1950, Club Med today is one of the largest vacation hosts in the world, serving nearly one million guests a year. Far from being "swinging singles," 50% of its GMs (gentils membres) are married.

One of the best reasons to rediscover the pleasures of Club Med is this stunning village set on not just one, but four of the most beautiful beaches on Tangolunda Bay. (Club Med's modus operandi when building a new resort is always to find the best beach in town.) The breathtaking architecture combines modern design with traditional Mexican elements—sort of "2001 meets the cliff dwellers." Accommodations are clustered in four separate *pueblitos* (small villages), each painted a flamboyant tropical color, such as laurel pink, lavender, or terra-cotta. Reflecting the changing nature of Club Med's clientele, the guest casitas, or little cottages, are cushier than ever before, with air conditioning and marble-trimmed sinks. Especially nice: the spacious terraces with hammocks for siestas. The only drawback for honeymooners is the fact that all accommodations feature two oversize single beds.

With Club Med's all-inclusive policy, rates cover everything from free tennis lessons to unlimited wine and beer with meals. The sports facilities are particularly extensive, with three swimming pools (including an Olympic-size one), three air-conditioned squash courts, a dozen tennis courts, as well as windsurfing, sailing, kayaking, snorkeling, boat rides, and lots more. Equipment and instruction are also included. At mealtimes, you can choose from five different excellent restaurants, including El Mirador for an Argentine-style barbecue, and La Kasbah for Moroccan cuisine. Each night, the staff puts on a different show, such as a lip-synch contest or fire dance, culminating in a sparkly fireworks display. Then everyone usually heads for the disco, where there's great music, accentuated by special effects such as lasers. Rates (all-inclusive including air transportation) range from $1,300 per person from Houston to about $1,420 per person from New York, plus membership fees of $55 to $90. Other departure cities are also available, so check with your travel agent.

Huatulco Sheraton Resort, Paseo de Tangolunda, Huatulco, Oaxaca, Mexico (tel. 958/1-00-55; U.S. reservations: toll free 800/325-3535). This brand-new 346-room luxury hotel (it opened in March 1989) lolls beside a long, broad beach on Tangolunda Bay. Built in updated Mexican colonial style, the appealing design incorporates traditional Mexican motifs and native materials. The glamorous circular lobby, for example, is accented by indigenous mahogany and marble. Open-air atrium corridors lead to the oversize rooms, resplendent and *muy simpatico* with their pale-pink tile floors and gray Mexican marble bathrooms. For accents, headboards and closet doors use local mahogany, while lamps and sculpture are crafted from black Oaxaca pottery. All rooms boast satellite color TVs, radios, air conditioning, telephones, safes, and minibars; nonsmoking rooms and king-size beds are available upon request.

You'll find plenty to do right on the property, since the Sheraton has a large free-form pool as well as a water-sports concession for sailing, windsurfing, and diving. To enjoy a spectacular sunset over the bay, sail off on their private yacht for a cocktail cruise. You'll also find four lighted tennis courts, plus a game room, gym, and health spa; sauna, steam room, and massage are also available. Each of the four restaurants spotlights a different cuisine, including Italian and Mexican. The very popular seafood/pizza café is housed under a giant palapa. A disco is slated to open early in 1990. Honeymoon package (BP): $290 per couple (three nights); $625 per couple (seven nights), low season. Includes breakfast daily, welcoming drinks, a bottle of domestic champagne, taxes and tips, and more.

---

3. Ixtapa/Zihuatanejo

Fifteen years ago this region consisted of nothing but Zihuatanejo (See-WHA-tah-nay-hoe), the quintessential Mexican "sleepy fishing village" with its picturesque boats and small harbor. Today, although its streets are all paved, and restaurants and boutiques flourish, you can still watch fishermen haul in the daily catch of oysters and marlin and see the local women shopping at open-air markets.

Ten minutes north is Zihuatanejo's glittery neighbor, Ixtapa, a resort as modern as Zihuatanejo is rustic. It stretches along six-mile-long Palmar Beach, covered with white sand and dotted with coconut palm trees. Here, the modern, high-rise hotels line up in a row, each offering deluxe accommodations, American-style service, and amenities (you can drink the water here), but each retaining a unique ambience. Most hotels have tennis courts, and you can partake of various water sports—parasailing, waterskiing, windsurfing—on the beach. Because of the rough surf at Palmar, the hotels all boast huge, fantastic swimming pools, with whimsical additions such as bridges, waterfalls, water slides, and swim-up bars.

Across from the hotel strip, the Palma Real Golf and Tennis Club features a Robert Trent Jones–designed 18-hole golf course winding along the base of the mountains and finishing at the edge of the ocean. Also across from the strip lies La Puerta, the area's largest shopping area, containing restaurants and a plethora of stores selling handcrafts from all over Mexico and designer resortwear.

Although a rental car can give you the freedom you may want, it's not a real necessity here. The hotels, restaurants, and discos are all an inexpensive cab ride away from one another. A cab ride from Ixtapa to Zihuatanejo is about US $3.

SHOPPING
Both towns offer better and better shopping each year.

Ixtapa's classy **malls** are the place to browse for fine men's and women's sportswear. At the Plaza Las Fuentes center you'll find top names such as **Polo/Ralph Lauren, ACA Joe,** and **Fila. Scruples** carries merchandise from **Calvin Klein, Christian Dior,** and **Bill Blass.** Mexico goes on safari at **African,** with sportswear, hats, and roomy tote bags perfect for globe-trotters. For handcrafts from Oaxaca, such as fanciful hand-painted wooden animals and woolen rugs, try **Laddi.** Also check out **Chiquita Banana,** a teeny boutique crammed with beautiful Mexican crafts; and **Go West,** with a huge selection of handmade boots priced about 25% to 30% less than in the United States.

At La Puerta shopping center, **Ferrioni** features men's and women's sportswear emblazoned with the line's Scottish terrier mascot. Stop by **Poco Loco** and **Bye-Bye** for T-shirts, **Creaciones Alberto's** for silver jewelry, and **Mic-Mac** for a selection of interesting Mexican crafts, women's sportswear, and leather goods. Serious art collectors will want to visit **Espacio P.K.** at the new Plaza Bugambilias mall (right behind La Puerta), which displays sculpture and jewelry by Pal Kepenyes.

Meanwhile, Zihuatanejo is known for its superb crafts shops such as **Coco Cabana** (Calle Vicente Guerrero), **Aramara** and **Bazar Xochilti** (both on Calle

Nicolas Bravo). All carry wares from throughout Mexico, such as hand-painted pottery from Puebla, black pottery from Oaxaca, Yucatecan hammocks, and more. There are more good finds at the **State** handcrafts store, near the zocalo. **Alberto's** (corner of Ejido and Cuauhtémoc) is known for its well-designed silver jewelry set with semiprecious stones such as turquoise, amethyst, and onyx.

ROMANTIC INTERLUDES

No honeymoon in Ixtapa is complete without a visit to primitive **Ixtapa Island,** a national park that shelters tropical birds and animals. There are some thatch-roofed restaurants serving fresh seafood just steps away from white-sand or pebble beaches. The gentle surf and underwater opportunities offer ideal opportunities for snorkeling or diving. Hotel desks can arrange excursions (about $15 per person including lunch), or you can take a little boat to the island from Playa Quieta, a short taxi ride from Ixtapa hotels.

Stroll through **Zihuatanejo** after dinner at one of the many seafood restaurants in town. Saunter along the beachfront to the main square, as the townsfolk do. Sometimes cruise ships dock in the harbor, providing a pretty sight with their clear lights streaming from their stacks. You can soak up the rustic beauty of the town by rambling up Calle Alvarez and other streets, visiting the small shops and sharing a drink at one of the local cantinas on the harbor, such as Los Amates, Bananas, or the Tango Bar.

Sometime during your honeymoon here you'll want to venture to some of Zihuatanejo's bevy of beautiful **beaches,** including the **Municipal Beach** right in the center of town; **La Madera,** with its gentle waves; and **Las Gatas,** accessible only by boat. But the biggest is best of all: **La Ropa,** a mile-long strand that curves like a smile. Here, you'll find a happy blend of Mexican families and gringo vacationers enjoying the gentle waves, perfect for swimming. You can bounce across the waves on a banana boat ($5.50 per person) or hover aloft on a parasail ($10 per person). And you can't find fresher seafood—or lower prices—than at the beachfront restaurants (see "Romantic Restaurants" section).

HONEYMOON HOTELS, INNS, AND HIDEAWAYS

Just as Zihuatanejo and Ixtapa are different in character, so are their accommodations. Modern, luxurious hotels line the hotel strip of Ixtapa, while Zihuatanejo's inns are more rustic and family-oriented. As in the rest of Mexico's beach resorts, rates from April through November (low season) are cut by as much as half. Some prices quoted reflect the spread between low- and high-season rates.

Camino Real, Playa Vista Hermosa, Ixtapa, Guerrero 40880, Mexico (tel. 743/4-33-00; U.S. reservations: toll free 800/228-3000). Another of the Westin chain's strikingly beautiful hotels, this one stands out for its angular design, which blends into the jungle hilltop and affords spectacular views of secluded Vista Hermosa Beach. Each of the hotel's 441 rooms has a view of the ocean from a large lanai that comes with chaise longue and hammock for private sunbathing, and a marble-topped table in the shade for dining or watching the sunset. The 13 suites also have their own swimming pools. Recreation focuses on the beach (you get to it by walking down the steep staircase cut in a cliff or by a private elevator) and a complex of four swimming pools connected by waterfalls and fountains. There are four lighted tennis courts. Jeeps are available to rent for those who want to explore the grounds and surrounding area. Honeymoon package: Four days/three nights (some meals): $405 per couple for a deluxe oceanview room; $790 for a junior suite with private Jacuzzi per couple. Includes buffet breakfast daily, flowers upon arrival, bottle of champagne, dinner for two including wine, one hour of tennis, welcoming cocktails. Available low season only. High-season rates: $205 per couple per night for a deluxe room.

Hotel Villa del Sol, Playa La Ropa, Apdo. 84, Zihuatanejo, Guerrero 40880, Mexico (tel. 743/4-22-39). It's difficult to beat the isolation and private atmosphere of this unusual hotel, conceived by Helmut Leins, a German engineer who discovered this area on vacation years ago and never left. The hotel consists of just 17 bungalow-type rooms laid out amid gardens and streams. Rooms have ceiling fans and canopied beds; bathrooms are lined in hand-painted Mexican tiles and there is a split-level living room area. Breakfast and dinner at the hotel restaurant—considered by many to be the finest in Ixtapa/Zihuatanejo—are included in the price. You can be guaranteed privacy and quiet here: Children under 14 are not allowed. The hotel is on one of Zihuatanejo's calm coves and best beaches. Warning: Because of its uniqueness and size, reservations are required a year ahead in high season. Honeymoon package: None. Rates (MAP): $145 to $175 per couple per night.

Krystal, Boulevard Ixtapa, Apdo. 68, Ixtapa, Guerrero 40880, Mexico (tel. 743/4-26-18; U.S. reservations: toll free 800/231-9860 nationwide; 800/392-4671 in Texas). This high-rise hotel—which resembles the bow of a ship thrusting toward the Pacific Ocean—is among the most sophisticated in Ixtapa. Chandeliers and polished Mexican granite accent the luxurious lobby. There are four tennis courts, a gigantic free-form pool with waterfall and toboggan slide, racquetball, and water sports. Honeymoon package: Eight days/seven nights (BP): $615 per couple, low season. Includes deluxe room, full breakfast daily, champagne and wedding cake in your room upon arrival, welcome cocktails, one candlelight dinner for two, room tax, and more. High-season rates (EP): $130 per couple per night.

Holiday Inn, Boulevard Ixtapa, Apdo. 55, Ixtapa, Guerrero 40880, Mexico (tel. 743/4-23-96; U.S. reservations: toll free 800-HOLIDAY), is an activity-oriented hotel with events planned all day around the huge tropical pool area. There is a tennis court and a lively disco. Honeymoon package: Eight days/seven nights: $670 per couple, low season. Includes deluxe room with king-size bed, American breakfast each day (one breakfast in bed with champagne), one dinner, and a welcome cocktail. High-season rates (EP): $130 per couple per night.

Sheraton, Boulevard Ixtapa, Ixtapa, Guerrero 40880, Mexico (tel. 743/4-31-84; U.S. reservations: toll free 800/325-3535). You'll get a terrific view of the Sheraton's towering atrium lobby—the centerpiece of this 358-room hotel—from the glass elevators leading to your room. There are four lighted tennis courts. Honeymoon package: Eight days/seven nights (BP): $715 per couple, low season. Includes deluxe room, welcoming drinks upon arrival, daily buffet breakfast, complimentary bottle of champagne, bottle of wine when dining at Casa Real restaurant, and discount on a rental car. High-season rates: $145 per couple per night for a deluxe room.

Stouffer Presidente, Boulevard Ixtapa, Apdo. 95, Ixtapa, Guerrero 40880, Mexico (tel. 743/4-20-13; U.S. reservations: toll free 800/HOTELS-1). This large hotel complex containing 440 rooms is both modern and traditional: Rooms in a newer, large tower building all face the ocean, while three hacienda-style buildings are set among tropical gardens and have a colonial flavor. There are a large swimming pool and two tennis courts. Honeymoon package: Seven days/six nights: $860 to $965 per couple. Includes room with king-size bed, American breakfast each day, welcome cocktails, one candlelight dinner, bottle of wine in room, fresh fruit basket, and discount on rental car.

ROMANTIC RESTAURANTS AND NIGHTSPOTS

From thatch-roofed local hangouts in Zihuatanejo to sleekly elegant hotel restaurants in Ixtapa, this area will have the dining spot to fit your mood.

Expensive

Villa del la Selva, Paseo del la Roca, near the Camino Real (tel. 4-20-96), advertises "private" sunsets, and as you sit at a small candlelit table on a terrace overlooking the sea, you might believe the sunset is, indeed, all yours. The setting is sublime, amid lush vegetation and the crashing surf far below. Seafood and meat dishes are the specialties (red snapper with hollandaise is one favorite), all served by candlelight. It's also one of the most expensive restaurants in Ixtapa. Dinner for two with wine will run $60 to $80. Open nightly from 6 to 11 p.m.

Moderate

Villa del Sol, at the Zihuatanejo hotel of the same name (see "Honeymoon Hotels" section), has a Swiss chef who prepares luscious European dishes. The menu changes each night, but always gives a choice of two entrées of meat or fish. The restaurant's candlelit tables overlook the ocean, and to make the atmosphere even more sumptuous, classical music accompanies the meal. The prix-fixe dinner costs $60 per couple. Open daily from noon to 11 p.m. **Coconuts** at Vicente Guerrero 4 (tel. 4-25-18) in Zihuatanejo offers a romantic setting of candlelit tables arranged in a garden under twinkling lights. Entrées such as red snapper cost $14 to $20. Open nightly from 6 to 11 p.m. Save room for delicious dessert specialties such as apple pie and coconut ice cream. **La Mesa del Capitán,** Nicolás Bravo 18 (tel. 4-20-87), run by an Englishman, Oliver Jones, and his wife, ranks as one of Zihuatanejo's most popular restaurants. Steak and lobster are the specialties, with dinner entrées running from $11 for a grilled fish filet to $32 for the surf 'n' turf combo. Open daily from 4 to 11 p.m. **Christine's** at the Krystal Hotel is a disco with electrifying special effects straight out of Star Wars. In Zihuatanejo try one of the thatch-roofed discos on the beach—**Ibiza** is one of the most popular.

Inexpensive

Emerald-green parrots jabber in English and Spanish, palm fronds rustle, waves break gently on the shore—that's the scene at the seaside restaurants on La Playa beach in Zihuatanejo. At favorite palapa-roofed eateries such as **La Perla, La Gaviota,** and **El Marlin,** you can treat yourself to a heaping platter (big portions are a matter of pride here) of garlicky shrimp ($5) or Pacific lobster ($10). They also serve ample breakfasts that might set you back $6 per couple. All are open daily for breakfast and lunch, 7:30 a.m. to 5 p.m.; no phones.

4. Manzanillo

In terms of mental outlook, Manzanillo is on the same latitude as Monaco, St. Tropez, Marbella, and other jet-set ports of call. Chitchat recaps auctions in Paris and skiing conditions in Aspen; 100-foot yachts with names such as *Knot to Work* and *Shangri-La* bear registries from hedonistic havens like Acapulco and Road Town, B.V.I.

Set in the center of the Gold Coast, Manzanillo is about 200 miles southeast of Puerto Vallarta. The lush area became a favorite of sun-worshipping aristocrats, movie stars, and other rich and famous glitterati when film director Blake Edwards used the Arabian Nights–inspired Las Hadas hotel as a setting for *10*.

Manzanillo presents an interesting split personality. The city itself is a working-class town, sprawled around the biggest and busiest seaport on Mexico's Pacific coast. But all the cachet comes from the self-contained luxury resorts and condominiums, where you just might find the subject of this week's *People* magazine's cover story lolling on the next beach chaise.

SHOPPING

For mercantile pursuits, your best bets are the elegant shops at **Plaza Puerto Las Hadas. Tane** and **El Taller** carry exquisite jewelry. Outposts of **Ellesse, Fila, Bye-Bye,** and **Ruben Torres** carry men's and women's sportswear. At the **Guess** boutiques, you'll find not only jeans but also fashion-right men's and women's clothes. **Jaramar Galerías** is a treasure trove for crafts, rugs, embroideries, masks, handbags, ceramic candlesticks from around the world. At Hotel Las Hadas, the **Aries** boutique features butter-soft leather goods and **Galleria de Arte Siles** showcases work by contemporary Mexican artists. In the nearby town of Santiago, **Grivil** offers some real finds, including onyx figurines and embroidered blouses.

ROMANTIC INTERLUDES

Because of Manzanillo's remoteness, many of the attractions here are a bit distant from one another, but the drive in between is rewarding—through verdant tropical landscape.

Rent a car and drive 35 miles north of Manzanillo along a modern highway bordered by tropical plantations to the quaint fishing village of **Barra de Navidad.** Along its long, curving beach, you'll find an authentic Mexican resort, with cantinas lining the beach and serving up the freshest seafood you'll find anywhere. Just spend the day dallying about here, soaking up the sun and the atmosphere of the laid-back town. Little boats on the lagoon at the east end of town will take you on private cruises for about $12 an hour.

Still by rented car, head inland on highway 110 about two hours to the quiet town of **Colima.** Along the way you'll see a spectacular active volcano and the Nevado de Colima mountains, which are sometimes snow-capped. Founded in 1523 on an Indian site, Colima is an attractive town of simple colonial buildings and gardens. At the **Museum of Western Mexico Indian Cultures** you'll see some pre-Columbian statues—for which this area is famous. You can buy reproductions in small shops in town. The museum is open Monday through Saturday, 10 a.m. to 1:30 p.m.; admission is free.

HONEYMOON HIDEAWAYS AND HOTELS

Hotels in this region stand out because of their uniqueness as romantic spots. Some rates quoted reflect the spread between low- and high-season rates.

Las Hadas, Apdo. Postal 442, Manzanillo, Colima 28200, Mexico (tel. 333/ 3-01-41; U.S. reservations: toll free 800/228-3000), is a fantasy come true for those who dream of a place where white spires rise out of green hillsides, where no cars are allowed, where fountains and statues greet you at every turn, and privacy is prized above all. The 203-room hotel is built in a style called by some Moorish, by some Mediterranean, and by others Disneyland. It was the dream of a Bolivian tycoon, Don Antenor Patino, who chose Manzanillo to build his "fairyland" retreat. Today, it's best known as the setting for the Dudley Moore–Bo Derek movie *10.* Rooms are in white and muted colors to match the exteriors, with private balconies, marble floors, and servi-bars. A true "self-contained" resort, Las Hadas has its own 70-vessel marina, golf course, and ten tennis courts. There are a lagoon-size swimming pool surrounded by islands and waterfalls, a private cove with white Arabian-style tents for shade, and a range of water sports available. Honeymoon package: Eight days/ seven nights: $1,235 per couple. Includes "Encantada" room with ocean view, sunset cruise, one dinner, bottle of champagne, flowers in room, and unlimited golf and tennis daily. High-season rate: $230 per couple per night.

Hotel La Posada, Apdo. 135, Manzanillo, Colima 28200, Mexico (tel. 333/ 2-24-04; U.S. reservations: toll free 800/252-0211). If Mexicans had invented bed-and-breakfast inns they would resemble this hotel. Small (24 rooms), low-key, and unpretentious, it exudes charm and relaxation, Mexican style. Surprise—it's actually owned and operated by an American, Bart Varelmann. The only aspect of the hotel that is even slightly outrageous is its exterior—painted in what the hotel calls "passionate pink." From the fan-cooled rooms, a tiled patio leads to the beach a few yards away, a small pool, and plenty of trees. The large lobby contains comfortable sofas and game tables with chess and backgammon boards and a bar where guests serve themselves on the honor system. The owner's three cats may even wander over for a nap on your laps. Honeymoon package: None. Rates: $44 to $55 per couple per night, with breakfast.

ROMANTIC RESTAURANTS

How can a restaurant help but be romantic along a stretch of coastline that is so beautiful and isolated?

L'Recif, Olas Altas, Manzanillo (tel. 3-06-24), actually hangs on the cliff next to the Vida del Mar Hotel. With one of the best ocean views of any restaurant in the area, L'Recif serves a cuisine that can best be described as French/continental. The bouillabaisse and seafood are outstanding (try the seafood combo plate). There is a large menu, as well as good choice of wines. If you come for lunch, you can also take a dip in the pool on the terrace. Serving lunch (1 to 5 p.m.) and dinner (7 to 11:30 p.m.) daily, about $40 to $60 per couple.

Carlos 'n' Charlie's, Avenida México 200, Km. 6.5 (tel. 3-11-50). The bar resembles a ship, plaster hippo heads decorate the dance floor, and stuffed fish and construction helmets dangle from the ceiling. There's only one place this could be —the Manzanillo edition of the irrepressible Carlos 'n' Charlie's chain. The menu features all the favorites: grilled snapper and shrimp, chicken enchiladas, pepper steak, and some of the most potent margaritas south of the Rio Grande. Alternate frenetic gyrations on the dance floor with strolls on the lovely beach right outside. Open daily from 6 p.m. to midnight (to 1 a.m. on weekends); $20 to $40 per couple plus drinks.

Willy's, Avenida Lázaro Cárdenas (tel. 2-34-15). Looking for a five-star view of the sunset, capped off by cocktails and a fresh seafood dinner? Then come to the extremely popular gathering place for vacationers in the know. Start off with the subtly seasoned guacamole or crab and shrimp terrine, followed by grouper mousseline, lobster, or—for landlubbers—meaty delights such as loin of pork in prune sauce. Desserts are something special, including a top-rate baked Alaska and flaky profiteroles, drizzled with chocolate sauce. Open for dinner only, 6:30 to 11:30 p.m.; $30 to $40 per couple.

Hotel Colonial Restaurant, Avenida México 100 (tel. 2-10-80). This atmospheric old hotel certainly lives up to its name, with oodles of Spanish colonial atmosphere. If the setting is a bit run down, it more than compensates with the intricately painted tiles on the floor, tall-back spool chairs, and massive wrought-iron chandeliers. You'll find superb renditions of Mexican classics: steak a la parrilla (grilled), octopus in its own ink, snapper Veracruz style (with spicy tomato sauce). Serving breakfast, lunch, and dinner daily from 9 a.m. to 11 p.m. Dinner will run $20 to $40 per couple.

Manzanillo is developing a happening disco scene. The número uno spot is **Enjoy,** while **Bacchus** and **Pip's** are also popular.

---

5. Puerto Vallarta

Once a remote fishing village, Puerto Vallarta has blossomed into one of Mexico's most popular resorts by virtue of its small-town charm and scenic beauty. Whitewashed stone houses with red-tile roofs and archways line the cobblestoned streets. The foothills of the Sierra Madres almost reach the ocean, and bougainvillea and other lush vegetation seem to meander across every balcony. Although today Puerto Vallarta is more of a city than a village, the sight of a farmer with his burro plodding along a busy downtown street won't let you forget its small-town origins.

Heading from the airport to Puerto Vallarta, you'll take Paseo Díaz Ordaz, the beachfront drive that passes most of the modern, deluxe hotels that line the road about a mile or two north of downtown. When you see the cobblestoned streets, the spire of the cathedral, and the oceanside promenade, you'll know you've arrived in Puerto Vallarta proper. The city center is bisected by the Río Cuale. In the middle of the river itself, you'll find five-acre Cuale River Island, linked to the town by two arched bridges. The island is packed with restaurants and dozens of chic shops such as Ralph Lauren and Gucci, as well as numerous little curio outlets—contributing to Puerto Vallarta's reputation for having the best shopping of any Mexican resort. At the mouth of the river, the waterfront promenade—the *malecón*—forms the hub of Puerto Vallarta's social life. From early afternoon to the wee hours of the morning, lively bars and restaurants throng with gringos toasting their newly acquired tans with margarita after margarita.

If you're seeking beaches, then you're sure to find one that will please you in Puerto Vallarta or a bit farther south. The action-packed main beach in town, Playa del Sol, bustles with sun-worshipping North Americans, snack stands, and even musical combos. You can try all the water sports here, including parasailing, windsurfing, and waterskiing, or rent horses for a ride on the beach. If you're both seeking quiet and seclusion, follow the cliff-hugging highway south along isolated stretches of ocean to remote caves that await exploration. Renting a car or, even more exhilarating, a four-wheel-drive Jeep for a day trip is the best way to take it all in. Driving south you'll come across some spectacular hillside villas before catching a glimpse of Playa las Estacas, a small inlet with beautiful white sand at the Camino Real hotel. Along the way you'll see the huge, craggy Los Arcos rock formations, which jut out from the sea. At Mismaloya, seven miles south, you can rent boats that will take you to Los Arcos for some of the best snorkeling in the area. Locals sell grilled fish in small stands on the Mismaloya beach. And on the hillside above, you can still see part of the set for the movie *Night of the Iguana,* which put Puerto Vallarta on the tourist map when Elizabeth Taylor dallied with Richard Burton during the filming.

Set aside a day to visit Yelapa, a village surrounded by jungle and ocean, and accessible only by boat. Hotel desks can arrange the trips, which leave each day for the 1½ hour cruise down the coast on the *Serape* and *Vagabundo* boats. When you get to Yelapa you'll find no roads and no electricity, only several small restaurants serving fresh seafood on the beach, a quaint Indian village, and a 150-foot waterfall, which you can explore by foot or by horseback. Cruises to Yelapa are about $22 per couple.

SHOPPING

Cognoscenti know that Puerto Vallarta boasts some of the best shopping in Mexico. For souvenirs and fashionable sportswear from big-name designers, the top shops are on Paseo Díaz Ordaz along the malecón, as well as on nearby Avenida Juárez. Puerto Vallarta is also emerging as a center for serious collectors of Mexican art. **Galería Uno** (Morelos 561) spotlights works by contemporary Mexican artists and foreign painters living in Mexico. **Sergio Bustamante** has a gallery at Juárez 275. For handcrafts, try **San Sebastián** (Mina 169), **St. Valentín** (Morelos 574), and **Galería de Artes Indigenes** (Lázaro Cárdenas 274).

ROMANTIC INTERLUDES

Puerto Vallarta's settings make a variety of options available.

Each morning, the *Bora Bora* trimaran **sails** to deserted Las Animas for a day of snorkeling and sunning at the kind of tropical beach you've probably fantasized about. You can also check at the Garza Blanca resort, where you can hire fishermen to take you to Las Animas in their private boats. For a three-hour cruise around Banderas Bay and to Los Arcos, natural arches formed in rock, sign on with El Vagabundo and Yelapa Yachts. Price is about $40 per couple, including lunch. At 5:30 p.m. each evening, the motor yacht *Serape* offers sunset cruises of the bay, with a buffet, live music for dancing, and two bars (about $28 per couple). Another day cruise is on the *Cielito Lindo* trimaran along the north shore, passing fishing villages, to isolated and beautiful Piedra Blanca (White Rock) beach. Price is about $30 per couple, including lunch. If you catch a fish, there is a cook on board who will prepare it for you. Hotel desks can arrange any of these and other sailing trips.

Stroll the **malecón.** Buy an ear of corn on a stick, or stop by for the best ice cream on the Mexican coast at **Helados Bing,** before taking a moonlight stroll along the **promenade,** where you can watch the waves break on the beach beyond the swaying palms. Then poke your heads into one of the many shops and galleries downtown before crossing the bridges to **Cuale River Island.** Saunter along pebbled paths winding through tropical gardens, then relax on one of the benches. At the foot of the steps of the southbound bridge, stop at the **Franzi Café,** which serves coffees, pastries, and exotic drinks, while a jazz band performs until midnight. Perhaps later, hop over to **Le Bistro Café,** where tiny lights twinkle in the trees along the banks of the river, and recorded jazz is played all evening long.

Not all the action centers on the city or on the beaches in Puerto Vallarta. The **jungle** inland is surprisingly accessible. It can be explored by horseback, by car or Jeep, and by organized tour. Day-long Jeep safaris ride across the back-country plantations of mangroves and through lush green forests (Jeep rental is $60 per day). A horseback tour at **Rancho Victoria**—a real working ranch—is accompanied by a "ranchero," a Mexican cowboy, who leads groups past small villages and along a river where you can take an invigorating swim. Cost is about $24 per couple. Check with hotel desks for arrangements for tours or Jeep rentals. One fun way to experience the Tarzan-like ambience is by lunching at one of the jungle restaurants south of town—such as Chico's Paradise (see "Romantic Restaurants" section). Here, you can splash around in pools and waterfalls before, during, or after lunch, and sunbathe to your heart's content amid trees and squealing birds and monkeys (most of them in cages).

HONEYMOON HOTELS AND HIDEAWAYS

Puerto Vallarta's hotels have kept pace with the phenomenal popularity of the resort. Almost all of the big modern hotels lie along the north shore, just outside of downtown. Becoming a big factor in Puerto Vallarta's accommodations scene are villas and condominiums, which offer all the amenities of a hotel, plus full kitchens. Unless otherwise indicated, difference in room rates reflects the spread between low- and high-season rates.

Expensive

Garza Blanca, Apdo. 58, Puerto Vallarta, Jalisco 48300, Mexico (tel. 322/2-10-23; U.S. reservations: toll free 800/331-0908 nationwide; 800/548-9121 in California). Puerto Vallarta's most exclusive—and expensive—hideaway is situated on a secluded stretch of Banderas Bay about ten minutes from downtown. Garza Blanca cannot be defined simply as a hotel. Yes, there are rooms, but none are "standard." The beachfront suites occupy two-story thatch-roofed huts, with living rooms overlooking the beach. Bedrooms contain king-size beds. Chalet suites sit higher up, on a hillside affording panoramic views of Los Arcos. Each contains a living room, a large bedroom, and a private pool shaded by bougainvillea and jungle-like trees. For the ultimate in romantic dining, reserve one of the three or four secluded and candlelit tables set out each night on the beach in front of the hotel's restaurant. Honeymoon package: Eight days/seven nights (EP): $1,120 per couple (chalet suite in low season). Includes welcome drinks, tropical flowers and fruit in room, bottle of champagne, and boat excursion to Yelapa. Call for high-season rates.

Moderate

Camino Real, Playa del las Estacas, Apdo. 95, Puerto Vallarta, Jalisco 48300, Mexico (tel. 322/2-00-02; U.S. reservations: toll free 800/228-3000), among the most luxurious of Puerto Vallarta's hotels, stands majestically on its own cove on Banderas Bay. The white-sand beach with its calm water is among the best in the area for swimming and water sports. Beautifully landscaped grounds greet guests even before they glimpse the bougainvillea-draped hotel from the highway. Each of its 250 rooms has views of the ocean. One of the two pools is a large free-form swimming pool lined in Mexican tile and crossed by wooden bridges. Standard rooms are spacious and have bright Mexican decor, while the icing on the cake here is the two-story penthouse suites considered by some to be the most elegant accommodations in Puerto Vallarta (Elizabeth Taylor used to forsake her house in town for one of these suites). Each has a private pool with glorious ocean views and a circular stairway leading to a mammoth bedroom with king-size bed and private terrace. Honeymoon package: Eight days/seven nights: $835 per couple. Includes deluxe oceanview room, daily full breakfast, one dinner, bottle of champagne, flowers in room, souvenirs, sunset cruise, and more. High-season rates: $175 per couple per night.

You need never to leave the **Krystal Vallarta**, Avenida de Las Garzas, Puerto Vallarta, Jalisco 48300, Mexico (tel. 322/2-14-59; U.S. reservations: 713/784-2682 in Houston; toll free 800/392-4671 in Texas; 800/231-9860 nationwide), to experience almost everything Puerto Vallarta has to offer. From Mexican fiestas on Saturday nights to bullfights in which guests can participate, the Krystal has it. Arched passageways, iron grillwork, red tile, low-rise buildings, and gushing fountains set a romantic mood. There is a host of daily activities from which to choose, including tennis classes with professionals, scuba lessons, basketball, soccer, and even donkey polo (participants whack a ball with a broom while astride a donkey). Six restaurants cater to a variety of moods and tastes, including a Japanese dining room and an Argentinian steakhouse. There is also a range in accommodations—a cluster of 38 villas with private swimming pools, master condominiums with kitchens, junior suites with king-size beds and living rooms, deluxe rooms with king-size beds and small sitting areas, and standard rooms. All have terraces or balconies overlooking gardens or the ocean, servi-bars, and TVs with reception of several U.S. channels. Baths in the suites and villas have large Roman-style bathtubs. Honeymoon package: Eight days/seven nights (BP): $615 per couple, low season. Includes deluxe accommodations with king-size bed, welcome tropical drinks, bottle of champagne and wedding cake brought to your room upon arrival, five full American breakfasts per couple during your stay (served in bed, if you desire), one candlelight dinner for two, hotel tax, and more. High-season rates (EP): $135 per couple per night.

Fiesta Americana, Apdo. 270, Puerto Vallarta, Jalisco 48300, Mexico (tel. 322/2-20-10; U.S. reservations: toll free 800/223-2332 nationwide; 212/949-7250 in New York). The dramatic lobby here—with its large, cone-shaped thatched roof and waterfall—sets a delightful tropical atmosphere at this hotel located just five minutes from downtown Puerto Vallarta. Brightly colored rooms have color TVs and servi-bars. Balconies with pretty potted flowers add splashes of color to the pale orange facade of the hotel. For more luxury, book a room in the Grand Fiesta, an 81-room adults-only section of the hotel whose rooms have amenities such as complimentary evening cordials and turn-down service, terry-cloth robes, private lounge for continental breakfast, and afternoon hors d'oeuvres. The hotel has all you could ask for from a deluxe resort, including a variety of restaurants and a prime location on one of Puerto Vallarta's most popular beaches. Honeymoon package: Eight days/seven nights: $840 per couple. Includes full American breakfast daily (one in bed with bottle of champagne), one dinner with wine, flowers in room, king-size bed. Available April 15 through December 15.

Los Tules Condominiums, Apdo. 169B, Puerto Vallarta, Jalisco 48300, Mexico (tel. 229/2-21-31; U.S. reservations: 206/537-7204 in Washington, or toll free 800/424-4441). Next door to the Fiesta Americana is Los Tules, a luxurious condominium village set amid 40 lushly gardened acres, with banana trees and winding cobblestoned streets. Units are attractively decorated and are ideal for honeymooners who would appreciate the at-home conveniences of kitchens and the other pluses of renting what are essentially fully equipped and fully furnished apartments. Master studios contain king-size beds and terraces or patios. There are five tennis courts and seven swimming pools, located right off the beach. Honeymoon package: None. Standard rates: $65 to $120 per couple per night for studios; $105 to $220 for one-bedroom units.

Bugambilias Sheraton, Apdo. 333, Puerto Vallarta, Jalisco 48300, Mexico (tel. 322/2-30-00; U.S. reservations: toll free 800/325-3535 nationwide; 800/392-3500 in Missouri). All the services you would expect from the Sheraton name are found at this sleek, modern hotel, whose six high-rise towers dominate the stretch of beach north of town. The largest hotel in Puerto Vallarta, the Sheraton is for couples who love being in the center of activity. There are four restaurants, five bars, Mexican fiestas each night, in addition to a daily roster of activities, most around the huge pool area. Five tennis courts are available. All rooms have ocean views and modern decor. Honeymoon package: Eight days/seven nights (BP): $685 per couple, low season. Includes deluxe oceanview room, full American breakfast daily, bottle of wine in room upon arrival, special discounts, and more. High-season rate (EP): $145 per couple per night.

Holiday Inn, Apdo. 555, Avenida De Las Garzas, Puerto Vallarta, Jalisco 48300, Mexico (tel. 322/2-17-00; U.S. reservations: 212/949-7250 in New York, or toll free 800/HOLIDAY). Two adjoining beachfront high-rises set the stage here for a modern first-class hotel. One tower contains 230 rooms and suites, while the second is more ideally suited for honeymooners with 236 more lavish suites with private terraces. Each room has a balcony, ocean view, cable TV, and servi-bar. A lovely pool area, three restaurants, two bars, a discothèque, and tennis are other pluses. There are plenty of activities: volleyball games, parasailing, and other water-based sports among them. Honeymoon package: Eight days/seven nights: $650 per couple (low season only). Includes upgraded room with king-size bed, welcome cocktails, American breakfast each day (one breakfast in bed with bottle of champagne), one dinner, flowers in room, and room tax.

Inexpensive

Puerto Vallarta's famed cobblestoned streets begin just outside the **Buenaventura,** Avenida México 1301, Puerto Vallarta, Jalisco 48300, Mexico (tel. 322/2-37-37; U.S. reservations: toll free 800/223-6764 nationwide; 800/522-5568 in New York), which manages to create a feeling of seclusion even though it's just steps away from the bustle of downtown. With all the services of a more luxurious hotel and such a prime location, this modern hotel offers a really good buy. An attractive five-story atrium lobby is the centerpiece of the hotel. Rooms are clean, comfortable, and nicely furnished. There are fashion shows and a Mexican Night once a week. Honeymoon package: Four days/three nights (BP): $205 per couple, low season. Includes bottle of champagne, welcome cocktails, breakfast daily, and one dinner for two. Call for high-season rates.

Molino de Agua, P.O. Box 54, Puerto Vallarta, Jalisco 48300, Mexico (tel. 322/2-19-07; U.S. reservations: toll free 800/826-9408 nationwide; 800/423-5512 in California), set among gardens accented by fountains, stone walkways, and cages with parrots squawking inside, this hotel lies hidden away beside the Río Cuale downtown. Older cabins are simple and clean with double beds and a terrace. There are also suites with ocean views in a new two-story addition on the beach. A casual, friendly atmosphere centers around and animates the two swimming pools. No frenzied activities or glitter of the high-rise resort hotels here. Honeymoon package: None. From $40 per couple per night for cabins; from $55 for suites.

ROMANTIC RESTAURANTS AND NIGHTSPOTS

Puerto Vallarta's restaurants can be blissfully quiet or fun and crazy, so there's a definite range from which to choose, both downtown and in the hotel zone.

Moderate

El Set, on the Mismaloya highway about two miles south of town (tel. 2-03-02). The hills of Puerto Vallarta afford many breathtaking views, but the setting of the El Set bar/restaurant, with its terraced seating and lush plants under a thatch roof, may afford the best of all. Famous for its "another lousy sunset in paradise" motto, El Set attracts Hollywood types and couples who enjoy watching the crashing ocean and twinkling of city lights, while sipping cool margaritas. Go for lunch and you can swim in the pool on the terrace. Seafood and steaks are specialties. Lunch for two from about $15; dinner about $35. Open daily from noon to 4 p.m. and from 7 to 10:30 p.m.

Chico's Paradise, off Mismaloya beach about 15 minutes south of town (no telephone, no electricity). Open daily from noon to 6 p.m., this is a place to spend the entire afternoon tucked away in the mountainous jungle. Wild, vibrant flowers, gushing waterfalls, and pools for swimming set the scene (make sure to bring swimsuits for a dip). Grilled steaks, spareribs, and Mexican food highlight the culinary offerings. Sample some of the delicious tequila and rum fruit-punch cocktails. Lunch for two with beer and wine is about $20 to $25.

La Hacienda, Aquacate 274 (tel. 2-05-90) is secluded from the hustle and bustle of town behind the walls of a former grand home. You've got the choice of a rustic, wood-beamed dining room or lush gardens for your dinner setting. Soft music and candlelight accompany such dishes as crêpes, French onion soup, Mexican platters, and grilled meats. Dinner starts at about $30 for two, plus wine, served from 7 to 10:30 p.m.

Daiquiri Dick's (tel. 2-05-66), Olas Altas 246, makes the perfect midday getaway spot after a morning on the beach. You can sit on the beach patio or in the indoor dining room decorated in a nautical motif while indulging in an extensive menu, including crêpes Suzette for dessert. Lunch for two (hamburgers, sandwiches) runs about $10; dinner with drinks about $25 to $30. Serving lunch, noon to 3:30 p.m.; and dinner, 6:30 to 10:30 p.m.

Carlos O'Brian's (tel. 2-14-44), Avenida Díaz Ordaz 786, is probably the wildest and most popular place in town, with live music and a party atmosphere. Lines to get in are not uncommon. Try the baked oysters, $4, or barbecued spareribs, $5. Open for lunch, noon to 3:30 p.m.; dinner, 6 to 11 p.m.

At **La Louisiane,** Lázaro Cárdenas 295 (tel. 2-53-27), Mexico meets the Big Easy with down-home, New Orleans–style seafood. Recommended dishes include the shrimp creole and the jambalaya, lightly spiked with Mexican chiles. Figure on $40 to $50 for dinner for two. Serving dinner from 6:30 to 10:30 p.m.

Moby Dick (tel. 2-06-55), just off the malecón on Cuale North, has a kitchen open to view that serves, arguably, the best seafood in town. Excellent fresh lobster ($20 to $25) and whole red snapper ($7) are the delights. Open nightly from 6:30 to 10:30 p.m.

When you enter **El Morocco** (tel. 2-20-10) at the Hotel Fiesta Americana, you'll feel as if you've stepped onto a movie set, thanks to the lavish, Casbah-like decor plucked straight from the Arabian Nights. Red snapper with orange sauce is delectable. Dinner about $40 for two. Open for dinner only, 6:30 to 10 p.m.

For dancing, head to **Capricco** (tel. 2-15-93), perched on a cliff and reached by funicular. A wild music-and-dance show erupts in the early morning hours (about 1:30 a.m.). It's on the highway to Mismaloya, about five minutes from downtown. You'll find live music for dancing or just listening at major hotels.

Downtown, the notable—and raucous—dancing spots are **Sundance** (tel. 2-22-96) and **City Dump** (tel. 2-07-19).

The new **Christine's** disco at the Krystal Hotel is fast becoming a favorite.

XI

MEXICO'S CARIBBEAN RESORTS

1. CANCÚN
2. COZUMEL

When Mexicans want to go on a beach vacation, they often head to a Caribbean island—without leaving their own country. Cancún and Cozumel, two tropical isles in the Caribbean Sea off the coast of the Yucatán peninsula, deliver practically goof-proof weather year-round, with temperatures averaging in the upper 80s and about 200 sunny days annually. The resorts abound in contemporary pleasures: from diving the second-longest coral reef in the world to dancing in laser-lit discos. The region is also one of Mexico's most historic, the setting for awesome ruins of the ancient Mayan civilization.

1. Cancún

This idyllic resort just off the tip of the Yucatán peninsula consists of mainland Cancún city and a narrow island of sand, almost 15 miles long, surrounded by lagoons and the sparkling waters of the Caribbean. The area receives little rain and maintains a steady 80° average temperature year-round.

Cancún provides a haven for water-lovers. The lagoons of Nichupte and Bojorquez to the west furnish secluded waters for waterskiing, windsurfing, and jet skiing, while the Caribbean side has the water sports as well as white, porous sand ideal for sunbathing. Abundant marine life makes for terrific snorkeling and scuba-diving everywhere on this coast. When you've had enough of the water, put on a pair of comfortable walking shoes, rent a car or join a day tour, and explore Mayan ruins. Chichen-Itza, the phenomenal and largest Mayan site in the Yucatán with its massive pyramids, makes a popular day trip (check hotel desks for tours, which run about $45 per person). If you can't find the time, don't despair: There are dozens of other Mayan sites, large and small, such as Coba, a jungle-covered city, and Tulum, 50 miles away (see "Romantic Interludes"). At night in Cancún, you can get a feel for traditional Mexico at the Ballet Folklórico (tel. 5-09-00), which entertains with music and dancing from all over the country. They perform every night except Sunday at the Inter-Continental Hotel; dinner and the show cost about $27 per person.

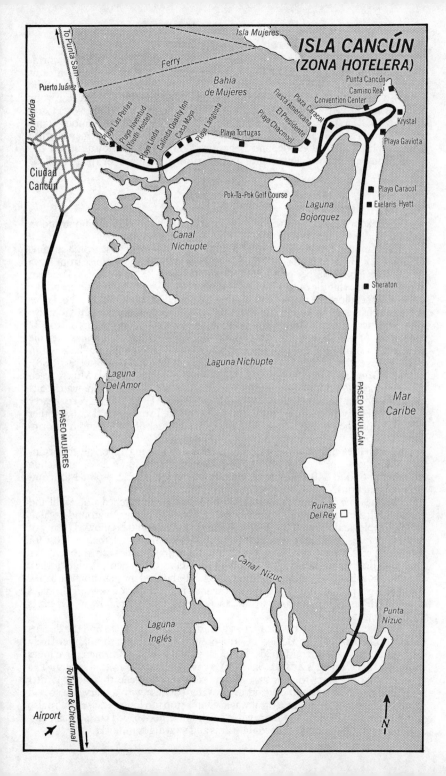

SHOPPING

Cancún has modern plazas and malls stocking goods from all over the world. **Ki-Huic,** downtown off Avenida Tulum, is one of the largest markets for Mexican handcrafts; stalls sell curios, serapes, and blouses, and bargaining is the order of the day. Also scope out the **flea market** just behind it. For top-notch sportswear, your best bets are the elegant shopping malls on Cancún Island, including Plaza Caracol, Plaza La Fiesta, and the new Flamingo. Here you can find famous-brand imports priced less expensively than back in the States, including merchandise from Ralph Lauren, ACA Joe, and Benetton. Don't miss the **boutiques** at the hotels: The ones at the Camino Real and Sheraton are known for their excellent selections.

ROMANTIC INTERLUDES

Water sports and the ancient ruins nearby nicely fill out any honeymoon agenda.

The islands of **Cozumel** and **Isla Mujeres** are just a short cruise from Cancún. Via an air-conditioned high-speed ferry, Cozumel is a 35-minute cruise from Playa del Carmen (about $5 per person round trip; tel. 4-64-33 or 4-69-35). The boat drops you in the middle of San Miguel, the main town; you can shop and spend the day there, or explore the many beaches (see "Cozumel" section). Various boat trips to tiny **Isla Mujeres** are offered by travel agencies. These usually take a total of five hours and include lunch, drinks, and on-board live music for dancing for $10 to $32 per person. At Isla Mujeres the boats dock at El Garrafón beach, which has a terrific coral reef for snorkeling. Several different boats depart daily, including the *Tropical,* which leaves each morning from the **Playa Langosta Tropical Dock** (tel. 3-14-88); the *Fiesta Maya* motor yacht—with a glass bottom—which visits Isla Mujeres each day from the **El Presidente** (tel. 3-18-04); and the *Aqua-quin* trimaran, which sails each day from the **Camino Real** (tel. 3-01-00, ext. 8703). There's even a party-hearty Pirate's Night adventure, complete with a dinner buffet, live show, and various other high jinks on the high seas (tel. 3-14-88). Check hotel desks for more information.

Cancún itself offers excellent snorkeling and scuba-diving, especially for beginners, since many fine reefs lie only 12 to 15 feet below the surface. For snorkeling trips (about $20 to $40 per person), contact **Ocean Sports** (tel. 4-60-34 for complete information).

Tulum is one of Mexico's most stunning Mayan cities. Perched atop a cliff and overlooking the turquoise of the Caribbean, it invites you to wander around its fascinating temples and ruins. If you take an organized tour, you'll be allowed plenty of time to explore, followed by lunch at the beachside Akumal Hotel, then let loose for snorkeling at **Xel-Ha** (pronounced shell-HA), a national park with seaside coves filled with brilliant tropical fish (you can rent snorkeling equipment, change clothes, and take showers here). An organized bus trip can be booked through hotel desks for about $25 per person. You can also rent a car and visit both on your own. Tulum lies about two hours down the coast from Cancún along a modern highway; Xel-Ha is practically next door to the ruins.

Rent a car and set out on the highway south of Cancún City to find the dozens of **hidden beaches** along Mexico's Caribbean coast. You'll pass through relatively developed areas of Puerto Morelos, Punta Bete, and Playa del Carmen. Five miles from Playa del Carmen is **Xcaret** (Shka-ret), a cove fed by underground springs. The grottos here have water so clear that you can see the rocks beneath. A little farther south is **Akumal,** a tranquil bay and underwater paradise with a marvelous beach protected from rough surf by a breakwater. Don't stop too long because you're also going to want to make it to **Chemuyil,** a small horseshoe-shaped cove. Its talcum-soft white sand is dotted with coconut palms and swaying hammocks.

HONEYMOON HOTELS AND HIDEWAYS

Because of its megasuccess, Cancún has been experiencing a building boom over the past two years. In addition to the opening of several spectacular new hotels, many of the older properties have undergone multimillion-dollar refurbishments. Cancún's hotels also are among the most expensive in all of Mexico, but honeymoon packages cut down on costs. During the off-season (mid-April through mid-December) prices drop by about a third. In particular, check out some of the newly opened hotels, many of which are offering low introductory rates.

Moderate

Camino Real, Paseo Kukulcán, Cancún, Quintana Roo 77500, Mexico (tel. 988/3-01-00; U.S. reservations: toll free 800/228-3000). Like the other hotels in the Camino Real chain, this one stands out for its bold architecture and setting. Shaped like a pyramid, the hotel sits on the tip of Punta Cancún so that it's bordered on three sides by the blue of the Caribbean. One of the property's unique features is the small Mayan ruin right on the cliffs fronting the sea. Thanks to a $9-million expansion and renovation project, the Camino Real looks more alluring than ever, with both a new lobby and a new 18-story tower. In the tower, you can treat yourselves to the select Royal Beach Club program, which includes concierge service, complimentary continental breakfast, cocktails and hors d'oeuvres each afternoon, and more. Throughout the hotel, every room has a private terrace from which to enjoy the sea views. A homey touch is the fresh flowers that are brought in each day. The suites contain living rooms and winding staircases leading to the bedrooms. The bevy of appetizing dining choices includes the new Calypso, Cancún's first restaurant spotlighting gourmet Caribbean cuisine. Honeymoon package: Seven days/six nights (EP): $990 per couple, low season. Includes lanai room with deluxe amenities and bathrobes, flowers and domestic champagne in your room upon arrival, one dinner for two with domestic wine. High-season rates: $215 per couple per night for a deluxe room.

Fiesta Americana Plaza Cancún and Villas, Paseo Kukulcán, Cancún, Quintana Roo 77500, Mexico (tel. 988/3-10-22; U.S. reservations: 212/949-7250 in New York; toll free 800/223-2332 nationwide). Your own private kingdom by the sea, a pink-walled minivillage that would fit right in on the French Riviera or alongside a desert oasis—that describes this captivating enclave. Accented by archways, towers, and minarets, the resort features accommodations in two main towers, as well as individual villas. Vacationers can enjoy the best of both worlds: the seclusion of private villas plus the services of a luxury hotel. Even the large and lovely standard rooms have the feeling of a suite, with a split-level design separating the sleeping and living areas. Expect pampering touches such as a marble stall shower and a bright hibiscus placed on your towel. All accommodations come with terraces or patios, satellite color TVs, and minibars. Although the beach is small, there are three swimming pools, plus three lighted courts for tennis buffs. In addition to the four excellent restaurants, the lounge in the impressive Italianate gray-and-rose marble lobby is the place to be seen sipping cocktails in the evening. Honeymoon package: Eight days/seven nights (BP): $1,125 per couple. Includes king-size bed in upgraded accommodations, full American breakfast daily (with one champagne breakfast in bed), welcome cocktails, fresh flowers in your room upon arrival, one dinner with half bottle of domestic wine. Available May through mid-December only.

Hotel Inter-Continental Cancún, Paseo Kukulcán, Cancún, Quintana Roo 77500, Mexico (tel. 988/5-07-55; U.S. reservations: toll free 800/327-0200). Crowning 52 acres of spectacular beachfront, the brand-new Inter-Continental caters to couples who want the best. The two interconnected nine-story towers incorporate Mexican design, with immense open areas and stunning corridors surrounding a soaring atrium. The spacious rooms certainly rank among the prettiest in Cancún. They're sophisticated yet very inviting, working off a soft beige palette with blond-wood cabinetry, adobe walls, and terra-cotta Mexican floor tiles spiced with brightly colored rugs. Furnishings come from the Mexican state of Jalisco, with the pottery crafted in Guadalajara. The marble bathrooms are outfitted with hairdryers, and you have use of terry-cloth robes during your stay. Of course, there's air conditioning—but for those who prefer their air au naturel, accommodations also feature ceiling fans and sliding louvered doors to the terrace. All rooms face either the Caribbean or Nichupte Lagoon. For water sports–lovers, there are two large swimming pools, plus sailing, windsurfing, scuba-diving, fishing, snorkeling, and jet skiing. On land, take advantage of the two lighted tennis courts, plus the fully equipped health club, which features Universal machines, free weights, and aerobics classes. Meanwhile, gourmets have a choice of four restaurants. Honeymoon package: Eight days/seven nights (BP): $1,190 per couple, low season. Includes deluxe oceanview room, breakfast in bed each morning, one dinner with domestic wine, bottle of domestic champagne upon arrival, bouquet of fresh flowers in your room, nightly turn-down service, and more.

Hotel Oasis, Paseo Kukulcán, Cancún, Quintana Roo 77500, Mexico (tel. 988/5-08-67; U.S. reservations: toll free 800/44-OASIS). With its steeply angled facades and pyramidal tower, this posh new hotel is a 21st-century descendent of the ancient Mayan cities of the Yucatán. Although the Oasis is the largest hotel in Mexico, with 1,200 rooms, it retains an intimate feeling because accommodations are divvied up among five different buildings. Since the property encompasses over 32 shorefront acres, you'll always have plenty of room. You'll be mesmerized by the quarter-mile-long swimming pool, Cancún's largest, a true aquatic playground with walk-through waterfalls and swim-up bars. The two-tone blue tiles that line the pool perfectly match the colors of the water lapping the wide beach. At the water-sports concession, you can rent equipment for snorkeling, windsurfing, sailing, jet skiing, and waterskiing, while four tennis courts, a pitch-and-putt golf course, and the spa/ health club help to keep you in tip-top shape. Especially eye-catching are the trompe l'oeil murals that adorn public areas and corridors. With their marble foyers, pale-pink stucco walls, and bright sapphire-blue spreads, the rooms pack plenty of flair (there's even a second phone extension in the marble bathroom). All accommodations have small balconies, as well as direct-dial phones, satellite color TVs, safes, and servi-bars. At mealtimes, you can choose from among 12 international restaurants. The hotel's outdoor amphitheater headlines razzle-dazzle Vegas-style shows, plus major stars such as Julio Iglesias. Honeymoon package: None. Rates: $120 to $190 per couple for a standard room; $145 to $210 for a deluxe room.

Exelaris Hyatt Regency, Paseo Kukulcán, Cancún, Quintana Roo 77500, Mexico (tel. 988/3-09-66; U.S. reservations: toll free 800/228-9000), is an elegant hotel, with an architecturally striking circular lobby where classical music is played in the evenings. All guest rooms feature private balconies with ocean views, air conditioning, color TVs, telephones, and minibars. For royal treatment, stay at the Regency Club on the top floors, where the personal service truly pampers. Here, you'll delight in such perks as a complimentary continental breakfast and free cocktails and hors d'oeuvres in the afternoon. A new fitness club has its own pool, gymnasium with Nautilus equipment, steam room, and Jacuzzi; in addition, there are two swimming pools and a large lagoon in which to swim. Honeymoon package: Eight days/seven nights (BP): $1,095 per couple, low season. "Temptingly Hyatt" package includes full American breakfast daily, welcome cocktails, rental car discounts, and more. High-season rates (EP): $220 per couple per night for an ocean-front room; $250 for Regency Club accommodations.

Hyatt Cancún Caribe, Paseo Kukulcán, Cancún, Quintana Roo 77500, Mexico (tel. 988/3-00-44; U.S. reservations: toll free 800/228-9000). After a multimillion-dollar renovation, this long-time favorite glitters with the panache of an all-new hotel. Waterfalls surround the driveway leading to the large and gracious lobby area, with see-through views toward the Caribbean. The property reflects a more Mexican verve, with a tile roof and pretty pink walls. Reconstruction has also tripled the size of the main swimming pool (there are also two smaller pools). The refurbished rooms are true knockouts, complete with lustrous beige marble floors and stylish new furniture. If you want to splurge, consider lodging in one of the villas, each with its own private terrace right beside the sea. For extra VIP service, there are also Regency Club accommodations. Three tennis courts and plenty of aquatic sports assure that you'll keep fit. The three restaurants include Blue Bayou for Cajun and creole cuisine. Honeymoon package: Eight days/seven nights (EP): $1,130 per couple, low season. Includes beachfront deluxe accommodations, bottle of champagne and tropical flowers in your room, breakfast in bed one morning, room tax, tour discounts, and more. High-season rates: $220 per couple for an oceanfront room.

Fiesta Americana, Cancún Boulevard, Cancún, Quintana Roo 77500, Mexico (tel. 988/3-14-00; U.S. reservations: toll free 800/223-2332). This hotel's quaint atmosphere makes it unique among Cancún's hostelries. The buildings, painted in pastel colors and topped with red-tile roofs, surround a striking pool area with tropical landscaping. At this five-star deluxe hotel, built to resemble a Mediterranean village, each of the 281 rooms is decorated with rattan furnishings counterpointed with bright tropical colors. In-room boons include color TVs, servi-bars, and private oceanview terraces, as well as plush terry robes to lounge in and turndown service to tuck you in at night. The tasty roster of restaurants includes lively Friday Lopez for drinks and barbecue specialties. Honeymoon package: Eight days/seven nights, $1,225 per couple, low season. Includes full breakfast each day (one in bed with a bottle of champagne), fresh flowers in the room, king-size bed, welcome cocktails, one dinner with half bottle of domestic wine, and more.

Cancún Sheraton Resort & Towers, Paseo Kukulcán, Cancún, Quintana Roo 77500, Mexico (tel. 988/3-19-88; U.S. reservations: toll free 800/325-3535). This is a big, activity-oriented, American-style hotel with a difference: namely, a small Mayan shrine right on the grounds. If you want plenty to see and do right at your hotel, this is the place. The Sheraton offers a full roster of daily events, from sightseeing excursions by bicycle to guacamole-making lessons. Loll around the large free-form swimming pool, join the gang for a round of water volleyball, hone your backhand on six lighted tennis courts, or go for a hole in one on the minigolf course. Set in pyramidal towers resembling Mayan temples, rooms treat guests to all the modern comforts, including telephones, color TVs, and minibars. The well-equipped gym features a sauna, steam room, and large whirlpool. Getting hungry? Take your choice of five restaurants and lounges. Honeymoon package: Eight days/seven nights (BP): $1,510 per couple, low season. Includes a deluxe oceanview room in Sheraton Towers, bottle of wine, two welcome cocktails, breakfast daily, and more. High-season rates (EP): $230 per couple per night for a junior suite with Jacuzzi.

Moderately Inexpensive

Cancún Palace, Paseo Kukulcán, P.O. Box 1730, Cancún, Quintana Roo 77500, Mexico (tel. 988/5-05-33; U.S. reservations: 305/375-9101 in Florida; toll-free 800/346-8225 nationwide). The name suggests the grandeur of this beachside resort: the striking statues of antelope poised in the reflecting pool, enormous champagne-colored marble lobby, "triplex" zigzag swimming pool. This five-star deluxe hotel—Mexico's highest rating—only opened in November 1988, and already it has become one of the leading places to see—and be seen in—in Cancún. Thanks to the sharply angled facade, each of the 421 rooms has a view of either the Caribbean or the lagoon—an outlook you can enjoy from your room's large terrace. Furnishings reflect the luxury touches you might find in a private hacienda. Mexican materials are used throughout: pale-blond marble for the floors, bleached caoba wood (the local mahogany) crafted into the delicately worked louvers and handmade bureaus. Original art adds color accents to the walls; a fully stocked servi-bar and satellite color TV give you all the comforts of home. The three restaurants are excellent, including Las Golondrias for Yucatecan cuisine. Honeymoon package: Eight days/seven nights (EP): $870 per couple, low season (high-season rates on request). Includes bottle of domestic champagne upon arrival, welcoming cocktails, flower arrangement in your room, transfers to and from Cancún airport, unlimited use of the gym, tips to bellhops and maids, special gift, and more.

Omni Cancún Hotel, Paseo Kukulcán, Cancún, Quintana Roo 77500, Mexico (tel. 988/5-07-14; U.S. reservations: toll free 800/THE OMNI). Luxury warmed by Mexican hospitality—that's what you'll find at the Omni, one of the most alluringly seductive of Cancún's new hotels. The people who designed this resort realize that details count, and you'll discern attention to beauty everywhere: from the lavish use of rose-colored marble for room floors and baths to the built-in closets crafted of mahogany. Upholsteries in pale hues of pink and celadon enhance views of the bright turquoise Caribbean. Accommodations feature balconies with views of either the sea or the lagoon, color TVs, servi-bars, and direct-dial telephones; room service functions around the clock. Meanwhile, the hotel sparkles with a distinctly Mexican vivacity; maids, for example, wear the traditional colorfully embroidered dress of the Yucatán. Set on an especially lovely stretch of beach, the Omni also features a sprawling succession of three interconnected swimming pools, including one with in-water lounge chairs—a boon for serious sunbathers. For recreation, there's a fitness center, as well as two lighted tennis courts. The three restaurants include the Fish Market, where you can savor fresh seafood tapas (hors d'oeuvres) while you watch the sunset. Honeymoon package: Eight days/seven nights (EP): $1,005 per couple, low season. Includes upgrade to a suite, complimentary welcoming cocktails, bottle of champagne, fresh flowers, one candlelight dinner, and tour of Tulum. Available mid-April through mid-December only. High-season rates: From $190 per couple per night.

Stouffer Presidente, Zona Hotelera, P.O. Box 451, Cancún, Quintana Roo 77500, Mexico (tel. 988/3-02-00; U.S. reservations: toll free 800/HOTELS-1). *"Muy impressionante"*—"Quite stunning"—was how one Mexican visitor described the Presidente, which recently reopened after a top-to-toe $15-million renovation. The refurbishments have earned the property a top-of-the-class, five-star deluxe rating. Consisting of a tower building and a low-slung pool unit, the 294-room hotel reposes along one of Cancún's nicest beaches, a crescent of sugar-white sand curving around the calm, outrageously blue water. The setting lends itself to every conceivable water sport, from waterskiing to windsurfing. There's also a lighted tennis court. Despite the striking architecture, the feeling is very friendly and welcoming. With its swim-up bar under a Mayan pyramid waterfall, the large pool area attracts one of the most convivial crowds in town. Facing either the lagoon or the sea, rooms are stylishly decorated with rattan furnishings and blue fabrics; all feature marble-walled baths, satellite color TVs, safes, and direct-dial telephones. The hotel has three restaurants, including the new, sumptuous Mediterranean, which highlights the specialties of Greece, France, Morocco, Spain, and Italy. Honeymoon package: Eight days/seven nights (BP): $980 per couple, low season (high-season rates on request). Includes room with king-size bed, breakfast daily, welcome cocktails, one candlelight dinner for two, bottle of white wine and fresh fruit basket in room, bottle of Damiana liqueur, special gift, and more.

Krystal Cancún, Paseo Kukulcán, Cancún, Quintana Roo 77500, Mexico (tel. 988/3-11-33; reservations: toll-free 800/231-9860 nationwide and in Canada). It has one of the most appealing swimming pools in Cancún—a swirly free-form design accentuated at its center by an island for sunbathing, with classical columns for a backdrop. Add in a fine stretch of beach, as well as the on-site presence of the wildly popular Christine's disco, and you'll understand why the Krystal has been a perennial top choice for Cancún-bound honeymooners. The 325 rooms have pleasant contemporary furnishings, plus such amenities as servi-bars and satellite color TVs. For extra pampering, chose accommodations on the new Krystal Club floors. In addition to an up-to-date health club, facilities include tennis and racquetball courts.

Of the five restaurants, Bogart's and Hacienda El Mortero (see "Romantic Restaurants" section) are among Cancún's standouts. Honeymoon package: Eight days/seven nights (CP): $825 per couple, low season. Includes Krystal Club accommodations, continental breakfast daily, welcome cocktails, champagne and cake in your room upon arrival, complimentary drinks and hors d'oeuvres each afternoon, one candlelight dinner at El Mortero, and more.

ROMANTIC RESTAURANTS AND NIGHTSPOTS

Chinese, German, Tex-Mex—these are some examples of the varied dining in Cancún. However, more than any other kind of cuisine, you'll find seafood, steak, and dishes of the Yucatán topping most menus.

Moderate

Restaurante du Mexique, Avenida Coba, Cancún City (tel. 4-10-77). Discover the true splendor of Mexican cuisine at this beautiful restaurant where the food, service, and ambience are absolutely impeccable. Although the setting is thoroughly contemporary, it is as supremely Mexican as the celebrations for Cinco de Mayo. Arched ceilings and stucco walls are accented by fine contemporary art (the pictures are for sale). Waiters wish you *"buen provecho"* ("good appetite") as they unfold napkins for ladies. The menu can best be described as Mexican nouvelle cuisine, using traditional ingredients (such as pumpkin, squash, jicama) in unusual ways to enhance meat, chicken, and seafood dishes. At the same time, many of the recipes are ancient, dating back to pre-Columbian times. Try a fine Mexican wine with your meal. Dinner for two, $40 to $50. Open for dinner only, 7 to 11 p.m.

L'Alternative, corner of Kukulcán and Avenida Bonampak, Cancún City (tel. 4-64-65). The elegant marble entryway, tall glass windows, and think-pink decor establish this as one of the most sumptuously romantic restaurants in Cancún. The fine French nouvelle cuisine soars, and afterward you can linger upstairs by the piano bar. Dinner for two, $50 to $60. Open nightly from 6 to 11:30 p.m.

La Dolce Vita, Avenida Coba, Cancún City (tel. 4-13-84). Pretty pastel colors and plush surroundings make this a favorite place to taste the sweet life, Italian style. Start off with a carpaccio romano or a fresh mixed green salad. Your dinner entrée might feature a filet mignon béarnaise, or tender calamari stuffed with shrimp mousse. For dessert, you'll have trouble choosing between the chocolate truffle cake and the lemon cheesecake. Dinner for two, $40 to $50. Open nightly from 6 to 11 p.m.

Hacienda El Mortero, Hotel Krystal, Cancún Island (tel. 3-11-33). A replica of a circa-1600 hacienda near Durango, El Mortero captures the romance of old Mexico. Built surrounding a fountain and plant-filled courtyard, the design incorporates graceful archways, mellowed-with-the-years tile floors, and heavy oak doors. The menu emphasizes favorite Mexican dishes. Begin with ceviche or Yucatecan lime soup, then choose from one of the specialties a la parrilla (grilled), including lobster, shrimp, and tenderloin steak. Team up dessert with a special coffee, laced with brandy, coconut liqueur, or xtabentum. Dinner for two, $60 to $100. Open for dinner only, 6 p.m. to midnight.

Bogart's, Hotel Krystal, Cancún Island (tel. 3-11-33). A kiss is still a kiss . . . a sigh is just a sigh . . . and as time goes by, lovers will have welcome memories of dinner at Bogart's. Certainly, you'll feel as if you've stepped into the film *Casablanca* as you walk through beaded curtains and enter a room filled with high-back rattan chairs and portraits of Humphrey Bogart. The cuisine is exotic, with offerings such as red snapper Bergman (with shrimp and hollandaise sauce) and duck Shanghai (flamed with Grand Marnier). Finish off with bananas Singapore or zabaglione. Dinner for two, about $60 per couple; open nightly from 7 p.m. to midnight.

Jalapeños, Hotel Zone, Cancún Island (tel. 3-28-96). No matter when you come, you'll feel as if you've walked into a fiesta at this party-happy restaurant beside the lagoon. They're known for their all-you-can-eat breakfasts (about $10 per couple), lunch specials such as grilled chicken or hamburgers ($15 per couple), and reasonably priced dinner entrées including spicy grilled shrimp ($20 to $30 per couple). There's mariachi music nightly from 5 to 7 p.m., and Monday night football on the big-screen TV in season. Open daily from 7 a.m. to midnight.

Perico's, 71 Yaxchilan, Cancún City (tel. 4-31-52). Pancho Villa and Emiliano Zapata would feel right at home at this lively cantina/restaurant. The decor reflects Mexican Revolution chic: hanging saddles, ancient rifles, and murals of real bandido-looking hombres slouching on the wall. An occasional papier-mâché skeleton sits propped on a bench for additional effect. Wear comfortable dancing shoes, because there's mariachi music in the afternoon, and a live band from 7 to 11 p.m. or so. The wide-ranging menu highlights steak and lobster dishes, priced $10 to $28. Open daily from 2 p.m. to 2 a.m.

Carlos 'n' Charlie's, Paseo Kukulcán, Cancún Island (tel. 3-08-46). The wacky furnishings include carousel horses out front, old photos of preening bullfighters and dandies on the walls, and a diver mobile dangling from the ceiling. And if you like, you can leave the restaurant something to remember you by—namely, by adding your autographed T-shirt to the collection hanging from the palapa roof. This wild and crazy branch of the hugely popular chain promises good times and good food. The large wooden menu divides selections into "peep" (chicken), "oink" (pork), and "moo" (beef) categories, with entrées ranging from $7.50 to about $30 for lobster. Plan to linger a while, because there's nonstop dancing on their pier fronting the lagoon. Open daily from 11:30 a.m. "until whenever," the manager says—"whenever" usually being way past midnight.

Looking for a cool, casual lunch stop while browsing through the boutiques at Plaza Caracol? Try **Casa Salsa,** right at the shopping center (tel. 3-11-14). Sample their Tex-Mex specialties, such as tacos or enchiladas, or an unusual entrée such as lobster in green sauce or jumbo shrimp with chayu (spinach) and flamed with xtabentum (a Mexican liqueur). Prices range from $20 to $60 per couple. Open daily for lunch, noon to 3 p.m.; dinner, 6 to 11 p.m.

Cancún's scintillating disco scene is starting to rival Acapulco's. **Christine's** at the Krystal Hotel is *the* place, with a dazzling light show that makes you feel as if you've been zapped into *Star Wars* or a computer-graphics program. Two newcomers—**Extasis** and **Daddy O**—have also started drawing crowds. **La Boom** in the Hotel Zone (tel. 3-11-52) attracts the younger, more casual set, while **Aquarius** (at the Camino Real) is the top choice of sophisticates.

Inexpensive

Los Almendros, downtown on Avenida Bonampak (tel. 4-08-07). When in Cancún, you may want to try dishes of the Yucatán, which are not fiery hot (no chiles are used). The cheerful dining room at Los Almendros sets the stage for such succulent fare as lime soup with chicken, and turkey in a white sauce of capers, olives, and almonds. Try the more famous Yucatecan specialties, such as cochinta pibil, which is beef marinated for 24 hours in a sauce with a variety of spices and then wrapped in banana leaves; or poc-chuc, slices of pork grilled with spices, orange juice, tomatoes, and onions. Or, better yet, order the combination plate. Lunch or dinner will run less than $15 per couple. Open daily from 11 a.m. to 9:30 p.m.

2. Cozumel

Cozumel lies like a jewel off the coast of the Yucatán. Mexico's largest island in the Caribbean, it is framed in white sand and pristine water that sparkle in the year-round sunshine. Physically, the island sprawls just 44 miles south of the sophisticated planned resort of Cancún, but in spirit, it's a world away. While Cancún is modern and luxurious, Cozumel is simple and relaxed—a haven for those just wanting to get away from it all.

Most of Cozumel is sparsely populated or uninhabited. All activity takes place on the west coast, where the major hotels dot the beaches south of the island's only town, San Miguel. Charming and still untouched by mass tourism, San Miguel provides plenty of people-watching in cafés and bars along the waterfront Avenida Rafael Melgar. There are dozens of small shops selling souvenirs, as well as designer resortwear and jewelry made from the black coral from the Palancar Reef.

SHOPPING

Cozumel attracts hundreds of happy cruisers (from ships) who hit the island's beaches, as well as the numerous stores in its main town, San Miguel. Consequently, despite the island's easygoing casualness, it features some fine shops. **El Mercado de Artesanías,** one block east of the square on Calle 1 Sur, is the place to pick up inexpensive souvenirs such as onyx chess sets, ceramic figurines, and woven belts. **La Concha** (Avenida 5 Sur) has unique made-in-Mexico items. **ACA Joe** (Calle 2 Norte) is another installation of the popular clothing chain. For more designer clothes, head for **Los Cinco Soles** on Melgar.

ROMANTIC INTERLUDES

There is much to explore and do on this island, 28 miles long and 11 miles across. Cozumel is perfectly located for excellent snorkeling and other **water sports.** At **Parque Chankanaab,** nine kilometers (5½ miles) south of town, you'll find a natural underwater park and botanical garden where you can spend a day exploring caves and the colorful life of a tropical reef (there is a small admission fee).

Off the shore of the south of the island is **Palancar Reef,** one of the longest coral reefs in the world, and thus a magnet for scuba-divers from all around the world. Cozumel is the closest Mexican resort to the Mayan ruins of **Tulum** and the lagoon of **Xel-Ha,** which are just across the water on the mainland (see the Cancún section).

On Cozumel itself, you can explore small, yet interesting, Mayan relics and ruins, such as **El Caracol,** a temple; and **El Cedral,** a tiny shrine. You can explore these by renting cars, Jeeps, or mopeds at hotels or in town.

So-called **Robinson Crusoe cruises**—all-day sailing and picnic lunch excursions—delight vacationers here. The most romantic of all journeys is to **Isla de la Pasion** (with a name like Island of Passion, it's got to be good) for a barbecue and day of seclusion on an islet just north of Cozumel. En route, the crew dives and fishes for your lunch, which is an orgy of red snapper, conch, and shellfish grilled on the beach. All-day adventures are about $30 per person, including lunch. Your hotel desk can sign you up for this and other boat excursions, including several to the breathtakingly vibrant coral reef, **Playa Palancar** (particularly fun are the glass-bottomed boat tours, both day and night, which run about $27.50 per person).

HONEYMOON HOTELS AND HIDEAWAYS

Cozumel does not have the luxury atmosphere of Cancún, but you'll still find hotels from deluxe to tourist class, and at lower prices. Like other resorts in Mexico the most modern, better hotels are located outside of town, while the less expensive and simpler properties are in the center of things. Special note for divers: All of the hotels listed offer diving packages, which might offer you better value.

Moderate

Plaza Las Glorias, Avenida Rafael E. Melgar, Cozumel, Quintana Roo 77600, Mexico (tel. 987/2-19-37; U.S. reservations: toll free 800/342-2644). Long known for its spectacular underwater scenery, Cozumel now lures visitors with a glamorous attraction on terra firma—the new and luxurious Plaza Las Glorías hotel. Painted sunny shades of ocher, terra-cotta, and pink, the red-roofed waterfront buildings look like a quaint village along the Riviera or Costa del Sol. Meticulous attention to detail assures that this is a class act: from the gray marble floors flecked with rose accents to the free-form pool deck thrust out over the limestone rocks and skirted by classical-motif columns. Rooms are designed to make guests feel pampered, with marble bathrooms, hand-sculpted shell-motif headboards, and rattan furnishings, set off by soft pastel colors. All accommodations face the sea, and a dive shop is right on the premises. San Miguel, with its lively shops and restaurants, is also close by. Honeymoon package: None. Rates: $95 to $120 per couple per night.

Sol Caribe, Playa Paraiso, Apdo. 259, Cozumel, Quintana Roo 77600, Mexico (tel. 987/2-07-00; U.S. reservations: toll free 800/233-2332). Dramatic Mayan architecture and an enormous free-form tropical pool mark this 310-room Mexican hotel, operated by the highly regarded Mexican hotel chain Fiesta Americana. Lush plants and trees spread over the grounds, giving a feeling of a newly discovered Mayan city. All units have servi-bars and spectacular views of the Caribbean. There is a nice cove for swimming and all the services of a deluxe hotel. Honeymoon package: Eight days/seven nights: $895 per couple, low season. Includes room with king-size bed, full breakfast each day (one in bed with bottle of champagne), one dinner with wine, fresh flowers in your room, and welcome cocktails. High-season rate: $155 per couple per night for a deluxe oceanview room.

Stouffer Presidente, Playa San Francisco, Cozumel, Quintana Roo 77600, Mexico (tel. 987/2-03-22; U.S. reservations: toll free 800/HOTELS-1), also is run by another prestigious Mexican chain. The island's first deluxe resort, it has 259 rooms divided between a beachfront tower and one-story wings. All rooms have colorful decor, ocean views, servi-bars and cable TVs; most have private terraces. The beach here is stunning. Honeymoon package: Eight days/seven nights: $900 per couple, low season. Includes deluxe room, breakfast each day, one candlelight dinner, fresh fruit in the room, welcome cocktails, bottle of wine, special gift, and more.

Mayan Plaza Hotel and Beach Club, P.O. Box 9, Cozumel, Quintana Roo 77600, Mexico (tel. 987/2-00-72). Although this is one of Cozumel's largest hotels, it retains a friendly, intimate feel. Accommodations are clustered in two low-rise buildings and a new 14-story tower (which contains marble-floored suites). Rooms feature contemporary rattan furnishings, telephones, two double beds, and terraces or balconies. From some of the downstairs rooms, you can walk right out to the nice spot of beach; there's also a large swimming pool. At mealtimes, take your choice of three restaurants. Honeymoon package: Eight days/seven nights (EP): $980 per couple, low season. Includes oceanview accommodations, round-trip airport transfers in Cozumel, welcome cocktails and a basket of fruit upon arrival, one dinner for two at Morgan's restaurant, souvenir T-shirts, and more. High-season rates: From $130 per couple per night.

Inexpensive

Cabañas del Caribe, P.O. Box 9, Cozumel, Quintana Roo 77600, Mexico (tel. 987/2-00-17). For sheer coziness, you won't find anything else quite like this on Cozumel. This casual inn about three miles north of town consists of 48 small bungalows on the beach—some older cabañas while others in the coconut grove are new units. Some have the added luxury of private terraces, and all are clean and comfortable with private baths and air conditioning. There are a small swimming pool, two restaurants, and a bar. Honeymoon package: Eight days/seven nights (EP): $765 per couple, low season. Includes oceanview accommodations, round-trip airport transfers in Cozumel, welcome cocktails and a basket of fruit upon arrival, one dinner for two at Morgan's restaurant, souvenir T-shirts, and more. High-season rates: From $95 per couple per night.

Casa del Mar, P.O. Box 129, Cozumel, Quintana Roo 77600, Mexico (tel. 987/2-16-65). Looking for a casual, congenial getaway in Cozumel? Casa del Mar

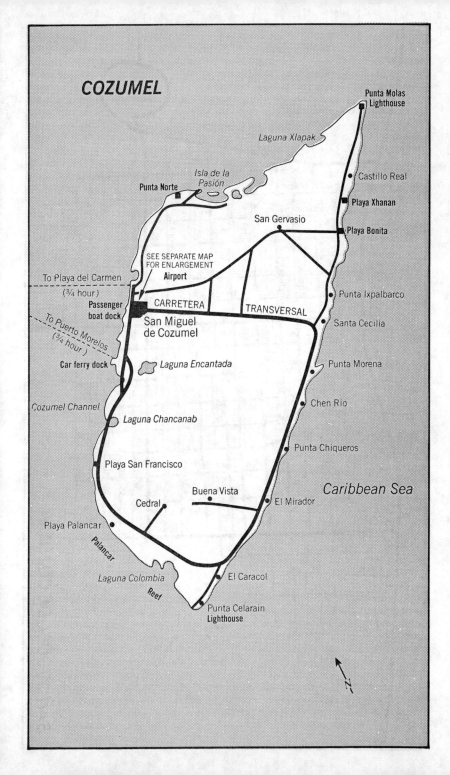

COZUMEL

Laguna Xlapak

Punta Molas
Lighthouse

Isla de la
Pasión

Punta Norte

Castillo Real

Playa Xhanan

San Gervasio

Playa Bonita

SEE SEPARATE MAP
FOR ENLARGEMENT

Airport

To Playa del Carmen
(¾ hour)

Passenger
boat dock

CARRETERA

TRANSVERSAL

Punta Ixpalbarco

Santa Cecilia

To Puerto Morelos
(¾ hour)

San Miguel
de Cozumel

Car ferry dock

Laguna Encantada

Punta Morena

Cozumel Channel

Chen Rio

Laguna Chancanab

Playa San Francisco

Punta Chiqueros

Buena Vista

Caribbean Sea

Cedral

El Mirador

Playa Palancar

Palancar

Laguna Colombia

Reef

El Caracol

Punta Celarain
Lighthouse

N

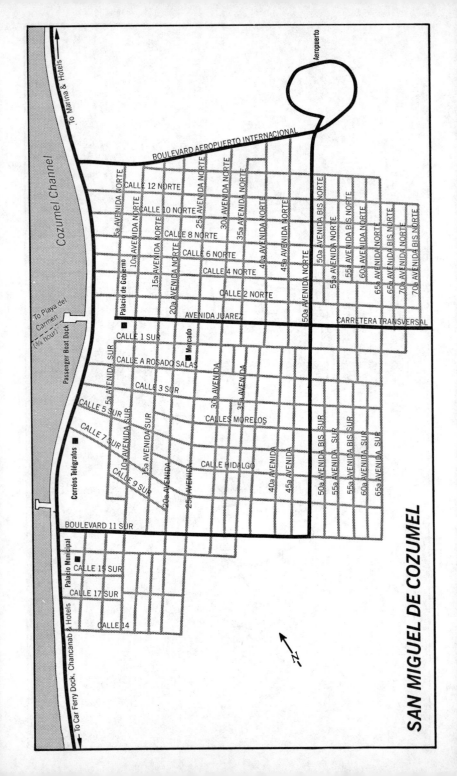

SAN MIGUEL DE COZUMEL

provides a perfect home away from home—especially for divers, thanks to its excellent Del Mar Aquatics facility. Built around a garden courtyard and fountain, the 106 rooms have plenty of Mexican charm, with latilla ceilings and yellow-tiled baths, plus both air conditioning and ceiling fans for comfort. The cabanas are especially appealing, with their stone walls and separate living/sleeping areas. Although there is no private beach, the property has a freshwater swimming pool and Jacuzzi. Shaded by a large palapa, the restaurant makes a popular gathering spot for swapping fish tales after a day's diving. Honeymoon package: None. Rates: $55 to $65 per couple per day for a double room; $90 to $100 for a cabana.

Hotel La Ceiba, P.O. Box 284, Cozumel, Quintana Roo 77600, Mexico (tel. 987/2-00-65; U.S. reservations: 214/692-5277 in Texas; toll free 800/621-6830 nationwide). Long ago, the ancient Maya considered the ceiba tree sacred, believing that it possessed magical powers for rejuvenation. Today, La Ceiba resort offers water-minded vacationers if not rejuvenation, at least revitalization. A longtime favorite of divers, La Ceiba also delights honeymooners with its list of amenities, including in-room telephones, color TVs, servi-bars, air conditioning, and ceiling fans, as well as on-site sauna and massage facilities. Accommodations are simple yet modern, and squeaky clean. Decorated with jumbo-size terra-cotta jars and carved cabinets, lobby areas are spacious and gracious. In addition to the freshwater pool, there's a small man-made beach; the restaurant is excellent. Honeymoon package: None. Rates (EP): $65 to $110 per couple per night for a standard room, depending on season.

ROMANTIC RESTAURANTS AND NIGHTSPOTS

Lunch in Cozumel will probably be at a small restaurant at the beach or at your hotel, while you'll probably want to walk along the waterfront in town for dinner and nightlife. A specialty in restaurants is conch—or, in Spanish, *caracol*—found mainly in this area.

Moderate

Morgan's (tel. 2-05-84) is the restaurant to choose for the special night out. It is one of the most elegant places to eat in Cozumel, and seafood and prime rib are the specialties. A dinner for two will be about $40. Open nightly from 8 to 11 p.m.

Inexpensive

Las Palmeras, on San Miguel's waterfront (tel. 2-05-32). This bistro-like restaurant is popular all day long as a people-watching hangout, probably because of its breezy location across from the ferry pier. You can get a reasonably priced breakfast or lunch, everything from hamburgers to Yucatecan specialties and there's often live music. Breakfasts of bacon and eggs will be about $2.50, while lunch and dinner entrées of seafood will run from $5 to $10. Open daily 8 a.m. to 11 p.m.

Pepe's Grill (tel. 2-02-13) entices with soft lights and tables open to the Caribbean breezes. Meat and fish specialties run $6 to $10 per entrée for dinner. Open nightly from 7:30 to 10 p.m.

Perhaps your most memorable meal of all will be lunch at **La Laguna** restaurant (no phone) at Parque Chankanaab. Here, shaded by thatch-roofed palapas and just a conch's crawl from the water, you can feast on specialties such as sopa de lima (chicken soup laced with strips of tortillas) and chicken mole. Lunch for two, $10 to $15 per couple. Open daily from noon to 5 p.m.

As in other Mexican resorts, most evenings you'll find a Fiesta Mexicana at one of the hotels, with mariachi bands and dancing along with a buffet. Inquire at the **Stouffer Presidente** and the **Sol Caribe**. For dancing, the popular clubs are **Scaramouche** (by the harbor), **Neptuno** (downtown), and **Maya 2000** (at the Sol Caribe).

PART THREE

THE CARIBBEAN, THE BAHAMAS, AND BERMUDA

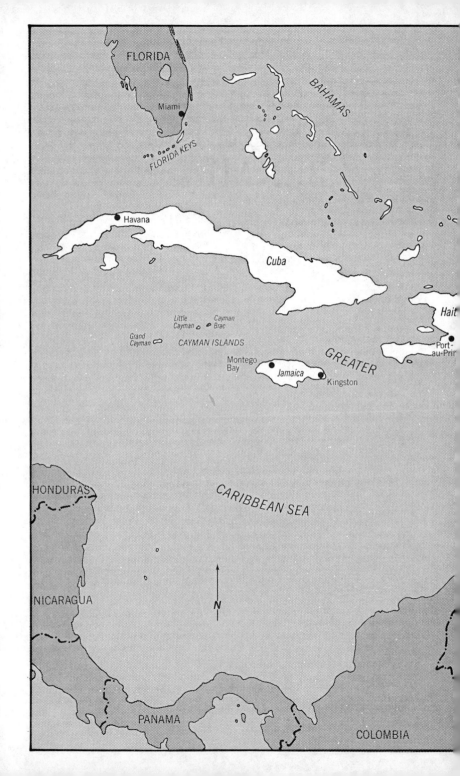

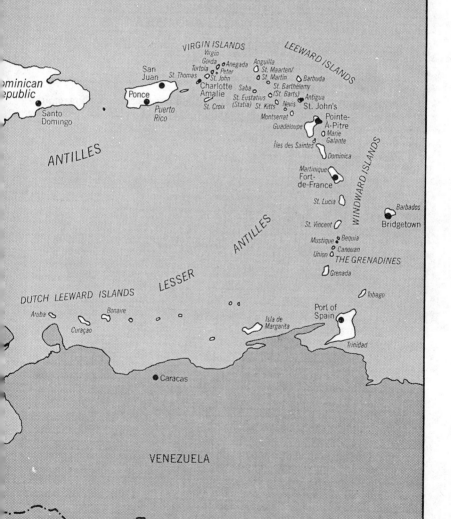

THE CARIBBEAN ISLANDS

| 0 | kms | 400 |
| 0 | miles | 200 |

ATLANTIC OCEAN

VIRGIN ISLANDS

LEEWARD ISLANDS

Dominican Republic

Santo Domingo

San Juan

Ponce

St. Thomas

Puerto Rico

Virgin Gorda

Tortola

St. John

Peter

Anegada

Charlotte Amalie

St. Croix

Saba

St. Eustatius (Statia)

Anguilla

St. Maarten/ St. Martin

St. Barthélemy (St. Barts)

St. Kitts

Nevis

Barbuda

Antigua

St. John's

Montserrat

Guadeloupe

Pointe-À-Pitre

Marie Galante

Îles des Saintes

Dominica

Martinique

Fort-de-France

St. Lucia

Barbados

Bridgetown

WINDWARD ISLANDS

St. Vincent

Mustique

Union

Bequia

Canouan

THE GRENADINES

Grenada

ANTILLES

LESSER

ANTILLES

DUTCH LEEWARD ISLANDS

Aruba

Bonaire

Curaçao

Isla de Margarita

Tobago

Port of Spain

Trinidad

Caracas

VENEZUELA

ANGUILLA

Exactly two hours ago on the airplane, your mind was busily scribbling reminders to itself. "Sell that stock." "Buy cat food the moment you get home." Now at the beach, you are completely mesmerized by the blue water, flat as glass and equally clear. A little wavelet froths up the powdery sands at the shoreline. Whoosh . . . as the ripple withdraws, the sea returns to absolute transparency. Somewhere in the distance, a calypso band rhythms into "Don't worry, be happy." You don't, you are.

That's the kind of tranquility you'll discover on the island of Anguilla. If you're looking for complete relaxation—in ultimate style—you've come to the right place. A little over ten years ago, the island had no electricity. No telephones. No roads. No real hotels—maybe just two cottages that took in guests. Today, it has become a "must" for the world's most fashionable vacationers, home to some of the most luxurious resorts in the Caribbean. Not that Anguilla has gone big-time metropolitan either. There are still only four traffic lights on the island, and the phone directory is thinner than most college alumni magazines. The shores of this northernmost of the British Leeward Islands are lapped by both the Caribbean Sea to the south and the Atlantic Ocean to the north. Because of the low annual rainfall, vegetation is sparse—some agave cactus here, a few sea grapes there. But Anguilla also has abundant treasure: its dazzlingly white coral-sand beaches and luminous blue waters—a contrast so scintillating that you can practically feel your nerve endings working overtime as your eyes try to adjust.

Lying low in the water (the island high spot, Crocus Hill, is only 212 feet above sea level), the flat profile differs markedly from the craggy peaks of St. Martin, which is only 5 miles away. Although the island is 16 miles long, it's only 3 miles wide. Because of its slender, squiggly shape, Christopher Columbus named the island Anguilla (which means "eel" in Italian) when he first sighted it in 1493. Because of the fierce, cannibalistic Carib Indians who inhabited the island, no Europeans attempted to establish a colony there for over 150 years. Finally, in 1650, English settlers moved over from nearby St. Kitts. They were followed by numerous Irish immigrants, who fled to the faraway West Indies to escape religious persecution under Cromwell. (Today, you can still detect an Irish brogue when Anguillans speak.) Notwithstanding French attempts to invade the island in 1745 and 1796, Anguilla remained British throughout the 18th- and 19th-century battles among the great European powers. To streamline management of its distant colonies, Britain merged Anguilla and St. Kitts into a federation in 1871; Nevis was grafted on to the group in 1882. Very independent and proud of their heritage—the plantation system (and consequently slavery) never really took hold here, and Anguillans have been independent landowners for generations—the Anguillans disliked being dominated by their larger Caribbean neighbors. And when Britain granted the St. Kitts–Nevis–Anguilla triumvirate independent statehood in 1967, matters led to one of the more peculiar political imbroglios of recent times. Carrying pitchforks and other farm implements, the Anguillans marched their St. Kittian governor off the island, then demanded that Great Britain take Anguilla back as a Crown Colony. This "mouse-that-roared" type of peaceful revolution worked. Today, Anguilla is a British Dependency, administered by a governor (appointed by the queen) as well as by ministers appointed from the elected members of the Legislative Assembly. Anguilla's population numbers only about 7,000.

Tourism is genuinely welcomed here. Until recently, the island had no industry to speak of other than fishing and some agriculture, and Anguillans had to move elsewhere in order to earn a living. Now, many have come home to work on their lovely island, and to enjoy sharing its beauty with visitors. Settlements dot the entire landscape. Anguilla's main town is known simply as "The Valley," located roughly at the island's center. Here you'll find the administration buildings and banks, as well as the gas station.

Many Caribbean islands claim to offer sun, sea, and sand. But no place gives you as much sunshine . . . such true-blue waters . . . such pearlescent beaches . . . as tiny Anguilla.

1. Practical Facts

ENTERING AND LEAVING

Proof of citizenship is required for both Americans and Canadians. Passports are preferred, although a photo ID (such as a driver's license), *plus* an authenticated birth certificate or voter registration card, is also acceptable. When you leave Anguilla, there is a per-person departure tax of $5.

GETTING THERE

Currently, there is no nonstop air service from the United States to Anguilla. The two main gateways are San Juan, Puerto Rico, and St. Martin. From San Juan, **American Eagle** offers frequent flights to Anguilla's Wallblake Airport; the trip takes about 50 minutes. **WINAIR (Windward Island Airways)** has regularly scheduled service from St. Martin; the flight lasts only 10 minutes. **LIAT** offers several flights a week from Antigua; WINAIR and **Air BVI** fly from St. Thomas in the U.S. Virgin Islands.

GETTING AROUND

There are two basic modes of transportation.

By Taxi

Taxis are readily available. Rates are fixed by the government; you should nevertheless always ask the driver how much the fare will be before you head off. Although prices are fairly reasonable, fares will really start adding up if you do a lot of exploring during the day and dining out at night. Consider renting a car.

Rental Cars

These are available both from several local agencies and from several of the major U.S. companies. Rates for an air-conditioned, compact car run about $40 a day. To drive, you will need a temporary Anguillan license; it costs $10 and is available from rental car agencies. You will need to show a valid U.S. driver's license to obtain it. Driving is on the left, British style. It is practically impossible to get lost, since there is only one main road on the entire island. Please observe the 30 mph speed limit, and watch for children and animals. Although the main road is good, the long driveways into even some of the poshest hotels tend to be what the Anguillans refer to as "natural" roads, i.e., unpaved. In addition to cars, you can rent motorbikes or minimokes (dune-buggy-like vehicles with canvas tops and open sides).

LANGUAGE AND MONEY
English is the official language, often accented by a West Indian lilt. Like the rest of the Leeward Islands, Anguilla uses the Eastern Caribbean dollar, known locally as the "Bee Wee." Currently, the official exchange rate is EC$2.60 to US$1. Practically all stores, taxi drivers, and restaurants will accept American currency, but ask in advance to be sure. Unless otherwise noted, all prices in this chapter are in U.S. dollars.

WEATHER
You couldn't ask for anything better, with temperatures averaging around 80°. Annual rainfall varies greatly, ranging from 22 to 50 inches a year.

CLOTHING
Anguilla embraces an easygoing lifestyle. During the day at your resort, you'll probably wear sports attire or bathing suits (with coverups for restaurants). Anguillans have a respect for proper decorum, so please do not wear swimsuits in public places or while sightseeing. Even at the ritziest places, dressing up at night means putting on long pants; men are not required to wear jacket and tie.

TIME
All year, Anguilla remains on Atlantic Standard Time, which is one hour ahead of Eastern Standard Time. This means that in winter, when it is noon in New York, it is 1 p.m. in Anguilla. In summer, when Daylight Saving Time is in effect in the United States, the times are the same.

TELEPHONES
You can call Anguilla direct from the mainland United States. First dial 809 (the area code), then the seven-digit phone number.

SHOPPING
Although you'll find some appealing crafts items, Anguilla is not the spot for megashoppers. Fortunately, St. Martin (just a 20-minute ferry ride away) offers some of the best duty-free buys in the entire Caribbean. See details that follow in "Romantic Interludes." One of your best shopping choices in Anguilla is the **Au Revoir Gift Shop** at the airport, which carries a good selection of ceramics and wood crafts by well-known island sculptor Courtney Devonish. The boutiques at The Mariners and Coccoloba resorts also feature interesting works by local artisans.

SPECIAL EVENTS
Several rousing celebrations highlight the Anguillan calendar. **Anguilla Day,** May 30, marks the start of the movement for separation from the St. Kitts/Nevis federation. But the biggest shebang of the year is **Carnival.** Held at the beginning of August, events include boat races, street dancing, calypso competition, beach barbecues, and the crowning of the Carnival queen.

HOW TO GET MARRIED IN ANGUILLA
The island makes it easy for couples who want to say their "I do's" here. You will have to be in Anguilla for at least 48 hours before you apply for a license. The license will be issued upon presentation of valid proof of citizenship from your

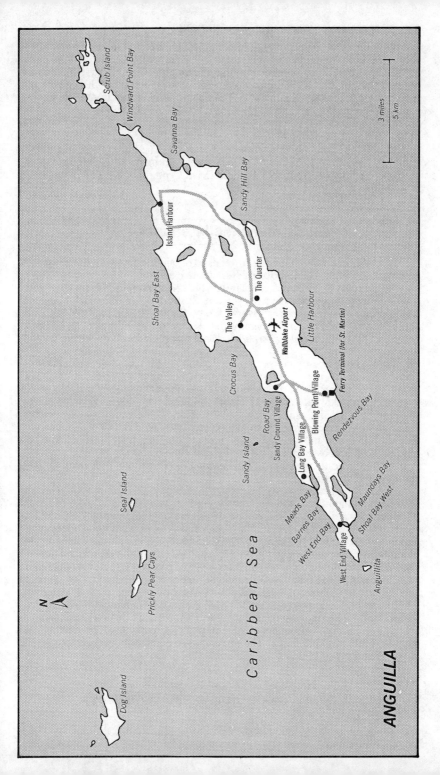

ANGUILLA

home country, such as a passport or authenticated birth certificate and a photo ID. If applicable, proof of divorce must be shown. The fee for the license is $188, plus a $12 stamp duty. (If you have been in Anguilla for more than 15 days, the costs are much less.) Your hotel can help you make all the arrangements with the registrar and magistrate; or contact a wedding service: **Sunshine Lady Productions,** Box 85, The Valley, Anguilla, Leeward Islands, B.W.I. (tel. 809/497-2911).

FOR FURTHER INFORMATION
Contact the **Anguilla Department of Tourism,** The Valley, Anguilla, B.W.I. (tel. 809/497-2759). In the U.S.: **Anguilla Tourism Information Office,** Medhurst & Associates, 1208 Washington Drive, Centerport, NY 11721 (tel. 516/673-0150).

---

2. Romantic Interludes

The laid-back pace on Anguilla extends to the sightseeing, with no "must-see" landmarks but plenty of near-deserted strands to explore.

Anguilla has over 30 beaches, many of which belong on any "best in the world" list. Even at the height of the season, you can usually discover a deserted cove somewhere on the island, perhaps at **Savannah Bay, Captain's Bay,** or **Shoal Bay** (nice snorkeling and great beach bars here). Ringed by coral reefs, Anguilla also offers excellent scuba-diving. Contact **Tamariain Watersports,** a PADI diving facility (tel. 497-2020).

If even these bounteous beaches are not enough for you, dozens of more pristine strands await on tiny cays just offshore from the Anguilla "mainland." Play castaways for the day on one of the popular **sailing/snorkeling cruises** that take you to islets such as **Prickly Pear** or **Sandy Island.** Sandy Island, for example, looks exactly like everyone's tropical fantasy, a tiny dollop of land completely ringed by beaches, with a few palm trees sprouting from its center. Here, you can view rainbow-hued tropical fish as you snorkel, and then enjoy a delicious picnic lunch of barbecued chicken, fish, or lobster (about $20 to $40 per couple). **Sandy Island Enterprises** (tel. 497-6395) can take you there for about $15 per couple; your hotel can also make arrangements for an excursion.

When Anguillans crave the bright lights and the big city, they hop aboard the ferry for a 20-minute cruise to **St. Martin.** For honeymooners also, a day trip to St. Martin makes an exciting change of pace from the languid, sunstruck spirit of Anguilla. Shared by both France and the Netherlands, St. Martin is known as both the shopping and the culinary capital of the Caribbean. Browse for duty-free bargains along Front Street in Philipsburg, on the Dutch side. In Marigot or Grand Case on the French side, linger for a *très français* dinner of pâté and coq au vin (chicken in wine sauce), topped off by chocolate mousse for dessert. Then hear the croupier call "Place your bets" at one of the island's glamorous casinos. (See the St. Maarten/St. Martin chapter for complete details.) The ferry departs from Blowing Point, Anguilla, and lands at Marigot, on the French side of St. Martin. The ferry runs approximately every half hour from 8 a.m. to 5:30 p.m.; a late-evening ferry also operates between Christmas and Easter. The trip costs $16 per person, round trip, plus the departure tax.

---

3. Honeymoon Hotels and Hideaways

Whether you want to live in the lap of luxury or in tropical simplicity, you'll enjoy a wide choice of accommodations on Anguilla. When looking at room rates, remember that a government room tax of 8% and a gratuity charge of 10% will generally be added to your bill. Unless otherwise noted, rates indicate the difference between high- and low-season prices.

VERY EXPENSIVE

Cap Juluca, P.O. Box 240, Anguilla, Leeward Islands, B.W.I. (tel. 809/497-6666 or 497-6779; U.S. reservations: 914/241-8770, or toll free 800/235-3505). If Scheherazade had taken up architecture rather than storytelling, the splendid buildings she would have designed would probably have resembled Cap Juluca. The resort enclave looks as if it had been plucked straight from the *Arabian Nights,* with stark-white turrets, domes, and minarets backdropped by a shocking-blue sea. The place is the dream-come-true of Robin and Sue Ricketts, the original co-creators of the exceptional Malliouhana (see write-up that follows). In designing their new resort (it opened in 1988), the Rickettses wanted to create a hideaway that was even more private . . . more romantic . . . more sexy. Indeed, everything at Cap Juluca helps enhance amorous impulses. As part of the nightly turn-down service, your maid lowers the lamps and lights a candle. Even the bathrooms feature dimmer switches (more about the bathrooms later on).

The resort encompasses some 180 acres, languidly arced along Maundays Bay and Cove Bay. Here, the sugar-white sand contrasts with the true-blue water, which glimmers turquoise near the shore, profound indigo farther out. In the distance, the silhouettes of St. Martin and Saba hover on the horizon, like a dusky mirage. While Malliouhana tends to attract people who want to be seen, Cap Juluca appeals to couples who want to hide. Privacy is treasured and nurtured. Breakfast is served on your private balcony, with only the tiny yellow-breasted sugar birds for chattering companions. No need to go out to dinner: Your meal can be delivered to your villa from Pimms Restaurant, or else a local cook can prepare a delicious West Indian dinner right in your kitchen. All 34 accommodations are ensconced in private villas, just a hop, skip, and jump from the sea. Nestled among the sea-grape trees in white villas, each of the accommodations is absolutely huge, comprising nearly 1,000 square feet of indoor and outdoor living space. With their grillwork and tiled courtyards, the villas would look equally at home in Casablanca. Strikingly exotic antiques—a Moroccan saddlebag here, a hand-embroidered "wedding belt" there—add character to the fine wicker furnishings. Louvered doors open onto large terraces, where archways frame the seaward views. The *pièces de résistance,* however, are the enormous (12-by-18-foot) bathrooms, lined with blond marble. The soaking tub for two comes thoughtfully provided with twin pillows on which to rest your heads; floor-to-ceiling windows front a small, extremely private garden where you can dry off au naturel. Even Aladdin with his magic lantern couldn't improve upon the impeccable service, with staff at guests' beck and call from dawn . . . to nearly dawn again. No need to keep your idylls idle: The resort offers three tennis courts, two lighted for night play. Sunfish and Hobie-Cat sailing, as well as windsurfing, are free for guests. "We wanted to build a fantasy," says Sue Ricketts. They succeeded. Honeymoon package: None. Rates (CP): $200 to $435 per couple per night for a beachfront double room. The resort closes in September and October.

Malliouhana Hotel, P.O. Box 173, Meads Bay, Anguilla, Leeward Islands, B.W.I. (tel. 809/497-6111; U.S. reservations: 212/696-1323). With its splashing fountains, Indian paintings, and tall archways, Malliouhana embodies the romance and beauty of the exotic East—a veritable oasis of luxury. Peace and tranquility are pervasive here. So is the desire to pamper guests to the hilt. Dramatically crowning a bluff overlooking two exquisite beaches, the resort encompasses 25 acres. The design can best be described as Moorish-modern, with archways, stark-white facades, and red-tile roofs. The 53 rooms are tucked into private villas as well as the main lodge. Understated island luxe characterizes the decor, with treasures from all over the world hobnobbing together. In the lobby lounge, huge Haitian-design murals depict an enchanted jungle with giraffes and cavorting monkeys. Louvered closets of

Brazilian walnut run practically the full length of the bedrooms. Some accommodations feature a honeymoon-worthy four-poster canopied bed. Bathrooms are a stunning symphony of beige marble, with large mirrors completely surrounded by lights. All accommodations feature telephones, minibars, and safe-deposit boxes; most are air-conditioned. You'll probably spend lots of time on your private terrace, designed for outdoor living with comfortable chairs, spacious tables, and a spectacular view of the sea. In addition to the two miles of white-sand beaches, Malliouhana offers three swimming pools: one for diving, one for swimming, and one that serves as a children's wading pool. Most water sports are complimentary for guests, and there are four tennis courts. For dining with a view, you can't surpass Malliouhana's clifftop terrace, where bright-coral bougainvillea frames views of the turquoise sea. Honeymoon package: None. Rates (EP): $230 to $460 per couple per night for a double room. Suites also available.

Coccoloba Plantation, P.O. Box 332, Barnes Bay, Anguilla, Leeward Islands, B.W.I. (tel. 809/497-6871; U.S. reservations: 212/696-4566, or toll free 800/225-4255). On one hand, you can describe Coccoloba by what it is: elegant, secluded, and sophisticated. But perhaps you can glean a better sense of its magnetic charms by a litany of what it's *not:* not pretentious, not isolated, and never, ever boring. Coccoloba is as refined and polished as any resort you'll encounter on this planet—and also one of the most fun. Crowning a low ridge right on the sea, the resort is blessed (not an overstatement) with two unbelievably long, blindingly white beaches. Unfurling for 1½ miles like a white satin ribbon, Barnes Bay is the "active" beach. Here, you'll find a lineup of Sunfish and Windsurfers, while waiters cheerfully prowl the sands in search of thirsty sunbathers, eager to fetch them a piña colada or a Coccoloba special (a heady potion made with rum and coconut). At the right end of the strand, there's a cave you can snorkel into (regular denizens include some pufferfish and a school of squid). Meanwhile, Meads Bay beach, just a five-minute stroll away from the main buildings, is for true escapists, with a mile of pristine sand. Throughout Coccoloba, the staff is super-friendly and accommodating. At how many other resorts in the world would a water-sports concession reopen after 6 p.m. to lend some just-arrived guests some snorkeling equipment?

There are only 51 accommodations, all with ocean views and both air conditioning and ceiling fans. Most of them are located in private villas that make you feel as if you have your own home in Anguilla for the week. Painted lemon yellow, the villas are very welcoming, with tall peaked roofs and winsome gingerbread trim on the front verandas. The proportions of the bi-level suites are spacious, with a sitting area downstairs and a large bedroom suite upstairs; the bamboo-edged furnishings and batik fabrics reflect tropical elegance. Help yourselves from the fully stocked refrigerator and minibar. Maid service is crackerjack. Dirty towels never tarried: Whenever we left our room for even five minutes, the maids would whisk a bevy of fluffy replacements into position. The tennis facilities are absolutely top-notch, with two courts under the direction of the Peter Burwash organization; every week, various guest tournaments are scheduled.

If wining and dining figure high on your list of vacation priorities, you'll find the Coccoloba restaurant superb. For breakfast, help yourself from the lavish continental buffet, with fruits, yogurts, cereals, and admirable croissants and brioches. At dinnertime, choose from exquisitely prepared European and Caribbean fare. Guests also enjoy complimentary afternoon tea, complete with finger sandwiches and melt-in-your-mouth walnut cookies—so delicious is the afternoon tea, in fact, that you'll wonder why we Americans abandoned the practice when we tossed out the Brits. And—best recommendation of all—the resort attracts many honeymooners each week. "We couldn't have found a more perfect place," commented one couple we talked with. "And the people are so friendly here." If you're considering launching your honeymoon with an island marriage, Coccoloba has just the spot: a small deck thrust out on a coral promontory, facing the setting sun. Honeymoon package: Seven days/six nights (BP): $1,320 to $1,780 per couple. Includes iced bottle of champagne, full American breakfast daily, use of sauna and two complimentary half-hour massages, three-day car rental, gift shop certificate, snorkeling trip to neighboring island. High-season rates (BP): $460 per couple per night.

MODERATE

The Mariners, Sandy Ground, Anguilla, B.W.I. (tel. 809/497-2671; U.S. reservations: 501/921-4237 in Arkansas or Alaska; toll free 800/223-0079 nationwide). One of the best small inns in the Caribbean—that describes this thoroughly captivating retreat on Road Bay. Everything is just so: from the plump pink-striped cushions arrayed on the poolside lounges to the framed Caribbean prints adorning cottage walls. Sandy paths edged with coral stone meander through the lovely gardens, a floral tapestry of bougainvillea, hibiscus, flamboyant, and oleander. Indeed, the eight-acre property flourishes like a veritable Garden of Eden, with ripe bananas, soursops, and paw-paws all ready to plop into your hands. The white gingerbread-trimmed cottages are true West Indian gems, primped by shutters painted dapper shades of red, aqua, yellow, and blue. Many different—but equally heart-winning —accommodations are available, poised cliffside or snuggled into the sea-grape trees; some are air-conditioned. Studio accommodations, for example, might feature pale-beige tile floors, white rattan furnishings, and white cotton fabrics patterned with the palest of pastels. Most of the cushions are handmade on Anguilla by local craftspeople. Bathrooms are absolute standouts, with their glass-enclosed showers, sparkling tiles, and thoughtful amenities basket. At night, eyelet-edged pillows grace the beds. Views will vary: Some accommodations face the sea, others the gardens.

During the day, you can play tennis, go Sunfish sailing or windsurfing, then relax in the Jacuzzis. At night, the restaurant seems made for romantic tête-à-têtes, with place settings embellished by embroidered tablecloths and lace-edged napkins. As you watch ships come and go in the harbor, dine on delicious snapper, grouper, lobster, or crayfish. Honeymoon package: None. Regular six-day/five-night package (some meals): $570 per couple for a room, $915 for a one-bedroom suite (low season). Includes breakfast daily, three dinners, two days' car rental, daytime tennis and water sports, all service charges and government taxes, and more. High-season rates (EP): $225 per couple per night for a room, $370 for a one-bedroom suite.

Cinnamon Reef Beach Club, P.O. Box 141, Little Harbour, Anguilla, B.W.I. (tel. 809/497-2727; U.S. reservations: toll free 800/223-1108). A bower of bougainvillea and hibiscus garlands the entrance to this serene resort nestled in the fashionable Little Harbour enclave. From the main lodge and some accommodations, you'll enjoy show-stopping views of St. Martin, just five miles away across the channel. Nice touches abound, such as the lending library and the complimentary afternoon tea (served with small cakes shaped like the resort's toucan mascot). The angled architecture is somewhat unusual—the villas resemble Egyptian pyramids with portholes. Inside, each of the 22 accommodations is extremely spacious. Deluxe villas really deliver on their name, with high, beamed ceilings, separate living and sleeping areas, and large bathrooms. Best of all, each terrace offers a hammock, a cozy spot to nap or read.

At the waterfront, take your pick among all the aquatic "toys," all free for guests, including paddleboats, small sailboats, and a fleet of Mistral sailboards. Now's a great time to learn a new sport, since lessons are offered free. The only drawback is the beach itself, which is small and partially man-made. A large pool, surrounded by a glamorous balustrade, helps compensate. Nearby, there's a sunken Jacuzzi hidden away in a gazebo, screened by latticework and hanging plants. For tennis players, the courts await. At the excellent restaurant, you'll enjoy stunning views of St. Martin as you savor specialties such as the grilled Black Angus steak, or a succulent lobster. Five nights a week, there's live entertainment. Honeymoon package: None. Regular eight-day/seven-night package (MAP): $2,080 per couple (low season). Includes round-trip transfers between hotel and airport or ferry, welcoming cocktails, champagne with dinner the evening of your arrival, full breakfast and dinner daily, government tax and service charge, and more. High-season rates: $330 per couple per night for a villa. Please note that credit cards are not accepted for accommodations.

Anguilla Great House, P.O. Box 157, Rendezvous Bay, Anguilla, B.W.I. (tel. 809/497-6061; U.S. reservations: 212/757-0225 in New York State; toll free 800/847-4249 nationwide in the U.S.; 800/255-3393 in Canada). Consisting of cozy white-painted cottages accented by jaunty red or blue shutters, this peaceful hideaway lolls on the palm-lined shores of Rendezvous Bay. Sea grapes twine across the dunes, while across the sapphire waters, the mountainous profile of St. Martin looms so near that you feel as if you could almost reach out and touch it. The cottages have a charming West Indian design, trimmed with gingerbread and latticework around the front porches. Inside, the accommodations are immaculate and inviting, furnished with Queen Anne–style furnishings and floral-print bedspreads. All are bright and airy, thanks to the traditional tray ceilings. Rooms feature ceiling fans, telephones, and clock radios; there's no air conditioning or television. Down at the beach, go windsurfing, sailing, or snorkeling; scuba-diving, deep-sea fishing, and waterskiing can all be arranged. Very good terrace restaurant. Honeymoon package: None. Rates (EP): $125 to $200 per couple per night for a room.

Shoal Bay Villas, P.O. Box 81, Anguilla, B.W.I. (tel. 809/497-2051; U.S. reservations: 212/535-9530, or toll free 800/223-5581). Here where the water is so clear that you can eye a parrot fish swimming dozens of yards out, a charming collection of villas offers easygoing escape. Outside your doorstep, two miles of diamond-white sand extend along Shoal Bay. The sea generally stays calm for swimming, thanks to the offshore reef (great for snorkeling). Most of the mere 13 units, set in white buildings with red roofs, have ocean views. All are sparkling clean, and decorated island style with tile floors and rattan furnishings. Each apartment features a separate living and sleeping area, as well as a fully equipped kitchen (the helpful staff will stock it for you if you request). In addition, the excellent Happy Jack's restaurant is right next door. Since you're definitely situated away from it all, you might want to consider renting a car; the staff can make all arrangements. Honeymoon package: None. Rates (EP): $125 to $225 per couple per night for a studio.

4. Romantic Restaurants

As you drive along the coast of Anguilla, you'll see trim boats everywhere—a sure sign that fresh fish and seafood head the list of specialties at most island restaurants. The catch of the day might include yellowtail, red snapper, grouper, bonito, hind, and oldwife. You'll also want to sample the local lobster and crayfish, as well as conch and whelks. Most of the other foodstuffs are imported from France. The good news is that the quality is extremely high, and you'll often find European delicacies such as tiny fraises du bois (wild strawberries) and white asparagus on menus. The bad news is that prices tend to be extremely high, even in "local" restaurants.

Pimms, Cap Juluca, Maunday Bay (tel. 497-6666). Run away to the Casbah—more precisely, to this exclusive Moorish-design resort that looks like an *Arabian Nights* fantasy come to life. With its dome, archways, and strategically placed palm trees, the restaurant resembles the perfect desert oasis. This haven, however, is set right on the dazzling blue sea. At night, they illuminate the crystalline waters, attracting various fish, turtles, and rays, which perform an impromptu water ballet as they retrieve tidbits. The five-course prix-fixe dinner menu featuring French and Caribbean specialties changes daily. Open daily for lunch, noon to 2 p.m.; about $40 per couple. Dinner served from 7 to 9:30 p.m.; $60 to $80 per couple plus drinks.

Johnno's Beach Stop Bar, Sandy Ground (tel. 497-2728). This is *the* island hot spot, attracting a ready-to-party mix of locals, expatriates, and vacationers who come to dance to live music. Every Sunday afternoon at around 2 p.m., an ebullient crowd gathers for a beach barbecue and rousing steel-band music. All week long, they serve tasty West Indian food and heady rum drinks. Open Tuesday, Thursday, and Friday from 10 a.m. to 6 p.m.; Wednesday and Saturday from 10 a.m. to 12:30 a.m.; Sunday from 10 a.m. to 7 p.m. Closed Monday. About $15 to $20 per couple.

The Barrel Stay, Sandy Ground (tel. 497-2831 or 497-3224). Located in a palm grove right by the water, this charmer conveys the proper castaway feeling, seemingly built of flotsam and jetsam. The restaurant's name, in fact, comes from the barrels that are used as tables. A cacophony of chirps and bleats emanates from chickens and goats strolling through the front yard; cats snooze peacefully in the corners. This down-home setting provides the backdrop for some first-rate cuisine. Start off with their famous fish soup, redolent of herbs from the south of France (it's been written up in *Gourmet* magazine). Then order one of their créole dishes, such as conch bouillabaisse, or a New York–cut Black Angus steak, served either grilled or with green-peppercorn sauce. Open daily for lunch, noon to 3 p.m.; dinner, 6:30 to 9:30 p.m.; about $50 to $80 per couple.

Happy Jack's, Shoal Bay (tel. 497-2051). Make a day of it at this thatch-roofed beachside restaurant where you can indulge in a swim between courses. The only concession to interior decoration is some fishnet strung across the ceiling. But who needs fancy furniture when the setting is heart-poundingly beautiful: a broad strand lapped by dead-calm water, with a swath of palm trees standing guard along the shore. Take a good look at the horizon: Your view is so clear that you can actually discern the curve of the earth. When you can tear your eyes away from the scenery, you'll find that the menu presents a wide array of American and West Indian favorites, ranging from hamburgers to lobster. Recommendations include the zesty pumpkin soup and the sautéed red snapper—so fresh that it probably swam in the bay the same morning. Every night except Wednesday, they offer a barbecue special. Either before or after your meal, you can rent lounge chairs or snorkeling gear, or sign on for a glass-bottomed boat ride. Open daily from 8 a.m. to 10 p.m.; lunch or dinner, $20 to $40 per couple (more if you order lobster).

Located just down the road from Happy Jack's, **Trader Vic's,** Shoal Bay (tel. 497-2091), is another fun base for a day at a beautiful beach. They're known for Caribbean lobster, as well as shrimp, whelks, conch, and fisherman pie. Open daily from 10 a.m. to 9 p.m.; dinner runs about $20 to $50 per couple. French-accented West Indian specialties—that's what you'll find at **Le Fish Trap,** Island Harbour (tel. 497-4488). Featured dishes include the fresh fish, such as snapper, grouper, or Caribbean lobster. Save room for dessert, especially one of the homemade pastries. Open nightly from 6:30 to 9:30 p.m.; $50 to $80 per couple.

XIII

ANTIGUA

1. PRACTICAL FACTS
2. ROMANTIC INTERLUDES
3. HONEYMOON HOTELS AND HIDEAWAYS
4. ROMANTIC RESTAURANTS

All Caribbean islands are not alike. Some earn renown for the kind of palm-fringed beaches that grace travel posters. Others become playgrounds for vacationing blue bloods, rock stars, and those who are just very, very rich. At some ports of call, an exuberant yachting crowd spreads good cheer, like seafaring Santa Clauses. In other fair oases, history and its heroes seem to come alive, as palpable as the afternoon trade winds. Amazing Antigua gives it all to you. Although it's a small island —just 108 square miles—it packs in an awe-inspiring rainbow of experiences.

Antigua (pronounced an-*tee*-ga) is the largest member of what is actually a three-island nation. The other components include Barbuda, known for its remarkable pink-sand beaches, and Redonda, an uninhabited rocky islet. Bathed by the Atlantic Ocean to the north and east, the Caribbean Sea to the south and west, the trio is located in the British Leeward Islands. Christopher Columbus was the first European to sight the island, sailing past it in 1493 and naming it after a statue of the Virgin in the Church of Santa Maria de la Antigua in Seville. The Spanish never established permanent settlements here, however. In 1632, English settlers colonized the island, starting up sugar plantations. Nevertheless, Antigua's importance was more strategic than agricultural. English Harbour, set on the island's south coast, is one of the safest harbors in the world. During the 18th century, the British built a major naval stronghold here to defend its prosperous colonies from enemy attack. The base is most closely associated with one Horatio Nelson, who served there as a young captain in 1784. He returned there as Admiral Nelson in 1805, when he pursued Napoleon's fleet across the Atlantic to a decisive victory at the Battle of Trafalgar. Today, legends of long-ago conflicts and courage still linger at Nelson's Dockyard and the remains of Fort Berkeley and Shirley Heights, which guard the entrance to English Harbour.

Although Antigua became independent from Great Britain in 1981, it remains a member of the Commonwealth, with the queen as head of state. The country has a population of 80,000. You'll still observe many Anglicisms. Afternoon tea is served promptly at 4 p.m., and cricket matches draw crowds from January through June. The proper British manner is buoyed by traditional West Indian warmth. Antiguans love to party, and this is most evident at the two biggest events of the year. Sailing

Week, a regatta held at the end of April, attracts sleek racing yachts from all over the world. Carnival, running from the end of July through the beginning of August, is celebrated with singing, dancing, and costume parades, and highlighted by a calypso and band show.

Antigua's coastline is as ruffled as the edges of a hibiscus blossom, edged by literally hundreds of diamond-white beaches—the island is said to have 365, one for each day of the year. You could spend an idyllic honeymoon looking for your favorite. Top contenders include Johnsons Point and Darkwood, which has a good beachside restaurant for an alfresco lunch. Another day, head for St. John's, Antigua's capital, and the center for commerce and shopping. It makes a good place for a stroll, especially on Saturday, which is market day. Farmers come from all over the island to hawk their fruits and vegetables. Colorful piles of breadfruit, papayas, and mangoes, plus fragrant baskets filled with nutmeg and cinnamon bark, line market stalls and overflow onto sidewalks. At least one evening, you'll want to try your luck in one of the island's five casinos.

Although Antigua is exotic, it is surprisingly close, less than a 4-hour flight from New York, only 2¼ hours from Miami. In fact, there's only one "problem." Antigua is so easy to get to—and so hard to leave.

1. Practical Facts

GETTING THERE

Citizens of the United States and Canada require proof of citizenship (such as a passport or authenticated birth certificate), as well as a return airline ticket. Airlines serving Antigua from North America include **American, B.W.I.A.,** and **Air Canada. American Eagle** offers frequent flights from San Juan, Puerto Rico. Several cruise lines also call at the island. Leaving Antigua, there is a departure tax of $6.

GETTING AROUND

It's easy, no matter how you choose to travel.

Taxis

Taxi rates are fixed by the government and are fairly reasonable. Always ask the driver how much the fare will be before you head off, since the taxis have no meters.

Rental Cars

Several major U.S. rental companies have branches in Antigua. From **Avis,** for example, a compact car with automatic transmission and air conditioning runs about $55 per day, $300 per week. You will need a temporary Antiguan driver's license; it costs $12 and is available from rental car agencies. You will need to show a valid U.S. driver's license to obtain it. Driving is on the left, British style. At traffic circles (known here as roundabouts), the vehicle on the right has the right of way. Keep an eye out for potholes, which often make Antigua's roads resemble a giant slalom course, as well as perambulating goats, chickens, and cows.

LANGUAGE AND MONEY

English has been the official tongue since the 1600s, and is kept sunny-side up by a West Indian lilt. Like the rest of the Leeward Islands, Antigua uses the Eastern Caribbean dollar, known locally as the "Bee Wee." Currently, the exchange rate is EC$2.60 to US$1. Practically all stores, taxi drivers, and restaurants will accept

American currency, but ask in advance to be sure. Unless otherwise noted, all prices in this chapter are in U.S. dollars.

WEATHER

Antigua is generally considered to have some of the best weather in the Caribbean. Temperatures hover around 85° F year-round, with only a 6° difference in average temperature between January and September.

CLOTHING

You're in the islands, so think casual. Bathing suits and short shorts are fine around the beach or pool, but shouldn't be worn for sightseeing or shopping around town. For some of the most elegant resorts and restaurants, gentlemen should wear a jacket (sometimes, jacket and tie) for dinner. Check in advance to be sure.

ELECTRICAL CURRENT

Although most parts of the island have 110 volts, the same as in the United States, some have 220 volts/60 cycles. Most of these hotels will have converters so that you can run your hairdryer and electric razor, but ask your travel agent to check this out.

TIME

Antigua remains all year on Atlantic Standard Time, which is one hour ahead of Eastern Standard Time. In winter, when it is noon in New York, it is 1 p.m. in Antigua. In summer, when Daylight Saving Time is in effect in the United States, the time in Antigua is the same as in the eastern U.S.

TELEPHONES

You can call Antigua direct from the mainland United States. First dial 809 (the area code), then the seven-digit phone number.

SHOPPING

Tops for hot shops is historic **Redcliffe Quay** in St. John's, where old stone-and-clapboard warehouses have been converted into chic boutiques. Check out **Island Woman,** which carries beautiful women's casualwear, plus one-of-a-kind fashions crafted in India, Indonesia, and Antigua itself. They also have a striking selection of accessories and costume jewelry that lend themselves well to gala tropical nights. Looking to exchange wedding presents? **The Goldsmitty** creates exquisite jewelry with gold, pearls, and precious gems, while **Colombian Emeralds** (Heritage Quay) offers more treasures in gold, silver, and gemstones. For a made-in-Antigua memento of your honeymoon, browse through the island ceramics at **The Pottery Shop. Dalila** displays lots of lovely batiks and exotic handicrafts from faraway Bali. Shopping hours generally run Monday through Friday, 9 a.m. to 4:30 p.m.; Saturday, 9 a.m. to 1 p.m.

Other shop stops include the new **Heritage Quay** complex, where you'll find 40 duty-free stores as well as a crafts arcade. Most of the larger resorts also feature noteworthy boutiques. **Island Arts** at the St. James's Club carries choice arts and crafts from throughout the Caribbean; the **boutique at Jumby Bay** specializes in eye-catching swimwear. If you love Caribbean art and handcrafts, don't miss **Harmony Hall** at Brown's Bay Mill near Freetown (tel. 463-2057). Set in a distinctive stone building by an old sugar mill, it displays original paintings, ceramics, and jewelry by some of the finest artists and craftspeople in the islands. The store is run by

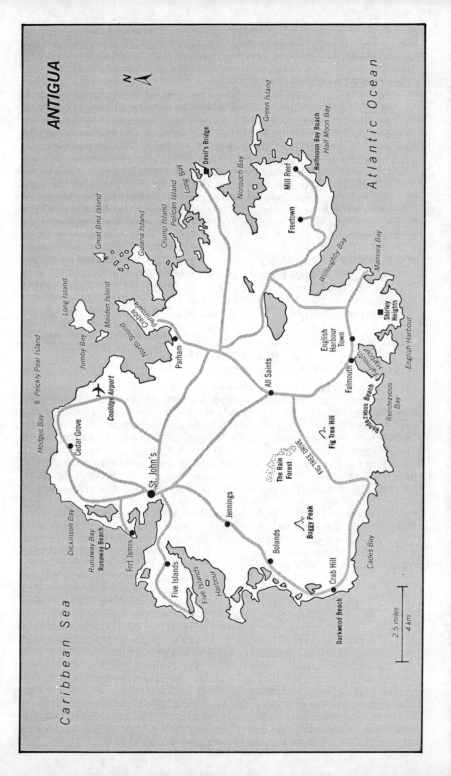

the same people who operate Harmony Hall in Ocho Rios, Jamaica. Open daily from 10 a.m. to 6 p.m.

HOW TO GET MARRIED IN ANTIGUA

The island warmly welcomes couples who want a tropical wedding. It's simple to make arrangements. Either the bride or the groom has to have been on Antigua for at least three days prior to the wedding ceremony. Upon arrival, the couple must first go to the Minister of Legal Affairs to fill out a marriage application. You both must present a passport or an authenticated birth certificate when you apply, and you'll both have to prove that you are not currently married. If you're single, you'll have to swear to an affidavit when applying for the marriage certificate. If either of you has been divorced or widowed, you must present a divorce or death certificate. Once you have the license, you go to the registrar of the High Court to set up a time and date to perform the ceremony. The ceremony costs $100 in Antiguan stamps if the ceremony takes place at the registrar's office (slightly more if the marriage is performed elsewhere).

FOR FURTHER INFORMATION

Contact the **Antigua-Barbuda Department of Tourism.** In Antigua: P.O. Box 363, St. John's, Antigua W.I. (tel. 809/462-0480). In New York: 610 Fifth Avenue, Suite 311, New York, NY 10020 (tel. 212/541-4117). In Miami: 121 S.E. First Street, Suite 508, Miami, FL 33131 (tel. 305/381-6762).

2. Romantic Interludes

Antigua lends itself well to explorations.

Step back in time at **Nelson's Dockyard,** a meticulously restored British Royal Navy complex built in 1725 on English Harbour. Extremely sheltered, the bay was a crucial "hurricane hole" and stronghold for English ships during the tumultuous 18th century, when the British, French, Spanish, and Dutch fought for control over a glittering prize: the fabulously wealthy West Indies. Today, you can walk along the waterfront past the weathered brick storehouses and armories, many now converted to atmospheric restaurants and intimate inns. Also visit the **Dockyard Museum,** which displays a fascinating collection of maritime artifacts: charts, models, and antiques.

For a splendid view of the harbor, head for **Shirley Heights Lookout,** atop a 500-foot ridge. The scene ranks as one of the most stunning panoramas in all of the Caribbean—bring your camera. Then stop for lunch at the excellent restaurant (see write-up that follows). Afterward, tour the **Shirley Heights Museum,** which retraces the story of the Army garrison during the late 18th century; open Monday through Friday, 10 a.m. to 4 p.m. Nearby, you can visit **Clarence House,** a mansion built in 1787 for Prince William Henry (later Duke of Clarence, subsequently King William IV) when he was stationed in Antigua to command the H.M.S. *Pegasus.* Today, the splendid Georgian-style house is used to entertain royalty and as the prime minister's country retreat. (Princess Margaret and Lord Snowdon spent part of their honeymoon here.) The house is open to the public for guided tours when the prime minister is not in residence; call 463-1026 for details.

For scuba enthusiasts, Antigua offers superb **diving.** Much of the island is surrounded by barrier reefs, and the choice of sites ranges from drop-offs to shipwrecks. Prime plunges include **Sunken Rock,** which starts just 30 feet below the surface. Here, you can glide along cave-like overhangs while remaining in open water. Interesting wreck dives include the remains of the *Andes* and the *Harbour of St. Johns,* both in **Deep Bay.** Two-tank dives cost about $80 per person. Contact the **Aquanaut Diving Centre** at the St. James's Club (tel. 463-1113).

Visit **Barbuda,** Antigua's sister island located some 28 miles to the north. Only 15 miles long and 5 miles wide, Barbuda is a haven for bird-lovers (over 170 indigenous species) and scuba-divers (countless ships have foundered on the shallow reefs). And practically everyone will fall in love with its miles of pristine beaches, including the second-longest unspoiled "pink-sand" shore in the world. You can reach Barbuda by a 15-minute flight; contact **LIAT** (tel. 462-0700), about $40 per person. You can also reach the island via the **Carib Link Ferry Service.**

3. Honeymoon Hotels and Hideaways

Antigua presents one of the most appealing blends of hotels in the Caribbean. Here you'll find posh private-island retreats. Luxury high-rise hotels. Casual tropical resorts. Personable historic inns where the footfalls of history seem to resound along brick walkways and in gabled bedrooms. When looking at room rates, also remember that a 7% government tax and a 10% service charge will be added to your bill. Unless otherwise noted, prices indicate the spread between low- and high-season costs.

VERY EXPENSIVE
Curtain Bluff, P.O. Box 288, Antigua, W.I. (tel. 809/463-1115; U.S. reservations: 212/289-8888). Even on an island known for sumptuous resorts, Curtain Bluff stands out as the creme de la creme. Self-assured in its preeminence, this is the kind of place that does not advertise, and that never name-drops about its celebrity clientele. The 20-acre resort is sequestered on a promontory overlooking Antigua's south coast. Owner Howard Hulford is the consummate perfectionist, shutting down the resort each summer to primp, paint, and completely refurbish each of the 60 rooms and suites. The attention lavished on detail really shows in the accommodations, where everything is *just so.* Original art decorates the walls; plump and inviting silk cushions balance on the sofas. Each room or suite has a secluded balcony overlooking the sea. The spectacular one-bedroom suites rank among the most beautiful hotel accommodations that we've seen anywhere. Decorated in soft pastels that match the shimmering afterglow of a sunset, they feature marble bathrooms and wide-open living areas.

For Curtain Bluff's guests, each day unfolds with a collection of delightful decisions. Which beach should we go to? (Curtain Bluff has two, one with surf, one without.) Shall we snorkel or sail (most water sports are free for guests)? With show-stopping views, the four championship tennis courts are the setting for tournaments such as the annual Antigua Tennis Week held in May; in addition, there's a weekly guest tournament. Every April, the resort sponsors Antigua Sailing Week, a regatta that attracts hundreds of sleek yachts from around the world. Curtain Bluff is as renowned for its excellent cuisine as it is for luxurious accommodations. (The same purveyor who supplies the White House and Lutèce also provides delicacies to Curtain Bluff.) Oenophiles should ask for a tour of the resort's wine cellars, which maintain over 25,000 examples of rare vintages at a consistent 55°. Honeymoon package: None. Rates (all inclusive): $400 to $545 per couple per night for a superior room with king-size bed. Includes all meals, drinks, water sports, laundry service, free postage, and—special for honeymooners—a bottle of champagne and a special dinner served in a garden gazebo. The resort closes annually from the end of June to the beginning of October.
Jumby Bay Resort, P.O. Box 243, Long Island, Antigua, W.I. (tel. 809/462-6000; U.S. reservations: toll free 800/421-9016). A plush—yet casual—playground, Jumby Bay occupies its own private Long Island just off Antigua's north coast, a cay extravagantly edged with magnificent beaches. Here, you can truly get away from it all, in style and luxury. There's no air conditioning. No telephones.

No TV. But what you'll find in abundance is barefoot elegance. You'll feel like the most privileged castaways, since there are only 38 rooms and 4 villas on the entire 300-acre island. The guest list scans like a Who's Who of the world's movers and shakers: Dan and Jean Rather, Lady Antonia Fraser and Harold Pinter. Robin Leach, supreme chronicler of the peregrinations of the rich and famous, has called it his favorite place to vacation. Everything bespeaks top-of-the-line quality and service, from the Italian tile floors to the twice-a-day delivery of fresh ice to your room. Jumby Bay zooms the concept of an all-inclusive resort to luxurious heights. Room tariffs cover all meals, unlimited bar drinks and vintage house wine, most water sports, and tennis. Even jaded globe-trotters enthuse about the free laundry service. Just toss your undies or rumpled polo shirts into the bathroom hamper, and *voilà,* they'll be returned, neatly washed and ironed, within 24 hours. Pampering and cosseting are assured, since there are three staff members to each guest.

With their stucco walls and red-tile roofs, the Mediterranean-flavored buildings create a dazzling juxtaposition against the ultrablue sea. The accommodations embody island chic, accented by rattan furnishings, original artwork, and pastel cottons. Wrap-around louvers encourage the caressing trade winds; doors open onto an expansive terrace canopied by bougainvillea. Some rooms have luxurious courtyard showers, facing a private tropical garden. In recognition that no man or woman is an island—even on his or her honeymoon—Jumby Bay proffers a tempting roster of activities. Sample the two beaches. Explore the walks and trails by foot or bicycle. Play Robinson Crusoe for a day with a picnic escape to a deserted island. It's all there for you to do—or not do—as you please. And as you sip cocktails at sunset, or partake of a sumptuous dinner at the Estate House, you'll know that you have chosen one of the Caribbean's great resorts for your holiday. Honeymoon package: None. Regular eight-day/seven-night package (all inclusive): $2,745 per couple (low season). High-season rates: From $775 per couple per night. The resort generally closes late August through mid-October. Please also be aware that because the resort is located across from the airport, you will hear planes on occasion.

St. James's Club, P.O. Box 63, St. John's, Antigua, W.I. (tel. 809/463-1430; U.S. reservations: 212/486-2575, or toll free 800/274-0008). A little corner of Paradise on Mamora Bay—that describes this all-so-posh retreat that arcs around one of Antigua's most photogenic harbors. From its star-studded opening bash to the present day, the property continues to draw a luminous clientele: Joan Collins, Liza Minnelli, Dustin Hoffman, and their Royal Highnesses Prince and Princess Michael of Kent, to name just a few.

Ensconced on a 100-acre peninsula between the lagoon-like bay and the Atlantic Ocean, St. James's remains intimate, with 105 rooms and 75 villas. The resort makes a perfect match for action-loving couples, since there is so much to see and do right at the resort—and practically everything is free for guests. Go deep-sea fishing on their own boat. Horseback ride at water's edge on their own well-schooled, Texas-bred quarter horses. Grab a mallet and play croquet. Work out with an aerobics class—or unwind with a massage. Tennis anyone? St. James's offers seven all-weather courts. Water sports? The shoreline pulsates with everything from aqua bikes to waterskiing. (Beach connoisseurs should be forewarned that although both strands are adequate, they do not rank among Antigua's finest.) Fun continues into the evening, with a lively nightclub and Antigua's most elegant casino.

St. James's offers guests nearly as varied a choice in accommodations as in activities. Deluxe rooms face the water; standard rooms, the gardens. All are air-conditioned. For couples who really want to spread out, there are two-story white bayside villas tucked within a floral jungle of bougainvillea, hibiscus, and oleander. Each of these suites is so amply proportioned, and so beautifully decorated with rattan furnishings and fine Caribbean art, that you'll probably want to move in permanently. Crave even more luxe? Several hilltop homes with private swimming pools are for rent. At mealtimes, take your pick from four fine restaurants. Honeymoon package: Eight days/seven nights (MAP): $1,825 to $2,080 per couple for a deluxe room (low season). Includes a bottle of champagne, complimentary water sports and tennis, and a $20 casino chip. High-season rates (MAP): $450 per couple per night for a deluxe room.

For something different—and romantic—for your honeymoon, how about chartering a yacht? Antigua is one of the principal yacht-charter centers in the Caribbean. Consistent trade winds, hundreds of good anchorages, and dozens of nearby islands add up to some great sailing. On a one-week charter, you could cruise down-island (south) to Guadeloupe, Les Saintes, Dominica, and Martinique. A northbound itinerary could take you to Barbuda, St. Barts, Anguilla, and St. Martin. Both crewed (with captain and cook) and bareboat (sail-it-yourself) charters are available. One of the largest charter operations is **Nicholson's Yacht Charters,** 432 Columbia St., Suite 21-A, Cambridge, MA 02141 (tel. 617/225-0555). They have a wide selection of luxury yachts available, starting at about $3,000 per couple for the week during the winter high season. You can also contact **Avery's Boathouse, Inc.,** P.O. Box 5248, St. Thomas, USVI 00801 (tel. 809/776-0113); **Le Boat, Inc.,** P.O. Box E, Maywood, NJ 07607 (tel. 201/342-1838, or toll free 800/922-0291); **Ocean Escapes,** P.O. Box 6009, 9 Ferry Wharf, Newburyport, MA 01960 (tel. 508/465-7116, or toll free 800/227-8633); **Ocean Voyages,** 1709 Bridgeway, Sausalito, CA 94965 (tel. 415/332-4681); **Regency International,** P.O. Box 9997, St. Thomas, USVI 00801 (tel. 809/776-5950, or toll free 800/524-7676); **Russell Yacht Charters,** 2750 Black Rock Turnpike, Suite 175, Fairfield, CT 06430 (tel. 203/372-6633).

MODERATE

Half Moon Bay Hotel, P.O. Box 144, St. John's, Antigua, W.I. (tel. 809/463-2101; U.S. reservations: 212/832-2277, or toll free 800/223-6510). Named for its luminescent arching beach, with the kind of soft, blindingly white sand you dream about (they even sweep it meticulously each morning), Half Moon Bay is a complete tropical resort. Sprawling over 150 acres, the property offers extensive tennis and golf facilities—yet is located a bit out of the way on Antigua's east coast, so you'll enjoy plenty of seclusion. (The water also tends to be a bit rougher, since this is the Atlantic side of the island.) There are only 100 rooms, set in two-story units that lounge along the shoreline—so close to the water, in fact, that you can hear the sound of the surf. In the morning, you can hop right from your room onto the beach for a wake-up dip. Decorated with simple, contemporary furnishings, the accommodations come with ceiling fans but no air conditioning; each has a patio or balcony facing the ocean. A full array of water sports awaits you, or you can play tennis on the five courts. There's also a nine-hole, par-34 golf course. And since the beach is long (nearly a mile in length), you've got plenty of room in which to find your own place in the sun. Honeymoon package: Eight days/seven nights (BP): $1,000 per couple (low season). Includes champagne with breakfast your first morning, fruit basket, rum punches daily, souvenir T-shirts, and more. High-season rates (MAP): $325 per couple per night.

The Inn at English Harbour, P.O. Box 187, St. John's, Antigua, W.I. (tel. 809/463-1014). Although many hotels claim that they're located on the beach, few express so genuine a reality as the Inn at English Harbour. Most of the accommodations here are located so close to palm-fringed Freeman's Bay that you can be out of bed and into the water in 30 steps (or fewer). Hidden away on ten acres just five minutes from Nelson's Dockyard, the inn was one of Antigua's first hotels. Set in trim, white-painted two-story units, each of the rooms offers simple, islandy furnishings. All have terraces or balconies; some feature kitchenettes. Right on the calm bay, you can go windsurfing, Sunfish sailing, or waterskiing; the resort can also arrange day sails or deep-sea fishing expeditions. With mother-country touches such as a first-rate afternoon tea, the inn is a fine choice for Anglophiles. Crowning a hilltop overlooking English Harbour, the Terrace Restaurant serves excellent meals; also try one of the fresh and formidable lime squashes from the bar. Honeymoon package:

None. Rates: Low season (EP): $105 to $165 per couple per night. High season (MAP): $375 to $412 per couple per night.

The **Royal Antiguan Resort & Casino,** P.O. Box 1322, St. John's, Antigua, W.I. (tel. 809/462-3733). Modern, sleek, and sophisticated, the nine-story Royal Antiguan is the first high-rise on the island. Despite its size, the resort maintains a country-club feel, thanks to its spacious setting on 150 acres alongside Deep Bay. Unlike many contemporary hotels whose architecture is as bland as bath water, the design here is eye-catching. A waterfall accents the Italian-marble lobby, with atrium and grand spiral staircase. There are 300 rooms, including villas and cottages. Euro-style elegance is the keynote here, with hand-tiled floors, wood detailing, and marble sinks in the bathrooms. Each of the accommodations is outfitted with all the modern comforts: remote-control color TV, VCR, minibar with refrigerator, direct-dial telephone, and air conditioning. For extra pampering, choose one of the white stucco cottages, which feature wrap-around patios and Jacuzzis.

The resort fronts two different bodies of water—a tranquil lagoon, perfect for Windsurfers, Sunfish, and pedalboats (all free to guests); and a Caribbean-front beach, with the kind of clear, true-blue water you dream about. By day, much of the activity centers around the large freshwater pool, which is shaped like a conch shell. Practically everything you might need during your holiday is available right on the property: boutiques, three restaurants, two bars, eight tennis courts plus a pro shop. At night, try your luck in the glamorous casino. Honeymoon package: Eight days/seven nights (MAP): $2,335 to $2,555 per couple (low season). Includes round-trip transfers between airport and hotel, oceanview or minisuite accommodations, welcome drinks, fresh flowers in room upon arrival, all hotel taxes and gratuities, and more. High-season rate: $300 per couple per night.

Halcyon Cove Beach Resort and Casino, P.O. Box 251, St. John's, Antigua, W.I. (tel. 809/462-0256; U.S. reservations: 212/661-4540 in New York State; toll free 800/223-1588 nationwide in U.S.; 800/531-6767 in Canada). Peace and quiet by day, followed by a lively night scene—that's what you'll find at this expansive, 40-acre resort surrounding mile-long Dickenson Bay. There are 135 rooms, all air-conditioned and set in low-slung stucco-and-stone buildings. For the top accommodations, choose the new beachfront suites and renovated oceanfront deluxe rooms, cheerily decorated with rattan furnishings and crisp island cottons, in sun-kissed hues of teal and peach. The serene waters of Dickenson Bay lend themselves to a wide array of water sports; play tennis day or night, or tee off at a nearby 18-hole golf course. In addition to the nightly entertainment, the Sunday beach barbecue is especially popular, served to the syncopations of a steel band. Take your choice of four restaurants, including Clouds. Considered one of the best dining spots on the island, Clouds offers breathtaking views across the Caribbean from its bluffside terrace—on a clear day, you can see all the way to St. Kitts. Top off your evening with dancing in the disco, and a whirl with Lady Luck in the casino. Honeymoon package: Eight days/seven nights (EP): $975 to $1,140 per couple (low season). Includes welcome cocktails, bottle of champagne, basket of tropical fruits, fresh flowers, glass-bottomed boat trip, $5 casino chip, and more. High-season rates (EP): $230 to $325 per couple per night.

Blue Waters Beach Hotel, P.O. Box 256, Soldier Bay, St. John's, Antigua, W.I. (tel. 809/462-0290; U.S. reservations: 212/696-1323 in New York State; toll free 800/372-1323 nationwide). You'll know where this hideaway gets its name the moment you see the water, and the electric color hits your eyes like a bolt of blue lightning. Among all the Caribbean islands, Antigua is famous for its scintillating seas—and on Antigua, Blue Waters' beach possesses the most breathtaking azure bay of them all. Snuggled along the island's verdant north coast, the resort is a perfect choice for couples who want to "discover" a gem-like oasis. Forty-six rooms and eight luxury villas loll beachside, nearly hidden from view by flamboyants, sea grapes, and coconut palms. The lush gardens are the pride and joy here, and bougainvillea scampers up the sides of units, then weaves a bower across second-floor balconies. Recently spruced up and refurbished, the accommodations are extremely welcoming, with rattan furnishings and spacious terraces or balconies facing the sea. All are air-conditioned and feature a minirefrigerator; the deluxe quarters are slightly larger and nearer to the water. Down at the spectacular beach, you can go windsurfing or sailing off on a Sunfish or Hobie-Cat—all free to guests. You have two excellent restaurants to choose from, and there's live entertainment nightly. Honeymoon package: Eight days/seven nights (EP): $770 per couple (low season). Includes dinner for two one night, champagne upon arrival, fruit basket, and upgrading to deluxe or villa accommodations whenever possible. High-season rates (MAP): $325 per couple per night for standard accommodations.

The **Hodges Bay Club Resort,** P.O. Box 1237, St. John's, Antigua, W.I. (tel. 809/462-2300; U.S. reservations: 212/535-9530 in New York State; toll free 800/223-5581 nationwide). For couples with a penchant for the lap of luxury—but with an aversion to high-flying prices, Hodges Bay Club provides a very appealing way to go. Surrounded by elegant estates in one of Antigua's most exclusive residential areas, the resort consists of privately owned one- and two-bedroom condos right by the sea. The decor reflects elegance and panache, with original Haitian paintings, Italian tile floors, and rattan furnishings handcrafted in the Dominican Republic. Thanks to the skillful layouts, you almost won't know that you have neighbors. All of the one-bedroom villas sit along the water and feature sea views and daily maid service. Although the beach is small, it offers diamond-bright sand and a bevy of happy-day water sports, with sailing, snorkeling, and windsurfing all free to guests. Challenge each other to a game of tennis—the resort has two courts. Each villa has a fully equipped kitchen, but when you don't want to cook (and who wants to overdo pots and pans on a honeymoon?), the waterfront Pelican Club restaurant is superb. All in all, it means a honeymoon haven that's easy to love. "When people go home," the managers report, "they give us hugs and kisses, and then say, 'We'll be back soon.'" Honeymoon package: None. Rates for a one-bedroom villa (EP): $165 to $335 per couple per night.

For history-buff honeymooners, the Nelson Dockyard area offers two extraordinary hostelries that reflect the charm and spirit of another era. Cross the threshold and you'll feel as if you've been whisked back 200 years in time. Although the English Harbour location precludes having a beach, the strands at Pigeon Point and Galleon Beach are about a five-minute drive away.

The **Copper and Lumber Store,** P.O. Box 184, St. John's, Antigua, W.I. (tel. 809/463-1058; U.S. reservations: 803/785-7411). When Lord Nelson was just Captain Horatio, this mellowed brick structure (completed in 1782) served as a naval warehouse. Today, the building has been exquisitely restored and converted into a one-of-a-kind inn. Rough-hewn beams soar across ceilings, almost like sculpture; corridors overlook quaint courtyards. There are only 14 suite accommodations, each with a private bathroom, fully equipped kitchen, and water views. Fling open your shutters in the morning, and you'll see the multimillion-dollar yachts coming and going on English Harbour. The real prize for honeymooners are the four deluxe Georgian suites, each named after a ship that participated in the Battle of Trafalgar. Here you'll find fine Persian rugs and exquisite antiques, such as mahogany washstands and Queen Anne wing chairs. Honeymoon package: Eight days/seven nights (CP): $875 to $1,590 per couple for a Georgian suite. Includes round-trip transfers between airport and inn, welcome cocktails, and a bottle of champagne.

INEXPENSIVE

The **Admiral's Inn,** P.O. Box 713, English Harbour, St. John's, Antigua, W.I. (tel. 809/463-1534 or 809/463-1027). Make your honeymoon a historic occasion at this waterfront inn that served as a British naval storehouse in the late 18th century. Built of brick, with windows framed by blue shutters, the inn has only 14 rooms. Although each of the accommodations is different, all look out over English Harbour. Two of the rooms have grand four-poster beds; some offer air conditioning.

When you want to go to the beach, the inn runs free shuttles to nearby strands. Adding to the warm and friendly atmosphere, the Admiral's Inn bar and restaurant are favorite gathering places for both locals and visiting yachtsmen. Honeymoon package: None. Rates (EP): $75 to $115 per couple per night for a room with a four-poster bed.

4. Romantic Restaurants

Variety—and quality—characterize the dining scene. You'll find everything from French haute cuisine to equally gourmet West Indian specialties. As you would expect with water, water, everywhere, ultrafresh seafood tops most menus. The local catch includes camry, rockfish, grouper, and snapper, as well as delectable Caribbean lobster. An island favorite is conch, often served curried or deep-fried with a spicy tomato sauce. Delicious side dishes include green bananas, boiled and served like mashed potatoes; christophene, a pale-green squash (also known as chayote); as well as sweet potato, plantains, and pumpkin. You'll also probably get hooked on roti, a puri (flat, Indian-type bread) stuffed with lightly curried beef, chicken, or fish. In addition to the bounteous fresh-fruit harvest of mangoes, paw-paws (papayas), and bananas, don't miss the famous Antigua "black" pineapples, said to be the sweetest in the world.

In general, Antiguan cuisine is robustly seasoned but not incendiary; the fireworks come from the hot sauces served on the side. For palate arsonists like ourselves (the types who think that if you don't cry, it's not hot enough), we recommend Susie's Hot Sauce, an orange-colored flame-thrower found in many local joints. (You can buy a big bottle for around $5 to take home.) Cool off with a drink made with Cavalier rum, Antigua's own. Speaking of beverages, you can drink the water in hotels and good restaurants; otherwise, order bottled beverages.

Study menus carefully—prices may be given in either EC$ or US$. Most restaurants add a 10% service charge to the bill; check to be sure.

The **Admiral's Inn,** Nelson's Dockyard (tel. 463-1534). True romantics are in their element at the Admiral's Inn, a 200-year-old building where Lord Nelson himself once stayed. Even if you spent hours dreaming, you couldn't come up with a more storybook setting than this frond-shaded terrace overlooking English Harbour. Stalwart stone pillars (once part of a boathouse) frame the postcard-perfect view; eucalyptus and genip trees shade the terrace. The lunch menu spotlights seafood specialties, such as conch chowder or sautéed red snapper, plus light bites, including hamburgers and omelets; about $20 to $40 per couple. In the evening, they offer a complete dinner of excellent value, with soup (pumpkin or gazpacho), steak or lobster entrée, salad, dessert, and coffee, all for about $30 per person. Open daily for breakfast, 7:30 to 10 a.m.; lunch, noon to 2:30 p.m.; dinner, 7:30 to 9:30 p.m.

The **Lookout,** Shirley Heights (tel. 463-1785). Poised on a 500-foot-high bluff, this restaurant provides a spectacular view over English Harbour. The 200-year-old stone buildings originally served as a British army garrison in the late 1700s. Today, seated on the terrace, gazing at the million-dollar seascape of yachts at anchor, you can savor excellent Antiguan and American favorites. Lunch selections range from chicken salad served in a pineapple shell and hamburgers to grilled lobster, or whelks simmered in wine sauce; $20 to $50 per couple. For dinner, the chef tempts you with steak and seafood dishes; about $50 per couple. Open daily from 10 a.m. to 10 p.m. On Sunday afternoons starting at about 1 p.m., folks from all over the island come here for a party-down good time, including a lavish barbecue and music from calypso and reggae bands.

Le Bistro, Hodges Bay (tel. 462-3881). Looking like a French country inn plunked into the Antiguan countryside, Le Bistro is located on Antigua's north shore in an exclusive residential enclave. With its beamed ceilings, latticework screens, and candlelit place settings, it's a top choice for a dinner rendezvous. Seafood is a specialty here, as well as rack of lamb and steaks, all beautifully presented in the classical manner. Open Tuesday through Sunday for dinner only, 7 to 10:30 p.m.; $60 to $80 per couple plus drinks. Closed May 1 to August 1.

The **Copper and Lumber Store Restaurant,** Nelson's Dockyard (tel. 463-1058). Set in a former Royal Navy warehouse, this hideaway captures all the romance of the 18th century. Old stone floors and heavy oak beams hint of the past, while tall doorways open onto the contemporary panorama of yachts at anchor on Freeman's Bay. At lunchtime, the restaurant features an English pub menu, highlighted by fare such as steak-and-kidney pie ($12) or a "Ploughman's lunch" (with English cheddar cheese, French bread, and various chutneys; about $5.50). For dinner, the cuisine has a French accent, including entrées such as grouper hollandaise or beef bourguignon. Dinner for two, about $80 per couple plus drinks. Open daily for lunch, 11:30 a.m. to 2:30 p.m.; dinner, 7 to 9 p.m.

Victory Restaurant & Bar, 3 Redcliffe Street, St. John's (tel. 462-4317). With its weathered stone-and-brick walls and lively bar scene, this makes a great place to stop for lunch when you are sightseeing in St. John's. Best bites include the lobster salad and the all-American hamburgers. Open Monday through Saturday for lunch, noon to 2:30 p.m.; $15 to $40 per couple.

If you love West Indian food, don't miss **"Gloria's Stand,"** a little sidewalk assemblage of plywood tables and aluminum roofing located across from the Admiral's Inn at Nelson's Dockyard. Gloria herself presides, and the food's the real thing—fried chicken, saltfish cakes, johnnycakes, and home-brewed ginger beer. Lunch for two might hit about $8—if you really pig out. Gloria's usually there Monday through Saturday, from 11:30 a.m. to about 3 p.m., or whenever the food runs out. When you're shopping in St. John's and you crave pepperpot soup, ducana and saltfish, curried conch, or a ginger beer, mosey over to **Brother B's,** on Long Street (tel. 462-0616). The outdoor courtyard provides a cool, breezy respite. Open Monday through Saturday, 8 a.m. to 10 p.m. Lunch or dinner for two, $20 to $40 per couple; higher for lobster. The **Curry House,** Redcliffe Quay (tel. 462-1895), serves savory beef, chicken, and conch rotis; about $7.50 per couple. Open Monday through Saturday for lunch, 11:30 a.m. to 2:30 p.m.

XIV

ARUBA

1. PRACTICAL FACTS
2. ROMANTIC INTERLUDES
3. HONEYMOON HOTELS AND HIDEAWAYS
4. ROMANTIC RESTAURANTS AND NIGHTSPOTS

Miles of sugary white-sand beaches. World-class resort facilities. Intimate restaurants. Las Vegas–type nightclubs. Whether your honeymoon plans include soft starry nights or bright disco lights—Aruba has it all.

The island is a tiny one, about 20 miles long and just 6 miles across at its widest point. Before it became a separate entity within the kingdom of the Netherlands in 1986, Aruba was part of the Dutch territories known as the Netherlands Antilles. Along with Bonaire and Curaçao, it had been included in the Leeward group of the Netherlands Antilles off the northern coast of South America—often referred to as the "ABC" islands. Aruba lies just 15 miles north of Venezuela and about 42 miles west of Curaçao. The country's political status is a form of "commonwealth" with Holland, along with Bonaire, Curaçao, and the three windward islands of the Netherlands Antilles—St. Eustatius, St. Maarten, and Saba, all located in the Caribbean more than 500 miles to the north of Aruba. Although Aruba has its own currency now, there haven't been any other changes that would affect couples who want to travel between Aruba and the other islands of the Netherlands Antilles.

Oranjestad, the capital city on the southwest coast, provides a number of clues to Aruba's early history. Fort Zoutman, built in 1796, and the Willem III Tower, built in 1868, are landmarks, and two of the earliest buildings in Aruba. The jumble of pastel-colored stucco walls topped with terra-cotta roofs and cupolas along Willhelminastraat aren't quite as old, but are fine examples of colonial shops and residences.

The island's first inhabitants were probably members of the Arawak Indian tribe that settled throughout the Caribbean. In 1499, Alonso de Ojeda, a Spaniard, was the first European to see the island. Subsequently, Aruba was visited by many pirates and buccaneers while its ownership was juggled between Spain, Holland, France, and England; the Dutch gained permanent possession in 1816.

Today, Aruba has a population of 65,000, made up of people of over 40 different nationalities. Despite their ethnic diversity, Arubans share a spirit of warmth and graciousness. "Bon Bini" means "welcome" in the native language, and Arubans will go out of their way to make you feel at home wherever you travel on the island.

They throw a weekly Bon Bini Festival, which introduces visitors to the Aruban people and their culture by showcasing the local arts, crafts, foods, and music. The festivities take place every Tuesday from 6:30 to 8:30 p.m. in the courtyard of the Aruba Historical Museum in Fort Zoutman. Tickets are available at all hotels; the $2 per person admission includes a folkloric dance show.

Take a day or so to explore the island. If you drive through the countryside, you'll probably see the ruins of the gold mines at Balashi and Bushiribana. Gold was discovered in Aruba in 1824; after that mining became Aruba's first industry. More than 3 million pounds of gold were brought to the surface before the mines ceased to be economical in 1916.

Most visitors to Aruba spend their time on the beaches in the resort area along the southwest coast. But the Aruban *cunucu* (countryside) is strangely beautiful, with many different areas to visit. For honeymoon couples, it provides unusual spots for private picnics and for leisurely or energetic exploration.

The north coast has a desolate beauty, and its crashing waves are a startling counterpoint to the limpid seas that lap the palm-fringed sand beaches of the resort area. The interior is stark and striking as well. No rain forests here. The land is brown and parched, much like the arid states of the southwestern United States.

The cunucu bristles with clumps of cactus, and many of the roads are practically fenced with the impenetrable, spiky plants. The hillsides are covered with divi-divi trees: The branches appear to be folded horizontally into 90° angles by the constant trade winds.

Roads that twist and turn through Aruba's interior lead to Yamanota, at 617 feet, Aruba's highest point. Drive right to the top, and you'll see panoramic views in every direction. A great place to greet a new day, or to pop open a bottle of champagne and watch a magnificent sunset.

---

1. Practical Facts

ENTERING AND LEAVING

U.S. citizens need proof of citizenship, and a return or continuing ticket. Although a passport is preferred, an authenticated birth certificate or a voter registration card is also acceptable. The departure tax is approximately $10 per person.

GETTING THERE

There's frequent air service to Aruba, and it's easy to reach the island from most places in the United States. **American Airlines** has flights to Aruba from New York (about a four-hour flight), as well as convenient connections from many major U.S. cities through Puerto Rico. **Continental** flies from Newark. There are also several daily inter-island flights from Curaçao and Bonaire to Aruba via **ALM Antillean Airlines.** All the hotels on Aruba are within a 15- to 30-minute drive from the Queen Beatrix International Airport; the taxi fare is approximately $12. Several cruise ships also call at Aruba. Ask your travel agent for details.

GETTING AROUND

Taxis don't have meters; the rates are based on your destination, rather than on the mileage. Rates are fixed by the government and are fairly inexpensive. Sample fares are posted at the airport; always confirm fares with the drivers before you ride.

Most U.S. **car-rental companies** have licenses in Aruba; there are also several reliable locally established companies. Jeeps are fun, but not necessary, even for a "safari" through the cunucu. Car rentals run approximately $30 to $40 per day; motor-scooter rentals are approximately $25 per day. Driving is on the right-hand side, as it is in the United States. Aruba uses international road signs.

Public **buses** make daily (including Sundays and holidays) loops from downtown Oranjestad to the main resort area, stopping on the L.G. Smith Boulevard in front of each of the high- and low-rise hotels. The bus fare is free from the hotels to town; about 50¢ from town to the hotels.

LANGUAGE

Aruba's native tongue is Papiamento, a language that evolved from Spanish, Dutch, and Portuguese, and combines a sprinkling of African and French, as well as Caribbean Indian dialects. You won't experience a language problem, though. Most Arubans are multilingual and speak several languages, including Dutch, Spanish, and English.

MONEY

The official currency of Aruba, introduced when the country gained equal status as a member within the Dutch Kingdom in 1986, is the Aruba florin (AFl), which fluctuates on the world market. At this writing, there are 1.80 florins to the U.S. dollar.

If you also travel to the nearby islands of Bonaire and Curaçao, make sure you don't confuse Aruba's square coin with the square coin of the Netherlands Antilles! In Aruba it's a 50-cent piece; in Bonaire and Curaçao it's a nickel.

U.S. dollars are accepted everywhere on the island. Although the hotels and the shops in the downtown shopping district accept major credit cards, many local restaurants require cash payment.

WEATHER

The climate in Aruba is dry and sunny, and it's always summer there! The trade winds are constant, and blow at a steady 15 miles per hour. So hold on to your hats —and forget about your hairdo!

The temperature in Aruba is almost always a warm 82°. There's only a slight change of temperature from day to night, and the temperature difference between summer and winter is only 2° or 3°. The average rainfall is 20 inches per year, which mainly occurs in brief showers during the months of October, November, and December. This isn't truly a rainy season, though, and if you do seek shelter, you'll be able to get right back onto the beach. The island lies completely outside the hurricane belt.

CLOTHING

Cool, casual, and informal summer clothes are the rule in Aruba, for both men and women. Dress-up clothes are fun, but not entirely necessary, for a night out in one of the elegant high-rise restaurants, nightclubs, or casinos. Dressing up for men usually means a jacket, although some places require ties; but it's not unusual to see jackets over polo-type shirts.

You should wear a coverup over bathing suits once you leave the beach; bathing suits aren't permitted in the shopping or business areas.

TIME

Aruba keeps Atlantic Standard Time all year long. That means that during the winter, it's one hour later in Aruba than it is in U.S. East Coast cities; during the summer, when eastern U.S. cities observe Daylight Savings Time, the time is the same.

TELEPHONES

You can dial Aruba direct from the mainland United States. The international dialing code is 011; the area code is 297-8; then dial the five-digit local number. When making calls in Aruba, just dial the five-digit local number. You can make local and international telephone calls through hotel operators.

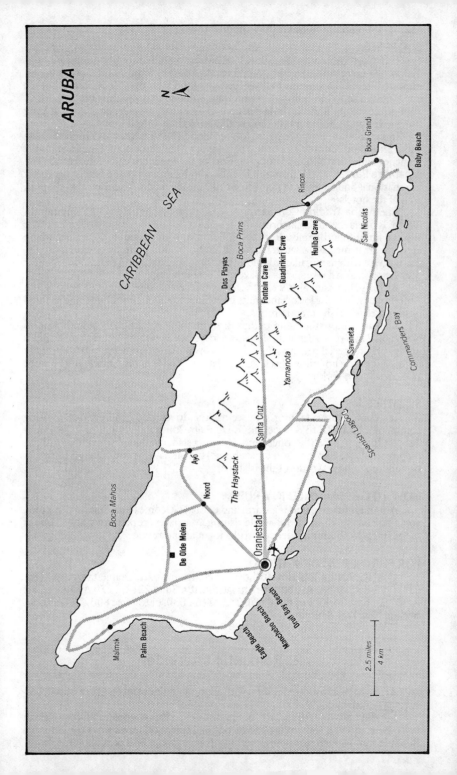

SHOPPING

U.S. Customs regulations allow U.S. citizens a $400 duty-free quota.

Aruba is considered a free port, since the country imposes little or no tax on imported items. This means that you can get good buys on specific items, but it's important to shop carefully before you leave home so that you can compare prices. Well-priced luxury items include perfume, table linens, china, crystal, and flatware; some jewelry and designer fashions are also attractively priced.

In Oranjestad, most shops are located along **Nassaustraat** and in the **Boulevard Shopping Center** opposite the harbor. Many stores in Oranjestad have branches in the **San Nicolas Shopping Center** at the eastern end of the island. The **Alhambra Bazaar,** across from the Divi Divi and Tamarijn Beach hotels, has many international boutiques with items from all over the world. There are also shops in each of the hotels.

The **Aruba Trading Company** on Nassaustraat is something of a tradition in Aruba. It offers the widest assortment of merchandise on the island, and some of the world's finest brand names. **Spritzer & Fuhrmann** is located at the corner where Hendrikstraat meets Nassaustraat. You'll find over 300 patterns of china, crystal, and flatware with names like Lalique, Waterford, Baccarat, and Wedgwood. Spritzer & Fuhrmann also has branches in several different hotels.

Aruba's shops are also well stocked with merchandise imported from South America; best bets for local handcrafts include pottery, ceramics, and hand-printed or silk-screened T-shirts and dresses.

Arubans follow the siesta tradition: shop hours are generally from 8 a.m. to noon and 2 to 6 p.m. Although shops are closed by law on Sundays, if a cruise ship is in the harbor, special permits allow them to open. Aruba has no sales tax. For more information on shopping, check out *A Shopper's Guide to the Caribbean* (Prentice Hall Press, New York).

SIGHTSEEING

It's easy to hire a taxi for sightseeing; the driver guide will provide running commentary for $15 to $20 per hour. **De Palm Tours** (tel. 24400 or 24545) and **Pelican Tours** (tel. 23888) offer tours of Oranjestad, combined with either full-day (approximately $40 per person for six hours) or half-day (approximately $16.50 per person for 2½ hours) tours of the island.

HOW TO GET MARRIED IN ARUBA

Although Aruba extends a warm and cordial welcome to just-married couples, you won't be able to say "I do" while visiting. Marriages are permitted only if one of the partners has been a resident of Aruba for at least one year.

FOR FURTHER INFORMATION

Contact: **Aruba Tourism Authority,** Schuttestraat 2A, Oranjestad, Aruba (tel. 011/297-8/21019); **Aruba Tourism Authority,** Suite 2212, 1270 Avenue of the Americas, New York, NY 10020 (tel. 212/246-3030, or toll free 800/TO ARUBA outside New York State).

---

2. Romantic Interludes

Aruba has sophisticated resorts with all the amenities and plenty of opportunity for adventure, too.

For **day sails,** the *Mi Dushi* ("my sweet one" in Papiamento), a 76-foot Danish ketch built in 1928 and restored to its original splendor, leaves from the Tamarijn Beach Hotel. You can purchase tickets in advance (about $40 per couple) at the De

Palm tour desk in all the hotels (tel. 24400 or 24545). The multihulled *Blue Melody* and the *Octopus* set sail from the **Pelican Watersports Center** at the Holiday Inn (tel. 23600, ext. 329); $40 to $80 per couple. Both companies offer **sunset cruises** as well, complete with rum punch and snacks for approximately $40 per couple.

The beaches are beautiful, but the **cunucu** (countryside) has much to recommend it too! Rent a car, Jeep, or motor scooter, pack a lunch, and don't miss the Natural Bridge, the highest and longest in the Caribbean; the massive boulder formations at Ayo and Casibari; and the caves with Indian inscriptions at Guadirikiri and Fontein. Ride through Frenchman's Pass, where Arawak Indians defended Aruba against the invaders in 1700; you'll have panoramic views of the countryside and abandoned aloe fields. The roads in the country are rough, and poorly marked, but it's literally impossible to become lost; the divi-divi trees point to the southwest, in the direction of the major hotels.

Whether you gamble, or just watch the action, a visit to Aruba wouldn't be complete without a visit to one of the island's **casinos.** Don't feel intimidated, even if you've never gambled before. The casinos are fun places, and in Aruba, the beach parties continue right into the gaming rooms. You don't have to dress up to gamble, but you won't look out of place if you do.

The **Alhambra Casino** (tel. 35000) is the only casino that's not attached to a hotel; it's in the Alhambra Bazaar, across from the Divi Divi and Tamarijn Beach hotels. The hotel casinos include: the **Americana Hotel & Casino,** the **Aruba Concorde Hotel & Casino,** the **Aruba Holiday Inn & Casino,** the **Aruba Palm Beach Hotel & Casino,** and the completely refurbished casino at the **Golden Tulip Aruba Caribbean Hotel & Casino.**

In addition to 5¢, 25¢, and $1 slot machines, the casinos usually offer games of chance, including blackjack, roulette, craps, wheel of fortune, and baccarat. Video poker is becoming increasingly popular. Persons under 18 years of age are not allowed in the casinos.

The **Seroe Colorado,** the residential area of the Exxon Corporation's Lago refinery, is in a beautiful location, well maintained, and open to the public. With the refinery closed, the executive homes and facilities are deserted. And so are the two sand beaches with their lush vegetation. **Baby Beach** and **Rodgers Beach** provide privacy and some of the best snorkeling on the island, with crystal-clear waters.

On the way back from Seroe Colorado, stop in at **Charlie's Bar** in San Nicolas (tel. 45086). You can get a light lunch, and take a look at the eclectic assortment of memorabilia that's been accumulating since 1941.

Try **island hopping.** Enjoy a touch of Holland on a one-day trip to Curaçao. **De Palm Tours** (tel. 24400 or 24545) runs a one-day excursion for approximately $175 per person, including airline tickets, airport transportation, sightseeing, lunch, and time to shop.

You can also make arrangements to spend a few days (or longer) on either Bonaire or Curaçao. Inter-island schedules change frequently, so plan to confirm your flight at least two days in advance. Since planes are small, with very limited luggage capacity, it's a good idea to pack light, check in early, and tote essentials in a small carry-on bag, just in case your luggage travels on a separate plane.

---

3. Honeymoon Hotels and Hideaways

There is a 5% government room tax and an 11% service charge on all room rates. The service charge on food and beverage is 10% to 15% in lieu of gratuities at the hotels. Some properties also charge a $3 energy surcharge per day.

All of the hotels in Aruba have package rates that are very attractive. Some packages include meal plans that represent good value, but you should decide in advance whether you'd rather experience a variety of restaurants and types of food. High season runs from mid-December to mid-April; low-season rates are about 20% to 50% lower. Prices quoted in this section reflect the range between low- and high-season rates.

Aruba has first-class hotels in its southwest coast resort area; casually elegant low-rise hotels are located on Druif and Manchebo beaches; stylish and sophisticated high-rise hotels are found on Palm Beach.

Divi Divi Beach Hotel, L.G. Smith Blvd. 93, Aruba (tel. 011/297-8/23300; U.S. reservations: 607/277-3484, or toll free 800/367-3484 nationwide). A sense of privacy prevails at this self-contained resort with outdoor pool and Jacuzzi, where the atmosphere reflects barefoot elegance. All of the luxury "Lanai" and "Casita" rooms have oceanfront balconies or patios, just a few steps from the private beach. Deluxe accommodations are set back in tri-level, bougainvillea-draped buildings made of white stucco with dark-wood trim that surround a free-form pool with a small island and a tea house accessible by a wooden footbridge. Inside your room, you'll find fresh flowers everywhere. Floral prints in deep tropical greens complement the room's dark-wood furnishings, providing a soft, cool, oasis-like retreat. Honeymoon package: Eight days/seven nights (EP): $1,015 to $2,570 per couple. Includes room taxes and gratuities, round-trip transfers between airport and hotel, bottle of wine, beach towel, and photo album.

Golden Tulip Aruba Caribbean Hotel & Casino, L.G. Smith Blvd. 81, Aruba (tel. 011/297-8/33555; U.S. reservations: 212/832-2277, or toll free 800/344-1212). The "Grand Dame" of the Caribbean is one of the only five-star deluxe hotels on the island. Everything is in tip-top condition after a $40-million refurbishment. The hotel is stately, and English tea is served every afternoon in the Lobby Lounge. But lavish use of turquoise accents throughout the building and grounds promotes an ambience of tropical informality that will have couples feeling right at home. Even the regular rooms are extremely spacious. Situated on 1,500 feet of white-sand beach, the resort has a water-sports center, a freshwater swimming pool with a sun deck, four floodlit tennis courts, a rooftop health and fitness center, a driving range, and a putting green. There are also four restaurants, a nightclub, and the most modern casino on the island. Honeymoon package: Eight days/seven nights (BP): From $1,160 per couple. Includes bottle of champagne, keepsake honeymoon photograph, use of designer bathrobes, sunset cruise, candlelight gourmet dinner, fruit basket, breakfast daily, and more. Four-day package also available. Packages not available in the high season, when rates (EP) range from $210 to $275 per couple per night.

Aruba Palm Beach Hotel, L.G. Smith Blvd. 79, Aruba (tel. 011/297-8/23900; U.S. reservations: 305/427-5488, or toll free 800/345-2782). Couples who want to experience a casual atmosphere while they enjoy high-rise conveniences will be more than happy in this centrally located 173-room hotel. The pretty rooms are large and airy, with comfortable modern furnishings and in-room TV; each has an ocean view and a private balcony. For daytime activity, there are a spacious beach with complete water-sports facilities, a freshwater swimming pool, and tennis. In the evening, the Club Galactica features international entertainers; there are also a disco and a casino. Honeymoon package: Eight days/seven nights (EP): $1,200 per couple. Includes deluxe room, bottle of champagne, round-trip transfers by limousine between airport and hotel, breakfast in bed the first morning, boat cruise, welcome cocktails, casino coupons, room tax and energy surcharge, and more. High-season rates (EP): $250 per couple per night.

Aruba Concorde Hotel & Casino, L.G. Smith Blvd. 77, Aruba (tel. 011/297-8/24466; U.S. reservations: 212/697-7405, or toll free 800/223-7944 or 800/442-8436 in NY). At 18 stories, this high-rise towers over everything else in Aruba. Soft rainbow hues decorate its southern wall, and with the little thatched sun umbrellas that line its beach, give the illusion of a tropical oasis with cosmopolitan conveniences. It's a lavish resort, and each of the 500 rooms has a terrace with ocean view, closed-circuit television, movies, radio with private-channel music, and an individual refrigerator. There are five restaurants and three cocktail lounges, a nightclub, and the Caribbean's largest casino. Outside, there are an open-air beachfront bar, an Olympic-size pool, facilities for water sports, and tennis courts. Honeymoon package: Eight days/seven nights (BP): $1,115 per couple (low season). Includes bottle of champagne, phone call home, welcome cocktails, two T-shirts, and more. High-season rates (EP): $230 to $255 per couple per night.

The **Holiday Inn Aruba Beach Resort & Casino,** L.G. Smith Blvd. 230, Palm Beach, Aruba (tel. 011/297-8/23600; U.S. reservations: toll free 800/HOLIDAY), on Palm Beach is like a miniature modern city. The lobby bustles with activity at all hours of the day and night, and there are more amenities than one couple could possibly make use of in a week. There are a beach, a pool, water sports facilities, four tennis courts, a health center with sauna, four restaurants and a deli, disco, casino, and the Palm Beach Room, famous for nightclub entertainment with international stars. The 602 newly decorated rooms feature private balconies and color TVs with free in-house movies. Honeymoon package: Eight days/seven nights (EP): $885 to $1,600 per couple. Includes round-trip transfers between airport and hotel, full American breakfast in bed one morning (includes service charge), welcome cocktails, bottle of champagne, trimaran cruise for two, his-and-her T-shirts, discount coupons, and more.

The **Bushiri Beach Hotel,** L.G. Smith Blvd. 35, Aruba (tel. 011/297-8/25216; U.S. reservations: 203/846-4140 in Connecticut; toll free 800/622-7836 nationwide). Take a tennis lesson . . . sip a rum punch . . . linger around the piano bar until the wee hours . . . and it won't cost you a bit extra, thanks to the Bushiri Beach resort's all-inclusive rates. Everything is covered by your room charge: airport transfers, three bountiful meals—plus snacks—daily, nightly entertainment, taxes and tips, plus a bevy of water sports ranging from paddleboats to windsurfing. The low-slung stucco buildings stretch alongside a wide (if somewhat pebbly) beach. Decorated in contemporary style, every room has an ocean view as well as air conditioning. Honeymoon package: Eight days/seven nights (all-inclusive): $1,355 per couple (low season); call for high-season rates. In addition to the regular resort features, package includes a bottle of champagne, a sunset cruise, and a telephone call home.

Americana Aruba Beach Resort & Casino, P.O. Box 218, Palm Beach Oranjestad, Aruba (tel. 011-297-8/24500; U.S. reservations: 212/661-4540 in NY; toll free 800/223-1588 nationwide). Sleek and sophisticated, the Americana offers elegance on one of Aruba's prettiest beaches. You'll find plenty to do right on the property, with a casino, a supper club, and a variety of water sports ranging from scuba-diving to windsurfing. After a $25-million construction and renovation project, all guest rooms have been completely refurbished, and tennis/racquetball facilities and a health club have been added. You'll want to linger beside the new swimming pool, a tropical playground with waterfalls and a swim-up bar. In addition to the two restaurants, you can cool out over sundaes at the ice-cream parlor in the lobby. Honeymoon package: Eight days/seven nights (EP): $1,275 per couple (low season). Includes round-trip transfers between airport and hotel, bottle of champagne, breakfast in bed one morning, fresh flowers in room, sunset cruise, two honeymoon nightshirts, and a photograph of the two of you. High-season rates (EP): $215 to $255 per couple per night.

4. Romantic Restaurants and Nightspots

Whether you're out for a ride in the country or a night on the town, you won't go hungry in Aruba.

The island has a wide variety of restaurants, ranging from the indoor and outdoor coffeeshops, main dining rooms, and specialty restaurants at the hotels, to moderate- and high-priced international and Aruban restaurants.

Restaurant prices are usually listed in both florins and U.S. dollars. A 10% to 15% service charge is almost always added to your bill.

EXPENSIVE

The Red Parrot, in the Divi Divi Beach Hotel (tel. 23300), is a casually elegant dining spot that comes complete with piano music every night except Tuesday. The menu is sophisticated, and the food is simply superb. Although the service tends to be rather formal, it's softened by a warm and friendly manner. A mural made of light-colored stained glass and large windows framed with greenery give the fully enclosed air-conditioned restaurant a breezy, open-air feeling. Hot and cold appetizers have international origins and are priced in the $7 range; the German potato salad and sausage was particularly good. Entrées are priced between $19 and $25; we enjoyed the veal Oscar and the flaming duck. The dessert cart has confections that are indescribably delicious. You won't be able to make up your mind—but you can have a taste of a few things for about $5. Open nightly from 6 to 9:15 p.m.

La Serre, in the Aruba Concorde Hotel (tel. 24466), sparkles and shimmers with bright glass and chrome against a deep-red and maroon decor. It overlooks the pool, where the reflections of hundreds of lights flicker in the water. As an appetizer, the escargots wrapped in flaky pastry are out of this world ($6). La Serre specializes in steaks and chops done to perfection, priced at $25 to $30. The wine list is extensive, and there's an excellent selection at $16 to $20 per bottle. Open nightly from 7 to 11 p.m.

Papagayo, upstairs at Boulevard Center, Oranjestad (tel. 24140), serves Italian specialties amid a profusion of lush plants and a number of brightly colored, jabbering parrots. Favorite dishes include the chicken in lemon sauce and the sirloin of beef, priced $16.50 to $22; about $30 for lobster. Open Monday through Friday for lunch, noon to 2:30 p.m.; Monday through Saturday for dinner, 5 to 9:30 p.m. They also offer an excellent value "early bird" dinner special from 5 to 7 p.m.; about $12 to $15 per person for a complete meal.

MODERATE TO INEXPENSIVE

Papiamento, on Wilhelminastraat in Oranjestad (tel. 24544). The setting for this intimate dining experience is one of Aruba's finest old mansions, where you'll have the undivided attention of your own personal chef. He'll prepare beef, chicken, or seafood specialties cooked to your individual taste on a sizzling marble tile, at your table. It's wonderful to watch, and delicious too. Or try chicken or seafood cooked just for the two of you in a pottery "egg" that's cracked open at your table. Dinner for two: about $65 plus drinks. Open Monday through Saturday, 6:30 to 10:30 p.m.

The Bali, Oranjested Harbor (tel. 22131). How about dining in a floating restaurant set in a typical Indonesian houseboat docked along the Oranjestad harbor? Indonesian specialties are priced at $15 to $20 each, or you can try the rijsttafel, an Indonesian smörgåsbord, for $16.50 to $27.50. If you don't want a full meal, chicken, beef, and pork satay (shish kebab) are served with drinks at the bar, which overlooks the harbor and a fleet of deep-sea fishing boats.

The New York Deli in the Alhambra Casino & Bazaar complex (tel. 25434) is the place to go when you want a taste of home. The overstuffed sandwiches really are; try to leave room for the cheese blintzes. Open 8 a.m. to 2 a.m.; $10 to $20 per couple. **Charlie's Bar** in San Nicolas (tel. 45086) is famous for its grilled shrimp ($15), but also serves light meals, sandwiches, and hamburgers priced at under $10. Open noon to 9 p.m.; closed Sundays and holidays. **Brisas del Mar** on the waterfront in Savaneta (tel. 47718) specializes in Aruban-style creole seafood dishes. Entrées priced from $10 to $20, although lobster runs higher. The restaurant is open daily from noon to 3 p.m. and from 6:30 to 10:30 p.m.

Don't miss Aruba's exciting nightlife. It starts late, and goes on till the early morning hours! Discos open after 10 p.m., including the **Roseland Ballroom** in the Alhambra Bazaar (tel. 35000), the **Scaramouche Disco** in the Boulevard Shopping Center (tel. 24954), and the **Visage Disco** on L.G. Smith Boulevard (tel. 33418) in Oranjestad.

During the high season, many nightclubs have an early show that starts close to midnight, and another in the early morning. Try the **Fandango Nightclub** in the Golden Tulip Aruba Caribbean Hotel & Casino (tel. 33555), the **Arubesque** in the Aruba Concorde Hotel & Casino (tel. 24466), and **L'Esprit Nightclub** in the Holiday Inn Aruba Beach Resort & Casino (tel. 23600).

XV

THE BAHAMAS

1. PRACTICAL FACTS
2. NASSAU/CABLE BEACH/PARADISE ISLAND
3. FREEPORT/LUCAYA
4. THE FAMILY ISLANDS: THE ABACOS, ELEUTHERA, THE EXUMAS
5. MORE SUGGESTIONS IN THE BAHAMAS

If variety is the spice of life, then The Bahamas couldn't be more highly seasoned. Starting only 50 miles off the coast of Florida, this chain of 700 islands (some not much larger than rocks) stretches into the Atlantic, almost reaching the Caribbean. The country's 200,000 people live on only a handful of these islands, leaving the rest uninhabited. The shapes and sizes of the islands and their offshore cays (pronounced "keys") are as varied as the lifestyles of their residents.

Which Bahamas are you looking for? The one that gives you something to do during every waking hour? Extensive shopping? Golf, tennis, and all kinds of water sports? Historical sights? Or the one that invites you to do nothing at all—except, of course, have beach after beach all to yourselves? The one that allows you to go barefoot or the one that tempts you to dress up every night? The one that lets you indulge in gourmet delights or the one that keeps you coming back for more homestyle local cooking? The best thing about honeymooning in The Bahamas is that you can have it all.

You may have heard it said that there are two sides to every story. Well, The Bahamas story has at least three: Nassau/Cable Beach/Paradise Island, Freeport/Lucaya, and the Family Islands. Each of these destinations is strikingly distinct. On the northern coast of the island of New Providence, Cable Beach, adjoining Paradise Island, and Nassau, the historic capital, offer more action than all the other Bahamian islands combined. While Grand Bahama's youthful Freeport/Lucaya can give Nassau a run for its money in the nightlife department, the pace here is generally more relaxed. Far removed from either New Providence or Grand Bahama are the rest of the Bahamian islands, collectively known as the Family Islands. Here life revolves around the blessings of nature, from the quiet empty beaches to the spectacular offshore reefs.

Columbus first brought The Bahamas to the attention of Europe when he arrived in 1492 to find Arawak Indians living peacefully on these predominantly flat, beach-rimmed islands. The exact place where he first landed in the New World is under dispute, but it is generally thought to be the southerly Bahamian island of San Salvador. (The islands are gearing up for a rousing party on October 12, 1992, celebrating the 500th anniversary of Columbus' arrival in the New World.) Spanish explorers soon lost interest in The Bahamas and the British began reshaping the islands. The first wave of Europeans came from Bermuda in 1648, settling on Eleuthera after fleeing religious persecution at home. For decades, ruthless pirates ruled the shores, hiding out in the quiet inlets and among the tiny cays. During the 17th and 18th centuries, Nassau was the home base of pirates who preyed on Spanish galleons transporting gold and silver from the New World to Europe. Then in 1718, Captain Woodes Rogers put an end to the plundering and became the first royal governor of The Bahamas.

Although The Bahamas gained its independence from Britain in 1973, there is still a marked British flavor to the country: You drive on the left, you can watch the changing of the guard at Government House in Nassau, and you can enjoy steak-and-kidney pie or fish-and-chips washed down with ale at many of the pubs. However, because of the proximity to the United States, Americans will also find much that is familiar. The Bahamian dollar, for instance, is on par with the U.S. dollar, so that the two currencies can be used interchangeably.

Now this is not to say that The Bahamas does not have a distinctly Bahamian character. The colorful lilt in the English spoken, the easygoing pace of life (even in bustling Nassau), and the home-grown Junkanoo and Goombay music—which gives rise to the festive Junkanoo parades at Christmastime and New Year's—are only a few examples of what the word "Bahamian" means.

Honeymooners who want to get an inside look at The Bahamas, from the point of view of its residents, should consider participating in the People-to-People Program. This free program introduces Bahamian couples to visitors with similar interests in picnics, shared meals, personalized sightseeing tours, or any other activities you'd like to arrange (contact a Bahamas tourist office).

No matter which island you choose—and to appreciate the variety of The Bahamas, you may decide to sample more than one—The Bahamas has a gentle way of helping romance thrive.

1. Practical Facts

ENTERING AND LEAVING
American and Canadian citizens are required to have proof of citizenship, such as a passport or birth certificate, as well as round-trip or onward-bound tickets. When flying home, you'll each pay a $7 departure tax.

GETTING THERE
Many airlines and cruise ships serve the Bahamas.

By Air
Flight time from Miami to Nassau is just over a half hour, and from New York to Nassau, about 2½ hours. Airlines serving The Bahamas include **Bahamasair, Delta, Midway, Pan American, TWA, USAir** and **Air Canada.** The new **Merv Griffin's Paradise Island Airways** offers several daily round trips between Paradise Island and both Miami and Fort Lauderdale. In addition, several small airlines fly from various Florida cities.

For interisland travel, **Bahamasair** has flights to almost all the Family Islands. **Chalk's International** will take you from Florida to Nassau, plus several different cays; **Aero Coach** flies from Florida to many of the Family Islands.

By Sea

If you want to ease into The Bahamas, a cruise provides a leisurely, fun-filled means of getting there. The kind of voyage you choose will depend on the size of the ship you want, the facilities (some of which are so extensive that you'll think you're in a resort hotel), and the ports of call. Some lines combine stops at Nassau and Freeport with visits to various Family Islands; others even give you a taste of Florida's Disney World along the way. Airfare from certain U.S. cities is often included in the package.

GETTING AROUND

Transportation is varied and convenient in The Bahamas.

By Taxi

In Nassau and Freeport: Taxis, which are metered, wait for passengers at airports and hotels. From Nassau International Airport to a hotel in Cable Beach, the two of you should expect to pay about $12; from the airport to Paradise Island, the ride will be about $20 including the $2 bridge toll. From Freeport's International Airport to the hotel districts, the fare will be from about $10. Taxis in the Family Islands are not metered and tend to be more expensive than in Nassau or Freeport. Taxi tours are available throughout The Bahamas for about $20 an hour.

By Car

Visitors with valid U.S. or Canadian driver's licenses can rent cars in The Bahamas. *Note that driving is on the left.* Daily rates range from about $55 to $95. You'll save money if you rent by the week. Agencies in Nassau and Freeport are at airports, hotels, and downtown locations. In high season, you may want to make a reservation before leaving home. In addition to local companies, **Avis, Budget, Dollar Rent-A-Car,** and **National** also have offices in The Bahamas. You can rent cars in the Family Islands (sometimes from taxi drivers), but many of the models have been battle scarred by years of use on bumpy roads. Be sure to check the condition of the car before starting out.

By Bus

Many Paradise Island and Cable Beach hotels provide free transportation to downtown Nassau. Freeport hotels that are not located on the beach offer frequent **shuttle** service to the shore. If you'd prefer to get around Nassau, Cable Beach, or Freeport/Lucaya the way Bahamians do, hop into a jitney, or minibus, for about 75¢. With reggae or calypso pulsing on the radio, you'll pass through residential neighborhoods and see a picturesque side of the islands that many tourists miss. For sightseeing tours in large or small air-conditioned buses, sign up at a hotel activity desk.

By Motor Scooter

Some hotels in Nassau, Paradise Island, and Freeport rent mopeds for about $30 a day plus $25 deposit. Be sure to wear helmets. Motor scooters are also available on some of the Family Islands, such as Exuma and Eleuthera.

By Bicycle

Especially on some Family Islands, bikes are a good way to get from one place to another. Some resorts rent bikes for about $10 a day; others make them available to guests at no cost.

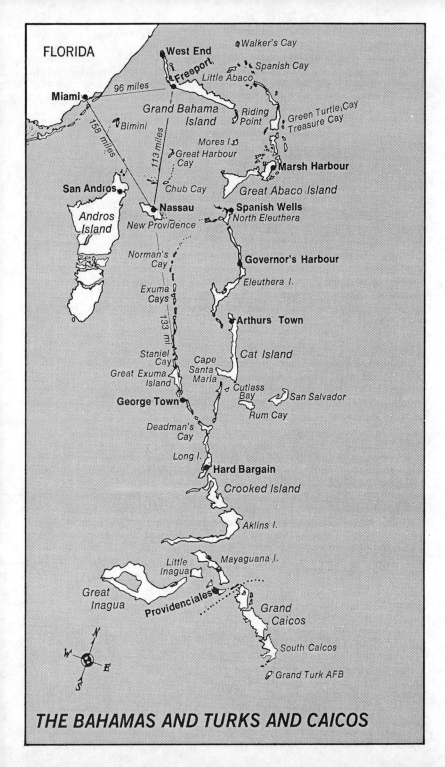

FLORIDA

West End
Freeport
Little Abaco

Walker's Cay
Spanish Cay

Miami   96 miles

Grand Bahama
Island

Riding
Point

Green Turtle Cay
Treasure Cay

Bimini

Mores I.
Great Harbour
Cay

Marsh Harbour

San Andros

Chub Cay

Great Abaco Island

Nassau

Spanish Wells
North Eleuthera

Andros
Island

New Providence

Norman's
Cay

Governor's Harbour

Eleuthera I.

Exuma
Cays

Arthurs Town

Cat Island

Staniel
Cay

Cape
Santa
Maria

Great Exuma
Island

Cutlass
Bay

San Salvador

George Town

Rum Cay

Deadman's
Cay

Long I.

Hard Bargain

Crooked Island

Aklins I.

Little
Inagua

Mayaguana J.

Great
Inagua

Providenciales

Grand
Caicos

South Caicos

Grand Turk AFB

N
W   E
S

THE BAHAMAS AND TURKS AND CAICOS

LANGUAGE

English is the national language. If you listen carefully, you'll hear Irish and Scottish influences along with the West Indian lilt. Also, Bahamians frequently interchange *v*'s with *w*'s, so don't be surprised if people say "You're velcome" when you thank them. This pronunciation is thought to date back to 18th-century English.

MONEY

Although The Bahamas has its own currency, U.S. dollars are also accepted throughout the islands. However, once you see the Technicolor Bahamian bills, you may want to forgo your monotonous American green. Since the U.S. dollar and the Bahamian dollar are equal in value, you'll often receive change consisting of both currencies.

The service charge is often included in restaurant checks. If not, tip about 15%. This percentage also goes for taxi drivers and tour guides. Porters are tipped about $1.

WEATHER

Temperatures average in the 70s during the winter season (December through April) and the 80s during the summer. Evenings tend to be slightly cooler. The summer months get a bit more rain, but showers are usually too brief to interfere with outdoor life.

CLOTHING

During the winter season, men will need jackets and ties at the more expensive restaurants at night. However, for the most part, even in high season, dress tends to be casual. Air conditioning and mild evenings can necessitate a shawl or jacket for women. Bahamians prefer that visitors confine beachwear and short-shorts to the shore or the pool only.

TIME

Eastern Standard Time is in effect in The Bahamas, and Daylight Saving Time is observed in the summer. Therefore, when it is 8 a.m. in New York, it is 8 a.m. in The Bahamas, year-round.

TELEPHONES

To call The Bahamas direct, dial 809 and the seven-digit local number.

SHOPPING

Although The Bahamas is not a duty-free territory, bargain hunters may have trouble parting company with Nassau, Paradise Island, and Freeport. Prices can be 25% to 45% lower than in the U.S. for some imports such as crystal, china, woolens, linens, French perfumes, watches, cameras, and liquor. You don't even have to leave the larger hotels to start dipping into your pocketbook—many have arcades with lots of tempting shops. But most visitors agree that it is more fun to venture out.

In Nassau, stores line **Bay Street,** the main thoroughfare, all vying for your attention. For Seiko and Rolex watches, jewelry, English bone china, Limoges porcelain, and much more, stop in at **John Bull** on Bay Street between East Street and Elizabeth Avenue. The **Brass & Leather Shop,** on Charlotte Street off Bay, sells wallets, belts, Bottega Veneta luggage, and the like. Other browse-worthy stores include the **Linen Shop** for lace tablecloths and pillowcases, and **Little Switzerland** for elegant jewelry and watches.

Many shops, boutiques, and restaurants in Freeport are clustered in the **International Bazaar.** Here you find stores featuring some of fashion's greatest names, including Gucci and Fendi. If you believe that emeralds are a girl's best friend, view the sparkling gemstones at **Colombia Emeralds.** Try **Island Galleria** for jewelry, art, and fine china; and the **London Pacesetter Boutique** for classy T-shirts.

For shopping, dining, and entertainment that are hot-hot-hot, scope out the new multimillion-dollar **Port Lucaya,** located across from the Holiday Inn and the Lucaya Beach Resort and Casino. The complex takes full advantage of its superb setting right on the water and marina. Built Bahamian style, with pastel-painted fronts accented by lattice trim, the shops run the gamut from Cartier and Gucci to market stalls selling smoothies and shell necklaces. Try **Inspiration** for beautiful men's and women's fashions. At the **Pusser's Co. Store,** you'll find ship-shape casual wear for both ladies and gentlemen, as well as bottles of their famous rum, souvenir grog mugs, and the like.

Handmade straw goods are sold on most Bahamian islands, but the variety is greatest in Nassau and Freeport. Pick up straw hats to keep the sun off, or buy straw bags to carry suitcase overflow on the way home. Don't be shy about bargaining— no one expects you to pay the first price you're quoted.

CASINOS

Visitors over age 21 are welcome to gamble in the casinos, which are located in Cable Beach, Paradise Island, and Freeport/Lucaya.

ABOUT ACCOMMODATIONS

New Providence, Paradise Island, and Grand Bahama offer every kind of hotel from big and brassy to quiet and unassuming.

Hotels add an 8% room tax to rates. Many also add a 15% service charge. High season runs from about December through April. During the summer (or "Goombay") season and autumn ("Discovery") season, rates are about 20% to 50% lower. The price ranges given for hotels in this chapter reflect the spread between low and high season. The **Bahamas Reservation Service** can help you book practically any hotel in the islands; toll free 800/327-0787 in the U.S. and Canada; 305/443-3821 in Miami.

DINING OUT

Throughout the islands, restaurants serve continental food along with local favorites. It is best to make reservations at most restaurants. Conch—the meat of that large shell you put to your ear to hear the roar of the ocean—is king on Bahamian menus. Pronounced "conk," it is served in a variety of forms: cracked (pounded tender and fried), raw as salad, in bite-size fritters, and in chowder. Other specialties are baked crab, local lobster, and okra soup. Grouper heads the list of fish—it's on breakfast, lunch, *and* dinner menus. Side dishes include mildly sweet johnny cake, peas and rice, and fried plantain. Try one of the country's prized rum cocktails: a Goombay smash, a yellow bird, or a Bahama Mama. For dessert, sample guava duff, made from slices of the fruit rolled in dough and boiled.

HOW TO GET MARRIED IN THE BAHAMAS

If you've always dreamed of an island wedding, why not make it happen? Although the procedure sounds a bit complicated, it all works very easily and smoothly. Your hotel or the Ministry of Tourism's People-to-People Program will help you handle all the details. Here's what you need to do. You both must be in The Bahamas at the time you apply for a marriage license, which costs $20. Request a waiver of the 15-day residency requirement from the Registrar General, P.O. Box N-532, Nassau, Bahamas (the waiver is always granted). You are required to spend three days in The Bahamas, and you can be married any time after the third day. If you're under 18 years of age, parental consent is necessary. While no blood test is required, you'll need to show proof of identity, such as a passport, and proof of divorce (if applicable).

FOR FURTHER INFORMATION

Contact: **The Bahamas Ministry of Tourism,** P.O. Box N-3701, Nassau, The Bahamas (tel. 809/322-7500). **The Bahamas Tourist Office,** 150 East 52nd St., New York, NY 10022 (tel. 212/758-2777), or one of the tourist offices in twelve other cities throughout the United States. **Grand Bahama Island Promotion Board,** 255 Alhambra Circle, Suite 1112, Coral Gables, FL 33134 (tel. 305/448-3386). The **Family Islands Promotion Board,** 255 Alhambra Circle, Suite 420, Coral Gables, FL 33134 (tel. 305/446-4111).

---

2. Nassau/Cable Beach/Paradise Island

Home of Nassau, the historic capital, New Providence Island is The Bahamas' most popular destination. Seven miles across at its widest point and 20 miles long, it is only an hour by air from Miami, Florida. Dreamy beaches, great snorkeling, scuba-diving, and other water sports, old forts, pastel-colored colonial homes, nonstop nightlife, casinos—it's all here.

The island has three main resort areas, all close to each other: Nassau, Cable Beach, and Paradise Island.

Nassau, the capital, is made for strolling. In particular, you'll want to check out Bay Street, the broad main thoroughfare, which is bordered by shops, boutiques, restaurants, banks, and the famed straw market. In addition to all kinds of straw goods, you'll see T-shirts and jewelry made from shells. Hone your bargaining skills with the friendly craftswomen—no one expects you to pay the first price you're quoted.

Near the straw market is flower-filled Rawson Square, across from the pink-and-white government buildings. In the courtyard formed by these buildings is a statue of a youthful Queen Victoria. Christopher Columbus has the honor of standing before nearby Government House, the colonial mansion that is the official residence of the British-appointed governor general. You may not be in London, but the changing of the guard does take place here every other Saturday at 10 a.m. Climb the 65 steps of the queen's staircase, hewn from solid limestone. At the top you'll find the crumbling remains of Fort Fincastle and you'll have a sweeping view. Still guarding the entrance to Nassau Harbour, Fort Charlotte, dating back to 1788, is one of the city's well-preserved forts.

The bridge that connects Paradise Island to New Providence arches majestically (the toll is $2 by car, 50¢ by moped, and 25¢ on foot, round-trip). For a spectacular vision, stand on the bridge at sunset. Not too long ago, Paradise Island was nothing but farmland and was known as Hog Island. Now its sparkling beaches are backed by high-rise hotels and its casino and Las Vegas-style nightlife draw travelers from all over. Secluded Cabbage Beach is a romantic cove that seems to have been carved into the eastern shore just for honeymooners. Ferries run between Nassau and Paradise Island (about $2 per person each way).

ROMANTIC INTERLUDES

For a romantic tour of historic downtown Nassau, sit back and relax in one of the **surreys** that leave from Rawson Square. Your driver will certainly entertain you with intriguing tales about the way things were.

You'll find a medieval cloister standing in **Versailles Gardens** on modern Paradise Island. These peaceful grounds with a dramatic view of the harbor invite hand-in-hand strolls. Near Fort Charlotte in Nassau, the **Botanical Gardens** (tel. 323-9575) attract nature-lovers. Open daily from 10 a.m. to 4 p.m.; admission is $1.25 per person. At **Ardastra Gardens** (tel. 323-5806) nearby, you can not only enjoy the flowers—trained flamingoes (the national bird of The Bahamas) put on a great show at 11 a.m., 2 p.m., and 4 p.m. Open daily from 9 a.m. to 4:30 p.m.; admission is $8.50 per person. When you need a break from shopping, board the 97-foot *Nautilus* ($40 per couple) for a two-hour, day-time cruise to the underwater **Sea Gardens** (tel. 325-2876).

Try **parasailing,** which is available at several hotels on Cable Beach or Paradise Island Beach. You'll be strapped to a parachute tied to a boat. As the boat takes off, you'll rise slowly into the air and the folks on the beach will grow as tiny as pebbles in the sand. What a view! Coming back to earth is no problem. You'll descend as gently as you rise. About $30 a ride.

Moray eels, bright parrot fish, sea turtles, spiny lobster, and sea cucumbers are just a few of the creatures you'll see on the multicolored coral reefs at **Coral World's Underwater Observatory** (tel. 328-1036). Get nose to nose with "man-eating" sharks—you'll peer at each other through the glass. Not far from the heart of downtown Nassau, Coral World is on a cay connected to the mainland by an arching bridge. Allow a couple of hours to visit the many exhibits and to stop for a bite at the oceanfront restaurant. Open daily from 9 a.m. to 6 p.m.; admission: $13.25 per person.

Most hotels can arrange **snorkeling and diving** excursions for the novice as well as for the experienced. Qualified scuba-divers can visit "James Bond Reef," which was featured in the movies *Never Say Never Again* and *For Your Eyes Only*.

One-tank dives run about $40; two-tank dives about $55. If you've never dived before, but think you would like to try, sign up for an introductory resort course, which runs approximately $80 per person.

Why not play Robinson Crusoe for a day and run off to a deserted island on a picnic sail? Several different boats offer castaway adventures; all run about $80 per couple. The triple-decker **Calypso I and II** party boats (Nassau Cruises Ltd., tel. 326-3577) take guests to Blue Lagoon Island, where secluded beaches, great snorkeling, and miles of nature trails await. The 50-foot **Sandy Cay** motor cruiser (Treasure Island Cruises Ltd., tel. 322-8184) anchors at Treasure Island, a postcard-perfect islet surrounded by beaches. For a real Bahamian party complete with calypso music, limbo contests, snorkeling, and complimentary rum punch, climb aboard the **Yellow Bird** or **Tropic Bird** catamaran (Majestic Tours Ltd., tel. 322-4941). Or perform your own feats of derring-do on a cruise to Discovery Island aboard the **El Buccanero II** (tel. 328-7772), designed after an 18th-century Spanish galleon. Most boats run evening cocktail/dinner cruises as well.

HONEYMOON HOTELS AND HIDEAWAYS

Whether your pleasure be a 200-year-old mansion or a modern high-rise, you'll find something to suit in Nassau, Paradise Island, and Cable Beach.

Very Expensive

Le Meridien Royal Bahamian, West Bay Street, P.O. Box N-10422, Nassau, New Providence, The Bahamas (tel. 809/327-6400; U.S. and Canadian reservations: toll free 800/543-4300). Quieter and more dignified than most Cable Beach hotels, this posh resort was born in 1946 as a private club. Peacocks grace the imaginatively landscaped grounds and afternoon tea is served. The lobby, with its marble floor and Georgian furnishings, opens onto a courtyard with a fountain in the center. The 170 individual rooms and villas, done in smoky pinks and bright blues, come equipped with terry-cloth robes, and the modern baths are stocked with all kinds of toiletries. Many have balconies; some look out over the sea. Relax by the pool, with its breezy café, or take advantage of the variety of water sports offered at the beach. If you prefer to be alone together when you take a dip, book one of the two villas with private pools. Pamper yourselves with mud baths or massages in the health spa; play tennis on two courts. Honeymoon package: Five days/four nights (BP): $1,540 per couple (standard room); $1,940 per couple (deluxe room). Includes breakfast daily, champagne and fruit basket upon arrival, Blue Lagoon island sightseeing cruise, polo shirts.

Expensive

Ocean Club, Box N-4777, Nassau, New Providence, The Bahamas (tel. 809/ 326-2501; U.S. reservations: toll free 800/321-3000). Before its transformation into a Resorts International hotel, this colonial-style mansion built in the 1960s was owned by millionaire Huntington Hartford and run as a private club. Each of the 70 guest rooms, including those in suites and villas, comes complete with thick terry-cloth bathrobes, sitting and dining areas, telephones in the bedrooms and baths, and both air conditioning and ceiling fans. After a $1.5-million enhancement program, the accommodations are lovelier than ever, with pastel furnishings and lavish use of marble. Try a villa if you'd like an enclosed patio with a Jacuzzi. The broad stark-white beach stretches for two miles. Slabs of flagstone create walkways through the flowering grounds and around the pool, which overlooks Versailles Gardens. This medieval cloister was imported from France and reconstructed here stone by stone. The garden's gazebo overlooking the harbor is a favorite spot for wedding ceremonies. Afternoon tea is served near the nine Har-Tru tennis courts, four of which are lit for evening games. Golfers have trouble staying away from the 18-hole championship golf course. Honeymoon package: Eight days/seven nights (EP): From $1,420 per couple. Includes welcome cocktails, admission to Le Cabaret Theatre revue, champagne breakfast in bed your first morning, champagne honeymoon reception, one complimentary round of golf, tote bag and sun visors, complimentary tennis, and more.

Coral World Villas, P.O. Box N-7797, Nassau, New Providence, The Bahamas (tel. 809/328-1036; U.S. reservations: toll free 800/221-0203). Honeymoon on a private island—just five minutes from downtown Nassau. Set on tiny Silver Cay, only a conch-shell toss away from the New Providence "mainland," these luxury villas sequester couples with utmost privacy . . . while high-stakes gambling excitement, top-name entertainment, and world-class restaurants lie within easy reach via free shuttle transportation; Coral World Bahamas marine park is right next door. Personal service is emphasized: A concierge supervises your check-in and helps arrange all the details of your stay—from car rentals to restaurant reservations. Stylish and sophisticated, each of the 22 roomy villas faces the sea and has a private plunge pool. The beige Italian-marble bathrooms are true knockouts, with floor-to-ceiling windows overlooking waves breaking on the ironshore. Remote-control satellite TVs, direct-dial telephones, and AM/FM radios link you to the rest of the world, if needed. A complimentary continental breakfast is delivered to your terrace each morning; refrigerators are thoughtfully stocked with top-quality frozen entrées. No wonder the management says that they sometimes don't see their guests for days. Honeymoon package: Eight days/seven nights (CP): $1,430 per couple. Includes complimentary bottle of champagne, tropical fruit basket, fresh flowers daily, unlimited free admission to Coral World marine park, admissions to Peanuts Taylor's island show, dinner for two one evening.

Moderate

Carnival's Crystal Palace Resort & Casino and **Carnival's Cable Beach Riviera Tower,** P.O. Box N-8306, Nassau, New Providence, The Bahamas (tel. 809/ 327-6200; U.S. reservations: 305/576-3506 in Miami; toll free 800/222-7466). Flashy and fun—that describes this razzle-dazzle new pleasure oasis at the center of the Cable Beach action. The resort encompasses two properties: the glittery 872-room Crystal Palace Resort & Casino and the slightly more laid-back Cable Beach Riviera Tower (formerly the Cable Beach Hotel). With art deco–design floors, mirrored ceilings, and tubular beams painted an outrageous—but curiously appealing —hue of bright purple, the public areas dazzle with high-tech glitz—sort of *Miami Vice* meets *2001: A Space Odyssey*. At night, rainbow-colored lights illuminate the facades, making the buildings look like slot machines making a gaudy payoff. Rooms are ultramodern, commodious, and comfortable, with kicky touches such as bright-green-and-purple-striped carpeting and bedside lamps that would look equally at home aboard the space shuttle. For sybarites who believe in indulging their imaginations, the Crystal Palace offers a choice of "super suites," including the $25,000-a-night Galactic Fantasy, which comes with its own robot, holograms on the wall (instead of paintings), plus such toys as a couch that swivels to face the screen when you turn on the TV. Sports facilities include tennis courts (clay and hard), racquetball and squash courts, an 18-hole golf course, a health club, swimming pools (one complete with 20-foot spiral water slide) . . . all this on the prime Cable Beach waterfront. Right on your doorstep, you have the Crystal Palace Casino, eleven restaurants (Le Grill is a favorite), bi-level discotheque, and a Las Vegas–style nightclub. Aside from the show-biz aspects, the nicest thing about the Crystal Palace is its top-notch staff: Everyone from bellhop to front-office manager is warm, friendly, and eager to help. Honeymoon package: Eight days/seven nights (BP): $1,350 to $1,885 per couple. Includes round-trip transfers from Nassau airport, deluxe oceanview accommodations with balcony, fruit basket and bottle of champagne, welcome drink upon arrival, breakfast daily, a dinner for two including wine, entrance to the casino show including two drinks, admission to the disco, match-play casino chips, special gifts, and more.

Paradise Island Resort & Casino, Box N-4777, Nassau, New Providence, The Bahamas (tel. 809/326-3000; U.S. reservations: toll free 800/321-3000). This extensive resort on three miles of stunning Paradise Island beach glitters and sparkles with revived flair under its new owner, entertainer and entrepreneur Merv Griffin. Griffin's aim is to turn this retreat into a true Fantasy Island . . . a true glamour destination in every sense of the word. The planned $25 million in renovations will completely refurbish all 1,200 rooms in both the Paradise Tower and Britannia Tower with oversize sofas and handcrafted furnishings made from wood, wicker, and bamboo. Bathrooms reflect movie-star panache, complete with white marble and sunken bathtubs; all accommodations feature a private balcony, refrigerator, and color TV. For sports fans, a new bar with 13 video monitors has recently opened. If you prefer active sports, take advantage of a dozen tennis courts, the 18-hole championship golf course, and aquatic fun such as snorkeling, windsurfing, waterskiing, and parasailing. In the afternoon, the beachside pool reverberates with activity. Bingo and other games follow entertainment by a live band. Twice a day, trained dolphins perform. There is no need to leave the hotel to go shopping, since you'll have a good selection of stores. Many consider the revue at Le Cabaret Theatre the hottest casino show in The Bahamas. Twelve restaurants serve up a variety of the world's great cuisines, from classic French to spicy Indian. Inquire about the Club Paradise program, an all-inclusive hotel package featuring a gourmet dining plan, all water sports, golf greens fees, weekly Bahamian night, beach barbecues, and daily cocktail parties; priced from $3,045 per couple. Honeymoon package: Eight days/seven nights (EP): From $1,020 per couple. Includes special honeymoon reception, bottle of champagne, his-and-her nightshirts, complimentary tennis day and night, one complimentary round of golf, and more.

Sheraton Grand, Box SS-6307, Paradise Island, The Bahamas (tel. 809/326-2011; U.S. and Canadian reservations: toll free 800/325-3535). This beachfront high-rise is a stone's throw from the Paradise Island casino. When you want action and excitement, just pop next door, then return to the peace and quiet of this elegant resort. The sunny lobby is decked out with a reflecting pool surrounded by plants, and high-backed wicker chairs stand next to the floor-to-ceiling windows. Delicious meals are served in several restaurants, including the bar and grill on the patio next to the swimming pool. The 360 colorful guest rooms have sitting areas, refrigerators, and balconies. Practically every water sport is available right on the property (there are tennis courts lighted for day or night play), and the hotel staff is always on hand to help with arrangements for any other activity. Honeymoon package: Eight days/seven nights (EP): $985 (low season); $1,485 (superior room) to $2,215 (Sheraton Towers) per couple (high season). Includes deluxe accommodations with guaranteed ocean view (upgraded to junior suite in low season), welcome cocktails, chilled bottle of champagne, special honeymooners' cocktail reception, special gift, two complimentary cocktails per person in Le Paon lounge, travel tote, two T-shirts, and more.

Paradise Paradise Beach Resort, P.O. Box SS-6259, Paradise Island, The Bahamas (tel. 809/326-2541; U.S. reservations: toll free 800/321-3000). Water sports are the main events at this casual, relaxed hotel in a quiet area. Some guests are convinced that the protected waters and the wide sandy expanse make this beach the best on Paradise Island. Even when the hotel is completely full, the beach and bean-shaped pool are far from crowded. All water sports and other activities (such as daily bike tours of the island) are included in room rates. Although the decor is bare-bones basic, all 100 rooms are equipped with minibars, color televisions, and king-size or double beds. Honeymoon package: Eight days/seven nights (EP): From $825 per couple. Includes a bottle of champagne, admission to the show at Le Cabaret Theatre, his-and-her nightshirts, manager's cocktail party, and complimentary land and water sports. Four-day/three-night package also available.

Graycliff, Box N-10246, West Hill Street, Nassau, New Providence, The Bahamas (tel. 809/322-2796). This 14-room hotel across the street from Government House has the distinction of being the only member of the prestigious Relais et Châteaux chain in The Bahamas. Set in a colonial mansion more than two centuries old, it has retained the feeling of an elegant private home. The large rooms, with colorful names such as Yellowbird and Hibiscus, are individually decorated with antiques and tile floors. Some have walk-in closets and dressing rooms; all are air-conditioned. Spacious bathrooms gleam with glass-enclosed stall showers and old-fashioned tubs that invite bubble baths. Rooms in the main house tend to have more atmosphere, even though the floors may squeak and the carpet looks a tad worn. The poolside cottages such as the Mandarino Suite are spiffier, newly refurbished and glamorous with such features as fine crystal chandeliers and palatially proportioned bathrooms with whirlpool tubs and saunas. Thriving gardens and a stone walkway surround the swimming pool. The excellent food, served in a variety of settings, draws a constant stream of diners. Honeymoon package: None. Rates (EP): $135 to $330 per couple per night.

With 411 plush rooms, the **Nassau Beach,** Box N-7756, Nassau, New Providence, The Bahamas (tel. 809/327-7711; U.S. reservations: toll free 800/225-5843), accommodates its guests in high style. The lobby sparkles with marble and tile floors. Recently refurbished, the guest rooms pamper visitors with white rattan upholstered furniture, marble baths, and dressing areas. For extra pampering, choose the all-inclusive Palm Club program, with perks that include all meals, complimentary wine and cocktails, boat excursions, free water sports, and more. The fare at the variety of restaurants ranges from all-American steak to Polynesian surprises. Accompanied by music and other entertainment, the weekly Junkanoo buffet eases visitors into the island spirit and allows them to sample Bahamian culinary specialties. At night the popular Out Island Bar is filled with couples shaking a leg or two. A tennis pro is on hand at the six-court tennis complex, and water sports are available on the hotel's wide strip of Cable Beach. A Trusthouse Forte property. Honeymoon package: Eight days/seven nights (EP): From $945 per couple (low season). Includes deluxe room, a bottle of champagne, a fruit basket, breakfast the first morning, a dinner for two at Frilsham Restaurant, nightly happy hour with hors d'oeuvres, taxes and gratuities on all included features, and more. Four-day/three-night package also available.

Pirate's Cove Holiday Inn, Box 6214, Paradise Island, Nassau, The Bahamas (tel. 809/363-2100; U.S. reservations: toll free 800/HOLIDAY). A top-to-toe $10-million renovation has transformed this lush oceanfront resort into one of the great beauties of Paradise Island. Graceful archways frame the elegant rose-granite–and–marble lobby; at stage center, the lively bar makes a popular after-hours gathering place. It's an action-oriented hotel, with something happening almost every hour of the day: scuba demonstrations, tennis tournaments, nature walks, swim races, aerobics classes. Decorated with tropical flair, rooms feature rattan furnishings and soft floral-print fabrics. The beach from which the property takes its name, Pirate's Cove, is picture-perfect, a small bay protected by rocky promontories and a jetty. Or pull up a lounge chair by the large freshwater pool, accented by waterfalls and small bridges. Honeymoon package: Eight days/seven nights (BP): $1,105 to $1,410 per couple. Includes deluxe oceanview room with balcony, full breakfast for two daily including gratuities, catamaran cruise for two, sightseeing tour for two, bottle of champagne with souvenir gift, weekly honeymoon party, tennis day or night.

Divi Bahamas Beach Resort & Country Club, P.O. Box N-8194, Nassau, New Providence, The Bahamas (tel. 809/362-4391; U.S. reservations: toll free 800/367-3484). This funloving property gives you the best of both worlds: access to all the exciting shopping, dining, and gaming options of Nassau, combined with the tranquility of a secluded, out-island setting. Located on the southwestern shore of Nassau, the 220-room Divi is tucked away from the major resort areas of Nassau, Cable Beach, and Paradise Island; thanks to a free bus that runs frequently between the hotel and town, however, getting around is easy. The expansive property rambles over 180 estate-like acres. Every day, different events are scheduled: snorkeling trips, volleyball games, a Bahamian buffet and dinner show complete with limbo competitions and fire dancers. Deluxe rooms merit their classification: They're large, attractively decorated with rattan furnishings, and trimmed with Bahamian wood doors and louvers. You'll have varied sports choices on land and sea, including tennis day or night, an 18-hole golf course, a fitness trail, as well as the superb Peter Hughes dive operation. Down at the beach, there are a new snackbar pavilion and a lovely free-form pool. Both restaurants are excellent. Honeymoon package: Eight days/seven nights (BP): $1,070 to $2,210 per couple. Includes deluxe accommodations with balcony or terrace, welcome drinks upon arrival, fresh flowers in room daily, one picnic lunch, bottle of wine with glasses, one dinner with champagne, breakfast daily, honeymoon photo album, complimentary beach towel, round-trip transfers between airport and hotel, taxes and gratuities.

Inexpensive

British Colonial Beach Resort, Box N-7148, No. 1 Bay Street, Nassau, New Providence, The Bahamas (tel. 809/322-3301; U.S. reservations: toll free 800/334-8484). This 325-room resort dating back to the 1920s is the dowager queen of Nassau, appealing to visitors who don't want to choose between sandy shores and city living. Affiliated with Best Western International, this is the largest downtown hotel and is the only one with a beach. Set in eight acres of gardens, it is right on Bay Street, the heart of Nassau's shopping district. An Olympic-size pool, three lighted tennis courts, and a nine-hole golf course are only a few of the many facilities. Rooms have been recently redone with contemporary furnishings and are very spacious. The property makes every effort to pamper honeymooners, booking them into the best accommodations in each price category. Honeymoon package: Eight days/seven nights (EP): $610 to $995 per couple (low season); $890 to $1,340 per couple (high season), depending on room category. Includes a bottle of champagne every night, floral arrangement in room, honeymoon photograph, his-and-her T-shirts, a complimentary bottle of Nassau Royale liqueur, and more. Four-night package also available.

ROMANTIC RESTAURANTS AND NIGHTSPOTS

Honeymooners have plenty of choices in Nassau, Paradise Island, and Cable Beach.

Expensive

Graycliff, Nassau (tel. 322-2796). This grandiose old mansion is one of the best places to dine in style. Begin lunch or dinner with cocktails in a drawing room furnished with antiques. Then get ready for the elegant gourmet fare served at tables sparkling with Royal Copenhagen china and silver imported from Britain. From the hot and cold hors d'oeuvres to the Italian pastries, each item on the elaborate menu is more tempting than the last. Bahamian crawfish in puff pastry with cream and saffron, pâté of Abaco wild boar with walnuts, filet mignon with mushrooms and tomatoes, roast duck with tropical fruit and calvados brandy—they all compete for your attention. Be sure to make reservations. Dinner for two will easily cost $100 or more. Jackets are required for men. Open Monday through Friday for lunch, noon to 3 p.m.; seven nights for dinner, 7 to 9:30 p.m.

Buena Vista, Delancy Street, Nassau (tel. 322-2811 or 322-4039). In the main dining room of this early 19th century manor house, plants hang in archways and the pink walls, trimmed in white, are decorated with paintings. Lush foliage surrounds the enclosed patio, with its terra-cotta tile floor. As candles flicker in hurricane lamps and ceiling fans gently stir the air, the pianist sings everything from "Waltzing Matilda" to songs from *Fiddler on the Roof*. Smoked dolphin with whipped horseradish sauce, avocado stuffed with lobster, or cream of garlic soup is a good way to begin. Memorable entrées follow, such as shrimp scampi, rack of lamb, duck in Grand Marnier sauce, and quail with wild mushrooms. Finish off with baked Alaska for dessert. Jackets—and reservations—are required. Dinner for two will cost about $80 to $100. Open nightly, December to April, 7 to 10 p.m. Closed Sunday the rest of the year.

At **The Courtyard Terrace,** Paradise Island (tel. 326-2501), in the luxurious Ocean Club resort, the sky makes a starry ceiling, tall palms rustle in the breeze, and a long rectangular pool with a fountain serves as a centerpiece. Candles flicker shadows over tables topped with Irish linen and Wedgwood china. Try goose liver pâté with truffles, Bahamian conch chowder, or cream of asparagus soup, and hearts of palm salad. House specialties include filet of beef stuffed with crabmeat, and well-seasoned pan-blackened red snapper. Pear belle Hélène (vanilla ice cream, pears, and chocolate sauce) or coconut cake is hard to resist. Live music floats down from the balcony above. Plan to spend $90 or more on dinner for the two of you. Open nightly for dinner, 7 to 10 p.m.

Frilsham House, next to the Nassau Beach Hotel (tel. 327-7639). Built in the 1940s by Lord Edward Mauger Iliffe, a British newspaper publishing magnate, this gray-and-white former mansion now houses one of Nassau's finest restaurants. Piano music, softly strummed, sets a romantic mood in the entrance foyer and bar. You can dine either on the glass-enclosed veranda overlooking the sea or in a more formal dining room, graced with Chippendale-style chairs and displays of antique china. The cuisine is sumptuous and memorable—all ingredients are absolutely fresh, and you can really taste the difference. Start off with a salade Pompadour, fresh seafood tossed with a creamy chive mayonnaise; or delectable Scottish salmon. Entrées include a whole grouper en croûte (wrapped in pastry) and a sirloin steak in pepper sauce. Finish off with a sweet treat from the dessert cart, such as lemon cheesecake or chocolate truffle cake. Count on spending $100 to $140 per couple, plus wine. Open nightly from 6:30 to 9:30 p.m.

Round House, Cable Beach (tel. 327-7921 or 327-7922). This intimate restaurant is housed in what was once a guard house for the surrounding homes. Nettie Symonette, your friendly host, ensures that patrons never forget her international treats. Various versions of shrimp, lobster, and conch are on the menu along with steak. Expect to pay about $80 to $90 for dinner for two, unless you go for one of their all-you-can-eat buffet nights—a steal at $11 per person. Open nightly from 6:30 to 9 p.m.

Café Martinique, Paradise Island (tel. 326-3000). When you're in the mood for a taste of France, reserve a table at Café Martinique. Wall-to-wall windows look out to the lagoon. Fans hang from a white latticework ceiling, and white wicker chairs surround the tables. Entrées include grilled Coho salmon or fruits de mer, a selection of seafood. Boneless veal sautéed with mushrooms, apples, and French apple brandy is also an excellent choice. Since the sinful desserts are so time-consuming to prepare, the dessert menu will be offered before the entrées. Consider chocolate soufflé or soufflé au Grand Marnier. Although the candlelit dinners are superb, Sunday brunch is just as popular. You can dine outdoors on the terrace. Expect to pay about $80 and way up for dinner for two. Men are required to wear jackets.

Moderate

Poop Deck, East Bay Street (tel. 393-8175). This place is so friendly that you'll feel like a beloved regular, even if you're dining here for the first time. Although the decor is casual (paper napkins, Formica tables), the restaurant features a one-in-a-million view of the harbor, as well as excellent Bahamian food. All of the local specials come highly recommended, especially conch chowder and Mother Mary's grouper, steamed in spices and served up with an ample helping of peas 'n' rice. Dinner for two, $40 to $50 plus drinks. Open daily for lunch and dinner from noon to 10:30 p.m.

Captain Nemo's, Deveaux Street Dock off Bay Street (tel. 323-8426). Jaunty blue-and-white captain's chairs enhance the nautical theme at this excellent seafood restaurant right on the harbor. Your best choices are any of the denizens of the deep —in the form of conch fritters, lobster salad, steamed grouper—which were probably swimming offshore just a few hours ago. For land-ho types, they also serve tasty hamburgers and steaks. Save room for the excellent desserts, most notably Key lime pie and guava duff. Lunch, $20 per couple; dinner, $40 per couple. Open daily from 11 a.m. to 10:30 p.m.

Local and imported seafood, from conch chowder to lobster, is on the menu at **Gulfstream,** Paradise Island (tel. 326-2431). Whether its Dover sole jetted in from the Continent or grouper that slept last night in the Caribbean, you'll find delectable fish and seafood served in elegant surroundings here. Begin by indulging yourselves with fresh cherrystone clams or oysters on the half shell. Main course selections include lobster thermidor, sautéed snapper, and grilled swordfish. Cap off the evening with a frothy Irish coffee. Open daily for dinner from 6:30 to 9 p.m.; $60 to $80 per couple.

Inexpensive

Parliament Terrace, 18 Parliament St. (tel. 322-2836). Just a half block—and several centuries—removed from the bustle of Bay Street, this is the place to enjoy an alfresco lunch of local specialties when shopping downtown. Shaded by palm fronds and perky umbrellas, the patio faces the pink-and-white government buildings. The menu features Bahamian fare such as baked chicken and stewed conch, as well as all-American hamburgers and sandwiches. Open daily from 8 a.m. to 10 p.m.; $10 to $30 per couple.

When you're shopping in Nassau, a good place to stop for a Bahamian buffet lunch is **Hotel Corona,** Nassau (tel. 326-6815). It's not fancy, but the food is good and plentiful. About $20 per couple. Open daily from 7:30 a.m. to 11 p.m. Ask a Bahamian to point you in the direction of the best "boil' fish" in town, and chances are you'll end up at the **Shoal,** Nassau (tel. 323-4400). They also serve other mouthwatering favorites such as stew fish, cracked conch, fried chicken, lobster, and mutton. Dinner for two should run $30 to $40. Open daily from 7:30 a.m. to 2 a.m.

Nassau, Cable Beach, and Paradise Island days stretch into the wee hours of the morning. Few leave New Providence without trying their luck at its two casinos. **Carnival's Crystal Palace Casino** (tel. 327-6200) is flashy and modern, with lots of neon. The Palace Theater here, whose 800 seats are often packed, hosts wildly entertaining musical extravaganzas (tel. 327-6200 for reservations; the dinner show runs about $90 per couple). You may think you've stumbled into Las Vegas at **Le Cabaret Theatre in the Paradise Island Casino** (tel. 326-3000). The revues here are full of feathers, sequins, and bare skin (dinner and the show will cost about $90 per couple; the show and two drinks will be about $60 for the two of you).

Most of the large hotels have nightspots. Some of the most popular among Bahamians as well as vacationers include **Tradewinds Lounge** and **Club Pastiche,** both in the Paradise Island Resort & Casino. In Nassau, **Peanuts Taylor's Drumbeat Supper Club,** West Bay Street (tel. 322-4233), presents an all-Bahamian revue, including limbo dancing and a fire ritual set to Afro-Bahamian music. There are two shows nightly, at 8:30 and 10:30 p.m. (at 8 and 10 p.m. on Tuesday and Saturday). Closed Sunday. Dance clubs of the moment are the **Palace** (Elizabeth Avenue, tel. 325-7733), **Waterloo** (East Bay Street, tel. 393-1108), and the **Ritz** (next to Captain Nemo's, tel. 322-7067).

---

3. Freeport/Lucaya

Dazzlingly modern, Freeport is barely three decades old. Together with adjoining Lucaya, it is known as The Bahamas' second city. Freeport/Lucaya sits on Grand Bahama, north of Nassau and only 80 miles (a half-hour flight) from Florida.

Freeport/Lucaya blends natural beauty with casinos, large-scale resorts, extensive shopping, scores of restaurants, nightspots, cruise-ship ports, and golf courses. The twin cities were certainly planned to be eye-pleasers: broad landscaped highways, glistening marinas, tall apartment buildings and condominiums, gardens, and parks. Many of its quiet beaches are free from the shadows of high-rise hotels, and the grounds surrounding the pretty private homes burst with flowering shrubs.

Almost everyone who lives here is from somewhere else—Nassau, the Family Islands, Canada, the United States, Europe. Celebrating the island's multicultural flavor, the International Bazaar in Freeport is one of the places few visitors miss. A Japanese *torii* gate stands at the entrance. Along narrow, winding alleyways lined with boutiques and restaurants, you'll travel around the world from Mexico to Morocco, China to Sweden, Ghana to France, and then some. Be sure to check out the markets selling Bahamian straw goods and arts and crafts. Shady plazas with fountains and cafés make pleasant rest stops. Not to be outdone, Lucaya now has a shopping and entertainment complex called Port Lucaya, across from the Holiday Inn and the Lucayan Beach Resort.

ROMANTIC INTERLUDES

Many of your most special moments will center on the superb beaches.

From the moment they lean their bottlenoses on your shoulder, your heart will turn to complete tuna fish. Who does this? Your rollicking swimming buddies at **The Dolphin Experience,** a research project that enables you to swim with trained Atlantic bottlenose dolphins. Like playful puppies, Stripe, Bimini, Romora, and friends retrieve rubber rings and execute precision leaps over your head. Often, they'll roll over on their backs so you can rub their sensitive bellies (which feel rather like an overinflated beach ball). It's an extraordinary experience, and one that will leave you with a big grin plastered across your face for hours. The swim sessions are held in the calm, protected waters of the training facility at the Underwater Explorers Society near Port Lucaya (see below). The hour-long program, which includes a 20-minute swim session, costs $55 per person; call 373-1250 for reservations. If you really get "hooked" on dolphins, you can sign on for the day as an assistant trainer and help teach and feed these fascinating mammals; $105 per person. Book way in advance—space is limited and the dolphin swims are super-popular.

In fact, getting wet is one of the best ways to plunge into the Grand Bahama fun. The crystal-clear waters offshore shelter some of the best scuba-diving in the world, with five-star sites such as **Ben's Cavern,** filled with stalactites, stalagmites, fossils, and flowstones; and **Edge of the Ledge,** where the continental shelf drops off abruptly from 80 feet—to over 2,000. And here, as *Skin Diver* magazine (the bible of the sport) reports, "UNEXSO is the most sophisticated and best-equipped diving facility in The Bahamas; and in fact, the world." The **Underwater Explorers Society,** commonly known as UNEXSO (tel. 373-1244), has its headquarters across from the Lucayan Beach Resort & Casino. Scuba-dive beginners will appreciate the thorough instruction and the opportunity to learn the basics in a tank that is 18 feet deep—far more helpful than the usual swimming pool lessons. The three-hour resort course is $89. Experienced divers will be thrilled by the excursions to a variety of dive sites, including wrecks, caves, and a one-mile drop off. One-tank dives cost $33; three-tank dives are $82; snorkeling trips, $22.

Said to be world's largest glass-bottomed boat, the *Mermaid Kitty* leaves from the dock near the Lucayan Beach Resort & Casino several times a day. You'll be treated to a diving show and visit sites teeming with brilliantly colored marine life. Make reservations at your hotel's activities desk or just show up at the dock. Cost is about $13.25 per person.

Pack a picnic and rent a car for a drive to the **Lucayan National Park,** at the eastern end of the island. These 40 secluded acres thrive with wild tamarind, cedar, and ming trees. The wonderfully wide beach is the star attraction. Off West End Road, at the **Rand Memorial Nature Centre,** you can take a guided tour and learn about some of the 200 species of birds and the varieties of plants. You probably won't be able to resist photographing each other by the pool filled with pink flamingoes. Call 352-5438 for tour times; closed Saturday. Admission is $2.25 per person. But Grand Bahamas' love affair with nature doesn't end here. The **Garden of the Groves,** also on West End Road, bursts with waterfalls and hanging gardens. At the entrance, be sure to stop at the **Grand Bahama Museum** ($2.25 per person), where fascinating artifacts of the Lucayan Indians are displayed. Open Tuesday through Sunday, 10 a.m. to 4 p.m.

Rent mopeds or a car, take a taxi (arrange with the driver to come back for you) —no matter how you do it, don't miss the unpeopled, palm-fringed **beaches** off Midshipman Road, such as Barbary, Churchill, and Fortune Bay. There is something about a deserted shore marked only by two sets of footprints—yours! The undulating turquoise and jade waters never looked so good, and it's difficult to remember sands that felt this soft.

As far as romantic fantasies go, it's hard to top riding **horses** along a quiet white-sand beach lined with palms, wispy pines, and glossy-leafed sea-grape trees. Bring this vision to life and try other equestrian adventures at **Pinetree Stables** (tel. 373-3600); about $30 an hour per person.

HONEYMOON HOTELS AND HIDEAWAYS

Modern is the key word here—after all, the resort is only 30 years old.

Bahamas Princess Resort & Casino, P.O. Box F-207, Freeport, Grand Bahama, The Bahamas (tel. 809/352-6721; U.S. reservations: 212/715-7079 in New York, or toll free 800/223-1834 nationwide). More than 960 rooms in two buildings make up this 2,500-acre tropical oasis near Freeport's famed International Bazaar, by far the luxury leader in Freeport. Although there is no beach at the hotel itself, complimentary shuttle buses whisk guests to the shore from both the low-rise Country Club and the high-rise Tower, across the street from each other. The Tower, next to the Princess Casino and the International Bazaar, is topped with striking Moorish minarets and this North African motif is echoed by the intricate hand-painted Portuguese tilework of the dramatic circular lobby. In addition to a ten-kilometer jogging trail, the Tower sports a pool, six tennis courts, and several good restaurants. The free-form pool at the Country Club, which also has six tennis courts and some fine eating spots, is known for its hot tub and free-form pool with a waterfall. At both the Country Club and the Tower, rooms reflect tropical elegance, with bleached wood furnishings and floral-design upholsteries. Honeymoon package: Four days/three nights (EP): $235 to $270 per couple (high season); $175 to $210 per couple (low season). Includes welcome rum swizzles, a bottle of champagne, a souvenir photo, a Princess discount booklet, all applicable taxes and gratuities. Extra nights available.

Xanadu Beach & Marina Resort, P.O. Box F-2438, Freeport, Grand Bahama, The Bahamas (tel. 809/352-6782). This 185-room resort was once the hideaway of Howard Hughes. With dark-wood paneling, backgammon tables, and a wrought-iron gate where you'd expect to find the door, his cozy private library is much the way he left it. When the reclusive millionaire dined in the hotel's gourmet Escoffier Room, no other guests were allowed. The nearby Persian Room, with muted lighting and hand-painted silk wall hangings, offers French selections. Guest rooms are comfortably contemporary. You can indulge in a variety of water sports at the excellent beach near the marina, or simply float in the pool. A taxi ride away from other hotels and the International Bazaar, Xanadu offers evening entertainment. Honeymoon package: Eight days/seven nights (EP): Up to $818 (or $1,203 for a one-bedroom suite) per couple. Includes a bottle of champagne, one breakfast in bed, a honeymoon photo, and a paddleboat ride.

The **Lucayan Beach Resort & Casino,** P.O. Box F-336, Lucaya, Grand Bahama, The Bahamas (tel. 809/373-7777; U.S. reservations: toll free 800/772-1227), a 247-room resort, is built around a lighthouse. Climb to the top for a sweeping view of the area. A lamplit walkway bordered by stone columns leads to the hotel and casino. The huge lobby is airy and elegant, with plush sofas and armchairs in various sitting areas. You'll cross a bridge over a wishing well to get to the circular main dining room. Each of the large rooms features a balcony or terrace and walk-in closets. Lush plantings dot the grounds. Sip cocktails at the poolside bar, play volleyball, or try some tennis or Ping-Pong. On the two miles of beach, you can enjoy every conceivable water sport. Also, be sure to check out the hotel's shops. Honeymoon package: Eight days/seven nights (EP): $965 per couple. Includes welcome drinks upon arrival, various discount vouchers, snorkeling trip with UNEXSO, manager's cocktail party, chilled split of champagne, his-and-her T-shirts.

Holiday Inn Lucaya Beach Resort, P.O. Box F-2496, Freeport, Grand Bahama, The Bahamas (tel. 809/373-1333; U.S. reservations: toll free 800/HOLI-DAY). A 503-room hotel, the Holiday Inn buzzes with activity day and night. Boutiques, restaurants, a liquor store, beauty parlors, water sports, poolside bingo, volleyball, shuffleboard, hat and balloon dances, nightly entertainment—you name it, they've got it. The low, four-story building surrounds a large pool with spacious sun deck that is the magnet for action during the day. Nearby, the small straw market allows for open-air shopping. As part of a $16-million renovation program, all accommodations have been completely refurbished. Fresh and inviting as a tropical breeze, the decor is accented by islandy bleached woods, orchid-print bedspreads, and jaunty paintings of flamingoes. Right at the resort, choose among three restaurants, including the new, gourmet Le Bouquet dining room. What you'll probably remember most about the resort, though, is the friendly, helpful staff. Honeymoon package: Eight days/seven nights (EP): $1,030 per couple. Includes deluxe room, bottle of champagne, snorkeling trip, round-trip airport/hotel transfers, champagne breakfast in bed, glass-bottomed boat tour, sightseeing tour, souvenir T-shirts, photo, and key rings, manager's cocktail party, room tax, and more. Three-night package also available.

Atlantik Beach Resort, P.O. Box F-531, Lucaya, Grand Bahama, The Bahamas (tel. 809/373-1444; U.S. reservations: toll free 800/622-6770). If this sleek tower right on Lucayan Beach immediately feels like your home away from home, there's a good reason: It was originally built for private apartments. Consequently, the 175 rooms and suites are especially large and well equipped, with air conditioning, telephones, and color TVs. The duplex one-bedroom suites with their compact kitchenettes offer very good value. Enjoy water sports at the beach, or unwind on the lovely pool deck or in the Jacuzzi. For golfers, the resort owns the par-72, 18-hole golf course at the Lucayan Golf and Country Club, and special golf rates are available for guests. In addition to the resort's own four restaurants, the lively Port Lucaya shopping and entertainment complex is just across the road. Honeymoon package: None. Rates (EP): $95 to $125 for a standard room; $125 to $155 for a one-bedroom suite.

Jack Tar, West End, Grand Bahama, The Bahamas (tel. 809/346-6211; U.S. reservations: 214/670-9888 in Texas, or toll free 800/527-9299). For a hideaway honeymoon, ensconce yourselves at this secluded West End property where the water shimmers in so many different shades of blue that it will give you goosebumps. Set on 2,000 semitropical acres, the Jack Tar is a perfect choice for the active sun-and-fun set because it's an all-inclusive resort. Paddleboats, fishing, tennis, golf, picnic sails, beach parties, live entertainment . . . enjoy them all, free of additional charge. Even all drinks, taxes, and gratuities are covered. If you just want to relax, that's fine too. Settle into a lounge chair on the sparkling white beach, or—better yet—cast yourselves adrift on one of the cushy floats in their gigantic saltwater pool. At mealtimes, you have four restaurants to choose from. The 424 rooms aren't fancy, but they're perfectly comfortable, furnished with two double beds, a telephone, and air conditioning; some have a terrace or balcony. Honeymoon package: Eight days/seven nights (all-inclusive land package): From $1,850 per couple. Ask your travel agent about special charter flights from many U.S. and Canadian cities.

ROMANTIC RESTAURANTS AND NIGHTSPOTS

Moonlight on the water, Vegas-style shows, and the casinos . . . who can ask for anything more?

Expensive

Luciano's, Port Lucaya (tel. 373-9100). For an elegant, pull-out-all-the-stops night on the town, this is the place. Certainly, Luciano's ranks as one of the prettiest restaurants in Grand Bahama, a symphony in black and pink, accented by black crystal on the tables and white French country–style furnishings. The menu highlights fine continental and Bahamian cuisine. Start off with Scottish salmon or fresh seafood in a pastry shell. Main course specialties include grilled island lobster as well as a prime filet mignon flamed with brandy-pepper sauce. Open Monday through Saturday, 6:30 to 11 p.m.; $70 to $100 per couple. Reservations and jackets are required.

Moderate

Blackbeard's, Fortune Beach (tel. 373-2960). Run away for the day to this magical spot poised right on the sparkling white smile of Fortune Beach. Thanks to close-in sandbars, you can saunter into the sea and head way off to the horizon . . . and still be just up to your knees in water. At the restaurant, driftwood, an aquarium, and nautical flags create a seafaring mood—your clue that the fish is "jumpin' fresh" here. Choices range from grouper fingers ($10) to a complete seafood dinner (lobster, salad, peas 'n' rice) for $27.50. The sunbathing and munching can't be beat! Open daily from 10 a.m. to 10 p.m. (until midnight on weekends).

I say there, old chap, know where we can get a pint and some shepherd's pie? How about **Pusser's Co. Store & Pub,** Port Lucaya (tel. 373-8450). Sit on the waterfront terrace while a robot piano player tinkles your favorite tunes, or cozy into the wood-paneled pub, so authentic that they even use Brit-style three-pronged forks. The fare includes sandwiches and hamburgers as well as various savory pies, including some with a Caribbean twist: stuffed with fish or chicken. Try one of their potent rum drinks, such as Pusser's Painkiller . . . guaranteed to mesmerize and immobilize. Lunch or dinner will run $15 to $30 per couple. Open daily from 11 a.m. to 1 a.m. (from noon on Sunday).

Scorpio's, Port Lucaya (tel. 352-6969). The ping of sailboat shrouds against the mast . . . the echoing call of gulls . . . the happy putt-putt of dinghies as boaters come ashore—these are just a few of the joyful sounds that fill the air at this harborfront restaurant. A longtime Grand Bahama favorite, Scorpio's boasts a scenic new location on a second-floor deck overlooking the marina. If you're coming for dinner, try to time your reservation so that you can watch the sun set over the island. You'll find memorable renditions of Bahamian dishes, such as minced lobster, steamed chicken, cracked conch, and fried grouper, served up with heaps of cole slaw and peas 'n' rice. Save room for dessert, especially the flaky apple pie. Open daily from 11 a.m. to 11 p.m. Lunch, $15 to $20 per couple; dinner, $30 to $40 per couple.

Pier One, Freeport Harbour (tel. 352-6674). Perched on stilts, this seafood restaurant is almost completely surrounded by water. At night, lights twinkle on the water. Sip cocktails on the balcony off the bar while watching the sun set. The ceiling beams are hung with plants and fishnets. Starfish, pots, and pans decorate the wood-paneled walls. Ask to be seated by the "Lovers' Lane" street sign. Dinner for two will be about $60 and up. Open daily for lunch, noon to 2 p.m.; dinner, 6:30 to 10 p.m.

The Stoned Crab, Lucaya (tel. 373-1442). Be sure to make reservations and to bring hefty appetites when you visit this crowd-pleaser on quiet Taino Beach. While you dine, you'll hear the waves lapping the shore as the moonlight dances on the water. The menu boasts all kinds of crab dishes, from crab and avocado salad to snow crab claws, plus fish and freshly baked raisin bread. They also feature an array of tempting lobster and steak choices. Only dinner is served. A meal for the two of you could cost $70 or more. Open nightly from 5 to 10:30 p.m.

Stop at **Café Valencia,** Freeport (tel. 352-8717), for lunch when you're ready for a break from shopping in the International Bazaar. You'll enter the restaurant through a tiled patio that leads to a bar/lounge with beige-tile floors and rattan furniture. Buffalo chicken wings, Caesar salad, pasta, and minced lobster (a Bahamian specialty). A complete lunch for two will run $20 to $40. Dinner will be about $50 for two. Open daily from 11 a.m. to 10 p.m.

Inexpensive

Surf Side, Taino Beach (tel. 373-1816). The only concession to interior decor is some fishnet on the ceiling and occasional driftwood propped in corners; "entertainment" comes in the form of rock 'n' roll blasting from the radio. But what you do find—in abundance—at this super-casual restaurant is great local food at low prices. Sandwiches start at about $4; steamed fish or cracked conch runs $7 to $8. Make a day of it—a good swimming beach lies right outside the door. Open daily from 8 a.m. to 11 p.m. (from 7 a.m. on weekends).

When touring the west coast of Freeport/Lucaya, make sure you stop for a bite at one of the excellent local restaurants. **Freddie's,** Hunters (tel. 352-3250), makes a good lunch spot. Although the emphasis is on shrimp, lobster tails, and other seafood, you'll also find pork chops and steak on the menu. Lunch for two will be about $30. At the **Buccaneer Club,** Holmes Rock (tel. 348-3794), dramatic sunsets accompany the Swiss and Bahamian dishes on the menu. Call for complimentary transportation from your hotel. Plan to spend about $60 per couple. Open nightly from 5 to 11 p.m. **The Star Club,** West End (tel. 346-6207), set in the oldest hotel in the island, is known for its delicious Bahamian specialties, including conch salad and fritters. About $20 per couple. Open from 11:30 a.m. to 3 p.m., 6 to 9 p.m. Another excellent West End choice is the **Harbour Hotel Restaurant** (tel. 346-6432), where you can savor excellent Bahamian and American food on a deck overlooking the sea. At night, the disco attracts a lively crowd. Open for lunch, 11 a.m. to 3 p.m.; $15 to $20 per couple. Dinner served from 6 to 9 p.m.; $20 to $30 per couple.

Nightlife

Now that you've taken a chance on love, how about a whirl with Lady Luck?

Grand Bahama beckons with two glittery high-stakes **casinos,** located at the Bahamas Princess Resort (tel. 352-6721) and at the Lucayan Beach Resort (tel. 373-7777). The excitement starts to build after 10 p.m.; Friday and Saturday nights, tables are packed practically shoulder to shoulder.

Flash and laughs—that's what you'll enjoy at the high-stepping Las Vegas–style revue at Casino Royale at the Bahamas Princess. Glittery costumes, sequin-clad (and unclad) showgirls, great one-liners from the stand-up comedians—all make for an evening of fun. Shows Tuesday through Sunday at 8:30 and 10:45 p.m.; $22 per person (tel. 352-6721, ext. 59, for reservations).

You'll move to disco, calypso, and reggae at **Sultan's Tent** in the Princess Tower. Other lively after-hours spots are **Panache** at the Holiday Inn and the **Palace II** on East Sunrise Highway. **Yellow Bird** at Castaways Resort headlines a lively Bahamian show.

---

4. The Family Islands: The Abacos, Eleuthera, The Exumas

The friendly Family Islands, full of natural splendor, are for those who like empty beaches, exceptional diving and snorkeling, and life at an easy, slow pace. They're for newlyweds who can make their own nightlife, who don't mind waiting until the weekend for most parties and musical entertainment, and who won't miss casinos. On some islands, one of the most popular and festive activities is helping to unload the weekly mail boat, which brings supplies—and livestock—from Nassau.

These islands are so friendly that many resorts don't even use keys for guest rooms (you can lock up your valuables in safe-deposit boxes, if you like). Although most dining out will happen in your hotel, there are also some excellent local restaurants specializing in fresh, home-style Bahamian fare. Most of the accommodations that follow are air-conditioned. Those that are not are cooled by trade winds and ceiling fans.

THE ABACOS

The northernmost part of the Bahamas, the Abacos are one of the most developed parts of the Family Islands. This 130-mile-long archipelago, shaped like an arm bent at the elbow, is about 75 miles north of Nassau and about 200 miles east of Miami, Florida. The Abacos have long been the shipbuilding center of The Bahamas and paradise for sailors. Your hotel staff will be pleased to make arrangements for you to charter a boat for sailing, fishing, or just plain exploring.

Many visitors are surprised by the New England flavor of three of the prettiest islands, Green Turtle Cay, Elbow Cay, and Man-O-War Cay. But once you learn the history of these islands, it all makes sense. The Abacos were settled by Loyalists, who, choosing to remain under the British Crown, fled New England and the Carolinas during and after the American Revolution. Today the fishing villages of New Plymouth on Green Turtle, Hope Town on Elbow Cay, and Man-O-War Cay are favorite sightseeing stops. Ferries will take you from Marsh Harbour to Elbow and Man-O-War cays (about $17.50 per person round trip); and from Treasure Cay to Green Turtle Cay (about $10 per person each way).

New Plymouth sports several beautifully restored historic homes, one of which houses a museum. Stop at a local restaurant to sample one of the Abacos specialties—wild boar or turtle steak.

South of Green Turtle, Hope Town is known for its red-and-white-striped lighthouse, which can be seen from almost any point in town, and for its long wide beaches with high grassy bluffs. Climb the 120 feet to the top of the lighthouse for a nonstop view of the area. Cars are banned from the center of town.

Romantic Interludes

For newlyweds with an adventurous spirit, the Abacos offer a variety of cays to explore.

While it's easy to stumble onto amazing **beaches** in The Bahamas, the Abacos have some of the country's most outstanding sandy shores. Treasure Cay, with its self-contained resort, sports a strip stretching almost four miles. Hilly Green Turtle Cay is surrounded by quiet bays and empty expanses where you can swim and relax undisturbed. The candy-striped Hope Town Lighthouse stands guard above Elbow Cay beaches; even those that border the picture-perfect town are never crowded.

Don't be fooled by the size of the **Albert Lowe Museum** in New Plymouth on Green Turtle Cay. This tiny museum is packed with intriguing memorabilia. The history of the Abacos is told through old photographs, model ships, paintings, antique furniture, and the architecture of the restored Loyalist home that houses the museum. Founded by Alton Lowe, one of the country's best-loved painters, the museum was named for his boat-building father. (Open from about 9:30 to 11:30 a.m., then from 1 to 3 p.m. Admission: $3.50 per person.)

Also in New Plymouth, stop in at **Miss Emily's Blue Bee Bar,** home of a renowned Goombay smash cocktail. Pump some coins in the jukebox, and leave behind a souvenir to join the business cards, old credit cards, driver's licenses—even undies—that cram the establishment.

If you're curious about **boat building,** take the ferry from Marsh Harbour to Man-O-War Cay (about $17.50 per person round trip). Craftsmen line the waterfront, where the marina is chock-full of bobbing boats. Nowadays most boats are made of fiberglass. But if you strike up a conversation with one of the men at work, he'll probably tell you a bit about the old days, when boats were painstakingly made of wood.

Honeymoon Hotels and Hideaways

You'll be surprised by the wide range of accommodations the Abacos offer.

Abaco Inn, Hope Town, Elbow Cay, Abaco, The Bahamas (tel. 809/367-2666). There are only 11 rooms in this peaceful, casually elegant hotel on a narrow strip of land a short drive from Hope Town. The ocean crashes on one side of the property and the calm bay bathes the other. You'll have a choice of three beaches. The main building, which houses the bar/lounge and dining room, is paneled in Abaco pine and has tiled floors and ceiling fans. Served on two waterfront terraces, the five-course gourmet dinners are delicious. Guest rooms, in cottages, are simple, most with their own hammock and private patio, and they come with books left by previous guests. Owner Ruth Maury and her staff are always happy to arrange water sports, including scuba-diving, snorkeling, sailing, windsurfing. Honeymoon package: None. Rates (EP): $105 to $140 per couple per night.

Hope Town Harbour Lodge, Hope Town, Elbow Cay, Abaco, The Bahamas (tel. 809/366-0095; U.S. reservations: toll free 800/626-5690). Not only is this lodge right in picture-perfect Hope Town, but it is also on a gorgeous beach. And you won't have to walk far to find a sandy stretch just for the two of you. The gray clapboard buildings, trimmed in red, are perched on a rise above the main road. From the front, the view is of the boat-filled harbor, and the back overlooks the pool and the ocean. Be sure to request a double bed when you make reservations. In addition to the 20 cheery guest rooms in the main house, a private cottage called Butterfly House is also available for rent. The food—prepared by Norris Smith, a young Bahamian chef who has trained in France, Switzerland, and Germany—is unforgettable. Honeymoon package: None. Rates (EP): $70 to $100 per couple per night.

Treasure Cay Beach Hotel and Villas, P.O. Box TC 4183, Treasure Cay, Abaco, The Bahamas (tel. 809/367-2847; U.S. reservations: toll free 800/327-

1584 nationwide; 800/432-8257 in Florida). On the east coast of Abaco, this 205-room, all-inclusive resort is a village in itself. When you check in you'll receive a map showing you how to find the tennis courts, four pools, the marina packed with yachts and other seacraft, and the shopping center, which boasts a bank, post office, pharmacy, and boutique. You can stay in an individual room, a suite, or a red-roofed villa. Best of all, thanks to the all-inclusive rates, you can relax and enjoy your vacation completely. Everything—all meals, drinks, water sports, scuba and snorkeling trips, even a complimentary bottle of wine—is covered as part of the price. Four miles of stark white beach await just outside your doorstep; in addition, the resort has its own second beach on Treasure Island, just a short cruise away. Dick Wilson designed the 18-hole golf course, and greens fees and carts are also included. Evening entertainment features poolside buffets, cocktail and disco cruises, and more. Honeymoon package: Seven days/six nights: $2,045 to $2,375 per couple, all-inclusive land (also covers taxes and gratuities). Packages including air fare are also available.

Green Turtle Club and Marina, P.O. Box 270, Green Turtle Cay, Abaco, The Bahamas (tel. 809/367-2572; U.S. reservations: tel. 305/833-9580, or toll free 800/327-0787). The ferry to Green Turtle Cay will let you off at a white clubhouse with a green awning at the edge of a marina. You'll be welcomed with Tipsy Turtles, the club's special brand of cocktail. Yachting club flags decorate the ceiling beams, and dollar bills, put there and signed by visitors, paper the walls. Guests stay in 31 individual rooms, suites, and waterfront villas. The roomy units have modern baths and sliding glass doors. A swimming pool is on the grounds and two beaches are short walks away. The snorkeling and diving in this area are excellent. Take one of the daily complimentary boat trips into the town of New Plymouth or stroll in for exercise. Honeymoon package: None. Rates (EP): $105 to $180 per couple per night.

Bluff House Club and Marina, Green Turtle Cay, Abaco, The Bahamas (tel. 809/365-4247; U.S. reservations: toll free 800/327-0787). Built on a hill high above a tantalizing beach, Bluff House offers deluxe, air-conditioned rooms, suites, villas, and even "treehouse" accommodations. Under new owners Martin Havill and his sister Barbara Bartey, the resort has blossomed into one of the Caribbean's prettiest getaways. All 32 units have been primped and refurbished. Sliding glass doors in the main house lead to the oceanview pool deck. Inside, the lounge is split-level, with a driftwood coffee table and colorful framed posters. Staff will arrange tennis, fishing, snorkeling, and diving excursions. Ferry rides to the town of New Plymouth are complimentary to guests—everyone goes along for the big dance on Saturday night. Back at Bluff House, the nightly candlelit dinners (with complimentary wine) offer delicious choices such as lobster or roast duckling with a secret sweet-and-sour sauce. Plan to diet after you leave! Honeymoon package: Eight days/seven nights (EP): $590 to $665 per couple for a room. Includes a bottle of champagne, welcome cocktails, complimentary hors d'oeuvres before dinner, free daytime tennis, and more.

ELEUTHERA

The pencil-thin arc called Eleuthera takes you back to the very beginning. Barely five miles across at its widest point, this island was where the first settlers, the Eleutherian Adventurers, set up camp in 1648. Since they had come to escape religious persecution in Bermuda, they used the Greek word for "freedom" when they named their new home. They were followed by other Bermudians and English settlers, many of whom brought their slaves, and later by British loyalists and freed slaves from America.

Just 70 miles east of Nassau, Eleuthera is 100 miles long. After New Providence and Grand Bahama, it is the most developed island in The Bahamas. Throughout Eleuthera you'll find blue holes (inland bodies of water teeming with fish), and caves awaiting adventurous souls. During the late 19th century, Eleuthera was a prime source of pineapples. A visit to the plantation in Gregory Town will allow you to sample pineapple rum. You may have heard about pink sand, but you've got to see Eleuthera's beaches to believe it. Many of the palm-shaded deserted beaches have a rosy hue from bits of coral and shells.

Harbour Island, off the northern coast, is famous for its pink-sand beaches and for charming Dunmore Town, the first capital of The Bahamas. Affectionately referred to as "Briland" by residents, this petite oasis is truly captivating. You'll think of Cape Cod when you see the small wooden houses, but the palm trees and the turquoise water will remind you that you are in The Bahamas.

Spanish Wells off the northern coast of Eleuthera received its name when Spanish galleons sent sailors ashore for fresh water. Today it is reminiscent of the suburban United States with brightly painted houses, colorful gardens, and neat lawns. Like Man-O-War Cay in the Abacos, the many blond-haired, blue-eyed residents may surprise you. Fishing is the island's main industry and you can buy some of the freshest lobster around.

A word to wise travelers: Make sure you fly into the correct Eleutheran airport. The island has three: North Eleuthera, Governors Harbour (central), and Rock Sound (south). A mistake could cost you a $100 taxi fare if you end up at the wrong end of the island.

Romantic Interludes

The action in Eleuthera revolves around water sports, but the land also holds some intriguing sights.

Ships were not the only victims of the Devil's Backbone, a magnificent spine of reefs off Eleuthera's northern coast. A **Civil War train** met its end here as well. This Union locomotive plunged into the depths from a barge on its way to Cuba in 1865. In a kaleidoscopic blast of color, fish and other sea creatures swim in and out of the rusted wreckage. This is one of the dive sites offered by the **Romora Bay Club** (tel. toll free 800/327-8286) and **Valentine's Dive Center** (tel. 333-2142), both on Harbour Island.

At least one day, rent a car (about $80) or hire a taxi ($150) to explore the island—a taxi makes a good choice since the island stretches 100 miles from top to toe and many of the best beaches and sights are unmarked, and known only to locals. In **Tarpum Bay,** browse through galleries that carry works by Eleuthera-based artists Mal Flanders and MacMillan Hughes; their prints and paintings of local scenes would make wonderful remembrances of your island honeymoon. Looking for a secluded beach? Near the southern tip of Eleuthera, **Millars Beach** offers excellent shelling, while **Ten Bay Beach** (an unmarked turnoff north of Savannah Sound) is great for swimming and sunbathing. Bring some bread when you visit a magical spot called **Ocean Hole,** a natural, inland saltwater pool near Rock Sound. Hungry jumbo-size snapper and grouper literally leap out of the water as they compete for morsels. Toward the northern end, the narrowest point on the island has come to be known as the **Glass Window.** Here the crashing surf has whittled the land down to a sliver, so that the dark blue of the ocean on one side is only a few feet from the turquoise of the shallower sound on the other side. A man-made bridge now crosses the gap where a natural rock arc once was.

For a real adventure, go spelunking in one of the many caves that dot the island. The entrance to one of the largest is marked by a sprawling fig tree said to have been planted as camouflage by pirates who had hidden treasure inside. Your hotel will put you in touch with a local guide, who will lead you through labyrinths of passageways, past stalagmites and stalactites in various configurations, and below bats (of the harmless variety) clinging to the ceilings.

Honeymoon Hotels and Hideaways

Eleuthera has some of the country's best accommodations, from the small and casual to luxurious resorts that receive royal patronage.

EXPENSIVE: Windermere Island Club, P.O. Box 25, Rock Sound, Eleuthera, The Bahamas (tel. 809/332-2538; U.S. reservations: tel. 212/839-0222 in New York state; toll free 800/237-1236 nationwide). If you want to follow in the footsteps of Prince Charles, Princess Diana, and Prince Andrew, Windermere Island is just the place for royal treatment. Notables and ordinary folk all come for seclusion and pampering. And privacy. When *Lifestyles of the Rich and Famous* requested permission to come and film here, they were turned down. Connected to the mainland by a bridge, this opulent resort is on its own private island. The beautifully decorated suites, villas, and private homes for rent are so distant from one another that you won't have any trouble finding a spot to be alone together. The same goes for the beaches. Since you have dozens of different strands to choose from, ranging from pocket-size coves to a spectacular 2½-mile-long strand, you'll feel like true island castaways. One favorite hideout is West Beach—"So quiet, you can hear the crabs cough," the manager joked. When you want activity, tennis, windsurfing, Sunfish sailing, glass-bottomed boat rides, bonefishing, and waterskiing are all available. If you're looking for a complete getaway, consider one of Windermere's private villas. These range in scale and grandeur from the simple Beach House studio right by the water ($200 per couple per night, EP) to the veritable lap of luxury, the four-bedroom Coriolana, an elegant beachside retreat equally suitable for black tie or bathing suits ($1,000 per night, EP). Begin breakfast with fresh pineapple or pawpaw served on your private balcony while you gaze at the deserted white beach. The day's end brings candlelit gourmet feasts. "I'm hoping this is what it's like in heaven," one blissful guest sighed. Honeymoon package: None. Rates (FAP): $270 to $385 per couple for a club room; $385 to $575 per couple for a one-bedroom suite.

MODERATE: Cotton Bay Resort Club, P.O. Box 28, Rock Sound, Eleuthera, The Bahamas (tel. 809/334-2101; U.S. reservations: toll free 800/223-1588 or 800/327-0787). Known for its spectacular Robert Trent Jones–designed golf course, Cotton Bay was once a private club catering to millionaires. Most of the 77 rooms look out to the Atlantic. After a multimillion-dollar renovation, the accommodations are sparkling fresh, with white tile floors, pickled mahogany furnishings, and crisp floral-print fabrics in candy-mint pastels. All feature both air conditioning and *Casablanca*-style fans. The maids seem to be blessed with either ESP or the powers of invisibility. As if by magic, fresh towels appear in your room, bedsheets are turned down . . . all seemingly without human intervention. The pièce de résistance, though, is the spectacular two-mile-long beach that arcs around a flat-as-glass bay protected by a coral reef just offshore. Here, the sand is so fine and think-pink in hue that it resembles face powder. Scuba-diving, tennis, and boating are among the sports available. A local guitarist entertains guests gathered in the octagonal lounge for drinks before dinner. Dining under the stars on the pool terrace couldn't be more romantic . . . or more delicious. The meals are exquisite here, whether the nightly five-course table d'hôte feast or the sumptuous Saturday-night buffet featuring barbecued steaks, shrimp, and more. Honeymoon package: Eight days/seven nights (MAP): $1,595 to $2,560 per couple. Includes bottle of champagne, souvenir poster, welcome cocktails, souvenir handmade straw basket with liqueur miniatures, free water sports, unlimited tennis, use of bicycles, and manager's cocktail party.

Winding Bay Beach Resort, P.O. Box 93, Rock Sound, Eleuthera, The Bahamas (tel. 809/334-4055; U.S. reservations: 212/661-4540 in New York State; toll free 800/223-1588 U.S. nationwide; 800/531-6767 in Canada). The name comes from the 2½-mile-long bay, fringed with pine trees and scalloped with tiny coves, that gets more beautiful as you walk along it. The resort itself is a honeymoon best bet, an all-inclusive property that offers especially good value. Everything—from meals and drinks to scuba-diving and Sunfish sailing—is covered by your room rate. Lounge by the lovely freshwater pool, or play tennis on one of the two courts. Surrounded by palm trees, rooms are modern and cheery, with rattan furnishings, air conditioning, ceiling fans, and patios. Good restaurant. Honeymoon package: None. Rates: Eight days/seven nights (all-inclusive): From $1,595 per couple for a standard room.

Runaway Hill, P.O. Box 31, Harbour Island, Eleuthera, The Bahamas (tel. 809/333-2150; U.S. reservations: toll free 800/327-0787). Staying at this small inn that was once a private home is like visiting old friends. The lounge is decorated with wicker furniture on a glossy black-and-white tile floor. Well-thumbed books have been left by previous travelers in the guest rooms, each of which is individually decorated. The fresh, delicious meals, which draw many visitors from other hotels, are served on the veranda above the swimming pool and pink-sand beach. Carol Becht, who runs this eight-room inn with her husband, Roger, writes the menu by hand every day. Honeymoon package: None. Rates (EP): From $140 per couple per night.

Romora Bay Club, P.O. Box 146, Harbour Island, Eleuthera, The Bahamas (tel. 809/333-2324; U.S. reservations: 305/760-4535, or toll free 800/327-8286). Overflowing with tropical flowers, bushes, and trees, Romora Bay borders both the beach and the harbor sides of the island. A popular activity, especially for honeymooners, is being marooned all day for an "X-rated" picnic on a deserted island. The 32 rooms run the gamut from comfortable to super-deluxe; all have private patios or balconies. There is an excellent dive program offered. Honeymoon package: Seven days/six nights (MAP): $1,240 to $1,330 per couple. Includes breakfast and dinner daily, picnic trip to a deserted island, wine with dinner, all taxes and gratuities.

INEXPENSIVE: Wykee's World Resort, P.O. Box 176, Governor's Harbour, Eleuthera, The Bahamas (tel. 809/332-2701). "Please don't write about this place," our friends begged. "We don't want it ruined." So we'll just whisper the facts about this gem of a hideaway—and only to very special travelers. Even if you spent hours daydreaming, you probably couldn't imagine as perfect a retreat as Wykee's World. You'll stay in your own private villa on an estate formerly owned by the late Sir Roland Symonette, Bahamian prime minister, which was used to house guests of the government. Built of coral stone with screened-in porches and plenty of jalousie windows to let in the breezes, each of the six cottages features a different layout. All have fully equipped kitchens as well as outdoor grills. (The nearest restaurants are in Governors Harbour, just three miles away. Many frequent guests fly in with favorite groceries from the mainland. Maid and cook services are available upon request.) Set on a hillside, the lushly gardened grounds slope down to miles of very private beach, with waters that reflect breathtaking shades of blue. Honeymoon package: None. Rates (EP): From $66 to $82 per couple for a one-bedroom cottage.

THE EXUMAS

Although the Exumas are said to have a cay for each day of the year, the population of this chain is concentrated on Great Exuma, the largest of the islands. Stretching for 100 miles between New Providence and Long Island, these islands are heaven for sailors and water-sports enthusiasts. When you fly in you'll see tiny islands strewn through swirls of turquoise in more shades than you thought existed. It's as if Mother Nature had pulled her fingers through the water, leaving a whimsical design.

In the center of George Town, the pink-and-white administration building resembles a dignified Government House in Nassau. The pastel-and-white color scheme of this and other buildings in town makes taking photos hard to resist. Women selling a multitude of straw goods set up shop in the shade of the huge fig trees that border the main road. A few scuba-diving operations, boutiques, and other stores are clustered here.

Rent a car or hire a taxi for a drive up north, and you'll pass tiny farming settlements and a few good home-style restaurants. Palm, banana, tamarind, and citrus trees grow along the road. Stop for a swim at deserted Three Sisters beach, where three huge dark rocks rise side by side out of the aquamarine water.

If your honeymoon happens to fall at the end of April, you'll be swept up in the excitement of the annual Family Island Regatta. The partying surrounding these three days of sailing races is stretched out for at least a week.

Romantic Interludes

Both on land and at sea, nature has given newlyweds plenty to discover in the Exuma cays.

Long, narrow Stocking Island lies across Elizabeth Harbour from George Town. Edged with some of the world's most powdery sand, this island lures romantics with countless **secluded coves** and inlets. Pack a picnic, or get hot dogs at the beach bar. The calm waters of the harborside are speckled with sailboats. You can walk out on a sandbar stretching at least 40 yards into the bay. Red and black starfish wash gently ashore. If you're into bonefishing, all you have to do is cast your lines off the dock. On the other side of the island, the shelling is excellent. Peace and Plenty Hotel provides daily complimentary ferry service to the island for its guests.

Lying on and around some of Exuma's most dramatic cays, the **Exuma Land and Sea Park** has been declared a national park. It encompasses more than 20 miles of striking coral reefs, brilliant fish, and other marine life, as well as nesting areas for flocks of birds. Since some of the colorful underwater spectacles are only three to ten feet down, snorkeling is extremely exciting here. To tour this region north of Great Exuma, make arrangements through your hotel to charter a boat.

Honeymoon Hotels and Hideaways

Once a sponge market and then a private home, **Peace and Plenty,** P.O. Box 55, George Town, Exuma, The Bahamas (tel. 809/336-2551; U.S. reservations: toll free 800/327-0787), has settled comfortably into its latest incarnation as a hotel. The hospitality here is truly Bahamian. Many residents socialize with visitors at the bar, which is decorated with anchors, nets, and other nautical touches. At breakfast, the grits and boiled fish—Bahamian specialties—are favorites. Weekend parties often take place on the pool patio and it seems as if the whole island turns out to wiggle their hips under the stars. Many of the 32 large rooms have sweeping views of Elizabeth Harbour, which attracts more than a few boaters. All rooms are air-conditioned. A complimentary ferry ride takes guests to the quiet beaches of Stocking Island, just across the water. Honeymoon package: None. Rates (EP): $90 to $105 per couple per night.

---

5. More Suggestions in The Bahamas

Some Bahama-philes are convinced that you've never really seen the Bahamas until you've taken a good look below its shimmering waters. At least two islands should not be missed by serious—or even semiserious—divers or snorkelers. Right off the beach-fringed eastern coast of Andros is an extraordinary 120-mile-long barrier reef, while on Long Island, divers can learn that sharks need not be frightening after all.

Small Hope Bay Lodge, P.O. Box N-1131, Nassau, New Providence, The Bahamas (tel. 809/368-2014; U.S. reservations: 305/463-9130, or toll free 800/223-6961). First, you'll forget to put on your watch. Soon, you won't even remember what day of the week it is. That describes the island euphoria which soon takes hold at Small Hope Bay Lodge, one of the few accommodations on massive, undeveloped Andros. You'll feel as if you're staying at a friend's home, not a hotel. You keep your own tab at the honor bar, and borrow books from the extensive lending library. At a rustic lodge, where jackets, ties, and shoes are virtually unheard of, soaking in a hot tub or having a massage might seem to be unlikely activities. However, not only is a hot tub right on the beach, but you can arrange for expert hands to relax your muscles after a hard day of diving, snorkeling, biking, or simply cooling out in a hammock. The palm-shaded beach begins just outside each cabin door. The 20 pine and coral units are decorated with distinctive batik wall-hangings and pillows. This colorful cloth is dyed at the local Androsia workshop, which makes resortwear sold throughout The Bahamas.

Since scuba-diving is the house specialty, nondivers are invited to take lessons free of charge, or they can learn to snorkel. The third-longest barrier reef in the world lies just offshore, as does the incredible Tongue of the Ocean—a chasm over a mile deep and 142 miles long. The superb dive operation at Small Hope Bay Lodge can take you to dozens of spectacular sites. For experienced divers, there's the ultimate plunge: "Over the Wall" to a ledge 185 feet down. Look over the brink—eerie blue nothingness stretches a mile down. "Like being in outer space" is how one diver described it. On land, take a fascinating "bush walk" with Dr. Bob, an Andros native who explains local herbs and potions. Meals, hearty and plentiful, are served at tables where various members of the Birch family dine with guests. Afterward, join fellow guests for Scrabble tournaments or spontaneous "jump up" dancing, or stake out one of the hammocks and watch the constellations peek out from behind the palm fronds. Honeymoon package: None. Rates: $1,715 to $1,750 (all inclusive). Includes round-trip airport transfers, welcome drinks, three meals daily, wine with dinner, use of resort facilities, taxes and tips.

Stella Maris Inn, P.O. Box SM-105, Stella Maris, Long Island, The Bahamas (tel. 809/336-2106; U.S. reservations: tel. 305/467-0466, or toll free 800/426-0466 or 800/327-0787). The waters off the coast of Stella Maris on Long Island provide a wealth of thrilling dive sites. For the adventurous, learning to dive (safely) with sharks is one of the special attractions of this 60-room German-owned inn. Sailing, windsurfing, waterskiing, deep-sea fishing, and snorkeling around the brilliant offshore reefs are also favorite pastimes—all free to guests. Cottages, apartments, and individual rooms dot the sprawling hilly grounds that border the ocean. You'll have a choice of three swimming pools and two tennis courts. On weekends, the Stella Maris is where the action is: Local musicians play up a "rake and scrape" storm. Honeymoon package: Eight days/seven nights: Winter season—$1,625 per couple (MAP, with breakfast and dinner); summer season—$1,045 per couple (EP, no meals). Includes one day's use of a rental car, one day's diving, one day's skiff fishing, welcome drinks, use of all facilities such as bikes and snorkeling gear. Taxes and service charges also included during the summer season.

XVI

BARBADOS

1. PRACTICAL FACTS
2. ROMANTIC INTERLUDES
3. HONEYMOON HOTELS AND HIDEAWAYS
4. ROMANTIC RESTAURANTS AND NIGHTSPOTS

Barbados is a little farther from U.S. shores than some other Caribbean locations—perhaps 45 or so extra minutes on a plane. But if you choose this extraordinary island for your honeymoon, you'll be well rewarded, since it combines the most delightful features of all the islands in one. It has more than its share of natural beauty—azure water, pristine beaches, graceful palm trees, warm, flower-scented breezes. But even more beguiling is the Barbadians' deeply personal approach to visitors. Although the hotels are sophisticated and know how to provide every amenity, you'll never be "processed" or shoved around in an impersonal way. Hotel managers greet you, check on you, coddle you until you feel like a guest in a private home. But much as visitors are cherished, Barbadians haven't sold out to big-time tourism; they mightily resist turning their island into an artificial, plasticized world designed to capture tourist dollars. They're proud of their native culture, which is vibrant, unspoiled, and, for the most part, devoid of grinding poverty and racial resentments. Even the simplest dwellings have a spruced-up dignity, and the humblest Bajan has the same sense of self-respect. They address you with an attitude that says "I'm a pretty terrific person. What about you?"

Barbados is one of the Windward Islands of the Lesser Antilles, an island chain that swings east from Puerto Rico, then south and back west again as it skims the coast of South America. The island is shaped rather like a pear that leans to the west —21 miles long (north to south) and 14 miles wide at the widest point (total area: 166 square miles).

Because it's the most easterly of all the Caribbean islands, it has three quite different seacoasts. The east coast, the northern end of which is aptly named the Scotland district, is a wild, forlorn area—hilly, picturesque, and populated mostly by farm animals that graze along the mountainsides. The rough, blue-gray Atlantic breakers start their shoreward roll from miles out, and as they crash, fill all the rocky bays with an eerie sea mist. In sharp contrast, the west coast, bathed by the much more gentle Caribbean Sea, has been sculpted and polished for the international visitor. One after another, elegant low-rise hotels and vacation homes (one of them belonging to Claudette Colbert) cozy up to the beach, the waves almost lapping their terraces. Guests wander across green lawns landscaped with hibiscus and bougainvillea, bathe in brilliant blue swimming pools, or sit in the sand under a palm tree and watch a glowing sunset. At the southwestern elbow of the island, you'll find Bridgetown, Barbados' capital, with its fine duty-free shops centered along Broad Street. Barbados' curving south coast (the bottom of the pear) is also peppered with pretty hotels, generally more moderate in price. The beaches are wider, breezier, and wavier than on the west coast. In the afternoons, colorful flotillas of windsurfers try to keep their boards balanced and sails high.

As early as 1511, Barbados was spotted by Spanish and Portuguese sailors, who named it "Isla de los Barbados" (Island of the Bearded Ones), perhaps referring to the native ficus tree whose aboveground roots grow down from its branches in a beard-like fashion. But it was a British trading party that took possession of the island in 1625, and England governed the island for the next 350 years. In 1627, the first settlers arrived to grow tobacco and cotton, but sugar proved to be a better economic bet. The island was deforested, sugar was planted everywhere, and plantation owners prospered. But since growing, harvesting, and refining sugar required a large work force, Africans were imported and the institution of slavery was established on the island.

In 1834, slavery was abolished on Barbados. Over the years, sugar became less lucrative and Barbadians turned to tourism and light industry to balance their economy. Sugar is still grown on the island, especially in the interior, and its by-products, molasses and rum, are among the island's major exports. Barbados became independent from Britain in 1966, but it still retains membership in the British Commonwealth. The Barbadians (also called "Bajans") maintain cultural links with England as well—they like cricket, polo, afternoon tea, and low-key good manners. Their parliamentary government is stable, and there is little crime. Bajans from all walks of life seem to get along with a minimum of racial and class tensions, probably because all people are free to advance in commerce and the professions as they wish. (Interracial marriages are not unusual.) As a tourist, you'll feel the goodwill and gentle interest of almost all Barbadians. Once when we asked directions in Bridgetown, an elderly woman walked us to our destination, delighted to point out the shortcut we surely would have missed. Her attitude is not unusual.

Barbados is not the place for hustle and bustle, glitz and glitter. No gambling here. The island's attractions are subtle and tasteful in the British tradition. This is paradise for honeymooners who enjoy natural beauty, water sports, history, and nightlife that's upbeat and elegant but not gaudy.

1. Practical Facts

ENTERING AND LEAVING

American and Canadian visitors will need proof of citizenship, plus a ticket for onward or return departure. Passports are always best, but you can get by with a birth certificate, along with a photo ID such as a driver's license. There is a departure tax of $8 U.S., payable when you check in for your return flight.

GETTING THERE

Barbados is a little over 4 hours from New York, 5 hours from Toronto, and 3 hours and 15 minutes from Miami. The island is easy to reach without stopping and changing planes, especially from the major East Coast United States cities. The following major air carriers serve Barbados nonstop (or one stop only) from the United States and Canada: **American Airlines, B.W.I.A., Pan American,** and **Air Canada.** You can connect from Midwest and West Coast cities via Miami or San Juan. From Barbados, it's also fun to island-hop to Martinique, Grenada, St. Lucia, and other nearby islands via **L.I.A.T., Air Martinique,** or **B.W.I.A.** Barbados' port of Bridgetown is also a popular stop for several cruise lines.

BARBADOS

0 | Miles | 4
0 | Kilometers | 5

North Point

ST. LUCY

Corben's Bay

N

1B 10

St. Nicholas Abbey
(plantation house)

1 Wildlife
Reserve

Farley Hill

Speightstown ST. ANDREW

ST. PETER Bellplaine

2

ATLANTIC OCEAN

Chalky Mount

2A

ST.
JAMES Flower
Forest Batsheba

1 ST. JOSEPH

St. James
Beach Welchman
Hall Gully 3A

Folkestone
Underwater
Park 1A ST. JOHN

Holetown ST. THOMAS 3B Ragged Point

2

4

3 St. George 4B ST. PHILIP

ST.
MICHAEL 4 5

1 5

Bridgetown CHRIST
CHURCH 6 Crane Beach

Carlisle
Bay 6

Hastings Rockley Beach St. Lawrence Oistins 7

Grantley Adams
International Airport

Oistin Bay Christ
Church

South Point

COBBLER'S REEF

CARIBBEAN SEA

GETTING AROUND

Barbados offers buses, taxis, rental cars, "mokes," and even motorbikes and bicycles for your convenience. To get the best transportation for your dollar, first find out where your hotel is located relative to other sights you'd like to see, restaurants where you'd like to dine, etc., then plan your vacation time accordingly.

By Bus

Buses give you most miles for your money all over the island (fare between any two points is $1 Bds. in exact change). They're comfortable and reliable, and the routes include many areas of interest. State-owned buses are blue with a gold stripe; those from the privately owned line are yellow with blue stripes. All buses run from 5 a.m. to 11 p.m. Routes and schedules are available from the Board of Tourism. Some hotels have courtesy van service to and from the airport and shuttle service to Bridgetown; check when you make your hotel reservations, or ask at the front desk once you arrive.

By Taxi

Taxis are always there when you need them, and the drivers friendly and eager to please. They are expensive, however, with fares from the airport to west coast hotels costing from $12 to $22 U.S. There are no meters; fixed rates are charged between various points on the island. Ask your taxi driver or the desk clerk at your hotel for a rate sheet. It's always wise to ask what the fare will be before you take a ride.

By Car

These are easy to come by from several local companies. Popular in Barbados are minimokes, dune buggy–like vehicles with canvas roofs and open sides. They rent for about $10 U.S. a day less than cars. A minimoke runs about $40 U.S. per day; a car, $45 to $50 U.S., plus tax and collision damage waiver. Use credit cards for car rental if you can: otherwise you must leave a large cash deposit. Rental car companies do not accept personal checks.

Even if you only drive for one day, you'll need a Barbados visitor's driving license (international licenses will not suffice). They are available through your rental car agency upon presentation of your valid license from home; the fee is $10 Bds.

Driving is on the left in Barbados and steering wheels are on the right; careful at those roundabouts (traffic circles)! Roads are generally (not always) well paved, but tend to be narrow and curvy (those on the mountainous east coast are often steep and like roller coasters). Driving is European style with lots of dodging and passing. Main arteries are well marked, but it's easy to get lost on secondary roads, especially at night. A couple of driving hints: Avoid traffic jams by steering clear of the Bridgetown area during rush hours. And if you wish to have dinner in a restaurant far away from your hotel, better visit the area in daylight first, spring for a taxi, or wait until the end of your stay when you know the roads better.

MONEY

The Barbados dollar is worth just about 50¢ U.S., and stays constant since it is officially tied to the U.S. dollar. To figure how much Barbadian goods and services cost in U.S. dollars, just divide the amount of the Barbadian price tag in half. Shops will accept U.S. and Canadian cash, plus traveler's checks. Some hotels, restaurants, and larger stores will take major U.S. credit cards, but ask first; don't assume. Hotels, stores, and banks all offer pretty much the same rate of exchange. All prices quoted in this section are in U.S. dollars, unless otherwise indicated.

LANGUAGE

English has been the official—and only—language since 1627, when the British landed and laid claim to the island. Bajans speak it with a lovely West Indian lilt—which tends to be catching.

WEATHER

Winter temperatures range from 68° to 85°, summer temperatures from 76° to 87°, but the island is constantly refreshed and cooled by steady northeast trade winds. The island boasts more than 3,000 hours of sunshine per year, the rainiest months being September, October, and November. February and March tend to have the driest weather. Rain seldom lasts long; the trade winds blow storm clouds quickly by.

CLOTHING

Bajans aren't stuffy about clothing, but they have the British regard for neatness and decorum. Bathing suits are for beach and pool area only; when you adjourn to the terrace for lunch, don a shirt or coverup. Tour the island in pants and a shirt, or an informal dress; no short shorts or halter tops, please. Many hotels and restaurants require men to wear jackets, some of the more elegant establishments also requesting ties during dinner; for special occasions during the winter season, some tony hotels require dinner jackets. Wardrobes are more casual in the summer. Check dress codes with hotels and restaurants in advance.

TIME

All year, Barbados is on Atlantic Standard Time, which is one hour ahead of Eastern Standard Time. In winter, when it's noon in New York, it's 1 p.m. in Barbados. However, when Daylight Saving Time is in effect, the time will be the same in both places.

TELEPHONES

You can reach Barbados direct from the United States by dialing area code 809 and the seven-digit number. The phone service on the island is good. Most hotels have phones in the rooms, and local calls are free. Minimum charge for a three-minute call to the United States is about $12.

SHOPPING

Do you want to fill out your English china or crystal pattern, or warm yourself in British woolens this winter? In Barbados you can buy these items at 20% to 40% less than in the United States! Excellent buys are also found on perfumes, Irish woolens and linens, Liberty silks and cottons, gold and silver jewelry, watches and liquor—especially Barbados rum. Hot spot for shopping: **Broad Street** in **Bridge-town,** where the finest department and specialty stores are located. Your number one stop should be **Cave Shepherd,** which carries just about everything a passionate shopper could desire, from Caribelle batiks to a bevy of treasures from Waterford, Wedgwood, and other famous names. **DaCosta's** pink-and-white atrium houses tempting boutiques selling a wide range of merchandise, including Rolex watches. Also prowl through **Intransit Barbados** for super-fashionable sports duds for men and women. Continuing along Broad Street, you'll also find **C.F. Harrison, Y. DeLima,** and **India House,** plus several fine jewelry stores. Nearby, **Origins** at the Careenage displays very sharp womenswear—bright and tropical for a night on the town. Shopping hours are 8 a.m. to 4 p.m. on weekdays (afternoons are less crowded), 8 a.m. to noon on Saturdays. Smaller branches of some of these stores are in the Barbados shopping malls. Many of the finest hotels have their own boutiques, as well.

When buying duty-free goods in Barbados, you can take your purchases with you immediately, *except* for liquor, tobacco, and electronic goods, which are sold "in bond." In-bond purchases will be delivered to the Chamber of Commerce section in the Departure Hall at the airport. You pick up your packages there before you leave. To take advantage of in-bond savings, you must make your purchases at least 24 hours before your departure time. Inform the sales clerk of your departure date plus your airline and flight number, and save any invoices to give to the airport official so that you can claim your packages. It all works very smoothly. When shopping, make sure you carry your identification and airline tickets with you, to verify that you are entitled to the duty-free prices.

Be sure to check out local Bajan handcrafts as well. Some of the most tasteful items—children's toys and clothes, basketry and other woven items, place mats, and ceramics—are to be found at the Best of Barbados shops (several different locations throughout the island). The owner and guiding spirit of **Best of Barbados** is designer Jill Walker, who is known throughout the island for her bright watercolors and hand-printed fabrics. Local straw work, batik, pottery of Arawak Indian design, and African-style jewelry made from shells can be seen at **Pelican Village,** Harbour Road, Bridgetown, with its individual thatch-roofed stalls. Also in Bridgetown, check out the **Handicraft Emporium,** Princess Alice Highway; and **West Indies Handcrafts and Articrafts,** Norman Center, Broad Street.

Don't forget that you can bring $400 worth of goods back to the United States duty free; a 10% duty will be collected on purchases over that amount. A hint when purchasing liquor: Although you can bring in only one quart of liquor duty free, you might consider buying several bottles of Barbados rum anyway. Even after you've paid the duty, you'll probably be spending less than you would in your local liquor store.

HOW TO GET MARRIED IN BARBADOS

Tying the knot in Barbados is easy but takes a bit of planning. Here's what to do. You must be on the island for three days before you apply for a marriage license. Ask your hotel to help you make arrangements for the ceremony with clergy or magistrate before you apply for your license. Also beforehand, purchase the special $12.50 stamp needed to make the license legal at a Barbados post office. On the fourth day after your arrival, you may apply for your license at the Ministry of Legal Affairs, Marine House, Christ Church (tel. 427-5420). Have identification with you —either a valid U.S. passport or a birth certificate plus a photo ID with signature, such as a driver's license. Also bring original or certified copies of divorce papers, if applicable. If one of you is widowed, bring proof of former marriage, plus death certificate of spouse. You will also need to show your airline tickets and the immigration cards you filled out on the aircraft. Your license will cost $50 and will be issued on the spot. There is a three-day waiting period before the marriage can take place. Most hotels will be delighted to help you handle all the details.

FOR FURTHER INFORMATION

Contact: **Barbados Board of Tourism.** Barbados: P.O. Box 242, Bridgetown, Barbados (tel. 809/427-2623, 2624). New York: 800 Second Ave., New York, NY 10017 (tel. 212/986-6516). Los Angeles: 3440 Wilshire Blvd., Suite 1215, Los Angeles, CA (tel. 213/380-2198/9). Or call toll free in the United States, 800/221-9831.

2. Romantic Interludes

Barbados waters are beautiful, clear, and warm—and there are so many ways you can enjoy them. Many hotels offer free **water sports** to their guests; this means that you can use their small sailboats, Windsurfers, and snorkeling gear—and maybe even go waterskiing—without charge. For divers, there are a number of fine dive shops on the island.

Arguably, the best reefs for snorkeling on the island can be found at **Folkestone Underwater Park,** next to the Coral Reef Club on the west coast. This sanctuary for underwater life is also devoted to marine research. Snorkelers can follow an underwater trail, while scuba-divers will find excellent reefs for steep, drop-off diving. If you think you'd like scuba, but you're not quite sure, call **Shades of Blue Diving** next to Folkestone Park (tel. 422-3215; evenings 432-2068). In addition to introductory dives ($45 per person), they conduct expeditions for intermediate and experienced divers as well ($40 per person, $50 per person for night dives). NAUI certified.

You don't even have to get wet to see Barbados' most spectacular underwater attractions, thanks to the **Atlantis II,** a 28-passenger submarine. You'll journey nearly 150 feet below the sea to view sponge gardens . . . even the eerie wreck of the *Stavronikita* cargo ship. The hour-long explorations cost $64 per person and depart from 9 a.m. to 9 p.m. A hint: Time your trip for about a half hour before sunset. That way, you'll get to view the large schools of fish active by day, as well as the fascinating "nightlife" of the reef, including vibrantly colored corals. For reservations and information, call 436-8929 or 436-8932.

Vistas of land and sea are spectacular on this island, and since Barbadians want visitors to see them to advantage, they have established a number of **gardens and walking paths** that you should not miss. The brick paths at **Flower Forest** (tel. 433-8152) meander up and down a mountainside covered with tropical trees and exotic flowers. Beyond the vegetation, lush green mountains loom. There's a lovely, romantic gazebo and benches where you can sit and soak it all up. Open daily from 9 a.m. to 5 p.m.; entrance fee, $3. Animal lovers must visit the **Barbados Wildlife Reserve** (tel. 422-8826). You stroll along a yellow brick path quietly observing the free-roaming animals—otters, raccoons, alligators, deer, tortoises, and a family of wallabies—while the lovely Barbados "green" monkeys soar overhead. Not smelly or confining, the reserve is beautifully kept by people who cherish animals. Open from 10 a.m. to 5 p.m.; entrance fee, $4.50. Be sure to visit the ruins of Farley Hill, an elegant old plantation house destroyed by fire in 1965 after it served as the site for the filming of *Island in the Sun,* starring Harry Belafonte. Behind the burnt-out mansion, you can walk up the hill under towering mahogany trees to the lookout, from where you can see the whole Scotland district, the Atlantic Ocean, and "Sleeping Napoleon," a strange cluster of huge rocks that simulate the profile face and belly of a reclining man. Take a picnic with you to Farley Hill; many hotels will prepare a box lunch if you ask them a day in advance. Admission fee, $1 per car.

Then continue to the northernmost point in Barbados and the **Animal Flower Cave,** so named because of the sea anemones found within the caverns. Looking like delicate underwater chrysanthemums, the long-"petaled" anemones are actually living animals—reach out to touch one and it will withdraw into a sheath. The caves themselves are magical, with eerie formations that resemble a skeleton, a frog. One cavern often fills with sea water, forming a one-of-a-kind swimming pool, perched on a cliff overlooking the wave-tossed north coast. Wear sneakers or rubber thongs for balance on the slippery rocks; bring a business card or ID to post in the snackbar, with walls papered with old credit cards, driver's licenses, and the like. Open daily from 9 a.m. to 5 p.m.; admission, $2 per person.

Barbados has a **beach** for every taste. Top contenders start with St. James Beach along the west coast. Lunch at **Sandpiper Inn** (tel. 422-2251) or **Treasure Beach** (tel. 432-1346), then walk down the curving strand, wading in the warm, gentle water and surveying all those elegant hotels. Crane Beach, south coast: This magnificent strip of pink sand beneath towering limestone bluffs is one of the most marvelously unspoiled beaches in the West Indies. Have a wonderful seafood lunch atop the bluff at the **Crane Hotel** dining room and enjoy the view. Every fish on the menu is highly recommended. Bathsheba Beach, east coast: When the poet John Keats wrote about "perilous seas in fairylands forlorn," he must have had in mind a beach like Bathsheba—foggy, mysterious, pounded by turbulent surf. Native surfers love it; you can see them far out on their boards, waiting for a wave. Wade only; rough surf and underwater rocks make swimming perilous.

Barbados even offers spectacular scenery underground, in the otherworldly forms of **Harrison's Cave** in St. Thomas. On your guided tour, an electric trolley takes you through the caverns, where stalactites and stalagmites glisten, and the roar of a tumbling waterfall reverberates against eons-old rock. Tours run every hour from 9 a.m. to 4 p.m.; admission is $5 per person.

Feeling footloose? No need to let a car come between you and the Barbados landscape. Most Sunday mornings, the Barbados National Trust, the Duke of Edinburgh Award Scheme, and the Barbados Heart Foundation host five-mile guided **hikes** through the countryside. Starting at 6 a.m., the walks are geared to three different speeds: fast, medium, and "stop-and-stare." It's a great way to get to know Barbados and the Barbadians. The program is free; call 426-2421 for schedules and locales.

Learning about Barbados' sugar economy is far more interesting than you would at first expect. Start by visiting the excellent **Barbados Museum** (tel. 427-0201 or 427-1956), housed in the old military prison at Garrison, St. Michael. You'll be able to view flora and fauna of the island as well as archaeological items, antiques, and artifacts from the plantation days. Open Monday through Saturday, 9 a.m. to 6 p.m. And do not miss **St. Nicholas Abbey,** St. Peter (tel. 422-8725 or 422-2446), a sugar plantation still in operation but open to the public. The owner, Lieut. Col. Stephen Cave, sometimes conducts tours himself and will give you the whole history of his family, closet skeletons and all. Sadly moving are the carefully written records of the plantation slaves, remembered only by their first names and estimated worth. A wonderfully detailed home movie, taken in 1935 by Cave's father, gives fascinating insights into the plantation culture and the techniques of harvesting and refining sugar. Open Monday through Friday, 10 a.m. to 3:30 p.m. Entrance fee, $3. Other privately owned "plantation great houses" are open to the public; of special interest are **Villa Nova** in St. John (tel. 433-1524) and **Sunbury Plantation House,** Highway 5, St. Philip (tel. 423-6270).

Half-day **sailing cruises** with lunch, drinks, and perhaps a stop for swimming and snorkeling will give you a wonderful lesson on how to be lazy in the tropics. Some hotels have their own boats (the Coral Reef Club owns the *Anna Kareena,* for example), and a cruise might be included as part of your honeymoon package. If not, you can call **Tiami Exclusive Sailing Cruises Ltd.** (tel. 436-5725) for a lunch or cocktail cruise on a graceful catamaran; $90 per couple. Adventure at sea is also available aboard the *Irish Mist II,* a spacious, 52-foot catamaran that offers lunch and dinner cruises along the west coast for approximately $90 per couple (tel. 436-9201). If you prefer lively parties and large boats, cruise on the pirate ship *Jolly Roger* (tel. 436-6424 or 436-6425). With her blood-red sails and skull-and-crossbones flag, the *Jolly Roger* is easily the best-known attraction in Barbados. Its jaunts offer nonstop fun for all, complete with a buffet feast and an open bar, plus such pirate pranks as walking the plank, rope swinging . . . even a mock pirate wedding on the nighttime cruise; $80 per couple. Meanwhile, the Mississippi-style riverboat *Bajan Queen* (tel. 436-2149) cruises off for four hours of seafaring adventures, including swimming, snorkeling, and dancing to red-hot calypso music; $80 per couple. Both the *Jolly Roger* and *Bajan Queen* also feature moonlight cocktail cruises for $80 per couple, including drinks, meal, and round-trip transportation. A guide called "Inns and Outs of Barbados," which you'll probably find in your hotel room, gives dates for full moons for a year . . . so take note!

Another night, have a great dinner, learn a little about Barbados history, and take in a show all at the same time by reserving a spot at a dinner theater performance, all run by the same outfit. *1627 and All That* (held Sundays and Thursdays) features a superb folk dance performance by members of the internationally acclaimed Barbados Dance Centre. The show is held in the courtyard of the Barbados Museum of Garrison, St. Michael, and the price of your ticket includes a museum tour. The musical comedy *Barbados, Barbados* (held Tuesdays) recreates the life and times of Rachel Pringle, said to be the island's first hotelier—and madame. Shows are presented in the aptly named Balls Boiling House, part of an old sugar mill. One price of $40 per person includes transportation to and from your hotel, hors d'oeuvres, buffet dinner, the show, and all drinks. Every Wednesday afternoon, the company also hosts *Where The Rum Come From,* a luncheon tour of the Mount Gay Bottling and Blending Plant. The program includes drinks and a buffet lunch, accompanied by entertainment from a steel band. It costs $25 per person. Call 435-6900 for reservations and information about all three shows.

3. Honeymoon Hotels and Hideaways

Barbados boasts some of the most romantic accommodations in the islands, with plenty of choices to suit all moods and inclinations.

Bajan prices are upscale; even moderate prices are a bit on the high side. But the good news is you don't have to be afraid of more modest places: They may be basic and no-frills (even romantically seedy), but they'll seldom be junky, cheap, or dirty. Except on the breezy south coast, most hotels give you a choice of air conditioning or a much more picturesque "punkah" ceiling fan. Telephones in the room are almost universal, but televisions are rare.

When trying to find the right place for you, remember that although posh resorts are found throughout the island, most of them are concentrated on the Caribbean (west) coast. The main buildings of many of these properties were once elegant estates or vacation homes. When the hoteliers bought them from their original owners, they added guest space by building free-standing cottages (or, more recently, low-rise condo-style units) on the surrounding land, which has been landscaped into a veritable Eden.

Several of Barbados' most prestigious west coast resorts have joined together to form "The Elegant Resorts of Barbados" collection. Among other features, guests staying at participating hotels can make arrangements to take their meals at any of the member resorts, and enjoy various social facilities. Special package rates are also available from May through mid-December. For details, contact "The Elegant Resorts of Barbados," P.O. Box 639, Bridgetown, Barbados, W.I.

On the south coast, the resorts around St. Lawrence Gap, a lively little harbor town of restaurants, night spots, and mall shops, are great for young, informal honeymooners who like action and the company of others. Some of the loveliest hotels are found farther east along the south coast, but they tend to be isolated from the rest of the island, best for honeymooners who want a leisurely pace, natural beauty, and privacy. Some of the least expensive hotels are found on the rugged east coast (where the Bajans themselves go on vacation), but this area is extremely secluded. If you go there, plan to do a lot of reading, hiking, or watching the waves roll in.

You'll get the best deals on hotel rates between mid-April and mid-December —from 30% to 50% lower than in the high season. Liveliest time during off-season is the Crop-Over Festival, which celebrates the completion of the sugar cane harvest. It's held during the last two weeks in July and positively busts loose with fairs, parades, and cultural events.

Prices in this chapter reflect the spread between low- and high-season prices. Unless otherwise indicated, the rates are European Plan (EP), which means there are no meals included. You can purchase a meal package in most hotels, or pay as you go. When figuring costs, remember that a 5% government tax and a 10% service charge will be added to your bill.

In addition to the major resort hotels, there are a number of small hotels, apartment hotels, and guesthouses. You can obtain a complete list by writing the Barbados Board of Tourism and requesting the brochure entitled "Hotel and Guest House Rates." Another way to go is to rent a luxury villa complete with housekeeper and/or cook. For information about villas, contact: West coast: **Bajan Services,** Seascape Cottage, Gibbs, St. Peter, Barbados (tel. 809/422-2618); or **Alleyne, Aguilar & Altman,** "Rose Bank," Derricks, St. James, Barbados (tel. 809/432-0840). South coast: **Ronald Stoute & Sons Ltd.,** Sam Lord's Castle, St. Philip, Barbados (tel. 809/432-6800).

WEST COAST

Expensive

One of the most venerated hotels on the island, **Coral Reef Club,** St. James Beach, Barbados (tel. 809/422-2372; U.S. reservations: 212/535-2445 or toll free 800/223-1108), combines British grace with West Indian warmth. You'll be met on arrival by at least one member of the O'Hara family; Budge and Cynthia have managed the hotel since 1956, and now are joined by their three attractive and friendly children. You'll have your own secluded cottage/suite, one of 75 on 12 beachfront acres, landscaped with palms and a multitude of flowering plants. The rooms have high ceilings, white coral-stone walls, and are decorated with splashy, cool-color native prints. You'll also enjoy such perks as hairdryers in the bathroom and in-room wall safes. Patio chairs and loungers are comfortable. You can play tennis on the property, or snorkel next door at Folkestone Park. The restaurant is just fine, with a wide variety of choices from continental cuisine to native fruits, vegetables, and fish. (The cooks regularly get creative with homegrown products, and the results are scrumptious.) Best of all, you get a meal plan that offers exchange dining with several other of the finest west coast hotels, so you can sample different restaurants without fuss and bother. Internationally known, Coral Reef Club is a member of the French group Relais et Châteaux and the British Prestige hotels. Honeymoon package (from April to mid-December): Eight days/seven nights (MAP): $1,320 per couple. Includes air-conditioned accommodations (upgraded to the best available on the day of your arrival); bottle of sparkling wine upon arrival, as well as flowers in room; cocktail cruise on hotel catamaran; bottle of rum; free windsurfing, snorkeling, and Sunfish sailing, plus reduced rates on waterskiing. Ten percent service charge and 5% government tax are also included. Winter-season rates (MAP): $380 to $565 per couple per night, depending on view.

Staying at the impeccable **Cobblers Cove,** St. Peter, Barbados (tel. 809/422-2291; U.S. reservations: 212/832-2277, or toll free 800/223-6510), is like renting a private villa with an attentive staff and sharing it with some people who turn into friends. This spiffy little resort consists of a small but elegant main house (formerly a plantation owner's vacation home) and 39 dew-fresh suites set in a U shape surrounding the terrace, pool, and bar. The living room of the suites opens onto outdoor sitting areas that are cleverly designed to give you a good view of beach and pool but without allowing others to see you. Are you seeking the perfect beginning for living happily ever after? Cobblers has just added the new and gorgeous Camelot Suite, fit for any king or queen of hearts. Poised overlooking the sea from the second story of the main great house, the suite pulls out all stops: lustrous Italian marble floors throughout, a patio that's really an outdoor living room, and a private plunge pool. But no matter which accommodations you choose, the picture-perfect beach is just a few steps away, curving around a tranquil bay edged with palm trees. Take advantage of the free water sports or curl up for a good read in a beach chaise or in a comfortable overstuffed armchair in the resort's antiques-filled lounge. Specially chosen European chefs make Cobblers' restaurant one of the best on the island, and the delicious drinks from Cobblers' bar have actually won awards! One of the Elegant Resorts of Barbados. Honeymoon package: Eight days/seven nights (BP): $1,320 per couple; $310 more for MAP. Includes superior garden suite accommodations; full American breakfast daily; flowers, fruit, and welcome drink upon arrival; bottle of sparkling wine "on ice"; lobster dinner for two one evening; souvenir beach bag; round-trip transfers between airport and hotel. Available mid-April to mid-December only. High-season rates (MAP): $475 to $560 per couple per night. Camelot Suite (MAP): $440 to $1,090 per couple per night, depending on season.

Sandy Lane Hotel & Golf Club, St. James, Barbados (tel. 809/432-1311; U.S. reservations: toll free 800/225-5843). Attention to detail . . . that's what distinguishes a great hotel from a merely good one. For those who believe there are just three rules for choosing a hotel—location, location, location—the Sandy Lane delivers nothing but the best. The resort (built around a former sugar plantation) occupies 380 sprawling acres of prime Caribbean coast real estate, with hundred-year-old mahogany trees fringing nearly 1,000 feet of beachfront. A Trusthouse Forte property, the hotel radiates the sparkling good health of $5 million in refurbishment and upgrading. All 110 units are equipped with such thoughtful niceties as hairdryers and toasters (so you can nibble warm breads and muffins on your terrace in the morning). The restaurants are excellent: The chef and the sous-chef studied in France with renowned masters of cuisine such as Roger Verger and Gabriel Le Nôtre. And with three staff members to every guest, personalized service is practically a religion here. Someone from the hotel greets you upon arrival at the airport (even before you go through Immigration), and you can be chauffeured to the resort in the hotel's own Rolls-Royce or Mercedes Benz (for an extra charge). Room service is ready when you are, 24 hours a day. For water-lovers, complimentary water sports include snorkeling, windsurfing, Hobie and Sunfish sailing. Back on land, there's a championship 18-hole golf course, plus five tennis courts (two lighted). Each evening on the seaside terrace, there's dancing under the stars (and on top of them . . . the floor incorporates a twinkling moon-and-stars motif). If you're considering getting married in Barbados, the hotel would love to help you make all the arrangements. One of the Elegant Resorts of Barbados. Honeymoon package: Eight days/seven nights (EP): $1,210 to $1,320 per couple (low season). Includes oceanfront room with terrace or balcony, welcome tray with rum and tropical fruit, champagne breakfast the morning after arrival, complimentary greens fees, a luncheon cruise aboard the *Bajan Queen* or *Jolly Roger,* and more. Call for high-season rates.

Royal Pavilion, Porters, St. James, Barbados (tel. 809/422-4444; U.S. reservations: 402/498-4307, or toll free 800/223-6510). This new resort easily lives up to its name: royal in the sumptuousness of its decor; pavilion-like in its architecture, with 75 rooms (all oceanfront) lolling along a glorious mile of beach. Painted the palest of seashell pinks, the buildings resemble Mediterranean palazzi with their archways, columns, courtyards, and campaniles . . . the Riviera, Barbados style. Even the line-up of boutiques in the shopping arcade (embracing the wares of Cartier, Nina Ricci, and Yves Saint Laurent, among others) expresses knowledgeable appreciation of The Good Life. The beautifully furnished rooms should set you scribbling memos to your interior decorator back home. Coral-stone walls and a pink marble entryway are enhanced by delicate pink, yellow, and Wedgwood-blue floral fabrics. Everything is designed to pamper: whisper-quiet central air conditioning, fully stocked minibar, a separate dressing area. Outdoors, there's a stunning pool deck that could serve as a role model even for Beverly Hills hotels, plus that incredible mile of beach, where you can indulge in a wide range of complimentary water sports, from snorkeling to waterskiing. Two tennis courts are lighted for night play. The Palm Terrace restaurant ranks among Barbados' best. Part of the Elegant Resorts collection, the property is the sister resort to its next-door neighbor, Glitter Bay. Honeymoon package: Eight days/seven nights (EP): $1,195 per couple. Includes oceanfront junior-suite accommodations, welcome drink upon arrival, flowers and champagne in room, champagne breakfast served in room first morning, *Jolly Roger* cruise, afternoon tea, personal gift, and more. Available mid-May through mid-December only. High-season rates (EP): From $440 per couple per night.

Glitter Bay, St. James, Barbados (tel. 809/422-4111; U.S. reservations: 402/498-4307, or toll free 800/223-6510). Coral sands that dazzle the eye by day, a certain silvery glint off the water on moonlit nights . . . these are the reasons behind the name Barbadian businessman George Manning bestowed on his secluded estate at the turn of the century. Blissfully, some things never change, and today the scintillating natural beauty of the locale is intensified by one of Barbados' great resorts. Gracious hospitality remains a tradition here. The property formerly belonged to Sir Edward Cunard of the wealthy shipping family; the hotel lobby is set in the great house where he entertained aristocrats and celebrities. Set on 15 acres, the resort retains the spacious ease of a residential enclave. The gardens are a triumph, with undulating expanses of emerald-green lawn dappled with palm trees and fountains; hibiscus grow in every conceivable color. Accommodations are clustered in two- and three-story Spanish-style whitewashed buildings with red-tile roofs. (All rooms and suites are slated for complete refurbishment in 1990.) The real treats here are the large, beautifully decorated terraces, screened by cascading ferns and bougainvillea . . . a cushy perch for curling up with a good book. For the active set, all water sports are complimentary, and there are two lighted tennis courts. When you work up an appetite, try one of the two fine restaurants. Every Friday night, there's a buffet barbecue followed by a show and dancing under the stars. Part of the Elegant Resorts collection, the property is the sister resort to its next-door neighbor, Royal Pavilion. Honeymoon package: Eight days/seven nights (EP): $1,375 per couple. Includes double room (upgraded to a suite wherever possible), welcome drink upon arrival, flowers and champagne in room, champagne breakfast served in room on first morning, *Jolly Roger* cruise, Monday-night buffet and Friday-night barbecue, afternoon tea and complimentary rum cocktails, special gift, and more. Package available mid-May through mid-December. High-season rates (EP): From $335 per couple per night.

If you want nothing less than total opulence for your honeymoon, **Grand Barbados Beach Resort,** P.O. Box 639, Bridgetown, Barbados (tel. 809/426-0890; U.S. reservations: 212/545-8469 in New York State; toll free 800/223-9815), is for you. This gorgeous seven-story pink edifice right on the water has recently been upgraded to offer guests everything their hearts desire, from valet parking to satellite TV and a hairdryer in every room. Are you hungry? There are three restaurants at Grand Barbados, including the Golden Shell (plush carpets, brocaded chairs) and The Boardwalk, offering Bajan-style lunches and snacks. Most striking are the pier lounge chairs, where you can enjoy view and sun; at the end of the pier is the Schooner Restaurant. The Honeymoon Suites are located out here, and Cupid himself couldn't have designed a more irresistible abode. Built out over the water and beautified with oceanside hues, the suites feature a spacious bedroom that opens onto a balcony—so near the water that you can drop in a fishing line. And the beach is sparkly white, with water so clear that you can eye little fish squiggling by. Water sports are complimentary here, including windsurfing, glass-bottomed boat rides, Sunfish sailing, snorkeling, and cruises aboard the resort's catamaran. One of the big advantages of the Grand Barbados is location—just a little over a mile from Bridgetown (depending on the tide, you can sometimes walk to town right along the shore). Honeymoon package: Eight days/seven nights (EP): Winter season: $1,920 per couple (deluxe room), $4,540 per couple (suite). Summer season: $1,190 per couple (deluxe room), $2,420 per couple (suite). Includes champagne, fruit basket, and fresh flowers upon arrival; welcome rum punch; bottle of rum; souvenir T-shirts; free tennis nearby (equipment provided); and more.

Treasure Beach, St. James, Barbados (tel. 809/432-1346; reservations: toll free 800/223-6510 in the U.S.; toll free 800/268-0424 in Canada). The best treasures are usually hidden—and true to form, this jewel of a hotel sits tucked away on the Caribbean. Since this is an owner-managed hotel, the emphasis is on quality and service. There are only 25 accommodations—all one-bedroom suites—and they are located in two- and three-story stucco villas that face pool, gardens, or ocean. Ingeniously designed and impeccably maintained, the suites mingle outdoor and indoor living. The louvered doors fronting your living room fold back, joining the sitting area to your terrace; just close them up when you want privacy. Exotic blooms always seem to be flaunting their colors in the lush gardens, and you can position your beach chaise either right on the pretty strand or on a shady lawn area facing the sea. To make your happiness complete, the restaurant is very good. One of the Elegant Resorts of Barbados. Honeymoon package: Eight days/seven nights (some meals): $1,100 per couple (low season). Includes welcome drink and bottle of champagne, full breakfast daily, two dinners for two, bottle of rum, souvenir beach bag, use of snorkeling equipment, tennis at nearby courts, and invitation to the manager's cocktail party. High-season rates (EP): $250 to $350 per couple per night, depending on view.

Sandpiper Inn, St. James Beach, Barbados (tel. 809/422-2251; U.S. reservations: toll free 800/223-1108). Intimate and inviting, this 46-room inn is so welcoming that bananaquits flit right through the open-air lobby. The grounds are lushly landscaped, and replete with blossoms of spectacular size and brilliance. The brand-new one-bedroom suites exemplify island elegance, with their white tile floors, pale tropical-flower fabrics, and French doors opening onto a large terrace— you'll certainly want to linger over breakfast here. Recently refurbished, the regular rooms maintain a more garden island feel: rattan furnishings, bougainvillea cascading over balcony railings. The property fronts a good stretch of calm Caribbean-coast beach, where you can enjoy free windsurfing, snorkeling, and Sunfish sailing; there's also a pretty, kidney-shaped freshwater pool. Award-winning restaurant. One of the Elegant Resorts of Barbados. Honeymoon package: Eight days/seven nights (MAP): $1,320 per couple (summer season). Includes air-conditioned accommodations (upgraded to the best available on the day of your arrival), bottle of sparkling wine upon arrival, flowers in room, cocktail cruise on hotel catamaran, a bottle of rum, reduced rates on waterskiing. Ten percent service charge and 5% government tax are also included. Winter-season rates (MAP): $370 to $400 per couple per night for a room; $480 to $510 for a suite.

Moderate

Colony Club, St. James, Barbados (tel. 809/422-2335; U.S. reservations: 212/696-1323 in New York State; toll free 800/372-1323 nationwide). A glamorous entrance driveway shaded by stately casuarinas, together with a choice location near some of the west coast's poshest private estates, enhances the relaxed but elegant mood at this hideaway. The property meanders over seven prime oceanfront acres that include a golden crescent-shaped beach. Mornings are especially soothing here, when white-jacketed waiters move smoothly over the pathways bearing breakfast trays, and gardeners rake an emerald-green lawn already as impeccably manicured as a golf-course fairway. The accommodations are located in two- and three-story buildings, and each of the 76 rooms features homey contemporary furnishings, with both air conditioning and ceiling fans. Best of all, there's a large terrace or balcony where you can savor an alfresco breakfast. And if you're lucky, you might spy some of the island's little green monkeys playing tag in the treetops. Take advantage of the free water sports (snorkeling, waterskiing, windsurfing, Sunfish and catamaran sailing) or try your mallet at croquet. Tennis, horseback riding, and golf are all available nearby. The open-air restaurant, with walls of rough-hewn coral stone, is quite good. Honeymoon package: Eight days/seven nights (BP): $990 to $1,180 per couple (summer season). Includes round-trip transfers between airport and hotel, bottle of sparkling wine in room, full English breakfast daily, welcome cocktail, manager's cocktail party weekly. Winter-season rates: $275 to $380 per couple per night. One of the St. James Beach Hotels.

Coconut Creek Club Hotel, St. James Beach, Barbados (tel. 809/422-2741;

U.S. reservations: 212/696-1323, or toll free 800/372-1323). This small (53-room) hotel is pretty, friendly, and gives you a lot for your money. Designed in Mediterranean style, with white walls and red tiles, the villas are built on a low bluff overlooking the Caribbean, so views from the rooms are marvelous. Guests walk to their beautiful beach down a short flight of limestone steps, and the strand itself is accented by dramatic limestone outcrops. Rooms have smooth tile floors and rattan furniture. The management tries to arrange for honeymooners to have oceanfront rooms, whatever price package they book, and gives couples who return for their anniversaries free bottles of champagne. Water sports are complimentary; exchange dining on the MAP enables you to eat at some of the west coast's finest hotel restaurants. One of the St. James Beach Hotels. Honeymoon package: Seven nights (BP): $865 to $1,050 per couple (mid-May through mid-December). Includes round-trip transfers between airport and hotel, bottle of sparkling wine in room, full English breakfast daily, welcome cocktail, manager's cocktail party weekly. Winter-season rates (MAP): $260 to $300 per couple per night.

SOUTH COAST

Moderate

Marriott's Sam Lord's Castle, St. Philip, Barbados (tel. 809/423-7350; U.S. reservations: toll free 800/228-9290). According to legend, the pirate Sam Lord used false beacons to lure ships onto the reefs. After the vessels foundered, he added their plunder to his treasure chest.

At any rate, Sam's marble-and-mahogany mansion with its Regency antiques is now the focal point of a 72-acre resort hotel, one of the plushest on the island. You might want to stay in one of the ten bedrooms in the castle itself and perhaps get a canopied four-poster bed covered with a brocade bedspread. Or you might choose a gaily decorated cottage room (or suite) with a king-size bed and a sliding glass door opening onto your own sunny terrace. It may take you your entire honeymoon to sample the four restaurants, walk the beach, play on the night-lighted tennis courts, swim in the three swimming pools, and just explore the property. Every night there's an extravaganza of some sort—seven-course feasts, folkloric shows, beach barbecues, rum punch parties. And the hotel's activities desk can arrange just about any other activity on the island you want to try. Honeymoon package: Eight days/ seven nights (EP): From $670 per couple (low season); from $2,180 per couple (high season). Includes welcome fruit basket and bottle of rum, round-trip transfers between airport and hotel, one dinner for two, bottle of champagne, two days' use of minimoke Jeep *or* breakfast and dinner for two for one day.

Ginger Bay Beach Club, St. Philip, Barbados (tel. 809/423-5810; U.S. reservations: 212/535-9530, or toll free 800/223-5581), is a little gem of a hotel where peace and quiet reigns. Each of the 16 suites (and there are suites only—no rooms) has wall-to-wall carpets, mahogany furniture, and a balcony (with hammock) facing the awesome sweep of Crane Beach. The entire hotel is decorated with exquisite taste; the exterior is painted pink, with island flowers delicately stenciled in white here and there. You reach the beach by walking down into the hotel's own limestone caves. There is a freshwater pool, Jacuzzi, tennis, and a fine restaurant, Ginger's, which specializes in smoked meats and fish. Honeymoon package: None. Suites: $132 to $275 per couple per day.

Crane Beach Hotel, St. Philip, Barbados (tel. 809/423-6220; Reservations: 416/674-1880, or toll free 800/387-3998). Have you ever dreamed of honeymooning in a high-ceilinged room with a four-poster bed and a door opening onto one of the world's most beautiful beaches? Crane Beach Hotel, high atop a bluff overlooking the famous beach, can match your fantasy. For sheer history and unsurpassed romance, the Crane is unrivaled. Built in the late 18th century (allegedly by old Sam Lord before he moved up the road), the house subsequently became the first resort in Barbados. Your first view of this white coral-stone hotel with its sapphire pool surrounded by Greek columns and a balustraded terrace will remind you more of an ancient temple than a full-service hotel. But it has two bars, four tennis courts, boutiques on the property, and a restaurant known for its excellent seafood. Every room is unique—adorned with mahogany antiques, pine-plank floors, and high tray ceilings. Honeymooners contemplating a splurge should consider room no. 2 in the East Wing, converted from a former private residence. It woos the senses with a big four-poster bed, captivating touches such as the small shell lamp in the bathroom, and a huge private balcony opening onto the broad lawn and the Atlantic. (Rolling Stone Mick Jagger often stays here.) And one of life's perfect moments comes on evenings when spotlights softly illuminate the sheer cliffs and white beach, and a full moon rises over the Atlantic. Honeymoon package: Eight days/seven nights (EP): $990 per couple for a room; $1,340 per couple for a suite (low season; call for high-season rates). Includes champagne breakfast in bed one morning, dinner with wine one evening, complimentary daytime tennis. Suite package also includes a luncheon or dinner boat cruise and use of a minimoke for two days.

Divi Southwinds Beach Resort, St. Lawrence, Christ Church, Barbados (tel. 809/428-7181; U.S. reservations: 607/277-3484, or toll free 800/367-3484). For the active sun 'n' fun set, the good times begin at this southside hotel where there's always something happening: from nature walks to introductory scuba lessons, fish fries to day sails. You even have three different freshwater pools to practice your strokes in. Surrounded by 20 verdant acres, the resort is conveniently near the shops and restaurants of St. Lawrence Gap. Ensconced in a six-story dazzling white building, the rooms are fresh, crisp, and clean, with white tiled floors, rattan furnishings, and ship-shape blue-and-white color scheme. Satellite TV, radio, and telephone help keep you in touch with the rest of the world; a fully equipped kitchenette allows you to brew up a cup of coffee in the morning, or chill champagne for a nightcap. Along the half-mile beach, a wide choice of water sports await: snorkeling, windsurfing, scuba diving. Two tennis courts are lighted for night play. Honeymoon package: Eight days/seven nights (EP): $1,235 (summer) to $2,545 (winter) per couple for an oceanfront suite. Includes round-trip airport transfers, tax and service charges on room, a bottle of wine, a beach towel, and a souvenir photo album.

Pink and white, airy and light, **Southern Palms Beach Club and Resort Hotel,** St. Lawrence Gap, Christ Church, Barbados (tel. 809/428-7171; U.S. reservations: toll free 800/223-6510), has the easy yet orderly atmosphere that typifies Barbados. Stroll along pathways studded with hand-painted Spanish tiles; gaze at the fish swimming in the lily pond. Rooms are bright and white-walled, with tables and headboards of blond bamboo, accented with flower-splashed fabrics. Their beach is long and beautiful; jog down the waterline or try sailing or windsurfing (water sports are free). If you prefer, there are two freshwater pools. Eat in the arcaded restaurant or walk a few steps to St. Lawrence Gap and enjoy the many eating spots there. The hotel's activities desk will arrange tours, trips, golf, and tennis. Honeymoon package: Eight days/seven nights (EP): $740 to $810 per couple (summer season). Includes round-trip transfers between airport and hotel, bottle of champagne and fruit basket upon arrival, weekly rum punch party, daytime tennis.

Inexpensive

If you like informality and a casual good time, you'll like **Sand Acres Hotel,** Maxwell Coast Road, Christ Church, Barbados (tel. 809/428-7141; U.S. reservations: toll free 800/223-1588), a simple, well-managed group of condos on a beautiful, breezy beach. The property is looking spiffier than ever after a recent refurbishment. Suites, which include living room, bedroom, and kitchen, are neatly furnished with touches of bleached rattan and bright bedspreads. Sliding glass doors lead to your own small terrace with views of pool and beach; bedrooms are air-conditioned. Sand Acres is not a full-service hotel, so unit rates are low, but it has a sparkling pool (the hotel's focal point), tennis, shuffleboard, and a fun, beach bar-style restaurant called Angie's. You're just a step from the beach, so you'll go to sleep lulled by the surf and the trade winds singing in the trees. If you want super restaurants and lively night spots, they're only a short walk away at St. Lawrence Gap. Honeymoon package: None. Standard rates per unit: Low season, $55 to $85 per couple per day; high season, $115 to $165 per day, depending on size.

EAST COAST

Inexpensive

A tiny seven-room hotel, truly far from the madding crowd, **Kingsley Club,** Box 297, Cattlewash, St. Joseph, Barbados (tel. 809/433-9422), has the relaxed atmosphere of a British colonial outpost. Its low room rates are attributable to its isolation on the wild coast of the Scotland district, never to its lack of charm, and its restaurant always gets good reviews. You'll love the breezy turn-of-the-century porch, with its wicker tables and chairs, rather like a veranda on a summer hotel in Maine. Honeymoon package: None. Rooms (EP): $60 to $72 per couple per day.

---

4. Romantic Restaurants and Nightspots

Food in Barbados is good—and getting even better. Hoteliers are ceasing to import the "right kind of fish," frozen, from Europe, and are taking advantage of the local catch, which is excellent. When you eat chubb, grouper, snapper, and dolphin, you can be sure it was swimming just a few hours before. Caribbean spiny lobsters are larger than their New England cousins and their meat is sweet and delicious. On the exotic side, try turtle or a local delicacy called "sea egg," which is actually the meat of a sea urchin. The Barbados equivalent of the American burger is the flying fish sandwich, typically served fried with french fries and cole slaw. Eat it with tartar sauce, to which you've added a tiny bit of spicy mustard sauce. Outstanding! Most restaurants offer Bajan specialties on their menu in addition to American or continental cuisine, so you'll have a good opportunity to try the local vegetable specialties: cou-cou (cornmeal and okra), eddoes (a potato-like vegetable), yams, cassava, and breadfruit. There will be a full array of tropical fruit as well, and a variety of marvelous drinks made with Barbadian rum, one of the smoothest in the world.

When you book a hotel, check whether it has exchange dining. If so, you can buy the meal package (either breakfast and dinner or all three meals) and eat dinner at other hotels and restaurants that participate in the plan.

This roundup will give you an idea of the great variety of restaurants Barbados has to offer.

EXPENSIVE

Built in 1645, **Bagatelle Great House,** Highway 2A, St. Thomas (tel. 425-0666), was the home of Barbados's earliest governors. Its entranceway, a picturesque double stairway with wrought-iron railing, makes it a favorite place for wedding receptions. The cuisine is an elegant mix of Bajan and continental. For appetizers you can have West Indian fish cakes with pepper dip or escargots bourguignon, homemade pumpkin soup or vichyssoise. Entrées feature braised pheasant, beef Wellington, shrimp creole, or local fish. Complete dinners run about $100 per couple for a five-course meal (tax, service charge, and liquor not included). Open Monday through Saturday (and alternate Sundays) for dinner, 7 to 9:30 p.m.

Josef's, St. Lawrence (tel. 428-3379). Dress up for Josef's. This small, exclusive hideaway is low-key, elegant, expensive—and reputedly has the best continental cuisine on the island. Especially well regarded is Josef's way with meat; try filet mignon with sauce béarnaise, rack of lamb, veal Cordon Bleu. Local fish (dolphin, kingfish, barracuda) are fixed continental style. Tempting appetizers (terrine of shrimp and salmon with green sauce, for example) are $3 to $8; entrées, $15 to $30. Open Monday through Friday for lunch, noon to 2 p.m.; Monday through Saturday for dinner, 6:30 to 9:30 p.m.

Palm Terrace, Royal Pavilion Resort, St. James (tel. 422-4444). With sheer oh-my-god glamour that looks as though it derived straight from a Hollywood movie set, the Palm Terrace lends itself to wining, dining, and hand-holding. Seeming acres of luscious pink marble cover the floor, and just steps away through the archways, the sea murmurs sweet nothings to the night. Potted palms placed here and there provide intimate screens for tables for two; soft jazz tinkles on the baby grand piano. The menu highlights "nouvelle Caribbean" cuisine, with an emphasis on steak and lobster. Save room for dessert, such as a flaky mille feuille pastry studded with mango, or pineapple crêpes flamed with kirsch. Prices are stratospheric, but worth it—this is where our Barbadian friends go when they want a super night on the town. Open nightly for dinner, 7 to 9 p.m.; count on spending $100 to $140 per couple plus drinks. For equivalent ambience at a gentler price bite, try the afternoon tea, 3:30 to 6 p.m.—about $20 per couple.

Reid's, Derricks, St. James (tel. 432-7623). Captivating gardens and cool, water-splashed fountains provide the perfect setting for romance at this fine west coast restaurant. Start off with a savory seafood crêpe or stuffed mushroom caps. Main courses are inventive and sumptuous, such as dolphin Rockefeller, first poached, then flamed with Grand Marnier, then served with spinach and cream. For sybarites, there's lobster italiano, sautéed in garlic butter and then tossed with fettuccine Alfredo. Reid's also features an ample selection of beef and chicken dishes, as well as an extensive wine list. Appetizers run $5 to $8.50 per person; entrées, $16.50 to $35. Open nightly from 7 to 9 p.m.

MODERATE

Shirley's Reddy Dun Restaurant, Queen Street, Speightstown, St. Peter (tel. 422-1316). Any gastronome has probably spent hours dreaming of such a place . . . where the instinctive genius of a born chef combines with the finesse of classic French cuisine. Well, *mes petits amis gourmets,* head on up to Speightstown, where Shirley Broome makes miracles happen. Born in the parish of St. Lucy, Shirley modestly admits that she comes from "a family of good cooks" and tells how she's been puttering about the kitchen since she was a little girl. The former sous-chef at Sandy Lane Resort, she was sent to study with famed chef Roger Verger in France. Now she runs her own restaurant right by the water on a small west coast beach. When you arrive, you'll probably be welcomed by Shirley herself, who greets you with a smile as warm as the Bajan sunshine. We advise that you surrender immediately to Shirley's advice as to what's best that day. It might be seafood pasta, exquisite enough to make the finest chefs in Venice beg for the recipe. Often, it's a sublime lobster—Shirley seems to have psychic communication with the crustaceans that convinces them that immortality awaits on your dinner plate. Don't miss dessert. For fun, Shirley experiments with new dishes, and one recent four-star success was the mango mousse, crowned with a creamy froth of mango purée. In short, plan on visiting Shirley's early during your stay in Barbados. You'll surely want to go back again . . . and again. Open Monday through Saturday for lunch, 11 a.m. to 3 p.m. (you can swim also on the beach); dinner, 7 to 9:30 p.m. Dinner for two, about $50 to $70. If you want more information, but can't reach Shirley at the restaurant, call her at home: 427-4641.

Pisces, St. Lawrence Gap, Christ Church (tel. 428-6558). As you sit at your candlelit table on Pisces' open terrace and watch the Gap's harbor lights twinkle, you'll know you're at Barbados' most romantic restaurant. Pisces features the freshest seafood, imaginatively prepared, Bajan style. For appetizers, try kingfish ceviche (pickled in a lime marinade) or filets of flying fish stuffed with caviar and chopped egg. For an entrée, try blackened dolphin, coated with Cajun spices and pan fried or a Pisces platter with a variety of local fish. There are also several excellent lobster dishes. Open nightly for dinner, 6:30 to 9:30 p.m.; about $40 per couple; $70 per couple if you order lobster.

Koko's, Prospect, St. James (tel. 424-4557). Enjoy superb Bajan *cuisine moderne* in this seaside bistro where you'll be serenaded by tree frogs, lulled by the swoosh of the surf—a honeymoon "must visit." Owners Steven and Sandra Toppin, a brother-and-sister duo, originally hail from Grenada, known as the "Spice Island." They remain true to their heritage with deft handling of seasonings: piquant enough to keep things interesting without needing to call in the fire engines. Menu entries sport perky names: "Spice Island Invaders" translates as stuffed local crab; "Limbo Three Degree" denotes a prime beef tenderloin flamed with rum and swathed with a trio of sauces. All come with expertly prepared peas 'n' rice plus fresh local veggies, such as christophene or plantains. Open nightly for dinner, 6:30 to 10 p.m.; about $60 per couple plus drinks.

Atlantis, Bathsheba Beach, St. Joseph (tel. 433-9445). Do not miss the extraordinary island buffet served Wednesday afternoons and after church on Sundays. Tourists and islanders line up near the buffet tables to see the food brought in, and each dish is labeled so you know what you're getting. This is Bajan food untouched by European hands—pepperpot, pumpkin fritters, salt-fish stew, yam pie, fried chicken, roast pork and more—all with creole spices. Fill up your plate and eat at your oilcloth-covered table overlooking Bathsheba's small fishing fleet and the pounding Atlantic surf. All you can eat: $30 per person. Drinks extra. Open daily for breakfast, 8 to 9 a.m.; lunch, 12:30 to 3 p.m.; dinner, 6 to 8 p.m.

Carambola, Derrick's, St. James (tel. 432-0832). Fine dining with a view is the specialty of the house here. A brick entryway leads to an expansive terrace poised on a small bluff over the Caribbean. Part of the deck is built right into the cliff so that the boulders seem more like sculpture, counterpointed by colorful flowers. Although the menu highlights fresh fish and seafood, there are plenty of tempting steak, chicken, and veal dishes for landlubbers. And on moonlit nights, the setting is pure magic. Dinner for two, $40 to $70 plus drinks. Open for dinner, 6:30 to 9:30 p.m.; closed Sunday. Reservations a must.

INEXPENSIVE

Bamboo Beach Bar, Paynes Bay, St. James (tel. 432-0910). Sun worshippers can stay at this barefoot bar through lunch and dinner and never leave the beach. Good, basic food is served here at reasonable prices, such as a toasted cheese, ham, and pineapple sandwich for $3.50. Luncheons in a basket—burgers, or shrimp with chips and salad—vary from $6 to $10. Dinner is a bit more expensive, but the food is just as healthful and basic. Try creole shrimp or a chicken casserole flavored with rum. Dinner for two, about $40. Open daily for lunch, noon to 3 p.m.; dinner, 7 to 10 p.m.

Barbados has a lot of great places when you just want to hang out. Sit at your harborside table and watch the boats go in and out of Bridgetown at the **Waterfront Café,** Cavans Lane, on the Careenage (tel. 427-0093). Open for lunch and dinner (dinners $40 to $50 per couple); live entertainment. Open daily from noon to 9:30 p.m.

Need a TV fix? **T.G.I. Boomers,** St. Lawrence Gap (tel. 428-8439), is a garden restaurant with a satellite television, and good American/Bajan meals that are reasonably priced. Off-season, get a bacon-and-egg breakfast for $5 per person. Lunches run about $8, while dinner will cost about $30 to $40 per couple, including soup, salad, entrée, rice or potatoes, and vegetables of the day. They also offer an excellent selection of Caribbean beers, including Red Stripe, Carib, and Barbados' own Banks brew. Open daily for breakfast, 8 to 11:30 a.m.; lunch, 11:30 a.m. to 3 p.m.; dinner, 5:30 to 9:45 p.m. A great pub-style bar and restaurant is **The Ship Inn,** St. Lawrence (tel. 428-9605). Meet island people, listen to impromptu performers, and sing along. Great bar snacks at $8 to $11. If you crave heartier fare, the adjoining **Carvery** serves up an ample grill buffet with five different meats, $18 per person. Open for lunch, noon to 3 p.m.; dinner, 6:30 to 10:30 p.m.; live entertainment nightly from 6 p.m. to 2 a.m. **The Barbados Windsurfing Club,** Oistin's Bay (tel. 428-7277), offers good, inexpensive food in a friendly atmosphere right on the beach. It's famous for its rotis—chicken, beef, or shrimp curry wrapped in a light pastry. Lunches $10 to $20 per couple. Open daily from 11 a.m. to 8:30 p.m.

For honeymooners on the go, what better destination than "the street that never sleeps," **Baxter's Road.** In the evening, the area pulsates with a friendly, good-times-bound blend of Barbadians and visitors, who come to move to the beat of live bands, "fire a grog" (drink), and sample Bajan specialties such as fish, chicken, and corn-on-the-cob, fresh-grilled over coalpots by the roadside. If your romancing includes dancing, point your shoes towards **Harbour Lights,** Marine Villa, Bay Street (tel. 436-7225), an open-air beachfront club overlooking Carlisle Bay which headlines top-name entertainers; open nightly. Another favorite when you want to step out is **Warehouse,** set in a 200-year-old building on Cavans Lane in Bridgetown (tel. 436-2897). They also showcase the Caribbean's hottest bands—and a cool, air-conditioned dance floor. Open Monday through Saturday; doors generally open at 9:30 p.m. The most elegant *boîte* in town is certainly **Secret Garden** (tel. 425-2222), next to Bagatelle Great House. On the air-conditioned dance floor, you can enjoy soft rock and oldies; at intimate tables, there's backgammon—all until the early hours of the morning. Also a restaurant, Secret Garden serves up cuisine redolent of faraway places . . . salmon à la russe, chicken tandoori, Thai pan beef, coconut fish curry, with entrées priced about $15 to $18. Open from 8:30 p.m. "till whenever."

BERMUDA

They tell the story about the famous watercolor artist who arrived in Bermuda and intended to remain two weeks. He ended up staying over 40 years. "I want to get the color of the water right," he explained. Certainly, capturing the proper nuance of Bermudian ocean blue is difficult, because at any given time, the sea reflects hundreds of shades—pale aqua, peacock turquoise, a most royal blue, and every gradation in between.

The colors are what you tend to remember most about Bermuda. Flowers bloom and burgeon everywhere: magenta bougainvillea tumbling over railings, pale pink oleander hedges lining roadways, fragrant purple passion flowers climbing up limestone walls. Both prim little cottages and large mansions are painted pastel shades of pink, lavender, mint, and yellow, and topped with white step roofs that positively sparkle in the sunshine. Bright green casuarinas bob in the breeze. And, of course, there are the blush-pink coral sand beaches, gently bathed by the surf.

The word "fairyland" might be overused, but it perfectly describes the ambience and landscapes of Bermuda. Contrary to what most people believe, Bermuda is not a Caribbean island, but rather lies in the Atlantic Ocean about 600 miles due east of North Carolina's Cape Hatteras. Although palm trees flourish, the climate is actually subtropical. Bermuda is not just one island, but rather is composed of approximately 150 different ones, many linked by bridges and causeways. When seen from the air, the island group resembles a fish hook, and the chain is about 22 miles long and 2½ miles wide at its broadest part. Built on the pinnacle of an extinct volcano, the islands are fairly flat, formed from lava, coral, and sandy limestone.

Ever since its earliest history, Bermuda has seemed tinged by magic. The islands were discovered in 1503 by a Spaniard, Juan de Bermúdez, who named the islands but did not settle them. Because of the treacherous reefs, early seafarers feared that the islands were inhabited by spirits. A shipwreck actually led to the settlement of Bermuda. In 1609, Admiral Sir George Somers was on his way to the new British colony in Jamestown, Virginia. Instead, he ran aground on Bermudian reefs in a hurricane, totally destroying his ship, the *Sea Venture*. Miraculously, everybody on board—some 150 people—were unharmed. Also to their wonder, the islands were richly stocked with food supplies—fish, birds, turtles, prickly pear, and even wild pigs (left by the Spanish). It took passengers and crew nearly a year to build two new, small pinnaces, constructed from the remains of the *Sea Venture* and native Bermudian cedar. These two ships, named the *Deliverance* and the *Patience,* sailed for Virginia in 1610. Tales of their adventures soon reached England, and William Shakespeare used these legends of "the still-vex'd Bermoothes" as the source for his play *The Tempest*.

The first formal settlement of Bermuda was established in 1612 at St. George's, at the eastern end of the island, and the first parliament sat in 1620 (making Bermuda's parliament the third oldest in the world, after Britain and Iceland). Slaves were brought to the islands in 1616, mainly to work as household servants and carpenters. Slavery was finally abolished in 1834.

Bermuda's population today numbers just over 57,000. It is Britain's oldest self-governing colony, administered by a governor who is the official representative of the queen, and a two-house parliament. The island is divided into nine parishes, all with names recalling the old country: St. George's, Hamilton, Smith's, Devonshire, Pembroke, Paget, Warwick, Southampton, and Sandys. Hamilton, Bermuda's capital, is located roughly in the middle of Bermuda, in Pembroke Parish. As you travel around the countryside, you'll observe the many links with British traditions: the white-uniformed cricket players, automobiles driving on the left, and the ritual of afternoon tea. Another local custom you'll notice is the gracious hospitality with which visitors are treated. Bermudians (known as "Onions") make everyone feel like honored guests, not mere tourists, and honeymooners receive especially warm welcomes.

Because Bermuda is so compact, you'll find it easy to explore from top to tip. Start your sightseeing in Hamilton, the capital, the center for shopping, dining, and nightlife. Take a photo of the Birdcage, where a Bermuda-shorts-clad bobby (policeman) directs traffic. Intersperse your shopping forays along Front Street with a bit of history. You'll want to see city hall, the Bermuda Cathedral, and Sessions House, where Parliament meets (you can attend sittings). Then stroll over to pretty Par-La-Ville Gardens on Queen Street. Here, the Bermuda Historical Society Museum at the Library has a collection of Bermuda newspapers dating back to 1787 and other memorabilia, such as a sea chest that belonged to Sir George Somers, considered Bermuda's founder. Stop by the Perot Post Office, named for William Bennett Perot, Bermuda's first postmaster. Mr. Perot, who designed Bermuda's first stamp, was a bit eccentric—he used to carry letters in the crown of his top hat while delivering mail.

Continue your explorations west to Somerset, east to St. George's, or down to the south shore beaches (see details under "Romantic Interludes"). As you whiz along on your scooters or in the pink-and-blue buses, you'll get the feel for the postcard-pretty scenery that characterizes the island. Honeymooners will be intrigued by Bermuda's moongates, round arches of coral stone shaped like a full moon. According to Chinese legend, moongates symbolize happiness and unity, and lovers who walk through them are assured good luck and happiness. The tradition was brought to Bermuda by a sea captain. You'll find moongates throughout Bermuda, and you'll surely want to walk through several different ones on your honeymoon.

Much of the charm of Bermuda comes from its love of traditions. Change is never undertaken lightly. After all, this is a place that did not permit private automobiles until 1946. Page one of the daily newspapers still announces "lighting up time"—the hour when carriage lanterns must be lit. Neon signs are expressly forbidden. Fifty years from now, if you return to Bermuda for your golden wedding anniversary, you'll probably find the gentle island very much like it is today.

Maybe those early mariners were right, and Bermuda is enchanted. Not by sea spirits, however—but because of the beautiful surroundings and the hospitable Bermudians themselves. Mark Twain, who often wintered here in the early 1900s, wrote, "Americans on their way to heaven call at Bermuda and think they have already arrived." It is a sentiment with which honeymooners still heartily agree today.

1. Practical Facts

GETTING THERE

Americans and Canadians must show proof of citizenship, such as a passport or birth certificate, as well as a return or ongoing ticket. Leaving Bermuda, there is a $10 departure tax at the airport; the $30 per-person port tax for cruise ship passengers is included in the ticket price.

You'll find Bermuda easy to reach by air or by sea from major east coast cities.

By Air

The following airlines fly nonstop to Bermuda: **Pan American, Continental, British Airways, Delta, American, Air Canada.** Flying time is so short, you'll barely have time to eat the meal and open your book: less than 1½ hours from New York.

By Ship

Start your honeymoon in Bermuda with a honeymoon to Bermuda—aboard a romantic cruise ship. From mid-April through the end of October, several different cruise lines regularly sail to Bermuda from New York and other ports, including **Kloster Cruises, Royal Caribbean Cruise Line,** and **Chandris Celebrity Cruises.** Ships call at the West End pier at Royal Navy Dockyard, St. George's, or right on Front Street, Hamilton—extremely convenient for shopping.

GETTING AROUND

Because Bermuda is so compact—only 21 square miles—you'll find it easy to get where you want to go. Please note that to prevent congestion and preserve Bermuda's unhurried lifestyle, visitors are not permitted to rent cars. We think you'll find this a veritable blessing.

By Taxi

Bermuda's taxis are absolutely tops: The drivers are extremely knowledgeable, and the vehicles themselves are meticulously maintained (you'll usually spot drivers polishing up their cars while they wait for fares). It's easy to find taxis at stands in Hamilton and in front of hotels. At restaurants, you telephone for a pickup and the cabs arrive promptly. Rates are fairly moderate: about $2.80 for the first mile, and $1.55 for each additional mile. For in-depth sightseeing, you can hire a taxi driver displaying the official blue Tour Guide flag. To qualify, drivers must pass an extensive exam, and there's hardly anything they don't know about Bermuda. The sightseeing rate for a cab is $22 per hour—extremely reasonable, especially if you choose to share the cost of the tour with another honeymoon couple.

By Moped

This is one of the most convenient, chipper, and fun ways to get around Bermuda. Mopeds (also known as scooters or motor-assisted bikes) can be rented from many different cycle liveries throughout the island. If you can ride a bicycle, you can ride a moped—practice a bit in the parking lot before you zoom off into rush-hour traffic. Both single-seater (about $25 per day; $73 per week) and two-seater ($32 per day; $125 per week) models are available. Remember—driving is on the left (use caution in the roundabouts), and wear your helmets.

BERMUDA

□ PARK

ATLANTIC OCEAN

ATLANTIC OCEAN

Miles
Kilometers

ST. GEORGE'S PARISH

Fort St. Catherine
St. Catherine Beach
Fort Albert
St. George's
St. George's Harbour
FERRY RD.
KINDLEY FIELD RD.
CAUSEWAY
Int'l Airport

Blue Grotto
Leamington Caves
Castle Harbour

Bermuda Pottery
Crystal Caves

Harrington Sound

HAMILTON PARISH

Pink Beach

Flatts
Devil's Hole

Spanish Rock

SMITH'S PARISH

Shelly Bay Beach

Aquarium, Museum & Zoo

NORTH SHORE RD.

MIDDLE RD.

DEVONSHIRE PARISH

Ft. Hamilton

Hamilton

PEMBROKE PARISH

PAGET PARISH

SOUTH RD.

Coral Beach

Flamingo Beach

WARWICK PARISH

Maritime Museum

Grassy Bay

HARBOUR RD.

MIDDLE RD.

Hamilton Harbour

Great Sound

Ferry

Ferry

Ferry

Little Sound

SOUTH RD.

SOUTHAMPTON PARISH

MIDDLE RD.

Ely's Harbour

Cambridge Beaches

Mangrove Bay

Somerset

SANDYS PARISH

SOMERSET BRIDGE

Ferry

By Bicycle

Bermuda is fairly flat, so bicycle riding makes for peaceful touring. Rates run about $15 per day for the first day; $6 for each additional day.

By Ferry

You'll definitely fall in love with Bermuda's jaunty ferries, which ply many different routes between the various islands, including Hamilton to Somerset or Hamilton to Ireland Island at Bermuda's northernmost tip. It's more like taking a sightseeing cruise than mere transportation. Fares are very inexpensive: from $1 to $2, depending on how far you are going. If you like, you can take your bikes or scooters on board, and then cycle back (a very popular excursion goes from Somerset back along the South Shore beaches).

By Bus

Bermuda's blue-and-pink buses provide another inexpensive, efficient way to get around the island. Bus rides run $1.25 to $2.50, based on distance. You must have exact fare in coins—paper money is not acceptable. You can also use tokens or tickets. You can get both tokens and fare information at your hotel.

LANGUAGE AND MONEY

Very proper English is spoken—you might even come home with a bit of an English accent. Although the U.S. dollar is accepted everywhere, the legal tender is the Bermuda Dollar (BD$), which is officially pegged to the American currency: 1 Bd$ = 1 US$. Also like the U.S. dollar, the Bermudian currency is divided into 100 cents. Traveler's checks and credit cards are accepted in most—but not all— restaurants, shops, and hotels. Be sure to ask in advance.

WEATHER

Bermuda is subtropical and has two real seasons: spring and summer. Summer temperatures prevail from late May until mid-November, the warmest months being July, August, and the beginning of September, with temperatures in the mid-80s (10° cooler in the evening). From November through April, temperatures range in the 60s and 70s. Rainfall is fairly evenly divided throughout the year and usually comes in the form of passing showers; all-day storms are very infrequent.

CLOTHING

During the warmer months, dress for summer—bring bathing suits and nice cotton sportswear. Also take along light sweaters or wraps for evenings. From December through March, bring spring and fall-weight clothing: light wools, plus a raincoat or windbreaker. Part of the fun of a Bermuda honeymoon is dressing up a bit—most restaurants require that men don a jacket and tie in the evenings, and women will have plenty of opportunities to wear trousseau finery. Dress is conservative—a legacy of Bermuda's British heritage. Bathing suits and bare feet are acceptable only at the beach and pool, not in town, public areas of hotels, nor aboard mopeds. Tennis whites are required on most courts.

TIME

Bermuda is on Atlantic Standard Time during the winter and observes Daylight Saving Time in the summer, so it is always one hour ahead of U.S. East Coast cities. When it is noon in New York, it is 1 p.m. in Bermuda.

TELEPHONES

You can call Bermuda direct from the United States. First dial 809 (the area code) and then the seven-digit phone number.

SHOPPING

The wide selection of stores and fine quality of merchandise make shopping a highlight of many Bermuda stays. Stores painted cheery shades of yellow, orange, pink, and green line Hamilton's Front Street, and you'll enjoy strolling from one to the other under the covered promenades. Many of Bermuda's best-known stores such as Cooper's, Smith's, and Trimingham's also have branches in St. George's and many hotels.

Although Bermuda is not a duty-free port, taxes are quite low, and you will find that prices are substantially lower than at home on many items, especially British imports. In addition, Bermuda has no sales tax. Best shopping bets include:

China and crystal: Consider using some of your wedding checks to fill out your patterns—all at substantial savings. Compared with U.S. prices, you can generally save 40% on fine bone china from Wedgwood, Royal Doulton, Aynsley, Royal Worcester, Spode, Minton, and other lines. On crystal, prices run about 30% lower on Waterford, Orreförs, Lalique, Baccarat, Galway, and others. You'll also find similar savings on decorative figurines from Lladró, Boehm, and Royal Copenhagen. The stores are all very experienced at packing purchases for you to carry to the United States. Also, they can arrange to ship items home for you. Although costs will be higher than if you carried items with you, you will still realize substantial savings over stateside prices.

Clothing and accessories: You'll find a large selection of classic sportswear, such as Shetland sweaters and Harris tweed jackets, which run about 30% to 50% less than in the United States. Ditto for cashmeres by Jaeger and Pringle, and raincoats from Burberry. Other good buys include cotton rugby shirts, wooly Icelandic sweaters, and authentic kilts and blazers.

Imported cosmetics and perfumes: Save from 20% to 30% on makeup from European companies, such as Orlane, Christian Dior, Chanel, Lancôme, and Yves Saint Laurent. Savings are similar on fragrances such as Chanel No. 5, Opium, L'Air du Temps, Joy, and other famous scents.

Watches and jewelry: Currently a very good deal in Bermuda, with savings on top-of-the-line designs by Concord, Movado, and others, as well as on more inexpensive, "fun" timepieces, such as Swatch watches.

Art and antiques: Bermuda has several well-known watercolor artists, and a painting of one of your favorite landscapes will always bring back fond memories of your honeymoon. You can also browse through old prints, nautical curios, and fine English and Bermudian antiques. Remember that you can bring back antiques over 100 years old and original art duty-free: Just make sure to get proper certificates when you make your purchases.

Wines, liquor, and liqueurs: You'll get the best savings (up to 40%) on English gin and scotch, as well as local Bermudian potions such as rum for swizzles. Please note that if you want to take liquor home, it is sold "in-bond"—you must purchase it at least 24 hours before your departure, and the store will deliver it to your airplane or cruise ship before you leave.

Linens and fabrics: To show off your new china and crystal, set your table with Irish linens, Brussels lace, or Portuguese hand-embroideries. If you sew, you can save on fabric by the yard: English tweeds, Scottish tartans, Italian and French provincial-style cotton prints.

Only in Bermuda: Look for unique items either made in Bermuda or specially designed for the country. One of the most popular choices include gold or silver charms or jewelry, shaped like the Bermuda longtail bird, surreys, or seashells. Many stores feature items made from local Bermuda cedar, including bookends, candlesticks, and classic Bermuda handbags, with a wooden handle and fabric cover that can be unbuttoned and changed with the season. For a fragrant souvenir of your honeymoon, consider perfumes made from Bermuda's own blossoms: lilies, passionflower, oleander, jasmine, and roses. You can buy them at Bermuda Perfumery and Gardens in Bailey's Bay, as well as many stores in town. To make an authentic Bermuda fish chowder or spike your Bloody Marys back home, pick up some spicy Outerbridge's Sherry Peppers. And when you want to brew up rum swizzles, you'll need Bermuda black rum, such as Black Seal. Also consider Bermuda Gold liqueur, made from loquats.

All of the following stores are located on Front Street, unless otherwise noted. Many also have several branches in hotels.

A.S. Cooper & Sons, Ltd.: The oldest china and glassware store in Bermuda, Cooper's carries Wedgwood, Royal Doulton, Belleek, Aynsley, Royal Copenhagen, Villeroy & Boch, and other fine china; Waterford, Orrefors, and Atlantis crystal; and Georg Jensen silver. They also have a fine men's shop, and their ladies' shop carries Jaeger sportswear.

H.A. & E. Smith Ltd.: Serving Bermudians for nearly 100 years, Smith's has the exclusive for Burberry raincoats and accessories, and has one of the widest selections of Shetland sweaters for both men and women, in up-to-date, fashion-right colors and designs. You'll also find bone china by Royal Doulton and Minton, Lladró figurines, and Waterford crystal. They also sell wool tartans and Liberty prints by the yard, cosmetics, and fragrances.

Trimingham's: You'll find one of the largest selections in Bermuda: sweaters, woolens, and other fashions, French perfumes, as well as china by Royal Worcester, Meissen, and Aynsley, Irish crystal by Waterford and Galway, Hermès and Liberty silk scarves, Italian leather accessories, as well as original-design gold jewelry.

Astwood Dickinson: Your stop for jewelry and watches, including timepieces from Patek Philippe, Omega, Movado, and Concord; plus a wide selection of Bermuda charms.

Bluck's: Carries Lalique, Baccarat, Waterford, Spode, Royal Doulton, Royal Worcester, Minton, and others.

Crisson's: Look through their selection of fine jewelry and gemstones, as well as watches from Rolex, Piaget, Baume & Mercier, Cartier, Ebel, Raymond Weil, and others.

Benetton: A new addition to Bermuda, this line found around the world features colorful casual clothes—knits and cottons, skirts and sweaters, you name it! All very well made, very fashionable—and priced about 30% less than back home.

Pegasus Prints and Maps (Pitts Bay Road across from the Hamilton Princess): Collectors of antique maps and prints will delight in browsing through their displays of maps and prints, including fine botanicals, caricatures, engravings of horses, fox-hunting, birds, and shells. Also a wonderful selection of inexpensive Bermuda map reproductions.

Irish Linen Shop: Fine linens from Ireland, to be sure, but also hand-embroideries from Madeira, Brussels lace, and an exclusive selection of the famous Souleiado line of French provincial cottons and accessories.

Bananas: Want something that says "Bermuda"? You can probably find it here —T-shirts, umbrellas, beach bags, and towels.

Bermuda Book Store (Baxters) Ltd.: Both a bibliophile's and a Bermuda-phile's paradise, with an extensive selection of books about Bermuda (from ghosts to antiques), as well as European periodicals, plus thrillers and romances for beach reading.

And for liquor: **Gosling Bros., Bermuda Wines & Spirits,** and **Frith's** all have extensive selections of the most popular brands, and can make complete arrangements for in-bond delivery.

Each U.S. citizen can bring back $400 worth of goods duty free, including one liter of liquor and one carton of cigarettes. If you bring back more, you'll have to pay Customs duty. On the first $1,000 worth of goods over your $400 duty-free allowance, you will be taxed at a flat rate of 10% of the retail value of the goods. For a complete explanation of U.S. Customs regulations, see the introduction to this book.

SPORTS

If you're interested in the sporting life, you'll have plenty of opportunities to enjoy your favorite pastimes in Bermuda.

Golf: Bermuda is especially well known for its eight challenging golf courses. Many of the holes at the tough **Castle Harbour Golf Club** (tel. 293-2040) feature breathtaking views of the Atlantic. Robert Trent Jones designed the courses at **Port Royal Golf Course** (tel. 234-0974) and **St. George's Golf Club** (tel. 297-8067). Other public courses include the **Belmont Hotel Golf & Beach Club** (tel. 236-1301); **Ocean View Golf & Country Club** (tel. 292-6758); and **Princess Golf Club** (tel. 238-0446). The **Riddells Bay Golf & Country Club** (tel. 238-1060) and **Mid Ocean Club** (tel. 293-0330) are private; introduction by a member is required. Daily greens fees run from about $15 to $65; if a hotel has a golf course, greens fees sometimes are reduced for guests.

Tennis: Tennis has been a Bermudian passion for over 100 years. In fact, it was a Bermudian, Mary Gray Outerbridge, who introduced the game to the United States. There are over 100 courts on the island, many lighted for night play. In the hotel listings that follow, we mention which properties have tennis courts; and many hotels permit both guests and visitors to play. Court time might be free or very inexpensive (about $5.50 per hour) for hotel guests; up to $13.50 per hour for visitors. Please note that tennis whites are preferred on all courts, and are mandatory on several.

Snorkeling and scuba-diving: Bermuda has the clearest water in the western Atlantic, and you'll be dazzled by the variety of fish and coral you can observe. Snorkelers might want to take one of the half-day boat trips offered by **Bermuda Water Sports** at the Grotto Bay Beach Hotel (tel. 293-2640), **Nautilus Diving** at the Princess Hotel (tel. 238-2332), **Bermuda Cruise & Bermuda Water Tours** in Hamilton (tel. 295-3727), **Blue Water Divers** at Somerset Bridge (tel. 234-1034), and **South Side Scuba** at the Sonesta Beach Hotel (tel. 238-1833). Half-day trips run about $30 and generally include snacks and rum swizzles. The reefs that surround Bermuda have claimed the lives of many a vessel, and scuba-divers will want to explore famous shipwrecks such as the *Mari Celeste*, an 1863 paddle steamer; and the *Minnie Breslauer*, an English ship that ran aground in 1783. Most of the above operators also run scuba-diving programs; a one-tank dive costs about $60. They also offer an introductory "learn to dive" program that will first teach you the basics, then take you out for a supervised shallow-water dive, about $85. Bermuda also has several unique "helmet-diving" operations, in which you wear a Jules Verne-style helmet and walk along the sea bottom (you do not have to know how to swim). It costs about $30 per person; contact **Hartley Helmet Diving Cruise** (tel. 292-4434) or **Hartley's Under Sea Adventure** (tel. 234-2861) for details. You can also relish a thrilling underwater adventure—without even getting wet. The submarine *Enterprise* (tel. 236-8000) takes passengers down to 70 feet below the surface to explore coral reefs, marine life, and eerie shipwrecks. Often, visibility reaches 200 feet. The *Enterprise* offers hourly dives from 9:30 a.m. to 3:30 p.m.; cost is $50 per person.

Other water sports: Bermuda has world-class conditions for other activities, such as sailing, deep-sea fishing, windsurfing, and waterskiing. Many Bermuda hotels have their own water-sports facilities, or can make outside arrangements for you. For complete information about all sports in Bermuda, get a copy of the free "Bermuda Sportsman's Guide," issued by the Bermuda Department of Tourism.

SPECIAL EVENTS

No matter what time of year you honeymoon, there's sure to be fun going on.

Bermuda Rendezvous Season: Every year from mid-November until early March, Bermuda welcomes vacationers with a series of special events: crafts demonstrations, fashion shows, golf tournaments, a performing arts festival. Every day, there are different free programs: a guided walking tour of Hamilton; a skirling ceremony with kilted pipers, drummers, and dancers at Fort Hamilton; tours through the Botanical Gardens or Camden, the official residence of the premier. Get complete details from the Bermuda Department of Tourism.

January through mid-February—Bermuda Festival. Spotlighting classical music, dance, jazz, drama, and entertainment.

January—Bermuda International Marathon. Attracts top runners; also a 10K race.

Late March to mid-May—Open Houses and Garden Tours. Every Wednesday, many residences are open to the public.

Good Friday. Traditional kite-flying day.

Late April—Invitational International Race Week. Yachtsmen from all over the world compete.

Late May—Bermuda Day. With dinghy races and the annual half-marathon.

Mid-June—The Queen's Birthday. Celebrated with a military parade in Hamilton.

Mid-June—Yacht Races. In even-numbered years, it's the Newport-to-Bermuda race; in odd years, the Annapolis-to-Bermuda contest.

Late July—Cricket Festival. Two days of matches.

October/November—Convening of Parliament. The governor opens Parliament amid traditional military ceremonies.

December 26—Boxing Day. Appearances of the Bermuda Gombey Dancers and various sporting events.

HOW TO GET MARRIED IN BERMUDA

It's hard to imagine a more romantic setting for a wedding than Bermuda, with its pink sands, aqua waters, and pretty gardens everywhere. If you want a church wedding, a favorite is the Bermuda Cathedral in Hamilton. Most nonchurch weddings can be performed in the registry (by appointment); other locales can be arranged with the consent of clergy. You might want to incorporate Bermudian traditions into your wedding, such as arriving at the ceremony in a horse-drawn carriage. It's also a custom for the bride and groom to have separate wedding cakes (which can be small): the groom's wrapped in gold paper (symbolizing prosperity), the bride's in silver. The bride's portion of the cake is kept until the christening of the first-born child. In addition, a tiny cedar tree is usually placed in the center of the top cake tier and later planted—with the idea that as the tree grows, so will love. Another tradition you'll surely want to follow is to walk through a moongate together for good luck. Here's how to make arrangements for a wedding in Bermuda.

1. No blood tests or health certificates are required.
2. Obtain a "Notice of Intended Marriage" form, available from the Bermuda Department of Tourism offices in New York, Boston, Chicago, Atlanta, and Toronto.
3. Send the completed form, along with $86 (must be a bank draft made payable to the Accountant General, Hamilton, Bermuda—personal checks not accepted) to: The Registrar General, Government Administration Building, Parliament Street, Hamilton HM 12, Bermuda.
4. The notice will be published by the registrar in Bermuda newspapers. Fourteen days later, the license will be issued. You do not have to be present in Bermuda during the waiting period. The license will be mailed to your home address, unless you request it to be held in Bermuda for your arrival. The license remains valid for three months.
5. The fee for a marriage in the registry is $89; the marriage certificate costs an additional $12 to $18.

Many hotels can help you make wedding arrangements; you can also contact the Bermuda Department of Tourism at one of the addresses below if you have specific questions.

FOR FURTHER INFORMATION

Contact the **Bermuda Department of Tourism.** Bermuda: Global House, 43 Church St., Hamilton HM12, Bermuda (tel. 809/292-0023). New York: Suite 201, 310 Madison Ave., New York, NY 10017 (tel. 212/818-9800, or toll free 800/BERMUDA nationwide; 800/223-6107 in New York State). Atlanta: Suite 2008, 235 Peachtree St., NE, Atlanta, GA 30303 (tel. 404/524-1541). Boston: Suite 1010, 44 School St., Boston, MA 02108 (tel. 617/782-0404). Chicago: Suite 1070, Randolph-Wacker Building, 150 North Wacker Dr., Chicago, IL 60606 (tel. 312/782-5486). Los Angeles: John A. Tetley, Inc., Suite 601, 3075 Wilshire Blvd., Los Angeles, CA 90010 (tel. 213/388-1151). Toronto: Suite 1004, 1200 Bay St., Toronto, ON, Canada M5R 2A5 (tel. 416/923-9600).

2. Romantic Interludes

Bermuda may only be 21 square miles in size, but every inch seems packed with romantic possibilities.

Yes, the **sands** really are pink—tinged a rosy hue by tiny specks of pink coral mingled in with the sand. Complete the pretty picture with crystal-clear waters the color of molten turquoise and stark limestone formations that jut out of the water like some strange, prehistoric sea dragons—and you know why Bermuda's beaches rank among the best in the world. Many of the beaches are public, and you'll have fun trying out the different strands. You'll soon note an unusual phenomenon—the beaches never seem to get crowded, mainly because there are over 20 fine ones to choose from.

Bermuda's most celebrated sands lie along the South Shore. Horseshoe Bay is a favorite—one of the longest sandy stretches on the island, it has a water-sports concession, snackbar, and toilet facilities. Warwick, just nearby, is another top choice. Honeymooners will want to get to Jobson's Cove early to set up their beach towels in one of the small caves that line the shore. Reef-enclosed Church Bay offers excellent snorkeling. Long Bay is shallow—perfect for sunbathers and nonswimmers. John Smith's Bay has some of the pinkest sands on the island.

What goes together as well as love and marriage? Certainly, a leisurely ride in a **horse-drawn Bermuda surrey,** which will slowly wend its way down Front Street, then softly clop along roads just outside of town (one popular route takes in the elegant residential area called Fairylands). As you mosey along, the driver will regale you with a delightful blend of Bermuda fact and fiction. A single horse-drawn carriage runs about $16.50 for a half hour for two; you can find carriages for hire along Front Street in Hamilton.

Perhaps you'd rather explore Bermuda from **horseback.** You'll trot along country lanes bordered by hibiscus and oleander, and wooded bridle paths. The caliber of the horses is generally excellent. **Spicelands Riding Center** on Middle Road in Warwick (tel. 238-8212 or 238-8246) offers a wide range of programs for both experienced and novice riders. We highly recommend the morning breakfast ride, which follows back roads to the beach for a long canter along the surf. Afterward, return to the stable for a hearty ranch-style breakfast. It costs $38.50 per person. Spicelands also runs guided rides along the historic Railway Trail, $22 per person for the one-hour excursion. All rides are accompanied by qualified instructors; long pants and shoes with hard heels are recommended. Escorted one-hour trail rides are also available through **Lee Bow Riding Centre** in Devonshire (tel. 292-4181).

One-and-a-half-million years of nature's handiwork has gone into sculpting

Crystal and Leamington Caves, high vaulted grottos eroded in the porous lime-stone rock from which Bermuda is formed. Crystal Caves were discovered in 1907 by two schoolboys looking for a lost cricket ball. What they found was a cavern filled with stalactites and stalagmites, and crystal-clear Cahow Lake. Located near Bailey's Bay, Crystal Caves are open daily except some holidays; admission is $2.50 per person (tel. 293-0640). Leamington Caves covers nearly two areas of crystal formations as well as several underground pools and a large grotto. Located near the Plantation Restaurant near Bailey's Bay, Leamington Caves are open Monday through Saturday, 9:30 a.m. to 4:30 p.m.; admission is $2.75 per person (tel. 293-0336).

Spend the day exploring the western part of Bermuda, **Sandys Parish.** From Hamilton, you (and your mopeds or bicycles) can hop aboard the ferry to the Dockyard complex on Ireland Island ($2 per person). If you're fascinated by legends of sunken galleons and pieces of eight, head for the **Maritime Museum** at the Royal Navy Dockyard (open daily from 10 a.m. to 4:30 p.m.; admission $5.50 per person). Here, you can view the treasure recovered from a ship that foundered on the reefs off Bermuda in 1595. Another must for history buffs is the multiprojector presentation of **"Attack on Washington"** at the Dockyard Theatre (tel. 238-0432 or 234-1709). Vivid with special effects, the film relates the role Bermuda played in the War of 1812, including the burning of the White House and the battle at Fort McHenry. Continuous shows run daily from 10 a.m. to 4 p.m.; admission is $2.75. Also visit the **Bermuda Arts Centre** (tel. 234-2809), which exhibits and sells works by local artists. Open Tuesday through Friday, 10 a.m. to 4:30 p.m.; Saturday and Sunday, 10 a.m. to 5 p.m.; admission is $1. Browse through the high-quality selection of made-in-Bermuda products at the **Craft Market** (tel. 234-3208) in Building 28 at the Dockyard. Here you'll find miniature furniture for doll houses, cedar work, jewelry, and many other handcrafts. Open daily from 10 a.m. to 4 p.m.

Then start wending your way back toward Hamilton. Perhaps stop to picnic near Ely's Harbour, or swim at Mangrove Bay (rumored to have been a smugglers' harbor). Visit **Fort Scaur**—once known as the Gibraltar of the west, Bermuda has had 22 forts built on its 21 square miles. From the ramparts, you'll enjoy sweeping views of the entire west end of the island. In Somerset, you'll want to pass by Somerset Bridge, the world's smallest drawbridge. For more great views, climb 117 feet up to the top of **Gibbs Hill Lighthouse** (tel. 238-0524; admission $1.75 per person). Built in 1846 of cast iron, this lighthouse affords some of the most panoramic vistas of Bermuda. Open daily from 9 a.m. to 4:30 p.m. Continue meandering back along South Road, stopping for refreshing swims at the beaches.

See Bermuda from the sea, aboard the luxurious 37-foot motor cruiser *Avalon.* A wide variety of sightseeing, swimming, and snorkeling cruises are available, including an especially amour-inspiring "sundowner" evening sail, on which you can nibble hors d'oeuvres and sip champagne (there's an open bar) while you voyage among the islands. Prices run $55 per couple for the cocktail cruise; $77 per couple for a snorkeling trip. For reservations and information, call 236-7435.

In 1620, the Pilgrims landed at Plymouth Rock. By that time, **St. George's** had already been settled for eight years, and the industrious residents had already built themselves a fort, a church, and the State House—which still stands today. Today, St. George's has been extensively restored, and visitors will delight in stepping back in time as they saunter along its narrow streets and alleyways, many with historic (or amusing) names, such as Blockade Alley, The King's Parade, and Old Maids' Lane. Start at Town Hall, where *Bermuda Journey,* a multimedia, audiovisual presentation, traces the history, culture, and heritage of Britain's oldest colony (admission $4 per person). Then go to Duke of York Street and climb the broad flight of brick stairs to white-painted St. Peter's Church, built on the site of the oldest Anglican church in the western hemisphere. View the silver communion service, a gift from King William III in 1698. You'll enjoy poking through the Tucker House Museum on Water Street, filled with wonderful antiques, such as a Waterford chandelier, a splendid Bermudian highboy, and a clock dating back to 1660 (it still keeps good time). Open Monday through Saturday, 10 a.m. to 5 p.m.; admission $2.25. The Carriage Museum on Water Street displays a wonderful collection of old conveyences—buggies, surreys, and shays. Open Monday through Saturday, 9 a.m. to 5 p.m.; admission is free; a small donation is suggested. In Kings Square, you'll want to have your photos taken in the stocks and pillory, used by early settlers to punish miscreants. Then cross the small bridge over to Ordnance Island, where you can view the life-size replica of the *Deliverance,* the vessel that carried the shipwrecked settlers from Bermuda to Jamestown. Open daily from 10 a.m. until 4 p.m.; admission is $2.25 per person. Nearby, check out the ducking stool—a replica of the instrument used to subdue suspected witches and nagging wives. Just a bit outside of town, stop by Fort St. Catherine, a 19th-century fortification. You'll probably feel a chill as you walk through the underground galleries and magazines and view the heavy muzzle-loading defense guns. There's also a fun display of replicas of the British Crown Jewels. Admission $2.75 per person; open daily from 10 a.m. to 4:30 p.m.

St. George's also has a fine selection of shops and boutiques. Frangipani carries very fashionable cotton sportswear for women. There are also outlets of Crisson's, Smith's, Trimingham's, Cooper's, Bluck's, and other top stores.

3. Honeymoon Hotels and Hideaways

Bermuda has some of the most unabashedly romantic hotels in the world. In addition to large, sophisticated self-contained resorts, you'll also find several uniquely Bermudian accommodations, such as elegant cottage colonies. Because of the wide selection, it is extremely important for you to decide exactly what kind of lodgings you want for yourselves—large or small, located in town or at the beach. Here's a brief overview of the kinds of accommodations available in Bermuda; they are grouped according to these categories in the hotel write-ups which follow.

Large resort hotels: These are usually complete worlds, with everything you need for honeymoon happiness right on the property: several restaurants, nightclubs, entertainment, boutiques, moped rentals, concierge service, tennis courts, often even golf courses. Most have their own beach or beach club, and many plan special daily activities for honeymooners. You usually have a choice of meal plans.

Small hotels: Although the services and facilities at the small hotels will be less extensive than at the major resort properties, they usually have a restaurant, bar, swimming pool, and water-sports equipment rental for snorkeling gear and small sailboats. Some small hotels lodge their guests within one main building; others have separate cottages surrounding the main house. Various meal plans are usually available.

Cottage colonies: A unique Bermudian institution, these feature separate cottages or cottage units scattered throughout landscaped grounds, affording maximum privacy. At the same time, the cottage colonies have all the facilities of a resort hotel, including a main "clubhouse" with dining room, bar, informal entertainment, beach and/or pool. Many of the cottages have small kitchens where you can prepare a light meal; at some, a maid comes in the morning to prepare your breakfast to order. Meal plans are generally BP or MAP.

"The Bermuda Collection": Seven of Bermuda's finest and most luxurious small hotels and cottage colonies have joined together to form "The Bermuda Collection": Cambridge Beaches, Glencoe, Lantana Colony Club, Newstead, Pompano Beach Club, The Reefs, and Stonington Beach Hotel. Each of these hotels is a true "gem," as you'll read in the write-ups that follow. By banding together, they have been able to plan joint social activities for their guests, and share services and facilities. In particular, guests at these hotels on the MAP (Modified American Plan) for meals can participate in "Carousel Dining," a dine-around program permitting them to take their meals at any of the seven different resorts—all of which are known for their superb restaurants. Contact the individual hotel or cottage colony for complete details.

Housekeeping cottages: These are similar to the cottage colonies in that lodgings are in separate cottages or wings, but there is no clubhouse. Some are apartment-type units with full kitchens. Rates usually are EP, without meals.

Guesthouses: Most of these occupy old Bermuda mansions, which have been refurbished and modernized to accommodate guests. Bedrooms might be in the main house or in separate units. Often, there is a dining room where some meals are served. The atmosphere tends toward the casual and informal; the meal plan will generally be CP.

When you compare Bermuda hotel prices with those in other destinations, remember that most Bermuda rates are MAP, including lunch and dinner daily. (Resorts in other parts of the world usually do not include any meals in their room rates.)

Although mid-November through March is considered the low season for Bermuda, not all hotels reduce their rates. On occasion, some facilities close temporarily for renovation during the winter, so be sure to check the hotel for details if you will be honeymooning at that time. Important—not all Bermuda hotels accept credit cards. Be sure to confirm your method of payment in advance. Also note that a 6% Bermuda government tax and a service charge to cover tipping (usually 10% or $8.50 per day for MAP guests) will be added to your final bill. Several hotels and guest houses also add an energy surcharge. Ask your travel agent for complete details.

LARGE RESORT HOTELS

Marriott's Castle Harbour Resort, P.O. Box HM 841, Hamilton, HM CX, Bermuda (tel. 809/293-2040; U.S. reservations: 212/603-8200, or toll free 800/228-9290). The drive in is impressive: The long road passes through the manicured fairways of the golf club and winds through tunnels formed by overarching palm trees, cedars, and casuarinas. When the car pulls up in front, a doorman wearing a white uniform with polished brass buttons and a feathered topee rushes to open the door for you. Yes, Marriott's Castle Harbour definitely belongs to the top rank of Bermudian resorts. The 402-room property occupies a 250-acre estate in the exclusive Tuckers Town area, with spectacular views of Castle Harbour and Harrington Sound. The main building has been returned to its original, old-world splendor. A cedar entranceway lined with gilt mirrors leads to a magnificent circular lobby, with marble floors and exposed cedar beams.

Castle Harbour boasts extensive sports facilities—most notably, the 18-hole, 71-par, 6,435-yard championship golf course designed by Robert Trent Jones. The first hole, where you tee off over the roadway towards the ocean, is considered among the most spectacular in the world. For your sporting pleasure, the resort also has three swimming pools (two of them heated), a complete assemblage of watersports facilities (including windsurfing, waterskiing, snorkeling, Hobie cat, and Sunfish rentals), and a beach club located just minutes away on one of Bermuda's finest beaches, next to Natural Arches. (A convenient beach shuttle runs constantly.) Stay in shape at their health spa, which boasts a Jacuzzi, saunas, Universal exercise equipment, as well as aerobics classes several times a week. One of the nicest places to sun yourself in winter is the Olympic-size Harbour pool, framed by the Romanesque limestone archways. Glass jalousies front the oceanside, acting as a windbreak to keep you toasty warm.

You'll have a tough time deciding whether you prefer the accommodations in the original building or in the new Harbour Wing. The latter, shaped like a futuristic white pyramid, cascades down the steep cliffside to the very edge of the water, and each room has a spacious balcony. In the original buildings, proportions are larger, and you'll find wonderful old-fashioned touches such as the huge walk-in closets.

However, most of the older rooms do not have balconies. All the accommodations are decorated in a classic contemporary style, with English-style furnishings, floral bedspreads in soothing shades of muted rose and slate blue, and walls tinged with the subtlest shade of pink. All rooms are air-conditioned and have color TVs. The property has three bars and six restaurants, including Mikado's—the only Japanese restaurant in Bermuda (see write-up that follows).

Honeymoon package (MAP): $360 to $425 per couple per night. Includes champagne and fresh flowers upon arrival, one day's use of moped, and souvenir gift.

Beach lovers, take note—the **Elbow Beach Hotel,** P.O. Box HM455, Hamilton, HM BX, Bermuda (tel. 809/236-3535; U.S. reservations: toll free 800/344-3526), is located on the longest, broadest, most exquisite strands in Bermuda, two miles of pale-pink sands and clear, cobalt waters. Overlooking the south shore in Paget Parish, the Elbow Beach provides perfect honeymoon headquarters for couples who want absolutely everything right on the property—from dancing under the stars to tennis to moped rentals. Shoppers will delight in prowling through the arcade that houses outposts of some of Bermuda's finest stores, including Trimingham's, Crisson's, and Cooper's. And, when you feel like wandering off, the property is conveniently located, just ten minutes from Hamilton.

Practically all of the 300 rooms are located in the four-story white hotel that crowns the hillside; there are also some lanai units and suites located in the gardens that line the paths down to the beach. The resort encompasses 35 lushly landscaped acres. At the water-sports concession at the beach, you can make arrangements for sailing, waterskiing, diving, or fishing charters. If you prefer a swimming pool, you'll have plenty of room to swim laps in the large free-form pool.

Most honeymooners choose either a junior suite or a superior room, each with king-size bed and an oceanview terrace. The two accommodations are virtually identical: The suite has a wall separating the living and bedroom areas. Elbow Beach has recently undergone a $5-million renovation. Rooms are done in soft tones of beige and off-white, with subtle accents of pale mauve, pink, and green.

You can dine in three different restaurants: The Surf Club down at the beach is especially nice for lunch, with its jaunty blue-and-white-striped umbrellas placed out on the terrace. There's entertainment every night, such as calypso music or a steel band, and every Saturday and Monday night in season, you can dance under the stars to live music at the Beach Terrace. Honeymoon package: Seven days/six nights (MAP): $2,250 per couple for a superior room. BP also available. Includes bottle of sparkling wine, Elbow Beach cookbook, welcoming drinks, invitation to weekly honeymooners' champagne party, invitation to weekly rum swizzle party, free admission to nightclub for one evening, souvenir honeymoon photograph album, and more.

Located on a peninsula thrust out into the ocean, the **Sonesta Beach Hotel,** P.O. Box HM1070, Hamilton HM EX, Bermuda (tel. 809/238-8122; U.S. reservations: toll free 800/343-7170), has not just one beach waiting for you, but three, all set on sheltered coves just off the Atlantic. The architecture is rather dramatic: the broad three-story, U-shaped building seems to embrace the sea from its rocky promontory. Lovers will want to stroll out to Honeymoon Point, a rocky spit that overlooks the ocean. On your way back, pass through the very pretty moongate, to assure yourselves good luck. Although the Sonesta has 403 rooms and spreads out over 25 acres, the feel remains intimate and personalized. By day, much of the activity centers on the three beaches, where you can rent equipment for windsurfing, snorkeling, or scuba-diving, or sign up for a glass-bottomed boat ride. Guests can play tennis on six courts, and golf on a Robert Trent Jones–designed course that lies just minutes away at the Port Royal Golf Course. Pamper yourselves at The Spa, which offers individually tailored health and fitness programs. Sign up for a facial or massage or work out in an aerobics class or on the exercise equipment.

One of the advantages of the Sonesta is that you are right on the beach—and since there are three sandy coves to choose from, they never seem crowded. You can also swim in a huge, heated outdoor pool—or a large indoor one, located under a glass dome. All of the rooms have a private balcony and all have recently been redone in very contemporary shades of mauve and aqua, with king-size beds available on request. All rooms have TVs; some have VCRs. Consider one of the split-level minisuites, with a sunken living room. There are three different restaurants: the Port Royal dining room, the Greenhouse restaurant, or in Lillian's, a new, art deco–style supper club serving grilled specialties. (On the MAP plan, you will have to pay extra to dine at the Greenhouse or Lillian's.) Every night, there's entertainment and music for dancing.

Honeymoon package: Eight days/seven nights (MAP): From $1,810 per couple. Includes: breakfast and dinner daily, with one breakfast in bed and one dinner in the Greenhouse Restaurant (the others are in the Port Royal), one bottle of wine at dinner, a honeymoon souvenir photograph, and more.

Grotto Bay Beach Hotel and Tennis Club, 11 Blue Hole Hill, Hamilton Parish CR 04, Bermuda (tel. 809/293-8333; U.S. reservations: toll free 800/225-2230 nationwide; 800/982-4770 in Massachusetts). If you're looking for a casual, laid-back place where outdoor good times provide the prevailing modus operandi, then Grotto Bay is your perfect honeymoon choice. This place is really fun. You'll feel right at home, thanks to the friendly, relaxed atmosphere. Grotto Bay offers all the amenities of the larger hotels, combined with the intimacy of a small (only 201 rooms) resort. There's always something going on—tennis clinics, a make-your-own-hat competition, photography lectures, or nature walks. In addition to the usual water sports (aquatrikes, snorkeling, waterskiing, and sailing), you can rent a Boston whaler (about $80 for half a day), and take off for one of the dozens of nearby uninhabited islands for a picnic. Back at Grotto Bay, you'll want to do your sunbathing at aptly named Honeymoon Beach, reached by passing through a moongate. Nearby, you can soak in the hot tub. And for honeymooners who really want something different, there's Cathedral Cave, with its very own underground lake. If you like, you can arrange to have yourselves locked in there for an hour, all by yourselves. At night, you can dance in one of the world's oldest discos—Prospero's Cave, set in another real, honest-to-goodness cavern complete with stalactites and stalagmites. No wonder Grotto Bay seems to have the happiest bunch of guests on the island.

Part of the outdoorsy, informal atmosphere comes because of the layout. Accommodations, located in nine separate lodges, are spread out over the 20 acres of gardens and beaches. Each room has a balcony with a water view. Thanks to a recent $4-million primping, Bermuda's friendliest, funnest resort is also becoming one of the island's spiffiest. Bathrooms sparkle after a complete refurbishment, and rooms have been redone with sand-and-sea tone pastels that reflect island sophistication. The honeymoon package includes so many goodies that you may need an extra suitcase to carry them all home. No wonder Grotto Bay is one of the most popular resorts for Bermuda-bound newlyweds. Honeymoon package: Seven days/six nights (BP): $1,235 to $1,775 per couple (summer season). Includes oceanview room, full English breakfast daily (with one champagne-and-caviar breakfast in bed), color honeymoon photo, use of two cycles for a day, boat cruise, scuba lesson or island sightseeing tour, china display plates, Grotto Bay coffee mugs, rum swizzles in Prospero's Cave Disco, honeymoon champagne party, manager's rum swizzle party, and walking tour of Bailey's Bay, with free admissions to the Dolphin Show, Crystal Caves, Bermuda Pottery, and Bermuda Perfumery. During the winter season, a four-day/three-night honeymoon package is available for $310 to $340 per couple. Features vary; ask your travel agent or Grotto Bay.

On the island of Bermuda, the **Southampton Princess Hotel, Golf, Beach, & Tennis Club,** P.O. Box HM1379, Hamilton HM FX, Bermuda (tel. 809/238-8000; U.S. reservations: 212/582-8100 in New York City; toll free 800/223-1818 nationwide; 800/442-8418 in New York State), is an island of luxury—and absolutely impeccable after a $20-million renovation. You'll find just about every creature comfort you could desire on the 100-acre estate that crowns a hillside on Bermuda's south shore. All 600 rooms have terraces that overlook either the Atlantic Ocean or Great Sound. As the name implies, the resort features complete golf, tennis, and beach facilities. For golfers, there's an 18-hole, par-3 course, with 2,600 yards of manicured terrain that challenge both the experienced and the novice golfer. Tennis players can work on their strokes on 11 courts (7 lit for night play). The private beach, reachable by shuttle from the main hotel, is one of Bermuda's finest. At the water-sports concession, you can rent snorkeling or scuba gear, or arrange fishing trips. There are also both outdoor and indoor swimming pools. For those whose favorite sport is shopping, the Southampton Princess' arcades contain 12 stores, including Smith's, Trimingham's, Calypso, and Cooper's.

All the rooms at the Southampton Princess are done in scrumptious pastels, the better to focus attention on the startling blue ocean seen through the sliding glass doors leading to the balcony. Rooms are all fairly similar, with a small, tea-rose-tone couch and a writing desk with rattan chair; all have air conditioning and a color TV (hooked up to a satellite dish) discreetly tucked in the armoire. For extra pampering, choose Port Club accommodations, which include concierge service, complimentary Continental breakfast and afternoon cocktails, and more.

If you like, you could dine at a different restaurant every day of the week, including two that are generally numbered among Bermuda's finest: the Newport Room with its nautical ambience, and the Waterlot, a 300-year-old inn. For entertainment, there's a spectacular dinner show and revue at the Empire Room, the island's largest nightclub; and dancing at the Neptune Lounge and Touch Club.

Honeymoon package: Five days/four nights. Winter: From $610 per couple (EP); summer: $1,475 per couple (MAP). Includes welcoming rum swizzles, admission to the "Follies" show plus two drinks (summer only), bottle of champagne upon arrival, honeymoon photo album, Princess totebag and Bermuda guidebook, airport transfers, taxes and gratuities.

The Princess Hotel, P.O. Box HM837, Hamilton HM CX, Bermuda (tel. 809/295-3000; U.S. reservations: 212/582-8100 in New York City; toll free 800/223-1818 nationwide; 800/442-8418 in New York State). For over 100 years, the Princess in Hamilton has epitomized gracious service. The hotel was named in honor of Princess Louise, the daughter of Queen Victoria who became the first member of the Royal Family to visit Bermuda. Today, thanks to a $14-million renovation to celebrate her centennial, The Princess reigns more regally than ever over Hamilton Harbour.

The Princess is located on Pitts Bay Road, just a few minutes' walk from all the Front Street shops. The imposing pink palace is set right on the edge of the harbour, surrounding lush gardens, palm trees, goldfish ponds, and large outdoor swimming pools. As is characteristic of older hotels, each of the 456 rooms has a slightly different layout and view. All have air conditioning and color TVs. Rooms, recently redecorated, have a substantial, British feel. Furnishings might include a moss-green velvet couch, captain's chest, or Bermuda prints on the walls; the modern bathrooms have a spring-like floral wallpaper. You definitely can enjoy the best of both worlds: proximity to Hamilton, plus complete use of all the beach, sports, and dining facilities at the Southampton Princess (weather permitting, a ferry runs between the two properties several times daily). The Princess in Hamilton itself has four excellent restaurants, and top-caliber shows in the Gazebo Lounge, which has a wraparound view of Hamilton's twinkling lights.

Honeymoon package: Five days/four nights (EP): $605 to $815 per couple. Includes welcoming rum swizzles, bottle of champagne upon arrival, honeymoon photo album, Bermuda Longtail wine glasses, Princess cookbook and tote bag, his-and-hers T-shirts, airport transfers, taxes and gratuities.

Overlooking Hamilton Harbour and Great Sound, the **Belmont Hotel, Golf & Beach Club,** P.O. Box WK251, Warwick WK BX, Bermuda (tel. 809/236-1301; U.S. reservations: toll free 800/225-5843), occupies a distinctly country-club–like setting, 110 acres of lush green verdure that undulate to the water's edge. All 150 rooms are located in the main building. If you love golf and tennis, this is your place. The hotel adjoins the fairways of its own 18-hole, par-70 championship course designed by Robert Trent Jones, with a complete pro shop on the property. Play tennis on three all-weather courts—the hotel also regularly schedules tournaments for guests. The very large heated sea-water pool that overlooks the harbor is not only fun to swim in, but also to watch—there are underwater portholes, so you can peek at the aquatic antics down under. For those who prefer to feel the pink sand squish under their toes, there's a private beach club just five minutes away by free shuttle. One of the biggest bonuses of the Belmont is its location—just a three-mile drive from Hamilton. Better yet—hop the ferry right at their private dock. After a scenic ten-minute cruise, you'll arrive right on Front Street.

Following its multimillion-dollar refurbishment, the Belmont radiates tip-top form. The lobby has the warmth of an English club, accented by Bermuda cedar paneling and brass chandeliers. Rooms, also all recently redone, face either the gardens, the golf course, or Hamilton Harbour. Furnishings evince distinguished elegance: a Queen Anne–style headboard and highboy, rattan armchairs, plush wall-to-wall carpeting, and a color cable TV. The Belmont is a Trusthouse Forte property. Honeymoon package (FAP): $275 per couple per night. Includes champagne upon arrival, dinner with wine nightly, complimentary motor scooter rental, one round of golf, free daytime tennis, hotel taxes and gratuities. BP also available.

SMALL HOTELS

For couples seeking an island of romance on the island of Bermuda, **Harmony Club,** P.O. Box PG299, Paget PG BX, Bermuda (tel. 809/236-3500; U.S. reservations: toll free 800/255-5843), provides the perfect getaway. Not only is Harmony Club Bermuda's first all-inclusive resort catering to couples only, it also weaves an ambience that is first-class all the way. Ensconced in a park-like enclave just two miles from Hamilton, the seven-acre luxury property has only 71 rooms. The property exudes Bermudian charm, with its columned entrance, pink-painted main building and cottages topped by white peak roofs, and showplace gardens—the head gardener has been with the property (formerly called Harmony Hall) for nearly 50 years, and he manages to coax snapdragons to grow to eye level. Personal, elegant touches abound. The main building is constructed around a 200-year-old residence, and you'll find fine architectural details impossible to replicate today—parquet floors, Bermuda cedar-paneled walls. All meals are served sit-down style, and you'll sup off fine crystal, silver, and china. Adding to the romantic glow, dinner is by candlelight every evening and there's live entertainment. With awareness of the kinds of privileges fun-loving honeymooners would appreciate, Harmony Club includes free use of a motor scooter throughout your stay. Among the places you might like to go are Oasis and The Club, two of Bermuda's hottest clubs, where Harmony Hall guests are admitted without a cover charge. For sports-lovers, there's tennis on two courts or a 1,000-foot blush-pink private beach at Discovery Bay. Right at Harmony Club, the swimming pool has been refurbished, with the addition of a California-style wooden sun deck, saunas, miniwaterfall, and a moongate that you can walk through for good luck. Since Harmony Club is a Trusthouse Forte hotel, guests enjoy special golf privileges at the Belmont Golf and Country Club.

The property lends itself particularly well to privacy, since most rooms are located in small cottages scattered around the gardens, lawns, and courtyard. (There are also some equally nice accommodations in the main house.) Rooms are big and airy; sunlight streams in the windows framed by tie-back drapes. Most rooms have private terraces or balconies; be sure to request a king-size bed if you prefer one, since some rooms have two doubles. In addition to color TVs, all rooms have coffee-and tea-making facilities. Honeymoon package (all-inclusive): Seven days/six nights: $1,560 to $2,230 per couple. Among the features the package covers: champagne and flowers upon arrival; traditional English afternoon tea daily; evening cocktail party with hors d'oeuvres; all meals, unlimited wines, beverages, and cocktails; island snorkeling party. Please note that the rate also includes all taxes, gratuities, and service charges.

The Reefs, 56 South Rd., Southampton SN 02, Bermuda (tel. 809/238-0222; U.S. reservations: toll free 800/223-1363). Casual elegance—that's what you'll find at this picturesque resort located on Bermuda's beach-studded south shore. The 65 rooms are set in two-story pink buildings that sashay down the coral bluffs toward the reef-sheltered sea. What makes The Reefs extra special is its private beach—a good-size stretch of pink sand, with that clear, aquamarine water beckoning you to jump on in. When you add in the personal attention given to guests by owners Bonnie and David Dodwell, you'll understand why The Reefs is usually booked solid all year, and 60% of its guests are returnees.

Recently refurbished, the clubhouse (built around a 200-year-old farmhouse) has a cozy piano bar, as well as that expansive outdoor terrace just made for sipping rum swizzles at sunset. All the rooms capture a warm, island ambience, with wicker and rattan furnishings, terra-cotta floors with area throw rugs, framed Bermuda maps and prints on the walls, and a color scheme incorporating nature's palette: seafoam greens, peaches, lilac, rose, and slate blue. Most rooms (except the Clubhouse and Poolside accommodations) face westward to the ocean, giving you on-the-brink views of the sunset from your balcony and terrace. In summer evenings, you can dine at Coconuts restaurant, poised on a beachside terrace. More music comes with the live entertainment nightly—singers, a combo, or a calypso band. The restaurants are known for their good food—guests rarely leave the hotel. A member of the Bermuda Collection. Rates: Winter (MAP); $160 per couple per night (poolside lanai), to $220 (surfside lanai). Summer (MAP): $260 per couple per night (poolside lanai) to $325 per couple per night (surfside lanai). Honeymoon package: $25 additional. Includes champagne upon arrival and half-day Sea Garden cruise.

Even in an island of beautiful locales, the **Pompano Beach Club,** 32 Pompano Beach Rd., Southampton SB 03, Bermuda (tel. 809/234-0222; U.S. reservations: tel. 617/237-2242 or 508/358-7737 in Massachusetts, or toll free 800/343-4155 nationwide), setting leaves you gasping at nature's handiwork. Poised at the edge of limestone cliffs, the pink buildings overlook a panoramic view of shoreline where reefs and sandbars color the water two startlingly different shades of blue. At low tide, the water often gets so shallow that you can walk over 250 yards out into the Atlantic—and still have your head well above water. Much of the warmth and hospitality of Pompano comes from David and Aimee Southworth (the family has owned and operated Pompano for over 30 years). They're young and enthusiastic, and know just the places and activities to recommend for newlyweds. Pompano itself offers seclusion and privacy on Bermuda's southwest coast in Southampton parish, about a half-hour's drive from Hamilton. The 54 rooms are located in seven separate units, all named for different sport fish. Each room offers that dramatic sea view, although layouts differ slightly: some have kitchenettes, others are studios, some have a separate bedroom or sitting area. The honeymoon package features a studio room with double bed, sitting area, private bath, and outdoor porch. The hotel has recently completed $4 million in renovations and improvements.

Thanks to the sandbar and protective reefs, Pompano offers excellent swimming, snorkeling, and windsurfing. The sand beach is rather small, so for sunbathing, you'll probably prefer the stunning white pool deck, thrust out toward the Atlantic. Park your lounge chair under a yellow umbrella, swim in the heated freshwater pool, or soak in the hot tub. There's also tennis on a clay court and golf at Port Royal Golf Course right next door (Pompano is only 500 yards from the first tee). The oceanview Cedar Room is an atmospheric place to dine, with its solid cedar furnishings, coral stone pillars, and excellent food. A member of The Bermuda Collection. Honeymoon package (MAP): Seven days/six nights: $1,245 to $1,640 per couple, depending on time of year. Includes studio accommodations, bottle of champagne, a gift for the bride, airport transfers, tickets to the Maritime Museum, round-trip ferry tickets to Hamilton. Package not available December and January, when rates for a studio are $82.80 per person per night (EP).

Waterloo House, P.O. Box HM333, Hamilton HM BX, Bermuda (tel. 809/ 295-4480; U.S. reservations: toll free 800/468-4100), occupies one of the most delightful settings you could possibly imagine. Two-story buildings painted a pale persimmon color and accented by trim white shutters surround a garden courtyard leading out to Hamilton Harbour. Although the inn is less than a three-minute walk from Hamilton's Front Street, you'll definitely feel more like you're a guest in an elegant English country house (the property was originally built as a private residence). There's a cozy, at-home ambience: You can sit down at the upright piano in the lounge, or challenge each other to a very British game of skittles (somewhat like billiards). Each of the 35 rooms is different—some have balconies and water views, others face the garden. All are very bright, cheerful, spacious, and well laid out, decorated with English-style furnishings, captains' chests, and overstuffed armchairs. When you wake up in the morning, the sun comes streaming in through the windows, and the colorful harbor throbs with activity. And because the rooms face onto the courtyard or harbor rather than busy Pitts Bay Road, the only sound you'll hear in the morning is the chirp of the bananaquits and the quack of the ducks. There's no beach, but you can take a dunk in the small pool in the courtyard. Guests also enjoy beach privileges at the very exclusive Coral Beach Club, for a small fee. Since Waterloo House is associated with Horizons & Cottages and Newstead resorts, guests enjoy exchange dining and other activities. Waterloo's own restaurant is excellent and, in summer, you can dine on the large terrace overlooking Hamilton Harbour. Honeymoon package: Seven days/six nights (MAP): $1,290 (garden view); $1,405 (harbor view). Includes a bottle of champagne upon arrival, a picnic lunch for two, one day's free tennis or golf, afternoon tea daily, a gift for the bride, a souvenir photo of the couple.

Rosedon, P.O. Box HM290, Hamilton HM AX, Bermuda (tel. 809/295-1640; U.S. reservations: toll free 800/225-5567). This white house with the aqua shutters set on a low hillside just minutes away from Hamilton's Front Street envelops you in turn-of-the-century graciousness. Built as a private residence in 1906, it is one of Bermuda's most captivating small hotels. A grand circular driveway edged with bright blooming flowers sweeps up to the front door, flanked by leaded-glass windows. When the mansion was built, no expense was spared. Fine woods such as oak, cherry, mahogany, and California redwood were imported for the paneling. This wealth of charm and detail is still appreciated by guests today. Pathways wind through lush gardens to the modern two-story wings where most of the 43 guest rooms are located. Accommodations are simple, comfortable, and clean, with bright quilted bedspreads, jalousie windows, floral-print drapes, and beige carpeting. All rooms have air conditioning and a minifridge. The wings surround a large garden courtyard that has a large heated pool at its center; all around, brick walkways meander past the palms, oleanders, and hibiscus that add color and fragrance to the grounds. For ocean swimming, Rosedon guests enjoy beach privileges at Elbow Beach Surf Club, with the hotel providing free transportation; golf privileges are available at a private club. Honeymoon package: Seven days/six nights (EP): From $430 to $570 per couple, depending on room category. Includes bottle of champagne upon arrival, gift for the bride, daily afternoon tea or a drink by the pool, a picnic lunch, rum swizzle party, half-day Sea Garden cruise.

Stonington Beach Hotel, P.O. Box HM523, Hamilton HM CX, Bermuda (tel. 809/236-5416; U.S. reservations: tel. 212/661-4540 in New York State; toll free 800/223-1588 nationwide). A modern luxury hotel, Stonington Beach occupies a prime location on one of Bermuda's finest south-shore beaches. It's the same two-mile strand shared with the Elbow Beach Hotel right next door, but much more tranquil, since Stonington is set at the far eastern end. Although the hotel attracts many honeymoon couples, the ambience is low-key: no group parties or games, but a lot of quiet enjoyment.

Because the property is small (only 64 rooms), it retains an intimate feel. The accommodations, all with panoramic ocean views, are situated in beige buildings with traditional Bermudian white step-style roofs, tucked amid the rolling lawns of the green hillside. Every room has attractive modern decor, an oceanfront balcony, and a ceiling fan as well as air conditioning. The public areas are especially inviting, including a Regency-style library where you can pick up copies of the *London Times* or the *Economist,* and settle in for a good read in front of the fireplace. The English-style Norwood Dining Room serves excellent cuisine. Outdoors, there's a large freshwater pool and two tennis courts screened behind bougainvillea. Both service and upkeep are superior, thanks to General Manager William Mulder, who was educated at the renowned Swiss Hotel School in Lausanne. You'll get doubly good attention, since the front-desk staff includes some students from Bermuda College's Department of Hotel Technology, all supervised in their duties by professional managers. A member of The Bermuda Collection. Honeymoon package: Seven days/six nights (BP): $836 to $1,660 per couple for a superior room. Includes a chilled bottle of champagne and fruit basket in your room upon arrival, airport transfers. MAP is also available.

Get a feel for the real Bermuda at **Glencoe,** P.O. Box PG297, Paget PG BX, Bermuda (tel. 809/236-5274; U.S. reservations: toll free 800/468-1500), an intimate resort located in a quiet residential area on the edge of Salt Kettle Bay. For the past 30 years, the property has been owned and managed by Reggie Cooper, who has nurtured its growth from a small guest house accommodating 22 people to its present 91-guest capacity. Although the property has grown, it hasn't really changed: It retains an informal but elegant atmosphere—a Bermuda-style country inn, centered around an historic 18th-century house that is now the main building. The rooms occupy graceful two-story pink buildings, with balconies and terraces trimmed with white latticework and wooden railings. No two rooms are alike, although most offer water views. Furnishings carry out the light tropical motif—many have open-beam cathedral ceilings, rattan chairs and dressers, and pastel floral print fabrics. Calla lilies and oleanders line the garden paths that lead to the two swimming pools and patios. If you prefer an ocean beach, Glencoe guests enjoy privileges at Elbow Beach. During the day, you can watch the yachts and Bermuda-fitted dinghies come and go from their moorings in the bay, or take off yourself aboard a Sunfish or Windsurfer. Deep-sea fishing, scuba-diving, tennis, and golf can all be arranged easily. At night, there's excellent dining both indoors and out, with sweeping views of sunset over Little Sound. Glencoe definitely offers the best of both worlds. Although it enjoys a secluded location, it is just five minutes away from Front Street, Hamilton, via the ferry that leaves from the nearby dock. A member of The Bermuda Collection. Honeymoon package: None. Rates (MAP): $210 to $270 per couple per night. BP also available.

Newstead, P.O. Box PG196, Paget PG BX, Bermuda (tel. 809/236-6060; U.S. reservations: toll free 800/468-4111). Imagine an English country manor with assorted guest houses transplanted to the edge of Hamilton Harbour, and you very much have the picture of Newstead, a pretty collection of moss-green-painted cottages just across the sparkling blue waters from Hamilton. The main building, dating back to the 19th century, contains a very grand ballroom-size living room, with exposed cedar beams, floral chintz couches, and exceptionally fine English antiques and original 19th-century oil paintings. Every afternoon, guests gather here for a traditional tea. Afterward, form a foursome for bridge in the card room, or take up skittles, an English game that resembles billiards. Hamilton is just a short drive or five-minute ferry ride away. This fine hotel is aiming to become even better, thanks to a renovation project that will refurbish public areas, modernize bathrooms, and add a new, outdoor dining terrace.

Rooms are located in different cottages that ramble down the hillside facing the harbor and Hamilton. (There are also 16 rooms in the main house.) There's a total of 49 rooms, each a unique gem: The most deluxe accommodations have private terraces right on the harbor. The furnishings seem to come from an English country manse: overstuffed wing chairs, Queen Anne headboards, and floral fabrics. And what would be a good country house without sports? In addition to two tennis courts, there are sailing and deep-water swimming from the private docks, as well as a large heated pool. For surf-bathing, Newstead guests enjoy privileges at the very posh Coral Beach Club for a small fee. Since Newstead is also a companion resort of Waterloo House and Horizons & Cottages, there's also a dine-around program with those properties. At Newstead's own dining room, you'll dine by candlelight beneath crystal chandeliers and open-beam ceilings. Newstead is also part of The Bermuda Collection. Honeymoon packages: Seven days/six nights (MAP): $1,520 per couple. Includes a bottle of champagne, free tennis, afternoon tea, and a rum swizzle party.

Mermaid Beach Club, P.O. Box WK250, Warwick WK BX, Bermuda (tel. 809/236-5031; U.S. reservations: toll free 800/441-7087 nationwide; 800/292-9695 in Pennsylvania). A millionaire's beach at a bargain price—that's what you get at this south shore hotel long known as one of Bermuda's best values. A favorite of college students at spring break, it offers a young, fun atmosphere year-round. The 86 rooms are located in two-story beige buildings that cozy up to a long stretch of soft pink sand, just a pebble's throw from other fine south-shore beaches, such as Warwick Long Bay and Jobson Cove. Most rooms have ocean views, as well as verandas or patios. After a recent refurbishment, the rooms are pretty and inviting, with rattan furnishings and soft pastel upholsteries. All are air-conditioned. Some rooms have small kitchenettes; there's a convenience store on the property where you can buy groceries, as well as a small restaurant. Tennis, golf, and all water sports can be arranged. Honeymoon package: Seven days/six nights (MAP): $1,450 to $1,730 per couple. Includes flowers for the bride, a two-hour Sea Garden cruise, a bottle of champagne, a free cocktail daily, complimentary snorkeling equipment, and free admission to a disco one evening.

COTTAGE COLONIES

Horizons and Cottages, P.O. Box PG198, Paget PG BX, Bermuda (tel. 809/236-0048; U.S. reservations: toll free 800/468-0022). Fresh as a summer's day, gracious as the "welcoming arms" stairway built of Bermuda sandstone, scenic as a longtail's view from on high—that describes Horizons, part of the crème de la crème of Bermuda cottage-colony society. The property crowns a hillock and offers you nearly 360° of horizons, including a postcard-perfect view of the very elegant Coral Beach Club. Because the resort encompasses nearly 30 acres, you'll feel completely secluded—yet Hamilton is less than three miles away. The clubhouse is built around a 17th-century farmhouse that once belonged to the Middleton family. Oriental carpets and valanced windows help complete the feeling of old Bermuda. Manager Wilhelm Sack runs a crack ship—one of the reasons that Horizons is the only Bermudian hotel that is part of the prestigious Relais et Châteaux group. Rooms in the main house use colors that come straight from a floral bouquet—soft peach and pistachio, with daffodil-yellow towels in the bathrooms. The rooms that will really win your hearts are in the ten delightful cottages, which have names such as "Morning Glory," "Sea Cloud," and "Wind Song." Each is unique: Some have fireplaces, others sunken living rooms with Mexican tile floors, all with islandy furnishings made of rattan, ceiling fans, and an Impressionist's palette of pastels—pink, aqua, yellow, and coral. All fabrics and accoutrements are crisp and new. Views overlook the water or gardens. Especially in the morning, you'll have time to savor your surroundings: A maid will prepare your breakfast to order in the separate kitchen, which you can then enjoy on your balcony. This, indeed, is the good life. And when you also want good sports, you'll find that Horizons has a heated swimming pool, three all-weather tennis courts, nine-hole mashie golf, and an 18-hole putting green. Full golf and all water sports can be easily arranged. Horizons is especially well known for its excellent cuisine, and many of the herbs and vegetables come from their own gardens. In summer, candlelit dinners are served outside on the terrace. Afterward, settle into a cozy, English-style pub with a dart board and skittles for some friendly competition. Three nights a week there's entertainment, and every Sunday evening you can dance underneath the stars. Guests at Horizons also can enjoy the facilities of its companion resorts, Newstead and Waterloo House. Honeymoon package: Seven days/six nights. Winter season: $990 per couple (BP); $1,230 per couple (MAP). Summer season: $1,200 to $1,900 per couple (BP); $1,505 to $2,140 per couple (MAP). Includes a bottle of champagne, complimentary golf and tennis on the property, and an introduction to a private beach.

Lantana Colony Club, SB 90, Sandys SB BX, Bermuda (tel. 809/234-0141; U.S. reservations: toll free 800/468-3733). Set on 20 acres of lushly gardened, lovingly tended grounds at Bermuda's west end, Lantana embraces guests with a feeling of elegant repose. Since there are only 65 rooms, the ambience is distinctly uncrowded. Very private pink cottages with the traditional white-step roofs sit discreetly tucked under palm trees, behind hibiscus hedges, along impeccably manicured lawns. The large pool area near the beach is exquisite: edged with tile and backed by a trim pink cabana. At the pink coral-sand beach, you can rent Sunfish and other small boats, Windsurfers, and snorkeling gear for exploring the clear-as-glass waters of Great Sound. It's easy to reach Hamilton without disrupting the relaxed pace—just hop the nearby ferry for a peaceful 40-minute cruise in. But you'll find plenty of pleasures right at Lantana: tennis on two all-weather courts, a putting green, and a superb croquet lawn (both John H. Young II and his wife, the owners, are international tournament-level players). Perhaps your favorite moments will come as you just stroll around the property, which has often been called a "museum without walls" because of the bronze sculptures by renowned artists such as Desmond Fountain and John Robinson that grace the lawns and glens. You'll also be captivated by some of the fanciful topiary creations. Accommodations—suites, one-, and two-bedroom units—are all differently delightful: You might find terracotta floors, rattan rugs, a ceiling fan, and fragrant cedar-wood armoires. Many have terraces, and some have water views.

For lunch, you'll enjoy the La Plage waterfront restaurant, shaded by the seagrape trees. Dinners are served in the formal dining room, with guests rotated night by night toward—and finally into—the Solarium, which has to be the most lavishly romantic dining spot in Bermuda. Chandeliers with their crystals formed like dangling bunches of grapes, spotlit hanging plants and white wrought-iron furniture; glimmering hurricane lanterns on the table weave a spell that is complemented by the exquisite cuisine. Part of The Bermuda Collection. Although there's no special honeymoon package, if you let them know that you're newlyweds, you'll receive a gift and an invitation to a private cocktail party. Rates (MAP) run from $165 to $285 per couple per night (winter); $240 to $350 per couple per night (summer), depending on proportions and views.

Cambridge Beaches, 30 King's Point, Sandys MA 02, Bermuda (tel. 809/234-0331; U.S. reservations: toll free 800/468-7300), is the type of place that can proclaim on its brochures, "Cambridge Beaches *is* Bermuda"—and nary a voice would beg to differ. The property is, in fact, Bermuda's original cottage colony, and it continues to reign as one of Bermuda's premier facilities for ambience and service. Owned by the Trott family (whose ancestors came over on the *Sea Venture*), the 25-acre estate is almost completely surrounded by water on a slender peninsula that curves out into Great Sound. The "Beaches" of the property's name actually number about six. Personalized service is the byword here—guests are always greeted by name. No wonder about 60% of the guests are repeat visitors. You'll have fun browsing through the plaques in the clubhouse that honor the returnees—some of whom have come for 60 years. The whole place has a substantial, old-guard Bermudian feel, from the cedar reception desk to the old beam ceilings and the crewel-work fabrics on the furniture.

Cambridge Beaches is that marvelous anachronism—a resort run exclusively for the pleasure of its guests. The 78 guest rooms are spacious, located in pink-painted, white-roofed cottages scattered hither and yon amongst the gardens, lawns, and shoreline. No two rooms are the same. Most have honest-to-goodness antiques: genuine cedar chests and secretary desks that are worth thousands. The decor recalls an English country house, with the comfortable feel of furnishings that have been passed down through generations. Some rooms have working fireplaces and Jacuzzis, and many have water views. The property recently completed a $5-million renovation project.

Sporting options include a large swimming pool stationed just at water's edge, all those fine beaches, three tennis courts, and all water sports are available right on the property. Meals are served either in the open-beam, cathedral-ceilinged dining room, or out on the terrace fronting Mangrove Bay, where white wrought-iron chairs surround a 300-year-old tamarind tree. Part of The Bermuda Collection. Honeymoon package: None. Rates (MAP): $260 to $425 per couple per night.

Pink Beach Club & Cottages, P.O. Box HM1017, Hamilton HM DX, Bermuda (tel. 809/293-1666; U.S. reservations: 212/696-1323 in NY; toll free 800/372-1323 nationwide). The name is appropriate, because this cottage colony fronts a third of a mile of the rosiest coral sands in Bermuda. The entire property radiates discreet elegance: Just a small brass plaque next to the cedar door announces "Pink Beach."

Pink cottages with green shutters and steep white roofs spread out over the expansive, 18-acre property filled with well-tended gardens. Whether you choose a cottage or studio, the rooms are big, all with private patios or terraces, and most with fine water views. The most spectacular accommodations are plunked right at the very edge of the sea, their coral-stone terraces merging gradually, perfectly with the jagged rocks. About 60% of the clientele are repeat guests.

Start off your day with an ample English breakfast (kippers, anyone?), cooked to order by your maid in the kitchen adjoining your cottage. Then head off for a game of tennis on the two all-weather courts, or golf at Marriott's Castle Harbour or the exclusive Mid Ocean Club (Pink Beach can arrange an introduction). Lunch is served under the graceful colonnade by the large saltwater pool. Dinner is a formal affair, with jackets and ties required for gentlemen every evening. Picture windows face out over the ocean, with guests gradually rotated to the windowside tables during the course of their stay. There's entertainment six evenings a week, and the beach is softly lighted at night; hand-in-hand strolls definitely encouraged. Honeymoon package: None. Rates (MAP): $280 to $345 per couple per night during the high season; 50% less during the off-season.

Fourways Inn, P.O. Box PG 294, Paget PG BX, Bermuda (tel. 809/236-6517; U.S. reservations: toll free 800/223-5581). This new cottage colony continues the tradition of elegance and excellence established by its neighboring Fourways Restaurant (see "Romantic Restaurants"). The two-story pink cottages sit atop a hillside on Middle Road, and each room has a sweeping view of Hamilton Harbour and Great Sound. Because of the central location, golf, tennis, the beach, and the ferry to Hamilton are conveniently nearby. Adding to the feeling of elegant intimacy, there are only ten guest rooms, and their classic, yet contemporary decor ranks them among Bermuda's finest. Floors are of cool pressed marble. Rattan sofas and traditional Bermudian open-beam cathedral ceilings mingle easily with English Chippendale-style chairs. The bathrooms win the award for best in Bermuda, hands down — they're huge, thoughtfully outfitted with niceties such as a scale and hairdryer. Movie stars and arbitragers, please note: These are the only hotel bathrooms in Bermuda equipped with phones. The downstairs rooms are one-bedroom suites, while upstairs you have deluxe studios; each has a kitchenette and a well-stocked private bar. To make your honeymoon home even more enjoyable, you get a continental breakfast of flaky rolls and croissants from the inn's pastry shop, the morning local paper, and fresh flowers. In your minifridge, you'll find fresh milk and orange juice daily. All this — plus Bermuda's finest restaurant next door. Honeymoon package: None.

Rates (CP): From $110 per couple per night (low season); $225 to $300 per couple per night (high season).

HOUSEKEEPING COTTAGES AND GUESTHOUSES

If you want seclusion—and you want it right on the beach, **Marley Beach Cottages,** P.O. Box PG278, Paget PG BX, Bermuda (tel. 809/236-1143; U.S. reservations: 201/236-1633 in New Jersey; toll free 800/247-2447), could be just the ticket. The small (11-unit) group of cottages clusters around a lovely pool and Jacuzzi, all perched on a bluff overlooking the south shore and Marley Beach. (Because of the breathtaking location, scenes from *Chapter Two* and *The Deep* were filmed here.) Marley Beach itself appears in many travel photos: It is a deep pocket of pink sand, sheltered by jagged boulders and casuarinas. The property is about five miles from Hamilton, two miles from the Southampton Princess. Every one of the pink cottages offers a spectacular view of the sea, rocks, and covelets. Owned and operated by June and Giff Stanton, the resort is personable, informal, and relaxed. Each of the rooms has slightly different layout and furnishings. All come with fully equipped kitchens—right down to the toaster and butter knives. Top choice for honeymooners would be the spacious Sandcastle Studio, with its beige tile floors, rattan furnishings, and jaunty awning that unfurls over the terrace facing the ocean. Or how about "Heaven"—a privately owned cottage that's often for rent. It has a fireplace and fantastic water views. Honeymoon package: Eight days/seven nights (EP): From $970 per couple. Includes a bottle of wine.

Clear View Suites, 10 Sandys Lane, Hamilton Parish CR 02, Bermuda (tel. 809/293-0484; U.S. reservations: toll free 800/468-9600), are romantic—and a good deal too! Located on Bermuda's north shore near Bailey's Bay and Flatts Village, and just five miles from St. George's, the pink-painted cottages face seaward from a rolling green hillside. Each of the 12 units is different—some are studios, others one-bedrooms, all have either full kitchens or kitchenettes, as well as verandas or patios (some even have fireplaces). Each is air-conditioned and comes with a TV. Rooms have an airy, Bermudian feel, with exposed-beam cathedral ceilings, peacock-style wicker chairs, and decorative wicker elephants that double as tables. Everything is fresh, clean, and inviting. Since no meals are included, you can cook your meals in the kitchen or the barbecue grills on the terraces, arrange to dine in Clear View's restaurant, or try any of the other fine dining spots on the island. Clear View has two large pools, there's good snorkeling and swimming in the waters just off shore and at nearby Shelly Bay Beach, plus a scenic route for jogging along the old railroad path down at the water's edge. Honeymoon package: Eight days/seven nights (EP): From $985 per couple. Includes bottle of champagne, souvenir gift, free admission to Crystal Caves and the Bermuda Aquarium, free tennis.

Astwood Cove, 49 South Rd., Warwick WK 07, Bermuda (tel. 809/236-0984; U.S. reservations: 617/879-8102, or toll free 800/225-2230 nationwide; 800/982-4770 in Massachusetts). Built around an 18th-century dairy farm (some of the original structures have been incorporated into the property), Astwood Cove is a cluster of 18 pristine white apartments that surround a free-form pool. Set on a low hill on Bermuda's south shore, the property overlooks woods and the sea. Astwood Cove is owned and operated by Gaby and Nicky Lewin, who make their guests feel welcome and comfortable. The accommodations include studios and suites, all with air conditioning, ceiling fans, and private terraces or patios. Fully equipped, the kitchens come with fine English bone china, wine glasses—even salt-and-pepper shakers. Standard rooms are at pool level; superior rooms occupy the second story and have high cathedral ceilings. Lush green gardens set off the crisp white paint of the buildings: You'll find not only brilliant flowers, but also herbs such as rosemary, thyme, and dill, while an orchard supplies fresh grapefruits, bananas, loquats, and peaches in season. Just across the road, you can swim at Astwood Cove beach, where you follow the footpaths through the casuarinas to pocket-size, private dollops of sand surrounded by limestone boulders. Honeymoon package:

None. Rates (EP): $60 to $80 per couple per night (winter); $90 to $110 per couple per night (summer).

Pretty Penny, P.O. Box PG 137, Paget PG BX, Bermuda (tel. 809/236-1194). Honeymoons that *begin* happily-ever-after start in these fairy-tale cottages nestled in gardens abloom with cherry blossoms and hibiscus. Pretty Penny combines the best of both worlds: the gracious charm of yesteryear for which Bermuda is known, plus newly renovated accommodations that are a perky delight. Located in a quiet neighborhood, the property was formerly a private residence. Painted a glistening shade of vanilla, accented by aqua shutters that match the peerless blue of a Bermudian sea, the cottages surround a gem-like freshwater swimming pool—a popular place for guests to congregate in the late afternoon. Each room is individually decorated with rattan furnishings and immaculate fabrics in floral pastels that resemble a bouquet garnered in the south of France. Although layouts vary, all accommodations have private patios, air conditioning (most also have ceiling fans), telephones, and fully equipped kitchenettes. The room known as "Play Penny" especially befits honeymooners, with a gate you can close off so as to enjoy a private lawn area. All this is just a few minutes' ride from Hamilton and the beach. Honeymoon package: Eight days/seven nights (EP): $540 to $755 per couple per night. Includes a bottle of champagne.

Grape Bay Cottages, P.O. Box PG 137, Paget PG BX, Bermuda (tel. 809/236-1194). So you want privacy. And you want a beach. And you want a prime location, tucked away amid some of Bermuda's most exclusive real estate. You'll find it all at Grape Bay. Privacy—there are only two cottages set on a quiet cul-de-sac. A beach—one of the island's most lovely, a pristine, pink half-mile-long strand that's reserved for area residents. Exclusivity—those aforementioned area residents on Rural Hill include several members of Parliament as well as the American Consul-General, who is your next-door neighbor. The cottages, painted soft pink with trim blue shutters, exude quintessential Bermuda charm. Furnishings combine wicker with contemporary touches—eminently comfortable, if not plush. Although there's no TV, a radio and telephone keep you in touch with the outside world . . . if needed. Maids come in to clean and bring fresh towels and linens daily, except Sunday. Conveniently located, Grape Bay is just minutes away from a grocery store, post office, and cycle livery (you'll probably want mopeds so you can get around readily). As you can imagine, these unique cottages book up way in advance, so make sure you reserve early! Honeymoon package: None. Rates (EP): $150 to $185 per couple per night.

Arlington Heights, Middle Road, Smith's Parish, Bermuda (tel. 809/292-1680). It's hard to say what will win your hearts the most at this flower-filled hideaway. Maybe it will be the gardens, lush with palm trees and hibiscus blossoms. Maybe it will be the large lovely swimming pool, surrounded by inviting pink and blue lounge chairs. Perhaps it will be your own room. Truly a home away from home, it features pleasant contemporary furnishings, a telephone and color TV, air conditioning, and a fully equipped kitchenette—there are even an iron and an ironing board. Several barbecues are set up around the property for impromptu grilling. Set smack-dab in the middle of the island chain that makes up Bermuda, Arlington Heights is near everything you want to do in Bermuda. Hamilton is an 8-minute drive away; the beach, about 10 to 15 minutes; St. George's, just 35 minutes. At the same time, the locale is tranquil, bucolic, with an occasional moo heard from cows in adjoining pastures. Honeymoon package: Eight days/seven nights (EP): $610 per couple. Includes a bottle of wine and fresh flowers upon arrival.

Loughlands Guest House and Cottage, 79 South Rd., Paget PG 03, Bermuda (tel. 809/236-1253). This big white house with green shutters on the crest of a hill in Paget exudes charm and character. The foyer is crammed with magnificent antiques—a towering grandfather clock, Chinese rugs, and bibelots tucked on the sideboard. The main house has 18 guest rooms; there are also seven rooms in the cottage. Although rooms differ slightly, all have private baths. You'll find richly old-fashioned touches such as chenille bedspreads, lace tablecloths, chintz draperies, and quilted floral bedspreads. Bathrooms retain their original 1920s mosaic tiles. The feeling is one of homey contentment; not posh, but eminently comfortable. Rooms in the cottages offer more privacy, but less ambience. Since the property rambles over nine acres, you'll definitely think of yourselves as staying at a private Bermudian estate. There are a new tennis court and a large swimming pool; Elbow Beach is just minutes away. Honeymoon package: None. Rates (CP): $66 to $105 per couple per night.

---

4. Romantic Restaurants in Hamilton

Bermuda offers everything from cozy British pubs where you can bend your elbow with a pint of Watneys on tap to elegant dining palaces that are truly international in scope.

Be sure to try some Bermudian dishes during your stay. Most menus feature "Bermuda fish"—the fresh catch of the day, usually grouper, snapper, or rockfish, generally served pan-fried or broiled. Another specialty is fish chowder, served with a flourishing addition of black rum and spicy sherry peppers. If you honeymoon between September and the end of March, you'll want to savor the succulent Bermuda lobster, or "guinea chicks"—small lobsters that are very tender and sweet. More local favorites include mussel pie, conch stew, Hoppin' John (black-eyed peas and rice), and shark hash—it's quite savory, and served on toast. To wash it all down, order rum swizzles (potent blends of rum and fruit juices) or Dark and Stormys (made with black rum and ginger beer). Because so many of the foodstuffs are imported, restaurant prices tend to be quite high: Figure that a lunchtime hamburger at the Bermudian equivalent of a coffee shop will run about $6.95 per person. Many restaurants require men to wear jackets and ties in the evenings; ask when you make reservations. Also note that some hotels offer dine-around programs with associated properties.

Most restaurants automatically add a service charge of 15% to your bill to cover gratuities. Ask the waiter if you are not sure. To whet your appetite, pick up a copy of *Dining Out in Bermuda,* sold in most local bookstores. It costs $2.75 and lists complete menus and prices for some of Bermuda's most popular restaurants.

For convenience, we've grouped all the Hamilton restaurants together, followed by other dining spots around Bermuda.

EXPENSIVE
Once Upon A Table, 49 Serpentine Rd., just off city hall (tel. 295-8585). Old Bermuda is alive and well at this charmer in Hamilton located in a former private residence. The Victorian surroundings seem made for romance: full-length lace portieres frame the windows, bentwood chairs surround tables set with pale-pink linens, archways separate the different rooms, paintings of flowers counterpoint blossoms on your table. Although the menu highlights continental dishes, you also will find intriguing Bermudian specialties, such as shark hash or corn fritters. The chef has a delicate hand with fish, such as the perfectly poached grouper in fresh sorrel sauce, accompanied by broccoli, new potatoes, and carrots. Other favorites include duck à l'orange, rack of lamb, or chateaubriand for two. The restaurant pulls out all stops for dessert: chocolate mousse, served with a sauce anglais; a pear poached in sauterne, aswim in raspberry sauce. Dinner for two, from $90 to $110 with drinks. Open nightly from 6:30 to 9:30 p.m.

MODERATE
Loquats, 95 Front St. (tel. 292-4507). Light and breezy, this is one of the few restaurants in Bermuda that feel distinctly tropical. Here, you'll enjoy a really nice

dinner that won't break your budget. Located on the second story of a Front Street building, Loquats takes advantage of its setting by placing a few tables out on the white-pillared terrace for alfresco dining with a glorious view of Hamilton Harbour. Inside, the main dining room is airy, with a high cathedral ceiling, light-wood floors, potted orchids, back-lit louvered Bermuda shutters, and stucco walls. The cuisine reflects Oriental and Mediterranean influences. Start off with the crunchy conch fritters or the Oriental "parcel" (pancakes stuffed with Chinese vegetables). For entrées, favorites include the prime rib of beef and the scampi provençale (grilled shrimp sauced with tomatoes, garlic, and white wine). Save room for one of the world's great desserts: profiteroles (like éclairs), nicely mounded with vanilla ice cream and drizzled with chocolate. Lunch, about $20 per couple; served Monday through Friday, noon to 2:30 p.m. Dinner, $50 to $60 per couple; served Monday through Saturday, 5:30 to 11 p.m.

Chopsticks, 63 Reid St. East (tel. 292-0791). For excellent Chinese food and a lively, fun-loving atmosphere, this is the place. The setting suggests Raffles-like foreign intrigue, with a smattering of high-backed wicker chairs, ceiling fans, and Oriental art spotlighted on the walls. Top appetizers include the shrimp toast and the baby-back ribs. Then move on to one of the house specials, such as Hunan pork with scallions, jade chicken (studded with broccoli), or moo goo scallops (stir-fried with Chinese cabbage, mushrooms, and bamboo shoots). Lunch, $15 to $20 per couple; served Monday through Friday, noon to 2:30 p.m. Dinner, about $50 per couple; served Monday through Sunday, 6 to 11 p.m.

Bombay Bicycle Club, 75 Reid St. (tel. 292-0048). The jewel in the crown of Bermuda's exotic restaurants, the Bombay Bicycle Club is known for its varied "homestyle" Indian cuisine, with more than 50 dishes on the menu—over 15 vegetarian side dishes alone. Whirring ceiling fans and rattan chairs seem to transport you to the time of the Raj, and the cuisine is authentic (practically all the chefs are Indian). Entrées travel the range of the Subcontinent's cuisine: from murg chilli korma (a mildly spiced chicken dish from Kashmir) to an incendiary beef curry from Madras certain to bring tears to your eyes. And if you're not in the mood for Indian food, they also offer a full English grill menu. Open for buffet lunch, Monday through Friday, noon to 2:30 p.m.; $10.95 per person. Dinner served Monday through Saturday, 6:30 to 11 p.m.; $30 to $40 per couple plus drinks.

The Conch Shell, Front Street (tel. 295-6969). This stylish and friendly rendezvous perched in a second-story roost over Front Street features aquariums filled with colorful tropical fish, and large windows to let in eyeful views of Hamilton Harbour. You can dine on the outside terrace, shaded by jaunty green umbrellas, or in the more sophisticated indoor dining room, decorated with black bentwood chairs and plenty of leafy green plants. The menu spotlights an intriguing blend of seafood and Asian dishes, with such offerings as St. David's seafood Newburgh, spicy Singapore chicken, ginger beef, as well as steaks, lamb chops, and duck. Dinner for two runs about $50 per couple. Open Monday through Saturday for lunch, noon to 3 p.m.; and snacks, 3 to 5 p.m. Dinner served Monday through Sunday, 6:30 to 10:30 p.m.

New Harbourfront, Front Street opposite the Ferry Terminal (tel. 295-4207 or 295-4527). In nice weather, dine on the terrace overlooking Front Street, watching horse-drawn carriages clop along the road and ferries chug into the landing. Indoors, the ambience is more formal, with French country tables and a baby grand piano contributing background music during the evening hours. Lunches can be casual—a tuna fish sandwich or broiled Bermuda fish ($20 to $40 per couple). For dinner, start off with the giant stuffed mushrooms, then move on to the scampi Riviera, sautéed in brandy with fresh tomatoes, baby clams, and herbs, or the grilled sirloin steak. Dinner for two, $60 to $70 plus drinks. Open Monday through Saturday for lunch, 11:45 a.m. to 3 p.m.; dinner, 6:30 to 10:30 p.m.

The Hog Penny, Burnaby Hill (tel. 292-2534). Bermuda's oldest English-style pub, and certainly one of its most popular, complete with wood paneling, half-

timbered trim, and antique copper and brass dangling over the bar, all producing
the proper dark, clubby feeling. If you fancy a pint, they have Watney Red, Webster's
Yorkshire Bitter, and John Courage Lager on tap. At lunchtime, choose a Hog Penny
burger, Shepherd's pie, or one of their excellent curry dishes ($20 to $30 per couple). Their early-evening special, a three-course dinner for $18 per person, is an espe-
cially good deal. For dinner, try the roast prime rib or Bermuda fish (about $40 per
couple). Open daily for lunch, 11:30 a.m. to 5:30 p.m.; dinner, 6 to 11 p.m. There's
lively entertainment each evening from about 9:15 p.m. until 1 a.m., and you can
sing along with the guitarist or make requests.

The Lobster Pot, Bermudiana Rd. (tel. 292-6898). When you want really
good seafood, head to this Hamilton restaurant with the hybrid England-by-the-
South Seas decor. A bamboo screen worthy of Sadie Thompson stands at the entrance, there's a British timbered ceiling and huge hearth, while an old fishing dory
and miscellaneous lobster traps loll here and there among the fishing nets. You'll
find all your favorite fish dishes on the menu: from fish 'n' chips to cold lobster salad
at lunch, Bermuda rockfish, tuna steak, and, of course, Bermuda lobster and guinea
chicks in season (about $32 per person). Lunch runs $30 to $40 per couple; dinner,
about $60 to $80 per couple. Open Monday through Saturday for lunch, 11:30 a.m.
to 5 p.m.; dinner, 6 to 11 p.m.

Fisherman's Reef, Burnaby Hill, opposite the Flagpole (tel. 292-1609). At
this nautical-motif restaurant, you'll feel as if you're dining 20,000 leagues under
the sea, thanks to the portholes and illuminated slides of fish that form the backdrop.
You can choose your own Maine lobster from the tank out front. The menu also lists
all your favorite fish, plus steak and veal specialties. Or order an aptly named "Bermuda Triangle," a combo plate with a filet mignon, broiled fresh fish, and grilled
scampi. Open Monday through Friday for lunch, noon to 2:30 p.m.; $20 to $40
per couple. Dinner, Monday through Sunday, 6:30 to 10:30 p.m.; $60 to $70 per
couple.

INEXPENSIVE

Prego, 63 Reid St. (tel. 292-0048). Take a look around you—most of your
fellow diners will be Bermudians, who come to this simple neighborhood trattoria
for the good food and reasonable prices. At lunchtime, they serve light dishes such
as pizza or pasta, about $15 to $20 per couple. For dinner, there's a wide range of
Italian favorites: veal scaloppine saltimbocca, rolled chicken breast stuffed with ham
and cheese, linguine in clam sauce, risottos, gnocchi, and more. Dinner for two, $25
to $40 plus drinks. Open Monday through Friday for lunch, noon to 2:30 p.m. Din-
ner, Monday through Saturday, 6:30 to 10 p.m.

Portofino, Bermudiana Road (tel. 292-2375 or 295-6090). Come for a touch
of the old country. A portrait of Mona Lisa grins from the wall, wine bottles hang
from the ceiling, and posters of pasta and the Piazza San Marco clue you in that the
name of the game here is pizza. Order up a Marathon, with tomatoes, mozzarella
cheese, ham, mushrooms, red and green peppers, and olives, or a vegetarian pie with
artichokes, green peppers, and mushrooms. All are excellent (about $9 to $10).
They also have reasonably priced pasta and veal dishes, priced $9 to $16. Open Monday through Friday, noon to 4 p.m. and 6 p.m. to 1 a.m.; Saturday, 6 p.m. to midnight; Sunday, 6 to 11 p.m.

5. Nightlife in Hamilton

Currently the hot spot in Bermuda is **Oasis,** with a disco nightclub. At 69 Front
St., tel. 292-3379 or 292-4978. **The Club** (tel. 295-6693) is also popular; it's on
Bermudiana Road above Little Venice restaurant. At each, the cover charge is about

$20 per couple; jackets required for men. At The Princess Hotel in Hamilton (tel. 295-3000), the **Gazebo Lounge** with its wrap-around views of the city offers different shows nightly. At 9:30 p.m., it's curtain's up on local performers such as singer/comedian Gene Steede, the Talbot Brothers, or the Bermuda Strollers, whose act combines calypso, reggae, R&B, and humor. At 10:45 p.m., there's a Broadway-style revue featuring singing and dancing. Cover charge is $30 per person, which includes two drinks.

---

6. Romantic Restaurants Elsewhere in Bermuda

EXPENSIVE
Tom Moore's Tavern, Harrington Sound Road, Walsingham's Bay (tel. 293-8020). It's hard to imagine a more poetically romantic locale than this Bermuda residence dating back to the 17th century. Here, under a giant calabash tree in the front yard, the Irish poet Thomas Moore is said to have written his farewell to the lady and the island he loved: "Farewell to Bermuda, and long may the bloom/Of the lemon and myrtle its vallies perfume . . ." The restaurant has been beautifully restored and refurbished, and everything reflects the utmost good taste. Seated in a tapestry-covered chair, you'll dine off the finest bone china from Luxembourg and crystal from Germany. The cuisine features superb renditions of classic French recipes, such as oysters poached in champagne and quail stuffed with pâté, truffles, and morels, and baked in a delicate puff pastry. Very expensive, but worth it. Count on spending at least $100 for two, plus wine. Open nightly from 7 to 10 p.m.

Built in 1727 of coral stone and cedar, **Fourways,** No. 1 Middle Rd., Paget (tel. 236-6517), was the private home of the Harvey family for two centuries. Today, meticulously restored, it retains its classic Bermudian charm and ranks as one of Bermuda's most celebrated restaurants. In the main dining room, polished brass chandeliers hang from the massive cedar beams, coral stone archways create intimate nooks, while candlelight, fresh flowers, and classical music complete the haute ambience. The food lives up to its reputation for finesse. The rich lobster bisque is flamed with cognac; ceviche gains a colorful new twist when made with white sea scallops, pearl-gray swordfish, and rosy salmon. Main dishes include a roast duckling with a poached pear, chateaubriand for two, or chicken breasts with a subtle chive, cream, and pink peppercorn sauce. For dessert, try pure ambrosia: the individually prepared soufflés, including a favorite made with Bermuda's own black rum. Open daily for dinner, 6:30 to 10 p.m.; Sunday brunch, 11:30 a.m. to 3 p.m. ($30 per person). Expect to pay $100 to $130 for two for dinner.

MODERATE
The Plantation, Harrington Sound Road, Bailey's Bay (tel. 293-1188). Under the ownership of Christopher and Carol West, this bright yellow 1930s home with the trim white shutters has become one of Bermuda's most captivating restaurants. Fresh, springtime colors create the sunny mood of an outdoor gazebo. Hanging baskets of philodendrons and ferns overhead, and little nosegays of daisies and freesias on the tables, complete the greenhouse picture. In nice weather, you can also dine outside under the bright yellow-and-white marquee surrounded by gardens (which are spotlit at night). The menu stars a string of delectable dishes at both lunch and dinner. Luncheons are light—an assortment of sandwiches, salads, and hamburgers (priced $7 to $14). Dinner choices reflect creativity and panache. Hot appetizers include a mousseline of Bermuda fish served with watercress sauce, and chicken and mushrooms served in a puff pastry. For your entrée, choose among such items as charcoal-broiled yellowfin tuna or lamb "loquat," a mignon of lamb grilled and accompanied by a loquat chutney. Dinner for two will run about $70 per couple plus

drinks. Open daily for lunch, noon to 2:30 p.m.; dinner, 7 to 9:15 p.m. The restaurant closes annually from mid-December through February.

Mikado Steak House, Marriott's Castle Harbour, Tucker's Town (tel. 293-2040). Tradition-loving Bermuda doesn't easily embrace trends—so it's the ultimate compliment that this new restaurant at Marriott's Castle Harbour has zoomed into prominence as Bermuda's "in" spot. Make reservations far in advance—it's *that* hard to get into. Mikado is Bermuda's only Japanese restaurant, and it is drop-dead gorgeous. The decor delights in the dramatic: The entranceway is filled with cherry blossoms and shoji screens; you enter over a little bridge that crosses a pond. Mikado features teppan-grilled items, with chicken, beef, and seafood dishes prepared by your chef right in front of you. Your four-course prix-fixe meal includes miso or clear soup, salad, a shrimp or scallop appetizer, as well as your main course. Complete dinner priced from $24 to $34 per person, depending on which entrée you choose. Whatever you do, don't miss the fried ice cream for dessert. It's rolled in a crunchy coating, quick fried, and topped with honey or chocolate sauce ($4.25). Open Tuesday through Sunday, 6:30 to 10 p.m.

Henry VIII Pub and Restaurant, South Shore Road, Southampton (tel. 238-0908 or 238-1977). For a fine evening, try this traditional inn located conveniently near the Southampton Princess and Sonesta hotels. The British atmosphere comes through nicely thanks to the exposed-beam ceilings hung with a miscellany of brass artifacts. At lunchtime, both the atmosphere and the menu are lighthearted. In addition to salad platters and sandwiches, you'll find good pub fare, such as fish-and-chips, steak-and-kidney pie, and an excellent rendition of Bermuda's own mussel pie. Lunch for two should run about $25 to $30 per couple plus drinks. In the evening, the setting is more formal. The royal menu specialties include the court jester (an array of broiled seafood); steak Anne Boleyn, flavored with Armagnac; and prime ribs with Yorkshire pudding. In season, Henry VIII features both Bermuda lobster and guinea chicks. Dinner for two: about $70 per couple plus drinks. Also check out the nightly entertainment at The Oak Room, the English pub right next door. Open daily for lunch, noon to 4 p.m.; dinner, 7 to 10:30 p.m.

Wharf Tavern, Somers Wharf, St. George's (tel. 297-1515). One of the nicest choices for seafood in Bermuda's east end. You'll know the catch is fresh—at the dock just outside, the fishing boats tie up, along with glamorous yachts from all over the world. In nice weather, you can dine outside overlooking the harbor; inside, the decor continues the nautical ambience with captain's chairs at the tables, and fish nets hanging from the ceiling. Start off with a Bermuda fish chowder, liberally laced with rum and sherry peppers, then savor some rockfish, guinea chicks, or a filet mignon and shrimp combo. They also serve a savory collection of pizzas. Dinner for two, $20 to $40 plus drinks. Open daily from 11:30 a.m. to 3 p.m. and 6 to 11 p.m.

7. Nightlife Elsewhere in Bermuda

When you want big-time entertainment and a lavish show, head over to the extravaganzas at the **Southampton Princess.** Greg Thompson's "Follies" is a glittering salute to the best of Broadway, with talented singers and dancers performing numbers from hit shows. Doors open at 9:30 p.m.; admission is $30 per person, which includes two drinks. For reservations, tel. 238-2555.

BONAIRE

If you crave an uncrowded and unspoiled island for your honeymoon—this is it! The flamingoes outnumber the people on Bonaire.

Located 50 miles off the coast of Venezuela, Bonaire is the second-largest island in the Netherlands Antilles. It ranks as one of the best diving destinations in the world, but not all of the arid coral reef's allure lies beneath the crystal-clear waters. Bonaire has couple-size coves, idyllic beaches, and dramatic vistas. Its greatest attraction, though, is a totally unhurried atmosphere.

The white-trimmed, ocher-colored buildings in the miniature capital of Kralendijk on the west coast provide a clue to the island's colonial heritage. Bonaire was discovered in 1499 by Amerigo Vespucci; Spain, Holland, France, and England vied for possession until 1816, when the Dutch took permanent possession. Kralendijk is just a few blocks long, but it provides the center for all activity on the island. One of its two main streets runs along the waterfront, where the casual open-air restaurants are located. Stop in at Karel's Beachfront Bar, overlooking the protected harbor and the uninhabited islet of Klein Bonaire. It's just the place to ease into your vacation, and to watch for the green flash at sunset.

Diving dominates the activity (and the conversation) on Bonaire, where you'll be able to see coral formations and improbably colored fish along the beach right in front of your hotel. This is a protected environment; the Bonaire Marine Park encompasses all land and water from the high-water tidemark to a depth of 200 feet. Many of the best dive sites lie immediately off-shore.

But there are things to see above the high-water mark too, so rent a car or jeep and head for the hills. Bring a mask and snorkel, though. The island is only 24 miles long and less than 7 miles at its widest point; all roads eventually lead to the beach, and there will be plenty of opportunities to stop for a swim.

The northwest part of the island is mountainous, with desert-like terrain studded with giant cactus that soar as high as 30 feet. The road out of town winds along the curving coast, before it begins to climb through the hills. At Gotomeer, a salt-water lake, you can usually spot hundreds of flamingoes flaunting their pink plumage quite close to the road. You'll continue to climb, until the road crests along a ridge called "Para Mira," where there's an observation point with panoramic views in all directions. Down below, you'll see the orange roofs of Rincon, Bonaire's oldest village, which was settled in the early 1600s, and the road that leads from the town to the entrance of Washington/Slagbaai National Park, a 13,500-acre wildlife preserve is clearly visible.

The park's northern coast is made up of volcanic rock cliffs and wildly desolate bays that are popular spots for hiking, picnicking, and sunbathing. It's impossible to swim off the rugged coral cliffs, but if you continue on to the secluded coves along the western edge of the park, you'll find a number of private, protected beaches.

The southern part of Bonaire is as flat as a pancake, except for the mounds of snow-white salt crystals of the Antilles International Salt Company. Within the salt-works property, there are protected breeding grounds for more than 10,000 flamingoes. Access is strictly prohibited, but from the road you can often see hundreds of the birds taking off for Venezuela in the sunset. At the southern tip of the island, the coral-hued sands of the Pink Beach attract beachcombers. Although this is the longest stretch of beach on Bonaire, it's not unusual to have it all to yourself. On the opposite coast, the shores of the almost completely landlocked Lac Bay are piled with conch shells, and its waters form a natural aquarium filled with exotic marine life.

There's not much nightlife on Bonaire, but that doesn't mean that everything stops when the sun goes down! The scuba-divers are still out there, and if you walk along the beach, you'll be able to see the torches of the night divers flickering underwater. In the evening, Kralendijk's two main streets throng with people, and the downtown area comes to life. Music spills from the alfresco bars and restaurants, and the town takes on a carnival air. It doesn't last long, though, and soon the only music you'll hear will be from E Wowo, Bonaire's only disco. If you're determined to stay up late, head for the casino at the Divi Flamingo Beach Resort.

1. Practical Facts

GETTING THERE

U.S. citizens need proof of citizenship and a return or continuing ticket. Although a passport is preferred, an authenticated birth certificate or a voter registration card is also accepted. The departure tax is $10 per person for those returning to the United States; the tax is $5.75 for interisland departures.

American Airlines provides daily flights from New York to Aruba and Curaçao, with an **ALM Antillean Airline** connection to Bonaire. ALM also offers flights from New York by way of Haiti. In addition, ALM has several interisland flights to Bonaire from Aruba and Curaçao. In season, you can also often find reasonably priced direct charters; ask your travel agent for details.

The Bonaire Government Tourist Office is hopeful that there will be more direct flights from the United States in the near future.

Bonaire's hotels are just minutes from the Flamingo International Airport; the taxi fare is approximately $5.

GETTING AROUND

Taxis don't have meters; the rates are based on your destination, rather than the mileage. Rates are fixed by the government; sample fares are posted at the airport. You should always confirm fares with drivers before you ride.

A **rental car** is almost a necessity on Bonaire; there's no public transportation, and taxi rides to scattered points of interest are expensive. There are a number of rental companies on Bonaire; car and Jeep rentals run approximately $30 a day; scooters are approximately $25 a day (plus insurance). Driving is on the right-hand side, as it is in the United States. Bonaire uses international road signs.

LANGUAGE

Bonaire's native tongue is "Papiamento," a language that evolved from Spanish, Dutch, and Portuguese and combines a sprinkling of African and French, as well as Caribbean Indian dialects. You won't experience a language problem, though. Most Bonaireans are multilingual, speaking several languages including Dutch, Spanish, and English.

MONEY

The currency of the Netherlands Antilles is the guilder (NAf), which fluctuates on the world market. At this writing, there are 1.77 guilders to the dollar.

The guilder is divided into 100 cents, and there are coins of 1 cent, 2½ cents, 5 cents (square nickel), 10 cents, 25 cents, and the 1 and 2½ guilder coins. Bank notes are issued in denominations of 1, 2½, 5, 10, 25, 50, 100, 250, and 500 guilders.

If you also travel to Aruba, don't let the square coin confuse you! In Bonaire and Curaçao the square coin is a nickel; in Aruban currency it's a 50-cent piece.

U.S. dollars are accepted everywhere on the island, but you may receive guilders as change. Although the hotels accept major credit cards, many restaurants and shops require cash payment.

WEATHER

The climate in Bonaire is dry and sunny, and it's always summer there. The temperature hovers at a warm 82°, cooled by pleasant trade winds. There's only a slight change of temperature from day to night, and the temperature difference between summer and winter is only 2° or 3°. The average rainfall is 22 inches per year, which occurs in brief showers during the months of October, November, and December. This isn't truly a rainy season, though, and if you do seek shelter, you'll be able to get right back onto the beach. The island lies completely outside the hurricane belt.

CLOTHING

Cool, casual, and informal clothes are the rule in Bonaire, for both men and women. You'll practically live in a bathing suit—so bring a couple with you. Although some women dress for dinner in sundresses, jackets for men are rarely seen.

TIME

Bonaire keeps Atlantic Standard Time all year long. That means that during the winter, it's one hour later than it is in U.S. East Coast cities; during the summer, when U.S. cities observe Daylight Saving Time, the time is the same.

TELEPHONES

You can call Bonaire direct from the mainland United States. The international dialing code is 011; the area code is 599-7; then dial the four-digit local number. When making local calls in Bonaire, just dial the four-digit local number.

You can make local and international telephone calls through hotel operators. The average price for a three-minute call to the mainland United States is approximately $10.

SHOPPING

U.S. Customs regulations allow U.S. citizens a $400 duty-free quota.

Most of Bonaire's shops are located along **Kaya Grandi** in Kralendijk. Although Spritzer & Fuhrmann and Littman Jewelers have small shops located there,

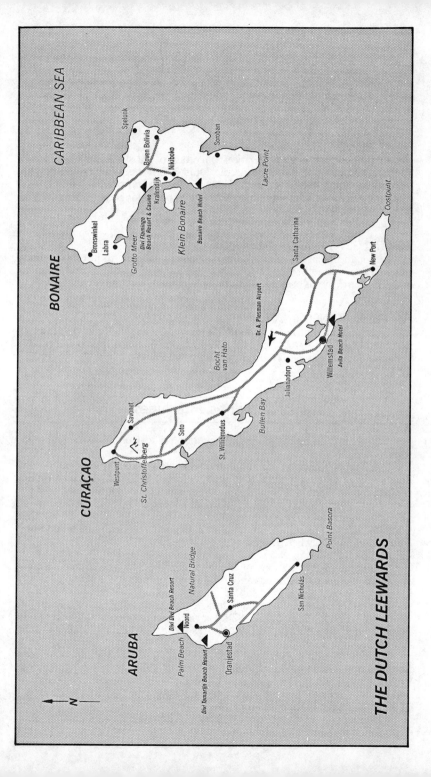

CARIBBEAN SEA

BONAIRE

Spelunk

Rowen Bolivia
Nikiboko
Kralendijk
Divi Flamingo
Beach Resort & Casino

Bronswinkel
Labra

Grotto Meer

Klein Bonaire

Soroban

Lacre Point

Bonaire Beach Hotel

CURAÇAO

Santa Catharina

New Port

Oostpunt

Dr. A. Plesman Airport

Bocht
van Hato

Savonet

St. Christoffelberg

Soto

St. Willibrordus

Bullen Bay

Juliahadorp

Willemstad

Avila Beach Hotel

Westpunt

ARUBA

Point Basora

Natural Bridge

Divi Divi Beach Resort

Noord

Santa Cruz

San Nicholás

Palm Beach

Oranjestad

Divi Tamarijn Beach Resort

N

THE DUTCH LEEWARDS

for the most part, the shopping in Bonaire is for inexpensive items, especially printed T-shirts. Two of the best boutiques are located in the Divi Flamingo Beach Resort and the Sunset Beach Hotel. Dive shops carry the latest in snorkeling, scuba-diving, and photography gear. Local arts and handcrafts include wood carvings and silver and gold jewelry decorated with flamingo motifs. Shop hours are from 8 a.m. to noon and 2 to 6 p.m., daily except Sunday.

SIGHTSEEING

A number of sightseeing operations offer tours of the island and Washington/Slagbaai National Park, including **Archie Tours & Transport** (tel. 8630), **Bonaire Sightseeing Tours** (tel. 8300, ext. 225), and **Flamingo Tours** (tel. 8310). Half-day island tours are priced at approximately $10 to $25; day-long excursions to the national park cost $45.

HOW TO GET MARRIED IN BONAIRE

Although Bonaire extends a warm and cordial welcome to just-married couples, you won't be able to say "I do" while visiting. Marriages are permitted only if one of the partners has been a resident of Bonaire for at least one year.

FOR FURTHER INFORMATION

Contact: **Bonaire Tourist Bureau,** Kaya Simon Bolivar 12, Kralendijk, Bonaire, N.A. (tel. 011/599-7/8322 or 011/599-7/8649). **Bonaire Tourist Office,** 275 Seventh Ave., New York, NY 10001 (tel. 212/242-7707).

---

2. Romantic Interludes

Bonaire is for couples who love the outdoors, above or below the high-water mark!

You'll probably get the urge to at least try **diving** while you're in Bonaire. Introductory dive programs and resort courses run about $80. You'll learn everything you need to know about equipment and technique in the morning, and you'll be diving in the afternoon. Contact **Sand Dollar Dive and Photo** at the Sand Dollar Condominiums (tel. 8738), **Dive Inn** at the Sunset Beach Hotel (tel. 8448), **Dive Bonaire** at the Divi Flamingo Beach Resort & Casino (tel. 8285), or **Captain Don's Habitat** (tel. 8290), where Dee Scarr takes divers on nature walks underwater (tel. 8529).

All of the dive operations on Bonaire offer specially priced dive packages; snorkelers and nondivers can go out on the dive boats on a space-available basis for approximately $12 per person.

You can bring home one-hour videos of your underwater escapades shot by a divemaster at **Photo Bonaire** (tel. 8285) at the Divi Flamingo Beach, or by Andre Nahr at **Sand Dollar Dive and Photo** (tel. 8738) at the Sand Dollar Condominiums.

Rent a Jeep (a car will do), and "safari" through the 13,500-acre **Washington/Slagbaai National Park,** located at the northern tip of the island. You'll discover an ever-changing landscape, waves crashing against coral cliffs on the northern coast, and idyllic beaches with mysterious caverns and caves to the west. The roads are rugged and dusty, but safe and well marked.

Flamingoes usually congregate near the beach at Playa Funchi (also one of the best picnicking, swimming, and snorkeling spots on the island) and in the brackish waters of Gotomeer. Whether you're a serious "birder" or not, you can't help but be awed by the unusually large number of birds (including brightly colored parakeets) that appear in the early morning and late afternoon at Put Bronswinkel, Posi Mangel, and Saliña Slagbaai.

The park is open seven days a week from 8 a.m. to 5 p.m., except for major holidays. Admission is $2 per person.

Your hotel activities desk can arrange for a water taxi to take you to the uninhabited island of **Klein Bonaire** for a picnic or barbecue. If you do go out to this 1,500-acre desert island, wear running shoes (not sandals) and a hat. There's a rough coral beach, and the cactus doesn't provide shade from the sun. They can also arrange full- or half-day sailing charters and sunset cruises. **Karel's Watersports** (tel. 8434) opposite the Zeezicht Restaurant, and run by its owners, rents couple-size motorboats for approximately $30 per hour, and everything you need for fishing for $60 for a half day. They also have jet skis ($25 for half an hour) and glass-bottomed-boat rides ($10 for an hour trip). **Windsurfing Bonaire** (tel. 8095) provides Windsurfers for $35 a half day or $15 an hour.

Pack a basket with Dutch cheese, bread, some wine or a bottle of champagne, and head for a picnic on your own **private beach.** There are so many spots on Bonaire that you can have all to yourselves, that it may be hard for you to choose. It could be at **Boca Cocolishi,** in the national park, with its protected swimming basin and black-sand beach. Perhaps you'd prefer Lac Bay or the Pink Beach at the southern end of the island.

The boulder-strewn white-sand beach at out-of-the-way Nukove, on the western coast, may be the most romantic spot on Bonaire. Waves lap the sands that seem to sparkle, and a cooling breeze rustles through the greenery shading the fringes. Off a little-used road, just before Playa Funchi, Nukove is well known to the scuba-divers who begin shore dives there. It has to be the diving community's best-kept secret.

---

3. Honeymoon Hotels and Hideaways

Bonaire offers a wide range of accommodations, from resort facilities to small waterfront bungalows, apartments, and condominiums. You won't find any highrises; most accommodations don't have telephones or TVs in the rooms; many aren't air-conditioned. There is a 5% government room tax and a 10% service charge on all room rates. The service charge on food and beverages is 10% to 15% in lieu of gratuities at the hotels.

All accommodations listed are within a mile of Krajendijk, the capital. High season runs from about December 15 to April 15; low-season rates are about 20% to 30% lower. Prices quoted reflect the spread between low- and high-season rates.

Relaxed and casual, the **Divi Flamingo Beach Resort & Casino,** Kralendijk, Bonaire, N.A. (tel. 011-599-7/8285; U.S. reservations: 607/277-3484, or toll free 800/367-3484), perfectly captures the mood and feeling that pervades Bonaire. The architecture is in Spanish style, with red-tile roofs, white stucco walls, and darkwood trim; the decor is tropical, with cool cotton fabrics in floral prints. All 145 rooms are air-conditioned, with sheltered patios or balconies. There's an intimate feel to this beachfront resort, which includes a freshwater swimming pool and secluded outdoor Jacuzzi. Its "barefoot casino" is housed in a beautifully restored manor house, a historic Bonairean landmark.

The dining facilities are outstanding. In particular, breakfast at the Calabas Terrace is a real treat: fresh muffins and pastries, and mounds of sliced tropical fruits are just the beginning. Dive Bonaire operates from a pier on the grounds. Honeymoon package: Eight days/seven nights (CP): From $946 up per couple. Includes deluxe oceanfront accommodations, one dinner with champagne, a picnic lunch, wine, two souvenir glasses, a beach towel, a photo album, and round-trip airport transfers. Dive packages available.

Sand Dollar Condominiums, near Kralendijk; mailing address: 50 George-town Rd., Bordentown, NJ 08505 (tel. 609/298-3844, or toll free 800/345-0805), when finished by 1990, will boast 83 spacious units, all with air conditioning, ceiling fans, immaculate kitchens, and ocean views. A new grocery store, restaurant, and casino will supplement the good-size swimming pool, cabana, and two tennis courts (with night lighting); in addition, André and Gabrielle Nahr will be operating a dive-and-photo shop, with opportunities to take the plunge directly off-shore. Olive, divi-divi, and flowering trees and shrubs already punctuate the grounds, which spread to eleven acres. You can take your choice from a studio unit with fold-up bed, a one-bedroom unit, a two-bedroom town house—or bigger if you want to get lost together. And let owners Sylvia Milton and her son, Gary Weisberg, know you're on your honeymoon: They'll add flowers and wine to the room in anticipation of your arrival. Honeymoon package: None. Rates: $125 to $245 per couple per night.

Sunset Beach Hotel, P.O. Box 333, Bonaire, N.A. (tel. 011-599-7/8448; U.S. reservations: toll free 800/223-9815). Formerly the Bonaire Beach Hotel & Casino, the Sunset Beach reopened under new ownership in June 1989. Besides refurbishing and redecorating all 120 air-conditioned rooms, the hotel brought in a beachful of white sand to supplement the existing 600-foot Playa Leche. Eleven buildings sprawl across 12 acres that include a new full-service dive and water-sports facility and a renovated beach bar and restaurant. The rooms now have minifridges, cable TVs, and two double beds set in a tropical-green and mustard decor. Honeymoon package: None at press time. Rates: $55 to $150 per couple per night.

Cap'n Don's Habitat/Hamlet, P.O. Box 88, Bonaire, N.A. (tel. 011-599-7/8290; U.S. reservations: 212/535-9530; toll free 800/223-5581 or 800/327-6709). "Habitat is a concept—an attitude—not a hotel," philosophizes Captain Don, who runs this unique diving- and nature-oriented retreat. Lush vegetation and landscaped palms, flowering plants, and bougainvillea ensure a sense of privacy for approximately 150 guests. Loll in a hammock, or enjoy the companionship of kindred spirits at the open-air restaurant and bar. Habitat offers comfort in a natural environment; there are 4 deluxe studio accommodations with private baths, 10 two-bedroom Mediterranean-style cottages, 16 deluxe doubles, 20 superior villa doubles, and 3 deluxe villa suites. The tidy villas look like a modern interpretation of traditional Spanish architecture with red-tile roofs and upstairs balconies highlighted by turquoise balustrades. The dive operation is staffed by expert dive masters and certified instructors and is considered one of the best in the Caribbean. Honeymoon package: Call for details. Standard eight day/seven night rate (CP): $664 to $980 per person includes buffet breakfast, six days of boat dives, unlimited off-shore diving, and airport transfers. Nondivers can use the à la carte plan with room rates from $423 to $690 per person per week.

---

4. Romantic Restaurants

There are a number of fine restaurants featuring a wide variety of international cuisine in Kralendijk and along the waterfront. The fish and seafood here are fresh, fresh, fresh!

Restaurant prices are usually listed in both guilders and U.S. dollars; a 10% to 15% service charge is frequently added to your bill. Unless otherwise noted, all restaurants are in Kralendijk.

Chibi Chibi, at the Divi Flamingo Beach Resort (tel. 8285/8485). Don't miss this trilevel open-air restaurant cantilevered over Calabas Reef—it's just spectacular! The reef is lighted from under the water, and you can toss bread to the best-fed fish in the Caribbean! We were hard-pressed to choose our favorite appetizer: The escargot in mushrooms ($6.50) in a light garlic butter sauce was superb, the gazpacho ($2.95) with crispy, crunchy, garden fresh vegetables was perfectly chilled. Seafood and steaks priced at $15 to $20. Open from 6 to 10 p.m. nightly. Reservations recommended.

Den Laman Aquarium Restaurant & Bar, between the Sand Dollar Condominiums and the Sunset Beach Hotel (tel. 8955). If you haven't had your fill of underwater scenes, come here. A giant aquarium with numerous colorful fish and lobsters forms one entire wall. The denizens are to look at, not to eat, however. Seafood entrées range from $11 to $26.50. The fresh-fish specials are always good, and the Coral Reef combo ($18.85) is out of this world. Desserts and appetizers will add another few dollars to the meal. Open from 6 to 11 p.m. daily except Tuesday. Reservations recommended.

Zeezicht Restaurant & Bar, Kaya Corsow, overlooking the harbor and Klein Bonaire (tel. 8434). This popular hangout exudes lots of character; it's been operated by the same family since 1929. Because of the fine views, prime tables are on the veranda; inside, the decor is crisp, white, and nautical, with lamps made of foot-long conch shells hanging over the bar. Seafood is the specialty here. If you can't make up your mind, try the Special II ($20)—a smorgasbord of lobster, conch, shrimp, fish, and octopus. Breakfast ranges from $2 to $4; lunch from $5 to $16; complete dinners from $5 to $20. The menu emphasizes seafood. Open daily from 8:30 a.m. to 11 p.m. No reservations taken.

Lisboa Terrace, in the Hotel Rochaline, Kaya Grandi (tel. 8286). The whitewashed walls with classic arches frame travel poster-like views of the fish market, the harbor, and Klein Bonaire. It's a casual place, featuring local seafood dishes and special pizzas. Go for the Rochaline Special Appetizer ($6.85), half of a melon-size avocado literally stuffed with shrimp, and the special broiled lobster ($28.50), indescribably delicious. Other appetizers priced from $4.85. Entrées priced from about $7 to $40 (paella for two). Open daily for breakfast, 7:30 to 11 a.m.; lunch, 11 a.m. to 3 p.m.; dinner, 6 to 11 p.m. Reservations recommended.

The Green Parrot, at the Sand Dollar Condominiums (tel. 8738), is run under the able hands of Americans Jim Hough and Sara Matera, who have created a restaurant that combines the best of both worlds: island flavors with U.S. service. Besides the nightly specials—which range from barbecued chicken, ribs, and Italian sausage to the local keshi yena to wonderfully fresh fish—the Green Parrot serves up U.S. steaks, homemade cakes, and killer frozen fruit drinks (Lora Berde, the Green Parrot Special, includes a take-home surprise). Lunch satisfies American tastes too, with good burgers, deli sandwiches, and salads. Be sure to reserve early and ask for one of the four tables directly on the water; you couldn't ask more for romance. Prices range from $3.50 to $9 per person for lunch and from $9.50 to $19.95 per person for dinner; a tropical drink will add another $3.50 or $4 to your bill. Wine list with champagne. Open daily from 8 a.m. to 10:30 p.m.

Egretta Bar & Restaurant, located in the Lac Bay area of Sorobon and well worth the 15-minute drive it takes from Kralendijk to get there. The decor is an eclectic mix of cactus, European antiques, and noisy macaws, and it works beautifully. The luncheon menu features homemade soups and Dutch-style sandwiches priced at about $5. Dinner entrées priced from about $15. There's no phone, but the restaurant is open daily Tuesday through Saturday from 11 a.m. to 11 p.m. and on Sunday from 5 to 11 p.m.

Bistro des Amis, on Kaya L.D. Gerharts (tel. 8003 after 5 p.m. or 8770 from 8 a.m. to 5 p.m.). Elegant, and excellent. Save room for the homemade ice cream. Dinner for two: $40 plus drinks. Open from 6:30 to 11:30 p.m. ; closed Sunday; reservations absolutely necessary. **Rendez Vouz,** on Kaya L.D. Gerharts (tel. 8454 or 8539). Vegetarian dinners around $8, seafood specialties from around $13. Dinner from 6 to 11 p.m.; closed Tuesday. Espresso and cappuccino served all evening at the bar.

5. Nightlife

Despite the focus on outdoor activities, the fun on Bonaire doesn't stop when the sun goes down. Bonaire's only disco, **E. Wowo** (tel. 8998), is located on Kaya Grandi, and opens for business every night. On Saturday, you can see the costumed dancers at the **Pirate House,** on the second level of the Zeezicht Restaurant (tel. 8434). There's also blackjack, roulette, and slot-machine action at the **Divi Flamingo Beach Casino** (tel. 8285 or 8485) from 6 p.m. till the early morning hours.

THE BRITISH VIRGIN ISLANDS

Sunset. The three-masted barquentine cruises across the horizon, her square-rigged sails silhouetted against the crimson sun. Overhead, a black-and-red frigate bird gyres slowly, its seven-foot wingspan catching the rising thermal. Along the shore, fishermen haul in huge seining nets, heavy with yellowtail and grouper.

It's a scene that could have happened 300 years ago—or one that you could witness today, honeymooning in the British Virgin Islands.

Located in the Caribbean Sea about 60 miles east of Puerto Rico and right next to the United States Virgin Islands, the B.V.I. encompasses about 50 different islands. These range in size from 12-mile-long Tortola, site of Road Town, the capital, to teeny lava rock outcrops like the Indians where only the seabirds roost. Only 16 of the islands are inhabited; only 7 even offer tourist accommodations.

What makes the B.V.I. so romantic? First of all, it's the sheer number of emerald-green, palm-thatched, bougainvillea-draped islands that surround you. All of the B.V.I. (with the exception of Anegada) surround the 22-mile-long Sir Francis Drake Channel—creating a veritable pleasure bowl for vacationers, especially sailors. Stand on the deck of a boat or atop a mountain and gaze around you—your glance can take in over 20 islands at a time. Then look again. On the fringes of many of these jungled, green islands, dazzling white, coral sand beaches catch your attention.

If your honeymoon agenda includes the search for the perfect beach, you'll find many candidates here. Strands like Cane Garden Bay on Tortola, White Bay on Jost Van Dyke, the Baths on Virgin Gorda, and Deadman's Bay on Peter Island easily belong on any "Best in the World" list. Meanwhile, the warm, transparent Caribbean Sea convinces all beholders that the color blue can exist in infinite gradations.

The division of the island chain into the United States and the British Virgin Islands owes more to the whims of history than the imperatives of geography—the two groups lie less than a 45-minute ferry ride from each other. The islands were discovered by Christopher Columbus in 1493. "Very mountainous," he recorded in his diary. "And very green down to the sea. A delight to see." He was so struck by their beauty and purity, he named them after the legendary followers of St. Ursula.

For the next hundred years, the islands snoozed peacefully, ignored by the major European powers until 1595, when Sir Francis Drake led a fleet through the channel that now bears his name. The English, Dutch, and Spanish disputed possession until 1672, when England annexed Tortola.

However, the major power in these islands was an international gaggle of pirates, cutthroats, and brigands who plundered treasure ships heading from Mexico and South America to Europe. Buccaneer legends still pervade the region. Robert Louis Stevenson reportedly based *Treasure Island* on tales about Norman Island. The island Jost Van Dyke is named for a Dutch pirate; on Dead Chest Island, the notorious Blackbeard is said to have marooned some of his men, giving rise to the "Yo, ho, ho, and a bottle of rum" ditty.

Toward the end of the 17th century, the islands regained middle-class stability when many English planters arrived to farm the land. Today, the B.V.I. has a population of about 11,000 and is a British territory, administered by a governor appointed by the queen. Although the official language is the queen's English, warmed by West Indian accents, and pub menus highlight traditional English favorites such as fish 'n' chips and Pimm's Cup, the official currency is the U.S. dollar.

The British Virgin Islands is perfect for couples who really want to get away. Very few hotel rooms have televisions; "air conditioning" usually comes via the trade winds or *Casablanca*-style ceiling fans; and you won't need to ride an elevator to get to the beach. This low-key lifestyle has attracted some high-powered vacationers. Paul McCartney, Steven Spielberg, and Neil Young have all cruised the B.V.I. aboard yachts. Princess Di along with a royal entourage vacationed on private Necker Island off Virgin Gorda, and a crowned monarch and his queen were recently spotted on a buffet line at Peter Island.

Honeymooners who love sports and the outdoors will find plenty to do in the B.V.I. Such as sailing. What Aspen is to skiers or Mount Everest is to climbers, the B.V.I. represents for sailors—namely, the best in the world. Even if you're not sailors yourselves, you can hop aboard one of the many day sails that embark for uninhabited cays, or charter a yacht with a skipper. Scuba-divers and snorkelers will also find top-class conditions, with visibilities of 60 to 150 feet, and varied sites to explore—from underwater caves to coral forests and shipwrecks. On land, you can play tennis, saddle up for horseback riding, or take a hike.

Wherever you go, you'll discover another natural resource of the B.V.I.—its friendly people. Some friends recently rented a car on Tortola, and told the rental agent that they wanted to return the vehicle later in the evening, when the office would be closed. Was that a problem? "No problem," the agent smiled. "Just leave the keys in the car—and don't lock the door."

Now, we're not recommending that people leave keys in unlocked cars. But the story illustrates the openness and the warmth of B.V.I. residents. As you motor along, other drivers will toot their horns in greeting; children wave as they ride home on donkeys. You'll feel very welcome here—almost as though you've come home yourself.

---

1. Practical Facts

GETTING THERE

Americans need proof of U.S. citizenship. A valid passport is preferred; however, an authenticated birth certificate or voter registration card is also acceptable.

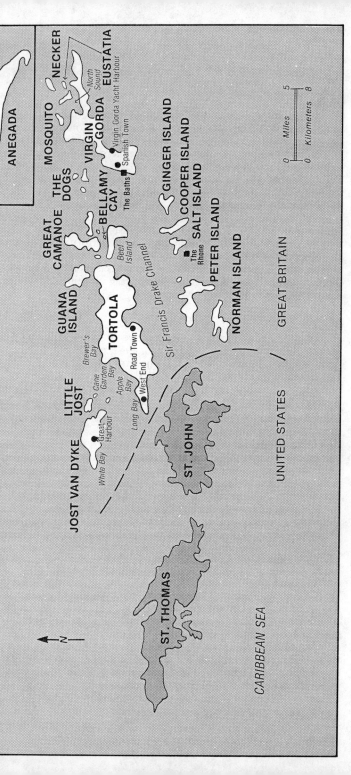

BRITISH VIRGIN ISLANDS

ANEGADA

NECKER
MOSQUITO
EUSTATIA
North Sound
VIRGIN GORDA
Virgin Gorda Yacht Harbour
Spanish Town
THE DOGS
The Baths

GREAT CAMANOE
BELLAMY CAY
Beef Island

GINGER ISLAND
COOPER ISLAND
SALT ISLAND
The Rhone

GUANA ISLAND
TORTOLA
Brewer's Bay
Road Town
Cane Garden Bay
Apple Bay
West End
Long Bay
Sir Francis Drake Channel
PETER ISLAND
NORMAN ISLAND

LITTLE JOST
JOST VAN DYKE
Great Harbour
White Bay

ST. JOHN

GREAT BRITAIN

UNITED STATES

ST. THOMAS

CARIBBEAN SEA

N

0   Miles   5
0   Kilometers   8

There is a departure tax of $5 per person if you leave by air, $3 per person if you depart by boat.

It's easy to reach the B.V.I. from most places in the United States.

By Air

Although there are currently no direct flights from the continental United States, you can take advantage of several convenient connecting flights daily from San Juan, Puerto Rico, and St. Thomas, in the U.S. Virgin Islands.

To Tortola: The airport is located on Beef Island, at the far eastern end of Tortola. From San Juan, you can fly into the Beef Island Airport on **American Eagle, Air BVI, Eastern Metro,** and **Crownair.** From St. Thomas, you can take Air BVI into the Beef Island Airport; the **V.I. Seaplane Shuttle** lands at West End. Consequently, the sea plane is more convenient if your hotel is on the western side of the island.

To Virgin Gorda: Air BVI, Eastern Metro, and American Eagle fly daily from San Juan; Air BVI and American Eagle fly daily from St. Thomas.

To Anegada: Air BVI flies from Beef Island, Tortola, several days a week.

Since the airplanes that fly into the B.V.I. are quite small, they have limited luggage capacity. To help assure that your luggage gets on the same flight that you do, check in early and pack light. To play it safe, take a bathing suit and personal essentials with you in a small carry-on bag.

By Sea

Frequent, convenient, and inexpensive **ferries**—including **Smith's Ferry Service,** Native Son, and Speedy's Fantasy—connect the B.V.I. with both St. Thomas and St. John in the U.S.V.I. The ferry ride takes about one hour from St. Thomas to Tortola (Road Town), about 20 minutes from St. John to Tortola (West End). To Virgin Gorda, the high-speed **North Sound Express** ferry runs from near Tortola's Beef Island Airport to North Sound. The ferries are your best bet if you have a lot of luggage. Fares run $13 to $15 per person each way.

GETTING AROUND

Once you arrive in the B.V.I., you have a wide choice of transportation.

By Taxi

Taxis are available only on Tortola and Virgin Gorda. Rates between destinations are fixed by law and are charged per person, and vary according to the number of people in the cab. Rates are moderate. For example, Road Town, Tortola, to the airport costs approximately $13.50 per couple. Although fares are reasonable, expenditures can add up if you take a lot of taxis.

Rental Cars

Once again, these are available only on Tortola and Virgin Gorda. Rentals run about $55 per day. Driving is on the left. You will need a temporary B.V.I. driver's license; it costs $10 and is available from rental car agencies. To obtain one, you will need to show a valid U.S. driver's license.

Jeeps are the most fun. Rental car companies do not permit their conventional two-wheel-drive cars on some of the island back roads, which can be steep, bumpy, and curving—but which also lead to the most beautiful scenery and vistas. Jeeps allow you to explore everywhere on the islands.

LANGUAGE AND MONEY

The queen's English is spoken, often with a West Indian lilt. The U.S. dollar is the official currency. Most hotels and restaurants accept major credit cards, but ask in advance just to be sure. Traveler's checks are widely accepted; personal checks are not.

WEATHER

The B.V.I. offers practically perfect year-round weather, with little variation between the seasons. Temperatures range from 77° to 85° in winter, 80° to 90° in summer. Evening temperatures run about 10° cooler. Constant trade winds provide breezy refreshment. Tropical storms might occur from late August through October. These usually pass through quickly and you can go right back to the beach.

CLOTHING

Dress tends to be very casual. Bring lightweight, comfortable clothing, including several bathing suits—you'll be living in them all day. Off the beach, local custom requires that you wear cover-ups over bathing suits. For men, jackets (no ties) are required for dinner at Little Dix Bay, Peter Island, and some other elegant restaurants, but these resorts are the exception in the B.V.I., not the rule.

TIME

The islands remain on Atlantic Standard Time all year. In winter, this means that when it is noon in New York, it is 1 p.m. in the B.V.I. In summer, when Daylight Saving Time is in effect, the time is the same in the B.V.I. as in U.S. East Coast cities.

TELEPHONES

You can call the B.V.I. direct from the mainland United States. First dial 809 (the area code), then the seven-digit phone number. All B.V.I. phone numbers begin with 49. When making local calls in the B.V.I., omit the 49 and just dial the last five digits.

SHOPPING

Like everything else in the B.V.I., shopping is a relaxed experience. You'll find some fine souvenir and gift items, but nothing like the enormous range of duty-free merchandise sold by stores in the U.S. Virgin Islands. If you're interested in some real "power shopping," plan on spending your last day in St. Thomas before flying home.

Best bets in the B.V.I. include unique island items—B.V.I. Sea Salt, dapper T-shirts emblazoned with the Union Jack, and Pusser's Rum, distilled according to the original recipe used by the Royal Navy. Also, since there is no duty levied on British imports, you can find bargains on English china, fabrics, and food (such as Fortnum and Mason teas). Liquor prices on scotch whisky are quite good, but you can only bring home one liter per person duty free. You'll find the best selection of merchandise in Road Town, Tortola; Spanish Town, Virgin Gorda; or in boutiques in the resorts.

In **Road Town,** many of the plantation-period buildings clustered around Main Street now house interesting boutiques. Browse through—you'll find a wide choice of items that might strike your fancy, from fashionable beachwear at **Pretty Things** to English antiques and books at **Past and Presents. Carousel** and the **Cockle Shop** stock china by Wedgwood and other English items. Go bonkers—to **Bonkers Gallery,** that is, for high-style casual clothing imported from France, Italy, and around the world. **The Shipwreck Shop,** located in one of the oldest buildings in Tortola, sells baskets, hammocks, and other tropical handcrafts from around the world. **Sunny Caribbee,** a spice and herb shop, offers such invaluable elixirs as "West Indian Hangover Cure" and "Arawak Love Potion." They also exhibit watercolors and paintings by local Caribbean artists. **Zenaida** specializes in fabrics, artifacts, and jewelry from the exotic corners of Africa, Asia, and the South Pacific. For Union Jack insignia mugs and shipshape sportswear decorated with their own bright logo, head for the **Pusser's Company Store** on Main Street in Tortola and at West End.

In **Virgin Gorda,** the **Pavilion at Little Dix Bay** is one of the nicest gift shops in the B.V.I., with merchandise selected with an eye to quality and detail. The **Reeftique** at the Bitter End Yacht Club features a jaunty array of seashell jewelry, cotton sportswear, and bright logo-print shirts and accessories. The boutiques at the Virgin Gorda Yacht Harbour display tempting treasures. At the **Pelican's Pouch,** you'll find up-to-the-minute fashions for beach and casual wear. And you could browse for hours at **Island Woman,** which carries exquisite crafts from around the world: Haitian art, wood carvings from Bali and Indonesia, baskets from Africa—in all price ranges.

Each person can bring home $400 worth of goods to the United States duty free. However, if you also stay in the U.S. Virgin Islands (where the duty-free allowance is $800 per person), you can buy $400 worth of merchandise in the B.V.I., plus $400 in goods in the U.S.V.I.

ABOUT ACCOMMODATIONS

That old expression about "running the gamut" applies to the assortment of accommodations available in the B.V.I.

High season runs approximately December 15 through April 15; low-season rates are about 20% to 50% lower. The price ranges quoted for hotels in this section reflect the low- and high-season rates.

At many hotels and resorts, especially in more secluded island areas, room rates are Full American Plan (AP), including breakfast, lunch, and dinner. Consider this when reviewing room rates, so you can compare the value you are getting for your money. A 7% accommodation tax, plus a 10% to 12% service charge, will be added to hotel bills. Even at the finest resorts, rooms seldom have air conditioning, and instead are designed to rely on the cooling trade winds and ceiling fans. If air conditioning is important to you, check in advance.

One of the most romantic B.V.I. honeymoons isn't on land, but aboard a luxury yacht. More than 300 charter boats are available, either crewed or bare boat, and rates compare to those at a luxury resort. For information about yacht charter in the B.V.I., contact: **The Moorings, Ltd.,** 1305 U.S. 19 South, Suite 402, Clearwater, FL 33546, tel. 813/530-5651 (in Florida), or toll free 800/535-7289; **CSY (BVI) Ltd.,** Box 157, Road Town, Tortola, B.V.I., tel. 809/494-2741; **Virgin Islands Charteryacht League,** Homeport, St. Thomas, U.S.V.I. 00802, toll free 800/524-2061.

DINING OUT

Practically every restaurant worth its salt shaker requires advance reservations. In high season, these should be made several days ahead. Some restaurants—especially those that cater to boaters—ask you to place your meal orders in advance by telephone or ship-to-shore radio. Many restaurants monitor VHF Channel 16.

If you like fish, the fresh local catch is always a best bet. Finny favorites include yellowtail snapper, "old wife," grouper, and dolphin (the fish, not the mammal). And thanks to the islands' British heritage, you'll find authentic renditions of fish 'n' chips, bangers 'n' mash, and roast beef with Yorkshire pudding.

HOW TO GET MARRIED IN THE B.V.I.

The territory warmly welcomes couples who want to say "I do," and planning a B.V.I. wedding is easy.

You must be in the territory three days before you can be married. You can get an application form then at the attorney general's chambers on Main Street, Road Town. Bring along proof of identity, such as passports, birth certificates, and certified proof of marital status. Blood tests are not necessary. You must have two witnesses with you to verify receipt of the license.

After obtaining the license, you go to the registrar's office in Road Town. You can be married either by the registrar (fee is $10), or by the officiant of your choice. For details, contact: **Registrar's Office,** P.O. Box 418, Road Town, Tortola, B.V.I. (tel. 809/494-3701 or 494-3492, ext. 303/304).

FOR FURTHER INFORMATION

Contact the **B.V.I. Tourist Board.** Tortola: P.O. Box 134, Road Town, Tortola, B.V.I. (tel. 809/494-3134). New York: 370 Lexington Ave., Suite 511, New York, NY 10017 (tel. 212/696-0400). San Francisco: 1686 Union St., San Francisco, CA 94123 (tel. 415/775-0344). Or call their toll free numbers: 800/835-8530 nationwide (except NY).

---

2. Tortola

Although Tortola is the center of commerce and the largest of the British Virgin Islands, is the site of the capital, and reigns as one of the premier yacht charter centers in the Caribbean, it remains far off the beaten path for tourists. Life's pace moves no faster than the shiny, plump brown cows that saunter home slowly for the afternoon milking. You'll find it a wonderful hideaway for relaxation—interrupted, perhaps, by some poke-around sightseeing.

What activity there is centers on Road Town, located about midway on Tortola's south coast. Road Town has been the capital of the B.V.I. since 1774; 80% of the country's population resides here. The town cheerfully and haphazardly blends the old and the new. On Main Street, where most of the shops are clustered, the many original buildings reflect traditional plantation architecture. Now restored, the wood-front structures are painted jaunty tropical colors such as hibiscus pink, ginger yellow, and passionflower purple. Meanwhile, along the waterfront state-of-the-art marina developments such as the Village Cay Marina and the Moorings boast everything for the visiting yachtsman—from haul-out and dry-dock facilities to gourmet provisioning (ripe brie, anyone?) and designer boutiques.

Tortola is easy to explore by car or Jeep. The island is small—about 12 miles long and 3 miles wide—and you could drive around it in about two hours if you didn't stop to sightsee or swim. Since Tortola is hilly inland, and flat along the coast, it's practically impossible to get lost. When in doubt, drive downhill, and you'll hit one of the main roads that circle the island.

Moving along Tortola's south coast from Road Town, the island tends to be more desert-like, bristling with loblolly pines, wild tamarind, and 12-foot-tall agave cactus that rise like sentinels across the hillsides. On the northern side, vegetation flourishes in lush profusion—mangroves along the shore, then, further inland, groves of banana trees and golden mangoes, accented by colorful outbursts of hibiscus, flamboyant, and bougainvillea. Here, small settlements like Apple Bay and Carrot Bay reflect a West Indian lifestyle.

Along Tortola's north shore, you'll also find the kind of beaches you fantasize about—broad, diamond-white, powder-soft swaths of fine, coral sands, rimmed with glossy green coconut palms that provide shade. Check out Long Bay, a sweeping strand toward Tortola's west end that's never crowded. If the surf's up, watch bronzed surfers at Little Apple Bay. Follow the steep, winding road past the ruins of an old sugar mill to Brewers Bay. The wide beach is perfect for Frisbee, while the protected harbor makes for a quiet swim.

ROMANTIC INTERLUDES

For honeymooners, Tortola is ripe with romantic promise—on land and at sea. At 1,780 feet, **Sage Mountain** is the highest point in the Virgin Islands. You'll need a four-wheel-drive vehicle to handle the steep terrain. Take along a bottle of champagne, then follow the trails through the rain forest. If you think you've gotten to the end of the road—you haven't. Keep going until you reach the clearing about a mile below the summit. As night falls, the tiny coqui frogs start their plaintive chirp, the lights of Road Town sparkle like diamonds below, and the wrap-around view takes in St. Thomas, St. John, and most of the B.V.I.

The **White Squall,** an 80-foot schooner, takes you to either the Baths (sea grottos) on Virgin Gorda or the caves on Norman Island (tel. 4-2564). The *Shadowfax,* an elegant 60-foot catamaran and one of the fastest boats in the islands, also calls at the Baths (tel. 4-2175). Both day cruises include lunch, libations, and time for snorkeling. They cost about $145 per couple.

Thanks to introductory **dive** programs, you can learn about scuba equipment and techniques in the morning, and be swimming with the fishes in the afternoon, on supervised, open-water dives. Cost for the introductory resort course runs about $85 per person. On Tortola, contact **Underwater Safaris,** P.O. Box 139, Road Town (tel. 4-3235, or toll free 800/537-7032), or **Baskin in the Sun,** P.O. Box 108, Road Town (tel. 4-2858/9, or toll free 800/233-7938). Full certification courses and trips for certified divers are also available.

A loaf of bread (French-style baguette), a jug of wine (some cabernet sauvignon, perhaps), and your own true love—what better way to spend a sun-kissed afternoon? Get all the gourmet fixin's at two shops that specialize in yacht provisioning: The **Ample Hamper** at West End (tel. 5-4684); and **The Gourmet Galley** at The Moorings (tel. 4-2332).

What a beach—a mile and a half of sparkling white sands, surrounding one of the truest, bluest harbors imaginable. It's popular, lively fun—yet very unspoiled. **Cane Garden Bay** bottom is sandy all the way out, making it perfect for water sports. Go waterskiing, or rent a Hobie cat or Windsurfer, and skitter across the bay. Then join the genial crowd that congregates under the shade of the palm trees at **Rhymer's Beach Bar** or **Quito's Gazebo.**

Rhymer's usually features live entertainment, and you can rent Windsurfers or arrange a glass-bottomed boat ride. Open daily, from 8 a.m. to 9:30 p.m.; tel. 5-4639.

HONEYMOON HOTELS AND HIDEAWAYS

Tortola offers about the widest range of accommodations in the B.V.I.—everything from full-scale resorts (with so many facilities, you might never want to leave the property), to campgrounds. In addition, room rates tend to be the most moderate in the B.V.I.

Rates quoted reflect the spread between low- and high-season prices.

Moderate

Sugar Mill Hotel, Box 425, Apple Bay, Tortola, B.V.I. (tel. 809/495-4355; U.S. reservations: 212/545-8437, or toll free 800/223-9815). Built on a hillside overlooking Apple Bay on Tortola's beach-fringed north shore, this intimate hideaway (only 20 rooms) surrounds the restored ruins of a 360-year-old rum distillery. You'll feel right at home thanks to the warmth of the American owners, Jinx and Jeff Morgan, who are also noted food and travel writers.

Contemporary, cheery, and comfortable, all rooms have balconies, kitchen facilities, and views of the sea or gardens. Decor reflects cool island casualness, with tile floors, rattan furnishings, and cotton spreads on the bed. Throughout the resort, you'll be charmed by the personalized touches: fresh flowers in the vases, original island watercolors by Jinx gracing the walls. You can borrow books from the little library, and the honor bar stays open 24 hours a day. The circular freshwater pool occupies the site of the old treadmill, and there's good snorkeling off the small but delightful beach. After a full day of activity (or serious sunbathing), the superb restaurant is a great place to come home to, making the Sugar Mill a superb perch for tropical gourmets. "The people who are happiest here," says Jinx, "are those who appreciate natural beauty and remain open to new experiences and people." Honeymoon package: Eight days/seven nights (EP): $865 to $1,106 per couple; (MAP): $1,280 to $1,520 per couple. Includes welcome cocktails, manager's cocktail party, bottle of champagne, half-day trip to Road Town for shopping, beach picnic for two, resort-course scuba lessons for beginners or two-tank dive for certified divers, full-day sail on a charter yacht, personally autographed cookbook (*Two Cooks in One Kitchen,* written by the Sugar Mill proprietors). Package not available mid-December through mid-April, when daily rates (EP) are $122 to $175 per couple. Hotel is closed August 1 through September 30.

Set in a 50-acre estate on aptly named Long Bay Beach near Tortola's West End, **Long Bay Hotel,** P.O. Box 433, Road Town, Tortola, B.V.I. (tel. 809/495-4252; U.S. reservations: toll free 800/537-6247), offers easygoing escape, seclusion, and a low-key lifestyle alongside one of the island's most spectacular beaches. There are only 37 rooms, located in small villas and cottages sheltered here and there among the palms and hibiscus on the knolls and by the water. For sweeping views, choose one of the air-conditioned hillside studios, with a kitchenette, dressing area, and large balcony overlooking the sea and neighboring islands. Beach buffs should opt for the cabanas, built on stilts and located just 30 feet from the water. The cabanas have amply proportioned decks and patios, as well as kitchenettes and ceiling fans. And for seaside luxury, check into the spacious new beachfront villas. In addition to deluxe features such as air conditioning and wet bars, the pink stucco villas offer absolutely smashing vistas of several other British Virgin Islands, including Jost Van Dyke, Sandy Cay, and Green Cay. In addition to the mile-long beach, there's a salt-water pool, a tennis court, nine-hole pitch-and-putt golf course, and two fine restaurants (the one at the beach occupies a former rum distillery). Honeymoon package: Eight days/seven nights (includes some meals): From $980 per couple (hillside studio); $1,090 per couple (beach cabana); $1,210 per couple (deluxe beachfront villa). Includes a bottle of champagne; all breakfasts; four dinners by candlelight; unlimited free tennis and use of snorkeling gear; round-trip transfers from the airport or ferry dock; and either an island tour or use of a self-drive Jeep for the day.

The following moderately priced properties, all located within minutes of Road Town, are especially convenient if you plan to pick up or drop off a charter yacht.

Treasure Isle Hotel, P.O. Box 68, Road Town, Tortola, B.V.I. (tel. 809/494-2501; U.S. reservations: tel. 212/355-6605, call collect; or toll free 800/221-4588). Nestled into the cliffside just a mile from Road Town, this self-contained resort overlooks the harbor and Sir Francis Drake Channel. Lush, tropical gardens surround the low-slung, contemporary-style buildings. Each room is air-conditioned and has a private balcony with view of the harbor. Treasure Isle appeals to many water-sports enthusiasts, since the Offshore Sailing School is located right on the premises. The facilities also include a mooring dock, squash and tennis courts, and a freshwater pool (complete with a porthole, so you can peer out from under water). Although there's no beach, the resort runs trips daily to different beaches. The property has recently been purchased by the Moorings, the world's largest yacht-charter organization, and is undergoing a top-to-toe refurbishment, scheduled for completion in 1990. Ask your travel agent or the hotel for a progress update. Honeymoon package: None. But for honeymooners intrigued by spending some time at sea, Treasure Isle's Club Mariner programs offers some enticing options. The "Shore 'N' Sail" package gives you the best of both worlds: three nights at Treasure Isle, plus four nights' sailing aboard a fully crewed Moorings 51, with a captain to chart your adventures in the British Virgin Islands and a cook to prepare delicious meals and snacks. Rates: From $1,860 per couple (summer); $2,570 per couple (winter). Includes airport transfers; bar, beverages, and most meals aboard the yacht; services of a professional skipper and cook. Gratuities and taxes not included.

Prospect Reef Resort, P.O. Box 104, Road Town, Tortola, B.V.I. (tel. 809/

494-3311; U.S. reservations: toll free 800/356-8937). This stylish, contemporary resort complex is the largest in the B.V.I. (131 rooms), yet it retains an open, spacious feeling thanks to its 40 acres of beautifully landscaped grounds. For scuba enthusiasts, a dive shop is located right on the premises. The resort also has marina facilities, six lighted tennis courts, a nine-hole pitch-and-putt course, two freshwater pools, a small but perfectly loungable man-made sand terrace—all just a few minutes from Road Town on Tortola's south coast. The low-rise white-painted buildings offer a range of accommodations, all tastefully decorated with rattan furniture, tile floors, and natural fabrics in cool blue and white tones. The garden rooms, facing the lagoon, are air-conditioned; the reef rooms command spectacular views across the channel. Louvered windows and sliding doors leading to terraces allow you to bring the outdoors in, complete with the rustle of palm leaves and the fragrance of oleander. Honeymoon package: Eight days/seven nights (EP): $765 to $1,140 per couple (garden rooms); $800 to $1,240 (reef studios). Includes welcome rum punches, a bottle of champagne and fruit basket, a full-day sail to nearby islands including lunch, round-trip transfers from airport to resort, and a scuba demonstration lesson. Also inquire about their packages that combine a four-night stay at Prospect Reef with three nights aboard a charter yacht (either crewed or noncrewed).

Ramada Nanny Cay Resort & Marina, P.O. Box 281, Road Town, Tortola, B.V.I. (tel. 809/494-4895; U.S. reservations: toll-free 800/228-9898). Ensconced on its own 25-acre islet surrounded by the blue Caribbean and linked to the Tortola "mainland" by a short causeway, this cheery new property is just minutes away from Road Town. The design is extremely winsome, combining West Indian motifs such as latticework, gingerbread, and open-beam ceilings with thoroughly modern room amenities. Certainly, the accommodations rank among the most appealing on Tortola. Decorated with rattan furnishings and tropical-floral fabrics, the spacious lodgings pamper you with such niceties as air conditioning and ceiling fans, glass-enclosed stall showers, minibars and refrigerators, plus well-equipped kitchenettes outfitted with toasters, coffee makers, and pots and pans. Most have terraces or balconies. The only drawback is that the buildings are landlocked, located at island center, rather than on the waterfront. Sports options include a sea wall–enclosed swimming area on the Caribbean, a freshwater pool, a dive shop, and a 231-slip, full-service marina, one of the largest in the region. In the late afternoon, the casual poolside bar (shirts and shoes optional) is a popular gathering place for watching yachts head in to their anchorages, and the Peg Leg Landing restaurant is an excellent choice for lunch or dinner. Honeymoon package: Seven days/six nights (EP): $960 to $1,480 per couple. Includes deluxe studio accommodations, welcome rum cocktails, bottle of champagne, fresh fruit basket, day sail with lunch to a deserted island, horseback ride to Sage Mountain, and two days' car rental.

Very Inexpensive

Brewers Bay Campground, Box 185, Tortola, B.V.I. (tel. 809/494-3463). If you crave the stars overhead and soft sands under your sleeping bag, then this is the place for you—located right on one of Tortola's most beautiful north-shore beaches. They have all the amenities—charcoal grills, a commissary, even a bar and restaurant. Honeymoon package: None. Bare sites cost $7.50 per night, prepared sites with tents are $17.50.

ROMANTIC RESTAURANTS

Tortola's fine selection of restaurants makes dining out well worthwhile.

The Sugar Mill, Apple Bay (tel. 5-4355). The setting—an old sugar mill—would be romantic enough. But add flickering candles on the tables, original—and extremely high-caliber—Haitian art on the coral stone walls, and innovative cuisine, and the Sugar Mill earns its reputation as one of the best restaurants in the islands. Caribbean—but with a California flair best describes the menu created by owners Jinx and Jeff Morgan, who have authored several cookbooks and write regularly for *Bon Appétit* magazine. Specialties include roast honey-lime duck with fried plaintains, seafood creole, and one of the tastiest conch stews around. Many of the ingredients—from fresh herbs to coconuts—are harvested right on the property. Prix-fixe four-course dinner for two: $55 plus drinks. Open nightly from 7 to 9 p.m. And, for a luncheon with a view, the Sugar Mill hosts light meals beachside at the Sand Bar Restaurant. In addition to tasty favorites such as sandwiches and burgers, the menu highlights daily local specials, such as a zingy conch chowder or patties (pastries stuffed with beef). Lunch served daily from noon to 2 p.m.; $15 to $20 per couple plus drinks.

Sky World, Meyers (tel. 4-3567). See how many islands you can count from your perch at this hilltop restaurant. On clear days, the views sweep all the way to Anegada, Virgin Gorda, and Puerto Rico. Located on Ridge Road, just ten minutes from Road Town, Sky World is open from 10 a.m. until 9 p.m. every day except Tuesday. We like it best for lunch, when the menu includes light entrées such as hearty fish chowder, conch fritters, or pasta of the day. About $15 to $20 per couple. Or come by for cocktails, when the setting sun blazes over the Caribbean, then linger for a six-course dinner feast starring different fish and lobster entrées every day, prix fixe at $36 per person.

The Last Resort, Bellamy Cay (tel. 5-2520). This unique pub-cum-music hall is a real B.V.I. institution, so popular with yachting folk that it's hard to find room for your dinghy at the dock. (The island is also reachable by ferry from Tortola.) It's known for it's wildlife—of all varieties. Chocolate the Donkey pokes her head in through the back door, cats snooze in armchairs, and a monster dwells in a corner of the ladies' room (you'll see what we mean). At 9:30 p.m., British entertainer Tony Snell puts on a wickedly funny show spoofing everything from charterboat captains to matadors and the Bermuda Triangle. The dinner menu includes homemade soups, roast beef with Yorkshire pudding, and a help-yourself hot buffet. Dinner is about $45 for two; you can also just have drinks and watch the entertainment (there's a $3.50-per-person cover charge). Open Monday through Saturday; dinner served from 7:30 to 9 p.m.

Santa Maria Restaurant, Village Cay Marina, Road Town (tel. 4-2771). Mariners—ancient and otherwise—consider this restaurant a prime anchorage for whiling away shoreside hours. From its outdoor deck, you can eye sleek sailboats bobbing at their moorings and pelicans diving for an on-the-fin snack. The decor isn't fancy—just some wooden tables and chairs—but what you'll find will be good food, and plenty of it. Choices range from a fried chicken sandwich or burger (about $5.50), all the way up to toothsome entrées such as Caribbean lobster ($27). In the evenings, enjoy jazz and pop-guitar music from 6 to 8 p.m., and live entertainment from 8 to 11 p.m. (except Monday). Open daily for breakfast, lunch, and dinner; 7 a.m. to 10 p.m.

Elena's, Main Street, Road Town (tel. 4-2790). With its pink-and-white lattice trim, cages of twittering finches and parakeets, and broad verandas shaded by palms fronds and pergolas, Elena's embodies island charm. At this family-run restaurant operated by Elena Reynolds, her son Patrick O'Donnell, and his wife Polly, the menu emphasizes English, Caribbean, and Oriental specialties. From the Far East come delicacies such as Mandarin shrimp crêpes and a Javanese rice melody studded with savory morsels of meat and seafood, and served with peanut sauce. Other international favorites include fresh island fish and English savory dishes such as shepherd's pie. Lunch, $15 to $20 per couple; dinner, $20 to $30 per couple. Open daily from 10 a.m. to 10 p.m.

Fort Burt Hotel, Road Town (tel. 4-2587), built around a 300-year-old fort, specializes in Old English favorites like steak-and-oyster pie as well as fresh lobster done up four different ways, including lobster Chaucer—fit for a king in a cream sauce with caviar ($32). There is also a three-course prix-fixe dinner priced from $20. Open daily for lunch, noon to 2:30 p.m.; dinner, 7:30 to 10 p.m. Reservations required.

In the British Navy, the "pusser" was the purser, who handed out the daily ration of grog. **The Pusser's Landing**—on Main Street, Road Town (tel. 4-2467); and right on the harbor in West End (tel. 5-4554)—carries out this nautical theme. The menu hits the spot with burgers, barbecued chicken, and other casual fare. Try the famous rum drinks such as "The Pusser's Pain Killer" or "Nelson's Blood"— sure to inspire feats of derring-do. Entrées priced from $8 to $15. Open daily for lunch, 11:30 a.m. to 2:30 p.m.; dinner, 6 to 10 p.m. (dinner not served Sundays at the Road Town restaurant).

For local dishes such as papaya soup, coconut chicken, and soursop sherbet, head to **Mrs. Scatliffe's** in Carrot Bay (tel. 5-4556). It's home-style cooking at its best: The restaurant is set on the second-floor terrace of the family home, and many of the herbs and vegetables come from their own garden. Following dinner, Mrs. Scatliffe, along with her husband, daughters, and son-in-law, put on a fungi performance. A complete dinner for two runs $40 to $50 plus drinks. Open daily for lunch, noon to 2 p.m.; dinner, 7 to 9 p.m. (reservations essential).

Granny Molyneaux, known as "the baddest thing in the kitchen," is the inspiration behind **The Apple in Little Apple Bay** (tel. 5-4437), set in a small West Indian cottage. Befitting its waterside locale, the restaurant specializes in local seafood dishes such as West Indian conch, whelk in garlic butter, fish steamed in lime butter, and more. Open daily from 4 to 10 p.m. or so; reservations essential. On Sunday and Wednesday, in season, there's live entertainment.

Brandywine Bay Restaurant, just outside Road Town (tel. 5-2301), is set on a former private estate overlooking Drake's Channel. Great views, and the sophisticated menu highlights grilled items, fresh herbs, and some excellent pastas. Dinner for two, about $50 plus drinks. Open nightly from 6:30 to 9 p.m.

---

3. Virgin Gorda

There are beaches, to be sure, about 20 of them. And an extraordinary seaside grotto formed from massive boulders that look like they tumbled from the hands of a giant. But what makes Virgin Gorda so special to visitors who return again and again is the sheer number of things you can do, all here on this little island most people never heard of.

Located at the eastern end of Sir Francis Drake Channel, Virgin Gorda is the second largest of the B.V.I. The island covers about 8.3 square miles and has a population of about 1,000. What makes this particular Virgin "gorda" ("fat" in Spanish) is Virgin Gorda Peak, the highest point on the island.

Most of Virgin Gorda's residents live on the southwest coast near Spanish Town, which was capital of the B.V.I. in the 18th century. But for vacationers, most of the action centers on the yacht harbors. North Sound (officially named Gorda Sound) throbs with activity. Windsurfers and Sunfish zip across the sapphire blue waters; power boats head out for deep-sea fishing or waterskiing. Along the shore, happy-hour tipplers gather in convivial waterfront bistros for some serious sunset watching. Virgin Gorda Yacht Harbour, on the island's southwest coast, lies just a short drive from Spanish Town. The waterfront shopping center caters to boaters, with good markets, wine stores, a dive shop, and several boutiques selling resortwear and island handcrafts. Just inland in "The Valley," you'll find most of the island's services (the airport, taxi rentals), and hotels and restaurants.

ROMANTIC INTERLUDES

Great water sports and a genial, gregarious life ashore make Virgin Gorda a favorite of both sailors and landlubbers.

The famous **Baths** on Virgin Gorda's southwest coast are sea caves and grottos formed from huge granite boulders—some as large as houses. The entrance to the caves is deceptively simple, set in a little circular palm grove that looks like a desert oasis from the tales of Ali Baba. Inside the caves, voices echo against eons of rock, and shafts of sunlight penetrate the shadows. From one cave, you can swim out to the bright turquoise sea, where more fallen stones create a surreal backdrop for snorkelers. Bring deck shoes or sneakers for rock climbing, a picnic lunch if you want to spend the day (no snackbars).

You'll find superb **snorkeling** sites all around the North Sound area. Long Beach reef has huge stands of elkhorn coral. The diving is so good, Jean Michel Cousteau takes groups here. Rocky Beach (at the northeastern end of Moskito Island) offers some wonderfully spooky underwater caves. Off Eustatia Island, you can spot an ancient anchor and three cannons. Half-day snorkeling trips run about $30; introductory scuba lessons cost from about $85 per person. For certified scuba-divers, two-tank dives are $65 per person. Contact **Kilbrides Underwater Tours** at North Sound (tel. 4-2746) or **Dive B.V.I. Ltd.,** at Virgin Gorda Yacht Harbor (tel. 5-5513).

For something different, board *Flipper,* a semisubmersible craft, for a one-hour underwater tour of Eustatia Reef (tel. 4-2746). The sea fans and gorgonians look so close, you feel that you could reach out and touch them.

Rent a Jeep—it's the best way to get to know Virgin Gorda. Head for **Virgin Gorda Peak,** a 1,370-foot summit. The peak area is in National Park and has good hiking trails. At the southeastern end of the island, you can visit **Copper Mine Point,** where the Spaniards who first settled the island mined the ore. To cool off, seek out some of the secluded **beaches** that dot the island. Favorites include Savannah Bay, Pond Bay, and Valley Trunk Bay, a long white strand dotted with coconut palms. Jeep rentals are available through **Speedy's Car Rental** for $50 per day (tel. 5-5235 or 5-5240).

HONEYMOON HOTELS AND HIDEAWAYS

The key words to describe Virgin Gorda resorts are "understated elegance." Accommodations are casual—but in the ultimate best taste. Rates quoted reflect the spread between low- and high-season prices. Also note that most hotels on Virgin Gorda offer Full American Plan (AP).

Expensive

To our way of thinking, **The Bitter End Yacht Club,** Box 46, Virgin Gorda, B.V.I. (tel. 809/494-2746; U.S. reservations: 312/944-5855, or toll free 800/872-2392), is the quintessential B.V.I. resort—exuberant, young, gregarious, with a seafaring, outdoors-loving outlook. It seems to be the Virgin Gorda good times center—dinghies chug, cocktail glasses clink, and Windsurfers whoosh through the waves. It's the perfect place for people who want a yachting atmosphere while living ashore. (If you do want to live aboard, they also have Cal 27 yachts complete with maid service.) Set on a hillside above North Sound, villas overlook the harbor; stone stairs, wooden walkways, and gravel paths crisscross gardens where hummingbirds hover near bougainvillea, frangipani, and oleander blossoms. A wide variety of accommodations are available. Private and luxurious, the peak-roofed cedar Chalets give off a wonderfully airy feeling. Each has a private balcony overlooking the harbor, tile floors, rattan furniture, a sitting area—and a huge shower surrounded by plants that could practically accommodate your entire wedding party. For your convenience and comfort, rooms are air-conditioned and outfitted with minifridges and coffee makers. If you crave a more casual, islandy atmosphere, choose a Beachfront or Hillside Villa, with a large thatch-roofed deck open to the views. Surrounded by tropical gardens, you'll feel as if you're living in a posh tree house. Paddle fans and trade winds provide natural coolness; every room is equipped with a refrigerator. Easygoing pontoon boats on the harbor shuttle guests around the property.

Best of all, take advantage of the water-sports facilities. Guests enjoy unlimited day sailing, with a choice of more than 80 boats—Lasers, Rhodes 19s, Sunfish, J-

24s—all with free instruction. The week-long package also includes sailing regattas, daily snorkeling trips, and all-day powerboat trips. The resort also offers three good beaches and two "in" restaurants. Honeymoon package: None. Standard eight days/seven nights package (Full AP): $1,730 to $2,925 per couple (Hillside Villas); $2,040 to $3,310 per couple (Beachfront Villas); $2,155 to $3,465 per couple (Chalets), depending on season. Includes unlimited day sailing and instruction, day sail to Anegada, sunset catamaran sail, Virgin Gorda Airport transfers, and more.

Biras Creek Hotel, P.O. Box 54, Virgin Gorda, B.V.I. (tel. 809/494-3555/6; U.S. reservations: toll free 800/223-1108). Very private, very elegant—that captures the ambience of this lush 130-acre estate at the southeastern corner of North Sound. Perched atop a narrow promontory of land separating the tranquil harbor from the pounding sea, the resort's main stone building seems almost like a medieval fortress. Down below, walkways and marked nature trails wind through lush, tropical gardens to the 32 secluded yellow stucco guest accommodations (all are L-shaped, two-room suites), screened by almond trees, palms, and sea-grape trees for privacy. The decor of the modern, ultracomfortable rooms creates a tropical feeling. Swim at secluded Deep Bay Beach or in the hexagonal freshwater pool overlooking the sea—a real knockout. Guests enjoy complimentary use of bicycles, snorkeling equipment, Windsurfers (plus instruction), and 12- to 14-foot sailboats, plus day trips to other beaches nearby. There's also free tennis and courtesy rackets; the two courts are lighted for night play. Gourmet restaurant. Honeymoon package: Eight days/seven nights (Full AP): $2,080 to $2,410 per couple (low season), depending on view. Grand Suite accommodations available for $3,070 per couple. Includes round-trip transfers between Virgin Gorda airport and the resort, a bottle of champagne, sunset cruise. Package not available in the high season; the resort is closed September and October.

Little Dix Bay, P.O. Box 70, Virgin Gorda, B.V.I. (tel. 809/495-5555; U.S. reservations: toll free 800/223-7637). This intimate retreat (a Rockresort property) is elegant—without being stuffy. Here is a place where you can relax completely, knowing that you will be cared for and catered to. Impeccably landscaped grounds sprawl over 500 acres, and even by Virgin Islands standards, the waters lapping the half-mile-long, crescent-shaped beach are an ultraclear turquoise marvel. The 102 accommodations, tucked here and there along the beach under sea-grape trees and palms, offer privacy. Built of native stone and fine hardwoods such as purple heart, locust, and ash, they harmonize with the beautiful setting. Some rooms have hexagonal layouts, others rectangular ones; all have private balconies or terraces, and plenty of louvers to let in the trade winds.

At the resort, the emphasis leans toward water sports and tennis. Guests enjoy free use of seven tennis courts, small sailboats, snorkeling gear, bicycles, and waterskis; horseback riding is available for a small fee. There are also three day-trips by Boston whaler to various secluded beaches and coves on Virgin Gorda; you can arrange to take along a picnic lunch. Both restaurants, the elegant Main Pavilion and the more informal Sugar Mill, are excellent. With all these amenities, you may never want to leave the property—but if you do, the shops and restaurants of the Virgin Gorda Yacht Harbor lie just over the hillside. Honeymoon package: Seven days/six nights (Full AP): $2,145 to $2,475 per couple. Includes deluxe oceanview accommodations, sunset cocktail cruise, champagne upon arrival, round-trip transfers to Virgin Gorda airport. Package not available December 20 through March 31.

Moderate

Drake's Anchorage, P.O. Box 2510, Virgin Gorda, B.V.I. (tel. 809/494-2254; U.S. reservations: toll free 800/624-6651). How about honeymooning on your own private island? Drake's Anchorage occupies a 125-acre isle at the entrance to North Sound, well known for its beaches and snorkeling. The neat and cozy cottages sit right on the beach; each has a white-railed balcony overlooking the harbor. The tropical furnishings are simple, but comfortable, and convey a classy, castaway feel—tile floors, wicker headboards, natural fabrics, stone walls, floor-to-ceiling louvers, and Haitian wallhangings. You'll feel like you have the whole island to yourselves because there are only ten rooms (two of these are suites), plus two luxury villas. (Reserve the villas way in advance, since they book up fast.) Guests have free use of all water-sports equipment—including snorkeling gear and day sailers—and there are boat trips to nearby deserted islands. Terrific restaurant. Honeymoon package: Eight days/seven nights (Full AP): $1,095 per couple (low season). Includes oceanfront accommodations, champagne upon arrival, taxes and service charges. Villas run $345 to $495 per couple per night.

    Olde Yard Inn, P.O. Box 26, Virgin Gorda, B.V.I. (tel. 809/495-5544; U.S. reservations: toll free 800/633-7411). If you're looking to get away from it all, check out the cozy and intimate Olde Yard Inn. Ensconced on 4½ acres of lawns and gardens, it reflects all the at-home comforts of a private estate. It's the kind of place where a musically inclined guest might strike up an impromptu serenade on the piano, and the two octagonal-shaped libraries are stocked with good reads by authors such as Rex Stout and P. D. James. Located inland near Little Dix Bay, the resort faces toward the cool, breezy Atlantic side of Virgin Gorda. The only noises you'll hear will be the bleat of some neighboring goats and the babble of chickens; flowers such as night-blooming jasmine perfume the air. There are only 14 rooms, set in low, two-story units. The simple contemporary furnishings are enhanced by original watercolors and homey features such as a fine antique or a Haitian bedspread. In the afternoon, guests gather in the bar to try their skills at chess, backgammon, and darts. You'll want to dine at the excellent restaurant—more than once perhaps. When you want to go to the beach, Savannah Bay and the Baths are just a short drive away. Honeymoon package: Eight days/seven nights (MAP): $1,195 to $1,655 per couple, depending on season. Includes accommodations in the honeymoon suite, a bottle of champagne, fresh flowers in your room daily, and a half-day sightseeing tour.

Inexpensive

    Guavaberry Spring Bay, P.O. Box 20, Virgin Gorda, B.V.I. (tel. 809/495-5227). Where do people who live in the Virgin Islands go for a vacation? Often, to this unique retreat run by Betty Row and her daughter Tina Goschler. The location is excellent, nestled amid massive boulders near the famous Baths, and just a few minutes from the white sands of Spring Beach. Each of the 16 individual, hexagonally shaped units (they are built on stilts) has complete living, kitchenette, and dining facilities—complete with king-size bed and daily maid service. Furnishings are modern, made of teakwood. Meanwhile, the wrap-around balconies let you take advantage of the panoramic views. There's a small commissary on the property where you can buy almost everything from steaks to freshly laid eggs from their own chickens, and town is quite close by. "Guavaberry is another name for heaven," reads the embroidery on a throw pillow. Many couples agree—the hideaway is a popular locale for weddings. Honeymoon package: None. Standard rates: $77 to $120 per couple per day for a one-bedroom villa.

    Leverick Bay Resort and Marina, North South Yacht Charter Ltd., P.O. Box 1077, Virgin Gorda, B.V.I. (tel. 809/495-7421; U.S. reservations: toll free 800/387-4964). Located on pleasure-loving North Sound, the villa residences at Leverick Bay offer vacationers cushy surroundings and a millionaire's view of a myriad of British Virgin Islands, sparkling like emeralds in a sapphire sea. Since you're set off from the other resorts, you'll enjoy plenty of seclusion. Nestled in hillside cottages, the beautifully decorated, expansive accommodations feature stylish enhancements such as open-beam ceilings, rattan furnishings, glass-block walls, balconies, and humongous walk-in closets; all are individually furnished and several offer air conditioning and kitchenettes. Daily maid service is provided. Sports-lovers can take advantage of the two beaches; freshwater swimming pool, tennis courts; Windsurfers, Hobie cats, and Sunfish are available for rent. At mealtimes, the Salty

Whale Pub and Eatery is a favorite stop for visiting yachts. Honeymoon package: None. Weekly rates (EP): $540 to $770 per couple for a bedroom; $615 to $960 per couple for a studio with kitchenette.

Fischers Cove Beach Hotel, P.O. Box 60, The Valley, Virgin Gorda, B.V.I. (tel. 809/495-5252; U.S. reservations: 312/699-7570 in Illinois; toll free 800/621-1270 nationwide). Built of stone and stucco, the low-rise cottages of Fischers Cove snuggle down into the greenery surrounding a pretty, sea grape–fringed beach, just a five-minute walk from Virgin Gorda Yacht Harbour. There are only 20 rooms, all perfectly clean and tidy, with private bathrooms (with showers), balconies, coffee makers, and ceiling fans; some offer kitchenettes. Fronting the Sir Francis Drake Channel, the good restaurant serves breakfast, lunch, and dinner daily, with live entertainment twice a week. Honeymoon package: None. But if you let the friendly staff know that you're newlyweds, you'll receive fresh flowers and a bottle of rum. Weekly rates, depending on time of year: $605 to $770 per couple for a cottage with kitchenette (EP); $945 to $1,265 per week for a room (MAP).

ROMANTIC RESTAURANTS

Ask charter-boat captains to name the best restaurant in the B.V.I.; **Drake's Anchorage** (Moskito Island, tel. 4-2254) will be the hands-down winner. It's located at water's edge, on a private island at the entrance to North Sound. This stone-walled restaurant with stunning Caribbean views serves up an elegant amalgam of West Indian and French cuisine. You'll have trouble deciding what to order. Should it be the rich tomato soup or a tender conch salad? Each entrée arrives cooked to perfection: coquilles St-Jacques in a light cream sauce; fresh Caribbean lobster served with drawn butter; filet of beef au poivre, flamed in cognac and cream, and served rare as requested. For your finale, save room for a member of the dessert Hall of Fame: the chocolate mousse. Five-course prix-fixe dinner from $60 to $80 per couple; lunch, about $20 to $30 per couple; good selection of reasonably priced French and Italian wines. Open daily from noon to 2 p.m. and from 7 to 9 p.m.

Biras Creek, North Sound (tel. 4-3555). Great views and gourmet cuisine—that describes your dinner at this luxury resort. First sip cocktails on the circular terrace with a 360° panorama of North Sound, the Atlantic Ocean, and the Caribbean Sea—then head inside to the batik-cushioned rattan armchairs and flickering hurricane lamps in the dining room. Specials for the table d'hôte gourmet dinner might include a scallop consommé, pâté maison, veal Cordon Bleu, lobster meunière, or shrimp scampi. Another favorite is the curry lunch, held every Sunday. Excellent, extensive wine list. Three-course lunch, $30 per couple; served daily from 1 to 2 p.m. Five-course prix-fixe dinner, $80 per couple plus drinks. Men are required to wear long pants and shirts with collars after 6 p.m.; no shorts for ladies.

The Grill, Bitter End, North Sound (tel. 4-2746). Whether you come for champagne breakfast, rum grog lunch, or full-course dinner, you'll enjoy the excellent food and animated crowd at this popular gathering spot overlooking North Sound. The dining room, under its thatch roof, is open to the trade winds, and every table offers ringside views of the magnificent yachts coming and going in the harbor. Colorful burgees (ship's flags) flutter in the breezes, gifts of visiting yachtsmen who wanted to leave a little of themselves behind at their favorite island watering hole. At lunchtime, the serving table positively groans under the weight of the hot and cold buffet, including chicken, ribs, roast meats, and seafood fritters. At night, first help yourself from the appetizer buffet, soup cauldron, and salad bar, then enjoy some fresh fish, grilled steak, or island specialty such as chicken coconut or lobster supreme, made from juicy lobsters, fresh from the restaurant's fish pens. Three-course prix-fixe lunch, about $35 per couple plus drinks, served daily from 12:30 to 2 p.m. Five-course prix-fixe dinner, $60 to $80 per couple plus drinks, served nightly from 6:30 to 9:30 p.m.

Little Dix Bay Hotel, near Virgin Gorda Yacht Harbour (tel. 5-5555, ext. 20-22). Taste the lifestyle of this chic resort at lunch or dinner. The main Pavilion Dining Room is a masterpiece of contemporary island architecture, with a shingle roof supported by Goliath-size purple heart timbers—some weighing more than 3,000 pounds. The Pavilion is completely open-sided to take advantage of the trade winds and a postcard-perfect view of shimmering Little Dix Bay. The luncheon smorgasbord serves up a luscious harvest of tropical fruits, chunky chicken salad, enough cold cuts (roast beef, ham, and turkey) to do a New York City deli proud, plus hot specials such as shrimp and pasta. For dessert, delights include a kiwi-banana cream pie, a molasses-rich pecan pie, and some very toothsome chocolate-chip cookies. At dinner, the menu highlights both continental and Caribbean specialties (jackets required for men most evenings). For more informal dining, try the stone Sugar Mill, which serves broiled lobster and other dishes. Start your meal with a potent Pelican Smash cocktail. Lunch, $45 per couple; served from 12:30 to 2 p.m. Dinner, $90 per couple plus drinks; served from 7 to 9 p.m.

Olde Yard Inn, near Little Dix Bay (tel. 5-5544). With its ceiling crafted from rolled banana leaves, its vibrant Caribbean art, and its pottery (made by owner Carol Kaufman), the Olde Yard embodies the warmth and friendliness of the islands. The menu favors zesty flavors and fresh ingredients, with selections such as local fish chowder, poached chicken breast with rum cream sauce, and coconut shrimp (with the coconuts in question plucked from the palms out in the garden). They make their own pastas, breads, rolls, and pastries daily with tender loving care. Classical music in the background enhances the romantic mood; there's also live entertainment twice a week, plus some spontaneous "jump ups," when guests push the tables aside to make room for dancing. Open for lunch (sandwiches and salads) from noon to 2 p.m.; about $20 per couple. Dinner seatings at 7 and 9 p.m.; from $40 per couple. Reservations please.

Chez Michelle, near Virgin Gorda Yacht Harbour (tel. 5-5510), is another island favorite. Owned by Eric and Michelle Noevere, the restaurant uses local ingredients to add pizzazz to recipes such as homemade fettuccine provençale, red snapper in ginger-lime butter, and roast breast of chicken stuffed with fresh fruits. Dinner for two, $60 to $80 plus drinks. Open nightly from 6:30 to 9:30 p.m.

The Bath and Turtle, Virgin Gorda Yacht Harbour (tel. 5-5239). According to the manager, the incongruous name comes from the confluence one evening of an old bathtub, a sea turtle, and a sizable hangover. True to such tipsy origins, this feisty pub attracts a hale and hearty yachting set for sandwiches and burgers (about $5 per person), and lobster ($30 per person). Open daily for breakfast, 7:30 to 10 a.m.; lunch, 11 a.m. to 2 p.m.; dinner, 6 to 9 p.m.

From fish fries to reggae fests—you can find out what's happening in Virgin Gorda by checking the bulletin board at the Yacht Harbour Shopping Centre.

---

4. Jost Van Dyke

No cars, no roads, no airport, and only about 130 permanent residents—yes, this is the island for honeymooners who crave escape. According to legend, the island is named after a Dutch pirate, a contemporary of Sir Francis Drake's. What the island lacks in amenities, it compensates for with its scenery. White Bay is one of the prettiest beaches you can encounter, with its long stretch of white sand edged by coconut palms, and two reefs to protect the waters and provide good snorkeling. Just around the bend, you'll find Great Harbour, a favorite yacht anchorage.

HONEYMOON HOTELS AND HIDEAWAYS

Because of its fine beaches and lively beach bars, Jost Van Dyke is a "must" for cruising charter boats. Although accommodations on land are limited, they are comfortable and offer the opportunity to get away from it all. Completely.

Rates quoted reflect the spread between low- and high-season prices.

White Bay Sandcastle, P.O. Box 540, Pawleys Island, SC (tel. 803/237-8999). There are only four cottages in this secluded resort situated snugly on beautiful White Bay. You'll almost expect to see Robinson Crusoe snoozing beneath a palm tree. Although there's no electricity, passive solar power and propane run the stereos, heat up the water for showers, and light your reading lamps, but you should leave hairdryers and electric shavers at home. Each of the octagonally shaped wooden cottages is cozy, tidy, and private, plunked right on the edge of the beach. All the furnishings and upholsteries have been completely updated—and the view through the big glass windows is worth a million dollars. Help yourself from the honor bar; borrow books or cassettes from the library. Guests also enjoy complimentary use of snorkeling gear; scuba-diving, day sails, and deep-sea fishing can all be arranged. Excellent restaurant; the beachside Soggy Dollar bar makes a great afternoon hangout. Honeymoon package: None. Room rate (Full AP): $260 to $325 per couple per day.

ROMANTIC RESTAURANTS

If your idea of romantic dining encompasses cocktails fueled by a fiery sunset, followed by a dinner under the stars, then you're in luck.

In Great Harbour, check out the string of casual, folksy beach restaurants that line the waterfront. Jost Van Dyke habitués speak of **Rudy's Mariners Rendezvous** with the same reverence that Scarlett O'Hara regarded Tara. It's a good place to down lobster, barbecued chicken, and a frosty beer; every Tuesday and Saturday night, there's a complete beachside pig roast ($20 to $40 per couple). **Foxy's Tamarind,** another Jost Van Dyke tradition, has a lobster dinner priced from $15 per person, and Foxy often entertains on the guitar. Or try **Happy Laury's,** with Laury himself behind the bar. The menu features lobster (starring a three-pound monster, for $40), barbecued chicken and ribs (about $15 to $20 per person), and you can shoot a game of pool between courses. None of these places has a telephone—just drop in.

5. Peter Island

Picture a perfect, half moon–shaped sweep of fine white coral sand that rolls on for a mile. The bay is calm, clear, the color of molten turquoise; palm trees curve gently, sculpted by the constant trade winds. This is Deadman's Bay, perhaps first among equals of exquisite B.V.I. beaches. Deadman's Bay is the crown jewel of Peter Island—and of the very exclusive Peter Island Resort.

Peter Island Hotel and Yacht Harbor, P.O. Box 211, Peter Island, B.V.I. (tel. 809/494-2561; U.S. reservations: toll free 800/346-4451 nationwide; 800/562-0268 in Michigan). Peter Island ranks—justly—among the world's most exclusive island retreats, a preferred port of call for yachtsmen, celebrities, and the jet set. The island is completely private. The resort owns most (1,800 acres) of the 1,956-acre island; there are also some private estates. A bevy of sports awaits right on your doorstep—tennis, snorkeling, windsurfing, and sailing—all complimentary for guests. Four secluded beaches around the island account for five miles of coastline.

For the most spectacular accommodations, choose one of the 20 cedar-and-stone beach house rooms in the two-story villas fronting Deadman's Bay. The spacious rooms are the most luxurious in the B.V.I., furnished with Mexican tile floors, peacock-style wicker armchairs, and pastel-colored fabrics. But the biggest star (next to the views from the huge balcony or terrace overlooking the bay) is the bathroom and adjoining plant-filled garden atrium.

The 32 Bay View rooms, situated between Sprat Bay and the Sir Francis Drake Channel, all have verandas or patios and are air-conditioned. The A-frame buildings have a modern Scandinavian design, warmed by cheery tropical decor. As you would expect, special touches pamper guests—accommodations have his and hers sinks in the bathroom, as well as a minirefrigerator, and you'll find a hibiscus on your pillow every night. Or if you really want to splurge, there are six private villas, including the spectacular Crow's Nest, commanding a superb view of the Caribbean. Honeymoon package: Eight days/seven nights (FAP): $2,190 to $2,575 per couple (low season). Includes welcome cheese and bottle of wine upon arrival, round-trip transfers from Tortola to Peter Island, bottle of rum, special gift, and either a day-sail to The Baths or day trip to Tortola. High season rates (FAP): $410 to $580 per couple per night.

Peter Island has two restaurants open to both guests and visitors. Advance reservations are very necessary (tel. 4-2561). In the Main Dining Room, candlelight flickers on the tables, accenting the rough-textured stone walls and colorful tropical motif paintings. The menu features continental favorites such as filet mignon with béarnaise sauce, as well as fresh fish (grouper, snapper) caught by the resort's "own" fishermen. Dinner served nightly from 7:30 to 9:30 p.m.; $80 to $90 per couple plus drinks. Jackets required for men. For casual lunches and dinners (highlighting barbecued chicken or steak, and a salad bar), try the open-air Beach Bar. The view of Deadman's Bay can't be beat. Open for lunch, 12:30 to 2 p.m.; $40 per couple. Dinner served most nights, 7:30 to 9:30 p.m.; $60 to $70 per couple plus drinks.

---

6. More Suggestions in the B.V.I.

Since the various isles and cays that make up the British Virgin Islands lie so close to each other, much of the fun comes from exploring different places. Join one of the day sails from the main islands, or charter a yacht yourselves. Here's a roundup of the most popular anchorages.

Norman Island reportedly provided Robert Louis Stevenson with the model for his *Treasure Island*. A French pirate supposedly hid his booty in one of the four huge sea caves on the island's northwest coast, so you can live out all your childhood fantasies of searching for buried treasure. Then head outside for what may be the best snorkeling of your lives. The water is absolutely transparent, with easily 100 feet of visibility, and hundreds of yellow-and-black sergeant majors and big yellowtail snappers greet you when you dive in. You can reach the island only by boat, with Norman Bight a favorite anchorage. At the bight, dinghy over to the *William Thornton*, an old (1915) Scandinavian freighter that's now a floating bar and restaurant (tel. 4-2564). Open daily from 11 a.m. to 11 p.m.

Salt Island is best known for the wreck of the R.M.S. *Rhone*, a royal mail vessel that sunk on the rocks during a violent hurricane on October 29, 1867. The wreck is probably the most popular dive site in the entire Caribbean, and underwater scenes for *The Deep* were filmed here. Because of the superb visibility (generally over 100 feet), snorkelers as well as scuba-divers can view the ship's shattered remains, which lie only 20 to 80 feet down. Since the wreck is a national park, and it is illegal to take catch here, you'll encounter lots of big, happy fish who nudge up against divers for handouts (they like potato chips).

Anegada sits apart from the main B.V.I. group, about 20 miles northeast of Tortola. Its Horseshoe Reef offers superb dives, especially shipwrecks. Over 100 vessels have foundered in the treacherous shallows, including the British frigate H.M.S. *Astra*, and the *Paramatta*, which sank over 100 years ago—both popular dive sites. The island lies so low in the water (its highest point is only 28 feet above sea level) that Spanish sailors named it "the drowned island." In addition to its diving, Anegada offers fine beaches on its north and west coasts. For total escape, book one of the 12 rooms at the **Anegada Reef Hotel,** or drop by for a barbecued lobster, chicken, or steak (tel. 5-8002). Dinners run from $35 to $70 per couple; served nightly at 7:30 p.m. Reservations essential.

Also consider **Great Dog,** which has wonderful coral forests for snorkelers to explore; and **Cooper Island,** with sparkling Manchioneel Bay and a good restaurant. Along the rocky shores of **Guana Island,** you can often catch your own lobster dinner. There's also fine snorkeling off of **Necker Island, Green Cay,** and the **Indians.** For more buccaneer tales, stop by **Deadman's Chest Island.** According to legend, Long John Silver buried his treasure here—along with the 15 men who carried it ashore.

XX

THE CAYMAN ISLANDS

1. PRACTICAL FACTS
2. GRAND CAYMAN
3. CAYMAN BRAC
4. LITTLE CAYMAN

Tucked in the British West Indies 480 miles south of Miami and 180 miles north-northwest of Jamaica, the Cayman Islands are a world unto themselves: properly British, yet seeming more like Florida than a foreign land. They are friendly, safe, comfortable—and above all, fun. Romantic? Oh yes. Do you want secluded beaches of talcum-fine, pure white sand? Hammocks swaying beneath the palms? Dinner by candlelight in an old Victorian home? Or do you prefer a little more action—limbo on the beach, party boats at sunset, feeding fish by hand?

You'll find it all on the three Cayman Islands—Grand Cayman, Cayman Brac, and Little Cayman. The islands hunker down close to the blue Caribbean—both Grand and Little Cayman are flat, and the ridge that runs along the spine of Cayman Brac rises only 140 feet above sea level. But don't let the low-slung profile fool you. These islands are actually the tops of a submerged mountain range cut by valleys that plummet 6,000 feet deep. The upper "slopes" are lined with some of the finest scuba reefs in the world: underwater forests of antler coral, canyons lined with blood-red sponges, tunnels filled with lobster, drop-offs so sheer you can't see bottom, and fish so friendly they nibble cheese from your fingers. All this in water clear enough to eye a clump of coral 200 feet away.

Back on land, the Caymans give you your choice of pace—slow, medium, or fast. Grand Cayman offers life in the fast lane—at least speedy by Cayman Islands standards. (After all, these are islands that have chosen the turtle as their official mascot.) On Grand Cayman, you'll have enough to keep you busy—yacht cruises, innumerable dive shops, nightclubs, and duty-free shopping—along with plenty of peace and quiet when you prefer. Cayman Brac provides even more of a chance to catch your breath—paired with fantastic diving and hiking. There are caves and quaint towns to explore, plus hotels where all-in-one packages do, indeed, take care of everything. And Little Cayman is the true escape, with simple cottages on the beach, tarpon ponds among the mangroves, and mile upon mile of sands.

Change has come so quickly here in the past two decades, it's hard to remember the Caymans were once just sleepy fishing villages; even harder to picture a time when bloodthirsty pirates roamed the islands. Christopher Columbus started it all in May 1503, stumbling across these three long, flat clumps of coral covered with iridescent-backed turtles and surrounded by translucent cobalt water. He promptly dubbed them Las Tortugas and sailed away. Twenty years later, Spanish sailors, mistaking the local iguanas for crocodiles, renamed the islands Caimanas, which turned to Caymans when the islands were ceded to Great Britain in 1670.

By the 17th century, these waters had become a highway for Spanish galleons laden with Inca gold—and a hideout for pirates. The vessels provided easy pickings for pirates the likes of Captain Henry Morgan and Blackbeard, whose treasure is rumored to lie in crevices of Cayman caves to this day. Despite their notoriety, the pirates' reign lasted barely 30 years, leaving a legacy of skull-and-crossbones beach names (Pirate's Point, Bloody Bay), an annual pirate festival (last week of October), and the official island symbol: a peg-leg turtle dressed in pirate's clothing.

By 1788, the piracy was long gone. In fact, when ten Jamaican ships foundered on a Grand Cayman reef, islanders slogged through treacherous seas to rescue the seamen. In gratitude, England's King George III granted the islands a tax-exempt status—which remains to this day. Today, the total lack of taxes has brought the Caymans more riches than any pirate could have dreamed of, the gold of business profits from banking and tourism.

The Caymans are a British crown colony, with a legislative assembly and a governor. And while the islanders' English comes with a decided Jamaican lilt, you'll find Whitbread's Ale, steak-and-kidney pie, and dart boards in the pubs.

For couples on a visit, the biggest problem is finding time for it all . . . time to nose about the pastel-pink towns and roam the beaches of Grand Cayman, to climb through the caves and hike the orchid trails of Cayman Brac, to bicycle the unpaved back paths and fish the tarpon ponds of Little Cayman.

Above all, share some time with the Cayman Islanders—friendly people who are never too busy for a chat or to help strangers find their way. Stop in a native restaurant and you'll probably leave with the family recipe for conch stew. Hire a cab and you'll like as not get a minitour of the island, complete with tips on the hottest night spots and restaurants of the moment. That friendliness and comfort, that feeling you're a member of the family come home for a visit, is what's most precious about a Cayman stay.

---

1. Practical Facts

GETTING THERE

Americans and Canadians can use various proofs of citizenship (passport, birth certificate, voter's registration, or certificate of naturalization). However, a valid passport will speed things along. An onward or return ticket is also required. Departure tax is $7.50.

Cayman Airways offers regularly scheduled jet service from New York, Miami, Houston, Atlanta, and Tampa to Grand Cayman and Cayman Brac, as well as interisland service to all three islands. Cayman Airways also arranges regular charter service from several major U.S. cities. Some of these charter flights operate only during the winter season, others year-round. For further information, telephone toll free 800/422-9626.

Northwest Airlines has regular jet service from Miami to Grand Cayman. Telephone toll free 800/447-4747.

Several cruise lines also call at Grand Cayman. Check with your travel agent for details.

GETTING AROUND

There are lots of transportation options on Grand Cayman, fewer on Cayman Brac, almost none on Little Cayman.

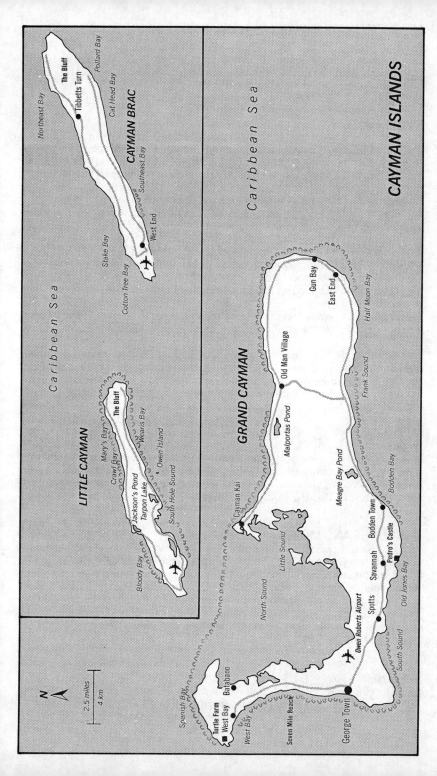

CAYMAN ISLANDS

CAYMAN BRAC

The Bluff
Tibbetts Turn
Northeast Bay
Pollard Bay
Cat Head Bay
Southeast Bay
West End
Stake Bay
Cotton Tree Bay

LITTLE CAYMAN

Caribbean Sea

Mary's Bay
The Bluff
Crawl Bay
Wearis Bay
Jackson's Pond
Tarpon Lake
Owen Island
South Hole Sound
Bloody Bay
Spanish Bay

GRAND CAYMAN

Caribbean Sea

Cayman Kai
Old Man Village
Malportas Pond
Gun Bay
East End
Half Moon Bay
Frank Sound
Meagre Bay Pond
Bodden Bay
Little Sound
Bodden Town
North Sound
Savannah
Pedro's Castle
Owen Roberts Airport
Spotts
Old Jones Bay
South Sound
Turtle Farm
Batabano
West Bay
Seven Mile Beach
George Town

N
2.5 miles
4 km

Taxis

Taxis are available on Grand Cayman and Cayman Brac. Taxi rates on Grand Cayman are controlled by the government and based on four people per taxi. Fares from the airport to Seven Mile Beach run $8.50 to $15.

Rental Cars

Auto, moped, and bicycle rentals are available on Grand Cayman and Cayman Brac. (On Little Cayman, you can arrange with the island hotels to take you around.) By law, rental cars cannot be picked up at the Grand Cayman airport (they can, however, be dropped off there). To get your rental car, you will have to take a taxi or walk to the rental car office (a few are located across from the airport). During the high season, make sure you reserve your vehicle way in advance.

Cars come big and small, standard shift and automatic, with air conditioning and without. In addition, you can rent vans and Jeeps. Rentals run from about $25 to $60 per day, $150 to $265 per week. You'll need your U.S. driver's license to obtain a temporary Cayman license (available at the rental car counter for a $3 fee).

Mopeds and scooters range from $45 to $78 for a three-day rental. Warning: Don't ride mopeds or scooters on Lighthouse Road on Cayman Brac. Some riders have been seriously injured on this undulating sand and rock road, which is no way to end a honeymoon.

On Grand Cayman, bicycles rent for about $8 a day ($12 for a tandem). Some hotels, especially on the smaller islands, make bikes available for guests free of charge.

A tip: Get the Esso road map, generally available at their gas stations. It's small and extremely detailed, including every paved road on Grand Cayman. Best of all, the plainly marked Esso gas stations make great landmarks when you're trying to figure where to make that critical left turn. Finally, whatever you are riding, remember: *Drive on the left.*

Buses

On Grand Cayman, private bus lines serve the Seven Mile beach area (where most hotels and condos are located), running hourly between West Bay on the north end and downtown George Town to the south. Buses are also available to eastern destinations (e.g., Bodden Town). The fare is $1.25.

LANGUAGE AND MONEY

English is the official tongue, spoken here with traces of Scottish and Welsh and flavored with a Caribbean lilt. The Cayman dollar (abbreviated CI$) is fixed at U.S. $1.25, making the U.S. dollar worth 80¢ Cayman. Prices in island shops and restaurants might be given in either Cayman or U.S. dollars, so be sure to ask. Unless otherwise noted, all prices given in this book are in U.S. dollars. American and Canadian currency is accepted virtually everywhere, as are major credit cards and traveler's checks. Personal checks are usually not accepted, unless drawn on a local or (sometimes) Miami bank.

WEATHER

The climate is delightfully balmy year-round. Winters average 75°, summers 80°. Most rainfall occurs in the summer months, but that's when you'll get the calmest conditions for scuba-diving. In fact, one dive operator on Grand Cayman is so confident of his ability to find good diving in summer that he promises a refund if you're blown out of the water between April and December. Winter brings an occasional "nor'wester" that shakes the palms and roughens the seas somewhat. But even when that happens, dive operators just trundle over to the lee side of the island.

CLOTHING

Casual dress is accepted virtually everywhere, meaning men can leave the coat and tie home. Even the fanciest restaurants will settle for a "casual but elegant" look. Skimpy beachwear is frowned on away from the beach, although the Caymanians are too polite to say anything. Occasional cool and breezy winter evenings make taking a light wrap or sweater a good idea.

TIME

The Cayman Islands remain on Eastern Standard Time year-round. In the summer, this means that honeymooners arriving from New York or Washington, D.C., should set their watches back one hour.

TELEPHONES

You can call the Caymans direct from the United States and Canada. First dial area code 809, then the seven-digit phone number. All Cayman phone numbers begin with "94," so when in the islands, you can omit the "94" and just dial the last five digits. The cheapest way to call the United States from the Caymans is via USA-Direct. Just dial 1-USA (1-872) from a Cayman telephone, and you'll be connected to an AT&T operator in the United States, who will place your credit-card or collect call.

SCUBA-DIVING

Some of the best diving and snorkeling in the world awaits you in the Caymans. Here all the elements come together: beautiful corals and sponges, colorful tropical fish, sheer walls with tunnels and caverns to explore, and, most important, knowledgeable and dependable dive operators.

On Grand Cayman, there are dozens of dive operators, ranging from the huge fleet and many locations of **Bob Soto's Diving** (whose founder virtually invented Caribbean dive vacations) to smaller, more personalized operations such as **Quabbin Dives.** Most are clustered around the Seven Mile Beach area, and many will pick you up on the beach behind your hotel or condo. But if you're staying in another area, "not to worry," as they say here. Most resorts located away from the mainstream have their own, or nearby, dive operators.

On Cayman Brac and Little Cayman, you'll be diving with the operator attached to your hotel. There's always a good choice of diving destinations, and the diving off Little Cayman is the best in the islands.

Most dive trips consist of two dives: the first on a wall to about 100 feet, and the second (after a suitable surface interval) on a shallower reef at 30 feet or so. You might want to bring something to feed the very friendly fish—Cheeze Whiz, hot dogs, or an ear of corn are good choices. Always ask your dive master first, however: Fish feeding is banned at several sites.

SHOPPING

Grand Cayman is no St. Thomas but you'd be surprised at the little treasures you can find here as well as on Cayman Brac.

Each of you can bring back $400 worth of merchandise from the Cayman Islands. The tax-free status means bargains, especially on European imported goods such as watches, gold chains, fine porcelain, exotic perfumes and, most notably, china and crystal, whose prices are 30% to 50% off those in the United States. Save your liquor shopping for the airport on Grand Cayman, since that's the only place spirits are sold duty free.

Grand Cayman has the serious shopping centered on George Town, the downtown area. The main shopping area is concentrated in a few blocks near the dock. In this cornucopia, several shops stand out. **Kirk Freeport,** with branches in town on both Cardinal Avenue and on Albert Panton Street, is the biggie when it comes to famous-name merchandise at duty-free prices. Here you'll find watches from Patek Philippe, Rolex, Baume & Mercier, and others; crystal from Lalique, Baccarat, and Waterford; fine china by Wedgwood; plus fabulous jewelry by Cartier and perfumes from all the great houses. In the Anchorage Centre, **Paper Unlimited** offers not only attractive postcards and Cayman turtle–design cocktail napkins, but also an intriguing selection of Caribbean spices—a perfect souvenir of your island holiday. Try **Colombia Emeralds International** in the Anchorage Centre for watches and gold chains; **Heritage Island Crafts** for all kinds of Caribbean craftwork from Caymanian palm baskets to Jamaican carvings. For an especially memorable trinket, look for pendants, rings, and bracelets incorporating genuine pieces of eight and gold doubloons salvaged from shipwrecks, some over 300 years old. **Finiterre, Pieces of Eight,** and **Smiths** carry many different exquisite designs.

Thanks to the new **Galleria Plaza minimall,** shoppers don't even have to bestir themselves from the Seven Mile Beach area in order to seek out bargains. The roster of boutiques includes branches of some of the most famous chains, as well as nifty sportswear emporiums such as **Tropical Trader** and **Pacesetter.**

Just south of town, don't miss **Pure Art Gallery and Gifts** on South Church Street, just a quarter of a mile before the Grand Old House Restaurant. In this charming Cayman cottage owned and run by artist Debbie van der Bol, you'll find a treasure trove of arts and crafts: watercolors, batiks, sculptures, embroideries, and more, all created by local artists. Prices start at about $5 and go up to $1,500 or more for major, collector-quality pieces. Open Monday through Saturday, 10 a.m. to 4 p.m.

And then, there's black coral, a dense, bushy growth taken from deep water. It polishes up to such a high luster that it looks like a gemstone. Craftspeople on most Caribbean islands dabble in black coral, but here, it is a true art. There must be 30 places on Grand Cayman that sell black coral, a dozen of them along Fort Street (downtown), alone. Also on Fort Street, you'll find a place called **Black Coral And . . . ,** where artist Bernard K. Passman has woven polished black coral and gold into exquisite forms. There's a tiny sports car, a saxophone with each key done in gold, a cancan dancer with gold stars in her skirt. It's museum-quality stuff, with prices to match. But go in for a look, even if you can't afford to buy. Mitzi, another black coral artist, also has a shop downtown. But if you want a tour of Mitzi's studio to boot, drive back to West Bay near the Turtle Farm area and just follow the signs that say **Coral Art Collections** (Old Fort Building, on the waterfront). Delicate pendants sell for as little as $20, hearts inlaid with gold for $60.

On your drive around the island, browse through **Dr. Carey's Black Coral Clinic,** located south of town about two or three houses up from the Crow's Nest restaurant. Here, surrounded by an array of snoozing kitties, you can select black coral jewelry "butchered" and crafted by Dr. Carey himself, a colorful chap almost completely tattooed from the waist up. When you reach the town of Pedro, keep an eye out for **Ralph Terry's** house. There's a sign out front and a porch filled with mugs, walking sticks, napkin holders, vases, even foot massagers, carved of everything from mahogany and cherry wood to poison ivy.

Cayman Brac has a half dozen tiny shops with local craftware scattered along the north shore road. The two that stand out are **Idalee's Black Coral and Jewelry** and **N.I.M. Things.** You can't miss Idalee's. It's the home of Eddie Scott, the woodshop teacher in the local high school. Eddie built half the house himself, carving the gingerbread trim and hand-making the two frontyard lighthouses in his workshop. Ask Eddie to show you the scuba-diver he carved in black coral with a knife (before electricity came to the island). It's so detailed that you can see the buckle on the diver's belt. Then indulge yourself in a piece of his black coral jewelry, which he sells for a fraction of the cost of comparable pieces on Grand Cayman. N.I.M. (Native Island Made) Things in Spot Bay specializes in caymanite. It's a layered stone that polishes up to a rainbow splash of pinks, oranges, blacks, and browns and makes great jewelry and paperweights.

ABOUT ACCOMMODATIONS

Except for a few knockout exceptions that are fairly new arrivals on these islands, Cayman accommodations tend to be the "white bread" of the Caribbean. Rooms are clean, attractive, and modern—but lacking in personality and character. You'll find no real surprises, but then, people choose the Caymans because of the water sports, beaches, and sightseeing—not the bedrooms. Really cheap accommodations in the way of campsites and cabins simply do not exist. Nor do those very exclusive, very expensive hideaways frequented by folks who don't mind spending $500 a day for their digs.

There are a handful of hotels, but mostly what you find are condos. And in truth, a condo is a good way to go. For virtually the same price as a single room, you get your own fully furnished apartment with a kitchenette, plenty of space, and daily maid service. By rustling up some of your own breakfasts and lunches, you can save enough for guilt-free dinner splurges at some of the islands' finer restaurants.

As a rule—but with plenty of exceptions—Cayman hotels offer honeymoon packages; condos do not. (When you make your condo reservations, however, let them know that you are honeymooners—often you'll get a complimentary bottle of champagne.) If you are scuba-divers, consider taking the dive package rather than the honeymoon package; it will probably offer you better value.

The hot spot of Grand Cayman is Seven Mile Beach, with its many hotels and condos, water-sports shops, barbecues, and door-to-door scuba pickup service. Those seeking a bit more quiet head for Spanish Cove (the northern nub of land above Seven Mile Beach) or, better yet, the north side of the island towards Rum Point.

High season is December 15 through May 15, with low-season rates running 20% to 35% lower. Most hotels and condos on Grand Cayman are European Plan (EP), meaning they don't provide meals. Hotels on Cayman Brac and Little Cayman, where restaurants are scarce, all offer Full American Plan (AP). A 6% accommodation charge and a 10% to 15% service charge are added to hotel bills. To facilitate making arrangements, the **Cayman Islands Reservations Service** has toll-free numbers: 800/327-8777 nationwide; 800/432-4858 in Florida.

DINING OUT

Casual is the byword here. Even the ritziest restaurants don't require a coat and tie. Reservations, however, are another story, especially during high season.

Restaurants run the gamut from gourmet French to Burger King with a marvelous conglomeration of native spots in between. Unfortunately, nothing is cheap. The top restaurants tend to be very good and very expensive—count on spending at least $100 per couple. The next down are good but still very expensive. Your best bet, especially if you like fish, are those native places that serve up a potpourri of conch stews, fritters, and fried fish.

HOW TO GET MARRIED IN THE CAYMANS

A Cayman marriage is the perfect start to a Cayman honeymoon. A special nonresident marriage license may be issued upon application to the governor and payment of a $225 fee.

At least one of you must apply in person and have been in the Caymans three days. Blood tests aren't necessary. You can use a minister or a lay marriage officer registered with the chief secretary's office.

For details, write to Administrative Secretary, Government Administration Building, George Town, Grand Cayman, B.W.I. (tel. 809/949-7900, ext. 2403).

If you want to add a spice that your friends back home are guaranteed not to have, arrange for all this to be done underwater, either in scuba gear or on a submarine. Both are becoming popular (see "Romantic Interludes").

FOR FURTHER INFORMATION

Contact: **Cayman Islands Department of Tourism.** Grand Cayman: P.O. Box 67, George Town, Grand Cayman, B.W.I. (tel. 809/949-7999). Atlanta: P.O. Box 900024, Atlanta, GA 30329 (tel. 404/934-3959). Chicago: One Magnificent Mile, 980 North Michigan Ave., Suite 1260, Chicago, IL 60611 (tel. 312/944-5602). Dallas: 9794 Forest Lane, Suite 569, Dallas, TX 75243 (tel. 214/931-2224). Houston: 2 Memorial City Plaza, 820 Gessner, Suite 170, Houston, TX 77024 (tel. 713/461-1317). Los Angeles: 3440 Wilshire Blvd., Suite 1202, Los Angeles, CA 90010 (tel. 213/738-1969). Miami: 250 Catalonia Ave., Suite 604, Coral Gables, FL 33134 (tel. 305/444-6551). New York: 420 Lexington Ave., Suite 2312, New York, NY 10017 (tel. 212/682-5582). Tampa: P.O. Box 824, Tarpon Springs, FL 34286 (tel. 813/934-9078). Toronto: Earl B. Smith Travel Marketing Consultants, 234 Eglington Ave. E., Suite 306, Toronto, ON M4P-1K5 (tel. 416/485-1550).

---

2. Grand Cayman

Here's where you'll find fun in the sun with a touch of sophistication—but not so much you can't just hole up and relax.

Actually, Grand Cayman is more than just a beachfront playground. Thanks to the total lack of taxes and complete privacy for business transactions, this clump of coral is home to over 500 banks, about the same number of insurance companies, and 18,000 other assorted corporations.

This business atmosphere brings a crack efficiency to this otherwise relaxed Caribbean isle. There's no looseness in, say, the scuba operations. Trips leave when they should. Equipment operates. Divemasters know the reefs. And it's the same with other island activities, from fishing to sightseeing tours.

Despite its weighty name, Grand Cayman is rather small—22 miles long and 8 miles wide—and flat. Its highest point reaches only 60 feet above sea level. The island looks like a reversed letter "L" on its back. The leg that sticks up along the western end embraces the powder-fine sands of Seven Mile Beach, the main resort area. This and the crook of the "L" where George Town (the Cayman Island capital) sits form the center of island life. You'll find most of the island's 2,000 condo and hotel rooms here, many of them conveniently located on the beach for that starlit, midnight swim.

What to do? Just about everything. Along the beach there's waterskiing, jet skiing, windsurfing, sailing, and paddleboating. Check with **Aqua Delights** at the Holiday Inn (tel. 7-4444) and **Red Sail Sports** (tel. 9-7965). Red Sail, at the Hyatt Regency Grand Cayman, also offers safe but thrilling parasail rides 300 feet above the crystal-clear waters ($33 per person). Perfect for hand-holding honeymooners, their Skyrider accommodates two people in a porch swing–like apparatus. You sit there comfortably (instead of dangling) and you don't even get wet: Takeoffs and landings occur on the tow boat.

Then, of course, there's diving and snorkeling (some of the best in the world). Most dive operators will pick you up on the beach. Many have representatives in the hotels, or stop in at their shops along West Bay Road. Farther out, there's fishing:

snapper, grouper, and barracuda year-round; dolphin, wahoo, and tuna in spring; and marlin in midsummer.

On land, there's tennis (free for guests, a small fee for nonguests) at the Holiday Inn, Cayman Kai, Caribbean Club, and other hotels. And there's golf at the Britannia. Jack Nicklaus designed a special "Cayman ball" that weighs a third of a regular ball and travels only half as far, so you can play 18 holes in the space that would generally accommodate 9.

If you can tear yourself away from all this, there's the rest of the island. Tight on time? Do a guided tour (two to six hours) via **Tropicana Tours Ltd., Gray Line, Rudy's Travellers Transport,** and **Elite Limousine Service.** (Make arrangements at your hotel front desk.)

Better yet, do it on your own. Start with a stroll through George Town, an incongruous mix of whitewashed colonial stone buildings and modern glass structures. (You'll be surprised how many of them house banks.) Then head over to the shopping district, which centers on a few blocks near the docks.

If you've always been fascinated by legends of buccaneers and pieces of eight, stop in at **Pirates World & Treasure Museum** (tel. 9-7470), just up from town on North Church Street. Here, an animated figure of Blackbeard recounts tales of piracy in the Caymans. You'll also see glittering treasures salvaged from *Nuestra Señora de las Maravillas,* which sank in 1656 carrying a cargo worth over $1.6 billion: gold doubloons, emeralds and diamonds, as well as a gold bar valued at over $50,000 that you can actually hold. Scuba enthusiasts will be especially interested in the collection of early dive equipment, including some rather grim-looking lead dive boots. Excellent gift shop. Open Monday through Friday, 9 a.m. to 5 p.m.; admission $5.50 per person.

Leaving George Town, continue past Seven Mile Beach to that eerie expanse of jagged, blackened coral called Hell. (Many couples mail their postcards here—the postmark, of course, will read "Hell.") Nearby, hit the Turtle Farm (tel. 9-3894), literally crawling with turtles (27,000 of them). The littlest critters are barely bird-size, and love to be tickled under the neck. Open daily from 9 a.m. to 5 p.m.; admission is $4.50 per person.

Now go back down Seven Mile Beach, past George Town, and head out around the island. It's hard to get lost, since there's only one road that circles the island plus a single cross-island route. The island is flat and sandy, covered with thick sea-grape scrub interlaced with coconut palms, the peeling, red-barked gumbo-limbo, breadfruit, and flaming poinciana.

You drive through tiny towns of low pastel houses, and offshore, the Caribbean sparkles with a half dozen shades of coral-studded blue.

On your tour of the island, you'll pass the Pirate Cave, with its antique lanterns and other leftover tools of early life; the Blow Holes, where waves spew 30 feet through coral cracks; the endless deserted beaches of the north shore; and, finally, Rum Point. Take the cross-island road to save time on the way back.

ROMANTIC INTERLUDES

Fast lane or slow, on land or at sea, it's all here on Grand Cayman.

You'll find plenty of **beaches** where you'll be totally by yourselves. Barkers lies north of Seven Mile Beach, past Spanish Cove along the top of the northernmost point. Turnoffs lead to its three miles of pure white sand shaded by sea-grape trees. To reach Smith's Cove, go south of George Town past the Grand Old House restaurant to find the crescent of sand surrounded by ruggedly beautiful ironshore (coral weathered a dark gray). East End is appropriately on the far east end of Grand Cayman, past the village of Gun Bay. Beyond the Tortuga Club, paths lead off to a string of deserted coves. Along North Side untouched beaches stretch all the way from Old Man Bay to Rum Point. Storms and sea currents bring driftwood and shells here, so picnic and then go beachcombing for treasures.

The *Atlantis* (tel. 9-7700), a 28-passenger vessel built especially for **underwa-**

ter touring, takes you along the top of the Cayman "wall" at 65 feet, then descends to about 150 feet past gardens of coral and tropical fish. Day trips $55 per person, night dives $60 per person. Ask about special honeymooner rates. Located next to Government Dock, downtown George Town. For something truly out of this world, ride the **Research Submersibles Ltd.** (RSL) (tel. 9-8296) sub to 800 feet down. You'll glide along the Cayman wall past rare black coral and perhaps pay a visit 790 feet down to the *Kirk Pride,* an island freighter that sank some ten years ago. It's still laden with cargo. These are genuine research subs: not for the claustrophobic. It costs $250 per person and is worth it. Office located next to the Burger King on the waterfront north of George Town.

The incomparable reefs, served by two dozen **dive** operators, draw most people to Grand Cayman. The famous Cayman Wall starts a scant 300 yards offshore. Closer in is Devil's Grotto, a twisting maze of coral-encrusted tunnels that *Skin Diver* magazine rates as one of the ten best shallow dives in the world. At the Aquarium, yellowtail and grouper are so tame that you can feed them by hand (Cheese Whiz in a can is best). One of the most magical dives (only 12 feet deep) for beginning scuba enthusiasts as well as snorkelers is Stingray City, where the gregarious fish hover around divers like underwater flying saucers, flapping their wingtips in anticipation of a morsel.

Boats give door-to-door service along Seven Mile Beach, picking up divers as they wait on the beach in front of their hotel. For certified divers, most hotels have special dive packages that include their trips to the reefs. If you want to learn, there's a one-day resort course ($95) or a full NAUI/PADI (National Association of Underwater Instructors/Professional Association of Diving Instructors) open-water certification that takes five days ($385).

One highly recommended dive shop is **Bob Soto's Diving, Ltd.** (tel. 9-2022). Not only is this the largest operator in the Caymans and its only PADI Five-Star facility, Soto is one of the pioneers of Caribbean diving, having established his shop way back in 1957. Another excellent outfit is **Quabbin Dives** (tel. 9-5597), known for its individualized services. **Red Sail Sports** at the Hyatt Regency (tel. 9-7965) also offers a wide range of water-sports options, from night and wreck dives (from $45) to full PADI certification course ($400) to snorkeling trips ($22) to deep-sea fishing excursions (from $440 for a half-day trip on a six- to eight-passenger vessel).

So that you can vividly look back upon your Cayman dives in years to come, have your exploits videotaped. Several different dive operators offer this service, or contact **Fisheye Photographic Services,** Trafalgar Place, West Bay Road (tel. 7-4209). A two-tank dive costs $50 per person; the videotape (VHS) of your dive, edited and titled with music, is $110.

Even if you don't dive, various boats, both power and sail, make North Sound **snorkeling trips.** One of the most elegant cruises is aboard the sleek 65-foot, wing-masted catamaran *Spirit of Ppalu* (the word means "navigator" in Polynesian). The boat itself is a knockout, with its twin glass-bottomed hulls for underwater viewing, and comfortable decks where you can hang out and improve upon your tan. On the snorkeling day trip, you'll get a chance to meet the friendly denizens of Stingray City, then enjoy lunch on board the vessel ($110 per couple, including lunch and snorkeling gear). They also offer sunset cocktail sails ($55 per couple), plus an elegant dinner cruise, complete with candles on the table ($125 per couple). For reservations, contact **Red Sail Sports** at the Hyatt Regency (tel. 9-7965).

For a **wedding** you'll really remember, tie the knot at 40 feet . . . or even 800. For scuba-divers, the wedding party plus divemaster goes down and runs through the ceremony using underwater slates to say their "I do's." Then you come back up to the boat and repeat the ceremony verbally before the clergy or justice of the peace (there are no scuba-certified marriage officers). You can even have the whole thing videotaped. Prices start at about $275 and go on up, depending on how lavish a wedding you want. **Red Sail Sports** will be happy to help you plan the details (tel. 9-7965).

For nondivers, there are the submarines. The RSL subs are a bit cozy, but you can squeeze in the pilot, minister, and couple in one sub and a small wedding party in another sub. You have the ceremony, then come up for the reception on a party boat. Figure the whole thing—subs, party raft, video—starting at about $2,750. Contact **RSL** (tel. 9-8296). The *Atlantis* sub holds 28 people and you can have it for 90 minutes for about $1,200 to $1,500. A month's advance notice is required, price subject to fluctuation. Contact ***Atlantis*** (tel. 9-7700).

HONEYMOON HOTELS AND HIDEAWAYS

Whether it's a condo or a hotel room, the center of parties and excitement or some private hideaway, Grand Cayman has it.

Prices quoted reflect the spread between low- and high-season rates. Package rates usually include tax and service while single day rates do not.

Expensive

Hyatt Regency Grand Cayman, Seven Mile Beach, Grand Cayman, B.W.I. (tel. 809/949-1234; U.S. reservations: toll free 800/233-1234). This luxurious 236-room hotel has everything: free-form pool with swim-up bar, waterfall in the courtyard, concierge on duty to help you with everything from renting a car to getting your clothes ironed, and (out back) the Britannia golf course. The resort is located just two miles from George Town. Gracious elegance, West Indian style, is the hallmark here from the moment you enter along the circular driveway and through the columned entrance. The lobby reflects the splendor and warmth of a great-house estate, with its mahogany pillars, 30-foot-high open-beam ceiling, and magnificent wrought-iron stairway depicting fish and coral, specially commissioned from artist Ivan Bailey. With their blue-and-white facades, the colonial-style buildings look like Wedgwood villas. All rooms and suites have their own verandas, with views of water, foliage, or the golf course. Decor blends refinement with an easygoing island flair. Look for natural furnishings of bleached ash, rattan, teak, and mahogany, plus all the niceties: air conditioning, satellite TV, and fully stocked minibars. And on an island where space is so tight even the golf balls are engineered to fall short, this place (hotel, golf course, beachfront complex with dive shop, hotel, and pools), sprawls across 88 acres, stretching from North Sound to Seven Mile Beach (the main buildings are across the road from the beach). And for those of you contemplating a Cayman Island wedding, the romantics-at-heart at the Hyatt have just the place: a small grotto framed by poincianas and backdropped by a waterfall. They'll be glad to help you plan all the details. Honeymoon package: Eight days/seven nights (EP): From $945 per couple (summer); from $1,895 per couple (winter). Includes bottle of champagne in your room, breakfast for two delivered to your room the first morning, sunset cruise on the 65-foot catamaran *Spirit of Ppalu,* and more.

Moderate

Ramada Treasure Island Resort, West Bay Road, P.O. Box 1817, Grand Cayman, B.W.I. (tel. 809/949-7777; U.S. reservations: toll free 800/228-9898). Looking for fun and lots of activity? Good times are practically guaranteed at this spiffy new resort that has quickly gained a reputation as the happeningest place in town. Much of that recognition comes because of the big-name entertainers who appear regularly in the nightclub. Owners of the hotel include country and western superstars Conway Twitty, Larry Gatlin, and Ronnie Milsap, among others; and they, along with other celebrity buddies, frequently headline in the state-of-the-art entertainment center. But even the illustrious talent lineup can't steal the scene from the glamorous resort facilities, which feature two freshwater swimming pools and whirlpools, two restaurants, tennis courts, water-sports center, dive shop, tour desk . . . even an art gallery. The 290 spacious accommodations are designed to pamper, with honor bars, satellite color TVs, telephones, air conditioning, and in-room safes. All of this is yours on 25 acres right on Seven Mile Beach, and just two miles from George Town. Honeymoon package: Eight days/seven nights (BP): $1,100 per couple (low season). Includes superior accommodations overlooking the pools or ocean, full breakfast each morning, bottle of champagne and fruit basket in room, unlimited daytime tennis, manager's rum punch party, and free nightclub admission. High-season rates (EP): $210 per couple per night for a garden-view room.

Holiday Inn Grand Canyon, P.O. Box 904, Seven Mile Beach, Grand Cayman, B.W.I. (tel. 809/947-4444; U.S. reservations: tel. 901/767-8050, or toll free 800/421-9999), is party central, with 213 beachfront rooms, the magnet for all hot action on the island. The rooms are pleasantly contemporary, and many have been stylishly redone with bleached rattan furnishings and delicate, shell-motif spreads. There are telephones, although no TVs. Outside, you'll find a huge beach studded with coconut palms and a bar shaded by casuarinas (the island spot for sunsets), a free-form swimming pool with stools in the water so you can sip your rum punch in ultimate weightless comfort, tennis courts, reservation booths for the Bob Soto dive operation, and Aqua Delights, a water-sports concession. George Novak, the Barefoot Man, does Cayman folk music nightly outside on the terrace, and every night, there's a beachside barbecue. Honeymoon package: Eight days/seven nights (EP): $1,690 per couple per night, low season. Includes oceanfront accommodations with king-size bed and balcony, 10% service charge and 6% government tax, one dinner for two with wine, bottle of champagne, two souvenir beach bags and T-shirts, free tennis, manager's cocktail party, complimentary admissions to Pirates World Museum. High-season rates (EP): $240 per couple per night for an ocean-front room.

Villas of the Galleon, P.O. Box 1797, Grand Cayman, B.W.I. (tel. 809/947-4433; U.S. reservations: toll free except Florida, 800/232-1034), is how you get close to the Seven Mile Beach action without drowning in it. You've got the Holiday Inn with its parties and beach bar while enjoying the quiet and convenience of a condo. The beige stucco-and-wood buildings look like something from a Florida resort community, with individual porches, modern furniture, and all the conveniences, including kitchens and comfy queen-size beds. All offer central air conditioning, dishwashers, and satellite TVs; some feature microwaves or VCRs. It's hardly 50 steps to the ocean and there are handy "dunk" tanks to rinse scuba gear. Best of all, this is a regular stop for the scuba boats: door-to-door service. There's no honeymoon package, but if you let someone know in advance you've just been married, you'll find a bottle of cold champagne in your room. Rates (EP): from $180 to $225 per couple per day for one-bedroom villa.

Villas Pappagallo, P.O. Box 952, Barkers, Grand Cayman, B.W.I. (tel. 809/ 949-3568; U.S. reservations: toll free except Florida, 800/232-1034). You don't *have* to go to the other side of the island for seclusion. You can have it right here in West Bay, on the peninsula north of Seven Mile Beach. There's nothing on either side of this 45-unit condo resort except empty beach and a bird sanctuary. (Because of the privacy, you'll need to rent a car or scooter.) With its beige stucco set off with black wrought-iron work and red-tile roofs, there's a Mediterranean feel. Loads of lush greenery—hibiscus, palms, sea grape—carpet the grounds. Inside, the units are a cut above those in the usual island condo, with central air conditioning, washers and dryers, dishwashers, ice makers in the refrigerators, and a rock coral wall that looks like a reef, with individual chunks of brain, star, even lettuce coral. All have terraces or balconies. As for activity, forget it. "No barbecues, no parties, no sailboat tours, none of that," says the manager, adding, "but we do have quiet . . . *real* quiet." Honeymoon package: None. Rates (EP): $180 to $225 per couple per day for one-bedroom villa.

Island Pine Villas, P.O. Box 2082, Grand Cayman, B.W.I. (tel. 809/949-6586). For prime location, you can't beat these casual condos in the heart of Seven Mile Beach. Although each of the one- and two-story buff-colored villas is individually decorated, expect to find attractive tropical touches such as rattan furnishings, as well as all the comforts of home: air conditioning, ceiling fans, satellite color TV, and a very workable kitchenette (no dishwasher, however). Everything is beautifully maintained and extremely clean. Many owners leave a guestbook for you to sign, and you'll delight in rummaging through the warm comments previous vacationers have left behind. The lending library might stock novels from an eclectic brew of writers ranging from P. D. James to D. H. Lawrence. Best of all, the condos are just 30 seconds from the beach along a pretty pathway bordered with oleander—and just 27 seconds from the excellent Don Foster dive operation. Honeymoon package: None. Rates (EP): $105 to $165 per couple per night.

Cayman Kai Resort, P.O. Box 1112, Grand Cayman, B.W.I. (tel. 809/947-9055). Oldtime island friendliness smiles over the north coast, where even Caymanians come when they want to vacation. After a recent primping, the Kai's 26 spacious Sealodge cottage accommodations are warm and inviting for honeymooners, with islandy rattan furnishings and large, screened-in patios. All have ocean views and fully equipped kitchens (send them your grocery list and they'll stock the refrigerator for your arrival). It's a perfect choice for divers, since the Kai has its own dive facility right here on the property, and the famous Northwall awaits right in your own backyard. In addition to a good restaurant serving international and local cuisine, there's satellite TV in the air-conditioned lounge, plus the popular Beach Reef bar, where a congenial mix of locals and guests gather to scrutinize the sunset. Most of all, you'll enjoy the hospitable staff, who delight in telling you the best spots to cast your fishing line, or explaining how to shuck a coconut. Honeymoon package: Eight days/seven nights (CP): $1,000 (summer) to $1,470 (winter) per couple. Includes welcome cocktails, one-bedroom Sealodge accommodations, daily maid service, snorkeling trip to Stingray City, continental breakfast daily, a dinner for two, souvenir T-shirts, all hotel taxes and service charges, round-trip airport transfers, plus a surprise gift. The Kai also rents out several elegant north coast villas —ask for details.

Retreat at Rum Point, Box 46, North Side, Grand Cayman, B.W.I. (tel. 809/947-9535; U.S. reservations: toll free 800/423-2422). Rum Point, located on the north side of the island, is where you come on Grand Cayman if you really want to get away from it all. The three-story beige stucco buildings are surrounded by a rainbow of tropical flowers: yellow oleanders, flame hibiscus, purple bougainvillea. Inside, the recently refurbished accommodations feature king-size beds, cane furniture, and modern kitchens—all overlooking a beach with talcum-fine sand and an offshore reef. There are tennis, racquetball, a sauna and fitness center, the resort's own dive shop, and a freshwater pool. Honeymoon package: None. Rates (EP): $160 to $200 per night per couple for one-bedroom villa.

ROMANTIC RESTAURANTS
This is where Grand Cayman shines, with a wide choice of restaurants—from fancy to footloose. As in many suburban U.S. cities, many of the most popular restaurants are located in shopping malls. For seaside dining, often your best chance is the hotel restaurants.

Expensive
Le Diplomat, Grand Pavilion Hotel, Seven Mile Beach (7-4666). With its crystal chandelier, etched-glass wall, flickering candlelight, and gourmet French food served on Villeroy & Bochu china, this place is easily the most elegant restaurant in the Caymans. French with a Caribbean touch is how you might best describe the food. Among their truly special dishes are the scallop mousse, lobster Caribe (lobster slices sautéed in whisky sauce), and the absolutely-not-to-be-missed bananas flambé (bananas flamed in liqueurs, brown sugar, butter, and citrus fruits, then poured—still burning—over ice cream). Dinner for two: about $100 plus drinks. Open nightly from 6:30 to 10 p.m.

Elegant with a native touch, **Ristorante Pappagallo,** West Bay Road (9-3479 or 9-1119), nestles beneath a huge palm-thatched roof (100,000 leaves) on a spit of land in the middle of a bird sanctuary. Inside, the walls are ringed with bay windows housing tropical birds; candlelight and fresh flowers add to the seductive ambience. The food here is northern Italian: pastas of all kinds, an array of seafoods, and absolutely the best veal on the island. For something really special, try the linguine in salsa di aragosta, a sinfully creamy lobster sauce, and finish with Caribbean Coffee: coffee, coconut rum, and Tia Maria, all set afire with a flourish. There's a four-course prix-fixe menu offered at $27.50 per person; an à la carte dinner for two will cost about $80 per couple plus drinks. Open nightly from 6 to 10:30 p.m.

Grand Old House, just south of George Town on South Church Street (9-2020). There's a genteel feel to this century-old Caymanian plantation house–turned–restaurant owned by the well-known TV personality German-born Chef Tell (Tell Erhardt), four-time winner of the Cordon Bleu award and Gold Medalist at the International Cooking Olympics. The white frame house with its veranda, ceiling fans, Tiffany lamps, and wrought-iron chairs is truly one of a kind. You can dine either on the gingerbread-trimmed porch with a lovely view of the Caribbean or in a cozy pink-and-white wainscotted café that recalls some of your favorite Parisian bistros. With his appreciation of the fresh ingredients the islands offer, combined with his impeccable classical cooking techniques, Chef Tell has crafted an inventive menu. Appetizers range from a *très français* pâté maison to unusual grouper beignets, marinated fish that is deep-fried and "puffed," then served with a minted yogurt-and-curry sauce. In addition to continental dishes such as Wiener Schnitzel and roast duck with red cabbage and spätzle, savory Cayman specialties are offered, including an outstanding turtle steak. Indicative of the care and finesse with which everything is prepared, even the fruit punch uses only fresh juices. Open Monday through Friday for lunch, 11:45 a.m. to 2:30 p.m.; Monday through Sunday for dinner, 6 to 10 p.m. Dinner for two will run $80 to $100 plus drinks.

Moderate to Inexpensive

Crow's Nest Eatery, just south of Grand Old House on the beach (tel. 9-6216). Okay, time for true confessions. We're going to climb out on that limb and admit that this is our favorite restaurant in Grand Cayman because of the food (delicious!), the views (sensational!), and the prices (a steal!). Set in a typical West Indian –style cottage painted white with blue trim, the Crow's Nest sits on its own private beach. From a table on the outdoor patio, you can watch wavelets break on the offshore reef and nearby Sand Cay. The menu highlights Cayman cuisine at its best. Although the meat dishes are quite good, the real "stars" are the local fish. It's unlikely that you could encounter a more beautiful piece of swordfish or snapper anywhere else in the world—so fresh, you almost think it will backstroke off your plate. Turtle steak with vermouth sauce is another winner. Warning: This is no place to get persnickety and watch your weight, because the desserts are worth every calorie. Surrender to the white-chocolate mousse crowned with raspberry sauce, or a Key lime mousse pie—actually a cold baked soufflé topped with fresh whipped cream and lime-custard sauce. Afterward, there's good snorkeling on the reef (that is, if you're not afraid of sinking after all that good food). Open Monday through Saturday for lunch, noon to 2:30 p.m.; $40 per couple. Dinner, 6 to 10 p.m.; $50 to $60 per couple.

Lighthouse Club, South Sound Road in Breakers (tel. 7-2047 or 7-0855). True to its name, this restaurant features an honest-to-goodness lighthouse-shaped contraption topping the roof, plus miscellaneous anchors and chains draped around the perimeter. It's located on an especially wild, indomitable stretch of coast where huge white-crested breakers come rolling into shore, sending mist into the air. From your cushion-strewn stone banquettes inside the restaurant, you'll have an open view of the sea. Luncheon fare is simple: shrimp or lobster cocktail, fresh catch of the day, turtle steak. In addition to fresh fish and conch, dinner choices include German specialties such as Wiener Schnitzel and Sauerbraten, plus some admirable apple fritters for dessert. Open daily for lunch, 11:30 a.m. to 3 p.m.; $25 per couple. Dinner, 6:30 to 10 p.m.; $50 to $80 per couple.

Hemingway's, Hyatt Regency, Seven Mile Beach (tel. 9-1234). Capturing the spirit of romance and adventure that the great novelist loved best, this beachside bistro serves up excellent food within a striking scenic ambience. Rattan furnishings and pale, sunset-hue pastels establish island elegance; tall potted palms and graceful columns on the terrace frame views of the pool, beach, and water. At lunchtime, the menu tends to lighter fare, such as a properly spicy pepperpot soup or beer-batter shrimp. After nightfall, you'll find continental cuisine accented by Caribbean flair. Try the fresh catch of the day, such as salmon or sea bass, served as you like it: poached, char-grilled, or sautéed. Another favorite is the spinach linguine, topped with tuna, shrimp, and scallops in a spicy garlic-cream sauce. The restaurant is also celebrated for its potent rum drinks, such as the Papa Dobles, reportedly created after Hemingway's own favorite recipe from the Floridita Bar in Havana. Open daily for lunch, 11:30 a.m. to 2:30 p.m.; $40 to $60 per couple. Dinner, 6 to 10 p.m.; $60 to $80 per couple. No shorts or collarless shirts for gentlemen, please.

Pirate's Den, Galleria Plaza, Seven Mile Beach (tel. 9-7144). Ahoy there, buccaneers and lasses. You'll be right at home at this rollicking pub (a.k.a. PD's), where the heavy plank walls make you feel as if you're climbing aboard a galleon and where pirate murals adorn the walls. They serve good, hearty fare: conch chowder, nachos, shrimp 'n' chips, Buffalo-style chicken wings. "Oh, this is a great place for honeymooners," the bartender commented when we told him about our subject. "It gets real dark in here at night." Lunch or dinner for two, about $20 to $25 plus drinks. Open Monday through Friday, 11:30 a.m. to 1 a.m.; Saturday, 11:30 a.m. to midnight; Sunday, 1 p.m. to midnight.

Cracked Conch, Selkirk Plaza, West Bay Road, Seven Mile Beach (tel. 9-5717). As the name suggests, a nautical theme predominates in the decor, a flotsam-and-jetsam assemblage ranging from a Jolly Roger flag to leftover Christmas lights and a stuffed marlin on the wall, plus, of course, a flotilla of conch shells perched over the bar. The tender pink mollusk stars in a number of the house dishes: stews, chowders, curries, as well as the namesake cracked conch, served lightly breaded and fried. They also have a tempting array of seafood and lobster entries, plus juicy T-bone steaks for confirmed landlubbers. Try one of their special drinks: tropically flavored daiquiris, kicky rum potions, even an aptly named Cupid's Cup cocktail. Open Monday through Saturday for lunch, 11:30 a.m. to 3 p.m.; $15 to $20 per couple. Dinner, 6 to 10 p.m.; $40 to $60 per couple.

West Bay Polo Club, Cayman Falls Shopping Centre (north of Holiday Inn), Seven Mile Beach (tel. 7-4581). For a small place, this restaurant packs in a big menu, with suggestions overflowing to a large blackboard. It's an especially good spot for downing drinks and munchies (known as "appeteasers" here), which circle the globe: Cuban black-bean soup, Indonesian chicken satay, fried mozzarella, quesadillas, French onion soup, all priced in the $7.50 range. For heartier appetites, they serve a full roster of fresh fish and steak dishes, plus a medley of stir-fries, about $16 to $22 each. They've also got the megapopular MVP Bar, hung with football and baseball banners, as well as some incongruous vintage skis and snowshoes. Drop by to view major sporting events on the satellite TV. Open for snacks, 2:30 to 6 p.m.; dinner, 6 to 10 p.m. nightly.

DJ's, Coconut Place, Seven Mile Beach (tel. 7-4234). With its jaunty checked tablecloths and kerosene lanterns on the tables, DJ's probably looks like your favorite trattoria back home—and the excellent food and friendly service will probably make it one of your favorite haunts in Grand Cayman. Since the menu changes to take advantage of fresh local ingredients, the daily offerings are written on the chalkboard. Start off with the chicken quesadillas or conch fritters, then choose among such delights as filet mignon, Caribbean lobster tail, chicken parmesan, and the fresh catch (the baked red snapper is memorable). They also have a good selection of reasonably priced French and California wines, as well as wine by the glass. If you just want to hang out, the casual and chummy bar area features sports events via satellite TV. Open nightly for dinner, 6 to 10 p.m.; to midnight or 1 a.m. at the bar.

Monkey Business, upstairs at Cayman Falls Shopping Center, Seven Mile Beach (tel. 7-4066). The second most fun you can have on land is an evening of high jinks at the hottest dance club in town, with a zap-happy video system plus large-screen TV for keeping up with the home-town sports showdowns. When you get hungry between sets, they serve tasty snacks such as jerk pork and jerk chicken. The cover charge is $7 per person; $4 at happy hour. Open Monday through Friday, 7 p.m. to 1 a.m.; on Saturday, 7 p.m. to 12 midnight. Closed Sunday. No shorts, faded jeans, sleeveless or collarless shirts, please.

The **Lone Star Bar & Grill,** Seven Mile Beach (tel. 9-5575), is Tex-Mex with a touch of fish and has one of the island's few big-screen TVs plus a lively happy hour. Tacos and enchiladas run about $10. Open daily from noon to midnight. Mondays and Thursdays, you get all-you-can-eat fajitas for $10 per person, 6:30 to 10 p.m. **Wrecks' View Craft Shop,** past Gun Bay on East End (tel. 7-7438), opens as a restaurant only on Sundays, noon to 3:30 p.m. This funky little spot on the sand serves down-home native chow: whelk, conch and turtle stew, ribs, chicken plus "heavy cake," a dense, sweet concoction not to be missed. You can get out of here for about $8 per person. Head to **Lord Nelson Pub,** Trafalgar Place, West Bay Road (tel. 7-4595), for the likes of steak-and-kidney pie, good British ale, and a jolly game of darts (about $10 to $20 per couple). Open Monday through Saturday for lunch, noon to 3 p.m.; Monday through Sunday for dinner, 6 to 10 p.m. Looking for good local food? **Island House,** West Bay (tel. 9-3017), is the place to find mouthwatering renditions of conch soup, turtle steak, curried chicken, and Caymanian fish, all prepared with love and at reasonable prices. Open daily for lunch, noon to 2:30 p.m.; about $25 per couple. Dinner served from 7 to 10 p.m.; $50 to $60 per couple.

And if you're staying in a Seven Mile Beach condo, you should know about **Foster's Food Fair,** in the Greenery on West Bay Road (near the Holiday Inn). It's a big American-style supermarket where you can stock up on all your needs. Complete bakery and deli department too—perfect for picnics. Open Monday through Saturday, 7 a.m. to 11 p.m.

---

3. Cayman Brac

Everyone talks about the good old days on Grand Cayman, when the beaches were empty, the hotels small, the pace of life turtle slow. But the Grand Cayman of 30 years ago still exists. To find it you need only head 86 miles northeast to the Brac.

Cayman Brac, 12 miles long and 1½ miles wide, has secluded beaches, but also enough creature comforts (meaning air conditioning, freshwater showers, restaurants, and some nightlife) to keep people happy. The island's 1,500 residents live in a scattering of small towns on the north coast, leaving the south side mostly empty except for a couple of interesting caves and fine beaches.

Fishing is fantastic, whether you borrow a rig from your hotel and cast for bonefish from the beach or go out with a guide (some of the Caymans' best fish guides live here) for tuna, wahoo, or marlin. Underwater, you'll find more of that fabulous Cayman diving, only here, it's practically untouched. Southside diving features great tunnels and caves, sandy chutes leading to sheer walls coated with coral and sponges, shallow forests of huge coral that looks like antlers. The north side has seven-foot-tall basket sponges in only 50 feet of water and the soft corals and tiny critters that macrophotographers love. In addition, the superb sites of Little Cayman are just a short boat run away.

Between dives and fishing, tour the island. The hotels offer guided trips, or you can rent a car or scooters. There's the **Brac Museum** in Stake Bay, an old house filled with lanterns, old dental tools, and other marvelous tidbits from turn-of-the-century Brac life. Open Monday through Friday, 9 a.m. to noon and 1 to 4 p.m.; Saturday, 9 a.m. to 12 noon. Also pass by Spot Bay on the northeast side, a town of little pastel houses ringed by breadfruit, bananas, and flaming poincianas.

ROMANTIC INTERLUDES

Great diving, great exploring, and great people make this island everyone's favorite.

"A *free* dive trip?" one scuba enthusiast asked hopefully. No, it's a *three*-dive trip that should prove to be the highlight of your Cayman vacation. Several times a week, the superb **Peter Hughes** dive operation at the Divi Tiara Beach Resort offers a three-tank extravaganza to the fabled walls offshore Little Cayman (tel. 8-7553; $90 per person). Depending on conditions, sites might include **Jackson's Bight,** packed with interesting coral formations and oodles of fish; and **Chimneys,** where a chute dense with corals and sponges plunks you out at 80 feet on a wall—rated one of the top three dives in the world by *Skin Diver* magazine. The dives are interspersed with an idyll on the little-known fourth island in the Cayman group, **Owen Island,** just off Little Cayman. Here, where the water iridesces to the most amazing shades of turquoise—like molten gemstones—you'll enjoy a picnic lunch beneath the seagrape trees. Since the waters are so clear and the walls begin at about 40 feet, the excursion is terrific for snorkelers as well as divers. Later that evening, a bunch of us who had gone on the trip sat around discussing the day's events. "You know," one man sighed, "this wasn't just a great dive—it was one of the best experiences of my entire life."

Take Bluff Road, turn off on Lighthouse Road, and you'll wind six miles down a roller-coastering rock path to the far eastern tip of the island. There you'll find the **Brac** (bluff in Gaelic), a coral spine that runs up the middle of the island, ending in a sheer, 140-foot-high cliff that plummets straight to the sea. There, surrounded by cactus and palms that seem to glow in the setting sun, you can pick your way across rugged, blackened coral or, better yet, just sit on the bluff's edge and watch the birds.

Caves honeycomb the limestone spine of the Brac. The Bat Cave (two miles east of the west-end cross-island road) is an abstract painting of muted colors: black, white, gray, coral, and green. A hole in the ceiling drips with vines and leaves, and somewhere in the farthest recesses are, indeed, bats. But the best of the caves is called, simply, Great Cave (at road's end on the southeast side of the island). Inside is a delicate lace of stalactites, fluted, crystallized walls, and the most profound silence on this earth. For the most comfort, wear sneakers and old, washable clothes, and bring a flashlight.

At the far east tip of the island, beyond the entrance to Great Cave, lies a very special **beach** that has no name. There's little sand. Instead, you walk on a carpet of marble-size pieces of perfectly preserved coral braided with vines and purple flowers. Off in the distance, the bluff hangs there, striped with the black, rust, and white of mineral drippings, its harsh edges softened by the mist of crashing waves.

HONEYMOON HOTELS AND HIDEAWAYS

There are only two tourist hotels on this island. Prices quoted reflect the spread between low- and high-season rates. Note some prices here include air fare from the U.S., all meals, and liquor.

Brac Reef Beach Resort, P.O. Box 235, Cayman Brac, B.W.I. (tel. 809/948-7323; U.S. reservations: toll free 800/327-3835, nationwide; 800/233-8880 in Florida), is the quieter and more elegant of the two southside hotels. There's no daily schedule of activities beyond diving and beachside barbecues. Instead, what this place has is a wide beach studded with coconut palms, flowering oleander, and cool forests of sea grape hung with hammocks. A recent renovation has glamorized all 41 rooms, all of which are air-conditioned; many also offer satellite color TVs. The downstairs accommodations are the ticket here—they have patios, and you can bound over to the beach in no time. Outside, there's not only a sparkling freshwater pool but a Jacuzzi. The Brac Reef has also just added a new, hard-surface tennis court and a lovely, air-conditioned dining room. Since the hotel next door had a bar over the water, the Brac Reef went one better, making their bar a double-decker with swinging loveseats.

Guests have unlimited use of paddleboats and Windsurfers. "Fantasy Flight" honeymoon package: Eight days/seven nights (Full AP): $1,985 per couple (low season). Includes round-trip air fare from Florida, round-trip airport transfers on the Brac, welcome rum swizzles, deluxe oceanfront accommodations, all meals plus alcoholic beverages and soft drinks, service charge and government tax. Slightly higher prices apply for air service from Houston or Atlanta. All-inclusive dive packages also available.

Think of the **Divi Tiara Beach Hotel, Resort,** P.O. Box 238, Stake Bay, Cayman Brac, B.W.I. (tel. 809/948-7313; U.S. reservations: 607/277-3484, or toll free 800/367-3484) as a low-key Club Med. Daily scheduled fun runs the gamut from crab races and sandcastle-building contests to snorkeling tours. But the jewel in the Tiara's crown is the absolutely top-notch Peter Hughes dive operation, which pampers scuba-divers every step of the way: loading gear on board, helping them on and off with their equipment, providing excellent briefings about the sites (see "Romantic Interludes," above). Meanwhile, nondivers can take advantage of the unlimited free water sports—not only snorkeling but windsurfing, use of paddleboats, bonefishing, and deep-sea fishing. Tennis is also available. The 70 rooms are spacious and comfortable, with telephones and air conditioning. Although some of the older rooms have bare-bones furnishings and hot water that gives out on occasion, renovations are scheduled to remedy any downsides by 1990. Don't let the quibbles put you off, however—this is a happy, fun resort, where guests sport permanent ear-to-ear grins, rather like kids at their first circus. And the food is superb and plentiful, with all meals served buffet style (a boon for divers who like to get in and get out fast). At breakfast, the omelet station does brisk business; for dinner, elegant entrées might include seafood Newburgh, roast beef, or shrimp curry. Afterward, settle into one of the hammocks slung between the palm trees and watch the world go by. Or peruse the marvelous collection of signs posted by the swimming pool, contributions of previous guests. A sample: "Bob and Peggy—forever returning." Best of all, this is a place where the staff goes that extra mile to make sure you have a great vacation. When one incoming traveler missed his air connections, for example, the general manager himself made new arrangements. That's just part of the reason why repeat guests (of whom the Tiara has many) advise that you should plan on staying a few extra days, because once you're here, you'll never want to leave. Honeymoon package: Eight days/seven nights (some meals): $970 per couple (low season); $1,670 per couple (high season). Includes deluxe oceanfront accommodations, breakfast daily, one dinner for two, a picnic lunch for two, a bottle of wine with souvenir glasses, round-trip transfers between hotel and airport, a beach towel, all applicable taxes and service charges.

ROMANTIC RESTAURANTS

If you're expecting gourmet French tidbits by candlelight, this is not your place. Native food and local atmosphere, however, are plentiful.

La Esperanza, north side (8-8531), looks like a wood shack on the sand with a scattering of picnic tables about under a thatched roof. Both inside and out, tables are set with ketchup, hot sauce, and dominoes—a giveaway that this is the main northside watering spot for locals. The menu stars Cayman fried fish, conch stew, turtle steak, as well as a sublime local lobster, sautéed with peppers and onions. After you eat too much (the food is so good, it's hard not to), you can recuperate in one of the thatch-shaded hammocks facing the sea. Lunch, $25 per couple; dinner, $40 to $50 per couple. Open Monday through Saturday, 9 a.m. to midnight.

Other spots to check out: **Ed's Place,** near the airport (tel. 8-7208), serves up a mean mix of local food and Chinese cuisine. For nightlife, try **Bar 29** in Spot Bay (tel. 8-8323), which features outdoor dancing to soca music; and **Coral Isle,** on the south shore (tel. 8-7213). All are closed Sunday.

---

4. Little Cayman

This island is the kind of place newlyweds dream about—ten miles of palms and orchids lined by talcum-fine, absolutely uninhabited sand.

Aside from 30 or so locals (including hotel staff), Little Cayman is deserted. There are no outside restaurants, no bars, no TV. Nothing but legendary fishing: bonefish practically at your front door, tarpon in a landlocked mangrove lake that boils with their frenzy.

Diving here is among the best in the world: walls of encrusted coral starting at barely 20 feet and plunging to infinity, stands of fragile staghorn fingers and sponge cups by the hundred, forests of rare black coral, and visibilities approaching 200 feet. The diving is so good that folks motor over from Cayman Brac five miles away.

For a break, swing in your hammock beneath the palms, island drink in hand. Or hike the cross-island nature trail, an ancient footpath used by early settlers, lined with orchids, cactus, and delicate bromeliads.

ROMANTIC INTERLUDES

Relax and enjoy, that's the key here.

All for you, a stretch of powder-fine pink sand, rimmed with coconut palms and protected by a ring of offshore coral. The lagoon is mirror calm, the water crystal clear. And there's nobody here at **Point O'Sand** on the far eastern tip of Little Cayman but the two of you.

Owen's Island, 11 acres of beach, trails, and mangrove forest, sits so close to the Southern Cross Club that you can actually walk to it (the water's only chest deep). Most folks, however, get a lift from the hotel, then spend their hours snorkeling, picnicking, and exploring the forest.

Have a day of **fishing** in the southside lagoon, where the bonefish sometime run so thick that their fins carpet the top of the water. Or go out in a small boat for snapper, jack, and grouper. Your guide ($75 to $85 a half day per couple) knows the best spots and has all the fishing gear. Then sit back while he cooks your fresh catch over a fire.

HONEYMOON HOTELS AND HIDEAWAYS

This is the ultimate getaway. Prices reflect the spread between low- and high-season rates and include all meals; fishing or diving may cost extra.

Pirates Point Resort Ltd., Little Cayman, Cayman Islands, B.W.I. (tel. 809/ 948-4210). Usually, divers come back from Little Cayman raving about the extraordinary sites, such as Jackson Wall and Bloody Bay. When a friend of ours returned home, all he wanted to talk about was the great food he had while staying at Pirates Point. Owner-manager Gladys Howard, a transplanted Texan with Cordon Bleu credentials (she studied with Julia Child, among others), cooks up a storm. Every evening she spotlights a different international cuisine: her home-bred Tex/Mex is one favorite, with sizzling fresh fajitas, her famous green enchiladas, creamy flan for dessert—and fluttering Mexican flags to add south-of-the-border ambience. Practically everything is made from scratch; Gladys even bakes her own baguettes. There are only six rooms, all oceanfront with islandy rattan furnishings and ceiling fans. Thanks to the desalinization facility, there's plenty of hot water for showers. Let the staff know that you're newlyweds and they'll try to accommodate you in the spacious, secluded honeymoon suite (the governor general also stays here whenever he visits). They've got their own PADI-affiliated dive operation, with a 28-foot boat. Evenings, folks gather around the bar, swap fish and dive yarns, and peruse the various signs designed by guests—there's an annual contest to choose the best one. "We're really a home," Gladys says in summary. Honeymoon package: None. Rates (Full AP): $320 to $350 per couple per night. Includes all meals, airport transfers, use of bicycles, plus two boat dives—and unlimited shore dives—daily.

The enduring favorite on this island, the **Southern Cross Club,** Little Cayman, Cayman Islands, B.W.I. (tel. 809/948-3255; U.S. reservations: 317/636-9501 in Indiana), is a very private collection of cabins on the beach—a bit of a glorified fish camp. The beds are clean and comfortable, the plumbing works (freshwater showers were recently added) and although there's no air conditioning, ceiling fans and the louvered windows let the breezes waft through—simplicity as you like it. The cabins are scattered about the sand, surrounded by palm trees strung with hammocks so you can lie back and watch the setting sun. What a place to be together!

Honeymoon package: None. Standard rate (Full AP): $200 to $275 per couple per night. Includes airport transfers, snorkeling, and bicycling. Please note that they do not accept credit cards.

XXI

CURAÇAO

1. PRACTICAL FACTS

2. ROMANTIC INTERLUDES

3. HONEYMOON HOTELS AND HIDEAWAYS

4. ROMANTIC RESTAURANTS AND NIGHTSPOTS

If city sights and balmy tropical nights rank high on your honeymoon agenda, "the little Europe" of the Caribbean is the place to go.

Located just 35 miles off the coast of Venezuela, Curaçao is the largest island in the Netherlands Antilles. Most of the 175,000 inhabitants live in and around the capital city of Willemstad. There, reconstructed colonial fortresses mix with modern highways and bridges, and with the futuristic superstructures of one of the largest crude oil refineries in the world.

Although Curaçao was discovered by the Spaniard Alonso de Ojeda in 1499, Spain, Holland, France, and England contended for its possession until 1815, when the Dutch established their dominance. One hundred years later, an oil refinery spurred Curaçao's prosperity. Today, the refinery is one of the largest, and Curaçao's harbor one of the busiest, in the world. A constant flow of traffic bustles in and out of Schottegat Bay, which also has one of the largest dry docks in the region.

The best way to see Willemstad is on foot; and one of the best places to start is at the Queen Emma Floating Bridge, which spans the entrance to Schottegat Bay. From the west, or Otrobanda side of the bay, you'll have a perfect view of Curaçao's Handelskaade, or ferry landing, surely one of the most easily identifiable waterfronts in the world. The pastel buildings on the Punda side of the bridge look like a multicolored Amsterdam. Each reflects the Dutch architectural heritage, but the white-trimmed facades, and the tiled, peaked roofs also display an unmistakable tropical influence. The pontoon bridge opens 20 to 30 times a day to allow ships to enter and leave Schottegat Bay, but you won't be stranded if it opens while you're admiring the Handelskaade. Free ferries shuttle pedestrians across the harbor entrance whenever the bridge is open.

When you cross over to the Punda side of Curaçao, you'll be in the midst of the downtown and shopping districts, and not far from the historical renovations at Fort Amsterdam, the current seat of government. A short walk brings you to the floating market, where small sailboats that have crossed the ocean from Venezuela tie up. There's a fish market there, too, where South American and local fishermen sell fresh snapper, grouper, yellowtail, and conch.

The floating market is proof positive that you're in the tropics. But where are the palm trees and the stretches of white-sand beach? The best beaches in Curaçao aren't in front of the hotels, so you'll have to venture away from Willemstad's urban sprawl. You won't find long stretches of sand, but there are 38 small coves and inlets along Curaçao's southern coast that are perfect for a day in the sun.

There are a number of public beaches on the southern coast to the west of Willemstad; only Santa Cruz has rest-room and changing facilities. Don't miss Knip Bay (local people refer to it as "love city"), where there are actually two separate coves. Both are lovely, but if you follow the trail that curves to the left, you'll end up at the more secluded one. To the east of Willemstad, there's a public beach with facilities at the Curaçao Seaquarium complex. The private beaches at Jan Thiel Bay and Santa Barbara have rest-room and changing facilities. Admission to each is under $5.

Back in the city, Curaçao has the kinds of attractions one would expect in a cosmopolitan center. There's the Curaçao Museum, the Botanical Gardens, and a zoo. The Center for Performing Arts serves up a full season of entertainment, and the Curaçao Stadium has regularly scheduled soccer and baseball games. Unique to Curaçao, though, is the Chobolobo Distillery, where the famous Curaçao of Curaçao Liqueur is prepared. Made from a recipe traced to the 18th century, the liqueur is distilled in antique copper vats that bristle with valves and levers. Bottling in the traditional blue delft containers is still done by hand. After touring the facility and sampling the orange-flavored liquid you'll know that you have found the perfect gift to bring home to family and friends.

1. Practical Facts

GETTING THERE

U.S. citizens need proof of citizenship and a return or continuing ticket. Although a passport is preferred, an authenticated birth certificate or a voter registration card is also acceptable. The departure tax is $10 per person.

There's frequent air service to Curaçao, and it's easy to reach the island from most places in the United States. **American Airlines** and **ALM Antillean Airlines** have daily flights from New York. ALM flies daily from Miami. There are also several daily interisland flights from Aruba and Bonaire via ALM. The hotels in the Willemstad area are about 20 minutes from the International Airport; the taxi fare is approximately $10.

GETTING AROUND

All points of tourist interest are easily accessible by paved roads, so you have various transportation options to choose from.

By Taxi

Taxis don't have meters; the rates are based on your destination, rather than on the mileage. Rates are fixed by the government and are fairly inexpensive. Sample fares are posted at the airport; ask your driver to confirm the rate before getting in the car. Sightseeing taxi costs $15 for a one-hour trip.

By Car

Many American rental car companies have licenses in Curaçao; there are also several reliable local companies. Rentals run approximately $30 to $40 per day.

Driving is on the right-hand side, as it is in the United States. Curaçao uses international road signs.

By Public Transportation

The hotels on the outer edge of Willemstad run free shuttle-bus transportation to and from the downtown area during the day. And there's a fleet of yellow buses that operate from Wilhelminaplein to most parts of Curaçao.

LANGUAGE

Curaçao's native tongue is "Papiamento," a language that evolved from Spanish, Dutch, and Portuguese and combines a sprinkling of African and French words, as well as Caribbean Indian dialects. You won't experience a language problem, though. Most Curaçaoans are multilingual, speaking several languages, including Dutch, Spanish, and English.

MONEY

The currency of the Netherlands Antilles is the guilder (NAf), which fluctuates on the world market. At this writing, there are 1.77 guilders to the U.S. dollar.

The guilder is divided into 100 cents, and there are coins of 1 cent, 2½ cents, 5 cents (square nickel), 10 cents, 25 cents, and the 1 and 2½ guilder coins. Bank notes are issued in denominations of 1, 2½, 5, 10, 25, 50, 100, 250, and 500 guilders.

If you also travel to Aruba, don't let the square coin confuse you! In the N.A. currency used in Curaçao and Bonaire the square coin is a nickel; in the Aruban currency it's a 50¢ piece.

U.S. dollars are accepted everywhere on the island. Although the hotels and shops in the downtown shopping district accept major credit cards, many local restaurants and shops require cash payment.

WEATHER

The climate in Curaçao is dry and sunny, and it's always summer there! The temperature stays a warm 80°, cooled by pleasant trade winds. There is only a slight change of temperature from day to night, and the difference between summer and winter is only 2° or 3°. The average rainfall is 20 inches per year, and it occurs in showers of short duration during the months of October, November, and December. This isn't truly a rainy season, though, and if you do seek shelter, you'll be able to get right back on the beach. The island lies completely outside the hurricane belt.

CLOTHING

Cool, casual, and informal summer clothes are the rule in Curaçao, for both men and women. Dress-up clothes are fun, but not entirely necessary, for a night out in the city or in the elegant hotel restaurants, nightclubs, or casinos. Dress-up for men usually means a jacket but no tie.

You should wear a coverup over bathing suits once you leave the beaches and pools of the resort hotels; bathing suits or revealing outfits aren't permitted in the shopping or business areas.

TIME

Curaçao keeps Atlantic Standard Time all year long. That means that during the winter, it's one hour later in Curaçao than it is in U.S. East Coast cities; during the summer, when U.S. cities observe Daylight Saving Time, the time is the same.

TELEPHONES

You can call Curaçao direct from the mainland United States. The international dialing code is 011; the area code is 599-9; then dial the five- or six-digit local number. When making calls in Curaçao, just dial the five- or six-digit local number.

You can make local and international telephone calls through hotel operators. The average price for a three-minute call to the mainland United States is approximately $10.

SHOPPING

U.S. Customs regulations allow U.S. citizens a $400 duty-free quota.

Although Curaçao no longer offers the kinds of bargains that made it a famous duty-free shopping destination, you can still get good buys on certain items: fragrances, jewelry and watches, designer clothing, china, crystal, flatware, and linens. Also on electronic goods, due to a recent change in the law. Shop carefully before you leave home, so that you can compare prices; don't forget that sales taxes on high-ticket items in the United States can raise prices considerably.

Start your shopping on **Breedestraat,** lined with elegant stores that are institutions in the city. At the foot of the street, in a landmark 1708 building, is **Penha & Sons,** the exclusive distributor for many famous perfumes, including Lanvin, Chanel, Patou, and Yves Saint Laurent. There are also two floors of designer clothing for men and women at excellent prices.

You'll find four **Spritzer & Fuhrmann** stores on Breedestraat. One showcases china tableware, crystal stemware, and china and porcelain figurines; another focuses on optical goods including chic frames, opera glasses, binoculars, and barometers. Their "house of watches" branch features an extensive selection of Swiss timepieces; the main store, with its revolving figurines and carillon chimes that sound every quarter hour, specializes in diamond and gold jewelry, prestige watches, and exquisite clocks.

As you continue up Breedestraat, you'll come to **Gandelman Jewelers,** the only manufacturing jeweler in the Netherlands Antilles. This is the place to purchase a genuine "made in Curaçao" memento of your honeymoon. Gandelman's creates contemporary designs and settings, but the intricate gold filigree pieces are uniquely Curaçaoan. The **Little Holland** store is nearby, with fabulous discounts on hand-embroidered linens. At **Kan,** housed in a beautifully renovated 18th-century gabled building, you'll find a splendid collection of Swiss watches, exquisite jewelry, and a fine selection of gift items. The ocher-and-white building with the balcony is the **Yellow House,** famous since 1887 for its selection of fragrances.

The centrally located **Gomezplein,** a popular plaza with sidewalk cafés, runs perpendicular to Breedestraat. Along with many adjacent narrow side-streets in Willemstad's shopping district, the Gomezplein has been closed to vehicular traffic and turned into a pedestrian shopping mall, where you'll find small boutiques with casual clothing and accessories, and gift shops carrying local items, including dolls dressed in traditional Curaçaoan costumes, and paintings by local artists. The famous Curaçao Liqueur in the traditional blue delft containers is also a good buy. This is something uniquely Curaçaoan; only a limited number of bottles are exported each year. Recently, many shops carrying electronic equipment have also moved into the Gomezplein area.

Stores are open Monday through Saturday from 8 a.m. to noon and from 2 to 6 p.m.

SIGHTSEEING

A number of sightseeing operations, including **Daltino Tours** (tel. 61400) and **Tabor Tours** (tel. 76637 or 76713), offer sightseeing excursions. Willemstad city tours cost approximately $30 per couple; half-day tours of the island cost approximately $30 per couple; full-day tours run $60 per couple.

HOW TO GET MARRIED IN CURAÇAO

Although Curaçao extends a warm and cordial welcome to just-married couples, you won't be able to say "I do" while visiting. Marriages are permitted only if one of the partners has been a resident of Curaçao for at least one year.

FOR FURTHER INFORMATION
Contact: **Curaçao Tourist Board,** Waterfront Plaza, Willemstad, Curaçao, N.A. (tel. 011/599-9/613397 or 011/599-9/611967). **Curaçao Tourist Board,** 400 Madison Ave., New York, NY 10017 (tel. 212/751-8266).

---

2. Romantic Interludes

Curaçao offers honeymoon couples all the attractions of a cosmopolitan city center, just minutes from exciting new recreational facilities.

Curaçao Underwater Park and Seaquarium, a 12.5-mile stretch of coral reef along Curaçao's southeast coast, is a paradise for scuba-divers. Permanent mooring buoys protect the fragile reef from being damaged by the anchor of dive boats at 16 sites, including a wreck dive and several wall dives.

The underwater park stretches from Koral Specht to East Point, with many points accessible by car. The park's headquarters, though, are located just east of the Princess Beach Hotel, where a brand-new recreational complex is located. There are a sandy beach with lifeguards (admission $1.50), changing facilities, lockers, and showers: an adults-only three-story wet-and-wild water slides open on weekends; and a shop that rents Windsurfers, Sunfish, and other water-sports equipment. Call tel. 624242 for information about a free slide show of the park.

Underwater Curaçao, a fully equipped dive shop in the recreation complex, can provide underwater equipment rentals and scuba-diving instructions (tel. 616666). Nondivers can follow the snorkel trail. You can also float over the reef in a glass-bottomed boat.

The unique Curaçao Seaquarium displays the world's largest collection of tropical fish and coral in their natural habitat. Admission is $5 for adults and $2.50 for children. The underwater park is a good place to unwind after a day in the city. There's often entertainment in the evening, and boats are available for sunset or moonlight excursions. The park has a first-class restaurant adjacent to the Seaquarium, and an open-air bar. New to Curaçao is an eight-person **submarine** that plunges for just $59 per person (tel. 625400).

Rent a Jeep (although a car will do) and drive 30 minutes from Willemstad to **Mount Christoffel National Park** (tel. 640363), a 4,500-acre wildlife preserve. There, a 35-mile network of well-marked roads winds through the hilly park leading to several breathtaking lookouts. Keep your arms inside your vehicle if your windows are open—much of the roadway is overgrown with spiny cactus and other scratchy vegetation. You can drive the shortest of four color-coded circuits in about an hour; the longest in under three hours. If you'd like to do some hiking, three of the routes provide access to footpaths that wind 1,239 feet up to the top of Christoffel—and the top of Curaçao—providing 360° panoramas. Although the path isn't difficult, it's best to go in the early morning, before it gets hot. You may want to bring your own refreshments, since there are only limited services within the park. Open Monday through Saturday from 8 a.m. to 5 p.m., Sunday from 6 a.m. to 3 p.m. Admission is $2.

---

3. Honeymoon Hotels and Hideaways

Curaçao's first-class hotels include a recently refurbished high-rise in the downtown area and a number of modern resort facilities on the outer edge of Willemstad. There is a 5% government room tax and a 10% service charge added to all room rates. The service charge on food and beverage is 10% to 15% in lieu of gratuities at the hotels. In general, the honeymoon packages include airport transfers, taxes, a welcome cocktail party, champagne, and casino chips.

The **Princess Beach Hotel & Casino,** Dr. Martin Luther King Boulevard, Willemstad, Curaçao, N.A. (tel. 011/599-9/614944; U.S. reservations: toll free 800/223-9815 or 800/44-UTELL), on the western edge of the Curaçao Underwater Park, is great for couples who like the outdoors, but don't want to give up any comforts! The Princess has recently undergone extensive renovations. One of its two old wings is now completely renovated; the other, torn down. And two new wings have sprung up to make a total room count of 202. Most rooms have sitting areas, patios, and king-size beds or two doubles. A full-service dive facility is part of the resort, so you can rent equipment or take diving instructions just a few steps from your room. When it's time for relaxing, head for the hotel beach, which adjoins the Seaquarium's sandy shoreline to make a 2½-mile stretch that's great for swimming, snorkeling, windsurfing, and other water sports. Thatch-roofed umbrellas, snack tables and chairs, and a freshwater play pool and swim-up bar complement the beach. The modern casino provides lively distraction at night in addition to live entertainment most evenings at the restaurant or in the bar area. Honeymoon package: Eight days/seven nights (EP): $869 to $1,199 per couple. Includes American breakfast daily, entrance to the Seaquarium, glass-bottomed boat ride, rental car for one day, Jeep safari, one dinner with wine at the Bistro le Clochard, and drinks at a local pub.

Holiday Beach Hotel & Casino, P.O. Box 2178, 31 Pater Eeuwensweg, Willemstad, Curaçao, N.A. (tel. 011-599-9/625400; U.S. reservations: toll free 800/223-9815). Each of the 202 rooms in this four-level, self-contained resort has a sliding glass door opening onto its own balcony with spectacular view of the ocean, pool, or countryside. It's located on Rif Beach, to the west of Willemstad. The rooms are comfortable and colorful; the white rattan furniture is accented with drapes and spreads in tropical shades of orange, yellow, brown, and green. You can loll on the private beach or around the pool, or enjoy unlimited water sports and tennis. The Holiday Beach also has dancing, entertainment, and gambling at the recently expanded Casino Royale. Honeymoon package: Eight days/seven nights (EP): $599 to $799 per couple. Includes one breakfast in bed, one scuba lesson each, complimentary passes to Naick's Place Disco, tennis—and a surprise.

Golden Tulip Las Palmas Hotel, Casino, & Vacation Village, P.O. Box 2179, Piscadera Baai, Willemstad, Curaçao, N.A. (tel. 011/599-9/625200; U.S. reservations: toll free 800/333-1212 or toll free 800/622-7836). This white stucco, orange-roofed village is made up of 100-room low-rise hotel and close to 90 one- and two-bedroom villas with kitchenettes, sliding glass doors, and terraces scattered across the property. The accommodations have a light and breezy feeling; most of the furnishings are built-in European style, and have orange lacquer accents. It's a casual, low-key resort on Piscadera Bay, on the outskirts of Willemstad, with a swimming pool and lighted tennis courts on the grounds. A short walk away lies the private beach with complete water-sports facilities. Honeymoon package: Eight days/seven nights: $1,099 to $1,159 (inquire for winter rates). Includes three meals daily, water sports, fresh flowers, and more.

In the heart of the Punda section of downtown Willemstad, the **Curaçao Plaza Hotel,** P.O. Box 229, Willemstad, Curaçao, N.A. (tel. 011/599-9/612500; U.S. reservations: 212/661-4540, or toll free 800/223-1588), is built on the foundation of one of the forts that guarded the entrance to Santa Anna Bay. Its architecture blends beautifully with Willemstad's colonial gable-roofed houses, but the hotel has a thoroughly modern and sophisticated atmosphere. It was recently remodeled and refurbished, and you'll enjoy the state-of-the-art disco and casino as well as in-room cable TV and 24-hour room service. Although the location rules out beach facilities, a free shuttle bus will transport you to nearby hotels, where you'll enjoy complete beach privileges. Honeymoon package: Eight days/seven nights (EP): $560 to $770 per couple. Includes a bottle of Curaçao liqueur, cheese tray, and rental car discount. Standard winter rates: $100 to $145 per night.

4. Romantic Restaurants and Nightspots

For a special dinner in a unique setting, search out a restaurant located in one of Willemstad's landmark buildings. Local fare has a strong Dutch influence, with many dishes using Dutch cheeses and Indonesian spices.

Restaurant prices are usually listed in both guilders and U.S. dollars; a 10% to 15% service charge is almost always added to your bill.

MODERATE

Fort Nassau, Fort Nassau, near Point Juliana, Willemstad (tel. 613086 or 613450). This unique restaurant perched high above the Schottegat Harbor provides a charming setting and spectacular views of the dollhouse-size buildings of the Punda. It's in the ruins of a 200-year-old fortress, and winding, low-ceilinged passageways lead to the many-windowed dining room. Entrées are truly international; we enjoyed scampi a l'Indienne, mildly seasoned with curry, and Hawaiian chicken breast, served with pineapple and melted cheese. Desserts include a number of ice cream confections, and there's an extensive yet reasonably priced wine list, with most selections in the $20 to $30 range. Dinner for two will run about $45 for two with appetizers. Open for lunch (noon to 2 p.m.) Monday through Friday. Dinner daily (7 to 11 p.m.). Reservations recommended.

Bistro Le Clochard, on the Otrabunda side of the pontoon bridge, Rif Fort, Willemstad (tel. 625666 or 625667). Set in the vaults of the 18th-century Rif Fort, the bistro's rustic interior is dark wood and white stucco; a picture window provides a sentry's view of the harbor and the Queen Emma Bridge. Gourmet Swiss and French cuisine includes creamy fondues, wonderful bouillabaisse from fresh local fish, and French onion soup. The desserts are out of this world; try the vanilla ice cream flavored with Cheri-Suisse liqueur or the crêpes with strawberries and Grand Marnier. Appetizers are approximately $10 or less. Entrées priced around $15 to $25. Wines range from $20 to $25. Open for lunch from noon to 2 p.m. and dinner from 6:30 p.m. on weekdays; dinner only, from 6:30 p.m. on Saturday; open on Sunday from approximately mid-December through March.

Bellevue Restaurant, Baai Macolaweg, in Parera, overlooking the Dutch naval base (tel. 54291). This family-owned and -operated restaurant is a hangout for local bigwigs and government officials, and you'll see lots of meeting and greeting, hand shaking and back slapping. The special Funchi Table is a bargain. It combines funchi (a white type of cornbread) with five local delicacies: Keshi Yena (gouda cheeseball stuffed with chicken and spices and baked), a stewed fishball, stewed goat meat, stewed codfish, and a vegetable stew of the day. Entrées run between $9 to $13. Open daily except Sundays for lunch from noon to 2 p.m. and for dinner from 7 to 10 p.m.

INEXPENSIVE

Jaanchie's, in Westpunt at the far end of Curaçao (tel. 640354). If you go to the national park, this is a "must stop" place for lunch. Jantje Christiaan runs a large, open-air family-style restaurant that his father started in 1939. Ask to see some of the guestbooks that date back to 1962, and don't forget to add your name to the current one. Although Jaanchie's provides standard steak, chicken, and pork-chop fare, this is the place for fish. Don't even ask for a menu—just order the daily special (wahoo is Jantje's favorite, but the catch of the day could be barracuda, red snapper, or grouper) with funchi and fried bananas. A generous portion is $6, an extra large serving is $9. Open seven days from 10 a.m. to 6 p.m., but call first to verify.

For nightclub shows or disco dancing, try **Infinity** (tel. 613450), located downstairs from the restaurant in Willemstad's Fort Nassau. Infinity has an intimate atmosphere in the midst of glittering lights. It's open every night from 9 p.m. to 2 a.m. **Naick's Place** (tel. 614640) in Saliña stays open from 10 p.m. til 4 a.m., and has a disk jockey spinning the latest European and U.S. hits, as well as occasional live entertainment (closed Tuesday).

More casual places include **Joe Cool** (tel. 618314) in Wilhelminaplein, where live music sessions are held in a former synagogue from 8 p.m. till . . . You can play cards or darts, or listen to music at **The Pub** on Saliña 144-A (tel. 612190), open from 9 p.m. until the wee hours. **The T Cafe** on Caracasbaaiweg 27 (tel. 615940) starts up at 5 p.m. and also stays open until the crowd disperses, but it is best known for its happy hour—from 5 to 7 p.m. on Tuesday and Friday. **Tap Maar In** on Santa Rosaweg (tel. 77344) is also popular during its Tuesday and Friday half-price happy hour, from 6 to 8 p.m.

GUADELOUPE

A far-flung piece of France, Guadeloupe attracts honeymooners seeking understated adventures. It is actually a butterfly-shaped pair of islands divided by a stream. Basse-Terre, the green, mountainous western wing, covers 312 square miles. Flatter, drier Grande-Terre, to the east, spreads over 218 miles. Along with Martinique and the rest of the French Caribbean, this Leeward Island in the Lesser Antilles is an overseas region of France. This means that its 330,000 residents are citizens of France and enjoy all the same rights as their European compatriots.

Most of Guadeloupe's larger hotels are clustered in Grande-Terre's centrally located Gosier. This beachfront village boasts several lively discos. The stores in nearby Pointe-à-Pitre, the main town, draw shoppers and browsers. Fish, fruit, and vegetables are piled high at the open-air market and ferries leave from the dock for offshore islands, such as peaceful Terre-de-Haut.

Along Grande-Terre's southern coast are old sugar mill towers, cane fields, and the stunning beaches of Sainte-Anne. Saint-François is a fishing village with another spectacular beach. An 18-hole golf course is near the Meridien, the only large hotel in the area.

More than half of fertile Basse-Terre, with its banana plantations, waterfalls, volcano, and cloud-topped mountains, consists of the Parc Naturel. Go hiking or take a drive through this scenic area, where fluffy pines stand next to palms and towering bamboo stalks.

Columbus came upon Guadeloupe in 1493. The resident Carib Indians valiantly fought off Spain's attempts to claim it. The island fell into French hands in 1635 and the French and British squabbled over control until 1763, when the island was restored to France. After the abolition of slavery in 1848, East Indians were brought in to work in the fields.

Since tourism was almost nonexistent in Guadeloupe before the 1970s, the calm lifestyle of the island is still very much as it has always been: French, accented with African and East Indian influences. People greet each other with kisses on both cheeks, and French wine flows with lunch and dinner. Topless bathing is the norm on most beaches. The local beguine music has a rousing African beat and the Creole spoken by almost everyone combines French with West African words.

A honeymoon in Guadeloupe means indescribably delicious food, water sports galore, quiet beaches, and a chance to get next to nature in the French version of the tropics.

Traveler's Alert

As we were preparing this edition for press in September 1989, Hurricane Hugo ripped through the Caribbean, causing considerable damage. Although rebuilding began almost immediately, if you are planning to honeymoon on Guadeloupe in early 1990, it is advisable to check out the island's status before completing your arrangements.

---

1. Practical Facts

GETTING THERE

In addition to a return or onward-bound ticket. Americans need proof of U.S. citizenship. While a valid passport (or one that has expired within the last five years) is best, an authenticated birth certificate or a voter registration card is also acceptable. For Canadians, a valid passport is required. A departure tax will be included in your air fare.

You'll have no problem reaching Guadeloupe, no matter how you travel.

By Air

Flying time is about three hours from Miami and just over four from New York. **American Airlines** jets in from New York, Newark, and other U.S. cities by way of San Juan. **Air France** will take you from Miami and San Juan. **LIAT,** the airline of the Caribbean, flies from many other Caribbean islands. Local airlines with flights to Les Saintes, St. Barts, and other islands include **Air Guadeloupe** and **Caraibes Air Tourisme.**

By Ship

Cruise ships dock downtown in Pointe-à-Pitre, near the shopping district. Immigration and customs officials board right away and passengers are cleared within a few minutes. The larger ships—more like aquatic resorts—have extensive facilities, such as swimming pools, health spas, and water-sports platforms. Some cruise lines include air fare to the point of embarkation in their rates. The 750-passenger *Cunard Countess,* for example, boasts an outdoor pool and a casino. Two different seven-night cruises leave year-round from San Juan for Tortola, St. Martin, St. Thomas, and other islands in addition to Guadeloupe. Rates range from $990 to $3,820 per couple. Contact **Cunard Line** (U.S. tel.: 212/661-7777, or toll free 800/221-4770). One of the most romantic cruises is on a 126-passenger yacht, the *Fantôme,* which was launched in 1927. Aristotle Onassis once purchased it as a wedding gift for Princess Grace and Prince Rainier. The year-round five-night cruises go from Antigua to Guadeloupe and other islands. Rates are $1,400 to $2,600 per couple. Contact **Windjammer Barefoot Cruises** (U.S. tel.: 212/686-4868).

GETTING AROUND

There are several convenient ways to get to know Guadeloupe.

By Taxi

You'll be able to find taxis at Raizet International Airport, in both Pointe-à-Pitre and Basse Terre, and at major hotels. Since most cabs do not have meters, check the rates, which are posted at taxi stands and the Office of Tourism, before getting into a cab. Many drivers don't speak much English, so if you don't speak French, take along a dictionary or phrase book. The fare from the airport to Gosier hotels runs about $10 for two people with luggage. From 9 p.m. to 7 a.m., a taxi ride will cost 40% more than during the day.

By Bus

If you want to save money and you're at least semicomfortable with a bit of French, climb into the vans that crisscross Guadeloupe. In downtown Pointe-à-Pitre, the jitneys at Gare Routière de Mortenol will take you to Grande-Terre hotels and other locales. The vans at Gare Routière de Bergevin are headed for places in Basse-Terre. From Pointe-à-Pitre all the way to southern Basse-Terre, the ride is only about $3 per person.

By Rental Car

The excellent road system makes driving a pleasure in Guadeloupe. Be forewarned, however, that local drivers always seem to be in a hurry. You're required to have a valid license or a temporary permit in order to rent a car. You'll save money by renting by the week. Using a credit card will allow you to avoid the $250 to $400 cash deposit. Especially if you're traveling during the winter season, you may want to make a reservation before you leave home. **Avis** (tel. 82-33-47), **Budget** (tel. 82-95-58), **Hertz** (tel. 82-00-14), and others have offices at Guadeloupe's international airport. Some also have branches in Pointe-à-Pitre, Basse-Terre, and many hotels. Local companies include **Guadeloupe Cars** (tel. 82-10-94) and **Agence Azur** (tel. 82-90-43).

By Ferry

You can fly to Terre de Haut, an offshore island in the group known as Les Saintes. But when the water is calm, the trip is wonderful by sea. Ferries depart from

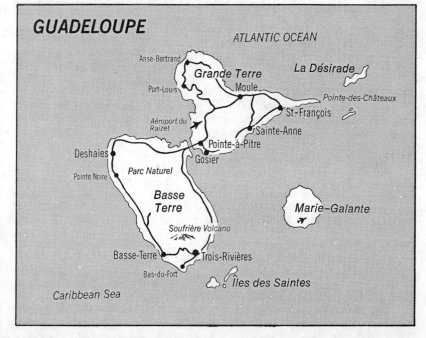

Pointe-à-Pitre on Grande-Terre (a 1¼-hour ride) and from Trois-Rivières on Basse-Terre (a 30-minute ride).

LANGUAGE

If you speak French but don't understand conversations you overhear, you're probably listening to Creole, Guadeloupe's second language. This patois combines French, Spanish, English, and words from West African languages. Unless you speak French, be sure to take along a phrase book and a dictionary. The larger hotels have English-speaking staff, but you'll need to know some French if you plan to venture beyond the tourist areas.

MONEY AND TIPPING

As in France, the franc is Guadeloupe's official currency. You'll get the best exchange rates at banks, which are open Monday through Friday from 8 a.m. to noon and from 2 to 4 p.m. U.S. dollars are accepted at some shops, restaurants, and hotels. Some stores give an additional 20% discount when you pay with traveler's checks.

Restaurant checks often include the tip, so ask if you're not sure. Hotel rates also frequently include the service charge for your room maid and other staff. Otherwise, a tip of 10% to 15% is fine. It is not necessary to tip porters, but if you are so inclined, you can give one franc per bag. Most taxi drivers, many of whom own their cabs, don't expect tips.

WEATHER

During the day, temperatures average in the high 70s and low 80s. Although the weather is warmest in the summer, there is very little variation in temperature throughout the year. Trade winds blow constantly, keeping the weather pleasant year-round. Rainfall is usually brief, followed by sunshine.

CLOTHING

Like life in general in Guadeloupe, dress is also a relaxed affair. Men hardly ever wear jackets at dinner and ties are almost nonexistent. However, evening attire tends to be somewhat dressier during the winter season than during the summer. Women should pack a shawl or light sweater for cool evenings or air-conditioned restaurants and clubs. Also, women won't need their bikini tops at hotel beaches, but can certainly wear them if they prefer. Beachwear should only be worn at the poolside or the ocean.

ELECTRICAL CURRENT

Electricity is 220 volts AC, 50 cycles, so you'll need converters and adapter plugs for your hairdryer or other appliances. Some hotels keep converters and adapters on hand, but it's best to bring your own.

TIME

Guadeloupe is on Atlantic Standard Time, which is an hour later than Eastern Standard Time. When it is 10 a.m. in New York during the winter, it is 11 a.m. in Guadeloupe. However, when Eastern Daylight Saving Time is in effect, the time is the same in Guadeloupe and U.S. East Coast cities. Time is told in the French way here; for example, 1 p.m. is called 13 hours.

TELEPHONES

To make direct calls to Guadeloupe, dial 011-590, then the six-digit local number.

SHOPPING

French imports such as cosmetics and perfumes are excellent buys, along with crystal and china. Mostly found in Pointe-à-Pitre, stores are open Monday through

Friday and Saturday mornings. During the week, they close for lunch from noon to 2:30 p.m. Try **Vendôme** (rue Frébault, Pointe-à-Pitre) for watches, jewelry, and imported fashions for men and women. With several locations in Pointe-à-Pitre and Basse-Terre, **Rosébleu** has a large selection of crystal and French cosmetics. If you'd like clothes made of the vibrantly colorful madras cloth used for head ties by some local women, visit **Le Bambou** (rue de la Liberté) in Saint-Franĉois. You are each allowed to take home $400 worth of purchases duty free. For a change of scenery and an appealing selection of shops, plan an excursion to St. Bart's, one of Guadeloupe's dependencies.

HOW TO GET MARRIED IN GUADELOUPE

If you are considering beginning your honeymoon in Guadeloupe with a wedding, you should know that one partner must have lived in the French West Indies for at least 30 days before filing the marriage license application. Applications are available at the local *mairie* (town hall). You'll need to have a birth certificate, proof of citizenship, proof of divorce (if applicable), and a medical certificate—all accompanied by French translations. (For the medical certificate, a list of qualified English-speaking doctors is available by contacting the American Consulate in Martinique, Immeuble Place Pere Labat, 14 rue Blenac, 97206 Fort-de-France; tel. 596/63-13-03, or your local French Consulate.) Allow at least ten days after filing the application for the publication and posting of the marriage banns (the official announcement of your intention to marry). You may be asked to take a blood test and witnesses will be necessary. A religious wedding may only be performed *after* the civil service. The minister, priest, or rabbi must be given a certificate of civil marriage *(certificat de célébration civile)* before performing the religious ceremony.

FOR FURTHER INFORMATION

Contact the **French West Indies Tourist Board,** 610 Fifth Ave., New York, NY 10020, 212/757-1125, or **Office Departemental du Tourisme de la Guadeloupe,** B.P. 1099, Angle des Rues Schoelcher et Delgrès, 97110 Pointe-à-Pitre, Guadeloupe, French West Indies, 590/82-09-30.

---

2. Romantic Interludes

According to Jacques Cousteau, **Pigeon Island,** off the western coast of Basse-Terre, is "one of the world's ten best" places for **scuba-diving.** You'll swim side by side with spotted, striped, and iridescent fish darting in and out of coral configurations and waving ferns. To see the deep, make arrangements at the **Nautilus Club** (tel. 98-85-69) or **Les Heures Saines** (tel. 98-86-63) on Malendure beach, or through dive operations at the Bas-du-Four Marina or the hotels in Gosier. The uninitiated can take lessons at many places, including **Aqua-Fari** (tel. 84-26-26) at La Créole Beach.

Snorkeling is particularly exciting along the western and southern coasts of Basse-Terre; at the Saint-François reef, near Grande-Terre's southern coast; and around Ilet de Gosier, just offshore from Gosier hotels, most of which provide equipment.

Much of the land in lush, mountainous Basse-Terre is part of the **Parc Naturel,** or Natural Park. Pack a picnic and go exploring. Near the entrance to the park in the north, follow a rocky path to **La Cascade aux Ecrevisses (Crayfish Falls)**—be sure to wear good walking shoes. The path is dappled with sunlight peeking through the thick, overhanging trees. The falls are great for a refreshing dip. There is a zoo and botanical garden in this area, where you'll find plants and animals native to Guadeloupe, from iguanas and land crabs to friendly raccoons.

Route de La Traversée highway cuts across the island from east to west, through tropical forests, past lakes and valleys, and between the pair of mountains aptly called Les Deux Mamelles (the Two Breasts). Going north along the west coast, you'll come to Deshaies. Here you'll find one of Guadeloupe's most prized beaches, in a bay enclosed by hills and mountains.

Head south on Basse-Terre toward the quiet, picturesque capital of Guadeloupe, also called Basse-Terre. Tiny villages, a flower nursery, and the Hindu temple of Changy dot the countryside. The most accessible part of the three-tiered **Carbet Falls** is reached on foot (about a 20-minute walk). The source of the river that feeds the falls is in the famed 4,813-foot **Soufrière volcano.** Steam and sulfurous fumes often burst from it. You can drive to the foot of the crater. Park at Savane-à-Mulet and touch the ground. You'll feel the intense heat of the subterranean lava. If you're ready for an adventure, climb to the edge of the volcano to peek into the boiling crater.

In Grande-Terre at Pointe-des-Châteaux, the narrowest part of Guadeloupe, the calm Caribbean meets the turbulent Atlantic. Here a dramatic series of rocks rises from the water looking like huge **abstract sculptures.** When you come to view this stunning example of nature's handiwork, be sure to bring your cameras and your appetites. Good casual seafood restaurants dot the road to Pointe-des-Châteaux. The coves off the road are good for secluded swimming and the beach at Pointe Tarare is reserved for nude bathing.

Deshaies, on the western coast of Basse-Terre, is a good place to charter a **sailboat.** Here a bay enclosed by hills is rimmed by Grande Anse, one of Guadeloupe's most inviting beaches. Try a romantic moonlight sail on the catamaran *Papyrus* (tel. 90-92-98). At the Marina de Saint-François, **Evasion Marine** (tel. 84-46-67) offers one-week and two-week sailing courses. Companies specializing in boat and yacht charters include **Locaraibes** (tel. 90-82-80) at the Bas du Fort Port de Plaisance, and **Basse-Terre Yachting** (tel. 81-11-45) at the Marina de Rivière-Sens. Check hotel desks for more information about bareboat or crewed sailboats.

For a change of pace, take a day trip to a **nearby island.** Beach-fringed Terre-de-Haut, in the group of tiny islands called Les Saintes, is anchored off the southern coast of Basse-Terre. You can fly here, but the breezy ferry ride is more romantic. At the dock where you arrive, children sell tourments d'amour, freshly baked coconut or banana tarts that are not to be missed. When you leave the colorful town square, you'll see far more pedestrians, goats, cows, and iguanas than cars along the narrow, roller-coaster roads. On the way to the beach, either on foot or in a minibus taxi, you'll pass small cottages with bright flowers spilling over their front fences. The unending view from Fort Napoleon and the gardens there are worth the steep trip. Fishing boats tie up in the bay in front of **Le Foyal Restaurant,** which serves unusual dishes like seafood pizza.

Fly over to **St. Barthélemy.** Those who have come to know this small island 140 miles north of Guadeloupe affectionately refer to it as St. Barts. The name of the capital, Gustavia, recalls the island's Swedish heritage. Especially during the annual August Festival of St. Barthélemy, boats fill the rectangular harbor. **La Langouste Restaurant** is the place to try fresh local lobster. Then visit some of the duty-free shops. Rent a minimoke (an open-air Jeep)—the island is so hilly that if you're not going up, it's only because you're going down. Even in high season, you'll have no trouble finding an empty beach. In some areas, old women wearing the starched white bonnets of their ancestors from Normandy sell tempting straw goods outside their homes.

3. Honeymoon Hotels and Hideaways

Most hotels are in seaside Gosier and nearby Bas du Fort. If you don't need to be near other hotels, try quieter areas like Saint-François on Grande-Terre and

Deshaies on Basse-Terre. Sprinkled throughout the island, the smaller hotels, many of which are charming family-run inns, are collectively known as Relais Créoles.

High season runs from about mid-December through mid-April; low season rates dip about 20% to 50%. The price ranges given for hotels in this chapter reflect the low- and high-season rates. A 10% or 15% tax and service charge is generally included in room rates. In some resort areas, you'll also pay an additional government tax of approximately $1 per person per day.

MODERATELY EXPENSIVE

Auberge de la Vieille Tour, Montauban 97190 Gosier, Guadeloupe, F.W.I. (tel. 590/84-23-23; U.S. reservations: 212/757-6500, or toll free 800/223-9862). The reception area of this comfortable hotel is in the tower of a sugar mill dating back to 1835. Equipped with balconies, minibars, and direct-dial telephones, the 80 modern rooms have been built onto this old structure. The property is scheduled to reopen in April 1990 after extensive renovations. Wander through the gardens surrounding the tower, float on your back in the freshwater pool, stretch out on the private beach, or join a volleyball game. Nude bathers are whisked over to the Ilet de Gosier, just offshore. Most nights during the high season, guests flock to the gourmet dining room, relax at the piano bar, or dance to the infectious music of a steel band at the beachside Ajoupa restaurant. Tennis courts are lit for night games. The small town of Gosier is a brief walk away. Honeymoon package: None. Rates (EP): $180 to $260 per couple per night.

Known as the Frantel Guadeloupe in its previous life, the **PLM Azur Marissol,** Bas du Fort, 97190 Gosier, Guadeloupe, F.W.I. (tel. 590/90-84-44; U.S. reservations: 212/757-6500, or toll free 800/223-9862), has 200 rooms, including 50 bungalows. About a ten-minute drive from Pointe-à-Pitre, it is within walking distance of a handful of restaurants, cafés, and other hotels. Glossy leaves of banana trees and other greenery decorate the grounds. The beach is man-made, but it's hard to tell, and the pool lets you take a break from the sand. Guests also amuse themselves with Sunfish sailboats, pedalboats, volleyball, tennis, and shopping in the boutiques. The tiled rooms have minibars, and baths are French style, with separate toilets. You'll find televisions in deluxe rooms. If you have a taste for pizza, the poolside snackbar is the place to go. Gourmet meals are served up at Le Grand Baie. After dark, Le Foufou reverberates with disco and island sounds. Honeymoon package: None. Rates (EP): $120 to $168 per couple per night.

Fleur d'Épée-Novotel, Le Bas du Fort, 97190 Gosier, Guadeloupe, F.W.I. (tel. 590/90-81-49; U.S. reservations: 914/472-0370, or toll free 800/221-4542). There always seems to be a flurry of fun-filled activity at this hotel. Located in three wings of a three-story building, most of the 180 attractive rooms have balconies. The Fleur d'Épée shares a beach with the PLM Azur Marissol, and like its neighbor, it attracts a casual, young crowd. A large swimming pool, pedalboats, all kinds of water sports, Ping-Pong, and volleyball keep guests moving. Shops in the lobby draw many browsers. Gosier hotels and Pointe-à-Pitre are each about a ten-minute drive from here. Honeymoon package: None. Rates (CP) $178 to $263 per couple per night.

Hamak, 97118 Saint-François, Guadeloupe, F.W.I. (tel. 590/88-59-99; U.S. reservations: 803/785-7411, or toll free 800/633-7411). In a quiet part of the island 25 miles from the airport, Hamak is conveniently located across from an 18-hole Robert Trent Jones–designed golf course and near the marina. Pamper yourselves in a luxurious beachfront bungalow. Reclining in your personal hammock on your front patio, you'll be lulled by the surf at the small beach. Out back is another patio and an outdoor shower (lush foliage ensures privacy). Furnishings include twin or double beds, sitting areas with a couch and a desk, and modern kitchenettes. Villas and duplexes are available. Jimmy Carter, Giscard d'Estaing, and other leaders knew what they were doing when they held the 1979 international summit at Hamak. Rainbow-colored Sunfish speckle the water, which sparkles an amazing

498 □ FROMMER'S HONEYMOON DESTINATIONS

shade of pale turquoise in this area. Many guests play tennis when they are not taking advantage of water sports. Closed June and September. Honeymoon package: Eight days/seven nights (EP): $2,030 to $2,520 per couple; three days/four nights (EP): $1,160 to $1,440 per couple. Includes fruit basket, fresh flowers, bottle of champagne on arrival, one lobster dinner for two, one day's free car rental.

Arawak, 97190 Gosier, Guadeloupe, F.W.I. (tel. 590/84-24-24; U.S. reservations: toll free 800/223-6510). At ten stories, the 160-room Arawak rises high on a nice stretch of private beach. A broad, breezy lobby welcomes visitors to the hotel. Water-sports facilities are available, and a pool and tennis courts also keep guests busy. Cheerfully furnished, the spacious rooms have minibars. Both superior and deluxe rooms come with televisions and closed-circuit video. Honeymoon package: None. Rates (CP): $145 per couple per night.

La Créole Beach Hotel, Pointe de la Verdure, 97190 Gosier, Guadeloupe, F.W.I. (tel. 590/84-26-26; U.S. reservations: 212/477-1600, or toll free 800/223-1510). At the end of the Gosier hotel strip, the 156-room Créole Beach has not one but two beaches, one of which has long attracted those who prefer to bathe in the buff. No matter what kind of water sport you want to get into, chances are you'll find it here—if not at the beach shared with the other hotels. Tennis courts can be used by day or night. Bursts of bougainvillea, hibiscus, and other colorful blossoms are sprinkled throughout the nicely landscaped grounds. All of the large guest rooms have televisions, telephones, and open onto balconies or terraces. Many have two double beds. Honeymoon package: None. Rates (CP): $186 to $248 per couple per night.

With 271 rooms, the **Hotel Méridien,** 97118 Saint-François, Guadeloupe, F.W.I. (tel. 88-51-00; U.S. reservations: 212/265-4494, or toll free 800/543-4300), is the largest hotel in drowsy Saint-François. This is a good choice for couples who want the bustle of a resort in low-key surroundings. A gorgeous beach and the Méridien's proximity to the 18-hole golf course and the marina add to its appeal. Tennis courts, extensive water sports, and a swimming pool are available to guests. Rooms are comfortably stylish, with tropical touches. You'll choose among several restaurants, from casual to gourmet, and nightlife on the premises can be quite lively. Honeymoon package: None. Rates (EP): $200 to $225 per couple per night.

MODERATE

Cap Sud Caraïbes Hotel, Chemin de la Plage, Petit Havre, 97190 Gosier, Guadeloupe, F.W.I. (tel. 590/85-96-02; U.S. reservations: 212/840-6636, or toll free 800/223-9815). In a tranquil residential neighborhood near Sainte-Anne, this 12-room hotel sits high above the water. A tiled staircase with a dark wooden bannister snakes around the outside of the pink building. While dining in the cozy breakfast room near the pool, you'll have a stunning view of the ocean far below. On a clear day—and there are many in Guadeloupe—you can see the islands of Les Saintes, Dominica, and Marie-Galante. The beach is not far from the hotel. Rooms are all decorated with color-splashed paintings. Some have terraces and sunken tiled bathrooms. Honeymoon package: None. Rates (CP): $100 to $110 per couple per night.

---

4. Romantic Restaurants and Nightspots

Guadeloupe's renowned creole cuisine combines the best of delicate French food with the spice of Caribbean cooking. Characterized by light sauces, dishes are flavored with lime, basil, thyme, and mint. Seafood steals the show on many menus, with favorites such as sunfish, red snapper, soudons (tiny clams), lambi (conch), langouste (clawless local lobster), and steamed baby shark. You can also sample roast duckling and fricassee of goat. For a sweet surrender, try coconut custard, mango sherbert, or a lemon soufflé.

If you're in Guadeloupe in August, don't miss the legendary Fête des Cuisinières (Festival of Women Cooks). Come hungry—food is free. Festivities include music, dancing, and a procession of the cooks, all decked out in traditional madras dresses. If you taste something you just can't get enough of, don't worry. Many of the cooks run local restaurants.

EXPENSIVE

Auberge de la Vieille Tour, Montauban Gosier (tel. 84-23-23). The old sugar-mill tower out front lets you know you've arrived at this gourmet hotel restaurant. Chandeliers hang from beamed ceilings in the main dining room. Waitresses wear colorful creole madras dresses. Table d'hôte and à la carte selections include seafood crêpes, roast lamb with saffron, and clams in escargot butter. The wine list is long and good. About $80 for dinner for two. Open every day for lunch, noon to 2 p.m.; dinner, 7 to 11 p.m.

La Canne à Sucre, Pointe-à-Pitre (tel. 83-58-48). Few people who like to eat leave Guadeloupe without spending at least one evening with Gérard and Marie Virginius. They have converted this old home into a gourmet restaurant with an international reputation. The dining area is a study in cool greens and white—green ceiling beams, green borders around the shuttered windows, white lace curtains. Paintings and elaborately framed mirrors decorate the walls, and ceiling fans stir the air. Flower bouquets sit beside lamps with fringed shades. The menu tempts diners with rich pumpkin soup, coquilles St-Jacques, pig's feet, red snapper cooked in coconut milk, chicken stuffed with conch, and grilled lamb chops. Side dishes include purée of bananas and purée of yams. Chocoholics won't be able to resist the chocolate mousse with amandine white sauce. Expect to spend about $80 per couple. Open for lunch, noon to 2:30 p.m.; dinner, 7:30 to 10:30 p.m. No lunch on Saturday; closed Sunday.

Hidden in an undistinguished shopping center, elegant **La Plantation,** Bas du Fort (tel. 90-84-83), is open for dinner only. The chef continually changes his highly creative nouvelle cuisine dishes—try the duck breast with pears. Reservations are essential. Open for lunch, noon to 2:15 p.m.; dinner, 7 to 10:30 p.m. No lunch on Saturday; closed Sunday. The cost is about $80 per couple, including wine. Hammocks are strung across the dining room ceiling at **Hamak,** Saint-François (tel. 88-59-99). Fish brochette with Indian rice is a delicious choice, and a favorite for dessert is vanilla ice cream topped with toasted almonds, pineapple, and caramel sauce. Plan to spend $70 and up per couple. Open every day for lunch, 12:30 to 2:30 p.m.; dinner, 7:30 to 9:30 p.m.

MODERATE

Fruit de la Passion, Bas du Fort, Gosier (tel. 91-81-91). There are not even ten tables in this roadside restaurant located on a front porch. The young chef-owner is always on hand to ensure that the creole food is as attractively presented as it is delicious. Diners feast on dishes such as freshly caught fish and beef brochette, accompanied by red rice and vegetable garnishes—and served on square wooden plates. Meals begin with light, puffed accras (cod fritters) or lobster bisque with a dash of sherry. Coconut or passionfruit ice cream are on the menu for dessert. Cooking is done on an outdoor grill. Hung with paintings and starfish, low bamboo and wood-paneled walls leave the dining area open to the sun or stars. Dinner for two: $35 to $55. Open for lunch, 12:30 to 2:30 p.m.; dinner, 7:30 to 10:30 p.m. Closed Sunday.

Le Karacoli, Deshaies (tel. 28-41-17). When you're touring northern Basse-Terre, plan to have lunch here. The breezy patio, set back from stunning Grand Anse beach, is shaded by tall palms pierced by shafts of sunlight. Tables are covered with red-and-white plaid or checkered tablecloths. Owner Lucienne Salcede has made sure that all meals here are memorable. Begin as Guadeloupeans do, with potent punch made with rum and pieces of tropical fruit. Conch or crab in a cream sauce comes in a clam shell. Try blood sausage, lobster salad, grilled kingfish, or curried lamb—all served with rice and peas. For a delicious finale, order a flambéed banana flanked by scoops of ice cream. Then stretch out on the beach. The cost is about $30 or $40 per couple. Open every day for lunch from 12:30 to 3 p.m.; no dinner.

Auberge du Vieux-Fort, Vieux-Fort (tel. 92-00-72), is the place for lunch when you're touring southern Basse-Terre. From the second-floor open-air terrace you have a view of the lighthouse at Pointe du Vieux Fort and the rounded green islands of Les Saintes. We found the grilled dolphin done to perfection, topped with a mildly spicy onion and hot pepper sauce; the side dish of lentils and rice was delicious! Lunch should run about $35 to $40 for two. Open for lunch, noon to 3 p.m.; dinner, 7:30 to 10 p.m. No dinner on Sunday; closed Monday.

At **Balata,** Gosier (tel. 90-88-25), the owners from Lyon combine the spice of creole with French regional cuisine. Save room for something from the dessert trolley. Dinner for two: $50 and up plus drinks. Open for lunch, 12:30 to 2:30 p.m.; dinner, 7:30 to 10:30 p.m. No lunch on Saturday; closed Sunday. Specialties at **L'Accras,** Sainte-Anne (tel. 88-22-40), include conch in a creamy white sauce, steak, and local vegetables. A meal for two will cost about $30 to $45. Open daily for lunch, noon to 2 p.m.; dinner, 7:30 to 10 p.m.

INEXPENSIVE

La Nouvelle Table Créole, Saint-Félix, Gosier (tel. 84-28-28). Before moving to these large oceanview quarters with ten vacation bungalows on the grounds, Jeanne Carmelita (known as Madame Jeanne) spent three decades running a small restaurant nearby. Try the red snapper grilled with ginger, blaff (a spicy fish stew), beef brochette, or lobster fricassée. Some evenings a steel band plays during dinner. The cost for two will be about $25 to $35. Open for lunch, noon to 3 p.m. (except Saturday); dinner, 7:30 to 10:30 p.m.

NIGHTLIFE

Nightlife is most active in the Gosier area. Some clubs charge an admission fee of about $10. At **Mandingo** (Gosier) live bands will show you what beguine is all about. If you want to combine dinner with discoing, check out **Elysées Matignon** (Bas du Fort), which plays a lot of European popular music.

JAMAICA

Irie. It's a word you'll see emblazoned on T-shirts, headlined on posters announcing festivals, and hear threaded through the sensuous, syncopated rhythms of the reggae music. Irie . . . it means a joyous welcome—and it neatly summarizes the happy mood of a honeymoon in Jamaica.

The name Jamaica comes from the Arawak Indian word *Xaymaca,* meaning "land of wood and water." Indeed it is. The country packs amazing geographic wallop into its 4,411 square miles. For vacationers, the chief attractions are the powdery coral-sand beaches that curve gracefully along the island's north coast—shores that have become the centerpieces for some of the most celebrated resorts in the Caribbean: Montego Bay, Ocho Rios, Port Antonio, and Negril. But in addition to its beaches, Jamaica has waterfalls, plateaus, plains, rivers, mineral springs, caves, coves, and the forest-clad Blue Mountains, which run through the island's interior. Soaring up to 7,402 feet tall, the peaks rise higher than any mountains in the United States east of the Mississippi.

Located in the northern Caribbean about 700 miles from Miami, 550 miles due north of the Panama Canal, Jamaica is one of the three islands that form the Greater Antilles. It is the third largest Caribbean island, measuring some 146 miles from east to west and 51 miles from north to south at its widest point. It has a population of about 2.5 million, making it the largest English-speaking island in the Caribbean.

Nature has treated Jamaica well. The countryside is lush, rich, bounteous. If ripe mangoes or bananas don't plop right into your hands, they—or other sweet tropical treats such as genip, papaya, and naseberry—never seem more than an arm's length away. When you drive along country roads Technicolor vistas succeed each other like scenes from a movie. You'll pass velvety green polo fields, undulating acres of sugarcane, old sugar-mill ruins, quiet coves, and rocky cliffs pounded by the sea.

Jamaica was originally settled by the peaceful Arawak Indians, who probably came to the island from the South American mainland some 1,300 years ago. Christopher Columbus was the first European to see it, sailing along the north coast in May 1494. He called it "the fairest isle that eyes have beheld, mountainous, and the land seems to touch the sky." In 1510, the Spanish cemented their claim to Jamaica by founding a permanent settlement at New Seville. The capital was moved to Villa de la Vega (now Spanish Town) in 1534. In 1655, a British expeditionary force of 6,000 soldiers trounced 500 Spaniards at Kingston Harbour, snatching the rich island prize for England.

Because of Jamaica's central location, the British used the island as a base for plundering Spanish treasure ships. This form of legalized piracy was known as privateering. The practice was so widely condoned that the notorious buccaneer Henry Morgan was named lieutenant governor of Jamaica—and even received a knighthood for his efforts. Jamaica's Port Royal (just south of Kingston) established itself as the pirate headquarters. Its swashbuckling reign as "the wickedest city on earth" came to an abrupt end on June 7, 1692, at 11:43 a.m., when a tremendous earthquake hurled one-third of the city into the sea.

The pirate era was over. In its place, the English turned to agriculture, growing indigo, tobacco, and cotton, before settling on sugar as the chief cash crop. During the 1700s, over 700 plantations flourished on the island, making Jamaica the richest British colony. Of course, there was a dark side to this prosperity. Sugar meant slavery, and thousands of Africans were brought to toil in the fields. Some slaves were freed, others escaped. They became known as the Maroons (from the Spanish word *cimarron,* meaning "untamed") and inhabited the thickly wooded reaches of Jamaica's backcountry. Slavery was finally abolished throughout the colony in 1838.

From 1866 until 1944, Jamaica was a British Crown Colony. In 1962, Jamaica became a fully independent nation within the British Commonwealth. The nation is a parliamentary democracy, with a well-established two-party system.

Jamaica's motto is "Out of Many, One People," which recognizes that the country is a true ethnic melting pot. Most of its citizens come from African or Afro-European descent, but there are also many British, Chinese, Indians, Portuguese, Germans, and other West Indians. Nowhere is this international hodgepodge more evident than in Jamaican cuisine. Saltfish—which along with ackee is the national dish—was a staple of Portuguese sailors. Goat curry, a frequent lunch special, uses Indian spices. And afternoon tea, a legacy of the British, is still an island tradition.

Because of Jamaica's variety, honeymooners can plan a trip that perfectly matches their interests. Since the island has over 200 miles of beaches, it is a prime area for water sports—swimming, windsurfing, waterskiing, deep-sea fishing, snorkeling, scuba-diving, and sailing. But couples can also hike along mountain trails, explore deep beneath the earth on a spelunking (caving) expedition, play golf or tennis at a luxury resort—or improve their polo game at a week-long clinic. At the same time, Jamaica's rich historical and cultural heritage makes sightseeing well worthwhile. You can visit old plantation great houses (maybe you'll meet one of the resident ghosts), browse through art galleries and crafts markets, climb to the top of a 600-foot waterfall, or spend a lazy afternoon drifting down a languid river aboard a bamboo raft.

---

1. Practical Facts

GETTING THERE

Proof of citizenship is required for both Americans and Canadians, such as a passport, or any two of the following documents: birth certificate, voter registration

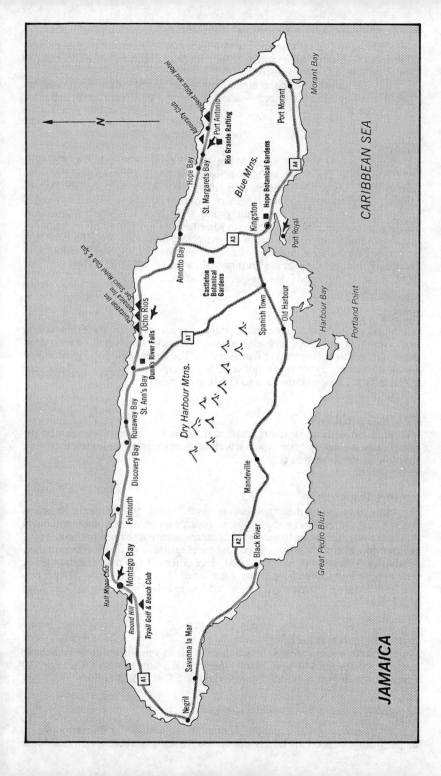

JAMAICA

card, affidavit, and driver's license with a photograph. A return or ongoing airline ticket is also necessary. Upon leaving Jamaica, there is a departure tax of about $8 per person, payable in Jamaican currency.

Frequent nonstop and direct flights from major United States cities means that you can leave home in a snowstorm—and be sunning yourself on a Jamaican beach a few hours later.

By Air

Jamaica is only 1½ hours from Miami, 3¾ hours from New York or Chicago, and 6 hours from Los Angeles. The country has two international airports: Manley International, about 20 minutes from downtown Kingston; and Sir Donald Sangster International, ten minutes east of Montego Bay. Most airlines fly to both airports. Sangster Airport serves Montego Bay, Ocho Rios, and Negril; Manley Airport is your best bet for hotels located in Kingston, Mandeville, and Port Antonio.

Air Jamaica, the island's national carrier, flies from New York, Philadelphia, Baltimore/Washington, Atlanta, Miami, Tampa, Los Angeles, San Francisco, and Toronto. **American Airlines** and **Continental** also serve the island. All international flights must be confirmed 72 hours before departure.

By Sea

Jamaica has become increasingly popular as a port of call for cruise ships sailing from New York and Port Everglades, Miami. The liners usually put in at Montego Bay or Ocho Rios; some stop at Port Antonio. The *Regent Star* (registered in The Bahamas) is currently the only major vessel based year-round in Jamaica. It also calls at Costa Rica, Cartagena, the Panama Canal, and Aruba.

GETTING AROUND

Since Jamaica's major resort areas are all located fairly near each other on the north coast, it's easy to get to know several of them during your honeymoon. You have several transportation choices.

Airport Transfers

How you get from the airport to your hotel depends on whether the transfer is included in your vacation package. If your package includes the hotel transfer, you will have a voucher to give to the company representative at the airport. Even if your package does not include the transfer, your travel agent can set up the transportation in advance. This is highly recommended, since otherwise you might be stranded or have to pay a high individual taxi fare. Sample taxi fares are from $6 to $17 per person from Sangster International Airport to Montego Bay hotels; $75 to Ocho Rios; and $65 to Negril.

Intra-island Air Travel

Trans-Jamaican Airlines, Ltd., links the island's major resort areas. Sample one-way airfares are $40 from Manley Airport (Kingston) to Port Antonio; $50 from Manley Airport to Negril. For reservations, call 809/923-8680.

Taxis

Taxis provide excellent, reasonably priced transportation for short trips (for example, from your hotel to a crafts market). You'll usually find several cabs available at hotels and resorts. If you're going to a remote location (like a great house or a rafting trip), arrange for the driver to return at a designated time to pick you up. Many well-known island restaurants in the resort areas also provide a free shuttle service from major hotels for their patrons. JUDA (Jamaica Union Drivers Association) is the main taxi service on the island; they have offices throughout the island, including Montego Bay (tel. 952-0813) and Ocho Rios (tel. 974-2292).

Although there are some metered cabs, most Jamaican taxis are "Contract Carriages" that charge fixed rates between points. Verify what the fare will be before you take the taxi; at your hotel, you can ask the doorman to double-check the rate. Away from hotels, you can summon a taxi either by telephone, or by flagging one down in the street. Contract carriages can be recognized by the bright red PPV (Public Passenger Vehicle) plates.

Many Jamaican cab drivers also make knowledgeable tour guides. Ask your hotel front desk to make arrangements with someone qualified. Rates are quite inexpensive if you share the ride with another couple.

Jamaica also has a system of public minibuses that ply various popular routes. Although they have no fixed schedules, they run frequently and are quite inexpensive. However, they tend to get crowded, and most visitors either call a cab or rent a car.

Rental Cars

These are a very popular option, since Jamaica has an excellent system of paved roads linking the entire country. Major rental car agencies have branches at airports and the resort areas. It's a good idea to reserve your car in advance, since popular models (especially air-conditioned vehicles) tend to be in short supply. To rent a car, you must be at least 21 years of age and have a valid driver's license.

Sample rates for a subcompact car with automatic transmission from **Avis Rent-A-Car** range from about $77 per day (for a one- or two-day rental) to about $365 for a one-week rental, all with unlimited mileage. In all cases, you pay for gas, which is quite expensive: about $2.50 per imperial gallon (an imperial gallon is about one-fifth bigger than a U.S. gallon). Gas stations are usually open from 7:30 a.m. until 7 p.m. Monday through Saturday. Many are closed on Sunday.

Driving is on the left; most rental cars have steering wheels on the right. You should adjust to this quickly. What takes a little more getting used to is the Jamaican driving style. Many Jamaican drivers seem to relish overtaking slower moving cars on blind curves, and avoid using directional signals with a relentless passion. In the country, cows and goats consider that they have equal rights to the asphalt. None of this is a major hazard nor should prevent you from enjoying your drive. Just maintain a sense of humor, practice good defensive driving techniques, and honk on blind curves.

Sightseeing Tours

Many different ground operators offer organized tours to Jamaica's most popular tourist attractions—Dunn's River Falls, Martha Brae or Rio Grande river rafting, Rose Hall great house, plus day trips to Negril. Ask at your hotel's front desk for details and costs.

LANGUAGE

English is the official language. You also might hear Jamaicans speaking a local patois, which mixes English with Caribbean words and cadences—quite difficult to understand. This dialect reflects the different nations that have influenced Jamaican culture. Shoes are called *shampatas,* adapted from the Spanish *zapatos.* The words *duppy* (ghost) and *bankra* (basket) come from Africa.

Jamaicans are also extremely polite. Whether you're in a shop or asking driving directions, always begin your conversation with "good morning," "good afternoon," or the like.

MONEY

The official currency is the Jamaican dollar, which is written: J$. As we go to press, the official exchange rate is $1 US equals about J$5.50. Check the Jamaica Tourist Board or your bank for the current exchange rate. Unless otherwise noted, all prices in the book are in U.S. dollars. When traveling in Jamaica, always double-check which dollar rate stores, taxi drivers, and others are quoting.

Jamaican currency laws are quite strict. Tourists must pay all bills in Jamaican dollars, and it is illegal to take Jamaican currency out of the country. Since you cannot exchange Jamaican dollars in the United States, make sure that when you return home, you allow sufficient time at the Jamaican airport for changing your money. Airport exchange bureaus are open to service all incoming and outgoing international flights. Save your currency exchange receipts—you must present them when exchanging extra Jamaican dollars at the end of your honeymoon.

The Jamaican currency system uses bills of various denominations: J$1, J$2, J$5, J$10, etc. Coins are 1¢, 5¢, 10¢, 20¢, 25¢, and 50¢. Banks are open from 9 a.m. until 2 p.m. Monday through Thursday; from 9 a.m. until noon and again from 2:30 until 5 p.m. on Friday. They are closed on Saturday, Sunday, and holidays. In addition, most island hotels, cruise ships, and duty-free shops can change your money; ask in advance. The exchange rate is about the same as you will get at the airport or the bank. Many hotels, restaurants, and shops accept major credit cards, but check beforehand to be sure. Your bill will be written up in Jamaican dollars, then charged to your account in U.S. dollars. Traveler's checks will usually be accepted, but you will get your change in Jamaican dollars.

Most Jamaican hotels and restaurants add a service charge of 10% to your bill. If this has not been done, tip waiters 10% to 15% of the bill; leave chambermaids $2 per couple per day. Give porters and bellboys $1 per bag. Taxi drivers get 15% of the fare.

WEATHER

From December through March, the coolest months, daytime temperatures range from the high 70s to the mid-80s. Summer temperatures run about 80° to 90°, somewhat warmer inland. Phrases like "black velvet" come to mind when describing the balmy evenings, which are about 5° to 10° cooler. Constant breezes moderate the climate; these blow from the water during the day, from the land at night. Remember that Jamaica is a mountainous country and temperatures are lower in the hills. The average daily temperature is 86° at sea level, 63° in the mountains.

From May through early June, and again from October until early November is generally the rainy season, although this pattern has wobbled a bit in recent years. Rains usually come in the form of passing showers.

CLOTHING

Dress casually by day in shorts, swimsuits, and lightweight sports cloths. Wear bathing suits and short shorts only at the beach—they are not appropriate garb for city streets. If you are going to the mountains, bring a light sweater or jacket.

At night, dress standards vary at the different resorts. In Negril, dressing up usually means putting on a clean T-shirt, while some of the posh grand resorts in Montego Bay, Ocho Rios, and Port Antonio require men to wear a jacket and tie to dinner—perhaps even black tie certain nights. Throughout the island, wardrobe codes tend to be more permissive in summer, when a jacket (no tie) admits men to most fine places. Ask your travel agent to check in advance.

Many hotels and beaches (especially those in Negril) have areas that are designated as "swimsuits optional." Nude beaches?! Perhaps the best feedback we've gotten about this au naturel phenomenon comes from the woman who said, "For the first ten minutes, I felt embarrassed because no one was wearing any clothes. For the next ten minutes, I felt embarrassed because I was the only one wearing clothes. Then I took my clothes off—and wondered what all the fuss was about anyway."

In any event, confine your nude sunbathing to the designated places—it's illegal elsewhere on the island.

TIME

Jamaica stays on Eastern Standard Time all year. In winter, Jamaican time is the same as New York's. In summer, when it is noon in New York, it is 11 a.m. in Jamaica.

TELEPHONES

You can call Jamaica direct from the United States; dial 809 (the area code), and then the number. When placing calls from Jamaica, be aware that a government tax of 15% will be added to hotel charges on all overseas calls. When making long-distance calls, it is a good idea to use a credit card or to call collect.

ELECTRICAL CURRENT

Although most hotels use 110 volts (just as in the United States), some have 220 volts, 50 cycles (as in Europe). Many hotels have converters available, but ask your travel agent to check this out.

SHOPPING

Jamaica offers tempting buys on both island-produced items and fine European imported goods. In general, store hours are from 8:30 a.m. until 5 p.m. on weekdays, from 8:30 a.m. until 6 p.m. on Saturday. For specific store recommendations, see the appropriate resort area information.

Imported Goods

Jamaica's in-bond prices mean that you can save from 20% to 50% on imported merchandise. Best buys include Swiss watches, French perfume, and English china, porcelain, and crystal. Most stores are clustered together in the main tourist areas; prices tend to be the same in the different resorts. Stores often have exclusivity, carrying different brand names and patterns, so shop around.

"In-bond" means that goods technically never enter the country, so no duty is charged on them. In some countries, you cannot take purchases with you from the store; instead, they will be delivered to your departing flight or cruise ship. However, in Jamaica, American tourists with proof of identity who pay in U.S. dollars, traveler's checks, or with credit cards, can take all their purchases with them except for consumables, such as liquor and cigars. These must be picked up upon departure at the cruise-ship pier or airport. Large in-bond shops such as Chulani's, which sells perfumes, cameras, crystal, and more, have outlets in most of the major resort areas.

Locally Made Items

Jamaica has a flourishing folk crafts tradition, rich with African, Indian, and

European influences. Goods include straw work, baskets, and paintings. Wood carvings made from lignum vitae, a native hardwood, are popular, formed into statues, bookends, and salad bowls. Also look for colorful resort fashions made from fabrics silk-screened on the island, and jewelry made from local agate, black coral, and semiprecious stones.

For the widest selection, check out the crafts market in Montego Bay; there are also crafts markets in Negril, Ocho Rios, and Port Antonio. Entrepreneurs also set up "shop"—or at least their wares—near major tourist attractions such as Dunn's River Falls and patrol the public beaches at the major hotels. Designs and prices tend to be similar at the different outlets, so browse around until you find something you like. Many of the merchants also can execute designs to order. At all outdoor markets, haggling is accepted. As a rule of thumb, start by offering the vendor (called a higgler) one-third to one-half of the asking price; the final price will be somewhere in the middle. Sometimes vendors will be overly persistent about hawking their merchandise; just politely but firmly say no.

Consider taking home a taste of Jamaica, such as Tía María, a coffee-flavored liqueur, other exotic liqueurs made from pimento (allspice) or ginger, or one of the mellow island rums. Although you can't bring Jamaica's succulent fresh fruits back to the United States, you can return with them preserved in tangy chutneys. Best of all, buy a couple of bags of rich Blue Mountain coffee—Jamaica's volcanic soil produces some of the finest beans in the world. (Make sure you buy the 100% brew.) Or perfume yourselves with Jamaica's own tropical scents: Royal Lyme or Royall Bay Rhum for the groom, White Witch perfume or Khus Khus toilet water for the bride. Also fun for women—getting their hair braided like Bo Derek in *10*. It can be done at little shacks along many Jamaican beaches; the braids stay in for a couple of days, if you take care of them. Depending on the elaborateness of the do, prices range between $15 and $40.

For fine art, the island center is Kingston. You can also view and buy works by well-known artists such as Edna Manley and Mallica "Kapo" Reynolds at Harmony Hall in Ocho Rios.

ABOUT KINGSTON

Kingston, Jamaica's capital, is a bustling metropolis with a population of about 700,000, making it the largest English-speaking city in the western hemisphere south of Miami. Although most vacationers bypass it in favor of the beach resorts, Kingston is well worth exploring because it represents the heart and soul of the nation. Many of the north coast resorts offer day trips to the capital, or you can stop by on your way back to the states, returning via Kingston's Manley Airport. Places to visit include:

The National Gallery of Art, 12 Ocean Blvd. (tel. 922-1563), down on the waterfront, with a superb collection of paintings and sculpture by contemporary Jamaican artists. It also exhibits portraits, engravings, and maps dating back to the 17th century. Open Monday through Saturday, 10 a.m. to 5 p.m.; admission $1.50 per person.

Devon House, 26 Hope Rd. (tel. 926-6867), was the 19th-century home of George Stiebel, one of the Caribbean's first black millionaires, who made a fortune mining in South America. It has been beautifully restored by the Jamaica National Trust, with elegant period furnishings and paintings. Small shops located in what once were the stables sell some of the best crafts on the island. Open Monday through Saturday, 10 a.m. until 5 p.m.; admission $3.50 per person. Then enjoy a delicious lunch on the brick patio under spreading mango and mahogany trees at the Devonshire Restaurant. The menu includes seafood crêpes, steamed snapper, and other Jamaican specialties. Open daily from noon to 2:30 p.m. and from 7 to 9 p.m.; $20 to $40 per couple. For dessert, head over to the little kiosk for some of the best ice cream in the world, if not the universe, in delectable flavors such as passionfruit and Blue Mountain coffee.

Port Royal, favorite lair of marauding buccaneers such as Henry Morgan and Blackbeard, was largely destroyed by earthquake and tidal wave in 1692. Today, a walk through what remains provides a fascinating glimpse back to the time when the Jolly Roger ruled the Caribbean. Stop by St. Peter's Church, which contains a silver plate rumored to be a gift from Morgan. Fort Charles, built in 1656, today houses the Maritime Museum. The Old Naval Hospital is now a museum displaying Port Royal artifacts recovered by divers and archeologists, including Spanish armor, guns, swords, and a watch that stopped at the exact moment of the cataclysmic earthquake. All are open daily from 9 a.m. until 5 p.m.; there are small admission fees. You can reach Port Royal by ferry from Kingston, or by driving west past the airport along the narrow Palisadoes peninsula.

Get an entirely different outlook on Jamaica from 3,000 feet up in the cool, misty **Blue Mountain highlands** above Kingston, less than an hour's drive. Ranges of forest-clad peaks undulate as far as the eye can behold, like waves upon a storm-tossed sea. This is prime coffee-growing country, and from November through May the red berries are harvested by hand to make the famous Blue Mountain brew. Savor a cup at **Pine Grove Chalet** (tel. 922-8705), which puts out a lovely afternoon coffee spread, accompanied by rich dessert cake. Served daily from 4 to 5:30 p.m.; about $10 per couple.

A trip to Kingston would be worth it just for dinner at the **Blue Mountain Inn** (tel. 927-1700 or 927-2606), located on Newcastle Road less than a half hour's drive from downtown. Built nearly 200 years ago as a coffee plantation, it is today one of Jamaica's finest restaurants. Peruse the menu while you enjoy cocktails on the terrace, soothed by the whoosh of the Hope River, coursing just beyond the garden. Inside, the dining room reflects formal elegance, with red French provincial–design chairs, timbered ceiling, and thick stone walls. The cuisine is inventive and sumptuous: an ackee quiche, perhaps, or smoked marlin stuffed with crabmeat, or melt-in-your-mouth grilled snapper, served with butter-orange sauce. For dessert, finish with a flourish—a flaming baked Alaska. Open Monday through Saturday for dinner, 7 to 9 p.m.; $80 to $100 per couple plus drinks.

SPECIAL EVENTS
Throughout the year, Jamaica serves up festivals, sports events, and happenings that delight both locals and visitors.

Negril Reggae Festival (January/February) is a series of concerts headlining major performers.

Chukka Cove Cup (late January) is a polo tournament near Ocho Rios with four competing teams, each with a high-handicap player.

Manchester Golf Week (March), held at the Manchester Club in Mandeville, is Jamaica's oldest golf tournament, and attracts leading local and international players.

Miami to Montego Bay Yacht Race (mid-March). Oceangoing yachts compete in this annual race.

Jamaica Sailing Week and Easter Regatta (late March/early April). Yacht crews compete in the week's races, while landlubbers will enjoy the beach parties and pig feasts.

Jamaica International Marlin Tournament (late May) is a marlin fishing tournament in Ocho Rios.

Trelawny Carnival (late May). Held at Falmouth (about midway between Montego Bay and Ocho Rios), the three-day festival features steel bands, drum corps parades, historical tours, Jamaican crafts and food markets, and three nights of concerts at Burwood Beach headlining top calypso, soca, and reggae performers.

Independence Day (first Monday in August). Parades, native dance, music, arts, and crafts animate the streets of Kingston and the parish capitals.

Reggae Sunsplash (late August). This is it—Jamaica's biggest musical event. Held in Montego Bay, it's part concert, part carnival, and part beach party. The festi-

510 □ FROMMER'S HONEYMOON DESTINATIONS

val turns on five nights of sizzling reggae and rock. The event is exuberant and authentic, and not toned down for most tourists' tastes. Advance hotel reservations are very necessary.

Junkanoo (Christmas). Brightly costumed dancers take to the streets throughout the country, whirling and twirling to the rhythms of Caribbean drums and bamboo fifes.

MEET-THE-PEOPLE PROGRAM

If you want to delve past the tourist level and join in Jamaican life, this superb program run by the Jamaica Tourist Board makes it possible. You'll be introduced to Jamaicans who share similar jobs, hobbies, or interests with your own—maybe even other newlyweds. You might join a couple for afternoon tea or dinner, play a game of tennis or golf, go horseback riding or birdwatching. Nearly 700 Jamaican families participate. The program is absolutely free, but you might want to bring your hostess a small gift (such as a bouquet), or pick up the restaurant bill or sightseeing admission fees. Contact the local Jamaica Tourist Board at one of the addresses that follow, giving your name, length of stay, main interests, and when you will be available.

ABOUT ACCOMMODATIONS

Jamaica boasts an extraordinary number of accommodations that are best in class—luxury resorts that revel in the graciousness of the plantation era, posh villas staffed by a retinue of servants, and all-inclusive resorts where you never need to spend a Jamaican dollar. But what makes Jamaica so remarkable is the wide choice of excellent accommodations available to suit all tastes and pocketbooks—including inexpensively priced, family-run hotels, and simple cottages right by the side of the sea.

The high season runs from mid-December through mid-April. Winter rates often include two or three meals a day (Modified American Plan or American Plan). During the low season (mid-April through mid-December), rates are about 25% to 50% lower, and hotels often offer the European Plan (no meals). A 10% service charge is usually added to the bill. Jamaica also levies a room tax of about $10 to $15 a day (winter), $5 to $10 a day (summer), depending on the hotel category.

The Elegant Resorts

Several of Jamaica's most exclusive properties have joined together to offer vacationers the opportunity to sample several different resorts. Guests can dine at the different resorts and even stay overnight, subject to availability. Participating properties include Half Moon Club, Round Hill, and Tryall Golf and Country Club in Montego Bay; Plantation Inn and Sans Souci in Ocho Rios; and Trident Hotel and Villas in Port Antonio. For details, call the "Elegant Resorts" hotline toll free, 800/237-3237 or 305/666-3566.

All-Inclusive Resorts

Jamaica is known for its all-inclusive properties, where everything—accommodations, meals, drinks, sports, entertainment—often even cigarettes—is covered by a single package price. The cost depends on the category of room you choose. The only additional expenses you will incur will be for souvenirs and perhaps some sightseeing excursions. Here are some points to consider when selecting an all-inclusive resort for your honeymoon.

□ What exactly is included? Price variations between resorts are usually explained by exactly what features are covered. How many meals a day are offered? Are menu choices limited or can you order à la carte? What sports are included—do you have to pay extra for diving or horseback riding? Are any sightseeing excursions included?

□ Couples resorts versus "everyone" resorts. Some resorts cater to couples only; others allow all comers—couples, singles, and families. Each setup creates a different ambience.

Villa Rentals

This is another popular option in Jamaica. Here, a villa is really any rental property, from cottage to mansion, going for anywhere between $800 and $4,500 a week. Many have a private swimming pool; most come complete with staff (maid, cook, gardener). The cooks are generally true treasures, equally adept at whipping up Jamaican pepperpot soup, soufflés, or hamburgers. Some villa owners have agreements with nearby hotels permitting house guests to use the resort facilities. To get a list of villa representatives in Jamaica, contact the Tourist Board or the **Jamaica Association of Villas and Apartments** (JAVA), 1320 South Dixie Hwy., Suite 1160, Coral Gables, FL 33146 (tel. 305/667-0179). They represent over 300 rental properties. Another excellent firm that specializes in luxury villas not only in Jamaica but also throughout the entire Caribbean and Mexico is **Travel Resources,** P.O. Box 1043, Coconut Grove, FL 33133 (tel. 305/444-8583 in Florida; toll free 800/327-5039 nationwide).

One particular rental villa that might tickle your fancy is Goldeneye, the beachfront house near Ocho Rios where Ian Fleming created Agent 007—James Bond—and wrote all 13 original Bond novels. It rents for $2,475 per week during the summer; about $3,300 per week in the winter. Contact **Denise Mills,** Island Communications, P.O. Box 118, Ocho Rios, Jamaica, W.I. (tel. 809/974-2489).

DINING OUT

Good food is one of the great pleasures of Jamaica. The island's ample dimensions and agricultural bounty means that most of the fruits, vegetables, meats, and fish that appear on menus are ultrafresh, often coming from the restaurant's own backyard. Visitors can find an international array of cuisines—from elegantly sauced French classics to perfectly British afternoon teas, fiery Indian curries, stir-fry Chinese—and delicious Jamaican specialties that combine the best of all worlds.

In recent years, more and more Jamaican hotels have instituted the European Plan, allowing guests to try the island's fine restaurants. Most restaurants include a 10% service charge in the bill; if not, tip waiters 10% to 15% of the total.

Both at your hotel and in restaurants, you'll often find Jamaican favorites appearing on the menu side-by-side with continental choices. One local delicacy is Caribbean rock lobster, served either simply grilled or dressed up with sauce thermidor or sauce américaine. For an appetizer, you might want to try one of the hearty soups —pepperpot, with spinach, okra, and meat; or callaloo, made with a leafy vegetable resembling spinach. Jamaica's national breakfast dish is saltfish and ackee—a savory concoction of cod cooked with a local vegetable that tastes like scrambled eggs, seasoned up with onions, garlic, and pepper. Goat curry reflects the Indian influence on Jamaican cuisine, *escaveche* (marinated fish) the Spanish. Popular side dishes include squash, yams, sweet potatoes, pumpkin (boiled or mashed with butter), green bananas or plantains (boiled or fried), plus rice and peas (rice simmered with red beans, onions, spices, and salt pork).

For a Jamaican-style lunch, try jerk chicken or pork, a dish that originated with the Maroons. The meats are seasoned with spices, then barbecued slowly over a pimento-wood fire. It's served at many hotel beach bars and food stands that line the north coast road. If you want a snack, get patties, pastries filled with highly seasoned meat and bread crumbs.

To quench your thirst, Jamaica has developed smooth, cooling beverages. First and foremost is Red Stripe beer, well rounded and "hoppy." If you want something nonalcoholic, try a fruit punch, blended from the island's harvest, or "bellywash"— the local name for lemonade. Finish your meal with Blue Mountain coffee, Tía María, or rum.

Then we get to jelly coconuts, the consumption of which combines refreshment with ritual. These young green coconuts are sold by roadside vendors whose salesmanship rivals that of P. T. Barnum. With a subtle flourish of their machetes, they first hack off the coconut top, leaving a small hole through which you drink the sweet liquid inside. For an encore, the coconut is cut in half so you can scoop out the delicate jelly in the center, using a thin piece of the shell.

HOW TO GET MARRIED IN JAMAICA

More and more couples are choosing to say their "I do's" in Jamaica. Favorite sites include beautiful gardens or beaches on your hotel grounds, and various island attractions, such as Dunn's River Falls and Shaw Park Gardens in Ocho Rios, or Athenry Gardens in Port Antonio. Most Jamaican hotels offer all-inclusive wedding packages (about $225) that cover the services of the officient, processing the license, witnesses, champagne, flowers, and the wedding cake. They can also arrange for a photographer.

No blood tests or physical exams are required. You must bring birth certificates and be on the island for 24 hours before filing for a license. There is a J$12.50 stamp duty fee. People who have been married before should bring certified copies of their divorce decrees. Once the license has been issued, it is valid for three months, and the couple can be married immediately. The Jamaica Tourist Board can assist you in meeting and making arrangements with a marriage officer. For approximately US $100 to $150, the marriage officer will obtain the license for you and perform the ceremony.

Most couples incorporate Jamaican traditions into their ceremony. You might be married under an arch made from braided coconut leaves festooned with hibiscus and other flowers. Brides can put a leaf of sweet basil or a leaf from the noo-noo bush in their shoes or stockings for good luck. Or arrange for a "show bread"—an elaborately braided loaf with a bird on top to symbolize peace or two birds to signify love.

FOR FURTHER INFORMATION

Contact the **Jamaica Tourist Board** at the following addresses: 21 Dominica Dr., New Kingston, Jamaica (tel. 809/929-8694); 3440 Wilshire Blvd., Los Angeles, CA 90010 (tel. 213/384-1123); 1320 South Dixie Hwy., Coral Gables, FL 33146 (tel. 305/665-0557); 36 South Wabash Ave., Chicago, IL 60603 (tel. 312/346-1546); 866 Second Ave., New York, NY 10017 (tel. 212/688-7650 or toll free 800/223-5225); 8411 Preston Rd., Suite 605, LB31, Dallas, TX 75225 (tel. 214/361-8778).

The Jamaica Tourist Board also maintains centrally located offices in the island's main tourist areas: Cornwall Beach, Montego Bay (tel. 952-4425); Visitors Service Bureau, Negril (tel. 957-4243); Ocean Village Shopping Centre, Ocho Rios (tel. 974-2570); City Centre Plaza, Port Antonio (tel. 993-3051); or Rafter's Rest, Port Antonio (tel. 993-2778).

---

2. Montego Bay

Montego Bay was Jamaica's original tourist destination. As early as 1908, the local citizens' association ran advertisements in American newspapers inviting tourists to "Come South—to Montego Bay, the most beautiful spot in Jamaica." From being Jamaica's first vacation resort, Montego Bay has become Jamaica's premier vacation resort, a magnet for royalty, rock stars, and honeymooners from around the world. The moment you set eyes on the broad, crescent-shaped harbor, you'll know why Montego Bay reigns as Jamaica's number one tourist destination. Partly, it's the splendid natural setting—clear aquamarine waters surrounded by lush green hills.

Mainly, it's the spirit—the knowledge that this place subscribes to the pleasure principle. Lazing on a soft white beach feels right here. So does dancing until dawn, bantering with the old fruit lady in the market, prowling for backstairs ghosts in 200-year-old great houses, or shopping till you drop. Whatever kind of honeymoon you crave, Montego Bay embraces and encourages your desires.

Located on the northwestern coast of Jamaica, the town is better known to both Jamaicans and just-arrived tourists as MoBay. The second largest city in the country, it is sometimes referred to as The Republic—a tribute to the independently minded local landowners who threatened to secede from the central government in Kingston during the 19th century.

It is significant that most of the town has developed around the beaches rather than the harbor, because life here revolves around the sea and sand. Some of the finest beaches in the Caribbean scallop the shoreline from Tryall east to Rose Hall. There's no one main resort area per se; the major tourist hotels have been built around the various strands.

Because of its excellent beaches and clear waters, the area lends itself to all water sports. Most of the major hotels offer snorkeling, scuba-diving, windsurfing, and sailing right on the property; there are also Windsurf rental shops at Doctor's Cave Beach. You can charter boats for deep-sea fishing from **Seaworld** (near Rose Hall, tel. 953-2180). On land, golfers can tee off on four 18-hole championship courses: Tryall, Ironshore Golf Club, Half Moon Golf Club, and the Wyndham Rose Hall Beach Hotel's Golf Club. Most hotels have tennis courts, several lighted for night play. Horseback riding can be arranged through the hotels or direct with various stables: **Seawind** (tel. 952-4070), **White Witch** (no phone), and **Good Hope Plantation** near Falmouth (tel. 954-3289).

Good roads link Montego Bay with other resort areas, permitting easy day trips. The seven-mile beach at Negril is about a two-hour drive (47 miles); spectacular Dunn's River Falls and the other Ocho Rios attractions also take about two hours to reach (67 miles, but it is a straighter road). But whether you use your resort as a base for exploring the rest of Jamaica, or never wander farther than the beach bar, Montego Bay will reward you with sun, fun, and honeymoon bliss.

SHOPPING

Since Montego Bay is the commercial and shopping hub of this northwest part of the island, it offers the widest selection of stores, boutiques, and crafts vendors. The **Crafts Market** near Harbour Street is perfect for picking up souvenirs—jipajapa hats, straw bags, wooden carvings, and more. For in-bond shopping for luxury items, try the shops at your hotel or the major shopping areas: **City Centre** and the **Casa Montego Arcade** in Montego Bay, and **Holiday Village** across from the Holiday Inn Hotel. At Casa Montego, for example, you can find major duty-free outlets such as **Swiss Stores** (watches from Rolex, Patek Philippe, Rado, and Swatch) and **Bijoux** (imported liquor and liqueurs, English bone china, including Wedgwood, Royal Doulton, and Aynsley; plus Lalique and Waterford crystal). City Centre features **La Belle Creole** (cameras and electronics, imported embroidered linens, and watches by Cartier, Corum, Seiko, and Swatch); **Chulani** (cameras by Nikon, Minolta, and Canon; crystal by Lalique and Baccarat; china; electronics; perfumes and cosmetics; and watches by Ebel, Girard-Perregaux, and Seiko); and others. Holiday Village offers **Casa de Oro** (cameras by Canon and Minolta; electronics; linens; and watches by Cartier); **China Craft** (china by Wedgwood, Minton, and Royal Worcester; crystal by Waterford, Lalique, and Baccarat; figurines by Lladró, Hummel, and Royal Doulton; embroidered linens); and **Tropicana** (jewelry and watches by Piaget, Concorde, Movado, and Seiko). The Holiday Inn, Half Moon, and Trelawny Beach Hotels all have especially fine shopping arcades. Very attractive with its stucco–and–red-tile design, the new **St. James Place** is one of the nicest places to browse. Seek out **Golden Nugget** for duty-free merchandise, **Coconut Joe** for T-shirts and sportswear.

Check out some shops that sell some uniquely Jamaican items. At **Blue Mountain Gems,** Mike O'Hara creates one-of-a-kind jewelry pieces made from exotic gemstones, such as agates, found in the riverbeds of the Blue Mountains. The shop also sells black-coral necklaces, batiks, and large wooden salad bowls (located at Holiday Village). On the north coast road just east of Falmouth, stop by **Caribatik,** where American Muriel Chandler designs and handcrafts clothing and wallhangings. Prices start at about $100 and climb into the thousands; the store is open Tuesday through Saturday, 10 a.m. until 3 p.m. A bit farther east, **Gallery Joe James** near Rio Bueno displays oil paintings by the owner, as well as fine crafts by other area artisans, including intricate straw work and fine wooden bowls. The Lobster Bowl Restaurant next door is perfect for lunch on an oceanside deck.

ROMANTIC INTERLUDES

In Montego Bay, your "problem" won't be deciding what to do, but rather finding the time to pack it all in.

If tales of ghosts and witchcraft tickle your fancy, don't miss **Rose Hall Great House.** The house's notoriety derives from Annie Palmer—a woman best known as "The White Witch of Rose Hall."

Fact and legend intermingle in the history of Annie. Born Annie Mae Patterson in England, she moved to Haiti with her parents. Orphaned at a young age, she became the protégé of a Haitian voodoo priestess. She moved to Jamaica, where she married John Rose Palmer—whom she allegedly poisoned soon afterward. Annie married several more times and took on several lovers—all of whom she murdered when they grew tiresome. Finally, she was strangled by her own slave/lover when she was 29.

Thanks to American millionaire John Rollins, Rose Hall has been beautifully and accurately restored. The house is part of the Jamaica National Trust. Knowledgeable guides lead you through the corridors and rooms, gleefully relating the most lurid details of Annie's life. It's all a tremendous amount of fun. Downstairs, there's a souvenir shop where you can buy books and postcards—there's even an Annie Palmer Frisbee.

Rose Hall (tel. 953-2323) is located just nine miles east of Montego Bay and is open daily from 9 a.m. until 6 p.m. Admission is $6 per person.

If ghost stories provide the literary motif for Rose Hall, poetry is the medium at **Greenwood Great House** (no phone), which was built by the family of Elizabeth Barrett Browning (she wrote "How Do I Love Thee," among other works). The Georgian-style house was built in 1780 by Sir Richard Barrett, a cousin of Elizabeth's father.

The house has been opened to the public by owners Bob and Anne Betton. At Greenwood, they have assembled one of the finest collections of period furnishings in the Caribbean. In addition, there's an appealingly quirky collection of antiques: a 16th-century court jester's chair, a chamber pot manufactured by Royal Crown Derby, and old musical instruments in perfect working order—including a player piano that tinkles out "Daisy, Daisy."

Greenwood (no phone) is open daily from 9 a.m. until 6 p.m.; admission is $5. This great house is 14 miles east of Montego Bay.

Maybe this is the ultimate Jamaican fantasy—drifting slowly down a sparkling river shaded by almond trees, picnicking on mangoes in leafy glades, swimming in freshwater pools so clear that you can see every pebble on the bottom. The raft trip on the **Martha Brae River** (tel. 952-0889) is one of the most soothing interludes you can have during your honeymoon. A skilled raftsman poles your two-seater craft down broad channels and gentle rapids. Be sure you wear bathing suits under coverups so you can swim. The raft trips depart from Martha Brae Rafter's Village, about three miles south of Falmouth. The rafts operate daily until about 4:30 p.m. and cost $30 per couple.

Make some fine feathered friends at the **Rocklands Feeding Station** bird sanctuary run by Lisa Salmon, one of Jamaica's best-known naturalists. Birds will eat right out of your hand, including doves, finches, and Jamaica's famous "doctor bird"—a type of hummingbird. If you want to learn more about Jamaica's birds, pick up a copy of the definitive *Field Guide to the Birds of the West Indies,* written by James Bond. (Ian Fleming, part-time Jamaica resident and creator of superspy 007, named his hero after the ornithologist.) Rocklands (tel. 952-2009) is located a mile from Anchovy, east of Montego Bay. It is open daily from 3:30 p.m. until sundown; admission is $4 per person.

Take advantage of that sparkling blue Caribbean and cruise off on the **Calico,** a 55-foot gaff-rigged wooden ketch that brings you to a secluded reef and beach for snorkeling and a picnic lunch. All snorkeling gear and instruction are provided; $80 per couple. A two-hour evening cocktail cruise is also available, $40 per couple (tel. 952-5860, North Coast Cruises Ltd., for reservations and information).

For Jamaica's newest adventure, sign up for one of the **rail tours,** which depart from Montego Bay Rail Station.

Governor's Coach Tour. All aboard a replica of the train once used for official travel by the governor of Jamaica. Complete with a calypso band and a professional guide, the train chugs 40 miles into the heartland of Jamaica. Stops include Catadupa, where seamstresses hang out rows of bright fabrics along the railroad tracks. Choose your favorite pattern for a shirt, sundress, or skirt—and the made-to-order garment will be ready for you on the afternoon return trip three hours later. You'll also explore Ipswich Caves, filled with stalactites and stalagmites; and tour Appleton Sugar Factory, where you'll learn how rum is made and then sample rums and liqueurs. The trip costs $38 per person, including snacks, rum punch, and round-trip transfers from Montego Bay Hotel. For schedules and reservations, call Jamaica Tours at 952-2887 or 952-1398.

Mandeville Rail Tour. Explore the cool mountain countryside of Mandeville, located 2,000 feet above sea level in the Manchester Mountains. En route, the train stops at Balacava, where you can have dresses and shirts made to order at the market. You can pick up your new wardrobe later that afternoon. Then, you continue to Williamsfield, where you'll board a bus for Mandeville, considered the most English town in Jamaica. After a visit to a private home garden filled with exotic orchids, you'll have a buffet lunch at the family-run Hotel Astra, where the specialties include Jamaican dishes. The train tour costs $50 per person; for departures and reservations, call 953-2859.

Known as the **Hilton High Day Tour,** this program gives you the chance to discover the interior regions of Jamaica—and get a bird's-eye view of it all from a hot-air balloon. You'll journey by motorcoach to St. Leonards, where you'll be greeted by Norma Hilton-Stanley at the 350-acre banana plantation that has been in her family for seven generations. Here, you can ascend over 300 feet into the air aboard a tethered hot-air balloon. After a real Jamaican breakfast, you can go horseback riding through the countryside or stroll to the German-style town of Seaford. At lunchtime, help yourself to the buffet spread that includes roast suckling pig, roasted breadfruit, rum punch, and other Jamaican specialties. The excursion costs $42 per person; for information, call 952-3343.

HONEYMOON HOTELS AND HIDEAWAYS

Since Montego Bay is the largest resort area in Jamaica, it also offers the widest range of accommodations—couples-only resorts, ultraelegant hotel compounds, high-rises, and guesthouses. Rates quoted reflect the spread between low- and high-season prices.

Ultraluxurious

The Half Moon Club, P.O. Box 80, Montego Bay, Jamaica, W.I. (tel. 809/953-2211; U.S. reservations: toll free 800/237-3237). Certain resorts feel right the instant you walk in. The Half Moon Club is one of them. From the moment you drive through the wrought-iron gate, you know this 400-acre resort is a class act. The reception area is located beneath a loggia surrounding an open-air courtyard, where two absolutely humongous palms tower overhead, and the patter of water from a hexagonal fountain soothes the senses. Service is impeccable, gracious yet friendly, thanks to the careful direction of longtime Managing Director Heinz Simonitsch. Simonitsch is one of the legendary hoteliers of the Caribbean, having served as president of both the Caribbean Hotel Association and the Jamaica Hotel Association, and the personal attention he lavishes on the resort really shows. Fresh hibiscus flowers brighten rooms daily, room service orders arrive promptly and piping hot, and a lady never has to glide out her own chair in the restaurant. No wonder the hotel has been named one of the 300 best in the world.

The resort takes its name from the perfect crescent-shaped beach it surrounds—a one-mile stretch of fine white coral sand and a tranquil bay, sheltered by a protective reef. At water's edge, a fleet of Windsurfers, Sunfish, and Hobie cats awaits your pleasure. Honeymooners usually opt for the deluxe oceanview rooms in the two-story wing fronting the beach on one side, lush gardens on the other. The downstairs rooms convey an English feeling, with Queen Anne–style furnishings and glossy parquet floors. Bathrooms are large, and there's a minifridge. The upstairs rooms reflect a more tropical motif, with tile floors and a huge eat-in terrace— perfect for breakfasts overlooking the sea. All rooms have air conditioning. If you want to splurge, reserve one of the generously proportioned private "cottages" that come with a swimming pool big enough to swim laps in.

Name your favorite sport, and you can probably indulge in it right on the property. Half Moon Club has 2 main pools, 13 tennis courts (4 lighted), 4 lighted squash courts, an aerobics room, sauna, massage room, Nautilus-equipped gym, and an 18-hole championship golf course just across the road. Introductory snorkeling and scuba lessons are provided free. You'll welcome the opportunity to work out, because the Seagrape Terrace restaurant is excellent. And if you want to mellow out completely, try one of the bartender's prizewinning concoctions, such as a Gold Label Float or a Top Hat. A member of "The Elegant Resorts of Jamaica." Honeymoon package: There's none per se; most couples take the Half Moon Plan, which includes accommodations, airport transfers, fruit basket, flowers, shell necklace, golf-greens fees, tennis, squash, glass-bottomed boat trip, and more. Eight days/ seven nights (EP): $1,035 to $1,890 per couple.

Tryall Golf, Tennis & Beach Club, Sandy Bay Post Office, Hanover Parish, Jamaica, W.I. (tel. 809/952-5110; U.S. reservations: 212/889-0761 in New York State; toll free 800/336-4571 nationwide). Luxe on a grand scale—that's what you'll find at this vast, 2,200-acre hilltop resort set on a former sugar plantation. An imposing entrance driveway curves up from the main road, flanked by stately royal palm trees and the 18th green of the golf course, where tournaments such as the Mazda Champions take place. Built in 1834, the original great house is a magnificent example of Jamaican architecture, with its intricate parquet floors, high cathedral ceilings, and fine English antiques, such as wing chairs and camelback sofas. Today, guests gather on the veranda for afternoon tea, and on the broad terrace for excellent dinners overlooking the Caribbean. From the great house, walkways draped by pale-lavender bauhinia blossoms lead to the guest accommodations.

The rooms in the great-house wing, part of the original estate, are characterized by amply gracious proportions. We prefer the downstairs rooms, where a stairway in the foyer leads to a huge bedroom and large, white-balustraded terrace. Although the upstairs rooms have no balconies, they feature picture windows overlooking the palm-dotted golf course and the north coast all the way to Montego Bay. Layouts and furnishings will vary, but all accommodations come with clock radios, telephones, air conditioning, and ceiling fans. In addition to the 52 recently refurbished rooms and suites, the resort also rents out several elegant villas, graced with evocative names such as Following Seas, Linger Longer, and No Problem. Many offer private pools and out-of-this-world ocean views. Throughout the resort, the housekeeping staff is absolutely crackerjack, under the watchful eye of the longtime head housekeeper, Mrs. Niles.

For tennis players, there are nine tennis courts (five lighted); for beach loungers, a lovely arcing strand dotted with thatch-roofed umbrellas plus a beach restaurant. Here, you can swim, windsurf, sail, snorkel, or cruise off on pedalboats. All in all, it adds up to a vacation nestled in the lap of luxury . . . which in Jamaica means very sumptuous indeed. A member of "The Elegant Resorts of Jamaica." Honeymoon package: Eight days/seven nights (BP): $1,245 to $1,480 per couple (low season). Includes round-trip transfers between airport and hotel, breakfast daily, bottle of champagne and flowers, dinner for two in Montego Bay (with transportation), river rafting, unlimited tennis, tax and service charges, and more. High-season rates (MAP): $310 to $400 per couple per night. During the summer, villa accommodations are available for eight days/seven nights (EP) for $2,055 per couple ($2,410 with the meal plan). Call for details.

Round Hill Hotel and Villas, P.O. Box 64, Montego Bay, Jamaica, W.I. (tel. 809/952-5150; U.S. reservations: 305/666-3566 in Miami; toll free 800/237-3237). Round Hill embodies all that gives Jamaica its sparkling pizzazz on the international tourism scene. First and foremost, it's an elegant retreat where the rich and famous can relax in virtual anonymity. Although the guest roster is terribly hush-hush, droppable names include Paul McCartney, Paul Newman, and Joanne Woodward. (Unmentionable vacationers include several members of European royalty.) Yet also, Round Hill remains a place of traditions, where guests sip cocktails around the same piano played by Noël Coward and Leonard Bernstein. The resort occupies a breathtaking location on a Caribbean-lapped promontory just eight miles west of Montego Bay. The half-mile-long entrance driveway spirals up what indeed is a round hill, bordered by Australian pine trees with impeccably manicured circular tops. Flowers bloom everywhere on the 98-acre estate, a rainbow palette of hibiscus, bougainvillea, and jasmine.

At Round Hill, you'll feel as if you are a treasured member of a very exclusive club, not a mere hotel guest. There are only 36 hotel rooms, plus suite accommodations available for rent in 27 exquisite private villas (many opening onto their own private pool). With their English-style furnishings and tiled floors, all of the regular rooms overlook the sea. Although there is no air conditioning, ceiling fans and louvers bring in the cooling trade winds. Enjoy a full English breakfast on your terrace, perhaps sharing a spot of toast with one of the shiny black kling-kling birds that beg for a tidbit. Loll around the swimming pool or swim at the nice (if a bit pebbly) beach. Hone your tennis game on the five courts (two are lighted for night play); three championship golf courses are nearby. In the evening, different events are held under the stars: a beachside barbecue, perhaps, or the legendary Saturday Galas (black-tie requested for gentlemen in the winter season). A member of "The Elegant Resorts of Jamaica." Honeymoon package: Eight days/seven nights (EP): $2,190 per couple (mid-April to mid-December). Includes villa accommodations with private pool, services of a cook and maid, dinner for two in Montego Bay (with transportation), rafting trip on the Great River, round-trip transfers between airport and hotel. High-season rates (BP): $285 to $295 per couple for a hotel room; $325 to $480 for a villa. Add $50 per couple per day for stays during December and February, when MAP (including breakfast and dinner) is mandatory.

All-Inclusive Resorts

If all the world loves lovers, then **Sandals Montego Bay,** P.O. Box 100, Montego Bay, Jamaica, W.I. (tel. 809/952-5510; U.S. reservations: tel. 305/284-1300, or toll free 800/327-1991), must rank as the most popular address in the universe. It definitely is to the couples who check into this luxurious all-inclusive resort for twosomes only. And not just any hand-holding pairs—at any given time, about 50% of the guests are honeymooners. The resort occupies a stellar location along the largest private beach in Jamaica.

Gordon "Butch" Stewart, the owner of Sandals, has designed a seemingly un-stoppable roster of activities. Absolutely everything is included in your room price —meals, snacks, drinks, entertainment, transfers, tips, and every sport you can name (plus some you probably couldn't, such as crab racing). Only cigarettes, massages, and day trips aboard the 45-foot catamaran cost extra. The list of things to do covers two sides of an elongated piece of paper: glass-bottomed boat rides, waterskiing, volleyball games, tennis, free scuba lessons and dives, and—literally—hundreds more. An enthusiastic and energetic young staff known as "Playmakers" make sure the fun keeps happening, whether it's the weekly Olympics or theme nights (centered on pirates, masquerades, or togas) that enliven evenings. At night, you dine by candlelight on the open-air, oceanfront terrace, then can head over to the Skydome nightclub, which headlines a different show every night, from reggae to magic. If you've overindulged at the ample buffet spreads, the gym stays open 24 hours a day.

Sandals has several different categories of rooms—all of which combine a breezy tropical feeling (high ceilings, white furniture, cotton spreads, jalousie windows, floral-patterned drapes) with the finer creature comforts (king-size beds, air conditioning, paddle fans, and in-room hairdryers). All rooms (except for 12 standard units) have balconies. As you'd expect, the most expensive accommodations sit right by the sea. Whichever kind you choose, you'll have plenty of elbow room, since the three-story units are spread out, and the resort occupies 19 acres of grounds. The complex is located just behind the Montego Bay airport, and it has become a Sandals tradition to wave at the departing planes.

Sandals not only specializes in honeymoons—it's also a popular place for weddings. They can make all the arrangements.

Sandals offers a wide variety of all-inclusive packages, ranging from four to eight nights. For an eight-day, seven-night package, sample rates for a standard room run $2,010 to $2,125 per couple.

Sandals Royal Caribbean, P.O. Box 167, Montego Bay, Jamaica, W.I. (tel. 809/953-2231; U.S. reservations: 305/284-1300 or toll free 800/327-1991). An entrance portico framed by graceful columns. Afternoon tea served daily. Buildings named after British royal homes. And the all-inclusive package includes . . . croquet? That gives you some idea of the upscale, Euro-style romantic atmosphere that pervades Sandals Royal Caribbean.

Like its sister property, Sandals Royal Caribbean is an all-inclusive resort for couples only. The party atmosphere begins the moment you arrive, when a calypso band breaks into song in the lobby. New arrivals receive a welcome basket brimming with goodies—scarves, suntan oil, Tía María, and Blue Mountain coffee. Much of the activity centers on the pearly-white beach that stretches the length of the property. Water sports run the aquatic gamut—sailing, windsurfing, waterskiing, pedaling an aquatrike, snorkeling (excellent near the offshore reef), and scuba-diving (the intro lesson and one dive a day are included). Beach buffs can tan all over at the swimsuit-optional private island reachable by boat (yes, you wear clothes on the boat). On land, there's tennis day or night on the lighted courts, volleyball, golf, and a health club with a weight room. Now's a good time to learn a new sport, because instruction and equipment are free. Even in the middle of a game, most guests stop to observe another Sandals tradition—waving at the planes taking off from nearby Montego Bay airport.

Sandals Royal Caribbean prides itself on its fine cuisine. Breakfast and lunch are served buffet style, but dinner is an elegant, sit-down, à la carte bash every night. Other gracious features here: You can order breakfast in bed, and you can have before-dinner drinks served on your porch or patio. At night, sing along at the piano bar, or head for the disco, where there's live entertainment every night.

The pink-painted guest units are spread out over the property, tucked in palm groves or sidling up to the sea. Rooms are large and cheery, air-conditioned, and king-size beds are available on request. Room layouts are fairly consistent throughout the resort; the top-of-the-line rooms are located on the oceanfront, away from the activity surrounding the main building.

If you'd like to combine your wedding with your honeymoon, Sandals Royal Caribbean will gladly oblige. They can set up the complete ceremony.

Sandals Royal Caribbean has all-inclusive packages ranging from four to eight days in length. For an eight days/seven nights package, sample rates for a standard room run $2,010 to $2,125 per couple.

Carlyle on the Bay, P.O. Box 412, Kent Avenue, Montego Bay, Jamaica, W.I. (tel. 809/952-4141; U.S. reservations: toll free 800/327-1991 nationwide; 305/284-1300 in Florida). Words like "gem-like" and "intimate" come to mind when describing this pristine resort located in Montego Bay, within walking distance of Doctor's Cave and the area's fine shopping. Situated on a tiny cul-de-sac just off the main road, the white colonial-style facade positively sparkles in the sunshine. The hotel's walkways and arcades surround a white tiled courtyard, with a large pool and Jacuzzi at its center. The resort is owned by Gordon "Butch" Stewart, the moving spirit behind Sandals and Sandals Royal Caribbean, and, like its sister properties, the Carlyle on the Bay is an all-inclusive, couples-only retreat. The atmosphere here, however, tends to be quieter and more intimate, since this is a small, in-town inn, not a sprawling resort. Compared with the other Sandals properties, the water-sports program is less expansive, since the Carlyle doesn't have its own beach, instead utilizing a small public strand across the street.

Although the hotel was built about 20 years ago, it conveys a gracious, Old Jamaica feeling. Original Jamaican art brightens the walls of the rooms, which have all been newly refurbished. Each of the 52 rooms has a slightly different layout, but each features air conditioning, a telephone, and a hairdryer in the bathroom. Not all rooms have balconies; the deluxe rooms have better views of the pool, ocean, or beach just beyond the coconut palms and the bougainvillea blossoms. There's tennis available right on the property, as well as a health spa; water sports include snorkeling, windsurfing, scuba-diving, sailing, and glass-bottomed boat rides. The Plantation Restaurant serves both native and continental cuisine, with live entertainment every night. Indicative of the charm and grace of this resort, you can opt for room service at no extra charge.

Because Carlyle on the Bay is just a block away from the heart of Montego Bay, guests can easily get involved with the local culture. Jamaican culture, in fact, is very much part of this resort. The "fruit lady" comes around selling paw-paw, soursop, or other fruits in season; local craftspeople visit several times a week to demonstrate wood-carving or straw-weaving techniques. It all adds up to an experience that is warm, intimate, and uniquely Jamaican. Honeymoon package: None. Standard eight-day/seven-night package: $1,445 to $1,465 per couple.

Jack Tar Village, Montego Beach Hotel, P.O. Box 144, Montego Bay, Jamaica, W.I. (tel. 809/952-4340; U.S. reservations: 214/670-9888, or toll free 800/527-9299). So you want an all-inclusive resort, you want to be in the center of Montego Bay and all its shopping and clubs, and you want a white-sand beach and waters so transparent you can play tag with a parrot fish 30 yards away? Then consider Jack Tar Village, Montego Beach, part of the famous all-inclusive chain with properties throughout the Caribbean. This four-story resort is located on the main Montego Bay thoroughfare, and right near Doctor's Cave Beach, probably the clearest stretch of waters in Jamaica. Given such a sublime aquatic positioning, much of the day's activities centers on the water: Windsurfers, pedalboats, waterskis, snorkeling gear, and Sunfish await your pleasure. (You can also retreat beneath the thatch-roofed sunshades that dot the sands.) Every day, there's a full roster of special events—from reggae lessons to toga parties and cooking classes. You can work on your serve on three tennis courts (free instruction included), then unwind with a massage or sauna (also included). Since there are only 130 rooms, you'll never feel crowded. The rooms here are really big; we prefer the accommodations in the Sunset Lodge, which have been recently refurbished and are even larger and nicer than the rest. All rooms have ceiling fans, air conditioning, balconies, and full-front ocean views; if you get a ground-floor room, you're literally on the beach. Honeymoon package: None. Standard rate: $310 to $330 per couple per night. Includes all meals, limited wine during lunch and dinner, unlimited drinks, most water sports (except deep-sea fishing, scuba lessons, and glass-bottomed boat rides), nightly entertainment, airport transfers, all applicable taxes, tips, and service charges. The resort admits a fun-loving mixture of couples, singles, and families.

Trelawny Beach Hotel, P.O. Box 54, Falmouth, Jamaica, W.I. (tel. 809/954-2450; U.S. reservations: 212/545-2222 in New York State, toll free 800/223-0888 nationwide), offers the best of both worlds—seclusion, plus plenty of activity when you want it. The 6-story, 350-room resort is located in Falmouth, just 23 miles from Montego Bay and 44 miles from Ocho Rios, permitting easy access to island "musts" such as Dunn's River Falls and rafting on the Martha Brae River. But in between sightseeing excursions, couples can relax on the fine beach, or indulge themselves to the hilt in the sports and activities programs at this all-inclusive resort. Complimentary activities for guests include snorkeling cruises, Sunfish sailing, windsurfing, waterskiing, and glass-bottomed boat rides. There's also tennis on four lighted Laykold courts and tennis instruction, aerobics and exercise classes, Jamaican dialect and reggae dance lessons, nightly entertainment, and daily shuttle service to Montego Bay for sightseeing and shopping. And if you've ever wanted to try scuba-diving, you can—for free. Trelawny's rates include both the introductory resort course and a one-tank dive daily, all under the supervision of certified dive masters. The resort bills itself as an "inclusive resort for everyone," and predominantly attracts a mix of families and couples, especially honeymooners. "Islanders," the name for the guest relations staff, make sure that the array of amusements continues nonstop. But one of the nicest aspects of Trelawny is that you'll never feel any pressure to participate and can opt for a snooze under the beachside palms if you prefer. Most meals are served buffet style; there are also theme dinners, such as a poolside Jamaican barbecue.

Thanks to the H-shaped layout, views are maximized, and the honeymoon package includes an oceanview room with king-size bed. All rooms are air-conditioned and have private balconies, radios, and telephones. Whenever possible, furnishings utilize wicker and floral-print Jamaican fabrics for island ambience, and the grounds are impeccably landscaped with palm trees, hibiscus, and bougainvillea. Honeymoon package: Eight days/seven nights (MAP): $1,460 to $2,060 per couple. Includes a horseback ride along the beach, "honeymoon dinner" with wine and wedding cake, champagne and a fruit basket with Jamaican liqueur in the room, his-and-hers T-shirts, gift coupon for use on a return visit, taxes and service charges. Different-length packages and Full AP are also available. If you want to tie the knot in Jamaica, Trelawny features a wedding package, which includes the services of a justice of the peace, marriage license, witnesses, domestic champagne, native flowers, and wedding cake.

First-Class Hotels

Definitely the first choice if you want to be at the center of the action, the **Holiday Inn Montego Bay,** P.O. Box 480, Montego Bay, Jamaica, W.I. (tel. 809/953-2485; U.S. reservations: toll free 800/HOLIDAY), is the largest hotel in Jamaica, with 516 rooms. Somehow, the hotel seems much smaller—almost folksy—because it is low-rise (only four stories) and is nicely sprawled along a fine stretch of golden sand just a few miles east of Montego Bay proper. There's always something happening—a poolside crab race, horseback riding down at the beach, snorkeling on the reef just offshore, volleyball, rum-swizzle parties, or a backgammon tournament. Tennis anyone? You can play day or night on four lighted courts. Need to buy some souvenirs? Just across the road, Holiday Village offers a wide variety of crafts shops as well as in-bond stores. When you get hungry, you can dine at your choice of four restaurants. There are three different bars, one set on an island in the center of the large free-form pool. And after dark, the Witch's Hideaway nightclub and the Thriller disco offer the most exciting nightlife in Montego Bay (even the locals come here).

The rooms have all the deluxe stateside amenities you expect from the Holiday Inn chain: radios, telephones, and air conditioning. Top-of-the-line choices for honeymooners are the King Leisure oceanfront rooms, with king-size beds and balconies thrust out over the ocean. Honeymoon package: Eight days/seven nights (EP): $1,050 to $1,495 per couple. Includes King Leisure oceanfront room, fruit basket, flowers in room, bottle of Tía María, a dinner for two, sightseeing excursions, T-shirts.

Moderately Priced

Lady Diane's Health and Fitness Resort, 5 Kent Ave., Montego Bay, Jamaica, W.I. (tel. 809/952-4415). What better place for a honeymoon than this tropical oasis where relaxation and harmonious balance are emphasized above all? Lady Diane's is indeed something different—a complete vacation retreat for body and mind. Although one would expect to find concern with tranquility and health at a California spa, not a Caribbean playground, the restful spirit transplants splendidly to Jamaica. All pink, purple, and pretty, the resort is set across the street from a quiet beach and glimmering turquoise sea. Like a pastel rainbow, wooden deck chairs painted variegated colors surround the swimming pool, facing out to sea. There are only 15 rooms plus a guest cottage—all simple, yet very islandy and inviting with rattan furnishings, Jamaican straw work, and colorful prints. Owners Beva and Dick Cherkiss soon make you feel like one of the family. Wander into the kitchen and see what's cooking . . . maybe even help chop up some vegetables, if you like. The restaurant serves gourmet food that tastes so delicious you'll be surprised to learn that it's healthy too, using macrobiotic, mostly vegetarian recipes. Right at the hotel, they offer pampering body treatments such as Shiatsu massages, facials, "skin glows," and ginger compresses. Attend yoga classes on the premises, or attend an aerobics workout nearby. Honeymoon package: Eight days/seven nights (FAP): $1,650 per couple. Includes three meals daily, two complimentary massages, round-trip transfers between airport and hotel, two picnic box lunches.

Fantasy, Gloucester Avenue, P.O. Box 161, Montego Bay, Jamaica, W.I. (tel. 809/952-4150; U.S. reservations: toll free 800/526-2422). Located across the street from Doctor's Cave Beach (Montego Bay's finest strand), Fantasy is sparkling fresh after a top-to-toe, $2-million renovation that completely remodeled the property. The motif is musical, reflected in the names of the public areas, such as the Tempo Terrace and the Harmony Bar. Every room in the nine-story tower offers an ocean view, with vistas of Montego Bay and the surrounding mountains getting better the higher you go. Decorated with contemporary white furnishings, accommodations feature all-new bathrooms that have been groomed and polished. Facilities include two tennis courts, an exercise room, and a swimming pool plus Jacuzzi. Honeymoon package: None. Rates (EP): $90 to $110 per couple per night.

Richmond Hill, Union Street, P.O. Box 362, Montego Bay, Jamaica, W.I. (tel. 809/952-3859). This 18th-century great house positively exudes old-world charm, with its pillars and awnings, timbered ceilings, oriental-design rugs, and Queen Anne–style antiques. It sits 500 feet above Montego Bay, an airy perch overlooking both town and harbor. During the 1700s, it belonged to the Dewars, members of the Scottish clan of whiskey fame. Today, although a bit of the grandeur has faded, the charm still remains. The rooms are of moderate size, most furnished with English-style furniture, wall-to-wall carpeting, and velvet drapes—atmospheric albeit a bit heavy for the tropics. Each room is different; some have air conditioning, but all open onto verandas. There's no beach, but the hotel compensates very nicely by running a shuttle to Doctor's Cave in town. Best of all, there's a large, sublimely photogenic pool on the outdoor terrace. Excellent restaurant (see "Romantic Restaurants"). Honeymoon package: None. Regular eight-day/seven-night package (EP): $615 to $825 per couple. Includes welcome drinks.

ROMANTIC RESTAURANTS

As Jamaica's most popular resort, Montego Bay offers the most dining choices, with everything from elegant hilltop restaurants to roadside stands selling jerk pork. Many of the restaurants listed below provide free shuttle transportation for patrons from their hotels; call them for details.

Expensive

The Georgian House, 2 Orange St. (tel. 952-0632). Located in a landmark 18th-century brick town house, the Georgian House earns our vote for the most romantic restaurant in town. Exquisitely restored, the mansion is replete with period details such as crystal chandeliers, lace curtains, and reproduction Gainsborough and Renoir paintings. The upstairs dining room is especially grand, opulently furnished with Queen Anne–style chairs and oriental-design carpets. On fine evenings (and Jamaica is known for them), you can also dine under the stars on the outdoor terrace, surrounded by fountains and statues. At lunchtime, choose from an extensive menu featuring sandwiches and salads; $30 to $40 per couple. For dinner, specialties include baked stuffed lobster and also tournedos Rossini, served with pâté, mushrooms, and a Madeira-wine sauce. Dinner for two, $60 to $80 plus drinks. Open Monday through Friday for lunch, noon to 3 p.m.; nightly for dinner, 6 to 9:30 p.m.

Sugar Mill Restaurant, The Half Moon Club, Half Moon Golf Course (tel. 953-2314). Set alongside a 150-year-old water wheel that once propelled an old sugar mill, this gracious restaurant overlooks the golf course and the Caribbean. At night, the setting looks especially romantic, with candlelight flickering on the tables. Luncheon fare is light, including sandwiches, hamburgers, omelets, and salads; about $20 per couple. For dinner, the Sugar Mill is especially well known for flambé specialties, including the lobster calypso, sautéed in rum and served with a subtle creole sauce. Another favorite is the daily roast, served from the traditional silver wagon; all pastas (including a notable fettuccine with smoked marlin) are made on the premises. For dessert, the flaming orange crêpes make for a grand finale. Dinner for two, about $80 per couple plus drinks. Be forewarned that the prices of imported wines are hazardously steep; better yet, try one of the good Jamaican wines or a Red Stripe beer. Open daily for lunch, noon to 3 p.m.; dinner, from 7 to 10 p.m. Reservations suggested for dinner.

Seagrape Terrace, Half Moon Club (tel. 953-2211). A perfect red hibiscus floats in a glass bowl. Flames flicker in the hurricane lamps. In the background, a trio plays numbers such as "Satin Doll," "Strangers in the Night," and "Yellow Bird," which fit this sophisticated atmosphere as much as the black velvet night and the lapping waves. This is part of the Jamaican good life at the Seagrape Terrace at the Half Moon Club. You'll dine at an elegantly set table on the outdoor gallery or terrace, which face the calm bay. At terrace center, gay Japanese lanterns bob in the branches of the giant sea-grape tree, for which the restaurant is named. As much as possible, the menu spotlights fresh Jamaican ingredients. Conch might substitute for veal in a traditional schnitzel; chicken is poached in coconut milk; a fresh snapper is filleted, then stuffed with lobster, callaloo, and cream sauce. Be sure to save room for the desserts, which might include mango or coconut mousse, or banana crêpes flamed with Jamaican rum and brown sugar. Five-course prix-fixe dinner for two: about $70 per couple plus drinks. Open nightly from 7 to 9:30 p.m.

An Evening on the Great River, just west of Montego Bay (tel. 952-5047 or 952-5097). As the fishing boat moves up the torchlit river, you start to hear the calypso rhythms. Once you arrive, you're handed a rum punch, and you settle in for the good times. "The Evening on the Great River" includes a buffet-style Jamaican dinner, open bar, dessert, and coffee. There's also entertainment by local dancers and musicians, plus a chance for you two to show off some fancy steps while you dance under the stars to the live band. Definitely a fun evening. Held Sundays, Tuesdays, and Thursdays, $80 per couple, including transportation to and from your hotel.

The Diplomat, 9 Queen's Dr. (tel. 952-3353). The setting has all the glamour of a 1930s movie set—Italian-marble floors, oversize sofas in the drawing room, and big French doors opening onto the veranda. Fred Astaire and Ginger Rogers would not look misplaced hoofing it to the Gershwin, Porter, and Berlin tunes played on the grand piano. If The Diplomat has the feel of a private villa, that's because it is—only the downstairs terrace area is open for dinner in the evening. You'll dine on the columned terrace overlooking the classic-motif swimming pool, which in turn overlooks all of Montego Bay, sparkling lights and moonlit harbor included. The well-prepared continental cuisine lives up to the setting. Start off with the lobster cocktail or the pepperpot soup (about $3.50). Entrées include fresh fish meunière, lobster, or steak (entrées about $20 to $30). Definitely worth the splurge. Open Monday through Saturday, 6:30 to 9:30 p.m.

Moderate

Calabash, 5 Queen's Dr. (tel. 952-3891). Another favorite perch for lunching or dining above Montego Bay, this one some 500 feet above the harbor. You'll be seated on a breezy terrace with flowerpots and white balustrades, which form a dazzling contrast to the turquoise Caribbean. For lunch, you'll find first-rate Jamaican favorites such as ackee and saltfish or curried goat, as well as classic dishes like chicken simmered in sherry (complete lunch $20 to $30 per couple). At dinnertime, the menu gets more elaborate and more expensive, with highlights such as Jamaican lobster, Caribbean fish, veal with peppers and sherry, or filet mignon, served with rice and peas or a potato casserole; $50 to $60 per couple. Open for lunch, 12 noon to 2 p.m.; dinner, 6 to 10 p.m.

Cascade Room at the Pelican, Gloucester Avenue, Montego Bay (tel. 952-3171). Spotlit grottos and waterfalls weave the magic at this rendezvous that is very popular with lovers, located within walking distance of most of the downtown hotels. In addition to the seductive atmosphere, the Cascade Room is also one of the best seafood restaurants in Montego Bay. The specialty here is every conceivable manifestation of lobster: Newburg, curry, or creole, served stuffed back in its own shell with a thermidor sauce, simply broiled, or arranged on a skewer for shish kebab (about $25). Landlubbers can opt for one of the steaks broiled to order (about $22), and you both might like to share a slice of their delectable coconut cream pie ($5). Open for dinner only, 6:30 to 9:30 p.m. When making reservations, be sure to specify the Cascade Room—the Pelican Restaurant out front is a casual diner.

Richmond Hill Inn, Union Street (tel. 952-3859). The attractions here are twofold—the once-upon-a-time charm of a plantation great house dating back to the 18th century, and the postcard-perfect views of Montego Bay, as seen from 500 feet up. Lunch and dinner are served on the broad, white-balustraded terrace that surrounds the pool, where a sculpted swan and cherubs provide just the right classic touch. Lunches are casual and not too expensive: The light fare of sandwiches or salads should run you about $20 per couple. If you're planning to come for dinner, time your arrival for sunset—Richmond Inn offers prime views. The special four-course dinner including soup, salad, lobster or fish, and dessert is a steal at $30 per person. Otherwise, entrées such as a sirloin steak are $25. Open daily for lunch, 11:30 a.m. to 3 p.m.; dinner, 7 to 10 p.m.

Lady Diane's, 5 Kent Ave. (tel. 952-4415). A hearty carrot soup . . . escaveche of fresh fish served with roasted breadfruit and a tossed salad . . . chocolate cake with coconut-cream topping . . . Not only does it sound good, this meal is good for you, too, at Lady Diane's, a gourmet macrobiotic, mostly vegetarian restaurant that's part of the health and fitness resort. Fish is offered, although meat and chicken are not. The food is so delicious that you won't feel like you're "missing" anything. Meals are served family style in the pink-and-purple-painted dining room or beside the swimming pool—help yourself from the oversize platters. Frequently, menus include renditions of Jamaican favorites, such as ackee and fish, or stewed rice and peas. Many herbs and vegetables come from the garden out back, or are specially grown by local families. Desserts often use Jamaican chocolate—grown in the mountains and hand-pounded and rolled on the island. Open nightly from 6:30 to 9 p.m.; about $50 per couple.

Siam, 25 Leader Ave. (tel. 952-5727). Montego Bay's roster of fine international cuisines now includes Thai food thanks to this restaurant on a hillside terrace overlooking the bay. Savor subtly spiced lobster, shrimp, and fish delicacies, counterpointed by live jazz. Open Tuesday through Sunday, 6 to 10 p.m. for dinner; until midnight at the bar.

A good place for your first taste of jerk chicken, pork, or fish is the **Cotton Tree Jerk House and Bar** on Queens Drive near Malvern Gardens (tel. 952-5329) or the **Pork Pit** on Gloucester Avenue in town (no phone). Portions run about $5 a person. Both are open daily from 11 a.m. to 10 p.m. If you want to dine under the stars and beside the water, check out **Marguerite's by the Sea** on Gloucester Avenue in Montego Bay (tel. 952-4777). Seated on a high-backed rattan chair, you can look out over the transparent blue waters near Doctor's Cave Beach. Choose from the fresh catch of the day, lobster, beef, or chicken dishes. Lunch, served from 11 a.m. to 3 p.m., about $30 per couple; dinner, served from 6 to 10 p.m., $45 to $65 per couple.

NIGHTLIFE

When you want to go out dancing, you'll have several hot spots to choose from. **Disco Inferno** at the Holiday Village (no phone) draws the most action, with its huge bar, large dance floor, and live acts (often three different bands a night). You can also try **Thriller Disco** across the street at the Holiday Inn (tel. 953-2485). Set in a huge, thatch-roofed building at water's edge, **Evita's** attracts a lot of couples. It's located west of town, and has inspiring views: indoors, there's an eight-foot TV screen; outdoors, you look over the Great River and lights of Montego Bay (tel. 952-2301). Ask about the special night-out packages, including pick-up from your Montego Bay hotel, dinner with wine, and dancing under the stars, priced at $35 per person.

Friday nights, *the* place to get a bit crazy is **Pier 1** on the Montego Bay waterfront (tel. 952-2452). There's dancing on the seaside deck on Friday nights only; $5-per-person cover charge. The rest of the week, Pier 1 is a popular restaurant, serving entrées such as Jamaican red snapper, lobster creole, and sirloin steaks, about $40 to $60 per couple. Open daily, 11 a.m. to 11 p.m.

---

3. Negril

The slightly hedonistic aura that pervades Negril is neatly summarized by the anonymous entry in a hotel guestbook: "Come to Negril and live, mon!" Negril, located at the western tip of Jamaica, is less a place than a state of mind—a mental condition characterized by sensuality and indolence. This is a place that bewitches vacationers, transforming them into folk for whom the most energetic event of the day is watching the sunset.

Negril is located about 47 miles west of Montego Bay, about two hours' drive. The area's supreme natural attraction is its seven miles of beach, coral sands as soft as talc that unfurl along the shores of two well-protected bays: Negril Harbour (formerly known as "Bloody Bay") and Long Bay. At West End on the island's very tip, the sands give way to dramatic ironshore (weathered coral) cliffs, explaining the spot's nickname as "The Rock."

What people commonly refer to as Negril stretches from the edge of Negril Harbour to the Lighthouse, at the very western tip of the island. "Town" is actually a modern minimall located on a roundabout; here you can buy picnic supplies at the supermarket or oil your hips at the very happening Com"pulse" on disco. If you follow Lighthouse Road west from the roundabout, you'll pass small wooden-front restaurants such as Chicken Lavish and Sweet Bite, and tiny, fancifully named cottage accommodations called Moon Glow, Home Sweet Home, Mirage, and Catch A Falling Star. The road ends at the Negril Lighthouse, located some 100 feet above sea level. At Lighthouse Park, steps lead down the cliff face to the sea.

The vibes in Negril are truly friendly. This is a "people place," a legacy of the time when hospitable rural families took in long-haired, flower-bedecked hippies who had discovered the fine beach. Since the area is also a popular vacation spot for islanders, you'll be able to get to know Jamaicans, not just other tourists. A love of reggae forms the common bond here—sensuous bursts of music waft suddenly from passing cars and beachside restaurants; video screens feature Tosh and Marley rather than Springsteen and George Michael. There's little shopping to speak of— you might be able to round up a couple of commemorative T-shirts at the shopping plaza in the village. But you will bring home memories of snorkeling together through a cave, sharing a Red Stripe beer and a fish fry under a palm tree, or rewarding a particularly boffo sunset with applause. If you want to truly relax and get away from it all, this is the place.

ROMANTIC INTERLUDES

Negril itself is the romantic interlude. In a place so completely committed to pleasurable lethargy, recommending any activity seems to be a contradiction. But here, nevertheless, are a few suggestions:

Named for the owner, with a tip of the fedora to *Casablanca* and Bogie, **Rick's Café** (tel. 957-4335) is the heart and soul of Negril. Vacationers don't just visit Rick's, they make a pilgrimage. Late afternoon every day, sun-bronzed bodies rouse themselves from along the seven-mile stretch of sand and slouch off to this watering hole out on the coral cliffs toward the West End of town. The main event, of course, is the setting sun, which earns a standing ovation when it puts on a particularly flashy crimson show. For a supporting cast, there are also amateur cliff divers, who hurl themselves off the rocks with either perfect swan dives or ridiculous belly flops.

The same superb views of shore and sea that make Rick's numero uno for sunset watching also make it a scenic choice for your meals. Light lunch entrées such as a lobster and veggie omelet, sandwiches, and burgers fall in the $7 to $10 range. At dinnertime, the menu gets more elaborate, with entrées such as red snapper baked in white wine ($20), steak kebab ($24), or a steak-and-lobster "surf'n'turf" combo topping off the list at about $30.

So you'll look like an experienced Negrilian when you arrive at Rick's, please note that you have to exchange your cash for bar beads at the desk out front—the bartender does not accept money. Credit cards are not accepted. Open noon to 10 p.m.

Because of its long isolation from the rest of Jamaica, Negril has no "must-see" historic sights. Its most interesting attractions are on, near, or under the **water**. **Snorkelers** will want to explore the caves along the ironshore at West End. **Scubadivers** can make arrangements through the **Negril Scuba Centre** at the Negril Beach Club Hotel (tel. 957-4223). For a bird's-eye view, sign up for **parasailing** at **Ray's Parasailing** (tel. 957-4349) on the beach, or at the **Negril Tree House Club** (tel. 957-4287). Various entrepreneurs along the beach can take you **waterskiing**.

Horseback riding isn't generally considered a water sport—but it is when you can canter along the surf's edge as you can in Negril. You can rent horses from **Horseman Riding Stables** (tel. 957-4216); about $30 per person for a two-hour ride.

For an adventure worthy of Robinson Crusoe, escape on a day sail to **Booby Cay,** an islet off the coast of Negril. The whole trip, including snorkeling gear, barbecued picnic lunch, and an open bar, costs about $35 per person. Contact **Aqua Nova Water Sports** at the Negril Beach Club (tel. 957-4323). Aqua Nova also runs half-day snorkeling trips for $25 per person.

The many restaurants along Negril's beaches are not just places to eat—they form the central focus of an entire day's nonactivity. In addition to having lunch or dinner, you can stake out a palm tree or a chaise longue, and practice your suntanning. For a lowdown on favorite hangouts, see the restaurant write-ups that follow.

HONEYMOON HOTELS AND HIDEAWAYS

Formerly an area of simple beach cottages, Negril is developing into a major resort area, with a wide range of different accommodations.

All-Inclusive Resorts

Grand Lido, Negril, Jamaica, W.I. (tel. 809/957-1317; U.S. reservations: 516/868-6924, or toll free 800/858-8009). As the glamorous name suggests, this spanking new (late 1989 opening) all-inclusive resort promises to be the splashiest and most luxurious ever to have hit Negril. Although complete details were not available as we went to press, here's how the $35-million property shapes up so far. Set on 22 acres, the Grand Lido is the only hotel on a beautiful bay fringed by seagrape trees. When it comes to making grand entrances, the marble-columned lobby is a drop-dead stunner, traversed by a stream leading to an indoor, working waterwheel. What differentiates the Grand Lido from a mere marble palace, however, is the dedication to personal service, with a high staff-to-guest ratio of nearly one-to-one. Your wish is their command. Valet service, 24-hour room service, free laundry service—even complimentary manicures—are among the amenities that await you. Each of the 200 rooms offers an ocean view from its terrace or patio. Among the perks you'll find in your honeymoon home: a sunken sitting area, color satellite TV, videocassette recorder, audiocassette player, and, of course, a telephone. At mealtimes, choose among three restaurants and nine bars; for night owls, there's a disco and a piano bar. Along the lovely beach, you can enjoy all water sports, plus some recreation fit for a millionaire—a 147-foot luxury motor yacht, used for sunset cruises and cocktail receptions. The Grand Lido is owned by SuperClubs, which also runs Couples and Jamaica, Jamaica. It welcomes both couples and singles (adults only). Honeymoon package: None. Eight days/seven nights (all-inclusive): $3,090 to $3,695 per couple.

Sandals Negril, Negril, Jamaica, W.I. (tel. 809/957-4216; U.S. reservations: 305/284-1300, or toll free 800/327-1991). Beach chairs face out toward the sunset, two by two. Fins churn out twin wakes as two hand-holding snorkelers trail an iridescent parrot fish. Like its sister resorts in Montego Bay and Ocho Rios, Sandals Negril is proving that togetherness is twice as much fun at an all-inclusive, couplesonly resort. One of the newest Sandals retreats (it opened in late 1988), the Negril property is also one of the loveliest. Built of stone and wood, the units snuggle into 17 acres of lush natural foliage. No building on the grounds stands taller than a coconut tree. Inside, each of the 186 rooms has a Caribbean feel. Each is air-conditioned, and features a clock radio, hairdryer in the bathroom, and, of course, a king-size bed. For the cushiest accommodations, choose the loft-style oceanfront suites. Down at the beach (one of the largest private strands on the island), you can try out a freewheeling array of water sports: scuba-diving, waterskiing, glass-bottomed boat rides, windsurfing, Sunfish sailing, canoeing, kayaking, and aquatriking. Flex some muscles in the health spa, or challenge each other to a tennis or racquetball match. There's also a large freshwater pool surrounded by tropical landscaping. Honeymoon package: None. Regular eight-day/seven-night package (all inclusive): $2,010 to $2,365 per couple for a standard room.

Negril Inn, P.O. Box 19, Negril, Jamaica, W.I. (tel. 809/957-4370; U.S. reservations: toll free 800/634-7456). A secret garden of delights practically hidden by hibiscus blossoms, Negril Inn combines charm and elegance on Negril's famous seven-mile beach. If you're looking for a laid-back, yet sophisticated all-inclusive resort, this could be just the ticket. There are only 46 rooms, tucked in two-story white buildings facing a garden courtyard. Perky cobalt-blue awnings screen the terraces (downstairs) and balconies (upstairs), providing guests with a cool, outdoor sitting area. Decor strikes precisely the right balance of island insouciance, with crisp white cotton bedspreads, tile floors, and wardrobes crafted from local wood. Accommodations are air-conditioned (no ceiling fans). For greater privacy, request a room upstairs. Down at the beach, you can enjoy windsurfing, Sunfish sailing, waterskiing, snorkeling and scuba-diving; tennis and a gym are also available. The food is delicious, with cuisine alternating each night: perhaps Jamaican dishes one night, followed by Chinese specialties the next. As at Jamaica's other all-inclusive resorts, meals, drinks, sports, and entertainment are all covered by the package price. Negril Inn welcomes both couples and singles. Honeymoon package: Eight days/seven nights (all-inclusive): $1,630 to $2,000 per couple.

Moderate to Inexpensive

Negril Cabins, Negril, Jamaica, W.I. (tel. 809/957-4350; U.S. reservations: toll free 800/526-2422). Looking part tree house, part *South Pacific,* this resort has zoomed into top-notch popularity since its 1987 opening. What you'll find here are ten cabins perched on stilts, surrounded by royal palm, mango, and almond trees. In the mornings, the only sound you'll hear will be the chirping of birds. Watch for a flurry of bright-green wings—often, wild parrots streak by. Entirely crafted of native Jamaican pine, the cabins feature soaring cathedral ceilings and humongous bathrooms. Letting you get the most out of outdoor living, doors to the balcony fold back completely, giving you an alfresco lifestyle when you want. Surrounded by louvers on three sides, accommodations are airy and cool, thanks to the trade winds and ceiling fans. Rooms all have garden views—the beach is across the road, where Negril Cabins enjoys prime frontage on that famous seven-mile beach. But what you'll probably remember most here is the friendly staff—you'll soon feel like family, not a hotel guest. Excellent restaurant. Honeymoon package: Eight days/seven nights (EP): $410 to $610 per couple. Includes bottle of wine, taxes and service charges.

Dream Scape, West End Road, Jamaica, W.I. (tel. 809/957-4495; U.S. reservations: 312/883-1020, or toll free 800/423-4095). When you enter the courtyard through a bower of flowers, you'll almost think you're seeing a mirage . . . small seaside cottages—yet complete with big-time luxuries, such as water beds and hot tubs. This intimate enclave has only six rooms (four with breathtaking sea views). On the terraces of the oceanview rooms, you can settle into peacock-backed wrought-iron chairs and let an hour or three slide by. Inside, the surroundings enfold you within low-key island elegance. Polished marble floors feel cool to your feet; the minifridge sits invitingly stocked with chilled champagne; most accommodations come with a Jacuzzi. Rooms offer both air conditioning and ceiling fans; each has a satellite color TV. All around, you're surrounded by palm trees and hibiscus blossoms. Beyond the lawn, stairways in the rocks zigzag across the ironshore to the sea, glittering like a pirate's ransom. Here you can swim or snorkel; the hotel can also make arrangements for all other water sports. It all adds up to living out a complete tropical fantasy. Honeymoon package: None. Regular eight-day/seven-night package (CP): $790 to $1,205 per couple.

Rock Cliff Club, West End Road, Negril, Jamaica, W.I. (tel. 809/957-4331; U.S. reservations: 203/438-3793, or toll free 800/243-9420). A new charmer out by Negril's West End, Rock Cliff reflects a trim, West Indian feel with white stucco walls, red-tile roofs, and balustraded terraces. Each of the 40 rooms has a private balcony with sea views. Since the resort is located near the western tip of the island, you'll enjoy ringside views of the sunset. All accommodations have air conditioning and ceiling fans, and are nicely decorated with contemporary furnishings. Although there's no sand beach here, stairways head down the dramatic ironshore to the crystal-clear water. You can also swim in the new, freshwater pool. There's a good restaurant; the weekly all-you-can-eat barbecues for $22 per person offer extremely good value. Honeymoon package: None. Rates (EP): From $65 per couple per night.

Charela Inn, P.O. Box 33, Negril, Jamaica, W.I. (tel. 809/957-4277), with its red-tile roof, arched walkways, wrought-iron grillwork, and garden courtyard, has a Spanish ambience. Owners Daniel Grizzle and his French-born wife Sylvie have created an inn with charm and personality right in the center of Negril's Long Bay beach. There are only 36 rooms, all with air conditioning, ceiling fans, wall-to-wall carpeting, and a queen-size four-poster bed on request. Every room has either a terrace or a balcony; we prefer the upstairs accommodations because of the high ceilings, which add an airy feel. Honeymoon package: None. Deluxe room (EP): $88 to $155 per couple per night. In winter, MAP (including full breakfast and a five-course dinner at the excellent restaurant) is also available; it costs an additional $28 per person per night.

Rockhouse, P.O. Box 24, West End, Negril, Jamaica, W.I. (U.S. reservations: toll free 800/423-4095). You may never have seen anything quite like it—at least, not east of Tahiti or west of Africa. Rockhouse is really a collection of Rockhouses—seven thatch-roofed, round villas planted at the very brink of the limestone cliffs. Catwalks and bridges traverse inlets where the sea has bitten deep into the rock. Some of the cottages even overhang the water, so you can hear the sea surging right under your feet. Very magical. Best news of all for escapists who like their creature comforts as well is that accommodations come complete with all the amenities: queen-size beds, rattan rugs, tables, chairs, and real bathrooms with open-air showers, well screened by lush greenery for privacy. Kerosene lanterns illuminate the property at night; there is also some limited electricity (yes, you can use your hairdryer). For lodgings, we recommend the villas, which are larger than the studios. Floor-to-ceiling glass windows take advantage of the views of cliffs and shimmering turquoise sea. When you want to swim, there's no sand beach—ladders descend from the rocks into the crystal-clear water, and skinny-dipping and all-over tans are encouraged. Snorkelers will want to poke around the underwater caves nearby. Although there's no restaurant on the premises, many local cafés also lie within easy walking distance, including Rick's. But since Rockhouse is near the very end of West End's Lighthouse Road, you'll probably want to rent a car, bike, or moped so you can get around. Honeymoon package: None. Villas (EP): $100 to $130 per couple per night.

ROMANTIC RESTAURANTS

Negril Tree House Club, Long Bay (tel. 957-4287), is a place where you'll be tempted to plunk your beach towel for the entire day. The Tree House Club is situated on one of the finest stretches of Negril beach, with shallow turquoise waters and that powdery white sand. (Designated nude beaches lie to the left and right.) For lunch, start off with a creamy banana daquiri—diligent research has determined it's the best in Negril. Then move on to the lobster sandwich, succulently crammed with shellfish. The lunch tab should run about $20 to $40 per couple; lobster dinners about $60 per couple. Open daily for breakfast, 8 to 11 a.m.; lunch, noon to 3 p.m.; dinner, 6 to 10 p.m.

Xtabi, West End (957-4336). Located at the far west of Negril, Xtabi has no beach; instead, you sunbathe on the flat rocks along the cliff. A circular stairway hewn from the rock wends its way down to the sea. There's excellent snorkeling, including some sea caves. When you get hungry, try one of their tender conch steaks or a toothsome lobster salad; about $25 to $30 per couple. For dinner, favorites include the charbroiled pork chops or a simple—but irreproachable—grilled lobster; $25 to about $60 per couple, if you order lobster. Open daily, 11:30 a.m. to 10 p.m.

Kaiser's Café, West End (no phone). After sunset, the party crowd clears out of Rick's and heads over to Kaiser's, just a wee bit down the road. What Rick's is to sunsets, Kaiser's is to nocturnal drinking and dancing. The bartender whips up a potent medley of tropical drinks, and there's a live band nearly every night. This is also the only club in Negril with videos, which feature reggae stars such as the late Peter Tosh and the late Bob Marley. Sit out on the plateaus of lava rock thrust out over the sea and enjoy. If you need some nourishment to fortify yourselves through the evening, Kaiser's serves Jamaican specialties such as curried chicken, plus various shrimp and lobster dishes. Dinner for two, $30 to $50 per couple. Open daily, 8:30 a.m. until after midnight.

Cafe au Lait, Lighthouse Road, West End (tel. 957-4277). Delicious French and Jamaican cuisine, enjoyed in the dining room or on a terrace overlooking the sea—that's what you'll find at this charming inn run by the Grizzle family (who also own Charela Inn). At lunchtime, you'll savor impeccably prepared light fare, such as pâtés and quiches. Those in the know order one of the famous pizzas, topped with vegetables; or, for true epicures, there's lobster. Dinner choices are especially creative, such as a cheese-and-callaloo crêpe, or a flaky fish run-down, simmered in fresh coconut milk. Then again, you can't beat the grilled lobster, served with butter-garlic sauce. For a sweet finish, order a Tía María ice-creme crêpe. Fine selection of French wines and champagne. Open daily for lunch, noon to 2:30 p.m.; $20 to $30 per couple. Dinner served from 7 to 9 p.m.; $30 to $60 per couple plus drinks.

Mariners Inn, West End (tel. 957-4348). If you've been yearning for a lobster that hangs over the side of your plate, head for Mariner's Inn, located out on the cliffs between Xtabi and Rick's. While you dine outdoors by candlelight, you can watch blowholes in the coral along the shore shoot columns of mist two to three feet up into the air. In addition to lobster, the menu features fresh fish, including an excellent pan-fried snapper. A complete dinner will cost you about $40 to $60 per couple. Open daily for breakfast, 8 to 11 a.m.; lunch, noon to 3 p.m.; dinner, 6 to 10 p.m.

Le Vendôme, Charela Inn (tel. 957-4277). Out front, water splashes in the fountain adorned with a sailfish. On the terrace, high-backed white wrought-iron chairs nestle beneath the plump coconut palms. In front of you, nothing impedes the view of Long Bay beach and the blue Caribbean. When you take into account the excellent food, a table for two at Le Vendôme makes a delightful place for honeymooners to hold hands. At both lunch and dinner, Le Vendôme specializes in Jamaican and Caribbean favorites. For lunch, try the steamed fish with ackee, goat curry, or roast chicken (about $5 to $15 for entrées). At dinner, choose from dishes such as lobster served grilled or creole style or a roast leg of lamb (entrées from $15 to $25). In addition, there's a different five-course dinner special nightly, a very good deal at $30 per person. Le Vendôme also has a fine, reasonably priced wine list. Open daily for breakfast, 8 to 10 a.m.; lunch, noon to 2 p.m.; dinner, 6:30 to 9:30 p.m.

Start off your day with breakfast at the **Silver Star** on Lighthouse Road in West End, just west of the roundabout (tel. 957-4345). Seated on a covered patio, you'll enjoy a hearty American-style meal, complete with eggs or pancakes, whole-wheat toast, jam, peanut butter, and great coffee. Best of all, for you late risers, they serve breakfast all day, adding choices of sandwiches and Italian cuisine for lunch or dinner. Breakfast will cost $15 to $20 per couple. Open daily, 8:30 a.m. to 10:30 p.m. For jerk chicken and other Jamaican dishes, check out **Chicken Lavish** (tel. 957-4410) over toward West End. Portions run about $7 per person. Open daily from noon to about 10 p.m. Satisfy your sweet tooth at the **Sweet Bite Café** in West End, just east of Kaiser's. Ask for two forks to share the enormous slices of chocolate or Grand Marnier cake (about $2.50 each). When you want to go dancing, there's the **Com"pulse"on** disco in town (tel. 957-4416). But some of the hottest action is on the floor of **Hedonism II.** Nonguests can buy a day pass for $40 per person, and enjoy dinner and dancing (tel. 957-4200 to make advance arrangements).

---

4. Mandeville

Situated practically in the center of Jamaica, on a plateau some 2,000 feet above sea level, Mandeville gives you a look at a different aspect of Jamaica from the beach resorts. Here, in the Manchester Mountains, you'll find wild orchids and some of the country's most prestigious schools, 19th-century buildings and a bustling street market. When you visit an old great house, you'll most probably be shown around by the owner himself. (It all adds up to that elusive quality so sought by discerning travelers—the "real Jamaica.")

The fact that Mandeville is located in a parish named Manchester seems appropriate, since Mandeville has often been called the most British town in Jamaica. Certainly, the landscape with its lush, green, rolling hills looks like the English countryside, and the town itself is named for a former British governor. Mandeville is built around a typical English green, and many fine Georgian buildings dating to the early 1800s remain intact, including St. Mark's Church and the Courthouse. Because of the high elevation, temperatures here remain much cooler than at the coastal resorts, averaging in the 70s in summer, the 60s in winter. This moderate climate helped establish Mandeville as one of Jamaica's first tourist areas, a popular "hill station" with the early British settlers, who would summer here.

With its central location and excellent network of highways, Mandeville makes a convenient base for exploring the rest of the island. Honeymooners in particular will want to explore the little-known south coast beaches, such as Great Pedro Bay and Treasure Beach. On the way, stop for a glimpse of Lover's Leap, a 1,500-foot sheer cliff that plunges to the Caribbean.

ROMANTIC INTERLUDES

If you share special interests, such as history, birdwatching, or horticulture, you can pursue them in the Mandeville area. **Marshall's Pen,** an 18th-century great house on a 300-acre cattle ranch, once belonged to the Earl of Balcarres, governor of Jamaica from 1795 to 1801. Its current owner, Arthur Sutton, will give you a personally guided tour, and explain the history of the antiques and paintings you'll see. The property also has hiking trails and a bird sanctuary. Contact Robert Sutton at 809/962-2260; tours cost $6 per person. **Mrs. Stephenson's Gardens** are known for their exquisite varieties of orchids and are the site of an annual flower show at the end of May. Mrs. Stephenson herself will show you around. To arrange visits for any of the above, contact Diana MacIntyre-Pike at the Hotel Astra, tel. 809/962-3265.

HONEYMOON HOTELS AND HIDEAWAYS

If you want to get beyond the usual tourist destinations and be treated like a friend—not a guest—this is the place.

The story of the **Hotel Astra,** 62 Ward Ave., Mandeville, Manchester, Jamaica, W.I. (tel. 809/962-3265 or 962-3377), is inseparable from that of its co-owner and manager, Diana MacIntyre-Pike, a one-woman dynamo and the area's unofficial tourist information center. Her family has been in the hospitality business in Jamaica for over 38 years, and ran some of the first guest cottages in Negril.

Diana's experience, warmth, and enthusiasm have created a friendly, homey hotel—personalized, but run with crackerjack efficiency. Each of the 20 rooms is modern and comfortable, with its own telephone and private bathroom. The hotel has a large pool and sauna; there are also some special health and fitness programs (aerobics, yoga, stress reduction, and massages) that can be arranged by appointment. Hotel service is especially impressive: A phone call to Europe came through in about one minute flat, and the Astra's guest information booklet (personally signed by Diana) tells you everything that you need to know not only about the hotel but about the Mandeville area as well.

Diana's personalized service goes as far as plopping you in her car and driving you off for an orientation tour—what has been called "Di's Whirl Around Mandeville." It's a perfect introduction to the area, and will help you decide which attractions you want to pursue in depth. Since Diana seems to know not only everyone in Mandeville but also everyone in Jamaica, she'll gladly help you arrange special sightseeing and visits. Honeymoon package (BP): $95 per couple per night.

ROMANTIC RESTAURANTS

The choices here aren't so much romantic as atmospheric, and you'll have many opportunities to try real Jamaican dishes.

Hotel Astra (tel. 962-3265). Whether you come for lunch or dinner, you're sure to find many Jamaican specialties on the menu. Meals are served in the Zodiac Dining Room, a pleasant, friendly spot with tapestry-design wall coverings and draperies. For starters, there might be pumpkin soup or a beef soup laden with vegetables. Your main course will center around beef, chicken, or fish, accompanied by different local dishes, such as rice and peas, or stamp and go (made with codfish), or akkra (vegetables). Everything is very, very good, and the friendly waiters will be glad to identify any unidentified objects on your plate. Complete lunch, from $40 per couple; dinner, $60 to $70 per couple. After dinner, you might want to sip some rum or brandy in the Revival Room, a Jamaican-style pub built from old oaken rum casks. Open daily from 6:45 a.m. to 10:30 p.m.

Located some 600 feet above Mandeville, the veranda of **Bill Laurie's Steak House,** Bloomfield Gardens (tel. 962-3116), offers one of the best vantage points for viewing the town and the softly rolling countryside. Every inch of the place is crammed with automotive memorabilia—license plates from around the world, old car photos, and various old cars. Inside the restaurant proper, a friendly, pub-like atmosphere prevails: The bar stools are old rum casks, and pewter tankards belonging to the regulars hang on the walls. The steaks and chops here are excellent, and should run you about $20 to $40 per couple, including salad, vegetable, and "chips" (french fries). Open for dinner only, 6:30 to 9:30 p.m.

---

5. Ocho Rios

If you know a little Spanish, you'll be surprised to learn that this town was not originally called "eight rivers." The Spanish first referred to this area as *choreras,* meaning waterfalls, for the cascades that tumble down the verdant hillsides. With time, the English settlers altered the spelling and the pronunciation, to the name we know today.

Like its name, Ocho Rios is not quite what it seems at first glance. Although high-rise luxury hotels line the harborfront, and multimillion-dollar villas dot the hillsides, the place still retains the friendly atmosphere of the fishing village and banana-shipping port it was just 20 years ago. Ochee, as Jamaicans affectionately call it, is just a small town at heart.

Ocho Rios is located on Jamaica's north coast, about midway between Montego Bay and Port Antonio, each about a two-hour drive (70 miles) away. True to its fishing village roots, Ocho Rios life still centers on the broad, curving harbor—only now, sleek cruise ships drop anchor, instead of tiny skiffs. The harbor also provides the focus for water sports, such as waterskiing, windsurfing, and sailing. Ocho Rios is one of Jamaica's most historic areas, dating back to Christopher Columbus, who is said to have landed at Discovery Bay, west of town. During the 20th century, Ocho Rios has been closely associated with movie stars and writers such as Noël Coward and Ian Fleming, both of whom owned houses in the vicinity. They were lured by the same secluded beaches, dense fern forests, and rushing waterfalls that captivate honeymooners today.

SHOPPING

Since Ocho Rios is so compact, you can walk to town from many of the most popular hotels and villas. **Pineapple Place,** on Main Street, has **Chulani** for in-bond shopping for cameras, electronics, perfumes, and crystal by Baccarat, Lalique, and Swarovski. **Casa de Oro** offers duty-free savings on watches by Piaget, Concorde, Cartier, and Movado; perfumes such as Giorgio and Obsession; plus jewelry, table linens, and cameras. The **Duty Free Complex,** opposite the Little Pub, carries figurines, watches, perfumes, and more.

Coconut Grove Shopping Centre, opposite Plantation Inn, specializes in local crafts items. In particular, check out **Selection** for hand embroidery and black-coral jewelry. Coconut Grove also has duty-free shops such as **Geeta** for electronic equipment.

At **Ocean Village Shopping Centre,** on Ocho Rios Bay, you'll find **The Swiss Store** for duty-free watches, including Omega, Tissot, Patek Philippe, and Rolex. **Mohan's** carries cameras by Nikon, Canon, Minolta, and Pentax. **Americana Shops** specializes in crystal by Lalique, Waterford, and Baccarat, plus china by Royal Doulton, Wedgewood, Royal Worcester, and Aynsley. **Hemisphere,** at the Americana and the Sheraton Hotels, carries Waterford, Wedgwood, and Sevres. For woven-straw items and wood carvings, check out the colorful stalls of the adjacent **Ocho Rios Crafts Market.** Opposite the crafts market, **Nancy's China and Crystal Palace** offers savings on a wide variety of in-bond goods: Lladro figurines, Waterford crystal, Royal Doulton china, and jewelry. You'll also find an excellent selection of popular crafts, especially wood carvings, hawked by vendors just inside the entrance to Dunn's River Falls. For the finest quality selection of local crafts and gift items, head over to **Harmony Hall** or **Cariñosa Gardens** (see details under "Romantic Interludes"). Most hotels also have shopping arcades.

ROMANTIC INTERLUDES

Near Ocho Rios, you'll find some of the most romantic places in all of Jamaica. **Dunn's River Falls,** a sparkling cascade, is perhaps the island's best-known sightseeing attraction, a beautiful spot where waters tumble and splash over wedding-cake tiers of smoothed rocks before ending at a white-sand beach and the Caribbean. So grab your spouse's hand, and start climbing! An experienced guide will lead you up the natural stone staircase to the top of the 600-foot falls. Along the way, you'll stop to swim in crystal-clear pools and relax in natural whirlpools. Be sure to bring a bathing suit (there's a changing room available at the base of the falls), and wear old sneakers to protect your feet. Admission to the falls area is about $1 per person; the guided climb costs an additional $1 a person.

More breathtaking waterfalls—14 in all—await at **Cariñosa Gardens,** 20 acres of flower-filled tropical splendor complete with lily ponds, quaint footbridges, and orchid-lined pathways. View soupbowl-size hibiscus blossoms in brilliant shades ranging from tender pink to flaming crimson, and stroll past lakes where statuesque East African crown cranes pose in the reeds. There's also an aquarium, as well as a walk-through aviary where you can watch canaries diligently build their nests and listen to blue-and-gold macaws jabbering from their perches. Afterward, lunch at the excellent restaurant set by a waterfall (see "Romantic Restaurants" section), then browse through the crafts shop, which features a top-notch selection of intricately worked wooden bowls, ceramic pitchers, and other Jamaican crafts, all reasonably priced. Open daily for tours from 9 a.m. to 5 p.m.; admission is $15 per person (tel. 974-5346).

Ocho Rios is known as the "garden of Jamaica." You'll understand why when you visit one of the area's working plantations that are open to the public. At **Prospect Plantation,** you'll learn how bananas grow "up," not down, and see where some of your favorite fruits, such as mangoes and pineapples, come from. You can tour the property by jitney ($8 per person)—or better yet, enjoy one of their horseback riding excursions ($20 to $32 per person) that take you across the hilltops above Ocho Rios, or along a tree-shaded gorge by the White River (tel. 974-2058). Also visit the **Fern Gully** rain forest, an officially protected reserve, running three miles along an old river bed. Over 550 varieties of native ferns flourish here, everything from the 30-foot-tall tree fern to the tiny film fern, with translucent leaves that are only one cell thick. The reserve is perfect for a short hike or picnic in the shade.

A Victorian house dating from 1886, **Harmony Hall** has been lovingly restored, right down to the very last curlicue in the gingerbread fretwork. Today, it serves as a gallery of arts and crafts, showcasing the work of some of Jamaica's best artists and craftspeople. The roster of painters and sculptors who have exhibited work here includes Edna Manley, Mallica "Kapo" Reynolds, and George Rodney. Styles of the works range from intuitive to highly sophisticated. You can also browse through beautiful batiks, shell jewelry, and antiques. Original oil paintings start at about $100, ceramic sculptures of Jamaican cottages are $5, or you can bring home a "taste of Jamaica" in the form of Blue Mountain coffee or island spices such as sage or nutmeg starting for about $4. Open daily from 10 a.m. to 6 p.m.; admission is free (tel. 974-4222).

Two different legends exist about the origins of **Runaway Bay.** According to one account, it was the place from which escaped slaves launched their dugout canoes and headed for freedom in Cuba, just 90 miles away. The alternate theory maintains that the Spanish governor of Jamaica hid here after the British took over the island in 1658. Whichever explanation you prefer, the spot is fascinating because of the nearby **Green Grotto Caves,** which you can visit. On the 45-minute tour, you'll go about 120 feet underground, passing natural rock formations that look like sculptures. There's also the underground lake that gives the caves their name. The caves are open daily from 9 a.m. to 5 p.m.; admission is $3.50 per person.

Firefly was the home of Noël Coward, the playwright, composer, and dramatist whose elegance and savoir faire seem so in tune with Jamaica. During his lifetime, Coward often entertained his celebrated friends here, including Winston Churchill, Laurence Olivier and Vivien Leigh, Katharine Hepburn, and the Queen Mother. Located 20 miles east of Ocho Rios in the hills above Oracabessa, the house is now part of the Jamaica National Trust. All the belongings remain exactly as they were on the day Coward died in 1973—right down to his silk shirts and bathrobe in the cupboard, and the sheet music ("Three Little Words") on the piano in the living room. The house itself is small and time-worn; the most appealing part of a visit here comes while strolling the grounds, which have extraordinary views of the north coast. The ruined lookout is said to date from Coward's time. Open daily from 10 a.m. to 4 p.m.; admission $2 per person.

Chukka Cove is the largest full-scale equestrian center in the Caribbean, and whether you're looking for an enjoyable **trail ride**—or a serious three-day event clinic, you'll find top-notch horses and facilities. Choose from a complete range of activities. On the one-hour trail ride, you'll head through a working coconut and banana plantation, Papillon Cove, where scenes from that movie were filmed ($25 per person). More experienced riders will enjoy the six-hour day trip up to a 2,000-foot-high mountain ridge, passing wild orchids and a coffee plantation en route ($85 per person). Other programs combine a stay at a luxury resort with a polo clinic, eventing clinic (Captain Mark Phillips, a former member of the British Olympic Team, has taught here), or trekking. Polo matches are held here every Thursday during the winter. For complete details and schedules, contact **Chukka Cove Farm**

Ltd., Richmond, Llandovery, P.O. Box 160, Ocho Rios, Jamaica, W.I. (tel. 972-2506).

HONEYMOON HOTELS AND HIDEAWAYS

Even in a country known for luxury resorts, Ocho Rios dazzles vacationers with elegant choices—grand and gracious Old Jamaica inns, sleeky modern high-rise hotels, all-inclusive couples resorts, personable small hotels and cottages, and private villas.

Ultraluxurious

Jamaica Inn, P.O. Box 1 Ocho Rios, Jamaica, W.I. (tel. 809/974-2514; U.S. reservations: 203/438-3793 in Connecticut; 212/697-2340 in NY; toll free 800/243-9420). A clean, fluffy towel awaits you, even after your umpteenth return from the beach. The bed is freshly made, even after an afternoon nap. It's details like these that move Jamaica Inn beyond the realm of merely beautiful hotels into the ranks of the truly great ones. Everything remain classically just so—white archways and columns lead to the reception area, white balustrades line the dining terrace overlooking the sea (a view that has often graced the Jamaica posters). At any given time, there are never more than 90 guests on the property, and since the two-story, U-shape inn spreads out over more than six acres, including 700 feet of beachfront, you'll enjoy plenty of elbow room around your chaise longue. Ambience is assured rather than showoffy—this is the kind of place where the only sport on the property is croquet. (Ah, yes, there's a lovely oval-shape freshwater pool and good snorkeling, and tennis, golf, and horseback riding can all be arranged.)

As you would expect, rooms are spacious and classic, with chenille bedspreads, floral chintz draperies, and mahogany headboards. But what really wins over guests lies just outside—the huge private terraces or balconies that are really outdoor living rooms, taking advantage of Jamaica's balmy climate. Ask for a downstairs room—the patios are larger, and you can pop right over the railing onto the sand from many of them. All rooms are air-conditioned, most have views of both the mountains and ocean, and the hotel is situated so that you'll generally have a four-star view of the sunset. Superb restaurant. Honeymoon package: Seven days/six nights (MAP): $1,535 per couple (low season). Additional nights available for $210 per couple per night. Includes all taxes and service charges, round-trip transfers between airport and hotel, trip to Dunn's River Falls, rafting trip on the White River, bottle of wine, bottle of rum, glass-bottomed boat ride, sailing excursion, and bottle of cologne. High-season rates (FAP): $375 to $400 per couple per night. And if we wanted to splurge, we couldn't think of any place more romantic than the White Suite—absolutely gigantic, completely surrounded by terraces, and very secluded on the brink of a promontory (Winston Churchill slept here). From $365 to $600 per couple per night.

Pretty and pink, **Sans Souci Hotel, Club, & Spa,** P.O. Box 103, Ocho Rios, Jamaica, W.I. (tel. 809/974-2353; U.S. reservations: 305/666-3566 in Florida; toll free 800/237-3237 nationwide), meanders down the cliffside above a tranquil, reef-protected cove on the Caribbean. The buildings combine West Indian and Italian architectural elements, with archways, white lattice-framed balconies, and a distinctive campanile-type structure that houses the elevator to the pool. The whole property positively sparkles after a $4-million renovation. There are only 80 rooms and suites, each different in size and layout. Pink and yellow predominate—in the soft floral print upholstery, oomphy cushions on the sofa, and original prints of native Jamaican flowers. Proportions are ample, and the rooms are so comfortable that you'll want to move right in.

A lot of care is lavished on guests, so that your stay will be truly *sans souci*—without care. Equally appealing are the fanciful touches at the resort. Rolly the Parrot (a.k.a. Sir Walter Raleigh) holds court amid the white wicker, chintz, and hanging plants of the reception area; there's a human-scale chessboard down by the pool;

and the new health club facilities have been named "Charlie's Spa" to honor the resident turtle mascot. The resort has some of the finest spa facilities in the Caribbean, with a complete roster of bodily indulgences: massages, facials, body scrubs, exercise classes. (One of life's most enchanted moments comes when you have a massage in one of their private cabanas overlooking the sea.) Water-lovers can avail themselves of the two swimming pools (one spectacularly thrust over the rocks), as well as the powdery white beach that's the focus for sailing, scuba-diving, snorkeling, and other sports. Tennis is complimentary on the two courts. And there's low-key entertainment nightly: piano music in the Balloon Bar, or perhaps a calypso trio syncopating to the rhythm of the surf. The Casanova Restaurant is excellent. A member of "The Elegant Resorts of Jamaica." If you want to launch your honeymoon with a wedding in Jamaica, Sans Souci has a charming gazebo at water's edge, perfect for exchanging vows at sunset. Honeymoon package: Eight days/seven nights (MAP): $1,525 to $2,275 per couple for a deluxe room; $1,755 to $2,580 per couple for a one-bedroom suite. Includes round-trip transfers between hotel and airport, basket of fruit, champagne, trip to Dunn's River Falls (admissions not covered), and more.

Plantation Inn, P.O. Box 2, Ocho Rios, Jamaica, W.I. (tel. 809/974-5601; U.S. reservations: 305/666-3566 in Florida; toll free 800/237-3237 nationwide). "Plantation Inn? I'd go back there in a minute," replied one dreamy-eyed woman, some four years after her honeymoon. Maybe it's the open-air corridors, thickly overhung with climbing vines. Maybe it's the proper English afternoon tea, served from a silver teapot, or the white columned entrance portico where Scarlett O'Hara would feel right at home. Probably it's the sum total of all these exquisite details that establishes Plantation Inn as one of Jamaica's great resorts.

Imagine an antebellum southern mansion transplanted to a low hillside above two fine north coast Jamaican beaches, and you've pretty much gotten the picture. At the far side of the lobby, latticework archways open onto a broad terrace. Here, seated in a graceful white wrought-iron chair, you can take high tea or dine overlooking the pool and beaches. Each of the 65 rooms and 14 suites is centrally air-conditioned, and each has a private balcony with a wrought-iron railing overlooking the sea. Ask for rooms in the new section. Recently refurbished, they are breezy and tropical with white bamboo furniture and rattan rugs. Junior suites come with large terrace living areas complete with couches and a dining table.

Plantation Inn doesn't just have a private beach, it has a private bay, edged by two crescent-shape beaches. Just 100 yards offshore, you can snorkel over a coral reef. Learn to windsurf, or sail a light dinghy. Back on land, there's tennis on two courts (one lighted for night play), and horseback riding and golf can be arranged. Superb restaurant. A member of "The Elegant Resorts of Jamaica." Honeymoon package: Eight days/seven nights (FAP): Low season—$1,695 to $2,505 per couple for a superior room; $2,125 to $3,150 per couple for a junior suite. Includes round-trip transfers between airport and hotel, fruit basket, bottle of champagne, service charges and taxes, trip to Dunn's River Falls, and more.

All-Inclusive Resorts

Couples, P.O. Box 330, Ocho Rios, Jamaica, W.I. (tel. 809/974-4271; U.S. reservations: tel. 516/868-6924 in New York State; toll free 800/858-8009). As the name implies, this all-inclusive resort located just east of Ocho Rios admits twosomes only. No singles. No families. No children.

Couples has been called a place created by romantics for romantics, and it lives up to its reputation. The mood is blissful, but lighthearted—part Garden of Eden, part summer camp, thanks to the amazing roster of sports available. Everything is included: sailing, windsurfing, snorkeling, and scuba-diving down at the beach; greens fees for golf; tennis, squash, racquetball; and a state-of-the-art gym with Nautilus equipment and free weights. Want to participate, but don't know how? Take advantage of the free lessons.

The romance comes not only from the clientele, but also from the tranquil setting on an 800-foot, half-moon-shaped beach. Just offshore, there's a tiny, vintage Robinson Crusoe island you can swim to (or take the launch): Tower Island, reserved for nude sunbathing. The white, red-roofed main hotel was constructed way back when—"when" being a time when people knew how to build things right. Accommodations are big, and even have walk-in closets. Rooms have been refurbished with lovers in mind: with king-size beds, air conditioning, and private balconies, each with a mountain or a sea view. Request a room on the fourth floor of the main building: although a tad smaller than the rest, they have lots of character, with sunken living areas and triangular bathrooms.

Breakfast and lunch are served buffet style on the veranda, with choices of both American and Jamaican dishes. Dinner is a sit-down affair at convivial tables of four or five couples, with a four-course table d'hôte menu that often includes steak or lobster (or both, if you prefer). With lunch and dinner, you get unlimited free wine. In fact, you could eat, drink, and be merry nearly 24 hours a day, if you like, what with afternoon hors d'oeuvres, free cocktails, midnight snacks, and a piano bar that doesn't close down until the last guest departs. And if you want to tie the knot in Jamaica, Couples can handle all wedding arrangements. Honeymoon package: None. Oceanview room: Eight days/seven nights: From $2,345 per couple. Mountainview rooms are $70 less per couple per week .

Sandals Ocho Rios, Ocho Rios, Jamaica, W.I. (tel. 809/974-5691; U.S. reservations: 305/284-1300 in Florida, or toll free 800/327-1991). What components do you seek in your portion of honeymoon paradise? A private, secluded beach? Sports such as tennis, waterskiing, and scuba-diving? The carefree spirit engendered by never having to ask how much something costs, never having to pay a tip or fee? That's what you'll find at Sandals, an all-inclusive, couples-only resort. Sandals packs in an energetic repertoire of sports and instruction. On the water, there's windsurfing and snorkeling, with instruction if you need to hone your skills. Back on terra firma, you can opt for tennis, horseback riding, or working out in the fitness center. During the day, an action-packed schedule can keep you on the move from sunup to well after moonrise: beach volleyball, aerobics classes—even jaunts to Dunn's River Falls or to Ocho Rios for shopping. If you want to get married in Jamaica, the folks at Sandals can arrange all the details of a dandy wedding party. Honeymoon package: None. Regular eight-day/seven-night package (all-inclusive): $1,925 to $2,340 per couple for a standard room.

Jamaica, Jamaica, P.O. Box 58, Runaway Bay, Jamaica, W.I. (tel. 809/973-2436; U.S. reservations: 516/868-6924 in NY; toll free 800/858-8009 nationwide). Sip wine on a hansom-cab ride through lanes close-hemmed by bougainvillea and oleander. Move to the beat of both reggae and rock 'n' roll in the disco. These are just some of the warm, colorful, and romantic aspects of the island you'll encounter at Jamaica, Jamaica, an all-inclusive resort located at Runaway Bay, about a half-hour drive (18 miles) west of Ocho Rios.

One could not ask for a more attractive natural setting, poised at the edge of one of the longest beaches on Jamaica's north coast. The architecture of the buildings is especially pleasing: none looms taller than the sheltering coconut palms, and the wings are angled to maximize views and privacy. Upstairs rooms have balconies, the downstairs ones have terraces; all are air-conditioned. Newly refurbished in a soft palette of sea green, peach, and lavender, the rooms are highlighted by beautiful cedar furniture handcrafted in Jamaica. The resort's lobby fulfills all your tropical fantasies, with waterfalls, squawking parrots, a jungle of plants, and hanging basket chairs.

Since Jamaica, Jamaica admits all adults over the age of 16, an upbeat, energetic atmosphere permeates the resort. Well-known Jamaican performers headline at the nightclub, and the disco packs 'em in until the early hours. For the sports-minded, there are three swimming pools: a gigantic free-form pool, a lap pool, and a volleyball pool. Down at that gorgeous beach, you can set sail on a Sunfish or Windsurfer, go snorkeling, or cruise aboard a 40-foot catamaran. Improve your tennis or golf game, or pump some iron in the Nautilus-equipped gym. Perhaps learn two of Jamaica's favorite national pastimes: soccer and cricket. In addition, you can sign up for the weekly tanning contests, fashion shows, beach Olympics, and goat racing. There's a daily shopping shuttle to Ocho Rios and excursions to Dunn's River Falls. If you prefer peace and quiet, Jamaica, Jamaica encompasses over 27 acres, so you can always get away to a hammock under a palm tree.

One of your favorite aspects of Jamaica, Jamaica is sure to be the food prepared by the resort's award-winning chefs, who prepare recipes from around the world. Breakfast and dinner are buffets, while dinner is generally sit-down, offering you a choice of continental, Jamaican, or low-calorie dishes. And for the unstoppable, there are also afternoon hors d'oeuvres and midnight snacks. Jamaica, Jamaica attracts many honeymooners, and the resort offers them his-and-hers T-shirts and invitations to a special all-newlyweds cocktail party. Here, everyone will want to sample the drink called "Matrimony," said to guarantee a long marriage and passionate nights. Honeymoon package: None. Standard eight-day/seven-night package: From $2,180 per couple.

Sleek, modern, and elegant, the 325-room **Americana Hotel,** P.O. Box 100, Ocho Rios, Jamaica, W.I. (tel. 809/974-2151; U.S. reservations: 212/661-4540 in New York State; toll free 800/223-1588 nationwide), has all the facilities and panache of the well-known chain. The property has recently adopted an all-inclusive plan. Couples can relax and enjoy their honeymoon completely, knowing that everything—airport transfers, three meals daily, drinks, taxes, and tips—is covered by the room rate. The high-rise hotel is set on a completely private beach on Mallards Bay, just a short walk from the heart of Ocho Rios and the crafts market, and right across from the Mallards Beach Hotel. The property has recently completed a million-dollar refurbishment, and everything looks spanking new. The pool area has been enlarged, and the water-sports facilities have been expanded, and now feature waterskiing, jetskiing, snorkeling, scuba-diving, fishing trips, and cruises. Most important, all the rooms have been redone and now have a breezy island feel, the white furniture accented by pretty pastel tones of pink, lavender, and blue. Framed paintings of local landscapes adorn the walls. All the rooms are basically the same, with oceanview balconies, air conditioning, telephones, and radios; they will try to honor requests for king-size beds. Room prices vary according to elevation: accommodations on the higher floors are considered more deluxe. The Americana has two restaurants, a snackbar, a cocktail lounge, two lighted tennis courts, freshwater swimming pool, and a shopping arcade. Honeymoon package: None. Double-room rates (EP): $415 to $965 per couple per week. Various meal plans are also available.

First-Class Hotels
Mallards Beach Hotel, P.O. Box 245, Ocho Rios, Jamaica, W.I. (tel. 809/974-2201; U.S. reservations: 305/667-8860, or toll free 800/526-2422). The Americana's neighbor on Mallards Bay, this 397-room hotel is similar in modernist, high-rise outlook. It, too, is practically a self-contained resort, with three restaurants, three bars, entertainment, and a shopping arcade. Thanks to the prime Mallards Bay location, a bevy of water sports awaits right on your doorstep: deep-sea fishing, snorkeling, scuba-diving, sailing, waterskiing, and glass-bottomed boat rides. You can team up for doubles on the two lighted tennis courts, or line up some players for volleyball. All rooms are air-conditioned and have been recently redecorated, and now sport cool, tropical fabrics. Sparkling, modern bathrooms feature "Hollywood-style" illuminated mirrors. Here, the various room categories do boast different amenities. The superior and deluxe rooms have balconies; the standard rooms do not. Different special events light up the nights: a beach party with reggae music, or a "Miss Mallards Beach" beauty contest. Honeymoon package: Eight days/seven nights (BP): $1,030 to $1,325 per couple for a deluxe room. Includes round-trip transfers between airport and hotel, welcome cocktails, taxes, and more. Several other room packages and meal plans are also available.

Eaton Hall Hotel & Villas, Runaway Bay, P.O. Box 112, Runaway Bay, Jamaica, W.I. (tel. 809/973-3503; U.S. reservations: 305/667-1776), is the kind of place where the guests write virtual love notes in the big register in the lobby: "Wonderful Jamaican hospitality!" "Thanks for all the smiles." "Fabulous!" If you're looking for an intimate-scale all-inclusive resort with plenty of warm Jamaican friendliness, Eaton Hall could be just your ticket to paradise. Part of the charm is the setting itself: The main building of the resort is a plantation great house dating to 1655. But what really makes the resort is General Manager Ned Wong, who positively delights in spoiling his guests—especially honeymooners.

Although the resort is small (only 52 rooms), you can choose from a wide range of accommodations. Couples who prefer something old-fashioned should request accommodations in the original great house, where some rooms have king-size four-poster beds. (Be sure you reserve these in advance.) More modern types will enjoy the villas, which each have three contemporary apartments with huge balconies overlooking the sea. There's a fine private beach, and the reefs just offshore teem with colorful fish. You can make friends with them while snorkeling or cruising aboard Sunfish, rafts, or a glass-bottomed boat. Practice your serve on the full-size tennis court (not lighted), play some tennis or chess, or unwind with a massage. At mealtime, you'll sit either on the outdoor terrace or in the formal dining room, decorated with Jamaican Victorian furniture. Most of the socializing centers around one of the two pools, especially the one near the shingle-roof gazebo bar at water's edge. Honeymoon package: None. Standard rate (MAP): $135 to $220 per couple per night. Includes round-trip transfers between airport and hotel, room taxes and service charges, and daily activities program.

Moderately Priced

Hibiscus Lodge Hotel, P.O. Box 52, Ocho Rios, Jamaica, W.I. (tel. 809/974-2676). Intimacy and oodles of charm—that's what you'll find at this small, personable inn steeped in the traditions of Old Jamaica. Although the property is conveniently near the center of town, you feel secluded from the hustle and bustle, since it is surrounded by three acres of lush gardens. Purple cattleya orchids snuggle in the crooks of trees; grapefruit and avocado trees flourish—a veritable Eden. Rooms are modern and simple to basic in decor, with private baths. Most have ceiling fans—no air conditioning. All the rooms face the Caribbean, but vary somewhat in layout: Some are closer to the water, others have larger balconies. Not fancy or posh, but completely endearing. Hibiscus does not have a sand beach, but there's a stone sundeck dramatically thrust out over the water, and you can swim in the crystal clear, reef-protected waters right from there. Honeymoon package: None. Double-room rates (EP): $50 to $60 per couple per night.

Runaway H.E.A.R.T. Country Club, P.O. Box 98, St. Ann, Jamaica, W.I. (tel. 809/973-2671; U.S. reservations: toll free 800/526-2422). "Beautiful." "I love it." "We were very impressed with the excellent service." Those are just a few of the rave reviews that the Runaway H.E.A.R.T. Country Club has been earning from guests. Poised on a plateau above the golf course and Runaway Bay, the resort is perfect for couples who want a quiet honeymoon haven—but one that's accessible to many different activities. The resort is built plantation style, with soft-pink walls accented by white balustrades. You'll enjoy strolling around the lush gardens (take special note of the splendid old ficus tree). There are only 20 rooms, all beautifully decorated with contemporary furnishings and equipped with air conditioning and color TV. French windows open onto a private balcony. During the day, a free shuttle runs to the golf club and private beach; you can also settle into a lounge chair by the freshwater pool right at the hotel. What makes the resort extra special is the employees. Many of them are students at the H.E.A.R.T. Academy, learning all aspects of the hotel industry under the careful supervision of professional staff. You'll find no greater personal attention anywhere else on the island . . . and the room rates are exceedingly reasonable. Honeymoon package: Eight days/seven nights (some meals): $825 per couple (low season). Includes seven breakfasts and three dinners, round-trip transfers between airport and hotel, sightseeing trip to Dunn's River Falls, bottle of wine, fresh flowers, taxes and service charges, and more. High-season rates (EP): $55 per couple per night.

ROMANTIC RESTAURANTS

Jamaica's black velvet nights seem particularly seductive in Ocho Rios, where most of the best restaurants also come with beautiful views.

The Ruins, on the Turtle River, Ocho Rios (tel. 974-2442 or 974-2789). Built around the ruins of an old sugar mill (it even has the requisite resident ghost), The Ruins has a setting that seems to be made for lovers, set in a glade shaded by palm trees by the edge of a waterfall. You can dine on an open terrace by the side of the waterfall and river, or beneath a thatch-roofed gazebo. The menu features an intriguing combination of Chinese, Jamaican, and continental specialties: everything from fish creole to a T-bone steak to Lotus Lily lobster, stir-fried with ginger and oyster sauce (entrées from $18 to $25). Either before or after your meal, you can wander up the paths and bridges that climb past the ferns and moss-covered boulders to the top of the falls, or browse through the gift shop that carries some pretty hand-painted *pareus* (sarongs). Given the fairy-tale setting, The Ruins is a perfect spot for a wedding, and Cleveland Hoo, the general manager, will be glad to help you with all the arrangements. Open Monday through Saturday for lunch, noon to 2:30 p.m.; Monday through Sunday for dinner, 6 to 9:30 p.m. Reservations recommended.

Almond Tree, Hibiscus Lodge (tel. 974-2813). For alfresco dining with a Caribbean view, head for the Almond Tree, set cliffside some 30 feet above the sea. The white wrought-iron railings and chairs on the terrace contrast with the bright blue of the sea, which laps against the rocky shoreline. The lunch menu features crisp, crunchy salads. For starters, you might want to sample one of Jamaica's classic soups, such as pumpkin or pepperpot. At dinnertime, the chef has a deft hand with both continental and Caribbean dishes such as veal scaloppine, breaded butterfly shrimp, or broiled red snapper. Reservations required. Open daily for lunch, noon to 2 p.m.; $20 to $40 per couple. Dinner is served from 6:30 to 10 p.m.; $40 to $60 per couple.

Cariñosa Restaurant, at Cariñosa Gardens (tel. 974-5346). For two lovers, the next best thing to dining in the Garden of Eden must be a table for two—with a waterfall—at the Cariñosa Gardens restaurant. Just as the grounds highlight Jamaica's beautiful flowers and wildlife, the restaurant features the best of the island's cuisine, with all ingredients fresh from the farm or the sea. Appetizers include coconut shrimp and Jamaican ackee, served in a delicate curry sauce. As your main course, you'll have trouble deciding between such dishes as chicken calypso, stuffed with callaloo (like spinach) and served with a ginger-honey sauce; and lobster Marguerite, sautéed in wine and Jamaican spices. For dessert, the smart money chooses the delectable homemade ice creams, in exotic flavors such as pineapple and mango. Plan on taking a stroll after dinner: the grounds are dramatically illuminated at night, spotlighting the rushing waterfalls and flowering vines. Open daily for lunch, 11:30 a.m. to 2:30 p.m.; about $40 per couple. Dinner served from 6 to 9 p.m.; about $60 per couple plus drinks.

Cardiff Hall Restaurant, Runaway H.E.A.R.T. Country Club (tel. 973-2671). The setting seems made for those balmy Jamaican nights—a broad terrace surrounded by archways and columns. Piano music plays quietly, counterpointed by the soft chirrup of tree frogs in the gardens. Hand-holding and shared secrets just seem to come naturally at this romantic restaurant perched in the tropical hills above Runaway Bay. The cuisine is excellent. Start off with the cool and creamy vichyssoise or some savory smoked marlin. Entrées include chicken Cordon Bleu, steamed lobster with callaloo mousse, or chateaubriand for two. For dessert, try the excellent chocolate mousse. Best of all, the service is extra-attentive and friendly, since the staff includes restaurant and hotel students from the H.E.A.R.T. Academy, a program training young people to work in the resort industry. Open for lunch, noon to 2:30 p.m.; $20 to $30 per couple. Dinner served from 7 to 10 p.m.; $40 to $60 per couple plus drinks.

The Little Pub Restaurant & Cocktail Bar, Little Pub Complex, 59 Main St., Ocho Rios (tel. 974-2324). The Little Pub calls itself the "Home of Lobsters and Fun," and it delivers nicely on both counts. The restaurant is set in the courtyard of this small shopping center, surrounding the oldest standing building in Ocho Rios (1871). You'll sit on white wrought-iron chairs under the palm trees. The lobsters come prepared in a variety of styles—thermidor, creole, or curried—but we prefer ours simply grilled and dipped in lots of butter (about $30). At lunch, you can get juicy burgers for about $6. Other than lobster, the dinner menu features a variety of grilled items: kingfish, sirloin steak, shish kebab, or chicken, priced from $15 to $20. For dessert, you can set your night afire with some bananas flambé ($5). The fun really gets going thanks to the evening entertainment: the Stone Fire Band nightly, plus special performances and shows by entertainers such as The Mighty Digger. Reservations recommended. Open daily for lunch, noon to 2 p.m.; dinner, 6:30 to 10 p.m.

Nights on the Rivers. In Ocho Rios, you'll find two special evening events that take advantage of the area's natural attractions. **Dunn's River Feast** (check your hotel desk or call 974-2619) is an evening of Jamaicana centered around the famous falls, which are illuminated by torchlight. There's an open bar and a Jamaican buffet feast served beachside, with the emphasis on local dishes. Then get ready to enjoy the live music and John Canoe (a kind of calypso) dancers, or join in yourself for the limbo contest or goat races. Held every Wednesday at 7 p.m.; price $33 per person.

A Night on the White River (tel. 974-2619) takes you by canoe up the torchlit river, frogs and crickets chirping in the jungly vegetation. You'll disembark for a buffet dinner—barbecued chicken and ribs, washed down with plenty of rum punches from the open bar. For entertainment, you'll enjoy limbo dancers, fire swallowers, and live music for dancing. Held Sunday and Tuesday evenings at 7 p.m.; price $35 per person.

Even if you're not staying at Jamaica Inn, Sans Souci, or Plantation Inn, you can drop over for lunch, afternoon tea, or dinner. At any one of the three, you'll enjoy excellent food, panoramic sea views, and experience the gracious service that is a Jamaican hallmark. **Jamaica Inn** (tel. 974-2514) offers a balustraded dining terrace under the rustling palm trees. The five-course prix-fixe dinner menu ($35 to $40 per person) spotlights both Jamaican and continental dishes. Open daily for lunch, 1 to 2:30 p.m.; dinner, 8 to 9:30 p.m. **Plantation Inn** (tel. 974-2501) serves an especially atmospheric high tea every afternoon on the open terrace from 4 to 5:30 p.m. Choices include sweet cakes and tiny tea sandwiches served from a mahogany and silver cart. About $5 per person complete with tea or coffee. The Plantation Inn also serves an elegant five-course prix-fixe dinner for about $40 per person; served nightly from 8 to 9:30 p.m. **Casanova at the Sans Souci** (tel. 974-2353) offers dining both outdoors on the poolside terrace and indoors in the main room (although the wide-open windows make you feel as if you're outdoors anyway). Dinner will cost about $40 per person. Open daily for lunch, noon to 2 p.m.; dinner, 7 to 9 p.m. Reservations required for all.

6. Port Antonio

The drive east from Ocho Rios along Jamaica's north coast plays hide-and-seek with the sea. Alternately, the road opens onto awesome vistas of mountain and sea coast, then plunges deep into bamboo forests and dense sugarcane fields, so close to the road that foliage swishes against the car windows as you pass. The route takes you through the towns of Oracabessa and Port Maria (with their busy markets on Fridays), and runs along the base of mountains that plummet straight to the sea. Some two hours and 67 miles after you leave Ocho Rios, you'll arrive in perhaps the lushest and most tropical part of Jamaica, what poet Ella Wheeler Wilcox called "the most exquisite port on earth"—Port Antonio.

Today, Port Antonio still retains a quiet, old-world charm, heavily tinged with movie-star and jet-set connotations. There are two ports actually—east and west harbors—both surrounded by steep, jungly hillsides. The town is a historic one, originally settled by the Spanish. It staked its initial claim to fame as the center for the banana trade in the 19th century. Because of the rich profits the bananas yielded, they soon became known as "green gold." According to legend, the banana planters grew so wealthy that on "Banana Day" (any day a ship was loading), they would light their cigars with $5 bills. Prosperity ended abruptly with the outbreak of Panama disease, which destroyed nearly the entire crop. The industry never recovered.

Into this sleepy ex-banana-port sailed the yacht *Zacca,* owned by Errol Flynn. The swashbuckling actor acquired substantial real estate holdings here, including Navy Island, which he supposedly won in settlement of a gambling debt. Flynn's widow, Patrice Wymore Flynn, still lives in the area. Another interesting footnote: Flynn receives credit for making river rafting a popular attraction for vacationers. The rafts were originally used to bring bananas to market, and Flynn, true to form, started racing them down the river and wagering on the results.

Another fascinating story concerns the Folly, a mansion built in 1906 by millionaire Alfred Mitchell for his wife Annie Tiffany (daughter of the founder of the Fifth Avenue store). By 1938, the entire structure collapsed: Seawater had been used in mixing the concrete, and the supporting iron rods rusted through. Today, only a jumbled pile of ruined columns remains, and the site makes a hauntingly beautiful spot for a stroll or a picnic.

Despite its reputation as an oasis for the rich and famous, Port Antonio remains refreshingly innocent, and is still largely unspoiled by tourism. For a uniquely Jamaican experience, stop by the market held Thursday through Saturday, and sample some savory jerk pork served with hard-dough bread. Perhaps pick up some Irish moss, which can be brewed into a tea said to be an aphrodisiac. No high-rise buildings mar the profile of the main town, which is dominated by the Georgian Courthouse and the brick parish church, Christ Church, which dates from 1840. Queen Street has some other good examples of Georgian architecture. The town is looking pretty spiffy these days, ironically thanks to Hollywood connections once again: It was used as the setting for the Robin Williams movie *Club Paradise.* It is precisely this interplay between show business and local Jamaican culture, glamour, and down-home roots that makes Port Antonio so intriguing to honeymooners.

SHOPPING

Your options are quite limited here. In town, there's **Sang-Hing's Freeport Giftland,** with a small selection of duty-free figurines and perfumes. For local crafts, try the **weekly market** or the **pier** on those days when cruise ships come to town. If you're really looking to buy, plan to spend time in Montego Bay, Ocho Rios, or Kingston.

ROMANTIC INTERLUDES

The choicest options center around Port Antonio's lush surroundings. For the best view of Port Antonio's twin harbors, cruise off aboard the **Lady Jamaica** glass-bottomed boat on a sunset cocktail cruise. The boat is equipped with lights, so you'll be able to see lots of different fish. It costs $14 per person; call 993-3318.

According to legend, the **Blue Lagoon** is bottomless; more scientific types have determined that it's about 180 feet deep. In any event, it's beautiful—crystal-clear, sapphire-blue waters fed by freshwater springs said to have amazing rejuvenating powers. Located a short drive west of Port Antonio, the lagoon is framed by white beaches and green cliffs. For a small charge, you can waterski or take a glass-bottomed boat ride to view the reef and colorful fish; better yet, bring your bathing suit and go for a swim (absolutely free). It's also a fine spot for a picnic.

The only sounds are the chirps of the June bugs in the surrounding jungle and the wind rustling through the stands of bamboo. For a true oasis of peacefulness and bliss, head over for the rafting trip down the **Rio Grande,** which has its headwaters in the Blue Mountains, and runs all the way to the Caribbean. This particular journey runs about eight miles, and takes about two to three hours. Seated on a bench just big enough for two, you'll float down the river on the 33-foot-long raft, propelled by an experienced skipper with a stout pole. Along the way, you can stop for a swim in the crystal waters (remember your bathing suits), or for a drink at a little riverside stand. To reach the embarkation point, you can either take an organized tour from your hotel or drive your rental car. If you drive, you can hire a licensed, insured driver to bring your car to the journey's end (this costs about $12). The raft trip itself costs $40 per couple (tel. 993-2778).

Located just east of Port Antonio a bit past the Blue Lagoon, the **Nonsuch Cave and Gardens of Athenry** (tel. 993-3740) are located on a 185-acre working coconut and banana plantation. The journey is worth it just for the drive: The road to the plantation winds up through the hills and offers splendid vistas of the mist-covered Blue Mountains. At Nonsuch Cave, you can catch up on the past 1½ million years of history. The caves were discovered in the 1950s by someone looking for a lost goat. During the guided tour of the caves, you'll pass stalactites, stalagmites, fossilized marine animals, and artifacts left by the Arawak Indians, the original inhabitants of Jamaica. Then, if you've ever wondered where many of your favorite kitchen spices came from, join the guided tour of the gardens. You'll view coconuts, thyme, pimiento (allspice), bay leaf, ackee, nutmeg trees, vanilla vines with their fragrant seed pods, and other plants and flowers typical of Jamaica. There's also a charming restaurant, where you can lunch alfresco and admire the views. The property is open 9 a.m. to 5 p.m., and $5 per person admits you to both the caves and gardens.

Waterfalls, rivulets, and deep rock pools make **Somerset Falls** a cool change of pace from the beach. Go swim and splash in the tumbling waters. The forests are lush and jungly, thick with croton, banana plants, bamboo, and huge red ginger lilies. Bring a picnic lunch; there's also a small restaurant. Located ten miles west of Port Antonio, just past Hope Bay.

HONEYMOON HOTELS AND HIDEAWAYS

Port Antonio offers a small, but select, collection of places to stay. In addition to the regular hotel and villa accommodations, the area also features some absolutely splendid private residences for rent. Some of the poshest are located on the "Millionaire's Row" near the Blue Lagoon. Weekly rentals run about $1,500 to $2,000 per couple per week, including services of a cook/housekeeper. Contact the **Jamaican Tourist Board** or **Air Train** (tel. 416/620-4666, or toll free 800/263-4354).

Ultraluxurious

Trident Villas and Hotel, P.O. Box 119, Port Antonio, Jamaica, W.I. (tel. 809/993-2602; U.S. reservations: tel. 212/308-3330 in New York State; toll free 800/235-3505), is the kind of place that makes you wish that your honeymoon could, in fact, go on forever. The 14-acre setting is a marvel, right on the brink of rocky bluffs at the edge of the Caribbean. And where the rocks end, the lovingly tended verdure of Trident's manicured lawns begin, dotted with palm trees, gazebos, and flowers. The one- and two-story white cottages and villas are scattered along the edge of the cliffs, providing maximum privacy and panoramic impact. Each of the 27 accommodations is different and delightful, and all come furnished with antiques and have large balconies or verandas. But the pièce de résistance will surely be the view of the pounding surf, just beyond your terrace. Each room has a large paddle fan, to enhance the cooling trade winds that usually comfort this coast.

The ambience is a gracious blend of Jamaican plantation hospitality and English country house tradition. Waiters in crisp uniforms walk along the paths, ferrying breakfasts to the guests. High tea becomes high art when served on white linen tableclothes on the brick terrace. Adding the final regal touch, white and blue peacocks and peahens strut regally across the ample lawn. No wonder the hotel attracts a regular clientele among the rich and famous, including Peter O'Toole, Jimmy Cliff, and Twiggy.

Trident has a small, private beach with a protected sand cove for swimming. If you get hungry or thirsty, the beach boy will whisk lunch and cocktails right to your chaise longue. In addition, there's a stunning free-form pool by the main house (it's been photographed for several magazines). The little gazebo at the end makes a cozy nook for two lovers to gaze out over the blue, blue Caribbean. A member of "The Elegant Resorts of Jamaica." Honeymoon package: Eight-day/seven-night "Elegant Platinum" package (FAP): Low season—$2,345 per couple for a junior suite; $2,960 per couple for a villa. Includes all meals, bar drinks, round-trip transfers between airport and hotel, bottle of champagne, fresh flowers and fruit basket, special gift, taxes and service charges, and more. High-season rates (MAP): $330 per couple per night for a junior suite; $440 for a villa.

All-Inclusive

Fern Hill Club, P.O. Box 100, Port Antonio, Jamaica, W.I. (tel. 809/993-3222; U.S. reservations: toll free 800/423-4095). "You've got to see this place," said the honeymoon couple we met while rafting on the Rio Grande. "We love it and are coming back for our first anniversary next year." We took their advice—and discovered Fern Hill Club, which must be one of the best-kept secrets in the Caribbean. A secret, at least, to most Americans—the property is Canadian-owned and is extremely popular with vacationers from Canada, especially honeymooners. Fern Hill Club is an all-inclusive resort, with accommodations both in deluxe and standard rooms, as well as extremely spacious, well-appointed, and modern villas. The villas are nestled in the foothills of the Blue Mountains, and offer travel-poster-caliber views of Port Antonio, just a ten-minute drive away. Villa accommodations each have different, but assuredly impeccable, furnishings, and fully equipped kitchens. Not that you'll have to cook—meals are served down at the main building on one of the three patios. Floor-to-ceiling louvers all around guarantee a breezy island ambience. (There's also air conditioning.)

Fern Hill's hillside location precludes a beach on the property, but they run a free shuttle to the beach at San San. There's complimentary snorkeling and windsurfing, as well as tennis. Every day, you can participate in special activities— sightseeing tours through Maroon country, trips to the Rio Grande for rafting, beach parties, and sunset cruises, as well as live entertainment nightly. And, our honeymooning friends ask us to add, "The staff really make the place. They'll help you with anything you need. Just great people!" Honeymoon package: None. Villas: From $1,585 per couple per week. Standard rooms: From $1,320 per week. Includes airport transfers; welcome rum punch; breakfast, lunch, and dinner daily; beer, local liquors, and wine with dinner; shuttle bus to beaches. A $150 per couple service charge will also be added.

Moderately Expensive

The **Admiralty Club at Navy Island,** P.O. Box 188, Port Antonio, Jamaica, W.I. (tel. 809/993-2667). A mere dollop of an island afloat in Port Antonio's west harbor, Navy Island embraces a more romantic history than that of many nations. Originally a British naval station, the cay was supposedly won by suave actor Errol Flynn in a card game, and used by him as a personal hideaway. Today, the Admiralty Club resort on the island ranks as one of the nicest spots in the world on which to be a castaway . . . 64 acres of paradise. Certainly, Robinson Crusoe never had it so good. The lifestyle here is decidedly casual and relaxed: leave those jackets and high heels at home. Sporting names such as Skylark and Enchantment, each of the thatch-roofed cottages is completely in tune with nature. There's no air conditioning; instead, all-around louvered windows and ceiling fans enhance the cooling trade breezes. Much of the furniture is handcrafted right on the premises—when we were visiting, for example, carpenters were turning and polishing a new table and chairs for one of the villas. Play tennis on the new court, or enjoy excellent snorkeling along one of the offshore reefs. Or just plunk your towel on one of the beaches: Navy Island has three, including a secluded "clothes-optional" strand. Watch the sun set over the Blue Mountains as you sip a drink at the Bounty Bar, or enjoy a fine meal in the Fountain Room or Orchid Terrace (local fishermen bring in the day's catch, flopping fresh). There's no need to get island fever—the ferry to the mainland runs 24 hours a day. And down at the waterfront, you can see the longboat that Errol Flynn reputedly used to ferry maidens to island trysts. Honeymoon package: None. Rates (BP): $155 to $215 per couple per night.

Goblin Hill Villas at San San, P.O. Box 26, Port Antonio, Jamaica, W.I. (tel. 809/993-3286 or 993-3049; U.S. reservations: toll free 800/423-4095). For escapists, one of Jamaica's most perfect hideaways is this 12-acre hilltop estate in Port Antonio's most exclusive residential area, where families with last names such as Woolworth and Molson (of the brewing fortune) maintain vacation retreats. There are just 28 serene two-story villas, each individually decorated with island touches such as Jamaican cedar furnishings and tropical flower fabrics. Bedrooms are air-conditioned. Best of all, each villa is staffed with a housekeeper who will come in and prepare your meals. Many of the cooks take pride in showing off their family recipes, so be prepared for some delicious renditions of Jamaican specialties. Pathways wind through the velvety lawns down to San San Beach, a magnificent strand (you can snorkel over to a small islet just offshore). Right at the resort, you can bronze yourselves by the pretty freshwater pool or play tennis (both courts are lighted). In the afternoon, guests gather for cocktails in the lounge, settling into the high-backed rattan chairs to discuss the day's activities. All in all, for independently minded honeymooners, it adds up to quite a nice way to go. Honeymoon package: None. Rates (EP): $1,190 to $1,850 per couple per week. Includes transfers by chauffeured car from Kingston airport, use of a rental car, and services of a housekeeper/cook.

Inexpensive

Bonnie View Hotel, P.O. Box 82, Port Antonio, Jamaica, W.I. (tel. 809/993-2752). As the sign out front will tell you, this is one of the oldest continuously operating hotels in Jamaica. The view, in fact, does live up to its name: Set some 600 feet above Port Antonio, the panorama encompasses the east and west harbors to the north, the Blue Mountains to the southwest. The rooms themselves are quite simple but very tidy, with plain tile floors, private bathrooms with showers, and jalousie windows, which take advantage of the cool upcountry breezes (no air conditioning, because it's usually 10° cooler here than in town). Each room has a private balcony facing the mountains or sea. There's a large freshwater pool, and the dining terrace makes a very attractive perch for a light lunch. In the evenings, you can dance to calypso music at the bar pavilion. Honeymoon package: None. Double room: $60 per couple per night year-round.

ROMANTIC RESTAURANTS

From elegant restaurants with white-glove service to casual stands by the sea, Port Antonio offers something to please everyone.

Expensive

Trident Hotel Restaurant (tel. 993-2602). A silver candelabra flames on the table set with English bone china and fine cutlery. Antique tapestries and crystal chandeliers adorn the white stone walls. Another world . . . almost another century

. . . that's the feeling captured when you dine at the Trident Restaurant. Dinner is served promptly at eight, a five-course fixed-menu gourmet treat that gracefully balances both Jamaican and continental dishes, exquisitely prepared. The waiter, wearing a red vest, starched white shirt, black bow tie, and—yes—white gloves, murmurs the name of each dish as he serves it. "Blinis, sir, served with Russian caviar." "How would you like your roast beef, madam?" (said as he wheels a silver trolley to your table). "Jamaica fruits flambéed." "Viennese pastries." After dinner, there's a musical combo at the bar, or an occasional spur-of-the-moment sing-along around the grand piano in the Oriental-carpeted lounge. The fixed dinner costs $45 per person; served nightly 8 to 10 p.m. Jackets and ties required for men in the winter season; jackets only, May to December; cocktail attire for ladies. Reservations required. They also serve an absolutely storybook afternoon tea on the seaside terrace, with the geometrically perfect sliced cheese sandwiches and melt-in-your-mouth raisin cookies. Served daily from 4:30 to 5:30 p.m.; about $10 per couple.

Inexpensive

Blue Lagoon Cafe, Blue Lagoon (no phone). If you've seen the movie *Club Paradise,* this thatch-roofed building with decks right on the Blue Lagoon might look familiar—it was built as one of the sets. Now, it's enjoying a new incarnation as a casual beach bar . . . a wonderful place to while away a languid afternoon. The food is Jamaican and wonderful, with tasty offerings such as pumpkin soup, fish escabeche, smoked marlin, and codfish fritters. Open daily from 10 a.m. to 6:30 p.m.; about $25 to $30 per couple.

Boston Bay Beach (no phones). The beachside stands at Boston Beach are generally conceded to have the best jerk pork and jerk chicken on the island. After all, the dish originated here, a staple of the Maroons who inhabited the nearby hinterlands. Portions are sold by weight—a half pound to three-quarters of a pound should do you nicely, and cost about $5. Just dig in with your fingers. Afterward, take a siesta, then cool off with a swim. Boston Beach, located east of Port Antonio and the Blue Lagoon, is a public beach, donated to the government during the 1950s by Robin Moore, author of *The Green Berets.*

The terrace at **Bonnie View Hotel** (tel. 993-2752) serves light sandwiches and salads for lunch, with a side order of the best views of Port Antonio and Navy Island. About $10 to $15 per person. Open daily for lunch, noon to 2:30 p.m.; dinner, 7 to 9:30 p.m. Built by an old sea captain in typical New England style, **DeMontevin Lodge** (tel. 993-2604) is the place to head for soul-satisfying Jamaican food—pepperpot soup, breadfruit, home-style chicken with vegetables, and desserts such as banana cream pie. Dinners about $20 per person. Open daily for lunch, noon to 2 p.m.; dinner, 7 to 9 p.m.

Into the night, one of the hottest, happening spots anywhere is the **Roof Club** (no phone), which attracts a party-happy blend of Portlanders plus visiting movie stars and miscellaneous blue bloods.

---

7. Elsewhere in Jamaica

Natania's Guest House, Little Culloden, Whitehouse P.O., Westmoreland, Jamaica, W.I. (no phone). If you really, really want to get away from it all, this could be the place—a secluded retreat on Jamaica's little-known south coast, about an hour's drive from Negril. There are only eight rooms, finished with coral stone (downstairs) and stucco (upstairs). Neatly furnished (all have king-size beds), the accommodations feature tile floors and louvered windows to let in the trade winds; all offer sea views and spic-and-span private bathrooms. When you want to relax, make yourselves cozy in the large hammock on your balcony or terrace. The beach is small but startlingly white, framed by dramatic limestone boulders. Deep-sea fishing and snorkeling are available. In the evening, enjoy cocktails at the Tiki bar (sublime sunset views), then dine in the excellent restaurant, specializing in lobster, fish, and steak. Natania's makes a great base for exploring the south coast. Head over to the town of Black River, where crumbling—yet still majestic—Victorian mansions line the waterfront; then stop in Whitehouse at one of the roadside stands that sell zingy pepper shrimp and fish, and fresh bammy. Yum . . . Honeymoon package: None. Rates (EP): $40 to $50 per couple per night.

XXIV

MARTINIQUE

1. PRACTICAL FACTS
2. ROMANTIC INTERLUDES
3. HONEYMOON HOTELS AND HIDEAWAYS
4. ROMANTIC RESTAURANTS AND NIGHTSPOTS

Nibbling freshly baked croissants, a newly married couple breakfasts at a seaside café. They think of the gourmet meal they had the night before prepared by an award-winning French chef. Snatches of French conversations float by as they gaze into the harbor filled with masted boats. That afternoon, they are planning to drive through the hilly countryside sprinkled with red-roof houses. No, they are not in the French Riviera. It's true that they are honeymooning on French soil, but they are not in France. The sun glistens on the Caribbean, not the Mediterranean. The ancestors of most of the people they see came from Africa, not Europe. And in addition to French, they've heard the musical patois called Creole. They are in Martinique, in the French West Indies.

Separated by Dominica from Guadeloupe, its sister island, 425-square-mile Martinique is in the eastern Caribbean. About 320,000 people call it home. Residents are quick to remind visitors that their mountainous island is as much a part of France as Hawaii is of the United States. While the serene Caribbean Sea soothes one side, the tumultuous Atlantic throws itself against the other.

Start getting acquainted with the island in Fort-de-France, the capital. Backed by mist-covered mountains, this city faces a busy harbor. Wander along the narrow, winding streets, past women selling fruits and vegetables by buildings with fretwork balconies. Ferries cruise across the bay to Pointe du Bout and Anse Mitan, the two main beach resorts. Some of the island's best restaurants are here, along with stunning beaches where snorkeling is particularly colorful, and there are hotels in all shapes and sizes. The only casino on the island is in Pointe du Bout.

A drive north of Pointe du Bout along the Caribbean coast will take you past sugarcane fields, banana plantations, and undulating hills. Small fishing villages dot the shore. Diamant, a small village in the south, is known for the massive rock that juts 600 feet out of the ocean just offshore. Some of the island's most attractive beaches are in this area.

As palm trees sway in the breeze and the clear water ripples turquoise, then navy, Martinique will give honeymooners more than a taste of France.

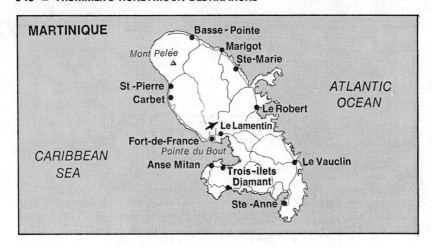

1. Practical Facts

GETTING THERE

Americans must have a valid passport, a passport that has expired within five years, a voter registration card, or an authenticated birth certificate. For Canadians, a passport is necessary. You'll also need to show a return or ongoing ticket. The departure tax will be included in your air fare.

Whether you fly or sail, traveling to Martinique is hassle-free.

By Air

Martinique is about three hours from Miami and just over four from New York. All international flights land at Lamentin Airport, about five miles from the capital of Fort-de-France. **American Airlines** offers flights from New York, Newark, and other U.S. cities via San Juan. **Air France** will fly you in from Miami or San Juan, and **Air Canada** from Montreal and Toronto. Both **Air Martinique** and **LIAT,** the Caribbean's local airline, connect Martinique with other Caribbean islands.

By Sea

If you decide to sail to Martinique, you'll have a wide choice of boats, from yachts with fewer than 100 passengers to enormous vessels with over a thousand. The pools, health spas, nightly entertainment, and seemingly endless meals make some of the larger ships seem like floating hotels.

Carnival Cruise Lines (tel. toll free 800/327-9501), for instance, offers seven-night cruises on the *Festivale*. Among the many facilities are three outdoor pools and a casino. Leaving from San Juan on Sundays, year-round, the ship stops at St. Thomas, St. Martin, and Barbados as well as Martinique. The cost is from $2,050 to $4,500 per couple, including air fare to San Juan from 100 U.S. cities.

If you prefer something smaller, the *Mandalay,* a 72-passenger yacht launched in 1923, takes 12-night sails throughout the year between Grenada and Antigua. In addition to Martinique, ports include Mustique in the Grenadines and Les Saintes off Guadeloupe. The cost is $2,730 and up per couple. Contact **Windjammer Barefoot Cruises** (U.S. tel.: 212/686-4868).

GETTING AROUND
With taxis, buses, and cars for rent, on-island transportation is convenient.

By Taxi
You'll find taxi stands at the airport, downtown Fort-de-France, and the larger hotels. Cabs are not metered, so be sure to check at your hotel to find out how much your ride should be. The fare from the airport to Pointe du Bout hotels runs about $25 for two people with luggage. Note that between 8 p.m. and 6 a.m., fares increase by 40%. If you speak some French and you want to save money, look for collective taxis (TCs). These eight-seat limousines and vans congregate at Pointe Simon on the waterfront in Fort-de-France and run from early morning to about 6 p.m.

Taxi tours are most economical when you join forces with another couple. A half-day sightseeing tour will run from about $50 to $75 for two to four passengers. Many drivers speak some English.

By Bus
For a half day or full day of sightseeing by bus, try **Madinina Tours** (tel. 73-35-35) in Fort-de-France or **Carib Tours** (tel. 66-02-56) in Pointe du Bout. Tours include historic sites, dramatic scenery, beaches, and often stops at restaurants for creole specialties.

By Ferry
Ferries, or *vedettes,* as they are called locally, go between the Quai d'Esnambuc at the Fort-de-France harbor and the resort areas of Pointe du Bout, Anse Mitan, and Anse-à-l'Ane. The fare is about $2 each way or $3 round trip. While the boats go to and from Pointe du Bout from early morning until about midnight, boats to the other two areas stop running in the late afternoon.

By Rental Car
You'll need a valid driver's license to rent a car. Most roads are well marked and well paved, but many of the most scenic are narrow and winding, so drive carefully. Especially during the winter season, it is best to make advance reservations for a rental car. In Martinique, you'll find rental agencies at the airport, in Fort-de-France, and at some hotels. As in France, agencies and other businesses close for lunch from about noon to 2:30 p.m.

The following companies are among those that have offices in both the United States and Martinique: **Avis** (airport: tel. 51-26-86; Fort-de-France: tel. 70-11-60), **Budget** (airport: tel. 51-22-88; Fort-de-France: tel. 70-22-75), and **Hertz** (airport: tel. 51-28-22; Fort-de-France: tel. 60-64-64). You'll save a few dollars at local companies, such as **Carib Rent-a-Car** (tel. 51-19-33) at the airport; **Royal Car** (tel. 70-62-49) and **Tropicar** (tel. 60-55-28), both in Fort-de-France; and **Safari Car** (tel. 66-06-26) in Anse Mitan. If you don't have plastic, be prepared to put down a cash deposit of between $180 and $300.

LANGUAGE
French is the official language. Creole, a patois incorporating words from French, Spanish, English, and West African languages, is also widely spoken. Front-desk staff members of some restaurants and the larger hotels speak some English, but you'll need to know at least a little French if you plan to do much exploring. If you don't speak French, be sure to take along a phrase book and a dictionary.

MONEY AND TIPPING
The French franc is the official currency of Martinique, and its value in relation to the dollar changes daily. Local banks give better exchange rates than hotels. Banks

are open Monday through Friday, from 7:30 a.m. to 4 p.m., and are closed for lunch from noon to 2:30 p.m. U.S. dollars are accepted at some shops, restaurants, and hotels. In addition, several stores give an additional 20% discount when you make purchases using certain credit cards or traveler's checks in dollar denominations. Most large hotels accept credit cards.

The tip (or service charge) is often included in restaurant checks and hotel rates, in which case it is not necessary to leave a tip for your room maid. Ask if you're not sure. Tip 10% to 15% when the service charge is not included. Porters don't usually expect tips, but if you'd like, you can give one franc per bag. Most cab drivers don't expect to be tipped either.

WEATHER

Daytime temperatures average in the high 70s and low 80s year-round, with the weather somewhat warmer during the summer months. Evening temperatures can be 5° to 10° cooler. Refreshing trade winds blow continually and rainfall is usually too brief to disrupt the beach scene for long.

CLOTHING

The attire in Martinique is generally casually chic. Women tend to wear dressier evening outfits during the winter season than during the summer. Pack a shawl or light sweater for cool nights or air-conditioned restaurants and clubs. Men rarely wear jackets at dinner, and ties are seldom seen. Bikini tops are scarce on most hotel beaches. Beachwear should be restricted to poolside and seaside.

ELECTRICAL CURRENT

Unlike the United States, electricity is 220 volts AC, 50 cycles, so you'll need converters and adapter plugs for your iron, razor, hairdryer, or any other electrical appliances you might bring. Some of the larger hotels will lend converters and adapters to guests, but it's best to bring your own.

TIME

Martinique is on Atlantic Standard Time, which is one hour later than Eastern Standard Time. During the winter this means that when it is 9 a.m. in New York, it is 10 a.m. in Martinique. However, when Daylight Saving Time is in effect, the time is the same in Martinique and U.S. East Coast cities. You'll notice that time is told in the French way here, so that, for example, 1 p.m. is called 13 hours.

TELEPHONES

To call Martinique from the United States directly, dial 011-596, then the six-digit local number.

SHOPPING

Martinique offers bargains on an array of honeymoon mementos. Although the island is not duty free, the 20% tax reduction discount on luxury items purchased with traveler's checks or credit cards makes for some excellent bargains. Together the two of you can take home up to $800 worth of goods duty free. The best buys by far are in French imports, including designer fashions, perfume, and fine wines. Local rum is also a popular purchase. The majority of the island's shops line the narrow side streets of Fort-de-France. Most stores close from about noon until 2:30 p.m. during the week. Unless you like crowds, avoid shopping when cruise ships are in, and on Saturdays, when stores are only open in the morning.

For a wide selection of crystal, china, cosmetics, jewelry, watches, and leather goods, head for **Roger Albert** (on rue Victor Hugo). The treasure trove at **Cadet Daniel** (on rue Antoine Siger) includes gold and silver jewelry, Lalique crystal, and Limoges china. Roger Albert and Cadet Daniel are two of the stores that give additional discounts on items bought with some credit cards and travelers' checks.

Near the cathedral, **Au Printemps** (on rue Schoelcher) is a branch of the famous Parisian department store. It carries a good selection of French fashions, fancy kitchen gadgets, gourmet foods, and other imports. You'll also find small boutiques in the capital selling French resortwear for both women and men, such as skimpy high-fashion bikinis and Cardin bathing trunks.

In addition to imports, Martinique has some tempting home-grown goods. **La Case à Rhum** (avenue de la Liberté) sells local rums and other alcohol. Take a stroll through **La Savane,** an attractively landscaped park where crafts are sold. You'll see handmade creole dolls clad in bright madras dresses and the island's trademark bakoua hat (pointed and wide-brimmed). Then recover from all your shopping by relaxing at a café along the Rue de la Liberté side of the park, or by the Statue of Empress Josephine.

While you're touring the Atlantic coast, stop in at **Ella,** a gourmet boutique specializing in local spices, homemade preserves, jams, and liqueurs. Just north of Trinité, this pleasant shop is in the village of Bézaudin, near Sainte-Marie. On the way back to the city on the road from Le Robert, stop in at **Laurent-Marie,** where you'll find clothing made of madras cloth (or decorated with silk-screened designs) and other items made by local artisans.

CASINOS

Feeling lucky? There's a casino at the Méridien hotel in Pointe du Bout. Men don't need jackets and ties, but dress tends to be elegantly casual. You may be asked to show some form of identification with a photograph. The casino is open nightly from 9 p.m. to 3 a.m.; admission is about $10. Proof of identity is required.

HOW TO GET MARRIED IN MARTINIQUE

In order to tie the knot on this tropical island, one partner must have resided in the French West Indies for at least 30 days prior to filing the marriage license application. Applications are available at the local *mairie* (town hall) upon presentation of a birth certificate, proof of citizenship, proof of divorce (if applicable), and a medical certificate—all accompanied by French translations. For the medical certificate, a list of qualified English-speaking doctors is available from the American Consulate in Martinique (Immeuble Place Père Labat, 14 rue Blenac, 97206 Fort-de-France, Martinique, F.W.I.; tel. 596-63-13-03) or your local French Consulate.

After filing the application, allow at least ten days for the publication and posting of the marriage banns (the official announcement of your intention to marry). You may be asked to take a blood test, and witnesses will be necessary. A religious wedding may only be performed *after* the civil service. The minister, priest, or rabbi must be given a certificate of civil marriage (*certificat de célébration civile*) before performing the religious ceremony.

FOR FURTHER INFORMATION

Contact the **French West Indies Tourist Board,** 610 Fifth Ave., New York, NY 10020, tel. 212/757-1125; **Office Departemental du Tourisme de la Martinique,** B.P. 520, 97206 Fort-de-France, Martinique, French West Indies, (001)596/63-79-60.

2. Romantic Interludes

The legacy of famous lovers, secluded natural wonders, and activities best done in pairs make Martinique perfect for newlyweds.

Le Jardin de Balata (tel. 64-48-73) is a tropical botanical garden deep in a thick rain forest. To get here from Fort-de-France, you'll drive for 20 to 30 minutes up a steep, winding road through the picturesque suburb of Didier and you'll look down on the busy capital. In the garden, paths are bordered by ferns as large as trees, fragrant multicolored flowers, and gurgling brooks. Their peaks caught in the clouds, mountains stand in the distance. The reception area, in the gracious 60-year-old vacation home of the owner's grandmother, is attractively decorated with antiques and old photographs of island residents. Dolls, colorfully decked out in madras outfits, are on display along with bright creole hats once worn by local women. Le Jardin de Balata is open every day from 9 a.m. to 5 p.m. and admission is about $5. On your way back to Fort-de-France, stop at **Sacre Coeur de Balata,** a lovely church that bears a startling resemblance to its Parisian namesake.

Following La Trace road to the Atlantic side of the island, you'll cross one of the most spectacular parts of the rain forest. Towering bamboo and high walls of vegetation in endless variations of green create a tunnel-like passageway.

Pack a **picnic lunch**—maybe some freshly baked croissants, cheese, a bottle of wine, a few ripe mangoes—and drive to **Caravelle,** a scenic peninsula that pokes out into the Atlantic near Trinité. There are marked hiking trails in this idyllic nature preserve, as well as the impressive **ruins of Dubuc Castle,** once the home of a wealthy 18th-century family. The only remains are the crumbling walls of the castle and slave cells, a dam, a mill, and sheep pens. You can tour the ruins every day from 8:30 a.m. to 12:30 p.m. and from 2:30 to 5:30 p.m. Admission is about $1. The view is truly breathtaking.

Martinique has several intriguing museums—all small enough to squeeze in between trips to the beach. Begin at the **Musée de la Pagerie** (tel. 68-34-55) near the village of Trois Ilets, a brief ferry ride from Fort-de-France. The museum sits on the grounds of the plantation where Napoleon's empress Josephine was born in 1763. Along with portraits of the Empress, her bed, and invitations to balls in Paris, you'll find a steamy love letter she received from Napoleon (with an English translation). The admission is about $1 per person, and the museum is closed on Mondays.

North of here, **Carbet** is the place where Columbus is said to have landed. This village is also known for its unusual dark-sand beaches. Here the **Gauguin Museum** (tel. 77-22-66) commemorates the work completed by the legendary French painter during his four-month stay on the island in 1887. The museum is open every day from 10 a.m. to 5 p.m. Admission is about $1.75.

Farther north, you'll come to **Saint-Pierre.** Once a sophisticated city called "the Paris of the West Indies," it was two centuries old in 1902 when the now-dormant Mont Pelée volcano erupted violently. Three minutes was all it took to destroy the entire city, killing the 30,000 inhabitants. At the **Musée Volcanologique** (tel. 77-15-16), remains of the disaster are on display—petrified spaghetti, a half-full bottle of perfume fused shut, a huge melted church bell, disfigured clocks all stopped at the same time. The museum is open every day from 9 a.m. to noon and from 3 to 5 p.m. Admission is about $1.

The golden expanse in southern Martinique known as **Les Salines** is easily one of the most stunning beaches in the Caribbean. At one end of the crescent, you'll see the silhouette of Le Diamant in the distance. You may find it difficult to tear yourselves away from these calm turquoise waters. But keep in mind that there are some excellent creole restaurants nearby that are great for lunch.

Trot on horseback through sugarcane fields, past banana plantations, and along scenic mountainsides and seashores. **Black Horse** (tel. 66-00-44) in La Pagerie will even have riders picked up in and returned to Pointe du Bout, about 15 minutes from the stables. The cost is about $25 per person for the 1½-hour ride.

For bareboat or skippered **yacht charters,** try **Star Voyages Antilles** (tel. 66-00-72) at the Pointe du Bout Marina or **Ship-Shop** (tel. 71-43-40) in Fort-de-France. Yacht charters range about $400 a weekend for a yacht with two double cabins to about $3,000 a week for one that sleeps eight.

3. Honeymoon Hotels and Hideaways

The hotel you choose will depend on whether you want to be in the thick of things, a stone's throw from the action, or as far away from it as possible. In addition to modern beachfront high-rises and medium-size hotels, there are cozy inns, collectively known as the Relais Créoles. Some are in historic homes; many are renowned for their excellent creole cuisine; all are friendly, casual, and best for visitors who speak at least a little French.

Most of Martinique's tourist hotels speckle the waterfront in the Pointe du Bout/Anse Mitan area, a brief ferry ride from the capital. This is where the nightlife is the liveliest—beginning with some of the island's most popular restaurants, a casino, and musical entertainment. If you're looking for seclusion, consider Leyritz Plantation, up north in Basse-Pointe, or Manoir de Beauregard, down south in Sainte-Anne near the island's most breathtaking beaches.

High season runs from about mid-December through mid-April; low-season rates dip about 20% to 50%. The price ranges given for hotels in this chapter reflect the difference between low- and high-season rates. A 10% or 15% tax and service charge is generally included in room rates. In some resort areas, you'll also pay an additional government tax of approximately $1 per person per day.

MODERATE

Leyritz Plantation, 97218 Basse-Pointe, Martinique, F.W.I. (tel. 596/75-53-92; U.S. reservations 212/477-1600, or toll free 800/223-1510). Tucked away at the northern end of the island, the 50-room Leyritz Plantation blends modern comforts with living history. The old rum distiller has been turned into a health spa where you can pamper yourselves in the solarium, Jacuzzi, or massage rooms. Dormitories for plantation workers have been transformed into guest rooms, and the main house is furnished with antiques including oriental rugs and day beds. Stone walkways wind past lush vegetation and old buildings with red-tile roofs. From the hotel, you can appreciate the sweeping vistas of banana groves and distant mountains. Hosts Charles and Yveline de Lucy de Fossarieu give people the personalized attention that brings guests back year after year. The restaurant draws people from all over the island for lunch. When you want a break from the swimming pool, transportation is provided to a nearby beach. Almost a two-hour drive from the capital or the airport, Leyritz Plantation is for people who want total relaxation. Honeymoon package: None. Rates (EP): $112 to $168 per couple per night. Health spa packages available.

Bakoua Beach Hotel, Pointe du Bout, 97229 Trois-Îlets, Martinique, F.W.I. (tel. 596/66-02-02; U.S. reservations: 914/472-0370, or toll free 800/221-4542). The name of this hotel comes from the pointed, broad-brimmed straw hats worn by fishermen. Swaying palms, frangipani, and other bright flowers surround the hillside and oceanfront buildings. Some of the 140 rooms have balconies that face the water while the patios of others are right on the beach. Many members of the friendly, accommodating staff have worked here for years, and the resort is a favorite of visiting celebrities (Jean-Paul Belmondo and Paul McCartney stayed here). Bakoua Beach offers a variety of water sports, tennis courts, and a pool perched high above the ocean. During the afternoons and evenings, the circular bar is a popular hangout. In the adjoining Châteaubriand, the large open-air beachfront dining room, a thatch roof covers the dance area. Dinner is accompanied by live music. The chef blends the best of French cooking with creole specialties. Once a week, an elaborate buffet is followed by a performance of Les Grands Ballets de la Martinique, which shows off the island's African roots. Honeymoon package: None. Rates (CP): $230 to $308 per couple per night.

PLM Azur Carayou, Pointe du Bout, 97229 Trois-Îlets, Martinique, F.W.I.

(tel. 596/66-04-04; U.S. reservations: 212/757-6500, or toll free 800/223-9862). Formerly the Frantel Martinique, this 200-room hotel sits at the edge of the bay facing Fort-de-France. The grounds, which resemble a botanical garden, are interlaced with footpaths. Balconied rooms in bungalows look out to the bay, the marina, or the flower-filled gardens. Guests can swim or sunbathe at the beach or float in the circular swimming pool and gaze at the bay. Sports include sailing and tennis. If you want TV and closed-circuit video, book a deluxe room. Boutiques on the premises make shopping convenient and Le Vesou discotheque is one of the island's hottest spots. Honeymoon package: None. Rates (EP): $120 to $168 per couple per night.

Hôtel Méridien–Trois Ilets, Fort-de-France CEDEX, 97229 P.O. Box 894, Martinique, F.W.I. (tel. 596/66-00-00; U.S. reservations: 212/265-4494, or toll free 800/543-4300). If you like being near other hotels and you don't want to go far to gamble, the Méridien, with a casino on the premises, is a good place to stay. Not only are there many other hotels within walking distance, but the Méridien is right near the dock for the ferry to Fort-de-France, just across the bay. The breezy lobby is open to the palm-shaded pool. At the small beach, Windsurfers and other water-sports equipment are free to guests. Take the full-day picnic sail on the *Old Nick* with Captain Cap at the helm, or board the glass-bottomed *Aquarius* for a snorkeling trip. Room service is available 24 hours a day in the 303 guest rooms, some of which have king-size beds. The Anthurium restaurant is known for its delicious gourmet food and Von Von disco is the place to shake a leg or two. Honeymoon package: Four days/three nights (CP): $640 per couple; or eight days/seven nights (CP): $1,560 per couple. Includes welcome punch and champagne on arrival, two T-shirts, cap and two introductory scuba lessons.

Le Calalou Hotel, 97229 Anse-à-l'Ane, Martinique, F.W.I. (tel. 596/68-31-78; U.S. reservations: 212/840-6636, or toll free 800/223-9815). On a beautiful beach a short drive from other hotels, Le Calalou attracts many guests from France and Canada. Visitors enter the open-air reception area after walking along a palm-lined path, under an awning, and through a wrought-iron gate. Her limbs elongated, the abstract statue of a woman holding a broken chain above her head stands in tribute to the abolition of slavery. Upholstered rattan decorates the beachfront bar/sitting area, while white garden furniture fills the breezy dining room. Tall palms and flowering bushes grow in abundance on the property. The 36 air-conditioned rooms in bungalows, some of which are right on the water, are cheerfully done in wicker and bright colors. Some rooms have double beds and terra-cotta tile patios. There is a barbecue every Friday night in season. Fort-de-France is a ferry ride away. Calalou is closed in October. Honeymoon package: None. Rates (MAP): $177 to $195 per couple per night.

Diamant-Novotel, Pointe de la Chéry, 97223, Le Diamant, Martinique, F.W.I. (tel. 596/76-42-42; U.S. reservations: 914/472-0370, or toll free 800/221-4542). This self-contained resort buzzes with activity. Staying here, you may not feel the urge to wander far. To get to the round dining room from the open lobby, you'll walk over a bridge stretching across the large pool. The 180 individual rooms and suites have recently been completely refurbished. The pristine accommodations now boast TVs and direct-dial telephones, and there's a new restaurant that overlooks both the protected bay and the ocean. Scuba facilities and licensed instructors are available at the hotel's beach, and other beaches are nearby. For many, evenings bring visits to the nightclub. When you make reservations, simply let the hotel know you're honeymooners and you'll receive V.I.P. treatment. Your room will be upgraded to a seaview accommodation and, along with a fruit basket, you'll find a bottle of chilled champagne in your room upon arrival. Honeymoon package: None. Rates (EP): $165 to $240 per couple per night.

Hôtel Relais Caraïbes, La Chéry, 97223 Le Diamant, Martinique, F.W.I. (tel. 596/76-44-65). This brand-new property is perched high above Martinique's southern coast, not far from the activity at Diamant-Novotel. From the patio around the pool you have a bird's-eye view of both Diamond Rock and Morne Larcher, a mountain formation that resembles the head and shoulders of a reclining woman. The main building, overlooking the pool and patio, houses the restaurant, lounge, and gift shop; 12 private bungalows with gingerbread fretwork and tiled patios cling to the hillside. Each three-room bungalow is decorated in cool pastel shades and has the most modern amenities, including air-conditioning, direct-dial telephones, and a TV in the sitting room. Identify yourselves as a honeymoon couple and you'll get extra-special treatment, including a celebratory bottle of champagne. Honeymoon package: None. Rates (EP): $110 per couple per night.

Manoir de Beauregard, 97227 Sainte-Anne, Martinique, F.W.I. (tel. 596/76-73-40; U.S. reservations: 212/832-2277, or toll free 800/223-6510). An ornate wrought-iron gate thrown wide invites you into this 18th-century manor house. The stark-white building with thick stone walls is set off by a weathered orange-tile roof. Wicker rockers, a wicker couch, a heavy dark-wood desk, and gray-and-white-checkered tiles made of marble decorate the reception area. The 27 air-conditioned rooms are furnished with high four-poster beds, tall armoires, and other antiques. All rooms have modern baths. Manoir de Beauregard has a swimming pool and the hotel is a short drive from Les Salines, considered by many to be the island's best beach. It is also within walking distance of the town of Sainte-Anne. Honeymoon package: None. Rates (CP): $126 per couple per night.

INEXPENSIVE

The first in the area, the **Auberge de l'Anse Mitan,** Anse-Mitan, 97229 Trois-Îlets, Martinique, F.W.I. (tel. 596/66-01-12; U.S. reservations: 212/840-6636, or toll free 800/223-9815), has long been popular with vacationing Martiniquais. The small white building sits at the edge of the bay and guests dine on the shaded veranda facing the water. The cozy dark-paneled lobby is shared with the bar and sitting room, whose walls are hung with maps. Tiled floors give this inn a European flavor. All of the 20 guest rooms are air-conditioned. Five are huge, and some have two double beds. Old photos and drawings decorate the walls, making the rooms truly home-like. Honeymoon package: None. Rates (EP): $65 per couple per night.

Saint-Aubin Hotel, B.P. 52, 97220 Trinité, Martinique, F.W.I. (tel. 596/69-34-77; U.S. reservations: 212/840-6636, or toll free 800/223-9815). Perched on a hill overlooking the Atlantic, a carpet of sugarcane fields, and colorful gardens, St. Aubin was once a private home. It was built around the turn of the century and has been painstakingly restored by Guy Foret, a former restaurant owner originally from Normandy. This small hotel is an excellent place to perfect the art of enjoying undisturbed peace and quiet. Wide, airy verandas, with gingerbread fretwork railings, surround both the ground floor and the second story. Just inside the salmon-colored building, high archways lead to a tiled sitting area furnished in blond wicker. Across the entranceway, the sunny dining room opens onto the front veranda. The hotel's 15 rooms, with double beds or twins, all have private baths. Take a dip in the pool or head for the beach in Trinité, a five-minute drive away. Honeymoon package: None. Rates (EP): $81 per couple per night.

---

4. Romantic Restaurants and Nightspots

For visitors and Martiniquais alike, eating out is a cherished activity. Whether you have a taste for elegant French cuisine, highly seasoned creole dishes, or a marriage of the two, you'll find a surprisingly wide selection of excellent restaurants. Most are in the Fort-de-France/Pointe du Bout/Anse Mitan area, connected by ferries. If you stay in another part of the island, dining out and evening entertainment will center around your hotel.

You'll need reservations for dinner at the most popular restaurants—and it's difficult to find a restaurant in Martinique that isn't popular. Escargots and soufflés will tempt you on some menus. On others you'll find creole specialties such as accras (bite-size cod or shrimp fritters), blaff (fish stew spiced with garlic, lime, and bay rum berries), crabes farcis (stuffed crabs), and langouste (clawless native lobster). Land-lubbers can begin with creole blood sausage or paté en pot (a thick mutton soup), then try tender beef or chicken dishes. Meals are accompanied by French wine and potent rum punch made with fruits such as coconut, guava, and pineapple.

La Grand' Voile, Pointe Simon, Fort-de-France (tel. 70-29-29). The high point of many a vacation in Martinique is a meal at this restaurant overlooking the bay. Near the Yacht Club, it is decorated with nautical touches, such as buoys suspended from the ceiling by the bar. Owners Muriel Palandri and Dominique Laval have imported the very best of the cuisine from their native Toulouse, known for its gourmet food. If you would like a sweeping view of the water to accompany your meal, try to be seated near the window. French and creole selections include scallops Grand Voile, stuffed crab, and mouth-watering beef dishes. About $75 and up per couple for dinner. Open for lunch, noon to 3:30 p.m.; dinner, 7:30 to 10:30 p.m. Closed Sunday.

The **Palais Créole,** 26 Perrinon (tel. 63-83-33), is a tiny new restaurant in the heart of Fort-de-France, facing the Law Court and its square and the statue of Victor Schoelcher. Established by Mounia, currently one of Yves Saint Laurent's favorite fashion models, it has quickly become the place for local movers and shakers to meet and greet each other. The freshest seafood and produce distinguish the imaginatively presented French and Créole cuisine. There's a prix-fixe lunch for $15; dinner for two should run $50 to $60. Open for lunch, noon to 3 p.m.; dinner, 7 p.m. to midnight. No lunch on Saturday; closed Sunday.

Le Tiffany, La Croix Bellevue, Anc. Rte. de Schoelcher (route de Bellevue), Fort-de-France (tel. 71-33-82), is comfortably situated in the former home of a prominent Martiniquais who was the mayor of Fort-de-France for 40 years. There is a complete à la carte menu, but you can't go wrong with either of the prix-fixe lunches ($10 and $22); the prix-fixe dinner ($25) offers choices from French and creole cuisines. The wine list is extensive, and expensive, but there's a good selection in the $15 to $25 range. On Friday evenings, several magicians are joined by the restaurant's owner to perform sleight of hand at your table. Lunch, noon to 2 p.m.; dinner, 7:30 to 10:30 p.m. No lunch on Saturday; closed Sunday.

La Biguine, route de la Folie, Fort-de-Folie, Fort-de-France (tel. 70-12-52), a small duplex restaurant, is in an old home in the capital. Downstairs, the informal grill serves light meals such as beef and chicken brochette. Upstairs, the more up-scale menu offers delights like escargots, crayfish in a creamy red sauce, lobster salad, and duck laced with pineapple sauce. For dessert, try fresh fruit sherbet. Presided over by Gérard Padra, formerly of the Bakoua Beach Hotel, La Biguine continues to grow in popularity. Reservations are a must. Dinner upstairs will be about $50 and up per person, including drinks and tip. Open for lunch 11:30 a.m. to 3 p.m.; dinner, 7:30 p.m. to midnight. No lunch on Saturday. Closed Sunday.

La Belle Époque, Didier (tel. 64-47-98). A handsome old home is the setting for this pleasant restaurant in a suburb of Fort-de-France. The emphasis is on French cuisine, with a smattering of creole thrown in. Entrées range from veal kidneys in mustard sauce to shrimp with passionfruit juice. Expect to pay about $70 for a complete dinner for two. Open for lunch, noon to 2 p.m.; dinner, 7:30 to 10 p.m. No lunch on Monday; closed Sunday.

L'Amphore—Anse Mitan (tel. 66-03-09). A short walk from the Bakoua Beach Hotel, this restaurant faces the water. At night, the music of crickets accompanies the mellow tunes of a guitarist who welcomes requests from diners. High-backed wooden chairs surround the small tables, and brick archways separate sitting areas. Choose your lobster fresh from the tank, or try tenderloin with green-pepper sauce, duck l'orange, or coquilles St-Jacques. Appetizers include creole blood sausage, accras (cod fritters), and sea urchins. But whatever you do, be sure to save room for dessert:

passionfruit and lemon mousse, bananas cooked in a cream sauce, sinfully rich chocolate cake with vanilla ice cream and hot fudge—you may have to dine here more than once. A complete dinner, including drinks and dessert, will be about $50 per couple. Open for lunch, noon to 2 p.m.; dinner, 7 to 10:30 p.m. Closed Monday.

If popularity with residents is a measure of a restaurant's worth, then **Le Matador** in Anse Mitan (tel. 66-05-36) is undoubtedly a winner. Surrounded by bright vegetation, this creole dining spot is owned by a former hotel chef. Home-style specialties include crabes farcis (stuffed crabs), red snapper, and for the adventurous, octopus and curried mutton. Dinner should be about $40 to $50 for two. Open for lunch, noon to 3 p.m.; dinner, 7 to 11 p.m. Closed Wednesday.

Two Anse Mitan creole restaurants well worth visits: **La Bonne Auberge** (tel. 66-01-15) has bright madras fabric draped artfully across white tablecloths. About $50 per couple for dinner. Open for lunch, noon to 2:30 p.m.; dinner, 7 to 11 p.m. Closed Wednesday. And **La Villa Creole** (tel. 66-05-53) is run by a brother and sister. She cooks and he strums the guitar. About $50 and up per couple for dinner. Open for lunch, noon to 2 p.m.; dinner, 7 to 10:30 p.m. Closed Sunday.

The stone buildings that now house the restaurant at **Leyritz Plantation,** on the north coast in Basse-Pointe (tel. 73-53-08), were once a chapel and storage room. Lunchtime tour groups make this restaurant busy at midday, but the food is worth a stop. The savory seafood, beef, and chicken dishes are accompanied by local vegetables such as taro root, breadfruit, and red beans. A complete lunch for two will be about $45. Open for lunch every day from 12:30 to 3 p.m.

When in the Les Salines area, take a break from the beautiful beaches with lunch at **Manoir de Beauregard,** 07227 Sainte-Anne (tel. 76-73-40). A large fishing boat sits in the dining room, which serves accras de crevette (shrimp fritters), avocado stuffed with crab, veal cutlets, broiled sirloin, and herbed lamb. Dinner for two should be about $50 and up. Open every day for lunch, noon to 2 p.m.; dinner, 7 to 10:30 p.m.

La Canne à Sucre, Le Marin (tel. 74-84-16), is another good lunch stop when you're touring the southern coast. It's a tiny place (there are only five tables) on the second floor; the view takes in most of downtown. It's cool and breezy, with wicker furniture and brightly patterned fuschia, pink, and avocado linens. Lunch will run about $15 to $20 per couple. Open for lunch, 11 a.m. to 3 p.m.; dinner, 7 to 10 p.m. Closed Saturday.

Martinique has many night spots where you can let your hip bones slip. They are located in and outside of hotels, and you'll hear American and European popular music as well as beguine (the local sound), reggae, and salsa. In Fort-de-France, try **Le New Hippo** (boulevard Allegre), **Le Must** (boulevard Allegre), **Le Carafe** (rue Lamartine), and **Le Jardin Brésilien** (Rond-Point du Vietnam Heroïque). Outside the city, there's **Number One** (in Trinité) and **L'Oeil** (in Ducos). In Pointe du Bout, you'll find nightlife at the hotels: **Von Von** (in the Méridien) and **Vesou** (at the PLM Azur Carayou). Most are closed Sunday and/or Monday nights. Try to catch the spirited **Les Grands Ballets de la Martinique,** a dance troupe that performs at various hotels after dark.

XXV

PUERTO RICO

1. PRACTICAL FACTS

2. ROMANTIC INTERLUDES

3. HONEYMOON HOTELS AND HIDEAWAYS

4. ROMANTIC RESTAURANTS

5. NIGHTLIFE

How do you like your romance? With a "salsa" beat and the seductive tug of a blackjack table? How about a deserted beach and the whisper of trade winds in the palms? Or perhaps accompanied by a coffee or a cognac in a moonlit 17th-century Spanish courtyard?

Nestled between the Dominican Republic and the U.S. Virgin Islands, a combination of history, size, and location has blessed Puerto Rico with variety—variety of everything—that is rarely found on a Caribbean island. Add to that its accessibility from the U.S. mainland—less than 3½ hours from New York—and you may find that Puerto Rico offers just the honeymoon you are looking for.

One thousand miles southeast of Florida on the northern rim of the Caribbean island chain, Puerto Rico is 100 miles long and 35 miles wide, with the Atlantic Ocean to the north and the Caribbean Sea on the south. But there really are two Puerto Ricos: San Juan, the island's lively capital, center of its tourism industry, and home to most of the hotels and resorts; and "out on the island," a local term referring to everything else. But within the two there is remarkable, even startling, variety. Old San Juan, for example, beautifully restored and dating back to the 16th century, lies gracefully only minutes away from the most dazzling, throbbing resorts and casinos in the Caribbean. Lovely coffee plantations–turned–paradors perch on dark, rich hillsides of the Central Cordillera, in contrast to the open, cactus-covered hills of the southwest rolling onto the miles of deserted beaches of Cabo Rojo. The choice is yours—which Puerto Rico appeals the most?

Puerto Rico's history, rather unique in the Caribbean, has contributed enormously to its present character. The island was discovered by Christopher Columbus in 1493. Unlike many other Caribbean islands, whose nationalities changed every time the powers of Europe fought a war, Puerto Rico was held by the Spanish for nearly 400 years. The Spaniards conquered the local Taino Indians as early as 1508, and Juan Ponce de León (who would later go on to seek the Fountain of Youth) became its first governor. Despite several attempts by Britain and Holland to change the course of history, the island remained Spanish until 1898, when the Spanish-American War gave Puerto Rico to the United States. Today, Puerto Rico is a U.S. Commonwealth, and its people are U.S. citizens.

This uninterrupted history of Spanish influence has left a lasting impact on Puerto Rico. It certainly is the most European of the Caribbean islands; in fact, much of it, particularly Old San Juan and some of the smaller historic towns such as

Ponce and San Germán, are strongly reminiscent of Spain. And it is not just in the landmarks that reflect the island's heritage. While influenced, of course, by Caribbean tastes and customs and later by American lifestyles, Puerto Rico's cultural life, its religious life, even the local cuisine, today remain strongly Spanish in character. Virtually no day in Puerto Rico goes by, for instance, without the celebration in some small town of its patron saint. In the luxuriant traditions of Europe, Christmas on the island is celebrated for weeks, rather than just one public holiday.

This is not to say that Puerto Rico has ignored its other influences. Its Indian ancestry is recognized in the preservation of several ceremonial and religious centers out on the island, including the Gaguana Indian Ceremonial Park, located on the central mountains near Utuado, and the Tibes Indian Ceremonial Center, on the south coast, just outside Ponce. The island's African heritage is particularly vibrant in the town of Loíza, dating back to the 16th century and still populated with residents descended from African slaves who were brought over to work in the sugar plantations. Using coconut *vejigante* masks, dances, and feasts, the town honors that heritage in a festival held once a year.

Puerto Rico's American heritage has produced the modern lifestyle of the island. Fast-food chains, for example, abound in new San Juan and the larger cities out on the island. English is widely spoken across the island. And American political ties—although Puerto Rico is internally self-governing—have resulted in many practical benefits. Roads are good, telephone communications plentiful. U.S. investments have contributed to the island's economy. But don't come here looking for Miami Beach; despite its American affiliation, which makes travel here virtually hassle-free, Puerto Rico is delightfully and decidedly foreign.

Puerto Rico's size and location also combine to create a variety of natural environments and attractions. Its Atlantic beaches have been described as the "Hawaii of the Caribbean" because of their excellent surf. The Caribbean National Forest—also known as El Yunque—is one of only two tropical rain forests in the United States. Portions of the tiny islands of Vieques and Culebra off Puerto Rico's east coast are preserved as wildlife sanctuaries. The Caribbean coastline is noted for its expansive and uncrowded beaches. In the northwest, Camuy Caves Park offers a glimpse of one of the world's largest and most beautiful underground cave systems.

Puerto Rico's variety is not limited to natural wonders and the contrasts of old and new. The range of activities, for example, is extensive. From casinos to history, art galleries to baseball, rum tasting to sunbathing, there is a remarkable choice of things to do. Water sports include sailing, snorkeling, scuba-diving, deep-sea fishing (some 40 world record catches were made offshore here), and the traditional resort activities such as windsurfing. Other sports include golf at some of the Caribbean's best-known courses, tennis on more than 100 courts, many of which are lighted for night play, horseback riding, hiking, and cycling. Spectator sports include Puerto Rico's famous winter baseball league action (where many of the mainland's stars spend their off-season), horse racing, the San Blas Marathon, sailing regattas, and fishing tournaments.

A trip to Puerto Rico has only two absolutes: the weather, regardless of the month, is honeymoon weather, and the hospitality is warm and genuine. After that, you're on your own. Don't come looking for ski lodges, but just about anything else is possible. In Puerto Rico you can plan the honeymoon you dream about.

Traveler's Alert

As we were preparing this edition for press in September 1989, Hurricane Hugo ripped through the Caribbean, causing considerable damage. Although rebuilding began almost immediately, if you are planning to honeymoon in Puerto Rico (especially around Fajardo and Luquillo or on Vieques or Culebra) in early 1990, it is advisable to check out the area's status before completing your arrangements.

1. Practical Facts

GETTING THERE

Because Puerto Rico is a U.S. Commonwealth, no passports or visas are required for U.S. citizens. However, it is always wise to travel with a valid form of personal identification. U.S. Customs regulations also apply to Puerto Rico and there are no duties on items purchased there and brought to the mainland. There is, however, inspection by the U.S. Department of Agriculture.

Nonstop and direct air service to Puerto Rico is available from a number of U.S. cities, including New York, Boston, Newark, Miami, Dallas/Ft. Worth, Chicago, Baltimore, Los Angeles, Atlanta, and St. Louis. **American Airlines** has made San Juan their hub for all Caribbean operations and offers the most convenient flights from many U.S. cities. Other carriers that fly there include **TWA** and **Delta.** Most flights are to San Juan, the island's capital, but there is also service available to Aguadilla on the northwest coast.

Puerto Rico is also a major port of embarkation for well over a dozen international cruise lines and nearly 20 other ships call there on a regular basis throughout the year. Ask your travel agent for details.

GETTING AROUND

Public transportation in Puerto Rico is plentiful and varied, and rental car companies are well represented, particularly in San Juan.

Taxis

All taxis authorized by the Public Service Commission use meters except for long-distance chartered trips. While more expensive than other means of public transportation, taxis are the most efficient way of getting around San Juan. Rates are roughly equivalent to those in major U.S. cities and there is a nominal extra charge for suitcases, home calls, and for waiting. Cab companies are listed in the telephone directory and taxi stands are plentiful at hotels and locations in the city. Taxis can also be hailed from the street. The approximate cost of a taxi from San Juan's international airport to the Condado area is $7 to $10, depending on your hotel. Be aware that some San Juan cab drivers have been getting a bit balky about using the meter and will instead propose a fixed fare. Practically always, the ride costs less by meter, so politely but firmly request that the driver pull down the flag before you depart for your destination. Similarly, if going via fixed fare, always agree to the amount before departing.

Rental Cars

Most of the major rental car companies are represented in Puerto Rico, including: **Avis** (toll free 800/331-1212), **Budget** (toll free 800/527-0700), **Hertz** (toll free 800/654-3131), **National** (toll free 800/227-7368), and **Thrifty** (toll free 800/367-2277), all of which can be booked in advance from the U.S. mainland with rates comparable to those in U.S. cities.

Carros Públicos

Automobiles with license plates ending in P or PD are public cars and operate as inexpensive taxis, often between towns on the island. They do not use meters, but the Public Service Commission requires that they be insured and fixes routes as well as reasonable rates.

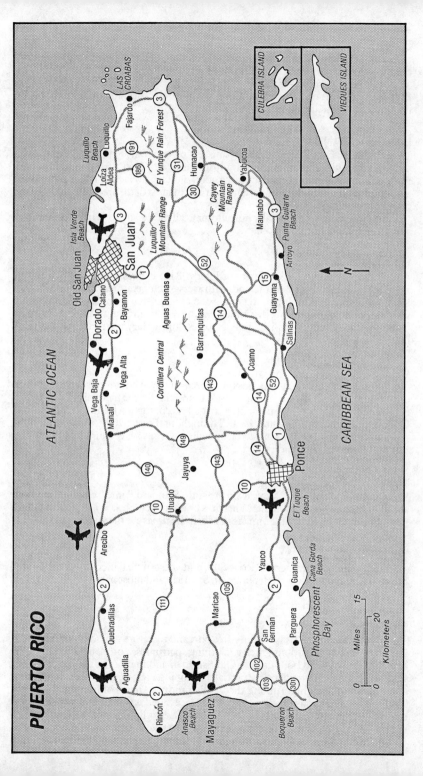

Buses

The San Juan metropolitan area is amply, though often erratically, served by a bus system that is inexpensive (25¢) and an excellent way to get a feel for the city. The most popular route for visitors runs from Rio Piedras to San Juan (use no. 1 or 2) and includes the hotel section of Condado, the university, and many of the historical attractions, including the Old City.

LANGUAGE AND MONEY

The language of Puerto Rico is Spanish. However, only in the smallest of towns is there any difficulty communicating in English, and even then goodwill usually makes all things known. Currency is the good old U.S. dollar and major credit cards are accepted almost everywhere in San Juan and in most of the areas out on the island that are visited by tourists.

Service charges are generally not automatically added to hotel or restaurant bills and 15% is standard tipping policy.

WEATHER

Decidedly tropical, the climate of Puerto Rico is favored by trade winds that make for pleasant weather year-round, with average temperatures in the high 70s and low 80s. The central mountain region is cooler and more humid, while the southwest part of the island is quite dry, much like the American Southwest. Evening temperatures drop about 10° to 15°. Temperatures during the winter months may reach into the low 70s.

CLOTHING

What you wear largely depends on where you stay. The large resorts in San Juan can be quite formal in the evenings—jackets and ties for the men, dresses and skirts for women—and short shorts are discouraged except for beach and recreational use. Out on the island, dress is quite casual. Throughout the year, light, summer clothing will suffice, but you might want to bring light coverups for restaurants and casinos, which are *very* well air-conditioned.

TIME

Puerto Rico operates all year on Atlantic Standard Time, which is one hour ahead of Eastern Standard Time. When it is noon in New York, it is 1 p.m. in Puerto Rico. When Daylight Saving Time is in effect, the times are the same.

TELEPHONES

The area code for Puerto Rico is 809, and you can dial direct from the United States. There are public pay telephones in San Juan and most of the towns and cities of the island.

SHOPPING

While Puerto Rico is not a duty-free port and therefore superdiscounts are rare, imported goods, including jewelry, clothing, perfumes, porcelain, and china, are available in shops and boutiques in Old San Juan and in most of the larger resorts. Old San Juan, in particular, is a pleasant shopping area, with stores often staying open late in the evening. Among the locally produced items of note are the *santos*, small wooden religious carvings; handmade lace called *mundillo*; and *quatros*, a guitar-like instrument that comes in several sizes. Puerto Rico also is the world's leading rum producer. Cigars are also a favorite gift to take home.

Standout shops in Old San Juan include **Galería Caliban,** 51 Cristo, for exquisite carved wooden masks from Ponce; and **Boveda,** 209 Cristo, for unusual women's clothing and accessories. The **Cristo Street Mall,** located at 202 Cristo in a beautifully restored 19th-century building, has several fine boutiques, including **Leather and Pearls,** featuring wares by Gucci and Majorica; and **Spicy Caribbee,** which carries aromatic herbs and spices of the Caribbean. Also on Cristo street, you'll find offshoots of some of fashion's toniest names, including **London Fog, Polo/Ralph Lauren,** and **Hathaway.** But the best discovery of all is **Amparo Cuellar's boutique** in her elegantly refurbished 300-year-old home at 53 Cristo. The Colombian-born artist hand-paints delicate designs on fine European porcelain, from miniature jewelry boxes to complete dinner sets, priced from $10 up. The store is open only Wednesdays and by appointment (tel. 722-1777), but it well merits your visit.

HOW TO GET MARRIED IN PUERTO RICO

There are no residency requirements. If either or both of you are under age 18, you'll need parental consent. Blood tests are necessary; a mainland U.S. blood test will suffice if it is not more than ten days old by the actual marriage date. Couples can apply for a marriage license at the Department of Health in San Juan or other cities. The license must be signed by a doctor after an examination of both the prospective bride and groom. Catholic ceremonies must be performed in a church; other ceremonies can be arranged at any number of romantic locations. For complete details, write: **Commonwealth of Puerto Rico Health Department,** Demographic Register, P.O. Box 9342, 26 Fernandez Juncos, San Juan, Puerto Rico 00908 (tel. 809/728-7980).

FOR FURTHER INFORMATION

Contact: **Puerto Rico Tourism Company.** In New York: 575 Fifth Ave., 23rd Floor, New York, NY 10017 (tel. 212/599-6262) or call toll free 800/223-6530. In Miami: 200 S.E. St., Suite 903, Miami, FL 33131 (tel. 305/381-8915). In Chicago: 11 East Adams St., Chicago, IL 60603 (tel. 312/922-9701). In Los Angeles: 3575 West Cahuenga Blvd., Suite 248, Los Angeles, CA 90068 (tel. 213/875-5991).

---

2. Romantic Interludes

In addition to such activities as golf, tennis, water sports, gambling, and fine dining, Puerto Rico offers some special opportunities to make a honeymoon all the more memorable.

The tiny **Old City of San Juan** (barely ten square blocks on the western tip of the metropolitan area) has been called "an architectural masterpiece in the Caribbean." Quite simply, there is nothing like it. Other islands have their museums and restored fortresses and buildings, Puerto Rico has an entire living, breathing city that is a step back several centuries in time. It has museums but it is not a museum itself; on the contrary, much of Puerto Rico's most exciting life takes place here, but in an atmosphere that is far more European than tropical.

Wander the narrow streets that are paved with stones originally used as ballast by the Spanish fleets. Climb the hill to **San Juan Cathedral** (no phone) in the center of the old city, first built in 1540 but continually restored, and containing the body of Ponce de León. Open daily from 6:30 a.m. to 5 p.m. Farther on, at the tip of the old city, is **El Morro Castle** (tel. 724-1974), which has protected the city's busy harbor for 400 years. This enormous, six-level fortress is open daily from 8 a.m. until 6 p.m., and guided tours are available. Follow the massive city walls along the cliffs overlooking the sea and stop in at the **Cristo Chapel,** built to commemorate a miracle. Hundreds of years ago, horse races were conducted through the narrow streets of Old San Juan. When a young jockey and his mount plunged over the city wall, a spectator vowed to build a chapel on the spot if his life was spared. According to the legend, he was, and the graceful chapel overlooks the harbor, usually filled with cruise ships.

Visit **La Fortaleza,** the oldest governor's mansion still in use in America. Built in 1540 and remodeled in 1848, the building is open Monday through Friday, 9 a.m. to 4 p.m. (tel. 721-7000). Or stop in at the many museums, including **Casa del Libro** (tel. 723-0354), with one of the Caribbean's finest collections of rare books, the **San Juan Museum of Art and History** (tel. 724-1875), or the **Casals Museum** (tel. 723-9185), commemorating Pablo Casals, the noted cellist and conductor. Or shop at the many stores and boutiques. Night or day, Old San Juan is a perfect interlude. But do it on foot; much of the old city is closed to all but pedestrian traffic.

Be big spenders and take the nighttime **ferry** from Old San Juan across the bay to Cataño. In the evening there is no reason to get off in Cataño, and each way will cost only a dime. There is no other view of San Juan's lights, castles, and churches by night quite like it.

Puerto Rico produces 14 different kinds of rum. Just across the bay from San Juan is the **Baccardi factory.** You can reach the free samples by public transportation, ferry, or by car. The plant can put out 100,000 gallons a day, so don't worry about it running out. Forty-five-minute free tours are offered Monday through Saturday between 9:30 a.m. and 3:30 p.m. (tel. 788-1500).

You might consider giving the casinos a rest and visit the nearby **U.S. Virgin Islands.** By plane, it's about a 30-minute flight; round-trip air fare runs about $90 per person on airlines such as American Eagle, American Airlines, Aero Virgin Airlines, TWA World Express, Eastern Metro, and Virgin Islands Seaplane Shuttle. The tour desk at every major San Juan hotel can set you up with a package.

Cabo Rojo and **Phosphorescent Bay** on Puerto Rico's southwest corner are some of the island's most romantic settings. Don't try them on a day trip from San Juan, but if you're out on the island for a few days, it is a must. Towering cliffs plunge into the sea from the edge of open country that resembles the American Southwest. Miles and miles of unnamed beaches make you wonder how something so perfect can have so few visitors. In the tiny village of Parguera, visit Phosphorscent Bay, which, on moonless nights, sparkles with an intensity most casino and disco operators can only wish for, as millions of microscopic animals light up the water. There are several paradors nearby for comfortable accommodations, including Villa Paraguera, on the bay itself.

You might consider a change of pace from the glamour and bustle of San Juan's 20th-century lifestyle and remove yourselves to a **country inn** where time seems to stand still. There's one with therapeutic baths, another on a tiny island, and several only seconds from the beach. See details under "Honeymoon Hotels and Hideaways."

There are two large islands off Puerto Rico's east coast, reachable by air from San Juan or by ferry from Fajardo. **Vieques** in the last few years has developed a reputation as an "in place" for romantic escapes, with a picturesque Parador Esperanza and lazy, secluded beaches. **Culebra** is, for the most part, a wildlife preserve and particularly interesting for day trips. Both provide a wonderful contrast to the sophistication of San Juan. In addition to these major islands, several smaller islets off Puerto Rico's coast offer exquisite beaches and colorful coral reefs for snorkeling. Several different operators offer day sails/snorkeling trips to islands such as **Icacos, Palominos,** and **Monkey Island** (so named because of the thousand-plus monkeys that roam free here). Rates, including a picnic lunch and soft drinks, run about $55 to $65 per person. Contact **Caribe Aquatic Adventure** at the Caribe Hilton (tel. 721-0303, ext. 2447); **Barefoot II** catamaran sales (tel. 791-6195 days, or 726-5752 evenings); **Island Safari** at the La Concha Hotel (tel. 723-4740); or **Palmas Sailing Yachts** in Humacao, near Palmas del Mar resort (tel. 736-9320 or 863-9742).

3. Honeymoon Hotels and Hideaways

The best honeymoon hotels in Puerto Rico come in two varieties: large, glamorous resorts with extensive facilities, private beaches, nightlife, and entertainment; and small, secluded country inns. With few exceptions, the hotels of San Juan are in the former category: high-rise structures along the beaches of Condado or Isla Verde, where the accent is on glittering activity—often 24 hours a day. Enormous casinos, swimming pools and beaches, tennis and nearby golf facilities, a choice of several restaurants, supper clubs and lounges are all standard features of these hotels, which differ only in style and decor. Rooms are fully air-conditioned and equipped with all the conveniences of home, including color TVs and VCRs at many of them. Such amenities as room service and special honeymoon packages are also standard. An additional benefit to a honeymoon hotel in San Juan is proximity to other resorts: Most of the larger hotels are within walking distance of several others so that restaurants and entertainment need not be limited only to your resort.

Out on the island the large resorts, too, have a wealth of facilities and services to offer the honeymooner, often including sailing marinas, deep-sea fishing, snorkeling and scuba-diving, horseback riding, tennis and golf. In contrast, the handful of gracious paradors scattered throughout Puerto Rico provide an escape from everything. Modest in accommodations as well as price but lacking nothing by way of appeal or service and local hospitality, these country inns are for the couple who need only each other, a good meal or two, and beautiful scenery to start off married life.

SAN JUAN

There are a number of perfect honeymoon hotels in San Juan and Old San Juan for you to choose from.

Expensive

The **El San Juan Hotel & Casino**, P.O. Box 2872, Isla Verde, San Juan, Puerto Rico 00902 (tel. 809/791-1000; reservations: toll free 800/468-2818), has become, if anything, even more glamorous since its recent $40-million renovation. It exudes all the sumptuous self-confidence of a pleasure palace built by a Roaring 20s tycoon, and a low-slung Hispano-Suiza convertible would not look misplaced purring along the palm tree-lined driveway. Spectacular chandeliers, brass, and polished wood help create an atmosphere of European sophistication in the tropics. The hotel features Puerto Rico's only wine bar (complete with cruvinet), and a Palm Court provides an air of almost sinful luxury. The countdown of in-room amenities rings like a chorus from "The Twelve Days of Christmas," with three telephones, two color TVs (yup, there's also one in the bathroom), and, if not a partridge in a pear tree, then at least goodies such as a marble-topped sink, separate vanity table with makeup mirror, and one of the nicest toiletries selections we've ever encountered, tucked into a jaunty bag that makes a great beach minitote. Some of the suites have their own private Roman baths, and private balconies add a touch of intimacy. Five restaurants, three clubs, a selection of lounges, and one of the largest casinos in the Caribbean offer the opportunity to make variety the theme of the honeymoon. Honeymoon package: Eight days/seven nights (EP): $1,320 to $1,590 per couple, low season; from $2,090 per couple, high season. Includes one dinner for two with wine, flowers and basket of fruit in your room upon arrival, city tour of Old San Juan, manager's cocktail party, and more.

Condado Plaza Hotel & Casino, 999 Ashford Ave., Puerto Rico 00907 (tel. 809/721-1000; reservations: toll free 800/468-8588). One of the largest hotels in San Juan, the Condado Plaza is not only action packed—it's the center of San Juan action, with five restaurants, several entertainment lounges, and one of the hottest discos in town, Isadora's. With an airy, tropical feel to it (accomplished by the use of pale-wood paneling and wicker furniture), the Condado Plaza is one of the only hotels on Puerto Rico's Condado strip that fronts both the Atlantic Ocean and the Condado Lagoon. For the aquatically inclined, the hotel features one saltwater pool, three freshwater pools, and a small beach on the Atlantic. The lagoon-side watersports concession offers aqua-trikes, jet skiing, windsurfing, and waterskiing. Other sports facilities are abundant, including two lighted tennis courts and a fitness center, with sauna, steam room, and exercise equipment (including a Lifecycle). Recently renovated, the casino sparkles with immense deco-style chandeliers and Hollywood-type lights. The thoroughly modern rooms feature cable TVs, minibars, safes, and both air conditioning and ceiling fans. Honeymoon package: Eight days/ seven nights (EP): $1,100 (low season, minimum room) to $2,210 (high season, deluxe room) per couple. Includes flowers and a basket of fruit upon arrival, welcome cocktails, a candlelight dinner for two, the first three minutes of the bride's call home, admission to a show and two cocktails, a $5 casino chip, and more.

Caribe Hilton International, P.O. Box 1872, San Juan, Puerto Rico 00903 (tel. 809/721-0303; reservations: toll free 800/223-1146), has long set the standards for all San Juan resorts. Muted pastel colors, tropical plants, and open spaces (about 17 gardened acres) give the hotel a soothing quality, and its location, perched on the beach across from the historic Fort San Jeronimo, is breathtaking. Because the hotel occupies its own small peninsula (like an island, really), it achieves the secluded tranquility of a countryside resort; however, it lies just minutes away from the charms of Old San Juan and the scintillating excitement of the Condado area. Constant primping and grooming have kept the property looking as if it had just opened for business last month, although it recently celebrated its 40th birthday. Sportslovers will appreciate the extensive facilities, which include courts for racquetball, tennis, and squash; two freshwater swimming pools plus a private beach; a state-of-the-art gymnasium with Universal/Nautilus training machines; and a water-sports center for scuba-diving, snorkeling, and waterskiing. And if you're considering getting married in Puerto Rico, the hotel has just the spot—a captivating gazebo set amid the sea-grape trees, with views of the fort and Caribbean. Juliana's, the hotel's disco and supper club, is considered "the" place to be seen in San Juan. Honeymoon package: Eight days/seven nights (BP): $1,186 per couple, low season. Includes welcome drinks, bottle of champagne, breakfast daily, two-for-one casino match chip ($20 per couple), T-shirts, souvenir gift, and more. High-season rates: From $225 per couple per night.

Sands Hotel & Casino, P.O. Box 6676, Loíza Station, Santurce, Puerto Rico 00914 (tel. 809/791-6100; reservations: toll free 800/443-2009). Located at 187 Isla Verde Rd., set alongside a two-mile stretch of beach—one of the finest strands in the San Juan area—this sleek high-rise hotel exudes all the razzle-dazzle fun you would expect of the sister resort to the Sands in Atlantic City. The gigantic free-form pool, site of wet 'n' wild volleyball tournaments, is one of the largest in the Caribbean. So is the 50-person-capacity outdoor hot tub. Ditto the glittery casino, where you can try your luck at everything from nickel slot machines to high-stakes baccarat. In the Calypso showroom, top entertainers such as Joan Rivers and Jay Leno headline nightly except Sunday. All 429 rooms are decorated with modern tropical flair, with white rattan furnishings, original prints on the walls, and marble sinks in the bathrooms. Oceanview rooms really deliver on their name, with a travel poster–caliber outlook over the palm-fringed Atlantic. Honeymoon package: None. Rates (EP): $145 to $230 per couple (low season); $270 to $350 (high season).

Radisson Normandie Hotel, Call Box 50059, San Juan, Puerto Rico 00902 (tel. 809/729-2929; reservations: toll free 800/333-3333). You couldn't have dreamed up a more amorous history if you tried. A wealthy young man from a well-respected Puerto Rican family travels to Europe and falls in love with a beautiful French chorus girl. They marry, and honeymoon aboard the luxury transatlantic cruise liner *Normandie*. Upon their return to Puerto Rico, he builds her an opulent hotel designed after the great ship where they spent so many blissful days. Fact or legend, it's a great story, and one that infuses this fabulously restored art deco masterpiece with almost palpable romance. After over $20 million in refurbishment, the Normandie reigns once again as one of San Juan's great hotels. Authentic deco details, such as stylized palm-motif columns and swirly marble lobby floor, make a stay here almost a step back in time. Built surrounding an atrium, the rooms are really large—a heritage of an era when corridors and closets had to accommodate massive steamer trunks. All rooms are thoroughly updated with modern features such as remote-control color TVs and stylish white-tile bathrooms, as well as sunroom-like sitting nooks. Honeymoon suites are especially seductive, semicircular in layout (they occupy the "prow" of the ship design), decked out with white carpets and bleached-wood furniture. There's a good stretch of beach plus an appealing pool area (also ship-shaped), and the restaurant is one of the best in town (see "Romantic Restaurants" section). When you want a change of scene—dinner shows, casinos—the Caribe Hilton is right next door. Honeymoon package: Eight days/seven nights (BP): $1,090, low season. Includes suite accommodations, breakfast daily, bottle of champagne, souvenir gift, room tax, and more. High-season rates: From $200 per couple per night.

Moderate

Condado Beach Hotel, 1071 Ashford Ave., Condado, Puerto Rico 00907 (tel. 809/721-6090; reservations: toll free 800/468-2775). The Condado Beach was built by no less than the Vanderbilts in 1919 and, nicely updated, still maintains that devil-may-care atmosphere. It is also smack-dab in the heart of Condado's late-night casino action. Built in Spanish hacienda design, with stucco walls, red-tile roof, and a grand double lobby stairway, the hotel has hosted the weddings of daughters and sons of San Juan high society for generations. Rooms (many with ocean view) are comfortably contemporary; the hotel is slated to undergo thorough refurbishment shortly. Private-floor Vanderbilt Club accommodations offer special perks, such as private check in/out, an honor bar, complimentary continental breakfast, nightly turn-down, and more. Honeymoon package: Eight days/seven nights: $1,375 to $1,830 per couple. Includes round-trip air-fare on TWA, junior suite if available, two welcoming drinks, a bottle of champagne, T-shirts, one dinner at the hotel restaurant, and various coupons and discounts.

Ramada El Convento, 100 Cristo St., San Juan, Puerto Rico 00901 (tel. 809/723-9020; reservations: toll free 800/468-2779), is a hotel like no other in Puerto Rico, set in what was a 17th-century convent across a cobblestoned street from the San Juan Cathedral in the Old City. Built around a courtyard that contains a gracious alfresco restaurant, this is the place for friendly European elegance, located within walking distance of all the historic old streets, the museums, restaurants, and bars that make Old San Juan unique in the Caribbean. In the lobby, old portraits of Spanish royalty, antique tapestries, and black-and-white marble floors enhance the graceful archways and wooden beams. Although the grandeur is a bit worn and faded, the atmosphere of the conquistadors still remains. All the rooms are different, with recently modernized bathrooms and contemporary furnishings that are comfortable, albeit rather bland. All feature telephones, air conditioning, and satellite color TVs. Since the in-town location precludes a beach, there's a swimming pool in the courtyard, and the hotel runs a daily shuttle to a public beach. Above all, a stay at the El Convento is more like being in Spain than being in the tropics. Honeymoon package: None. Rates (EP) are $130 to $165 per couple per night for a superior room.

Inexpensive

El Canario Inn, 1317 Ashford Ave., San Juan, Puerto Rico 00907 (tel. 809/722-3861). **El Canario by the Sea,** 4 Condado Ave., San Juan, Puerto Rico 00907 (tel. 809/722-8640 or 722-8632). **El Canario by the Lagoon,** 4 Clemenceau, San Juan, Puerto Rico 00907 (tel. 809/722-5058). If you're looking for budget-priced accommodations in San Juan, El Canario inns have been the classic choice of savvy penny-counters for over a generation. Nicely updated, all continue to keep pace with the times, with such amenities as air conditioning, color TVs, telephones, plus complimentary continental breakfast daily. Furnished simply in contemporary style, rooms are clean and welcoming if a bit basic. All three hotels boast convenient central locations. El Canario Inn is on a prime stretch of Ashford Avenue, near restaurants and shopping. Just a half block from the beach, El Canario by the Lagoon is also near some of Condado's most glittery hotels and casinos. The newest property in the group, El Canario by the Lagoon is also in the heart of the Condado area; some rooms have a lagoon view. Honeymoon package: None. Rates: Approximately $65 (low season) to $95 (high season) per couple per day.

OUT ON THE ISLAND

Dorado is 25 miles west (a 40-minute drive) of San Juan. Here Hyatt Hotels has recently spent some $50 million to renovate and improve two self-contained resorts. A mile apart and connected by a free shuttle bus system, the hotels' guests can make use of both properties' extensive facilities and amenities, including restaurants.

Hyatt Dorado Beach Hotel, Dorado, Puerto Rico 00646 (tel. 809/796-1234; reservations: toll free 800/228-9000 nationwide; 800/228-9001 in ME), the smaller and slightly more exclusive of the two, sits in tropical splendor on the ocean's edge, seemingly centuries away from the pace of life back home. The focus here is on the resort's natural beauty, which is unmatched on the island. Beyond two long, golden, crescent-shaped beaches, palm-crowned mountains recede into the distance as far as the eye can see. Rock jetties protect the beaches, creating tranquil coves for swimming. As you float on your back in the dead-calm water, the contrast with the white caps surging against the breakwaters is breathtaking. From the lower-level, beachfront rooms, you can literally saunter out your door, pass quickly through the palms and sea-grape trees, and be out on the beach for a sunrise—or sunset—swim. Back in your cushy room, you'll admire the ample proportions, bleached-wood furniture, beige marble bathroom with distinctive leaf-motif sconces. Some accommodations feature a magnificent four-poster bed worked from bamboo. Everyone on the staff, from bellhop to front-desk manager, is extremely courteous, friendly, and helpful, extending the warm hospitality for which Puerto Rico is known. In addition to the large lap pool and jogging and bike trails, two Robert Trent Jones–designed golf courses and seven all-weather tennis courts have made Dorado a favorite among athletically inclined honeymooners. Honeymoon packages: Eight days/seven nights (MAP): from $2,345 to $2,650 per couple for a standard room, low season. Includes airport transfers, breakfast and dinner daily, air-conditioned room with private balcony, welcoming drinks, champagne and fresh flowers upon arrival, one hour of tennis or greens fees for one round of golf daily, use of bicycles, all applicable taxes and gratuities for meals, souvenir T-shirts, one day's use of exercise equipment at Spa Caribe, $10 casino chip per person. High-season rates (EP): $320 per couple per night.

Hyatt Regency Cerromar Beach Hotel, Dorado, Puerto Rico 00646 (tel. 809/796-1010; reservations: toll free 800/228-9000), may be the splashiest resort in the Caribbean, with the recent installation of the world's longest swimming pool (1,776 feet), which winds through the hotel's splendid grounds. This aquatic playground wins honors as the most-fun pool in the world, bubbling with toys and surprises such as water slides, swim-up bars, Jacuzzis-in-a-cave, and tributaries with currents that keep you floating gently down the stream. Almost twice the size of Dorado (504 rooms), Cerromar also provides the best in sporting facilities in a breathtaking natural surrounding. Two golf courses, 14 tennis courts, a private casino, a supper club, as well as a disco, plus a health club ensure that honeymooners may become pleasantly exhausted but never bored. Open-air corridors lead to the rooms in the seven-story structure. Airy and bright, accommodations have white-tile floors and rattan furnishings; most have water views (the higher the story, the better the panorama). Honeymoon package: Eight days/seven nights (EP): $1,430 to $2,000 per couple, low season. Includes deluxe oceanview room, airport transfers, welcoming drinks, one hour of tennis daily or greens fees for one round of golf, $10 casino chip per couple, one day's use of exercise equipment at Spa Caribe, and more. High-season rates (EP): $240 per couple per night for a standard room.

Horned Dorset Primavera Hotel, Apdo. 1132, Rincón, Puerto Rico 00743 (tel. 809/823-4030; reservations: 315/855-7898). Alice must have felt an equivalent sense of delicious amazement when she tumbled into Wonderland. Here you are, about as far out *en la isla* as it is possible to get, a place where satellite dishes vanish from backyards and you have to drive while keeping an eye out for skittery baby goats and perambulating chickens. And amid all this rustic simplicity, you come across pastoral splendor—the very luxe Horned Dorset Primavera Hotel, Puerto Rico's first and only elegant country inn. Owners Harold Davies and Kingsley Wratten (they also run the much-loved Horned Dorset Inn in Leonardsville, New York) have created the perfect setting for a lovers' tryst. The 26 accommodations—all suites—occupy sparkling white, Mediterranean-suffused villas, embellished with archways and red-tile roofs. Decorated with an eye to beauty and romance, the rooms feature four-poster beds crafted from hand-turned Puerto Rican mahogany. The glamorous marble bathrooms, with gilt-toned faucets and fixtures imported from France, earn oohs and aahs themselves. From most of the ballustraded terraces, you'll enjoy sea views. In addition to the small but perfect beach, there's a classic Roman-style pool that's so lovely it could serve as the setting for the *Sports Illustrated* swimsuit issue. Assuring the aura of blissful escape, there are no TVs or radios; children are not permitted. As if to prove that getting away from it all need not mean roughing it, the dining room serves some of the *haute*-est cuisine in Puerto Rico (see "Romantic Restaurants" section). And the secluded region around Rincón is perhaps the island's best-kept, most beautiful secret, with dramatic mountains-embrace-the-sea vistas that rival those of Hawaii. Honeymoon package: None. Rates (EP): $120 to $145 per couple per night (low season); $190 to $210 per couple per night (high season).

Palmas del Mar, P.O. Box 2020, Humacao, Puerto Rico 00661 (tel. 809/852-6000; reservations: toll free 800/221-4874 nationwide; 212/983-0393 in New York State). "At Palmas a high-rise is a seaside cliff, not a condominium tower. And no building can be taller than the tallest tree," is the way the architect of this lovely 2,700-acre resort puts it, and quite accurately. There may be no resort in the Caribbean that is more beautifully suited to its natural environment. And that's what people come here for—to enjoy Puerto Rico's beauty and its bountiful sports activities. In addition to one of the island's most comprehensive sailing and fishing marinas, Palmas has a golf course, tennis courts, riding stables, a casino, five freshwater pools, a fitness center, and three miles of perfect beaches. Although all these activities await literally on your doorstep, Palmas del Mar isn't one of these gung-ho, everybody-in-the-pool-for-volleyball places that specialize in organized fun. Privacy is not only respected—it's encouraged. For your honeymoon nest, you have a choice of accommodations either in a Mediterranean-style split-level villa or at the lovely Palmas Inn. Imagine a charming New England country inn come to the tropics, and you pretty much get the picture of this intimate, 23-suite hideaway. With its tinkling fountain, hand-painted Puerto Rican tiles, and wide-open views, the lobby immediately establishes the inn as the kind of intimate Caribbean retreat you've been dreaming of. Service is personalized, and each suite features TV, radio, refrigerator, and a balcony overlooking tropical gardens. Honeymoon package: Four days/three nights (EP): $610 per couple at the Palmas Inn, low season. Includes a bottle of champagne, a sunset trail ride on horseback along the beach, greens fees for a round of golf, two hours' tennis court time, two hours' use of bicycles, and round-trip transfers to the San Juan airport. High-season rates: $265 per couple per night at the Palmas Inn; $1,100 to $1,980 per couple per week for a one-bedroom villa.

Paradores puertorriquenos, Puerto Rico Tourism Company, 1290 Avenue of the Americas, New York, NY 10104 (tel. 212/541-6630, or toll free 800/223-6530; reservations: toll free 800/443-0266). Modeled after Spain's successful system, the paradors of Puerto Rico are a collection of government-sanctioned and monitored country inns. Each must be situated in a historic building or a site of exceptional beauty, and all are noted for their fine kitchens. These are not luxury resorts: Service is simple and gracious, and there are no large-scale facilities, although a number do have tennis courts, swimming pools, and access to some of the island's most spectacular beaches. What they afford the honeymoon couple is an unforgettable opportunity to see the island of Puerto Rico, meet its people, sample its cooking —all in great comfort, with the assurance of being well cared for. Rates vary from roughly $40 to $80 per night per couple, with meals as little as $15 for two.

The great charm of the paradors lies in their contrast to the bustle and glamour of San Juan and their individual character. Some are perched on cliffs overlooking the ocean, others are in small fishing villages. The paradors are generally quite small and have become extremely popular with American as well as European visitors, so book well in advance. Contact the Puerto Rico Tourism Company for a complete list and description of these hotels. Meanwhile, here are some of our favorites:

Parador Vistamar, Route 113, Quebradillas. High atop a cliff overlooking the sandy beaches of the Atlantic Ocean on Puerto Rico's northwest coast, Vistamar has 35 air-conditioned rooms, a restaurant, two swimming pools, and a tennis court as well as beach access. There is even live entertainment on weekends. Rates: $50 to $60 per couple per night.

Parador Hacienda Juanita, Route 105, Maricao. A restored coffee plantation high in the Central Mountains of Puerto Rico. The 21-room inn was originally built in 1830 and, while renovated, the historic atmosphere remains intact. A swimming pool and tennis court blend in nicely with the surrounding lush forests, towering palms, waterfalls, and flowers. Excellent restaurant (see comments that follow). From $45 per couple per night.

Villa Parguera, Route 304, Lajas, is in the fishing village of Parguera on the southwest coast. This is the site of Phosphorescent Bay, which sparkles like millions of stars on moonless nights, and the hotel itself, with 50 air-conditioned rooms and a swimming pool, offers the opportunity to sample rural life in Puerto Rico at its best. The restaurant specializes in seafood. From $60, per couple per night.

Parador Baños de Coamo, Route 546, Coamo, is built on the oldest thermal springs in America, which were once visited by Franklin D. Roosevelt in the 1920s. The Indian cultures of Puerto Rico discovered the medicinal waters more than 300 years ago. The hotel has 48 rooms, a swimming pool, and a tennis court in addition to the baths. Coamo is on the south coast. Rates: $65 per couple per night.

4. Romantic Restaurants

You may think that all you need is love on a honeymoon, but a bite of food now and then is not a bad idea. Here, too, Puerto Rico means choices. The larger hotels and resorts all have an assortment of restaurants, ranging from inexpensive coffeeshops to elegant supper clubs complete with floor shows. In San Juan, the choice of restaurants is unlimited: Italian, French, Chinese, continental, nouvelle cuisines, and, of course, Caribbean dishes and Puerto Rico's own *cocina criolla* (creole-style cooking).

Out on the island the dining rooms of the paradors are noted for their excellent quality, particularly the local dishes, and a dinner can cost as little as $15 for two. Along the coast, especially in the southeast, southwest, and northwest, don't hesitate to try the tiny seaside cafés where seafood may be only minutes from the water and two can dine for practically nothing.

SAN JUAN

Normandie, Muñoz Rivera Avenue and Rosales Street at the Radisson Normandie (tel. 729-2929). With its original gold-leaf ceiling and illuminated fountains topped by clear obelisks, the Normandie recaptures the drop-dead glamour of the art deco era to which it belongs. Not to be outdone, the artistic presentation of the French-accented cuisine rivals the sumptuous setting. A rose petal (actually a carved tomato peel) adorns a salmon pâté appetizer; stuffed calamari float on a sea of swirled sauces. For a grand finale, there's the Ultimate Chocolate Dessert: chocolate mousse and gelati, encased in what appears to be a gilded cage (actually spun caramel). Dinner for two, $80 to $100 per couple. Open for lunch Monday through Friday, noon to 3 p.m.; dinner Monday through Saturday, 7 to 11 p.m.

Amadeus, 106 San Sebastián, Old San Juan (tel. 772-8635). Set in a magnificently restored old building across from Plaza San José, Amadeus earns bravos for its exquisite renditions of nouvelle Puerto Rican dishes as well as continental cuisine. The menu covers such unusual entries as yautía fritters (made from a kind of taro) stuffed with cheese, as well as a classic grilled veal chop . . . even hamburgers. Candles and fresh flowers on the tables enhance romance; upbeat jazz music and lively bar action up front create a good-times mood. Lunch or dinner for two, $20 to $50 per couple. Open Tuesday through Sunday, noon to 1 a.m.

El Patio de Sam, 102 San Sebastián, Old San Juan (tel. 723-1149). What Rick's Cafe represents in the movie *Casablanca,* El Patio de Sam means to life in Old San Juan. Located across the plaza from San José Church, it's a popular hangout for a friendly brew of locals, expatriates, and visiting gringos. Ensconce yourselves at a table near the animated bar area up front, or in the enclosed (and air-conditioned) garden area out back. The well-prepared food offers good value, with a wide variety of sandwiches, fish, steaks, and daily specials such as lasagna. Lunch, $15 to $20 per couple; dinner, $15 to $30 per couple. Open daily from 12:30 p.m. to 10 p.m. (to 2 a.m. or later at the bar).

La Mallorquina, 207 San Justo, Old San Juan (tel. 722-3261). Patios and ceiling fans enhance the tropical mood in what is reputed to be the oldest restaurant in San Juan. La Mallorquina specializes in local favorites, the cocina criolla dishes served with sophistication, including asapao (chicken and rice soup), paella, and grilled lobster. About $40 for two plus drinks. Open daily except Sunday, 11:30 a.m. to 10 p.m.

La Zaragozana, 356 San Francisco, Old San Juan (tel. 723-5103), may be the place for the extraspecial romantic meal with full flourishes. Tableside guitars or strolling violins are just the beginning at this elegant hacienda complete with a splash of fountains in a courtyard. Traditional Spanish and Cuban dishes, as well as typical Puerto Rican favorites, including many "flambées" for dessert. Dinner runs $50 and up for two plus drinks. Open daily from 11:30 a.m. to 11:30 p.m.

Los Galanes, 65 San Francisco, Old San Juan (tel. 722-4008). Take a step or two back in time and dine in this restored town house nestled in the heart of the old city. Both continental cuisine and Puerto Rican favorites are served with a Spanish colonial flair, including antique-looking tableware. Dinner will be $50 and up for two plus drinks. Open Tuesday through Saturday, 7 to 11 p.m

ON THE ISLAND

Horned Dorset Primavera Hotel, Apdo. 1132, Rincón (tel. 809/823-4030). Glamour? The dining room at this sumptuous country inn sizzles with enough pizzazz to mollify even the most persnickety Hollywood screen queen. The twin stairways leading to this second-story restaurant seem made for grand entrances; the black-and-white checkerboard-design floors, Oriental carpets, and antique tapestries provide a fitting backdrop for lingering tête-à-têtes. Best described as French inspired by Caribbean flair, the cuisine sparkles with such offerings as a hearty sancocho stew (made with beef, pumpkin, yams, and other vegetables), fresh lobster crêpes, chateaubriand. On the cheese tray, you might find a fresh Puerto Rican chèvre (goat cheese); or if you feel sweetly self-indulgent, try the likes of chocolate mousse cupped in a meringue shell. Six-course prix-fixe dinner, $40 per person. Serving nightly from 6:30 to 9:30 p.m.; advance reservations required, especially for nonguests at the inn.

The **Puerto Rico Tourism Company** features a restaurant program for "mesones gastronómicos" (gastronomic inns), modeled after the successful parador system. This program gives a seal of approval to eating places out on the island. Selected for their authenticity, these restaurants specialize in traditional Puerto Rican cooking, featuring such favorites as asopao and lechon asado, roast suckling pig.

Hacienda Juanita, Route 105, Km. 23.5, Maricao (tel. 838-2550). As if on cue, a chorus of coquis break into melodious chirps as you walk through the gardens to the restaurant set in an 18th-century coffee plantation, part of a gracious parador. Here, local cooks (most of them ladies who live in the mountains nearby) prepare Puerto Rican specialties at their best, including beef escabeche (marinated) or sancocho. For dessert, try the five-star flan. You can eat either inside, sheltered by thick stone walls; or out on the terrace, where a bunch of ripening plantains dangles from the portico, backdropped by the verdant rain forest. Breakfast, lunch, or dinner for two: $10 to $20 plus drinks. Open daily from 7:30 a.m. to 8:30 p.m.

El Buen Cafe, Hatillo (tel. 898-3495), was one of the first members of the "mesones gastronómicos" program. The restaurant, on the northern coast road from San Juan and only a half hour from the Camuy Caves, features such dishes as goat and veal fricassee, Puerto Rican steak and onions, and fresh fish and seafood. It is open for lunch and dinner, about $20 to $30 per couple. Open daily from 6 a.m. to 10 p.m.

Villa Parguera Hotel, Route 304, Parguera (tel. 899-3975), is one of the better seafood specialty restaurants on Puerto Rico's south coast. For those visiting the Phosphorescent Bay, lunch and dinner here are real treats; expect to pay $15 to $30 for two plus drinks. Open daily from 7 a.m. to 9:30 p.m.

---

5. Nightlife

The island's gambling casinos must, by law, be part of a hotel. Conveniently, most of the major resorts in San Juan are contained in the Condado and Isla Verde sections of the city, and it is not only possible but common for visitors to stroll along in the moonlight from one to another until the money runs out. Puerto Rico's casinos are all large, noisy, glittering, and glamorous, so try them all. Most of the larger hotels have casinos, as do the two Hyatts in nearby Dorado and the self-contained Palmas del Mar resort in Humacao.

Supper clubs and discos, too, are found in the larger hotels of San Juan for the most part, although a few are located in other parts of the city. Many of the supper clubs feature big-name entertainment as well as folkloric shows. Consult your hotel concierge or the weekly guides to entertainment available in hotels for up-to-date information on who's appearing where. Among the more popular are **Club Caribe** in the Caribe Hilton, **Club Tropicoro** at the El San Juan, and the Condado Plaza's **Copa Room.**

ST. LUCIA

Deeply furrowed, jungled with dense foliage, St. Lucia looks like the quintessential tropical island. True, there are taller mountains in the Caribbean, but certainly St. Lucia's twin peaks, called the Pitons, are the most awesome, rising a sheer-faced half mile above the sea. Other islands may have more native flowers, but none can surpass the profusion of St. Lucia's blossoms—orange flamboyant, magenta bougainvillea, pink oleander . . . even rainbow-hued rose gardens. Although other islands boast longer beaches or more beaches, vaster rain forests or taller waterfalls, none other offers such extravagant vistas as this small jewel in the Windward Islands chain. In St. Lucia, you'll encounter the most spectacular tropical scenery this side of the South Pacific. Lines of mountains pierce the sky, as sharp as dragon's teeth. Palm trees fringe black-sand beaches; sweet mangoes—ready to be plucked—dangle by roadsides. The exoticism continues, undiminished, into the night. Thousands of tiny crickets and tree frogs launch into a symphony so all-consuming that the air itself seems to vibrate.

St. Lucia is located just 21 miles south of Martinique, and 26 miles north of St. Vincent. The eastern (windward) coast is washed by the Atlantic Ocean, the western (leeward) shore by the calm Caribbean Sea. Although the island measures only 27 miles long and 14 miles wide, it packs in over 100 beaches, including some with glistening black sands. The highest point on the island is Mount Gimie, 3,117 feet above sea level. But the most famous landmarks are the Pitons—double summits soaring perpendicularly from the sea on St. Lucia's west coast, formed by a volcanic eruption about 15,000 years ago. The pinnacles are actually the tops of a collapsed volcano; the waters just offshore cover part of the crater. They plunge an incredible 11,000 feet down—one of the deepest spots in the Caribbean.

St. Lucia has been dubbed "the Helen of the West"—in part because of the island's beauty, in part because the British and French fought bloody battles to reign over her shores for nearly 200 years, recalling the ancient Trojan wars. The island was first settled around A.D. 200 by the peaceful Arawak Indians. Later, the fearsome Caribs conquered the island, going on to dominate the entire region. No one is certain which of the Europeans first gazed upon St. Lucia's soaring mountains: Some say Christopher Columbus; others give the honor to his mapmaker, Juan de la Cosa.

In 1605, a group of 67 Englishmen attempted to settle the island, purchasing land from the resident Caribs. Apparently, mercantile interests weren't all that motivated the Caribs: Within five weeks, all but 19 of the English were killed and/or eaten by the cannibalistic tribe. St. Lucia wasn't successfully colonized until 1650, when two enterprising Frenchmen purchased the island, along with Grenada and Martinique, for the then-exorbitant sum of 1,660 pounds sterling. But peace didn't come to the island. For the next 150 years, British and French contended for sovereignty, trading possession 14 times. Finally, in 1814, the island was definitively ceded to the English as part of the Treaty of Paris, which marked the end of Europe's Napoleonic Wars.

Over 175 years later, both English and French influences continue to mark St. Lucia's culture and traditions. The legacy of the French includes many place names (Vieux Fort, Gros Islet), as well as zesty Créole recipes and a Gallic-based patois still spoken in the countryside. From the British, the St. Lucians have retained a tradition of stable, parliamentary government and the rules of the road—everyone drives on the left. St. Lucia gained independence in 1979, and is today a part of the British Commonwealth. In addition to tourism, the major industry is agriculture—the island exports coconuts, cocoa, mace, nutmeg, citrus fruits, and bananas (some 127 varieties flourish here).

St. Lucia has a population of about 130,000 people, about 40% of whom live in or near Castries on the northwest coast. The island capital, Castries is known for its busy harbor and Columbus Square, with its spreading 150-year-old saman tree. It's a bustling town, caught in transition between being a sleepy West Indian port and a harried commercial center. The most interesting (albeit traffic-jammed) time to visit is on Friday and Saturday, the liveliest market days. Vendors come from all over the island to sell their harvest. Plantains, bananas, cabbages, mangoes, and paw-paws (papayas) are piled on planks and overflow from baskets, in a riotous display of colors and fragrances. For the best view of Castries, drive up the hill of Morne Fortune (Hill of Good Fortune). Here, the contending English and French soldiers alternately defended—and stormed—Fort Charlotte, which guarded the city. As the road corkscrews up through the lush landscape, you'll enjoy panoramic vistas of Castries—especially at the lookout just below the home of the British governor general, which is topped by an intricate wrought-iron crown.

Because of the island's volcanic past, you won't find the diamond-bright beaches that characterize some other Caribbean islands. Similarly, runoff from the island's several rivers mingles with the sea, so you don't have the transparent blue waters found in Anguilla or The Bahamas. But for unmitigated scenic splendor, St. Lucia can't be topped. The island's best beach is the St. Lucian, located about ten miles north of Castries. Nearby Rodney Bay is the magnet for tourist action on the island, with several first-class hotels and the largest, best-equipped marina south of St. Thomas. Here, luxury yachts bob at anchor, and a bevy of happy-go-lucky bars and restaurants attracts crowds late into the night. "Let's go for a lime," you might hear St. Lucians say to each other. "Limin'" is a compound concept, meaning to hang out with friends, to party, to have a good time. It's a word you'll discover—and practice—on a honeymoon in St. Lucia.

1. Practical Facts

ENTERING AND LEAVING

Proof of citizenship is required for Americans and Canadians. A passport is preferred, but an authenticated birth certificate, a voter registration card, or other valid identification is also acceptable. You must also show a return or onward-bound ticket. Leaving St. Lucia, there is a departure tax of about $4 (EC$10) if you are flying to

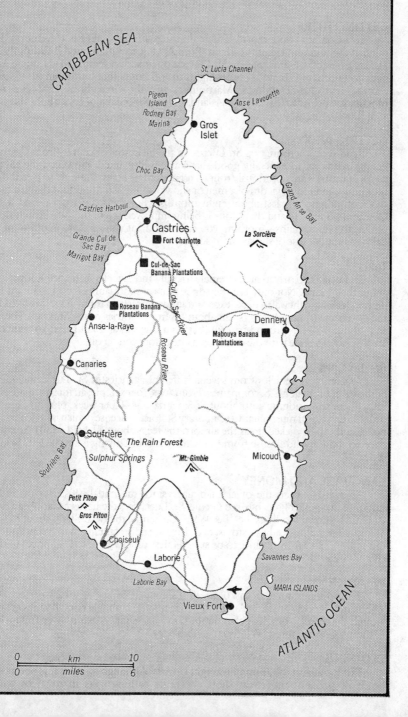

ST. LUCIA

CARIBBEAN SEA

St. Lucia Channel

Pigeon
Island
Rodney Bay
Marina

Anse Lavouette

● Gros
Islet

Choc Bay

Grand Anse Bay

Castries Harbour

● Castries

Grande Cul de
Sac Bay

Fort Charlotte

La Sorcière

Marigot Bay

Cul-de-Sac
Banana Plantations

Cul de Sac River

Roseau Banana
Plantations

● Anse-la-Raye

Dennery

Mabouya Banana
Plantations

Roseau River

● Canaries

● Soufrière

The Rain Forest

Soufrière Bay

Sulphur Springs

Mt. Gimbie

Micoud ●

Petit Piton

Gros Piton

● Choiseul

● Laborie

Savannes Bay

Laborie Bay

MARIA ISLANDS

ATLANTIC OCEAN

Vieux Fort ●

0   km   10
0   miles   6

another Caribbean island, $8 (EC$20) if you are flying to the U.S. mainland, Canada, or other destination. This tax must be paid in EC dollars.

GETTING THERE

St. Lucia has two airports. The main international facility is Hewanorra, located at the southern tip of the island. Both **American Airlines** and **B.W.I.A.** fly to St. Lucia from the United States; **Air Canada** offers service from Canada. Vigie Airport, just north of Castries, handles flights to and from other Caribbean islands, including Barbados, Dominica, Martinique, and the Grenadines. **LIAT** and **Air Martinique** provide frequent intra-island service. Several major cruise lines also call at St. Lucia.

GETTING AROUND

Road-wise, there are two St. Lucias. In the main tourist center (from Castries north), roads are in generally good shape and well marked. However, the routes south of Castries are notoriously rough and pocked by holes; some are so pitted that they look like a recent victim of a meteor shower. (One taxi driver said that his car's shock absorbers only last about eight months.) But the main tourist road from Castries to Soufrière and the Pitons is being improved. Here the path switchbacks across steep mountains—nothing you can't handle if you go slow. You'll want to dally anyway because of the splendid scenery.

Taxis

St. Lucian taxi drivers are extremely friendly and eager to share their knowledge about their island. Not only can they drive you on short jaunts (to a restaurant for dinner, let's say), they also make excellent guides for island tours. Rates are fixed by the government; sample tariffs run about $8 from Castries to the St. Lucian beach area; about $80 for a round-trip run between Castries and Soufrière, to view the Pitons. Always agree with the driver on a rate before you set off.

Rental Cars

You can rent vehicles from several different agencies in St. Lucia, including branches of the major U.S. companies. From **Avis,** for example, an intermediate-size car with air conditioning costs about $55 per day, $440 per week, plus mileage. In order to drive, you must obtain a temporary St. Lucian license, which is issued by the police and can be picked up at the airport; the fee is about $12 (EC $30). You will need to show a valid license from home to obtain it. Driving is on the left, British style.

LANGUAGE AND MONEY

English has been the official language since the mid-1800s. But many St. Lucians also speak a French-based Creole. St. Lucia uses the Eastern Caribbean dollar (EC$), known locally as the "Bee Wee." Currently, the EC dollar is about 37¢ in U.S. currency. Practically all stores, taxi drivers, and restaurants will accept American dollars, but ask in advance to be sure. Unless otherwise noted, all prices in this chapter are in U.S. dollars.

WEATHER

Temperatures range from 70° to 90° Fahrenheit, averaging a bask-perfect 78°. The wettest months are from August to November, and annual rainfall varies greatly around the island, from 60 inches on the north and south coasts to over 160 inches in the interior rain forest. Winters tend to be dry.

CLOTHING

Bring comfortable, summer-weight clothes. Although swimwear is fine at the beach or pool, do not wear short shorts or bathing suits in town or while sightseeing. A few of the more elegant restaurants require a jacket (sometimes jacket and tie) for gentlemen.

TIME

All year, St. Lucia remains on Atlantic Standard Time, which is one hour ahead of Eastern Standard Time. In winter, when it is noon in New York, it is 1 p.m. in St. Lucia. In summer, when Daylight Saving Time is in effect in the United States, the time is the same as in the U.S. East Coast.

TELEPHONES

You can call St. Lucia direct from the mainland United States. First dial 809 (the area code), then the seven-digit local phone number. When you're on the island, you need dial only the last *five* digits of the number (not the 45 that precedes them).

ELECTRICITY

You will generally need dual-voltage appliances or converters, since St. Lucian voltage is 220 to 230 volts AC/50 cycles, the same as in Europe (U.S. and Canadian current is 110). Also bring plug adapters, since outlets are shaped differently from those in North America. Some hotels also have converters available, or have certain sockets that accept North American appliances. Check in advance to be sure.

SHOPPING

The new and elegant **Pointe Seraphine Shopping Centre** is your best bet for one-stop shopping, with over 20 stores and a crafts market. Built right on Castries Harbour, the pretty West Indian–style complex has white stucco walls and red roofs. **Bagshaw's** offers unique fabrics, silk-screened by hand and beautifully crafted into place mats, handbags, and other gift items. At **Windjammer,** you'll find fashionable men's and women's sportswear, all island-made. For duty-free liquor and perfumes, stop in at **J.Q. Charles.** Pick up your souvenir T-shirts at **Island Connection.** As its name indicates, **The Gallery** displays handsome wood carvings, paintings, and other crafts.

St. Lucia has earned its reputation for high-quality crafts. One of the island's leading national treasures is Joseph Eudovics, who has been carving wood for nearly 40 years. Born in St. Lucia, he started out by making his own tools out of old knives and nails. He has studied art in Africa, England, and Haiti. You can visit his studio and gallery, **Goodlands,** Morne Fortune (tel. 452-2747). Here, you'll view works in progress as well as the dazzling finished designs. Everything is done by hand—no electric tools are used. Mr. Eudovics gets ideas from the shape of the wood he works with, and the finished products have the soaring quality associated with sculptors such as Brancusi. Many pieces draw their inspiration from the outdoors: Sculptures have titles such as "Bird" or "Nature." Prices start at about $100 and climb to well over $2,000 for the most elaborate works. MasterCard and Visa are both accepted, and the shop can pack and ship your purchases home for you. Artwork can enter the United States duty free. The studio is open Monday through Friday, 8 a.m. to 4:30 p.m.; Saturday, 8 a.m. to noon.

Also nearby on The Morne, **Caribelle Batik** has its own workshop in 80-year-old Howelton House. Each individually waxed and dyed, the lovely cotton batiks are used for sundresses, scarves, and pareos, or they can be framed for wall hangings. South of Castries, **Tapion Craft** occupies a 19th-century gun emplacement. It carries top-quality handmade pottery and woodwork, leather, jewelry, needlework, and prints.

HOW TO GET MARRIED IN ST. LUCIA

A wedding in paradise is simple to arrange, and your hotel can generally help you handle all the details. After both of you have been in St. Lucia for 48 hours, you can apply to the governor general for a marriage license. You will each need your passport or authenticated birth certificate. If either of you has been divorced or widowed, you must present an original divorce decree or death certificate. If either of you is under the age of 21, evidence of parental consent (such as a sworn affidavit) is required. It usually takes an additional four days to process all the paperwork. Fees will run approximately $130 for a lawyer (needed to make the application to the governor general), $25 for the registrar to perform the ceremony, and $40 for the license.

FOR FURTHER INFORMATION
Contact the **St. Lucia Tourist Board.** In St. Lucia: Point Seraphine, Castries, St. Lucia, W.I. (tel. 809/452-4094). In New York: 820 Second Avenue, New York, NY 10017 (tel. 212/867-2950, or toll free 800/456-3984).

---

2. Romantic Interludes

St. Lucia's 238 square miles encompass some of the most magnificent scenery you'll encounter in this hemisphere.

One day, rent a car—or hire a taxi (about $120)—and explore the southern part of St. Lucia, including the volcano at Mount Soufrière and the Pitons. The drive from Castries to Soufrière, St. Lucia's third-largest town, takes about 2½ hours. The road corkscrews so much that one mile of geographic north-south distance will log eight miles on your odometer.

Everywhere you go, you'll see glossy green banana trees. Known as "green gold," they are not only St. Lucia's major agricultural export—they account for about 80% of the island's economy. Stop en route at **Marigot Bay,** one of the most photogenic yacht harbors in the Caribbean. It was here that the British admiral Samuel Barrington hid his fleet from the French fleet, camouflaging the warships by binding palm fronds to the masts. If you're getting hungry, stop for a bite at the harborside Doolittle's Restaurant, named for the movie *Dr. Doolittle,* which was filmed here. Continuing on, you'll pass quiet fishing villages where time seems to have stood still for centuries. In the town of **Canaries,** for example, you'll view women washing clothes down by the river, pounding the laundry on rocks just as their grandmothers, and great-grandmothers, did years ago. Just beyond Canaries, the road starts climbing into the mountains and soon you'll notice the temperature dropping. You are entering St. Lucia's **rain forest,** a lush and mysterious world where tiny wild orchids snuggle in the crooks of trees, and flaming-red anthuriums grow larger than your hand. Giant ferns tower overhead; ripe mangoes plop onto the roadsides. In the distance, lines of mountains undulate toward the horizon, like waves on a storm-tossed sea. Watch for a flurry of green wings—it might be one of the colorful St. Lucian parrots.

Just after the rain forest, the road hurtles sharply toward the coast—and you'll enjoy your first magnificent vista of the **Pitons.** Located at the base of Petit Piton, the town of **Soufrière** is only lightly touched by tourism. Around its central plaza, you'll see many weathered West Indian–style wooden buildings embellished with intricate gingerbread trim, designed in the patterns of snowflakes or flowers. North of Soufrière, visit the Caribbean's only drive-in volcano—the simmering cauldron of **Sulphur Springs,** hot springs that are remnants of ancient volcanic activity. A little farther down the hill (just below the bridge), the sulfur pools flow into a cool river. If you like, you can swim here (the waters are said to have curative powers). Open daily from 9 a.m. to 5 p.m.; admission, $1.50 per person. Nearby, visit the gardens at **Diamond Falls,** where your guide will point out many of the different flowers that grow on St. Lucia. Diamond Falls themselves are truly gem-like, with lacy cascades tumbling some 50 feet into a lush grotto shaded by giant trees and ferns. Both the gardens and the waterfall make great backdrops for photographs, so be sure to bring your camera. Near the falls, view the elaborate mineral baths, constructed in 1785 under the orders of Louis XVI in order to strengthen and fortify his troops in their battles with the British. Today, the baths have been restored and you can enjoy a relaxing soak in the mineral-rich waters for a small fee.

Another way to reach the awe-inspiring natural wonders of the south coast is by boat. Several different operations offer cruises that depart from Castries. Aboard the **Cahoni,** a 34-foot sailboat, you'll enjoy a leisurely sail down the west coast to Soufrière, where you'll have a splendid view of the Pitons. From here, you'll go on a guided tour of the Sulphur Springs and Diamond Falls. Return to the *Cahoni* for lunch, followed by a swim at a secluded beach. View picturesque Marigot Bar before returning to Castries Harbour, clinking glasses in a champagne toast as you head into port. The *Cahoni* takes a maximum of 10 passengers; the excursion costs $50 per person (tel. 452-0693). The motor yacht **Vigie** runs a similar cruise for $60 per person, including lunch at the Hummingbird in Soufrière (tel. 452-3762). One of the most popular trips is aboard the brig **Unicorn,** a 140-foot-long "tall ship" with over 6,000 square feet of sail that was used in the filming of *Roots.* About $60 per person (tel. 452-6811).

Some other day, bring a picnic lunch to **Pigeon Point National Park,** at the northern part of the island. Actually an island, the conical outcrop is now connected to the St. Lucia "mainland" by a causeway. From here, the pirate Jambe de Bois ("wooden leg") kept watch for ships to plunder, and England's Admiral Rodney set sail in 1782 to defeat the French in the decisive Battle of the Saints. (Rodney also accounts for the island's name: He used to breed pigeons here.) Climb to the top to view the remains of the old fort, which once guarded St. Lucia from enemy attack. From the summit, you'll have a panoramic view of the Gros Islet area; on clear days, you can see all the way to Martinique. Pigeon Point also features a good swimming beach, plus a small museum tracing the geological and natural history of St. Lucia.

Although St. Lucia is just becoming widely known as a vacation destination, there's one group of people who have flocked here for years—scuba-divers. Several island sites frequently appear on any "world's best" list. The most famous dives include **Coral Gardens** and the **Piton Wall,** a dramatic drop-off thick with sea whips, gorgonia, and delicate soft corals. Top operation on the island is **Scuba St. Lucia,** a PADI five-star training facility located at Anse Chastanet (tel. 809/454-7000). They're absolutely crackerjack, and run their dives with a concern for protecting the reefs. One-tank dives cost $27.50; a six-dive package costs $130; resort courses and full certification courses are also available.

"Jump up"—that's the Caribbean expression to describe a party, especially one with a lot of dancing. And that's exactly what you'll find Friday nights at Gros Islet, a small town just eight miles north of Castries. Part carnival, part street fair, the weekly festival attracts an ebullient combination of vacationers, along with what seems like the entire population of St. Lucia. The town streets are closed to cars from 9 p.m. on Friday until 1 a.m. on Saturday, so people can literally dance in the streets to calypso, reggae, and U.S. pop hits. From roadside stalls, you can feast on lambi (roast conch), as well as grilled snapper, roast corn, fish cakes, barbecued chicken. Also sample island beverages such as sea moss (made from—obviously enough—sea moss spiked with rum) or fruit punch, with guava and passionfruit nectars. The festival makes a great way to meet the friendly St. Lucians.

With so much to see and do in St. Lucia, you'll be tempted never to leave. But just a few miles away other ports beckon, and **island hopping** is easy. On a jaunt to the Grenadines, you can fly to Union Island, then board a yacht that will call at Petit St. Vincent and Palm Island. About $165 per person. Or spend the day in Martinique, just a 15-minute flight away. The $145 per-person excursion includes air fare and an island tour. Many different companies offer excursions; ask at your hotel activities desk for details.

3. Honeymoon Hotels and Hideaways

St. Lucia is known for its wide range of hotels, including a good number of choices in a moderate price range. If you're on a budget, you can book even "no frills" accommodations with peace of mind, since St. Lucian hotels are invariably spotless—especially the bathrooms. Although some of the following hotel prices look high, check carefully at what the rates cover. Several of the following are all-inclusive properties; for at least one hotel, the package also includes air fare from the United States. When looking at room rates, also remember that a government room tax of 8% and a 10% gratuity charge will generally be added to your bill. Unless otherwise noted, rates indicate the difference between high- and low-season prices.

EXPENSIVE

Cunard Hotel La Toc & La Toc Suites, P.O. Box 399, Castries, St. Lucia, W.I. (tel. 809/452-3081; U.S. reservations: toll free 800/222-0939). Ensconced in a secluded valley just ten minutes from Castries, La Toc sets the standards for luxury in St. Lucia. The resort consists of 155 hotel rooms plus 54 of the fabled La Toc Suites, known for their privacy and elegance. With its five tennis courts and nine-hole golf course, the resort ranks as a top choice for sports-lovers. Flowers bloom everywhere on the manicured 110-acre property: as an especially nice touch, most of the plants and trees are labeled, so you can learn the names of the different exotic varieties.

Set into the hillside fronting a half-mile-long beach, the pink-painted Hotel La Toc incorporates three large, interconnected wings. Pretty and romantic, the hotel rooms feature different decors. Some come with white-tile floors and bleached-wood furniture enhanced by jungle-leaf bedspreads; others have pink wicker chairs, pine headboards, and Indian rugs. Spiffily maintained, all accommodations look daisy-fresh; each comes with telephone, air conditioning, and radio, as well as a balcony. Views take in the garden, swimming pool, or ocean. Arrayed atop a ridge or beachside, the La Toc Suites display the kind of harmonious beauty seen in home-furnishings magazines. Everything is just so: the delicate beige-and-pastel color scheme, comfortable rattan sofas, Dhurrie rugs. In addition to minifridges and wet bars, accommodations have color TVs and VCRs; some also have ultraprivate plunge pools. Service aims to pamper, with a concierge as well as personal chamber-maids available to help with unpacking, laundry, refreshments, or breakfast in bed.

Long and golden, the La Toc beach offers a protected swimming area. Wind-surfing, Sunfish sailing, waterskiing, and snorkeling are all free to guests. The large swimming pool is accented by a small island with its own palm tree—a popular lo-cale for weddings. Honeymoon package: Eight days/seven nights (EP): $2,300 to $2,935 per couple for a seaview room; $3,245 to $4,455 per couple for a suite with private plunge pool. Includes round-trip air fare from New York or Miami to St. Lucia (other departure cities available at extra cost), round-trip transfers between airport and hotel, flowers and fruit basket in your room upon arrival, bottle of cham-pagne, half-hour tennis or golf lesson for two, souvenir photograph, special gift, dis-count coupons for Cunard cruises, and more.

Couples, Malabar Beach, P.O. Box 190, Castries, St. Lucia, W.I. (tel. 809/452-4211; U.S. reservations: toll free 800/544-2883). Couples isn't just the loveli-est couples-only, all-inclusive resort we've ever encountered—its sumptuous ac-commodations contend for top honors in any class. Fittingly for honeymooners, the property offers something old and something new. As the link with the past, a mag-nificent 200-year-old saman tree occupies a position of honor in the entrance gar-dens. The new comes from an array of contemporary pleasures, which can keep couples on the go from dawn . . . to dawn again. Whether you crave a go-getter honeymoon or long snoozes under the palm trees, Couples gives you any kind of vacation you want. Every day, the activities blackboard announces the day's events. The resort offers nearly as many sports as the Olympics, with everything from waterskiing and scuba-diving to horseback riding available free for guests. Other highlights include a day sail and a picnic at historic Pigeon Point. At mealtime, expect a lavish spread—from expansive buffets to delectable sit-down dinners. All bar drinks and wine with both lunch and dinner are included as part of your package. Evening entertainment might center on a beach barbecue, toga party, or guest talent show.

Throughout the seven-acre property, the lush gardens are a throwback to the original paradise—you can literally pluck ripe bananas from trees that line the paths. Cascades of bougainvillea and oleander screen the 100 accommodations, which are designed West Indian style, with white stucco walls, red-tile roofs, and plenty of French doors to admit both views and cool trade winds. For top-of-the-line honeymoon headquarters, choose one of the splendiferous oceanfront luxury suites. Built to pamper, they feature pink marble floors, four-poster beds, glass-brick walls in the bathroom, Jacuzzi tubs, plus a private gazebo with hammock . . . all this right on the beautiful beach. (Reserve these early—they book up fast!) Honeymoon package: None. Rates: Eight days/seven nights (all inclusive): $1,970 to $2,440 per couple for a superior room; $2,660 to $3,135 per couple for an oceanfront luxury suite in the height of the winter season.

Le Sport, Cariblue Beach, P.O. Box 437, St. Lucia, W.I. (tel. 809/452-8551; U.S. reservations: toll free 800/544-2883). No body's better than one that has been toned, bathed, massaged, buffed, tanned, wrapped, and primped at Le Sport, St. Lucia's first world-class spa facility. Tucked away on what was once a private estate, Le Sport brings together three great concepts: body treatments, sports, and an all-inclusive resort. It adds up to a total honeymoon—for both you and your body. Nestled into a hillside above Cariblue Beach, Le Sport opened in December 1988 after a lavish $15-million renovation. The 128 air-conditioned rooms are set in pink buildings with white trim aligned on a gentle rise above the beach. Cariblue Beach itself is idyllic, a dark-sand cove with calm water that shines like a blue mirror. In the background, the cone-shaped summit of Pigeon Point reaches toward the heavens.

As its name suggests, Le Sport offers all the pleasurable pastimes of a vacation resort. If you've ever thought about dabbling in a new sport, now's a great time to begin. Active options include horseback riding, fencing, and archery, with equipment and instruction all included. In addition, you can partake of some more customary pursuits, such as golf on the nine-hole course, or tennis. Daily aerobics classes and weight training help you keep in shape. In early 1990, Le Sport is slated to open its stunning new spa facility. Crowning a hillock overlooking the water, the spa looks like a pink Taj Mahal, with reflecting pools, friezework, and marble floors. Here, you can indulge yourselves with treatments such as thalassotherapy, thermal jet baths, and various massages. At mealtimes, Le Sport follows through with a choice of regular menus or special cuisine légère, which keeps count of calories—so you don't have to. Honeymoon package: None. Rates (all-inclusive): $385 to $640 per couple per night for an oceanview room in season. Price includes all meals, drinks, and use of the spa facilities. Off-season rates are a bit lower.

Why enjoy just one island on your honeymoon when you can explore several? St. Lucia is one of the leading yacht-charter centers of the Caribbean, with many sleek boats available for both bareboat ("sail it yourself") and crewed charter (with a captain and cook to tend to your needs). The premier destinations here are the Grenadines, unspoiled islets ringed by iridescent blue waters, including Petit St. Vincent, Canouan, Bequia, and Mustique. Bareboat charters cost about $1,430 to $3,400 per couple per week; crewed charters (which include all meals) run around $4,820 to $6,360. One of the largest—and best—charter operations in the Caribbean is **The Moorings,** 1305 U.S. 19 South, Suite 402, Clearwater, FL 34624 (tel. 813/538-8760, or toll free 800/535-7289). The Moorings also operates the fine Marigot Bay Resort, and offers an unusual "Shore 'n' Sail Vacation" that gives you two nights on land at Marigot Bay, followed by four nights aboard a crewed charter, sailing through the Grenadines. Eight-day/seven-night rates (including most meals) run $1,850 to $2,455 per couple (based on four people sharing a yacht).

Other companies offering yacht charters in St. Lucia include **Stevens Yachts,** Rodney Bay, Box 928, Castries, St. Lucia, W.I. (tel. 809/452-8648).

MODERATELY EXPENSIVE
Anse Chastanet, P.O. Box 216, Soufrière, St. Lucia, W.I. (tel. 809/454-7355; U.S. reservations: 212/535-9530, or toll free 800/223-5581). Maybe it's the nearness to the Pitons, which soar heavenward from the water. Perhaps it's the black-sand beach, which sparkles like dusky diamonds. Or the sea itself, bright blue and shallow near shore, profound blue and plummeting thousands of feet deep just a few hundred feet out. Whatever the cause, the effect remains: Anse Chastanet seems magical, magnetic, a supreme example of the right resort in the right place. If you want to escape from the rest of the world, there is no more spectacular place to do it than this 400-acre plantation. The resort is about a 15-minute ride from Soufrière—a drive that seems more like a safari because of the pothole-strewn road.

Sculpted into the cliff, the villas and hilltop restaurant overlook the picturesque beach and a bay so clear that you can eye the outlines of the coral reef below the surface. From the villas, a stone stairway zigzags down the hill to the beach ("Better than aerobics class," one guest commented about the 150-step climb). Everything at the resort is handled with an eye to island elegance. At the beach restaurant, a local artisan has carved the cedar columns with fanciful fish and sea horses. In the rooms, furniture is crafted from island woods such as cedar, greenheart, and wild breadfruit; bedspreads are made from colorful Madras fabrics from Martinique. There are only 37 accommodations, tucked into villas surrounded by flamboyant and bougainvillea. You'll feel as if you're dwelling in a posh treehouse in the superior rooms, set in octagonal villas with wrap-around jalousie windows. The accommodations are very spacious and downright sexy—there's even a dimmer switch for the lights. Or how about a honeymoon au naturel in an open-air deluxe one-bedroom suite? Set high upon the hillside, the villa is completely screened from view by a jungle of bougainvillea and frangipani, banana trees and coconut palms. There's no one to see you except for the hummingbirds.

Fortunately for active honeymooners, Anse Chastanet is more than just a pretty place. Take advantage of the free water sports, including snorkeling, Sunfish sailing, and windsurfing; there's also a tennis court. Of course, Anse Chastanet is also world-famous as a scuba-diving destination, with Scuba St. Lucia, a P.A.D.I. five-star training facility right on the premises (see "Romantic Interludes" above). Both restaurants are excellent. At the beachside Trou-au-Diable café, enjoy specials such as kingfish for lunch. For dessert, be sure to try one of the homemade ice creams in luscious tropical flavors such as guava, passionfruit, and banana. The hilltop Pitons Restaurant offers dinner with a sunset view; from some tables, you can see the Pitons. If you want to get married in St. Lucia, Anse Chastanet has just built a new wedding chapel, backdropped by the Pitons. Honeymoon package: Eight days/seven nights (EP): $985 to $1,580 per couple. Includes round-trip transfers between airport and hotel; welcoming cocktails; complimentary sightseeing tour of the volcano, Sulphur Springs, and mineral baths; bottle of champagne; resort scuba-diving course; and more.

MODERATE
The St. Lucian, P.O. Box 512, Reduit, St. Lucia, W.I. (tel. 809/452-8351; reservations: 201/842-7677, or toll free 800/221-1831). For beach-lovers, action lovers, and just plain lovers, the St. Lucian is the number one choice for fun in the sun. The resort basks along the golden sands at Reduit, the finest beach on St. Lucia, with the craggy profile of Pigeon Point looming in the distance. The property strikes exactly the right balance between elegance and island informality. With its white-tile

floors, columns, and archways, the lobby reflects West Indian graciousness. At the same time, the mood is friendly and personable. Guests soon feel as if the St. Lucian is "their" hotel. For example, take a look at the little plaques in the gardens. The resort gives frequent guests small trees to plant, identified with their names.

Although there are 223 rooms, the hotel never seems crowded because the units are spaced apart, fronting a broad lawn and the sea. Spritely and inviting, rooms are indeed delights to come home to, with their white-tile floors, beige-and-pink color schemes, and modern bathrooms. All come with air conditioning and direct-dial telephones; most look out toward the sea. At the tawny beach, zoom off for windsurfing, waterskiing, or sailing—all free for guests. Parasailing, scuba-diving, and snorkeling are available through the water-sports center for an extra charge. Back on land, there are two tennis courts (both lighted). Shop for local crafts in the small market next to the hotel; you can also enhance your wardrobe at one of the St. Lucian's fashion-conscious boutiques. At mealtimes, take your choice of two restaurants and four bars, including the island's most-happening disco, Splash. Planning a tropical wedding? The St. Lucian's white gazebo is the setting for many ceremonies. Honeymoon package: None. Rates (BP): $105 to $240 per couple per night.

Halcyon Beach Club, Choc Bay, P.O. Box 388, St. Lucia, W.I. (tel. 809/452-5331). In ancient legends, the halcyon was a bird believed to bring calm and tranquility over the seas. Exactly that same feeling of peace and serenity characterizes this resort located just ten minutes from Castries. After an extensive renovation, the property ranks among the loveliest in St. Lucia. A driveway edged by stately palm trees creates an imposing entrance. With its high peaked roof supported by stone columns and marble reception desk, the open-air lobby embodies tropical chic. The 180 rooms occupy two-story stone-and-stucco units, their fronts completely twined with flowering vines. Broad green lawns undulate toward the sea, their emerald perfection interrupted by an occasional mango tree. The rooms themselves are as refreshing as a morning dip, appealingly decorated with white rattan or local mahogany furniture. Some face the sea, others the swimming pool; all offer terraces or balconies, air conditioning, telephones, and clock radios. Although the mood is low-key, you'll find plenty to do right on the property. The new, large pool deck and swim-up bar serve as the nucleus for congenial resort activity. Play a set on the tennis courts. At the beach, take advantage of the free water sports, such as windsurfing, parasailing, waterskiing, snorkeling, and more. The resort offers two fine restaurants, including Fisherman's Wharf, built out over the water. Every night, different performers entertain: a steel band, perhaps, or a limbo show. Honeymoon package: Eight days/seven nights (EP): $885 to $1,270 per couple for an oceanview room. Includes a bottle of champagne, tropical fruit and flowers in your room, dinner for two one evening.

INEXPENSIVE

The Islander Hotel, P.O. Box 907, Castries, St. Lucia, W.I. (tel. 809/452-0255; U.S. reservations: 212/840-6636 in New York State; toll free 800/223-9815 nationwide in U.S.; 800/468-0023 in Ontario and Québec). Make yourselves at home at this friendly complex located at lively Rodney Bay. The Islander consists of 40 rooms and 20 studios (the studios feature a fully equipped kitchenette), set in one-story bungalows facing lawns and gardens. Furnishings are comfortable and contemporary, if not fancy; all accommodations offer air conditioning, telephones, and terraces. Everything is geared to give you a hassle-free stay: The large pool stays open 24 hours a day, and the tour desk can set up car rentals or day trips to the Grenadines. Best of all, the staff will bend over backward to make your holiday perfect, arranging everything from room service to island weddings. Although the Islander isn't located right on the beach, their club facilities at the St. Lucian beach are just a three-minute stroll away. In addition to the beach bar and grill, the Islander has a fine restaurant at the resort. Friday nights, their barbecue attracts an energetic crowd for excellent grilled steak, chicken, ribs, and fish, and "jump up" music from a steel band. Honeymoon package: None. Rates (EP): $70 to $105 per couple per night. Different meal plans are also available.

East Winds Inn, P.O. Box 1477, Castries, St. Lucia, W.I. (tel. 809/452-8212). Hide away at this ten-cottage retreat, where only the seabirds can find you. The enclave surrounds La Brelotte Bay, located roughly midway between Castries and Cap Estate. When you first turn off the main highway onto the long, extremely rutted road marked "East Winds," you'll almost think that you've made a wrong turn. Continue on—and five minutes or so later, you'll come upon this charming collection of octagonal cottages shaded by palm trees. The effect is rather like stumbling across a hidden oasis. Here you'll find seclusion, not isolation. With their eight-sided design, all of the cottages have plenty of louvers and jalousie windows to admit the trade winds (rooms are not air-conditioned). Decor is simple but comfortable, with rattan chairs and sisal rugs, and accents of bright Caribbean colors; all come with radios and cassette players. Newly redone, the bathrooms are spotless. Other new features include a beautiful swimming pool edged in stone, and a peak-roofed "fun house," where guests can borrow games or play cards. The small, rocky beach features good snorkeling just offshore; windsurfing, sailing, and canoeing are all free to guests. Good seaside restaurant. Honeymoon package: None. Rates: $80 per couple per night (EP); $130 per night (FAP, including bar drinks).

4. Romantic Restaurants

Although the English may have won the battle for control over St. Lucia's political allegiance, the French retained dominance over the island's culinary fortunes—luckily for gastronomes. St. Lucian food is generally superb. In addition to classic French cuisine, you'll also find savory creole dishes, such as stuffed crabs. Just as calypso music blends Spanish songs, French ballads, and African tribal rhythms, West Indian cooking combines international cuisines: from French mousse to Chinese stir-fries. Island dishes worth discovering include pumpkin soup, callaloo (a soup made with spinach, dumplings, and salted beef), and pouile Dudon, a zesty chicken stew. The local fish and seafood here are invariably delicious. If you see St. Lucian crayfish on the menu, don't hesitate: Taken fresh from island rivers, they are sweet and tender. Study menus carefully—prices may be given in either E.C. dollars or American dollars. Most restaurants add a 10% service charge to the bill; check to be sure.

EXPENSIVE

San Antoine, Castries (tel. 452-4660). The setting—a wonderful old stone mansion nearly hidden behind flowers high above Castries. The cuisine—island delicacies impeccably prepared in the classic French manner. A step back into the past, plus a meal you'll remember for a lifetime . . . that's what awaits you at this historic restaurant that wins the five-heart award for ultimate romance. Originally built in 1860 as a private manse, the building was converted in 1921 into a hotel (the island's first), attracting a glittering clientele during its heyday. After the structure was almost totally destroyed by fire in 1970, it remained empty for nearly 15 years. Then the property was purchased by Michael and Alison Richings, who had previously owned the excellent Inn at English Harbour in Antigua. They have meticulously restored the estate to its former glory and established the restaurant as one of the culinary stars of the Caribbean. Set amid 11 acres of gardens, the restaurant overlooks Castries and Pigeon Point, with views extending all the way to Martinique in clear weather.

In the same way that San Antoine rises high above Castries, the food here soars over the dispirited recipes that pass for gourmet food in much of the Caribbean.

First, enjoy a drink in the bar terrace while you peruse the menu and wine list. (Restrain the impulse to make an entire meal of the melt-in-your-mouth cheesesticks that accompany your apértif.) Host Michael Richings will come by to offer recommendations and take your order. Start off with a savory appetizer such as the peppered ham with mango coulis and sour cream, or Russian eggs topped with caviar and served with an icy glass of vodka. Main courses reflect international influences: pam pam shrimp stir-fried with vegetables and Pernod, steak béarnaise, or an unusual beef "Pont Cheval," napped with a cream sauce zested by sherry, raisins, and black peppercorns. All breads and desserts are homemade. In fact, San Antoine could earn top ranking just on the basis of its impeccable coconut cheesecake. Kudos should also be bestowed on the knowledgeable and discreet staff. Finished platters disappear at the appropriate time. Ditto extraneous silverware. All in all, it adds up to an exquisite remembrance. Dinner for two, $80 to $100 per couple plus drinks. Open Monday through Friday for lunch, 11:30 a.m. to 2:30 p.m. Dinner served Monday through Saturday, 6:30 to 10:30 p.m. Closed Sunday, April to November.

MODERATE

The Green Parrot, Red Tap Lane, Morne Fortune (tel. 452-3399 or 452-3167). At this hilltop perch near where the British and French fought so bitterly over the years, you'll enjoy a sweeping panorama of the glittering prize—the broad harbor of Castries. From the outdoor terrace, you'll gaze out over the entire capital. Indoors, the decor tends toward haute funk, with ornate velvet-flocked wallpaper and a stuffed crocodile posing on the piano. Either way, you'll savor delicious St. Lucian cuisine—which is to say, very delectable indeed. They serve an excellent four-course prix-fixe dinner for $33 per person, which might include seafood quiche, lobster bisque, grilled steak or shrimp Provençale for your main course, topped off with a crème caramel or trifle for dessert. Wednesday and Saturday evenings, live entertainment adds to the fun. Open daily for breakfast, 7 to 10 a.m.; lunch, noon to 3 p.m.; dinner, 6:30 to 11:30 p.m.

The Hummingbird, Soufrière (tel. 454-7232). If we had to name our favorite restaurants in the Caribbean, Hummingbird would definitely place at the top of the list. Certainly, the view ranks among the most spectacular in the world: a black-sand beach fringed by palm trees, with the awesome peaks of the Pitons jutting sheer from the sea just beyond. This is the sort of friendly, casual place where you'll want to make lunch stretch out for hours. In addition to some tables underneath palm-thatched umbrellas by the swimming pool, there's additional seating in the open-air restaurant itself. Flags and burgees from visiting yachts hang from the ceiling; batiks and wood carvings decorate the walls. While you contemplate the menu, sample one of their famous drinks, such as a Pitons Peril or Hummingbird Wallbanger. Choose among superb West Indian favorites: pepperpot, beef or chicken curry, Caribbean fish. But the house specialties are definitely the seafood: whelks, crab, octopus, lobster, or—most sublime delicacy of them all—St. Lucian crayfish, served with a garlic-butter sauce. Bring lots of film and a hearty appetite. Open daily from 8 a.m. to 10 p.m. or so; $25 to $50 per couple.

Rain, Columbus Square, Castries (tel. 452-3022). Named for the famous Somerset Maugham story (Maugham had frequently vacationed in St. Lucia), this white-and-green gingerbread-trimmed mansion with a tin roof looks as if it had been transported straight from the South Seas. Rain is known for its homemade ice creams and pizzas, as well as its potent rum drinks. In the evening, an elaborate seven-course champagne banquet is highlighted by four different wines and sumptuous entrées such as chicken Romanoff or steak. Open Monday through Saturday, 9 a.m. to 11 p.m.; about $20 to $30 per couple for lunch; $70 per couple for the prix-fixe banquet.

Rodney Bay is the hot spot for island action, with several good restaurants. Try the **Eagles Inn** (tel. 452-0650) for fresh seafood such as snapper or lobster, as well as creole cuisine; about $30 to $50 per couple for dinner. Open Sunday through

Thursday, 7 a.m. to midnight; Friday, 7 a.m. to 5 p.m.; Saturday, 5 p.m. to midnight. As its carefree name suggests, **The Lime** (tel. 452-0761) provides an open-air, informal setting for either lunch or dinner. At lunch, they offer light tidbits, such as roti, sandwiches, fish lasagna, or steak-and-kidney pie; about $20 to $40 per couple. The dinner menu highlights everything from seafood and chicken to steaks and chops, about $30 to $50 per couple. Open daily (except Tuesday) from 11 a.m. to 1 a.m. Overlooking the yacht harbor, **The Charthouse** (tel. 452-8115) is so chock-full of plants that it almost resembles a greenhouse. Along with the verdant milieu, harbor views add a handsome backdrop for enjoying steak and lobster, as well as other dishes. Come hungry—portions are generous. Open for dinner only, 5 p.m. to midnight; $30 to $50 per couple plus drinks (prices higher if you order lobster). When you want to dance, head to the **Splash** at the St. Lucian Hotel. **Monroe's** in Grande Rivière is more of a local place, featuring good reggae.

INEXPENSIVE
Chinese Wok, 91 Chausée Rd., Castries (tel. 453-1744). Connoisseurs of that West Indian specialty called roti will be in culinary heaven here. What exactly is it? It's a pancake-like Indian bread called puri stuffed with lightly curried chicken, beef, or vegetables. Chinese Wok makes the best in St. Lucia—all freshly prepared—and the portions are huge. Cool your palate with one of their excellent fresh tropical juices, such as passionfruit, soursop, or tamarind. They also do delicious Chinese take-out. Please remember—you're coming here for food, not ambience. The atmosphere is zilch (unless you think that Formica counts), but the entire establishment is sparklingly clean. Open Monday through Saturday, 11:30 a.m. to 9:30 p.m.; about $5 to $10 per couple.

ST. MAARTEN/ST. MARTIN

1. PRACTICAL FACTS
2. ROMANTIC INTERLUDES
3. HONEYMOON HOTELS AND HIDEAWAYS
4. ROMANTIC RESTAURANTS
5. NIGHTLIFE

Listen carefully and you'll hear the sugar birds as you wend your way along the beach past the blossoming oleander and bougainvillea to the two narrow main streets of the island's largest city—Philipsburg. Even here, where cars still pass in slow single file, the noises evoke a land that echoes its history: the gentle lapping of waves; the fluid mix of English, French, and Dutch; and the calling of men from the boats that ply the harbor combine to form a picture that overlaps century-old traditions with modern vitality.

France and the Netherlands share this small, 37-square-mile island, the smallest land mass in the world to be governed by two separate countries. When honeymooning here you have choices you won't find anywhere else, for this island is unique. Here you can opt to spend time exploring the quiet green pasturelands and fields of the French side for half the day, then join the bustle and excitement of the developing towns and their casinos on the Dutch side.

Situated in a string of three islets called the Dutch Windwards, St. Maarten/St. Martin lies 144 miles east and just barely south of Puerto Rico. To the immediate northeast are Saba and Sint Eustatius (also known as Statia), sister islands ruled by the Dutch. South and west lies St. Barthélemy, fondly referred to as St. Barts, kin to the French side of St. Martin.

Before the island claimed its dual nationality, Columbus supposedly anchored off its shores on November 11, 1493, the feast day of St. Martin of Tours (some historians claim he landed offshore of Nevis). Until the French corsairs arrived in the 1500s, the island was virtually left alone; only the Amerindians lived on its flatlands and rolling hills. The pirates liked the many bays and coves of St. Martin; the irregularities of its near-heart shape hid their ships when they retreated after plundering Spanish galleons bearing golden treasures from Mexico.

An early Dutch exploratory team landed in the 1600s but didn't stay long; nor did the French who took refuge on the island in 1629 after they were shipwrecked by a hurricane.

Later that year, however, the French returned, having been driven off of St. Kitts by the Spaniards. The Dutch came again too, two years later, and initiated the unique plan of cohabitation that exists in slightly altered form to this day. These early settlers picked the salt from the Grand Case salt pond, following in the historical footsteps of the Amerindians, who called the island *Salouiga*, "the land of salt."

The somewhat peaceful coexistence became marred by a Spanish takeover a few years later that produced one of the United States' earliest figureheads. Dutchman Peter Stuyvesant, who governed New York City when it was known as Nieuw Amsterdam, lost his leg in a battle to capture St. Maarten for his native country.

The year 1648 marks the true colonization of the island. On a day in late March the two countries signed a Partition Treaty at Mont des Accords (Mount Concordia), a site you can still hike to. One hundred and twenty-four years later a boundary—a stone wall—was established. Today there is only a small stone monument and back-to-back signs that say "Welkam aan de Nederlandse Kant" and "Bienvenue en Partie Française." Actually, legend tells that two men, one French and one Dutch and both drunk, paced off the island. The Frenchman had the greater stride apparently, but the Dutchman got the more valuable property.

Through sugar boom, slavery, and growing cotton, the island has survived with a certain spunk and a generous amount of friendly sophistication. Foreigners have always played a large part in the island's growth. Even in 1775 plantation owners and other inhabitants were speaking English as a common language. The population of outsiders now outnumbers the indigenous population.

Philipsburg, the capital of Dutch St. Maarten, stands on a slender strip of land outlined on one side by the Great Bay of the Caribbean and on the other side by the large Salt Pond. Its alleyways, called *steegjes*, join Front Street to Back Street, the only two main thoroughfares in town. It's a busy city compared to the relatively calmer maze of streets that comprise Marigot, the capital of the French side. The harborside ambience permeates this very French town, even on the more built-up streets, where the international boutiques are. Women pass by with baguettes under their arms, and a small cart with a red-and-white-checked umbrella, an *île aux glaces,* sells ice cream at the edge of the water. Grand Case, the only other developed village on the island, is a few minutes past Marigot. It's a one-street main town known for its many international restaurants.

Outside of the cities the land is a bit scrubby, with a smattering of cactus mixed in. When you head inland toward Colombier or Paradise Peak, however, you see a part of the island many tourists miss. This is where the land turns lush and tropical. Although bougainvillea, hibiscus, and frangipani grow by the sea, the growth in the interior surrounds you with a cool, almost tactile presence. This diversity appeals to many sports-minded vacationers. Thirty-seven inviting crystal-clear beaches draw scuba and snorkel aficionados, while the peaks here and on Saba and Statia lure hikers.

---

1. Practical Facts

GETTING THERE

For St. Maarten, Americans need to show proof of citizenship. A valid passport is preferable, but you can also use one that is expired, provided that it's not more than five years out of date. An original birth certificate with a raised seal, or a photocopy with a notary seal, or a voter registration card will also suffice. St. Martin requires one piece of identification with a photo, but there are no customs stops between the two sides of the island, so it is highly unlikely that you would be required to show your picture ID. You also must have a confirmed room reservation and a return ticket.

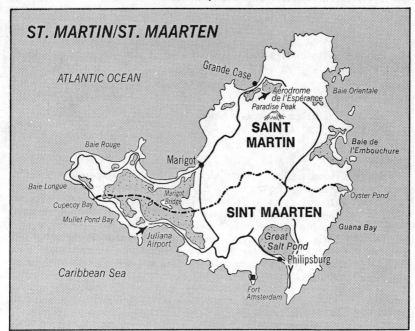

ST. MARTIN/ST. MAARTEN

ATLANTIC OCEAN

Grande Case

Baie Orientale

Aérodrome
de l'Espérance
Paradise Peak

SAINT
MARTIN

Baie de
l'Embouchure

Baie Rouge

Marigot

Baie Longue

Marigot
Bridge

Oyster Pond

Cupecoy Bay

SINT MAARTEN

Mullet Pond Bay

Juliana
Airport

Guana Bay

Great
Salt Pond

Philipsburg

Caribbean Sea

Fort
Amsterdam

There is a departure tax of $5 per person, which you do not have to pay if you are going from St. Maarten to Saba or Statia or are "in transit" to St. Barts.

The island is one of the most popular in the Caribbean, so you can reach it easily by plane, usually with only one change or by a direct flight.

By Air

All flights to and from the United States use Juliana Airport on the Dutch side of the island. **American Airlines** now offers some nonstop flights from New York and San Juan and one-stop or connecting flights from Boston, Chicago, Miami, and Dallas. **Pan Am** and **ALM Antillean Airlines** also have nonstop service from New York, and **Continental** wings its way nonstop between Newark and St. Maarten. Continental and Pan Am—like American—also offer a number of convenient connections to St. Maarten from several U.S. cities.

The other Dutch islands—Aruba, Bonaire, and Curaçao—connect with St. Maarten via ALM, and **Windward Islands Airways (WINAIR)** has regularly scheduled service from half a dozen other Caribbean islands.

The island has another, much smaller airfield outside of Grand Case. Esperance Airport serves **Air Guadeloupe** for its daily flights to and from St. Barthélemy and Guadeloupe.

Take note if you're flying from Puerto Rico or the ABC (Dutch) islands that baggage has been known to get delayed sometimes. The bags usually show up the next day by midafternoon. Plan accordingly if it's at all possible.

To Saba and Sint Eustatius: Regularly scheduled flights leave Juliana International Airport via Windward Islands Airways International (tel. 599/5-44237).

By Sea

Ferries and **sightseeing boats** ply the waters between St. Maarten and St. Barts, Anguilla, and Saba. Most of the boats to St. Barts—the *White Octopus* and *Quicksilver* are two—and the *Style,* which takes you to Saba, are day sails primarily for tourists. Rates run about $45 to $60 per person. More specific information is available at your hotel activities desk or at the tourism offices in Philipsburg and Marigot.

The ferry to Anguilla leaves from and returns to Marigot six days a week (not on Monday), catering as much to islanders as to tourists. Inquire in Marigot at the tourist office for schedules.

GETTING AROUND

You can explore the French or the Dutch side by taxi or by rental car. Following are the details.

By Taxi

Taxi fares are set, rather than metered, and are based on two-person occupancy. If you're coming from the airport, you should know that additional passengers raise the fare only $1 more per person. The daytime fares are reasonable, ranging from $4 to $15 from the airport to most major hotels and guest houses. Past 10 p.m. the rates go up 25% until midnight, when the fares become 50% more than daytime rates (until 6 a.m.). There are two main taxi centers, one in Philipsburg by the harbor and the other in the center of Marigot. Either can arrange for a 2½-hour island tour ($37.50 for two) or you can hire a taxi for $10 an hour, plus $2.50 for each additional 15 minutes.

By Rental Car

A valid driver's license is all that's needed. Although you can make a reservation for a car from the United States, once you get to the airport in St. Maarten, you must check in at the rental car counter (**Budget, Avis,** and **Hertz** are represented on the island). Even then you might not be able to drive away immediately. Regulations require that the car be delivered to your hotel. The regulations are not strict, however, and you sometimes may find that you can indeed drive away from the airport in your rented car.

Japanese and Korean cars are common, although Peugots do show up. Make sure the car you rent is fitted with seatbelts, and check tires, lights, etc., before you take the car out. And don't be shy if you'd like to exchange the car for another one; that is, if one is available.

Driving can be hazardous, as there are embankments and gutters along the sides of some of the roads. Drivers are more casual here than in the United States, and it's not uncommon for cars to pass, barely missing oncoming traffic. Also, be aware that most insurance companies do not cover accidents on dirt roads, which is a problem because many of the major hotels lie at the end of some unpaved pathway.

Don't be surprised either at the goats and cows wandering by the side of the road. After wondering whether they ever get hit, I saw a small goat buckle under a van. Miraculously, he fit directly under the wheels and bounced back up with only a forlorn bleat. Still, they do stray into cars' paths, and you might not be as lucky as the driver of that van.

By Bus

The bus system runs infrequently but regularly from 7 a.m. to midnight (fare 85¢). Opt for a rental car or taxi for island exploration; you'll be able to go farther, into more interesting places, and you can set your own pace.

LANGUAGE AND MONEY

Although Dutch is the official tongue and Papiamiento is the local dialect in St. Maarten, English is the prevailing language. You should have no problems communicating with people. On the French side, however, you may run into a few people who don't speak English, but they'll be the rarities. However, if you're unfamiliar with French food, you may find it handy to bring along a menu translation guide.

The money situation is also very simple. Although the Netherlands Antilles florin (or guilder) (NAf) and the French franc are the official currencies for the Dutch and French sides, respectively, the dollar is accepted throughout the island. In fact, the dollar is used more widely than the guilder. Even some vending machines accept American coins.

WEATHER

Temperatures remain at a pleasant 80° or 85° year-round, with the added comfort of breezy trade winds.

CLOTHING

Dress is casual, even in the casinos, although a few people do don evening apparel for special nights out. Bring at least two bathing suits for the beach, and a coverup for hotel common areas. A sweater or light wrap for women and a lightweight jacket for men will be sufficient for the occasional cool night.

TIME

The island is on Atlantic Standard Time, which means that in winter there is a one-hour time difference between St. Maarten/St. Martin and the East Coast of the United States; when it is noon in New York, it is 1 p.m. in Philipsburg and Marigot. When Daylight Saving Time goes into effect on the East Coast, the island then keeps the same time as New York.

TELEPHONES

To call Dutch St. Maarten from the United States, use the international calling code 011, then dial 599-5, then the local five-digit number. For French St. Martin, it's 011-590 plus the local six-digit number you want. Calling long-distance from the island to home is not always easy, so plan ahead if you can, with enough time to try again. If you're staying on the Dutch side and you want to call Marigot or Grand Case, dial 06, then your local number. Calls originating from the French side must begin with 3.

SPORTS

St. Maarten is a sports-lover's paradise on land and at sea. If you're interested in exploring the waters around the island, ask **Ocean Explorers** (tel. 45252) for their free diving guide. It's not only a good beginner's booklet, but a great introduction to the offshore treasures of the island, describing underwater caves as well as the sunken ship the H.M.S. *Proselyte,* a British frigate that went down in 1801. **Maho Watersports** (tel. 44387) and **Under the Waves** at the Grand Case Beach Club also offer resort courses and scuba-diving. It's $40 for one dive, equipment included; $100 for a three-dive package.

Sailors make use of the numerous marinas, at the same time that Windsurfers, waterskiers, and parasail adventurers are frolicking on the calm waters of Simpson Bay Lagoon and Orient Bay. **Lagoon Cruises** at Mullet Bay (tel. 42898) takes you 200 feet up in the air to ride the winds by parachute, for $25. Windsurfer rental around the island runs about $10 an hour, more for lessons.

On the shores of the lagoon within the Mullet Bay Resort is the island's only golf course, an 18-hole layout designed by Joseph Lee, exclusively for Mullet Bay guests. For tennis, visitors can play on one of the approximately 50 courts on the island. Serious athletes may appreciate the new sports center outside of L'Habitation; **Le Privilège** (tel. 873737) offers tennis, squash, archery, body-building, aerobics, yoga, and more. It's a complete sports village with restaurant, studio lodging, and nightclub.

SHOPPING

Because of its duty-free status, St. Maarten offers some of the best shopping buys in the Caribbean, especially on high-priced items such as jewelry, watches, fine crystal, porcelain, and silver—from all over the world and at prices usually between 20% and 60% off what you'd find in the United States. More than 500 shops on the Dutch-held side of the island alone are duty free. Most accept traveler's checks and credit cards, and almost all price their goods in dollars. Hours are generally from 8 a.m. to noon and from 2 to 6 p.m. (Monday through Saturday), although the shops by the casinos tend to keep later hours.

Philipsburg is a shopper's paradise. It's as if **Front Street** exists only for tourists with money to spend. Mirrored and chromed emporiums vie with small gingerbread-trimmed cottages to get travelers' attention.

If you're planning to buy a watch, dinnerware, camera, or appliance, do a little research before you get on the plane. Write down model numbers and names of specific items, with the price (including tax). Although the savings can be big, they can also be disappointing, especially on cameras and appliances where savings can be better in New York discount houses.

Two of the biggest and most-recognized names on the island offer jewelry and watches at huge discounts, and both have offices in New York that can service the timepieces when necessary. **H. Stern Jewellers** on Front Street offers savings of 20% to 40%. Open half-circle earrings in 14k gold with 16 emeralds for each ear sell for $280; a ¼-inch thick solid 14k gold bracelet with a Florentine finish, for $625. Sapphires, diamonds, aquamarines, tourmalines, pearls, lapis—the jewelry within these doors is both bold and staid; you can take your choice. Many name watches are here: Raymond Weil, Piaget, Concorde, Corum, Baume & Mercier, and more. **Spritzer & Fuhrmann** tempts shoppers at three locations (Mullet Bay by the casino, Marigot, and the airport). Watches, with as full a range as H. Stern, are usually 25% to 40% off U.S. prices; jewelry, 20% to 35% off; and Limoges, Lalique, Lladró, and other fine crystal and china, from 40% to 60% off.

Oro de Sol Jewelers in Marigot offers a similar line of watches, jewelry, and porcelain in addition to perfume and a good selection of china. (Their staff is also exceptionally nice.) You can get a full dinner service at 35% or more below their normally low prices if you take advantage of their occasional sales. The price range is enormous; for example, one five-piece place setting of Limoges "Monet" china— which at press time sold at Tiffany for $420—sold here for $238; a Villeroy & Boch "Mariposa" china place setting went for $68. The range is also evident in the flat-ware: a Christofle "Perles" silverplate five-piece place setting sold for $141, while a sterling setting of Puiforcat "Deauville" went for $4,900.

Colombian Emeralds (in Philipsburg and Marigot) is another well-known Caribbean jeweler that offers substantial discounts on watches and fine gems. A men's black Jaeger Le Coultre "Heraion" watch, normally $3,650, sold for $2,190.

Little Switzerland (in Philipsburg and Marigot) also has china, crystal, and watches. An 18k Rolex Lady Presidential was selling for $6,750 in St. Maarten.

The perfumes on the island in general can be as much as half off what you'd pay in the United States. Chanel No. 5 practically jumps off the shelves for $80 for ½ ounce, compared to the $110 price quoted in New York. Opium at ¼ ounce brings in $67.50 at home but only $55 on the island. There are many perfume and figurine shops on Front Street, or nearby, including **Penha** and **Yellow House**. Most of the prices are similar, varying perhaps by a few dollars. It's probably not worth your time comparison shopping.

International boutiques include **La Romana** (on Front Street, in Marigot, and in Mullet Bay), where you can indulge in designer fashions—Fendi, Krizia, Gianni Versace, Giorgio Armani, and Bottega Veneta among them—often at savings of 25% to 30%. **Leda of Venice** draws you in with Missoni ties, Missoni sweaters and cotton Polo shirts. For leather goods, try **Maximoflorence** in Philipsburg, which offers briefcases and handbags primarily, with a smaller selection of shoes and belts.

Marigot's other boutiques worth checking out carry fashions by Gucci, Guy Laroche, Yves Saint Laurent, Christian Dior, and Sonia Rykiel.

Stéphane Kélian, whose shoes from Paris include designs by Claude Montana, Maud Frizon, and Charles Jourdan, is represented at a shop in Mullet Bay. Next door, **Optiques Caraïbes** had Vuarnet glasses, and neighboring **Lolita Lingerie** boasts two windows full of silky, satiny, and sexy follies.

What you really want is a souvenir of the island; head for **Impressions** in Philipsburg. Batik pareus sell for $28, and you can walk away with striking hand-painted Haitian pegboards for $29 to $39. The store specializes in handcrafts and can package items for shipping and mailing. Only a few stores away, **Caribelle Batik** has smaller souvenir items such as T-shirts for a variety of prices, and sand dollars and whelks for $2.95. It's also a source for *USA Today,* the *Wall Street Journal,* and other U.S. papers.

Recently developed **Old Street,** off of Front Street, is Philipsburg's newest shopping area. Besides a fur salon, a Venetian glass shop, and clothing boutiques, the mall has a number of good snack places including a yogurt shop, a crêperie, and a sports bar and restaurant with a giant 46-inch satellite TV screen.

One last note for those of you going on to Saba. In the 1870s, one of the Saban women who had gone to study in a convent in Caracas, Venezuela, came back with the skills to make "Spanish work," or what has now become known as "Saba lace." After a brief period when the islanders almost lost their knowledge of how to make this delicate lacework, Saba again produces it for tourists. The prices vary greatly.

ABOUT ACCOMMODATIONS

If you know what you want, you can probably get it here. The island's dual identity encourages differences. You'll find an assortment of accommodations to suit a variety of tastes and budgets.

For those who have never visited the island, the general rule has been that St. Maarten had the big, casino-oriented resorts while St. Martin was known for quiet, small hotels. There's a grain of truth in that, but only a grain. The Dutch side of the island has two of the most attentive and most beautiful small hotels on the island—the Caravanserai and the Oyster Pond Yacht Club—not to mention the even smaller guesthouses in and around Philipsburg. At the same time, St. Martin has been developing larger, sophisticated resorts such as L'Habitation, La Belle Créole and condominium complexes not mentioned here. Still, the French side of the island for the most part is quieter and somewhat more isolated.

The prices listed in this section reflect the range from low season to high season. Generally, high season runs from December 15 through April 15. Some hotels have instituted a shoulder season, with corresponding midrange rates, so if you're traveling within a week or two of the beginning or end of high season, it might be worth your while to delay the trip until the hotel's official low season starts. The summer rates can be as much as 30% to 50% lower than winter rates for the same accommodations.

European Plan (EP) rates—with no meals included in the cost—seem to be the most widespread, although Modified American Plan (MAP, breakfasts and dinners included) rates are surfacing here and there.

All hotel bills include a 5% room tax in St. Maarten, and most also add a 10% to 15% service charge in lieu of tipping. St. Martin's hotels may—or may not—add a $1 per day per person room tax. A few hotels on the island add an energy surcharge, especially for air conditioning. Ceiling fans, however, are very effective; and some of the nicest accommodations are cooled only by the gentle whirr of their blades. Also, the current in most hotels matches that of the United States (many of the French hotels provide double-duty outlets for appliances using European or American current), so there's no need to bring adapters. In addition, some of the bigger, newer resorts come equipped with individual built-in hairdryers, so if you plan to travel with one, you might ask and save yourself the extra few pounds.

DINING OUT

St. Martin is known as the culinary capital of the Caribbean. The quality, consistency, and variety of the restaurants are truly remarkable, especially considering that many of the ingredients are flown in from all over the world. No matter what season you're traveling, make dinner reservations as soon as possible, preferably when you're making the hotel reservation. During high season, reserve at least one week in advance if at all possible; in summer, it's still a good idea to make reservations beforehand because the hours and days of operation may change depending on the numbers of tourists and the whim of the owners.

In most cases, a 15% service charge will be added to the bill, so tip only if you feel that your service was above the norm. Skim the menu, however, to double-check that service is indeed included as part of the total cost of the meal.

Don't get confused. In some restaurants *entrée* means "appetizer" rather than "main course." The main course dishes are usually listed under the headings *poissons* (fish) and *viandes* (meat).

HOW TO GET MARRIED ON ST. MAARTEN/ST. MARTIN

On the Dutch side, you'll have to establish residency one year prior to the wedding date. True to the romance of the French, you don't have to wait quite so long—only 30 days. Either you or your spouse have to have lived on St. Martin for the 30-day period prior to your application for a license. Once that is established you need to present proof of American citizenship, such as a valid passport or birth certificate. Or you can present proof of divorce, if that is applicable.

Even though you may not qualify for a civil or legal marriage on St. Maarten, you may still opt for a church wedding once you have a license granted by a U.S. official. The **Chamber of Commerce** (tel. 23590) can help you arrange the ceremony as well as many of the details, including flowers, catering, photographer, and the like.

FOR FURTHER INFORMATION

Contact **Mallory Factor Inc.,** 275 Seventh Ave., New York, NY 10001 (tel. 212/242-0000). **St. Maarten Tourist Information Office,** C. Wathey Square, Philipsburg, St. Maarten (tel. 22337). The **French West Indies Tourist Board,** 610 Fifth Ave., New York, NY 10020 (tel. 212/757-1125). **French Government Tourist Office,** 9454 Wilshire Blvd., Beverly Hills, CA 90212 (tel. 213/272-2661). **St. Martin Tourist Information Bureau,** Waterfront, 97150 Marigot, St. Martin, F.W.I. (tel. 875326).

---

2. Romantic Interludes

With lively casinos, lush mountain peaks, and hidden coves, the island offers one of the most diverse arrays of romantic activities in the Caribbean.

It's wonderful and exceedingly tempting! All of the island's **beaches** are open to the public. Many of the famous—and not so famous—hotels front the beaches but anyone can wander onto their strands and revel in their distinctive characters. Some of the more spectacular include Cupecoy, nestled into the cliffs; horseshoe-shaped Guana, isolated and quiet, known for its good body-surfing waves; and more lively Baie Rouge, a long semicircle of sand with a wave-washed arched rock at one end. Also notable are the nude beach at Orient Bay and the fine-sanded, good swimming beach by the Caravanserai; the latter, which lies at the end of the airport runway, provides unusual entertainment—you can watch the planes come in right overhead, with their landing gear already out and ready to touch down.

No beaches! Yet verdant **Saba,** an extinct volcanic peak that juts its nose up above water, draws a steady stream of curious travelers who want to spend an active day hiking the steps carved out of the rock mountain or scuba-diving at one of the most well-known sites in the Caribbean. Only four Hansel-and-Gretel-like villages house a total population of 950. Day trips by boat, on the *Style* (tel. 22167), depart at 9 a.m. six days a week from the **Great Bay Marina** in Philipsburg. For $45 per person, you'll be back by 5 p.m. the same afternoon. For longer stays, contact **WINAIR** (tel. 44237) about flights and fares.

Sister island to Saba and St. Maarten, **Sint Eustatius** (fondly known as Statia) lies 17 minutes away by **WINAIR** (tel. 44237). While there, take in the historic sights of the second-oldest synagogue in the Western Hemisphere, the **St. Eustatius Museum** in the 18th-century Doncker/De Graaff House, and the remains of warehouses once stacked with arms for the American colonists during the revolution. The other highlight not to be missed is the **Quill;** this extinct volcano is topped by a tropical rain forest dignified with majestic giant cedar trees and memorable iridescent hummingbirds.

In addition to Saba, Anguilla, and other neighboring inhabited islands, you may want to sail or motor to a smaller islet just for the **snorkeling.** Tintamarre and Pinel fill the bill well; their superb reefs are supplemented by the sunken hull of an old tugboat. Leave from the harbor by **L'Habitation** (tel. 873333, ext. 1382), or from **Bobby's Marina** (tel. 22366) for a longer sail. With full lunch and use of snorkeling equipment and 110 underwater camera, the trips cost approximately $55 per person.

The 46-foot red-and-white ketch *Gabrielle* departs **Bobby's Marina** in Philipsburg Harbor every day at 9 a.m. for a refreshing sail to a secluded beach for swimming, snorkeling, and picnicking. They provide the snorkeling equipment and underwater camera; you bring the 110 film. The $55-per-person fee includes lunch, beer, and soda but not the port tax. For information and reservations, call 22366 or 26016, or contact your hotel activities desk. Sunset and moonlight sails are also available at Bobby's Marina and other ports.

Right off the beach, within walking distance, the shallow reefs of **Dawn Beach** begin. This is a good spot for beginning snorkelers, who haven't become accustomed to submerging themselves yet—when the surf is calm. You may want to call the Dawn Beach Hotel (tel. 22929) and ask their water-sports center about surf conditions. Snorkeling equipment there costs $5 to $10 per person.

Saddle up and ride into the waves. The Dutch side's **Crazy Acres Riding Center** (tel. 22061) offers bracing 2- to 2½-hour horseback-riding excursions that venture through verdant countryside to a crystalline beach. The regularly scheduled morning trip ($45 per person) leaves at 9 a.m. with no more than eight people plus experienced escorts; the more private afternoon ride can be for just the two of you. **Caid and Isa** (tel. 873292), the French-side equivalent, outfit you with a beautiful Paso Fino horse. The rides leave from near L'Habitation at Anse Marcel and go to a secluded beach, unreachable by road, called Adam's Apple Cove (Anse de la Pomme d' Adam). It's $40 for a 2½-hour romp.

It's late in the day and the horizon is clear: take note that you may be witness to an exceptional **sunset.** The bright orange disc renders the turquoise water translucent for the most extraordinary effect. Head for the **Caravanserai** hotel near the airport in St. Maarten (tel. 42510) for a civilized drink in their newly renovated oceanfront gazebo or climb into the ruins of **Fort Marigot,** high on a hill just north of town.

Between Marigot and Grand Case you'll see a sign for **Paradise Peak,** the highest point on St. Martin. The 1,500-foot summit lies at the end of a narrow, curving road that passes through some of the lushest landscapes on the island. The vista once you get there is quite spectacular too, with clear views of Anguilla, Marigot, and Philipsburg. Plan the journey for the early morning—you won't want to hike the last few steps in the heat of the noon sun.

3. Honeymoon Hotels and Hideaways

You'll find a wide choice of accommodations on the island—from resort villages with casinos, shopping centers, and discos to quiet hideaways known for their tranquility and exclusivity. The rates quoted below reflect the spread between low- and high-season prices. Also, most packages include airport transfers.

THE FRENCH SIDE
Here are the choices for St. Martin.

Very Expensive
La Samanna, Baie Longue, P.O. Box 159, 97150 St. Martin, F.W.I. (tel. 590/875122; U.S. reservations: 212/696-1323, or toll free 800/372-1323 outside New York State.). Tucked into 55 acres of greenery at Baie Longue, this intimate, Mediterranean-inspired resort welcomes an exclusive but ever-so-casual crowd. The white stucco buildings and thatch-roofed terraces create an atmosphere that is known to soothe even the most savage business executive. Power brokers the world over have supped quietly in anonymous glory here. Nothing offensive meets the eye. Each of the 74 rooms—whether the air-conditioned main-house chambers or the spacious beachfront "apartments" cooled by ceiling fans—is fitted with a fully equipped kitchen, tasteful natural wicker and rattan appointments, chaise longues on the terraces, fresh flowers, and lovely tiled sinks. As of 1987, the resort switched over to a mandatory Modified American Plan (breakfasts and dinners) in season, with European Plan (no meals) available in summer. The price includes all water sports (except for lessons), use of the three tennis courts, and easy access to the 1½-mile stretch of isolated beach. Fine restaurant. Honeymoon package: None. Rates (MAP): $300 to $1,550 per couple per day plus $78 per person MAP. Closed September 1 to November 1.

Expensive
La Belle Créole, P.O. Box 118, Pointe des Pierres a Chaux, Marigot 97150, St. Martin, F.W.I. (tel. 590/875866; U.S. reservations: toll free 800/HILTONS). This extravagant resort complex was once the dream of Claude Philippe (former vice president and general manager of the Waldorf-Astoria), who envisioned it as an elegant retreat. He planned for it to resemble a French Mediterranean village with a central square and cobblestoned streets. His dream was not immediately fulfilled and the property lay abandoned until a few years ago. Conrad International (of Hilton fame) rehired Robert Cabrera, the original architect, to complete the 21 guest buildings on 25 acres of land. The hotel opened in December 1987 and offers five categories of rooms, twice-daily maid service, and full concierge desk. Breakfast is French continental-style, with croissants and brioche. A lovely tropical expanse with a three-acre lagoon marks it as a place to watch. Honeymoon package: Eight days/seven nights (BP): From $1,165 per couple. Includes champange and chocolates upon arrival, oceanview room with king-size bed, round-trip airport transfers, and more.

L'Habitation de Lonvilliers, P.O. Box 230, Marcel Cove, 97150 St. Martin, F.W.I. (tel. 590/873333; U.S. reservations: 212/757-0225, or toll free 800/847-4249 outside New York State). The magnificent approach to L'Habitation winds its way up to a spectacular vista, then curves down again to sea level at Marcel Cove. Standing on the flat of the land is an imposing mix of architecture with Disneyesque color and eclecticism: rustic lodge, balconied buildings à la New Orleans, and an elaborate Georgian plantation-style main house. To complete the fantasy, the planners installed a gazebo surrounded by flower-lined blue pebble walks. In the main house, a broad double staircase of marble leads down to the reception area and lounges. The 250 good-size rooms, inspired by the same imagination, flaunt fanciful headboards, geometric bedspreads, and pink marble sinks. All the rooms have either an efficiency or full kitchen, private balcony, and air conditioning. For privacy away from the central areas, request the quiet one-bedroom apartments by the marina causeway, where birdsong from the nearby 150-acre nature reserve replaces the murmur of more active guests. At your disposal is a freshwater pool, a children's playground, shuffleboard, volleyball on the 1,600-foot beach, and for a fee, tennis, squash, fitness equipment, and water sports. There are also international boutiques and two restaurants. Honeymoon package: Eight days/seven nights (BP): $1,539 to $2,134 per couple from April to December. Includes a bottle of champagne on arrival, daily breakfast, a dinner for two and wine at their restaurant, La Belle France, and a honeymoon souvenir. Five-day package also available.

Moderate
Grand Case Beach Club, Grand Case, 97150 St. Martin, F.W.I. (tel. 590/ 875187; U.S. reservations: 212/661-4540, or toll free 800/531-6767 outside New York State). New Yorker Michael Acciani and his family bring an upbeat atmosphere to this lively 76-room beachfront hotel just outside of Grand Case. Choose between studio and one-bedroom accommodations; the latter offer king-size beds with bamboo headboards, sitting area partitioned by a folding door, and balconies off the living room and bedroom. If you opt for a studio, request double beds (some are twin-bedded). Both types of rooms come with air conditioning, equipped kitchenette, and dining area. Beach buffs will prefer the oceanview, where you can hear the surf as a gentle lullaby through the night. A nice touch much appreciated by the guests is the inviting two-person hammocks strung along a strip of planted land just above the beach. Good restaurant. Water-sports center on the property. Honeymoon package: Eight days/seven nights (CP): $655 to $2,069 per couple. Includes a bottle of champagne at dinner, flowers, continental breakfast daily, use of artificial grass Omnicourt tennis court day and night. Four-day package also available.
Le Galion, Baie de l'Embouchure, 97150 St. Martin, F.W.I. (tel. 590/ 873177; U.S. reservations: toll free 800/223-9815). Tucked into a corner of the island near the nude beach at Orient Bay, Le Galion attracts a laid-back young set who don't mind a little sand on the floor. One honeymooning couple remarked, "We're treated like family guests rather than clients. They've been gracious, warm, hospitable." Manager Georges Bernard has been known to open a bottle of champagne spontaneously to welcome newlyweds, but it's an action of the moment. Here you're likely to see the guests windsurfing and sailing in the quiet bay, playing cards in front of the restaurant, or playing tennis. The renovated capacious one-bedroom cottages make a nice splurge for romantics. Air conditioning, kitchenettes or refrigerators, televisions, and patios bring high-tech comfort to an otherwise low-key and understated resort of only 63 units. Honeymoon package: None. Rates (EP): $85 to $470 per couple per day.
Club Le Grand Beach Resort, P.O. Box 582, Marigot, 97150 St. Martin, F.W.I. (tel. 590/875791). Nestled into the back streets of Marigot, Club Le Grand is just a seven-minute walk from the restaurants and shopping area around the harbor. Club Le Grand's claim to fame, however, is its billing as the only all-inclusive resort for couples on the island. The compact resort expanded in 1989 and now has 150 rooms under its wings and an enlarged pool area. The nicest units, with high ceilings and four-poster cane-and-wood beds, look out onto Gallis Bay. The bulletin board by the restaurant reflects the real draw here, for activities abound. Besides a bus to the casinos one night, a tour of the island, a boat trip to the snorkeling haven of Pinel Island, and nightly dancing, honeymooners will occasionally find posted a

call for players for the club's own version of the *Newlywed Game,* volleyball in the pool, or Ping-Pong. And, of course, there's an array of water sports. Honeymoon package: None. Rates: Four days/three nights (all-inclusive): From $780 to approximately $1,240 per couple, including all activities, three meals a day, unlimited drinks, airport transfers, tips, and taxes.

Inexpensive
Bertine's Guest House, Savana Grand Case, 97150 St. Martin, F.W.I. (tel. 590/875839). Open all year, but call to confirm. Friendly and charmingly modest, Bertine's appeals to the casual bed-and-breakfast crowd. The five petite rooms have a half-size refrigerator, ceiling fan, and folding aluminum chairs made cozy with patterned fabric cushions. Owners Bernard and Christine Poticha, originally from Chicago, and their small staff add a personal air that makes up for what the place lacks. The restaurant, which overlooks the untouched beauty of the hills above Grand Case and offers a grand, sweeping view of the bay from afar, welcomes the public. Continental breakfast is included in the rates, and coffee's available to early risers. Honeymoon package: None. Rates: From $45 per couple per day.

THE DUTCH SIDE
Here are the selections for St. Maarten.

Expensive
Mullet Bay Resort, SunResorts Ltd., N.V., St. Maarten, Netherlands Antilles (tel. 42801; U.S. reservations: 212/593-8600, or toll free 800/468-5538). A megaresort with over 600 rooms and suites, casino, disco, six restaurants, and eight bars, Mullet Bay feels more like an expatriate village on the island than a hotel. A country-club atmosphere predominates, primarily because of the resort's 18-hole, recently extended, Joseph Lee golf course—the only course on the island—which sprawls throughout the property, giving an open, landscaped effect to the 172 acres. Whether you're sports-minded or not, the emphasis here is on leisure. Besides the golf pro and staff, the facility offers 14 all-weather tennis courts and pro shop, two salt-water pools, jogging path with exercise stations, and for the more sedentary crowd, a major tax-free shopping center with international boutiques, food stores, and gift shops. The water-sports activities take advantage of the ¾-mile stretch of beach in addition to the lagoon and Mullet Pond, the two bodies of water that define the inner horseshoe shape of the resort. To ease guests' explorations, a courtesy bus calls at designated stops every 15 or 20 minutes. All accommodations have air conditioning, wall-to-wall carpeting, and king-size beds (or twins); many have a terrace. The one- and two-bedroom suites feature separate parlor/living rooms and full kitchens. Medical clinic on grounds. Honeymoon package: Eight days/seven nights (some meals): From $1,695 per couple during the summer; inquire for winter rates. Includes champagne and cheese tray on arrival, honeymoon dinner with wedding cake, rental car for one day, two rounds golf and tennis lesson, breakfast daily, three additional dinners. Four-day package also available.

Reserved and romantic, **Oyster Pond Yacht Club,** P.O. Box 239, St. Maarten, Netherlands Antilles (tel. 599-5/22206 or 23206; U.S. reservations: 212/696-1323, or toll free 800/372-1323 outside New York State), is a newlywed's dream. Just a few minutes from the French border on the eastern coast of the island, the yacht club sits on a spit of land with Oyster Pond on one side and the Caribbean on the other. You're more isolated here than at most of the other accommodations on the island, and tranquility is supreme. Children under 10 are not welcome, a policy that reflects the attitude and lifestyle of this sophisticated 20-room resort. Fashioned after a villa with a central courtyard and tower (with a lovely suite in it), the stone-and-stucco buildings were constructed in the 1960s; then in the early 1980s everything but the main structures underwent extensive renovation. The result: an impeccable vacation hideaway embellished with pastel-cushioned, white wicker, and rattan appointments, arched patios, and blooms and greenery everywhere. Take note of the door plaques, another example of the evident attention to detail. Each carries the name of a beloved or famous boat—*Fandango, Harlequin, Passage* (for *Windward Passage,* one of the greatest racing boats of its time)—and was carved in Newport in 1983 during the Americas Cup race. Good restaurant. Tennis. Swimming pool. Adjacent watersports center. Honeymoon package: None. Rates (EP): $190 to $370 per couple per day.

Moderate

The Caravanserai, P.O. Box 113, Maho Bay, Philipsburg, St. Maarten, Netherlands Antilles (tel. 599-5/42510; U.S. reservations: toll free 800/223-9815). Yes, it's right next to the airport, but it's situated so perfectly that you can take delight in watching the planes come in to land—usually between 9 a.m. and 9 p.m. One of the treasures of this tasteful but stylish 85-unit hotel is room no. 19, whose unique terrace dramatically juts out into an outcrop of highly textured rock carved out by the crashing ocean. Then there are the *caravanserai,* ten rooms built around a courtyard, reminders of the sleeping quarters in the 1600s for Eastern caravans. Other views overlook the ocean or the garden. At 4:30 you'll want to relax in a wicker couch by the arched colonnades of the beautiful Palm Court, where tea is laid out. The service is friendly and indulgent; what you can't find here—water sports, casino, golf course, disco—you'll find at sister establishment Mullet Bay, just minutes away. The Oasis restaurant is a well-known spot for watching the sunset, especially from within the delicate framework of the wrought-iron gazebo bar. Honeymoon package: Eight days/seven nights (MAP): $1,785 per couple in spring, summer, and fall. Includes welcome bottle of champagne, breakfast and dinner daily (at Caravanserai or Mullet Bay's restaurant), use of Mullet Bay's Tennis Village and golf course, rental car, even a wedding cake! Four-day package also available.

The Dawn Beach Hotel, P.O. Box 389, Oyster Pond, St. Maarten, Netherlands Antilles (tel. 599-5/22929; U.S. reservations: 212/840-6636, or toll-free 800/351-5656 outside New York State), rightly boasts about its beach, a long, superb stretch of aquamarine water with great close-to-shore reefs for snorkeling in addition to its swimming areas. Situated on the quiet eastern coast of the island, 155 recently redecorated guest rooms sit on 16 landscaped acres rising from the shore to the crest of a high hill, so all but a few rooms benefit from a water view. The oceanside rooms best befit a newlywed couple, with vaulted ceiling highlighting white exposed beams set against pink wainscotting. Sitting areas feature cable TVs and casual couches; kitchenettes, terraces or patios, and louvered, screened side windows make these rooms eminently comfortable. Tennis and a pretty pool complement the grounds. Whether you're snorkeling or staying overnight, stop in at the open-to-the-breezes bar and restaurant overlooking the pool for a romantic setting. Honeymoon package: Eight days/seven nights (EP): $714 to $785 per couple. Includes beachside room with use of rental car free for one day, snorkeling equipment for one day, tennis clinic and use of courts during the day, champagne and cheese platter, fresh flowers in the room, plus more.

Point Pirouette Villa Hotels, P.O. Box 484, St. Maarten, Netherlands Antilles (tel. 599-5/44207; U.S. reservations: 212/840-6636, or toll-free 800/351-5656 outside New York State). Five different villa communities make up this luxury complex of 51 units on 18 acres. Although there is no beach, each villa sports its own swimming pool, boat dock, and spacious, clean, and sophisticated surroundings. The decor will differ from villa to villa because each is individually owned, but all come with daily housekeeping service, use of the tennis court, and complimentary croissants and coffee each morning. Happy to arrange boat rentals and delivery, water sports, and TV or VCR rentals, the main office stands as a friendly focal point. Perhaps more than any other place on the island, Point Pirouette has the potential to become your home-away-from-home. The beaches at Mullet Bay and Cupecoy are just a short drive away, and although many of the larger hotels and casinos are nearby, these villas repose in relative quiet and seclusion. Honeymoon package: None. Rates: $90 to $455 per couple, or more if you want more than a one-bedroom villa.

Inexpensive

Mary's Boon, P.O. Box 278, Simpson Bay, St. Maarten, Netherlands Antilles (tel. 599-5/44235; U.S. reservations: 212/986-4373). At the gate, two painted sentries keep guard in front of black-and-white painted gatehouses. The garden path leads up to a cozy guesthouse that would fit as easily in Provincetown, Massachusetts, as it does here. The breezy front room attracts bibliophiles with eclectic tastes. Books are everywhere, backgammon tables stand ready in the bar room, and local art fills the wall space, occasionally broken by the delicate frame of a wicker bird cage. The 12 rooms on the ocean and by the airport (you *can* hear the planes) sport simple, urbane, and unadorned furnishings. You'll find twin beds pushed together, twin burners, and a one-sink efficiency kitchenette. This has the feel of a New England bed-and-breakfast turned tropical. Request the balconied upper-floor rooms that overlook the beach. Although children will be absent from the scene, you'll probably meet one of Rush Little's six dogs. Honeymoon package: None. Rates (EP): $75 to $150 per couple per day. Closed September and October. No credit cards or checks accepted.

The Pasanggrahan, P.O. Box 151, Front Street, Philipsburg, Netherlands Antilles (tel. 23588; U.S. reservations: 800/223-9815), features the comforts of a relaxed but well-run guesthouse right on Front Street. The veranda invites people watching, while the interior induces guests to share stories and sit back. This is a place that will please diehard city dwellers who crave being able to step out of their hotel into a bustling world of tourists and islanders. Personal attention, air conditioning, and beachside lounging out beyond the tropical backyard are the pluses here. Rates range from $57 for the standard beachfront room to $110 for the more romantic Queen's Room.

SABA AND STATIA

Captain's Quarters, Windwardside, Saba, Netherlands Antilles (tel. from St. Maarten 04-2201; U.S. reservations: toll free 800/223-9815). A quaint ten-room inn that was a sea captain's house in the 19th century, Captain's Quarters hides its guests away in either wood-frame guest cottages or in the main house where the honeymoon suite is located. Antiques and four-poster beds make the secluded stay a joy, as does the remarkable pool, the only one on the island. Honeymoon package: None. Rates (EP): $75 and up per couple per day. For MAP rates, add $25.

The Old Gin House, P.O. Box 172, Lower Town, St. Eustatius, Netherlands Antilles (tel. from St. Maarten 03-2319; U.S. reservations: 212/535-9530, or toll free 800/223-5581). If you like black-sand beaches, *quiet* nights, and the feel of being truly away from it all, you'll love Statia. The 20 rooms of this made-for-romance hideaway give you two choices: Six face the beach, the others, across the street, front the pool. The charming inn stands on the site of a building that once housed a cotton gin. Although the building is a modern reconstruction, it captures the feel of the past without neglecting the amenities of the present. Run by a former art director of a major advertising company and his wife, who taught art, the many-beamed inn flourishes under their care. Each room is individually decorated with comfortable and interesting antiques. The restaurant serves up notable gourmet fare on beautiful Spode china. Honeymoon package: None. Rates (EP): $130 to $180 per night for two.

4. Romantic Restaurants

The island's restaurants deserve their world-class reputations. As much as you like one restaurant, be adventurous and go someplace new the next time. From Chinese and Indonesian to the finest French and Italian, the restaurants alone will lure you back to St. Martin/St. Maarten.

EXPENSIVE

Le Poisson d'or, Marigot (tel. 877245). Water laps gently at the base of the dining terrace, capturing the best of a romantic moonlit night. Inside, stone walls with arched entrances provide a backdrop for a changing exhibit of original art. But it's the cuisine here that draws crowds from every corner of the world. From the simple to the sublime, the food is in a word—wonderful. Lobster and vegetables in a light vanilla cream sauce. Puff pastry with flawless scallops. The inspired combinations work with a sensitivity rarely found outside the best restaurants of New York City and France. As beautiful to the eye as to the palate, the creations at Poisson d'Or merit the expense. Dinner for two with appetizers, dessert, and wine runs from about $130 per couple and up. Open daily from noon to 2 p.m. and from 6:30 to 10 p.m. in season; from 6:30 to 10 p.m. off-season; closed Sunday, May to December.

Messalina, Marigot (tel. 878039). A classic beauty that oozes romance, this impeccable restaurant overlooking the square and harbor in Marigot enfolds its diners in a skyscape of blue with white clouds. The fresco-like painting is set off by gold moldings that are in turn accentuated by delicate peach and sand wall colors. The ambience and food match the decor. Classical music plays softly in the background, while crystal chandeliers add a soft light to the scene. Choose from a diversity of Italian specialties, from salmon carpaccio to fresh trenette in pesto sauce to snapper poached in marsala wine. Selections for lunch are more limited but no less delicious. Lunch for two with soft drinks and antipasti, about $50; dinner, appetizers from $7.50 to $14, pasta appetizers from $9.50 to $17.50 ($17.50 for pasta as a main course), entrées from $15 to $26.50, salads from $7.50 to $9.50. Open daily from noon to 2 p.m. and from 6 to 10 p.m.; closed Tuesday off-season.

Casual and chummy, both the tourists and the staff at **Sebastiano's,** on the outskirts of Grand Case (tel. 875886), seem to have a good, high-spirited time. Here you'll find down-home northern Italian cooking. The chef, Sergio, hails from Milano and makes a mean matriciana sauce and a superb scaloppine alla pizzaiola. The fresh pasta dishes are priced from $11 to $14 (add $5 if served as a main course or shared); the appetizers run from $6 to $11; entrées, from $17 to $26. Dessert will add another $5 or so to the bill. MasterCard and Visa accepted, but not American Express. Call for hours.

Hévéa, Grand Case (tel. 875685). Located on the main street, Hévéa boasts an elegant intimacy that begins at the door, which is flanked by two simple topiary trees. Once inside, you'll find the table set with pink linen, Aynsley Pembroke china, and a single taper in a glass chimney. The food ranks among the best on the island, with a mixed greens and foie gras salad that should not be missed. Save room, too, for the desserts, which taste as wonderful as they look. Appetizers from $8, main courses from $20, and desserts from $6.50; Hévéa also offers two prix-fixe menus, for $27 and $36. Call for hours (usually 6:30 to 10 p.m. daily); the owners also occasionally leave a reservations notebook on the porch for guests to indicate their preferred dining hours.

Le Tastevin, Grand Case (tel. 875545). Chef Daniel Passeri brought treats from Burgundy to Grand Case at L'Auberge Gourmande; now across the street and on the water, at Le Tastevin he and chef Philippe Cassan are offering delicious, well-prepared nouvelle cuisine to tempt even the most diehard traditional *saucier*. The beachfront terrace drips with bougainvillea and is especially nice for lunch. The smooth pâté of tuna in a sweet pepper ring is garnished beautifully with a tomato rose. The grilled langouste Tastevin and the charred chicken present simple but elegant fare executed by a knowing hand—and it is this simple elegance that makes Tastevin the gem that it is. Lunch for two with appetizers, beverage, and a shared dessert: about $60; dinner, from about $70. Their superb wine list starts at $15 and includes such extravagances as a Château Margaux 1971 for $285 and a Château d'Yquem 1979 for $210; the wine list maps each grape-producing region and now also offers wines by the glass. Open from noon to 2:15 p.m. and from 6:30 to 10 p.m.; closed Wednesday (and they usually close for vacation during September). MasterCard and Visa accepted, but not American Express.

La Rhumerie, Colombier (tel. 875698). The best of French Créole cooking awaits you in this charming house set in the lush interior of the island. Madame Le Moine, who brought fame to Marigot's Cas' Anny restaurant (then called Chez Lolotte), has outdone herself here; with an herb and vegetable garden out back, she uses the freshest of ingredients for such delectable items as conch creole style and court bouillon of crayfish. For an authentic taste of the French West Indies, try the accras (fish fritters) and the house's special homemade—and potent—fruit-imbued rums. Take a stroll down the pastoral road before you head in to eat; the scents and sights outside are a perfect complement to cuisine indoors. Dinner for two with appetizers, dessert, and two rum drinks, from about $90 up. No credit cards accepted; traveler's checks and personal checks with passport or picture license are welcomed. Call for hours; usually two sittings at dinner.

La Samanna, Baie Longue (tel. 875122). This most exclusive and picture perfect of resorts on the island opens its doors to the public for breakfast, lunch, dinner, and drinks. The atmosphere bespeaks relaxed gentility, taste, tranquility. The backdrop: aquamarine water and perennial blossoms. Straw chairs with blue-fringed cushions, ceiling fans, white stucco walls—each element helps to evoke a lifestyle of leisure and pleasure. Even the table setting, a blue-and-white Rosenthal wave pattern, adds to the effect. Feast on sautéed foie gras with truffle sauce, osetra caviar, rack of lamb, roasted free-range chicken, and the like; dieters will appreciate the dinner menu, which notes low-calorie dishes. If you just want a peek at the place, go for the continental breakfast ($13 per person) from 8 a.m. to 10 a.m. Figure on at least $50 for two for lunch and $140 for dinner, not including drinks or wine. American Express accepted, but not MasterCard or Visa. Closed September 1 to November 1. Open for lunch from 12:30 to 2:30 p.m.; dinner from 7 to 9:30 p.m. Reservations suggested.

Oasis, at the Caravanserai (tel. 42510). Thoroughly romantic oceanside dining and a great place for a sunset drink. Since the polygonal Oasis juts out into the sea, many tables look right out over the wave-washed lava rock directly to the horizon. Muted greens and pinks color an interior gazebo bar that offers such "potent potions" as a Cheri Love Kiss. Lunch entrées begin at $7.50, with soups a little less; dinner entrées start at $15, soups and salads at $4, and appetizers at $7. Open for breakfast from 7:30 to 10:30 a.m.; lunch from noon to 2:30 p.m.; dinner from 7 to 10 p.m.; Sunday brunch from 11 a.m. to 2:30 p.m. Or come for the happy hour, which runs from 5 to 7 p.m.

MODERATE

West Indian Tavern, Philipsburg (tel. 22965). It's a little touristy but loads of fun late at night. The West Indian Tavern has a funky, somewhat offbeat air, with brightly colored parrot planters, lots of greenery, vivid red, green, and white gingerbread trim and trellises, and parasol-covered ceiling lights. On Sunday, Tuesday, and Thursday nights, strolling guitar players wander from the terraced tables to the backgammon barroom and tropical veranda. Fresh fish dinners are served until midnight; the bar and veranda stay open until 12:30 or 1 a.m. Appetizers from $5.95; main dishes from $14.95. Happy hour drinks are two-for-one from 4 to 6 p.m.

Bamboo Garden, at the Mullet Bay Resort (tel. 2801, ext. 367). Delicious gourmet Chinese food, New York style, is what you'll get here. Manager Lawrence Lo moved from the heart of Manhattan to work his wonders here—the Peking duck and crisp beef with orange rind are standouts. The restaurant, in the resort's hillside building (ask for directions at the front desk), sports a fantasy-like Polynesian decor that's at once festive and genial. Appetizers start at $5.50, main dishes at $14.75; the restaurant also offers two "dinners for 2," for $65 and $82. Open daily except Tuesday from 5:30 to 10:30 p.m. year-round.

INEXPENSIVE

On the Dutch side, most likely you'll be sitting next to locals at Callaloo (no phone), Promenade Arcade, off Front Street next to Impressions. For an inexpensive lunch, grab a slice of pizza or quiche or hamburger at this Philipsburg institution. Hours noon to 3 p.m. for lunch, 7 to 11 p.m. for dinner. **Zemi-by-the-Sea**, on Front Street in Philipsburg (tel. 25221), also offers low-priced ultracasual lunches —and you get the bonus of overlooking the harbor from a pleasant wood deck. The place features health foods and delicious fresh fruit drinks at prices that can't be beat: breakfasts from $3, lunches from $4. Open 8:30 a.m. to 9:30 p.m. At the U.S.–style **Cheri's Cafe,** next to the Casino Royale, you can relax under the white pavilion and order munchies such as fried zucchini, buffalo wings, and mozzarella sticks for $3.50 and up. They have seven-ounce hamburgers, kosher hot dogs, and salads too! Soca, jazz, or other live entertainment charges the area from 8 p.m. till the midnight closing. Don't expect to use your credit cards, though. Further indulge yourself at the nearby shopping center's **Ben and Jerry's Ice Cream** store or at the **West Indies Yogurt Co.,** which tempts passersby with Häagen-Dazs and French crêpes as well as frozen yogurt; cones and cups start at $1.75 and $1.50, respectively. Both places are usually open 9:30 a.m. to 10 p.m. (until 1 a.m. on weekends).

The French side has a few good inexpensive retreats as well. **Le Panoramique Restaurant and Grill** (tel. 875187), located near the Grand Case Beach Club in a polygonal building that juts out into the sea, serves up fresh fish specials as well as hamburgers and other classic American sandwiches; prices start at $5.25. Open for breakfast from 8 to 10 a.m.; lunch from noon to 3 p.m.; dinner from 7 to 9:30 p.m. In Grand Case proper, settle in to people-watch at one of the outdoor tables at **Restaurante Típico Português,** where you can get a very unpretentious prix-fixe lunch for $12. If you're strolling in Marigot, stop in at one of the cafés for the lunch special; prices vary but most are under $10. Then, at **Etna par dolce vita** (on Kennedy Avenue), finish lunch or dinner with homemade ice cream and cookies. Flavors run from the expected chocolate and coffee to the unusual: soursop, passionfruit, and rose.

5. Nightlife

If it's nightlife you want, you'll find plenty of it at the island's eight casinos in and around Philipsburg.

For discos, head to **L'Atmosphere** (tel. 875024) in Marigot, **Studio Seven** above the Casino Royale (tel. 42115), or **Le Club** (tel. 42801) at Mullet Bay. **Boîte Privilège,** at Le Privilège (tel. 873737) has a dance floor high above Anse Marcel, and **Night Fever,** a disco in Colombier, is an interesting adventure into island life. St. Maarten now even has its own **Comedy Club,** with shows Tuesday through Sunday, at the Maho Beach Resort. *St. Maarten This Month,* a free tourist guide, includes up-to-date listings of where and when to go for live music—from steel bands and calypso to traditional piano-bar fare.

UNITED STATES VIRGIN ISLANDS

"Isle 95 weather. Mostly sunny today, high about 82°. Mostly clear tonight, temperatures around 75°. Winds from the east at about 12 knots per hours. Sunny tomorrow." That's the weather report you'll hear on the radio practically every day of the year in the United States Virgin Islands.

Blessed with about 300 sunny days a year, crystal-clear waters the color of molten turquoise (and sapphire, and aquamarine), plus pure white, powder-fine beaches, the U.S. VI has become known as America's Paradise. The island group is composed of St. Thomas, St. John, and St. Croix, plus about 50 tiny islets and cays, most of them uninhabited. St. Thomas turns on the glamour full force, tempting visitors with a cosmopolitan array of duty-free shopping bargains and fast-lane nightlife. Life centers on its red-roofed capital, Charlotte Amalie, which arcs around a harbor as famous as that of Rio de Janeiro or Monte Carlo—and equally pleasure-loving. Nature reigns on St. John, the lushest of the isles, where two-thirds of the land is national park, and a string of unspoiled beaches with evocative names such as Hawksnest and Cinnamon Bay are strung like pearls along the northern coastline. Life's pace moves mighty slow here—the whole island seems to have hung up a "Do Not Disturb" sign. St. Croix combines a rich history with modern pleasures. Christiansted, its capital, looks very much as it did 300 years ago, with its yellow-painted fort and arcaded promenades lining the waterfront. But it is also thoroughly up-to-date: Many of those old buildings now house duty-free shops and gourmet restaurants, and you'll enjoy coming home to your luxury hotel after a full day of explorations. St. Croix also packs in the most geographical diversity of the islands, with everything from cactus-strewn desert on its far eastern end to dense rain forest on the west. And exotic as the vistas are, you'll feel right at home, because the U.S. VI is an American territory. English is spoken, the currency is the dollar, you don't need a passport, and satellite dishes pick up all the big televised games from the United States.

Located about 18° north of the equator, the island group spreads out over 14,000 square miles of sparkling blue waters. Puerto Rico lies 40 miles to the east, the British Virgin Islands immediately to the west. St. Thomas and St. John are neighbors, less than three miles apart from each other across Pillsbury Sound; St.

Croix is 35 miles to the south. While both St. Thomas and St. John have their north shores bathed by the Atlantic, and south coasts lapped by the Caribbean Sea, St. Croix is completely surrounded by the Caribbean. It's easy to travel between the islands: St. Thomas and St. John are linked by a 20-minute ferry ride, while St. Croix is joined to its sister islands by both seaplane and regular air service.

Whether you approach the region by sea or air, you'll be amazed by the sheer number of mountainous green islands you'll see looming out of the water—about 100 in all, between the U.S. and British Virgin Islands. The islands look exactly as you imagine Caribbean isles should, with glossy coconut palms, sugar-white beaches, and colorful flowers everywhere: white and pink oleander, orange flamboyant, scarlet poinsettia, and bougainvillea blossoms in magenta, crimson, and orange.

Although jungly vegetation covers most of the hillsides, you can still discern the jagged contours, testimony to the islands' fiery volcanic past. You'll wonder how they looked to Christopher Columbus, when he sailed through the channel after so many days at sea. "Very mountainous," he recorded in his 1493 diary, "and very green down to the sea. A delight to see." In appreciation of the islands' beauty and number, he named them Las Virgines, after the legendary followers of St. Ursula. Columbus didn't stay long—the resident Carib Indians gave him a fierce welcome—but he did christen St. Croix, St. Thomas, and St. John.

For the next 400 years, possession of the islands seesawed between the great European powers—Spain, the Knights of Malta, France, England, Holland, and Denmark. Because of the lack of any strong government, piracy flourished during the late 16th and early 17th century. The islands' many bays and secret coves became hiding places for the likes of Captain Kidd and Edward Teach, better known as Blackbeard. (Blackbeard clearly was one of the first to realize the importance of public image. To terrify his victims, he braided his chest-length beard with colored ribbons and stuck lighted matches in his hair so that he would look truly fiendlike.)

Finally the Danes established domination and a modicum of control, taking over St. Thomas (1672) and St. John (1683), and finally buying St. Croix from the French in 1733. The diligent Danes set about organizing the islands for profit. To encourage trade, St. Thomas became a free port in 1724, while St. John and St. Croix devoted themselves to sugarcane cultivation. For nearly 100 years, sugarcane ruled as king in what was called the Danish West Indies. But cane cultivation was only profitable when dependent on the cruelties and horrors of slavery. After the abolition of slavery in 1848, the sugar industry dwindled.

In 1917, the Danes sold the islands to the United States for the then-exorbitant sum of $25 million, and the Stars and Stripes began flying over Government House and other public buildings. Today, the United States Virgin Islands are an American territory, presided over by an elected governor and legislature, and residents are U.S. citizens (although they cannot vote in federal elections).

The best thing about a honeymoon in the U.S. VI is the wide range of possibilities open to you. If you enjoy sports, you'll want to take advantage of the world-class conditions for scuba-diving, snorkeling, and fishing. In particular, consistent trade winds and deep cruising waters make the U.S. VI and neighboring B.V.I. a spectacular pleasure for sailors. You can also play tennis, golf on championship courses, saddle up for a ride through the rain forest or along the shore, or perhaps take up windsurfing or waterskiing. Meanwhile, lazy bodies can bronze themselves on a bevy of beaches, many of which—such as Magens Bay on St. Thomas, Trunk Bay on St. John, and Buck Island near St. Croix—show up on various "Most Beautiful in the World" lists. In fact, relaxation is so much a way of life hereabouts, that Virgin Islanders have a special expression to describe it—"just limin'," they say. Count on doing plenty of "limin'" on your honeymoon.

---

1. Practical Facts

GETTING THERE

No passports are required for U.S. or Canadian citizens. However, you will need proof of citizenship, such as an original birth certificate or notarized copy, or a voter registration card, for re-entry into the U.S. mainland.

Frequent flights from throughout the United States make it easy to reach paradise. In addition, the islands are one of the most popular Caribbean ports of call for cruise ships.

By Air

To St. Thomas: **American, Pan Am, Delta, TWA,** and **Midway** all serve the island (some via connecting service from San Juan).

To St. Croix: **American, Pan Am,** and **Midway** all serve the island, first stopping in St. Thomas.

To St. John: You must fly to St. Thomas, then take the **Virgin Islands Seaplane Shuttle** or the **Red Hook ferry** (see details which follow) to St. John. Some of the St. John hotels run private ferry shuttles for their guests.

Commuter carriers flying from San Juan to the islands include **American Eagle, Eastern Metro, Aero Virgin Islands, Crown Air, VI Seaplane Shuttle/Trans World Express.**

By Ship

Charlotte Amalie in St. Thomas is the number one port in the U.S. VI. Over 700,000 cruise passengers a year visit this sparkling blue harbor surrounded by steep green hillsides, and they rate it as their favorite port of call. Among the lines calling at St. Thomas are **Carnival, Norwegian, Caribbean, Princess,** and many, many others. Ask your travel agent for details. St. Croix has become increasingly popular, with ships putting in either at Christiansted or Frederiksted. No large ships call at St. John, only the ultra-yachts, such as Cunard's *Sea Goddess.*

INTER-ISLAND TRAVEL

Because each of the three U.S. Virgins has such a different personality, it's fun to island-hop during your honeymoon. Convenient seaplane and ferry service makes it convenient, too.

By Seaplane

The **Virgin Islands Seaplane Shuttle** (affectionately known to area residents as "The Goose") links St. Thomas, St. Croix, St. John, Tortola (British Virgin Islands), and San Juan (Puerto Rico). The flight is really nifty, and you get great views of the islands from the air. A flight from St. Thomas to St. Croix costs about $35 one way and $70 round trip. For reservations and information, see your travel agent or call 809/773-1776.

By Ferry

The Virgin Islands ferries provide another scenic, convenient way to do island sightseeing. The St. Thomas–St. John ferry runs between Red Hook, St. Thomas, and Cruz Bay, St. John every hour between 7 a.m. and 10 p.m.; fare is $2.25 per

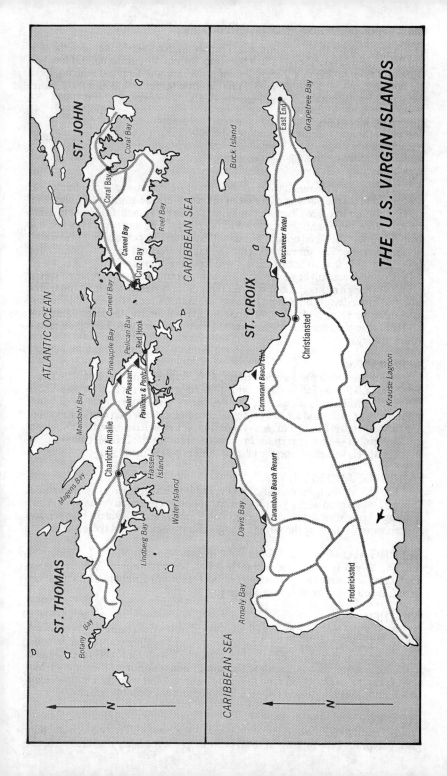

THE U.S. VIRGIN ISLANDS

ST. JOHN

ATLANTIC OCEAN

Coral Bay

Coral Bay

Caneel Bay

Cruz Bay

CARIBBEAN SEA

Reef Bay

ST. THOMAS

Mandahl Bay

Magens Bay

Pineapple Bay

Caneel Bay

Pelican Bay

Red Hook

Point Pleasant

Pavilions & Ponds

Charlotte Amalie

Hassel Island

Water Island

Lindberg Bay

Botany Bay

N

Buck Island

East End

Grapetree Bay

Buccaneer Hotel

Christiansted

ST. CROIX

Cormorant Beach Club

Krause Lagoon

Carambola Beach Resort

Davis Bay

Annaly Bay

Frederiksted

CARIBBEAN SEA

N

person each way for the 20-minute ride. There is also ferry service between the U.S. and British Virgin Islands: from St. Thomas to Tortola, Virgin Gorda, and Jost Van Dyke; and from St. John to Tortola. For information about fares and schedules, call the **Native Son** (tel. 809/774-8685) or **Smith's** ferries (tel. 494-4430). Note: Proof of citizenship is required to enter the B.V.I.

GETTING AROUND

Good taxi service and widely available rental cars make it easy to get around all three islands.

By Taxi

Taxis are available on all three islands. Rates are fixed by law and charged per person, based on the number of people in the cab. Rates are quite reasonable: From the St. Thomas airport to Charlotte Amalie will be $6 per person; from the airport to the Red Hook ferry to St. John, about $12 per person. The most expensive taxi ride from the airport to a hotel on St. Thomas will be about $22 per couple. There will be an extra charge of 75¢ for each suitcase. Drivers are required to carry copies of the designated taxi rates, so ask to see it if you have any questions. Tipping is not required, though you might want to give something extra if you have received special service. Although tariffs are inexpensive, taxi fares really start to add up if you will be taking several a day. If you plan on bopping around a lot, rent a car. On St. John, taxi service gets a bit spotty after 9 p.m. If you are arriving on the island from the mainland later than that, make sure you make arrangements with your hotel for a pickup from the ferry dock.

By Rental Car

The major rental car agencies (**Hertz, Avis, Budget,** and **National**) are represented on St. Thomas and St. Croix, with desks right at the airport. Rates run $22 to $85 per day, unlimited mileage. Jeeps are definitely the way to go on the steep, winding roads of St. John and are fun on any of the three islands; Jeep rentals run about $60 to $65 per day. In order to rent a car or Jeep, you *must* have your driver's license.

Remember—*driving is on the left,* a holdover from the Danish colonial days. Steering wheels will also be on the left, the same as on the mainland.

LANGUAGE AND MONEY

The U.S. dollar is the official currency, and English is the language, sometimes warmed and flavored with a West Indian lilt. You might hear a bit of "talkin' broad" —using Creole dialect, which mixes in Portuguese, French, Dutch, English, and African words, reflecting the varied heritages that have influenced these islands.

GETTING ALONG

The Virgin Islanders are extremely polite, reserved people. A simple "good day" is a must when dealing with them, rather than starting right in with a question. In return you will be treated with courtesy.

WEATHER

With such a blessedly perfect climate, you almost wonder why they bother with a daily weather report. The U.S. VI has sunny, warm weather year-round. Summer temperatures average about 82°, winters, around 77°—just a 5° difference. Thanks to the cooling trade winds, the islands remain comfortable during the summer. May and September to December tend to get the most rain, but even then, most precipitation tends to fall in passing showers. Days without any sunshine are rare.

CLOTHING

No matter which island you visit, casual is the byword. Pretty much anything goes, except for bathing suits in town or in shops. Some fancy restaurants require jackets and ties for gentlemen in the winter season (usually jackets only in summer), but such guidelines are rare. You will be most comfortable in lightweight cotton clothing. Because of the balmy climate, you probably won't need a cotton sweater or sweatshirt, even at night.

TIME

The U.S. VI remains on Atlantic Standard Time all year. In winter, when it is noon in New York, it is 1 p.m. in the U.S. VI. In summer, when the mainland observes Daylight Savings Time, the hour is the same in East Coast cities as it is in the U.S. VI.

TELEPHONES

You can dial the U.S. VI direct from the mainland; the area code is 809. Once in the islands, the phone system functions pretty much as it does back on the mainland. Coin-operated pay phones are everywhere; local calls cost 25¢ for the first five minutes.

POSTAGE

Once again, you're in familiar territory. The islands are part of the U.S. postal system and use the same rates and stamps as the rest of the country.

SHOPPING

America's paradise is also a shopper's paradise. From the time of the Danes, the islands, and most notably St. Thomas, have been duty-free ports. Not only does the U.S. VI offer low prices and a wide selection, Americans also get double the U.S. Customs exemption permitted from other Caribbean islands—$1,600 per couple. For details, see the section on U.S. Customs, which follows.

Charlotte Amalie on St. Thomas has the widest selection and the most shops, which line Main Street and the quaint alleyways leading to the harbor, as well as at **Havensight Mall,** at the West Indian cruise-ship dock. Many of the best-known stores, such as Little Switzerland and Colombian Emeralds, have branches both in St. Thomas and St. Croix. Meanwhile, St. John is known for island-made fashions, fine handcrafts, and gifts. When shopping, look for stores that belong to the V.I. Retailer's Association: Members display the logo, which depicts a gift-wrapped box. Member stores agree to offer the highest-quality goods at the lowest possible price, and stand behind their merchandise. In the islands, most stores are open 9 a.m. to 5 p.m., Monday through Saturday. Hotel boutiques often close later. In St. Thomas, the Havensight Mall stores stay open until 9 p.m. on Fridays.

Here's a general introduction to the shopping bargains you can find in the U.S. VI. For details about where to shop, see the write-ups on each of the islands.

China, porcelain, and crystal. Fill out your china and crystal patterns, at prices about 40% to 60% lower than back home. You'll find all the most prestigious lines, including Wedgwood, Royal Worcester, and Villeroy & Boch china; as well as crystal from Waterford, Lalique, Baccarat, and Orrefors. Porcelain figurines by Lladró, Goebel-Hummel, and Royal Copenhagen are also good value. Note: Even if a store carries a certain line, it may not stock your particular pattern. To find out who carries what, contact: In St. Thomas/St. John: **Virgin Islands Retailers Association,** P.O. Box 1275, St. Thomas, USVI 00804 (tel. 809/774-7305). In St. Croix: **St. Croix Visitors Bureau,** P.O. Box 4538, Christiansted, USVI 00822 (tel. 809/773-0495). You might also want to check out a copy of *A Shopper's Guide to the Caribbean* (Prentice Hall Press, New York).

Table linens. Set your table with fine linens. Take your choice—stores carry everything from delicate laces and hand embroideries to easy-care drip-dries.

Jewelry and watches. Savings can run up to 50% on classic timepieces from Rolex, Movado, Patek Philippe, Piaget, Concord, and other famous lines; also gold chains, jewelry, and unset gemstones.

Leather goods. Gucci, Fendi, Bottega Veneta, and Louis Vuitton all have out-lets in St. Thomas, with savings of about 30%.

Perfume and cosmetics. Save from 20% to 30% on your favorite brands, such as Yves Saint Laurent's Opium and Paris, Chanel No. 5, Oscar de la Renta, and Nina Ricci L'air du Temps. Stock up on your favorite cosmetics too—prices are about 20% lower.

Liquor, wines, and liqueurs. These are the best value of all, often sold at up to 60% off the U.S. mainland prices. You'll get especially good values on Scotch whisky and English gin, Russian vodkas, and imported liqueurs. In addition, the U.S. Cus-toms allowance is particularly generous. Each of you can bring home, duty free, one gallon of liquor, plus a sixth bottle, provided that the latter is made in the U.S. VI, such as the justly celebrated Virgin Islands rums. So you don't have to lug the bottles around with you, the various retailers can deliver your purchases to your airplane or cruise ship, upon your departure. (Note: Check your home state about excise taxes.)

Clothing. From Courrèges and Guy La Roche to Benetton, you can update your wardrobe in style. You'll find very good selections of bathing suits and casual cotton clothing—an especially good bet if you had trouble finding these items back home before your honeymoon.

Cameras and accessories. All the big-name brands are here: Nikon, Vivitar, Canon, Minolta. Stores also stock binoculars, video cameras, stereo components, calculators, etc. On all these items, you should shop very carefully: Sometimes, prices are comparable to what you would pay at a discount outlet back home. Also make sure that your purchases are covered by a guarantee and that you can get them serviced on the mainland.

Art and antiques. Original art and antiques over 100 years old are exempt from Customs duty. Make sure you get a certificate of authenticity at the time of purchase.

Made in the U.S. VI. For a very special memento of your honeymoon, bring home items made in the islands. In addition, locally made merchandise is duty free (ask for a certificate of origin if your purchases exceed $25). Things you might want to bring home include leather sandals, silk-screened or batik fashions, shell jewelry, straw hats and bags, and wood carvings. Another pleasing souvenir—tropical scents for him and her made from local flowers and spices. To help you re-create some of your favorite island recipes, browse through the good selection of local cookbooks. You can also pick up island-made seasonings, spices, and teas.

ABOUT U.S. CUSTOMS

Because the Virgin Islands are part of the United States, returning citizens have certain privileges. As mentioned previously, each of you has a duty-free allowance of $800 worth of goods—which translates as $1,600 per couple (you can "pool" your allowance). If you buy more, you can each bring back an additional $1,000 worth of merchandise and pay a flat 5% duty on its value. Over that amount, you will pay duty as assessed by U.S. Customs. If you want to send gifts to friends and family back home, you can mail presents (valued at $100 per recipient per day). This is over and above your duty-free allowance.

Another convenience: When returning home to most U.S. states, you clear Customs in the islands before boarding your plane.

ABOUT ACCOMMODATIONS

The U.S. VI has the largest lineup of hotels in the Caribbean, and whatever kind of accommodations you crave, you're sure to find something to suit: from luxury suites to a bare tent site with ocean view, with lots of choices in between, and at all price ranges. High season generally runs from December 15 to April 15; low-season rates will be about 20% to 50% lower. Rates do not include the 7½% government tax, which will be added to your bill.

If you want to do something different—and very romantic—on your honeymoon, how about chartering a yacht? The U.S. and neighboring British Virgin Islands offer some of the premier cruising waters in the world, and St. Thomas is the home port for one of the world's largest sailing fleets. You don't even have to know an anchor from a mizzenmast. You can charter a crewed yacht, with a captain and crew who do everything for you, from navigating through straits to giving snorkeling lessons or whipping up some poached grouper with tarragon sauce. Rates are comparable to those of a luxury resort. For information about chartering a yacht in the U.S. VI, contact: **Virgin Islands Charteryacht League,** Homeport, St. Thomas, U.S. VI 00802 (tel. toll free 800/524-2061); **Le Boat, Inc.,** P.O. Box E, Maywood, NJ 07607 (tel. 201/342-1838 in New Jersey, or toll free 800/922-0291 nationwide); **Dragon Yachts,** 1151 Aquidneck Ave., Suite 445, Middletown, RI 02840 (tel. 401/846-7850, or toll free 800/752-5257); **Lynn Jachney Charters,** P.O. Box 302, Marblehead, MA 01945 (tel. 617/639-0787, or toll free 800/223-2050); **The Moorings, Ltd.,** 1305 U.S. 19 South, Suite 402, Clearwater, FL 34624 (tel. 813/535-1446, or toll free 800/535-7289 outside of FL); **Nicholson Yacht Charters,** 9 Chauncy St., Cambridge, MA 02138 (tel. 617/661-8174, or toll free 800/662-6066); **Ocean Escapes,** P.O. Box 6009, 9 Ferry Wharf, Newburyport, MA 01950 (tel. 508/465-7116, or toll free 800/227-8633 outside of MA); **Russell Yacht Charters,** 2750 Black Rock Turnpike, Suite 175, Fairfield, CT 06430 (tel. 203/372-6633).

DINING OUT

From French haute cuisine to mama mia's veal scaloppine or local lobster, you'll find most nationalities represented in the U.S. VI's fine restaurants. The fresh catch of the day is usually excellent, especially yellowtail snapper and dolphin (the fish, not the mammal). You'll probably soon become addicted to the delicious Caribbean lobster (sometimes called langoustine), and conch, served in fritters, salads, and chowders. Although it would seem logical that since you are on an island, the fish will always be fresh, that is not always the case. Ask before you order.

Also try some of the Virgin Islands' West Indian–style dishes, which are spicy, but not hot. Popular main courses are curries (especially goat or lamb) or garlic chicken. These might be accompanied by fungi (little dumplings made from cornmeal). You'll also want to try callaloo soup, a stick-to-your-ribs concoction with ham, crab, and greens. More West Indian treats are the patés (pronounced "patties"), spicy little meat pies. Wash it all down with mauby, brewed from tree bark (believe us, it tastes great), or soursop juice, a smooth, sweet-tart drink made from the delicious fruit.

Speaking of fruits, you'll want to sample whatever the islands have in season. In addition to the aforementioned soursop, try star apples, fig bananas, guavas, and papayas. Perhaps the best reason on earth for June brides—and June honeymoons—are mangoes, which are in peak season then.

HOW TO GET MARRIED IN THE U.S. VI

If you've always fantasized about having your wedding in a tropical paradise, here's your chance. You can get married in a church or courthouse, or have an outdoor ceremony at the beach or in a beautiful garden. Many Virgin Islands hotels or wedding services can help you make all the details, including arranging for flowers, a photographer, etc.

1. No blood tests or physical examinations are necessary.

2. Obtain an "Application for Marriage" form from the Territorial Court of the Virgin Islands. For St. Thomas and St. John: P.O. Box 70, Charlotte Amalie, St. Thomas, USVI 00801, Attention: Viola E. Smith, Clerk of the Court. For St. Croix: P.O. Box 9000, Kingshill, St. Croix, USVI 00850, Attention: Family Division.

3. Mail the $25 license fee, along with the completed form, which must be notarized (include a copy of the county clerk's certificate verifying that the commission of the notary public has not expired), back to the territorial court.

4. There is an eight-day waiting period before the marriage license can be issued; during this time, the application is posted for public inspection. (This waiting period can be waived; inquire in advance.)

5. If you want to be married by a judge of the territorial court, a date and time will be scheduled by the court office; the fee is $50. If you prefer a religious ceremony, write directly to the officiant.

Various wedding services can help you plan the perfect ceremony, whether you want a quiet marriage at sunset or a lavish bash that includes getting whisked off by helicopter to a private island. Contact **Weddings the Island Way,** P.O. Box 11694, St. Thomas, USVI 00801 (tel. 809/776-4455); or **Virgin Islands Wedding Consultants,** P.O. Box 11192, St. Thomas, USVI 00801 (tel. 809/775-9203, or toll free 800/843-3566).

FOR FURTHER INFORMATION

Contact the **Virgin Islands Department of Commerce,** P.O. Box 6400, Charlotte Amalie, USVI 00801 (tel. 809/774-8784), or the **Virgin Islands Tourist Information Office.** In Atlanta: 235 Peachtree Center, Suite 1420, Atlanta, GA 30303 (tel. 404/688-0906). In Chicago: 122 South Michigan Ave., Suite 1270, Chicago, IL 60603 (tel. 312/461-0180). In Miami: 2655 LeJeune Road, Suite 907, Coral Gables, FL 33134 (tel. 305/442-7200). In New York: 1270 Avenue of the Americas, New York, NY 10020 (tel. 212/582-4520). In Los Angeles: 3450 Wilshire Blvd., Los Angeles, CA 90010 (tel. 213/739-0138). In Washington, D.C.: 1667 K St., N.W., Suite 270, Washington, DC 20006 (tel. 202/293-3707).

---

2. St. Thomas

Neat white houses with bright red roofs step-placed on the verdant hillsides. A broad blue harbor where million-dollar yachts bob at anchor, awaiting the whims of pleasure-seekers. A street where all that glitters in shop windows is real gold—bejeweled treasures gathered from the four corners of the globe. Tranquil turquoise bays, long white beaches, the flashing lights of a disco, insinuatingly sensuous steelband rhythms—these are the sights and sounds that come to mind when you mention, "St. Thomas."

St. Thomas is the most cosmopolitan of the Virgin Islands, as known for its nightlife and duty-free shopping as it is for its beautiful beaches. The second-largest island in the group, it measures 13 miles long and 3 miles wide. Most of the action centers on Charlotte Amalie, the capital of the U.S. VI, located practically in the middle of the island's south shore. Charlotte Amalie is, deservedly, one of the most photographed harbors in the world, a sapphire gem set in the midst of emerald-green hills. Just off the harbor, quaint alleyways are lined with elegant, duty-free boutiques selling luxury goods from all over the world. Many of these shops are located in thick-walled 300-year-old warehouses, where merchants once stored rum and molasses for trade—and pirates hid their ill-gotten booty. Reflecting the town's Danish origins, many streets still have Danish names, such as Kongen's Gade and Dronningens Gade—better known as Main Street.

Intersperse your shopping forays with visits to Charlotte Amalie's historic sights. Founded in 1691 and named for a Danish queen, the town has many beautifully restored buildings that will whisk you back in time. Stop by Fort Christian, the oldest structure in St. Thomas, dating back to the late 17th century. The fort is now a museum of Virgin Islands' history. (Open Monday through Friday, 8 a.m. to 5 p.m.; Saturday, 9 a.m. to 4 p.m.; Sunday, 9 a.m. to 12 noon; admission is free.) Visit Government House, a typical 19th-century West Indian structure. Today, it is the official residence of the governor, but the second-floor reception room is open Monday through Friday, 8 a.m. to noon, and 1 p.m. to 5 p.m.; admission is free (tel. 774-0001). Take each others photographs on the 99 Steps, which clamber up Government Hill to Lille Tarne Gade. Nearby, view Blackbeard's Tower, where the cutthroat pirate supposedly kept watch for treasure galleons to plunder (today it is part of a hotel and restaurant).

Sightseeing around the rest of St. Thomas is covered under "Romantic Interludes." Now, let's turn our attentions to one of St. Thomas' most renowned attractions: the duty-free bargains.

Traveler's Alert

As we were preparing this edition for press in September 1989, Hurricane Hugo ripped through the Caribbean, causing considerable damage. Although rebuilding began almost immediately, if you are planning to honeymoon on St. Thomas in early 1990, it is advisable to check out the island's status before completing your arrangements.

SHOPPING

St. Thomas offers some of the biggest shopping values in the Caribbean. Many of the best-known stores have branches both in town (along Main Street, the alleyways, and the waterfront); as well as at the Havensight Mall complex at the West Indian dock. Charlotte Amalie stores are open 9 a.m. to 5 p.m., Monday through Saturday; the Havensight shops also stay open late and on Sundays if cruise ships are in town. To plan your shopping expeditions, pick up a free copy of *St. Thomas This Week*, which has the most complete, up-to-date listing of stores and the merchandise they carry. Here's a rundown on some of the largest shops and their specialties. All stores are in town, unless otherwise indicated.

Animal Crackers Fun Factory: For the child in us all, delightful stuffed monkeys that jabber and roll up their tails, bright cotton parrots, teddy bears dressed up in three-piece suits, pinafores, doctors' uniforms, and other delights (Royal Dane Mall in town).

Boolchand's Linen Center: For embroidered sheets, pillowcases, and tableclothes.

Boolchand's: Cameras and accessories, including lines by Minolta, Canon, Nikon.

Cardow Jewelers: The treasure chests of Blackbeard or Captain Kidd could not have glittered more brightly than the display cases of this jewelry store, offering adornments to suit all budgets. There's a special 100-foot-long chain bar, featuring 14k and 18k gold chains.

Caribbean Marketplace (Havensight Mall): Wonderful selection of "Made-in-the-U.S. VI" products that will help you bring the sunshine home: Caribbee Hot Sauce, guava jelly, papaya chutney, Virgin Islands cookbooks, and two mixes you might find handy: Arawak Love Potion and the West Indian Hangover Cure—purported to bring peace to mind and body.

Cartier (Les must de Cartier): A boutique carrying their most popular items: the watches, lighters, pens, wallets, and jewelry.

Circe (Palm Passage): Displays one-of-a-kind jewelry—ancient Egyptian scarabs, Chinese seals, black pearls from Tahiti, and lots more.

Colombian Emeralds: Both uncut and set emeralds and other gemstones. Note: unset emeralds enter the U.S. duty free.

Down Island Traders: For island-made items such as jellies, candies, seasonings, and teas.

The English Shop: Fine tableware from all over the world: Spode, Wedgwood,

Limoges, Minton, and Noritake china; Swarovski, Gorham, and Stuart crystal; figurines by Lladró, Bing & Grøndahl, Belleek; and much more.

Gucci: In their own boutique on the waterfront near the entrance to Riise's Alley, this outlet carries one of the most comprehensive Gucci collections in the Caribbean.

The Leather Shop: Fine goods from the best manufacturers, including Fendi and Bottega Veneta. Selection covers handbags, wallets, attaché cases, and more.

Linen House: Specializing in decorative tablecloths, place mats, and hand-embroidered goods in all styles and colors.

Lion in the Sun: High-fashion clothes for men and women from Kenzo, Yamamoto, Saint Laurent Rive Gauche, Sonia Rykiel.

Little Switzerland: For jewelry, watches, and crystal, including watches by Rolex, Baume & Mercier, and Concord; Waterford, Lalique, and Baccarat crystal; china from Wedgwood, Aynsley, Royal Worcester, and Villeroy & Boch; and Lladró and Goebel-Hummel figurines. They have four shops, including one devoted to the Rosenthal Studio line. (For information, call toll free 800/524-2010.)

Polo—Ralph Lauren: Clothing for men, women, and boys, as well as furnishings for the home.

Purse Strings: Excellent selection of handbags, wallets, and other items, including eel-skin accessories.

Purse Strings Boutique: Specializes in one-of-a-kind accessories: belts, jewelry, shoes, and sweaters.

A.H. Riise: In their several different stores, they carry watches (Patek Philippe, Ebel, Concord, Heuer, and Swatch), original art, china and crystal (Royal Copenhagen, Herend, Wedgwood, Lalique, Baccarat, Orreförs), jewelry, flatware, perfumes, and cosmetics. Also an excellent liquor store.

Royal Caribbean: For cameras and accessories from Yashica, Vivitar, Canon, and others.

Scandinavian Center: Contemporary designs from Georg Jensen, Royal Copenhagen, Bing & Grøndahl, as well as sterling silver jewelry.

The Silver Vault: A wide selection of sterling silver jewelry, from designer pieces to West Indian bangles.

H. Stern: The internationally known jeweler has five outlets in St. Thomas, selling spectacular jewelry, and fine watches from Concord, Corum, and Movado.

Sweet Passion: Carries one-of-a-kind antique pieces (in Royal Dane Mall in town).

Mr. Tablecloth: Fine linens, lace dresser scarfs, and place mats.

Towel & Sun: Great selection of knock-your-socks-off beach towels.

Tropicana Perfume Shoppes: Perfume and cosmetics—and nothing but—including Opium, Shalimar, Ralph Lauren, Anais Anais.

Louis Vuitton: This is the only Vuitton shop in the Caribbean, and they carry the entire line from France: handbags, luggage, and accessories.

ROMANTIC INTERLUDES

With its beautiful beaches and crystal-clear waters, St. Thomas is indeed a tropical paradise.

Red-roofed Charlotte Amalie is only part of the St. Thomas experience. The sightseeing jaunt outlined below is based on renting a car and doing it yourselves; there are also several tour companies that can take you around (ask at your hotel; rates run about $20 per person).

For a new perspective of the lovely Virgins, either soar above or explore below the crystal-clear waters. Get a gull's-eye view on a thrilling helicopter "flightseeing" tour, swooping over deserted beaches and mountaintops. It costs $100 per couple for a 10-minute flight, $210 for a 30-minute flight over St. Thomas' south shore beaches plus the island of St. John. Contact **Antilles Helicopters** (tel. 776-7880) or **Air Center Helicopters** (tel. 775-7335). Or enjoy a Jules Verne–like adventure aboard the *Atlantis,* a 46-passenger submarine that takes you 90 feet below the surface to view colorful fish and coral reefs. The one-hour underwater voyage costs $105 per couple for a day dive; $125 for the night plunge, when the sponges and coral seem to glow with otherworldly luminescence. Contact **Atlantis Submarines** at Havensight Mall (tel. 776-5650).

See more wonders down under—without getting wet—at **Coral World** (tel. 775-1555), a unique underwater observation tower that descends 15 feet under the ocean surface. Through the huge glass windows, you can view the colorful coral reef and the abundant fish. Try to time your visit for the daily fish feeding (including sharks) at 11 a.m. Open daily from 9 a.m. to 6 p.m.; admission is $11 per person.

You'll definitely want to see—and swim at—**Magens Bay,** which usually appears on the "Most Beautiful in the World" list of beach connoisseurs. The broad, U-shaped harbor is edged by a mile of sugar-white sand. With its full facilities—food, beverages, and water-sports equipment rentals—Magens is highly popular, and gets a bit crowded. If you honeymooners want to escape from the world a bit, just stroll on down to the far ends. There's a small admission charge: 50¢ per car, plus 50¢ a person. (It's located off of Rte. 35 on the north shore.)

To get a bird's-eye view of where you've just been, take Rte. 40 to **Drake's Seat,** where Sir Francis himself is supposed to have kept watch for Spanish galleons. The view of Magens Bay, and the rugged outlines of about 100 U.S. and British Virgin Islands in the distance, is truly breathtaking.

If you want to linger over the splendid vistas, head over to **Mountain Top,** off Rte. 33. They are known for their high-octane banana daquiries, and also have a small gift boutique.

Your sense of wanderlust will undoubtedly get piqued by the views of all these lovely deserted islands that rise out of the blue Caribbean. How about getting a closer look—on a **day sail** that takes you out to a deserted island where you can swim and snorkel, then enjoy a picnic lunch? Many different charters are available. **Sea Adventures** at Frenchman's Reef Hotel (tel. 774-9652) offers a deluxe sail for $72 per person, which includes lunch, snacks, plus free snorkeling equipment and instruction. Snorkel sites include the wreck of the *Cartanser Sr.,* a 191-foot World War I freighter. Other day trips include the yacht *My Way,* which cruises to uninhabited Little Hans Lollick island. It costs $65 per person, which includes all snorkeling equipment and instruction, lunch and all-day bar, and free use of an underwater camera (tel. 776-9547).

What two newlyweds could resist a splendid stretch of white coral sands named **Honeymoon?** This excursion is a bit off the beaten path, but very simple to accomplish from Charlotte Amalie. Honeymoon Beach is located on the western side of Water Island, in the middle of Charlotte Amalie Harbor. Water Island has some private residences and is linked to Charlotte Amalie by a ferry that departs from Sub Base, just west of Charlotte Amalie. The ferry runs every half hour; 7 a.m. to midnight from St. Thomas, 7:30 a.m. to 12:30 a.m. from Water Island. The fare is $3.85 per person. With its palm trees and beach bar, Honeymoon makes a great place to while away a day. Since the beach faces west, it provides ringside views of the sunset.

HONEYMOON HOTELS AND HIDEAWAYS

Although St. Thomas has one of the widest selections of hotels in the Caribbean, you'll be pleasantly surprised to find that there is no one big "strip" of high-rise hotels. In fact, with only one exception, there are no high-rises at all. Hotels are found all around the island, both in town (Charlotte Amalie) and along the north and east coasts. In St. Thomas, a beachfront hotel really is right on the beach—and usually, that beach is exclusive (at most, two hotels might share a stretch of sand). Many properties are located on quiet coves. Remember—no spot on St. Thomas is more than a half hour's drive from Charlotte Amalie. Whichever hotel you choose, you'll be near to the fine shops and restaurants in town.

High season runs approximately December 15 to April 15; summer season rates can be up to 50% lower. Prices quoted here reflect the difference between low and high season rates.

Moderately Expensive

Even in an island known for magnificent vistas, you won't quite believe the views you'll see from your private balcony at **Point Pleasant Resort,** Estate Smith Bay, St. Thomas, USVI 00802 (tel. 809/775-7200; reservations: toll free 800/524-2300): the almost blindingly blue waters of Pillsbury Sound, the Windward Passage, and Sir Francis Drake Channel, with emerald-green isles such as Thatch Cay, Tortola, Jost Van Dyke, St. John, and dozens of others dotting the sea all the way to the horizon. Set on a steep hillside on Water Bay, on St. Thomas' northeastern shore, Point Pleasant Resort is a very special place run by a very special woman, Ruth Pfanner. She and her late husband Gunther envisioned a resort that would do justice to the spectacular 15-acre locale. They succeeded brilliantly. Nature paths wind down the cliffside past serrated boulders that date back to the island's earliest formation, bright orange hibiscus blossoms where hummingbirds dart and hover, and tall agave cactus.

Accommodations are set in white buildings with cedar-shingled roofs, angled into the cliffs to take maximum advantage of the dazzling views. Rooms have quarry-tile floors, rattan furnishings, sisal area rugs, tropical flower-print fabrics, and all have kitchenettes and large private balconies with water views. The studios are slightly larger than the efficiency units, and have a separate bedroom area screened off by louvered doors. Although rooms have air conditioning, you'll probably prefer to rely on the trade winds and ceiling fans, with the soothing tempo of the waves to lull you to sleep. If you'd rather not walk down (or more probably, back up) the rather steep paths, a jitney shuttles guests around the property. Point Pleasant has three freshwater pools and a small sand beach tucked amid boulders; you can also stroll over to neighboring Pineapple Beach and Coki Point. Tennis, Sunfish, snorkeling equipment, Windsurfers, and an introductory scuba lesson are all complimentary for guests. Point Pleasant gives guests free use of a car for four hours daily—just sign up on the sheet and you've got your wheels for exploring the island. There's plenty going on right at the resort too, with excellent dining at the Agave Terrace restaurant, overlooking the water, and different events daily, from a manager's cocktail party to a calypso steel band. Honeymoon package: Eight days/seven nights (EP): $1,400 to $1,920 per couple. Includes airport transfers, champagne, room, full-day sail to a neighboring island including lunch. MAP available for $90 per couple per day.

Bolongo Beach Resorts, P.O. Box 7337, St. Thomas, USVI 00801 (tel. 809/775-1800; reservations: toll free 800/524-4746). A beautiful, secluded bay . . . the intimacy of a small resort . . . sports facilities galore. . . . That's what you'll find at Bolongo Beach Resorts, not one but three very unique honeymoon retreats just a ten-minute drive from Charlotte Amalie. Dick and Joyce Doumeng, the owner/managers, are warm and caring hosts, and their enthusiasm and attentiveness pervade the entire operation. The whole resort positively radiates relaxation and good times, and even first-time guests feel like long-lost friends from the moment they check in. You'll soon feel right at home, waving at Debbie, the manager, or asking Mr. Green, the head bartender, to whip you up one of his mysterious tropical concoctions, such as a Blue Caribbean. Best of all, Bolongo offers a wide range of vacation options—from luxury villas to an all-inclusive club.

Bolongo Bay Beach & Tennis Club is one of the most popular honeymoon retreats in the Caribbean. The 78 rooms are set right on a lovely bay, sheltered by a coral reef that makes for excellent snorkeling (gear and instruction are free). Sportslovers will also want to take advantage of the free Sunfish sailboats and lessons, four tennis courts (two of which are lighted), plus a day sail aboard the club yacht. If you've ever wanted to learn how to scuba-dive, now's your chance—a free scuba lesson is included, and the on-premises St. Thomas Diving Club is recognized as one of the best scuba operations in the U.S. VI. Every day, you can participate in different guest activities.

Your room is a perfect honeymoon haven. The two-story white buildings are right on the beach: All you have to do is scamper down the stairs (from upstairs), or hop off the balcony (downstairs), and you can go for that refreshing morning dip. All rooms have beachfront views, private balconies, 22-channel color TVs, telephones, wet bars and kitchenettes, air conditioning and ceiling fans. Honeymoon package: Eight days/seven nights (some meals): $1,220 to $1,645 per couple for a superior room. Includes welcoming rum cocktail, flowers and champagne in your room, continental breakfast daily, and three dinners (including one with a bottle of wine).

Bolongo Villas offer all the advantages of the Beach & Tennis Club right next door, along with the extra space and privacy that come from staying in a suite. The villas share the same beach as their neighbor, and guests enjoy all the same fun—free snorkeling and Sunfish sailing (even lessons), tennis day or night, yacht cruise to St. John, and more. Each of the oceanview suites is individually decorated, and each features a huge balcony, complete kitchen, telephone, cable TV, fully stocked minibar, and both air conditioning and ceiling fans. Honeymoon package: Eight days/seven nights (some meals): $1,375 to $1,800 per couple for a minisuite; $1,570 to $2,145 per couple for a full one-bedroom suite. Includes welcoming rum punch, flowers and champagne in your room, continental breakfast each morning, three dinners (including one with bottle of wine).

Limetree All-Inclusive proves that the next-best thing to a free vacation is one where you don't have to worry about money. The first all-inclusive resort in St. Thomas, Limetree gives you everything: all meals and drinks galore, activities ranging from aquacize to volleyball, a scuba resort course or two free dives, day sail to St. John, half-day catamaran sail, one day's use of a rental car, nightly entertainment with steel bands and mocko jumbies, and . . . the list could tumble on for at least two more pages. You'll have plenty of space, because the property encompasses 24 acres. Even better, rooms are beachfront on one of St. Thomas' loveliest strands. The accommodations feature telephones, cable TVs, plus fully stocked minibars. Back outdoors, you'll want to make friends with Limetree's mascots: the giant iguanas who bask by the pool. They are very tame, handsome in a prehistorically suave way, and they'll munch hibiscus blossoms right from your hand. Honeymoon package: Eight days/seven nights (all-inclusive): $2,375 to $2,915 per couple for a deluxe room. Gratuities are covered; the government room tax is not.

Frenchman's Reef Beach Resort, P.O. Box 7100, Charlotte Amalie, St. Thomas, USVI 00801 (tel. 809/776-8500; reservations: toll free 800/524-2000). Set spectacularly on a promontory that guards the entrance to Charlotte Amalie harbor, Frenchman's Reef is top choice for couples who want the luxury and amenities of a self-contained resort. Right on the property, you'll find 7 excellent restaurants, 24 shops in an air-conditioned mall, 4 lighted tennis courts overlooking the beach, 2 Olympic-size swimming pools, and the largest water-sports and scuba-diving center on St. Thomas. The property fronts Morning Star Beach, a long, slim strand lapped by the Caribbean. Charlotte Amalie is only five minutes away by car; ten minutes by shuttle ferry that drops you right downtown. Frenchman's is the closest St. Thomas comes to having a big hotel, with 424 rooms. The main building is eight stories tall and built into the cliff. There are also 96 cushy units in the luxury Morning Star Beach Club villas. All are air-conditioned and come with color TVs, in-room safes, and minibars. The property looks lovelier than ever after over $15 million in renovations to lobbies, restaurants, and rooms. Accommodations in the main building reflect tropical elegance, with white-tile floors, pale-pink stucco walls, marble-topped sinks, and spring-fresh floral bedspreads that look borrowed from a Monet painting. Room rates vary according to view: hillside, harbor, or ocean. If you can, opt for the Morning Star accommodations, which are located in five two-story buildings right on the beach. Rooms are really BIG, and you'll enjoy the pampering touches, such as a concierge for personalized service, telephones in the bathroom, and use of plush bathrobes. All the facilities of the main resort are right on your doorstep. And if you'd like to get married in the Virgin Islands, the social activities staff can help you with all the arrangements. Honeymoon package: Eight days/seven nights (EP): Low season: $1,820 per couple for an oceanview room; $1,975 to $2,245 for the Morning Star Beach Club. Call for high-season rates. Includes welcoming cocktails, tennis court use, a moonlight cruise, champagne, his-and-hers T-shirts. Frenchman's Reef also offers an all-inclusive honeymoon package covering breakfast or lunch and dinner daily, five drinks per person daily, water sports, welcome rum punches, a moonlight cruise, T-shirts, and all applicable taxes and gratuities. Eight-day/seven-night all-inclusive package: $2,440 per couple for a room; $2,935 per couple at Morning Star (low season). Call for high-season rates.

Bluebeard's Castle, P.O. Box 7480, St. Thomas, USVI 00801 (tel. 809/774-1600; reservations: toll free 800/524-6599). There might—or might not—have been a swashbuckling pirate named Bluebeard. But whether or not he really existed, the legends of his exploits have left a romantic tradition—one that is continued by this top-notch hotel that commands a sweeping view of Charlotte Amalie and its harbor. The white-painted, red-roofed buildings and the stone watchtower are a St. Thomas landmark, perched on their hillock just above the town. After a $6-million program of construction and renovation, the 20-acre resort complex is in tip-top condition. Both the studios and the one-bedroom suites have been beautifully re-done with beige-tile floors, rattan furnishings, and fabrics done in soft beiges and jungly floral prints. From the large balconies, you can behold the postcard-perfect view of Charlotte Amalie from many rooms. All rooms have air conditioning, ceiling fans, and color cable TVs; most also have wet bars and minifridges. For something really unique, consider the honeymoon room located in "The Castle"—the 300-year-old stone watchtower. Although the room is small, it is perfect for couples with a penchant for history and romance ($175 to $225 per couple per night).

Bluebeard's has two hard-surface tennis courts, both lighted for night play. There is a beautiful saltwater pool overlooking the town and cruise ships docked at the harbor. Because its in-town location precludes having a beach, the hotel runs a shuttle to Magens Bay twice a day. Bluebeard's has two fine restaurants; in particular, Entre Nous Restaurant offers stellar views of the harbor (see "Romantic Restaurants" section). Honeymoon package: Eight days/seven nights (EP): $1,205 to $1,475 per couple (low season); $1,525 to $1,830 per couple (high season). Includes welcome cocktail, bottle of champagne at dinner one evening, souvenir Royal Copenhagen plaquette, his-and-hers terry velour robes, introductory scuba lesson, cocktail reception, $25 gift certificate, full-day tour with lunch to St. John.

The **Stouffer Grand Beach Resort,** P.O. Box 8267, St. Thomas, USVI 00801 (tel. 809/775-1510; reservations: toll free 800/HOTELS 1), has to rate as one of the most stunning hotels on St. Thomas. It sprawls out over gardens, hillsides, and beachfront on Pineapple Bay, on St. Thomas' northeastern shore. The low-rise hotel has a decided island flavor, using natural wood shingles and West Indian–style windows and archways. As its centerpiece, the resort surrounds one of the most glamorously spectacular pools on the island, with free-form angles and fountains to add pizzazz. Rooms are decorated with equal panache, done in dusky rose and forest green, with the light touch of rattan furnishings. Amenities will vary: Some will have balconies, wet bars, or Jacuzzis. If you prefer the cooling trade winds to air conditioning, be aware that not all rooms have windows that open, so make sure you check things out in advance. For sports enthusiasts, the resort has a fitness center, lighted tennis courts, Sunfish, Windsurfers, and snorkeling gear, all free to honeymoon guests. Excellent restaurants. Honeymoon package: Six days/five nights (EP): $1,065 (regular room) to $1,450 (deluxe) per couple. Includes champagne upon arrival, guided tour of St. Thomas, sunset cruise with cocktails and hors d'oeuvres, special gift. An ultraposh package featuring accommodations in a one-bedroom suite with Jacuzzi and lots more is available for $2,320 per couple.

Sapphire Beach Resort & Marina, P.O. Box 8088, St. Thomas, USVI 00801 (tel. 809/775-6100; reservations: toll free 800/524-2090). You'll know where this brand-new resort gets its name the moment you walk into the lobby and view the gem-like hues of the sea through the archways. One of the biggest assets here is the beach, regarded by St. Thomas cognoscenti as one of the best on the island. Lined by sea grapes, it offers terrific snorkeling out at the point, and steady breezes for windsurfing. Want to pack a lot of excitement into your honeymoon? This activity-oriented resort is the place to do it, with different events scheduled daily, such as trips to the Baths on Virgin Gorda, sails to St. John, a manager's cocktail party, volleyball tournaments. Snorkeling equipment, Sunfish sailing, windsurfing, and tennis are all free. When you want to relax, the spacious accommodations—all suites and villas—are especially nice to come home to. Decorated with white-tile floors, rattan furnishings, and blue fabrics (the better to enhance the seascapes), they feature kitchenettes and color TVs, as well as both ceiling fans and air conditioning. If you're looking to splurge, the duplex villas are worth it, with their cedar cathedral ceilings and sea-forever views over the palms. Thanks to the 67-slip marina, the resort is a favorite with visiting yachtsmen, especially in August, when it hosts the U.S.VI Marlin Tournament. Honeymoon package: Eight days/seven nights (EP): $1,330 to $2,100 per couple for a suite; $1,715 to $2,715 per couple for a villa. Includes champagne and hors d'oeuvres upon arrival, fresh flowers in room, day yacht trip for two, two T-shirts, and round-trip airport transfers.

Pavilions & Pools, Route 6, St. Thomas, USVI 00802 (tel. 809/775-6110). Privacy? Sometimes guests check in here and the staff won't see them for the entire week. As the name of the resort suggests, much of the seductive charm here comes from the oh-so-secluded swimming pool that each room has . . . literally three steps from the large master bedroom. Surrounded by a large deck and dense plantings of oleander, hibiscus, frangipani, and flamboyant, the pools lend themselves to nude sunbathing. Set in low white units, each of the 25 "pavilions"—villas, really—have slightly different layouts and furnishings. Decorated with rattan furnishings and tile floors, the accommodations each feature a large bathroom with a garden and a skylight, wonderfully tropical in feel. In fact, an easygoing island ambience pervades the entire resort. When you want to go to the beach, Sapphire is less than a ten-minute stroll away. If you're looking for a casual escape, this could be just the ticket. Honeymoon package: Eight days/seven nights (EP): $1,270 to $1,425 per couple (low season). Includes round-trip airport transfers or one day's use of a rental car, champagne, welcome cocktails, flowers in room, use of snorkeling gear, and discount on a day sail. High-season rates: $235 to $265 per couple per night.

Mark St. Thomas, Blackbeard's Hill, Charlotte Amalie, St. Thomas, USVI 00802 (tel. 809/774-5511; reservations: toll free 800/343-4085). Step back in time to the era when sugar was king and horse-drawn carriages clattered down Charlotte Amalie's cobblestoned streets. Built over 200 years ago, the Mark St. Thomas is a shimmering West Indian gem, with filigreed cast-iron balconies, hibiscus-motif gingerbread trim, teak floors, and nine-foot-tall mahogany doors. Snuggled amid lush hillside gardens, the inn commands a smashing view of the harbor. Originally a private residence, the house was meticulously restored in 1988 and converted into a small, intimate bed-and-breakfast, with an attention to detail that rivals the finest European traditions. Each of the eight rooms is uniquely captivating. If pressed to name our favorites, we'd certainly include the Blue Room, featuring a king-size mahogany four-poster bed, plus a large, beautifully furnished terrace screened by white trelliswork and frangipani. For privacy, choose the stone-walled Library, with a queen-size mahogany four-poster bed and a silk patchwork quilt sewn by the owner's grandmother.

In contrast to the vintage surroundings, all the amenities are thoroughly state-of-the-art, with color cable TVs, air conditioning, ceiling fans, direct-dial telephones, and daily maid service. Stroll down the historic 99 Steps to Main Street shopping; you can drive to fine beaches in about ten minutes (the inn also has a lovely free-form pool). In the evening, the Mark's Great Room restaurant serves exquisite cuisine, accompanied by a stellar vista of Charlotte Amalie (see "Romantic Restaurants" section). Honeymoon package: Seven days/six nights (BP): $985 per couple (low season). Includes airport transfers, bottle of champagne, first-night dinner (excluding beverages and gratuity), polo shirts, day sail with buffet lunch and drinks. High-season rates (BP): $165 to $215 per couple per night.

Moderate

Carib Beach Hotel, P.O. Box 340, Lindburg Bay, St. Thomas, USVI 00801 (tel. 809/774-2525; reservations: tel. 212/832-2277 in New York State; toll free 800/223-6510 nationwide), is a casual resort with a warm island friendliness, and also offers the advantage of being right on a beach—yet only ten minutes away from Charlotte Amalie. All 96 accommodations are air-conditioned and carpeted, and are expected to reopen in Spring 1990 after refurbishment. It is definitely worth springing for the superior rooms, which all have ocean views; the standard accommodations face the parking lot. Although the property is near the airport, the noise is not obtrusive, but you do hear the planes. Lindburg Beach is small, but sparkling, and you can rent Sunfish, snorkeling gear, and Windsurfers from the water-sports concession. You can also sun yourselves on the large deck surrounding the freshwater pool. At least one evening, you'll want to dine at the new Tonga Reef restaurant, where the carved totems, wooden masks, and waterfall make you feel like you've been swept off to the South Pacific rather than the Caribbean. Menu choices include Polynesian, West Indian, and all-American dishes. Honeymoon package: Eight days/seven nights (EP): From $945 per couple for a superior room. Includes welcome drink, manager's cocktail party, fresh flowers in room, $10 gift certificate at Cardow's (jewelry), use of snorkeling gear, bottle of champagne at the restaurant, 25% discount on auto rental, special gift, and more.

ROMANTIC RESTAURANTS

What's your choice—elegant French cuisine, piquant West Indian specialties, or casual fare with a seaside view? You'll find something to please in St. Thomas. Reservations are a must at all the better restaurants. Not all places accept credit cards, so ask in advance.

Expensive

Fiddle Leaf Restaurant, Watergate Villas (tel. 775-2810). Exquisite cuisine and stunning art deco surroundings establish Fiddle Leaf as one of the best restaurants in St. Thomas—and the whole Caribbean, for that matter. Owner Pat LaCorte uses only the freshest ingredients for imaginative recipes that combine the best of American and French regional cuisines. The restaurant itself is beautiful, done in black and white, with red-tile floors and trelliswork adding a dramatic accent. From appetizer to desserts, all dishes come with elegant touches that make a meal memorable, such as the ethereal seafood boudin (like a sausage), which arrived draped in a spinach leaf and adorned by a "rose" carved from a tomato. Entrées include filet mignon stuffed with brie cheese and served with a red-wine sauce, New Orleans blackened fish, or a Santa Fe roast game hen cooked with chiles and cilantro and served with black bean fritters and pumpkin flan. For dessert, indulge in the velvety smooth délice au chocolate or a fresh fruit cobbler. For both its cuisine and its ambience, Fiddle Leaf was a gold medal winner in the recent "Great Events" restaurant awards. Open nightly from 6 to 10 p.m.; $80 to $100 per couple plus drinks.

Hotel 1829, Kongens Gade (near Government Hill), Charlotte Amalie (tel. 776-1829), is one of St. Thomas' best and most historic restaurants. Originally constructed in 1829 for a French sea captain, the hotel is now owned by Baron Vernon and Eva Ball—the baron actually being a self-made American millionaire who bought the title some years ago. (Backgammon players, take note: The baron is also the former World Backgammon Champion. You can sometimes pick up a game with him.) Under head chef Gerhard Hofmann, who has been with the hotel for 20 years, the menu features continental specialties such as rack of lamb, flambéed peppersteak filet mignon, and fresh (and nothing but fresh) fish, such as a sautéed yellowtail with lime or succulent Caribbean lobster. For dessert, make sure to place your order for one of the sublime soufflés: chocolate, Grand Marnier, or raspberry spiked with whipped cream. Since entrées are priced from $25, count on spending about $80 to $100 per couple for dinner, plus drinks. The excellent wine list includes some good, moderately priced "finds" as well as the famous labels. Open daily for dinner, 6:30 to 10 p.m.

Au Bon Vivant, Government Hill (tel. 774-2158). Romantic? This restaurant is so alluring that it's likely to spark marriage proposals . . . all over again. Set in a former private town house, Au Bon Vivant surrounds you with the fine details, such as mellow Mexican tile floors and weathered stone walls; lovely batik paintings add a hint of faraway places. You'll dine on an open-air deck poised just above the start of Main Street in Charlotte Amalie. Time your reservation so that you can watch the sky glow pink at sunset and see the lights start to twinkle over the harbor. The menu is inventive and sumptuous. Start off with conch flan with saffron sauce, or a cold langoustine and endive salad. For your main course, recommendations include the sautéed shrimp in muscat and basil sauce, and medallions of veal served with crabmeat and sauce béarnaise. The rich desserts are famous, especially the soufflés and hot lemon pie. Open Monday through Saturday for lunch, 11:30 a.m. to 3 p.m.; $30 to $40 per couple. Dinner, 6:30 to 10 p.m.; $70 to $100 per couple plus drinks.

Entre Nous, Bluebeard's Castle (tel. 776-4050). No view better captures the glamour of Charlotte Amalie than that from this perch high over the harbor, with yachts and cruise ships lit up as gaily as Christmas trees. Music wafts in at just the right decibel level from the piano bar; small lights tucked among the foliage, as well as flickering hurricane lamps, encourage hand-holding. Knowledgeable waiters help you choose from the night's selections—and the food is very, very good indeed. Caesar salad is prepared tableside with flourish and showmanship. The proper slight after-explosion of jalapeños lingers when you taste the ceviche. Rack of lamb arrives tender and pink; a glorious flounder francese incorporates a fish so fresh it obviously spent the morning swimming laps in the channel. Finish off festively with a baked Alaska for two. Open nightly 6:30 to 9:30 p.m.; $80 to $100 plus drinks. Interesting wine list with good range of moderate selections.

Club Z Nightclub and Restaurant, 41 Contant, above Charlotte Amalie (tel. 776-4655). With its striking black-and-white decor, Club Z is, quite simply, the most drop-dead gorgeous restaurant on the island—with elegantly executed Italian cuisine and seafood that soars to the occasion. The dining pavilion opens to the outside, allowing oleander-scented breezes to waft through the air. Fine china, crystal stemware, and hurricane lamps cast a romantic spell over the tables. The staff is always helpful, considerate, and knowledgeable. The list of specialties will certainly whet your appetite. As an appetizer, try the steamed mussels or share one of the homemade pastas. Entrées include grilled tuna with ginger and shallot-lime vinaigrette, and veal medallions sautéed with wild mushrooms, priced $16.50 to $30. Top off your meal with one of the pastries from the dessert cart, then boogie on out to the dance floor, which has an excellent stereo and light system. Couples who dine at the restaurant do not have to pay the disco cover charge of $11 per person. Open Monday through Saturday; dinner, 7 to 9:30 p.m.; disco, 9:30 p.m. to 4 a.m.

Moderate

Gregerie East, east of Frenchtown at 17 Crown Bay (tel. 774-2252). If you didn't know it was there, you wouldn't find it, tucked among the sail shops and marine supply stores on the waterfront. But once you park your car and head up the ramp to their waterfront deck, you'll have a million-dollar view—literally. Some of the priciest yachts on the seven seas moor here, thanks to the deep-water harbor. In season, it is not uncommon to see five or more 200-foot motor cruisers tied up—

ships belonging to corporate CEOs, European royalty, oil moguls. As you would imagine, these chaps like to eat well—and hence the resounding success of Gregerie's. The setting is simple: an open-air deck, wainscotted walls behind the bar, good rock music to launch a party mood. For both lunch and dinner, the menu highlights the freshest ingredients, perfectly prepared. Start off with conch fritters or their celebrated Caesar salad (locals swear it's the best on the island). Follow up with Dover sole or grilled steak. Plan on lingering a while—the lively bar is a great place for spinning seagoing yarns. Want an even more laid-back atmosphere? Right next door, there's the "boatie bar"—same food, but no shirts or shoes required, so it's popular with the boat crews. Open daily for lunch, 11:30 a.m. to 3 p.m.; $15 to $30 per couple. Dinner served Tuesday through Sunday, 6:30 to 10 p.m.; $60 to $80 per couple.

L'Escargot, near the sub base, just west of Charlotte Amalie (tel. 774-6565). Located just a short drive out of town, the garden setting provides a tranquil oasis for relaxed lunches and dinners. The salad bar is a favorite ($4 as an appetizer, or $8 by itself). Entrées include beef Wellington, seafood, pasta, and grilled specialties. Dinner for two should run $50 to $70 plus drinks. Excellent wine selection. Open daily for lunch, 11:45 a.m. to 2:30 p.m.; dinner, 6 to 10:30 p.m.

Piccola Marina Café, at the Red Hook ferry landing (tel. 775-6350). From your table on the outdoor deck of Piccola Marina, you'll look out at the million-dollar sailing yachts moored at the docks. Here the atmosphere is definitely casual, attracting a congenial group of folks waiting for the St. John ferry, yachtspeople, and locals coming by for good food and good times. Favorite dishes include homemade pastas and sauces, as well as mesquite-grilled specialties. Open daily for lunch, 11:30 a.m. to 3 p.m.; $13.50 to $22 per couple. Dinner, 6:30 to 10 p.m.; $40 to $50 per couple plus drinks.

St. Thomas has so many good restaurants, this list can go on and on. Here are some more favorites, grouped according to atmosphere or location.

FOR LUNCH IN CHARLOTTE AMALIE: William and Daniels, Main Street, above Scandinavian Center (tel. 776-8877). Located on the second floor overlooking the hustle and bustle of Main Street, William and Daniels is known for its impeccable attention to detail, excellent food, and moderate prices. There's a different quiche of the day each day and a fresh-fish special, as well as international dishes such as chicken français and steak tartar. Open for lunch only Monday through Saturday, 11:30 a.m. to 3 p.m.; about $40 to $50 per couple. Café Amici, Riise's Alley (no phone). Located in the brick-walled open-air alleyway, shaded by palm trees, the place feels like an Italian sidewalk café transplanted to the tropics. Excellent light fare—veal, pasta, fresh fish, and salads, priced from about $8 to $15. Open Monday through Saturday, 7:30 a.m. to 4 p.m.

DINNERS WITH A VIEW: Agave Restaurant, Point Pleasant (tel. 775-4142). Perched on the cliffs overlooking Pillsbury Sound on St. Thomas' north shore, Agave specializes in local and nouvelle cuisine. Specialties include chicken Martinique and stuffed Caribbean lobster; entrées priced from $16 to $30. A gold medal winner in the recent "Great Restaurants Event." Open daily for lunch, noon to 2 p.m.; dinner, 6:30 to 10 p.m. Blackbeard's Castle, above town (tel. 776-1234). The sign outside that announces "Since 1679" isn't joking. A long flight of stairs leads to a stone tower where, according to local lore, the notorious pirate Blackbeard kept watch for ships to plunder. Today, this stunning setting continues to present a four-star view of St. Thomas harbor, along with fine American regional cuisine. Open shutters frame vistas of Charlotte Amalie; lace tablecloths and pink-painted hurricane lamps enhance the elegant mood. Open Monday through Friday for lunch, 11:30 a.m. to 2:30 p.m.; $20 to $40 per couple. Dinner served Tuesday through Sunday, 6:30 to 10:30 p.m.; $80 to $100 per couple.

Mark St. Thomas, Blackbeard's Hill (tel. 774-5511). St. Thomas has discovered a delicious new tradition: tapas, Spain's savory hors d'oeuvres served with evening cocktails. If you were to search the world far and wide, you probably could not find a more panoramic place for whetting your appetite than the curlicued veranda at the Mark St. Thomas, an exquisitely restored 200-year-old mansion overlooking Charlotte Amalie. Nibble pan-fried crab cakes with pimiento and watercress mayonnaise, or carrot blini with sour cream and caviar. Having such a wonderful time that you don't want to leave? No problem—the Mark is also a superb restaurant, weaving Caribbean magic into such dishes as a roast game hen with mango chutney, and braised red snapper with corn-and-green-papaya ragoût. Open nightly from 5:30 to 10 p.m. Tapas, $4.50 to $9.50 per dish; dinner, $60 to $80 per couple. Piano music on Friday and Saturday evenings from 7 to 10 p.m.

Tavern on the Beach, Frenchman's Reef (tel. 776-8500). Soft piano music counterpoints the lapping surf. Graceful louvers open full to frame the lovely water views. That describes the West Indian idyll that awaits at this elegant waterfront restaurant. The menu emphasizes unusual American regional recipes. Start off with the L.A. pasta—fettuccine mingled with smoked turkey and goat cheese, then tossed with a creamy garlic-tomato sauce. Grilled quail is also excellent, stuffed with apples and pecans. Memorable entrées include the "Black Jack" duck, marinated in Jack Daniels and mesquite-grilled. Don't miss their ultracreamy homemade ice cream for dessert. Open nightly for dinner, 6:30 to 10:30 p.m.; $70 to $90 plus drinks.

IN FRENCHTOWN: This district just west of Charlotte Amalie gets its name from the French fishermen from St. Barts who migrated here in the late 19th century. Today, the area retains a fishing village atmosphere; it also boasts several excellent restaurants. **Alexander's Café** (tel. 774-4349). Café-style chairs and pink walls create a cozy, bistro feeling. In addition to fresh seafood and pastas, the menu highlights Austrian dishes including an excellent wienerschnitzel and apple strudel. Open Monday through Saturday for lunch, 11:30 a.m. to 3 p.m.; $20 to $40 per couple. Dinner, 6 to 10 p.m.; $40 to $60 per couple plus drinks. **Café Normandie,** ruedo St. Barthélemy (tel. 774-1622). Candlelight sets the romantic mood at this small, air-conditioned restaurant. The four-course prix-fixe dinner (starting at $21 per person, depending on entrée) includes soup, salad, sorbet, and a choice of specialties such as Bombay duck, Caribbean lobster, veal, or rack of lamb. For dessert, take the word of the wise, and order a slice of the memorable chocolate fudge pie. Since the restaurant is located on the way to the airport, it's a great place to stop for a meal and end your vacation with a flourish. Open Monday through Friday for lunch, 11:30 a.m. to 2:30 p.m.; Monday through Sunday for dinner, 6:30 to 10 p.m.; Sunday brunch, 11 a.m. to 3 p.m. Reservations are a must.

Hook, Line, and Sinker (tel. 776-9708). Casual, with an exuberant seafaring spirit, the open-air restaurant overlooks a small harbor where many yachts tie up. Seated in wooden booths, surrounded by a convivial crowd (many of the people come off the charter boats), you can enjoy favorites such as hamburgers, sandwiches, or tacos for lunch. Dinner choices include more burgers, as well as heartier fare: an excellent London broil, sautéed coconut shrimp, or specials such as yellowtail creole or a lobster stir-fry. Lunch, $20 per couple; dinner, $20 to $60 per couple. Open Monday through Saturday, 11 a.m. to 10 p.m.; Sunday, 5 to 10 p.m.; the bar stays open till around midnight. Closed Sunday in the off-season. **Famous** (tel. 774-8651). This funky 30-seat hideaway owned by Vincent DeVingo specializes in fresh pastas (including a mean fettuccine Alfredo), yellowtail français (sautéed in batter and served with a lemon butter sauce), and an oriental stir-fry with chicken, shrimp, beef, or lobster. Entrées are all priced $13 to $19. Open nightly from 6 to 11 p.m.

LOCAL FOOD: Daddy's, near the Red Hook dock (tel. 775-6590), is known for its conch in lemon butter sauce, conch fritters, fish dishes (try the fresh catch fried or West Indian style), or fresh lobster served with fungi and rice. For dessert, sample the Key lime pie. Meals are served on the garden patio. Open Monday through Saturday for dinner only, 6:30 to 10:30 p.m.; about $50 per couple. **Eunice's Terrace,** just east of the Coral World turnoff (tel. 775-3975). Enjoy a feast of local specialties on the open-air veranda—conch fritters; broiled, boiled, or fried fish; lobster; and steak. All are served with local sweet potato, and a choice of peas and rice, or fungi; green banana or fried plaintains. On Saturday nights, try the specials, including souse and callaloo. Honeymooners might like to try "The Eunice Romance"—a rum potion rumored to have aphrodisiac powers. Lunch, about $40 per couple; dinner, about $50 per couple. Open daily from 9 a.m. to 10 p.m.

And—would you believe honest-to-goodness Texas barbecue? Austin native Bill Collins has two barbecue stands, one on the St. Thomas waterfront, the other in Red Hook. **The Texas Pit** pork ribs, beef ribs, brisket, and chicken cook slowly over a cool fire, for maximum flavor and juiciness. They're served with cole slaw and potato salad. The stands open up about 6:30 p.m., and close at about 10 p.m., when everything is sold out. About $8 for a heapin' portion. Call (tel. 776-9579) for details.

---

3. St. Croix

Located roughly 35 miles south of St. Thomas and St. John, St. Croix is literally a place apart—and an island of contrasts. It has all the attributes you would expect of a tropical isle: sugar-white beaches, palm trees, and cascades of colorful flowers everywhere you look: bougainvillea, oleander, and the yellow ginger thomas, the territorial flower. But it also has vistas you would not anticipate: rolling meadows where contented cows graze, arid plains where only cactus can grow amid the rocks, and a damp, shady rain forest where ferns grow nearly as large as trees, and vines dangle from mahogany tree limbs. A strong feeling of history pervades the entire island. Ruins of sugar mills dot the landscape. The town of Christiansted, with its waterfront arcades and massive yellow fort guarding the harbor, remains virtually unchanged from 200 years ago, when it reigned as capital of all the Danish West Indies. Main roads make frequent 90° turns, since their routes skirt what had been the boundaries of early estates. At the same time, St. Croix offers a sizable amount of very contemporary pleasures: Old waterfront buildings now house duty-free boutiques and gourmet restaurants, rock music reverberates down narrow alleyways, and luxury resorts cater to the body and soul.

About 6 miles wide and 23 miles long, St. Croix is the largest of the Virgin Islands. The original inhabitants were the cannibalistic Carib Indians, who called the land Ay Ay. The island's recorded history formally began on November 13, 1493, when Christopher Columbus landed at what is now Salt River on the north coast, his first stop in the Virgin Islands. If you look at old maps of the estates on St. Croix, some plantation names recall the nationalities who settled here: Frederikshaab, Campo Rico, Tipperary, Oxford, and Bonne Esperance. Other names reflect the hopes of the early settlers—and the sober realities they encountered: Wheel of Fortune, Prosperity, Barrenspot, Adventure, and Little Profit.

St. Croix's basically flat terrain proved admirably suited to sugarcane production, and by 1800, the island was one of the wealthiest in the Caribbean. However, the collapse of sugar prices and the abolition of slavery ended the prosperity of the plantation era, and, like Sleeping Beauty, St. Croix peacefully dozed for nearly 100 years. In many ways, this slumber was a blessing, because it helped preserve the rich architectural heritage of the island.

You'll have fun exploring St. Croix because of its variety. The two main towns, Christiansted, on the north coast, and Frederiksted, on the west, lie at opposite ends of the island, with most of the attractions and resorts spread out in between. Sightseeing features many changes of pace—from plantation great houses, to botanical gardens, to spectacular beaches such as Grape Tree and Davis Bay. Although you

won't find the go-go lifestyle of St. Thomas, St. Croix offers one of the tastiest assortment of restaurants in the Caribbean, and evening entertainment that ranges
from mellow jazz to rock and reggae, or perhaps a performance by the island's Quad-
rille dancers, who curtsy and follow French calls, much as Crucians did 100 years
ago. And whether you're filling in your china pattern at a duty-free shop, or sunning
yourself by the side of a sparkling blue bay, you'll have plenty of elbow room, so you
can truly enjoy. This feeling of intimacy amid wide-open spaces is exactly what
makes St. Croix so appealing to honeymooners.

Traveler's Alert

As we were preparing this edition for press in September 1989, Hurricane
Hugo ripped through the Caribbean, causing considerable damage. Plans immediately were underway to rebuild, but St. Croix was especially hard hit, so if you are
planning to honeymoon there in 1990, it is advisable to check out the island's status
before completing your arrangements.

SHOPPING

St. Croix's stores offer just the right blend of famous names and serendipitous
finds. Like St. Thomas, St. Croix features duty-free prices on a wide range of items,
with china, crystal, jewelry, watches, perfume, and liquor ranking among the best
buys. Prices tend to be the same on both islands, and some stores, such as Little
Switzerland, have outlets on both. Because the St. Croix stores are less crowded,
shopping tends to be a much more relaxed experience. You'll also be able to browse
through an interesting selection of island-made crafts and designs. Although
Frederiksted has a few small boutiques, practically all the noteworthy shopping is in
Christiansted. Most of the shops are located on the waterfront, on King Street, or in
the arcades off of Strand Street. Top Christiansted choices include:

Colombian Emeralds: Both unset and mounted gemstones, as well as Omega
watches. 43 Queen Cross St.

Crucian Gold: Handmade, island-designed 14k and 18k gold jewelry. 57A
Company St.

Happiness Is: For locally crafted items, such as silk-screened clothing, seashell
wind chimes, wood carvings, and jewelry. Pan Am Pavilion.

Many Hands: Handmade arts and crafts, pottery, jewelry, plus original works
by local artists on display. Pan Am Pavilion.

Lion in the Sun: Top choice for fashion-forward womens wear. Strand Street.

Little Switzerland: The place to go for fine china (Aynsley, Rosenthal, Wedgwood), crystal (Lalique, Baccarat, Waterford), watches (Rolex, Baume & Mercier),
and many other elegant lines. On King Street.

Spanish Main: Hand-screened, island-designed fabric, both by the yard and in
ready-to-wear fashions. Pan Am Pavilion.

Violette's: Carries the largest selection of perfume in St. Croix, as well as cosmetics (Orlane, Lancome, Clarins), Dupont and Dunhill lighters, gold and costume
jewelry, Seiko watches, men's and ladies' fashions—all at duty-free prices. 38 Strand
St., Caravelle Arcade.

ROMANTIC INTERLUDES

With its rich history and varied geography, St. Croix offers many pleasant dalli-
ances for lovers.

Located off the northeastern coast of St. Croix, **Buck Island** is a national monument, administered by the National Park Service. It's reached by a 45-minute sail

from Christiansted. Both neophyte and expert snorkelers will relish the opportunity to explore the underwater wonders of the coral reef. Off the east end of the island, there's a fascinating, marked underwater trail that takes you over huge stands of elkhorn and staghorn coral, past bright-purple sea fans, and through coral grottos. You'll spot multicolored parrot fish and damselfish, schools of yellow-and-black-striped sergeant majors, and some very dignified French angelfish, who generally cruise by in pairs. Afterward, the boat sails over to the west side of Buck Island, where you can swim and sun on the pristine white coral-sand beach and picnic under the shade of the sea-grape trees.

Many different cruises to Buck Island are available. In particular, honeymooners will enjoy the trips offered by Captain Mark Sperber of **Mile-Mark Charters,** headquartered at the King Christian Hotel, King's Wharf (tel. 773-2285, 773-2628, or toll free 800/524-2012). He's young and fun, and will delight in sharing his knowledge of St. Croix with you. In addition to his sleek six-passenger trimaran, Mark has a new, specially designed glass-bottomed motor cruiser that will give you a sneak preview of the underwater world. Because this vessel takes less than half an hour to reach the Buck Island trail, it also includes time at the west-end beach (most other half-day excursions do not). Rates for half-day trimaran sails run $38.50 per person; full-day excursions cost $45 per person. Aboard the glass-bottomed motor cruiser, the half-day rate is $22 per person. All trips include snorkeling gear, instruction, and a guided tour along the underwater trail. During the full moon, Mark also runs evening sails out to the island; call for details. Other boats that go to Buck Island include the **Serenity,** a 39-foot Gulfstar sloop (tel. 773-3030); and the **Diva,** a 35-foot Beneteau (tel. 778-4675). Each takes a maximum of six passengers; $65 for a full-day sail.

One of the best ways to appreciate the lush, primeval beauty of St. Croix's **rain forest** is from **horseback.** Get into the saddle with **Jill's Equestrian Stables** (tel. 772-0305), run by Jill Hurd, whose family runs Sprat Hall Hotel. Both beginning and experienced riders will appreciate Jill's well-schooled mounts, which range from Crucian ponies to thoroughbreds. On your guided ride, you'll pass the remains of old sugar plantations, and pass beneath towering mahogany trees. Jill will explain the history of the area, and point out the tropical fruits in season, which you'll be able to sample en route. Bring your cameras—saddlebags are provided—and you'll want to take photos of the spectacular views, which take in the beach at Sandy Point, Frederiksted, and Mahogany Valley. The 1½-hour ride costs $45 per person. During the full moon, Jill sometimes runs romantic evening rides; call for details. For a different perspective, settle into a cozy horse-drawn carriage for a saunter through the Frederiksted environs, sipping champagne as you tour along the palm-fringed shore. It costs $100 per couple for a private ride, $40 per couple if you go with four other people. Contact **Seahorse Stables** (tel. 772-1264 or 772-0365). They offer sunset and moonlight rides too!

"Better diving than the wall in Grand Cayman!" That's how one experienced diver described the extraordinary sites off St. Croix. Best of all, getting to the **dives** is easy—many of the prime sites lie just a few dozen feet offshore. Along the north shore, the Cane Bay Wall, a 1,200-foot drop-off, runs from Salt River to Ham's Bluff. On the west coast, divers can explore three shipwrecks near Butler Bay. Bring your macro lenses to photograph the tiny seahorses at Frederiksted pier. On St. Croix, you can choose from several excellent operators, including **Peter Hughes Dive St. Croix** (tel. 773-3434) and **Sea Shadows Scuba** (tel. 778-3850). One-tank dives cost $45, two-tank dives about $82. Never been diving before but think you might like to give it a try? Intro courses, including instruction and a supervised open-water dive, cost about $82.

Step back in time on a walking tour through **Christiansted,** much of which has remained virtually unchanged for over 200 years. The wharf building, the fort, and several other buildings are a national historic site. Your first stop should be the Visitor's Bureau located in the Scalehouse, a 19th-century building where imports and exports were once weighed. Here, you can pick up walking tour maps of Christiansted and Frederiksted. Highlights include:

Fort Christiansvaern. Built of yellow brick brought from Denmark as ballast in sailing ships, the fort was completed in 1749. Here, you can pick up maps for a self-guided walking tour. You'll shudder when you view the cells, only four feet high, and the tiny dungeon, which held the worst offenders. Then come back to the daylight, and the splendid view of the harbor from the ramparts of the Water Battery—a great place to take photos of the cannon and the harbor. Open Monday through Saturday, 8 a.m. to 5 p.m.; admission is $1.

Steeple Building. Completed in 1753, this was the first Lutheran Church on St. Croix. It is now a small museum tracing the history of St. Croix—from the Indians through the reign of the Danish West India and Guinea Company. Open Monday through Friday, 9 a.m. to 4:30 p.m.; Saturday, 9 a.m. to noon; admission is free.

Government House. If you have any susceptibility to atmosphere, you'll be enthralled by the 18th-century Government House, facing King Street. For over 100 years, this was the seat of the Danish colonial government in the West Indies. The most impressive room is the second-floor ballroom, lined with tall gilt mirrors and lighted by sconces—you'll almost imagine that you can see dancers sweeping across the floor. Also pause in front of the portrait of Peter von Scholten, who served as governor general from 1828 to 1848. Von Scholten's story is a rather poignant one. A far-sighted man and a humanitarian, he instituted many reforms, including free, compulsory education for slave children. No doubt, von Scholten's views were influenced by Anna Heegaard, the former slave who became his mistress after his Danish wife deserted him. During an uprising in 1848, von Scholten issued a proclamation freeing all the slaves in the Danish West Indies. Although the Danish king had previously agreed to emancipation, von Scholten was recalled to Denmark and convicted of acting without authority. He never returned to St. Croix, nor ever again saw the woman he loved. The portrait of von Scholten that hangs in the Assembly Room is a fine one, and it almost seems to communicate the full weight of this tale.

Site of the Crugar hardware store. Born on the nearby island of Nevis, Alexander Hamilton worked as a clerk at this store from about 1766 to 1773, before leaving for America. The store was located on King Street, across from Government House, where the Little Switzerland shop now stands.

Because of St. Croix's sprawling dimensions, it is best to divvy up your sightseeing. The island's **west end** offers an interesting blend of historic great houses and forts, natural beauty, and white-sand beaches. Driving from Christiansted, your stops could include:

The St. George Village Botanical Gardens. The gardens display the exotic flowers and trees of the island against the coral stone and brick walls of what was once a 19th-century African workers' village. Depending on what month you visit, you might view one of the spectacular annual displays, such as the quarter-acre bed of red and white poinsettias, which bloom every winter. Various parts of the original village are also being restored, and on Thursdays, volunteers demonstrate metal-forging techniques in the blacksmith shop. The gardens are also a popular spot for weddings. If you would like to get married here, contact the St. Croix Visitors Bureau to arrange permission. Located just off Centerline Road (Rte. 70), the gardens are open Monday through Saturday, 9 a.m. to 3:30 p.m.; Sunday, 10 a.m. to 3 p.m.; admission is $2.25 per person.

Cruzan Rum Distillery. Learn how rum is made at this working distillery—and get to sample some of the product. You'll walk through the plant surrounded by wooden kegs, and get a whiff of the intoxicating fumes from the distillery. Finally, you'll be able to quaff some of the potent rum (they make a 151 proof), and try their drink of the day. The free guided tours run Monday through Friday, 8:30 to 11:15 a.m. and 1 to 4:15 p.m. Located on West Airport Road (tel. 772-0799).

Estate Whim Plantation Museum. Get a feel for the plantation era of the late 1700s, when St. Croix was one of the richest sugar-producing islands in the Caribbean. Built by Christopher Mac Evoy, Jr., in the late 18th century, the three-room great house is built of stone and coral, mortared together by molasses. It combines architectural features of the famous châteaux of Europe, modified to accommodate tropical living (for example, a dry moat surrounds the house, to reduce humidity). The great house has been beautifully restored with period furnishings. Then stop by the cookhouse for some piping hot johnnycakes (fried breads), before strolling around the rest of the property, which includes a stone windmill and a steam mill. Stop by the gift shop, where you'll find some charming souvenirs and gift items. The great house is a national historic site managed by the St. Croix Landmarks Society. Located on Centerline Road near Frederiksted; open daily from 10 a.m. to 5 p.m.; admission is $4.50 per person.

Frederiksted. While Christiansted retains a decidedly Danish colonial feel, the ambience at Frederiksted is very Victorian, with many buildings boasting elaborate fretwork and gingerbread trim. Although the town was founded in 1751, much of it was destroyed in a fire in the late 1800s, and houses were reconstructed in the curlicued style of the time. Today, the excellent harbor makes Frederiksted a popular cruise-ship port, but it still retains a sun-washed, almost sleepy, mood. Start your explorations with a visit to the visitors bureau, located in the old Customs House at the corner of Strand and Custom House Streets. Here, you can pick up maps for a self-guided tour. Stop in at historic Fort Frederik, where the first foreign salute to the new stars and stripes flag supposedly occurred in 1776. Here too, in 1848, Governor Peter von Scholten issued his proclamation emancipating the slaves: "All not free in the Danish West Indies are from today free." Many elegantly restored buildings line Strand Street, fronting the harbor, including the fine Victoria House (7–8 Strand St.). There are also several shops for browsing, and cafés for relaxing.

The rain forest. From the tropical sunshine, escape to the cool of St. Croix's rain forest. Take Creque Dam Road just north of Frederiksted. You'll pass beneath towering mahogany trees and yellow cedar. At St. Croix Leap in the rain forest, you'll come across a group of talented woodcarvers with their works for sale. Don't hesitate about buying a large sculpture or some chairs—they can arrange to ship items home for you. From here, you can return towards Christiansted on the Scenic Road, which runs along the island's mountainous backbone.

Sandy Point. Five miles of sand and sea, and nothing but . . . that's what you'll find at this breathtaking promontory where land and sea swirl together. Since this is the westernmost part of St. Croix, the sunsets are outstanding. Go here with someone who knows the road: The correct route through the dunes is practically impossible to follow. Since the beach is usually deserted, it is also recommended that you go with a group of at least four people.

Turtle Watch. Blackness blankets the forest night. Suddenly, your nostrils smell damp, churned-over earth—and your eyes can just barely discern a hawksbill turtle scooping out her nest. This is no TV nature documentary: you're actually there, and doing your part to help preserve one of the wonders of nature. Both St. Croix and Buck Island Reef National Monument are important nesting places for several endangered turtle species. From April through July, leatherback turtles lay their eggs at Sandy Point, and hawksbill turtles nest from July through September in the beach forests at Buck Island. Volunteers are crucially needed to assist park rangers and biologists in two different tagging, measuring, and behavioral studies. Even one evening can help. Contact the **U.S. Fish and Wildlife Service** for information about leatherback turtle research at Sandy Point (tel. 772-0274), the **St. Croix Environmental Association** for details about the Buck Island Hawksbill Project (tel. 773-1989).

HONEYMOON HOTELS AND HIDEAWAYS

St. Croix has a wide range of places to stay—from breezy, island-style inns to a brand-new, superluxurious resort. If you decide to stay in Christiansted, you'll have its bevy of fine restaurants and shops right on your doorstep. Although there's no beach in town, you can take advantage of lovely beach and excellent water-sports facilities at Protestant Cay, in the middle of the harbor; it's just two minutes away by ferry.

Rates quoted reflect the difference between low- and high-season prices.

Moderately Expensive

The Buccaneer, Box 25200, Gallows Bay Station, St. Croix, USVI 00824 (tel. 809/773-2100; reservations: tel. 212/586-3070, or toll free 800/223-1108). This pink-painted colonnaded resort occupies one of the most historic sites on St. Croix, part of a 17th-century estate belonging to Charles Martel, a Knight of Malta. Today, owned by the Armstrong family, it is still St. Croix's premier luxury resort, located just a mere wink (about two miles) from Christiansted. The Buccaneer offers guests the best of both worlds: a rolling green hilltop location (great views) that undulates its way down to not one, but three of St. Croix's finest beaches. After its recent redecoration, the lobby has a great house feel, with its ceiling fans and new wicker furnishings. All rooms have just undergone a thorough refurbishment, and each features a minifridge, air conditioning, and a private terrace or balcony. Many of the accommodations have lavish pink-marble bathrooms. If you're looking for something really special, choose one of the elegant Ridge Rooms, set in stone structures that once were plantation outbuildings. They've been entirely renovated and feature glossy marble floors, king-size four-poster beds, and French doors leading to spacious stone terraces. The Buccaneer is a complete, self-contained resort with eight tennis courts overlooking the Caribbean, an 18-hole golf course, and water-sports facilities for snorkeling and scuba-diving. At the new health spa, you can indulge in various treatment programs such as massage and acupressure, as well as work out on the exercise equipment. For couples considering getting married in St. Croix, the Buccaneer has just the spot—its landmark sugar-mill tower overlooking the sea. Honeymoon package: Eight days/seven nights (some meals): $1,190 per couple (superior room); $1,650 per couple (deluxe room). Includes breakfast daily, bottle of champagne, Tuesday night buffet, one hour tennis court time daily, sunset cocktail cruise, snorkel lesson, daytime shuttle transportation to Christiansted, 7½% government tax, and more. Package is not available during the high season, when rates (EP) range from $260 to $330 per couple per night.

Carambola Beach Resort and Golf Club, P.O. Box 3031, Kingshill, St. Croix, USVI 00850 (tel. 809/778-3800; reservations: toll free 800/447-9503). Located on the north shore, the Carambola Beach occupies 28 secluded acres on Davis Bay, a spectacular strand that attains an awesome solemnity that recalls the coast of Hawaii. A grove of palm trees slants toward the sea; deeply furrowed cliffs recede to the west—a splendid counterpoint to the sunset. The striking thing about Carambola is not only its luxury, but also the concern for the environment (one could almost say reverence) with which it was developed. Built of stucco, wood, and stone, the resort incorporates both Danish and West Indian architectural motifs. The 156 guest accommodations occupy two-story, six-unit clusters, completely surrounded by palm trees, hibiscus, and bougainvillea. The rooms are huge; each has an ocean view, and a separate sitting and sleeping area. There's also a room-size screened-in porch with built-in banquettes where guests can read, relax, and enjoy the scenery and trade winds—exactly like the treehouse you wished you'd had as a child. Accommodations are air-conditioned. In addition to the splendid beach, guests can cool off in the large free-form swimming pool, play tennis on four courts, or tee off on the 18-hole, Robert Trent Jones–designed Carambola Golf Course (formerly known as Fountain Valley). Carambola has two excellent restaurants: Saman, the main dining room; and the Mahogany Room, which showcases gourmet continental and Caribbean cuisines. Honeymoon package: Seven days/six nights (FAP): $2,035 per couple (low season). Includes three meals daily, bottle of champagne, Tiffany picture frame, and tour of St. Croix. Package not available mid-December to April, when rates (FAP) run $520 to $630 per couple per night.

Cormorant Beach Club, 108 La Grande Princesse, St. Croix, USVI 00820 (tel. 809/778-8920); reservations: 212/696-1323 in New York State; toll free 800/372-1323 nationwide). Tucked in a palm grove near Christiansted, the Cormorant is the most elegant small hotel in St. Croix—a treat for discerning travelers. There are only 38 accommodations, located in handsome buildings crafted of stone and stucco. Extremely spacious, rooms are beautifully decorated with rattan furnishings and quilted floral bedspreads. Each has a terrace or patio; on clear days, views from your oceanfront quarters extend all the way to St. Thomas. At night you can lull yourself to sleep to the murmur of waves breaking on the offshore reef (terrific for snorkeling). The personal service really pampers, with maids primping your room three times a day. Maintaining the ambience of restful escape is the absence of televisions in the rooms. During the day, different activities are planned, including water aerobics, snorkeling instruction, and tennis—all complimentary to guests. The unusual meal plan includes breakfast, lunch, and all drinks until 5 p.m., allowing couples the freedom to sample St. Croix's many tempting restaurants for dinner. Meanwhile, the Cormorant's own restaurant, right at surf's edge, is excellent. Honeymoon package: Eight days/seven nights (most meals and drinks): $1,485 to $2,885 per couple per night. Includes champagne, sailing/snorkeling trip to Buck Island, upgrade to suite when available.

Traveler's Alert

As we were preparing this edition for press in September 1989, Hurricane Hugo ripped through the Caribbean, causing considerable damage. Plans immediately were underway to rebuild, but St. Croix was especially hard hit, so if you are planning to honeymoon there in 1990, it is advisable to check out the island's status before completing your arrangements.

St. Croix by the Sea, P.O. Box 248, Christiansted, St. Croix, USVI 00821 (tel. 809/778-8600; reservations: toll free 800/524-5006 or 800/223-5695). "Everything was like we dreamed it would be." "It was great!" These are just a few of the happy comments vacationers write in the guestbook here, at St. Croix's only all-inclusive resort. With 65 rooms, the two-story pink-painted building faces the island's north shore, where the white foam of the breaking surf stretches as far as the eye can see. Surfing and windsurfing are excellent; since the water gets a bit rough for swimming, there's a large saltwater pool carved into the coral reef along the shore. In addition to all meals and drinks at the bar, the all-inclusive package covers many sightseeing options, such as a full-day sail to Buck Island, an island tour, Christiansted sightseeing. The feeling is intimate and laid back, with an emphasis on individual enjoyment rather than group activity. All rooms feature contemporary island furnishings, as well as air conditioning, cable TVs, and telephones; rates vary according to view. Entertainment enlivens the nighttime scene, especially on the West Indian buffet and barbecue nights. Facilities include four tennis courts and a shopping arcade. If possible, they try to upgrade honeymooners to an oceanview room. Honeymoon package: Eight days/seven nights (all-inclusive): $1,950 to $2,300 per couple (low season); $2,310 to $2,770 per couple (high season).

Moderate

Colony Cove, Suite 11, Caravelle Arcade, Christiansted, St. Croix, USVI 00820 (tel. 809/773-9780; reservations: toll free 800/524-2025). Make yourself at home at Colony Cove, an elegantly furnished beachfront condo resort just a three-minute drive from Christiansted. Set in three-story stucco buildings, all of the accommodations have at least a partial ocean view. Each of the big, airy units is two-bedroom, two-bath, so you can really spread out. Although decor varies, expect lots of islandy touches, such as rattan furnishings and white-tile floors. You'll enjoy all the modern comforts: color TV, fully equipped kitchen with microwave oven, washer/dryer, plus daily maid service. The bedroom is air-conditioned, although the living room is not. Some of the units are plunked right down on the beach: These are booked on a first come, first served basis, so ask! At the water-sports center, you can sign on for floats, snorkeling gear, Windsurfers, and catamarans, or play a game of tennis. For honeymooners who want tranquil surroundings and a central location, it's a perfect choice.

Colony Cove is managed by Antilles Resorts, which also handles Schooner Bay resort condominiums. Honeymoon package: Eight days/seven nights (EP): $1,035 to $1,570 per couple. Includes gift basket with fruit, cheese, sausage, and more upon arrival; bottle of champagne; half-day sail to Buck Island; souvenir honeymoon photo and frame; press release and honeymoon photo sent to your home-town newspaper.

Inexpensive

Chenay Bay Beach Resort, P.O. Box 24600, Christiansted, St. Croix, USVI 00824 (tel. 809/773-2918; reservations: toll free 800/548-4457). Remember how in *Cinderella* the fairy godmother turns a pumpkin into a magnificent coach? The same type of transformation has happened at Chenay Bay, a 30-acre resort on a serene cove about ten minutes from Christiansted. Here, the magic is being worked by Vicki and Richard Locke, veteran Caribbean hoteliers who recently bought the property. They're creating an intimate, casual resort—one of the most captivating in the Caribbean. Sheltered under the genip trees, each of the cottages reflects winsome, West Indian charm, with gray-painted woodwork and white lattice trim. Inside, the immaculate accommodations have been redone with new quarry-rock floors, wicker furnishings, and art deco–flavored Erté prints on the walls; each also has a fully equipped kitchenette. Some offer air conditioning.

Getting away from it all doesn't mean that you can't enjoy big-time amenities. The property features two new tennis courts and a sparkling swimming pool right by the water; a Mistral sailboard school is on the premises. The seaside beach pavilion serves breakfast, lunch, and dinner daily—the grilled fish and barbecued chicken are excellent, but there are many other choices as well. Honeymoon package: Eight days/seven nights (EP): $625 to $705 per couple (low season); $1,280 to $1,360 per couple (high season). Includes accommodations with king-size bed, bottle of champagne and tropical flowers in room, discount coupon book.

King Christian Hotel, P.O. Box 3619, Christiansted, USVI 00822 (tel. 809/773-2285; reservations: toll free 800/524-2012). Friendly and hospitable, this landmark inn usually appears in the photos you see of Christiansted harbor. The three-story hotel is located right on the dock, and its yellow-painted facade, blue shutters, and shopping arcade fit right in with the historic structures that surround it. About the only thing old-fashioned at the King Christian itself, however, is the attention to detail and dedication to personal service. Owner Betty Sperber and her staff will help you plan excursions to suit your interests—from sails to Buck Island to golf at the Carambola course. All rooms are air-conditioned and have private baths. Each of the superior rooms has a modern decor and features two double beds, color cable TV, minifridge, room safe, and a large dressing area. Best of all, each has a spacious balcony overlooking the waterfront, providing ringside seats for watching yachts come and go in the harbor and spectating at sunsets. Although the minimum rooms have neither a balcony nor a harbor view, the price is certainly right. Whichever accommodations you choose, you can swim and sun yourselves in the freshwater pool in the central courtyard shaded by towering palms. Thanks to the hotel's superb location, you're right in the middle of Christiansted activity. The hotel is also the center for St. Croix water-sports fun, with Mile-Mark Charters located right on the premises, and dive packages available through the excellent Peter Hughes operation. Honeymoon package: Eight days/seven nights (EP): $725 to $950 per couple for a superior room. Includes airport transfers, sail to Buck Island, a dinner by candlelight, welcome drinks, a $10 gift certificate, his-and-her T-shirts.

Club Comanche, 1 Strand St., Christiansted, USVI 00820 (tel. 809/773-0210), exudes plenty of character and charm. No two rooms are alike, but many have romantic mahogany four-poster beds; all have color TVs and most are air-conditioned. There are two sections: an original building (dating to the mid-1700s), which has been updated with contemporary amenities but still has plenty of West Indian atmosphere ($60 to $110 per couple per night for a room with a king-size bed); and more modern additions, which are located by the pool and the harbor. If you favor one-of-a-kind accommodations, choose the honeymoon suite that occupies the landmark sugar-mill–design structure on the harborfront. Your sleeping quarters, complete with a king-size bed, have a little spiral stairway leading to the balcony on the roof, where you can sun yourselves or watch Christiansted harbor shimmer in the moonlight ($110 to $160 per couple per night).

Sprat Hall Plantation, Route 63 (P.O. Box 695), Frederiksted, St. Croix, USVI 00840 (tel. 809/772-0305). Step back in time to all the romance of the plantation era at Sprat Hall, the oldest great house in the Virgin Islands. Dating from about 1670, the house is indeed a beauty, with a gracious front porch surrounded by archways, and rooms decorated with fine mahogany antiques. All rooms in the great house have four-poster beds. In room no. 5, the four-poster is an especially fine specimen, with a carved pineapple design. Room no. 3 is currently the only air-conditioned part of the great house (the breezes alone usually keep everything cool, but air conditioning will soon be added throughout). Only nonsmokers can stay in the great house—a rule that is strictly enforced. The place is run by Joyce Hurd, whose family is one of the oldest on St. Croix. She supervises the excellent kitchen (see "Romantic Restaurants" write-up that follows) and shares oldtime hospitality and warmth with her guests. Sprat Hall is located at St. Croix's west end, just north of Frederiksted. Beachgoers will enjoy the fine stretch of sand at the Sprat Hall Beach Club, and horseback riders will appreciate the easy proximity to the stables, run by Joyce's daughter, Jill. Don't expect modern luxuries or conveniences per se: Its charms are casual rather than highly refined. But for couples who want to experience a long-ago way of life, Sprat Hall could be just the ticket. (If you prefer a little more modernity in your lives, there are also Sprat Hall's Arawak cottages, which are air-conditioned and decorated simply.) Honeymoon package: None. Rates (EP): $99 to $132 per couple per night for great house rooms; $110 to $155 per couple per night for cottages.

Traveler's Alert

As we were preparing this edition for press in September 1989, Hurricane Hugo ripped through the Caribbean, causing considerable damage. Plans immediately were underway to rebuild, but St. Croix was especially hard hit, so if you are planning to honeymoon there in 1990, it is advisable to check out the island's status before completing your arrangements.

ROMANTIC RESTAURANTS

St. Croix seems to specialize in open-air eateries with a lively, convivial atmosphere. Some of the most attractive restaurants are set in the second stories of the old buildings that line Christiansted's narrow streets. Unless otherwise noted, all restaurants are in Christiansted. Reservations are a necessity, and since not all places take credit cards, you should ask in advance.

Moderate

Set right on King's Wharf overlooking the harbor, the **Chart House,** King Christian Hotel, King's Wharf, Christiansted (tel. 773-7718), is a great favorite with locals and visitors alike. Try to get a table by the window so that you can watch the passing parade of old salts and assorted glitterati. The restaurant is part of the well-regarded U.S. chain, but it far and away surpasses the ordinary with its excellent food and nautical ambience. The first and biggest hit is its 40-item salad bar, the largest in the islands. For an entrée, seafaring types will want to try one of the teriyaki platters, with shrimp and/or lobster; landlubbers will happily dig into the juicy prime rib. For dessert, request two forks, and start excavating into the huge slab of chocolate mud pie. Dinner for two, about $70 plus drinks. Open nightly 6 to 10 p.m.

Tivoli Gardens, 39 Strand St., Pan Am Pavilion (tel. 773-6782), a second-story charmer upstairs on Strand Street, recalls its Copenhagen namesake with the trellises, hanging plants, and tiny white lights that create a fairy-tale—yet tropical—atmosphere. Owner Gary Thomson often strums old favorite songs on the guitar, and the sounds of classics from the 1930s, 1940s, and 1950s somehow seem right in the island atmosphere. The menu spotlights an international array of dishes, from lobster-stuffed mushroom caps to steak Diane, fresh fish, stir-fry chicken orientale, and even a warming rendition of Hungarian goulash. Dinner entrées include salad, bread, and fresh vegetables. For dessert, everybody's favorite is the chocolate velvet. Dinner for two, about $60 plus drinks. Open Monday through Saturday for lunch, 11:15 a.m. to 2:30 p.m.; Monday through Sunday for dinner, 6 to 9:30 p.m.

Comanche, 1 Strand St. (tel. 773-0210), is actually two restaurants: one on the second story of the hotel; the other directly across the street and facing the waterfront. Open for breakfast, lunch, and dinner, Comanche has been St. Croix's most popular restaurant for nearly 40 years. For breakfast, head over to the hotel side and try to snare one of the tables on the outdoor balcony (these are a favorite with regulars, so it might take some persistence). From this perch, you can watch the comings and goings of citizens down below on Strand Street, and the acrobatics of the bananaquits (sugar birds), zooming in for a sweet treat from the bird feeders. Breakfast is served from 7 to 11 a.m.; about $15 per couple (very good eggs Benedict). At dinnertime, the waterfront side wins out for the atmosphere. Here, the most romantic seating comes in the peacock-backed wicker chairs. The menu offers a combination of down-island and continental specialties, from callaloo to duck à l'orange. They are especially well known for their curries. Dinner for two, about $70 plus drinks; served from 6 to 10 p.m. nightly.

Anchor Inn, 58A King St. (tel. 773-0263). When it's dining with a water view that you're after, head straight for Donn's Anchor Inn with its second-floor open-air deck overlooking Christiansted harbor. It's a pleasant stop for breakfast, lunch, or dinner. For a leisurely breakfast, make your selection from 14 different omelets or opt for the memorable french toast, topped with real whipped cream (about $8). The lunch menu is casual, with burgers and salads (about $10 per person). At dinnertime, the fresh fish is the way to go: conch fritters or conch salad for starters, followed by fresh Caribbean lobster. Finish off your meal with a slice of the homemade cheesecake. Dinner for two will run about $60 to $70 plus drinks. A bonus here is the extended hours. Breakfast served daily, 7:30 a.m. to 2:30 p.m.; lunch, 11 a.m. to 2:30 p.m.; dinner, 6:30 to 11 p.m. or so.

Kendrick's, Queen Cross Street at King Street (tel. 773-9199). You'll feel as if you've been whisked to the French countryside at this charming boîte run by David and Jane Kendrick, a husband-and-wife team (he's the chef, she manages the dining rooms). Crisp blue tablecloths, nosegays of fresh flowers, and hanging baskets of plants create a tranquil mood; etched-glass panels set off the different rooms, enhancing privacy. The cuisine is innovative and delicious. Specialties include the medallions of beef with sauce béarnaise, pecan-crusted pork loin, or sautéed shrimp topped with two sauces: pesto cream and sweet red-pepper cream. For dessert, they're famous for the white-and-dark chocolate mousse cake and liqueur-spiked coffees. Serving dinner from 6 to 10:30 p.m., $60 to $70 per couple. Closed Tuesday.

Banana Bay Club, Caravelle Hotel, Queen Cross Street (tel. 778-9110). Surprisingly enough for a harbor town, Christiansted has few seaside restaurants—except for this favorite, where you can dine right down by the water. For lunch, choose one of their tasty burgers or a heaping platter of fried shrimp or chicken; $15 to $20 per couple. Dinner entrées include pasta Alfredo and blackened swordfish; about $40 per couple for a complete dinner. Don't miss dessert, especially one of the namesake banana creations—from soufflés to pies. Their dinner specials offer exceedingly good value. On Thursdays, there's a complete Maine lobster dinner for $19 per person; on Fridays, folks line up for the all-you-can-eat pasta bar starring 20 different variations—$10.95 per person. Open for breakfast, 7:30 a.m. to 10:30 a.m.; lunch, 11:30 a.m. to 5:30 p.m.; and dinner, 5:30 to 11:30 p.m.

Stixx, upstairs at the Pan Am Pavilion (tel. 773-5157). Sushi with a view—that's what you'll find at this popular restaurant overlooking Christiansted harbor. All the fish is fresh-caught from local waters: tuna, dolphin, wahoo, snapper, and grouper. In addition to sushi rolls and sashimi, the menu covers teriyaki steak, chicken, and shrimp; stir-fries; and tempura. To accompany your meal, you can choose from a range of sakes and Japanese beers. Please note that the menu is Westernized at lunchtime, offering a selection of sandwiches and burgers on the outdoor deck. Open Monday through Saturday for lunch, 11:30 a.m. to 5 p.m.; $20 per couple. Serving dinner nightly from 6 to 10 p.m.; $30 to $40 per couple.

Le Strand Café, Strand Street, Frederiksted (tel. 772-0607). You couldn't ask for a setting more redolent with island romance, tucked in the recently restored 19th-century Sea View Inn. The full-bodied cuisine radiates all the sunshine of a sunny day in the south of France. Lunch is simple: salmon quiche, perhaps, or a duck salad . . . maybe even a hamburger. For dinner, try the tuna Provençale or duck à l'orange. Every dish is meticulously prepared: their steak tartare, for example, is hand-chopped. Finish with a flourish—chocolate mousse or a fresh-fruit tart. Open Tuesday through Sunday for lunch, 11:30 a.m. to 2:30 p.m.; $20 to $40 per couple. Dinner served Tuesday through Saturday, 6:30 to 10 p.m.; $50 to $70 per couple.

Nolan's, Queen's Cross Street (tel. 773-7885), is known for succulent Caribbean seafood such as lobster and conch; they also do a mean chicken curry. Save plenty of room for garlic bread and johnnycakes to accompany your order. Try one of their rum drinks—they carry many different brands. About $40 to $50 per couple. Open nightly from 5 to 9 p.m.

Sprat Hall Plantation and **Sprat Hall Beach Club,** one mile north of Frederiksted (tel. 772-0305). If the thought of West Indian specialties such as conch chowder, chicken curry, or pork loin in orange sauce makes your mouth water, this is the place for you. Joyce Hurd, whose family has lived on St. Croix for generations, dishes out authentic island cuisine. Lunch is served on the terrace at the Sprat Hall Beach Club, set on a very lovely white-sand beach on St. Croix's west coast. Lunch features conch soup, salads, the fresh catch of the day—and some ambrosial pumpkin fritters. After lunch, you're welcome to spread out your beach towels on the sand

and enjoy the crystal-clear waters here on St. Croix's lee shore. Lunch will run about $30 per couple; open noon to 2:30 p.m. daily.

For a very special dinner that will whisk you 300 years back in time, make reservations for the dining room at Sprat Hall Great House, the oldest plantation great house in the Virgin Islands. Many of the fruits and vegetables come right from Sprat Hall's own gardens. Do not pass up the conch, steeped in butter and spiked with just a hint of sherry. The menu constantly changes to take advantage of what's fresh, but might include fish and lobster dishes, beef burgundy, or leg of lamb, all accompanied by rice or potatoes and four or five different fresh vegetables. Cap off your meal with one of Mrs. Hurd's specialties, such as soursop ice cream or soursop pie. Reservations at the great house are absolutely essential, since you are, in effect, dining in a private home. A very special experience. Dinner for two, about $50.

Sundowner Beach Bar, north of Frederiksted pier (tel. 772-9906). It's not much to look at—just a beach shack, really. But it's *the* place to go for sunsets, especially on Sundays starting at about 5 p.m., when the live entertainment could be strumming country and western or simmerin' up some mean reggae. As you watch for the "green flash" when the sun slips beyond the horizon, down some "Cruzan painkillers," wicked concoctions of coconut and rums, topped with nutmeg . . . definitely not for the fainthearted. Sustain yourselves with some gen-u-ine Texas-style fajitas, marinated beef and chicken and sautéed vegetables crammed into a flour tortilla—a steal at $3.50 each. Open seven days a week. Breakfast served Monday through Saturday from 6 to 11 a.m. and on Sunday from 9 a.m.; about $10 per couple. Lunch is served Monday through Saturday, 11 a.m. to 4 p.m.; $10 to $20 plus drinks. The Sunday band starts at 5 p.m., and won't stop until you drop. No reservations, no credit cards.

4. St. John

If you ask a St. Johnian how far his island is from St. Thomas, the populous Virgin Islands capital, a slow grin may spread over his face. "About twenty minutes . . . and a hundred years," he'll reply, only half joking.

St. John is the most truly virgin of the U.S. islands, a smidgen of unspoiled paradise surrounded by sapphire-blue seas. Located about two miles east of St. Thomas across Pillsbury Sound, it measures only nine miles long and five miles wide, making it the smallest of the major islands. About two-thirds of St. John is national park, donated to the U.S. government in 1956 by Laurance Rockefeller to preserve its pristine beauty for generations to come. If your top honeymoon priority is beaches, you've come to the right place. A necklace of several line the island's north shore, all blessed with crystal-clear turquoise bays and white sands so soft they're almost fluffy.

Long before Christopher Columbus came, St. John was inhabited by Indians —first, the gentle Arawaks, who were subsequently displaced (and/or devoured) by the ferocious Caribs. Many Indian artifacts have been found, and you can view mysterious petroglyphs (rock carvings) along trails through the island's interior (see details, which follow). The Danes settled at the protected harbor of Coral Bay in 1718. Viewing St. John's rather siesta pace today, you'll find it hard to believe that the island was once one of the most prosperous sugar-producers in the region. A violent slave rebellion in 1733, and the subsequent abolition of slavery in 1848, ended the plantation era. For nearly 100 years, the island remained virtually undisturbed, while old coral stone walls crumbled and lianas entangled themselves in the vanes of sugar mills. In recent years, nature-loving vacationers have discovered St. John's serene beauty, and they have made it a haven for peaceful escape.

What action there is centers on Cruz Bay, the main town located on St. John's west coast, where the St. Thomas ferry puts in. Here, time seems to have politely decided to stand still. Roosters crow and scamper across the main square, dogs snooze under the benches, and the town's original rental car agency still operates out of a hut. The whole place is about three blocks long and two blocks wide. Don't be misled by the funky side, however. St. John is a preferred port of call for the rich and famous, who anchor their yachts in secluded bays, or ensconce themselves in luxury resorts. St. John attracts a mixed-bag clientele—CEOs and craftspeople, campers and yachtsmen, movie stars and, of course, starry-eyed honeymooners. All come to immerse themselves in the sun, the seclusion, and the magnificent beaches. St. John is the kind of place you'll feel like you've "discovered"—and you'll sincerely hope it never fully joins the 20th century.

SHOPPING

The Cruz Bay shops are one of the better-kept secrets of the Virgin Islands. You won't find large duty-free emporiums; instead, individualistic boutiques specialize in fine, one-of-a-kind crafts items.

Many of the best shops are clustered in **Mongoose Junction,** a minimall built of coral stone and ballast brick to resemble the ruins of the sugar plantations that dot the island. Here **The Canvas Factory** carries canvas bags in all different sizes. **R&I Patton Goldsmithing** makes original-design gold and silver jewelry on the premises. Many pieces incorporate island motifs such as scallop shells, seahorses, or petroglyph symbols. **Wicker, Wood, and Shells** sells all that—as well as St. John basketwork, straw hats, and some charming bird feeders made from coconut shells. **The Fabric Mill** offers framed wall-hangings, Haitian cottons, and batiks imported from Indonesia and the Netherlands. **The Clothing Studio** displays hand-painted clothing. **The Donald Schnell Ceramic Studio** has a beautiful selection of hand-crafted platters, mirrors, and wind chimes, as well as exquisite hand-blown Christmas ornaments.

Probably no shops in the world face a more spectacular view than those at **Wharfside Village,** a new double-decker minimall right on the Cruz Bay waterfront. Noteworthy boutiques include **Let's Go Bananas** for bright, tropical clothing for women, and **Colombian Emeralds** for jewelry and gemstones.

At the **Lemon Tree Mall** on Backstreet, **Caribbean Casting Company** displays original jewelry designed by craftspeople from the islands as well as the mainland. **Pink Papaya,** also at the Lemon Tree, features an excellent selection of crafts and gifts. **Batik Caribe,** on Backstreet, carries hand-painted T-shirts by local artists (the large ones make great beach coverups) and brilliantly colored batik *pareus* (sarongs) and wall-hangings from Barbados. For T-shirts, head for **Stitches** or the **Art Project.**

ROMANTIC INTERLUDES

To best appreciate St. John, rent a Jeep and follow the winding roads, taking in the scenic lookouts over the north shore beaches and heading for the top of **Bordeaux Mountain,** the island high point. As you travel along, keep your eyes open for the furry mongooses, which often scurry across your path. Here are some attractions you might like to take in.

Ask a knowledgeable **beach** connoisseur to name the ten best beaches in the world—and it's possible that five of them will be on St. John. Part of the pleasure of a St. John sojourn involves trying out the different strands that fringe the island's north shore. You'll want to check out:

Hawksnest: A big, beautiful bay where scenes from Alan Alda's *The Four Seasons* were filmed. Facilities include toilets, picnic tables, and barbecue pits.

Trunk Bay: Ringed by sea-grape trees, this broad white beach and calm blue bay with a tiny islet in the middle must be one of the most-photographed sites on St. John. Part of the national park, the beach is also known for its marked underwater snorkeling trail. Snorkeling gear rental, a snackbar, and showers are located right at the beach.

Cinnamon Bay: Characterized by its long sweep of sand with cast-up, sun-bleached driftwood pieces, Cinnamon also has a teeny offshore island that's a favorite with snorkelers. Novice snorkelers will enjoy exploring the shallow reef at the bay's eastern end. Cinnamon is part of the national park campground and offers a snackbar, water-sports equipment rental, and guided snorkeling tours several times a week. Call (tel. 776-6201) for details.

Big and Little Maho Bays: Ringed by manchineel trees, these tranquil, horseshoe-shaped harbors have no public facilities—just beautiful beaches.

Francis Bay: Because it's the most isolated of the beaches, it usually is the least crowded—a sparkling white crescent that seems to roll on forever. Toward the east end at Mary Point, you can often spot turtles.

If you want to take along a picnic lunch, you can get all the fixin's at the **St. John Supermarket and Deli,** Centerline Road (Rte. 10) just outside of town across from the Texaco station (tel. 776-7373). In addition to tasty meats, seafood, and cheeses, they have the island's best wine collection. **Cruz Bay Provision Co.,** Wharfside Village in Cruz Bay (tel. 776-2157), also has a complete deli, bakery, and wine selection.

Next to the sheer beauty of the island, the thing that will surprise you most about St. John is the very visible and caring presence of the National Park Service, which administers about two-thirds of the island. In addition, park rangers run a wide variety of **hikes, historic tours,** and **snorkeling tours** that enable visitors to get the most out of their stays on St. John. Program schedules vary; write or call for details: **Virgin Islands National Park,** P.O. Box 710, St. John, USVI 00830 (tel. 809/776-6201). Events include:

Historic bus tour: The three-hour tour retraces the island's story from the time of the Arawak Indians to the Danish colonists through to the present. Along the route, the park ranger will fill you in on local lore, such as plants used in folk medicine, or the story of Easter Rock, a huge boulder said to march itself to the sea every Easter. You'll also learn about St. John's unofficial mascot, the mongoose. The tour is free, but the bus transportation costs about $13.50 from Cruz Bay. No charge if you bring your own car or Jeep.

Guided hikes: A favorite is the guided walk down Reef Bay Trail. It's the best kind of hike—downhill all the way—and concludes with a cooling swim and a boat ride back to Cruz Bay. Along the way, hikers pass a rain forest and mango groves, as well as ruins of an old sugar plantation and intriguing petroglyphs (rock carvings) attributed to the early Arawak settlers. The return boat ride costs $9 per person. The park service also publishes excellent hiking trail maps of the island; you can pick them up at the Cruz Bay Visitor Center.

Snorkeling trips: Held at Cinnamon Beach, the program teaches you safe snorkeling techniques and provides an excellent introduction to the fish that live on the coral reef. (Bring snorkeling gear, which you can rent at Cinnamon Bay.) Ask about the schedules for the boat tours around the island, usually held on Sunday.

"The best part of our trip!" That's how two honeymooners described the **snorkeling day trip** they had taken. Cruises head to the British Virgin Islands or some uninhabited cay. Popular day sails from St. John include **Water Lemon Cay,** a postage-stamp-size islet in Leinster Bay with superb snorkeling; and also **Sandy Cay, Great Thatch,** and **Tobago.** Crewed charters that take six to eight passengers are available out of the major resorts as well as at **Cruz Bay Watersports** (tel. 776-6234) and **St. John Watersports** (tel. 776-6256), both in Cruz Bay. Costs run about $65 to $70 for the full-day sail (includes lunch).

The waters off St. John also offer superb scuba-diving and snorkeling. Of special interest are three wreck dives, including the *Major-General Rogers,* a sunken Coast

Guard vessel, and the celebrated *Wreck of the Rhone*, a Royal Mail Steamer that sank in 1867 off the British Virgin Islands. Dive operators who can take you there: **Cruz Bay Watersports** (tel. 776-6234), a P.A.D.I. five-star training facility; **St. John Water Sports** (tel. 776-6256); and **Low Key Watersports** (tel. 776-7048). Two-tank dives cost about $72 per person; $105 for the *Rhone*.

At the beautiful **Annaberg Sugar Mill** overlooking Leinster Bay and the British Virgin Islands, you can retrace the history of St. John's plantation era. You can pick up a self-guided-tour map at the entrance and walk through the ruins of the slave quarters, mill, and outbuildings. Several times a week, St. Johnians demonstrate island cookery or crafts, such as basketweaving.

HONEYMOON HOTELS AND HIDEAWAYS

Although St. John does not have a vast number of different hotels, it offers an extremely wide choice of accommodations: everything from ultraposh resorts to seaside sites where you can pitch your own tent. The amazing thing is—all are, in their own way, superb. Rates quoted reflect the difference between low-and high-season prices.

Expensive

Caneel Bay, Virgin Islands National Park, St. John, USVI 00830 (tel. 809/776-6111; reservations: 212/765-5950 in New York State; toll free 800/223-7637 nationwide). St. John owes much of its luxury-hideaway cachet to this elegant Rockresort, which spreads out over not just one, but seven, diamond-white beaches on the island's north shore. The resort encompasses a broad, 170-acre peninsula that seems to reach out to embrace the sea. Located within the boundaries of the national park, Caneel Bay is designed to enhance the beautiful natural environment. Guest accommodations are unobtrusive, screened by palm trees (15 different varieties) and color-splashed gardens bright with hibiscus, oleander, bougainvillea, and ixora. Ruins of an 18th-century sugar mill have been incorporated into one of the restaurants. There are only 168 rooms, all in low-profile buildings situated around the property. The decor utilizes coral stone walls, dark bamboo furnishings, and ceiling fans. There are no in-room telephone, television, or air conditioning. Thanks to this combination of luxury and seclusion, Caneel Bay has become a preferred hideaway for the famous. Mrs. Vincent Astor, Mel Brooks and Anne Bancroft, and Henry Kissinger all stayed here.

Honeymooners will appreciate the fact that the Caneel Bay experience is all-inclusive. The sports facilities are superb, with guests enjoying complimentary use of the eleven tennis courts, a fleet of small sailboats, snorkeling equipment and instruction, and bicycles. With seven beaches to choose from, you're sure to be able to find one where yours will be practically the only sets of footprints in the sand. One beach you'll want to check out—the strand appropriately enough named Honeymoon. Day sails, deep-sea fishing, horseback riding, waterskiing, scuba-diving, and windsurfing are all available at an extra charge. In addition, all meals are included, with guests having their choice of Caneel's three excellent restaurants: the Beach Terrace, Turtle Bay Estate, or the Sugar Mill. Honeymoon package: Seven days/six nights (Full AP): $2,180 to $2,475 per couple. Includes deluxe accommodations, transfers from St. Thomas, a sunset cocktail cruise, a bottle of champagne, manager's reception, a half-day sail, and more. Also inquire about packages that combine stays at Caneel Bay with a holiday on Little Dix Bay, its sister Rockresort on Virgin Gorda; Carambola, on St. Croix; or with a crewed or bareboat charter of a luxury Hinckley yacht. Packages not available mid-December through April 1, when the rate (Full AP) is $440 to $630 per couple per night. Rates do not include gratuities or the 7½% U.S. VI hotel tax.

Virgin Grand St. John, Great Cruz Bay, St. John, USVI 00830 (tel. 809/776-7171; reservations: 212/661-4540, or toll free 800/223-1588). Built into the hillside, the 264-room luxury resort overlooks Great Cruz Bay (which is a mile outside of the town). The feeling is very much that of a plush country club. The striking modern design combines New England–style shingles, West Indian louvers and fan-motif windows, and future-forward magenta awnings and trim. Rolling green lawns undulate around both beach and hillside accommodations, tempting you to run barefoot across the expanse. The resort aims to go first class all the way, offering guests special features such as use of an exclusive airport lounge in St. Thomas, private ferry transport to St. John, plus an array of room amenities: air conditioning, cable color TVs, wet bars and refrigerators, and marble bathrooms with baskets containing not only shampoo and soap but also sunscreen. Sports facilities are extensive, including a huge free-form swimming pool (complete with its own islands, palm trees, and waterfall) and six lighted tennis courts. The beach is adequate, although not one of St. John's finest. Here guests can zip off on sailboats, Windsurfers, or a private yacht, and snorkeling gear is available for rent. At mealtime, you have a choice of three restaurants including Fronds, the art deco–style gourmet restaurant. Honeymoon package: Eight days/seven nights (Full AP): $2,470 (superior room) to $2,855 (deluxe) per couple (low season). Call for high-season rates. Includes welcome cocktails, three meals daily, nonalcoholic beverages, flowers in room, use of water-sports equipment, a beachbag, sunset sail, his-and-her bathrobes.

Moderate

Gallows Point, P.O. Box 58, St. John, USVI 00831 (tel. 809/776-6434; reservations: toll free 800/323-7229). Try island living at this villa resort perched in the headlands of Cruz Bay. With gray clapboard siding, fan-motif windows, jalousies and louvers, the buildings look a bit like Cape Cod come to the tropics. Each of the 60 rooms overlooks either the harbor or the sapphire-blue sweep of Pillsbury Sound, where you can watch ferries and sailboats skittering across the waves. The accommodations are truly luxurious and BIG, with tile floors, rattan furnishings, soaring ceilings, fully equipped kitchens, and terraces or balconies. For an extremely plush nest, choose one of the duplex Loft Suites, with a large bedroom upstairs, a living room downstairs, and a lushly planted bathroom where you'll feel as if you're showering in the Garden of Eden. For swimming, there are a small beach and several small coves, as well as a freshwater pool. Right at the resort, there's the excellent Ellington's restaurant (the upstairs deck is perfect for watching the sunset); the fun-loving townlet of Cruz Bay is less than a five-minute stroll away. Honeymoon package: None. Rates (EP): $140 to $155 per couple per night (summer); $220 to $275 per couple per night (winter).

Estate Zootenvaal, Hurricane Hole, St. John, USVI 00830 (tel. 809/776-6321; reservations: 216/861-5337). Your own kingdom by the sea—that's what you'll find at Estate Zootenvaal, a collection of four beach cottages right on the water on St. John's secluded east coast. You couldn't ask for a more pristine location, within the very boundaries of the U.S. Virgin Islands National Park, and near the small town of Coral Bay. Each of the simple stucco cottages awaits in move-in condition, with inviting rattan furnishings, flower-print draperies, and plenty of jalousie windows to let in the trade winds. Each comes with a fully equipped kitchenette and barbecue grill; beach towels, coolers, and irons are all provided. Cottage no. 1, poised at water's edge, is especially romantic. Brown Bay, the nearest good swimming beach, is just a short stroll away. Honeymoon package: None. Rates: Eight days/seven nights (EP): $800 per couple.

Inexpensive

Maho Bay, P.O. Box 310, Cruz Bay, St. John, USVI 00830 (tel. 809/776-6240; reservations: 212/472-9453 in New York State; toll free 800/392-9004 nationwide). For couples who love an easygoing, natural lifestyle amid incredibly beautiful surroundings, Maho Bay offers the best honeymoon value in the entire Caribbean. The resort is a community of 100 ultracomfortable tent cottages located within a private preserve in the national park. It's camping—with real beds and plumbing. The cozy tents are set on wooden decks overlooking the sea, and have three rooms: living room, bedroom (some with a double bed draped behind mosquito netting), and a cooking area, plus an open porch for sunbathing. Centrally located bathhouses are equipped with modern toilets, sinks, and showers. The guiding spirit behind Maho, Stanley Selengut, has created a resort that lives harmoniously with its surroundings. Frangipani and hibiscus flowers splash scarlet against the jungle greenery, orchids nestle in the crooks of tree branches, and peacocks strut along the walkways. At mealtime, guests can cook on the propane stoves in their tents (you can pick up supplies at Maho's convenience market), or head over to the breezy pavilion-deck restaurant. A special treat is Sunday night dinner, when St. Johnians bring in food that they have prepared in their own homes; a rich, cheese-laden lasagna, perhaps, or poached mahimahi (fish), or spicy West Indian chicken. The Maho cottages are perched just above some of St. John's finest beaches, Little Maho and Francis Bay. The resort runs extensive water-sports programs, with Windsurfers, Sunfish, and day sails all available. Maho is also the cultural center of St. John, hosting an eclectic series of special events throughout the year, ranging from jazz festivals to health, photography, and astronomy workshops—all free to guests. It all adds up to a very unique experience—and isn't that what honeymoons are all about? Honeymoon package: $50 to $80 per couple per night, based on a seven-night stay. Includes a bottle of champagne. They'll also give you one of the more secluded cottages with a superb view and a double bed.

Cinnamon Bay Campground, P.O. Box 120, Cruz Bay, St. John, USVI 00831-0720 (tel. 809/776-6330; reservations: 212/586-4459 in New York City; toll free 800/223-7637 nationwide). The soft lap of the waves, starlit nights, and sunny days on one of the most beautiful of St. John's beaches—the best things in life, if not free, are a very good deal at Cinnamon Bay Campground. The word "campground" is a bit misleading here, since the area has three different kinds of accommodations, all suitable to couples with different thresholds of "roughing it." Cottages are indeed real—albeit basic—apartments, with two concrete walls and two screened walls. They come provided with electricity, real beds (twins, so you'll have to resort to some ingenuity), and linens (changed weekly), plus a picnic table, barbecue grill, two-burner propane gas stove, ice chest, water container, cooking and eating utensils ($44 to $75 per couple per night). The tents are extremely commodious and comfortable, built on platforms and equipped with camp cots and pads, linens (changed weekly), and the other features of the cottages, except electricity ($30 to $60 per couple per night). Bare sites are just that: a cleared area with a picnic table and a built-in charcoal grill; you bring everything else ($11 per couple per night). The four bath houses with showers and flush toilets are kept clean and sparkling. If you don't feel like cooking yourselves, the Raintree Terrace cafeteria serves breakfast, lunch, and dinner.

ROMANTIC RESTAURANTS

Whether you're dining elegantly at a posh resort, or just limin' at a local hangout, you'll find that St. John's restaurants have plenty of personality and downright great food. Only the Sugar Mill at Caneel Bay is romantic in a soft candlelight/tropical flower sense; instead, the rest of these recommendations exude plenty of energy and fun—romanticism at its most spirited and adventure-loving best. Reservations are necessary all over, and not all places accept credit cards.

Expensive

Sugar Mill, Caneel Bay (tel. 776-6111). Sample the elegant Caneel Bay lifestyle at this restaurant built around the ruins of an old sugar mill—the only restaurant on the property that is open to nonguests. At lunchtime, you'll be treated to the four-star views from the Sugar Mill terrace, with panoramic vistas of (or so it seems) all 100 of the U.S. and British Virgin Islands. The restaurant has been completely renovated for 1990 and now specializes in pastas and seafood. Thanks to the open kitchen, the chef is part of the show. All in all, the new Sugar Mill promises to become the new "in" spot in St. John. Open daily for lunch, 11:30 a.m. to 3 p.m.; dinner, 7 to 8:30 p.m. Price information for the new menus were unavailable as we went to press; call for details.

Moderate

Pusser's, Wharfside Village, Cruz Bay (tel. 774-5489). Clink a toast with the one you love most at this good-times restaurant and bar—the "happeningest" place in town. Pusser's revives a 300-year-old tradition of Britain's Royal Navy: the daily ration of rum, issued by the "Pusser" (purser). Today, both landlubbers and old salts can down that same mellow blend of five West Indian rums that helped Admiral Nelson win the Battle of Trafalgar. Inside the restaurant, there's a wood-and-brass Victorian-style bar; outside, the deck boasts wrap-around views of the bay. A nautical theme prevails, especially on the drinks menu, which highlights the Pusser's Pain-killer, a smooth and sneaky concoction with rum, cream of coconut, pineapple and orange juices. On the hearty bill of fare, best bets include the prime rib of beef—perhaps with a lobster tail for companionship. Lunch, $20 per couple; dinner, $40 to $60 per couple. Open daily, 11 a.m. to 10 p.m.

Old Gallery, Centerline Road in Cruz Bay (tel. 776-7544). If the thought of local specialties such as boiled fish, baked chicken, plantains, sweet potatoes, and fungi makes your mouth water, mosey on over to this friendly, casual restaurant run by Winston and Alecia Wells. You can dine inside or on the small balcony, watching the passing parade to and from town. Open Monday through Saturday, 11 a.m. to 10 p.m.; $20 to $30 per couple.

Lime Inn, Lemon Tree Mall on Backstreet, Cruz Bay (tel. 776-6425). Punning on the West Indian expression "just limin'" (hanging out), this folksy restaurant is perfect for doing exactly that. Shaded by trees and a corrugated aluminum roof, a happy-go-lucky mix of regulars and tourists mingle together (along with some snoozing cats and an occasional sightseeing chicken). The bill of fare is light, featuring an array of tasty burgers, sandwiches, salads, and quiches, as well as an excellent fresh-squeezed lemonade. Open Monday through Friday, 11:30 a.m. to 10 p.m.; Saturday, 5:30 to 10 p.m.; $20 to $30 per couple.

Cruz Quarters Restaurant and Bar, Cruz Bay (tel. 776-6908). Located right behind Cruz Bay Park and across from the ferry dock, this seems to be the favorite local hangout—probably because the broad terrace and comfortable cast-iron chairs make this a prime spot for people watching. The food's pretty good too, with a selection of sandwiches, chicken, roast beef, and Mexican favorites such as burritos. Open daily from 7 a.m. to 10 p.m.; $20 to $40 per couple.

The Backyard, Cruz Bay (tel. 776-8553), is another favorite local gathering spot, the kind of place where residents thumb through stateside magazines to catch up on the latest news (of about two weeks ago), dogs doze off in the corners, and the bartender asks you if you want a glass with your beer. If you're the type of person who doesn't need a glass, you'll fit right in with the crowd. The best eats come on Monday, Tuesday, and Wednesday, when Miss Maggie cooks up real West Indian treats such as chicken curry or stewed conch. It's a fun way to plug into the local lifestyle. Lunch, about $20 per couple; dinners, about $30. Open daily from 11 a.m. "till whenever."

Inexpensive

Mongoose Restaurant, Café, and Bar, Mongoose Junction, Cruz Bay (tel. 776-7586). Decks clamber between the levels, residents trade gossip at the bar, and a stream adds its rushing rhythms to the general hubbub—that describes the animated atmosphere at this local favorite that is open for breakfast, lunch, and dinner. It's an especially convenient lunch spot if you're shopping in town. Choose from fresh salad platters, sandwiches, or burgers (priced $10 to $12). Open daily from 8:30 a.m. to 10 p.m.

Some of the best eating in St. John isn't in restaurants—it's from a trio of roadside vendors in Cruz Bay. **Hercule Pâté Delight,** Cruz Bay (tel. 776-6352), is just a casual sidewalk stand, but its food is high art. They serve meat, chicken, and fish pâtés (deep-fried pies), only about $2.25 each. As a beverage, try ginger beer (tart and tingly), mauby, or soursop juice. For savory conch fritters, head for **Cap's Place,** a stand opposite the Post Office. For dessert, stroll across the street to the **Nature's Nook** fruit stand, where you can get the pick of the harvest—papaya, mangoes, genip, whatever is in season. The stands are generally open Monday through Saturday, 7 a.m. to 5 p.m.

SUGGESTED READING

Now that you have selected your honeymoon destination, here's a list of other specialized touring guides you may wish to consult in planning your itinerary. They are all published by Prentice Hall Travel in New York and are available in bookstores or directly from the publisher.

THE UNITED STATES

NEW ENGLAND

Frommer's Boston, by Faye Hammel
Frommer's New England, by Tom Brosnahan
Gault Millau: The Best of New England, directed by André Gavot
Marilyn Wood's Wonderful Weekends, by Marilyn Wood

CALIFORNIA

Frommer's California, by Mary Rakauskas
Frommer's Los Angeles, by Mary Rakauskas
Frommer's San Francisco, by Mary Rakauskas
Gault Millau: The Best of Los Angeles, directed by André Gayot
Gault Millau: The Best of San Francisco, directed by André Gayot
The Serious Shopper's Guide to Los Angeles, by Jennifer Merin

FLORIDA

Frommer's Florida, by Marylyn Springer and Donald A. Schultz
Frommer's Orlando, Disney World, and EPCOT, by Marylyn Springer

HAWAII

Frommer's Hawaii on $60 a Day, by Faye Hammel and Sylvan Levey
Frommer's Hawaii, by Faye Hammel
Frommer's Cruises, by Marylyn Springer and Donald Schultz

NEW YORK

Frommer's New York State, by John Foreman
Frommer's New York on $60 a Day, by Joan Hamburg and Norma Ketay
Frommer's New York, by Faye Hammel
Marilyn Wood's Wonderful Weekends, by Marilyn Wood

PENNSYLVANIA
Frommer's Mid-Atlantic States, by Patricia Tunison Preston and John Preston
Frommer's Philadelphia, by Jay Golan
Marilyn Wood's Wonderful Weekends, by Marilyn Wood

MEXICO

Frommer's Mexico on $35 A Day, by Tom Brosnahan
Frommer's Cancún, Cozumel, and the Yucatán, by Tom Brosnahan
Frommer's Mexico City and Acapulco, by Tom Brosnahan
Frommer's Cruises, by Marylyn Springer and Donald A. Schultz

THE CARIBBEAN, THE BAHAMAS, AND BERMUDA

Frommer's Bermuda & The Bahamas, by Darwin Porter
Frommer's Caribbean, by Darwin Porter
Frommer's Cruises, by Marylyn Springer and Donald A. Schultz
Caribbean Hideaways, by Ian Keown
A Shopper's Guide to the Caribbean, by Jeanne and Harry Harman

THE DOLLARWISE
TRAVEL CLUB

In this book we'll be looking at how to get your money's worth as well as enjoyment from your honeymoon, but there is a "device" for saving money and determining value on *all* your trips. It's the popular, international Frommer's Dollarwise Travel Club, now in its 30th successful year of operation. The Club was formed at the urging of numerous readers of the $-a-Day and Frommer Guides, who felt that such an organization could provide continuing travel information and a sense of community to value-minded travelers in all parts of the world. And so it does!

In keeping with the budget concept, the annual membership fee is low and is immediately exceeded by the value of your benefits. Upon receipt of $18 (U.S. residents), or $20 U.S. by check drawn on a U.S. bank or via international postal money order in U.S. funds (Canadian, Mexican, and other foreign residents) to cover one year's membership, we will send all new members the following items.

(1) Any two of the following books
Please designate in your letter which two you wish to receive:

Frommer $-A-Day Guides
Europe on $40 a Day
Australia on $30 a Day
Eastern Europe on $25 a Day
England on $50 a Day
Greece on $30 a Day
Hawaii on $60 a Day
India on $25 a Day
Ireland on $35 a Day
Israel on $40 a Day
Mexico (plus Belize and Guatemala) on $35 a Day
New York on $60 a Day
New Zealand on $40 a Day
Scandinavia on $60 a Day
Scotland and Wales on $40 a Day
South America on $35 a Day
Spain and Morocco (plus the Canary Is.) on $40 a Day
Turkey on $30 a Day
Washington, D.C., & Historic Virginia on $40 a Day

($-A-Day Guides document hundreds of budget accommodations and facilities, helping you get the most for your travel dollars.)

Frommer Guides
Alaska
Australia
Austria and Hungary
Belgium, Holland, and Luxembourg

Bermuda and The Bahamas
Brazil
California and Las Vegas
Canada
Caribbean
Egypt
England and Scotland
Florida
France
Germany
Italy
Japan and Hong Kong
Mid-Atlantic States
New England
New York State
Northwest
Portugal, Madeira, and the Azores
Skiing USA—East
Skiing USA—West
South Pacific
Southeast Asia
Southern Atlantic States
Southwest
Switzerland and Liechtenstein
Texas
USA

(Frommer Guides discuss accommodations and facilities in all price ranges, with emphasis on the medium-priced.)

Frommer Touring Guides

Australia
Egypt
Florence
London
Paris
Scotland
Thailand
Venice

(These new, color illustrated guides include walking tours, cultural and historic sites, and other vital travel information.)

Gault Millau

Chicago
France
Hong Kong
Italy
London
Los Angeles
New England
New York
San Francisco
Washington, D.C.

(Irreverent, savvy, and comprehensive, each of these renowned guides candidly reviews over 1,000 restaurants, hotels, shops, nightspots, museums, and sights.)

Serious Shopper's Guides
    Italy
    London
    Los Angeles
    Paris
(Practical and comprehensive, each of these handsomely illustrated guides lists hundreds of stores, selling everything from antiques to wine, conveniently organized alphabetically by category.)

A Shopper's Guide to the Caribbean
(Two experienced Caribbean hands guide you through this shopper's paradise, offering witty insights and helpful tips on the wares and emporia of more than 25 islands.)

Beat the High Cost of Travel
(This practical guide details how to save money on absolutely all travel items—accommodations, transportation, dining, sightseeing, shopping, taxes, and more. Includes special budget information for seniors, students, singles, and families.)

Bed & Breakfast—North America
(This guide contains a directory of over 150 organizations that offer bed-and-breakfast referrals and reservations throughout North America. The scenic attractions, and major schools and universities near the homes of each are also listed.)

California with Kids
(A must for parents traveling in California, providing key information on selecting the best accommodations, restaurants, and sightseeing attractions for the particular needs of the family, whether the kids are toddlers, school-age, pre-teens, or teens.)

Caribbean Hideaways
(Well-known travel author Ian Keown describes the most romantic, alluring places to stay in the Caribbean, rating each establishment on romantic ambience, food, sports opportunities, and price.)

Frommer's Belgium
(Arthur Frommer unlocks the treasures of a country overlooked by most travelers to Europe. Discover the medieval charm, modern sophistication, and natural beauty of this quintessentially European country.)

Frommer's Cruises
(This complete guide covers all the basics of cruising—ports of call, costs, fly-cruise package bargains, cabin selection booking, embarkation and debarkation—and describes in detail over 60 or so ships cruising the waters of Alaska, the Caribbean, Mexico, Hawaii, Panama, Canada, and the United States.)

Frommer's Honeymoon Destinations
(A special guide for that most romantic trip of your life, with full details on planning and choosing the destination that will be just right in the U.S. [California, New England, Hawaii, Florida, New York, Pennsylvania, etc.], Mexico, and the Caribbean.)

Frommer's Skiing Europe
(Describes top ski resorts in Austria, France, Italy, and Switzerland. Illustrated with maps of each resort area. Includes supplement on Argentinian resorts.)

Marilyn Wood's Wonderful Weekends
(This very selective guide covers the best mini-vacation destinations within a 200-mile radius of New York City. It describes special country inns and other accommo-

dations, restaurants, picnic spots, sights, and activities—all the information needed for a two- or three-day stay.)

Manhattan's Outdoor Sculpture
(A total guide, fully illustrated with black-and-white photos, to more than 300 sculptures and monuments that grace Manhattan's plazas, parks, and other public spaces.)

Motorist's Phrase Book
(A practical phrase book in French, German, and Spanish designed specifically for the English-speaking motorist touring abroad.)

Paris Rendez-Vous
(An amusing and *au courant* guide to the best meeting places in Paris, organized for hour-to-hour use: from power breakfasts and fun brunches, through tea at four or cocktails at five, to romantic dinners and dancing till dawn.)

Swap and Go—Home Exchanging Made Easy
(Two veteran home exchangers explain in detail all the money-saving benefits of a home exchange, and then describe precisely how to do it. Also includes information on home rentals and many tips on low-cost travel.)

The Candy Apple: New York with Kids
(A spirited guide to the wonders of the Big Apple by a savvy New York grandmother with a kid's-eye view to fun. Indispensable for visitors and residents alike.)

The New World of Travel
(From America's #1 travel expert, Arthur Frommer, an annual sourcebook with the hottest news and latest trends that's guaranteed to change the way you travel—and save you hundreds of dollars. Jam-packed with alternative new modes of travel that will lead you to vacations that cater to the mind, the spirit, and a sense of thrift.)

Travel Diary and Record Book
(A 96-page diary for personal travel notes plus a section for such vital data as passport and traveler's check numbers, itinerary, postcard list, special people and places to visit, and a reference section with temperature and conversion charts, and world maps with distance zones.)

Where to Stay USA
(By the Council on International Educational Exchange, this extraordinary guide is the first to list accommodations in all 50 states that cost anywhere from $3 to $30 per night.)

(2) Any one of the Frommer City Guides
Amsterdam
Athens
Atlantic City and Cape May
Boston
Cancún, Cozumel, and the Yucatán
Chicago
Dublin and Ireland
Hawaii
Hong Kong
Las Vegas
Lisbon, Madrid, and Costa del Sol

London
Los Angeles
Mexico City and Acapulco
Minneapolis and St. Paul
Montréal and Québec City
New Orleans
New York
Orlando, Disney World, and EPCOT
Paris
Philadelphia
Rio
Rome
San Francisco
Santa Fe, Taos, and Albuquerque
Sydney
Tokyo
Washington, D.C.

(Pocket-size guides to hotels, restaurants, nightspots, and sightseeing attractions covering all price ranges.)

(3) A one-year subscription to *The Dollarwise Traveler*

This quarterly eight-page tabloid newspaper keeps you up to date on fastbreaking developments in low-cost travel in all parts of the world, bringing you the latest money-saving information—the kind of information you'd have to pay $35 a year to obtain elsewhere. This consumer-conscious publication also features columns of special interest to readers: **Hospitality Exchange** (members all over the world who are willing to provide hospitality to other members as they pass through their home cities); **Share-a-Trip** (offers and requests from members for travel companions who can share costs and help avoid the burdensome single supplement); and **Readers Ask . . . Readers Reply** (travel questions from members to which other members reply with authentic firsthand information).

(4) Your personal membership card

Membership entitles you to purchase through the club all Frommer publications for a third to a half off their regular retail prices during the term of your membership.

So why not join this hardy band of international budgeteers and participate in its exchange of travel information and hospitality? Simply send your name and address, together with your annual membership fee of $18 (U.S. residents) or $20 U.S. (Canadian, Mexican, and other foreign residents), by check drawn on a U.S. bank or via international postal money order in U.S. funds to: Frommer's Dollarwise Travel Club, Inc., 15 Columbus Circle, New York, NY 10023. And please remember to specify which *two* of the books in section (1) and which *one* in section (2) you wish to receive in your initial package of members' benefits. Or, if you prefer, use the order form at the end of the book and enclose $18 or $20 in U.S. currency.

Once you are a member, there is no obligation to buy additional books. No books will be mailed to you without your specific order.

INDEX

Oahu (*continued*)
inexpensive, 210–11; moderate, 209–10
sights and attractions, 204–5
Ocho Rios (Jamaica), 531–40
accommodations, 534–9; all-inclusive resorts, 535–7; first-class, 537–8; moderately priced, 538–9; ultra-luxurious, 534–5
restaurants, 539–40
shopping, 532
sights and attractions, 532–4
Orlando (Florida), 161; map, 161

Pacific Coast resorts (Mexico), 287–307
Acapulco, 287–94; accommodations, 290–3; nightlife, 294; restaurants, 293–4; shopping, 288; sights and attractions, 289–90
Huatulco, 294–7
Ixtapa/Zihuatanejo, 297–300
Manzanillo, 300–2
Puerto Vallarta, 302–7: accommodations, 304–6; restaurants, 306–7; shopping, 303; sights and attractions, 303–4
see also California
Pacific Grove (California), 93–6
accommodations, 93–5
restaurants, 95–6
Palm Springs (California), accommodations, 137–8
Paradise Island (Bahamas), 364–72
accommodations, 367–9
restaurants, 370–2
sights and attractions, 365
Passports, 13–14
Pebble Beach (California), 96–8
Pennsylvania: *see* Poconos
Peter Island (B.V.I.), 460–1
Phone calls from abroad, 15
Planning your honeymoon, 3–8
checklist, 3–4
choosing your destination, 4–6
glossary of travel terms, 6, 8
travel agents, 6
Poconos, the (Pennsylvania), 263–76
accommodations, 269–76; Caesars resorts, 270–1; Mount Airy/Strickland's/Pocono Gardens, 273–5; Penn Hills, 275–6; Summit Resort, 275
getting there and around, 264, 266
map, 265
practical facts, 264, 266–8
restaurants, 267–8
shopping, 266–7
sights and attractions, 268–9
tourist information, 268
wedding planning, 268
Port Antonio (Jamaica), 540–5
accommodations, 542–4

restaurants, 544–5
shopping, 541
sights and attractions, 541–2
Puerto Rico, 558–72
accommodations, 565–70; expensive, 565–7; inexpensive, 567–8; out on the island, 568–70; moderate, 567; San Juan, 565–8
getting there and getting around, 560, 562
map of, 562
nightlife, 572
practical facts, 560, 562–3
restaurants, 570–2
sights and attractions, 563–4
shopping, 562–3
tourist information, 563
wedding planning, 563
Puerto Vallarta (Mexico), 302–7
accommodations, 304–6
restaurants, 306–7
shopping, 303
sights and attractions, 303–4
Restaurants: *see specific places*
Rhode Island, map of, 30

Saba, accommodations, 600
St. Croix, 624–35
accommodations, 628–33; inexpensive, 631–3; moderate, 630–1; moderately expensive, 629–30
restaurants, 633–5
sights and attractions, 625–8
shopping, 625
St. John, 635–42
accommodations, 638–40
restaurants, 640–2
sights and attractions, 636–8
shopping, 636
St. Lucia, 573–86
accommodations, 580–4; expensive, 580–2; inexpensive, 583–4; moderate, 582–3; moderately expensive, 582
getting there and getting around, 574, 576
map of, 575
practical facts, 574, 576–8
restaurants, 584–6
sights and attractions, 578–9
shopping, 577
tourist information, 578
wedding planning, 577–8
St. Maarten/St. Martin, 587–603
accommodations, 593–4, 596–600; Dutch side, 598–600; expensive, 596–9; general information, 593–4; inexpensive, 598, 600; moderate, 597–600; Saba and Statia, 600
getting there and getting around, 588–90
map of, 589

NOW!
ARTHUR FROMMER LAUNCHES HIS SECOND TRAVEL REVOLUTION
with

The New World of Travel

The hottest news and latest trends in travel today—heretofore the closely guarded secrets of the travel trade—are revealed in this new sourcebook by the dean of American travel. Here, collected in one book that is updated every year, are the most exciting, challenging, and money-saving ideas in travel today.

You'll find out about hundreds of alternative new modes of travel—and the many organizations that sponsor them—that will lead you to vacations that cater to your mind, your spirit, and your sense of thrift.

Learn how to fly for free as an air courier; travel for free as a tour escort; live for free on a hospitality exchange; add earnings as a part-time travel agent; pay less for air tickets, cruises, and hotels; enhance your life through cooperative camping, political tours, and adventure trips; change your life at utopian communities, low-cost spas, and yoga retreats; pursue low-cost studies and language training; travel comfortably while single or over 60; sail on passenger freighters; and vacation in the cheapest places on earth.

And in every yearly edition, Arthur Frommer spotlights the 10 GREATEST TRAVEL VALUES for the coming year. 448 pages, large-format with many, many illustrations. All for $16.95!

ORDER NOW
TURN TO THE LAST PAGE OF THIS BOOK FOR ORDER FORM.

NOW, SAVE MONEY ON ALL YOUR TRAVELS!
Join Frommer's™ Dollarwise® Travel Club

Saving money while traveling is never a simple matter, which is why the **Dollarwise Travel Club** was formed 31 years ago. Developed in response to requests from Frommer Travel Guide readers, the Club provides cost-cutting travel strategies, up-to-date travel information, and a sense of community for value-conscious travelers from all over the world.

In keeping with the money-saving concept, the annual membership fee is low —$18 (U.S. residents) or $20 (residents of Canada, Mexico, and other countries)— and is immediately exceeded by the value of your benefits, which include:

1. Any TWO books listed on the following pages.
2. Plus any ONE Frommer City Guide.
3. A subscription to our quarterly newspaper, *The Dollarwise Traveler.*
4. A membership card that entitles you to purchase through the Club all Frommer publications for 33% to 50% off their retail price.

The eight-page *Dollarwise Traveler* tells you about the latest developments in good-value travel worldwide and includes the following columns: **Hospitality Exchange** (for those offering and seeking hospitality in cities all over the world); **Share-a-Trip** (for those looking for travel companions to share costs); and **Readers Ask . . . Readers Reply** (for those with travel questions that other members can answer).

Aside from the Frommer Guides, the Serious Shopper Guides, and the Gault Millau Guides, you can also choose from our Special Editions. These include such titles as **California with Kids** (a compendium of the best of California's accommodations, restaurants, and sightseeing attractions appropriate for those traveling with toddlers through teens); **Candy Apple: New York with Kids** (a spirited guide to the Big Apple by a savvy New York grandmother that's perfect for both visitors and residents); **Caribbean Hideaways** (the 100 most romantic places to stay in the Islands, all rated on ambience, food, sport opportunities, and price); **Honeymoon Destinations** (a guide to planning and choosing just the right destination from hundreds of possibilities in the U.S., Mexico, and the Caribbean); **Marilyn Wood's Wonderful Weekends** (a selection of the best mini-vacations within a 200-mile radius of New York City, including descriptions of country inns and other accommodations, restaurants, picnic spots, sights, and activities); and **Paris Rendez-Vous** (a delightful guide to the best places to meet in Paris whether for power breakfasts or dancing till dawn).

To join this Club, simply send the appropriate membership fee with your name and address to: Frommer's Dollarwise Travel Club, 15 Columbus Circle, New York, NY 10023. Remember to specify which single city guide and which two other guides you wish to receive in your initial package of member's benefits. Or tear out the next page, check off your choices, and send the page to us with your membership fee.

FROMMER BOOKS
PRENTICE HALL TRAVEL
15 COLUMBUS CIRCLE
NEW YORK, NY 10023
212-373-8125

Date_____

Friends:
Please send me the books checked below:

FROMMER™ GUIDES

(Guides to sightseeing and tourist accommodations and facilities from budget to deluxe, with emphasis on the medium-priced.)

☐ Alaska	$14.95	☐ Germany	$14.95
☐ Australia	$14.95	☐ Italy	$14.95
☐ Austria & Hungary	$14.95	☐ Japan & Hong Kong	$14.95
☐ Belgium, Holland & Luxembourg	$14.95	☐ Mid-Atlantic States	$14.95
☐ Bermuda & The Bahamas	$14.95	☐ New England	$14.95
☐ Brazil	$14.95	☐ New York State	$14.95
☐ Canada	$14.95	☐ Northwest	$14.95
☐ Caribbean	$14.95	☐ Portugal, Madeira & the Azores	$14.95
☐ Cruises (incl. Alaska, Carib, Mex, Hawaii, Panama, Canada & US)	$14.95	☐ Skiing Europe	$14.95
		☐ South Pacific	$14.95
☐ California & Las Vegas	$14.95	☐ Southeast Asia	$14.95
☐ Egypt	$14.95	☐ Southern Atlantic States	$14.95
☐ England & Scotland	$14.95	☐ Southwest	$14.95
☐ Florida	$14.95	☐ Switzerland & Liechtenstein	$14.95
☐ France	$14.95	☐ USA	$15.95

FROMMER $-A-DAY® GUIDES

(In-depth guides to sightseeing and low-cost tourist accommodations and facilities.)

☐ Europe on $40 a Day	$15.95	☐ New York on $60 a Day	$13.95
☐ Australia on $30 a Day	$12.95	☐ New Zealand on $45 a Day	$13.95
☐ Eastern Europe on $25 a Day	$13.95	☐ Scandinavia on $60 a Day	$13.95
☐ England on $50 a Day	$13.95	☐ Scotland & Wales on $40 a Day	$13.95
☐ Greece on $35 a Day	$13.95	☐ South America on $35 a Day	$13.95
☐ Hawaii on $60 a Day	$13.95	☐ Spain & Morocco on $40 a Day	$13.95
☐ India on $25 a Day	$12.95	☐ Turkey on $30 a Day	$13.95
☐ Ireland on $35 a Day	$13.95	☐ Washington, D.C. & Historic Va. on	
☐ Israel on $40 a Day	$13.95	$40 a Day	$13.95
☐ Mexico on $35 a Day	$13.95		

FROMMER TOURING GUIDES

(Color illustrated guides that include walking tours, cultural and historic sites, and other vital travel information.)

☐ Australia	$9.95	☐ Paris	$8.95
☐ Egypt	$8.95	☐ Scotland	$9.95
☐ Florence	$8.95	☐ Thailand	$9.95
☐ London	$8.95	☐ Venice	$8.95

TURN PAGE FOR ADDITONAL BOOKS AND ORDER FORM.

FROMMER CITY GUIDES

(Pocket-size guides to sightseeing and tourist accommodations and facilities in all price ranges.)

☐ Amsterdam/Holland	$7.95	☐ Minneapolis/St. Paul	$7.95
☐ Athens	$7.95	☐ Montréal/Québec City	$7.95
☐ Atlantic City/Cape May	$7.95	☐ New Orleans	$7.95
☐ Barcelona*	$7.95	☐ New York	$7.95
☐ Belgium	$7.95	☐ Orlando/Disney World/EPCOT	$7.95
☐ Boston	$7.95	☐ Paris	$7.95
☐ Cancún/Cozumel/Yucatán	$7.95	☐ Philadelphia	$7.95
☐ Chicago	$7.95	☐ Rio	$7.95
☐ Denver/Boulder*	$7.95	☐ Rome	$7.95
☐ Dublin/Ireland	$7.95	☐ San Francisco	$7.95
☐ Hawaii	$7.95	☐ Santa Fe/Taos/Albuquerque	$7.95
☐ Hong Kong*	$7.95	☐ Seattle/Portland*	$7.95
☐ Las Vegas	$7.95	☐ Sydney	$7.95
☐ Lisbon/Madrid/Costa del Sol	$7.95	☐ Tokyo*	$7.95
☐ London	$7.95	☐ Vancouver/Victoria*	$7.95
☐ Los Angeles	$7.95	☐ Washington, D.C.	$7.95
☐ Mexico City/Acapulco	$7.95	*Available June, 1990	

SPECIAL EDITIONS

☐ A Shopper's Guide to the Caribbean	$12.95	☐ Manhattan's Outdoor Sculpture	$15.95
☐ Beat the High Cost of Travel	$6.95	☐ Motorist's Phrase Book (Fr/Ger/Sp)	$4.95
☐ Bed & Breakfast—N. America	$11.95	☐ Paris Rendez-Vous	$10.95
☐ California with Kids	$14.95	☐ Swap and Go (Home Exchanging)	$10.95
☐ Caribbean Hideaways	$14.95	☐ The Candy Apple (NY with Kids)	$12.95
☐ Honeymoon Destinations (US, Mex & Carib)	$12.95	☐ Travel Diary and Record Book	$5.95

☐ Where to Stay USA (Lodging from $3 to $30 a night) $10.95
☐ Marilyn Wood's Wonderful Weekends (Conn, Del, Mass, NH, NJ, NY, Pa, RI, VT) $11.95
☐ The New World of Travel (Annual sourcebook by Arthur Frommer for savvy travelers) $16.95

SERIOUS SHOPPER'S GUIDES

(Illustrated guides listing hundreds of stores, conveniently organized alphabetically by category.)

☐ Italy	$15.95	☐ Los Angeles	$14.95
☐ London	$15.95	☐ Paris	$15.95

GAULT MILLAU

(The only guides that distinguish the truly superlative from the merely overrated.)

☐ The Best of Chicago	$15.95	☐ The Best of Los Angeles	$14.95
☐ The Best of France	$16.95	☐ The Best of New England	$15.95
☐ The Best of Hong Kong	$16.95	☐ The Best of New York	$14.95
☐ The Best of Italy	$16.95	☐ The Best of Paris	$16.95
☐ The Best of London	$16.95	☐ The Best of San Francisco	$14.95

☐ The Best of Washington, D.C. $14.95

ORDER NOW!

In U.S. include $2 shipping UPS for 1st book; $1 ea. add'l book. Outside U.S. $3 and $1, respectively.
Allow four to six weeks for delivery in U.S., longer outside U.S.

Enclosed is my check or money order for $_____

NAME _____

ADDRESS _____

CITY _____ STATE _____ ZIP _____

0190